T0137026

Lecture Notes in Computer Science 12697

More information about this subseries at http://www.springer.com/series/7410

Anne Canteaut · François-Xavier Standaert (Eds.)

Advances in Cryptology – EUROCRYPT 2021

40th Annual International Conference on the Theory and Applications of Cryptographic Techniques
Zagreb, Croatia, October 17–21, 2021
Proceedings, Part II

Editors
Anne Canteaut
Inria
Paris, France

François-Xavier Standaert
UCLouvain
Louvain-la-Neuve, Belgium

ISSN 0302-9743 ISSN 1611-3349 (electronic)
Lecture Notes in Computer Science
ISBN 978-3-030-77885-9 ISBN 978-3-030-77886-6 (eBook)
https://doi.org/10.1007/978-3-030-77886-6

LNCS Sublibrary: SL4 – Security and Cryptology

This Springer imprint is published by the registered company Springer Nature Switzerland AG
The registered company address is: Gewerbestrasse 11, 6330 Cham, Switzerland

Preface

Eurocrypt 2021, the 40th Annual International Conference on the Theory and Applications of Cryptographic Techniques, was held in Zagreb, Croatia, during October 17–21, 2021.[1] The conference was sponsored by the International Association for Cryptologic Research (IACR). Lejla Batina (Radboud University, The Netherlands) and Stjepan Picek (Delft University of Technology, The Netherlands) were responsible for the local organization.

We received a total of 400 submissions. Each submission was anonymized for the reviewing process and was assigned to at least three of the 59 Program Committee (PC) members. PC members were allowed to submit at most two papers. The reviewing process included a rebuttal round for all submissions. After extensive deliberations the PC accepted 78 papers. The revised versions of these papers are included in this three-volume proceedings.

The PC decided to give Best Paper Awards to the papers "*Non-Interactive Zero Knowledge from Sub-exponential DDH*" by Abhishek Jain and Zhengzhong Jin, "*On the (in)security of ROS*" by Fabrice Benhamouda, Tancrède Lepoint, Julian Loss, Michele Orrù, and Mariana Raykova and "*New Representations of the AES Key Schedule*" by Gaëtan Leurent and Clara Pernot. The authors of these three papers received an invitation to submit an extended version of their work to the *Journal of Cryptology*. The program also included invited talks by Craig Gentry (Algorand Foundation) and Sarah Meiklejohn (University College London).

We would like to thank all the authors who submitted papers. We know that the PC's decisions can be very disappointing, especially rejections of good papers which did not find a slot in the sparse number of accepted papers. We sincerely hope that these works will eventually get the attention they deserve.

We are indebted to the PC and the external reviewers for their voluntary work. Selecting papers from 400 submissions covering the many areas of cryptologic research is a huge workload. It has been an honor to work with everyone. We owe a big thank you to Kevin McCurley for his continuous support in solving all the minor issues we had with the HotCRP review system, to Gaëtan Leurent for sharing his MILP programs which made the papers assignments much easier, and to Simona Samardjiska who acted as Eurocrypt 2021 webmaster.

Finally, we thank all the other people (speakers, sessions chairs, rump session chairs…) for their contribution to the program of Eurocrypt 2021. We would also like to thank the many sponsors for their generous support, including the Cryptography Research Fund that supported student speakers.

April 2021

Anne Canteaut
François-Xavier Standaert

[1] This preface was written before the conference took place, under the assumption that it will take place as planned in spite of travel restrictions due to COVID-19.

Preface

Eurocrypt 2021

The 40th Annual International Conference on the Theory and Applications of Cryptographic Techniques

Sponsored by the *International Association for Cryptologic Research*
Zagreb, Croatia
October 17–21, 2021

General Co-chairs

Lejla Batina	Radboud University, The Netherlands
Stjepan Picek	Delft University of Technology, The Netherlands

Program Committee Chairs

Anne Canteaut	Inria, France
François-Xavier Standaert	UCLouvain, Belgium

Program Committee

Shweta Agrawal	IIT Madras, India
Joël Alwen	Wickr, USA
Foteini Baldimtsi	George Mason University, USA
Marshall Ball	Columbia University, USA
Begül Bilgin	Rambus - Cryptography Research, The Netherlands
Nir Bitansky	Tel Aviv University, Israel
Joppe W. Bos	NXP Semiconductors, Belgium
Christina Boura	University of Versailles, France
Wouter Castryck	KU Leuven, Belgium
Kai-Min Chung	Academia Sinica, Taiwan
Jean-Sébastien Coron	University of Luxembourg, Luxembourg
Véronique Cortier	LORIA, CNRS, France
Geoffroy Couteau	CNRS, IRIF, Université de Paris, France
Luca De Feo	IBM Research Europe, Switzerland
Léo Ducas (Area Chair: Public-Key Crypto)	CWI, Amsterdam, The Netherlands
Orr Dunkelman	University of Haifa, Israel
Stefan Dziembowski (Area Chair: Theory)	University of Warsaw, Poland
Thomas Eisenbarth	University of Lübeck, Germany
Dario Fiore	IMDEA Software Institute, Spain
Marc Fischlin	TU Darmstadt, Germany

Benjamin Fuller	University of Connecticut, USA
Adrià Gascón	Google, UK
Henri Gilbert	ANSSI, France
Shai Halevi	Algorand Foundation, USA
Annelie Heuser	Univ Rennes, CNRS, IRISA, France
Naofumi Homma	Tohoku University, Japan
Kristina Hostáková	ETH Zürich, Switzerland
Tetsu Iwata	Nagoya University, Japan
Marc Joye	Zama, France
Pascal Junod (Area Chair: Real-World Crypto)	Snap, Switzerland
Pierre Karpman	Université Grenoble-Alpes, France
Gregor Leander (Area Chair: Symmetric Crypto)	Ruhr-Universität Bochum, Germany
Benoît Libert	CNRS and ENS de Lyon, France
Julian Loss	University of Maryland, College Park, USA
Christian Majenz	CWI, Amsterdam, The Netherlands
Daniel Masny	Visa Research, USA
Bart Mennink	Radboud University, The Netherlands
Tarik Moataz	Aroki Systems, USA
Amir Moradi	Ruhr-Universität Bochum, Germany
Michael Naehrig	Microsoft Research, USA
María Naya-Plasencia	Inria, France
Claudio Orlandi	Aarhus University, Denmark
Elisabeth Oswald (Area Chair: Implementations)	University of Klagenfurt, Austria
Dan Page	University of Bristol, UK
Rafael Pass	Cornell Tech, USA
Thomas Peyrin	Nanyang Technological University, Singapore
Oxana Poburinnaya	University of Rochester and Ligero Inc., USA
Matthieu Rivain	CryptoExperts, France
Adeline Roux-Langlois	Univ Rennes, CNRS, IRISA, France
Louis Salvail	Université de Montréal, Canada
Yu Sasaki	NTT Laboratories, Japan
Tobias Schneider	NXP Semiconductors, Austria
Yannick Seurin	ANSSI, France
Emmanuel Thomé	LORIA, Inria Nancy, France
Vinod Vaikuntanathan	MIT, USA
Prashant Nalini Vasudevan	UC Berkeley, USA
Daniele Venturi	Sapienza University of Rome, Italy
Daniel Wichs	Northeastern University and NTT Research Inc., USA
Yu Yu	Shanghai Jiao Tong University, China

Additional Reviewers

Mark Abspoel
Hamza Abusalah
Alexandre Adomnicai
Archita Agarwal
Divesh Aggarwal
Shashank Agrawal
Gorjan Alagic
Martin R. Albrecht
Ghada Almashaqbeh
Bar Alon
Miguel Ambrona
Ghous Amjad
Prabhanjan Ananth
Toshinori Araki
Victor Arribas
Gilad Asharov
Roberto Avanzi
Melissa Azouaoui
Christian Badertscher
Saikrishna Badrinarayanan
Karim Baghery
Victor Balcer
Laasya Bangalore
Magali Bardet
James Bartusek
Balthazar Bauer
Carsten Baum
Christof Beierle
James Bell
Fabrice Benhamouda
Iddo Bentov
Olivier Bernard
Sebastian Berndt
Pauline Bert
Ward Beullens
Benjamin Beurdouche
Ritam Bhaumik
Erica Blum
Alexandra Boldyreva
Jonathan Bootle
Nicolas Bordes
Katharina Boudgoust
Florian Bourse
Xavier Boyen
Elette Boyle
Zvika Brakerski
Lennart Braun
Gianluca Brian
Marek Broll
Olivier Bronchain
Chris Brzuska
Benedikt Bünz
Chloe Cachet
Matteo Campanelli
Federico Canale
Ignacio Cascudo
Gaëtan Cassiers
Avik Chakraborti
Benjamin Chan
Eshan Chattopadhyay
Panagiotis Chatzigiannis
Shan Chen
Yanlin Chen
Yilei Chen
Yu Chen
Alessandro Chiesa
Ilaria Chillotti
Seung Geol Choi
Arka Rai Choudhuri
Michele Ciampi
Daniel Coggia
Benoît Cogliati
Ran Cohen
Andrea Coladangelo
Sandro Coretti-Drayton
Craig Costello
Daniele Cozzo
Ting Ting Cui
Debajyoti Das
Poulami Das
Bernardo David
Alex Davidson
Gareth Davies
Lauren De Meyer
Thomas Debris-Alazard
Leo de Castro
Thomas Decru
Jean Paul Degabriele
Akshay Degwekar
Amit Deo
Patrick Derbez
Itai Dinur
Christoph Dobraunig
Yevgeniy Dodis
Jack Doerner
Jelle Don
Benjamin Dowling
Eduoard Dufour Sans
Yfke Dulek
Frédéric Dupuis
Sylvain Duquesne
Avijit Dutta
Ehsan Ebrahimi
Kasra Edalat Nejdat
Naomi Ephraim
Thomas Espitau
Andre Esser
Grzegorz Fabiański
Xiong Fan
Antonio Faonio
Sebastian Faust
Serge Fehr
Patrick Felke
Rune Fiedler
Ben Fisch
Matthias Fitzi
Antonio Flórez-Gutiérrez
Cody Freitag
Georg Fuchsbauer
Ariel Gabizon
Nicolas Gama
Chaya Ganesh
Rachit Garg
Pierrick Gaudry
Romain Gay
Peter Gaži
Nicholas Genise
Craig Gentry

Marilyn George
Adela Georgescu
David Gerault
Essam Ghadafi
Satrajit Ghosh
Irene Giacomelli
Aarushi Goel
Junqing Gong
Alonso González
S. Dov Gordon
Louis Goubin
Marc Gourjon
Rishab Goyal
Lorenzo Grassi
Elijah Grubb
Cyprien de Saint Guilhem
Aurore Guillevic
Aldo Gunsing
Chun Guo
Qian Guo
Felix Günther
Iftach Haitner
Mohammad Hajiabadi
Mathias Hall-Andersen
Ariel Hamlin
Lucjan Hanzlik
Patrick Harasser
Dominik Hartmann
Eduard Hauck
Phil Hebborn
Javier Herranz
Amir Herzberg
Julia Hesse
Shoichi Hirose
Martin Hirt
Akinori Hosoyamada
Kathrin Hövelmanns
Andreas Hülsing
Ilia Iliashenko
Charlie Jacomme
Christian Janson
Stanislaw Jarecki
Ashwin Jha
Dingding Jia
Daniel Jost
Kimmo Järvinen
Guillaume Kaim
Chethan Kamath
Pritish Kamath
Fredrik Kamphuis
Ioanna Karantaidou
Shuichi Katsumata
Jonathan Katz
Tomasz Kazana
Marcel Keller
Mustafa Khairallah
Louiza Khati
Hamidreza Khoshakhlagh
Dakshita Khurana
Ryo Kikuchi
Eike Kiltz
Elena Kirshanova
Agnes Kiss
Karen Klein
Michael Klooß
Alexander Koch
Lisa Kohl
Vladimir Kolesnikov
Dimitris Kolonelos
Ilan Komargodski
Yashvanth Kondi
Venkata Koppula
Adrien Koutsos
Hugo Krawczyk
Stephan Krenn
Ashutosh Kumar
Ranjit Kumaresan
Po-Chun Kuo
Rolando L. La Placa
Thijs Laarhoven
Jianchang Lai
Virginie Lallemand
Baptiste Lambin
Eran Lambooij
Philippe Lamontagne
Rio Lavigne
Jooyoung Lee
Alexander Lemmens
Nikos Leonardos
Matthieu Lequesne
Antonin Leroux
Gaëtan Leurent
Jyun-Jie Liao
Damien Ligier
Huijia Lin
Benjamin Lipp
Maciej Liskiewicz
Qipeng Liu
Shengli Liu
Tianren Liu
Yanyi Liu
Chen-Da Liu-Zhang
Alex Lombardi
Patrick Longa
Vadim Lyubashevsky
Fermi Ma
Mimi Ma
Urmila Mahadev
Nikolaos Makriyannis
Giulio Malavolta
Damien Marion
Yoann Marquer
Giorgia Marson
Chloe Martindale
Ange Martinelli
Michael Meyer
Pierre Meyer
Andrew Miller
Brice Minaud
Ilya Mironov
Tal Moran
Saleet Mossel
Tamer Mour
Pratyay Mukherjee
Marta Mularczyk
Pierrick Méaux
Yusuke Naito
Joe Neeman
Patrick Neumann
Khoa Nguyen
Ngoc Khanh Nguyen
Phong Nguyen

Tuong-Huy Nguyen
Jesper Buus Nielsen
Ryo Nishimaki
Abderrahmane Nitaj
Anca Nitulescu
Lamine Noureddine
Adam O'Neill
Maciej Obremski
Cristina Onete
Michele Orru
Emmanuela Orsini
Carles Padro
Mahak Pancholi
Omer Paneth
Dimitris Papachristoudis
Sunoo Park
Anat Paskin-Cherniavsky
Alice Pellet-Mary
Olivier Pereira
Léo Perrin
Thomas Peters
Duy-Phuc Pham
Krzyszof Pietrzak
Jérôme Plût
Bertram Poettering
Yuriy Polyakov
Antigoni Polychroniadou
Alexander Poremba
Thomas Prest
Cassius Puodzius
Willy Quach
Anaïs Querol
Rahul Rachuri
Hugues Randriam
Adrian Ranea
Shahram Rasoolzadeh
Deevashwer Rathee
Mayank Rathee
Divya Ravi
Christian Rechberger
Michael Reichle
Jean-René Reinhard
Joost Renes
Nicolas Resch
João Ribeiro
Silas Richelson
Tania Richmond
Doreen Riepel
Peter Rindal
Miruna Rosca
Michael Rosenberg
Mélissa Rossi
Yann Rotella
Alex Russell
Théo Ryffel
Carla Ràfols
Paul Rösler
Rajeev Anand Sahu
Olga Sanina
Pratik Sarkar
Alessandra Scafuro
Christian Schaffner
Peter Scholl
Tobias Schmalz
Phillipp Schoppmann
André Schrottenloher
Jörg Schwenk
Adam Sealfon
Okan Seker
Jae Hong Seo
Karn Seth
Barak Shani
Abhi Shelat
Omri Shmueli
Victor Shoup
Hippolyte Signargout
Tjerand Silde
Mark Simkin
Luisa Siniscalchi
Daniel Slamanig
Benjamin Smith
Fang Song
Jana Sotáková
Pierre-Jean Spaenlehauer
Nicholas Spooner
Akshayaram Srinivasan
Damien Stehlé
Marc Stevens
Siwei Sun
Mehrdad Tahmasbi
Quan Quan Tan
Stefano Tessaro
Florian Thaeter
Aishwarya Thiruvengadam
Mehdi Tibouchi
Radu Titiu
Oleksandr Tkachenko
Yosuke Todo
Junichi Tomida
Ni Trieu
Eran Tromer
Daniel Tschudi
Giorgos Tsimos
Ida Tucker
Michael Tunstall
Akin Ünal
Dominique Unruh
Bogdan Ursu
Christine van Vredendaal
Wessel van Woerden
Marc Vauclair
Serge Vaudenay
Muthu Venkitasubramaniam
Damien Vergnaud
Gilles Villard
Fernando Virdia
Satyanarayana Vusirikala
Riad Wahby
Hendrik Waldner
Alexandre Wallet
Haoyang Wang
Hoeteck Wee
Weiqiang Wen
Benjamin Wesolowski
Jan Wichelmann
Luca Wilke
Mary Wootters
David Wu
Jiayu Xu
Sophia Yakoubov

Shota Yamada
Takashi Yamakawa
Sravya Yandamuri
Kang Yang
Lisa Yang
Kevin Yeo
Eylon Yogev
Greg Zaverucha
Mark Zhandry
Jiayu Zhang
Ruizhe Zhang
Yupeng Zhang
Vassilis Zikas
Paul Zimmermann
Dionysis Zindros

Contents – Part II

Masking and Secret-Sharing

Leakage, Faults and Tampering

Quantum Constructions and Proofs

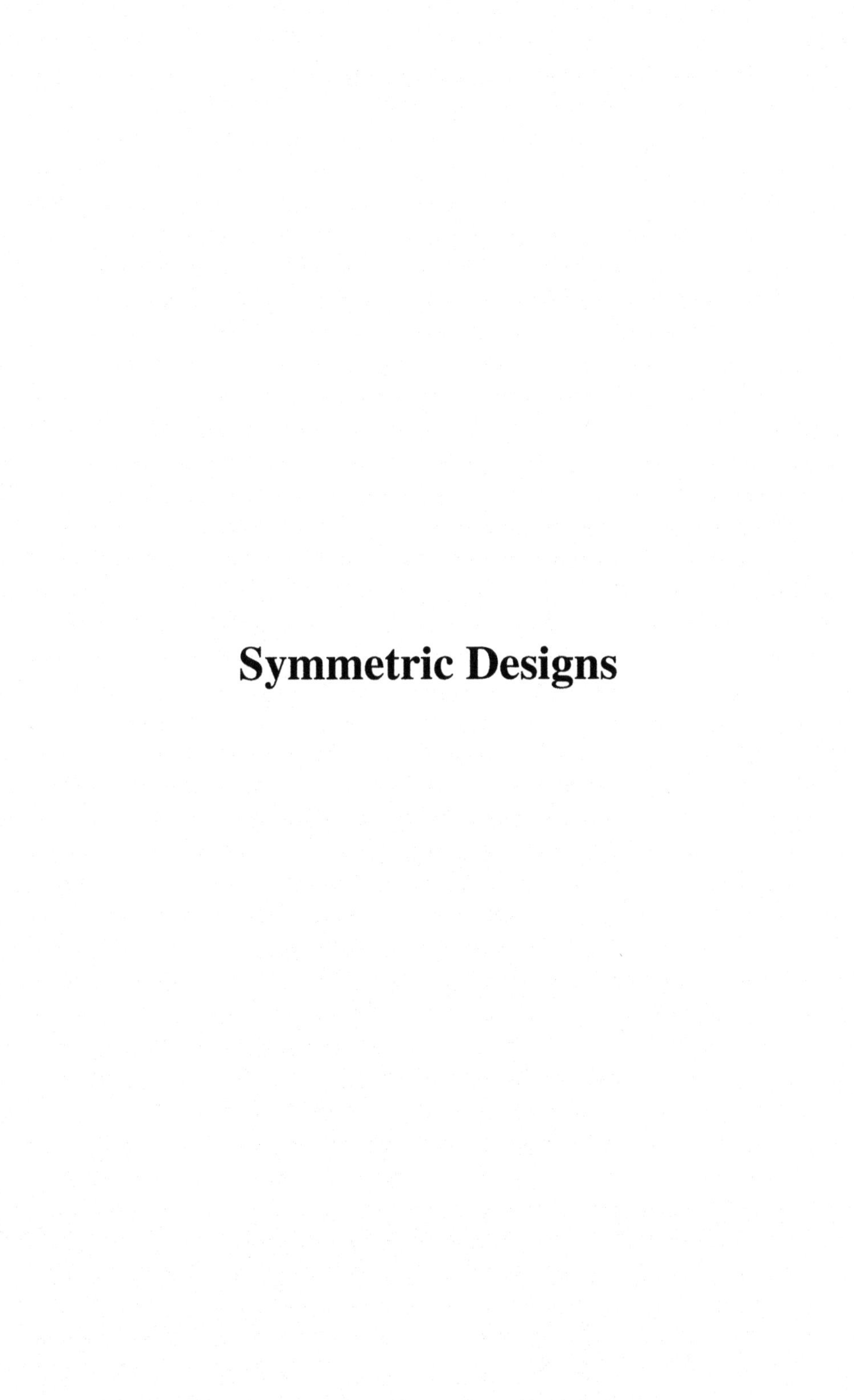

Symmetric Designs

CIMINION: Symmetric Encryption Based on Toffoli-Gates over Large Finite Fields

Christoph Dobraunig[1,2(✉)], Lorenzo Grassi[3(✉)], Anna Guinet[3(✉)], and Daniël Kuijsters[3(✉)]

[1] Lamarr Security Research, Graz, Austria
christoph.dobraunig@lamarr.at
[2] IAIK, Graz University of Technology, Graz, Austria
[3] Digital Security Group, Radboud University, Nijmegen, The Netherlands
lgrassi@science.ru.nl, email@annagui.net, Daniel.Kuijsters@ru.nl

Abstract. Motivated by new applications such as secure Multi-Party Computation (MPC), Fully Homomorphic Encryption (FHE), and Zero-Knowledge proofs (ZK), the need for symmetric encryption schemes that minimize the number of field multiplications in their natural algorithmic description is apparent. This development has brought forward many dedicated symmetric encryption schemes that minimize the number of multiplications in $\mathbb{F}_{2^n}$ or $\mathbb{F}_p$, with p being prime. These novel schemes have lead to new cryptanalytic insights that have broken many of said schemes. Interestingly, to the best of our knowledge, all of the newly proposed schemes that minimize the number of multiplications use those multiplications exclusively in S-boxes based on a power mapping that is typically x^3 or x^{-1}. Furthermore, most of those schemes rely on complex and resource-intensive linear layers to achieve a low multiplication count. In this paper, we present CIMINION, an encryption scheme minimizing the number of field multiplications in large binary or prime fields, while using a very lightweight linear layer. In contrast to other schemes that aim to minimize field multiplications in $\mathbb{F}_{2^n}$ or $\mathbb{F}_p$, CIMINION relies on the Toffoli gate to improve the non-linear diffusion of the overall design. In addition, we have tailored the primitive for the use in a Farfalle-like construction in order to minimize the number of rounds of the used primitive, and hence, the number of field multiplications as far as possible.

Keywords: Symmetric encryption · Low multiplicative complexity

1 Introduction

Recently, several symmetric schemes have been proposed to reduce the number of field multiplications in their natural algorithmic description, often referred to as the multiplicative complexity. These ciphers fall into two main categories. The first one contains ciphers that minimize the use of multiplications in $\mathbb{F}_2$, for instance, Flip [54], Keyvrium [22], LowMC [4], and Rasta [33]. The second category is comprised of ciphers having a natural description in larger fields, which are mostly

A. Canteaut and F.-X. Standaert (Eds.): EUROCRYPT 2021, LNCS 12697, pp. 3–34, 2021.
https://doi.org/10.1007/978-3-030-77886-6_1

binary fields $\mathbb{F}_{2^n}$ and prime fields $\mathbb{F}_p$. Examples include MiMC [3], GMiMC [2], Jarvis [8], Hades [41], Poseidon [40] and Vision and Rescue [6]. The design of low multiplicative complexity ciphers is motivated by applications such as secure Multi-Party Computation (MPC), Fully Homomorphic Encryption (FHE), and Zero-Knowledge proofs (ZK). These recent ciphers based on specialized designs highly outperform "traditionally" designed ones in these applications. The search of minimizing the multiplicative complexity while providing a sufficient security level is an opportunity to explore and evaluate innovative design strategies.

The sheer number of potentially devastating attacks on recently published designs implies that the design of schemes with low multiplicative complexity has not reached a mature state yet. Indeed, we count numerous attacks on variants of LowMC [32,59], Flip [35], MiMC [36], GMiMC [15,19], Jarvis [1], and Starkad/Poseidon [15]. Attacks that are performed on schemes defined for larger fields mostly exploit weaknesses of the algebraic cipher description, e.g., Gröbner bases attacks on Jarvis [1] or higher-order differential attacks on MiMC [36]. Nonetheless, attack vectors such as differential cryptanalysis [17] and linear cryptanalysis [52] do not appear to threaten the security of these designs. Indeed, the latter two techniques seem to be able to attack only a tiny fraction of the rounds compared to algebraic attacks.

Interestingly, the mentioned ciphers working over larger fields are inspired by design strategies proposed in the 1990s to mitigate differential cryptanalysis. For example, MiMC resembles the Knudsen-Nyberg cipher [56], Jarvis claims to be inspired by the design of Rijndael [27,28], while Hades, Vision, and Rescue take inspiration from Shark [60]. The latter ciphers have a linear layer that consists of the application of a single MDS matrix to the state. An important commonality between all those examples is a non-linear layer that operates on individual field elements, e.g., cubing single field elements or computing their inverse. Furthermore, design strategies naturally working over larger fields easily prevent differential cryptanalysis. However, algebraic attacks seem to be their main threat. Therefore, it is worth exploring different design strategies to increase the resistance against algebraic attacks.

Our Design: Ciminion. In that spirit, CIMINION offers a different design approach in which we do not apply non-linear transformations to individual field elements. Instead, we use the ability of the multiplication to provide non-linear diffusion between field elements. Our cipher is built upon the Toffoli gate [62], which is a simple non-linear bijection of field elements that transforms the triple (a, b, c) into the triple $(a, b, ab + c)$. The binary version of the Toffoli gate is used as a building block in modern ciphers, such as FRIET [61], which inspired our design. In addition to this, the S-box of Xoodoo [26] can also be described as the consecutive application of three binary Toffoli gates. With respect to the linear layer, we learned from ciphers like LowMC [4] that very heavy linear layers can have a considerably negative impact on the performance of applications [31]. Therefore, we decide to pair the Toffoli gate with a relatively lightweight linear layer to construct a cryptographic permutation on triples of field elements. Compared to the designs that use a non-linear bijection of a single field element, e.g., cubing in $\mathbb{F}_{2^n}$ for odd n, we can define our permutation on any field, and then provide a thorough security analysis for prime fields and binary fields.

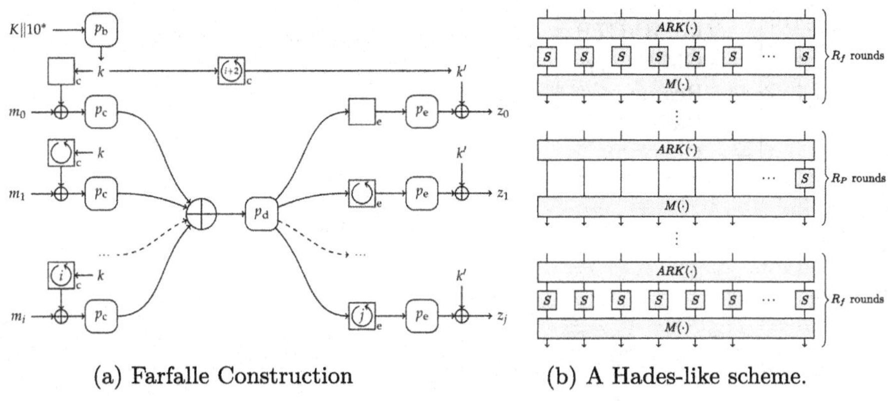

(a) Farfalle Construction (b) A Hades-like scheme.

Fig. 1. Comparison of a Farfalle construction and a Hades-like scheme.

We do not use a bare primitive in the applications, but we employ primitives in a mode of operation. Indeed, instead of constructing a primitive of low multiplicative complexity, our goal is to provide a cryptographic function of low multiplicative complexity. We achieve this by using a modified version of the Farfalle construction to make it possible to perform stream encryption. Farfalle [12] is an efficiently parallelizable permutation-based construction with a variable input and output length pseudorandom function (PRF). It is built upon a primitive, and modes are employed on top of it. The primitive is a PRF that takes as input a key with a string (or a sequence of strings), and produces an arbitrary-length output. The Farfalle construction involves two basic ingredients: a set of permutations of a b-bit state, and the so-called rolling function that is used to derive distinct b-bit mask values from a b-bit secret key, or to evolve the secret state. The Farfalle construction consists of a *compression layer* that is followed by an *expansion layer*. The compression layer produces a single b-bit accumulator value from a tuple of b-bit blocks representing the input data. The expansion layer first (non-linearly) transforms the accumulator value into a b-bit rolling state. Then, it (non-linearly) transforms a tuple of variants of this rolling state which are produced by iterating the rolling function, into a tuple of (truncated) b-bit output blocks. Both the compression and expansion layers involve b-bit mask values derived from the master key.

We slightly modify Farfalle (see Fig. 3) and instantiate it with two different permutations: p_C for the compression part, and p_E for the expansion part. Those two permutations are obtained by iterating the same round function, but with a different number of rounds. In our construction, the permutation p_C takes an input that is the concatenation of a nonce $\aleph$ and a secret key, and it derives a secret intermediate state from this input. Then, the intermediate state is updated by using a simple rolling function, and fixed intermediate keys. From this intermediate state, the keystream for encrypting the plaintext is derived by using the permutation p_E. In order to prevent backward computation, the outputs of the expansion layers are truncated. Our security analysis that is

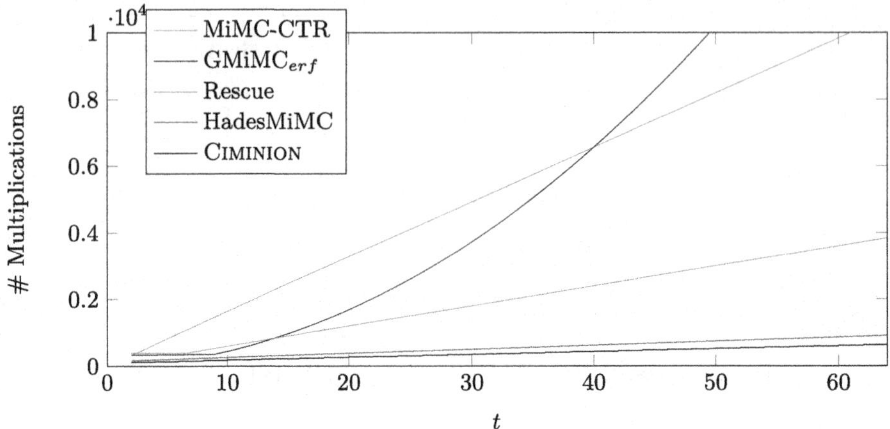

Fig. 2. Number of MPC multiplications of several designs over $(\mathbb{F}_p)^t$, with $p \approx 2^{128}$ and $t \geq 2$ (security level of 128 bits).

presented in Sect. 4 shows that p_E requires a significantly lower number of rounds than p_C. The relatively low number of multiplications that is used per encrypted plaintext element leads to a remarkably overall low multiplicative complexity. The full specification for CIMINION is presented in Sect. 2. A detailed rationale of the choices made during the design process is given in Sect. 3. A reference implementation can be found at https://github.com/ongetekend/ciminion.

A Concrete Use Case: Multi-party Computation. The primary motivation of our design is to explore the limits on the use of non-linear operations in cipher design, while limiting the use of linear operations, and ensuring a secure design. The main body of our paper is thus dedicated to cryptanalysis which is accompanied by one specific use-case, namely Secure Multi-Party Computation.

MPC is a subfield of cryptography that aims to create methods for parties to jointly compute a function over their inputs, without exposing these inputs. In recent years, MPC protocols have converged to a linearly homomorphic secret sharing scheme, whereby each participant is given a share of each secret value. Then, each participant locally adds shares of different secrets to generate the shares of the sum of the secrets. In order to get data securely in and out of a secret-sharing-based MPC system, an efficient solution is to directly evaluate a symmetric primitive within such system. In this setting, "traditional" PRFs based on, e.g., AES or SHA-3 are not efficient. Indeed, they were designed with different computing environments in mind. Hence, they work over data types that do not easily match the possible operations in the MPC application. As developed in [43], "traditional" PRFs like AES and SHA-3 are rather bit/byte/word-oriented schemes, which complicate their representation using arithmetic in $\mathbb{F}_p$ or/and $\mathbb{F}_{2^n}$ for large integer n, or prime p.

From a theoretical point of view, the problem of secure MPC is strongly connected to the problem of masking a cryptographic implementation. This observation has been made in [45,46]. The intuition behind is that both masking and MPC aim to perform computations on shared data. In more detail, the common strategy behind these techniques is to combine random and unknown masks with a shared secret value, and to perform operations on these masked values. Only at the end of the computation, the values are unmasked by combining them, in a manner that is defined by the masking scheme. In our scheme, we use a linear sharing scheme, because affine operations (e.g., additions, or multiplications with a constant) are non-interactive and resource efficient, unlike the multiplications that require some communication between the parties. The number of multiplications required to perform a computation is a good estimate of the complexity of an MPC protocol.

However, in practice, other factors influence the efficiency of a design. For instance, while one multiplication requires one round of communication, a batch of multiplications can be processed into a single round in many cases. In that regard, CIMINION makes it possible to batch several multiplications due to the parallel execution of p_E. Another alternative to speed up the processing of messages is to execute some communication rounds in an offline/pre-computation phase before receiving the input to the computation. This offline phase is cheaper than the online rounds. For example, in the case of CIMINION, precomputing several intermediate states is possible by applying p_C to different nonces $\aleph$. As a result, for the encryption of arriving messages, those intermediate states only have to be expanded, and processed by p_E to encrypt the plaintext.

Section 5 demonstrates that our design CIMINION has a lower number of multiplications compared to several other schemes working over larger fields. The comparison of the number of multiplications in MPC applications to the ciphers that are presented in the literature, is shown in Fig. 2, when working over a field $(\mathbb{F}_p)^t$ with $p \approx 2^{128}$ and $t \geq 1$, and with a security level of 128 bits (which the most common case in the literature). It indicates that our design needs approximately $t + 14 \cdot \lceil t/2 \rceil \approx 8 \cdot t$ multiplications compared to $12 \cdot t$ multiplications that are required by HadesMiMC, or $60 \cdot t$ multiplications that is needed by Rescue. These two schemes that have recently been proposed in the literature are our main competitors. Additionally, our design employs a low number of linear operations when compared with other designs present in the literature. Indeed, CIMINION grows linearly w.r.t. t, whereas the number of linear operations grows quadratically in HadesMiMC and Rescue. That is because their rounds are instantiated via the multiplication with a $t \times t$ MDS matrix. Even if the cost of a linear operation is considerably lower than the cost of a non-linear one in MPC applications, it is desirable to keep both numbers as low as possible. Our design has this advantage.

2 Specification

2.1 Mode

In order to create a nonce-based stream-encryption scheme, we propose to work with the mode of operation described in Fig. 3. First, the scheme takes a nonce

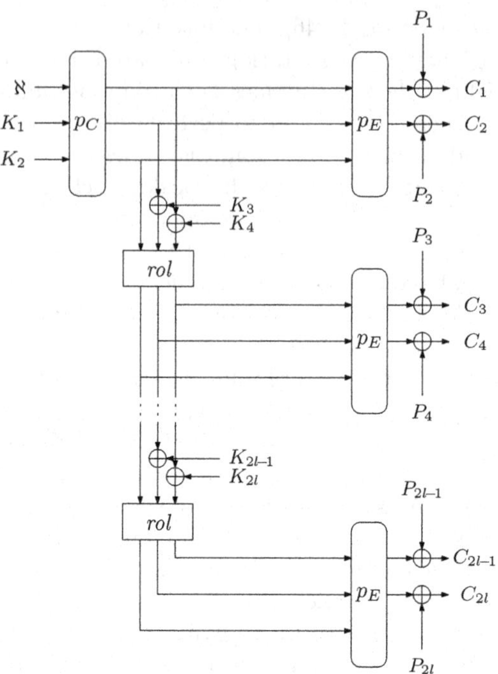

Fig. 3. Encryption with CIMINION over $\mathbb{F}_{2^n}$. The construction is similar over $\mathbb{F}_p$ ($\oplus$ is replaced by $+$, the addition modulo p).

ℵ along with two subkey elements K_1 and K_2 as input, and processes these input with a permutation p_C to output an intermediate state. This intermediate state is then processed by a permutation p_E, and truncated to two elements so that two plaintext elements P_1 and P_2 can be encrypted. If more elements need to be encrypted, the intermediate state can be expanded by repeatedly performing an addition of two subkey elements to the intermediate state, then followed by a call to the rolling function *rol*. After each call to the rolling function *rol*, two more plaintext elements P_{2i} and P_{2i+1} can be encrypted thanks to the application of p_E to the resulting state. We consider the field elements as atomic, and therefore, our mode can cope with a different number of elements without the need for padding. The algorithmic description of the mode of operation that is described in Fig. 3, is provided in [34, App. A. I].

2.2 Permutations

We describe two permutations of the vector space $\mathbb{F}_q^3$. They act on a *state* of triples $(a, b, c) \in \mathbb{F}_q^3$. The first permutation is defined for a prime number $q = p$ of $\log_2(p) \approx n$ bits, while the second permutation is specified for $q = 2^n$. Both permutations are the result of the repeated application of a round function. Their only difference is the number of repeated applications that we call *rounds*.

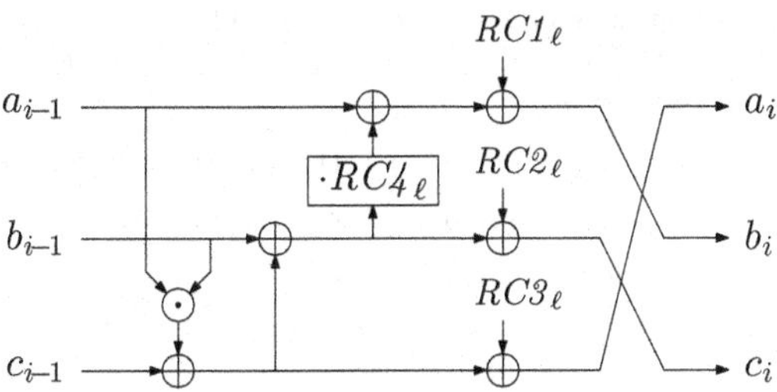

Fig. 4. Round function f_i.

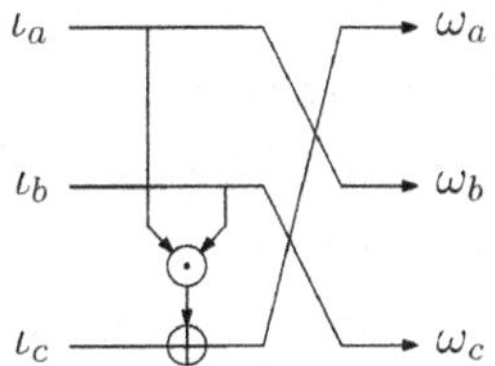

Fig. 5. *rol.*

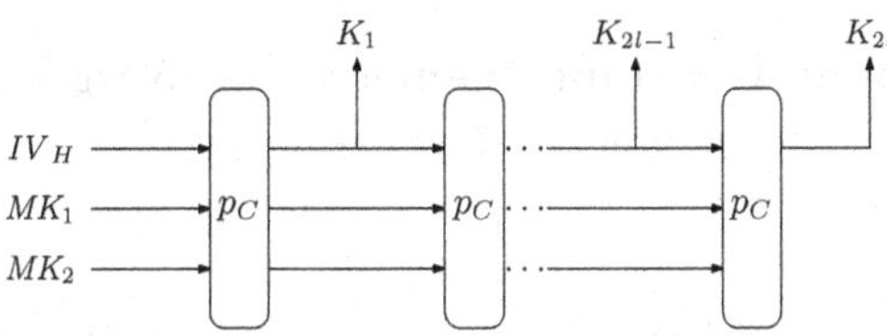

Fig. 6. Key generation.

As presented in Fig. 3, we employ two permutations p_C and p_E that have respectively N and R rounds.

Round Function. We write f_i for round i (Fig. 4). It uses four round constants RC_ℓ, with $\ell = i$ for p_C, and $\ell = i + N - R$ for p_E. We assume that $RC4_\ell \notin \{0, 1\}$. For each $i \geq 1$, f_i maps a state $(a_{i-1}, b_{i-1}, c_{i-1})$ at its input to the state (a_i, b_i, c_i) at its output, where the relation between these two states is

$$\begin{bmatrix} a_i \\ b_i \\ c_i \end{bmatrix} := \begin{bmatrix} 0 & 0 & 1 \\ 1 & RC4_\ell & RC4_\ell \\ 0 & 1 & 1 \end{bmatrix} \cdot \begin{bmatrix} a_{i-1} \\ b_{i-1} \\ c_{i-1} + a_{i-1} \cdot b_{i-1} \end{bmatrix} + \begin{bmatrix} RC3_\ell \\ RC1_\ell \\ RC2_\ell \end{bmatrix} .$$

2.3 The Rolling Function

Our rolling function *rol* is a simple NLFSR as depicted in Fig. 5. The rolling function takes three field elements ι_a, ι_b, and ι_c at the input. It outputs three field elements: $\omega_a := \iota_c + \iota_a \cdot \iota_b$, $\omega_b := \iota_a$, and $\omega_c := \iota_b$. The latter variables form the input of the permutation p_E in our Farfalle-like mode Fig. 3.

2.4 SubKeys and Round Constants

SubKeys Generation. We derive the SubKey material K_i from two master keys MK_1, and MK_2. As a result, the secret is shared in a compact manner, while the expanded key is usually stored on a device, and used when needed. To expand the key, we use the sponge construction [13] instantiated with the

Table 1. Proposed number of rounds based on f. The security level s must satisfy $64 \leq s \leq \log_2(q)$, and $q \geq 2^{64}$, where q is the number of elements in the field.

Instance	p_C	p_E (two output words per block)
Standard	$s+6$	$\max\left\{\left\lceil \frac{s+37}{12} \right\rceil, 6\right\}$
Data limit $2^{s/2}$ elements	$\frac{2(s+6)}{3}$	$\max\left\{\left\lceil \frac{s+37}{12} \right\rceil, 6\right\}$
Conservative	$s+6$	$\max\left\{\left(\left\lceil \frac{3}{2} \cdot \frac{s+37}{12} \right\rceil\right), 9\right\}$

permutation p_C (Fig. 6). The value IV_H can be made publicly available, and is typically set to one.

Round Constants Generation. We generate the round constants $RC1_\ell$, $RC2_\ell$, $RC3_\ell$, and $RC4_\ell$ with Shake-256 [14,55]. The detail is provided in [34, App. A].

2.5 Number of Rounds and Security Claim for Encryption

In this paper, we assume throughout that *the security level of* s *bits satisfies the condition* $64 \leq s \leq \lfloor \log_2(q) \rfloor$. This implies that $q \geq 2^{64}$.

In Table 1, we define three sets of round numbers for each permutation in our encryption scheme:

- The "standard" set guarantees s bit of security; in the following sections, we present our security analysis that supports the chosen number of rounds for this case.
- For our MPC application, we propose a number of rounds if the data available to the attacker is limited to $2^{s/2}$; our security analysis that supports the chosen number of rounds for this case is presented in [34, App. F].
- Finally, we present a "conservative" number of rounds where we arbitrarily decided to increase the number of rounds by 50% of the standard instance.

Since many cryptanalytic attacks become more difficult with an increased number of rounds, we encourage to study reduced-round variants of our design to facilitate third-party cryptanalysis, and to estimate the security margin. For this reason, it is possible to specify toy versions of our cipher, i.e., with $q < 2^{64}$ which aim at achieving, for example, only 32 bits of security.

3 Design Rationale

3.1 Mode of Operation

In order to provide encryption, our first design choice is to choose between a mode of operation that is built upon a block cipher or a cryptographic permutation. In either case, a datapath design is necessary. However, a block cipher requires an additional key schedule, unlike a cryptographic permutation. If a designer opts

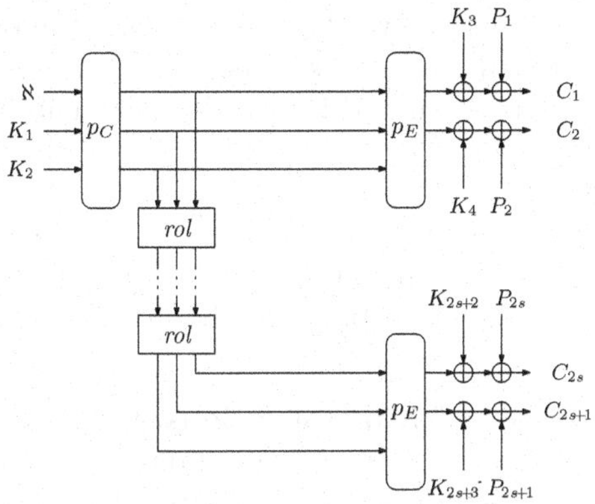

Fig. 7. Intermediate step in constructing Fig. 3

for a block cipher, the key schedule can be chosen to be either a non-linear, an affine, or a trivial transformation, where the round keys are equal to the master key apart from round constants. In this case, the designer has to be careful, because a poor key schedule leads to weaknesses and attacks [19]. Considering that the research in low multiplicative complexity ciphers is a relatively new research area, we decided to limit our focus to the essential components of a primitive. Therefore, we opted for permutation-based cryptography.

Since we consider the application of low multiplicative ciphers in areas that have enough resources to profit from parallel processing, we base our mode of operation on the Farfalle construction [12] as depicted in Fig. 1a. The Farfalle construction is a highly versatile construction that provides many functionalities.

A Modified Version of Farfalle. As already mentioned in the introduction, our mode of operation resembles the Farfalle construction. In this section, we explain and support the modifications that we performed on the original Farfalle construction, as depicted in Fig. 1a. The aim of those modifications is to both increase the resistance of the construction against algebraic attacks which are the most competitive ones in our scenario, and to increase its efficiency in our target application scenario, that is to say to minimize the number of multiplications. We focus first on the security aspect, before explaining in further detail how we reach our efficiency goal.

Our first modification is for simplicity. Since the functionality provided by the Farfalle construction to compress information is not needed, we merge p_c and p_d to a single permutation p_C.

Our second modification is to truncate the output. This prevents meet-in-the-middle style attacks that require the knowledge of the full output.

The third modification is to manipulate different keys K_i (see Fig. 7) instead of employing the same key k' for each output block. Since we aim to have a permutation with a low degree, Gröbner bases are the main threat. For the scheme that is depicted in Fig. 7, an attacker has to exploit equations of the form $f(x) + K_i = y$ and $f(x') + K_i = y'$, with $f(x) - f(x') = y - y'$ for a Gröbner basis attack. We describe this scenario in more detail in Sect. 4.4.

Our last modification is to move the keys K_i from the output of p_E to the input of our rolling function, and hence, effectively to the input of p_E (Fig. 3). Figure 3 is our final construction, and it provides two main benefits. First, having the keys at the input does not make it possible to easily cancel them by computing the difference of the output as described before. Hence, this adds an additional barrier in mounting successful Gröbner basis attacks. Second, we can use a simple non-linear rolling function, because the addition of the key stream during the rolling function prevents the attacker from easily detecting short cycles within it.

Minimizing the Number of Multiplications. One main reason to use the Farfalle construction is that its three permutations p_c, p_d, and p_e do not have to provide protection against all possible attack vectors. Indeed, the permutation p_e alone does not have to provide resistance against higher-order differential attacks [48,50]. The latter are particular algebraic attacks that exploit the low degree polynomial descriptions of the scheme. Resistance against higher-order differential attacks (higher-order attacks in short) can be provided by the permutations p_c, and p_d, and it inherently depends on the algebraic degree that a permutation achieves. Hence, requiring protection against higher-order attacks provides a lower bound on the number of multiplications that are needed in a permutation. In a nutshell, since p_e does not have to be secure against higher-order attacks, we can use a permutation with fewer multiplications. This benefits the multiplication count of the scheme, since the permutations p_c and p_d are called only once independently of the number of output words.

The Rolling Function. An integral part of the Farfalle construction is the rolling function *rol*. The permutations p_c and p_e (Fig. 1a) in the Farfalle construction are usually chosen to be very lightweight, such that the algebraic degree is relatively low. Hence, to prevent higher-order attacks, the rolling function is chosen to be non-linear. In our modified version, the same is true up to the intermediate construction as depicted in Fig. 7. In this case, *rol* has to be non-linear in order to use a permutation p_E of low degree. For our final construction (Fig. 3), we do not see any straightforward way to exploit higher-order attacks due to the unknown keys at the inputs of p_E. Thus, we could use a linear rolling function *rol*, but we rather choose to use a simple non-linear *rol* for CIMINION. That is because it makes it possible to analyze the security of Fig. 7, and to keep the same conclusion when we opt for the stronger version of Fig. 3. In addition, we present AIMINION in [34, App. B], a version of our design that does not follow this line of reasoning. AIMINION uses a linear rolling function, and nine rounds of p_E. We deem this version to be an interesting target for further analysis that aims to evaluate the security impact of switching from a non-linear to a linear rolling function.

Generating the Subkeys. Instead of sharing all subkeys K_i directly by communicating parties to encrypt messages, we specify a derivation of the subkeys K_i from two master keys MK_1, and MK_2. These subkeys can be generated in a single precomputation step. For the storage of the subkeys, trade-offs can be made to store as many subkeys as needed, and to split messages into lengths that match the stored subkey lengths.

3.2 The Round Function

Our round function is composed of three layers: a non-linear transformation, a linear transformation, and a round constant addition. Like classical designs, we employ the same non-linear and linear transformations for each round, but with different round constant additions. This makes it easier to implement, and to reduce code-size and area requirements. Nonetheless, some primitives that have been designed to lower the multiplicative complexity use a different linear layer for each round, like in LowMC [4].

Non-linear Transformation. Most primitives operating in large fields have a variant of powering field elements, e.g., x^3 or x^{-1}. These mappings became popular to guard against linear and differential cryptanalysis due to their properties [56]. The most popular design that uses such mappings is the AES [28], where x^{-1} is used as part of its S-box. For ciphers that aim at a low multiplicative complexity, these power mappings are interesting because they often have an inverse of high degree, which provides protection against algebraic attacks. However, they impose some restrictions, e.g., the map $x \mapsto x^\alpha$ for integer $\alpha \geq 2$ is a bijection in $\mathbb{F}_q$ if and only if $\gcd(q-1, \alpha) = 1$ (e.g., $x \mapsto x^3$ is a permutation over $\mathbb{F}_{2^n}$ for odd n only). Hence, one has to consider several power values α in order for x^α to stay a permutation for any field. In a design that should make it possible to be instantiated for a wide variety of fields, considering those special cases complicates the design of the cipher.

Instead of a power mapping, the non-linear element in our designs is the Toffoli gate [62]. Indeed, algebraic attacks are the main threat against designs aiming to lower the multiplicative complexity, and the multiplications are the main cost factor in our design. It thus seems counter intuitive to spend the non-linear element on simply manipulating a single field element, as is the case for power mappings. Therefore, we choose to multiply two elements of the state, instead of operating on a single state element, in order to increase the non-linear diffusion. Furthermore, the Toffoli gate is a permutation for any field, and therefore we are not restricted to a specific field. We mitigate potential negative effects of the property of the Toffoli gate to provide the same degree in forward and backward direction by mandating its use only in modes that truncate the permutation output, and that never evaluate its inverse using the secret key.

Linear Transformation. We present the linear transformation in its matrix form, the coefficients of which must be carefully chosen. One possibility is to use an MDS matrix. Since an MDS matrix has the highest branch number [24] among all possible matrices, it plays an important role in proving lower bounds on the linear and differential trail weight. However, we do not need to rely on MDS matrices as the field multiplications already have advantageous properties against linear and differential attacks.

Another option is to randomly choose the coefficients of the matrix for each round, and then verify that the matrix is invertible. This strategy was used in one of the first low multiplicative complexity designs, namely LowMC [4]. However, the drawback is that random matrices contribute significantly to the cost of the primitive in some scenarios, and the security analysis becomes more involved. Hence, we have decided to use a much simpler linear layer.

In order to provide sufficient diffusion, complex equation systems, and low multiplicative complexity, the degree of the functions that output equations depending on the input variables must grow as fast as possible. By applying a single multiplication per round, the degree doubles per round in the best scenario. However, this also depends on the linear layer. For instance, this layer could be a simple layer permuting the elements (e.g., the 3×3 circulant matrix $circ(0,0,1)$), for which the univariate degree of a single element only grows according to a Fibonacci sequence. To ensure that the univariate degree of a single element doubles per round, the result of the previous multiplication has to be reused in the multiplication of the next round. This is also applicable to the inverse of the permutation. Hence, we decided to use the following matrix for the linear layer:

$$M = \begin{bmatrix} 0 & 0 & 1 \\ 1 & RC4 & RC4 \\ 0 & 1 & 1 \end{bmatrix} \qquad \text{(and} \qquad M^{-1} = \begin{bmatrix} 0 & 1 & -RC4 \\ -1 & 0 & 1 \\ 1 & 0 & 0 \end{bmatrix} \text{)},$$

Here, $M_{0,2}, M_{1,2}, {M^{-1}}_{0,2}, {M^{-1}}_{1,2} \neq 0$ with $M_{i,j}$ denoting the element of the matrix M at row i and column j. The use of the round constant $RC4 \notin \{0,1\}$ is motivated by aiming to improve the diffusion, and to avoid a weakness with respect to linear cryptanalysis that we discuss in Sect. 4.1.

About Quadratic Functions. In addition to the matrix multiplication, another (semi-)linear transformation[1] over a binary field $\mathbb{F}_{2^n}$ is the quadratic permutation $x \mapsto x^2$. This transformation can be exploited as a component in the round function (e.g., as a replacement of the multiplication by $RC4$) to both increase the diffusion and the overall degree of the function that describes the scheme. However, we do not employ it for several reasons. First, even if the quadratic permutation is linear over $\mathbb{F}_{2^n}$, its cost in an application like MPC might not be negligible. Indeed, the quadratic permutation costs one multiplication as detailed in [43]. As a result, even if it makes it possible to reduce the overall number of rounds due to a faster growth of the degree, the overall number of multiplications[2] would not change for applications like MPC. Secondly, the quadratic function is not a permutation over $\mathbb{F}_p$ for a prime $p \neq 2$. Thus, its introduction implies having to work with two different round functions: one for the binary case and one for the prime case. Since our goal is to present a simple and elegant general scheme, we decided not to use it.

Round Constants. The round constants break up the symmetry in the design. They prevent the simplification of the algebraic description of the round function. However, as we manipulate many round constants, and since they influence

[1] A function f over $(\mathbb{F}, +)$ is semi-linear if for each $x, y \in \mathbb{F}$: $f(x+y) = f(x) + f(y)$. It is linear if it is semi-linear and if for each $x \in \mathbb{F}$: $f(\alpha \cdot x) = \alpha \cdot f(x)$.

[2] A minimum number of multiplications is required to reach maximum degree, which is one of the property required by a cryptographic scheme to be secure.

the rounds in a complex manner, we use an extendable output function to obtain round constant values without an obvious structure. We performed some experiments where we added round constants to one or two state elements. These instances provided simpler algebraic descriptions. Considering the small costs of manipulating dense round constants, we decide to use three round constants to complicate the algebraic description of the cipher, even after a few rounds.

4 Security Analysis

We present our security analysis of CIMINION with respect to "standard" application of the attacks that are found in the literature. This analysis determines the required number of rounds to provide some level of confidence in its security. Due to page limitation, further analysis is presented in the full version of the paper.

First and foremost, the number of rounds that guarantees security up to s bits are computed under the assumption that the data available to the attacker is limited to 2^s, except if specified in a different way. Moreover, we do not make any claim about the security against related-key attacks and known- or chosen-key distinguishers (including the zero-sum partitions). The latter are out the scope of this paper.

We observe that the attack vectors penetrating the highest number of rounds are algebraic attacks. On the contrary, traditional attacks, such as differential and linear cryptanalysis, are infeasible after a small number of rounds. As detailed in the following, in order to protect against algebraic attacks and higher-order differential attacks, we increase the number of rounds proportionally to the security level s. A constant number of rounds is added to prevent an adversary from guessing part of the key or the initial or middle state, or to linearize part of the state. Hence, the numbers of rounds for p_C and p_E are respectively $s+6$ and $\lceil \frac{s+19}{12} + 1.5 \rceil$ for the standard security level.

4.1 Linear Cryptanalysis

Linear cryptanalysis [52] is a known-plaintext attack that abuses high *correlations* [25] between sums of input bits and sums of output bits of a cryptographic primitive. However, classical correlation analysis is not restricted to solely primitives operating on elements of binary fields. In this section, we apply the existing theory developed by Baignères et al. [9] for correlation analysis of primitives that operate on elements of arbitrary sets to the permutations defined in Sect. 2.

General Correlation Analysis. An application of the theory to ciphers operating on elements of binary fields is presented by Daemen and Rijmen [29]. In this section, we apply the theory to the more general case of primitives operating on elements of $\mathbb{F}_q$ where $q = p^n$. Henceforth, we suppose that $f : (\mathbb{F}_q)^l \to (\mathbb{F}_q)^m$.

Correlation analysis is the study of *characters*, and their configuration in the l-dimensional vector space $L^2((\mathbb{F}_q)^l)$ of complex-valued functions $(\mathbb{F}_q)^l \to \mathbb{C}$. The space $L^2((\mathbb{F}_q)^l)$ comes with the inner product $\langle g, h\rangle = \sum g(x)\overline{h(x)}$, which defines the norm $\|g\| = \sqrt{\langle g, g\rangle} = q^{\frac{l}{2}}$.

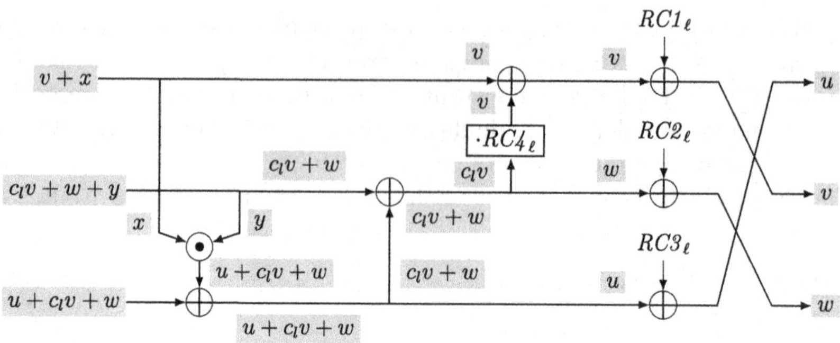

Fig. 8. Mask propagation in f

A character is an additive homomorphism from $(\mathbb{F}_q)^l$ into $S := \{z \in \mathbb{C} : |z| = 1\}$. It is well-known that *any* character on $(\mathbb{F}_q)^l$ is of the form

$$\chi_u(x) = e^{\frac{2\pi i}{p}\operatorname{Tr}_p^q(u^\top x)},$$

for some $u \in (\mathbb{F}_q)^l$. We recall that for $q = 2$ we have that $\chi_u(x) = (-1)^{u^\top x}$, which appears in classical correlation analysis. Here, $\operatorname{Tr}_p^q(x) = x + x^2 + \cdots + x^{p^{l-1}} \in \mathbb{F}_p$ is the *trace function*. For this reason, $u^\top x$ is called a *vectorial trace parity* and u a *trace mask vector*. We call the ordered pair (u, v) a linear approximation of f, where u is understood to be the mask at the input and v to be the mask at the output of f.

We define the vectorial trace parity correlation in the following definition.

Definition 1 (Correlation).

$$\mathrm{C}_f(u, v) = \frac{\langle \mu_u, \mu_v \circ f\rangle}{\|\mu_u\|\|\mu_v \circ f\|} = \frac{1}{q^l}\sum_{x\in(\mathbb{F}_q)^l} e^{\frac{2\pi i}{p}\operatorname{Tr}_p^q(u^\top x - v^\top f(x))}$$

This helps us to define a more general linear probability metric as follows.

Definition 2 (Linear probability). $\mathrm{LP}_f(u, v) = |\,\mathrm{C}_f(u, v)|^2$

The idea is then to consider the permutation as a circuit made of simple building blocks. Those blocks correspond to the operators that we apply, and for which we attach to each edge a trace mask vector. Importantly, these trace mask vectors are in one-to-one correspondence with characters. The goal of the attacker is to construct a linear trail from the end of the permutation to the beginning, with the goal of maximizing the linear probability of each building block. A list of the linear probabilities of each such building block can be found in [34, App. C.2] to deduce the result of the analysis.

On Three-Round Linear Trails. Figure 8 illustrates how the linear masks propagate through the round function when the linear probabilities of all building blocks are maximized. In this Figure, $c_\ell := RC4_\ell$. The attacker is able to choose

u, v, and w freely at the beginning of the first round, and afterwards, a mask at the input of the next round is determined by a mask at the output of the former round. We write R_i for the i'th round function. Moreover, we use the notation $c_{ij} := c_i c_j$ and $c_{ijk} := c_i c_j c_k$, where the subscript refers to the round number. The masks evolve as follows:

$$\begin{pmatrix} u \\ v \\ w \end{pmatrix} \xrightarrow{R_0} \begin{pmatrix} v \\ c_1 v + w \\ u + c_1 v + w \end{pmatrix} \xrightarrow{R_1} \begin{pmatrix} c_1 v + w \\ u + (c_1 + c_{12})v + (1 + c_2)w \\ u + (1 + c_1 + c_{12})v + (1 + c_2)w \end{pmatrix}$$

$$\xrightarrow{R_2} \begin{pmatrix} u + (c_1 + c_{12})v + (1 + c_2)w \\ (1 + c_3)u + (1 + c_1 + c_{12} + c_{13} + c_{123})v + (1 + c_2 + c_3 + c_{23})w \\ (1 + c_3)u + (1 + 2c_1 + c_{13} + c_{12} + c_{123})v + (2 + c_2 + c_3 + c_{23})w \end{pmatrix}.$$

An implicit assumption in both Fig. 8, and the mask derivation above, is that the masks at the output of the multiplication and at the input of the third branch are equal. However, an attacker can only make sure that this assumption is valid if the following system of equations has a non-zero solution:

$$\begin{pmatrix} 1 & c_1 & 1 \\ 1 & 1 + c_1 + c_{12} & 1 + c_2 \\ 1 + c_3 & 1 + 2c_1 + c_{13} + c_{12} + c_{123} & 2 + c_2 + c_3 + c_{23} \end{pmatrix} \begin{pmatrix} u \\ v \\ w \end{pmatrix} = \begin{pmatrix} 0 \\ 0 \\ 0 \end{pmatrix}.$$

If we denote by A the matrix above, then this happens if and only if the matrix is singular, i.e., if $\det(A) = c_2 c_3 + 1 = 0$. If either c_2 or c_3 is equal to zero, then the condition does not hold. If both are non-zero, then the condition is equivalent to requiring that $c_2 = -c_3^{-1}$. In this case, we can freely choose one value, which determines the other. Hence, the probability that the condition holds is equal to $\frac{q-1}{q^2} < \frac{1}{q}$. Since $\log_2(q)$ is the security parameter, this probability is negligible and there exists no three-round trail with a linear probability of 1.

Clustering of Linear Trails. We have $\mathrm{LP}_f(u, v) \geq \sum_{Q \in \mathrm{LT}_f(u,v)} \mathrm{LP}(Q)$, where $\mathrm{LT}_f(u, v)$ is the set of linear trails contained in (u, v). If we suppose now that an attacker is able to find more than q linear trails, i.e., if $|\mathrm{LT}_f(u, v)| > q$, then we have $\mathrm{LP}_f(u, v) > \frac{1}{q}$. However, $\log_2(q)$ is the security parameter, therefore the latter condition is not feasible. In a nutshell, three rounds are sufficient to resist against linear cryptanalysis.

Round Constant Multiplication Necessity. If the multiplication by the round constant is not present, or $RC4_\ell = 1$, then the masks evolve as follows over a single round:

$$\begin{pmatrix} u \\ v \\ w \end{pmatrix} \xrightarrow{f^{-1}} \begin{pmatrix} v + x \\ v + w + y \\ u + v + w \end{pmatrix} \xrightarrow{\text{if } u=v \text{ and } x=y=w=0} \begin{pmatrix} v \\ v \\ 0 \end{pmatrix} \xrightarrow{f^{-1}} \begin{pmatrix} v \\ v \\ 2v \end{pmatrix},$$

where (x, y) is the mask vector at the input of the multiplication function, which, like u, v, and w, can be freely chosen. Hence, if we choose $u = v$, and $x = y = w = 0$, and since the characteristic of the field is equal to two, then a one-round approximation with a linear probability of one can be chained indefinitely. This is the reason behind including a multiplication by a non-trivial constant.

4.2 Differential Cryptanalysis

Differential cryptanalysis exploits the probability distribution of a non-zero input difference leading to an output difference after a given number of rounds [17]. As CIMINION is an iterated cipher, a cryptanalyst searches for ordered sequences of differences over r rounds that are called *differential characteristics/trails.* A differential trail has a Differential Probability (DP). Assuming the independence of the rounds, the DP of a differential trail is the product of the DPs of its one-round differences (Definition 3).

Definition 3 (One-round differential probability). *Let* $(\alpha_a, \alpha_b, \alpha_c) \in (\mathbb{F}_p)^3$ *be the input of the round, and* $(\alpha_a^*, \alpha_b^*, \alpha_c^*) \in (\mathbb{F}_p)^3$ *the chosen non-zero input difference. The probability that an input difference is mapped to an output difference* $(\beta_a^*, \beta_b^*, \beta_c^*) \in (\mathbb{F}_p)^3$ *through one iteration of the round function* f *is equal to*

$$\frac{|f(\alpha_a^* + \alpha_a, \alpha_b^* + \alpha_b, \alpha_c^* + \alpha_c) - f(\alpha_a, \alpha_b, \alpha_c) = (\beta_a^*, \beta_b^*, \beta_c^*)|}{|(\mathbb{F}_p)^3|}.$$

The operation $+$ *is replaced by* $\oplus$ *in* $\mathbb{F}_{2^n}$*.*

However, in general, the attacker does not have any information about the intermediate differences of the differential trail. Hence, the attacker only fixes the input and the output differences over r rounds, and works with *differentials.* A differential is a collection of differential trails with fixed input and output differences, and free intermediate differences. The DP of a differential over r rounds is the sum of all DPs of the differential trails that have the same input and output difference over the same number of rounds as the differential.

In this paper, we perform the differential cryptanalysis by grouping fixed differences in *sets.* Those sets impose some conditions to satisfy between the differences of the branches of the round, and/or specify that some differences at the input of the branches equal zero. Then, given an input difference, we study the possible sets of output differences after a round, and we determine the DP that an input difference is mapped into an output difference over a round. The goal is to find the longest differential trail with the highest DP.

Toward this end, we build a state finite machine (more details in [34, App. C.3]) that represents all the encountered sets of differences as states associated to their differential probabilities. To construct the graph, we start with a difference of the form $\{(0, 0, x) | x \neq 0\}$, and we search for the possible sets of output differences until we have explored all the possibilities from each newly reached set. Hereafter, let us assume that the difference x is not zero. We see that an input difference from $\{(0, 0, x)\}$ is mapped into an output difference of the form $\{(x, RC4_\ell x, x)\}$ after one round with probability one. Indeed, since the input difference goes through the non-linear operation and stays unchanged, the output difference is simply the result of the linear operation applied to the input difference. For the other cases, a non-zero input difference propagates to an output difference over one round with probability equal to p^{-1} in $\mathbb{F}_p$, or 2^{-n} in $\mathbb{F}_{2^n}$. From those results, we determine the differential over three rounds with the highest DP.

On Three-Round Differentials. The differential trail in $\mathbb{F}_p$ with the highest DP is

$$\{(0,0,x)\} \xrightarrow{\text{prob. } 1} \{(x, RC4_\ell x, x)\} \xrightarrow{\text{prob. } p^{-1}} \{(-RC4_\ell x, x, 0)\} \xrightarrow{\text{prob. } p^{-1}} \{(0,0,x)\},$$

where the fixed input difference x is equal to another fixed value in the following rounds, and satisfies the conditions imposed by the set (for details see [34, App. C.3]). Additionally, this differential trail holds if and only if the round constant $RC4_\ell$ introduced by the first round is equal to the round constant $RC4_\ell$ of the third round.

In $\mathbb{F}_{2^n}$, we obtain almost the same state finite machine as in $\mathbb{F}_p$. The only exception is that the set of differences $\{(-RC4_\ell x, x, 0)\}$ corresponds to $\{(RC4_\ell x, x, 0)\}$, because $-z$ is equal to z for each $z \in \mathbb{F}_{2^n}$. Hence, the differential trail in $\mathbb{F}_{2^n}$ with the highest DP is

$$\{(0,0,x)\} \xrightarrow{\text{prob. } 1} \{(x, RC4_\ell x, x)\} \xrightarrow{\text{prob. } 2^{-n}} \{(RC4_\ell x, x, 0)\} \xrightarrow{\text{prob. } 2^{-n}} \{(0,0,x)\},$$

under the same conditions that in $\mathbb{F}_p$.

In summary, a fixed difference from $\{(0,0,x)\}$ is mapped to the difference of the form $\{(x, RC4_\ell x, x)\}$ after one round with probability one in $\mathbb{F}_{2^n}$ and in $\mathbb{F}_p$. Moreover an input difference can be mapped to an output difference of the form $\{(0,0,x)\}$ with DP p^{-1} (resp. 2^{-n}) if and only if this difference is of the form $\{(-RC4_\ell x, x, 0)\}$. This means that the *only* possible differential trail over three rounds with input and output differences of the form $\{(0,0,x)\}$ are the ones given before. The DP of this differential trail is expressed in the following Lemma.

Lemma 1. *A differential trail over three rounds has a probability at most equal to p^{-2} in $\mathbb{F}_p$ and 2^{-2n} in $\mathbb{F}_{2^n}$.*

The DP of all other differential trails over three round are at most equal to p^{-3} in $\mathbb{F}_p$ and 2^{-3n} in $\mathbb{F}_{2^n}$. Since the security level s satisfies $s \leq \log_2(p)$ in $\mathbb{F}_p$ and $s \leq n$ in $\mathbb{F}_{2^n}$, we therefore conjecture that three rounds are sufficient to guarantee security against "basic" differential distinguishers. We thus choose to have at least six rounds for the permutations p_E and p_C, which is twice the number of rounds necessary to guarantee security against "basic" differential/linear distinguishers. The minimal number of rounds for the permutations should provide security against more advanced statistical distinguishers.

4.3 Higher-Order Differential and Interpolation Attacks

If a cryptographic scheme has a simple algebraic representation, higher-order attacks [48,50] and interpolation attack [47] have to be considered. In this part, we only focus on higher-order differential attacks. We conjecture that the number of rounds necessary to prevent higher-order differential attacks is also sufficient to prevent interpolation attacks (see details in [34, App. D]). This result is not novel, and the same applies for other schemes, like MiMC, as further explained in [36].

Background. We recall from Fig. 3 that an attacker can only directly manipulate a single element, and the two other elements are the secret subkeys. We therefore operate with this single element to input value sets, while keeping the two other elements fixed. Each output element is the result of a non-linear function depending on the input element x, and two fixed elements that are the input of the permutation. Thus, we have $f_N(x) = p(x, const, const)$ in $\mathbb{F}_{2^n}$, and $f_p(x) = p(x, const, const)$ in $\mathbb{F}_p$.

A given function f_p over prime fields $\mathbb{F}_p$ is represented by $f_p(x) = \sum_{i=0}^{p-1} \kappa_i x^i$ with constants $\kappa_i \in \mathbb{F}_p$. The degree of the function $f_p(x)$ that we denote by $d_{\mathbb{F}_p}$, corresponds to the highest value i for which $\kappa_i \neq 0$. The same holds for a function f_n working over binary extension fields $\mathbb{F}_{2^n}$. For the latter, $f_N(x) = \bigoplus_{i=0}^{d} \kappa_i x^i$ with $\kappa_i \in \mathbb{F}_{2^n}$, and $d_{\mathbb{F}_{2^n}}$ is the degree of the function $f_n(x)$. Like previously, the degree is the highest value i for which $\kappa_i \neq 0$. In $\mathbb{F}_{2^n}$, the function can as well be represented by its algebraic norm form (ANF) $\overrightarrow{f_n}(x_1, \ldots, x_n)$, whose output element j is defined by its coordinate function $f_{n,j}(x_1, \ldots, x_n) = \bigoplus_{u=(u_1,\ldots,u_2)} \kappa_{j,u} \cdot x_1^{u_1} \cdot \ldots \cdot x_n^{u_n}$ with $\kappa_{j,u} \in \mathbb{F}_2$. The degree $d_{\mathbb{F}_2^n}$of $\overrightarrow{f_n}$ corresponds to the maximal Hamming weight of u for which $\kappa_{j,u} \neq 0$, that is to say $d_{\mathbb{F}_2^n} = \max_{i \leq d}\{hw(i) \mid \kappa_i \neq 0\}$.

For the last representation, as proved by Lai [50] and in[48], if we iterate over a vector space $\mathcal{V}$ having a dimension strictly higher than $d_{\mathbb{F}_2^n}$, we obtain the following result: $\bigoplus_{v \in \mathcal{V} \oplus \nu} f_n(v) = 0$. A similar result has also been recently presented for the prime case in [36, Proposition 2]. More precisely, if the degree of $f_p(x)$ is $d_{\mathbb{F}_p}$, then iterating over all elements of a multiplicative subgroup $\mathcal{G}$ of $\mathbb{F}_p^t$ of size $|\mathcal{G}| > d_{\mathbb{F}_p}$ leads to $\sum_{x \in \mathcal{G}} f_p(x) = f_p(0) \cdot |\mathcal{G}|$. The last sum is equal to zero modulo p since $|\mathcal{G}|$ is a multiple of p.

In order to provide security against higher-order differential attacks based on the presented zero-sums, we choose the number of rounds of our permutation to have a function of a degree higher than our security claim.

Overview of our Security Argument. In our construction, we assume that an attacker can choose the nonce $\aleph$, which is the input of the permutation p_C. For the first call of this permutation, we want to prevent an attacker to input value sets that always result in the same constant after the application of the permutation p_C. This requirement is necessary, since we assume in the remaining analysis that the output values of p_C are unpredictable by an attacker. We emphasize that if the output of the permutation p_C is guaranteed to be randomly distributed, then this is sufficient to prevent higher-order differential attacks. That is because the inverse of the final permutations p_E is never evaluated, and the attacker cannot construct an affine subspace in the middle of the construction.

Estimating the Degree of p_C: Necessary Number of Rounds. We study the evolution of the degrees $d_{\mathbb{F}_p}$ and $d_{\mathbb{F}_{2^n}}$ for the permutation p_C for which the round function f (Fig. 3) is iterated r times. We conclude that the degree of the permutation p_C remains unchanged for two rounds, if an input element is present at branch a, and the input at the branch b is zero. For a higher number of rounds, the degree increases. We have chosen the affine layer to ensure that the output of the multiplication can affect both inputs of the multiplication in the next round. This should make it possible for the maximal possible degree of the output functions to increase faster than having affine layers without this property. In the best case, the maximal degree of the function can be doubled per round.

Considering both previous observations, a minimum of $s + 2$ rounds are required to obtain at least $d_{\mathbb{F}_p} \approx 2^s$, or $d_{\mathbb{F}_{2^n}} \approx 2^s$. As we want to ensure that the polynomial representation of p_C is dense, it is then advisable to add more rounds as a safety margin. In order to reach this goal, we arbitrarily decided to add four more rounds.

4.4 Gröbner Basis Attacks

Preliminary. To perform a Gröbner basis [21] attack, the adversary constructs a system of algebraic equations that represents the cipher. Finding the solution of those equations makes it possible for the attacker to recover the key that is denoted by the unknown variables $x_1, ..., x_n$ hereafter. In order to solve this system of equations, the attacker considers the *ideal* generated by the multivariate polynomials that define the system. A *Gröbner basis* is a particular generating set of the ideal. It is defined with respect to a total ordering on the set of monomials, in particular the lexicographic order. As a Gröbner basis with respect to the lexicographic order is of the form

$$\{x_1 - h_1(x_n), \ldots, x_{n-1} - h_{n-1}(x_n), h_n(x_n)\},$$

the attacker can easily find the solution of the system of equations. To this end, one method is to employ the well-known Buchberger's criterion [21], which makes it possible to transform a given set of generators of the ideal into a Gröbner basis. From a theoretic point of view, state-of-the-art Gröbner basis algorithms are simply improvements to Buchberger's algorithm that include enhanced selection criteria, faster reduction step by making use of fast linear algebra, and an attempt to predict reductions to zero. The best well-known algorithm is Faugère's F5 algorithm [11,37].

Experiments highlighted that computing a Gröbner basis with respect to the lexicographic order is a slow process. However, computing a Gröbner basis with respect to the grevlex order can be done in a faster manner. Fortunately, the FGLM algorithm [38] makes it possible to transform a Gröbner basis with respect to the grevlex order to another with respect to the lexicographic order. To summarize, the attacker adopts the following strategy:

1. Using the F5 algorithm, compute a Gröbner basis w.r.t. the grevlex order.
2. Using the FGLM algorithm, transform the previous basis into a Gröbner basis w.r.t. the lexicographic order.
3. Using polynomial factorization and back substitution, solve the resulting system of equations.

Henceforth, we consider the following setting: let K be a finite field, let $A = K[x_1, \ldots, x_n]$ be the polynomial ring in n variables, and let $I \subseteq A$ be an ideal generated by a sequence of polynomials $(f_1, \ldots, f_r) \in A^r$ associated with the system of equations of interest.

Cost of the F5 Algorithm. In the best adversarial scenario, we assume that the sequence of polynomials associated with the system of equations is *regular.*[3] In this case, the F5 algorithm does not perform any redundant reductions to zero.

Write $F_{A/I}$ for the *Hilbert-Series* of the algebra A/I and $H_{A/I}$ for its *Hilbert polynomial.* The *degree of regularity* D_{reg} is the smallest integer such that $F_{A/I}(n) = H_{A/I}(n)$ for all $n \geq D_{\text{reg}}$. The quantity D_{reg} plays an important role in the cost of the algorithm. If the ideal I is generated by a regular sequence of degrees $d_1, \ldots, d_r$, then its *Hilbert series* equals $F_{A/I}(t) = \frac{\prod_{i=1}^{r}(1+t+t^2+\cdots+t^{d_i-1})}{(1-t)^{n-r}}$. From this, we deduce that $\deg(I) = \prod_{i=1}^{r} d_i$, and $D_{\text{reg}} = 1 + \sum_{i=1}^{r}(d_i - 1)$.

The main result is that if $f_1, \ldots, f_r$ is a regular sequence in $K[x_1, \ldots, x_n]$, then computing a Gröbner basis with respect to the grevlex order using the F5 algorithm can be performed within

$$\mathcal{O}\left(\binom{n + D_{\text{reg}}}{D_{\text{reg}}}^{\omega}\right)$$

operations in K, where $2 \leq \omega \leq 3$ is the matrix multiplication exponent.

Costs of Gröbner Basis Conversion and of Back Substitution. FGLM is an algorithm that converts a Gröbner basis of I with respect to one order, to a Gröbner basis of I with respect to a second order in $\mathcal{O}(n \deg(I)^3)$ operations in K. Finally, as proved in [39], the cost of factorizing a univariate polynomial in $K[x]$ of degree d over $\mathbb{F}_{p^n}$ for a prime p is $\mathcal{O}(d^3 n^2 + d n^3)$.

Number of Rounds. After introducing the Gröbner Basis attack, we analyze the minimum number of rounds that is necessary to provide security against this attack. However, we first emphasize that:

- there are several ways to set up the system of equations that describes the scheme. For instance, we could manipulate more equations, and thus more variables, of lower degree. Alternatively, we could work with less equations, and thus less variables, of higher degree. In addition, we could consider the relation between the input and the output, or between the middle state and the outputs, and so on. In the following, we present some of these strategies, that seem to be the most competitive ones;
- computing the exact cost of the attack is far from an easy task. As largely done in the literature, we assume that the most expensive step is the "F5 Algorithm". If the cost of such a step is higher than the security level, we conclude that the scheme is secure against the analyzed attack.

[3] A sequence of polynomials $(f_1, \ldots, f_r) \in A^r$ is called a regular sequence on A if the multiplication map $m_{f_i} : A/\langle f_1, \ldots, f_{i-1}\rangle \to A/\langle f_1, \ldots, f_{i-1}\rangle$ given by $m_{f_i}([g]) = [g][f_i] = [gf_i]$ is injective for all $2 \leq i \leq r$.

A Weaker Scheme. Instead of using the model that is described in Fig. 3, we analyze a weaker model as illustrated in Fig. 7. In the latter, the key is added after the expansion part, instead of before the rolling function application. This weaker model is easier to analyze, and makes it possible to draw a conclusion regarding the security of our scheme. Thus, *we conjecture that if the scheme proposed in Fig. 7 is secure w.r.t. Gröbner Basis attack, then the scheme in Fig. 3 is secure.* Indeed, in the scheme proposed in Fig. 7, it is always possible to consider the difference between two or more texts to remove the final key addition. For instance, given $f(x) + K = y$ and $f(x') + K = y'$, it follows that $f(x) - f(x') = y - y'$. As a result, the number of variables in the system of equations to be solved remains constant independently of the number of considered outputs. However, in Fig. 3, given $g(x+K) = y$ and $g(x'+K) = y'$, this is not possible except if $g(\cdot)$ is inverted. Nevertheless, since it is a truncated permutation, this does not seem feasible, unless the part of the output which is truncated is either treated as a variable (that results to have more variables than equations) or guessed by brute force (that results in an attack whose cost is higher than the security level, and $2^s \leq q$). Such consideration leads us to conjecture that the number of rounds necessary to make the scheme proposed in Fig. 7 secure is a good indicator of the number of rounds necessary to make the scheme in Fig. 3 secure as well.

Input-Output Relation. The number of rounds must ensure that the maximum degree is reached. Based on that, we do not expect that the relation that holds between the input and the output, makes it possible for the attacker to break the scheme. In particular, let N be the nonce, and k_1, k_2 be the secret keys. If we assume that a single word is output, then an equation of degree 2^r can be expressed between each input $(N, k_1, k_2) \in (\mathbb{F}_q)^3$, and the output $T \in \mathbb{F}_q$ with r the number of rounds. Hence, if there are two different initial nonces, then the attacker has to solve two equations in two variables. In that case, $D_{reg} = 1 + 2 \cdot (2^r - 1) \approx 2^{r+1}$. The cost of the attack is thus lower bounded by $\left[\binom{2+2^{r+1}}{2^{r+1}}\right]^\omega \geq \left[\frac{(1+2^{r+1})^2}{2}\right]^\omega \geq 2^{2r+1}$, where $\omega \geq 2$. Consequently, $2^{2r+1} \geq 2^s$ if the total number of rounds is at least $\lceil \frac{s-1}{2} \rceil$ (e.g., 64 for $s = 128$). Since the number of rounds for p_C is $s + 6$, this strategy does not outperform the previous attacks as expected.

Finally, we additionally consider a strategy where new intermediate variables are introduced to reduce the degree of the involved polynomials. We concluded that this strategy does not reduce the solving time as it increases the number of variables.

Middle State-Output Relation. There is another attack strategy that exploits the relation between the middle state and the outputs. In this strategy, only p_E is involved, and several outputs are generated by the same unknown middle state. For a given nonce N, let $(x_0^N, x_1^N, x_2^N) \in (\mathbb{F}_q)^3$ be the corresponding middle state. Since the key is added after the permutation p_E, we first eliminate the key by considering two initial nonces, and taking the difference of the corresponding output. This makes it possible to remove all the secret key material at the end, at the cost of having three more unknown variables in the middle.[4]

Hence, independently of the number of outputs that are generated, there are six variables, and thus simply the two middle states. That means that we need at least six output blocks, and an equivalent number of equations. Since two words are output for each call of p_E, we have six equations of degree 2^{r-1} and 2^r for the first two words, 2^r and 2^{r+1} for the next two words, and so on. We recall that every call of the rolling function increases the degree by a factor two, while the function that describes the output of a single block has a maximum degree, namely 2^r after r rounds for one word, and 2^{r-1} for the other two words. Hence, $D_{reg} = 1 + (2^{r-1} - 1) + 2 \cdot \sum_{i=0}^{1} (2^{r+i} - 1) + (2^{r+2} - 1) = 21 \cdot 2^{r-1} - 5 \approx 2^{r+3.4}$, and the cost of the attack is lower bounded by

$$\left[\binom{6 + 2^{r+3.4}}{2^{r+3.4}}\right]^{\omega} \geq \left[\frac{(1 + 2^{r+3.4})^6}{6!}\right]^{\omega} \geq 2^{12(r+3.4)-19},$$

where $\omega \geq 2$. Therefore, $2^{12(r+3.4)-19} \geq 2^s$ if the number of rounds for p_E is at least $\lceil \frac{s+19}{12} - 3.4 \rceil$ (e.g., 9 for $s = 128$). Like previously, potential improvement of the attack (e.g., an enhanced description of the equations) can lead to a lower computational cost. We thus decided to arbitrarily add five rounds as a security margin. We conjecture that at least $\lceil \frac{s+19}{12} + 1.5 \rceil$ rounds for p_E are necessary to provide some security (e.g., 14 for $s = 128$).

In addition, in order to reduce the degree of the involved polynomials, we studied the consequences of introducing new intermediate variables in the middle, e.g., at the output of the rolling function or among the rounds[5]. In that regard, we did not improve the previous results. Moreover, we also considered a scenario in which the attacker accesses more data, without being able to improve the previous results.

4.5 On the Algebraic Cipher Representation

Algebraic attacks seem to be the most successful attack vector on ciphers that have a simple representation in larger fields, while restricting the usage of multiplications. Until now, we have mainly focused on the growth of the degree to estimate the costs of the algebraic attacks that we considered. However, this is not the only factor that influences the cost of an algebraic attack. It is well known that such attacks (including higher-order, interpolation, and Gröbner basis attacks) can be more efficient if the polynomial that represents the cipher

[4] Another approach would be to involve the keys in the analysis. However, since the degree of the key-schedule is very high, the cost would then explode after few steps. It works by manipulating the degree of the key-schedule, or by introducing new variables for each new subkeys while keeping the degree as lower as possible. This approach does not seem to outperform the one described in the main text.

[5] For example, new variables can be introduced for each output of the rolling state. It results in having more equations with lower degrees. Our analysis suggests that this approach does not outperform the one described in the main text.

Table 2. Number of monomials of a certain degree for $\mathbb{F}_p$.

Output		Degree																											
Round	Variable	0	1	2	3	4	5	6	7	8	9	10	11	12	13	14	15	16	17	18	19	20	21	22	23	24	25	26	27
	Max	1	3	6	10	15	21	28	36	45	55	66	78	91	105	120	136	153	171	190	210	231	253	276	300	325	351	378	406
2	a	1	3	4	3	1																							
	b	1	3	4	3	1																							
	c	1	3	4	3	1																							
3	a	1	3	6	8	11	8	6	3	1																			
	b	1	3	6	8	11	8	6	3	1																			
	c	1	3	6	8	11	8	6	3	1																			
4	a	1	3	6	10	15	19	24	28	33	28	24	19	15	10	6	3	1											
	b	1	3	6	10	15	19	24	28	33	28	24	19	15	10	6	3	1											
	c	1	3	6	10	15	19	24	28	33	28	24	19	15	10	6	3	1											
5	a	1	3	6	10	15	21	28	36	45	53	62	70	79	87	96	104	113	104	96	87	79	70	62	53	45	36	28	21
	b	1	3	6	10	15	21	28	36	45	53	62	70	79	87	96	104	113	104	96	87	79	70	62	53	45	36	28	21
	c	1	3	6	10	15	21	28	36	45	53	62	70	79	87	96	104	113	104	96	87	79	70	62	53	45	36	28	21

is sparse. Consequently, it is necessary to study the algebraic representation of the cipher for a feasible number of rounds.

To evaluate the number of monomials that we have for a given degree, we wrote a dedicated tool. This tool produces a symbolic evaluation of the round function without considering a particular field or specific round constants. Nevertheless, it considers the fact that each element in $\mathbb{F}_{2^n}$ is also its inverse with respect to the addition. Since we do not instantiate any field and constants, the reported number of monomials might deviate from the real number of monomials here, e.g., due to unfortunate choices of round constants that sum to zero for some monomials. As a result, the entries in the tables are in fact upper bounds, but we do not expect high discrepancies between the numbers reported in the tables and the "real" ones.

Prime Case. First, we consider iterations of the round function f over $\mathbb{F}_p$. In Table 2, we evaluate the output functions at a_i, b_i, and c_i depending on the inputs a_0, b_0, and c_0 after a certain number of rounds $i \geq 2$. We count in Table 2 the number of monomials for a certain multivariate degree up to a fixed degree $d_{\mathbb{F}_p}$. Higher degree monomials might appear, but they are not presented in the table. To report this behavior, we do not input 0 in the table after the highest degree monomial. The column 'max' indicates the maximal number of monomials that can be encountered for three variables. As reported in Table 2, the number of monomials increases quite quickly, and we do not observe any unexpected behavior, or missing monomials of a certain degree.

Binary Case. Table 3 provides the number of monomials of a certain degree in $\mathbb{F}_{2^n}$. We notice that the diffusion is slower than in $\mathbb{F}_p$, and it may be because of the behavior of the addition that is self inverse in $\mathbb{F}_{2^n}$. More discussions on the algebraic cipher representation in the binary case can be found in [34, App. D].

5 Comparison with Other Designs

In this section, we compare the performance of our design with other designs that are presented in the literature for an MPC protocol using masked operations. We

Table 3. Number of monomials of a certain degree for $\mathbb{F}_{2^n}$.

Output		Degree																											
Round	Variable	0	1	2	3	4	5	6	7	8	9	10	11	12	13	14	15	16	17	18	19	20	21	22	23	24	25	26	27
	Max	1	3	6	10	15	21	28	36	45	55	66	78	91	105	120	136	153	171	190	210	231	253	276	300	325	351	378	406
2	a	1	3	4	2	1																							
	b	1	3	4	2	1																							
	c	1	3	4	2	1																							
3	a	1	3	6	7	7	3	3	0	1																			
	b	1	3	6	7	7	3	3	0	1																			
	c	1	3	6	7	7	3	3	0	1																			
4	a	1	3	6	9	15	14	19	12	13	5	6	2	3	0	0	0	1											
	b	1	3	6	9	15	14	19	12	13	5	6	2	3	0	0	0	1											
	c	1	3	6	9	15	14	19	12	13	5	6	2	3	0	0	0	1											
5	a	1	3	6	9	15	18	28	28	39	35	41	36	39	24	26	16	19	9	10	7	9	3	3	0	3	0	0	0
	b	1	3	6	9	15	18	28	28	39	35	41	36	39	24	26	16	19	9	10	7	9	3	3	0	3	0	0	0
	c	1	3	6	9	15	18	28	28	39	35	41	36	39	24	26	16	19	9	10	7	9	3	3	0	3	0	0	0

mainly focus on the number of multiplications in an MPC setting, which is often the metric that influences the most the cost in such a protocol. In addition, we discuss the number of online and pre-computation/offline rounds, and we compare those numbers to the ones specified for other schemes. The influence of the last two metrics on the overall costs highly varies depending on the concrete protocol/application, and the concrete environment, in which an MPC protocol is used, e.g., network of computers vs. a system on chip. Finally, we consider the advantages and the disadvantages of our design w.r.t. the other ones.

5.1 MPC Costs: CIMINION and Related Works

We compare the MPC cost of CIMINION with the cost of other designs that are published in the literature with $q \approx 2^{128}$, and $s = 128$ bits. We assume that the amount of data available to the attacker is fixed to $2^{s/2} = 2^{64}$, which is the most common case. Due to page limitation, we limit our analysis to CIMINION and HadesMiMC. The latter is the main competitive design currently present in the literature for the analyzed application. The detailed comparison with other designs (including MiMC, GMiMC, Rescue and Vision) is provided in [34, App. G]. A summary of the comparison is given in Table 4 and 5 for the binary and prime case, respectively.

Our design has the lowest minimum number of multiplications w.r.t. all other designs, in both $\mathbb{F}_p$ and $\mathbb{F}_{2^n}$. In $(\mathbb{F}_q)^t$ for $q \approx 2^{128}$, our design needs approximately $t + 14 \cdot \lceil t/2 \rceil \approx 8 \cdot t$ multiplications w.r.t. $12 \cdot t$ multiplications required by HadesMiMC or $60 \cdot t$ by Rescue. Additionally, our design has a low number of linear operations compared to other designs. For instance, for large $t \gg 1$, our design needs approximately $50 \cdot t$ affine operations (sums and multiplications with constants) while HadesMiMC requires approximately $12 \cdot t^2 + (157 + 4 \cdot \max\{32; \lceil \log_3(t) \rceil\}) \cdot t$ affine operations. However, this advantage comes at the price of having more online rounds than the other schemes. In particular, $104 + \lceil t/2 \rceil$ online rounds are required by our design whereas HadesMiMC and Rescue have respectively 78 and 20 online rounds.

Table 4. Comparison on the MPC cost of schemes over ${\mathbb{F}_{2^n}}^t$ for $n = 128$ (or 129), and a security level of 128 bits. With the exception of Vision (whose number of offline rounds is equal to $\max\left\{20, 2 \cdot \left\lceil \frac{136+t}{t} \right\rceil\right\}$), the number of offline rounds for all other schemes is zero.

Scheme	Multiplications (MPC)		Online rounds
	Element in ${\mathbb{F}_{2^n}}^t$	Asymptotically ($t \gg 1$)	
CIMINION	$8 \cdot t + 89$	8	$104 + \lceil t/2 \rceil$
MiMC-CTR	$164 \cdot t$	164	82
Vision	$t \cdot \max\left\{70, 7 \cdot \left\lceil \frac{136+t}{t} \right\rceil\right\}$	70	$\max\left\{50, 5 \cdot \left\lceil \frac{136+t}{t} \right\rceil\right\}$

Table 5. Comparison on the MPC cost of schemes over ${\mathbb{F}_p}^t$ for $p \approx 2^{128}$, and a security level of ≈ 128 bits. With the exception of Rescue (whose number of offline rounds is equal to $\max\{30; 6 \cdot \left\lceil \frac{32.5}{t} \right\rceil\}$), the number of offline rounds for all other schemes is zero.

Scheme	Multiplications (MPC)		Online rounds
	Element in ${\mathbb{F}_p}^t$	Asymptotically ($t \gg 1$)	
CIMINION	$14 \cdot \lceil t/2 \rceil + t + 89$	8	$104 + \lceil t/2 \rceil$
MiMC-CTR	$164 \cdot t$	164	82
GMiMC$_{erf}$	$4 + 4t + \max\left\{4t^2, 320\right\}$	$4 \cdot t$	$2 + 2t + \max\left\{2t^2, 160\right\}$
Rescue ($\alpha = 3$)	$t \cdot \max\{60; 12 \cdot \left\lceil \frac{32.5}{t} \right\rceil\}$	60	$\max\{20; 4 \cdot \left\lceil \frac{32.5}{t} \right\rceil\}$
HadesMiMC	$12t + \max\{78 + \lceil \log_3(t^2) \rceil; 142\}$	12	$\max\{45 + \lceil \log_3(t) \rceil; 77\}$

Ciminion. For $q \approx 2^{128}$, and a security level of 128 bits with data limited to 2^{64}, the permutation p_C counts 90 rounds. In order to output $2t' - 1 \leq t \leq 2t'$ words, we call t' times the permutation p_E that is composed of 14 rounds, and $(t' - 1)$ times the rolling function. Therefore, for the binary and the prime case, the cost of CIMINION in MPC applications to generate t words is

$$
\begin{aligned}
\#\,\text{multiplications:} &\quad 14 \cdot \lceil t/2 \rceil + (t-1) + 90 \approx 8 \cdot t + 89\,,\\
\#\,\text{online rounds:} &\quad 104 + \lceil t/2 \rceil\,,\\
\#\,\text{affine operations:} &\quad 99 \cdot \lceil t/2 \rceil + 629 \approx 50 \cdot t + 629\,.
\end{aligned}
$$

The number of online rounds depends on t, because the rolling function is serial. It is noteworthy that the expansion part can be performed in parallel. We emphasize that the number of sums and multiplications with a constant[6] (denoted as "affine" operations) is proportional to the number of multiplications. That is one of the main differences w.r.t. to the Hades construction as we argue afterwards.

HadesMiMC. HadesMiMC [41] is a block cipher that is proposed over $(\mathbb{F}_p)^t$ for a prime p such that $\gcd(p-1, 3) = 1$, and $t \geq 2$. It combines $R_F = 2R_f$ rounds with a full S-box layer (R_f at the beginning, and R_f at the end), and R_P rounds with a partial S-box layer in the middle. Each round is defined with $R_i(x) = k_i + M \times S(x)$, where M is a $t \times t$ MDS matrix, and S is the S-box layer. This layer is defined as the concatenation of t cube S-boxes in the rounds

[6] Each round counts six additions and one multiplication with a constant.

with full layer, and as the concatenation of one cube S-Box and $t-1$ identity functions in the rounds with partial layer.

In addition, hash functions can be obtained by instantiating a Sponge construction with the Hades permutation, and a fixed key, like Poseidon & Starkad [40]. In [15], the authors present an attack on Starkad that exploits a weakness in the matrix M that defines the MixLayer. The attack takes advantage of the equation $M^2 = \mu \cdot I$. This attack can be prevented by carefully choosing the MixLayer (we refer to [44] for further detail). There is no attack that is based on an analogous strategy that has been proposed for the cipher[7].

In order to guarantee some security, R_F and R_P must satisfy a list of inequalities [41]. There are several combinations of (R_F, R_P) that can provide the same level of security. In that regard, authors of [41] present a tool that makes it possible to find the best combination that guarantees security, and minimizes the computational cost. For a security level of approximately $\log_2(p)$ bits, and with $\log_2(p) \gg t$, the combination (R_F, R_P) minimizing the overall number of multiplications is

$$(R_F, R_P) = \left(6, \max\left\{\left\lceil\frac{\log_3(p)}{2}\right\rceil + \lceil\log_3(t)\rceil ; \lceil\log_3(p)\rceil - 2\lfloor\log_3(\log_2(p))\rfloor\right\} - 2\right).$$

In MPC applications ($p \approx 2^{128}$ and $s = 128$ bits), the cost of HadesMiMC is

$$\begin{aligned}
\#\,\text{multiplications:} \quad & 2 \cdot (t \cdot R_F + R_P) = 12t + \max\{78 + \lceil\log_3(t^2)\rceil\,; 142\},\\
\#\,\text{online rounds:} \quad & R_F + R_P = \max\{45 + \lceil\log_3(t)\rceil ; 77\},\\
\#\,\text{affine operations:} \quad & 2 \cdot t^2 \cdot R_F + (4 \cdot R_P + 1) \cdot t - 2 \cdot R_P\\
& \approx 12 \cdot t^2 + (157 + 4 \cdot \max\{32; \lceil\log_3(t)\rceil\}) \cdot t\,.
\end{aligned}$$

Parallel S-boxes can be computed in a single online round[8]. To compute the number of affine operations, we considered an equivalent representation of the cipher in which the MixLayer of the rounds, with a partial S-box layer, is defined by a matrix. In this matrix, only $3t-2$ entries are different from zero, that is to say the ones in the first column, in the first row, and in the first diagonal. (A $(t-1) \times (t-1)$ submatrix is an identity matrix.) The details are presented in [41, App. A]. Therefore, the total number of affine operations required grows quadratically w.r.t. the number of rounds with full S-box layer, and thus w.r.t. the number of multiplications.

Finally, we highlight that the number of multiplications is minimized when HadesMiMC takes as input the entire message. Indeed, let us assume that the input message is split into several parts, and that HadesMiMC is used in CTR mode (as suggested by the designers). In the analyzed case in which the security level is of the same order of the size of the field p, the number of rounds

[7] The main problem, in this case, regards the current impossibility to choose texts in the middle of the cipher by bypassing the rounds with full S-Box layer when the secret key is present.

[8] We refer to [43] on how to evaluate $x \to x^3$ within a single communication round.

is almost constant, and independent of the parameter $t \geq 2$. It follows that using HadesMiMC in CTR mode would require more multiplications, because every process requires the computation of the rounds with a partial S-box layer, whereas this computation is needed only once when the message size equals the block size. We stress that a similar conclusion holds for Rescue/Vision, for which the total number of multiplications would barely change when they are used in CTR mode, rather than when the message size is equal to the block size.

5.2 Ciminion Versus Hades: Advantages and Similarities

The previous comparison highlights that the two most competitive designs for MPC applications with a low multiplicative complexity are CIMINION and HadesMiMC. Referring to Fig. 1, we further develop the similarities and advantages between a block cipher based on a Hades design, and a cipher based on Farfalle. We present a brief comparison between our new design and the "Fork-Cipher" design that is proposed in [7] in [34, App. G.2].

Similarities: Distribution of the S-Boxes. We focus our attention on the *distribution of the S-boxes, or more generally, the non-linear operations.* Both strategies employ a particular parallelization of the non-linear operations/S-boxes to their advantage, in order to minimize the number of non-linear operations. More precisely, each step is composed of t parallel non-linear operations in the external rounds, i.e., the rounds at the end and at the beginning. Furthermore, each step is composed of a single non-linear operation in the internal rounds.

Both strategies take advantage of an attacker that cannot *directly* access the state in the middle rounds, because the state is masked both by the external rounds or phases, and by the presence of a key. In a Farfalle design, the attacker knows that each output of the expansion phase always employs the same value at the input, without accessing those inputs. In a Hades design, the attacker is able to skip some rounds with a partial S-box layer by carefully choosing the texts (see [15]). However, they cannot access the texts without bypassing the rounds with the full S-box layer that depends on the key.

Having middle rounds with a single S-box makes it possible to reduce the overall number of non-linear operations. In addition, they ensure some security against algebraic attacks. Indeed, even a single S-box makes it possible to increase the overall degree of the scheme. For a concrete example, let (R_c, R_m, R_e) be the rounds for respectively the compression part, middle part and expansion part of Farfalle. Like previously, let (R_F, R_P) be the number of rounds with respectively a full and a partial S-box layer in Hades. The number of multiplications is respectively $(R_c+R_e)\cdot t+R_m$ and $R_F\cdot t+R_P$. If $R_P \gg R_F$ and $R_m \gg R_c + R_e$. For a similar number of round, i.e., proportional to $\approx R_P + R_F$ or/and $\approx R_m + R_c + R_e$, it is then necessary to reach the maximum degree. Our number of multiplications is lower compared to a classical design where the rounds have a full S-box layer.

Advantages. There are major differences between Farfalle-like designs and Hades-like designs, because of their primary intention. The Farfalle-like design aims to behave like a Pseudo-Random Function (PRF), and the Hades-like design like a Pseudo-Random Permutation (PRP). The latter is used as a PRF in the Counter mode (CTR).[9] Under the assumption that affine operations are cheaper than non-linear ones, designers of Hades defined the MixLayer as the multiplication with a $t \times t$ MDS matrix. Consequently, each round with full S-box layer counts t^2 multiplications with constants. However, when $t \gg 1$, linear operations cannot be considered as free anymore, and their presences influence the overall performance.

This problem is not present in a Farfalle-like design. Indeed, by construction, in the first R_c and the last R_e rounds, the MixLayer is not required. That implies that the first three words are never mixed with the following ones. On the contrary, the elements are simply added together to generate the input of the compression phase. In addition, the expansion part's input is generated through a non-linear rolling function whose cost grows linearly with t. Finally, since invertibility is not required, the number of input words can be lower than the number of output words to design a function from $(\mathbb{F}_q)^3$ to $(\mathbb{F}_q)^t$ for any $t \geq 1$. Thus, independently of the number of output words, one multiplication per round is present in the compression phase, contrary to $\mathcal{O}(t)$ of a Hades-like scheme.

Acknowledgements. We thank Joan Daemen for his guidance and support and the reviewers of Eurocrypt 2021 for their valuable comments that improved the paper. This work has been supported in part by the European Research Council under the ERC advanced grant agreement under grant ERC-2017-ADG Nr. 788980 ESCADA, the European Research Council (ERC) under the European Union's Horizon 2020 research and innovation programme (grant agreement No 681402), and the Austrian Science Fund (FWF): J 4277-N38.

References

1. Albrecht, M.R., et al.: Algebraic cryptanalysis of STARK-friendly designs: application to MARVELLOUS and MiMC. In: Galbraith, S.D., Moriai, S. (eds.) ASIACRYPT 2019. LNCS, vol. 11923, pp. 371–397. Springer, Cham (2019). https://doi.org/10.1007/978-3-030-34618-8_13
2. Albrecht, M.R., et al.: Feistel structures for MPC, and more. In: Sako, K., Schneider, S., Ryan, P.Y.A. (eds.) ESORICS 2019. LNCS, vol. 11736, pp. 151–171. Springer, Cham (2019). https://doi.org/10.1007/978-3-030-29962-0_8
3. Albrecht, M.R., Grassi, L., Rechberger, C., Roy, A., Tiessen, T.: MiMC: efficient encryption and cryptographic hashing with minimal multiplicative complexity. ASIACRYPT. LNCS **10031**, 191–219 (2016)
4. Albrecht, M.R., Rechberger, C., Schneider, T., Tiessen, T., Zohner, M.: Ciphers for MPC and FHE. In: Oswald, E., Fischlin, M. (eds.) EUROCRYPT 2015. LNCS, vol. 9056, pp. 430–454. Springer, Heidelberg (2015). https://doi.org/10.1007/978-3-662-46800-5_17

[9] This means that, in both cases, the cost of encryption and decryption is the same. That is because Farfalle-like and Hades-like designs are used as stream ciphers.

5. Aly, A., Ashur, T., Ben-Sasson, E., Dhooghe, S., Szepieniec, A.: Design of symmetric-key primitives for advanced cryptographic protocols. Cryptology ePrint Archive, Report 2019/426 (2019)
6. Aly, A., Ashur, T., Ben-Sasson, E., Dhooghe, S., Szepieniec, A.: Design of symmetric-key primitives for advanced cryptographic protocols. IACR Trans. Symmetric Cryptol. **2020**(3), 1–45 (2020)
7. Andreeva, E., Lallemand, V., Purnal, A., Reyhanitabar, R., Roy, A., Vizár, D.: Forkcipher: a new primitive for authenticated encryption of very short messages. In: Galbraith, S.D., Moriai, S. (eds.) ASIACRYPT 2019. LNCS, vol. 11922, pp. 153–182. Springer, Cham (2019). https://doi.org/10.1007/978-3-030-34621-8_6
8. Ashur, T., Dhooghe, S.: MARVELlous: a STARK-friendly family of cryptographic primitives. Cryptology ePrint Archive, Report 2018/1098 (2018)
9. Baignères, T., Stern, J., Vaudenay, S.: Linear cryptanalysis of non binary ciphers. In: Adams, C., Miri, A., Wiener, M. (eds.) SAC 2007. LNCS, vol. 4876, pp. 184–211. Springer, Heidelberg (2007). https://doi.org/10.1007/978-3-540-77360-3_13
10. Bar-Ilan, J., Beaver, D.: Non-cryptographic fault-tolerant computing in constant number of rounds of interaction. In: ACM Symposium, pp. 201–209. ACM (1989)
11. Bardet, M., Faugère, J., Salvy, B.: On the complexity of the F5 Gröbner basis algorithm. J. Symb. Comput. **70**, 49–70 (2015)
12. Bertoni, G., Daemen, J., Hoffert, S., Peeters, M., Van Assche, G., Van Keer, R.: Farfalle: parallel permutation-based cryptography. IACR Trans. Symmetric Cryptol. **2017**(4), 1–38 (2017)
13. Bertoni, G., Daemen, J., Peeters, M., Van Assche, G.: Sponge functions. In: Ecrypt Hash Workshop 2007 (2007)
14. Bertoni, G., Daemen, J., Peeters, M., Van Assche, G.: The Keccak SHA-3 submission (Version 3.0) (2011)
15. Beyne, T., et al.: Out of oddity – new cryptanalytic techniques against symmetric primitives optimized for integrity proof systems. In: Micciancio, D., Ristenpart, T. (eds.) CRYPTO 2020. LNCS, vol. 12172, pp. 299–328. Springer, Cham (2020). https://doi.org/10.1007/978-3-030-56877-1_11
16. Biham, E., Biryukov, A., Shamir, A.: Cryptanalysis of skipjack reduced to 31 rounds using impossible differentials. In: Stern, J. (ed.) EUROCRYPT 1999. LNCS, vol. 1592, pp. 12–23. Springer, Heidelberg (1999). https://doi.org/10.1007/3-540-48910-X_2
17. Biham, E., Shamir, A.: Differential cryptanalysis of DES-like cryptosystems. In: Menezes, A.J., Vanstone, S.A. (eds.) CRYPTO 1990. LNCS, vol. 537, pp. 2–21. Springer, Heidelberg (1991). https://doi.org/10.1007/3-540-38424-3_1
18. Bogdanov, A., Wang, M.: Zero correlation linear cryptanalysis with reduced data complexity. In: Canteaut, A. (ed.) FSE 2012. LNCS, vol. 7549, pp. 29–48. Springer, Heidelberg (2012). https://doi.org/10.1007/978-3-642-34047-5_3
19. Bonnetain, X.: Collisions on Feistel-MiMC and univariate GMiMC. Cryptology ePrint Archive, Report 2019/951 (2019)
20. Boura, C., Canteaut, A., De Cannière, C.: Higher-order differential properties of Keccak and *Luffa*. In: Joux, A. (ed.) FSE 2011. LNCS, vol. 6733, pp. 252–269. Springer, Heidelberg (2011). https://doi.org/10.1007/978-3-642-21702-9_15
21. Buchberger, B.: A theoretical basis for the reduction of polynomials to canonical forms. SIGSAM Bull. **10**(3), 19–29 (1976)
22. Canteaut, A., et al.: Stream ciphers: a practical solution for efficient homomorphic-ciphertext compression. J. Cryptol. **31**(3), 885–916 (2018)
23. Carter, L., Wegman, M.N.: Universal classes of hash functions (extended abstract). In: STOC, pp. 106–112. ACM (1977)

24. Daemen, J.: Cipher and hash function design, strategies based on linear and differential cryptanalysis, Ph.D. Thesis. K.U. Leuven (1995)
25. Daemen, J., Govaerts, R., Vandewalle, J.: Correlation matrices. In: Preneel, B. (ed.) FSE 1994. LNCS, vol. 1008, pp. 275–285. Springer, Heidelberg (1995). https://doi.org/10.1007/3-540-60590-8_21
26. Daemen, J., Hoffert, S., Van Assche, G., Van Keer, R.: The design of Xoodoo and Xoofff. IACR Trans. Symmetric Cryptol. **2018**(4), 1–38 (2018)
27. Daemen, J., Rijmen, V.: The block cipher Rijndael. In: Quisquater, J.-J., Schneier, B. (eds.) CARDIS 1998. LNCS, vol. 1820, pp. 277–284. Springer, Heidelberg (2000). https://doi.org/10.1007/10721064_26
28. Daemen, J., Rijmen, V.: The design of Rijndael. AES - The Advanced Encryption Standard. Springer, Heidelberg (2002). https://doi.org/10.1007/978-3-662-04722-4
29. Daemen, J., Rijmen, V.: Correlation analysis in GF 2^n. The Design of Rijndael. ISC, pp. 181–194. Springer, Heidelberg (2020). https://doi.org/10.1007/978-3-662-60769-5_12
30. Damgård, I., Fazio, N., Nicolosi, A.: Non-interactive zero-knowledge from homomorphic encryption. In: Halevi, S., Rabin, T. (eds.) TCC 2006. LNCS, vol. 3876, pp. 41–59. Springer, Heidelberg (2006). https://doi.org/10.1007/11681878_3
31. Dinur, I., Kales, D., Promitzer, A., Ramacher, S., Rechberger, C.: Linear equivalence of block ciphers with partial non-linear layers: application to LowMC. In: Ishai, Y., Rijmen, V. (eds.) EUROCRYPT 2019. LNCS, vol. 11476, pp. 343–372. Springer, Cham (2019). https://doi.org/10.1007/978-3-030-17653-2_12
32. Dinur, I., Liu, Y., Meier, W., Wang, Q.: Optimized interpolation attacks on LowMC. In: Iwata, T., Cheon, J.H. (eds.) ASIACRYPT 2015. LNCS, vol. 9453, pp. 535–560. Springer, Heidelberg (2015). https://doi.org/10.1007/978-3-662-48800-3_22
33. Dobraunig, C., et al.: Rasta: a cipher with low ANDdepth and Few ANDs per bit. In: Shacham, H., Boldyreva, A. (eds.) CRYPTO 2018. LNCS, vol. 10991, pp. 662–692. Springer, Cham (2018). https://doi.org/10.1007/978-3-319-96884-1_22
34. Dobraunig, C., Grassi, L., Guinet, A., Kuijsters, D.: Ciminion: symmetric encryption based on toffoli-gates over large finite fields. Cryptology ePrint Archive, Report 2021/267 (2021). https://eprint.iacr.org/2021/267
35. Duval, S., Lallemand, V., Rotella, Y.: Cryptanalysis of the FLIP family of stream ciphers. In: Robshaw, M., Katz, J. (eds.) CRYPTO 2016. LNCS, vol. 9814, pp. 457–475. Springer, Heidelberg (2016). https://doi.org/10.1007/978-3-662-53018-4_17
36. Eichlseder, M., et al.: An algebraic attack on ciphers with low-degree round functions: application to full MiMC. In: Moriai, S., Wang, H. (eds.) ASIACRYPT 2020. LNCS, vol. 12491, pp. 477–506. Springer, Cham (2020). https://doi.org/10.1007/978-3-030-64837-4_16
37. Faugère, J.C.: A new efficient algorithm for computing Gröbner bases without reduction to zero F5. In: ISSAC, pp. 75–83. ACM (2002)
38. Faugère, J., Gianni, P.M., Lazard, D., Mora, T.: Efficient computation of zero-dimensional Gröbner bases by change of ordering. J. Symb. Comput. **16**(4), 329–344 (1993)
39. Genovese, G.: Improving the algorithms of Berlekamp and Niederreiter for factoring polynomials over finite fields. J. Symb. Comput. **42**(1–2), 159–177 (2007)
40. Grassi, L., Khovratovich, D., Rechberger, C., Roy, A., Schofnegger, M.: Poseidon: a new hash function for zero-knowledge proof systems. In: USENIX Security 2021. USENIX Association (2021)

41. Grassi, L., Lüftenegger, R., Rechberger, C., Rotaru, D., Schofnegger, M.: On a generalization of substitution-permutation networks: the HADES design strategy. In: Canteaut, A., Ishai, Y. (eds.) EUROCRYPT 2020. LNCS, vol. 12106, pp. 674–704. Springer, Cham (2020). https://doi.org/10.1007/978-3-030-45724-2_23
42. Grassi, L., Rechberger, C., Rønjom, S.: A new structural-differential property of 5-round AES. In: Coron, J.-S., Nielsen, J.B. (eds.) EUROCRYPT 2017. LNCS, vol. 10211, pp. 289–317. Springer, Cham (2017). https://doi.org/10.1007/978-3-319-56614-6_10
43. Grassi, L., Rechberger, C., Rotaru, D., Scholl, P., Smart, N.P.: MPC-friendly symmetric key primitives. In: CCS, pp. 430–443. ACM (2016)
44. Grassi, L., Rechberger, C., Schofnegger, M.: Weak linear layers in word-oriented partial SPN and HADES-like ciphers. Cryptology ePrint Archive, Report 2020/500 (2020)
45. Grosso, V., Standaert, F., Faust, S.: Masking vs. multiparty computation: how large is the gap for AES? J. Cryptograph. Eng. **4**(1), 47–57 (2014)
46. Ishai, Y., Sahai, A., Wagner, D.: Private circuits: securing hardware against probing attacks. In: Boneh, D. (ed.) CRYPTO 2003. LNCS, vol. 2729, pp. 463–481. Springer, Heidelberg (2003). https://doi.org/10.1007/978-3-540-45146-4_27
47. Jakobsen, T., Knudsen, L.R.: The interpolation attack on block ciphers. In: Biham, E. (ed.) FSE 1997. LNCS, vol. 1267, pp. 28–40. Springer, Heidelberg (1997). https://doi.org/10.1007/BFb0052332
48. Knudsen, L.R.: Truncated and higher order differentials. In: Preneel, B. (ed.) FSE 1994. LNCS, vol. 1008, pp. 196–211. Springer, Heidelberg (1995). https://doi.org/10.1007/3-540-60590-8_16
49. Knudsen, L.R.: DEAL - a 128-bit block cipher (1998)
50. Lai, X.: Higher order derivatives and differential cryptanalysis. In: Blahut, R.E., Costello, D.J., Maurer, U., Mittelholzer, T. (eds.) Communications and Cryptography. The Springer International Series in Engineering and Computer Science (Communications and Information Theory), vol. 276. Springer, Boston, MA (1994). https://doi.org/10.1007/978-1-4615-2694-0_23
51. Biham, E., Dunkelman, O., Keller, N.: Differential-linear cryptanalysis of serpent. In: Johansson, T. (ed.) FSE 2003. LNCS, vol. 2887, pp. 9–21. Springer, Heidelberg (2003). https://doi.org/10.1007/978-3-540-39887-5_2
52. Matsui, M.: Linear cryptanalysis method for DES cipher. In: Helleseth, T. (ed.) EUROCRYPT 1993. LNCS, vol. 765, pp. 386–397. Springer, Heidelberg (1994). https://doi.org/10.1007/3-540-48285-7_33
53. McGrew, D.A., Viega, J.: The security and performance of the Galois/Counter mode of operation (full version). Cryptology ePrint Archive, Report 2004/193 (2004)
54. Méaux, P., Journault, A., Standaert, F.-X., Carlet, C.: Towards stream ciphers for efficient FHE with low-noise ciphertexts. In: Fischlin, M., Coron, J.-S. (eds.) EUROCRYPT 2016. LNCS, vol. 9665, pp. 311–343. Springer, Heidelberg (2016). https://doi.org/10.1007/978-3-662-49890-3_13
55. NIST: FIPS PUB 202: SHA-3 standard: permutation-based hash and extendable-output functions (August 2015)
56. Nyberg, K., Knudsen, L.R.: Provable security against a differential attack. J. Cryptol. **8**(1), 27–37 (1995)
57. Procter, G.: A security analysis of the composition of ChaCha20 and Poly1305. Cryptology ePrint Archive, Report 2014/613 (2014)
58. Procter, G., Cid, C.: On weak keys and forgery attacks against polynomial-based MAC schemes. J. Cryptol. **28**(4), 769–795 (2015)

59. Rechberger, C., Soleimany, H., Tiessen, T.: Cryptanalysis of low-data instances of full LowMCv2. IACR Trans. Symmetric Cryptol. **2018**(3), 163–181 (2018)
60. Rijmen, V., Daemen, J., Preneel, B., Bosselaers, A., De Win, E.: The cipher SHARK. In: Gollmann, D. (ed.) FSE 1996. LNCS, vol. 1039, pp. 99–111. Springer, Heidelberg (1996). https://doi.org/10.1007/3-540-60865-6_47
61. Simon, T., et al.: Friet: an authenticated encryption scheme with built-in fault detection. In: Canteaut, A., Ishai, Y. (eds.) EUROCRYPT 2020. LNCS, vol. 12105, pp. 581–611. Springer, Cham (2020). https://doi.org/10.1007/978-3-030-45721-1_21
62. Toffoli, T.: Reversible computing. In: de Bakker, J., van Leeuwen, J. (eds.) ICALP 1980. LNCS, vol. 85, pp. 632–644. Springer, Heidelberg (1980). https://doi.org/10.1007/3-540-10003-2_104
63. Wagner, D.: The boomerang attack. In: Knudsen, L. (ed.) FSE 1999. LNCS, vol. 1636, pp. 156–170. Springer, Heidelberg (1999). https://doi.org/10.1007/3-540-48519-8_12

Mind the Middle Layer: The HADES Design Strategy Revisited

Nathan Keller[1(✉)] and Asaf Rosemarin[2]

[1] Mathematics Department, Bar Ilan University, Ramat Gan, Israel
nkeller@math.biu.ac.il

[2] Department of Computer Science, Bar-Ilan University, Ramat Gan, Israel

Abstract. The HADES design strategy combines the classical SPN construction with the Partial SPN (PSPN) construction, in which at every encryption round, the non-linear layer is applied to only a part of the state. In a HADES design, a middle layer that consists of PSPN rounds is surrounded by outer layers of SPN rounds. The security arguments of HADES with respect to statistical attacks use only the SPN rounds, disregarding the PSPN rounds. This allows the designers to not pose any restriction on the MDS matrix used as the linear mixing operation.

In this paper we show that the choice of the MDS matrix significantly affects the security level provided by HADES designs. If the MDS is chosen properly, then the security level of the scheme against differential and linear attacks is significantly higher than claimed by the designers. On the other hand, weaker choices of the MDS allow for extremely large invariant subspaces that pass the entire middle layer without activating any non-linear operation (a.k.a. S-box).

We showcase our results on the Starkad and Poseidon instantiations of HADES. For Poseidon, we significantly improve the lower bounds on the number of active S-boxes with respect to both differential and linear cryptanalysis provided by the designers – for example, from 28 to 60 active S-boxes for the $t = 6$ variant. For Starkad, we show that for any variant with t (i.e., the number of S-boxes in each round) divisible by 4, the cipher admits a huge invariant subspace that passes *any number* of PSPN rounds without activating any S-box (e.g., a subspace of size 2^{1134} for the $t = 24$ variant). Furthermore, for various choices of the parameters, this invariant subspace can be used to mount a preimage attack on the hash function that breakes its security claims. On the other hand, we show that the problem can be fixed easily by replacing t with any value that is not divisible by four.

Following our paper, the designers of Starkad and Poseidon amended their design, by adding requirements which ensure that the MDS matrix is chosen properly.

Research supported by the European Research Council under the ERC starting grant agreement number 757731 (LightCrypt) and by the BIU Center for Research in Applied Cryptography and Cyber Security in conjunction with the Israel National Cyber Bureau in the Prime Minister's Office.

A. Canteaut and F.-X. Standaert (Eds.): EUROCRYPT 2021, LNCS 12697, pp. 35–63, 2021.
https://doi.org/10.1007/978-3-030-77886-6_2

1 Introduction

1.1 Background

Substitution-permutation network (SPN) is a classical design strategy of cryptographic permutations, used in the AES [14] and in numerous other modern cryptosystems. An SPN iterates many times a sequence of operations called 'round', which consists of a layer of local non-linear operations (S-boxes) and a global linear mixing layer. The *wide trail strategy*, employed in the AES, allows designing SPNs with an easily provable lower bound on the number of active S-boxes in any differential or linear characteristic, thus providing a security guarantee with respect to the most common statistical cryptanalytic attacks.

In 2013, Gerard et al. [9] proposed the Partial SPN (PSPN) construction, in which the S-box layer is applied to only a part of the state in each round (in exchange for somewhat increasing the number of rounds). This approach, that has obvious performance advantages in various scenarios, was used in the block ciphers Zorro [9] and LowMC [1]. A drawback of this approach is that 'clean' security arguments (like the wide trail strategy) are not applicable for PSPNs, and thus, the security of these designs was argued by more ad-hoc approaches. These turned out to be insufficient, as Zorro was practically broken in [2] and the security of the initial versions of LowMC was shown in [7,8] to be significantly lower than claimed by the designers.

At Eurocrypt 2020, Grassi et al. [12] proposed the HADES design strategy that combines the classical SPN construction with the PSPN construction. In a HADES design, a middle layer of PSPN rounds is surrounded by two layers of SPN rounds. The scheme allows enjoying 'the best of the two worlds' – the efficiency provided by the PSPN construction, along with the clean security arguments applicable for the SPN construction. Specifically, the security arguments of the cryptosystem with respect to statistical (e.g., differential and linear) attacks are provided *only* by the SPN (a.k.a. 'full') rounds, using the wide trail strategy. The security arguments with respect to algebraic attacks use also the PSPN rounds, and take advantage of the fact that a partial non-linear layer increases the algebraic degree in essentially the same way as a 'full' non-linear layer. The linear layer in the HADES design is implemented by an MDS matrix (see [14]), which guarantees that if the number of S-boxes in any full round is t, then any differential or linear characteristic over two full rounds activates at least $t + 1$ S-boxes. Since the PSPN rounds are not used in the security arguments with respect to statistical attacks, the HADES designers do not impose any restriction on the MDS used in the scheme. As a specific example, they propose using *Cauchy matrices* over finite fields (to be defined in Sect. 2).

The designers of HADES presented applications of their strategy for securing data transfers with distributed databases using secure multiparty computation (MPC). Subsequently, Grassi et al. proposed Starkad [10, initial version] and Poseidon [11] – hash functions whose underlying permutations are instantiations of the HADES methodology, aimed at applications for practical proof systems, such as SNARKs, STARKs, or Bulletproofs. The HADES family of algorithms (including various Starkad and Poseidon variants) was a candidate in the STARK-Friendly Hash Challenge [17].

1.2 Our Results

In this paper we study the effect of the MDS matrix on the security level of HADES designs. We show that when the MDS is chosen properly, the PSPN rounds can be taken into consideration in the security arguments against differential and linear attacks, leading to a very significant improvement in the lower bound on the number of active S-boxes in differential and linear characteristics. On the other hand, we show that a weaker choice of the MDS matrix may lead to existence of huge invariant subspaces for the entire middle layer that do not activate any S-box (for any number of PSPN rounds). Furthermore, for certain instances (albeit, not for the specific instances chosen in [10, initial version] and [17]), these invariant subspaces allow breaking the hash function with a Gröbner-basis [3] preimage attack.

To be specific, we focus on the variants of Starkad and Poseidon suggested in [10, initial version]. Interestingly, our results point out a sharp difference between the cases of a prime field (Poseidon) and a binary field (Starkad).

Analysis of Poseidon. In the case of Poseidon (which operates over a prime field $GF(p)$), for all variants proposed in [10,11], we significantly improve the lower bound on the number of active S-boxes in differential and linear characteristics. The improvement is especially large for variants with a small number of S-boxes in each round (denoted in [12] by t). For example, for $t = 6$ (which is the main reference variant provided in the supplementary material of [10]), the designers claim a lower bound of $4 \cdot (6 + 1) = 28$ active S-boxes, based on application of the wide trail strategy to the 'full' rounds. We prove that the PSPN rounds must activate at least 32 S-boxes, thus more than doubling the lower bound on the number of active S-boxes to 60. For the $t = 2$ variant, the improvement is most striking: there are at least 41 active S-boxes in the PSPN rounds, while the designers' bound for the SPN rounds is 12 S-boxes. We obtain the new lower bounds using an automated characteristic search tool for PSPNs proposed in [2]. A comparison of our new lower bounds and the lower bounds of the designers is presented in Table 1.

Analysis of Starkad. In the case of Starkad (which operates over a binary field $GF(2^n)$), perhaps surprisingly, there is a significant difference between different values of t. For $t = 24$ (which is the main reference variant provided in the supplementary material of [10, initial version]), we show that there exists an invariant subspace U of size $2^{18 \cdot 63} = 2^{1134}$ that does not activate the S-box in the PSPN rounds. This means that U passes *any number* of PSPN rounds, without activating any S-box! On the other hand, for $t = 47$ and $t = 51$ (the other variants of Starkad considered in [10, initial version]), there are no t-round

Table 1. The lower bound on the number of active S-boxes in a differential/linear characteristic, for the full rounds (shown by the designers) and for the PSPN rounds (our results), for various versions of Poseidon

Security level	t	R_F = full rounds	R_P = partial rounds	S-boxes in R_F	S-boxes in R_P	S-boxes in total
128	2	8	82	12	41	53
128	4	8	83	20	36	56
128	6	8	84	28	32	60
256	8	8	127	36	42	78
128	16	8	64	68	12	80

differential or linear characteristics that do not activate any S-box.[1] We show that these results are not a coincidence, but rather follow from properties of Cauchy matrices over binary fields. Specifically, we prove the following:

Theorem 1. *Let $\mathbb{F} = GF(2^n)$ be a binary field. Let $t = 2^k \cdot s$ where $s \in \mathbb{N}$. Let M be a t-by-t Cauchy matrix over $\mathbb{F}$ constructed according to the Starkad specification. Then there exists a linear subspace $U \subset \mathbb{F}^t$ of dimension at least $(1 - \frac{k+1}{2^k})t$ such that for any $\ell \in \mathbb{N}$ and for any $x \in U$, the top n bits of $M^\ell x$ are equal to zero. Consequently, application of any number of PSPN rounds to any $x \in U$ does not activate any S-box.*

Theorem 1 implies that for any t that is divisible by 4, there is a huge subspace U of size at least $2^{nt/4}$ that passes any number of PSPN rounds without activating any S-box. (This follows from applying the theorem with $k = 2$ and $s = t/4$.) In fact, we conjecture that the lower bound on the dimension of the subspace in Theorem 1 can be improved to $(1 - \frac{2}{2^k})t$ (which would fully explain the size of the invariant subspace for the $t = 24$ variant of Starkad). We verified this conjecture experimentally for many values of n and t, including all variants of Starkad proposed in [10, initial version]. The sizes of the invariant subspace for $n = 63$ and several representative values of t are given in Table 2.

An especially notable case is Starkad variants with $t = 2^k$. For such variants, we show that the MDS is essentially an *involution*.

Theorem 2. *Let $\mathbb{F} = GF(2^n)$ be a binary field, and let $t = 2^k$ for $k \in \mathbb{N}$. Let M be a t-by-t Cauchy matrix over $\mathbb{F}$ constructed according to the Starkad specification. Then $M^2 = \alpha I$, where $\alpha = (\sum_{j=2^k}^{2^{k+1}-1} j^{-1})^2$. Consequently, there exists a linear subspace $U \subset \mathbb{F}^t$ of dimension at least $t - 2$ such that for any $\ell \in \mathbb{N}$ and for any $x \in U$, the top n bits of $M^\ell x$ are equal to zero.*

[1] We note that for the specific variants with $t = 47, 51$ proposed in [10], there does exist a large subspace that does not activate any S-box in the PSPN rounds, since the number of these rounds (25 for $t = 47$ and 24 for $t = 51$) is smaller than t. While this might be undesirable, this is an inevitable result of the choice of the number of PSPN rounds, that does not depend on the MDS matrix.

Table 2. The dimension of the invariant subspace whose elements do not activate S-boxes for any number of PSPN rounds, as a function of t (the number of S-boxes in each round), for a Starkad cipher over the field $GF(2^{63})$

t	Dimension of invariant subspace	t	Dimension of invariant subspace	t	Dimension of invariant subspace
4	2	6	0	8	6
10	0	13	0	16	14
18	0	21	0	24	18
28	14	32	30	42	0
46	0	47	0	48	42
50	0	51	0	52	26
56	42	64	62	70	0

As can be seen in Table 2, Theorem 2 is tight for all checked variants (i.e., $n = 63$ and $t = 4, 8, 16, 32, 64$).

We obtain Theorems 1 and 2 via an extensive study of properties of Cauchy matrices over binary fields.[2] As Cauchy matrices are widely used (e.g., for error correcting codes, see [15]), these linear-algebraic results are of independent interest.

Of course, a crucial question is whether these invariant subspaces can be used to actually attack Starkad. We show that they indeed can be used to mount a Gröbner-basis preimage attack proposed by Beyne et al. [6, Sec. 6.2], and that for certain choices of the parameters (e.g., a variant over the field $GF(2^{127})$ aimed at a 256-bit security level, like the variant proposed in the STARK-Friendly Hash Challenge [17], with 16 S-boxes in each round instead of 14), the resulting attack breaks the security claims of the hash function.

On the other hand, our results show that this deficiency can be fixed easily: it is sufficient to choose a value of t that is not divisible by 4 (see Table 2). Furthermore, we show that various other mild changes (such as slightly altering the way in which the sequences $\{x_i\}, \{y_j\}$ used in the construction of the Cauchy matrix are selected) are also sufficient for avoiding the existence of an invariant subspace.

Hence, our results (both on Poseidon and on Starkad) suggest that properly designing the MDS matrix and taking it into consideration in the analysis allows significantly improving the security guarantee of HADES constructions with respect to statistical attacks.

[2] We note that a variant of the easier Theorem 2 was independently and concurrently obtained in [6, Appendix A].

1.3 Practical Impact of Our Results and Subsequent Work

In the short time since the initial version of this paper appeared on eprint, its results had a practical impact:

Our Results for Strong MDS Matrices. The designers of Starkad and Poseidon accepted our results and included them in the amended security analysis presented in [10, updated version, Sec. 5.4.1] and [11]. In particular, the authors of [10,11] agreed with our claim that as far as statistical attacks are concerned, several full rounds could be replaced by partial rounds without reducing the security claims. Nevertheless, they decided to not reduce the number of full rounds in the amended version, since the full rounds are advantageous over partial rounds also with respect to certain algebraic attacks, such as Gröbner basis attacks (see [10, updated version, Sec. 5.4.1]).

Our Results for Weak MDS Matrices. Following our results, the designers of Starkad and Poseidon amended the design in such a way that invariant subspaces that pass an infinite number of PSPN rounds would not be possible (see [10]). To this end, they adopted the amednments we proposed (and in particular, required t to be odd), along with other amendments.

In addition, the STARK-Friendly Hash Challenge [17] cryptanalytic committee used our results, alongside other results, to motivate their recommendation to remove Starkad from consideration in the challenge (see [4, Sec. 4]).

Subsequent Work. Motivated by our results, Grassi et al. [13] presented a systematic study of linear layers for which the cipher admits an invariant subspace that passes all PSPN rounds for free. The results of the analysis were used to determine the requirements on the MDS matrix used in the amended variant of Starkad and Poseidon [10, updated version].

1.4 Organization of the Paper

This paper is organized as follows. We briefly describe the HADES construction and its instantiations, Starkad and Poseidon, in Sect. 2. In Sect. 3 we present our results on variants of Poseidon. In Sect. 4 we explore a special class of matrices over binary fields (which includes Cauchy matrices of the type used in Starkad) and obtain the linear-algebraic results required for proving Theorems 1 and 2. In Sect. 5 we present our results on variants of Starkad, and in particular, prove Theorems 1 and 2. We conclude the paper with a discussion and open problems in Sect. 6.

2 The HADES Construction

In this section we briefly describe the structure of a HADES permutation [12].

A block cipher/permutation designed according to the HADES strategy employs four types of operations:

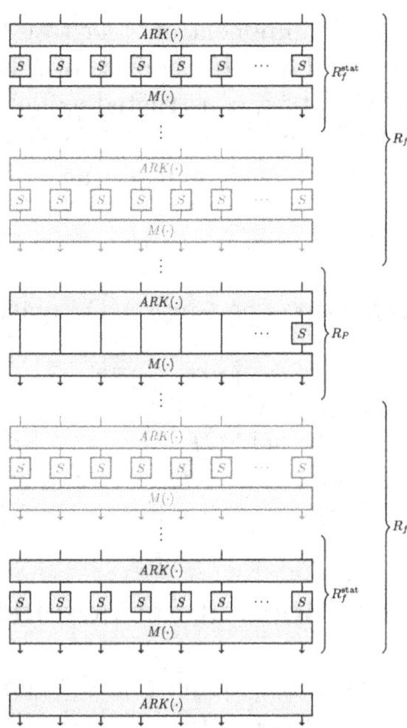

Fig. 1. The HADES construction

1. AddRoundKey, denoted by $ARK(\cdot)$ – a bitwise XOR of a round subkey (or a round constant for unkeyed designs) with the state;
2. Full S-box Layer, denoted by $S(\cdot)$ – parallel application of t copies of an identical S-box to the entire state;
3. Partial S-box Layer, denoted by $S^*(\cdot)$ – application of a single S-box to a part of the state, while the rest of the state remains unchanged;
4. Mixing Layer, denoted by $M(\cdot)$ – multiplication of the entire state by an MDS matrix.

A full round is defined as $M \circ S \circ ARK(\cdot)$, and a partial round is defined as $M \circ S^* \circ ARK(\cdot)$. The cipher consists of R_f full rounds, followed by R_P full rounds, followed by R_f full rounds, where the parameters R_P, R_f are chosen by a complex rule intended mainly to thwart algebraic attacks. The structure of HADES is demonstrated in Fig. 1.

In this paper, we study the Poseidon and Starkad permutations [10], built according to the HADES design strategy. Poseidon works over a finite field $GF(p)$, while Starkad works over a binary field $GF(2^n)$. Starkad uses only the S-box $S(x) = x^3$, while Poseidon uses also x^{-1} and x^5. For our purposes, the choice of the S-box is not relevant.

The block ciphers are parameterized by R_P, R_f (as in HADES), n – the logarithm of the field size, and t – the number of S-boxes applied in each full round.

The MDS Matrix. The design component on which we focus in this work is the MDS matrix used in the linear layer. In the case of a binary field $GF(2^n)$, the matrix is a so-called Cauchy matrix, constructed as follows.

First, a constant r is chosen. Then, one sets up two sequences $\{x_i\}, \{y_j\}$ of length t, by choosing a staring point x_0 and setting

$$\forall i \in [t] : x_i \triangleq x_0 + i - 1, y_i \triangleq x_i + r,$$

where + denotes integer addition. The t-by-t MDS matrix M is set as

$$M_{i,j} = (x_i \oplus y_j)^{-1},$$

where the inversion is taken in the field $GF(2^n)$. In all Starkad variants presented in [10], the parameters x_0, r are set to $0, t$, respectively. The construction for a prime $\mathbb{F}_p$ (on which we do not focus) is similar to the binary case.

3 Improved Security Bounds for Poseidon Permutations

In this section we show that the lower bounds on the number of active S-boxes in a differential or a linear characteristic obtained by the designers of Poseidon, can be improved significantly by taking into consideration active S-boxes in PSPN rounds and lower bounding their number.

In order to lower-bound the number of active S-boxes, we use a generic characteristic search algorithm for PSPNs, presented by Bar-On et al. [2] at Eurocrypt 2015. For a parameter a, the algorithm allows computing the (provably) minimal number r of rounds such that any r-round differential/linear characteristic must activate at least $a + 1$ S-boxes.

The idea behind the algorithm is to enumerate patterns of active/non-active S-boxes and to check the validity of each pattern by posing a homogeneous linear equation on each non-active S-box, and linearizing the output of active S-boxes by introducing new variables. As for checking an r-round variant, the algorithm has to sieve $\binom{rt'}{<a}$ possible patterns of active S-boxes, where t' is the number of S-boxes in each PSPN round, the running time of the algorithm is determined by the parameters a, r, t'. In addition, the complexity depends on t – the number of S-boxes in each full round, which affects the complexity of multipication by the MDS matrix (an operation used extensively in the algorithm). As a result, for smaller values of t, we were able to run the algorithm up to larger values of a.

For $t = 2$, the algorithm is not needed. Indeed, the MDS property of the matrix guarantees that both S-boxes are active every second round, and hence, the lower bound on the number of active S-boxes in an r-round characteristic is at least $r/2$. The $t = 2$ variant of Poseidon has 82 PSPN rounds, and thus, any characteristic over the PSPN rounds has at least 41 active S-boxes. Interestingly, the lower bound obtained by the designers using the wide trail strategy is much lower – only 12 active S-boxes.

For $t = 6$, which is the main variant proposed by the designers, we were able to run the algorithm up to $a = 8$, showing that there is no characteristic with at most 8 active S-boxes for 22 rounds. As this variant of Poseidon contains 84 possible rounds, our result implies that any characteristic for the PSPN rounds of Poseidon activates at least 32 S-boxes. This number is higher than the lower bound proved by the designers – 28 active S-boxes in the SPN rounds. Combining the bounds, we obtain a provable lower bound of 60 active S-boxes for the entire cipher, more than doubling the bound proved by the designers.

For large values of t (e.g., $t = 16$), the lower bound that follows from the wide trail strategy becomes much more effective, and on the other hand, the number of PSPN rounds is reduced. As a result, our lower bound for the PSPN rounds is less effective for these variants.

It should be emphasized that for all variants and for all values of a we were able to check, the minimal number of rounds for which any characteristic must activate at least $a + 1$ S-boxes is $t + 2a$ – matching exactly the generic estimate of [2]. This suggests that in this respect, the MDS matrices of all Poseidon variants achieve the effect of 'random' matrices.

The lower bounds we obtained on the number of active S-boxes for different variants of Poseidon, along with the maximal values of a we were able to check, are presented in Table 3. The code we used is publicly available.[3] The exact description of the algorithm is given in Appendix A.

Table 3. Lower bounds on the number of active S-boxes in a differential or a linear characteristic over the PSPN rounds, for variants of Poseidon. The column 'a' denotes the number of active S-boxes checked by our algorithm.

Security level	t	R_F	R_P	Field	a	S-boxes in R_f	S-boxes in R_P	S-boxes in total
128	2	8	82	$GF(p)$	-	12	41	53
128	4	8	83	$GF(p)$	12	20	36	56
128	6	8	84	$GF(p)$	8	28	32	60
256	8	8	127	$GF(p)$	7	36	42	78
128	16	8	64	$GF(p)$	5	68	12	80

4 A Class of Matrices over a Binary Field and Its Properties

In this section we study the properties of a certain class of matrices over commutative rings with characteristic 2 (e.g., binary fields $GF(2^n)$). As we will show in

[3] The link to the code is: https://anonymous.4open.science/r/bc580cca-659f-4e8f-b8c1-9dfcd5fb75a2/.

Sect. 5, the MDS matrix used in Starkad belongs to this class (for all variants of Starkad), and thus, the results of this section will allow us to study the security of the middle layer of Starkad constructions.

4.1 Special Matrices and Their Basic Properties

Special matrices[4] are matrices of order 2^k (for $k \in \mathbb{N} \cup \{0\}$) over a ring R, defined in the following inductive way.

Definition 1. *For $k = 0$, any 1×1 matrix over R is a special matrix. For $k \geq 1$, a matrix $M \in R^{2^k \times 2^k}$ is a special matrix if $M = \begin{bmatrix} A & B \\ B & A \end{bmatrix}$, where A and B are special matrices.*

The following proposition summarizes some basic properties of special matrices. Most importantly, it shows that special matrices commute.

Proposition 1. *Let R be a ring, let $k \geq 0$, and let S_k be the set of all $2^k \times 2^k$ special matrices over R. Then S_k is a commutative subring of $R^{2^k \times 2^k}$.*

Proof. We have to show that for any $k \geq 0$, if $M_1, M_2 \in R^{2^k \times 2^k}$ are special matrices, then:

1. $-M_1, M_1 + M_2$, and $M_1 \cdot M_2$ are special matrices;
2. M_1 and M_2 commute.

The proof is a simple induction on k; we provide it for the sake of completeness. For $k = 0$ the claim is obvious. For $k > 0$, assume the claim holds for $k - 1$, and let

$$M_1 = \begin{bmatrix} A & B \\ B & A \end{bmatrix}, M_2 = \begin{bmatrix} C & D \\ D & C \end{bmatrix}$$

be $2^k \times 2^k$ special matrices. We have $M_1 + M_2 = \begin{bmatrix} A+C & B+D \\ B+D & A+C \end{bmatrix}$. As by the induction hypothesis, $A+C$ and $B+D$ are special matrices, $M_1 + M_2$ is a special matrix as well.

Similarly, for any $c \in R$ (and in particular, for $c = -1$),

$$c \cdot M_1 = \begin{bmatrix} c \cdot A & c \cdot B \\ c \cdot B & c \cdot A \end{bmatrix},$$

and thus by the induction hypothesis, $c \cdot M_1$ is a special matrix.

Furthermore, we have

$$M_1 \cdot M_2 = \begin{bmatrix} A \cdot C + B \cdot D & A \cdot D + B \cdot C \\ B \cdot C + A \cdot D & B \cdot D + A \cdot C \end{bmatrix} = \begin{bmatrix} X & Y \\ Y & X \end{bmatrix},$$

[4] We refrain from giving a meaningful name to this class of matrices, since most probably it was already considered in previous works (which we were not able to find so far).

where $X = A \cdot C + B \cdot D$ and $Y = A \cdot D + B \cdot C$. By the induction hypothesis X and Y are special matrices, and thus, $M_1 \cdot M_2$ is a special matrix as well.

To show that special matrices commute, we first observe that they are symmetric. Indeed, we have

$$M_1^T = \begin{bmatrix} A^T & B^T \\ B^T & A^T \end{bmatrix} = \begin{bmatrix} A & B \\ B & A \end{bmatrix} = M_1,$$

where the middle equality follows by induction on k. Now, let M_1, M_2 be special matrices. We have

$$M_1 \cdot M_2 = (M_1 \cdot M_2)^T = M_2^T \cdot M_1^T = M_2 \cdot M_1,$$

where the first equality uses the fact that $M_1 \cdot M_2$ is a special matrix, and hence, is symmetric. This completes the proof.

4.2 Special Matrices over Commutative Rings of Characteristic 2

When R is a commutative ring of characteristic 2 (i.e., a commutative ring such that for any $x \in R$, we have $x + x = 0$), special matrices over R have more interesting structural properties, as is shown in the following two propositions.

In particular, a special matrix has a single eigenvalue and is 'almost' an involution, and we have $\det(M_1 + M_2) = \det M_1 + \det M_2$ for any pair M_1, M_2 of special matrices over R.

Proposition 2. *Let R be a commutative ring of characteristic 2, let $k \in \mathbb{N} \cup \{0\}$, and let $M \in R^{2^k \times 2^k}$ be a special matrix. Then:*

1. *M has exactly one eigenvalue, which is the sum of elements in each of its rows. Consequently, the characteristic polynomial of M is*

$$f_M(x) = (x - \lambda(M))^{2^k},$$

   where $\lambda(M)$ is the unique eigenvalue of M, and $\det(M) = \lambda(M)^{2^k}$.
2. *We have $M^2 = \lambda(M)^2 \cdot I$.*

Proof. By induction on k. For $k = 0$ the claim is obvious. For $k > 0$, assume the claim holds for $k - 1$, and let $M = \begin{bmatrix} A & B \\ B & A \end{bmatrix}$ be a $2^k \times 2^k$ special matrix. The characteristic polynomial of M, which we denote by $f_M(\lambda)$, satisfies

$$\begin{aligned} f_M(\lambda) = \det(\lambda \cdot I - M) &= \det(\begin{bmatrix} \lambda \cdot I - A & -B \\ -B & \lambda \cdot I - A \end{bmatrix}) \\ &= \det(\lambda \cdot I - A + B) \cdot \det(\lambda \cdot I - A - B), \end{aligned}$$

where the last equality uses the well-known formula

$$\det(\begin{bmatrix} X & Y \\ Y & X \end{bmatrix}) = \det(X + Y) \cdot \det(X - Y),$$

which is a special case of Theorem 3 below. As $\mathrm{char}(R) = 2$, we have

$$f_M(\lambda) = \det(\lambda \cdot I - A + B) \cdot \det(\lambda \cdot I - A - B) = \det(\lambda \cdot I - (A + B))^2.$$

Since $A + B$ is a special matrix by Proposition 1, we can use the induction hypothesis to deduce

$$f_M(x) = f_{A+B}(x)^2 = (x - \lambda(A + B))^{2^k}.$$

Thus, $\lambda(A+B)$ is the only eigenvalue of M, and so we have $f_M(x) = (x-\lambda(M))^{2^k}$ and $\det(M) = \lambda(M)^{2^k}$, as asserted.

Since $\mathrm{char}(R) = 2$, and as special matrices commute by Proposition 1, we have

$$M^2 = \begin{bmatrix} A^2 + B^2 & AB + BA \\ BA + AB & A^2 + B^2 \end{bmatrix} = \begin{bmatrix} (A + B)^2 & 0 \\ 0 & (A + B)^2 \end{bmatrix}.$$

Since $A + B$ is a special matrix, we can use again the induction hypothesis to deduce

$$M^2 = \begin{bmatrix} (A + B)^2 & 0 \\ 0 & (A + B)^2 \end{bmatrix} = \begin{bmatrix} \lambda(A + B)^2 \cdot I & 0 \\ 0 & \lambda(A + B)^2 \cdot I \end{bmatrix} = \lambda(M)^2 \cdot I.$$

Finally, note that in any special matrix, the sums of elements in all rows are equal. Hence, the sum of elements in each row is an eigenvalue, that corresponds to the eigenvector $(1, 1, \ldots, 1)$. This completes the proof.

Proposition 3. *Let R be a commutative ring of characteristic 2, let $k \in \mathbb{N} \cup \{0\}$, and let $M_1, M_2 \in R^{2^k \times 2^k}$ be special matrices. Then*

1. $\det(M_1 + M_2) = \det(M_1) + \det(M_2)$;
2. $\lambda(M_1 + M_2) = \lambda(M_1) + \lambda(M_2)$;
3. $\lambda(M_1 \cdot M_2) = \lambda(M_1) \cdot \lambda(M_2)$,

where $\lambda(M)$ denotes the unique eigenvalue of the special matrix M.

Proof. Let

$$M_1 = \begin{bmatrix} A & B \\ B & A \end{bmatrix}, M_2 = \begin{bmatrix} C & D \\ D & C \end{bmatrix} \in R^{2^k \times 2^k}.$$

We have

$$\lambda(M_1 + M_2) = \lambda(A + B + C + D) = \lambda(A + B) + \lambda(C + D) = \lambda(M_1) + \lambda(M_2),$$

where the first and last transitions follow from the fact that $\lambda(M) = \lambda(A + B)$ as was shown in the proof of Proposition 2, and the middle transition uses the induction hypothesis.

Since $\mathrm{char}(R) = 2$ and R is commutative, we have

$$\begin{aligned} \det(M_1 + M_2) &= \lambda(M_1 + M_2)^{2^k} = (\lambda(M_1) + \lambda(M_2))^{2^k} \\ &= \lambda(M_1)^{2^k} + \lambda(M_2)^{2^k} = \det(M_1) + \det(M_2). \end{aligned}$$

Finally, as $(1, 1, \ldots, 1)$ is an eigenvector of both M_1 and M_2, corresponding to the eigenvalues $\lambda(M_1)$ and $\lambda(M_2)$, respectively, it follows that $\lambda(M_1) \cdot \lambda(M_2)$ is an eigenvalue of $M_1 \cdot M_2$, corresponding to the same eigenvector. As $M_1 \cdot M_2$ is a special matrix, Proposition 2 implies $\lambda(M_1 \cdot M_2) = \lambda(M_1) \cdot \lambda(M_2)$. This completes the proof.

4.3 Nilpotent Special Matrices over Commutative Rings with Characteristic 2

In this subsection we consider the subring N_k of S_k which consists of the special matrices M that are nilpotent (i.e., $N_k = \{M \in S_k : \exists t, M^t = 0\}$). By Proposition 2, N_k has a simple characterization: $N_k = \{M \in S_k : \lambda(M) = 0\}$. We aim at showing that the product of *any* $k + 1$ matrices in N_k equals zero. To this end, we need a somewhat complex inductive argument, which uses the following auxiliary operator.

Definition 2. *For any $k \geq 1$, the operator $* : S^k \to S^{k-1}$ is defined as follows. For any special matrix $M = \begin{bmatrix} A & B \\ B & A \end{bmatrix} \in S_k$, we define $M^* = A + B$. (Note that $M^* \in S_{k-1}$ since the sum of special matrices is a special matrix.)*

Basic properties of the operator $*$ are described in the following proposition. The easy proof is provided for the sake of completeness.

Proposition 4. *Let $M_1, M_2 \in S_k$ for some $k \geq 1$. We have:*

1. $(M_1 + M_2)^* = M_1^* + M_2^*$;
2. $(M_1 \cdot M_2)^* = M_1^* \cdot M_2^*$;
3. $\lambda(M_1^*) = \lambda(M_1)$.

Proof. Let $M_1 = \begin{bmatrix} A & B \\ B & A \end{bmatrix}$ and $M_2 = \begin{bmatrix} C & D \\ D & C \end{bmatrix}$ be special matrices. Then

$$(M_1 + M_2)^* = A + B + C + D = M_1^* + M_2^*.$$

Furthermore, $M_1 \cdot M_2 = \begin{bmatrix} AC + BD & AD + BC \\ AD + BC & AC + BD \end{bmatrix}$, and hence,

$$(M_1 \cdot M_2)^* = AC + BD + AD + BC = (A + B) \cdot (C + D) = M_1^* \cdot M_2^*.$$

Part (3) was shown in the proof of Proposition 2.

We now define, by induction on $k + \ell$, the notion of a special matrix $M \in S_k$ which is a *depth-ℓ zero*.

Definition 3. *For $\ell = 0$ and for any $k \in \mathbb{N}$, a matrix $M \in S_k$ is a depth-0 zero if and only if $\lambda(M) = 0$.*

For any ℓ, k such that $\ell \geq k$, a matrix $M \in S_k$ is a depth-ℓ zero if and only if it is the zero matrix.

For all $k > \ell \geq 1$, a matrix $M = \begin{bmatrix} A & B \\ B & A \end{bmatrix} \in S_k$ is a depth-ℓ zero if:

1. A and B are depth-($\ell - 1$) zeros, and
2. $M^* = A + B$ is a depth-ℓ zero.

The zero depth *of a matrix $M \in S_k$ is the maximal ℓ, such that M is a depth-ℓ zero.*

Intuitively, the higher is the zero depth of $M \in S_k$ related to k, the 'closer' is M to the zero matrix. In particular, if the zero depth of M is 0, we only know that $\lambda(M) = 0$. If the zero depth of M is $k-1$, then M is 'almost zero', in the sense that $M = \begin{bmatrix} X & X \\ X & X \end{bmatrix}$, where $X \in S_{k-1}$ has zero depth $k-2$. If the zero depth of M is k, then M is the zero matrix.

The two following propositions relate the zero depth of the sum and the product of special matrices to their zero depths.

Proposition 5. *Let $M_1, M_2 \in S_k$ be special matrices over a commutative ring R with characteristic 2 that are depth-ℓ zeros, and let $c \in R$. Then $c \cdot M_1$ and $M_1 + M_2$ are depth-ℓ zeros as well.*

Proof. For $\ell = 0$, the assertion follows immediately from Proposition 3 (i.e., additivity of the eigenvalue for special matrices).

For $\ell \geq 1$, the proof is an easy induction on k. For $k = 0$ the claim is obvious. Assume the claim holds for $k-1$ and let

$$M_1 = \begin{bmatrix} A & B \\ B & A \end{bmatrix}, M_2 = \begin{bmatrix} C & D \\ D & C \end{bmatrix} \in S_k$$

be depth-ℓ zeros. By definition, A, B, C, D are depth-($\ell - 1$) zeros, and thus, by the induction hypothesis (or by Proposition 3, in the case $\ell = 1$), $A + C, B + D$ (which are the blocks of $M_1 + M_2$) are depth-($\ell - 1$) zeros as well. Furthermore, $M_1^* = A + B$ and $M_2^* = C + D$ are depth-ℓ zeros, and thus, by the induction hypothesis, $(M_1 + M_2)^* = A + B + C + D$ is a depth-ℓ zero as well. Hence, $M_1 + M_2$ is a depth-ℓ zero. The proof for $c \cdot M_1$ is similar.

Proposition 6. *Let $M, L \in S_k$ be special matrices over a commutative ring R with characteristic 2, and assume that:*

1. M is a depth-ℓ zero for some $\ell < k$;
2. L is a depth-0 zero.

Then $M \cdot L$ is a depth-($\ell + 1$) zero.

Proof. We prove the claim by induction on $k + \ell$. For the base case, we consider $k = 1, \ell = 0$. In this case, since $k = 1$ and $\lambda(M) = \lambda(L) = 0$, M and L must be of the form

$$M = \begin{bmatrix} a & a \\ a & a \end{bmatrix}, L = \begin{bmatrix} b & b \\ b & b \end{bmatrix},$$

for some a, b. In such a case, $M \cdot L = 0$, which is a depth-1 zero, as asserted.

Assume the assertion holds for all k', ℓ' with $k' + \ell' < k + \ell$, and let

$$M = \begin{bmatrix} A & B \\ B & A \end{bmatrix}, L = \begin{bmatrix} C & D \\ D & C \end{bmatrix} \in S_k$$

be such that M is a depth-ℓ zero and $\lambda(L) = 0$. We have

$$M \cdot L = \begin{bmatrix} AC + BD & AD + BC \\ AD + BC & AC + BD \end{bmatrix} = \begin{bmatrix} X & Y \\ Y & X \end{bmatrix}.$$

We consider several cases:

Case 1: $0 < \ell < k - 1$. First, we show that $X + Y = (M \cdot L)^*$ is a depth-$(\ell + 1)$ zero. By Proposition 4, we have $(M \cdot L)^* = M^* \cdot L^*$. M^* is a depth-ℓ zero by definition and $\lambda(L^*) = \lambda(L) = 0$. Thus, by the induction hypothesis (which can be applied since $\ell < k - 1$), $M^* \cdot L^*$ is a depth-$(\ell + 1)$ zero.

Now we show that X and Y are depth-ℓ zeros. As $\lambda(M) = 0$, we have $\lambda(C) = \lambda(D)$. Denote $\lambda(C) = \lambda(D) = \gamma$, and let $C' = C + \gamma \cdot I, D' = D + \gamma \cdot I$. We have

$$X = A \cdot (C' + \gamma \cdot I) + B \cdot (D' + \gamma \cdot I) = A \cdot C' + B \cdot D' + \gamma \cdot M^*.$$

By Proposition 5, $\gamma \cdot M^*$ is a depth-ℓ zero and by the induction hypothesis (which can be applied since $\ell > 0$), $A \cdot C'$ and $B \cdot D'$ are depth-ℓ zeros as well. Hence, by Proposition 5, X is a depth-ℓ zero. The proof for Y is similar.

Case 2: $\ell = 0$. In this case, the proof that $X + Y$ is a depth-1 zero works like in Case 1.

We now prove that X is a depth-0 zero; the proof for Y is similar. Since M and L are depth-0 zeros, we have $\lambda(A) = \lambda(B)$ and $\lambda(C) = \lambda(D)$. Hence, Proposition 3 implies

$$\lambda(X) = \lambda(AC + BD) = \lambda(A)\lambda(C) + \lambda(B)\lambda(D) = 0,$$

and thus, X is a depth-0 zero, as asserted.

Case 3: $\ell = k - 1$. In this case, the proof that X and Y are depth-ℓ zeros works like in Case 1. As $X, Y \in S_{k-1}$, this means that $X = Y = 0$, and thus, $M \cdot L$ is the zero matrix, which is of course a depth-$(\ell + 1)$-zero. This completes the proof.

Now we are ready to prove that the product of any $k + 1$ elements of N_k is the zero matrix.

Proposition 7. *Let $M_1, ..., M_{k+1}$ be 2^k-by-2^k nilpotent special matrices over a commutative ring R with characteristic 2. Then*

$$\prod_{i=1}^{k+1} M_i = 0.$$

Proof. By applying Proposition 6 on the sequence of products $P_j = \prod_{i=1}^{j} M_i$, we deduce that for all $j \geq 1$, P_j is a depth-$(j - 1)$ zero. In particular, $P_{k+1} = \prod_{i=1}^{k+1} M_i$ is a depth-k zero, which means that it is the zero matrix by the definition of zero depth.

4.4 Block Matrices with Special Blocks

In this subsection we consider s-by-s block matrices over a commutative ring R with characteristic 2, in which each block is a special 2^k-by-2^k matrix. We aim at showing that the *minimal polynomial* of any such matrix is of degree at most $s(k+1)$. As an intermediate result, we show that the characteristic polynomial of any such matrix has a very specific structure.

We use the following classical result (see, e.g., [16, Theorem 1]) on determinants of block matrices with commuting blocks.

Theorem 3. *Let $\ell, m \in \mathbb{N}$. Let R be a commutative ring and let S be a commutative subring of $R^{\ell \times \ell}$. Let $X \in S^{m \times m}$ be an m-by-m block matrix over R with ℓ-by-ℓ blocks in S. Then $\det_R(X) = \det_R(\det_S(X))$.*

The theorem asserts that if the blocks of the matrix commute, then in order to compute its determinant, we can first compute the determinant of the 'matrix of blocks' (an m-by-m matrix over the ring S), which in itself is an ℓ-by-ℓ matrix over R, and then compute the determinant (over R) of this determinant.

In the case of block matrices over a commutative ring with characteristic 2 whose blocks are special matrices, the computation of the determinant can be further simplified.

Proposition 8. *Let $k, s \in \mathbb{N}$. Let R be a commutative ring with characteristic 2, and let M be an s-by-s block matrix over R, each of whose blocks is a 2^k-by-2^k special matrix. Denote the blocks of M by $\{M_{i,j}\}_{i,j=1}^{s}$. Let $M' \subset R^{s \times s}$ be defined by $M'_{i,j} = \det(M_{i,j})$. Then $\det(M) = \det(M')$.*

The proposition asserts that for block matrices with special blocks, in order to compute the determinant, we can replace each block with its determinant and compute the determinant of the resulting s-by-s matrix.

Proof. By Theorem 3, we have $\det(M) = \det_R(\det_S(M))$. The expression $\det_S(M)$ is a sum-of-products of special matrices. As in the subring S_k of special matrices, the determinant is multiplicative *and additive* by Proposition 3, the expression $\det_R(\det_S(M))$ does not change if we replace each matrix in $\det_S(M)$ with its determinant. The result is exactly $\det(M')$. Thus, $\det(M) = \det(M')$, as asserted.

We are now ready for computing the characteristic polynomial of a block matrix whose blocks are special matrices.

Proposition 9. *Let $k, s \in \mathbb{N}$. Let R be a commutative ring with characteristic 2, and let M be an s-by-s block matrix over R, each of whose blocks is a 2^k-by-2^k special matrix. Denote the blocks of M by $\{M_{i,j}\}_{i,j=1}^{s}$. Let $M'' \subset R^{s \times s}$ be defined by $M''_{i,j} = \lambda(M_{i,j})$, where $\lambda(M_{i,j})$ is the unique eigenvalue of the special matrix $M_{i,j}$. Denote by $p(x) = f_M(x)$ and $q(x) = f_{M''}(x)$ the characteristic polynomials of M and M'', respectively. Then $p(x) = q(x)^{2^k}$.*

Proof. Since $\text{char}(R) = 2$, we have $p(\lambda) = f_M(\lambda) = \det(\lambda \cdot I + M)$. As the blocks of $\lambda \cdot I + M$ are special matrices (over the commutative ring $R[\lambda]$ that has characteristic 2), by Proposition 8 the expression $\det(\lambda \cdot I + M)$ does not change if we replace each block with its determinant. For non-diagonal blocks $M_{i,j}$, the replacement yields $M'_{i,j}$, where M' is as defined in the proof of Proposition 8. For diagonal blocks $M_{i,i}$, by Proposition 3 we have

$$\det(\lambda \cdot I + M_{i,i}) = \det(\lambda \cdot I) + \det(M_{i,i}) = \lambda^{2^k} + M'_{i,i}.$$

Therefore, we have

$$p(\lambda) = \det(\lambda \cdot I + M) = \det(\lambda^{2^k} \cdot I + M') = f_{M'}(\lambda^{2^k}).$$

Denote $f_{M'}(x) = \sum_{l=0}^{s} f_l(\{M'_{ij}\}) \cdot x^l$, where each $f_l(\{M'_{ij}\})$ is a sum of products of M'_{ij}'s. Recall that for any i, j,

$$M'_{i,j} = \det(M_{i,j}) = (\lambda(M_{i,j}))^{2^k} = (M''_{i,j})^{2^k}.$$

As $\text{char}(R) = 2$ (and so, the function $x \mapsto x^{2^k}$ is linear over R), it follows that for each l, $f_l(\{M'_{i,j}\}) = f_l(\{M''_{i,j}\})^{2^k}$. Hence,

$$f_{M'}(\lambda^{2^k}) = \sum_{l=0}^{s} f_l(\{M''_{i,j}\})^{2^k} (\lambda^{2^k})^l = (\sum_{l=0}^{s} f_l(\{M''_{i,j}\})\lambda^l)^{2^k}.$$

Finally, as $\sum_{l=0}^{s} f_l(\{M''_{i,j}\})\lambda^l = f_{M''}(\lambda)$, we obtain

$$p(\lambda) = f_{M'}(\lambda^{2^k}) = (f_{M''}(\lambda))^{2^k} = q(\lambda)^{2^k}.$$

This completes the proof.

We are now ready to show that the degree of the minimal polynomial of a block matrix whose blocks are special matrices is much lower than the degree of its characteristic polynomial. Specifically, we prove that its degree is at most $s(k+1)$, while the degree of the characteristic polynomial is $s \cdot 2^k$.

Proposition 10. *Let $k, s \in \mathbb{N}$. Let R be a commutative ring with characteristic 2, and let M be an s-by-s block matrix over R, each of whose blocks is a 2^k-by-2^k special matrix. Denote the blocks of M by $\{M_{i,j}\}_{i,j=1}^{s}$. Let $M'' \subset R^{s \times s}$ be defined by $M''_{i,j} = \lambda(M_{i,j})$, where $\lambda(M_{i,j})$ is the unique eigenvalue of the special matrix $M_{i,j}$. Denote by $q(x) = f_{M''}(x)$ the characteristic polynomial of M''. Then $q(M)^{k+1} = 0$.*

Proof. First, we claim that $q(M)$ is a block matrix whose blocks are *nilpotent* special matrices (equivalently, special matrices whose unique eigenvalue is 0). Indeed, the blocks of $q(M)$ are special matrices, since they are sums-of-products of special matrices. Hence, we can represent each such block $(q(M))_{i,j}$ in the form $\sum \prod A_i$, where all A_i are special matrices. By Proposition 3, we have

$$\lambda(q(M)_{i,j}) = \lambda(\sum \prod A_i) = \sum \prod \lambda(A_i) = (q(M''))_{i,j} = 0,$$

where the last equality holds since $q(M'') = 0$ by the Cayley-Hamilton theorem.

Now, we can apply Proposition 7. Consider the matrix $q(M)^{k+1}$. Each block of this matrix is a sum of products of $k+1$ nilpotent 2^k-by-2^k special matrices. By Proposition 7, each such product is the zero matrix. Hence, each block of $q(M)^{k+1}$ is the zero matrix, and thus, $q(M)^{k+1} = 0$, as asserted.

4.5 A Stronger Conjectured Bound

We conjecture that Proposition 10 can be further improved, and that in fact, the following holds:

Conjecture 1. Let $k, s \in \mathbb{N}$. Let R be a commutative ring with characteristic 2, and let M be an s-by-s block matrix over R, each of whose blocks is a 2^k-by-2^k special matrix. Denote the blocks of M by $\{M_{i,j}\}_{i,j=1}^{s}$. Let $M'' \subset R^{s \times s}$ be defined by $M''_{i,j} = \lambda(M_{i,j})$, where $\lambda(M_{i,j})$ is the unique eigenvalue of the special matrix $M_{i,j}$. Denote by $q(x) = f_{M''}(x)$ the characteristic polynomial of M''. Then $q(M)^2 = 0$.

We proved this conjecture for $s = 2$ by a direct computation (which we omit here, being not sufficiently illuminating), and verified it experimentally for many values of t, over various binary fields (including the field $GF(2^{33})$ used in Starkad with $t = 47$). In particular, it matches all sizes of invariant subspaces presented in Table 2. However, we were not able to prove the conjecture in general at this stage.

5 A Large Invariant Subspace in the Middle Layer of Starkad Permutations

In this section we apply the results on special matrices obtained in Sect. 4 to show that for many choices of t (i.e., the number of S-boxes in each round), the Starkad permutation admits a huge invariant subspace that allows bypassing any number of PSPN rounds without activating any S-box. We then explain how the invariant subspace can be used to mount a Gröbner basis preimage attack on Starkad, using an attack strategy proposed by Beyne et al. [6]. Subsequently, we show that these invariant subspaces can be easily avoided, by a careful choice of parameters, or by very mild changes in the design.

5.1 The Starkad MDS and Special Matrices

In this subsection we show that *for any choice of the parameters*, the Starkad MDS is a block matrix over a binary field $GF(2^n)$ (which is, in particular, a commutative ring with characteristic 2), whose blocks are special matrices. This will allow us to deduce Theorems 1 and 2 from the results on special matrices obtained in Sect. 4.

We start with the case $t = 2^k$.

Proposition 11. *Let $M \in GF(2^n)^{2^k \times 2^k}$ be a Cauchy matrix generated from the sequences $\{x_i\}, \{y_j\}$, where for each $1 \leq i \leq 2^k$, we have $x_i = i - 1$ and $y_i = x_i + r$ (integer summation), for some r such that $2^k | r$. Then M is a special matrix.*

Proof. In the following, we use the symbols $\boxplus$ and $\boxminus$ to denote integer addition and subtraction and $\oplus$ to denote bit-wise XOR, which is addition in the field.

We prove the claim by induction on k. For $k = 0$ the claim is obvious, assume the claim holds for $k-1$. Let $M = \begin{bmatrix} A & B \\ C & D \end{bmatrix} \in \mathbb{F}^{2^k \times 2^k}$ be a Cauchy matrix generated as described above. A is obviously a $2^{k-1} \times 2^{k-1}$ Cauchy matrix with

$$x_i = i \boxminus 1, y_i = x_i \boxplus r,$$

and thus, by the induction hypothesis, is a special matrix.

D is a $2^{k-1} \times 2^{k-1}$ Cauchy matrix with

$$x_i = 2^{k-1} \boxplus i \boxminus 1, y_i = x_i \boxplus r,$$

for all $1 \leq i \leq 2^{k-1}$. Using the range of the $i \boxminus 1$'s, we conclude that $x_i = 2^{k-1} \boxplus (i \boxminus 1) = 2^{k-1} \oplus x'_i$ for $x'_i = i \boxminus 1$. Similarly, as $2^k | r$, $y_i = x_i \boxplus r = x_i \oplus r$. Thus,

$$\begin{aligned} D_{ij} &= (x_i \oplus y_j)^{-1} = (x'_i \oplus 2^{k-1} \oplus x_j \oplus r)^{-1} = (x'_i \oplus 2^{k-1} \oplus x'_j \oplus 2^{k-1} \oplus r)^{-1} \\ &= (x'_i \oplus x'_j \oplus r)^{-1} = (x'_i \oplus (x'_j \boxplus r))^{-1} = A_{ij}. \end{aligned}$$

Hence, $D = A$.

Define $r' \triangleq 2^{k-1} \oplus r$. Notice that B is a Cauchy matrix with $x_i = i \boxminus 1, y_i = x_i \boxplus r \boxplus 2^{k-1}$. As $0 \leq x_i < 2^{k-1}$ and $2^k | r$, we have

$$y_i = x_i \oplus 2^{k-1} \oplus r = x_i \oplus r' = x_i \boxplus r'.$$

As r' is divisible by 2^{k-1}, we can use the induction hypothesis to conclude that B is also a special matrix.

C is a Cauchy matrix with $x_i = 2^{k \boxminus 1} \boxplus (i \boxminus 1) = 2^{k-1} \oplus (i-1), y_i = r \boxplus (i \boxminus 1) = r \oplus (i \boxminus 1)$. Thus $C_{ij} = (x_i \oplus y_j)^{-1} = ((i-1) \oplus (j-1) \oplus r')^{-1} = B_{ij}$. Hence, $C = B$. We proved that A, B are special and that $C = B, D = A$. Thus, M is a special matrix, as asserted.

Corollary 1. *For any $t = 2^k$, the MDS in Starkad with t S-boxes in each SPN round is a special matrix.*

Corollary 1 follows immediately from Proposition 11, since the sequences $\{x_i\}$ and $\{y_j\}$ used in Starkad to generate the Cauchy matrix are exactly those considered in the proposition, and since the parameter r is chosen in Starkad to be equal to t.

Now we consider variants of Starkad with any number t of S-boxes in each round.

Proposition 12. *Let $t = 2^k \cdot s$, for $k \geq 0$ and $s \geq 1$. Let $M \in GF(2^n)^{t \times t}$ be a Cauchy matrix generated from the sequences $\{x_i\}, \{y_j\}$, where for each $1 \leq i \leq 2^k$, we have $x_i = i - 1$ and $y_i = x_i + r$ (integer summation), for some r such that $2^k | r$. Then M is an $s \times s$ block matrix of $2^k \times 2^k$ special matrices.*

Proof. Divide the matrix M into $s \times s$ blocks of $2^k \times 2^k$ matrices. Denote the blocks by $M_{p,q}, 1 \leq p, q \leq s$. Let $M_{p,q}$ be one of the blocks and we will prove that it is a special matrix. $M_{p,q}$ is a Cauchy matrix with

$$x_i = (i \boxminus 1) \boxplus p2^k = (i \boxminus 1) \oplus p2^k, y_i = (i \boxminus 1) \boxplus q2^k \boxplus t = (i \boxminus 1) \oplus (q2^k \boxplus t).$$

Define $t' \triangleq p2^k \oplus (q2^k \boxplus t)$. We have

$$\begin{aligned}(M_{p,q})_{ij} &= ((i \boxminus 1) \oplus (j \boxminus 1) \oplus (p2^k \oplus (q2^k \boxplus t)))^{-1} \\ &= ((i \boxminus 1) \oplus (j \boxminus 1) \oplus t')^{-1} = ((i \boxminus 1) \oplus ((j \boxminus 1) \boxplus t'))^{-1}.\end{aligned}$$

Notice that $2^k | t'$, and thus, $M_{p,q}$ satisfies the assumption of Proposition 11, and thus, is a special matrix. This completes the proof.

Corollary 2. *For any $t = 2^k \cdot s$, the MDS in Starkad with t S-boxes in each SPN round is an s-by-s block matrix, each of whose blocks is a special matrix.*

Corollary 1 follows immediately from Proposition 11, since $\{x_i\}, \{y_j\}$, and r used in Starkad satisfy the assumption of the proposition.

5.2 A Large Invariant Subspace in Starkad with 4ℓ S-Boxes in Each Full Round

In this subsection we prove Theorems 1 and 2. The former shows that for any $t = 4\ell$, Starkad with t S-boxes in each SPN round admits a large invariant subspace. The latter asserts that if t is a power of 2, then the MDS of Starkad with t S-boxes in each SPN round is essentially an involution.

First, we prove Theorem 1. Let us recall its statement.

Theorem 1. Let $\mathbb{F} = GF(2^n)$ be a binary field. Let $t = 2^k \cdot s$ where $s \in \mathbb{N}$. Let M be a t-by-t Cauchy matrix over $\mathbb{F}$ constructed according to the Starkad specification. Then there exists a linear subspace $U \subset \mathbb{F}^t$ of dimension at least $(1 - \frac{k+1}{2^k})t$ such that for any $\ell \in \mathbb{N}$ and for any $x \in U$, the top n bits of $M^\ell x$ are equal to zero. Consequently, application of any number of PSPN rounds to any $x \in U$ does not activate any S-box.

Proof. Let M be a matrix that satisfies the assumptions of the theorem. By Corollary 2, it is an s-by-s block matrix, where each block is a 2^k-by-2^k special matrix. Hence, by Proposition 10, there exists a polynomial q' of degree $s(k+1)$ such that $q'(M) = 0$.

Let

$$U = \{x \in GF(2^n)^t : \forall 0 \leq i \leq s(k+1) - 1, (M^i x)_1 = 0\},$$

where $(X)_1$ stands for the top n bits of X that enter the unique S-box in the PSPN rounds. Clearly, U is a linear subspace of dimension at least $s(2^k - (k+1)) = (1 - \frac{k+1}{2^k})t$. We claim that for any $\ell \in \mathbb{N}$ and for any $x \in U$, the top n bits of $M^\ell x$ are equal to zero. Indeed, using division of polynomials we can write $M^\ell = q'(M) \cdot q_0(M) + q_1(M)$, where $\deg(q_1(M)) < \deg(q'(M)) = s(k+1)$. We have

$$(M^\ell x)_1 = (q'(M) \cdot q_0(M)x + q_1(M)x)_1 = (q_1(M)x)_1 = 0,$$

where the second equality holds since $q'(M) = 0$ and the last inequality holds since $\deg(q_1(M)) < s(k+1)$ and $x \in U$. This completes the proof.

As for any $k \geq 2$ we have $(k+1)/2^k \leq 3/4$, Theorem 1 implies that whenever the number t of S-boxes in each full round of Starkad is divisible by 4, there exists a linear subspace of dimension at least $t/4$ that does not activate any S-box for any number of PSPN rounds. If t is divisible by 8, the lower bound on the dimension of the subspace increases to $t/2$, if $16|t$, it increases to $11t/16$, etc.

In the cases where t is a power of 2, the structure of the Starkad MDS is surprisingly simple, as is shown in Theorem 2. Let us recall its statement.

Theorem 2. Let $\mathbb{F} = GF(2^n)$ be a binary field, and let $t = 2^k$ for $k \in \mathbb{N}$. Let M be a t-by-t Cauchy matrix over $\mathbb{F}$ constructed according to the Starkad specification. Then $M^2 = \alpha I$, where $\alpha = (\sum_{j=2^k}^{2^{k+1}-1} j^{-1})^2$. Consequently, there exists a linear subspace $U \subset \mathbb{F}^t$ of dimension at least $t-2$ such that for any $\ell \in \mathbb{N}$ and for any $x \in U$, the top n bits of $M^\ell x$ are equal to zero.

Proof. Let M be a matrix that satisfies the assumption of the theorem. By Corollary 1, M is a special matrix. By Proposition 2, we have $M^2 = \alpha \cdot I$, where $\alpha = \lambda(M)^2$, and $\lambda(M)$ (i.e., the unique eigenvalue of M) is the sum of elements in each row of M. By the construction of the Starkad MDS, these elements are the inverses of $\{2^k + i\}_{i=0}^{2^k-1}$. Hence,

$$\alpha = (\sum_{j=2^k}^{2^{k+1}-1} j^{-1})^2,$$

as asserted. Finally, the dimension of the subspace U is at least $t-2$, since it is sufficient to require $x_1 = 0$ and $(Mx)_1 = 0$, by the argument used in the proof of Theorem 1. This completes the proof.

5.3 Using the Invariant Subspaces for a Preimage Attack

In [6, Sec. 6.2], Beyne et al. showed that if the linear layer of Starkad or Poseidon was an involution, this could be used to mount a Gröbner basis preimage attack on the scheme.

Brief Description of the Attack of [6]. The basic idea behind the attack is simple. Assuming that the linear layer is involutionary, it is easy to show that there exists an invariant subspace of dimension $t-2$ over the field (where t is the number of S-boxes in each round) that passes all PSPN rounds without activating any S-box. Hence, if we restrict ourselves to plaintexts whose intermediate values lie in the invariant subspace, a Gröbner basis attack on the scheme can bypass all PSPN rounds for free. The condition that the intermediate value resides in the invariant subspace can be added as a set of linear constraints to the system of equations in the Gröbner basis attack, without increasing its complexity significantly. The preimage is then found by representing the full rounds as a system of equations, adding the linear constraints, and solving the resulting system of equations using Gröbner basis methods.

The authors of [6] conclude that a preimage can be found in time

$$2\gamma(2\pi)^{-\omega/2}(c+2)^{2-\omega/2}e^{\omega(c+2)}3^{(\omega(c+2)+1)(R_F-1)}, \tag{1}$$

where the parameters γ and ω are such that the computational cost of computing the row-reduced echelon form of an m-by-n matrix is γmn^{ω} (see [6, Appendix A]).[5]

Application of the Attack in our Scenario. The preimage attack of [6] is presented in terms of the multiplicative order of the linear layer (which is actually very high in Starkad, unless t is a power of 2). However, it is easy to see by going over the proof of [6, Lemma 2], that the multiplicative order of the matrix can be replaced by the co-dimension of the invariant subspace that passes the PSPN rounds without activating any S-box. (In other words, there is no difference between the case where $M^k = \alpha I$ for some constant α and the more general case where the minimal polynomial of M is of degree at most k).

Therefore, the attack described above can be applied to Starkad, where in the formula of the time complexity (i.e., Eq. (1) above) $c+2$ is replaced with $c+d'$, where d' is the degree of the minimal polynomial of M. In particular, if we take a variant of Starkad with the binary field $GF(2^{127})$ as was proposed in the Starkware Challenge [17] for 256-bit security, and take t to be any power of 2, then the scheme admits a preimage attack of complexity about 2^{220}, which breaks the 256-bit security bound.

We note however that for all actually proposed sets of parameters, the complexity of the preimage attack we described does not break the security bound.

[5] Note that these results are weaker than the results claimed in [6, Sec. 6.2]; specifically, we replace c by $c+2$, which affects the results significantly. In particular, this means that among the results presented in [6, Table 5], the complexity of the attack on the variant 128-e is increased from $2^{44.2}$ to about 2^{115}, the complexity of the attack on 256-b is increased from $2^{150.9}$ to about 2^{220}, and the attack on 128-c becomes infeasible. In addition, the attack on the variant 256-a fails as well, since for that variant we have $c = t/2$, while the attack applies only for $c < t/2$, as is explained in [6, Sec. 6]. The authors of [6] admitted (in private communication [5]) that the formula they wrote was incorrect, and agreed with our correction.

5.4 The Invariant Subspaces Can Be Avoided Easily

While it is not clear whether the invariant subspaces presented above can be exploited to attack the Starkad hash function, it seems clear that their existence is an undesirable feature. The 'good news' are that these subspaces can be easily avoided, by a careful choice of parameters. We present below three possible ways to make sure that the middle layer of Starkad cannot be bypassed without activating any S-box.

Choosing the Value of t Carefully. One possible way is to choose t that is not divisible by 4. As was exemplified in Table 2 for several values of t, in most cases[6] where t is not divisible by 4, there is no invariant subspace of the form described above. Furthermore, given a value of t, we can use the tool described in Sect. 3 to guarantee that any t-round characteristic indeed activates at least one S-box.

Changing the Parameter r. Another possible way is to change the parameter r used in the generation of the MDS matrix. Recall that the MDS matrix is a Cauchy matrix, generated by the sequences $\{x_i\}, \{y_j\}$, where $x_i = i - 1$ and $y_i = x_i + r$ (integer addition). The designers fixed $r = t$.

The relation of the Starkad matrix to special matrices, proved in Proposition 12, assumes that r is divisible by 2^k (which is obviously satisfied by $r = t$). This suggests that choosing a different value of r might avoid the invariant subspace. Our experiments, performed with $n = 2^{63}$ and $t = 24$, indicate that indeed, whenever r is not divisible by 4, there is no invariant subspace of the form described above (see Table 4). As before, given such a value of r, we can use the strategy described in Sect. 3 to guarantee that any t-round characteristic indeed activates at least one S-box.

Table 4. The dimension of the invariant subspace whose elements do not activate S-boxes for any number of PSPN rounds, as a function of r, for a Starkad permutation over the field $GF(2^{63})$ with $t = 24$

r	Dimension of invariant subspace	r	Dimension of invariant subspace	r	Dimension of invariant subspace
24	18	25	0	26	0
27	0	28	12	29	0
30	0	31	0	32	20
40	18	47	0	52	12
64	20	101	0	128	20

[6] We checked this experimentally, with numerous values of t and n. The only 'counterexamples' we are aware of occur for small values of n, that is, over small-sized binary fields.

Shifting the Sequence $\{x_i\}$. A third possible mild change is shifting the sequence $\{x_i\}$, namely, taking $x_i = x_0+i-1$ for some $x_0 \neq 0$. In this case, our experiments (performed with $n = 2^{63}$ and $t = 24$, see Table 5) indicate that non-divisibility of x_0 by 4 is not a sufficient condition. However, there exist many values of x_0 for which there is no invariant subspace of the form described above, and as before, for such values of x_0 we can guarantee that any t-round characteristic indeed activates at least one S-box using the technique of Sect. 3.

Table 5. The dimension of the invariant subspace whose elements do not activate S-boxes for any number of PSPN rounds, as a function of x_0 (the initial element of the sequence $\{x_i\}$ used in the construction of the Cauchy matrix), for a Starkad cipher over the field $GF(2^{63})$ with $t = 24$

x_0	Dimension of invariant subspace	x_0	Dimension of invariant subspace	x_0	Dimension of invariant subspace
0	18	1	6	2	0
3	0	4	12	5	0
6	0	7	12	8	18
9	6	10	0	11	0
12	12	13	0	14	0
15	12	16	18	17	6

6 Discussion and Open Problems

We conclude this paper with a discussion on the implication of our results on the HADES design strategy, and with a few open problems.

6.1 Discussion: PSPN Rounds Vs. SPN Rounds

In this paper we showed that the MDS matrix used in HADES constructions significantly affects the security level provided by the cryptosystem. This emphasizes the need of choosing the MDS matrix in the construction carefully, but also gives rise to a more general question regarding the design strategy.

Specifically, we showed in Sect. 3 that when the MDS matrix is chosen properly (which is the case for all suggested variants of Poseidon, an instantiation of HADES for prime fields), the lower bound on the number of active S-boxes in differential and linear characteristics can be significantly improved by taking into consideration the PSPN rounds. In some of the cases, the lower bound we obtain on the number of active S-boxes in the PSPN rounds is *much larger* than the lower bound obtained by the designers using the wide-trail strategy.

This gives rise to the question, whether full SPN rounds are 'cost effective' compared to PSPN rounds, in scenarios where the complexity is dominated by the number of S-boxes in the construction (which are the target scenarios of the HADES design strategy).

As was emphasized by the HADES designers, PSPN rounds are more cost-effective with respect to algebraic attacks, since when the linear layer is an MDS, the increase of the algebraic degree obtained by a PSPN round is the same as the increase obtained by an SPN round which uses t times more S-boxes. It should be noted (and was also emphasized by the HADES designers) that security with respect to algebraic attacks is determined not only by the algebraic degree, and thus, a single PSPN round provides less security with respect to algebraic attacks than an SPN round. However, it seems clear that t PSPN rounds provide a much larger security increase than a single SPN round, while employing the same number of S-boxes.

The HADES designers motivate the use of the SPN rounds by protection against statistical – mainly differential and linear – attacks, and in particular, by the ability to use the wide trail strategy for proving lower bounds on the number of active S-boxes in differential and linear characteristics. It turns out however that when the MDS matrix is chosen properly, the number of active S-boxes in a characteristic over PSPN rounds is not much smaller than the respective number for SPN rounds that employ the same number of S-boxes. Indeed, the wide trail strategy provides a tight lower bound of $t+1$ active S-boxes over two rounds which employ $2t$ S-boxes in total. For PSPN rounds with a single S-box in each round, the analysis of [2] suggests that for a 'good' MDS, the minimal number of active S-boxes over m rounds (which employ m S-boxes) is $\frac{m-t}{2}+1$. While the ratio $\frac{t+1}{2t}$ obtained by SPN rounds is somewhat larger than the ratio $\frac{m-t+2}{2m}$ obtained for PSPN rounds, the asymptotic difference between the ratios is small.

The wide trail strategy has the advantages of being generic, and of applicability to any number of active S-boxes (compared to the algorithm of [2] we use in this paper, which depends on the specific structure of the cipher and on the available computational resources). However, if indeed the advantage of SPN rounds with respect to statistical attacks[7] is small, while the advantage of PSPN rounds with respect to algebraic attacks is very large, then it might make sense to change the balance between the numbers of rounds in favor of PSPN rounds.

6.2 Open Problems

Finding Better Ways to Exploit the Invariant Subspace in Starkad. The first open problem arising from this paper is, whether there are more efficient ways

[7] It should be noted that in our analysis, we considered only differential and linear attacks, and not other types of statistical attacks. However, for all other classes of attacks, the security arguments provided for SPN constructions are heuristic, and hence, there is no clear way to decide whether r full SPN rounds provide a better security guarantee against those attacks, compared to tr PSPN rounds. Therefore, we focus on differential and linear attacks, for which the results are 'measurable'.

to exploit the large invariant subspaces found for variants of Starkad to mount attacks on the schemes.

Optimal Bound on the Size of the Invariant Subspace. Another open problem is to prove Conjecture 1 – namely, to show that the dimension of the invariant subspace for $t = 2^k \cdot s$ is at least $t - 2s$. Numerous experiments suggest that the conjecture (which would be tight if proved) indeed holds, and it seems that a proof is not out of reach.

Improved Cryptanalysis Techniques for PSPN Rounds. As was pointed out by the HADES designers, the cryptanalysis tools available for PSPN designs are very scarce. Developing new tools (and improving existing ones, like that of [2] we used) may enable a wider use of PSPN rounds, and further development of designs based on them. In particular, it seems unclear whether a design that contains *only PSPN rounds* with a few S-boxes in each round is necessarily problematic, despite the mixed success of previous designs of this class (Zorro and LowMC).

The recent paper [13] is a first step in this direction, but the main problems in the understanding of PSPN designs are still open.

Balancing the Number of SPN vs. PSPN Rounds in HADES Designs. As was mentioned in the above discussion, our results may suggest that one can design more efficient instantiations of HADES by choosing the MDS properly, taking into consideration the middle layer, and changing the balance between SPN and PSPN rounds. It will be interesting to find out whether this is indeed possible. To be concrete, we suggest studying the following variant.

Question 1. Consider a variant of Poseidon in which the $2R_f$ SPN rounds are replaced by tR_f PSPN rounds (and so, the cipher has only PSPN rounds, and the total number of S-boxed is reduced by tR_f). What is the security level of the new variant, compared to the initial variant?

If the security level of the new variant is not lower, this allows to speed up variants of Poseidon without reducing their security level, and suggests that using only PSPN rounds is advantageous over combining SPN and PSPN rounds, provided that the linear transformation is chosen properly.

Acknowledgements. The authors are grateful to Tim Beyne, Itai Dinur, Lorenzo Grassi and Christian Rechberger, for helpful discussions and suggestions.

A Detailed Description of the Pattern Search Algorithm

In this appendix we describe in detail the pattern search algorithm we applied to variants of the Poseidon permutation. The code of the algorithm is publicly available at: https://anonymous.4open.science/r/bc580cca-659f-4e8f-b8c1-9dfcd5fb75a2/.

A.1 Checking a Single Pattern

In order to check whether there exists a differential characteristic following a specific pattern, one can use the following algorithm:

algorithm **Check-Pattern**(pattern), pattern $\in \binom{[n]}{a}$

1. $ST := (I_t; 0_{a+t})$
2. $E := \emptyset$
3. $s := t + 1$
4. for every $i = 1 : n$
   (a) if $i \in$ pattern: $ST_1 \leftarrow e_s, s \leftarrow s + 1$
   (b) if $i \notin$ pattern: $E \leftarrow E \cup ST_1$
   (c) $ST \leftarrow M \cdot ST$
5. Solve the equation system E, return TRUE if and only if there exists a nontrivial solution

Explanation of the Algorithm. Each row of the state corresponds to the coefficients in the linear combination of the $t + a$ variables. Thus, the beginnings of the rows consist of the unit vectors $e_1, \ldots, e_t$.

On a non-active S-box, we get a linear restriction by the coefficients in the first row. On an active S-box, we replace the first row by a new variable, which is represented by e_s.

The state is updated after the S-box layer, using the MDS matrix. When we finish posing the linear equations, we can solve the system E using Gaussian elimination and check whether there exists a solution. We note that for linear characteristics, the same algorithm can be used, with the matrix $(M^T)^{-1}$ instead of M.

A.2 Checking All r-Round Patterns with a Active S-boxes

We can also iterate over all the patterns of length r with a active S-boxes, using the following simple recursive algorithm:

function **Search-Pattern**(pref, s, a, i, n):

1. if $i \geq n - 1 \wedge$ Check-Pattern(pref) : output pref
2. if $i < t + 2s$: Search-Pattern(pref,$s, a, i + 1, n$)
3. if $s < a \wedge 2s < i$: Search-Pattern(pref $\cup \{i\}, s + 1, a, i + 1, n$)

Explanation of the Algorithm. The word "pref" denotes a prefix of the pattern, s is the number of active S-boxes in the prefix, i is the length of the prefix and n is the total number of S-boxes (i.e., the length of the final pattern). It should thus always hold that $s \leq a, s \leq i$.

The function should be called with pattern $= \emptyset, s = 0, a, i = 2, n = t + 2a$.

Note that we assume that the function was already called for each $a' \leq a$ and that no differential characteristic was found. We use this fact to reduce the number of checked patterns, since if a pattern contains a previously checked pattern as a substring, then we do not have to check it.

The condition for a non active S-box is: $i < t + 2s$. Indeed, if $i \geq t + 2s$, then the prefix already cannot contain active S-boxes (this is the case of a lower a that was already checked), and thus we do not need to check this prefix at all.

The condition for an active S-box is: $s < a \wedge 2s < i$. Indeed, the condition $s < a$ is obvious. The condition $2s < i$ appears, since if $2s \geq i$ then the suffix (starting from $i + 1$) is a pattern that was already checked, as it corresponds to $a' = a - s, n' = n - 2s = t + 2(a - s) = t + 2a'$, and thus we do not need to check this prefix.

The stopping condition is at $n - 1$, as the last two S-boxes must be non-active or otherwise the prefix will correspond to $a' = a - 1$. By the same reasoning, we start from $i = 2$, meaning that the first two S-boxes are also inactive.

References

1. Albrecht, M.R., Rechberger, C., Schneider, T., Tiessen, T., Zohner, M.: Ciphers for MPC and FHE. In: Oswald, E., Fischlin, M. (eds.) EUROCRYPT 2015. LNCS, vol. 9056, pp. 430–454. Springer, Heidelberg (2015). https://doi.org/10.1007/978-3-662-46800-5_17
2. Bar-On, A., Dinur, I., Dunkelman, O., Lallemand, V., Keller, N., Tsaban, B.: Cryptanalysis of SP networks with partial non-linear layers. In: Oswald, E., Fischlin, M. (eds.) EUROCRYPT 2015. LNCS, vol. 9056, pp. 315–342. Springer, Heidelberg (2015). https://doi.org/10.1007/978-3-662-46800-5_13
3. Becker, T., Weispfenning, V.: Gröbner bases - a computational approach to commutative algebra, 1st edn., p. 576. Springer, New York, USA (1993). https://doi.org/10.1007/978-1-4612-0913-3
4. Ben-Sasson, E., Goldberg, L., Levit, D.: STARK friendly hash - survey and recommendation. Cryptol. ePrint Arch. Rep. **2020**, 948 (2020). https://eprint.iacr.org/2020/948
5. Beyne, T.: Personal communication (2020)
6. Beyne, T., et al.: Out of oddity – new cryptanalytic techniques against symmetric primitives optimized for integrity proof systems. In: Micciancio, D., Ristenpart, T. (eds.) CRYPTO 2020. LNCS, vol. 12172, pp. 299–328. Springer, Cham (2020). https://doi.org/10.1007/978-3-030-56877-1_11
7. Dinur, I., Liu, Y., Meier, W., Wang, Q.: Optimized interpolation attacks on LowMC. In: Iwata, T., Cheon, J.H. (eds.) ASIACRYPT 2015. LNCS, vol. 9453, pp. 535–560. Springer, Heidelberg (2015). https://doi.org/10.1007/978-3-662-48800-3_22
8. Dobraunig, C., Eichlseder, M., Mendel, F.: Higher-order cryptanalysis of LowMC. In: Kwon, S., Yun, A. (eds.) ICISC 2015. LNCS, vol. 9558, pp. 87–101. Springer, Cham (2016). https://doi.org/10.1007/978-3-319-30840-1_6
9. Gérard, B., Grosso, V., Naya-Plasencia, M., Standaert, F.-X.: Block ciphers that are easier to mask: how far can we go? In: Bertoni, G., Coron, J.-S. (eds.) CHES 2013. LNCS, vol. 8086, pp. 383–399. Springer, Heidelberg (2013). https://doi.org/10.1007/978-3-642-40349-1_22

10. Grassi, L., Kales, D., Khovratovich, D., Roy, A., Rechberger, C., Schofnegger, M.: Starkad and poseidon: new hash functions for zero knowledge proof systems. IACR Cryptol. ePrint Arch. **2019**, 458 (2019). https://eprint.iacr.org/2019/458
11. Grassi, L., Khovratovich, D., Rechberger, C., Roy, A., Schofnegger, M.: Poseidon: a new hash function for zero-knowledge proof systems. In: USENIX Security Symposium. USENIX Association (2021)
12. Grassi, L., Lüftenegger, R., Rechberger, C., Rotaru, D., Schofnegger, M.: On a generalization of substitution-permutation networks: the HADES design strategy. In: Canteaut, A., Ishai, Y. (eds.) EUROCRYPT 2020. LNCS, vol. 12106, pp. 674–704. Springer, Cham (2020). https://doi.org/10.1007/978-3-030-45724-2_23
13. Grassi, L., Rechberger, C., Schofnegger, M.: Weak linear layers in word-oriented partial SPN and hades-like ciphers. IACR Cryptol. ePrint Arch. **2020**, 500 (2020). https://eprint.iacr.org/2020/500
14. NIST: Advanced Encryption Standard, Federal Information Processing Standards publications No. 197 (2001)
15. Roth, R.M., Lempel, A.: On MDS codes via Cauchy matrices. IEEE Trans. Inf. Theory **35**(6), 1314–1319 (1989). https://doi.org/10.1109/18.45291
16. Silvester, J.R.: Determinants of block matrices. Math. Gaz. **84**(501), 460–467 (2000)
17. StarkWare: Stark-friendly hash challenge (2019–2020). https://starkware.co/hash-challenge

Password Hashing and Preprocessing

Pooya Farshim[1(✉)] and Stefano Tessaro[2]

[1] University of York, York, UK
pooya.farshim@gmail.com
[2] University of Washington, Seattle, USA
tessaro@cs.washington.edu

Abstract. How does the cryptanalytic effort needed to compromise t out of m instances of hashed passwords scale with the number of users when arbitrary preprocessing information on the hash function is available? We provide a formal treatment of this problem in the *multi-instance setting with auxiliary information.* A central contribution of our work is an (arguably simple) transcript-counting argument that allows us to resolve a fundamental question left open by Bellare, Ristenpart, and Tessaro (BRT; CRYPTO 2012) in multi-instance security. We leverage this proof technique to formally justify unrecoverability of hashed salted passwords in the presence of auxiliary information in the random-oracle model. To this end we utilize the recent pre-sampling techniques for dealing with auxiliary information developed by Coretti et al. (CRYPTO 2018). Our bounds closely match those commonly assumed in practice.

Besides hashing of passwords through a monolithic random oracle, we consider the effect of iteration, a technique that is used in classical mechanisms, such as bcrypt and PBKDF2, to slow down the rate of guessing. Building on the work of BRT, we formulate a notion of KDF security, also in the presence of auxiliary information, and prove an appropriate composition theorem for it.

Keywords: Password hashing · Multi-instance security · Preprocessing · KDF security

1 Introduction

Password hashing plays a central role in the design of secure systems. We store a password hash $H(pw)$ in lieu of a password pw for authentication purposes. Moreover, whenever key-management is too complex (e.g., in hard-drive encryption), one typically uses $H(pw)$ as a *secret key.* Generally, one assumes that the hash function is by itself secure in a standard cryptographic sense, and the real threat are attacks which exploit the limited entropy of humanly generated passwords and only evaluate the hash function in the *forward* direction on a sequence of password guesses. Several approaches have been adopted to make this task as hard as possible – these typically consist of making the computation of H as expensive as acceptable (e.g., via *iteration*, as in PKCS#5 [Kal00]

A. Canteaut and F.-X. Standaert (Eds.): EUROCRYPT 2021, LNCS 12697, pp. 64–91, 2021.
https://doi.org/10.1007/978-3-030-77886-6_3

or bcrypt [PM99], or by making the computation memory hard as in e.g., [PJ16, AS15]).

Our contributions, in a nutshell. This paper focuses on a crucial aspect of password-cracking attacks, namely the role of *pre-processing*. For example, *rainbow tables* [Oec03] are a well-known type of data structures that help speed up password-cracking attacks. The common wisdom is that *salting* defeats such pre-processing – one uses $H(sa, pw)$ instead of $H(pw)$, for a fresh salt sa. Indeed, recent works (cf. e.g. [Unr07, DGK17, CDGS18, CDG18]) analyze the security of random oracles under auxiliary information, and partially validate the benefits of salting.

Still, these results do not consider important aspects which are specific to password hashing. First, they focus on protecting a *single* password. Bellare, Ristenpart, and Tessaro (BRT) [BRT12] however point out that the security study of password hashing must consider *multi-instance security metrics*, to ensure that the hardness of password cracking grows with the number of passwords under attack. Second, existing results focus on monolithic random oracles, as opposed to constructions using them (e.g., by iterating them). Third, they focus on cryptographic hardness for uniformly chosen secrets, as opposed to using arbitrary distributions, with correlations across instances.

In this paper, we address all of the above, and extend the provable-security treatment of password-hashing (following BRT) to the pre-processing setting. On the way, of independent interest, we resolve open problems in the characterization of the hardness of password distributions via guessing games. We elaborate on our contributions next.

1.1 Guessing Games

The first set of contributions are independent of pre-processing, and revisit password-recovery hardness *metrics* in the multi-instance setting. For example, consider a vector $\mathbf{pw} = (\mathbf{pw}[1], \ldots, \mathbf{pw}[m])$ of m passwords sampled from a distribution $\mathcal{P}$, and our aim is to guess *all* of them. Then, the optimal guess is the *most likely* vector $\mathbf{pw}^*$ output by $\mathcal{P}$, and the success probability is captured *exactly* by the *min-entropy* $\mathbf{H}_{\infty}(\mathcal{P})$.

It is not immediately clear whether min-entropy, however, is a good metric in the password-hashing setting – there, one is additionally given m hashes

$$H(\mathbf{sa}[1], \mathbf{pw}[1]), \ldots, H(\mathbf{sa}[m], \mathbf{pw}[m]) \;, \tag{1}$$

where $\mathbf{sa}$ is a public vector of salts – which we assume to be distinct and sufficiently long for this discussion – and is asked to recover *the entire vector* $\mathbf{pw}$. The availability of the hashes themselves allows for verification of individual password guesses. Following [BRT12], this can be abstracted as an *interactive password guessing game* which initially samples $\mathbf{pw} \twoheadleftarrow \mathcal{P}$, and the adversary can issue user-specific queries $\textsc{Test}(i, pw)$, and learn whether or not $\mathbf{pw}[i] = pw$. The adversary wins if a query $\textsc{Test}(i, \mathbf{pw}[i])$ is made for *every* $i \in [m]$.

BRT suggest that the best probability of winning this game with a given budget T of $\textsc{Test}$ queries—which we denote as $\mathbf{Adv}^{\mathrm{guess}}_{\mathcal{P}}(T)$—is by itself a good metric of hardness for password distributions. However, it is very hard to evaluate. Our first contribution is a bound of the form

$$\mathbf{Adv}^{\mathrm{guess}}_{\mathcal{P}}(T) \leq \left(\frac{eT}{m}\right)^m \cdot 2^{-\mathbf{H}_\infty(\mathcal{P})} , \tag{2}$$

which only depends on the min-entropy of the distribution $\mathcal{P}$. This resolves the main open question of [BRT12], which only gave a bound for the case where (1) the passwords are *independent* and (2) we know separate and a-priori fixed bounds T_i on the number of $\mathrm{TEST}(i, \cdot)$ queries for each $i \in [m]$. We note that (2) is a strong assumption, since an optimal attacker generally stops using queries for a particular password when successful. For the case where the passwords are drawn independently from a set of size N, for example, our bound is $\left(\frac{eT}{mN}\right)^m$, which is clearly tight (the optimal strategy makes T/m distinct guesses for each $i \in [m]$).

In fact, our framework studies a more general metric $\mathbf{Adv}^{\mathrm{sa\text{-}guess}}_{\mathcal{P},\ell,\mathsf{Gen}}(T, c)$ which considers a general salt generator Gen (which may generate colliding salts, or salts with low entropy), allows for a password to be re-used across ℓ salts, and enables the adversary to learn c passwords via *corruption queries*. On special case of interest is that of *no salts*, i.e., $\mathsf{Gen} = \perp$ outputs m empty strings as salts (and thus $\ell = 1$ without loss of generality). Here, we prove that

$$\mathbf{Adv}^{\mathrm{sa\text{-}guess}}_{\mathcal{P},1,\perp}(T) \leq T^m \cdot 2^{-\mathbf{H}_\infty(\mathcal{P})} . \tag{3}$$

While this bound appears natural, the main technical challenge in the proof (which exploits a combinatorial counting argument) is to deal with distributions which yield collisions across passwords. It is worth noticing here that the effort needed to compromise all passwords, for example, increases by a factor of m – this is because every individual query can be helpful to guess any of the passwords.

1.2 Unrecoverability Bounds

We then turn to our first contribution in the pre-processing model. Here, we give tight bounds on the success probability of recovering all of $\mathbf{pw}$ in the setting of (1), when H is a random oracle with n-bit outputs (in the following, we let $N = 2^n$) to which the adversary can issue T queries, and where additionally the adversary is given S bits of pre-processed information about the random oracle H. This model is often referred to as the *random-oracle model with auxiliary information*, or AI-ROM for short. This generalizes in particular prior works on studying one-wayness in the AI-ROM [GT00, Wee05, Unr07, DTT10, DGK17, CDGS18] in that we consider both general pre-image distributions as well as (most importantly) *multi-instance* security.

Our analyses rely on a reduction to the bounds for guessing games discussed above, combined with the *bit-fixing random oracle model* (BF-ROM) of [Unr07, CDGS18]. In the BF-ROM, one analyzes unrecoverability in a setting where P input-output pairs of the random oracle are chosen arbitrarily (the rest of the random oracle is truly random) – here, P is a parameter. In [CDGS18] it is shown that replacing P with (roughly) ST, and multiplying the recovering probability by 2, gives a corresponding AI-ROM bound. We will slightly relax this paradigm, and realize that setting $P = ST/m$, while multiplying the probability by 2^m, allows us to obtain the right bound.

UNRECOVERABILITY IN THE UNSALTED CASE. For example, for the case where passwords are chosen uniformly from a set of size N (which is equal to the output size of the random oracle), we show that if no salts are used, then the probability of recovering all passwords is of order (assuming S is large enough)

$$\left(\frac{ST}{mN}\right)^m .$$

We also obtain a corresponding bound for arbitrary distributions. This is interesting, because it means that if we want to recover all passwords with probability *one*, then we need to invest time $T = mN/S$, in other words, the complexity of recovering multiple passwords *without* salts, even given a rainbow tables, grows linearly in the number of passwords. This is in contrast to the setting *without* auxiliary information, where in time $T = N$ we can recover essentially any number of passwords. In Appendix A, we give a self-contained and straightforward extension of Hellman's space-time trade-off for multi-instance security, where one can exactly see that computation needed to break one password cannot be recycled for another one.

UNRECOVERABILITY IN THE SALTED CASE. For the case with salts, in contrast, the expectation is that the S bits of pre-processing is not helpful. We confirm this via a bound, which depends on the salt size K, and prove that the probability of recovering all m passwords is roughly

$$\left(\frac{T}{N}\right)^m + \frac{m\ell}{K}\left(\frac{eST}{m^2N}\right)^m + \frac{m^2}{K}$$

for the special case of passwords drawn independently from an N-element set. (Again, our final bound is more general.) In other words, the first term becomes the leading one if K is sufficiently large.

1.3 AI-KDF Security of Iteration

Finally, we consider a simulation-based notion of KDF security which extends the notion introduced by BRT [BRT12] to the AI-ROM setting. The basic idea of KDF security is to see the functionality provided by a key-derivation function as providing m keys to honest users and giving an attacker the ability to test passwords guess for correctness. Thus, this notion requires that for any (real-world) attacker against a KDF function with salted passwords and auxiliary information there is a simulator against the ideal functionality that has essentially the same advantage. This notion in particular justified the use of password-based KDFs to replace uniform keys with those derived from (salted) passwords.

BRT's notion was inspired by the indifferentiability framework [MRH04, CDMP05], and restricts it to a particular ideal KDF functionality. Directly using indifferentiability as the target security notion, however, suffers from two drawbacks: the indifferentiability of iterated constructions (from RO) in general, remain unclear. Second, concrete security bounds for indifferentiability, due to the attack surface exposed, often fall short of providing the guarantees that are needed in practice to provably set salt sizes.

To prove our result, we first formulate a notion of KDF security in the bit-fixing random-oracle model. In this model we can present a simulator that simulates the primitive oracle by looking for about to complete chains of length $r-1$, where r in the iteration count, and if so, using the Test oracle provided in the ideal game to handle the query. As with BRT, we require that when the number of queries made by the adversary to the primitive oracle is T, the number of queries made by the simulator to its Test oracle is only T/r. This restriction will allow us to conclude that in applications an adversary needs to place r queries to the random oracle to check whether or not a candidate guess for a password was correct. Finally, we lift this BF-ROM result to the AI-RO model using [CDGS18, Theorem 5].

APPLICATIONS. We prove a composition theorem for AI-KDF security for a range of games beyond IND-CPA security as considered by BRT and extended to encompass a preprocessing phase. This result shows that uniform values used in a game can be replaced with those derived from *salted* passwords via an AI-KDF-secure function, even in the presence of preprocessing. This result can thus be seen as formal justification of "salting defeats preprocessing in password-based cryptography." As with BRT, our simulation-based notion allows us to reduce security to the full difficulty of the multi-instance password-guessing game.

1.4 Structure of the Paper

We start by recalling the necessary preliminaries in Sect. 2. We define our basic measures of unguessability of passwords in Sect. 3, where we establish our basic bounds. In Sect. 4 we define unrecoverability of hashed passwords and relate them to unguessability, both in the salted and unsalted settings. In Sect. 5 we study iterated hashing under KDF security in the presence of auxiliary information and show how to apply this result (and in general KDF security) to securely replace uniform keys with password-derived ones in various applications in the presence of preprocessing.

2 Preliminaries

NOTATION. Throughout the paper $\mathbb{N}$ denotes the set of nonnegative integers including zero, $\{0,1\}^n$ the set of all bit strings of length n, and $\{0,1\}^*$ denotes the set of all finite-length bit strings, and ε the empty string. For two bit-strings X and Y, $X|Y$ denotes string concatenation and (X,Y) denotes a uniquely decodable encoding of X and Y. The length of a string X is denoted by $|X|$. For a finite, non-empty set S we write $s \twoheadleftarrow S$ to mean that s is sampled uniformly at random from S. Overloading the notion, for a randomized algorithm A with input(s) x we write $y \twoheadleftarrow A(x)$ to mean that y is sampled from the outputs of A according to the distribution induced by running A on uniform random coins. We denote adversarial procedures, which may be randomized and/or stateful, by $\mathcal{A}$, honest stateless procedures with C, and honest stateful procedures with $\mathcal{S}$.

FACTORIALS AND FRIENDS. Recall that $(n/3)^n \leq n! \leq \mathrm{e} \cdot (n/2)^n$ and that $n! \sim \sqrt{2\pi n}(n/\mathrm{e})^n$. Further, for all $1 \leq m \leq T$,

$$\binom{T}{m} \leq \frac{T^m}{m!} < \left(\frac{\mathrm{e}T}{m}\right)^m .$$

We let $(T)_m := \binom{T}{m} m!$ denote the falling factorial. The Stirling numbers of the second kind $\left\{ {m \atop k} \right\}$ count the number of partitions of a set of size m into k non-empty sets. For these numbers we have,

$$\sum_{k=0}^{m} \left\{ {m \atop k} \right\} (T)_k = T^m \qquad \text{and} \qquad \left\{ {m \atop k} \right\} \leq \binom{m}{k} k^{m-k} .$$

We also have that $\left\{ {m \atop 0} \right\} = 0$ for $m \geq 1$.

THE RO MODEL. We denote the set of all functions from a domain D to a finite range R by $\mathrm{Fun}(D, R)$. The random-oracle model $\mathsf{RO}(D, R)$ is a model of computation where parties are given oracle access to a uniformly random function $\mathsf{H} \twoheadleftarrow \mathrm{Fun}(D, R)$.[1] We denote an adversary $\mathcal{A}$ with access to H by $\mathcal{A}^{\mathsf{H}}()$.

THE BF-RO MODEL. An assignment (or pre-set) list L is a list of pairs of points $(x, y) \in D \times R$ that respects the property of defining a function, i.e., for each x there is at most one y such that $(x, y) \in L$. For $P \in \mathbb{N}$, the *bit-fixing* random-oracle model $\mathsf{BF\text{-}RO}(P, D, R)$ grants oracle access to a uniformly chosen random function $\mathsf{H} \twoheadleftarrow \mathrm{Fun}(N, M)$ compatible with L, where $(\sigma, L) \twoheadleftarrow \mathcal{A}_0()$ is chosen by an initial (aka. offline or preprocessing) adversary $\mathcal{A}_0()$ and has size at most P. Note that $\mathcal{A}_0$ does *not* get access to H. We denote the online phase of the attack by $\mathcal{A}_1^{\mathsf{H}}(\sigma)$, which gets access to H and σ, the information passed from $\mathcal{A}_0$. Thus, σ does not depend on H. We use $\mathsf{H}[L]$ for a random oracle conditioned on L. Note that in the BF-RO model, there is no upper bound on the size of σ.

THE AI-RO MODEL. For $P \in \mathbb{N}$, the *auxiliary-input* (AI) random-oracle model $\mathsf{AI\text{-}RO}(S, D, R)$ grants oracle access to a random function $\mathsf{H} \twoheadleftarrow \mathrm{Fun}(D, R)$ together with oracle-dependent auxiliary information $\sigma \twoheadleftarrow \mathcal{A}_0(\mathsf{H})$, where $|\sigma| \leq P$. We denote the online phase by $A_1^{\mathsf{H}}(\sigma)$.

GAMES. A game is a randomized stateful algorithm $(y, st) \leftarrow \mathrm{G}(x; r; st)$, where x is the input, r the randomness, and st the state, which is initialized to ε. The output y is returned to a stateful adversary $(x, st') \twoheadleftarrow \mathcal{A}_1(y, st')$, which then calls the game x and so on. This interaction terminates by the game returning a flag

[1] Note the distribution is well-defined when $D = \{0,1\}^*$ and can be formalized in the language of measure theory.

win indicating win/loss. For indistinguishability games, the advantage metric takes the form $\mathbf{Adv}_{\mathrm{G}}^{\mathrm{ind}}(\mathcal{A}_1) := 2 \cdot \Pr[\mathsf{win}] - 1$ and for unpredictability games it takes the form $\mathbf{Adv}_{\mathrm{G}}^{\mathrm{pred}}(\mathcal{A}_1) := \Pr[\mathsf{win}]$. We can lift this definition to ideal models of computation by sampling a random oracle $\mathsf{H} \twoheadleftarrow \mathrm{Fun}(D, R)$, which both G and $\mathcal{A}_1$ can access, and passing auxiliary information computed by $\mathcal{A}_0$, as described above, to $\mathcal{A}_1$. We define $\mathbf{Adv}_{\mathrm{G},\mathsf{AI\text{-}RO}}^{\mathrm{ind}}(S, T)$ by taking the maximum of $\mathbf{Adv}_{\mathrm{G}}^{\mathrm{ind}}(\mathcal{A}_0, \mathcal{A}_1)$ over all $(\mathcal{A}_0, \mathcal{A}_1)$ that output at most S bits of auxiliary information and place at most T queries to the random oracle. Unpredictability advantages and advantages in the BF-RO model are defined analogously.

Coretti, Dodis, Guo, and Steinberger [CDGS18, Theorems 5 and 6] prove the following result, which bounds adversarial advantage in the AI-RO model in terms of that in the BF-RO model.

Theorem 1 ([CDGS18, Theorems 5 and 6]). *For any $P \in \mathbb{N}$ and any $\gamma > 0$ and any game* G *in the AI-RO model,*

$$\mathbf{Adv}_{\mathrm{G},\mathsf{AI\text{-}RO}}^{\mathrm{ind}}(S, T) \leq \mathbf{Adv}_{\mathrm{G},\mathsf{BF\text{-}RO}}^{\mathrm{ind}}(P, T_{\mathrm{G}} + T) + \frac{(S + \log \gamma^{-1}) \cdot (T_{\mathrm{G}} + T)}{P} + \gamma\ ,$$

where T_{G} is the query complexity of G*. Furthermore, for any unpredictability game* G*,*

$$\mathbf{Adv}_{\mathrm{G},\mathsf{AI\text{-}RO}}^{\mathrm{pred}}(S, T) \leq 2^{(S + \log \gamma^{-1}) \cdot (T_{\mathrm{G}} + T)/P} \cdot \mathbf{Adv}_{\mathrm{G},\mathsf{BF\text{-}RO}}^{\mathrm{pred}}(P, T_{\mathrm{G}} + T) + \gamma\ .$$

3 Unguessability

PASSWORD SAMPLERS. A password sampler is a randomized algorithm $\mathcal{P}$ that takes no input and outputs a vector of passwords $\mathbf{pw} = (\mathbf{pw}[1], \ldots, \mathbf{pw}[m])$ and some leakage z on the passwords.[2] We assume that $\mathcal{P}$ always outputs the same number of passwords m. To make this explicit we call the sampler an m-sampler. We note that password samplers in our work do not get access to the random oracle.[3]

A basic measure of the unguessability of a password sampler is its min-entropy. We consider an average-case notion over leakage z, as this will not be under the control of the adversary:

$$\tilde{\mathbf{H}}_\infty(\mathcal{P} \mid \mathcal{Z}) := -\log \mathbb{E}_{\mathcal{Z}}(2^{-\mathbf{H}_\infty(\mathcal{P} \mid \mathcal{Z} = z)})\ ,$$

Here $\mathcal{Z}$ denotes the random variable corresponding to the leakage.

UNGUESSABILITY. Following [BRT12], we consider a guessability game which allows for testing and adaptive corruptions of guessed passwords. The goal of

[2] This is *not* the preprocessing information, only some partial information related to passwords.

[3] In this work we do not consider password samplers that have oracle access to an ideal primitive.

the adversary is to guess *all* passwords. More precisely, for an adversary $\mathcal{A}$ we define

$$\mathbf{Adv}^{\text{guess}}_{\mathcal{P}}(T, c) := \max_{\mathcal{A}} \Pr\left[\text{GUESS}^{\mathcal{A}}_{\mathcal{P}}\right] ,$$

where game $\text{GUESS}^{\mathcal{A}}_{\mathcal{P}}$ is defined in Fig. 1 and the maximum is taken over all $\mathcal{A}$ that place at most T queries to TEST, and at most c queries to COR. Observe that the test oracle takes an index i. This signifies the fact that guesses are *user-specific* and thus cannot be amortized over all users. Our definition also includes some side information z for generality, which was not present in BRT.

Game $\text{GUESS}^{\mathcal{A}}_{\mathcal{P}}$:	Proc. $\text{TEST}(i, pw)$:	Proc. $\text{COR}(i)$:
$(\mathbf{pw}, z) \twoheadleftarrow \mathcal{P}$	$\mathsf{win}_i \leftarrow (pw = \mathbf{pw}[i])$	$\mathsf{win}_i \leftarrow \mathsf{true}$
$y \twoheadleftarrow \mathcal{A}^{\text{TEST},\text{COR}}(z)$	return win_i	return $\mathbf{pw}[i]$
return $\bigwedge_{i=1}^{m} \mathsf{win}_i$		

Fig. 1. The guessing game.

SIMPLIFYING ASSUMPTIONS. We assume, wlog, that $\mathcal{A}$ does not call $\text{COR}(i)$ on any index i for which TEST returned true. Similarly, we assume that $\mathcal{A}$ does not call TEST with an index i which was queried to $\text{COR}(i)$. Moreover, for $c' \leq c \leq m$, any adversary $\mathcal{A}$ that places c' queries to COR can be transformed to an adversary $\mathcal{B}$ that places $c \geq c'$ queries to COR without any loss in advantage.[4] Thus, throughout the paper we may assume, wlog, that adversaries that place at most c corrupt queries place exactly c corrupt queries. Furthermore, the set of corrupted indices and those for which TEST was successful are disjoint.

A BASIC MEASURE OF UNGUESSABILITY. It follows from the definitions of unguessability and average-case min-entropy that

$$\mathbf{Adv}^{\text{guess}}_{\mathcal{P}}(m, 0) = 2^{-\tilde{\mathbf{H}}_\infty(\mathcal{P}|\mathcal{Z})} .$$

To see this, note that given any $\mathcal{P}$ and any $\mathcal{A}$ in GUESS we can build an adversary $\mathcal{B}$ with *no* oracle access as follows. $\mathcal{B}$ runs $\mathcal{A}$ on the leakage that it receives and answers all its TEST queries with true, and outputs the set of passwords queried to TEST sorted according to their index. For all password vectors where $\mathcal{A}$ is successful, these queries are answered correctly. Thus, $\mathcal{B}$ runs $\mathcal{A}$ perfectly in the

[4] Algorithm $\mathcal{B}$ runs $\mathcal{A}$ and forwards its TEST and COR queries to its own respective oracles. It stops $\mathcal{A}$ from making further queries to TEST once $m - c$ queries to TEST return true. $\mathcal{B}$ corrupts the remaining indices. By the previous assumption, the passwords for these indices have not been found due to a corrupt or a test query so far. Clearly, the number of TEST queries of $\mathcal{B}$ is less than those of $\mathcal{A}$. Further $\mathcal{B}$ places in total at most c queries to COR. To see this let c_0' be the number of corrupt queries by $\mathcal{A}$ when it was stopped. At this point $c_0' + m - c$ passwords were found. Hence there are $m - (c_0' + m - c) = c - c_0'$ passwords that were not found at that stage. Thus, $\mathcal{B}$ places $c_0' + (c - c_0') = c$ queries to its COR oracle after $\mathcal{A}$ was stopped.

environment that it expects. Thus, $\mathcal{B}$ is successful whenever $\mathcal{A}$ is. Inequality in the opposite direction is trivial and we obtain the result. We note that in the presence of adaptive corruptions, it is unclear how to relate the above game-based notion of unguessability to a standard information-theoretic notion. Thus,

$$\mathbf{Adv}^{\text{guess}}_{\mathcal{P}}(m-c, c)$$

will form our basic measure of unguessability of passwords, which we call c-unguessability.

THRESHOLD SECURITY. Consider a *threshold* notion of unguessability whereby the adversary's goal is to guess t out of m of the passwords, while having access to TEST oracle, but no longer a COR oracle. The advantage of any such adversary is easily upper bounded by the advantage of an adversary that before termination simply corrupts the $m-t$ users for which recovery was not attempted. Thus,

$$\mathbf{Adv}^{t\text{-guess}}_{\mathcal{P}}(T) \leq \mathbf{Adv}^{\text{guess}}_{\mathcal{P}}(T, m-t) .$$

In the reverse direction, however, an inequality does not hold in general.[5] However, when the password sampler is a *product sampler* in the sense that for some $\mathcal{P}_i$ it computes $(\mathbf{pw}[i], z_i) \twoheadleftarrow \mathcal{P}_i$ (run on independent coins) and returns the vector $((\mathbf{pw}[1], \ldots, \mathbf{pw}[m]), z)$ where $z := (z_1, \ldots, z_m)$, we have

$$\mathbf{Adv}^{\text{guess}}_{\otimes \mathcal{P}_i}(T, c) \leq \mathbf{Adv}^{(m-c)\text{-guess}}_{\otimes \mathcal{P}_i}(T) .$$

Using an argument similar to [BRT12, Lemma F.1] the independence of the passwords allows for a perfect simulation of COR(i). Run the corrupting adversary and answer its test oracle using its own test oracle. When a COR(i) query is placed, return a value distributed according to $\mathcal{P}_i$, conditioned on auxiliary information z_i and output not matching any pw for which TEST(i, pw) previously responded with false.

Thus for product samplers, recovering t out of m passwords without corruptions is equivalent to recovering t passwords while corrupting $m-t$ of them. Since for non-product distributions the corrupting adversaries are stronger, we work with such adversaries.[6]

Our first result relates the unguessability of passwords to c-unguessability.

Theorem 2 (Unguessability). *For any m-sampler $\mathcal{P}$ and any $T, c \in \mathbb{N}$,*

$$\mathbf{Adv}^{\text{guess}}_{\mathcal{P}}(T, c) \leq \binom{T}{m-c} \cdot \mathbf{Adv}^{\text{guess}}_{\mathcal{P}}(m-c, c) .$$

[5] Consider m identical passwords, where the common password is uniformly distributed within a large set. With corruptions, guessing the common value is trivial; without, it can be done with small probability.

[6] Note however that for correlated passwords, this may imply that there is no security, whereas in practice we would like to argue that there is some security. We leave the treatment of this intermediate notion to future work.

Proof. By our simplifying assumptions, $\mathcal{A}$ makes exactly c corrupt queries and of the T test queries, exactly $m - c$ are successful. Consider an adversary $\mathcal{B}$ against GUESS that runs $\mathcal{A}$ as follows. At the onset, $\mathcal{B}$ guesses which of the $m - c$ queries among the T queries will result in true. There are $\binom{T}{m-c}$ such choices. It then runs $\mathcal{A}$ and answers all TEST queried for the guessed indices with true. The corruption queries are relayed. If the set of indices guessed is correct, the algorithm $\mathcal{B}$ runs $\mathcal{A}$ perfectly. We obtain the claim inequality by maximizing over $\mathcal{A}$. □

Despite its simplicity, this argument is novel and in particular resolves a problem left open by BRT on upper bounds for guessability with only a *global* bound on the total number of TEST queries (and not a priori bounds on the number of user-specific guesses, as treated by BRT).

SALTED GUESSABILITY. Following BRT, we consider an extension of GUESS that incorporates *salts*. We allow for multiple salts per password (as required in applications such as password-based encryption) and consider a TEST oracle which is *salt-specific* rather than user-specific. This test procedure thus *amortizes guessing* over all users who share a salt value. The rationale for this choice is that given salted *hashes* of passwords—whose security we will be ultimately analyzing—once a password is recovered, it is also recovered for all users for which password-salt pairs match. Crucially, a *single* query is needed to deduce this information.

Our formal definition, which is shown in Fig. 2, differs from that of BRT in a number of aspects. First, we allow for an arbitrary salt-generation algorithm Gen that takes a user index i and a counter j. (This choice allows for stateful generation of salts, which may be possible in certain contexts.) Second, under TEST we set win_i to true for *all* matching i, rather than only the first i for which a match is found as in BRT. This ensures that password-salt collisions do not result in an unwinnable game. We also release the set of all passwords indices for which password-salt matches the query (rather than the first such index). This choice more closely matches the setting of hashed passwords. Finally, we leak the *collision pattern* of the password-salt pairs. This is formalized via an algorithm $\mathsf{Colls}(\mathbf{pw}, \mathbf{sa})$ that takes a vectors of passwords $\mathbf{pw}$ of length m and an $m \times \ell$ matrix of salts and returns an $m\ell \times m\ell$ matrix whose $((i_1, j_1), (i_2, j_2))$ entry is set to 1 iff $(\mathbf{pw}[i_1], \mathbf{sa}[i_1, j_1]) = (\mathbf{pw}[i_2], \mathbf{sa}[i_2, j_2])$. We define the advantage of (T, c)-adversaries analogously to the GUESS game.

A direct reduction shows that for any password sampler $\mathcal{P}$, any salt-sampler Gen, and any number of salts per password ℓ,

$$\mathbf{Adv}^{\mathrm{guess}}_{\mathcal{P}}(T, c) \leq \mathbf{Adv}^{\mathrm{sa\text{-}guess}}_{\mathcal{P},\ell,\mathsf{Gen}}(T, c) \ .$$

In order to prove a result in the opposite direction, for a salt sampler Gen, we define

$$\mathbf{Coll}_{\mathsf{Gen}}(m, \ell) := \Pr[\exists (i, j) \neq (i', j') \in [m] \times [\ell] : \mathsf{Gen}(i, j) = \mathsf{Gen}(i', j')]$$

Game $\text{SA-GUESS}^{\mathcal{A}}_{\mathcal{P},\ell,\mathsf{Gen}}$:	Proc. $\text{TEST}(pw, sa)$:	Proc. $\text{COR}(i)$:
$(\mathbf{pw}, z) \twoheadleftarrow \mathcal{P}$	$S \leftarrow \{i : \exists j (pw, sa) =$	$\mathsf{win}_i \leftarrow \mathsf{true}$
for $(i,j) \in [m] \times [\ell]$ do	$= (\mathbf{pw}[i], \mathbf{sa}[i,j])\}$	return $\mathbf{pw}[i]$
$\mathbf{sa}[i,j] \twoheadleftarrow \mathsf{Gen}(i,j)$	for $i \in S$ do	
$z_{\mathsf{coll}} \leftarrow \mathsf{Colls}(\mathbf{pw}, \mathbf{sa})$	$\mathsf{win}_i \leftarrow \mathsf{true}$	
$y \twoheadleftarrow \mathcal{A}^{\text{TEST},\text{COR}}(\mathbf{sa}, z, z_{\mathsf{coll}})$	return S	
return $\left(\bigwedge_{i=1}^{m} \mathsf{win}_i\right)$		

Fig. 2. The password-guessing game with salts where the collision pattern of password-salt pairs is always leaked. win_i are initialized to false.

as the probability of obtaining $m\ell$ distinct salts. For uniform salts in $[K]$,

$$\mathbf{Coll}_{\mathsf{Gen}}(m,\ell) = 1 - \frac{K!}{K^{m\ell}(K-m\ell)!} \leq \frac{m^2\ell^2}{K} .$$

We note that in some settings, the distinctness of salts may be guaranteed. For instance, by appending (i,j) to salts, where i is a "user-id" and j is an application-specific "session-id," one can guarantee distinctness. As we shall see, to defeat preprocessing the salts must also be unpredictable. Hence (i,j,sa) for a random $sa \twoheadleftarrow [K]$ can be used in these settings.

The next theorem relates salted unguessability of passwords to their user-specific guessability.

Theorem 3. *For any m-sampler $\mathcal{P}$, any* Gen, *and any $\ell, T, c \in \mathbb{N}$,*

$$\mathbf{Adv}^{\text{sa-guess}}_{\mathcal{P},\ell,\mathsf{Gen}}(T,c) \leq \mathbf{Adv}^{\text{guess}}_{\mathcal{P}}(T,c) + \mathbf{Coll}_{\mathsf{Gen}}(m,\ell) .$$

Proof. Given a (T,c)-adversary $\mathcal{A}$ against SA-GUESS we build a (T,c)-adversary $\mathcal{B}$ against GUESS as follows. Algorithm $\mathcal{B}(z)$ picks $m\ell$ salts via $\mathsf{Gen}(i,j)$ and terminates if the salts are not distinct. Algorithm $\mathcal{B}$ sets z_{coll} to be the identity matrix (if the salts do not collide, certainly password-salt pairs will not), runs $\mathcal{A}(\mathbf{sa}, z, z_{\mathsf{coll}})$ and answers its corrupt queries using its own equivalent oracle. $\text{TEST}(pw, sa)$ queries are handled by first checking if $sa = \mathbf{sa}[i,j]$ for some (i,j). If not, $\mathcal{B}$ returns $\perp$; else it finds the *unique* (i,j) such that $sa = \mathbf{sa}[i,j]$. Such an index pair is unique due to the distinctness of salts. Algorithm $\mathcal{B}$ then queries $\text{TEST}(i, pw)$ and returns $S := \{i\}$ if it receives true, and the empty set otherwise. (We note that the loss is additive, rather than multiplicative, since $\mathcal{A}$ might be successful exactly when there is a collision among the salts.) □

THE UNSALTED SETTING. Unsalted hashing of passwords is interesting from both a historical and theoretical point of view. Unsalted unguessability is closely linked to *amplification of hardness*. Second, unguessability of passwords without salts constitutes a "worst-case" scenario and can be used to upper-bound unguessability with respect to *any* other salt generator.[7] When there are no salts, all

[7] The proof of this fact follows from the observation that the collision pattern of passwords and the collision pattern of salts (which is publicly available) are sufficient to infer the collision pattern of password-salt pairs.

passwords fall under a single (empty) salt, and in order to check if a candidate password matches any of the sampled passwords a reduction analogous to one given above would need to call $\text{TEST}(i, pw)$ for *all* $i \in [m]$. This, however, results in a blow up in the number of test queries, which we aim to avoid in this work.

Let us, by a slight abuse of notation, denote the salt generator Gen that always returns ε by $\perp$. We directly prove an upper bound on $\mathbf{Adv}^{\text{sa-guess}}_{\mathcal{P},\ell,\perp}(T, c)$. This extends [BRT12, Theorem 3.2] in two aspects: first, and as mentioned above, the number of queries to $\text{TEST}(i, \cdot)$ for each index i are no longer a priori fixed. Second, $\mathcal{P}$ no longer comprises independent and identically distributed samples from some base single-password distribution. Proving such a result was left open by BRT.

Theorem 4. *For any m-sampler $\mathcal{P}$ and any $\ell, T \in \mathbb{N}$,*

$$\mathbf{Adv}^{\text{sa-guess}}_{\mathcal{P},\ell,\perp}(T, 0) \leq T^m \cdot \mathbf{Adv}^{\text{guess}}_{\mathcal{P}}(m, 0) \ .$$

Proof. Observe that ℓ does not affect unguessability and thus we may assume, wlog, that $\ell = 1$. We now fix a *deterministic* adversary $\mathcal{B}$ and count the number of vectors $(\mathbf{pw}[1], \ldots \mathbf{pw}[m])$ on which $\mathcal{B}$ *wins*. Call this number N. Then, the final bound will be $N \cdot \mathbf{Adv}^{\text{guess}}_{\mathcal{P}}(m, 0)$.

Consider a vector $(\mathbf{pw}[1], \ldots \mathbf{pw}[m])$ on which $\mathcal{B}$ wins with T queries, and suppose the m passwords are distinct. These can be represented uniquely by a permutation giving the order in which the uncorrupted passwords appear. There are $(m-c)!$ such permutations. There are $\binom{T}{m-c}$ such indices and thus $N = (m-c)!\binom{T}{m-c} = (T)_{m-c}$.

In general, the collision pattern induces a partition of passwords into k groups. Suppose there are no corruptions. Then the number of password vectors $(\mathbf{pw}[1], \ldots \mathbf{pw}[m])$ on which $\mathcal{B}$ wins is at most

$$\left\{ {m \atop k} \right\} \cdot k! \cdot \binom{T}{k} \ ,$$

where $\left\{ {m \atop k} \right\}$ are the Stirling numbers of the second kind. Thus, the total number of representations is at most

$$N \leq \sum_{k=1}^{m} \left\{ {m \atop k} \right\} \cdot (T)_k \ = T^m \ ,$$

where the last equality is by an identity for Stirling numbers. □

We now deal with the general case with corruptions. We consider a non-adaptive guessability game NA-GUESS, where corruptions are carried out non-adaptively at the beginning of the game in parallel. This potentially lowers unpredictability advantage and thus strengthens upper bounds using it. Unpredictability in the adaptive game can be bounded by that in the non-adaptive game by guessing at the onset the $\binom{m}{c}$ indices that will be corrupted. However, below we carry a direct reduction to NA-GUESS to avoid multiple losses.

Theorem 5. *For any m-sampler $\mathcal{P}$ and $\ell, T, c \in \mathbb{N}$,*

$$\mathbf{Adv}^{\text{sa-guess}}_{\mathcal{P},\ell,\perp}(T-c,c) \leq (T^{m-c} + \mathcal{O}(T^{m-c-1})) \cdot \mathbf{Adv}^{\text{na-guess}}_{\mathcal{P}}(m-c,c) .$$

Proof. Once again, wlog, $\ell = 1$. We prove the bound for a modified game where $\text{Cor}(i)$ leaks the set of all indices j for which $\mathbf{pw}[j] = \mathbf{pw}[i]$. In this game, wlog, we may assume that Test and Cor oracles return *disjoint* sets that form a partition of $[m]$. This game is equivalent to the unmodified game where the adversary after a corrupt query places a test query on the password just revealed to learn its equality pattern. This results in c additional Test queries.

We now count the number of successful transcripts.

- The number of sets in the partition, $k \geq c$.
- A partition of $[m]$ into k sets: $\left\{ {m \atop k} \right\}$ choices.
- Which c of the k sets will be corrupted: $\binom{k}{c}$ choices. (No ordering of the guesses is needed, since the queried index will be contained in exactly one set.
- The order of the remaining $k-c$ sets that will be returned as responses to Test queries: $(k-c)!$ choices.
- The T test queries which these $k-c$ sets will be responses for: $\binom{T}{k-c}$ choices. (The rest of the queries are answered $\emptyset$.)

Hence,

$$\mathbf{Adv}^{\text{sa-guess}}_{\mathcal{P},1,\perp}(T-c,c) \leq \sum_{k=c}^{m} \left\{ {m \atop k} \right\} \binom{k}{c} (k-c)! \binom{T}{k-c} \cdot \mathbf{Adv}^{\text{na-guess}}_{\mathcal{P}}(m-c,c) .$$

When $c = 0$, this bound matches that stated in Theorem 4. Using (computer) algebra we have that,

$$\sum_{k=c}^{m} \left\{ {m \atop k} \right\} \binom{k}{c} (k-c)! \binom{T}{k-c} = \sum_{k=0}^{m-c} C(m-c,k,c) \cdot T^{m-c-k} = T^{m-c} + \mathcal{O}(T^{m-c-1}) ,$$

where the coefficients $C(n,k,c)$ are defined recursively via

$$C(n,k,c) := \begin{cases} 1 & \text{if } k=0 \text{ ;} \\ \left\{ {n+c \atop c} \right\} & \text{if } k=n \text{ ;} \\ c \cdot C(n-1,k-1,c) + C(n-1,k,c) & \text{otherwise.} \end{cases}$$

When there is a single corruption ($c = 1$), the sum bounding the advantage has the simple closed form $(T+1)^{m-1}$. □

4 Unrecoverability

We now define two notions of unrecoverability for *hashed* passwords in the AI-RO and the BF-RO models respectively. In the AI-RO model the adversary

Game AI-REC$^{\mathcal{A}_0,\mathcal{A}_1}_{\mathcal{P},\ell,\mathsf{Gen},\mathsf{KD}}$:	Game BF-REC$^{\mathcal{A}_0,\mathcal{A}_1}_{\mathcal{P},\ell,\mathsf{Gen},\mathsf{KD}}$:
$\mathsf{H} \twoheadleftarrow \text{Fun}(D, R)$	$\mathsf{H} \twoheadleftarrow \text{Fun}(D, R)$
$\sigma \twoheadleftarrow \mathcal{A}_0(\mathsf{H})$	$(\sigma, L) \twoheadleftarrow \mathcal{A}_0()$
$(\mathbf{pw}, z) \twoheadleftarrow \mathcal{P}$	$(\mathbf{pw}, z) \twoheadleftarrow \mathcal{P}$
for $(i, j) \in [m] \times [\ell]$ do	for $(i, j) \in [m] \times [\ell]$ do
$\quad \mathbf{sa}[i, j] \twoheadleftarrow \mathsf{Gen}(i, j)$	$\quad \mathbf{sa}[i, j] \twoheadleftarrow \mathsf{Gen}(i, j)$
$\quad \mathbf{k}[i, j] \leftarrow \mathsf{KD}^{\mathsf{H}}(\mathbf{pw}[i], \mathbf{sa}[i, j])$	$\quad \mathbf{k}[i, j] \leftarrow \mathsf{KD}^{\mathsf{H}[L]}(\mathbf{pw}[i], \mathbf{sa}[i, j])$
$\mathbf{pw}' \twoheadleftarrow \mathcal{A}_1^{\mathsf{H},\text{COR}}(\mathbf{sa}, \mathbf{k}, \sigma, z)$	$\mathbf{pw}' \twoheadleftarrow \mathcal{A}_1^{\mathsf{H}[L],\text{COR}}(\mathbf{sa}, \mathbf{k}, \sigma, z)$
return $(\mathbf{pw}' = \mathbf{pw})$	return $(\mathbf{pw}' = \mathbf{pw})$
Proc. COR(i):	Proc. COR(i):
return $\mathbf{pw}[i]$	return $\mathbf{pw}[i]$

Fig. 3. The password recoverability games in the AI-RO model (left) and the BF-RO model (right).

can carry out an initial stage of the attack and obtain arbitrary preprocessing information on the entire table of the random oracle. Formally, we define

$$\mathbf{Adv}^{\text{ai-rec}}_{\mathcal{P},\ell,\mathsf{Gen},\mathsf{KD}}(S, T, c) := \max_{\mathcal{A}_0,\mathcal{A}_1} \Pr\left[\text{AI-REC}^{\mathcal{A}_0,\mathcal{A}_1}_{\mathcal{P},\ell,\mathsf{Gen},\mathsf{KD}}\right] ,$$

where game AI-REC is defined in Fig. 3 (left) and the maximum is taken over all $\mathcal{A}_0$ that output at most S bits of auxiliary information, and all $\mathcal{A}_1$ that place at most T queries to the random oracle and at most c queries to the corrupt oracle.

Similarly, we define

$$\mathbf{Adv}^{\text{bf-rec}}_{\mathcal{P},\ell,\mathsf{Gen},\mathsf{KD}}(P, T, c) := \max_{\mathcal{A}_0,\mathcal{A}_1} \Pr\left[\text{BF-REC}^{\mathcal{A}_0,\mathcal{A}_1}_{\mathcal{P},\ell,\mathsf{Gen},\mathsf{KD}}\right] ,$$

where game BF-REC is defined in Fig. 3 (right) and the maximum is taken over all $\mathcal{A}_0$ that output a list L of size at most P and all $\mathcal{A}_1$ that place at most T queries to the random oracle and at most c queries to the corrupt oracle.

We start by showing that for any salt generator the BF-RO advantage can be upper bounded by that in the salted unguessability game. Here we will rely on the fact that the collision pattern z_{coll} is known in the SA-GUESS game.

Theorem 6. *Let* $\mathsf{KD}^{\mathsf{H}}(pw, sa) := \mathsf{H}(pw|sa)$ *for random oracle* H. *Then for any* m*-sampler* $\mathcal{P}$, *any salt generator* Gen, *and any* $\ell, P, T, c \in \mathbb{N}$,

$$\mathbf{Adv}^{\text{bf-rec}}_{\mathcal{P},\ell,\mathsf{Gen},\mathsf{H}}(P, T, c) \leq \mathbf{Adv}^{\text{sa-guess}}_{\mathcal{P},\ell,\mathsf{Gen}}(T + P, c) .$$

Proof. Let $(\mathcal{A}_0, \mathcal{A}_1)$ be a (P, T, c)-adversary in the BF-REC game. We construct a $(T+P, c)$-adversary $\mathcal{B}$ in the SA-GUESS game as follows. Algorithm $\mathcal{B}(\mathbf{sa}, z, z_{\mathsf{coll}})$ receives a salt vector $\mathbf{sa}$, z and a collision pattern z_{coll}. It then runs $\mathcal{A}_0()$ to obtain (σ, L).

Algorithm $\mathcal{B}$ now needs to prepare the challenge key vector $\mathbf{k}$ for $\mathcal{A}_1$. To this end, it will use its access to a TEST oracle to find out whether or not a password-salt pair appears on L. If it does, it uses the provided value in L. Else it will pick the answer randomly, ensuring consistency using the collision pattern of password-salt pairs z_{coll}.

In more detail, for each $(pw|sa, y) \in L$ with $sa = \mathbf{sa}[i, j]$ for some (i, j), algorithm $\mathcal{B}$ queries $\textsc{Test}(pw, sa)$ and obtains a set S of indices. If S is non-empty, it contains indices i for which $(\mathbf{pw}[i], sa[i, j]) = (pw, sa)$ for some j. For these indices, algorithm $\mathcal{B}$ uses y as the challenge value. If S is empty, $\mathcal{B}$ does nothing (the (pw, sa) pair on L is not one of the challenge password-salt pairs). For indices (i, j) such that $(\mathbf{pw}[i], sa[i, j])$ does not appear on L, algorithm $\mathcal{B}$ generates uniform values compatible with z_{coll} as the corresponding challenge keys. Note that for these lazily sampled values the domain point is only partially known. Note also that at this point $\mathcal{B}$ places at most P queries to $\textsc{Test}$.

Let $\mathbf{k}$ be the set of challenge keys sampled as above. Algorithm $\mathcal{B}$ runs $\mathcal{A}_1^{\mathsf{H}[L],\textsc{Cor}}(\mathbf{sa}, \mathbf{k}, \sigma, z)$ as follows. It relays all its $\textsc{Cor}(i)$ queries to its own $\textsc{Cor}(i)$ oracle. For the $\mathbf{pw}[i]$ received, $\mathcal{B}$ updates the corresponding unknown entry part of the domain point with $\mathbf{pw}[i]$. Note that $\mathcal{B}$ places at most c queries to $\textsc{Cor}$.

To answer a random-oracle query $\mathsf{H}[L](pw, sa)$ outside L, if sa does not match $\mathbf{sa}[i, j]$ for any (i, j) it chooses a random value. If $sa = \mathbf{sa}[i, j]$ for some (i, j), algorithm $\mathcal{B}$ queries $\textsc{Test}(pw, sa)$ to get a set of indices S. If this set is empty, $\mathcal{B}$ returns a random value. If S is non-empty, then $\mathbf{pw}[i]$ for $i \in S$ are discovered and the random value generated at the challenge phase is used. Note that for $i \in S$ this value was set consistently using z_{coll}. (Algorithm $\mathcal{B}$ also updates the corresponding unknown half of the domain point.) Note also that $\mathcal{B}$ places at most T queries to $\textsc{Test}$ during this phase. □

The estimated extra P queries to $\textsc{Test}$ queries during challenge preparation may indeed arise for example when passwords are predictable and there are no salts. On the other hand, for large random salts, with overwhelming probability no queries to $\textsc{Test}$ will be made at this stage. Our next theorem formalizes this.

Theorem 7. *Let* $\mathsf{KD}^{\mathsf{H}}(pw, sa) := \mathsf{H}(pw|sa)$ *for random oracle* H*. Then for any* m*-sampler* $\mathcal{P}$*, any salt generator* $\mathsf{Gen} := [K]$ *that outputs uniform salts in a set of size* K*, and any* $\ell, P, T, c \in \mathbb{N}$*,*

$$\mathbf{Adv}^{\text{bf-rec}}_{\mathcal{P},\ell,[K],\mathsf{H}}(P, T, c) \le \left(\binom{T}{m-c} + \frac{m\ell}{K}\binom{T+P}{m-c}\right) \cdot \mathbf{Adv}^{\text{guess}}_{\mathcal{P}}(m-c, c) + \frac{m^2\ell^2}{K} .$$

Proof. Let $(\mathcal{A}_0, \mathcal{A}_1)$ be a (P, T, c)-adversary in the BF-$\textsc{Rec}$ game. We construct an adversary $\mathcal{B}$ in the $\textsc{Guess}$ game. Algorithm $\mathcal{B}(z)$ receives z and runs $\mathcal{A}_0()$ to obtain (σ, L). It then generates a salt vector $\mathbf{sa}$ of size $m \times \ell$. If there is a collision among these salts, $\mathcal{B}$ terminates. Otherwise, $\mathcal{B}$ sets z_{coll} to be the all-zero collision pattern and prepares the challenge key vector $\mathbf{k}$ as follows. The difficulty in preparing these values lies in that the values need to be consistent with those specified in L. Let S denote an ordered list of salts and let P_{sa} for $sa \in [K]$ denote the number of passwords which together with sa appear in L. Since L is of size P we have that

$$\sum_{sa \in [k]} P_{sa} = P .$$

To prepare the challenge vector consistently, $\mathcal{B}$ calls its $\text{TEST}(i, pw)$ oracle on each password pw appearing on the L together with some salt $\mathbf{sa}[i, j] \in S$. If a password-salt pair is discovered to be on L, algorithm $\mathcal{B}$ uses the value provided in L, else it picks a random value. At this phase algorithm $\mathcal{B}$ makes $\sum_{sa \in S} P_{sa}$ queries to TEST.

Algorithm $\mathcal{B}$ now runs $\mathcal{A}_1(\mathbf{sa}, \mathbf{k}, \sigma, z)$ and answers its corruption queries by queries its own corruption oracle. Primitive queries on (pw, sa), which wlog can be assumed to be outside L, are handled by first querying $\text{TEST}(i, pw)$ if $sa = \mathbf{sa}[i, j]$ for some (i, j) and accordingly using either a value from the challenge phase, or a uniform value. Thus,

$$\mathbf{Adv}^{\text{bf-rec}}_{\mathcal{P},\ell,[K],\mathsf{H}}(P, T, c) \leq \frac{m^2\ell^2}{K} + \sum_{S \in [K]^{(m\ell)}} \frac{1}{K^{m\ell}} \cdot \mathbf{Adv}^{\text{guess}}_{\mathcal{P}}(T + \sum_{sa \in S} P_{sa}, c) \ ,$$

where $[K]^{(m\ell)}$ denotes all ordered lists of size $m\ell$ with *distinct* entries in K.

By Theorem 2 each summand above can be bound as

$$\mathbf{Adv}^{\text{guess}}_{\mathcal{P}}(T + \sum_{sa \in S} P_{sa}, c) \leq \binom{T + \sum_{sa \in S} P_{sa}}{m - c} \cdot \mathbf{Adv}^{\text{guess}}_{\mathcal{P}}(m - c, c) \ .$$

Now for fixed m and c the right-hand side is a convex function. Thus, by Jensen's inequality, the sum attains its maximum at one of the extremal values where $P_{sa} = P$ for a single salt $sa = sa^*$, and $P_{sa} = 0$ elsewhere. Since the advantage terms are symmetric, without loss of generality, we may assume that $sa^* = 1$.

For this particular distribution of passwords in L, we have that for $(m\ell)!\binom{K-1}{m\ell}$ terms the number of additional queries, $\sum_{sa \in S} P_{sa}$, is zero: choose $m\ell$ salts in $[K] \setminus \{sa^*\}$ and order them. For these cases $\mathcal{B}$ places T queries in total. For $(m\ell)!\binom{K-1}{m\ell-1}$ terms the number of additional queries is $\sum_{sa \in S} P_{sa} = P$: choose one salt to be sa^*, the rest in $[K] \setminus \{sa^*\}$, and order. For these cases $\mathcal{B}$ places $T + P$ queries in total.

Hence we obtain that

$$\begin{aligned}\mathbf{Adv}^{\text{bf-rec}}_{\mathcal{P},\ell,[K],\mathsf{H}}(P, T, c) \leq \frac{m^2\ell^2}{K} &+ \frac{(m\ell)!}{K^{m\ell}} \cdot \binom{K-1}{m\ell} \cdot \binom{T}{m-c} \cdot \mathbf{Adv}^{\text{guess}}_{\mathcal{P}}(m - c, c) \\ &+ \frac{(m\ell)!}{K^{m\ell}} \cdot \binom{K-1}{m\ell-1} \cdot \binom{T+P}{m-c} \cdot \mathbf{Adv}^{\text{guess}}_{\mathcal{P}}(m - c, c) \ .\end{aligned}$$

Using the upper bound on the binomial coefficients we have

$$\frac{(m\ell)!}{K^{m\ell}} \cdot \binom{K-1}{m\ell} \leq 1 \quad \text{and} \quad \frac{(m\ell)!}{K^{m\ell}} \cdot \binom{K-1}{m\ell-1} \leq \frac{m\ell}{K} \ .$$

The theorem follows. □

4.1 Main Theorems

In this section we derive upper bounds on the adversarial advantage in the AI-REC game based on the bounds established in the previous section.

Theorems 8–10 below upper-bound unrecoverability of hashed passwords in three different settings. We will use Theorems 2–4 to prove these results.

We start with the case of unsalted passwords. We focus on the case with no corruption; the case with corruptions can be dealt with similarly using our results but the involved bounds are more complex.

Theorem 8 (No salts). *Let $\mathcal{P}$ be an m-sampler and consider the empty salt generator. Then for any adversary in the* AI-REC *game outputting at most S bits of side information, making at most T queries to the random oracle and no corruption queries, for any $\gamma > 0$ and $m \leq T$ we have that*

$$\mathbf{Adv}^{\text{ai-rec}}_{\mathcal{P},\ell,\perp,\mathsf{H}}(S,T,0) \leq 2^m \cdot \left(T + \frac{2T(S+\log\gamma^{-1})}{m}\right)^m \cdot \mathbf{Adv}^{\text{guess}}_{\mathcal{P}}(m,0) + \gamma\,.$$

Proof. Theorems 4 and 6 together yield

$$\mathbf{Adv}^{\text{bf-rec}}_{\mathcal{P},\ell,\perp,\mathsf{H}}(P,T,0) \leq (T+P)^m \cdot \mathbf{Adv}^{\text{guess}}_{\mathcal{P}}(m,0)\,.$$

Using the second (i.e., the unpredictability) part of Theorem 1, noting that in our setting there are $m+T$ calls to H, and assuming that $m \leq T$ for any $\gamma > 0$, we may set

$$P := \frac{(S+\log\gamma^{-1})(m+T)}{m} \leq \frac{2T(S+\log\gamma^{-1})}{m}$$

to deduce the stated bound for any $\gamma > 0$.[8] □

We next consider the case of distinct and potentially low-entropy salts. This is for example the case when salts are an index and consequently the domain of the hash function is separated for different users.

Theorem 9 (Known distinct salts). *Let $\mathcal{P}$ be an m-sampler and consider a salt generator that always outputs distinct, but potentially low-entropy, known salts. Then for any adversary in the* AI-REC *game outputting at most S bits of side information, making at most T queries to the random oracle and no corruption queries, for any $\gamma > 0$ and $m \leq T$ we have that*

$$\mathbf{Adv}^{\text{ai-rec}}_{\mathcal{P},\ell,\mathsf{Gen},\mathsf{H}}(S,T,0) \leq 2^m \cdot \left(\frac{\mathrm{e}T + 2\mathrm{e}T(S+\log\gamma^{-1})/m}{m}\right)^m \cdot \mathbf{Adv}^{\text{guess}}_{\mathcal{P}}(m,0) + \gamma\,. \quad (4)$$

Proof. In the case of salted passwords with distinct salts, Theorems 3 and 6 together yield

$$\mathbf{Adv}^{\text{bf-rec}}_{\mathcal{P},\ell,\mathsf{Gen},\mathsf{H}}(P,T,0) \leq \binom{T+P}{m} \cdot \mathbf{Adv}^{\text{guess}}_{\mathcal{P}}(m,0) \leq \left(\frac{\mathrm{e}(T+P)}{m}\right)^m \cdot \mathbf{Adv}^{\text{guess}}_{\mathcal{P}}(m,0)\,.$$

Using the second part of Theorem 1, we may set P as in the unsalted case (which is close to the optimal) to deduce that the stated bound for any $\gamma > 0$. □

[8] Via differentiation, this value of P is close to the optimal choice.

We finally consider the case of uniform salts.

Theorem 10 (Uniform salts). *Let $\mathcal{P}$ be an m-sampler and consider a salt generator that always outputs uniformly random salts in a set of size K. Then for any adversary in the* AI-REC *game outputting at most S bits of side information, making at most T queries to the random oracle and no corruption queries, for any $\gamma > 0$ and $m \leq T$ we have that*

$$\mathbf{Adv}^{\text{ai-rec}}_{\mathcal{P},\ell,[K],\mathsf{H}}(S,T,0) \leq 2^m \cdot \left(\left(\frac{eT}{m}\right)^m + \frac{m\ell}{K} \cdot \left(\frac{eT + 2eT(S + \log \gamma^{-1})/m}{m}\right)^m\right) \cdot \mathbf{Adv}^{\text{guess}}_{\mathcal{P}}(m,0) + \frac{m^2\ell^2}{K} + \gamma \,.$$

Proof. Using Theorems 3 and 7 for uniform salts in $[K]$ we get

$$\mathbf{Adv}^{\text{bf-rec}}_{\mathcal{P},\ell,[K],\mathsf{H}}(P,T,0) \leq \left(\left(\frac{eT}{m}\right)^m + \frac{m\ell}{K}\left(\frac{e(T+P)}{m}\right)^m\right) \cdot \mathbf{Adv}^{\text{guess}}_{\mathcal{P}}(m,0) + \frac{m^2\ell^2}{K} \,.$$

We may set P as in the previous cases, which is again close to optimal, to deduce the stated bound for any $\gamma > 0$. $\square$

We summarize the above discussion for the case of uniform passwords in $[N]$ in the table below. We have assumed $\log \gamma^{-1} \leq m$ and have removed the additive "$+\gamma$" terms, and in the uniform case "$+\frac{m^2\ell^2}{K}$" terms, to help readability.

	No salts	Known distinct salts	Uniform salts
$S = 0$	$\left(\frac{6T}{N}\right)^m$	$\left(\frac{6eT}{mN}\right)^m$	$\left(1 + \frac{m\ell}{K}\right) \cdot \left(\frac{6eT}{mN}\right)^m$
"Large" $S \geq 3m$	$\left(\frac{6ST}{mN}\right)^m$	$\left(\frac{6eST}{m^2N}\right)^m$	$\left(\frac{2eT}{mN}\right)^m + \frac{m\ell}{K} \cdot \left(\frac{6eST}{m^2N}\right)^m$

5 Iterated Hashing

A well-known method for reducing vulnerabilities to brute-force attacks is to compute *iterated* hashes of salted passwords. The effects of iteration will be hardly noticeable by the honest users, but for the adversary the cryptanalytic effort will increase by a factor proportional to the number of iteration rounds (converting weeks of effort to years). This mechanism has been used, for example, in classical password-hashing mechanisms such as PBKDF and bcrypt.

The r-iterated construction is

$$\mathsf{KD}^{\mathsf{H}}_r(pw, sa) := \underbrace{\mathsf{H} \circ \cdots \circ \mathsf{H} \circ \mathsf{H}}_{r}(pw|sa) \,,$$

where $r \in \mathbb{N}$ is the number of rounds, and $\mathsf{H} : \{0,1\}^* \to \{0,1\}^n$ is a hash function that we will model as a random oracle. We also assume that $pw|sa$ is never of length n (and hence such values cannot be a hash output).

Game AI-KDF-REAL$^{\mathcal{D}_0,\mathcal{D}_1}_{\mathcal{P},\ell,\mathsf{Gen},\mathsf{KD}}$:	Game BF-KDF-REAL$^{\mathcal{D}_0,\mathcal{D}_1}_{\mathcal{P},\ell,\mathsf{Gen},\mathsf{KD}}$:
$\mathsf{H} \twoheadleftarrow \mathrm{Fun}(D,R)$ $\sigma \twoheadleftarrow \mathcal{D}_0(\mathsf{H})$ $(\mathbf{pw}, z) \twoheadleftarrow \mathcal{P}$ for $(i,j) \in [m] \times [\ell]$ do $\quad \mathbf{sa}[i,j] \twoheadleftarrow \mathsf{Gen}(i,j)$ $\quad \mathbf{k}[i,j] \leftarrow \mathsf{KD}^{\mathsf{H}}(\mathbf{pw}[i], \mathbf{sa}[i,j])$ $b' \twoheadleftarrow \mathcal{D}_1^{\mathrm{PRIM}}(\mathbf{pw}, \mathbf{sa}, \mathbf{k}, z, \sigma)$ return b'	$\mathsf{H} \twoheadleftarrow \mathrm{Fun}(D,R)$ $(\sigma, L) \twoheadleftarrow \mathcal{D}_0()$ $(\mathbf{pw}, z) \twoheadleftarrow \mathcal{P}$ for $(i,j) \in [m] \times [\ell]$ do $\quad \mathbf{sa}[i,j] \twoheadleftarrow \mathsf{Gen}(i,j)$ $\quad \mathbf{k}[i,j] \leftarrow \mathsf{KD}^{\mathsf{H}}(\mathbf{pw}[i], \mathbf{sa}[i,j])$ $b' \twoheadleftarrow \mathcal{D}_1^{\mathrm{PRIM}}(\mathbf{pw}, \mathbf{sa}, \mathbf{k}, z, \sigma)$ return b'
Proc. PRIM(w): return $\mathsf{H}(w)$	Proc. PRIM(w): return $\mathsf{H}[L](w)$
Game BF/AI-KDF-IDEAL$^{\mathcal{D}_1}_{\mathcal{P},\ell,\mathsf{Gen},\mathcal{S}_0,\mathcal{S}_1}$:	Proc. PRIM(w):
$(\sigma, st) \twoheadleftarrow \mathcal{S}_0()$ $(\mathbf{pw}, z) \twoheadleftarrow \mathcal{P}$ for $(i,j) \in [m] \times [\ell]$ do $\quad \mathbf{sa}[i,j] \twoheadleftarrow \mathsf{Gen}(i,j)$ $\quad \mathbf{k}[i,j] \twoheadleftarrow \{0,1\}^k$ $b' \twoheadleftarrow \mathcal{D}_1^{\mathrm{PRIM}}(\mathbf{pw}, \mathbf{sa}, \mathbf{k}, z, \sigma)$ return b'	$(y, st) \twoheadleftarrow \mathcal{S}_1^{\mathrm{TEST}}(w; st)$ return y Proc. TEST(pw, sa): $S \leftarrow \{i \in [m] : \exists j \in [\ell]$ st. $\quad (\mathbf{pw}[i], \mathbf{sa}[i,j]) = (pw, sa)\}$ return $\mathbf{k}[S]$

Fig. 4. Simulation-based notion of KDF security in the AI-RO and BF-RO model. Note that the ideal games are syntactically identical.

Following BRT, in this section we adopt a more modular approach to security and formulate two simulation-based notions of security for KDF. In the next section we will then show how to use KDF security to argue for the security of password-based protocols.

AI-KDF SECURITY. Our first definition is a (simulation-based) notion of KDF security which extends that of [BRT12, Sect. 3.1] to the AI-RO model. We define the KDF advantage of an adversary $\mathcal{D} = (\mathcal{D}_0, \mathcal{D}_1)$ in the AI-RO model with respect to a simulator $\mathcal{S} = (\mathcal{S}_0, \mathcal{S}_1)$ as

$$\mathbf{Adv}^{\text{ai-kdf}}_{\mathcal{P},\ell,\mathsf{Gen},\mathsf{KD},\mathcal{S}_0,\mathcal{S}_1}(\mathcal{D}_0,\mathcal{D}_1) := \Pr\left[\text{AI-KDF-REAL}^{\mathcal{D}_0,\mathcal{D}_1}_{\mathcal{P},\ell,\mathsf{Gen},\mathsf{KD}}\right] - \Pr\left[\text{AI-KDF-IDEAL}^{\mathcal{D}_1}_{\mathcal{P},\ell,\mathsf{Gen},\mathcal{S}_0,\mathcal{S}_1}\right],$$

where games AI-KDF-REAL and AI-KDF-IDEAL are defined in Fig. 4.

Our definition differs from that of BRT in a number of aspects. First, it includes a preprocessing stage via $\mathcal{D}_0$ in the real game and a simulated preprocessing stage via $\mathcal{S}_0$ in the ideal game. Second, our games sample salts via Gen, whereas in BRT an arbitrary joint distribution on passwords-salt pairs was considered. Such a notion is infeasible to achieve in the presence of preprocessing as salts need to have entropy. Finally, the TEST procedure in the ideal game returns the set of all indices i for which the i-th password matches the queried password and some salt associated with it matches the queried salt. We note that, as in BRT, the simulator does *not* get access to the collision pattern of the password-salt pairs: the purpose of the ideal KDF game is to translate security to a setting where keys are truly random, and their collision patterns are not necessarily known.

BF-KDF SECURITY. We now define an analogous notion of KDF security in the BF-RO model. We set

$$\mathbf{Adv}^{\text{bf-kdf}}_{\mathcal{P},\ell,\mathsf{Gen},\mathsf{KD},\mathcal{S}_0,\mathcal{S}_1}(\mathcal{D}_0,\mathcal{D}_1) := \Pr\left[\text{BF-KDF-REAL}^{\mathcal{D}_0,\mathcal{D}_1}_{\mathcal{P},\ell,\mathsf{Gen},\mathsf{KD}}\right] - \Pr\left[\text{BF-KDF-IDEAL}^{\mathcal{D}_1}_{\mathcal{P},\ell,\mathsf{Gen},\mathcal{S}_0,\mathcal{S}_1}\right],$$

where games BF-KDF-REAL and BF-KDF-IDEAL are defined in Fig. 4. Note that the ideal AI and BF games are syntactically identical.

Using Theorem 1, we first show that KDF security in the BF-RO model implies KDF security in the AI-RO model.

Theorem 11 (BF-to-AI KDF Security). *Let* KD^{H} *be a key-derivation where* H *is a random oracle and let* Gen *be a salt generator. Then for any AI-KDF distinguisher* $(\mathcal{D}_0,\mathcal{D}_1)$*, where* $\mathcal{D}_0$ *outputs* S *bits of auxiliary information and* $\mathcal{D}_1$ *places at most* T *queries to its* PRIM *oracle, and any* $P \in \mathbb{N}$ *and* $\gamma > 0$ *there is a BF-KDF distinguisher* $(\tilde{\mathcal{D}}_0,\tilde{\mathcal{D}}_1)$*, where* $\tilde{\mathcal{D}}_0$ *output a string of length at most* S *and a list of size at most* P*, and such that for any BF-KDF simulator* $(\mathcal{S}_0,\mathcal{S}_1)$ *and any* $\ell \in \mathbb{N}$,

$$\mathbf{Adv}^{\text{ai-kdf}}_{\mathcal{P},\ell,\mathsf{Gen},\mathsf{KD},\mathcal{S}_0,\mathcal{S}_1}(\mathcal{D}_0,\mathcal{D}_1) \leq \mathbf{Adv}^{\text{bf-kdf}}_{\mathcal{P},\ell,\mathsf{Gen},\mathsf{KD},\mathcal{S}_0,\mathcal{S}_1}(\tilde{\mathcal{D}}_0,\tilde{\mathcal{D}}_1) + \frac{(S+\log\gamma^{-1})\cdot(rm\ell+T)}{P} + \gamma .$$

Proof. Let $(\mathcal{D}_0,\mathcal{D}_1)$ be an AI-indifferentiability adversary. We apply the first part of Theorem 1 to the real AI-KDF game and obtain a BF-KDF distinguisher $(\tilde{\mathcal{D}}_0,\tilde{\mathcal{D}}_1)$. In the real game there are in total at most $rm\ell+T$ queries to H. Now let $(\mathcal{S}_0,\mathcal{S}_1)$ be a BF-KDF simulator for $(\tilde{\mathcal{D}}_0,\tilde{\mathcal{D}}_1)$. Then $(\mathcal{S}_0,\mathcal{S}_1)$ is also an AI-KDF simulator as the ideal BF- and AI-KDF games are syntactically identical. □

We now prove that salted iteration of a random oracle achieves KDF security in the BF-RO model. The technical challenge here is to show that the results of [BRT12] can be "lifted" to a setting with auxiliary information. To do so, we can follow the generic approach of Coretti et al. [CDGS18] (i.e., Theorem 1), but this results in a different construction where *every* primitive call in the construction is salted. Standard iterated constructions, however, only salt the innermost call.

We thus directly establish the *bit-fixing* KDF security of the iterated construction when $pw|sa$ are never an n-bit string where n is the output length of H. We then translate this result to the auxiliary-input setting using the above theorem. The length restriction on $pw|sa$ allows us to decouple the innermost call to H from the rest of the calls.[9]

Theorem 12 (Bit-fixing KDF security). *Let* $\mathsf{KD}_r^{\mathsf{H}}$ *be the* r*-iterated key-derivation function where* $\mathsf{H} : \{0,1\}^* \to \{0,1\}^n$ *is a random oracle, and let* Gen *be a salt generator that outputs uniform salts in a set of size* K. *Let* $N := 2^n$. *Then for any BF-KDF distinguisher* $(\mathcal{D}_0, \mathcal{D}_1)$ *where* $\mathcal{D}_1$ *outputs a list of size* P *and makes at most* T *primitive queries, there is a simulator* $(\mathcal{S}_0, \mathcal{S}_1)$ *such that for any* $\ell \in \mathbb{N}$

$$\mathbf{Adv}^{\text{bf-kdf}}_{\mathcal{P},\ell,\mathsf{Gen},\mathsf{KD}_r,\mathcal{S}_0,\mathcal{S}_1}(\mathcal{D}_0,\mathcal{D}_1) \le \frac{(r+1)m\ell T}{N} + 3 \cdot \left(\frac{rm\ell(rm\ell+P)}{N} + \frac{m\ell P}{K} + \frac{m^2\ell^2}{K}\right) .$$

Furthermore, $\mathcal{S}_1$ *places at most* T/r *queries to* RO *and runs in time* $\tilde{\mathcal{O}}(r)$.

We start with a high-level overview of our simulator, which we define in Fig. 5. The initial stage of the simulator $\mathcal{S}_0$ simply runs $\mathcal{D}_0$ to get (σ, L), and populates table H with assignments in L. It passes H (which is essentially L) onto $\mathcal{S}_1$ via state st. The online simulator simulates H via lazy sampling using H and detecting completed chains (as is common in indifferentiability proofs). For a query w, it looks for a *chain* of queries $w_0, w_1, \ldots, w_{r-1}$ such that the chain starts at $w_0 = pw|sa$ for a one of salts (note that the simulator knows the salts) and ends at $w_{r-1} = w$, and furthermore along the chain there were no collisions in H (and hence the chain, if defined, is unique). If a chain is found, the simulator uses the random oracle RO to answer the query; else a fresh random string is chosen. This simulator makes a TEST query as a result of a chain completion. Hence it makes at most T_2/r queries.[10]

Proof (Sketch). We now give an overview of the game transitions used in the proof of BF-KDF security and refer the reader to the full version of the paper for the details.

G_0: In this game we initially populate a table H (used for lazy sampling) with entries in L. We compute the challenge vector using lazy sampling and also answer primitive queries using H.

G_1: In this game we "optimistically" sample the outputs of the random oracle for the challenge values. We also set a bad flag bad if while computing chains we encounter a penultimate value whose hash has already been set. We still use the value already set, but in the next game we would like to set this value to the optimistically chosen one. G_1 and G_0 are identical.

---

[9] In particular, we do not run into "hash-of-hash" problems as in [DRST12] as *not* every H call is salted.

[10] We emphasize that without the length restriction on password-salt pairs, this simulator can fail. Consider a differentiator that gets $w_r \leftarrow \textsc{Const}(pw, sa)$, $w'_{r+1} \leftarrow \textsc{Prim}(w_r)$, and $w'_1 \leftarrow \textsc{Prim}(pw|sa)$. It the parses w'_1 as (pw', sa'), gets $w_{r+1} \leftarrow \textsc{Const}(pw', sa')$, and checks if $(w_{r+1} = w'_{r+1})$. This attack corresponds to the computation of two overlapping chains. Our $\mathcal{S}_1$ fails as it simulates the two PRIM queries randomly since it won't be able to detect any chains.

Algo. $\mathcal{S}_0()$:	Algo. $\mathcal{S}_1^{\text{TEST}}(w)$:	Sub. $\mathsf{FindChain}(w)$:
$(\sigma, L) \twoheadleftarrow \mathcal{D}_0()$	if $H[w] \neq \perp$: return $H[w]$	$w_{r-1} \leftarrow w$
for $(w, y) \in L$ do	$(pw, sa) \leftarrow \mathsf{FindChain}(w)$	for $i = 1$ to $r-1$ do
$H[w] \leftarrow y$	if $(pw, sa) \neq \perp$:	$S[w_{r-i}] := \{x : H[x] = w_{r-i}\}$
$st \leftarrow H$	$y \leftarrow \text{TEST}(pw, sa)$	if $\lvert S[w_{r-i}]\rvert \neq 1$: return $\perp$
return (σ, st)	if $y \neq \perp$ then $H[w] \leftarrow y$	$w_{r-i-1} \twoheadleftarrow S[w_{r-i}]$
	else $H[w] \twoheadleftarrow \{0,1\}^n$	if$\exists(pw, \mathbf{sa}[i,j]) : w_0 = pw\lvert\mathbf{sa}[i,j]$:
	return $H[w]$	return (pw, sa)
		return $\perp$

Fig. 5. Simulator for the bit-fixing KDF security of the r-iterated random oracle.

G_2**:** In this game, even if the hash of a penultimate value is already defined and the flag bad gets set, we set the hash of the penultimate value to the optimistically chosen one. (Note that the primitive oracle has not been changed.) G_2 and G_1 are identical until bad.

G_3**:** In this game we introduce two conceptual changes: (1) We no longer set the entry in H for the penultimate values; and (2) We modify the primitive oracle to check if a query is a penultimate value. If so, the primitive oracle uses the optimistically sampled value. G_2 and G_3 are identical.

G_4**:** In this game we change the way the primitive oracle operates by first checking if there is a chain of values of length $r-1$ leading to the query w. (This is done by maintaining a set of edges E for the graph resulting from the queries. If so, we set the hash of w to the optimistically chosen one. Otherwise if the query w matches a penultimate value, we set a flag bad_2 and set hash value to the optimistically chosen one. G_3 and G_4 are identical until bad.

G_5**:** In this game if bad_2 is set, we do not use the optimistically set value, but rather a random value. The two games are identical until bad_2.

G_6**:** This game removes code in computing the challenge keys and setting of bad_2. It also moves populating H with L to the primitive oracle. This game is identical to G_5.

G_7**:** In this game we modify the way chains are detected. Now of course the simulator does not know the password-salt pairs. Hence, we modify this chain detection procedure so that it uses a TEST oracle to check if a password-salt pair that traces to the queried point is indeed one of the challenge password-salt pairs. This game is identical to the ideal AI-KDF game with the simulator in Fig. 5.

Such a path, if it exists, will be unique as long the paths are isolated (that is there are no edges (u, v) on graph of execution E such that v is on the path but u is not) and the path has no loops. Here we use the fact that password-salt pairs have length different than n-bit, so that the adversary cannot "slide" the path.

These conditions ensure that there is at more one path for a given w. In particular the simulator makes at most T/r such paths and thus the simulator's number of queries to TEST is also at most T/r times.

We now bound the distinguishing advantage in the transitions above. The games G_1–G_4 are all identical until bad. So we can bound this difference with a *single* game hop. (G_2 and G_3 were used for reasoning.) The probability of bad is *upper bounded* by the probabilities of (1) hitting a bad starting point with a non-fresh salt, that is $m\ell P/K$; (2) two salts colliding, $m^2\ell^2/K$ (here we do not make any assumptions about the entropy of $\mathcal{P}$ and in particular it could be that the sampled passwords are not distinct); and (3) any value generated collides with a value generated before, or one of the pre-sampled values, i.e., $(rm\ell)(rm\ell + P)/N$. Thus, the overall bound is

$$\frac{m\ell P}{K} + \frac{m^2\ell^2}{K} + \frac{(rm\ell)(rm\ell + P)}{N} .$$

The distance between G_4 and G_5 is bounded by the probability of setting bad_2. We have that $\Pr[\mathsf{bad}_2] \leq \Pr[\mathsf{bad}] + \Pr[\mathsf{bad}_2|\neg\mathsf{bad}]$. Now under $\neg\mathsf{bad}$ the values that provoke bad_2 are uniform. Since there are $rm\ell$ of them we get that $\Pr[\mathsf{bad}_s|\neg\mathsf{bad}] \leq rm\ell T/N$.

We now bound the distance between G_6 and G_7. The probability that input-outputs defining the paths from password-salt pairs of length $r-1$ stay disjoint and outside L is given by the bound displayed above. Thus, we pick up three $\Pr[\mathsf{bad}]$ terms in total. The probability that no other queries enter into these paths is at most $rm\ell T/N$. The theorem follows by collecting terms. □

We note our bound above does not involve birthday terms of the form T^2 or $T \cdot P$, which would translate to salt sizes that are too large to be acceptable in practice. We may now apply Theorem 11 to deduce that for any AI-KDF adversary $(\mathcal{D}_0, \mathcal{D}_1)$ that outputs at most S bits of auxiliary information and places at most T queries to the primitive oracle, there is a simulator (namely the simulator for the BF-KD notion) such that for any $\gamma > 0$

$$\mathbf{Adv}^{\text{ai-kdf}}_{\mathcal{P},\ell,\mathsf{Gen},\mathsf{KD}_r,\mathcal{S}_0,\mathcal{S}_1}(\mathcal{D}_0,\mathcal{D}_1) \quad \leq \quad \frac{S'T'}{P} \; + \; 3P\left(\frac{rm\ell}{N} + \frac{rm\ell}{K}\right) \; + \; \cdots \quad ,$$

where $S' := S + \log\gamma^{-1}$ and $T' := rm\ell + T$ and the omitted terms do not involve P. For the optimal P, we set the two terms involving P to a common value and obtain (up to constant factors) that

$$P = \sqrt{\frac{S'T'NK}{3rm\ell(N+K)}} .$$

Plugging this back into the bound we finally obtain that

$$\mathbf{Adv}^{\text{ai-kdf}}_{\mathcal{P},\ell,\mathsf{Gen},\mathsf{KD}_r,\mathcal{S}_0,\mathcal{S}_1}(\mathcal{D}_0,\mathcal{D}_1) \leq 6 \cdot \sqrt{\frac{S'T'NK}{3rm\ell(N+K)}} \cdot \left(\frac{rm\ell}{N} + \frac{rm\ell}{K}\right) + \frac{3m^2\ell^2}{K} + \frac{3r^2\,m^2\ell^2 + (r+1)m\ell T}{N} + \gamma .$$

Game ai-multi-$G^{\mathcal{A}_0,\mathcal{A}_1}_{G,\mathcal{P},\mathsf{Gen},\mathsf{KD}}$:	Proc. GAME(i,x):
$\mathsf{H} \twoheadleftarrow \mathrm{Fun}(D,R)$	$(y, st_i) \leftarrow \mathrm{G}(x; (\mathbf{k}[i,1],\ldots,\mathbf{k}[i,1], b_i, r_i); st_i)$
$\sigma \twoheadleftarrow \mathcal{A}_0(\mathsf{H})$	return y
$(b_1,\ldots,b_m) \twoheadleftarrow \{0,1\}^m$	
$(\mathbf{pw}, z) \twoheadleftarrow \mathcal{P}$	Proc. COR(i):
for $(i,j) \in [m] \times [\ell]$ do	return $\mathbf{pw}[i]$
$\quad \mathbf{sa}[i,j] \twoheadleftarrow \mathsf{Gen}(i,j)$	
$\quad \mathbf{k}[i,j] \leftarrow \mathsf{KD}^{\mathsf{H}}(\mathbf{pw}[i], \mathbf{sa}[i,j])$	Proc. $\mathsf{H}(w)$:
for $i \in [m]$ do	return $\mathsf{H}(w)$
$\quad (x_i, st_i) \leftarrow \mathrm{G}(\varepsilon; (\mathbf{k}[i,1],\ldots,$	
$\quad\quad \ldots, \mathbf{k}[i,\ell], b_i, r_i); \varepsilon)$	
$b' \twoheadleftarrow \mathcal{A}_1^{\mathrm{GAME},\mathrm{COR},\mathsf{H}}(\mathbf{sa}, x_1,\ldots,x_m,\sigma,z)$	
return $(b' = \oplus_{i=1}^m b_i)$	

Fig. 6. Security game for the password-based multi-instance extension of G in the presence of auxiliary information on H. States st_i are initialized to ε and r_i are independent random coins of appropriate length. ℓ is the number of random strings that need to be replaced in each instance of G.

6 KDF Security in Applications

Given a game G, as defined in Sect. 2, we consider a multi-instance extension that runs a *central* adversary $\mathcal{A}_1$ with respect to m independent instances of G. Let

$$\mathbf{Adv}^{\mathrm{single}}_{\mathrm{G}}(\mathcal{A}) := 2 \cdot \Pr\left[\mathrm{G}^{\mathcal{A}}\right] - 1 ,$$

be the single-instance advantage. Suppose G uses randomness $(k_1,\ldots,k_\ell,b,r)$ for some ℓ. We are interested in replacing the values k_j with those that are derived from passwords through a KDF (see game ai-multi-G in Fig. 6). Let

$$\mathbf{Adv}^{\text{ai-multi}}_{\mathrm{G},\mathcal{P},\mathsf{Gen},\mathsf{KD}}(\mathcal{A}_0,\mathcal{A}_1) := 2 \cdot \Pr\left[\text{ai-multi-}\mathrm{G}^{\mathcal{A}_0,\mathcal{A}_1}_{\mathrm{G},\mathcal{P},\mathsf{Gen},\mathsf{KD}}\right] - 1 .$$

We show that if KD^{H} is a secure KDF in the AI-RO model, this advantage can be upper bounded by those in the single-instance game G and the salted guessing game.

Theorem 13. *Let* G *be a game with ℓ keys, $\mathcal{P}$ an m-sampler,* KD^{H} *a key-derivation function in the RO model, and* Gen *a salt generator. Then for any adversary $(\mathcal{A}_0,\mathcal{A}_1)$ in* ai-multi-G *with $\mathcal{A}_0$ outputting at most S bits of auxiliary information, and $\mathcal{A}_1$ placing at most T queries to* H *and at most c queries to* COR, *there is a AI-KDF distinguisher $(\mathcal{D}_0,\mathcal{D}_1)$ where $\mathcal{D}_0$ also outputs at most S bits of auxiliary information and $\mathcal{D}_1$ places at most T queries to its* PRIM *oracle, and an adversary $\mathcal{B}$ against* G *in the single instance setting (with uniform randomness) that uses S bits of non-uniformity and runs in time that of $\mathcal{A}_1$ plus* *the time need to run $m-1$ instances of* G *such that for any AI-KDF simulator* $(\mathcal{S}_0, \mathcal{S}_1)$,

$$\mathbf{Adv}^{\text{ai-multi}}_{\mathrm{G},\mathcal{P},\mathsf{Gen},\mathsf{KD}}(\mathcal{A}_0, \mathcal{A}_1) \leq 2 \cdot \mathbf{Adv}^{\text{ai-kdf}}_{\mathcal{P},\ell,\mathsf{Gen},\mathsf{KD},\mathcal{S}_0,\mathcal{S}_1}(\mathcal{D}_0, \mathcal{D}_1) + \\ 2 \cdot \mathbf{Adv}^{\text{sa-guess}}_{\mathcal{P},\ell,\mathsf{Gen}}(T, c) + m \cdot \mathbf{Adv}^{\text{single}}_{\mathrm{G}}(\mathcal{B}) .$$

Proof. The proof follows that of [BRT12, Theorem 3.4], except that we need to deal with general games and also auxiliary information on H.

Let ai-multi-G_0 be identical to ai-multi-G. Let $(\mathcal{S}_0, \mathcal{S}_1)$ be the AI-KDF simulator. We modify ai-multi-G_0 to a game ai-multi-G_1 that uses random keys instead of keys derived from passwords, and where σ and H are stimulated via the AI-KDF simulator $(\mathcal{S}_0, \mathcal{S}_1)$. This transition is justified using AI-KDF security as the inputs and oracles provided in each of the two AI-KDF games (that is, all passwords, real/random keys, and salts) are sufficient for an AI-KDF distinguisher $\mathcal{D}_0, \mathcal{D}_1$ to simulate ai-multi-G_0 or ai-multi-G_1. In this transition the distinguisher also picks coins r_i and bits b_i. When $\mathcal{A}_1$ returns b', the distinguisher returns $(b' = \oplus_{i=1}^{m} b_i)$. Thus,

$$\Pr[\text{ai-multi-G}_0] - \Pr[\text{ai-multi-G}_1] \leq \mathbf{Adv}^{\text{ai-kdf}}_{\mathcal{P},\ell,\mathsf{Gen},\mathsf{KD},\mathcal{S}_0,\mathcal{S}_1}(\mathcal{D}_0, \mathcal{D}_1) .$$

We now modify ai-multi-G_1 to ai-multi-G_2 that sets flag bad and terminates if the simulator queries *all* passwords to its TEST oracle. The two games are identical until bad. We can upper-bound the probability of bad by building a SA-GUESS adversary as follows. Run the initial simulator $\mathcal{S}_0$ to generate σ. (Note that this step entails that the SA-GUESS adversary that we build is potentially unbounded.) Pick randomness (including keys) to simulate the m instances of the games. The COR oracle is simulated by relaying queries to and the corruption oracle provided in SA-GUESS. For the TEST query, use the TEST oracle in SA-GUESS to get a set S of indices. If this set is non-empty, return the corresponding set of keys $\mathbf{k}[S]$; otherwise return $\perp$. Whenever bad is set, SA-GUESS is won and thus

$$\Pr[\text{ai-multi-G}_1] - \Pr[\text{ai-multi-G}_2] \leq \mathbf{Adv}^{\text{sa-guess}}_{\mathcal{P},\ell,\mathsf{Gen}}(T, c) .$$

We now bound the probability of winning ai-multi-G_2 in terms of winning a single instance of G with random keys. This is done via a simple guessing argument. In game ai-multi-G_2 at the onset an adversary $\mathcal{B}$ guesses an index i^* among the m instances which won't be corrupted. By the bad flag introduced in the previous game, if an index remains uncorrupted, i^* will be a good guess with probability $1/m$. For the reduction, $\mathcal{B}$ chooses σ, passwords, salts, and randomness for all games except for the i^*-th game. All games except the i^*-th instance are simulated using these values. The i^*-th instance is simulated using the provided game G. If i^* is corrupted, $\mathcal{B}$ returns a random bit. When $\mathcal{A}_1$ terminates with b', algorithm $\mathcal{B}$ returns $b' \oplus_{i \neq i^*} b_i$ as its guess in the single instance game. This guess is correct guess whenever $b' = b_{i^*}$. Thus,

$$\Pr[\mathrm{G}] = 1/m \cdot \Pr[\text{ai-multi-G}_2] + (1 - 1/m) \cdot 1/2 ,$$

and hence

$$\Pr[\text{ai-multi-G}_2] - 1/2 = m \cdot (\Pr[\text{G}] - 1/2) = m/2 \cdot \mathbf{Adv}_{\text{G}}^{\text{single}}(\mathcal{B}) \ .$$

The theorem follows by collecting the terms above and using the definitions of the advantage functions. Note that $\mathcal{B}$ uses $|\sigma|$ bits of non-uniformity in this reduction. □

Our result generalizes [BRT12, Theorem 3.4] to a larger class of games, which among others includes IND-CPA security for symmetric encryption (as considered by BRT without auxiliary information), as well as other games such as AE or CCA security for symmetric encryption, unforgeability for MACs, and may others all in the presence of auxiliary information. We emphasize that this result does not extend to games that access H (i.e., the random oracle in G and that used by the KD are shared). Indeed, when attempting to prove such a result, the initial two sequence of games above go through, but the last step fails: the oracle access in instance i^* cannot be simulated. (And indeed, attacks do exist.) Despite this, if the domains of access for H are separated for G and KD such an extension can be established.

Acknowledgments. Tessaro was partially supported by NSF grants CNS-1930117 (CAREER), CNS-1926324, CNS-2026774, a Sloan Research Fellowship, and a JP Morgan Faculty Award. Farshim was supported in part by EPSRC grant EP/V034065/1.

A Multi-instance Hellman

We present a simple adaptation of Hellman's space-time trade-off algorithm for inverting random permutations. Consider the cycle graph of the permutation $\pi : [N] \to [N]$. We pick S points that are roughly equidistant on the graph. We store each such point together with a pointer to a point T/m steps behind. Now given $\pi(x) = y$, where x is within distance T/m from one of the S points on the cycle graph, we can successfully recover x in T steps: We apply π iteratively to y until we reach one of the S points. We then jump backwards by T/m steps (following the stored pointer), and apply π until we reach x. This process takes exactly T/m evaluations of π. (This is as in the single-instance case except for the T/m instead of T).

Now, in the multi-instance setting with m points $x_1, \ldots, x_m$, if all of the x_i's land within distance T/m from one of the S points, we can recover each x_i by evaluating π for T/m times, and thus in the worst case we make at most $m \cdot T/m = T$ queries. The probability that this happens is $(ST/mN)^m$. With c corruptions, we first reduce m to $m - c$. Thus, for uniform passwords in $[N]$,

$$\mathbf{Adv}^{\text{ai-rec}}_{[N]^m,\ell,\perp,\pi}(S,T,c) \geq \left(\frac{ST}{(m-c)N}\right)^{m-c} \ .$$

With no corruptions, if we have sufficiently large side information, we may well need time $T = mN/S$. In particular, this means that we have a *direct sum* situation (without introducing salts). That is, the time to break m instances scales linearly with m.

References

[AS15] Alwen, J., Serbinenko, V.: High parallel complexity graphs and memory-hard functions. In: Servedio, R.A., Rubinfeld, R. (eds.) 47th ACM STOC, pp. 595–603. ACM Press (June 2015)

[BRT12] Bellare, M., Ristenpart, T., Tessaro, S.: Multi-instance security and its application to password-based cryptography. In: Safavi-Naini, R., Canetti, R. (eds.) CRYPTO 2012. LNCS, vol. 7417, pp. 312–329. Springer, Heidelberg (2012). https://doi.org/10.1007/978-3-642-32009-5_19

[CDG18] Coretti, S., Dodis, Y., Guo, S.: Non-uniform bounds in the random-permutation, ideal-cipher, and generic-group models. In: Shacham, H., Boldyreva, A. (eds.) CRYPTO 2018. LNCS, vol. 10991, pp. 693–721. Springer, Cham (2018). https://doi.org/10.1007/978-3-319-96884-1_23

[CDGS18] Coretti, S., Dodis, Y., Guo, S., Steinberger, J.: Random Oracles and non-uniformity. In: Nielsen, J.B., Rijmen, V. (eds.) EUROCRYPT 2018. LNCS, vol. 10820, pp. 227–258. Springer, Cham (2018). https://doi.org/10.1007/978-3-319-78381-9_9

[CDMP05] Coron, J.-S., Dodis, Y., Malinaud, C., Puniya, P.: Merkle-Damgård revisited: how to construct a hash function. In: Shoup, V. (ed.) CRYPTO 2005. LNCS, vol. 3621, pp. 430–448. Springer, Heidelberg (2005). https://doi.org/10.1007/11535218_26

[DGK17] Dodis, Y., Guo, S., Katz, J.: Fixing cracks in the concrete: random oracles with auxiliary input, revisited. In: Coron, J.-S., Nielsen, J.B. (eds.) EUROCRYPT 2017. LNCS, vol. 10211, pp. 473–495. Springer, Cham (2017). https://doi.org/10.1007/978-3-319-56614-6_16

[DRST12] Dodis, Y., Ristenpart, T., Steinberger, J.P., Tessaro, S.: To hash or not to hash again? (In)differentiability results for H^2 and HMAC. In: Safavi-Naini, R., Canetti, R. (eds.) CRYPTO 2012. LNCS, vol. 7417, pp. 348–366. Springer, Heidelberg (2012)

[DTT10] De, A., Trevisan, L., Tulsiani, M.: Time space tradeoffs for attacks against one-way functions and PRGs. In: Rabin, T. (ed.) CRYPTO 2010. LNCS, vol. 6223, pp. 649–665. Springer, Heidelberg (2010). https://doi.org/10.1007/978-3-642-14623-7_35

[GT00] Gennaro, R., Trevisan, L.: Lower bounds on the efficiency of generic cryptographic constructions. In: 41st FOCS, pp. 305–313. IEEE Computer Society Press (November 2000)

[Kal00] Kaliski, B.: Pkcs# 5: password-based cryptography specification version 2.0 (2000)

[MRH04] Maurer, U., Renner, R., Holenstein, C.: Indifferentiability, impossibility results on reductions, and applications to the random oracle methodology. In: Naor, M. (ed.) TCC 2004. LNCS, vol. 2951, pp. 21–39. Springer, Heidelberg (2004). https://doi.org/10.1007/978-3-540-24638-1_2

[Oec03] Oechslin, P.: Making a faster cryptanalytic time-memory trade-off. In: Boneh, D. (ed.) CRYPTO 2003. LNCS, vol. 2729, pp. 617–630. Springer, Heidelberg (2003). https://doi.org/10.1007/978-3-540-45146-4_36

[PJ16] Percival, C., Josefsson, S.: The scrypt password-based key derivation function. RFC 7914 (Informational) (August 2016)

[PM99] Provos, N., Mazières, D.: A future-adaptable password scheme. In: Proceedings of the FREENIX Track: 1999 USENIX Annual Technical Conference, 6–11 June 1999, Monterey, California, USA, pp. 81–91. USENIX (1999)

[Unr07] Unruh, D.: Random Oracles and auxiliary input. In: Menezes, A. (ed.) CRYPTO 2007. LNCS, vol. 4622, pp. 205–223. Springer, Heidelberg (2007). https://doi.org/10.1007/978-3-540-74143-5_12

[Wee05] Wee, H.: On obfuscating point functions. In: Gabow, H.N., Fagin, R. (eds.) 37th ACM STOC, pp. 523–532. ACM Press (May 2005)

Compactness of Hashing Modes and Efficiency Beyond Merkle Tree

Elena Andreeva[1(✉)], Rishiraj Bhattacharyya[2], and Arnab Roy[3]

[1] Technical University of Vienna, Vienna, Austria
elena.andreeva@tuwien.ac.at
[2] NISER, HBNI, Jatani, India
rishirajbhattacharyya@protonmail.com
[3] University of Klagenfurt, Klagenfurt, Austria
arnab.roy@aau.at

Abstract. We revisit the classical problem of designing optimally efficient cryptographically secure hash functions. Hash functions are traditionally designed via applying modes of operation on primitives with smaller domains. The results of Shrimpton and Stam (ICALP 2008), Rogaway and Steinberger (CRYPTO 2008), and Mennink and Preneel (CRYPTO 2012) show how to achieve optimally efficient designs of $2n$-to-n-bit compression functions from non-compressing primitives with asymptotically optimal $2^{n/2-\epsilon}$-query collision resistance. Designing optimally efficient and secure hash functions for larger domains ($>2n$ bits) is still an open problem.

To enable efficiency analysis and comparison across hash functions built from primitives of different domain sizes, in this work we propose the new *compactness* efficiency notion. It allows us to focus on asymptotically optimally collision resistant hash function and normalize their parameters based on Stam's bound from CRYPTO 2008 to obtain maximal efficiency.

We then present two tree-based modes of operation as a design principle for compact, large domain, fixed-input-length hash functions.

1. Our first construction is an Augmented Binary Tree (ABR) mode. The design is a $(2^\ell + 2^{\ell-1} - 1)n$-to-$n$-bit hash function making a total of $(2^\ell - 1)$ calls to $2n$-to-n-bit compression functions for any $\ell \geq 2$. Our construction is optimally compact with asymptotically (optimal) $2^{n/2-\epsilon}$-query collision resistance in the ideal model. For a tree of height ℓ, in comparison with Merkle tree, the ABR mode processes additional $(2^{\ell-1} - 1)$ data blocks making the same number of internal compression function calls.
2. With our second design we focus our attention on the indifferentiability security notion. While the ABR mode achieves collision resistance, it fails to achieve indifferentiability from a random oracle within $2^{n/3}$ queries. ABR$^+$ compresses only 1 less data block than ABR with the same number of compression calls and achieves in addition indifferentiability up to $2^{n/2-\epsilon}$ queries.

Both of our designs are closely related to the ubiquitous Merkle Trees and have the potential for real-world applicability where the speed of hashing is of primary interest.

A. Canteaut and F.-X. Standaert (Eds.): EUROCRYPT 2021, LNCS 12697, pp. 92–123, 2021.
https://doi.org/10.1007/978-3-030-77886-6_4

1 Introduction

Hash functions are fundamental cryptographic building blocks. The art of designing a secure and efficient hash function is a classical problem in cryptography. Traditionally, one designs a hash function in two steps. In the first, one constructs a *compression function* that maps fixed length inputs to fixed and usually smaller length outputs. In the second step, a *domain extending* algorithm is designed that allows longer messages to be mapped to a fixed-length output via a sequence of calls to the underlying compression functions.

Most commonly compression functions are designed based on block ciphers and permutations [10,13–15,32,34]. For a long time block ciphers were the most popular primitives to build a compression function and the classical constructions of MD5 and SHA1, SHA2 hash functions are prominent examples of that approach. In the light of the SHA3 competition, the focus has shifted to permutation [12] or fixed-key blockcipher-based [3,4] compression functions. Classical examples of domain extending algorithms are the Merkle–Damgård [21,28] (MD) domain extender and the Merkle tree [27] which underpins numerous cryptographic applications. Most recently, the Sponge construction [11] that is used in SHA-3 has come forward as a domain extender [5,13,16,33] method for designs which directly call a permutation.

<u>Efficiency of Hash Design: Lower Bounds.</u> Like in all cryptographic primitives, the design of a hash function is a trade-off between efficiency and security. Black, Cochran, and Shrimpton [14] were the first to formally analyze the security-efficiency trade-off of compression functions, showing that a $2n$-to-n-bit compression function making a single call to a fixed-key n-bit block cipher can not achieve collision resistance. Rogaway and Steinberger [35] generalized the result to show that any mn-to-ln bit compression function making r calls to n-bit permutations is susceptible to a collision attack in $(2^n)^{1-\frac{m-l/2}{r}}$ queries, provided the constructed compression function satisfies a "collision-uniformity" condition. Stam [37] refined this result to general hash function constructions and conjectured: if any $m+s$-to-s-bit hash function is designed using r many $n+c$-to-n-bit compression functions, a collision on the hash function can be found in $2^{\frac{nr+cr-m}{r+1}}$ queries. This bound is known as the Stam's bound and it was later proven in two works by Steinberger [38] and by Steinberger, Sun and Yang [39].

<u>Efficiency of Hash Design: Upper Bounds.</u> The upper bound results matching Stam's bound focused on $2n$-to-n-bit constructions from n-bit non-compressing primitives. In [36], Shrimpton and Stam showed a (Shrimpton-Stam) construction based on three n-to-n-bit functions achieving asymptotically birthday bound collision resistance in the random oracle model. Rogaway and Steinberger [34] showed hash constructions using three n-bit permutations matching the bound of [35] and assuming the "uniformity condition" on the resulting hash construction. In [25], Mennink and Preneel generalized these results and identified four equivalence classes of $2n$-to-n-bit compression functions from n-bit permutations and XOR operations, achieving collision security of the birthday bound asymptotically in the random permutation model.

In comparison, upper bound results for larger domain compressing functions have been scarce. The only positive result we are aware of is by Mennink and Preneel [26]. In [26], the authors considered generalizing the Shrimpton-Stam construction to get $m+n$-to-n-bit hash function from n-bit primitives for $m > n$, and showed $n/3$-bit collision security in the random oracle model. For all practical purposes the following question remains open.

If an m+n-to-n-bit hash function is designed using r many n+c-to-n-bit compression functions, is there a construction with collision security matching Stam's bound when $m > n$?

<u>Beyond Collision Resistance: Indifferentiability.</u> *Collision resistance* is undoubtedly the most commonly mandated security property for a cryptographic hash function. Naturally, all the hash function design principles and respective efficiencies are primarily targeting to achieve collision resistance. More recently, for applications of hash functions as replacement of random oracles in higher-level cryptographic schemes or protocols, the notion of indifferentiability has also gained considerable traction. The strong notion of indifferentiability from a random oracle (RO) by Maurer, Renner and Holenstein [24] has been adopted to prove the security of hash functions when the internal primitives (compression functions, permutations etc.) are assumed to be ideal (random oracle, random permutation, etc.). An important advantage of the indifferentiability from a random oracle notion is that it implies multiple security notions (in fact, all the notions satisfied by a random oracle in a single stage game) simultaneously up to the proven indifferentiability bound. The question of designing an optimally efficient hash function naturally gets extended also to the indifferentiability setting.
If an m+n-to-n-bit hash function is designed using r many n+c-to-n-bit compression functions, is there a construction with indifferentiability security matching Stam's bound when $m > n$? Note that, a collision secure hash function matching Stam's bound may not imply the indifferentiability notion up to the same bound.

1.1 Our Results

<u>New measure of efficiency.</u> Comparing efficiency of hash functions built from primitives of different domain sizes is a tricky task. In addition to the message size and the number of calls to underlying primitives, one needs to take into account the domain and co-domain/range sizes of the underlying primitives. It is not obvious how to scale the notion of rate up to capture these additional parameters.

We approach the efficiency measure question from Stam's bound perspective. We say an $m+s$-to-s-bit hash function construction designed using r many $n+c$-to-n-bit compression functions is optimally efficient if Stam's bound is tight, that is one can prove that asymptotically at least $2^{\frac{nr+cr-m}{r+1}}$ queries are required to find a collision. Notice that the value in itself can be low (say $2^{s/4}$), but given the proof, we can argue that the parameters are *optimal* for that security level.

Given that the collision-resistance requirement for a hash function is given by the birthday bound ($2^{s/2}$ queries), we can say that a hash function construction achieves optimal security-efficiency trade-off if $\frac{nr+cr-m}{r+1} = \frac{s}{2}$ and Stam's bound is asymptotically tight. Then one can focus on schemes which achieve the asymptotically optimal collision security, and normalize the efficiency of the construction. We hence propose the notion of *compactness* as the ratio of the parameter m and its optimal value $(\frac{2nr+2cr-sr-s}{2})$ as an efficiency measure of a hash function construction C. In Sect. 3 we formally define the notion and derive compactness of some popular modes.

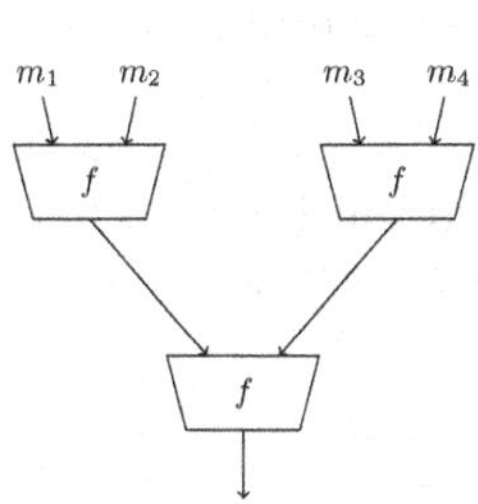

(a) Merkle tree hashing 4 input messages

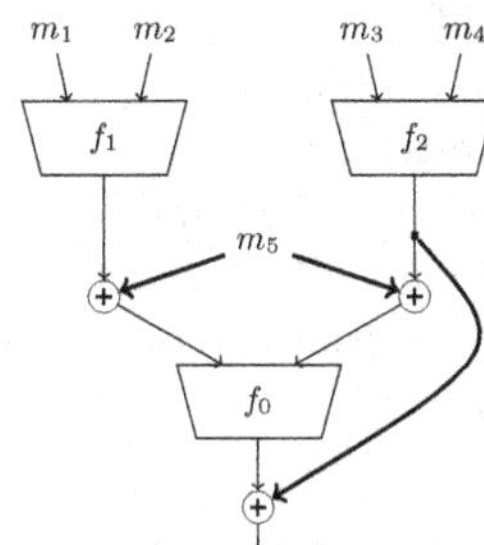

(b) ABR mode hashing 5 input messages

Fig. 1. Merkle Tree and ABR mode for height $\ell = 2$

OPTIMALLY COMPACT ABR MODE. We present a new tree-based mode ABR. ABR of height ℓ implements a $(2^\ell + 2^{\ell-1} - 1)n$-to-$n$-bit function making only $(2^\ell - 1)$ calls to the underlying $2n$-to-n-bit compressing primitives. Assuming the underlying primitives to be independent random oracles, we show that the ABR mode is collision resistant up to the birthday bound asymptotically. The parameters of ABR mode achieve maximum compactness. In Sect. 4 we formally present the ABR mode and prove its collision resistance.

A natural comparison with Merkle tree is in order. We show that Merkle Tree can achieve only 2/3 of the optimal compactness and thus our mode is significantly more efficient. For a tree of height ℓ, in comparison to the Merkle tree, the ABR mode can process an additional $(2^{\ell-1} - 1)$ message blocks with the same number of calls to the underlying compression functions.

ABR DOES NOT SATISFY INDIFFERENTIABILITY. Our next target is to consider the notion of indifferentiability. Specifically, how does the ABR compression score in the indifferentiability setting? The primary objective of this question is twofold. If we can prove the ABR construction with height $\ell = 2$ to be indifferentiable from a random oracle up to the birthday bound, then we could use the indifferentiability composition theorem and replace the leaf level compression function of ABR by $5n$-to-n-bit ideal compression function. Then by recursively applying the proof of collision resistency of ABR with height $\ell = 2$, we could extend the collision resistance proof to arbitrary large levels. Secondly, the proof of indifferentiability implies simultaneously all the security notions satisfied by a random oracle in single stage games. Unfortunately, we show that the ABR mode with height $\ell = 2$ does not preserve indifferentiability. We show an indifferentiability attack of order $2^{\frac{n}{3}}$ in Sect. 5. The attack can easily be generalized to ABR of arbitrary levels.

SALVAGING INDIFFERENTIABILITY. Next, in Sect. 5.2 we propose an almost optimally compact ABR^+ mode design which salvages the indifferentiability security (up to birthday bound) of the original ABR mode. In principle, our second construction ABR^+ (see Fig. 4a) tree merges two left and right ABR mode (of possibly different heights) calls by an independent post-precessor. Using the H-coefficient technique, we prove the indifferentiability of the ABR^+ construction up to the birthday bound.

Compared to ABR mode, ABR^+ compresses 1 less message block for the same number of calls. For large size messages, this gap is extremely small. In comparison to the Merkle Tree, the ABR^+ mode, improves the efficiency significantly and still maintains the indifferentiability property.

1.2 Impact of Our Result

Merkle trees were first published in 1980 by Ralph Merkle [27] as a way to authenticate large public files. Nowadays, Merkle trees find ubiquitous applications in cryptography, from parallel hashing, integrity checks of large files, long-term storage, signature schemes [8,9,18,19], time-stamping [23], zero-knowledge proof based protocols [7,22], to anonymous cryptocurrencies [6], among many others. Despite their indisputable practical relevance, for 40 years we have seen little research go into the rigorous investigation of how to optimize their efficiency, and hence we still rely on design principles that may in fact have some room for efficiency optimizations.

In view of the wide spread use of Merkle trees, we consider one of the main advantage of our construction as being in: *increased number of message inputs (compared to the classical Merkle tree) while maintaining the same tree height and computational cost (for both root computation and node authentication).* Our trees then offer more efficient alternatives to Merkle trees in scenarios where the performance criteria is *the number of messages hashed* for: 1. a fixed computational cost – compression function calls to compute the root, or/and 2. fixed authentication cost – compression function calls to authenticate a node.

Regular hashing is naturally one of the first candidates for such an applications. Other potential use cases are hashing on parallel processors or multi-core machines, such as authenticating software updates, image files or videos; integrity checks of large files systems, long term archiving [17], memory authentication, content distribution, torrent systems [1], etc. A recent application that can benefit from our ABR or ABR^+ mode designs are (anonymous) cryptocurrency applications. We elaborate more on these in Sect. 6.

2 Notation and Preliminaries

Let $\mathbb{N} = \{0, 1, \ldots\}$ be the set of natural numbers and $\{0, 1\}^*$ be the set of all bit strings. If $k \in \mathbb{N}$, then $\{0, 1\}^k$ denotes the set of all k-bit strings. The empty string is denoted by ε. $[n]$ denotes the set $\{0, 1, \cdots, n-1\}$. $f : [r] \times \mathsf{Dom} \to \mathsf{Rng}$ denotes a family of r many functions from Dom to Rng. **We often use the shorthand f to denote the family $\{f_0, \cdots, f_{r-1}\}$ when the function family is given as oracles.**

If S is a set, then $x \stackrel{\$}{\leftarrow} S$ denotes the uniformly random selection of an element from S. We let $y \leftarrow \mathsf{A}(x)$ and $y \stackrel{\$}{\leftarrow} \mathsf{A}(x)$ be the assignment to y of the output of a deterministic and randomized algorithm A, respectively, when run on input x.

An *adversary* A is an algorithm possibly with access to oracles $\mathcal{O}_1, \ldots, \mathcal{O}_\ell$ denoted by $\mathsf{A}^{\mathcal{O}_1,\ldots,\mathcal{O}_\ell}$. The adversaries considered in this paper are computationally unbounded. The complexities of these algorithms are measured solely on the number of queries they make. Adversarial queries and the corresponding responses are stored in a transcript τ.

Hash Functions and Domain Extensions. In this paper, we consider Fixed-Input-Length (FIL) hash functions. We denote these by the hash function $H : \mathcal{M} \to \mathcal{Y}$ where $\mathcal{Y}$ and $\mathcal{M}$ are finite sets of bit strings. For a FIL H the domain $\mathcal{M} = \{0, 1\}^N$ is a finite set of N-bit strings.

Note that, modelling the real-world functions such as SHA-2 and SHA-3, we consider the hash function to be unkeyed. Typically, a hash function is designed in two steps. First a compression function $f : \mathcal{M}_f \to \mathcal{Y}$ with small domain is designed. Then one uses a domain extension algorithm C, which has a blackbox access to f and implements the hash function H for larger domain.

Definition 1. *A domain extender C with oracle access to a family of compression functions $f : [r] \times \mathcal{M}_f \to \mathcal{Y}$ is an algorithm which implements the function $H = C^f : \mathcal{M} \to \mathcal{Y}$.*

Collision Resistance. Our definitions of collision (Coll) security is given for any general FIL hash function H built upon the compression functions f_i for $i \in [r]$ where f_is are modeled as ideal random functions. Let $\text{Func}(2n, n)$ denote the set of all functions mapping $2n$ bits to n bits. Then, for a fixed adversary A and for all $i \in [r]$ where $f_i \stackrel{\$}{\leftarrow} \text{Func}(2n, n)$, we consider the following definition of collision resistance.

Definition 2. *Let A be an adversary against $H = C^f$. H is said to be (q, ε) collision resistant if for all algorithm A making q queries it holds that*

$$\mathbf{Adv}_H^{\text{Coll}}(\mathsf{A}) = \Pr\Big[M', M \stackrel{\$}{\leftarrow} \mathsf{A}^f(\varepsilon) \ : \ M \neq M' \ \textit{and} \ H(M) = H(M') \Big] \leq \varepsilon.$$

Indifferentiability

In the game of indifferentiability, the distinguisher is aiming to distinguish between two worlds, the *real* world and the *ideal* world. In the real world, the distinguisher has oracle access to $(C^{\mathcal{F}}, \mathcal{F})$ where $C^{\mathcal{F}}$ is a construction based on an ideal primitive $\mathcal{F}$. In the ideal world the distinguisher has oracle access to $(\mathcal{G}, S^{\mathcal{G}})$ where $\mathcal{G}$ is an ideal functionality and S is a simulator.

Definition 3 (Indifferentiability [24]**).** *A Turing machine C with oracle access to an ideal primitive $\mathcal{F}$ is said to be $(t_A, t_S, q_S, q, \varepsilon)$ indifferentiable (Fig. 2) from an ideal primitive $\mathcal{G}$ if there exists a simulator S with an oracle access to $\mathcal{G}$ having running time at most t_S, making at most q_S many calls to $\mathcal{G}$* per invocation, *such that for any adversary* A, *with running time t_A making at most q queries, it holds that*

$$\mathbf{Adv}^{\text{Indiff}}_{(C^{\mathcal{F}},\mathcal{F}),(\mathcal{G},S^{\mathcal{G}})}(\mathsf{A}) \stackrel{def}{=} \left|\Pr[\mathsf{A}^{(C^{\mathcal{F}},\mathcal{F})} = 1] - \Pr[\mathsf{A}^{(\mathcal{G},S^{\mathcal{G}})} = 1]\right| \le \varepsilon$$

$C^{\mathcal{F}}$ is computationally indifferentiable from $\mathcal{G}$ if t_A is bounded above by some polynomial in the security parameter k and ε is a negligible function of k.

In this paper, we consider an information-theoretic adversary implying t_A is unbounded. We derive the advantage in terms of the query complexity of the distinguisher. The composition theorem of indifferentiability [24] states that if a construction $C^{\mathcal{F}}$ based on an ideal primitive $\mathcal{F}$ is indifferentiable from $\mathcal{G}$, then $C^{\mathcal{F}}$ can be used to instantiate $\mathcal{G}$ in any protocol with single-stage game. We note, however, the composition theorem does not extend to the multi-stage games, or when the adversary is resource-restricted. We refer the reader to [31] for details. We refer to the queries made to $C^{\mathcal{F}}/\mathcal{G}$ as construction queries and to the queries made to $\mathcal{F}/S$ as the primitive queries.

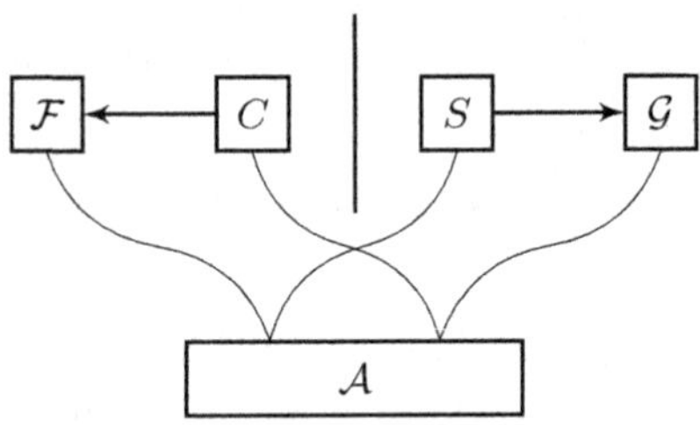

Fig. 2. The indifferentiability notion

Coefficient-H Technique. We shall prove indifferentiability using Patarin's coefficient-H technique [30]. Fix any distinguisher $\mathcal{D}$ making q queries. As the distinguisher is computationally unbounded, without loss of generality we can assume it to be deterministic [20,29]. The interaction of $\mathcal{D}$ with its oracles is described by a transcript τ. τ contains all the queries and the corresponding responses $\mathcal{D}$ makes during its execution. Let Θ denote the set of all possible transcripts. Let $X_{\texttt{real}}$ and $X_{\texttt{ideal}}$ denote the probability distribution of the transcript in the real and the ideal worlds, respectively.

Lemma 1. *[30] Consider a fixed deterministic distinguisher $\mathcal{D}$. Let Θ can be partitioned into sets Θ_{good} and Θ_{bad}. Suppose $\varepsilon \geq 0$ be such that for all $\tau \in \Theta_{good}$,*

$$\Pr[X_{\texttt{real}} = \tau] \geq (1-\varepsilon)\Pr[X_{\texttt{ideal}} = \tau]$$

Then $\mathbf{Adv}^{\mathit{Indiff}}_{(C^{\mathcal{F}},\mathcal{F}),(\mathcal{G},S^{\mathcal{G}})} \leq \varepsilon + \Pr[X_{\texttt{ideal}} \in \Theta_{bad}]$

Markov Inequality. We recall the well known Markov inequality.

Lemma 2. *Let X be a non-negative random variable and $a > 0$ be a real number. Then it holds that*

$$\Pr[X \geq a] \leq \frac{\mathbf{E}[X]}{a}$$

3 Compactness: Normalizing Efficiency for Optimally Secure Constructions

In Crypto 2008, Stam made the following conjecture (Conjecture 9 in [37]): If $C^f : \{0,1\}^{m+s} \to \{0,1\}^s$ is a compression function making r calls to primitive $f : \{0,1\}^{n+c} \to \{0,1\}^n$, a collision can be found in the output of C by making $q \leq 2^{\frac{nr+cr-m}{r+1}}$ queries. The conjecture was proved in two papers, the case $r = 1$ was proved by Steinberger in [38], whereas the general case was proved by Steinberger, Sun and Yang in [39]. The result, in our notation, is stated below.

Theorem 1 ([39]). *Let $f_1, f_2, \ldots, f_r : \{0,1\}^{n+c} \to \{0,1\}^n$ be potentially distinct r many compression functions. Let $C : \{0,1\}^{m+s} \to \{0,1\}^s$ be a domain extension algorithm making queries to $f_1, f_2, \ldots, f_r$ in the fixed order. Suppose it holds that $1 \leq m \leq (n+c)r$ and $\frac{s}{2} \geq \frac{nr+cr-m}{r+1}$. There exists an adversary making at most $q = \mathcal{O}\left(r2^{\frac{nr+cr-m}{r+1}}\right)$ queries finds a collision with probability at least $\frac{1}{2}$.*

In other words, if one wants to construct a hash function that achieves birthday bound collision security asymptotically, the query complexity of the attacker must be at least $2^{s/2}$. Then the parameters must satisfy the following equation:

$$\frac{nr+cr-m}{r+1} \geq \frac{s}{2}$$

Next, we rearrange the equation and get

$$m \leq \frac{2nr+2cr-sr-s}{2}$$

Thus we can analyze the security-efficiency trade-off across different constructions by considering only the schemes secure (asymptotically) up to the birthday bound and describe the efficiency by the ratio $\frac{2m}{2nr+2cr-sr-s}$. Then we argue that the optimal efficiency is reached when the parameters satisfy

$$m = \frac{2nr + 2cr - sr - s}{2}$$

Now we are ready to define compactness of hash functions based on compressing primitives.

Definition 4 Compactness. *Let $f_1, f_2, \ldots, f_r : \{0,1\}^{n+c} \to \{0,1\}^n$ be potentially distinct r many compression functions. Let $C : \{0,1\}^{m+s} \to \{0,1\}^s$ be a domain extension algorithm making queries to $f_1, f_2, \ldots, f_r$ in the fixed order. We say C is α-compact if*

- *for all adversary* A *making q queries, for some constant c_1, c_2, it satisfies that*

$$\mathbf{Adv}_C^{\mathrm{Coll}}(\mathsf{A}) \leq \mathcal{O}\left(\frac{s^{c_1} r^{c_2} q^2}{2^s}\right),$$

-

$$\alpha = \frac{2m}{2nr + 2cr - sr - s}$$

Clearly for any construction, $\alpha \leq 1$. For the rest of the paper, we consider constructions where $s = n$. Thus, we derive the value of α as

$$\alpha = \frac{2m}{2cr + nr - n}$$

In Sect. 3.1, in Examples 1 and 3 we estimate that both Merkle–Damgård and Merkle tree domain extenders with $2n$-to-n-bit compression function primitives have a compactness of $\approx 2/3$.

3.1 Compactness of Existing Constructions

Example 1. We consider the textbook **Merkle–Damgård** (MD) domain extension with length padding and fixed IV. Let the underlying function be a $2n$-to n-bit compression function f. Let the total number of calls to f be r. At every call n-bits of message is processed. Assuming the length-block is of one block, the total number of message bits hashed using r calls is $(r-1)c$. Hence, we get $m = (r-1)c - n$. Putting $c = n$ we compute

$$\alpha = \frac{2n(r-1) - 2n}{2nr + nr - n} = \frac{2nr - 4n}{3nr - n} < \frac{2}{3}$$

Example 2. For binary **Merkle tree** with $c = n$, let the number of f calls at the leaf level is z. Then the total number of message bit is $2nz$. Let the total number of calls to the compression function f is $r = z + z - 1 = 2z - 1$. Comparing with the number of message bits we get $m + n = (r+1)n$ which implies $m = rn$. So we calculate the compactness of Merkle tree as

$$\alpha = \frac{2rn}{3nr - n} = \frac{2r}{3r - 1} < \frac{2}{3}$$

Example 3. Next we consider **Shrimpton-Stam** $2n$**-to-**n compression function using three calls to n-to-n-bit function f. Here $m = n$ and $c = 0$. Then $\alpha = \frac{2n}{3n-n} = 1$. The **Mennink-Preneel** generalization [25] of this construction gives $2n$-to-n-bit compression function making three calls to n-bit permutations. Thus in that case $\alpha = \frac{2n}{3n-n} = 1$ as well.

Example 4. Consider again MD domain extension with length padding and fixed IV but let the underlying function be a $5n$-to n-bit compression function f. At every (out of r) f call $4n$-bits are processed (the rest n-bits are the chaining value). As we have one length-block, the total number of message bits hashed is $(r-1)4n$. Hence, we get $m = (r-1)4n - n$ and compute:

$$\alpha = \frac{2 \times 4n(r-1) - 2n}{2 \times 4r + nr - n} = \frac{8nr - 6n}{9nr - n} \approx \frac{8}{9}$$

Example 5. The 5-ary Merkle tree with $5z$ leaf messages has $5nz$ bit input in total. Thus $r = \frac{3(5z-1)}{4}$ and $m = n(5z-1)$. The compactness is given by

$$\alpha = \frac{2n(5z-1)}{2nr + nr - n} = \frac{5z-1}{3r-1} = \frac{8(5z-1)}{9(5z-1)-4} \approx \frac{8}{9}$$

4 ABR Mode with Compactness $\alpha = 1$

In this section we present the ABR domain extender. We prove its collision resistance in the random oracle model and show that it is optimally ($\alpha = 1$)-compact. Our ABR mode collision-resistance-proof is valid for FIL trees. That means that our result is valid for trees of arbitrary height but once the height is fixed, all the messages queried by the adversary must correspond to a tree of that height. We remind the reader that the majority of Merkle tree applications rely *exactly* on FIL Merkle trees.[1] The parameter of our construction is ℓ which denotes the height of the tree. The construction makes $r = 2^\ell - 1$ many independent $2n$-to-n-bit functions and takes input messages from the set $\{0,1\}^{\mu n}$, where $\mu = 2^\ell + 2^{\ell-1} - 1$. $f_{(j,b)}$ denotes the bth node at j^{th} level. The parents of $f_{(j,b)}$ are denoted by $f_{(j-1,2b-1)}$ and $f_{(j-1,2b)}$. We use the following notations for the messages. Let M be the input messages with μ many blocks of n-bits. The corresponding input to a leaf node $f_{(1,b)}$ is denoted by $m_{(1,2b-1)}$ and $m_{(1,2b)}$. For the internal function $f_{(j,b)}$, $m_{(j,b)}$ denotes the message that is xored with the previous chaining values to produce the input. We refer the reader to Fig. 3b for a pictorial view. Note, the leaves are at level 1 and the root of the tree is at level ℓ. The message is broken in n-bit blocks. 2^ℓ many message blocks are processed at level 1. For level $j(>1)$, $2^{\ell-j}$ many blocks are processed. The adversary A has query access to all functions, and it makes q queries in total.

[1] Although VIL Merkle tree exists with collision preservation proof, that is done at the cost of an extra block of Merkle-Damgård-type strengthening and padding schemes. As Stam's bound is derived for FIL constructions, we restrict our focus on FIL constructions only.

```
y ← ABR mode(m_1, ..., m_{2^ℓ+2^{ℓ-1}-1})
i ← 1, j ← 1
do
    y_{1,j} = f_{1,j}(m_i, m_{i+1})
    i ← i + 2, j ← j + 1
while i < 2^ℓ
count ← 2^ℓ
for j in{2, ..., ℓ}
i ← 1, s ← count
    do
        y_{j,i} = f_{j,i}(m_{s+i} ⊕ y_{j-1,2i-1},
                m_{s+i} ⊕ y_{j-1,2i}) ⊕ y_{j-1,2i}
    while i < 2^{ℓ-j}
count ← count + 2^{ℓ-j}
endfor
return y_{ℓ,1}
```

(a) Algorithm for computing ABR mode hash value with height ℓ

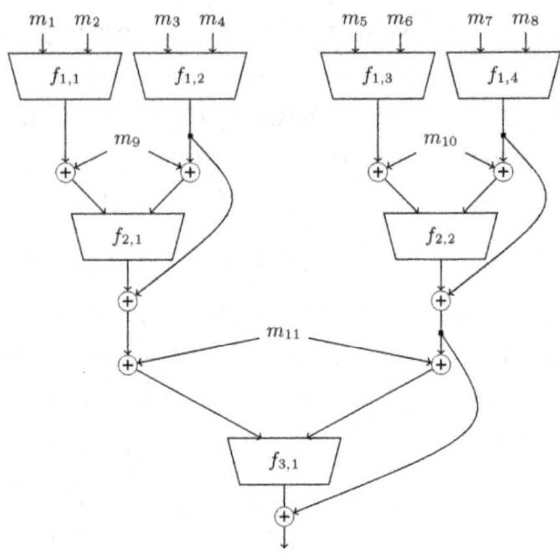

(b) ABR mode of height $\ell = 3$ with 2^3 leaf message inputs (valid for Merkle tree), $r = 7$ compression function calls, and total of $2^\ell + 2^{\ell-1} - 1 = 11$ input blocks.

Fig. 3. ABR mode algorithm and instantiation

Theorem 2. *Let $\ell \geq 2$ be a natural number and $r = 2^\ell$. Let $f : [r] \times \{0,1\}^{2n} \rightarrow \{0,1\}^n$ be a family of functions. Let* A *be an adversary against the collision resistance of ABR mode. If the elements of f are modeled as independent random oracles, then*

$$\mathbf{Adv}^{\mathrm{Coll}}_{ABR}(\mathsf{A}^f) = \mathcal{O}\left(\frac{rn^2q^2}{2^n}\right).$$

where q is the number of queries A *makes to f satisfying $q^2 < \frac{2^n}{2e(n+1)}$.*

4.1 Warmup: ABR Mode with Height 2

First, we prove the security of the case $\ell = 2$. In this case ABR mode implements a $5n$-to-n-bit compression function with 3 calls to $2n$-to-n-bit compression functions. For convenience of explanation, we refer the three functions as f_0, f_1, f_2 (see Fig. 1b).

Construction 3. *Let $f_0, f_1, f_2 : \{0,1\}^{2n} \rightarrow \{0,1\}^n$ be three compression functions. We define ABR mode for $\ell = 2$ as $ABR^f : \{0,1\}^{5n} \rightarrow \{0,1\}^n$ where*

$$ABR(m_1, m_2, m_3, m_4, m_5) = f_2(x_3, x_4) \oplus f_0(m_5 \oplus f_1(x_1, x_2), m_5 \oplus f_2(x_3, x_4))$$

Theorem 2 can be restated for this case as the following proposition.

Proposition 4. *Let* $f_0, f_1, f_2 : \times\{0,1\}^{2n} \rightarrow \{0,1\}^n$. *Let* A *be an adversary against the collision resistance of* ABR. *If* f_i*s are modeled as independent random oracles, then*

$$\mathbf{Adv}^{\text{Coll}}_{ABR}(\mathsf{A}^f) = \mathcal{O}\left(\frac{n^2q^2}{2^n}\right)$$

where q *is the maximum number of queries* A *makes to the oracles* f_0, f_1, f_2*s.*

Proof of Proposition 4. The proof strategy closely follows [36].
MOVING TO LEVEL-WISE SETTING. In general, one needs to consider the adversary making queries in some adaptive (and possibly probabilistic) manner. But for the case of $5n$-bit to n-bit ABR, as in [36], we can avoid the adaptivity as f_1 and f_2 are independent random oracles.

Lemma 3. *For every adaptive adversary* $\hat{\mathsf{A}}$, *there exists an adversary* A *who makes level-wise queries and succeeds with same probability;*

$$\mathbf{Adv}^{\text{Coll}}_{ABR}(\hat{\mathsf{A}}) = \mathbf{Adv}^{\text{Coll}}_{ABR}(\mathsf{A}).$$

COLLISION PROBABILITY IN THE LEVEL-WISE QUERY SETTING. From this point on, we assume that the adversary is provided with two lists L_1 and L_2 at the start of the game. L_1 and L_2 have q uniformly sampled points and they should be considered as the responses of the queries made by the adversary to f_1 and f_2, respectively. The adversary only needs to query f_0.

Let A be an adversary that can find a collision in ABR. Two cases may arise. In the first case, A can find collision in the leaf nodes (f_1 or f_2). In that case, there is a collision in either L_1 and L_2. In the other case, there is no collision among the outputs of f_1 or f_2, and the collision is generated at the final output. Let Coll_i denote the event that A finds a collision in L_i. Let Coll denote the event that A finds a collision in ABR.

$$\begin{aligned}\mathbf{Adv}^{\text{Coll}}_{\text{ABR}}(\mathsf{A}^f) \leq \Pr[\mathsf{Coll}] &= \Pr[\mathsf{Coll} \wedge (\mathsf{Coll}_1 \vee \mathsf{Coll}_2)] + \Pr[\mathsf{Coll} \wedge \neg(\mathsf{Coll}_1 \vee \mathsf{Coll}_2)] \\ &\leq \Pr[\mathsf{Coll}_1 \vee \mathsf{Coll}_2] + \Pr[\mathsf{Coll} \mid \neg(\mathsf{Coll}_1 \vee \mathsf{Coll}_2)] \\ &\leq \Pr[\mathsf{Coll}_1] + \Pr[\mathsf{Coll}_2] + \Pr[\mathsf{Coll} \mid \neg(\mathsf{Coll}_1 \vee \mathsf{Coll}_2)].\end{aligned}$$

As the functions are independent random oracles, $\Pr[\mathsf{Coll}_1]$ and $\Pr[\mathsf{Coll}_2]$ are bounded above by $\frac{q^2}{2^n}$. In the remaining, we bound the probability of the third term.
DEFINING THE RANGE. For every query (u_i, v_i) made by the adversary to f_0, we define the following quantity

$$Y_i \stackrel{def}{=} |\{(h_1, h_2) \mid h_1 \in L_1, h_2 \in L_2, h_1 \oplus u_i = h_2 \oplus v_i\}|.$$

where $f_0(u_i, v_i)$ is the ith query of the adversary. While Y_i counts the number of valid or more precisely consistent with the ABR structure pairs (h_1, h_2) that were already queried to f_1 and f_2, Y_i also denotes the number of possible ABR hash outputs produced by the adversary by making $f_0(u_i, v_i)$ query. Notice, that Y_i inputs to f_0 generate Y_i outputs. Each of these outputs are XORed each with only one corresponding consistent h_2 value determined by the equation $h_1 \oplus u_i = h_2 \oplus v_i$, hence producing Y_i ABR outputs on Y_i consistent number inputs to f_0. Let $Y = \max_i Y_i$.

Bounding Collision by range. Now, we show how bounding the range will help us bounding the collision probability. Let E_i denotes the probability that after making the ith query $f_0(u_i, v_i)$ produces a collision in the output of ABR. Suppose after making $i-1$ queries, adversary is not able to produce a collision for ABR. Hence, the adversary has produced $\sum_{j=1}^{i-1} Y_j$ many hash outputs. We bound the probability that i^{th} query response produces a collision.

$$\Pr\left[E_i \mid \wedge_{j=1}^{i-1} \neg E_j\right] \leq \frac{Y_i \sum_{j=1}^{i-1} Y_j}{2^n}$$

Now we can bound the collision probability as

$$\Pr\left[\mathsf{Coll} \mid \neg(\mathsf{Coll}_1 \vee \mathsf{Coll}_2)\right] \leq \sum_{i=1}^{q} \frac{Y_i \sum_{j=1}^{i-1} Y_j}{2^n} \leq \sum_{i=1}^{q} \sum_{j=1}^{i-1} \frac{Y^2}{2^n} \leq \frac{q^2 Y^2}{2^{n+1}}$$

We shall use the following lemma, which we prove later.

Lemma 4.

$$\Pr\left[Y > k \mid \neg(\mathsf{Coll}_1 \vee \mathsf{Coll}_2)\right] \leq \frac{q^{2k}(2^n - k)!}{k!\,(2^n - 1)!}$$

Using Lemma 4, we get

$$\begin{aligned} \Pr\left[\mathsf{Coll} \mid \neg(\mathsf{Coll}_1 \vee \mathsf{Coll}_2)\right] &\leq \Pr\left[\mathsf{Coll} \wedge Y \leq k \mid \neg(\mathsf{Coll}_1 \vee \mathsf{Coll}_2)\right] \\ &\quad + \Pr\left[Y > k \mid \neg(\mathsf{Coll}_1 \vee \mathsf{Coll}_2)\right] \\ &\leq \frac{k^2 q^2}{2^{n+1}} + \frac{q^{2k}(2^n - k)!}{k!\,(2^n - 1)!} \end{aligned}$$

Putting $k = n$ we get the probability as

$$\begin{aligned} \Pr\left[\mathsf{Coll} \mid \neg(\mathsf{Coll}_1 \vee \mathsf{Coll}_2)\right] \leq \frac{n^2 q^2}{2^{n+1}} + \frac{q^{2n}}{n!\,(2^n - 1) \cdots (2^n - n + 1)} &\approx \frac{n^2 q^2}{2^{n+1}} + \frac{q^{2n}}{2^{n^2}} \\ &= \mathcal{O}\left(\frac{n^2 q^2}{2^n}\right) \end{aligned}$$

Hence, we get the theorem. □

Proof of Lemma 4. Let $(h_{i_1}, h'_{j_1}), (h_{i_2}, h'_{j_2}), \cdots, (h_{i_k}, h'_{j_k})$ be the set of k pairs such that each $h_{i_l} \in L_1$ and $h'_{j_l} \in L_2$, and

$$h_{i_1} \oplus h'_{j_1} = h_{i_2} \oplus h'_{j_2} = \cdots = h_{i_k} \oplus h'_{j_k} = a \text{ (say)}$$

The condition $\neg(\mathsf{Coll}_1 \vee \mathsf{Coll}_2)$ implies that there is no collision in L_1 and L_2. The total number of ways to choose each of L_1 and L_2 such that there is no collision is $q!\binom{2^n}{q}$.

Next we count the number of ways of choosing L_1 and L_2 such that the k equalities get satisfied. The number of ways we can choose $i_1, i_2, \cdots, i_k$ is $\binom{q}{k}$. Fixing the order of $i_1, i_2, \cdots, i_k$, the number of ways to pair $j_1, j_2, \cdots, j_k$ is $k!\binom{q}{k}$. Observe that there can be 2^n many possible values of a. Fix a value of a. Thus for each value of h_{i_l}, there is a single value of h'_{j_l}. Hence the total number of ways we can select L_1, L_2 such that the equalities get satisfied is $q!\binom{2^n}{q} \times q!\binom{2^n-k}{q}$. Hence the probability that for independently sampled L_1 and L_2,

$$\Pr[Y > k \mid \neg(\mathsf{Coll}_1 \vee \mathsf{Coll}_2)] = \frac{k!\left(\binom{q}{k}\right)^2 2^n q!\binom{2^n}{q} \times q!\binom{2^n-k}{q}}{\left(q!\binom{2^n}{q}\right)^2}$$

After simplification, we get the probability as

$$\Pr[Y > k \mid \neg(\mathsf{Coll}_1 \vee \mathsf{Coll}_2)] = \frac{(q!)^2 2^n (2^n-k)!}{((q-k)!)^2\, k!\,(2^n)!} \leq \frac{q^{2k} 2^n (2^n-k)!}{k!\,(2^n)!}$$

At the last step, we upper bound $\frac{(q!)^2}{((q-k)!)^2}$ by q^{2k}. The lemma follows. □

4.2 Proof of Theorem 2

Proof Overview. Now we prove the general case. We start with an overview of the proof. Unlike the case for $\ell = 2$, we have to consider adaptive adversaries. Specifically, we can no longer assume that the adversary makes the queries level wise. Indeed, a query at a non-leaf level is derived from the previous chaining values (part of which is fed-forward to be xored with the output) and the messages. We can no longer "replace" the query without changing the chaining values. To the best of our knowledge, no proof technique achieving $2^{n/2}$ security bound asymptotically, exists in the literature for this case.

The intuition of our proof follows. Like in the previous case, our analysis focuses on the yield of a function. Informally, the yield of a query (u, v) to a function f is the number of chaining values created by the query. For example, consider a query (u, v) made to function $f_{j,z}$, z^{th} function of level j, and let y be the output of the query. How many chaining values does this query create? A cursory inspection reveals that the number of created chaining values are the number of "legal" feedforward (chaining value from the previous level function $f_{j-1,2z}$) values h. Indeed a feedforward value h can extend the chain, if there exists a chaining value h' from the set of chaining values created from $f_{j-1,2z-1}$ (the other parent of (j, z)) such that $h' \oplus u = h \oplus v$.

Naturally, if we can bound the total yield of a function (denoted as load), we can bound the probability of collision among the chaining values generated by the function. The load of a function $f_{j,z}$ gets increased in two ways. The first one is by a query made to $f_{j,z}$, as encountered in the previous section. The other one is by a query made to $f_{j',z'}$ where $j' < j$ and (j', z') is in the subtree of (j, z). To see why the second case holds, observe that the query to $f_{j',z'}$ increases the yield of the function, and thus creating new chaining values. Some of those newly created chaining values can be "legal" feedforward values for some queries already made to the next level, and thus increasing the yield of that query as well. Moreover, this in turn again creates new chaining value at the level $j' + 1$. The effect continues to all the next levels and eventually affects the load of all the functions in the path to the root, including (j, z).

We bound the load of functions at each level starting from the leaves. At each level, we bound the probability of having a transcript which creates the load on a function (of that level) over a threshold amount, conditioned on the event that in none of the previous level the load exceeded the threshold.

Formal Analysis. Our formal analysis involves the transcript of the queries and the corresponding responses. Each entry of the transcript contains a query response pair, denoted by $(u, v, y)_{(j,b)}$ which indicates that y is the response of the query $f_{j,b}(u, v)$. τ denotes the (partial) transcript generated after the q many queries. $Q_{(j,b)}$ denotes the set of queries made to the function $f_{(j,b)}$. $\mathcal{L}_{(j,b)}$ holds the responses.

YIELD SET. For each function $f_{(j,b)}$, we define a set $\Gamma_{(j,b)}$ holding the possible chaining values. Note, a chaining value $h \in \Gamma_{(j-1,2b)}$ can be a valid feedforward value for entry $(u, v, y)_{(j,b)}$ if there exists a matching $h' \in \Gamma_{(j-1,2b-1)}$ such that for some m', it holds that $m' \oplus h' = u$ and $m' \oplus h = v$. Such a m' can exist only if $h' \oplus u = h \oplus v$.

$$\Gamma_{(1,b)} \stackrel{def}{=} \{y \mid (u, v, y)_{(1,b)} \in \tau\}$$

$$\Gamma_{(j>1,b)} \stackrel{def}{=} \{y \oplus h \mid (u, v, y)_{(j,b)} \in \tau, h \in \Gamma_{(j-1,2b)}, \exists h' \in \Gamma_{(j-1,2b-1)}, h' \oplus u = h \oplus v\}.$$

FEEDFORWARD SET. For each function $f_{(j,b)}$, we define a set $F_{(j,b)}$ containing the possible elements that can be used as feedforward and xored with the output of $f_{(j,b)}$ to generate valid chaining values. It is easy to verify that $F_{(j,b)} = \Gamma_{(j-1,2b)}$, where $\Gamma_{(0,b)} = \emptyset$.

Let Coll denotes the event that the adversary finds collision in ABR mode. Let $M = (m_{1,1}, m_{1,2} \cdots, m_{1,2^\ell}, \cdots, m_{\ell,1})$ and $M' = (m'_{1,1}, m'_{1,2} \cdots, m'_{1,2^\ell}, \cdots, m'_{\ell,1})$ be the two distinct messages that produce the collision. We use $(u, v, y)_{(j,b)}$ and $(u', v', y')_{(j,b)}$ to be the corresponding queries made to function $f_{(j,b)}$ in the evaluation respectively.[2]

Proper Internal Collision. The transcript is said to contain a *proper internal collision* at (j, b), if the transcript contains two distinct queries $(u, v, y)_{(j,b)}$ and $(u', v', y')_{(j,b)}$ and there exists $h, h' \in \Gamma_{(j-1,2b)}$ such that $y \oplus h = y' \oplus h'$.

[2] We assume the adversary makes all the internal queries before producing a collision. Indeed we can always add the missing queries in the transcript without significantly changing the query complexity.

Lemma 5. *Collision in tree implies a proper internal collision.*

Proof. The proof follows the Merkle tree collision resistance proof. Without loss of generality, we assume that there is no collision at the leaf. Now, consider a collision in the tree. This implies that there exist $(u, v, y)_{(\ell,1)}, (u', v', y')_{(\ell,1)} \in \tau$ and $h, h' \in \Gamma_{(\ell-1,2)}$ such that

$$y \oplus h = y' \oplus h'$$

If $(u, v)_{(\ell,1)} \neq (u', v')_{(\ell,1)}$, then we get our proper internal collision at $(\ell, 1)$, and we are done. Otherwise $(u, v)_{(\ell,1)} = (u', v')_{(\ell,1)}$, which in turn implies $y = y'$. This implies $h = h'$. Moreover, we get $h \oplus u \oplus v = h' \oplus u' \oplus v'$. The above two equalities give us collision in the both left and the right subtree. As $M \neq M'$, the messages differ in one of the subtrees. Repeating the above argument in the appropriate tree, we indeed find a (j, b) with distinct inputs $(u, v)_{(j,b)} \neq (u', v')_{(j,b)}$. □

Bounding Probabilities of a Proper Internal Collision

YIELD OF A QUERY. Consider an element $(u, v, y)_{(j,b)} \in \tau$. We define the following quantity as the yield of the query $f_{(j,b)}(u, v)$.

$$Y_{u,v,j,b} \stackrel{def}{=} \begin{cases} \mid \{(h_1, h_2) \mid h_1 \in \Gamma_{(j-1,2b-1)}, h_2 \in \Gamma_{j-1,2b}, h_1 \oplus u = h_2 \oplus v\} \mid & \text{if } j > 1 \\ 1 & \text{if } j = 1 \end{cases}$$

LOAD ON A FUNCTION. The load on a function $f_{(j,b)}$ is defined by the total yield of the queries made to that function.

$$L_{(j,b)} \stackrel{def}{=} \sum_{(u_i,v_i) \in Q_{j,b}} Y_{u_i,v_i,j,b}.$$

Observe that if no internal collision happens at a function, the size of the yield set is the load on that function; $L_{(j,b)} =\mid \Gamma_{j,b} \mid$

For the rest of the analysis we use the variable k which is equal to $(n+1)^{\frac{1}{\ell}}$.
BAD EVENTS. In this section we define the notion of bad event. We observe that with every query, the load on the functions in the tree change. Two types of contributions to load happen with each query.

1. **Type I** A new $(u, v)_{(j,b)}$ query contributes to $L_{(j,b)}$. The contribution amount is $Y_{(u,v,j,b)}$.
2. **Type II** A new $(u, v)_{j',b'}$ query increases the load of (j, b) where $j > j'$ and (j', b') is in the sub-tree rooted at (j, b).

$\delta^1_{(j,b)}$ and $\delta^2_{(j,b)}$ denotes the total type-I and type-II contributions to $L_{(j,b)}$ respectively. We consider the following two helping Bad events.

1. $\mathsf{Bad1}$ happens at function (j, b) such that for some $(u, v, y)_{(j,b)} \in \tau$, such that $Y_{(u,v,j,b)} > k^{\ell}$. This event corresponds to the Type I queries.

2. Bad2 happens at function (j, b), if $\delta^2_{(j,b)} > k^\ell q$.

$\mathsf{Bad1}_j$ and $\mathsf{Bad2}_j$ denotes the event that Bad1 or Bad2 respectively happens at some node at level j. We define Bad_j as $\mathsf{Bad1}_j \cup \mathsf{Bad2}_j$. Let Bad denote the event that for the generated transcript Bad_j holds for some level j.

$$\mathsf{Bad} \stackrel{def}{=} \bigcup_j \mathsf{Bad}_j$$

The following proposition holds from the definitions.

Lemma 6.

$$\neg\mathsf{Bad}_j \implies \forall b \in [2^{\ell-j}] \text{ it holds that } L_{(j,b)} \leq 2k^\ell q$$

Deriving Collision Probability. Let Coll_j denote the event of a proper internal collision at (j, b) for some $b \in [2^{\ell-j}]$.

$$\begin{aligned}
\Pr[\mathsf{Coll}] &\leq \Pr[\mathsf{Coll} \cup \mathsf{Bad}] \\
&\leq \Pr[\mathsf{Coll}_1 \cup \mathsf{Bad}_1] + \sum_{j>1} \Pr\left[(\mathsf{Coll}_j \cup \mathsf{Bad}_j) \cap \cap_{j'<j} \neg\mathsf{Coll}_{j'} \cap \cap_{j'<j} \neg\mathsf{Bad}_{j'}\right] \\
&\leq \Pr[\mathsf{Coll}_1 \cup \mathsf{Bad}_1] + \sum_{j>1} \Pr\left[\mathsf{Bad}_j \cap \cap_{j'<j} \neg\mathsf{Coll}_{j'} \cap \cap_{j'<j} \neg\mathsf{Bad}_{j'}\right] + \\
&\quad \sum_{j>1} \Pr\left[\mathsf{Coll}_j \cap \cap_{j'<j} \neg\mathsf{Coll}_{j'} \cap \cap_{j'\leq j} \neg\mathsf{Bad}_{j'}\right]
\end{aligned}$$

Using the fact that $\Pr[A \cap B] = \Pr[A \mid B]\Pr[B] \leq \Pr[A \mid B]$,

$$\begin{aligned}
\Pr[\mathsf{Coll}] \leq &\Pr[\mathsf{Coll}_1 \cup \mathsf{Bad}_1] + \sum_{j>1} \Pr\left[\mathsf{Bad}_j \mid \cap_{j'<j} \neg\mathsf{Coll}_{j'} \cap \cap_{j'<j} \neg\mathsf{Bad}_{j'}\right] \\
&+ \sum_{j>1} \Pr\left[\mathsf{Coll}_j \mid \cap_{j'<j} \neg\mathsf{Coll}_{j'} \cap \cap_{j'\leq j} \neg\mathsf{Bad}_{j'}\right] \qquad (1)
\end{aligned}$$

Bounding. $\Pr[\mathsf{Coll}_1 \cup \mathsf{Bad}_1]$. As all the functions are modeled as a random function, for all $b \in [2^{\ell-1}]$, we have $\Pr[\mathsf{Coll}_{1,b}] \leq \frac{q^2}{2^n}$. Hence,

$$\Pr[\mathsf{Coll}_1] \leq \frac{2^{\ell-1} q^2}{2^n}$$

In order to find $\Pr[\mathsf{Bad}_1]$, we recall that $F_{1,b} = \emptyset$. In other words the nothing is xored with the output of the functions at the leaf level. Hence, $Y_{(u,v,1,b)} = 1$ for all $b \in [2^{\ell-1}]$ and $(u, v, y)_{1,b} \in \tau$. Hence $\Pr[\mathsf{Bad}_1] = 0$. Hence we get,

$$\Pr[\mathsf{Coll}_1 \cup \mathsf{Bad}_1] \leq \frac{2^{\ell-1} q^2}{2^n} \qquad (2)$$

Bounding. $\sum_{j>1} \Pr[\mathsf{Coll}_j \mid \cap_{j'<j} \neg\mathsf{Coll}_{j'} \cap \cap_{j'\leq j} \neg\mathsf{Bad}_{j'}]$. Fix $b \in [2^{\ell-j}]$ and thus fix a function at the jþ level. As analyzed in the previous section, given

$\cap_{j' \leq j} \neg \mathsf{Bad}_{j'}$, the proper internal collision probability for (j, b) is $\frac{L^2_{(j,b)}}{2^n}$. From Lemma 6, it holds that for each $b \in [2^{\ell-j}]$, $L_{(j,b)} \leq 2k^\ell q$. Hence for each $j > 1, b \in [2^{\ell-j}]$,

$$\Pr\left[\,\mathsf{Coll}_{(j,b)} \mid \cap_{j'<j} \neg \mathsf{Coll}_{j'} \cap \cap_{j' \leq j} \neg \mathsf{Bad}_{j'}\,\right] \leq \frac{4k^{2\ell} q^2}{2^n}.$$

Taking sum over all $j > 1, b \in [2^{\ell-j}]$,

$$\begin{aligned}
\sum_{j>1,b} \Pr\left[\,\mathsf{Coll}_{(j,b)} \mid \cap_{j'<j} \neg \mathsf{Coll}_{j'} \cap \cap_{j' \leq j} \neg \mathsf{Bad}_{j'}\,\right] &\leq \sum_{j=2}^{\ell} \sum_{b=1}^{2^{\ell-j}} \frac{4k^{2\ell} q^2}{2^n} \\
&= \sum_{j=2}^{\ell} 2^{\ell-j} \times \frac{4k^{2\ell} q^2}{2^n} \\
&= \frac{2^{\ell+2} k^{2\ell} q^2}{2^n} \times \left(\sum_{j=2}^{\ell} \frac{1}{2^j} \right)
\end{aligned}$$

In the next step we shall use the fact that $\sum_{j=2}^{\ell} \frac{1}{2^j} < \frac{1}{2}$. Finally we get,

$$\sum_{j>1,b} \Pr\left[\,\mathsf{Coll}_{(j,b)} \mid \cap_{j'<j} \neg \mathsf{Coll}_{j'} \cap \cap_{j' \leq j} \neg \mathsf{Bad}_{j'}\,\right] \leq \frac{2^{\ell+2} k^{2\ell} q^2}{2^{n+1}} \tag{3}$$

Bounding Pr [Bad]. Now we bound the probabilities of the two bad events. We bound the probabilities level-wise. Let $\mathsf{Bad1}_{j,b}$ denote that $\mathsf{Bad1}$ happens at node b of level j. Similarly, let $\mathsf{Bad2}_{j,b}$ denote that $\mathsf{Bad2}$ happens at node b of level j. Clearly, $\mathsf{Bad1}_j = \cup_{b \in [2^{\ell-j}]} \mathsf{Bad1}_{j,b}$ and $\mathsf{Bad2}_j = \cup_{b \in [2^{\ell-j}]} \mathsf{Bad2}_{j,b}$

Bounding $\mathbf{Bad1}_j$

Lemma 7. *For any $(u, v, y)_{(j,b)}$ for $b \in [2^{\ell-j}]$*

$$\Pr[\mathbf{Bad1}_{j,b} \mid \cap_{j'<j} \neg \mathsf{Coll}_{j'} \cap \cap_{j'<j} \neg \mathsf{Bad}_{j'}] \leq 2^n \left(\frac{ek^\ell q^2}{2^n} \right)^{k^\ell}$$

Proof. We bound the probability for any possible input $(u, v)_{(j,b)}$ that $Y_{(u,v,j,b)} > k^\ell$. Fix $u \oplus v = a$. Consider any entry $(u_1, v_1, y_1)_{(j-1,2b)}$ from τ. This entry contributes to $Y_{(u,v,j,b)}$ if there exists a $h \in F_{(j-1,2b)}$ and $x \in \Gamma_{(j-1,2b-1)}$ such that $y_1 \oplus h \oplus v = x \oplus u$. Rearranging, we get that $y_1 = h \oplus x \oplus a$. Probability of that event is $\frac{Y_{(u_1,v_1,j-1,2b)} |\Gamma_{(j-1,2b-1)}|}{2^n}$. As $\neg \mathsf{Bad}_{j'}$ holds for all $j' < j$, we have $|\, \Gamma_{(j-1,2b-1)} \,| \leq k^\ell q$, and $Y_{u_1,v_1,j-1,2b} \leq k^{j-1}$. Hence, the probability that

$(u_1, v_1, y_1)_{(j-1,2b)}$ contributes to $Y_{u,v,j,b}$ is at most $\frac{k^{\ell+j-1}q}{2^n}$. As there are at most q choices for $(u_1, v_1, y_1)_{(j-1,2b)}$ and each choice contributes one to $Y_{u,v,j,b}$,

$$\Pr\left[Y_{u,v,j,b} > k^\ell\right] \le \binom{q}{k^\ell}\left(\frac{k^{\ell+j-1}q}{2^n}\right)^{k^\ell}$$

Next, we use the inequality $\binom{a}{b} \le \left(\frac{ea}{b}\right)^b$, where e is the base of natural logarithm.

$$\Pr\left[Y_{u,v,j,b} > k^\ell\right] \le \left(\frac{ek^{j-1}q^2}{2^n}\right)^{k^\ell} \le \left(\frac{ek^\ell q^2}{2^n}\right)^{k^\ell}$$

Now, taking union bound over all possible choice of a, we get that for any possible input (u, v) to $f_{(j,b)}$,

$$\Pr\left[Y_{u,v,j,b} > k^\ell\right] \le 2^n\left(\frac{ek^\ell q^2}{2^n}\right)^{k^\ell}$$

□

Bounding $\mathbf{Bad2}_j$

Lemma 8. *Fix $b \in [2^{\ell-j}]$ and thus fix a function at the jþ level.*

$$\Pr[\mathbf{Bad2}_{j,b} \mid \cap_{j'<j}\neg\mathsf{Coll}_{j'} \cap \cap_{j'<j}\neg\mathsf{Bad}_{j'} \cap \neg\mathbf{Bad1}_{j,b}] \le \frac{2^\ell k^\ell q^2}{2^n}$$

Proof. Consider a query $(u, v, y)_{j',b'}$ where (j', b') is in the sub-tree of (j, b). As $\cap_{j'<j}\neg\mathsf{Bad}_{j'}$ holds, we argue $\neg\mathsf{Bad1}_{j'}$ holds. Thus the number of chaining value created by $(u, v, y)_{j',b'}$ query at the output of j', b' is at most k^ℓ, we have $Y_{u,v,j',b'} \le k^\ell$.

Next we calculate the increase in the load of the next node $f_{(j'+1,\lceil\frac{b'}{2}\rceil)}$ due to query $(u, v, y)_{j',b'}$. Consider any chaining value h created due to the query $(u, v, y)_{j',b'}$. h increases the load of $(j'+1, \lceil\frac{b'}{2}\rceil)$ if there exists $h_1 \in \Gamma_{j',b'-1}$ and $(u_1, v_1, y_1)_{j'+1,\lceil\frac{b'}{2}\rceil} \in \tau$ such that $h = h_1 \oplus u_1 \oplus v_1$. For a fixed h_1 and query $(u_1, v_1, y_1)_{j'+1,\lceil\frac{b'}{2}\rceil}$, probability the equation gets satisfied is $\frac{1}{2^n}$. There can be at most $|Q_{j'+1,\lceil\frac{b'}{2}\rceil}|$ many queries made to the function $j'+1, \lceil\frac{b'}{2}\rceil$ in the transcript, implying at most q many choices for candidate $(u_1, v_1, y_1)_{j'+1,\lceil\frac{b'}{2}\rceil}$.

$$\mathbf{E}\left[\delta^2_{(j'+1,\lceil\frac{b'}{2}\rceil)}\right] \le \frac{Y_{u,v,j',b'}\left|\Gamma_{(j',b'-1)}\right|\left|Q_{j'+1,\lceil\frac{b'}{2}\rceil}\right|}{2^n}$$

As $\neg\mathsf{Bad}_{j'}$ holds in the given condition, $\left|\Gamma_{(j',b'-1)}\right| = L_{(j',b'-1)} < 2k^\ell q$. Moreover, $Y_{u,v,j',b'} \le k^\ell$; thus the expected increase in the load of $f_{(j'+1,\lceil\frac{b'}{2}\rceil)}$ is at most $\frac{2k^{2\ell}q^2}{2^n}$.

We extend this argument to the next levels. For a random element from $Q_{j'+1,\lceil \frac{b'}{2} \rceil} \times \Gamma_{(j',b'-1)}$ the expected number of matched elements in $Q_{j'+2,\lceil \frac{b'}{4} \rceil} \times \Gamma_{(j'+1,\lceil \frac{b'}{2} \rceil -1)}$ is $\frac{\left|\Gamma_{(j'+1,\lceil \frac{b'}{2} \rceil -1)}\right|\left|Q_{j'+2,\lceil \frac{b'}{4} \rceil}\right|}{\left|\Gamma_{(j',b'-1)}\right|\left|Q_{j'+1,\lceil \frac{b'}{2} \rceil}\right|}$. Using $\neg\mathsf{Bad}_{j'}$ for all $j' < j$, we bound the expected increase of load for $f_{(j'+2,\lceil \frac{b'}{4} \rceil)}$ as

$$
\begin{aligned}
&\mathbf{E}\left[\delta^2_{(j'+2,\lceil \frac{b'}{4} \rceil)}\right] \\
&\leq \frac{Y_{u,v,j',b'} \mid \Gamma_{(j',b'-1)} \mid\mid Q_{j'+1,\lceil \frac{b'}{2} \rceil} \mid}{2^n} \times \frac{\mid \Gamma_{(j'+2,\lceil \frac{b'}{2} \rceil -1)} \mid\mid Q_{j'+1,\lceil \frac{b'}{4} \rceil} \mid}{\mid \Gamma_{(j',b'-1)} \mid\mid Q_{j'+1,\lceil \frac{b'}{2} \rceil} \mid} \\
&\leq \frac{Y_{u,v,j',b'} \mid \Gamma_{(j'+1,\lceil \frac{b'}{2} \rceil -1)} \mid\mid Q_{j'+1,\lceil \frac{b'}{4} \rceil} \mid}{2^n} \\
&\leq \frac{2k^{2\ell}q^2}{2^n}
\end{aligned}
$$

Inductively extending the argument

$$
\mathbf{E}\left[\delta^2_{(j,b)}\right] \leq \frac{2k^{2\ell}q^2}{2^n}.
$$

As there q many queries in the transcript, the expected total type II contribution for a function (j,b) is $\frac{2^\ell k^{2\ell} q^3}{2^n}$. By using Markov inequality we get that

$$
\Pr\left[\delta^2_{(j,b)} > k^\ell q\right] \leq \frac{\mathbf{E}\left[\delta^2_{(j,b)}\right]}{k^\ell q} \leq \frac{2k^\ell q^2}{2^n}
$$

□

Finishing the Proof. From Lemma 6, Lemma 7, and Lemma 8, we bound the probability of bad as

$$
\sum_{j>1} \Pr\left[\mathsf{Bad}_j \mid \cap_{j'<j}\neg\mathsf{Coll}_{j'} \cap \cap_{j'<j}\neg\mathsf{Bad}_{j'}\right] = \sum_{j>1, b\in[2^{\ell-j}]} \left(2^n \left(\frac{ek^\ell q^2}{2^n}\right)^{k^\ell} + \frac{2k^\ell q^2}{2^n}\right) \tag{4}
$$

$$
= \frac{2^{\ell+1}k^\ell q^2}{2^n} + 2^{\ell+n}\left(\frac{ek^\ell q^2}{2^n}\right)^{k^\ell} \tag{5}
$$

From Eq. 1, Eq. 2, Eq. 3, and Eq. 5, we get,

$$
\Pr\left[\mathsf{Coll}\right] \leq \frac{2^{\ell-1}q^2}{2^n} + \frac{2^{\ell+1}k^{2\ell}q^2}{2^n} + \frac{2^{\ell+1}k^\ell q^2}{2^n} + 2^{\ell+n}\left(\frac{ek^\ell q^2}{2^n}\right)^{k^\ell} \tag{6}
$$

$$
\leq \frac{2^{\ell+1}q^2(1+k^\ell+k^{2\ell})}{2^n} + 2^{\ell+n}\left(\frac{ek^\ell q^2}{2^n}\right)^{k^\ell} \tag{7}
$$

Finally, putting $k = (n+1)^{\frac{1}{\ell}}$, and assuming $q^2 < \frac{2^n}{2e(n+1)}$, we get

$$2^{\ell+n}\left(\frac{ek^{\ell}q^2}{2^n}\right)^{k^{\ell}} < \frac{2^{\ell}e(n+1)q^2}{2^n}$$

Putting $k^{\ell} = (n+1)$ in Eq. 7,

$$\Pr[\,\mathsf{Coll}\,] = \mathcal{O}\left(\frac{2^{\ell}(1+n+n^2)q^2}{2^n}\right) = \mathcal{O}\left(\frac{rn^2q^2}{2^n}\right).$$

This finishes the proof of Theorem 2. □

Corollary 1. *The compactness of* ABR *is* 1.

5 Achieving Indifferentiability Efficiently

Below we first consider the basic ABR compression function and analyze its security with respect to the indifferentiability notion. We show that while ABR fails to achieve indifferentiability, a simple modification can restore the indifferentiability. We call that modified tree ABR^+ mode construction. ABR^+ mode is the merge of two ABR modes (trees), not necessarily of the same height $\ell \geq 2$ each, and feeding their inputs to a final compression function (omitting the final message injection and feedforward).

5.1 Indifferentiability Attack Against ABR Mode

Our main result of this section is the following.

Theorem 5. *Consider the* ABR *mode with* $\ell = 2$. *There exists an indifferentiability adversary* A *making* $\mathcal{O}(2^{\frac{n}{3}})$ *many calls such that for any simulator* S *it holds that*

$$\mathbf{Adv}^{\mathrm{Indiff}}_{(\mathsf{ABR},f),(\mathcal{G},S^{\mathcal{G}})}(\mathsf{A}) \geq 1-\epsilon$$

where ϵ *is a negligible function of* n.

Theorem 5 can be extended for $\ell > 2$ as well.

Principle Behind the Attack. Recall the ABR with $\ell = 2$ from Fig. 1b. The idea is to find collision on the input of f_0 for two distinct messages m, m'. If the adversary finds such a collision, then the output of the simulator on this input needs to be consistent with the random oracle ($\mathcal{F}$) responses on two distinct messages. That is impossible unless there is a certain relation at the output of $\mathcal{F}$, making that probability negligible.

The Attack. The adversary A maintains three (initially empty) query-response lists L_0, L_1, L_2 for the three functions f_0, f_1, f_2, respectively. A chooses $2^{n/3}$ messages $(x_1^{(1)}, x_2^{(1)}) \in \{0,1\}^{2n}$, queries to f_1, and adds the query-response tuple to L_1. Similarly, A chooses $2^{n/3}$ messages $(x_1^{(2)}, x_2^{(2)}) \in \{0,1\}^{2n}$, queries to f_2, and adds the query-response tuple to L_2. A checks whether there exists $(x_1^{(1)}, x_2^{(1)}, h_1^{(1)}) \in L_1$, and $(x_1^{(2)}, x_2^{(2)}, h_1^{(2)}) \in L_1$, and $(x_3^{(1)}, x_4^{(1)}, h_2^{(1)}) \in L_2$, and $(x_3^{(2)}, x_4^{(2)}, h_2^{(2)}) \in L_2$ such that

$$h_1^{(1)} \oplus h_1^{(2)} \oplus h_2^{(1)} \oplus h_2^{(2)} = 0 \tag{8}$$

If such tuples do not exist, A outputs 1 and aborts. If there is collision in the lists, A outputs 1 and aborts. Otherwise, it chooses a random $\hat{m} \in \{0,1\}^n$. The adversary sets $m = h_1^{(1)} \oplus h_1^{(2)} \oplus \hat{m} = h_2^{(1)} \oplus h_2^{(2)} \oplus \hat{m}$, adversary computes $u = m \oplus h_1^{(1)} = \hat{m} \oplus h_1^{(2)}$ and $v = m \oplus h_2^{(1)} = \hat{m} \oplus h_2^{(2)}$. Finally, adversary queries $z = f_0(u, v)$ and outputs 1 if $z \neq \mathcal{F}(x_1^{(1)}, x_2^{(1)}, x_3^{(1)}, x_4^{(1)}, m) \oplus h_2^{(1)}$ or $z \neq \mathcal{F}(x_1^{(2)}, x_2^{(2)}, x_3^{(2)}, x_4^{(2)}, \hat{m}) \oplus h_2^{(2)}$. Else adversary outputs 0.
The full probability analysis is straightforward and skipped in this version.

5.2 Almost Fully Compact and Indifferentiable ABR$^+$ Mode

In this section, we show that the generalized ABR$^+$ mode without the additional message block at the last level is indifferentiable (up to the birthday bound) from a random oracle. For ease of explanation, we prove the result for three-level (see Fig. 4b) balanced tree. The proof for the general case follows exactly the same idea. The generalized ABR$^+$ mode can be viewed as the merge of two ABR mode instances, one being the left ABR$^+$ branch and the other being the right branch. Both their root values are input to a final $2n$-to-n-bit compression function to compute the final value of the ABR$^+$ tree. The ABR$^+$ tree can be either balanced or unbalanced depending on whether it uses two ABR modes of identical or distinct heights (see Fig. 4a), respectively.

Our main result here is the following theorem. The result can be generalized to ABR$^+$ with arbitrary height. However, the simulator description will be more detailed. For ease of explanation we consider the mode with $\ell = 3$.

Theorem 6. *Let $f : [7] \times \{0,1\}^{2n} \to \{0,1\}^n$ be a family of random functions. Let $C^f : \{0,1\}^{10n} \to \{0,1\}^n$ be the ABR$^+$ mode as in Fig. 4b. (C^f, f) is (t_S, q_S, q, ϵ) indifferentiable from a random oracle $\mathcal{F} : \{0,1\}^{10n} \to \{0,1\}^n$ where*

$$\epsilon \leq \mathcal{O}\left(\frac{n^2 q^2}{2^n}\right).$$

where q is the total number of queries made by the adversary. Moreover $t_S = \mathcal{O}(q^2)$ and $q_S = 1$

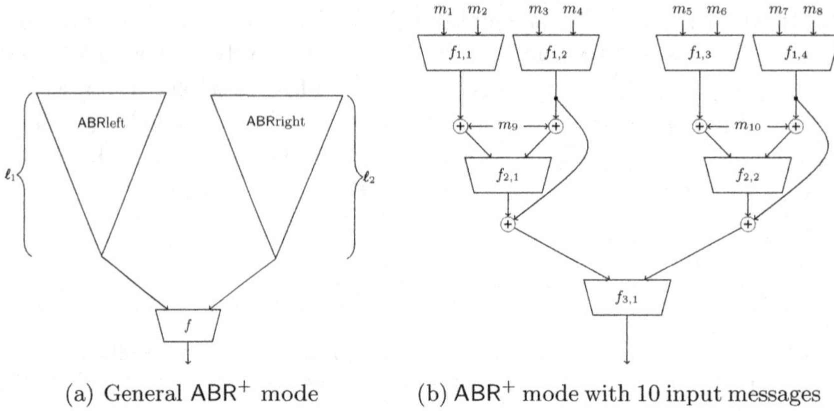

(a) General ABR^+ mode

(b) ABR^+ mode with 10 input messages

Fig. 4. ABR^+ mode examples

5.3 Proof of Theorem 6

We assume that the distinguisher $\mathcal{D}$ makes all the primitive queries corresponding the construction queries. This is without loss of generality as we can construct a distinguisher $\mathcal{D}'$ for every distinguisher $\mathcal{D}$ such that $\mathcal{D}'$ satisfies the condition. $\mathcal{D}'$ emulates $\mathcal{D}$ completely, and in particular, makes the same queries. However, at the end, for each construction queries made by $\mathcal{D}$, $\mathcal{D}'$ makes *all* the (non-repeating) primitive queries required to compute the construction queries. At the end, $\mathcal{D}'$ outputs the same decision as $\mathcal{D}$. As a result, in the transcript of $\mathcal{D}'$, all the construction query-responses, can be reconstructed from the primitive queries. Hence, it is sufficient to focus our attention on only the primitive queries and compare the distribution of outputs. If $\mathcal{D}$ makes q_1 many construction queries and q_2 many primitive queries, then $\mathcal{D}$ makes q_1 many construction queries and $q_2 + q_1 l$ many primitive queries in total where l is the maximum number of primitive queries to compute C.

The Simulator. We start with the high-level overview of how the simulator S works. For each $j \in [3]$, $b \in [2^{3-j}]$ the simulator maintains a list $L_{(j,b)}$. The list $L_{(j,b)}$ contains the query-response tuples for the function $f_{(j,b)}$.
MESSAGE RECONSTRUCTION. The main component of the simulator is the message reconstruction algorithm `FindM`. In the case of traditional Merkle tree, the messages are only injected in the leaf level. We have, in addition, the message injection at each (non-root) internal node. The message reconstruction in our case is slightly more involved.

The algorithm for message reconstruction is the subroutine `FindM`. It takes (u_0, v_0), the input to $f_{(3,1)}$, as input. Let $M = m_1||m_2||\cdots||m_{10}$ be the message for which $f_{(3,1)}(u_0, v_0)$ is the hash value. Also, suppose all the intermediate queries to $f_{(j,b)}(j < 3)$ has been made. In the following, we describe how the (partial) messages corresponding to chaining value u_0 is recovered. The other half of the message, corresponding to v_0, is recovered in analogous way.

Recall that there is no message injection at the final node. Hence, if all the intermediate queries related to M is made by the adversary, then m_9 must satisfy all the following relations, $\exists(u,v,y)_{(2,1)} \in L_{(2,1)}$, such that

$$y = u_0 \oplus v \oplus m_9 \qquad (m_1, m_2, u \oplus m_9) \in L_{(1,1)} \qquad (m_3, m_4, v \oplus m_9) \in L_{(1,2)}$$

We find a candidate m_9 by xoring u_0 with $y \oplus v$ for all the (so far) recorded entries $(u,v,y)_{(2,1)} \in L_{(2,1)}$. To check the validity of the candidate, we check the other two relations. If indeed such query tuples exist, we can recover the message.

SIMULATION OF THE FUNCTIONS. For every non-root function $f_{(j,b)}$, $j < 3$, the simulator simulates the function perfectly. Every query response is recorded in the corresponding list $L_{(j,b)}$. The simulation of $f_{(3,1)}$ is a little more involved, albeit standard in indifferentiability proof. Upon receiving a query (u_0, v_0) for $f_{(3,1)}$, the simulator needs to find out whether it is the final query corresponding to the evaluation for a message M. Suppose, all other queries corresponding to M has been made. The simulator finds M using the message reconstruction algorithm. If only one candidate message M is found, the simulator programs the output to be $\mathcal{F}(M)$. If the list returned by `FindM` is empty, then the simulator chooses a uniform random string and returns that as output. The first problem, however, arises when there are multiple candidate messages, returned by `FindM`. This implies, there are two distinct messages M, M' for both of which $f_{(3,1)}(u_0, v_0)$ is the final query. The simulator can not program its output to both $\mathcal{F}(M)$ and $\mathcal{F}(M')$. Hence, it aborts. In that case, there is a collision at either u or v, implying that the adversary is successful in finding a collision in ABR mode. The probability of that event can indeed be bounded by the results from the previous section. The second problem occurs in the output of non-root functions. Suppose for a $f_{(3,1)}(u_0, v_0)$ query the `FindM` algorithms returns an empty set. Intuitively, the simulator assumes here the adversary can not find a message M, for which the final query will be $f_{(3,1)}(u_0, v_0)$. Hence, the simulator does not need to maintain consistency with the Random Oracle. Now the second problem occurs, if later in the interaction, the output of some $f_{(j,b)}$ query forces a completion in the chaining value and a message M can now be recovered for which the final query will be $f_{(3,1)}(u_0, v_0)$. This will create an inconsistency of the simulator's output and the response of the Random Oracle. In the following, we bound the probability of these two events.

The description of the simulator is given in Fig. 5. The message reconstruction algorithm finds a candidate m_9 (and resp. m_{10}) for each entry in $L_{(2,1)}$ (and resp. $L_{(2,2)}$), and checks the validity against every entry of $L_{(1,1)}$ along with $L_{(1,2)}$ (resp. $L_{(1,3)}$ along with $L_{(1,4)}$). Thus the time complexity of message reconstruction algorithm is $\mathcal{O}(q^2)$. As the simulator invokes the message reconstruction algorithm at most once for each query, we bound $t_s = \mathcal{O}(q^2)$. Similarly, we find $q_s = 1$ as the simulator has to query $\mathcal{F}$ only once per *invocation*.

Procedure $S(3, 1, u, v)$

if $(u, v, z) \in L_{(3,1)}$ **return** z
$\mathcal{M} = \texttt{FindM}(u, v)$
if $|\mathcal{M}| > 1$**return** $\perp$
if $|\mathcal{M}| = 0$
  $z \xleftarrow{\$} \{0,1\}^n$
  $L_{(3,1)} = L_{(3,1)} \cup (u, v, z)$
  return z
endif
$M \leftarrow \mathcal{M}$
 $z = \mathcal{F}(M)$
 $L_{(3,1)} = L_{(3,1)} \cup (u, v, z)$
 return z

Procedure $S(j, b, u, v)$ where $j < 3$

if $\exists(u, v, z) \in L_{(j,b)}$
  return z
else
  $z \xleftarrow{\$} \{0,1\}^n$
  $L_{(j,b)} = L_{(j,b)} \cup (u, v, z)$
  return z
endif

Procedure $\texttt{FindM}(u, v)$

// Recovering message from u part
 $\mathcal{M}_1 = \emptyset$
 for each $(u', v', h') \in L_{(2,1)}$
  $m_9 = h' \oplus u \oplus v'$
 endfor
 if $\exists(m_1, m_2)$ such that $(m_1, m_2, u' \oplus m_9) \in L_{(1,1)}$
 $\wedge\, \exists(m_3, m_4)$ such that $(m_3, m_4, v' \oplus m_9) \in L_{(1,2)}$
  $\mathcal{M}_1 = \mathcal{M}_1 \cup (m_1, m_2, m_3, m_4, m_9)$
 endif
// Recovering message from v part
 $\mathcal{M}_2 = \emptyset$
 for each $(u', v', h') \in L_{2,2}$
  $m_{10} = h' \oplus v \oplus v'$
 endfor
 if $\exists(m_5, m_6)$ such that $(m_5, m_6, u' \oplus m_{10}) \in L_{(1,3)}$
 $\wedge\, \exists(m_7, m_8)$ such that $(m_7, m_8, v' \oplus m_{10}) \in L_{(1,4)}$
  $\mathcal{M}_2 = \mathcal{M}_2 \cup (m_5, m_6, m_7, m_8, m_{10})$
 endif
// Combining the messages
 for each$(m_1, m_2, m_3, m_4, m_9) \leftarrow \mathcal{M}_1$
 $\wedge$ each$(m_5, m_6, m_7, m_8, m_{10}) \leftarrow \mathcal{M}_2$
 $\mathcal{M} = \mathcal{M} \cup (m_1, m_2, \cdots, m_{10})$
 endif
 return $\mathcal{M}$

Fig. 5. Description of the simulator

The Bad Events. We shall prove the theorem using the H-coefficient technique. We consider the following Bad events.

Bad0: The set $\mathcal{M}$, returned by the message reconstruction algorithm has cardinality more that one. This implies, one can extract two message M_1, M_2 from the transcript such that the computation of $\mathsf{ABR}^+(M_1)$ and $\mathsf{ABR}^+(M_2)$ makes the same query to $f_{(3,1)}$.

Bad1: There exists an i, such that for the ith entry in the transcript $h_i = f_{(j,b)}(x_i, y_i)$ with $j < 3$, there exists a message M such that $C^f(M)$ can be computed from the first i entries of the transcript, but can not be computed from the first $i - 1$ entries. This in particular implies that there exists a i' with $i' < i$, such that:

- i'^{th} query is a query to $f_{(3,1)}$. $h = f_{(3,1)}(u_{i'}, v_{i'})$

- By setting $h_i = f_{(j,b)}(x_i, y_i)$ with $\ell > 0$, we create a message M such that all the other chaining values of $C^f(M)$ are present in the first $i-1$ queries with $f_{(3,1)}(u_{i'}, v_{i'})$ as the final query.

Lemma 9. *For adversary $\mathcal{A}$ making q many queries,*

$$\Pr[\,\text{BAD}\,] \le \mathcal{O}\left(\frac{n^2q^2}{2^n}\right).$$

Bounding Pr [BAD]. We bound the probabilities of the BAD events.

- **Case** BAD0**:** If there is a collision in the final query of the computations for two different messages, then there is a collision in the u part or v part of the chain. This implies a collision in one of the ABR mode output. Hence, by Proposition 4

$$\Pr[\text{BAD0}] \le \mathcal{O}\left(\frac{n^2q^2}{2^n}\right)$$

- **Case** BAD1**:** We first consider a query $f_{(j,b)}(u, v)$ with $j = 2$. Let $Y_{(u,v,j,b)}$ denote the yield of this query (recall that yield of a query denotes the number of new chaining values a query creates, see page 17). As there can be at most q many queries to $f_{(3,1)}$ done before this, probability that such a query raises the BAD1 is bounded by $\frac{Y_{(u,v,j,b)}q}{2^n}$. Taking union bound over all the queries at $f_{(j,b)}$, the probability gets upper bounded by $\frac{q\sum Y_{(u,v,j,b)}}{2^n}$. As we showed in the previous section this probability can be bounded by $\mathcal{O}\left(\frac{n^2q^2}{2^n}\right)$. Finally, we consider the case of BAD1 raised by some queries at the leaf level. As in the proof of collision resistance, the expected number of new chaining values created at the output by the leaf level queries is $\frac{nq^3}{2^n}$. Hence, by Markov inequality, the probability that the total number of new chaining values created is more that q is at most $\frac{nq^2}{2^n}$. Finally, conditioned on the number of new chaining values be at most q, the probability that it matches with one of the $f_{(3,1)}$ queries is at most $\frac{q^2}{2^n}$. Hence, we get

$$\Pr[\text{BAD1}] \le \mathcal{O}\left(\frac{nq^2}{2^n}\right)$$

Good Transcripts Are Identically Distributed. We show that the good views are identically distributed in the real and ideal worlds. Note that the simulator perfectly simulates f for the internal node. The only difference is the simulation of the final query. In case of good views, the queries to f_0 are of two types:

1. The query corresponds to the final query of a distinct message M, such that all the internal queries of $C^f(M)$ have occurred before. In this case, the simulator response is $\mathcal{F}(M)$. Conditioned on the rest of the transcript the output distribution remains same in both the worlds.

2. There is no message M in the transcript so far for which this is the final query. In this case, the response of the simulator is a uniformly chosen sample. As BAD1 does not occur, the property remains true. In that case as well, the output remains same, conditioned on the rest of the transcript.

Hence, for all $\tau \in \Theta_{good}$

$$\Pr[X_{\texttt{real}} = \tau] = \Pr[X_{\texttt{ideal}} = \tau]$$

This finishes the proof of Theorem 6.

Corollary 2. *The compactness of ABR$^+$ making r calls to underlying $2n$-to-n-bit function is $1 - \frac{2}{3r-1}$.*

6 Efficiency and Applications

In this section, we discuss the compactness of our proposed designs, possible applications and use cases.

6.1 Efficiency and Proof Size

Below we discuss and compare our designs with the Merkle tree regarding efficiency of compression and authentication and proof size: the number of openings to prove a membership of a node in a tree.

EFFICIENCY OF COMPRESSION AND AUTHENTICATION. To measure efficiency of compression we consider the amount of message (in bits) processed for a fixed tree height or a fixed number of compression function calls. As mentioned earlier, compared to a Merkle tree of height ℓ which absorbs $n2^{\ell}$ message bits, the ABR or ABR$^+$ modes process an additional $n(2^{\ell-1}-1)$ message bits. Thus, asymptotically the number of messages inserted in our ABR (or ABR$^+$) mode increases by 50% compared to Merkle tree. Additionally, the cost of authentication (number of compression function calls to authenticate a node) in a Merkle tree is $\log N$ where $N = 2^{\ell}$. Here as well the ABR or ABR$^+$ modes compress 50% more message bits compared to Merkle tree keeping the same cost of authentication as in Merkle tree as shown in Lemma 10.

PROOF SIZE. We refer to the tree chaining and internal message nodes as the tree *openings*. The proof size in a tree is determined by the number of openings. In a Merkle tree, the proof of membership of *all* (leaf) inputs requires $\log N$ compression function evaluations and openings each. More precisely, to prove the *membership of an arbitrary leaf input*, $\log N - 1$ chaining values and one leaf input are required. Note that while counting the number of openings, we exclude the input for which the membership is being proved.

Lemma 10. *In ABR mode, to prove the membership of any node (message block): leaf or internal, we require $2\log N - 1$ (n-bit) openings and $\log N$ compression function computations.*

Proof. To prove the membership of a leaf input in the ABR mode $2(\log N - 1)$ openings are required together with one leaf input. This makes a total of $2\log N - 1$ openings. To obtain the root hash $\log N$ computation must be computed. To prove the membership of an internal node, we need $2(\log N - 1)$ openings, excluding any openings from the level at which the internal node resides. Additionally, one more opening is required from the level of the node. Thus, in total we need again $2\log N - 1$ openings. The number of compression calls remains $\log N$.

Compared to Merkle tree, in ABR^+ the proof size increases by $\log N - 1$. Admittedly, for Merkle tree applications where the proof size is the imperative performance factor, the ABR^+ modes do not provide an advantage.

6.2 Applications and Variants

ZK-SNARKs. We briefly point out here the potential advantages of using the ABR mode in zk-SNARKS based applications, such as Zcash. In a zk-SNARK [22] based application, increasing the number of inputs or transactions in a block means that we need to increase the size of the corresponding Merkle tree. The complexity of the proof generation process in zk-SNARK is $C \log C$ where C is the circuit size of the underlying function. In ABR^+ modes the additional messages are inserted without increasing the tree height or introducing additional compression function calls. Since the messages are only injected with xor/addition operation, this does not deteriorate the complexity of the proof generation. Zcash uses a Merkle tree with height $\approx$29 and 2^{34} byte inputs. By using either one, ABR or ABR^+ modes, an additional of $\approx 2^{33}$ byte inputs can be compressed *without* making any extra calls to the underlying compression function. Asymptotically, ABR or ABR^+ provides 50% improvement in the number of maintained (in the tree structure) messages compared to a Merkle tree.

Further Applications. Our modes can be useful in applications, such as hashing on parallel processors or multicore machines: authenticating software updates, image files or videos; integrity checks of large files systems, long term archiving [17], content distribution, torrent systems [1], etc.

Variants. We continue with possible variants of utilizing the ABR compression function in existing constructions, such as the Merkle–Damgård domain extender and a 5-ary Merkle tree, and discuss their compactness and efficiency.

Merkle–Damgård (MD) Domain Extender with ABR. When the compression function in MD is substituted by ABR ($\ell = 2$) compression function, the collision resistance preservation of the original domain extender is maintained. We obtain compactness of $\approx 8/9$ of such an MD variant (see Sect. 3.1).

For all our modes, the high compactness allows us to absorb more messages at a fixed cost or viewed otherwise, to compress the same amount of data (e.g. as MD or Merkle tree) much cheaper. We elaborate on the latter trade-off here. To compress 1 MB message with classical MD that produces a 256-bit hash value and uses a 512-to-256-bit compression function, around 31250 calls to the underlying (512-to-256-bit) compression function are made. In contrast, ABR in MD requires just ≈7812 calls to the (512-to-256) compression function, that is an impressive 4-fold cost reduction.

5-ary Merkle Tree with ABR. One can naturally further construct a 5-ary Merkle tree using ABR with compactness <8/9 (see Sect. 3.1). That means to compress 1MB data with a 5-ary ABR mode with $5n$-to-n-bit ($n = 256$) compression functions will require ≈23437 calls to the 512-to-256-bit compression functions. Using the Merkle tree the number is 31250 compression function calls. On the other hand, the ABR and ABR^+ modes require *only* ≈20832 calls.

We have also considered simpler versions of ABR (e.g. when the feed forward from f_2 is omitted) to show how they fail to achieve collision security (in the extended version [2]).

7 Discussion and Conclusions

The ABR mode is the first collision secure, large domain, hash function that matches Stam's bound for its parameters. The ABR+ is also close to optimally efficient and achieves the stronger indifferentiablity notion, both completed in the ideal model. Based on our security results we can conclude that the ABR^+ mode is indeed the stronger proposal that achieves all the 'good' function properties up to the birthday bound. Driven by practical considerations for suitable replacements of Merkle tree, the ABR mode appears to be the more natural choice. This is motivated by the fact that the majority of Merkle tree uses are indeed FIL, namely they work for messages of fixed length.

Indeed, for such FIL Merkle trees collision preservation in the standard model holds but it fails once message length variability is allowed (for that one needs to add MD strengthening and extra compression function call). The ABR mode is proven collision secure in the ideal model. Our result confirms the structural soundness of our domain extenders in the same fashion as the Sponge domain extender does it for the SHA-3 hash function.

We clarify that simple modifications of ABR lead to the same security results. These variants are when one uses for feed-forward the left chaining value (instead of the right as in the ABR mode) *or* when the internal message itself (instead of the right chaining value) are fed-forward into the output of f_0. The collision security proofs for these two variants follow exactly the same arguments and are identical up to replacement for the mentioned values. Similarly, an extended tree version of the latter constructions can be shown collision or indifferentiability secure when it is generalized in the same fashion as the ABR^+ mode.

An interesting practical problem is to find and benchmark concrete mode instantiations. From a theory perspective, finding compact double length constructions is an interesting research direction.

Acknowledgements. We thank Martijn Stam for reading an earlier version of the draft and providing valuable comments. We would like to also thank Markulf Kohlweiss for discussion on the zksnarks and other applications of this work. We sincerely thank the reviewers of this and the earlier version of this paper for their insightful comments. Rishiraj is supported by *SERB ECR/2017/001974*.

References

1. http://bittorrent.org/beps/bep_0030.html
2. Andreeva, E., Bhattacharyya, R., Roy, A.: Compactness of hashing modes and efficiency beyond Merkle tree. IACR Cryptol. ePrint Arch. (2021)
3. Andreeva, E., Mennink, B., Preneel, B.: On the indifferentiability of the Grøstl hash function. In: Garay, J.A., De Prisco, R. (eds.) SCN 2010. LNCS, vol. 6280, pp. 88–105. Springer, Heidelberg (2010). https://doi.org/10.1007/978-3-642-15317-4_7
4. Andreeva, E., Mennink, B., Preneel, B.: Security reductions of the second round SHA-3 candidates. In: Burmester, M., Tsudik, G., Magliveras, S., Ilić, I. (eds.) ISC 2010. LNCS, vol. 6531, pp. 39–53. Springer, Heidelberg (2011). https://doi.org/10.1007/978-3-642-18178-8_5
5. Andreeva, E., Mennink, B., Preneel, B.: The parazoa family: generalizing the sponge hash functions. Int. J. Inf. Sec. **11**(3), 149–165 (2012)
6. Ben-Sasson, E., et al.: Zerocash: decentralized anonymous payments from bitcoin. IACR Cryptol. ePrint Arch. **2014**, 349 (2014)
7. Ben-Sasson, E., Chiesa, A., Tromer, E., Virza, M.: Succinct non-interactive zero knowledge for a von Neumann architecture. In: Fu, K., Jung, J. (eds.) USENIX Security 2014, pp. 781–796. USENIX Association (August 2014)
8. Benjamin, D.: Batch signing for TLS (2019). https://tools.ietf.org/html/draft-davidben-tls-batch-signing-02
9. Bernstein, D.J., Hülsing, A., Kölbl, S., Niederhagen, R., Rijneveld, J., Schwabe, P.: The SPHINCS$^+$ signature framework. In: ACM CCS 2019, pp. 2129–2146. ACM Press (November 2019)
10. Bertoni, G., Daemen, J., Peeters, M., Van Assche, G.: Duplexing the sponge: single-pass authenticated encryption and other applications. Cryptology ePrint Archive, Report 2011/499 (2011). http://eprint.iacr.org/2011/499
11. Bertoni, G., Daemen, J., Peeters, M., Van Assche, G.: Keccak. In: Johansson, T., Nguyen, P.Q. (eds.) EUROCRYPT 2013. LNCS, vol. 7881, pp. 313–314. Springer, Heidelberg (2013). https://doi.org/10.1007/978-3-642-38348-9_19
12. Bertoni, G., Daemen, J., Peeters, M., Van Assche, G.: On the indifferentiability of the sponge construction. In: Smart, N. (ed.) EUROCRYPT 2008. LNCS, vol. 4965, pp. 181–197. Springer, Heidelberg (2008). https://doi.org/10.1007/978-3-540-78967-3_11
13. Bertoni, G., Daemen, J., Peeters, M., Van Assche, G.: Duplexing the sponge: single-pass authenticated encryption and other applications. In: Miri, A., Vaudenay, S. (eds.) SAC 2011. LNCS, vol. 7118, pp. 320–337. Springer, Heidelberg (2012). https://doi.org/10.1007/978-3-642-28496-0_19
14. Black, J., Cochran, M., Shrimpton, T.: On the impossibility of highly-efficient Blockcipher-based hash functions. In: Cramer, R. (ed.) EUROCRYPT 2005. LNCS, vol. 3494, pp. 526–541. Springer, Heidelberg (2005). https://doi.org/10.1007/11426639_31
15. Black, J., Rogaway, P., Shrimpton, T.: Black-box analysis of the block-cipher-based hash-function constructions from PGV. In: Yung, M. (ed.) CRYPTO 2002. LNCS, vol. 2442, pp. 320–335. Springer, Heidelberg (2002). https://doi.org/10.1007/3-540-45708-9_21

16. Bogdanov, A., Knežević, M., Leander, G., Toz, D., Varıcı, K., Verbauwhede, I.: SPONGENT: A Lightweight Hash Function. In: Preneel, B., Takagi, T. (eds.) CHES 2011. LNCS, vol. 6917, pp. 312–325. Springer, Heidelberg (2011). https://doi.org/10.1007/978-3-642-23951-9_21
17. BSI. https://www.bsi.bund.de/SharedDocs/Downloads/EN/BSI/Publications/TechGuidelines/TR03125/TR-03125_M3_v1_2_2.pdf
18. Buchmann, J., Dahmen, E., Klintsevich, E., Okeya, K., Vuillaume, C.: Merkle signatures with virtually unlimited signature capacity. In: Katz, J., Yung, M. (eds.) ACNS 2007. LNCS, vol. 4521, pp. 31–45. Springer, Heidelberg (2007). https://doi.org/10.1007/978-3-540-72738-5_3
19. Buchmann, J., García, L.C.C., Dahmen, E., Döring, M., Klintsevich, E.: CMSS – an improved Merkle signature scheme. In: Barua, R., Lange, T. (eds.) INDOCRYPT 2006. LNCS, vol. 4329, pp. 349–363. Springer, Heidelberg (2006). https://doi.org/10.1007/11941378_25
20. Chen, S., Steinberger, J.: Tight security bounds for key-alternating ciphers. In: Nguyen, P.Q., Oswald, E. (eds.) EUROCRYPT 2014. LNCS, vol. 8441, pp. 327–350. Springer, Heidelberg (2014). https://doi.org/10.1007/978-3-642-55220-5_19
21. Damgård, I.B.: A design principle for hash functions. In: Brassard, G. (ed.) CRYPTO 1989. LNCS, vol. 435, pp. 416–427. Springer, New York (1990). https://doi.org/10.1007/0-387-34805-0_39
22. Gennaro, R., Gentry, C., Parno, B., Raykova, M.: Quadratic span programs and succinct NIZKs without PCPs. In: Johansson, T., Nguyen, P.Q. (eds.) EUROCRYPT 2013. LNCS, vol. 7881, pp. 626–645. Springer, Heidelberg (2013). https://doi.org/10.1007/978-3-642-38348-9_37
23. Haber, S., Stornetta, W.S.: How to time-stamp a digital document. J. Cryptol. **3**(2), 99–111 (1991). https://doi.org/10.1007/BF00196791
24. Maurer, U., Renner, R., Holenstein, C.: Indifferentiability, impossibility results on reductions, and applications to the random oracle methodology. In: Naor, M. (ed.) TCC 2004. LNCS, vol. 2951, pp. 21–39. Springer, Heidelberg (2004). https://doi.org/10.1007/978-3-540-24638-1_2
25. Mennink, B., Preneel, B.: Hash functions based on three permutations: a generic security analysis. In: Safavi-Naini, R., Canetti, R. (eds.) CRYPTO 2012. LNCS, vol. 7417, pp. 330–347. Springer, Heidelberg (2012). https://doi.org/10.1007/978-3-642-32009-5_20
26. Mennink, B., Preneel, B.: Efficient parallelizable hashing using small non-compressing primitives. Int. J. Inf. Secur. **15**(3), 285–300 (2015). https://doi.org/10.1007/s10207-015-0288-7
27. Merkle, R.C.: Protocols for public key cryptosystems. In: Proceedings of the 1980 IEEE Symposium on Security and Privacy, Oakland, California, USA, 14–16 April 1980, pp. 122–134. IEEE Computer Society (1980)
28. Merkle, R.C.: A certified digital signature. In: Brassard, G. (ed.) CRYPTO 1989. LNCS, vol. 435, pp. 218–238. Springer, New York (1990). https://doi.org/10.1007/0-387-34805-0_21
29. Nandi, M.: A simple and unified method of proving indistinguishability. In: Barua, R., Lange, T. (eds.) INDOCRYPT 2006. LNCS, vol. 4329, pp. 317–334. Springer, Heidelberg (2006). https://doi.org/10.1007/11941378_23
30. Patarin, J.: The "Coefficients H" technique. In: Avanzi, R.M., Keliher, L., Sica, F. (eds.) SAC 2008. LNCS, vol. 5381, pp. 328–345. Springer, Heidelberg (2009). https://doi.org/10.1007/978-3-642-04159-4_21

31. Ristenpart, T., Shacham, H., Shrimpton, T.: Careful with composition: limitations of the indifferentiability framework. In: Paterson, K.G. (ed.) EUROCRYPT 2011. LNCS, vol. 6632, pp. 487–506. Springer, Heidelberg (2011). https://doi.org/10.1007/978-3-642-20465-4_27
32. Ristenpart, T., Shrimpton, T.: How to build a hash function from any collision-resistant function. In: Kurosawa, K. (ed.) ASIACRYPT 2007. LNCS, vol. 4833, pp. 147–163. Springer, Heidelberg (2007). https://doi.org/10.1007/978-3-540-76900-2_9
33. Rivest, R.L., Schuldt, J.C.N.: Spritz - a spongy RC4-like stream cipher and hash function. IACR Cryptol. ePrint Arch. **2016**, 856 (2016)
34. Rogaway, P., Steinberger, J.: Constructing cryptographic hash functions from fixed-key blockciphers. In: Wagner, D. (ed.) CRYPTO 2008. LNCS, vol. 5157, pp. 433–450. Springer, Heidelberg (2008). https://doi.org/10.1007/978-3-540-85174-5_24
35. Rogaway, P., Steinberger, J.: Security/efficiency tradeoffs for permutation-based hashing. In: Smart, N. (ed.) EUROCRYPT 2008. LNCS, vol. 4965, pp. 220–236. Springer, Heidelberg (2008). https://doi.org/10.1007/978-3-540-78967-3_13
36. Shrimpton, T., Stam, M.: Building a collision-resistant compression function from non-compressing primitives. In: Aceto, L., Damgård, I., Goldberg, L.A., Halldórsson, M.M., Ingólfsdóttir, A., Walukiewicz, I. (eds.) ICALP 2008. LNCS, vol. 5126, pp. 643–654. Springer, Heidelberg (2008). https://doi.org/10.1007/978-3-540-70583-3_52
37. Stam, M.: Beyond uniformity: better security/efficiency tradeoffs for compression functions. In: Wagner, D. (ed.) CRYPTO 2008. LNCS, vol. 5157, pp. 397–412. Springer, Heidelberg (2008). https://doi.org/10.1007/978-3-540-85174-5_22
38. Steinberger, J.: Stam's collision resistance conjecture. In: Gilbert, H. (ed.) EUROCRYPT 2010. LNCS, vol. 6110, pp. 597–615. Springer, Heidelberg (2010). https://doi.org/10.1007/978-3-642-13190-5_30
39. Steinberger, J., Sun, X., Yang, Z.: Stam's conjecture and threshold phenomena in collision resistance. In: Safavi-Naini, R., Canetti, R. (eds.) CRYPTO 2012. LNCS, vol. 7417, pp. 384–405. Springer, Heidelberg (2012). https://doi.org/10.1007/978-3-642-32009-5_23
40. Wagner, D.: A generalized birthday problem. In: Yung, M. (ed.) CRYPTO 2002. LNCS, vol. 2442, pp. 288–304. Springer, Heidelberg (2002). https://doi.org/10.1007/3-540-45708-9_19

Real-World Cryptanalysis

Three Third Generation Attacks on the Format Preserving Encryption Scheme FF3

Ohad Amon[1], Orr Dunkelman[2(✉)], Nathan Keller[3], Eyal Ronen[1], and Adi Shamir[4]

[1] Computer Science Department, Tel Aviv University, Tel Aviv, Israel
{ohad.amon,eyal.ronen}@cs.tau.ac.il

[2] Computer Science Department, University of Haifa, Haifa, Israel
orrd@cs.haifa.ac.il

[3] Department of Mathematics, Bar-Ilan University, Ramat Gan, Israel
nkeller@math.biu.ac.il

[4] Faculty of Mathematics and Computer Science, Weizmann Institute of Science, Rehovot, Israel
adi.shamir@weizmann.ac.il

Abstract. Format-Preserving Encryption (FPE) schemes accept plaintexts from any finite set of values (such as social security numbers or birth dates) and produce ciphertexts that belong to the same set. They are extremely useful in practice since they make it possible to encrypt existing databases or communication packets without changing their format. Due to industry demand, NIST had standardized in 2016 two such encryption schemes called FF1 and FF3. They immediately attracted considerable cryptanalytic attention with decreasing attack complexities. The best currently known attack on the Feistel construction FF3 has data and memory complexity of $O(N^{11/6})$ and time complexity of $O(N^{17/6})$, where the input belongs to a domain of size $N \times N$.

In this paper, we present and experimentally verify three improved attacks on FF3. Our best attack achieves the tradeoff curve $D = M = \tilde{O}(N^{2-t})$, $T = \tilde{O}(N^{2+t})$ for all $t \leq 0.5$. In particular, we can reduce the data and memory complexities to the more practical $\tilde{O}(N^{1.5})$, and at the same time, reduce the time complexity to $\tilde{O}(N^{2.5})$.

We also identify another attack vector against FPE schemes, the *related-domain* attack. We show how one can mount powerful attacks

O. Amon—is supported in part by Len Blavatnik and the Blavatnik Family foundation and by the Blavatnik ICRC.

O. Dunkelman—was supported in part by the Center for Cyber, Law, and Policy in conjunction with the Israel National Cyber Bureau in the Prime Minister's Office and by the Israeli Science Foundation through grants No. 880/18 and 3380/19.

N. Keller—was supported by the European Research Council under the ERC starting grant agreement n. 757731 (LightCrypt) and by the BIU Center for Research in Applied Cryptography and Cyber Security in conjunction with the Israel National Cyber Bureau in the Prime Minister's Office.

E. Ronen—is a member of CPIIS.

A. Canteaut and F.-X. Standaert (Eds.): EUROCRYPT 2021, LNCS 12697, pp. 127–154, 2021.
https://doi.org/10.1007/978-3-030-77886-6_5

when the adversary is given access to the encryption under the same key in different domains, and show how to apply it to efficiently distinguish FF3 and FF3-1 instances.

1 Introduction

Standard block ciphers such as DES [19] and AES [11] are designed to encrypt and decrypt fixed length binary strings. However, there are many cases in which the data we want to encrypt has a different format such as a decimal number (e.g., a social security number) or a string of English letters (e.g., a name). While we can try to map such inputs to binary strings, we are usually faced with the problem that the number of possible inputs is not a perfect power of 2. In these cases, the size of the encrypted values will be larger than the size of the original values. This can pose a severe problem when we try to protect existing databases or communication packets which have a fixed format and whose fields cannot be expanded even by a single bit, since we will not be able to simply replace each original value by its encrypted version.

A solution to the problem was proposed 23 years ago by Brightwell and Smith who introduced the concept of *Format-Preserving Encryption (FPE)* [10]. More precisely, FPE is a cipher that encrypts any predefined domain into itself, even when it is not represented as a fixed length binary string. For example, we want that the encryption of a credit card number to look like another credit card number, following the same syntactic restrictions on its format. FPE has been used and deployed by numerous companies, e.g., Voltage, Veriphone, Ingenico, Cisco, as well as by major credit-card payment organizations.

In the last 20 years, numerous FPE schemes were proposed. The first cipher to support the FPE functionality was the AES candidate Hasty Pudding Cipher [22] which was submitted by Schroeppel and Orman. In 2002, Black and Rogaway [8] proposed three different methods for offering FPE functionality: Cycle walking, prefix cipher, and a Feistel-based construction, where in cycle walking schemes we iteratively encrypt the plaintext under the secret key, until a ciphertext that resides in the domain is found. In 2008, Spies proposed the Feistel Finite Set Encryption Mode (FFSEM) [24], which is an AES based balanced Feistel network that uses the idea of cycle walking. This has become the underlying approach for many FPE schemes.

In the subsequent years, several groups submitted to the US National Institute of Standards and Technology (NIST) proposals for FPE schemes: Bellare et al. proposed FFX [2,3] (called by NIST "FF1"), Vance [25] proposed VAES3 (called by NIST "FF2") and Brier, Peyrin and Stern [9] proposed BPS (whose central component was called by NIST "FF3"). All these proposals are block ciphers, based on types of a Feistel network.

In 2016, NIST published a special publication (SP800-38G [13]) that specified the aforementioned FF1 and FF3 as two modes of operation for format-preserving encryption. The domain in these schemes consists of $M \times N$ possible inputs, but for the sake of simplicity we assume that $M = N$ in all our complexity estimates.

The first analysis of FF3 was published shortly afterwards by Bellare et al. [1] who developed an efficient message recovery attacks for small domains. A year later, Durak and Vaudenay [12] presented at Crypto'17 a new slide attack [7] against the FF3 scheme. The attack makes it possible to compute new ciphertexts, but without finding the scheme's 128-bit cryptographic key (note that in FPE's the number of possible keys is typically much larger than the number of possible plaintexts). Its data complexity of $O(N^{11/6})$ is slightly smaller than the N^2 size of the codebook, and its time complexity is $O(N^5)$, regardless of the schemes's key size. The attack is based on the fact that the tweak-key schedule allows for a simple related-tweak attack that reduces the number of rounds we have to attack from 8 to only 4 rounds.

Following this attack, NIST had revised their recommendation by modifying the way the tweak is used in the scheme, calling the new scheme FF3-1 (see SP 800-38G Rev. 1 [14]). Despite this revision, the security of the original FF3 against slide attacks continued to stir a great deal of interest. In particular, at Eurocrypt 2019, Hoang, Miller and Trieu [17] presented a second generation slide attack which improved the first generation attack of Durak and Vaudenay by using better algorithms for detecting slid pairs. The resulting attack has the same data complexity of $O(N^{11/6})$ but a greatly reduced time complexity of $O(N^{17/6})$.

1.1 Our Contributions

In this paper we present three third generation slide attacks on FF3:

1. A *symmetric slide attack* that follows the general strategy of Hoang et al.'s attack [17] but simultaneously improves all its complexity measures – from $D = M = N^{11/6}$ and $T = N^{17/6}$ to $D = M = \tilde{O}(N^{7/4})$ and $T = \tilde{O}(N^{5/2})$. It can be generalized to any point along the time/data tradeoff curve $D = M = \tilde{O}(N^{7/4-t})$ and $T = \tilde{O}(N^{5/2+2t})$, for any $0 \leq t \leq 1/4$.
2. A new type of *asymmetric slide attack* which exploits the asymmetry of the classical distinguisher on 4-round Feistel schemes to reduce the complexity even further – to $D = M = \tilde{O}(N^{3/2})$ and $T = \tilde{O}(N^{5/2})$, and more generally, to the tradeoff curve $D = M = \tilde{O}(N^{2-t})$ and $T = \tilde{O}(N^{2+t})$, for all $0 \leq t \leq 1/2$ (including the point $D = M = T = \tilde{O}(N^2)$). The reduction in data complexity is especially important, since it pushes the amount of required data significantly farther from the entire codebook ($\tilde{O}(N^{3/2})$ instead of $O(N^{11/6})$, out of N^2), while keeping the time complexity at $\tilde{O}(N^{5/2})$ – lower than the complexity of Hoang et al.'s attack.
3. A *slide attack using the cycle structure* which matches the second attack at the lowest overall complexity point – $D = M = T = N^2$. This attack is particularly interesting since it is the first practical application of the *slide attack using the cycle structure* technique [4], which was previously believed to be purely academic due to its huge data complexity, but can be applied in the context of FPE schemes due to their small input domains. Its successful application demonstrates the importance of developing new "theoretical" attack

techniques which are often criticized for having hopelessly high complexities, since they may suddenly become practical in a different setting.

Our new attacks also utilize an improved PRF reconstruction phase. Durak and Vaudenay presented that the actual round functions can be reconstructed given $\tilde{O}(N^{10/6})$ input/output pairs in time $O(N^3)$ [12]. The time complexity of the reconstruction attack was improved by Hoang, Miller, and Trieu to $O(N^{5/3})$. Both algorithms rely on finding cycles of length 3 in a graph (defined by the data). We show an improved cycles detection algorithm (based on meet in the middle approach), that allows finding longer cycles (in our case of length 4 and 5) while reducing the data complexity of this phase to $\tilde{O}(N^{3/2})$ as well as the time complexity to $\tilde{O}(N^{3/2})$.

A comparison of the complexities of our complete attacks with the complexities of previous attacks is presented in Table 1.

Table 1. Comparison of complete attacks on FF3

Attack & source	Complexity		
	Data	Time	Memory
First generation [12]	$O(N^{11/6})$	$O(N^5)$	$O(N^{11/6})$
Second generation [17]	$O(N^{11/6})$	$O(N^{17/6})$	$O(N^{11/6})$
Symmetric slide (Sect. 4.1)	$\tilde{O}(N^{7/4-t})$	$\tilde{O}(N^{5/2+2t})$	$\tilde{O}(N^{7/4-t})$
Cycle detection slide (Sect. 4.2)	N^2	$\tilde{O}(N^2)$	N^2
Asymmetric slide (Sect. 4.3)	$\tilde{O}(N^{2-t})$	$\tilde{O}(N^{2+t})$	$\tilde{O}(N^{2-t})$

We experimentally verified all of our attacks and their complexity (source code is available at https://github.com/OhadAm7/FF3-code). Table 2 compares the concrete number of data queries required for our asymmetric slide attack and the second generation attack. We show that our attack outperforms the previous state-of-the-art in all parameters.

In the last part of the paper, we introduce a new class of distinguishing attacks that can only be applied to FPE schemes, which we call *related domain attacks*. We first show that if the cipher uses cycle walking *during the encryption process* of a block, then one can offer a simple key recovery attack. We then

Table 2. A comparison of our asymmetric slide attack (with $t = 0.5$ and $L = 3$) and the previous second generation attack

N	Asymmetric slide (Sect. 4.3)			Second generation [17])		
	Number of queries	Time complexity	Success rate	Number of queries	Time complexity	Success rate
2^7	13752	2^{18}	0.58	16384	2^{20}	0.39
2^8	48302	2^{20}	0.69	52012	2^{23}	0.5
2^9	161676	2^{23}	0.69	165140	2^{26}	0.33

show that it is possible to apply use this type of an attack to offer efficient and practical distinguishers on FF3 and FF3-1 using related-domain attacks. Finally, we identify a very simple design principal which can protect any FPE scheme from such attacks. This design principal was already used in various FPE schemes, e.g., FF1 [14].

1.2 Paper Organization

The paper is organized as follows: We describe FF3 in Sect. 2. The existing attacks against FF3 are summarized in Sect. 3. Our new attacks are given in Sect. 4. The experimental verification of these attacks is given in Sect. 5. We introduce the related-domain attack on cycle walking FPE schemes in Sect. 6, and discuss a specific set of distinguishing attacks for the case of FF3 and FF3-1 in Sect. 7. Finally, Sect. 8 concludes this paper.

2 FF3

FF3 is a Format Preserving Encryption based on the FFX methodology proposed by Brier, Peyrin, and Stern [9]. It is a Feistel construction which accepts a plaintext in a domain of size $N \times M$ and produces a ciphertext in that domain. The plaintext P is divided into two parts (which we refer to as halves even though they may have different sizes) L and R, each composed of u and v, respectively, characters over some alphabet. In each round one half enters a PRP (a full AES encryption) together with a tweak, the key, and a round constant (which is equal to the round number). The output is numerically added modulo the respective size to the other half, their roles are then swapped for the next round.[1]

Formally, the encryption algorithm takes a 64-bit tweak $T = T_L||T_R$, where T_L and T_R are 32-bit each. Then, an 8-round Feistel construction is used, as depicted in Algorithm 1. In each round, half of the data is encoded into 96 bits (padding it with 0's if needed) using the naive lexicographic transformation.[2]

The encoded value is appended to the XOR of the 32-bit tweak and the round constant. The resulting 128-bit string is then encrypted under AES with the key K. The AES' output is then added using modular addition to the other half.

It is important to note that following the previous attacks of [12], a new version of FF3 called FF3-1 had been proposed in [14]. In FF3-1, the tweaks T_L and T_R are chosen such that they always have 0 in the 4 bits which accept the round counter i. This tweak destroys the related-tweak slide property which lies in the core of the slide distinguishers, and thus prevents the attack of [12], as

[1] As the two halves may not be of equal size, following previous works that try to avoid possible confusion, throughout this paper we avoid the swap after the round function.

[2] FF3 is defined for strings over some alphabet; it uses the transformation *Encode*96(X) which computes the location of X in the lexicographic order of all the possible strings, and encodes this number as a 96-bit binary string.

Algorithm 1: The Encryption Algorithm of FF3

Input : Message P of domain of size $M \times N$, Key K, Tweak $T = T_L||T_R$
Output: Ciphertext C of domain size $M \times N$

$(L, R) \leftarrow P$;
for $i \leftarrow 0$ **to** 7 **do**
  if $i \mod 2 = 0$ **then**
    $L \leftarrow L \boxplus AES_K(Encode96(R)||T_R \oplus i) \mod M$;
  else
    $R \leftarrow R \boxplus AES_K(Encode96(L)||T_L \oplus i) \mod N$;
return $C \leftarrow L||R$;

well as its extensions [17] and our results presented in Sect. 4. All these attacks are only applicable to the original FF3 scheme.

On the other hand, our results presented in Sect. 7 are independent of the tweak schedule. Hence, the related-domain distinguishing attack applies both to FF3 and to FF3-1.

2.1 Our Notations

Throughout the paper we use several notations related to FF3: We use the term plaintexts and ciphertexts to refer to the inputs and outputs of 8-round FF3. As our attacks are usually mounted on 4-round FF3, we use the term inputs and outputs to denote those.

In addition, a plaintext is $P = (L_0, R_0)$, where the values after the ith round are (L_i, R_i), i.e., the ciphertext are (L_8, R_8). We use $LH(\cdot)$ to denote the left half of a value, and similarly $RH(\cdot)$ to denote the right half of a value.

The notation $\binom{n}{2}$ is the binomial coefficients for n choose 2, which is the number of possible pairs in a group of size x.

3 Previous Attacks

We now describe the previously published attacks against FF3. We note that they exploit the relatively small size of the input domain, and do not attempt to recover the 128-bit cryptographic key of the AES function. Consequently, their complexity is stated as a function of the scheme's domain size (which is N^2 when $M = N$) rather than as a function of the key size.

3.1 A Message Recovery Attack [1]

The first work analyzing FF3 is by Bellare, Hoang, and Tessaro [1]. The proposed attack is a message recovery attack for small domain sizes. The attack takes $3 \cdot 24 \cdot (n+4) \cdot 2^{6n}$ data to attack FF3 with $2n$-bit blocks (where each triplet is encrypted using a single tweak value). It is based on a simple differential distinguisher—given an input difference $(x, 0)$ the output difference is also $(x, 0)$ with a slightly higher probability than the expected probability (which is $1/(2^{2n} - 1)$).

The differential characteristic is quite straightforward. Given an input difference $(x, 0)$, the first round maintains the $(x, 0)$ difference with probability 1. The second round has a non-zero input difference, but with probability 2^{-n} (or $1/M$ of M if not a power of 2) the round function which is a PRF has an output difference of 0. This is an iterative differential, which suggests that the plaintext difference $(x, 0)$ becomes the ciphertext difference $(x, 0)$ with probability $1/(2^{2n} - 1) + 2^{-4n}$ for the 8-round FF3.

The attack is given a plaintext $X' = (L', R)$ and tries to recover the plaintext $X = (L, R)$ for some unknown $L \neq L'$. This is done by asking for the encryption of (X, X') under many different tweaks (the adversary in this scenario does not know X but can still obtain the corresponding ciphertexts). The differential characteristic suggests that the difference of the left half of the ciphertexts is equal to the difference in the left half of the plaintexts. As the ciphertexts can be observed, the adversary can compute the ciphertext difference. Since the input X' is known to the adversary, then the value of the left half of X can be recovered.

A similar idea can be used to recover the right hand side. The main difference is that only ciphertexts for which the left halves agree are used in the counting process (as the differential characteristic in use is based on the left hand side). The two attacks can be combined to recover an unknown X by probing its ciphertext together with two related plaintexts X' and X^* under many tweaks. Using the relation between X and X' one can recover its left half, and using the between X and X^* one can recover the right half.

3.2 A First Generation Related-Tweak Slide and PRF Recovery [12]

The original idea of the related-tweak slide attack was proposed at Crypto'17 by Durak and Vaudenay [12]. It can reconstruct the full table of $AES_K(x)$ for different inputs and for a given tweak, allowing the encryption/decryption of all plaintexts/ciphertexts with that tweak (and in some cases even under additional tweaks which are related to the original tweak).

The attack itself uses $O(N^{11/6})$ adaptive chosen plaintexts (for domains of size $N \times N$) which are encrypted under two tweaks: $T = T_L || T_R$ and $T' = T_L \oplus 4 || T_R \oplus 4$. As seen in Fig. 1, for the same key, if one can write the 8-round encryption under K with the tweak T as $g \circ f$ (each of 4 rounds), then the encryption under K with the tweak T' is equal to $f \circ g$.

As a result, if a plaintext P is partially encrypted under f (the first four rounds of the encryption under K and T) into P', then its corresponding ciphertext, C is equal to the evaluation of g on P'. This property continues (as C', the ciphertext corresponding to P' is the result of applying f to C), and allows constructing long slid chains, as suggested by Furuya [16]. For such a slid chain, the adversary is left with attacking a 4-round Feistel construction, for which

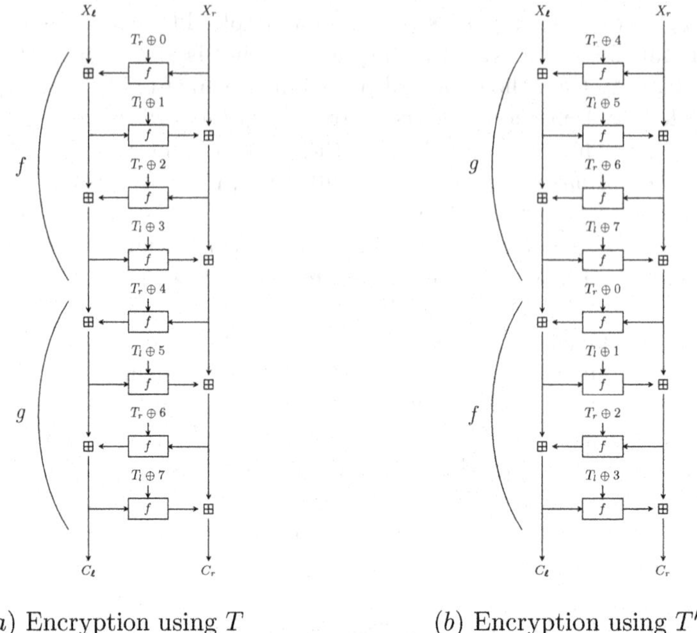

(a) Encryption using T (b) Encryption using T'

Fig. 1. Encryption under related-tweaks

Durak and Vaudenay present a known plaintext attack with $O(N^{10/6})$ data and $O(N^3)$ time.[3]

The attack algorithm, given in Algorithm 2 is as follows: First,[4] $N^{1/6}$ possible chains of $2N^{10/6}$ values are generated by picking a random x_0^i value, and iteratively encrypting it under K, T, i.e., $x_1^i = FF3_{K,T}(x_0^i)$, $x_2^i = FF3_{K,T}(x_1^i), \ldots$. Similarly, $N^{1/6}$ chains of $2N^{10/6}$ values are generated from random y_0^i values, iteratively encrypted under K, T', i.e., $y_1^i = FF3_{K,T'}(y_0^i)$, $y_2^i = FF3_{K,T'}(y_1^i), \ldots$.

Then, the attack tries each pair of starting points (x_0^i, y_t^j) (for all possible i, j, and $0 \leq t \leq N^{10/6}$) as if they constitute the beginning of a slid chains. If indeed x_0^i and y_s^t are slid pairs (which suggests that $f(x_0^i) = y_t^j$) then so are the rest of the chain (i.e., $f(x_s^i) = y_{t+s}^j$). Hence, the adversary obtains at least N pairs of values for the recovery attack. If the recovery attack succeeds, then the considered chains were indeed slid chains (not that it matters, as the recovery part succeeded). Similarly, the attack can be applied against $g(\cdot)$ with the corresponding changes.

---

[3] There are other reconstruction attacks against Feistel ciphers, such as [20] or [6], but these usually require a chosen plaintext attack scenario, whereas in this case, a known plaintext attack is needed.

[4] We alert the reader that [12, Sect. 5] suggests that $\sqrt{N}$ chains of length $2N$ values are needed. However, given that the function recovery attack needs $N^{10/6}$ known plaintexts, then we report, similarly to [17] the correct values.

Algorithm 2: The Basic Attack algorithm on FF3 by Durak and Vaudenay [12]

```
Pick at random N^{1/6} values x_0^i. Pick at random N^{1/6} values y_0^i. for all 1 ≤ i ≤ N^{1/6} do
    for j = 0 to 2N^{10/6} − 1 do
        Compute x_{j+1}^i = FF3_{K,T}(x_j^i) Compute y_{j+1}^i = FF3_{K,T}(y_j^i)
for all 1 ≤ i ≤ N^{1/6} do
    for all 1 ≤ j ≤ N^{1/6} do
        for all 0 ≤ t ≤ N^{10/6} do
            Assume that (x_0^i, y_t^j) generate slid chains.
            Call the Function Recovery attack on f with (x_0^i, y_t^j).
```

The function recovery attack is based on trying to recover the input/output values for 4-round Feistel (each with a different round function). Specifically, let the input/output of the 4-round FF3 be denoted by (L_0, R_0) and (L_3, R_4), respectively, then this input/output pair defines four input/output pairs to the corresponding round function. We follow previous work (and the description of [13]) and do not perform the swap after each Feistel round):

$$\begin{aligned} L_1 &= L_0 + F_0(R_0) \\ R_2 &= R_0 + F_1(L_1) \\ L_3 &= L_1 + F_2(R_2) \\ R_4 &= R_2 + F_3(L_3) \end{aligned}$$

where the F_i represent the keyed and tweaked round function.

The recovery attack starts with $N^{3/2+1/2L}$, for a parameter L set to 3, input/output pairs $((L_0^i, R_0^i), (L_3^i, R_4^i))$ with equal L_3, i.e., $L_3^i = L_3^j$ (for which there is no difference in the input or output of $F_3(\cdot)$) and with the right hand difference $R_4^i - R_4^j = R_0^i - R_0^j$. Furthermore, a set of *good pairs* is defined as pairs for which $L_1^i = L_1^j$. For these pairs

$$F_0(R_0^j) - F_0(R_0^i) = L_0^j - L_0^i \tag{1}$$

holds as well. In other words, for the good pairs, one obtains information about the outputs of $F_0(\cdot)$.[5]

Now, the attack tries to identify the good pairs using the following idea: Let the set of vertices be all the pairs for which $L_3^i = L_3^j$. A directed edge (i, j) is added to the graph if $L_3^i = L_0^j$ with the label $L_0^j - L_0^i$. The graph has cycles in

[5] We alert the reader that there are multiple solutions to the problem of recovering F_0, F_1, F_2, F_3. However, by fixing one value for F_0 (or any other F_i), the solution becomes unique.

it if the sum of labels on the edges is zero (as $\sum_{(i,j)\in cycle} L_0^j - L_0^i = 0$). If the cycle is composed only of good pairs, then we also obtain information about the outputs of F_0 (as the label on the edges that sum to zero is also the output of the round function F_0, following Eq. 1).

Hence, the attack tries to find such cycles of length L. Each R_0 input that appears in such cycles can then be part of the reconstruction phase, and thus we need all of them to be covered (i.e., appear in the graph). Moreover, we need that any R_0 input value will be connected (possibly via different cycles) to any other R_0 input value (as Eq. 1 is differential in nature). Once enough inputs to F_0 are present, one can assign one output F_0 arbitrarily (which defines all the other outputs). Once F_0 is (partially) recovered, the attack needs to recover F_1, F_2, F_3, which is a much simpler problem (which is solved either by Patarin's attack [21] and/or ideas very similar to the ones for the 4-round recovery attack). Hence, the adversary takes the largest connected component found in the attack, and runs the 3-round attack for the values that can be recovered (if the 3-round attack fails, then at least one of the values is wrong).

Given $O(N^{3/2+1/2L})$ known plaintexts, we expect $O(N^{3+1/L})$ pairs, out of which $O(N^{1+1/L})$ satisfy the differential conditions (zero difference in the left half of the ciphertext and the input of the right half of the plaintext equal to that of the ciphertext). Hence from any of $O(N)$ vertices, we expect about $O(N^{1/L})$ edges. In their analysis, Durak and Vaudenay show that a cycle of length $L = 3$ is sufficient. To detect these cycles, they just use the Floyd-Warshall algorithm [15] that takes $O(N^3)$ for $L = 3$.

Finally, Durak and Vaudenay noted that there is a non-trivial tradeoff between the number of vertices/edges in the graph and the success rate: If there are too few edges (i.e., too little pairs to begin with), then the chance that F_0 is recovered is small (as there are only small connected components). On the other hand, if there are too many edges, then besides the cycles of good pairs, we expect to find many cycles of bad pairs as well (which cause the failure of the recovery attack and waste time).

3.3 A Second Generation Related-Tweak Slide and PRF Recovery [17]

The attack of Hoang, Miller and Trieu [17] improves the attack of Durak and Vaudenay using two main ideas: The first idea is to improve the detection of slid chains. The second idea is an improved (and more suitable) cycles detection algorithm, which allows for better complexity.

The improved detection of slid pairs is done using the ideas presented in [4] of identifying the respective offset of a slide using a differential distinguisher (which were further developed in [5]). They rely on the existence of a bias in the probability of the differential characteristics $(x, 0) \to (x, 0)$, as for the correct shift between the chains, the number of pairs with input difference $(x, 0)$ having ciphertext difference $(x, 0)$ is higher than when the shift is wrong.

Hence, the slid chains are identified not by running an attack but rather by an auxiliary distinguisher. Instead of running the full recovery attack for each possible slid chains and possible offsets, the attack is repeated fewer times (about $O(N)$ for the parameters considered in [17]).

The combination of the slide with the differential is as follows: Collect $O(N^{1/6})$ chains of length $O(N^{5/3})$ each under T and under T'. For each pair of candidate slid chains (and respective offset) check whether the differential distinguisher succeeds, namely, check whether the input difference $(x, 0)$ leads to the output difference $(x, ?)$ with probability of $(2N-1)/N^2$ which is about twice as high as for the random case.

The distinguisher accepts m candidate input/output pairs (the inputs encrypted under T and the outputs under T'). These m input values are then divided into d bins according to the value of R_0^i. In each bin, all the inputs have the same value in the right hand side, and thus, input difference of 0 in that half. We note that bins with many such values offer many pairs, and thus can be used for the next step of the attack. For each bin with many inputs, the distinguisher checks how many times the difference in the left half of the inputs is equal to the difference in the left half of the outputs. The threshold was chosen to be $1/5 \cdot \frac{2N-1}{N^2} + 4/5 \cdot \frac{N}{N^2-1}$ of the number of candidate pairs.

We note that this threshold was chosen so that the probability of right slid chains to fail is negligible (i.e., $O(1/\sqrt{N})$) and that chance for a random permutation to pass the distinguisher is also $O(1/\sqrt{N})$. The latter claim is obtained using Chebyshev's inequality that suggests that the probability that the counter is k standard deviations larger than the mean value is at most $1/k^2$. The standard deviation is then upper bounded using the Cauchy-Schwartz inequality based on the sizes of the different bins.

The chains in use are of length $O(N^{5/6})$ and as in Durak and Vaudenay's attack one needs to consider $O(N^2)$ possible pairs of chains and corresponding offsets. Moreover, for each such possible chains and offsets, one can apply the same distinguisher for the last four rounds of FF3 (i.e., treating the outputs as inputs to four round FF3). Hence, a wrong chain/offset is expected to pass the two distinguishers with probability of at most $O(1/N)$. The time complexity of this part is $O(N^{17/6})$ and it dominates the running time of the attack.

The second idea is to offer a better PRF reconstruction attack that runs in time $O(N^{5/3})$ instead of Durak and Vaudenay's original $O(N^3)$. As it targets cycles of length 3, the *Triangle-Finding* algorithm puts the input/output pairs in a hash table indexed by $L_3^i \oplus L_0^i || R_0^i$. Any collision in the table offers a pair of input/output pairs

$$((L_0^i, R_0^i), (L_3^i, R_4^i)), ((L_0^j, R_0^j), (L_3^j, R_4^j))$$

Each of them has an edge in the graph.

The attack then starts from an edge in the graph. This edge defines the two nodes which are connected. In the case of a triangle, the two nodes define the requirement from the third node (as the sum of the labels is 0). Hence, it is a simple matter to check whether there is such a third node in the data, i.e., whether the edge the attack starts from is indeed part of a good triangle.

As the attack is repeated $O(N)$ times, and takes $O(N^{5/3})$, this part of the attack takes $O(N^{8/3})$ time in total.

4 Improved Attacks on FF3

Similarly to Hoang et al.'s attack, our attack uses two subroutines: Identification of the correct slid chains and a PRF reconstruction phase. We offer three methods to identify the correct slid chains: The first method follows Hoang et al.'s approach which we call symmetric slide attack. Our improved version uses $\tilde{O}(N^{7/4})$ data and $\tilde{O}(N^{5/2})$ time, and is described in Sect. 4.1. We also extend this distinguisher with a time-memory tradeoff attack for which $\tilde{O}(N^{7/4-t})$ data is used with time of $\tilde{O}(N^{5/2+2t})$ for $t \in [0, 1/4]$. The second method, described in Sect. 4.2, uses a cyclic structure of slid pairs (as proposed in [4]), resulting in data and time complexities of $O(N^2)$. The third method uses an asymmetric slide attack, it also offers a time-data tradeoff with $\tilde{O}(N^{2-t})$ data and $\tilde{O}(N^{2+t})$ running time. Its memory complexity is $\tilde{O}(N^2)$, and is described in Sect. 4.3.

The PRF reconstruction, described in Sect. 4.4, is the same for all slid chain identification variants. Our PRF reconstruction procedure follows the same general idea suggested by [12,17], i.e., based on cycles. At the same time, we introduce a meet in the middle approach to the recovery itself, which significantly reduces its running time, thus allowing the use of larger cycles (which results in reducing the data, and hence, the time complexities).

4.1 Symmetric Slide Attack

In this attack, our data is composed of 2 sets of $\tilde{O}(N^{1/4})$ chains, each containing $\tilde{O}(N^{3/2})$ plaintexts. Similarly to [12,17], the first set of chains are encrypted under K and T and the second set is encrypted under K and T'.

We iterate over all $\tilde{O}(N^{1/2})$ pairs of chains created by taking a chain from each set. For each such pair of chains, we slid the first chain across the second one for $\tilde{O}(N^{3/2})$ different offsets. For each of the $\tilde{O}(N^2)$ resulting offsets, we utilize a distinguishing attack to checking whether the candidate slid chains (with offset) corresponds to 4 rounds of FF3 or not.

Actually, the distinguisher we use is very similar in nature to that of [17]. We rely on the fact that the truncated differential characteristic $(x, 0) \to (x, ?)$ for 4-round FF3 has probability of about $2/N$ rather than $1/N$ for the random case. Unlike [17] that divided the datasets between bins (according to the x value) and counted how many of them had "more pairs than expected in the random case", we argue that a single counter is sufficient (and more efficient). Namely, given m pairs with input difference $(x, 0)$ we expect $2m/N$ pairs with output difference $(x, ?)$ (compared with m/N for a random permutation).

The number of pairs that follow the truncated differential is distributed according to the Poisson distribution. Hence, $m = O(N \log(N)) = \tilde{O}(N)$ is sufficient to distinguish between the two distributions—one Poisson distribution with parameter $\lambda = m/N$ and another with parameter $\lambda = 2m/N$.

The above fact can also be explained by the following probabilistic explanation: Each pair with the required input difference has probability of about $2/N$ for 4-round FF3 or $1/N$ for a random permutation to have the required output difference. Hence, we can assign an indicator variable to whether a given pair satisfies the differential. As all the indicators are independent (recall that 4-round Feistel is a PRP [18]) we can use the Chernoff bound: For the random permutation, the probability that the sum of indicators (which in our case corresponds to the number of pairs that satisfy the differential) is greater than $(1+\delta)m/N$ is no more than $(e^{\delta}/(1+\delta)^{1+\delta})^{m/N}$. For $m = c \cdot N \log N$ this bound is $(e^{\delta}/(1+\delta))^{c}$. Setting $\delta = 0.5$ this upper bound becomes $0.897^{c \cdot \log N}$. For example, taking $c > 5$ means that less than $1/\sqrt{N}$ of the sums of indicators for random permutations are greater than $1.5 \cdot 5 \cdot \log N$. The optimal threshold between the two distributions can be found either experimentally or by analyzing the Poisson distribution.

We note that similarly to [17], we can run the distinguisher twice: Once for the first 4 rounds, and another time for the second 4 rounds. Hence, the probability of a wrong slid chain to pass the distinguisher is less than $1/N$.

In contrast, for a 4-round FF3, the mean value for the sum of indicators is $2 \cdot c \log N$. Again, the number of right pairs is expected to be higher than $1.5 \cdot c \log N$ with high probability. This again can be achieved by a Chernoff analysis or by studying the Poisson distribution. However, as mentioned before, it is sufficient to set the threshold based on experiments (which confirm the Poisson distribution).

The attack follows the footsteps of [17], but with a significantly smaller number of pairs needed for the distinguisher as the statistical significance is larger. Hence, we start by taking $\tilde{O}(N^{1/4})$ chains of length $\tilde{O}(N^{3/2})$ each.

In each such chain, we insert all values (L_0^i, R_0^i) into a hash table according to the value of R_0^i. As there are $\tilde{O}(N^{3/2})$ values in the chain, we expect one of the bins to contain about $\tilde{O}(N^{1/2})$ values, which suggest $\tilde{O}(N)$ pairs, all with input difference $(x, 0)$. In practice, we need to take a constant number of bins.[6]

We take the actual values of L_0^i, and use them as the candidate inputs.

Then for each candidate chain (out of $\tilde{O}(N^{1/4})$ of them) and candidate offset (out of possible $\tilde{O}(N^{3/2})$ offsets) we extract the corresponding $\tilde{O}(N^{1/2})$ values which may serve as the candidate outputs for the above $\tilde{O}(N^{1/2})$ inputs, denoted by $(\hat{L}_3^i, \hat{R}_3^i)$. Then, for each bin, we store in a hash table the values $\hat{L}_3^i - L_0^i$, where each collision suggests a pair of inputs with difference $(x, 0)$ (the right hand zero difference is guaranteed by the way the inputs were chosen) and the corresponding outputs have difference x in the left hand side. Hence, we can test in time $\tilde{O}(N^{1/2})$ whether two chains are slid chains in a given offset.

The resulting algorithm, given in Algorithm 3 takes $\tilde{O}(N^{3/2})$ data and $\tilde{O}(N^{2.5})$ time.

Offering a Time-Data Tradeoff. We can offer a time-data tradeoff for the improved symmetric slide attack. The distinguisher takes $\tilde{O}(N^{7/4-t})$ data and has a running time of $\tilde{O}(N^{5/2+2t})$ for $t \in [0, 1/4]$.

The attack is based on taking shorter chains as in [17], but more of them. Given that the chains are shorter (of length $\tilde{O}(N^{3/2-2t})$) we need to collect plaintexts from N^{4t} bins to obtain enough pairs for the distinguisher. Then,

[6] Taking the 8 largest bins is empirically shown to suffice.

Algorithm 3: Improved Symmetric Slide Distinguisher for FF3

Input : $\tilde{O}(N^{1/4})$ chains C^r of $\tilde{O}(N^{3/2})$ plaintexts encrypted under K and $T = T_L||T_R$

Input : $\tilde{O}(N^{1/4})$ chains $\hat{C}^s$ of $\tilde{O}(N^{3/2})$ plaintexts encrypted under K and $T' = T_L \oplus 4||T_R \oplus 4$

Output: Slid chains $C^i, \hat{C}^j$ and their respective offset

for *all chains* C^r **do**
    Initialize a hash table H_1
    Insert all the plaintexts $(L_0^i, R_0^i) \in C^r$ into H_1 indexed by R_0^i
    Take a constant number d of bins (each with $O(\sqrt{N})$ plaintexts)
    Denote the plaintexts by $X_{i_1}, X_{i_2}, \ldots, X_{i_v}$
    for *all chains* $\hat{C}^s$ **do**
        for *all respective offsets* $u = 0, \ldots, N^{3/2}$ **do**
            Extract $(\hat{L}_0^{u+i_1}, \hat{R}_0^{u+i_1}), (\hat{L}_0^{u+i_2}, \hat{R}_0^{u+i_2}), \ldots, (\hat{L}_0^{u+i_v}, \hat{R}_0^{u+i_v})$ from $\hat{C}^s$
            Denote these values as "ciphertexts" $C_{i_1}, C_{i_2}, \ldots, C_{i_v}$
            Initialize d hash tables H_2^j
            for *all* k*=1,...,*v **do**
                if X_{i_k} *is from bin* j **then**
                    Store in H_2^j the value $LH(C_{i_k}) - LH(X_{i_k})$
            Count the number of collisions in all H_2^j
            if *number of collisions is greater than* $\frac{1.6}{N} \cdot \Sigma_{B \in bins} \binom{|B|}{2}$ **then**
                Call the PRF-recovery procedure with C^r as inputs and $\hat{C}^s$ shifted by u as the outputs.

---

when we process the second chain, we only consider a pair of outputs if they correspond to plaintexts from the same bin.

Repeating the above analysis shows that each step has to deal with shorter chains, but repeated more times. The result is indeed an attack whose data complexity is $\tilde{O}(N^{7/4-t})$ data and has a running time of $\tilde{O}(N^{5/2+2t})$ for $t \in [0, 1/4]$. The resulting algorithm is given in Algorithm 4.

The extreme case, with the minimal amount of data $\tilde{O}(N^{3/2})$, uses all the bins. The resulting attack uses $\tilde{O}(N^{1/2})$ chains of length $\tilde{O}(N)$. For each such chain, we insert all the plaintexts into a hash table indexed by the value of R_0^i, identify the $\tilde{O}(N)$ pairs (out of $\tilde{O}(N^2)$ possible ones) with input difference $(x, 0)$. Then, for any candidate chain counterpart (and any of the $\tilde{O}(N)$ possible offsets), we take the $\tilde{O}(N)$ corresponding values as ciphertexts, and check how many times the output differences are indeed x in the left half.

In other words, for each pair of candidate slid chains and offset, we just collect all the $\tilde{O}(N)$ pairs of inputs with difference $(x, 0)$ and test whether the corresponding outputs have difference x with the bias predicted for 4-round FF3. Identifying the pairs can be done in time $\tilde{O}(N)$ using a hash table. Hence, as there are $\tilde{O}(N)$ pairs of slid chains, each with $\tilde{O}(N)$ possible offsets, the total running time of the distinguisher is $\tilde{O}(N^3)$.

There are two technical details to note: First, the PRF reconstruction attack described in Sect. 4.4 requires $\tilde{O}(N^{3/2})$ input/output pairs for the 4-round FF3 construction. As a result, in attacks that use shorter chains, we need to ask for the extension of the identified slid chains. Luckily, in an adaptive chosen plaintext and ciphertext attack scenario, that merely means we need to ask for at most two chains of $\tilde{O}(N^{3/2})$.

Second, while previous distinguishing attacks were sufficiently good when the probability of a wrong chain to pose a slid chain was $1/\sqrt{N}$, we need a better filter. This filter is needed as to avoid the increase in the data complexity explained earlier. Hence, we need to ask that the probability of a wrong candidate to pass the distinguisher is no more than $(1/N^{1-t})$. The distinguisher can be applied twice, and thus out of the N^2 wrong slid chains/offsets, we get $\tilde{O}(N^{2t})$ candidate slid chains. This is sufficient to ensure the complete attack does not use more than $\tilde{O}(N^{7/4-t})$ data and $O(N^{5/2+2t})$ time.

Algorithm 4: Time-Data Tradeoff Variant of the Symmetric Slide for FF3

Input : $\tilde{O}(N^{1/4+t})$ chains C^r of $\tilde{O}(N^{3/2-2t})$ plaintexts encrypted under K and $T = T_L||T_R$

Input : $\tilde{O}(N^{1/4+t})$ chains $\hat{C}^s$ of $\tilde{O}(N^{3/2-2t})$ plaintexts encrypted under K and $T' = T_L \oplus 4||T_R \oplus 4$

Output: Slid chains $C^i, \hat{C}^j$ and their respective offset

for *all chains* C^r **do**
- Initialize a hash table H_1
- Insert all the plaintexts $(L_0^i, R_0^i) \in C^r$ into H_1 indexed by R_0^i
- Take $O(N^{4t})$ bins (each with $O(N^{1/2-2t}$ plaintexts)
- Denote the plaintexts by $X_{i_1}, X_{i_2}, \ldots, X_{i_v}$
- **for** *all chains* $\hat{C}^s$ **do**
  - **for** *all respective offsets* $u = 0, \ldots, N^{3/2-2t}$ **do**
    - Extract $(\hat{L}_0^{u+i_1}, \hat{R}_0^{u+i_1})$, $(\hat{L}_0^{u+i_2}, \hat{R}_0^{u+i_2})$,..., $(\hat{L}_0^{u+i_v}, \hat{R}_0^{u+i_v})$ from $\hat{C}^s$
    - Denote these values as "ciphertexts" $C_{i_1}, C_{i_2}, \ldots, C_{i_v}$
    - Initialize $O(N^{4t})$ hash tables H_2^j
    - **for** *all k=1,...,v* **do**
      - **if** X_{i_k} *is from bin* j **then**
        - Store in H_2^j the value $LH(C_{i_k}) - LH(X_{i_k})$
    - Count the number of collisions in all H_2^j
    - **if** *number of collisions is greater than* $\frac{1.6}{N} \cdot \Sigma_{B \in bins} \binom{|B|}{2}$ **then**
      - Ask for the extension of C^r and $\hat{C}^s$ to $\tilde{O}(N^{3/2})$ values.
      - Call the PRF-recovery procedure with C^r as inputs and $\hat{C}^s$ shifted by u as the outputs.

4.2 Cycle Structure Attack

The second attack follows the footsteps of [4] to find candidate slid chains. Consider a related-tweak slid pair (L_0, R_0) and $(\hat{L}_0, \hat{R}_0)$, i.e., 4-round FF3 with the key K and T partially encrypts (L_0, R_0) into $(\hat{L}_0, \hat{R}_0)$. If we start a chain of encryption from (L_0, R_0), we are assured to reach (L_0, R_0) again after some number of encryptions $t \leq N^2$. Due to the slid property, the same is true also for $(\hat{L}_0, \hat{R}_0)$, i.e., after t encryptions under K and T', we are assured to reach $(\hat{L}_0, \hat{R}_0)$ again. It is easy to see that this value does not repeat before t encryptions (as otherwise, (L_0, R_0) would also close the chain earlier). Hence, there is no point to check whether two chains can be slid chains, if their cycle length is not equal.

The attack thus tries to find chains which are actually cycles, of length $\tilde{O}(N^{3/2})$ (as this is the amount of data needed for the PRF reconstruction). We note that following Shepp and Lloyd's results [23] it is reasonable to assume that (a) such a cycle exists, and (b) that it is unique. Of course, if by chance the unlikely event happens, and there are two cycles in the encryption under K and T of exactly the same length of $\tilde{O}(N^{3/2})$, we can just try all pairs of chains, or just take the next larger cycle.

Once this pair of cycles is identified, one can run the distinguisher used before for all possible $\tilde{O}(N^{3/2})$ offsets. As the cost of the distinguisher is $\tilde{O}(N^{1/2})$, the total time complexity needed to identify the exact offset between the chains is $\tilde{O}(N^2)$. When the correct offset is identified, it is possible to run the PRF reconstruction attack as we have obtained $\tilde{O}(N^{3/2})$ input/output pairs for 4-round FF3.

Given that the PRF reconstruction takes $\tilde{O}(N^{3/2})$ time, we can call it at most $\tilde{O}(\sqrt{N})$ times. This requires that the filtering is set such that the probability of a random permutation to pass the threshold be below $\tilde{O}(1/\sqrt{N})$ (as the distinguisher can be applied twice in each offset, this rate is sufficient to discard all but a fraction of $\tilde{O}(1/N)$ of the wrong offsets).

The data complexity of the attack is about $O(N^2)$ encryptions: An adaptive chosen-plaintext attack would be based on picking a random plaintext, generating a cycle from it, and then, check whether the cycle has the right length. If not, an unseen plaintext needs to be picked, and the process is repeated. It is easy to see that the process is expected to finish after exploring almost all plaintexts (as most of the values lie in the larger cycles, e.g., the largest one of size about $(1 - 1/e) \cdot N^2$). A simple analysis suggests that about $\tilde{O}(N^{3/2})$ of the values remain "unseen" once the cycle of length $\tilde{O}(N^{3/2})$ is identified.

Another approach is to collect $N^2 - \sqrt{N}$ known plaintext pairs. If all the values in the cycle of length $\tilde{O}(N^{3/2})$ are not in the missing $\sqrt{N}$ ones, which happens with constant probability, then the cycle can be identified and used for the attack.

Hence, to conclude, this first phase of the attack (for the detection of slid pairs) takes data $O(N^2)$ and time $\tilde{O}(N^2)$. The resulting attack algorithm is given in Algorithm 5 (we describe the known plaintext variant, but it is very similar to the adaptive chosen plaintext one).

Algorithm 5: The Cycle Structure Slide Distinguisher for FF3

Input : $N^2 - N$ known plaintexts (P^i, C^i) encrypted under K and $T = T_L || T_R$
Input : $N^2 - N$ known plaintexts $(\hat{P}^i, \hat{C}^i)$ encrypted under K and $T' = T_L \oplus 4 || T_R \oplus 4$
Output: Slid chains $C, \hat{C}$

Initialize a bitmap B of N^2 bits to 0.
while *no cycle C of size $\tilde{O}(N^{3/2})$ was found* **do**
    Pick the first plaintext whose bit is not set in B — P_0.
    Set $B[P_0] = 1$, Set $t = 0$
    repeat
        Set $P_{t+1} = C_t (= E_{K,T}(P_t))$
        if *P_{t+1} is not in the dataset* **then**
            break (goto 2)
        Set $B[P_{t+1}] = 1$; Set $t = t + 1$
    until $P_t = P_0$;
    if $t = \tilde{O}(N^{3/2})$ **then**
        Set C to be $P_0, P_1, \ldots, P_{t-1}$

Initialize a bitmap B of N^2 bits to 0.
while *no cycle $\hat{C}$ of size t was found* **do**
    Pick the first plaintext whose bit is not set in B — $\hat{P}_0$.
    Set $B[\hat{P}_0] = 1$, Set $s = 0$
    repeat
        Set $\hat{P}_{s+1} = \hat{C}_s (= E_{K,T}(\hat{P}_s))$
        if *$\hat{P}_{s+1}$ is not in the dataset* **then**
            break (goto 2)
        Set $B[\hat{P}_{s+1}] = 1$; Set $s = s + 1$
    until $\hat{P}_s = \hat{P}_0$;
    Set $\hat{C}$ to be $\hat{P}_0, \hat{P}_1, \ldots, \hat{P}_{t-1}$

for *all possible offsets* **do**
    Call the differential distinguisher for any offset between C and $\hat{C}$
    if *the distinguisher succeeds* **then**
        Call the PRF reconstruction attack with C,$\hat{C}$, and the offset

4.3 Asymmetric Slide Attack

The new attack follows the footsteps of the low data distinguisher presented in Sect. 4.1, but offers an improved distinguishing algorithm as well as a tradeoff curve. The data and memory complexity of the attack is $\tilde{O}(N^{2-t})$ with time complexity $\tilde{O}(N^{2+t})$ for $t \in [0, 1/2]$.

This related-tweak slide differential distinguisher uses the minimal amount of pairs ($O(N \log N)$) similarly to the one of Sect. 4.1. The key element in it is the algorithmic gain, coming from searching the pairs from *the plaintext's side.*

Consider an input chain of $\tilde{O}(N)$ values. We preprocess the chain by computing for each of the $\tilde{O}(N)$ input pairs with a common right half P_i, P_j the value $LH(P_j) - LH(P_i), j - i$ and storing it in a hash table. In other words, we store for each pair the difference in the left half and the location difference. To prepare this table, we need $\tilde{O}(N)$ memory, where each cell contains about $\tilde{O}(1)$ values.[7] The table can be calculated in $\tilde{O}(N)$ time by using a supporting hash table keyed according to the right-hand-side of the plaintexts.

From the output side, we take a chain of length $\tilde{O}(N)$. We initialize $\tilde{O}(N)$ counters to zero. Then, we can compute for each such pair $(C_{i'}, C_{j'})$ the value $(LH(C_{j'}) - LH(C_{i'}), j' - i')$, and find the offset it proposes in the table. We then increment the $\tilde{O}(1)$ counters related to the offset.[8] For the correct offset the amount of pairs that "succeed" is expected to be $2m/N$ out of m pairs, compared with m/N for wrong offsets (or wrong chains). If the preprocessed input chains are all keyed into the same hash table, this search can be done simultaneously against all $\tilde{O}(N^{1-t})$ of them, taking only $\tilde{O}(N^2)$ time per output chain.

The attack is thus based on taking $\tilde{O}(N^t)$ output chains of length $\tilde{O}(N)$ and $\tilde{O}(N^{1-t})$ input chains of length $\tilde{O}(N)$. For each input chain we perform $\tilde{O}(N)$ preprocessing. Then we try $\tilde{O}(N^t)$ chains in time $\tilde{O}(N^{2+t})$, i.e., a time of $\tilde{O}(N^2)$ per output chain. This results in time complexity of N^{2+t} and data complexity which is $\max\{\tilde{O}(N^{1+t}), \tilde{O}(N^{2-t})\}$ (which if $t \in [0, 1/2]$ suggests $\tilde{O}(N^{2-t})$. The memory complexity is comprised of $\tilde{O}(N^{1-t})$ preprocessed plaintext tables of size $\tilde{O}(N)$ each, meaning $\tilde{O}(N^{2-t})$ in total (the amount of counters in the in the sliding part of the attack is also $\tilde{O}(N^{2-t})$).

The full attack algorithm is given in Algorithm 6.

4.4 The PRF Reconstruction Procedure

Our PRF reconstruction procedure follows the foot steps of Durak and Vaudenay and of Hoang et al. We use a graph where cycles are searched for. We follow Hoang et al.'s approach, and call the PRF reconstruction fewer times than there are candidate slid chains. However, to reduce the data and time complexities of our attack (which is needed as our slid chain detection is more efficient) we use cycles of larger size, i.e., we pick $L = 4$ and $L = 5$ rather than $L = 3$.

This means that for finding sufficiently large connected component between all the values, it is sufficient that from any node in the graph, there will be only $\tilde{O}(N^{1/L})$ outgoing edges (instead of $\tilde{O}(N^{1/3})$ needed for $L = 3$).

Hence, we are left with the problem of finding cycles of length L in a graph of $\tilde{O}(N)$ nodes, with an average out degree of $\tilde{O}(N^{1/L})$. Our algorithm just

[7] The number of actual values per cell follows a Poisson distribution, i.e., there may be a few cells with $\tilde{O}(\log N)$ values.

[8] We note that the table is expected to have 1 value on average in each cell. However, the actual number is distributed according to a Poisson distribution with this mean. Hence, some cells will be empty, and a few will have several possible offsets. When there are multiple offsets, we just increment all the counters corresponding to the offsets.

Algorithm 6: The Asymmetric Slide Distinguisher for FF3

Input : $\tilde{O}(N^{1-t})$ chains C^r of $q = \tilde{O}(N)$ plaintexts encrypted under K and $T = T_L||T_R$
Input : $\tilde{O}(N^t)$ chains $\hat{C}^s$ of $q = \tilde{O}(N)$ plaintexts encrypted under K and $T' = T_L \oplus 4||T_R \oplus 4$
Output: Slid chains $C^i, \hat{C}^j$ and their respective offset

Initialize a hash table H_1
for *all chains* $C_k^r \in C^r$ **do**
  for *all* i, j *where* $R_k^j = R_k^i$ **do**
    Store in H_1 in location $(j - i, L_k^j - L_k^i)$ the value (k, i)
for *all chains* $\hat{C}_{k'}^s \in \hat{C}^s$ **do**
  Initialize $\tilde{O}(N^{2-t})$ counters
  for *all* $i' = 0, 1, \ldots, \tilde{O}(N)$ **do**
    for *all* $j' = i' + 1, i' + 2, \ldots, \tilde{O}(N)$ **do**
      for *all* $k, i \in H_1[j' - i', L_{k'}^{j'} - L_{k'}^{i'}]$ **do**
        if $i' < i$ **then**
          Increment the counter of chain k and offset $i - i'$
  Identify k, v such that $counter[k][v]$ is maximal
  if $counter[k][v] > 1.6 \cdot \binom{q}{2} \cdot \frac{1}{N^2}$ **then**
    Ask for the extension of C_k^r and $\hat{C}_k^s$ to $\tilde{O}(N^{3/2})$ values.
    Call the PRF reconstruction with the chains $C_k^r, \hat{C}_{k'}^s$, with offset v

performs a simple meet in the middle procedure: From each node we detect all possible $\tilde{O}(N^{1/L})^{\lfloor L/2 \rfloor}$ nodes in distance $\lfloor L/2 \rfloor$, and then detect all the possible $\tilde{O}(N^{1/L})^{\lceil L/2 \rceil}$ nodes in distance minus $\lceil L/2 \rceil$ (i.e., when walking on the reversed edges graph) and find a collision between these sets (which correspond to a cycle of length L).

Similarly to [12,17], once the cycles are found, all the involved nodes are assumed to be good nodes, and they can be used to determine values for F_0. Heuristically, we found out that filling in $1/3 \cdot log(N)\sqrt{N}$ values of F_0 gives a high chance of success for the recovery attack on F_1, F_2, F_3 (exactly as proposed in [17]). If indeed the reconstruction is consistent with the slid chains, then we continue to reconstruct the missing values in F_0 (as we know the full F_1, F_2, F_3), and apply the recovery attack to the second half (i.e., swapping the order of the slid chains w.r.t. input/output).

On the other hand, if the results are inconsistent with the slid chain, we try a different value to start the assignment from (from a different connected component), or try a different slid chain (when there are other candidates). This part is similar to that of [17].

5 Experimental Verification

We implemented all of our attacks and experimentally verified their correctness and success probability. The code and instructions to reproduce our results is available at https://github.com/OhadAm7/FF3-code.

5.1 Experimental Verification of the Symmetric Slide Attack

We experimentally verified the full implementation of the symmetric slide attack (described in Sect. 4.1) for both $t = 0.25$ and $t = \frac{3}{4log(N)}$ (which leads to using 8 bins in the distinguisher). We tested the attacks for various values of $N = 2^n$ (n is half the bit size of the encryption domain) and various cycle sizes L. To calculate each attack's overall success probability for each parameter choice, we repeated the attacks 100 times using different random keys and tweaks. The results can be seen in Table 3 and Table 4.

"PRF Reconstruction" in the following tables denotes the success rate of the PRF Reconstruction subroutine over all calls. "Combined Reconstruction" denotes the rate at which both calls to the PRF Reconstruction subroutine for a single slide succeed, resulting in the full codebook being recovered.

Note that the PRF reconstruction rate for smaller domain sizes is lower than expected. This is due to overlap between the different chains that mean there is a correlation between multiple reconstruction attempts. As we continue trying different chains after failed reconstruction attempts but stop after the first successful one, the reconstruction rate is skewed to lower values.

5.2 Experimental Verification of the Cycle Structure Attack

We also tested the cycle structure attack (described in Sect. 4.2) for various values of $N = 2^n$ and L. These experiments were also repeated 100 times each using random keys and tweaks. The results are presented in Table 5.

Note that the success rate has a slight drop above $N = 2^9$. This is due to runs that fail to find a cycle of length between q and e^2q (where q is some $\widetilde{O}(N^{\frac{3}{2}})$ required for the distinguisher). With our parameters, $e^2q > N^2$ so there is no upper bound, and the probability of finding a cycle is very high. For $N > 2^9$ the probability drops to a constant but lower probability.

5.3 Experimental Verification of the Asymmetric Slide Attack

We also performed experimental verification of the Asymmetric Slide Attack (described in Sect. 4.3). This was tested both for a constant number of ciphertext chains (3) and for $t = 0.5$. We ran both experiments for 100 times each on random keys and tweaks. The results are presented in Table 6 and Table 7, respectively.

Table 3. Symmetric slide attack experiment results (*num bins* = 8.0)

N	L	Queries	Success rate	PRF reconstruction	Combined reconstruction	Distinguisher (cipher)	Distinguisher (Rand)
2^6	3	3679	0.26	0.527	0.286	0.919	1.0
2^7	3	12631	0.35	0.798	0.614	0.891	1.0
2^8	3	41578	0.37	0.963	0.925	0.93	1.0
2^9	3	203414	0.79	1.0	1.0	0.952	1.0
2^{10}	3	695431	0.76	1.0	1.0	1.0	1.0
2^6	4	3679	0.12	0.34	0.128	0.922	1.0
2^7	4	12631	0.14	0.484	0.226	0.912	1.0
2^8	4	41546	0.22	0.744	0.564	0.929	1.0
2^9	4	201246	0.75	0.963	0.926	0.953	1.0
2^{10}	4	670125	0.75	1.0	1.0	1.0	1.0
2^6	5	3679	0.0	0.042	0.0	0.922	1.0
2^7	5	12631	0.0	0.07	0.0	0.901	1.0
2^8	5	41546	0.0	0.025	0.0	0.93	1.0
2^9	5	201246	0.02	0.182	0.015	0.971	1.0
2^{10}	5	670125	0.31	0.557	0.32	1.0	1.0

Table 4. Symmetric slide attack experiment results ($t = 0.25$)

N	L	Queries	Success rate	PRF reconstruction	Combined reconstruction	Distinguisher (cipher)	Distinguisher (Rand)
2^6	3	3608	0.24	0.53	0.242	0.915	0.999
2^7	3	13472	0.49	0.765	0.59	0.896	0.999
2^8	3	48432	0.66	0.971	0.943	0.928	1.0
2^9	3	173349	0.69	1.0	1.0	0.921	1.0
2^{10}	3	594010	0.73	1.0	1.0	1.0	1.0
2^6	4	3492	0.11	0.283	0.096	0.909	0.998
2^7	4	12932	0.26	0.5	0.255	0.892	0.999
2^8	4	44252	0.5	0.799	0.61	0.924	1.0
2^9	4	154090	0.67	0.965	0.931	0.921	1.0
2^{10}	4	516131	0.74	1.0	1.0	1.0	1.0
2^6	5	3416	0.0	0.031	0.0	0.908	0.999
2^7	5	12438	0.0	0.021	0.0	0.895	0.999
2^8	5	42902	0.0	0.057	0.0	0.929	1.0
2^9	5	150015	0.04	0.163	0.033	0.949	1.0
2^{10}	5	488380	0.31	0.548	0.27	0.984	1.0

Table 5. Cycle structure attack experiment results (*num bins* = 8.0)

N	L	Queries	Success rate	PRF Reconstruction	Combined reconstruction	Distinguisher (cipher)	Distinguisher (Rand)
2^6	3	3851	0.24	0.542	0.289	0.874	1.0
2^7	3	15386	0.61	0.824	0.67	0.929	1.0
2^8	3	60686	0.89	0.954	0.908	0.98	1.0
2^9	3	244674	0.99	1.0	1.0	0.99	1.0
2^{10}	3	948308	0.9	1.0	1.0	0.978	1.0
2^{11}	3	3825251	0.85	1.0	1.0	0.988	1.0
2^{12}	3	16303811	0.86	1.0	1.0	1.0	1.0
2^6	4	3851	0.05	0.307	0.06	0.874	1.0
2^7	4	15386	0.18	0.462	0.198	0.929	1.0
2^8	4	60686	0.7	0.837	0.714	0.98	1.0
2^9	4	244674	0.91	0.965	0.929	0.99	1.0
2^{10}	4	948308	0.78	1.0	1.0	0.975	1.0
2^{11}	4	3923124	0.88	1.0	1.0	1.0	1.0
2^{12}	4	16366382	0.88	1.0	1.0	0.989	1.0
2^6	5	3851	0.01	0.072	0.012	0.874	1.0
2^7	5	15386	0.0	0.027	0.0	0.929	1.0
2^8	5	60686	0.01	0.102	0.01	0.98	1.0
2^9	5	244674	0.04	0.187	0.04	0.99	1.0
2^{10}	5	948308	0.2	0.538	0.256	0.975	1.0
2^{11}	5	3923124	0.62	0.841	0.705	1.0	1.0
2^{12}	5	16366382	0.86	0.989	0.977	0.989	1.0

6 A New Class of Attacks on Cycle Walking FPE Schemes

In this section we point out that generic FPE schemes which are based on the cycle walking idea may be highly vulnerable to a new class of attacks which we call *Related Domain Attacks.* These attacks are similar to related key or related tweak attacks, but can only be applied to FPE schemes in which we can dynamically change the declared size of the input domain.

To demonstrate the basic form of these attacks, consider an iterated FPE scheme which consists of an arbitrarily large number k of round functions, each one of which is a different keyed permutation over the input domain. Furthermore, we assume that the round function itself takes a value from a domain of size N and processes it using the cycle walking idea. In other words, the round function may cause the value to be outside the domain, in which case the same round function is applied again and again until the value resides again in the domain. For the sake of discussion, we assume that extracting the secret key from known or chosen plaintext/ciphertext pairs is infeasible, but that each keyed round function by itself is sufficiently simple that finding the key from the two-round version of this scheme is practically doable (this assumption is similar in nature to that of the slide attack [7]).

Table 6. Asymmetric slide attack experiment results with constant number of 3 ciphertext chains

N	L	Queries	Success rate	PRF reconstruction	Combined reconstruction	Distinguisher success rate
2^6	3	3863	0.31	0.5	0.295	0.417
2^7	3	13883	0.47	0.709	0.527	0.368
2^8	3	52526	0.63	0.921	0.9	0.326
2^9	3	193894	0.7	0.959	0.959	0.339
2^{10}	3	752222	0.63	0.955	0.955	0.304
2^{11}	3	2946123	0.7	1.0	1.0	0.344
2^6	4	3828	0.12	0.303	0.101	0.436
2^7	4	13775	0.2	0.451	0.194	0.373
2^8	4	51264	0.51	0.794	0.637	0.327
2^9	4	190204	0.68	0.929	0.883	0.347
2^{10}	4	733040	0.64	0.97	0.97	0.302
2^{11}	4	2874664	0.7	0.986	0.986	0.344
2^6	5	3824	0.0	0.035	0.0	0.435
2^7	5	13622	0.0	0.047	0.0	0.39
2^8	5	51099	0.0	0.078	0.0	0.34
2^9	5	189543	0.07	0.225	0.069	0.354
2^{10}	5	733453	0.28	0.562	0.35	0.297
2^{11}	5	2868815	0.53	0.813	0.639	0.355

Assume further that the permutation P used in each round follows the cycle walking paradigm: If we declare that the input domain is $\{1, 2, \ldots, N\}$, then for any input x which is in this domain, we output the first value y that follows x along its cycle in P which is in the domain (possibly going all the way until we reach x again). This guarantees that all the intermediate values encountered during the encryption are valid values in the domain, and that any such y can be uniquely decrypted to x.

The related domain attack uses two very similar domains: The first one is defined as $\{1, 2, \ldots, N\}$ and the second one is defined as $\{1, 2, \ldots, N-1\}$. When we use a keyed round permutation on the first domain, we skip over all the possible values of the permutation which are larger than N. When we use the same keyed round permutation on the second domain, we skip over all the values which are larger than $N-1$. The two permutations are almost identical, and the only difference between them is related to the single value N which is allowed in the first permutation but forbidden in the second permutation. More specifically, given the preimage of N in the first permutation, we compute its output as N in the first permutation, but as the postimage of N in the second permutation.

To apply our new adaptive chosen message attack, we perform the full k-round encryption of N in the first domain, getting the ciphertext $z = E_1(N)$. With high probability, z is different than N, and thus we can request its

Table 7. Asymmetric slide attack experiment results ($t = 0.5$)

N	L	Queries	Success rate	PRF reconstruction	Combined reconstruction	Distinguisher success rate
2^6	3	3856	0.34	0.47	0.252	0.408
2^7	3	13752	0.58	0.766	0.615	0.268
2^8	3	48302	0.69	0.934	0.908	0.182
2^9	3	161676	0.69	0.932	0.932	0.142
2^{10}	3	543516	0.77	0.891	0.885	0.129
2^{11}	3	1769542	0.79	0.975	0.975	0.09
2^6	4	3828	0.18	0.315	0.116	0.404
2^7	4	13757	0.26	0.432	0.195	0.292
2^8	4	46880	0.54	0.787	0.621	0.181
2^9	4	153589	0.68	0.914	0.895	0.139
2^{10}	4	504930	0.8	0.982	0.976	0.128
2^{11}	4	1624932	0.81	0.988	0.988	0.092
2^6	5	3808	0.0	0.04	0.0	0.418
2^7	5	13702	0.0	0.047	0.0	0.296
2^8	5	47486	0.01	0.081	0.007	0.194
2^9	5	153608	0.08	0.25	0.068	0.137
2^{10}	5	498716	0.3	0.5	0.254	0.111
2^{11}	5	1564668	0.7	0.863	0.737	0.087

decryption $w = E_2^{-1}(z)$ as a member of the second domain (using the same unknown key and known tweak). Consider now the composition of these functions $w = E_2^{-1}(E_1(N))$. With high probability, none of the intermediate values will be N, and thus we can cancel almost all the $2k$ rounds in matching pairs. The only thing left will be the two round version of the problem in which N encrypted by the first round of E_1 and then decrypted by the first round of E_2 is equal to w. By repeating this process several times with shrinking domains, we can get sufficiently many input/output pairs, which are presumably enough to find the key used by this first round of the original scheme. If each round permutation uses a different key, we can easily repeat the process in order to find the keys of all the subsequent rounds. Note that this kind of attack can also be used against Feistel structures.

To protect FPE schemes against this new kind of attack, we propose to use the declared size of the domain as part of the tweak in each round function. This is a very simple modification which costs almost nothing but will make sure that any change in the domain size will result in a new and unrelated round function.

7 A Related Domain Distinguishing Attack on FF3 and FF3-1

We now present a distinguishing attack on both FF3 and FF3-1. The distinguishing attack is a related-domain attack that highlights the importance of domain separation between different instances of the encryption algorithm. For example, FF1 [14] uses the input size parameters as an input to the round function, thus avoiding this attack.

The distinguishing attack is quite efficient. Given about $c \cdot 2^4$ pairs of chosen plaintexts, we can distinguish whether two FF3 or FF3-1 instances were applied with related domain sizes (using the same key and tweak) for binary domains. Note that FF3 supports plaintexts encoded in any base (denoted as *radix* in the standard). One can easily expand the distinguishing attack to use $c \cdot radix^4$ pairs of chosen plaintext to handle different *radix*-sizes.

Hence, for the sake of simplicity we will describe an attack on a binary domain. As mentioned before, one can easily extend it to any *radix*. Let D_1 be a domain that includes $2n$-bit plaintexts, whereas domain D_2 includes $2n+1$-bit plaintexts. In other words, in D_1, the plaintexts have n-bit halves, whereas in D_2 the halves are n-bit and $n+1$-bit, respectively.

The adversary is given access to two encryption oracles $\mathcal{O}_1$ (over D_1) and $\mathcal{O}_2$ (over D_2). Similarly to the related cipher scenario [26], either these two oracles are two independent random permutations (of different sizes), or they are $FF3$ instantiated with the same key K and tweak T. We note that the attack also works against FF3-1 without any change, since the only difference between them is in the way they deal with the tweak.

Consider a plaintext (x, y) encrypted using FF3 (or FF3-1) in the smaller domain D_1 to (z, w). During its encryption, there are 8 invocations of the AES function using the same key K and tweak T, but with different inputs and round constants. When we encrypt $(0||x, y)$ in the larger domain D_2, we also get 8 invocations of AES. In the first round, we get the same input (y in both cases), but this time, $n+1$ bits of the AES output are used in the modular addition (instead of the previous n). Let the n-bit output (for D_1) be denoted by α and for the $n+1$-bit output be denoted by $b||\alpha$. It is easy to see that if $x + \alpha < 2^{10}$ then $(0||x) + (b||\alpha) \bmod 2^{11} = (b||x+\alpha)$, otherwise, $(0||x) + (b||\alpha) \bmod 2^{11} = (\overline{b}||x + \alpha \bmod 2^{10})$. It is easy to see that independent of the value of b, with probability of $1/2$, the addition's output is $(0||x + \alpha \bmod 2^{10})$. When this happens, the actual input to the AES invocation in the second round is the same for both the smaller domain D_1 and the larger domain D_2, which suggests the same output of the second round function. Hence, the input to the third round is also the same. The third round is similar to the first, and indeed, with probability $1/2$, the MSB of the output of addition is also 0. This also repeats in rounds 5 and 7. In other words, with probability $1/16$, if $(0||x, y)$ is encrypted to $(0||z, w)$ in the larger domain, when $(x||y)$ is encrypted to (z, w) in the smaller domain.

It is easy to see that the probability that this holds for two random permutation (over $2n$-bit and $2n+1$-bit values, respectively) is much smaller (namely 2^{-2n}). This produces a very efficient distinguisher: Pick $c \cdot 16$ random plaintexts $P_i = (x_i, y_i) \in D_1$, and ask for their encryptions under $\mathcal{O}_1$, resulting in C_i. Then, ask for the encryptions of the $c \cdot 16$ plaintexts $(0||x_i, y_i)$ under $\mathcal{O}_2$, resulting in $\hat{C}_i$. If for about $c/16$ of the ciphertexts $\hat{C}_i = 0||C_i$, conclude that this is FF3; otherwise, conclude that the two oracles are independent random permutations. For small values of c, where the probability of obtaining a right pair in the random case is negligible, the success rate of the attack is about $1 - e^{-c}$. Hence, setting $c = 2$ (and using 32 pairs in total) results in a success rate of 86.5%.

The generalization of the above attack to larger radices is trivial. We just need to assume that the most significant character (rather than bit) is 0, which happens with probability $1/radix$. Hence, one can construct an efficient distinguisher with data and time complexity of $c \cdot radix^4$ chosen plaintext pairs.

8 Conclusions

In this paper we studied the FF3 format preserving encryption algorithm. Building on top of the previous ideas of using related-tweak slide attack against FF3, we presented three attacks: An improved symmetric slide attack which enjoys better time, data and memory complexity compared with previous results, a cycle detection slide attack, and a asymmetric slide attack which outperforms the symmetric one.

We also presented two related-domain attacks. The first, a generic attack against cycle walking schemes, which reduces the problem of breaking them into the problem of attacking two rounds of the construction. The second, which is applicable to FF3 (and FF3-1) offers efficient distinguishing and shows how to expand the knowledge on the encryption in the smaller domain, to recover the PRFs used in the bigger one.

References

1. Bellare, M., Hoang, V.T., Tessaro, S.: Message-recovery attacks on Feistel-based format preserving encryption. In: Weippl, E.R., Katzenbeisser, S., Kruegel, C., Myers, A.C., Halevi, S. (eds.) Proceedings of the 2016 ACM SIGSAC Conference on Computer and Communications Security, Vienna, Austria, 24–28 October 2016, pp. 444–455. ACM (2016)
2. Bellare, M., Ristenpart, T., Rogaway, P., Stegers, T.: Format-preserving encryption. In: Jacobson, M.J., Rijmen, V., Safavi-Naini, R. (eds.) SAC 2009. LNCS, vol. 5867, pp. 295–312. Springer, Heidelberg (2009). https://doi.org/10.1007/978-3-642-05445-7_19
3. Bellare, M., Rogaway, P., Spies, T.: The FFX mode of operation for format-preserving encryption (draft 1.1) (2010). http://csrc.nist.gov/groups/ST/toolkit/BCM/documents/proposedmodes/ffx/ffx-spec.pdf
4. Biham, E., Dunkelman, O., Keller, N.: Improved slide attacks. In: Biryukov, A. (ed.) FSE 2007. LNCS, vol. 4593, pp. 153–166. Springer, Heidelberg (2007). https://doi.org/10.1007/978-3-540-74619-5_10

5. Biham, E., Dunkelman, O., Keller, N.: A unified approach to related-key attacks. In: Nyberg, K. (ed.) FSE 2008. LNCS, vol. 5086, pp. 73–96. Springer, Heidelberg (2008). https://doi.org/10.1007/978-3-540-71039-4_5
6. Biryukov, A., Leurent, G., Perrin, L.: Cryptanalysis of Feistel networks with secret round functions. In: Dunkelman, O., Keliher, L. (eds.) SAC 2015. LNCS, vol. 9566, pp. 102–121. Springer, Cham (2016). https://doi.org/10.1007/978-3-319-31301-6_6
7. Biryukov, A., Wagner, D.: Slide attacks. In: Knudsen, L. (ed.) FSE 1999. LNCS, vol. 1636, pp. 245–259. Springer, Heidelberg (1999). https://doi.org/10.1007/3-540-48519-8_18
8. Black, J., Rogaway, P.: Ciphers with arbitrary finite domains. In: Preneel, B. (ed.) CT-RSA 2002. LNCS, vol. 2271, pp. 114–130. Springer, Heidelberg (2002). https://doi.org/10.1007/3-540-45760-7_9
9. Brier, E., Peyrin, T., Stern, J.: BPS: a format-preserving encryption proposal (2010). http://csrc.nist.gov/groups/ST/toolkit/BCM/documents/proposedmodes/bps/bps-spec.pdf
10. Brightwell, M., Smith, H.: Using datatype-preserving encryption to enhance data warehouse security, pp. 141–149 (1997). http://csrc.nist.gov/niccs/1997
11. Daemen, J., Rijmen, V.: The Design of Rijndael: AES - The Advanced Encryption Standard. Information Security and Cryptography. Springer, Heidelberg (2002). https://doi.org/10.1007/978-3-662-04722-4
12. Durak, F.B., Vaudenay, S.: Breaking the FF3 format-preserving encryption standard over small domains. In: Katz, J., Shacham, H. (eds.) CRYPTO 2017. LNCS, vol. 10402, pp. 679–707. Springer, Cham (2017). https://doi.org/10.1007/978-3-319-63715-0_23
13. Dworkin, M.: Recommendation for Block Cipher Modes of Operation: Methods for Format-Preserving Encryption. NIST Special Publication, 800-38G (2016)
14. Dworkin, M.: Recommendation for Block Cipher Modes of Operation: Methods for Format-Preserving Encryption. NIST Special Publication, SP 800-38G Rev. 1 (2019)
15. Floyd, R.W.: Algorithm 97: shortest path. Commun. ACM **5**(6), 345 (1962)
16. Furuya, S.: Slide attacks with a known-plaintext cryptanalysis. In: Kim, K. (ed.) ICISC 2001. LNCS, vol. 2288, pp. 214–225. Springer, Heidelberg (2002). https://doi.org/10.1007/3-540-45861-1_17
17. Hoang, V.T., Miller, D., Trieu, N.: Attacks only get better: how to break FF3 on large domains. In: Ishai, Y., Rijmen, V. (eds.) EUROCRYPT 2019. LNCS, vol. 11477, pp. 85–116. Springer, Cham (2019). https://doi.org/10.1007/978-3-030-17656-3_4
18. Luby, M., Rackoff, C.: How to construct pseudorandom permutations from pseudorandom functions. SIAM J. Comput. **17**(2), 373–386 (1988)
19. National Bureau of Standards. Data Encryption Standard (DES). Technical report. Federal Information Processing Standards Publication 46 (1977)
20. Patarin, J.: Generic attacks on Feistel schemes. IACR Cryptol. ePrint Arch. **2008**, 36 (2008)
21. Patarin, J.: Security of balanced and unbalanced Feistel schemes with linear non equalities. IACR Cryptol. ePrint Arch. **2010**, 293 (2010)
22. Schroeppel, R., Orman, H.: The hasty pudding cipher. AES candidate submitted to NIST, p. M1 (1998)
23. Shepp, L., Lloyd, S.: Ordered cycle lengths in a random permutation. Trans. Am. Math. Soc. **121**(2), 340–357 (1966)
24. Spies, T.: Feistel Finite Set Encryption Mode. NIST submission (2008)

25. Vance, J.: VAES3 scheme for FFX: An addendum to "The FFX Mode of Operation for Format-Preserving Encryption": a parameter collection for encipher strings of arbitrary radix with subkey operation to lengthen life of the enciphering key (2010). http://csrc.nist.gov/groups/ST/toolkit/BCM/documents/proposedmodes/ffx/ffx-ad-VAES3.pdf
26. Wu, H.: Related-cipher attacks. In: Deng, R., Bao, F., Zhou, J., Qing, S. (eds.) ICICS 2002. LNCS, vol. 2513, pp. 447–455. Springer, Heidelberg (2002). https://doi.org/10.1007/3-540-36159-6_38

Cryptanalysis of the GPRS Encryption Algorithms GEA-1 and GEA-2

Christof Beierle[1(✉)], Patrick Derbez[2(✉)], Gregor Leander[1(✉)], Gaëtan Leurent[3(✉)], Håvard Raddum[4(✉)], Yann Rotella[5(✉)], David Rupprecht[1(✉)], and Lukas Stennes[1(✉)]

[1] Ruhr University Bochum, Bochum, Germany
{christof.beierle,gregor.leander,david.rupprecht, lukas.stennes}@rub.de

[2] Univ Rennes, CNRS, IRISA, Rennes, France
patrick.derbez@irisa.fr

[3] Inria, Paris, France
gaetan.leurent@inria.fr

[4] Simula UiB, Bergen, Norway
haavardr@simula.no

[5] Laboratoire de Mathématiques de Versailles, Université Paris-Saclay, UVSQ, CNRS, Versailles, France
yann.rotella@uvsq.fr

Abstract. This paper presents the first publicly available cryptanalytic attacks on the GEA-1 and GEA-2 algorithms. Instead of providing full 64-bit security, we show that the initial state of GEA-1 can be recovered from as little as 65 bits of known keystream (with at least 24 bits coming from one frame) in time 2^{40} GEA-1 evaluations and using 44.5 GiB of memory.

The attack on GEA-1 is based on an exceptional interaction of the deployed LFSRs and the key initialization, which is highly unlikely to occur by chance. This unusual pattern indicates that the weakness is intentionally hidden to limit the security level to 40 bit by design.

In contrast, for GEA-2 we did not discover the same intentional weakness. However, using a combination of algebraic techniques and list merging algorithms we are still able to break GEA-2 in time $2^{45.1}$ GEA-2 evaluations. The main practical hurdle is the required knowledge of 1600 bytes of keystream.

Keywords: GPRS Encryption · Stream cipher · Algebraic attacks · GEA

1 Introduction

General Packet Radio Service (GPRS) is a mobile data standard based on the GSM (2G) technology. With its large deployments during the early 2000s worldwide, GPRS (including EDGE) was the technology for many of us, which provided us the first mobile Internet connection. While some countries are about to

A. Canteaut and F.-X. Standaert (Eds.): EUROCRYPT 2021, LNCS 12697, pp. 155–183, 2021.
https://doi.org/10.1007/978-3-030-77886-6_6

sunset 2G technology (or have already done so), other countries rely on GPRS as a fallback data connection. Consequently, the security of those connections *was and still is* relevant for a large user base. In the wireless medium, an attacker conducts an eavesdropping attack by merely sniffing the traffic in the victim's vicinity. To protect against eavesdropping GPRS between the phone and the base station, a stream cipher is used and initially two proprietary encryption algorithms `GEA-1` and `GEA-2` were specified.

Design Process of the GPRS Encryption Algorithm. A dedicated encryption algorithm for GPRS, now known as `GEA-1`, was designed by ETSI Security Algorithms Group of Experts (SAGE) in 1998. A technical report on the design process is available at [15]. The total budget spent was 429 man days and six organizations have been involved in the process. As seen in [15, Section 8], the following requirements were set for the design:

> The algorithm should be a stream cipher which gets a 64-bit key (Kc), a 32-bit IV, and a 1 bit flag to indicate the transfer direction as inputs and outputs a stream of 1,600 bytes.

It was explicitly mentioned as a design requirement that *"the algorithm should be generally exportable taking into account current export restrictions"* and that *"the strength should be optimized taking into account the above requirement"* [15, p. 10]. The report further contains a section on the evaluation of the design. In particular, it is mentioned that the evaluation team came to the conclusion that, *"in general the algorithm will be exportable under the current national export restrictions on cryptography applied in European countries"* and that *"within this operational context, the algorithm provides an adequate level of security against eavesdropping of GSM GPRS services"* [15, p. 13].

A successor algorithm, called `GEA-2`, was designed later. An official requirement specification by ETSI as for `GEA-1` is not publicly available. According to Charles Brookson in 2001, *"GEA2 was defined about a year later than GEA1 and was an improvement, which was allowed by the easing of export control legislation"* [8, p. 4].

The particular restrictions that `GEA-1` should fulfill in order to be exportable are not specified in the requirements.

Export Regulations. For a detailed survey on national and international regulations concerning the use, supply, import and export of cryptographic algorithms in the '90s, we refer to the *Crypto Law Survey* of Bert-Jaap Koops [23]. In France, rather strict regulations have been in place. In particular, until the late '90s, the use, supply, import and export of cryptography for providing confidentiality was subject to authorization by the prime minister. The requirements for obtaining such an authorization were not publicly available. To quote from [23], *"It was unclear to what extent the restrictive regulation was enforced in practice; it was rumoured to be widely ignored. It seemed impossible for individuals or enterprises to obtain authorisation for 'strong' cryptography. Even for state-owned industry, cryptography that does not serve military or high-grade security purposes had to be breakable. SCSSI, the office dealing with authorisation, rendered decisions without motivation."*

In 1998, the French Decrees[1] 98-206 and 98-207 were announced, in which exceptions from such authorization or declaration have been defined. The three most interesting exceptions defined in Decree 98-206 with regard to our work can be translated as follows:

- Means and services of Cryptology for *"mobile phones for civil use that do not implement end-to-end encryption"* are exempt from authorization or declaration for supply, use, import and export.
- Means and services of Cryptology for *"Commercial civil base towers with the following characteristics: a) Limited to connection with cell phones that cannot apply cryptographic techniques to traffic between terminals, excepted on the direct link between cell phones and base stations b) And not allowing the use of cryptographic techniques to traffic excepted on the radio interface"* are exempt from authorization or declaration for supply, use and import (but not export).
- Means and services of Cryptology in which *"exhaustive search of all possible keys does not require more than* 2^{40} *trials with a simple test"* are exempt from authorization or declaration for use and import (but not for supply and export).

Interestingly enough, we will show later in Sect. 3 that `GEA-1` offers only 40-bit security.

1.1 Related Work and Reverse Engineering

In 2011, Nohl and Melette analyzed the security of GPRS traffic and showed that GPRS signals could easily be eavesdropped [29]. This was reported as a serious weakness, especially since some providers did not activate encryption at all. However, according to the authors, most operators at that time employed the proprietary encryption algorithms `GEA-1` or `GEA-2` for encrypting the GPRS traffic.

In the same talk, Nohl and Melette also reported the reverse-engineering of those encryption algorithms. Without presenting all of the specification details, the following properties of the design of `GEA-1` have been shown:

- It is a stream cipher which works on an internal state of 96 bits and uses a 64-bit key.
- A non-linear function is employed for initialization.[2]
- The state is kept in three registers of sizes 31, 32, and 33 bits.[3]

[1] Available via https://www.legifrance.gouv.fr/jorf/id/JORFTEXT000000753702 and https://www.legifrance.gouv.fr/jorf/id/JORFTEXT000000753703, accessed Oct-06, 2020.

[2] See minute 32:15 of the recorded talk.

[3] The size of the registers are visible in the live state-recovery attack, see minute 48:25 of the recorded talk.

- The state update function is linear, i.e., the registers are LFSRs.
- The function that generates the output stream has algebraic degree 4.

The structure of the GEA-1 stream cipher as known from [29] is depicted in Fig. 1. For GEA-2, it was reported that it employs a similar algebraic structure to its predecessor GEA-1. While the key size for GEA-2 is 64 bits as well, the internal state was reported to be of size 125 bits.

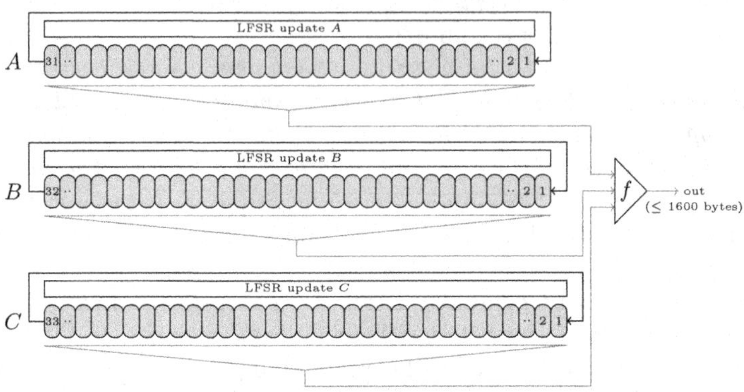

Fig. 1. The structure of the GEA-1 stream cipher with its 96 bit state known from [29]. The algebraic degree of the output function is 4.

In their talk, the authors claimed that GEA-1 has severe weaknesses against algebraic attacks, mainly due to the nonlinearity of the state update function and the availability of a long keystream to the adversary. Live on stage, a state-recovery attack was performed that took less than 15 minutes using "a Gaussian equation solver based on some SAT solver ideas" (minute 48:40 of the recorded talk).[4] However, details of this attack are not available.

Interestingly, the ETSI prohibited the implementation of GEA-1 in mobile phones in 2013, while GEA-2 and the non-encrypted mode are still mandatory to be implemented today [16].

Despite the hints of deliberately weakening GEA-1 for export and a demonstrated attack, a public cryptanalysis of GEA-1 and GEA-2 is still missing to date. This puts us in a position where we are uncertain about the algorithm's security guarantees. In this paper, we fill this gap with the first public cryptanalysis of GEA-1 and GEA-2. As part of this we also describe the design of those two proprietary algorithms, which we obtained from a source that prefers to stay anonymous.

[4] The authors acknowledged Mate Soos for ideas and also admitted that the live attack did not apply the SAT solver yet.

1.2 Our Contribution

After describing the stream ciphers GEA-1 and GEA-2 and their internal building blocks, we start by analyzing the security of GEA-1.

The main observation is that after the linear initialization process the *joint initial state of* 64 *bits* of two of the three LFSRs is guaranteed to be in one of only 2^{40} states (rather than close to 2^{64} as should be expected).

This property immediately allows to conduct a Divide-and-Conquer state-recovery attack in time 2^{40} GEA-1 evaluations by using only 65 bits of known keystream (with at least 24 bits in the same frame). The attack needs the pre-computation of a (sorted) table of size 44.5 GiB, which can be done in time of roughly 2^{37} GEA-1 evaluations. Once this table has been computed, the attack can be performed in time of roughly 2^{40} GEA-1 evaluations for each new 64-bit session key.

Further, we experimentally show that for randomly chosen LFSRs, it is very unlikely that the above weakness occurs. Concretely, in a million tries we never even got close to such a weak instance. Figure 2 shows the distribution of the entropy loss when changing the feedback polynomials of registers A and C to random primitive polynomials. This implies that the weakness in GEA-1 is unlikely to occur by chance, indicating that the security level of 40 bits is due to export regulations.

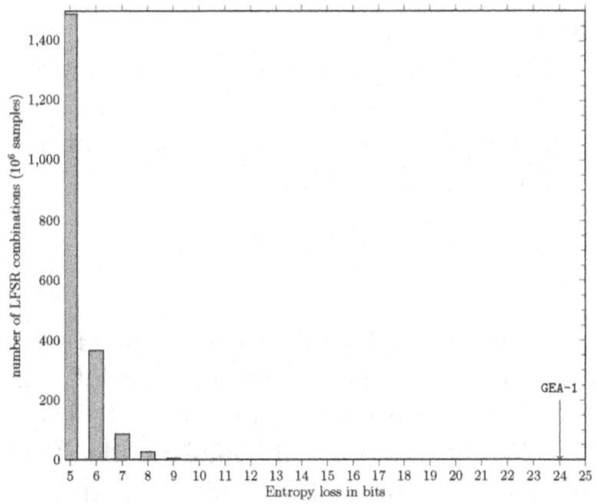

Fig. 2. The distribution of the entropy loss within the joint initial 64-bit state of registers A and C after the linear initialization in GEA-1 for a random sample of 10^6 combinations of primitive LFSRs. The occurences of entropy losses up to 4 bits are omitted.

As a last part of this work, we look into the security of the successor algorithm GEA-2. We conduct a state-recovery attack that does not target the initialization process, but rather the keystream generation itself. The idea is to mix a list merging algorithm, combined with algebraic techniques. The attacks works in time equivalent to $2^{45.1}$ GEA-2 evaluations. The required memory is roughly 32 GiB. Rather than only 65 bit of known keystream as for GEA-1, this attacks needs all of the keystream available per frame, i.e., 1,600 bytes, and it cannot exploit information coming from multiple frames.

We demonstrate the practical feasibility of the attack against GEA-1 on standard hardware. Further, we discuss the real-world requirements and attack implications for today's mobile phone network. Eventually, we are dedicated to eliminating weak ciphers in current and future mobile phones—improving mobile network security.

2 Description of GEA-1 and GEA-2

In this section, we give a detailed description of the two algorithms GEA-1 and GEA-2, which we obtained from a source. Therefore we verify the correctness of the algorithms by *a*) using test vectors that are available on github [28] and *b*) verify the algorithm by checking the interoperability with commercial phones using the osmocom project [31]. Both experiments confirm the correct functionality; thus, we can assume that the provided algorithms are accurate with a high degree of certainty.

For the encryption, the GEA algorithms take the following input parameters: the plaintext, which is the GPRS LLC (Logical Link Control) frame, the key (K), the direction bit (uplink/downlink), and the IV (Input) that consists of an increasing counter for each frame.

As we will see, GEA-2 is an extension of GEA-1– with slight but crucial exceptions. For this reason, we first describe GEA-1 first and explain the differences and extensions for GEA-2 in a second step. An overview of the keystream generation of GEA-1 and GEA-2 is shown in Fig. 3.

2.1 GEA-1

GEA-1 is built from three linear feedback shift registers over $\mathbb{F}_2$, called A, B and C, together with a non-linear filter function, called f. The registers A, B, C have lengths $31, 32$ and 33, respectively, and f is a Boolean function on seven variables of degree 4. The registers work in Galois mode. This means that if the bit that is shifted out of a register is 1, the bits in a specified set of positions in the register are flipped. The specification of $f = f(x_0, x_1, \ldots, x_6)$ is given in algebraic normal form as follows:

$$\begin{aligned}
&x_0x_2x_5x_6 + x_0x_3x_5x_6 + x_0x_1x_5x_6 + x_1x_2x_5x_6 + x_0x_2x_3x_6 + x_1x_3x_4x_6\\
&+ x_1x_3x_5x_6 + x_0x_2x_4 + x_0x_2x_3 + x_0x_1x_3 + x_0x_2x_6 + x_0x_1x_4 + x_0x_1x_6\\
&+ x_1x_2x_6 + x_2x_5x_6 + x_0x_3x_5 + x_1x_4x_6 + x_1x_2x_5 + x_0x_3 + x_0x_5 + x_1x_3\\
&+ x_1x_5 + x_1x_6 + x_0x_2 + x_1 + x_2x_3 + x_2x_5 + x_2x_6 + x_4x_5 + x_5x_6 + x_2 + x_3 + x_5
\end{aligned}$$

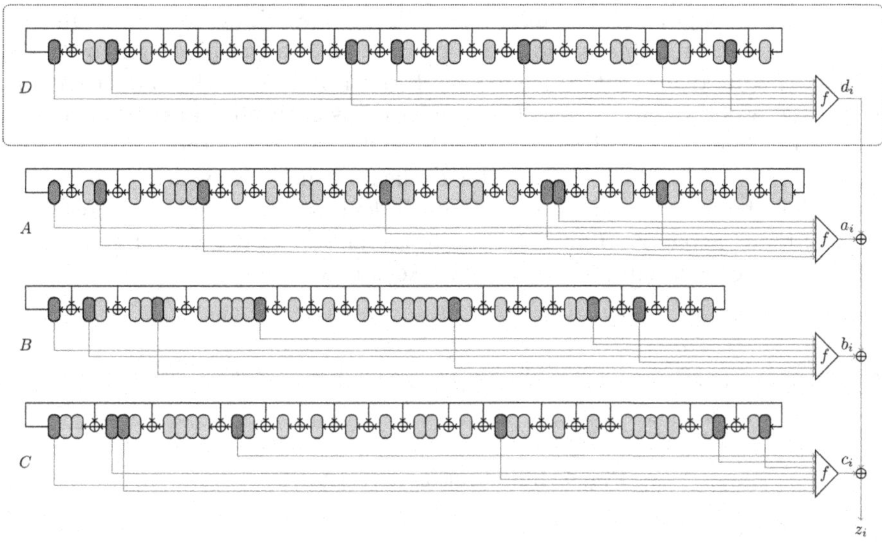

Fig. 3. Overview of the keystream generation of GEA-1 and GEA-2. The D register is only present in GEA-2.

Initialization. The cipher is initialized via a non-linear feedback shift register of length 64, denoted as S. This register is filled with 0-bits at the start of the initialization process. The input for initializing GEA-1 consists of a public 32-bit initialization vector IV, one public bit dir (indicating direction of communication), and a 64-bit secret key K. The initialization starts by clocking S 97 times, feeding in one input bit with every clock. The input bits are introduced in the sequence $IV_0, IV_1, \ldots, IV_{31}, dir, K_0, K_1, \ldots, K_{63}$. When all input bits have been loaded, the register is clocked another 128 times with 0-bits as input. The feedback function consists of f, xored with the bit that is shifted out and the next bit from the input sequence. See Fig. 4 for particular tap positions.

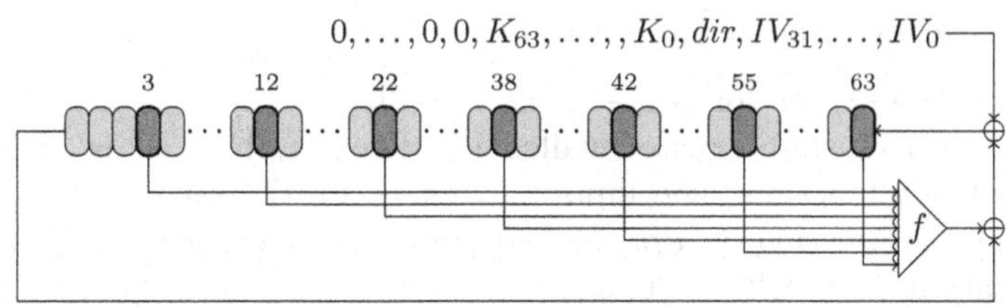

Fig. 4. Initialization of register S

After S has been clocked 225 times, the content of the register is taken as a 64-bit string $s = s_0, \ldots, s_{63}$. This string is taken as a seed for initializing

A, B and C as follows. First, all three registers are initialized to the all-zero state. Then each register is clocked 64 times, with an s_i-bit xored onto the bit that is shifted out before feedback. Register A inserts the bits from s in the natural order $s_0, s_1, \ldots, s_{63}$. The sequence s is cyclically shifted by 16 positions before being inserted to register B, so the bits are entered in the order $s_{16}, s_{17}, \ldots, s_{63}, s_0, \ldots, s_{15}$. For register C the sequence s is cyclically shifted by 32 positions before insertion starts. Figure 5 depicts the process for register B. If any of the registers A, B or C end up in the all-zero state, the bit in position 0 of the register is forcibly set to 1 before keystream generation starts.

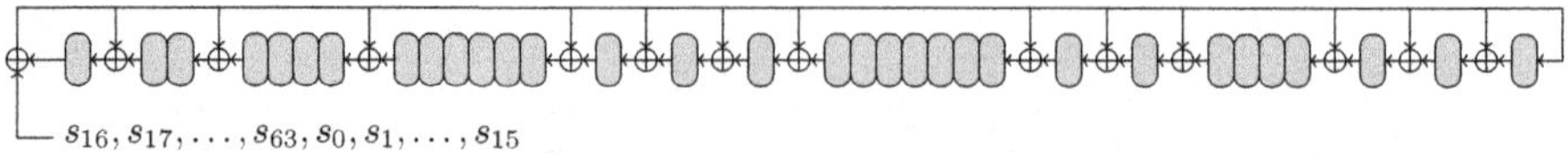

Fig. 5. Initialization of register B

Keystream Generation. When all registers have been initialized, the actual keystream generation starts. This is done by taking the bits in seven specified positions in each register to be the input to f. The three outputs from the f-functions are xored together to produce one bit of the keystream. Figure 3 shows the particular feedback positions of each register, as well as showing which positions form which input to f. In Fig. 3, the topmost arrow in the input to f represents x_0, and the input at the bottom is x_6. After calculating the keystream bit, all registers are clocked once each before the process repeats.

2.2 GEA-2

The cipher GEA-2 is a simple extension of GEA-1. A fourth register of length 29, called D, is added to the system together with an instance of f. During keystream generation, the output of f from the D register is added to the keystream together with the three others at each clock, as shown in Fig. 3. The initialization process of GEA-2 follows the same mode as for GEA-1, but it is done in a longer register that is clocked more times.

Initializing GEA-2. As for GEA-1, the initialization of GEA-2 is done via a non-linear feedback shift register, called W. The length of W is 97, and uses f as its feedback function. The input to GEA-2 are the same as for GEA-1; a 32-bit IV and a direction bit dir that are public, and a secret 64-bit key K.

Initialization starts with W being set to the all-zero state. Next, it is clocked 97 times, inserting one bit from the input sequence for each clock. The order for inserting IV, dir and K is the same as for GEA-1. After K_{63} is inserted, W is clocked another 194 times, with 0 as input. This process, together with the particular tap positions for f, is shown in Fig. 6.

The content of W is now taken as a 97-bit string $w = w_0, \ldots, w_{96}$, and inserted in A, B, C and D in much the same way as with GEA-1. The four

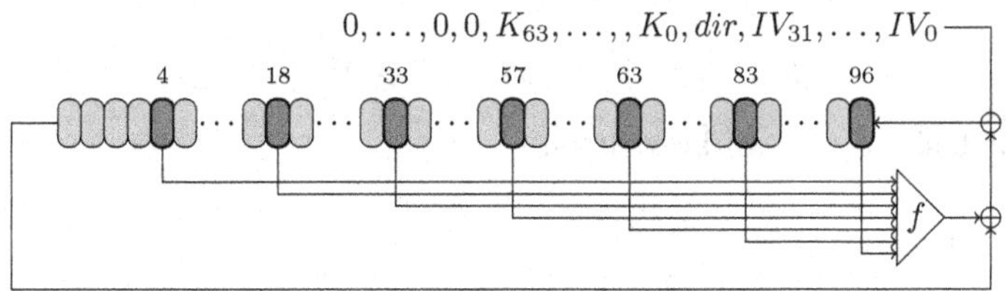

Fig. 6. Initialization of register W

registers starts from the all-zero state, and are filled with the bits of w in the same way as shown in Fig. 5. The offsets of where in the sequence w each register starts is different than for GEA-1. Register D inserts the bits of w in the natural order $w_0, \ldots, w_{96}$, whereas the registers A, B and C start with bits w_{16}, w_{33} and w_{51}, respectively. Again, if any of the registers happens to end up in the all-zero state after initialization, the bit in position 0 is hard-coded to 1 before key generation start.

2.3 Deconstructing the Filter Function

The filter function $f : \mathbb{F}_2^7 \to \mathbb{F}_2$ has a very particular Walsh (or Fourier) spectrum. Namely

$$\widehat{f}(\alpha) = \sum_{x \in \mathbb{F}_2^7} (-1)^{f(x)+\langle \alpha, x \rangle} \in \{0, \pm 2^{\frac{7+1}{2}}\},$$

for all $\alpha \in \mathbb{F}_2^7$. Several ways to construct such a Boolean function are known (we refer to Claude Carlet's treatment [9] for a detailed presentation of the required theory of Boolean functions). They appear as component functions of almost bent functions or can be constructed using bent functions in one dimension smaller. While we do not know how f was actually designed, it can certainly be decomposed into two bent functions

$$f_i : \mathbb{F}_2^6 \to \mathbb{F}_2$$

as

$$f(x) = (1 + x_6) f_0(x_0, \ldots, x_5) + x_6 f_1(x_0, \ldots, x_5).$$

Furthermore, the functions f_i are linearly equivalent to Maiorana-McFarland bent functions [27] (as actually all bent functions in 6 bits are classified in [32]). Indeed, we can decompose f_0 further into

$$f_0(x_0, \ldots, x_5) = g_0(x_0, x_1 + x_2, x_2, x_3, x_4, x_5)$$

where g_0 is a Maiorana-McFarland bent function given as

$$g_0(x_0, \ldots, x_5) = \left\langle \begin{pmatrix} x_2 \\ x_3 \\ x_4 \end{pmatrix}, \begin{pmatrix} x_0 + x_1 x_5 + x_5 \\ x_0 x_1 + x_0 x_5 + x_0 + x_1 + 1 \\ x_0 x_1 + x_5 \end{pmatrix} \right\rangle + h_0(x_0, x_1, x_5),$$

where

$$h_0(x_0, x_1, x_5) = x_0 x_5 + x_1 x_5 + x_1 + x_5.$$

In a similar fashion, f_1 can be written as

$$f_1(x_0, \ldots, x_5) = g_1(x_0 + x_2 + x_5, x_1, x_2, x_3, x_4 + x_5, x_5).$$

That is, f_1 is linearly equivalent to g_1 where g_1 is again a Maiorana-McFarland bent function. The function g_1 can be written as

$$g_1(x_0, \ldots, x_5) = \left\langle \begin{pmatrix} x_0 \\ x_3 \\ x_4 \end{pmatrix}, \begin{pmatrix} x_1 x_5 + x_2 x_5 + x_2 \\ x_1 x_5 + x_1 + x_2 + 1 \\ x_5 + 1 \end{pmatrix} \right\rangle + h_1(x_0, x_1, x_5),$$

where

$$h_1(x_0, x_1, x_5) = x_1 x_2 + x_1 x_5.$$

We like to note that those insights in the filter function do not play any role in our attacks and, for all we know, do not point at any weakness of the cipher. Rather, they indicate that the filter was generated following known and valid principles.

3 An Attack on GEA-1

First we recall some basic facts about LFSRs in Galois mode, as depicted in Fig. 7. For further reading we refer to ([34, p. 378 ff.], [20, p. 227]).

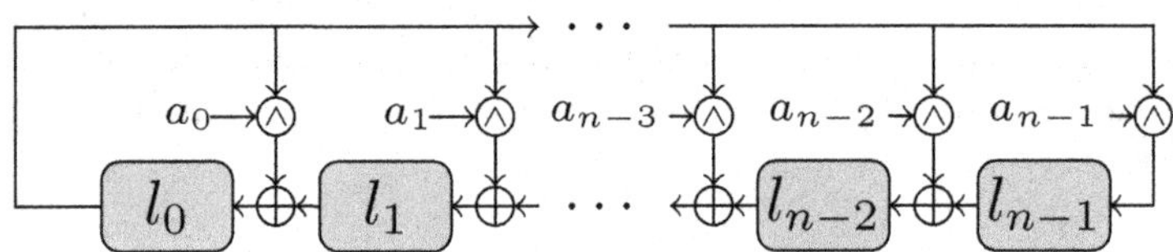

Fig. 7. An LFSR in Galois mode.

Given an LFSR L in Galois mode of degree n with entries in $\mathbb{F}_2$, clocking the inner state $l = l_0, \ldots, l_{n-1}$ is equivalent to the matrix-vector multiplication

$$G_L \cdot l := \begin{pmatrix} a_0 & 1\,0 \ldots 0 \\ a_1 & 0\,1 \ldots 0 \\ \vdots & \vdots\,\vdots\,\ddots\,\vdots \\ a_{n-2} & 0\,0 \ldots 1 \\ a_{n-1} & 0\,0 \ldots 0 \end{pmatrix} \cdot \begin{pmatrix} l_0 \\ l_1 \\ \vdots \\ l_{n-2} \\ l_{n-1} \end{pmatrix} = \begin{pmatrix} a_0 l_0 + l_1 \\ a_1 l_0 + l_2 \\ \vdots \\ a_{n-2} l_0 + l_{n-1} \\ a_{n-1} l_0 \end{pmatrix}$$

and the characteristic polynomial of G_L is

$$g(X) := X^n + a_0 X^{n-1} + \cdots + a_{n-2}X + a_{n-1}.$$

Throughout this work, we consider the case in which g is primitive. The characteristic polynomial $g(X)$ is equal to the minimal polynomial of G_L if and only if $a_{n-1} = 1$. Vice versa, given a primitive polynomial $g(X) := X^n + a_0 X^{n-1} + \cdots + a_{n-2}X + a_{n-1}$, then

$$G_L := \begin{pmatrix} a_0 & 1\,0 \ldots 0 \\ a_1 & 0\,1 \ldots 0 \\ \vdots & \vdots\ \vdots\ \ddots\ \vdots \\ a_{n-2} & 0\,0 \ldots 1 \\ a_{n-1} & 0\,0 \ldots 0 \end{pmatrix}$$

is the companion matrix of an LFSR in Galois mode with minimal polynomial g. We call such a matrix the *Galois matrix* and the corresponding minimal polynomial the *Galois polynomial* in the sequel. Moreover, given an LFSR L in Galois mode with minimal (primitive) polynomial g, we denote the Galois matrix with G_g. In the case of GEA-1 the Galois polynomials are

$$\begin{aligned} g_A(X) =& X^{31} + X^{30} + X^{28} + X^{27} + X^{23} + X^{22} + X^{21} + X^{19} + X^{18} + X^{15} \\ &+ X^{11} + X^{10} + X^8 + X^7 + X^6 + X^4 + X^3 + X^2 + 1, \\ g_B(X) =& X^{32} + X^{31} + X^{29} + X^{25} + X^{19} + X^{18} + X^{17} + X^{16} + X^9 + X^8 \\ &+ X^7 + X^3 + X^2 + X + 1, \\ g_C(X) =& X^{33} + X^{30} + X^{27} + X^{23} + X^{21} + X^{20} + X^{19} + X^{18} + X^{17} + X^{15} \\ &+ X^{14} + X^{11} + X^{10} + X^9 + X^4 + X^2 + 1. \end{aligned}$$

The initialization process of the registers A, B and C with the string s is obviously linear. Hence there exist three matrices $M_A \in \mathbb{F}_2^{31\times 64}$, $M_B \in \mathbb{F}_2^{32\times 64}$ and $M_C \in \mathbb{F}_2^{33\times 64}$ such that

$$\begin{aligned} \alpha &= M_A s, \\ \beta &= M_B s, \\ \gamma &= M_C s, \end{aligned}$$

where α, β and γ denote the states of the three LFSRs after the initialization phase. We exclude here the unlikely case that α, β or γ is still in the all-zero state after the shifted insertion of s.

We are now interested in the number of possible starting states of the registers after this initialization. For those considerations, we used the computer algebra system sagemath [37]. The corresponding code is attached in Appendix A. The first observation is that all the three matrices have full rank. This implies that the number of possible starting states after initialization is maximal when each LFSR is considered independently, i.e. there are 2^{31} possible states for register A,

2^{32} possible states for register B, and 2^{33} possible states for register C, as should be expected. However, when considering pairs of registers, the picture changes drastically. In particular, the number of possible joint states after initialization of the registers A and C is much smaller than expected. For this it is convenient to consider the kernels of the linear mappings. Clearly, the corresponding linear mappings represented by M_A, M_B and M_C have kernels of dimension of at least 33, 32 and 31, respectively. If we denote $T_{AC} := \ker(M_A) \cap \ker(M_C)$ and $U_B := \ker(M_B)$ then, curiously enough, we have

1. $\dim(T_{AC}) = 24$ and $\dim(U_B) = 32$,
2. $U_B \cap T_{AC} = \{0\}$.

From this it directly follows that $\mathbb{F}_2^{64}$ can be decomposed into the direct sum $U_B \oplus T_{AC} \oplus V$, where V is of dimension 8. Thus, for the key-dependent and secret string s, there exists a *unique* representation $s = u + t + v$ with $u \in U_B$, $t \in T_{AC}$, $v \in V$ and

$$\begin{aligned}\beta &= M_B(u + t + v) = M_B(t + v)\\ \alpha &= M_A(u + t + v) = M_A(u + v)\\ \gamma &= M_C(u + t + v) = M_C(u + v).\end{aligned}$$

From this decomposition, s can be computed with a Divide-and-Conquer attack with a complexity[5] of 2^{37} GEA-1 evaluations to build (and sort) 2^8 tables with 2^{24} entries of size 89 bits and a brute-force step of complexity 2^{40} GEA-1 evaluations for each new session key $K_0, \ldots, K_{63}$. The details will be given in Sect. 3.1.

In other words, the joint state of A and C can be described with only 40 bits and thus can take only 2^{40} possible values. This is the key observation of the attack and the weakness that is highly unlikely to occur unintentionally.

Once s is determined, $K_0, \ldots, K_{63}$ can be recovered as follows. Let S_i denote the state of register S after i clocks of initialization. So $S_0 = (0, 0, \ldots, 0)$ and $S_{225} = (s_0, s_1, \ldots, s_{63})$ where all the s_j are known (see also Fig. 4). The last 128 clocks of S all insert 0-bits from the string containing K, dir and IV, so it is straightforward to clock S_{225} backwards 128 times and find the content of S_{97}. Let $S_{97} = (a_0, a_1, \ldots, a_{63})$, where all the a_i are known.

Starting from the other side, the first 33 clocks of S_0 only insert the known bits $IV_0, IV_1, \ldots, IV_{31}, dir$, so the content of S_{33} is fully known. The next clock inserts $K_0 + b_0$ at position 63 of S_{34}, where b_0 is a known bit. Further clocking do not change the content of this cell, but only shifts it further positions to the left, so after 63 clockings starting from S_{34} we have $S_{97} = (K_0 + b_0, \ldots)$. Equating S_{97} from the forward direction with S_{97} from the backward direction gives us $K_0 = a_0 + b_0$.

With K_0 known, position 63 of S_{35} can now be given as $K_1 + b_1$, where b_1 is known. Clocking S_{35} forward 62 times gives $S_{97} = (K_0 + b_0, K_1 + b_1, \ldots)$ and

[5] The complexity will be measured by the amount of operations that are roughly as complex as GEA-1 evaluations (for generating a keystream of size $\leq$ 128 bit).

again equating with S_{97} from the backwards side gives $K_1 = a_1 + b_1$. Continuing this way recovers the whole session key K. Hence, the attack has to be conducted only *once per GPRS session* and is done in 2^{40} operations once the table has been established.

3.1 A Simple Divide-and-Conquer Attack on GEA-1

A table *Tab* is built by exhaustive search over the 2^{32} values

$$\beta_{t,v} = M_B(t+v), t \in T_{AC}, v \in V,$$

plugging $\beta_{t,v}$ into register B and clocking it ℓ times. The parameter ℓ will be determined later. The table is divided into 2^8 sub-tables $Tab[v]$ indexed by v; the output bits $b_{t,v}^{(0)}, \dots, b_{t,v}^{(\ell-1)}$ (after applying the filter f), together with t, are stored in $Tab[v]$. We then sort each $Tab[v]$ according to $b_{t,v}^{(0)}, \dots, b_{t,v}^{(\ell-1)}$ interpreted as an ℓ-bit integer. The table has 2^{32} entries of size $\ell + 24$ bits, so it can be generated and sorted with a complexity of $32 \cdot 2^{32} = 2^{37}$ operations if the size of ℓ is negligible (which it is, as we will see below).

Given ℓ bits of keystream z_i, the sequence s is recovered as follows. First, an exhaustive search is conducted over the 2^{40} values

$$\alpha_{u,v} = M_A(u+v),\ \gamma_{u,v} = M_C(u+v),\ u \in U_B,\ v \in V,$$

plugging $\alpha_{u,v}$ into A, $\gamma_{u,v}$ into C and clocking both registers ℓ times. We denote by $a_{u,v}^{(0)}, \dots, a_{u,v}^{(\ell-1)}$, resp., $c_{u,v}^{(0)}, \dots, c_{u,v}^{(\ell-1)}$, the output stream of register A, resp., C after applying the filter f. For each (u, v), the output stream

$$a_{u,v}^{(0)} \oplus c_{u,v}^{(0)} \oplus z_0, \dots, a_{u,v}^{(\ell-1)} \oplus c_{u,v}^{(\ell-1)} \oplus z_{\ell-1}$$

is generated and it is checked whether there is a match in $Tab[v]$. In the positive case, this gives candidates for u, t and v and finally for $s = u \oplus t \oplus v$ if and only if the entry is found in $Tab[v]$. The overall complexity of this step is 2^{40}, assuming that generating ℓ bits of keystream, together with a search in the sorted table is below the complexity of one GEA-1 evaluation (for generating a keystream of size 128 bit).

The correct key will always be identified, but this procedure can also suggest some wrong keys, depending on the value of ℓ. There is a trade-off between the amount of known plaintext available, the size of table, and the number of remaining keys. A wrong partial key $u \oplus v$ yields a bitstream stored in $Tab[v]$ with probability $\frac{1}{2^\ell}$ for each entry, if we assume the widely accepted hypothesis that an ℓ bit output of a filtered LFSR behaves like uniformly distributed random bits as long as ℓ is below its period (which will be the case here). We have 2^{24} entries in $Tab[v]$, thus there are at most 2^{24} possible correct entries per partial key. In other words, the probability that a wrong partial key does not cause a hit in $Tab[v]$ is $\left(1 - \frac{1}{2^\ell}\right)^{2^{24}}$ and therefore the probability that none of the wrong partial keys cause a hit is

$$\left(\left(1-\frac{1}{2^{\ell}}\right)^{2^{24}}\right)^{(2^{40}-1)} \approx \left(1-\frac{1}{2^{\ell}}\right)^{2^{64}}.$$

If we want the probability for no false hit to be larger than or equal to $\frac{1}{2}$, we can choose $\ell = 65$, for which we get $\left(1-\frac{1}{2^{\ell}}\right)^{2^{64}} \approx 0.607$. The corresponding size of the table *Tab* with this choice for ℓ is only 44.5 GiB and it can be built in time 2^{37}.

If we only have $n < 65$ known plaintext bits, we obtain a set of roughly 2^{64-n} remaining keys; if $n \geq 24$ we expect less than 2^{40} candidate keys, and can try each of them without increasing significantly the complexity of the attack. The key candidates can be verified using redundancy in the frame (*e.g.* checksums), or known bits in a different frame (*e.g.* headers). We need 65 known bits of information in total, but they can be spread over several frames as long as one frame has 24 bit of known plaintext. In practice, there are many GPRS frames with predictable content, so that intercepting a ciphertext with some known plaintext bits is not an issue (see Sect. 5.1 for details). Thus the attack is fully practical.

Note that the attack presented is rather straightforward and can probably be optimized. Moreover, several trade-offs are possible. For instance, one can alternatively apply the attack by building a table corresponding to the 2^{40} choices of $\alpha_{u,v}, \gamma_{u,v}$ and then performing an exhaustive search over 2^{32} values for $\beta_{t,v}$. This way, one would need 2^{32} `GEA-1` evaluations as the online time complexity, but much more memory for storing the table. For example, the memory needed to store 2^{40} values of 65-bit length is 8.125 TiB.

On the Likelihood that $\dim(T_{AC}) = 24$. We did an extensive computer search to answer the question if the situation in `GEA-1` is unlikely to occur. To do so, over 10^6 samples, we randomly generated two primitive polynomials g_1, g_2 of degrees d_1, d_2, built the corresponding Galois matrices G_{g_1}, G_{g_2}, computed the representation matrices $M_{G_{g_1}}, M_{G_{g_2},cs}$ for the initialization and computed the dimension of the intersection $T_{G_{g_1},G_{g_2},cs}$. Here, the parameter cs denotes the cyclic shift applied in the initialization process of the register. In Tables 1, 2, and 3, the results for the parameters as in `GEA-1` are given, i.e., for the parameters $d_1 = 31$ and $d_2 = 32$, $d_1 = 31$ and $d_2 = 33$, $d_1 = 32$ and $d_2 = 33$ with the corresponding shifts. A Sage program that allows the reader to repeat those experiments is provided in Appendix B.

Table 1. Behavior of intersections for randomly generated LFSRs of lengths $d_1 = 31$, $d_2 = 32$ and $cs = 16$ (10^6 tries)

Dimension of intersection	<5	5	6	7	8	9	10	11
# of spaces	996,027	3,002	742	171	49	6	1	2

Table 2. Behavior of intersections for randomly generated LFSRs of lengths $d_1 = 31$, $d_2 = 33$ and $cs = 32$ (10^6 tries)

Dimension of intersection	<5	5	6	7	8	9	10	11
# of spaces	998,027	1,490	366	86	26	5	0	0

Table 3. Behavior of intersections for randomly generated LFSRs of lengths $d_1 = 32$, $d_2 = 33$ and $cs_1 = 16, cs_2 = 32$ (10^6 tries)

Dimension of intersection	<5	5	6	7	8	9	10	11
# of spaces	999,065	701	181	39	10	3	1	0

Recall that in GEA-1, the intersection is of dimension 24. Thus, in general, our attack is avoided almost automatically when choosing random primitive feedback polynomials and further research needs to be conducted to better understand the design of GEA-1.

Experimental Verification. In this section we address our C++ implementation of the simple Divide-and-Conquer attack on GEA-1.

We first utilized sage to generate V and bases for T_{AC} and U_B. We then built a table Tab of 2^{32} entries, similarly as described above. Notice that each sub-table $Tab[v]$ is implemented as an array of 2^{19} sorted vectors containing entries consisting of 64 bits for $b_{t,v}$ and 24 bits representing t. The remaining bit of $b_{t,v}$ is implicitly stored as an index in $Tab[v]$. Tab is stored on disk such that it can be loaded when the attack gets executed again.

Given 65 bits of keystream z_i, the recovery of the initial state s is implemented as follows. For each combination of $u \in U_B$ and $v \in V$ the output stream is generated using a bitsliced implementation of A and C. To check whether there is a match in Tab we search through the vector at $Tab[v][idx]$ where idx represents the 19 most significant bits of the output stream. If there is a match we restore t from Tab and return $s = u \oplus t \oplus v$. To speed things up we parallelized both the generation of Tab and the recovery of s using OpenMP [10].

To test our implementation we first picked random values for t, u, v. After this we determined suitable values for K, IV and dir by clocking the register S backwards. Then we used the GEA-1 implementation that we were provided with to generate 65 keystream bits. Finally we checked if our attack restores the correct initial state $s = u \oplus t \oplus v$.

We executed the attack on a cluster made up of four AMD EPYC 7742 64-Core Processors. Generating and storing Tab takes 30 minutes whereas loading it from disk only takes five minutes. Tab is 46 GiB in size and the recovery of s has a running time of 25 minutes averaged over six runs.

4 An Attack on GEA-2

GEA-2 does not suffer from the same problems as GEA-1 for initialization. However, it is still possible to mount an attack on GEA-2 that does not target initialization, but keystream generation. The idea is to combine a list merging algorithm and algebraic techniques.

4.1 Algebraic Cryptanalysis

The algebraic degree of the filtering function f is 4. The filtering function also has an algebraic immunity of 4. But, as the 4 registers are never mixed, the number of monomials present in the system of equations formed by the relations between the keystream and the initial state is very limited. More precisely, this number is upper bounded by

$$1 + \sum_{i=1}^{4} \binom{29}{i} + \binom{31}{i} + \binom{32}{i} + \binom{33}{i} = 152682\,.$$

This relatively small number would directly imply a powerful attack, just by using a linearisation technique, or, even more powerful, by applying the Berlekamp-Massey algorithm [2,26], as this value is naturally an upper bound to the linear complexity of the output sequence (a direct consequence of Blahut's Theorem [5]).

However, each session in GEA-2 (or GEA-1) is limited to 1600 bytes, that is 12800 bits. This data limitation frustrates direct algebraic cryptanalysis, as the linearization technique is impossible when we have less equations than monomials.

4.2 Guess-and-Determine

The Guess-and-Determine technique seems to have its origin already in the cryptanalysis of A5/1 cipher [1,18]. It can be a powerful technique, specially for analyzing stream ciphers. In the context of algebraic cryptanalysis, it has been shown in [13] that Guess-and-Determine can really help to provide much simpler systems of equations. In a context of general multivariate system solving algorithms, this technique is known as the hybrid approach [3].

For GEA-2, we mainly want to reduce the number of monomials present in our system below 12800. By guessing n_d, n_a, n_b and n_c bits in the registers D, A, B and C respectively, we find that the number of non-constant monomials in the equations is upper bounded by

$$\sum_{i=1}^{4} \binom{29-n_d}{i} + \binom{31-n_a}{i} + \binom{32-n_b}{i} + \binom{33-n_c}{i}\,.$$

To get a system of equations of size below 12800 one needs to guess at least 59 bits of the initial state. One choice is $n_d = 29 - 16 = 13$ bits in the first register, $n_a = 31 - 16 = 15$ bits in the second register, $n_b = 32 - 17 = 15$ bits in the third register and $n_c = 33 - 17 = 16$ bits in the fourth register.

This leads to an attack complexity of 2^{59} times the cost of solving a linear system of size 12800, which is much more than the cost of the exhaustive search. We therefore need to combine guessing with other techniques.

4.3 Divide-and-Conquer Technique

The sum of the output of the four filtered registers frustrates the specific Divide-and-Conquer cryptanalysis described by T. Siegenthaler in 1985: correlation attacks [36].

However, Divide-and-Conquer techniques can also be applied when we adapt it for the following problem. We are given two sets S_1 and S_2, as well as two functions $f_1 : S_1 \to \mathbb{F}_2^c$ and $f_2 : S_2 \to \mathbb{F}_2^c$. For a given $t \in \mathbb{F}_2^c$ the problem is to find all $s_1 \in S_1$ and $s_2 \in S_2$ such that $f_1(s_1) + f_2(s_2) = t$. This problem arises quite often in cryptography and started in [35] with the cryptanalysis of the knapsack-based cryptosystem. Since then, advanced solving techniques have shown they can be a powerful tool for the cryptanalyst [6,12,22,24,33].

One way to solve this problem is to use a hash table H. Typically, for all $s_1 \in S_1$ we compute $f_1(s_1)$ and add s_1 to $H[f_1(s_1)]$. Then for each $s_2 \in S_2$ we compute $f_2(s_2)$ and check the corresponding values for s_1 in $H[t + f_2(s_2)]$. Using the right structure for H the complexity of exhausting all the solutions is $\mathcal{O}(|S_1| + |S_2|)$ in time and $\mathcal{O}(|S_1|)$ in memory.

Remark. This algorithm performs $|S_2|$ random accesses to H. If the table is too large to fit in RAM it may be faster to build the two lists, then to sort them and finally to sequentially go through them to find matches.

4.4 Description of the Attack

The techniques involved in our attack do not work in practice when used alone. However, they can be combined in an elegant way to recover the initial state with complexity significantly lower than 2^{64}. Our attack works as follows.

1. Guess $n_a + n_d$ bits in both registers A and D (note that the choice of values for n_a and n_d is not the same as in Sect. 4.2). The choice of registers A and D has been done with respect to their length, so as the choice of n_a and n_d that lead to the smallest number of guesses.
2. Using linearization technique, derive linear combinations of the keystream bits that are independent of the remaining variables in registers A and D. This corresponds to a set a linear masks m_i, for $1 \leq i \leq c$, such that for all i, $m_i \cdot s_{A+D}$ is constant, where s_{A+D} denotes the xor-sum of the sequences generated by the registers A and D, and $\cdot$ is the scalar product.
3. Apply the Divide-and-Conquer technique described previously, with S_1 covering all initial states β in register B and S_2 covering all initial states γ in

register C, with f_1 and f_2 being defined by the linear masks, and t_i defined as $m_i \cdot z \oplus m_i \cdot s_{A+D}$, where z is the known keystream, and $m_i \cdot s_{A+D}$ is known:

$$f_1 : \beta \mapsto (m_1 \cdot s_B, \dots, m_c \cdot s_B)$$
$$f_2 : \gamma \mapsto (m_1 \cdot s_C, \dots, m_c \cdot s_C)$$

First, we build polynomials corresponding to the output of each filtered register, with the initial value of the register bits as variables. We use register C as an example since it is the largest one. Since the LFSR is linear, we can write the state as a matrix representing the linear expression of each bit in terms of the 33 variables; clocking the LFSR is just a matrix product with a total cost of at most $12800 \times 33^3 = 2^{28.8}$. This could probably be improved further, but will be a negligible cost in the attack anyway.

Next, we notice that guessing $n_d = 9$ bits from register D and $n_a = 11$ bits from register A decreases the number of possible non-constant monomials in the 20+20 remaining variables from A and D to

$$\sum_{i=1}^{4} \binom{20}{i} + \binom{20}{i} = 12390$$

which is smaller than the amount of data available per session. Thus we can perform a Gaussian elimination on the system of equations to derive at least $12800 - 12390 = 410$ linear masks m_i on the output of A and D, such that every non-constant monomial vanishes. On a 64-bit computer the cost of this step is around $12800 \times 12390 \times 12390/64 = 2^{34.8}$ simple operations on 64-bit words.

In order to evaluate f_1 and f_2 efficiently, we write them as polynomials in the B and C variables, respectively. To do so we first choose $c = 64$ masks and we compute the corresponding polynomial expressions of outputs from B and C. This corresponds to multiplying a binary matrix of size $12800 \times (\sum_{i=1}^{4} \binom{32}{i} + \binom{33}{i})$ by a binary matrix of size 64×12800. This requires $64 \times 12800 \times 88385/64 = 2^{30.1}$ simple operations on 64-bit words. We also apply the masks to the keystream sequence with a negligible cost.

At the end of the previous step we have 64 equations of the form $P_B^i = P_C^i$ where P_B^i and P_C^i are polynomials in variables from registers B and C respectively and we can apply the Meet-in-the-Middle technique to retrieve the possible values for B and C. First we evaluate $(P_B^0, P_B^1, \dots, P_B^{63})$ for all the 2^{32} possible initial states of register B and store the result in a hash table H. Then we evaluate $(P_C^0, P_C^1, \dots, P_C^{63})$ for all the 2^{33} possible starting states of C and get the corresponding values for B by looking into the hash table. Using the enumeration technique of [7], we can evaluate the 64 degree-4 polynomials on all 2^n states for a cost of only $2^n \times 64 \times 4$ bit operation. Therefore, the cost of this step is roughly $(2^{32} + 2^{33}) \times 4 \times 64/64 = 2^{35.6}$ operations on 64-bit words plus $2^{32} + 2^{33} = 2^{33.6}$ random accesses to the hash table.

Finally, for all the remaining values for registers B and C we solve the system of equations in variables from A and D. As it was already echelonized in the first step of the attack we only have to check whether it is consistent or not, requiring approximately 12390 bit-operations. Since there are only a few remaining key candidates, this step is negligible.

Overall the attack requires:

- $2^{20} \times (2^{34.8} + 2^{30.1} + 2^{35.6}) = 2^{56.3}$ operations on 64-bit words
- $2^{20} \times (2^{33.6}) = 2^{53.6}$ memory accesses

In terms of GEA-2 operations, we assume that one encryption requires at least 64 word operations[6], and that one memory access is comparable to an encryption call. Therefore the complexity is equivalent to $2^{53.7}$ GEA-2 encryptions. The memory complexity corresponds to $2^{32} \times 64 = 2^{38}$ bits.

4.5 Improved Attack

We have developed two tricks to decrease the complexity of our attack against GEA-2. The first one is based on the observation that we perform the same computations several times and that this can be avoided by reorganizing them. The second improvement is highly inspired from classical time/data trade-offs where a sequence of n keystream bits can be seen as k (shifted) sequences of $n - k$ keystream bits.

Gaussian Elimination Only Once. The first Gaussian elimination is performed 2^{20} times, once for each guessed value of the 20 chosen bits of registers A and D. But since the polynomials are of degree 4, guessing a variable cannot *create* a monomial of degree 4. Thus, before starting to guess variables, it is possible to partially echelonize the system by removing all degree 4 monomials which do not contain a variable that will be guessed. This removes $\binom{20}{4} + \binom{20}{4} = 9690$ equations and requires $12800 \times (\sum_{i=1}^{4} \binom{29}{i} + \binom{31}{i}) \times 9690/64 = 2^{36.9}$ operations on 64-bit words. Then for each guess the first Gaussian elimination is performed on a matrix with $12800 - 9690 = 3110$ rows and $\sum_{i=1}^{3} \binom{20}{i} + \binom{20}{i} = 2700$ columns. As a consequence, the time complexity of the attack becomes:

- $2^{36.9} + 2^{20} \times (2^{28.4} + 2^{30.1} + 2^{35.6}) = 2^{55.6}$ operations on 64-bit words
- $2^{20} \times (2^{33.6}) = 2^{53.6}$ memory accesses

Reducing Number of Guesses. We can improve the attack using the classical trick of targeting the internal state at several different clocks, instead of focusing only on the initial state. The novelty here is that we can find masks which simultaneously work for several shifted keystream sequences.

First, we use $n_d = 10$ and $n_a = 11$, so that the number of non-constant monomial from A and D is only $\sum_{i=1}^{4} \binom{19}{i} + \binom{20}{i} = 11230$. We target one of the 753 first internal states, therefore we extract shifted keystream sequences of length 12047 produced by each of those states. The initial state produces

[6] In a brute-force search, the initialization requires at least 195 clocking of the W register per key.

keystream $z_0 \cdots z_{12046}$, the state after one clock produces keystream $z_1 \cdots z_{12047}$, and so on. We define V as the vector space of masks m (of length 12047) such that $m \cdot z$ is independent of z for all the 753 sequences considered; V has dimension $12047 - 753 + 1 = 11295$.

Using the strategy of the previous attack, for each guess of the 21 bits in registers A and D, we can deduce a vector space of dimension $12047 - 11230 = 817$ of masks such that $m_i \cdot s_{A+D}$ is constant. We intersect this vector space with V to obtain a space of dimension 65 of masks such that both $m_i \cdot s_{A+D}$ and $m_i \cdot z$ are constant, and we run the previous attack with 64 independent masks from this space.

The probability that the guess of the 21 bits is correct for at least one of the 753 first internal states is $1 - (1 - 2^{-21})^{753} \approx 2^{-11.4}$. Thus we have to repeat this step with $2^{11.4}$ different guesses on the average, and the time complexity becomes:

- $2^{36.9} + 2^{11.4} \times (2^{27.9} + 2^{30.1} + 2^{35.6}) = 2^{47}$ operations on 64-bit words
- $2^{11.4} \times (2^{33.6}) = 2^{45}$ memory accesses

This is equivalent to roughly $2^{45.1}$ GEA-2 encryptions.

4.6 Recovering the Master Key

This attack recovers the internal states of the registers A, B, C and D, either at the beginning or after a few clocks. From this we can easily recover the sequence w, because the initialization and the update of the LFSRs are linear functions. As in the case of GEA-1, we can also recover the master key by clocking the W register forwards from the zero state, and backwards from the recovered state w. Therefore, we only have to perform the attack once per GPRS session; we can decrypt all the messages in a session if we have one known message of length 1600 byte.

4.7 Using Less Data

Our attack can be applied with less data than 12800 bits of keystream. In that case the time complexity is increased as shown in Fig. 8. To reach a complexity below 2^{64} (the complexity of an exhaustive search on the key), we need around 1468 consecutive keystream bits.

4.8 Experimental Verification

We now briefly describe our proof of concept implementation of the attack on GEA-2. The implementation consists of a sage and C++ part which is made accessible to sage using Cython.

In an initial step we built matrices that represent polynomials corresponding to the filtered output of B and C by evaluating B and C symbolically in sage. Here we enumerated the 12 most significant bits and therefore we do not have one

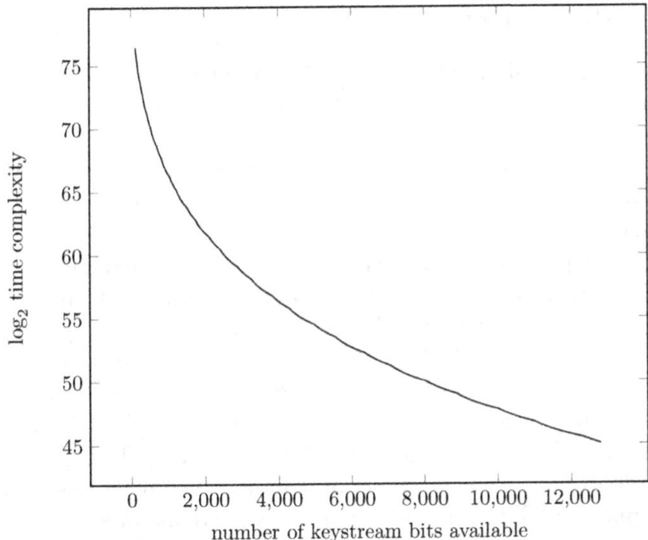

Fig. 8. Time complexity of our attack against GEA-2 as a function of the number of consecutive keystream bits available.

but 4096 matrices for each register. This allows straightforward parallelization of the Divide-and-Conquer step when using the enumeration technique of [7]. The matrices are stored on disks such that they can be loaded when the attack gets executed again.

Given the keystream we first compute V as described above. Then we start guessing 21 bits in A and D. For each guess we compute 64 corresponding masks. These are then handed over to the C++ part which builds upon the M4RI [25] library to apply the Divide-and-Conquer technique. Candidates for β and γ are returned to sage to check if they lead to consistent solutions for the remaining bits in registers A and D.

To test our implementation we picked random values for K, IV and dir and computed the keystream with the GEA-2 implementation we were provided with. We also determined the first 753 internal states such that we can directly check whether a guess of the 21 bits in A and D was correct or not.

We executed the attack on the same hardware as for the GEA-1 attack. It takes about one hour to perform the calculations on one guess and therefore we get roughly four months as the runtime of a full attack.

5 Discussion

In the following, we discuss the real-world attack feasibility, the attack severity and the attack implications.

5.1 Attack Requirements

To recover the full session key of a GEA-1 encrypted connection, the attacker must meet the following conditions: The attacker must *i*) sniff the encrypted radio traffic of the victim's phone and *ii*) know 65 bits of the keystream, preferably at the beginning of the keystream. As shown by Nohl and Melette [29], sniffing the encrypted traffic can be conducted with the osmocom-bb project [31] using ordinary hardware.

Meeting the requirement of knowing 65 bits of the keystream can be achieved by exploiting predictable SNDCP (Subnetwork Dependent Convergence Protocol) and IP header patterns. A GPRS data connection encapsulates each IP packet with the SNDCP, which is then encrypted by the LLC (Logical Link Control) protocol. In a small experiment, we study patterns that remain stable and predictable over multiple GPRS connections in the SNDCP and IP header. Header fields like the SNDCP NSAPI, the IP Version, TTL, ToS, and destination IP address fields remain stable over multiple connections. Consequently, guessing 65 plaintext bits and obtaining 65 keystream bits is plausible by an entirely passive attacker.

In contrast, the attack on GEA-2 requires the attacker to know the whole 1600 bytes of keystream to recover the session key with complexity $2^{45.1}$ GEA-2 evaluations. Accordingly, the attacker must correctly predict 1600 bytes of plaintext. Depending on the attacker's capabilities, this can be within the area of possibility. If the attacker controls a server that the victim visits, he can access the bytes sent or receives, and consequently, the attack can predict 1600 bytes. The recovered key is then valid for the whole GRPS session, including other traffic of interest. Such an attack may require some social engineering, e. g., a phishing attack, to convince the victim to visit the website.

5.2 Attack Severity

In GPRS the operator chooses the encryption algorithm, i. e., GEA-1, GEA-2, GEA-3 (based on KASUMI with a 64-bit key), or GEA-4 (based on KASUMI with a 128-bit key). According to a study by Tomcsányi et al. [11], that analyzes the use of the ciphering algorithm in GRPS of 100 operators worldwide, most operators prioritize the use of GEA-3 (58) followed by the non-encrypted mode GEA-0 (38). Only a few operators rely on GEA-2 (4), while no operator uses GEA-1 (0). Consequently, the likelihood for an attack based on the GEA-1 and GEA-2 vulnerabilities is *nowadays* comparably small.

To draw a complete picture, we additionally analyze the support of both algorithms in mobile phones. Since 2013, ETSI prohibits implementing GEA-1 in mobile stations, while GEA-2 and the non-encrypted mode (GEA-0) are still mandatory to be implemented [16]. We tested a range of current phones if they follow the specification regarding disabling the GEA-1 cipher. We use an osmocom GPRS setup which we extended with the support of GEA-1 and GEA-2 [31]. Table 4 shows a selection of phones in which we cover a wide range of baseband manufacturers. Those manufacturers are responsible for implementing the standard accordingly. Surprisingly, all tested phones support the vulnerable ciphers GEA-1, thereby clearly disrespecting the specification.

Table 4. Overview of the phones and basebands supporting (●) GEA-X

Phone	Year	Baseband	GEA-1	GEA-2
Apple iPhone XR	2018	Intel XMM 7560	●	●
Apple iPhone 8	2017	Intel XMM 7480	●	●
Samsung Galaxy S9	2018	Samsung Exynos 9810	●	●
HMD Global Nokia 3.1	2018	Mediatek MT6750	●	●
Huawei P9 lite	2016	HiSilicon Kirin 650	●	●
OnePlus 6T	2018	Qualcomm Snapdragon 845	●	●

Once the key is recovered, the attacker can decrypt all traffic for the complete GPRS session until the key gets invalid, which happens in the GPRS authentication and ciphering procedure triggered by the network. The start of this procedure depends on the operator's policy. Usually, the procedure starts on an expired timer, e. g., 1–24 h, or the change of a location area, which is a regional group of base stations.

5.3 Attack Implications

GEA-1 provides 40-bit security and is breakable by today's standard hardware. This fact causes severe implications for our mobile Internet connection during the early 2000s and now.

During the early 2000s, Internet connections were barely secured by any transport layer security, such as TLS. Under the assumption that an operator used GEA-1 for the network, the entire traffic was accessible to a passive attacker. In contrast, nowadays connections are mostly secured by TLS. However, if the network encryption can be bypassed (as with GEA-1), metadata is still accessible, such as DNS requests, IP addresses, and hostnames when using the TLS SNI extension. Consequently, the use of GEA-1 has still far-reaching consequences on the user's privacy and should be avoided at all costs.

Even if the operator uses a stronger cipher like GEA-3, the support of GEA-1 by the phone allows an attacker to recover a previous session key. A requirement for this attack is that the operator also relies on GSM authentication. GSM authentication is not replay protected, and thus the attacker can replay the previous authentication request with a fake base station and instruct the phone to use the vulnerable cipher (Authentication and Ciphering Request). After a complete attack procedure, sending the ciphering request forces the phone to use a weak cipher (i.e. GEA-1) for the next data uplink packet. At that point, the attacker can guess the plaintext to recover parts of the keystream and thus also the previous session key. Consequently, the attacker can decrypt the previous session, which was encrypted with a stronger cipher, e. g., GEA-3. This shows that even when operators do not actively use GEA-1, the weak GEA-1 design affects the security of today's communication.

Time/Memory Trade-Off Attack against GEA-2. While the present attack against GEA-2 has a complexity of 2^{45} GEA-2 evaluations and requires a large amount of known keystream, we could also think of a time/memory trade-off attack against GEA-2. However, in contrast to A5/1 where this could be applied [21], the initial state of 125 bits prohibits any such attack aiming for the initial state. Building a time/memory trade-off, using e.g. rainbow-tables, (see [30]) targeting directly the 64 bits secret key would only work for a fixed IV. While it would indeed reduce the amount of known keystream needed, it turns the attack into a chosen IV attack, which limits its practical interest.

5.4 Responsible Disclosure and Industry Implications

Following the guidelines of responsible disclosure, we have disclosed the vulnerability to the GSMA and ETSI Coordinated Vulnerability Disclosure programme [14,19]. We, thereby, followed two aims: In short term, we want to disable the support of GEA-1 from all mobile phones and thereby restore the specifications conformity. For mitigating the mid-risk of exploiting the GEA-2 vulnerabilities, we advocate for removing the support of GEA-2 from the specification.

The main objective of the GSMA CVD program was to disable the support of GEA-1. The GSMA informed the affected baseband vendors, phone manufacturers, including Google and Apple, through the CVD program. Further, the GSMA liaised with GCF (Global Certification Forum) [17], the mobile industry's globally recognized certification scheme for mobile phones and wireless devices based on 3GPP standards. The GCF included two test cases as part of version 3.81.0 of the certification criteria, which became available for certification in January 2021. These are: Conformance test case 44.2.5.2.5 Ciphering mode/Non-support of GEA-1 from 3GPP TS 51.010-1 and field trial test case 5.6.5 GPRS functionality – Non-support of GEA-1 from GSMA TS.11. Those test cases now allow to verify that the support of GEA-1 is *disabled* by devices before entering the market.

In contrast, the submission to the ETSI CVD program followed the mid-term goal to remove the support of GEA-2 from the specification and consequently also from mobile devices. At the time of paper finalization, the ETSI has accepted our CVD submission and considers whether any standards related measures need to be taken. Specification changes usually require the consent of several parties and take accordingly longer. We will continue to fight for removing the support of GEA-2 from the specification.

6 Conclusion

We have shown that the first version of the GPRS Encryption Algorithm, GEA-1, only offers 40-bit (out of 64) security. We have further shown that it is very unlikely for a random instance to suffer from such weaknesses. Since GEA-1 was designed to be exportable within the export restrictions in European countries in the late 1990s, this might be an indication that a security level of 40 bits was a barrier for cryptographic algorithms to obtain the necessary authorizations. Ultimately, the weak design of GEA-1 brings security problems for today's communication, even if it is not being actively used by the operators.

The successor algorithm GEA-2 seems to be a stronger design, in which the weaknesses of GEA-1 are not present anymore. Still, the cipher does not offer full 64-bit security and we have shown an attack of complexity $2^{45.1}$ GEA-2 evaluations. Although such an attack is more difficult to be applied in practice, we think that GEA-2 does not offer a high enough security level for todays standards. Therefore, we strongly recommend that only the much more secure GPRS Encryption Algorithms, starting from GEA-3, should be implemented.

Acknowledgment. This work was supported by the German Research Foundation (DFG) within the framework of the Excellence Strategy of the Federal Government and the States - EXC 2092 CASA - 39078197, and by French Agence Nationale de la Recherche (ANR), under grant ANR-20-CE48-0017 (project SELECT). Patrick Derbez was supported by the French Agence Nationale de la Recherche through the CryptAudit project under Contract ANR-17-CE39-0003.

Most of all, we give thanks to Dieter Spaar and Harald Welte for their support and contact persons of the osmocom project.

Appendix A Source Code to Compute the Kernels

Listing 1.1. gea1_kernels.sage

```
def getInitMatrix(p,keyLength,shift):
    P.<x> = PolynomialRing(GF(2))
    l = p.degree()
    #construct transformation matrix A for LFSR in Galois mode
    A = companion_matrix(p, "left")
    M = zero_matrix(GF(2),keyLength,l)
    for c in range(keyLength):
        x = zero_vector(GF(2),l)
        k = zero_vector(GF(2),keyLength)
        k[c] = 1
        for j in range(keyLength):
            x[0] = x[0] + k[(j+shift) % keyLength]
            x = A*x
        M[c] = x
    return M

#for GEA-1
```

```
P.<x> = PolynomialRing(GF(2))
keyLength = 64
pA = x^31+x^30+x^28+x^27+x^23+x^22+x^21+x^19+x^18+x^15
+x^11+x^10+x^8+x^7+x^6+x^4+x^3+x^2+1
shiftA = 0
pB = x^32+x^31+x^29+x^25+x^19+x^18+x^17+x^16+x^9+x^8+x^7+x^3
+x^2+x+1
shiftB = 16
pC = x^33+x^30+x^27+x^23+x^21+x^20+x^19+x^18+x^17+x^15+x^14
+x^11+x^10+x^9+x^4+x^2+1
shiftC = 32

MA = getInitMatrix(pA, keyLength, shiftA)
MB = getInitMatrix(pB, keyLength, shiftB)
MC = getInitMatrix(pC, keyLength, shiftC)

U_B = MB.kernel()
T_AC= MA.kernel().intersection(MC.kernel())
print(U_B.dimension())          #has dimension 32
print(T_AC.dimension())         #has dimension 24
print(T_AC.intersection(U_B).dimension()) #has dimension 0
```

Appendix B Source Code to Compute the Dimensions

Listing 1.2. random_kernels.sage

```
set_random_seed()
P.<x> = PolynomialRing(GF(2))

def get_random_primitive(l):
  V = VectorSpace(GF(2),l)
  v = list(V.random_element())
  p = P(v+[1])
  while (not p.is_primitive()):
    v = list(V.random_element())
    p = P(v+[1])
  return p

#parameters to set
keyLength = 64
l1 = 31
l2 = 33
shift1 = 0
shift2 = 32
samples = 1000000

dim = [0]*40
for i in range(samples):
  #get random primitive polynomials p1 and p2
  p1 = get_random_primitive(l1)
  p2 = get_random_primitive(l2)
  M1 = getInitMatrix(p1, keyLength, shift1)
```

```
M2 = getInitMatrix(p2,keyLength,shift2)
T = M1.kernel().intersection(M2.kernel())
dim[T.dimension()] = dim[T.dimension()]+1
if (((i+1)%1000)==0):
   print('runs =',i+1)
   print(dim)
```

References

1. Anderson, R.J.: A5 (was hacking digital phones). Newsgroup Communication (1994). http://yarchive.net/phone/gsmcipher.html. Accessed 4 Mar 2021
2. Berlekamp, E.R.: Algebraic Coding Theory. McGraw-Hill Series in Systems Science. McGraw-Hill (1968). http://www.worldcat.org/oclc/00256659
3. Bettale, L., Faugère, J., Perret, L.: Hybrid approach for solving multivariate systems over finite fields. J. Math. Cryptol. **3**(3), 177–197 (2009). https://doi.org/10.1515/JMC.2009.009
4. Biryukov, A., Gong, G., Stinson, D.R. (eds.): SAC 2010. LNCS, vol. 6544. Springer, Heidelberg (2011). https://doi.org/10.1007/978-3-642-19574-7
5. Blahut, R.E.: Theory and Practice of Error Control Codes. Addison-Wesley, Boston (1983)
6. Bogdanov, A., Rechberger, C.: A 3-subset meet-in-the-middle attack: cryptanalysis of the lightweight block cipher KTANTAN. In: Biryukov et al. [4], pp. 229–240. https://doi.org/10.1007/978-3-642-19574-7_16
7. Bouillaguet, C., et al.: Fast exhaustive search for polynomial systems in $\mathbb{F}_2$. In: Mangard, S., Standaert, F.-X. (eds.) CHES 2010. LNCS, vol. 6225, pp. 203–218. Springer, Heidelberg (2010). https://doi.org/10.1007/978-3-642-15031-9_14
8. Brookson, C.: GPRS Security (2001). https://web.archive.org/web/20120914110208/www.brookson.com/gsm/gprs.pdf. (snapshot of 14 September 2012)
9. Carlet, C., Crama, Y., Hammer, P.L.: Boolean functions for cryptography and error-correcting codes. In: Crama, Y., Hammer, P.L. (eds.) Boolean Models and Methods in Mathematics, Computer Science, and Engineering, pp. 257–397. Cambridge University Press (2010). https://doi.org/10.1017/cbo9780511780448.011
10. Dagum, L., Menon, R.: OpenMP: an industry standard API for shared-memory programming. IEEE Comput. Sci. Eng. **5**(1), 46–55 (1998)
11. Tomcsányi, D.P., Weyres, M., Simao, P.: Analysis of EGPRS Ciphering Algorithms used Worldwide. https://www.umlaut.com/en/analysis-of-egprs-ciphering-algorithms-used-worldwide. (to appear)
12. Dunkelman, O., Sekar, G., Preneel, B.: Improved meet-in-the-middle attacks on reduced-round DES. In: Srinathan, K., Rangan, C.P., Yung, M. (eds.) INDOCRYPT 2007. LNCS, vol. 4859, pp. 86–100. Springer, Heidelberg (2007). https://doi.org/10.1007/978-3-540-77026-8_8
13. Duval, S., Lallemand, V., Rotella, Y.: Cryptanalysis of the FLIP family of stream ciphers. In: Robshaw, M., Katz, J. (eds.) CRYPTO 2016. LNCS, vol. 9814, pp. 457–475. Springer, Heidelberg (2016). https://doi.org/10.1007/978-3-662-53018-4_17
14. ETSI: ETSI – Coordinated Vulnerability Disclosure. https://www.etsi.org/standards/coordinated-vulnerability-disclosure. Accessed 4 Mar 2021

15. ETSI: Security algorithms group of experts (SAGE); report on the specification, evaluation and usage of the GSM GPRS encryption algorithm (GEA). Technical report (1998). https://www.etsi.org/deliver/etsi_tr/101300_101399/101375/01.01.01_60/tr_101375v010101p.pdf. Accessed 8 Oct 2020
16. ETSI: Digital cellular telecommunications system (phase 2+) (GSM); security related network functions (3GPP TS 43.020 version 15.0.0 release 15). Technical Specification (2018). https://www.etsi.org/deliver/etsi_ts/143000_143099/143020/15.00.00_60/ts_143020v150000p.pdf. Accessed 8 Oct 2020
17. GCF: GCF – Global Certification Forum. https://www.globalcertificationforum.org/. Accessed 4 Mar 2021
18. Golić, J.D.: Cryptanalysis of alleged A5 stream cipher. In: Fumy, W. (ed.) EUROCRYPT 1997. LNCS, vol. 1233, pp. 239–255. Springer, Heidelberg (1997). https://doi.org/10.1007/3-540-69053-0_17
19. GSMA: GSMA – Coordinated Vulnerability Disclosure Programme. https://www.gsma.com/security/gsma-coordinated-vulnerability-disclosure-programme/. Accessed 4 Mar 2021
20. Hoffman, K., Kunze, R.A.: Linear Algebra. PHI Learning (2004). http://www.worldcat.org/isbn/8120302702
21. Kalenderi, M., Pnevmatikatos, D.N., Papaefstathiou, I., Manifavas, C.: Breaking the GSM A5/1 cryptography algorithm with rainbow tables and high-end FPGAS. In: Koch, D., Singh, S., Tørresen, J. (eds.) 22nd International Conference on Field Programmable Logic and Applications (FPL), Oslo, Norway, 29–31 August 2012, pp. 747–753. IEEE (2012). https://doi.org/10.1109/FPL.2012.6339146
22. Khovratovich, D., Naya-Plasencia, M., Röck, A., Schläffer, M.: Cryptanalysis of Luffa v2 components. In: Biryukov et al. [4], pp. 388–409. https://doi.org/10.1007/978-3-642-19574-7_26
23. Koops, B.J.: Crypto law survey (2013). http://www.cryptolaw.org. Accessed 8 Oct 2020
24. Lamberger, M., Mendel, F., Rechberger, C., Rijmen, V., Schläffer, M.: Rebound distinguishers: results on the full whirlpool compression function. In: Matsui, M. (ed.) ASIACRYPT 2009. LNCS, vol. 5912, pp. 126–143. Springer, Heidelberg (2009). https://doi.org/10.1007/978-3-642-10366-7_8
25. Albrecht, M., Bard, G.: The M4RI Library. The M4RI Team (2021). http://m4ri.sagemath.org. Accessed 4 Mar 2021
26. Massey, J.L.: Shift-register synthesis and BCH decoding. IEEE Trans. Inf. Theory **15**(1), 122–127 (1969). https://doi.org/10.1109/TIT.1969.1054260
27. McFarland, R.L.: A family of difference sets in non-cyclic groups. J. Comb. Theory Ser. A **15**(1), 1–10 (1973). https://doi.org/10.1016/0097-3165(73)90031-9
28. MediaTek: Test Vector GEA1/2 – MediaTek-HelioX10-Baseband. https://github.com/Dude100/MediaTek-HelioX10-Baseband/blob/591772a0d659ef0f7bba1953d18f8fe7c18b11de/(FDD)MT6795.MOLY.LR9.W1423.MD.LWTG.MP.V24/driver/cipher/include/gcu_ut.h. Accessed 4 Mar 2021
29. Nohl, K., Melette, L.: GPRS intercept: Wardriving your country. Chaos Communication Camp (2011). Slides http://events.ccc.de/camp/2011/Fahrplan/attachments/1868_110810.SRLabs-Camp-GRPS_Intercept.pdf. Accessed 8 Oct 2020. Recorded talk https://media.ccc.de/v/cccamp11-4504-gprs_intercept-en#t=1744. Accessed 8 Oct 2020
30. Oechslin, P.: Making a faster cryptanalytic time-memory trade-off. In: Boneh, D. (ed.) CRYPTO 2003. LNCS, vol. 2729, pp. 617–630. Springer, Heidelberg (2003). https://doi.org/10.1007/978-3-540-45146-4_36

31. osmocom: osmocom – Cellular Network Infrastructure. https://osmocom.org/projects/cellular-infrastructure. Accessed 4 Mar 2021
32. Rothaus, O.S.: On "bent" functions. J. Comb. Theory Ser. A **20**(3), 300–305 (1976). https://doi.org/10.1016/0097-3165(76)90024-8
33. Sasaki, Y.: Meet-in-the-middle preimage attacks on AES hashing modes and an application to Whirlpool. In: Joux, A. (ed.) FSE 2011. LNCS, vol. 6733, pp. 378–396. Springer, Heidelberg (2011). https://doi.org/10.1007/978-3-642-21702-9_22
34. Schneier, B.: Applied Cryptography - Protocols, Algorithms, and Source Code in C, 2nd edn. Wiley (1996). http://www.worldcat.org/oclc/32311687
35. Schroeppel, R., Shamir, A.: A $\mathrm{T}=\mathrm{O}(2^{\mathrm{n}/2})$, $\mathrm{S}=\mathrm{O}(2^{\mathrm{n}/4})$ algorithm for certain np-complete problems. SIAM J. Comput. **10**(3), 456–464 (1981). https://doi.org/10.1137/0210033
36. Siegenthaler, T.: Decrypting a class of stream ciphers using ciphertext only. IEEE Trans. Comput. **34**(1), 81–85 (1985). https://doi.org/10.1109/TC.1985.1676518
37. The Sage Developers: SageMath, the Sage Mathematics Software System (2020). https://www.sagemath.org

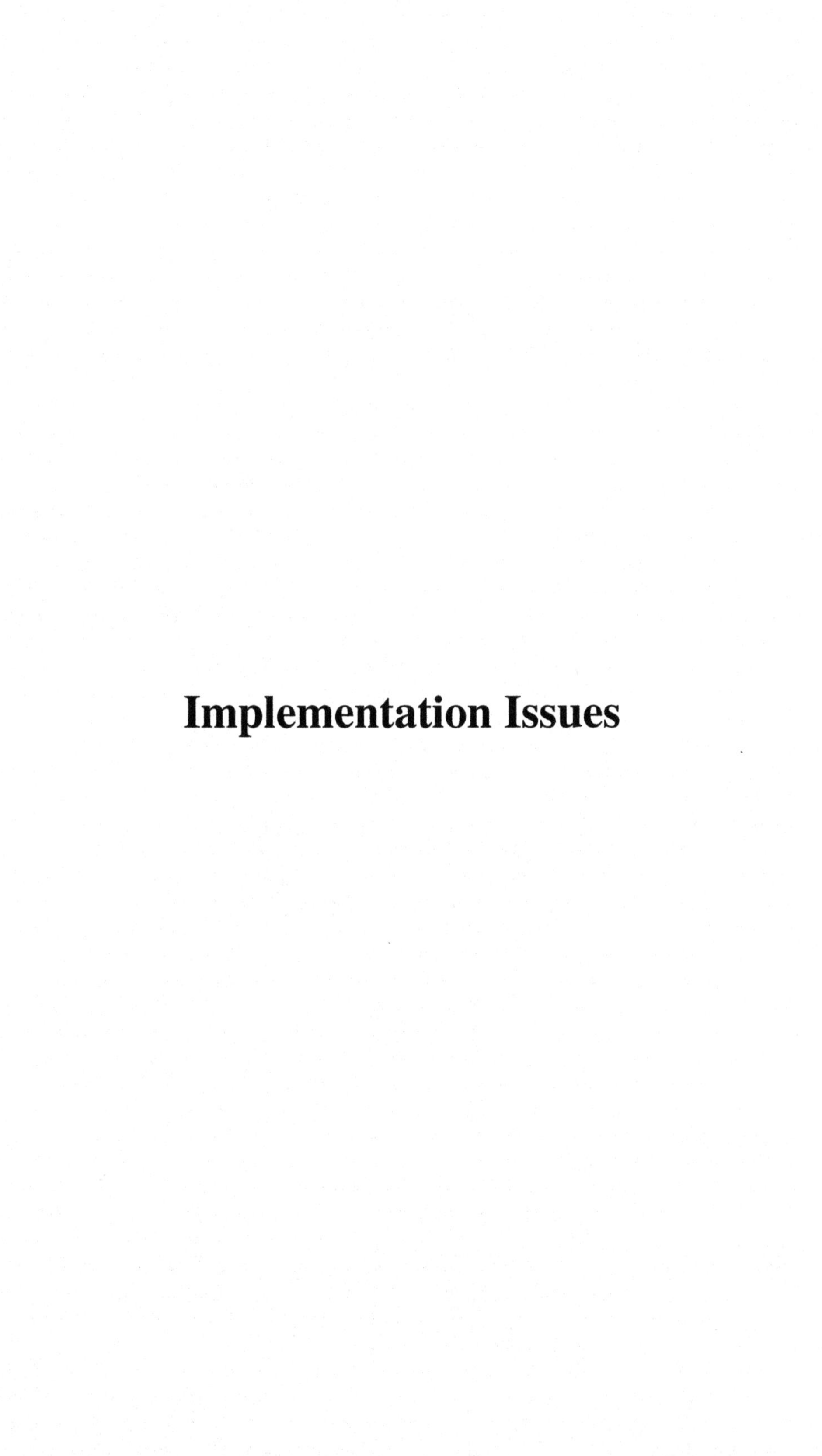

Implementation Issues

Pre-computation Scheme of Window τNAF for Koblitz Curves Revisited

Wei Yu[1(✉)] and Guangwu Xu[2,3(✉)]

[1] State Key Laboratory of Information Security, Institute of Information Engineering, Chinese Academy of Sciences, Beijing 100093, China
yuwei@iie.ac.cn, yuwei_1_yw@163.com

[2] Key Laboratory of Cryptologic Technology and Information Security of Ministry of Education, Qingdao 266237, Shandong, China
gxu4sdq@sdu.edu.cn

[3] School of Cyber Science and Technology, Shandong University, Qingdao 266237, Shandong, China

Abstract. Let $E_a/\mathbb{F}_2 : y^2 + xy = x^3 + ax^2 + 1$ be a Koblitz curve. The window τ-adic non-adjacent form (window τNAF) is currently the standard representation system to perform scalar multiplications on $E_a/\mathbb{F}_{2^m}$ utilizing the Frobenius map τ. This work focuses on the pre-computation part of scalar multiplication. We first introduce $\mu\bar{\tau}$-operations where $\mu = (-1)^{1-a}$ and $\bar{\tau}$ is the complex conjugate of τ. Efficient formulas of $\mu\bar{\tau}$-operations are then derived and used in a novel pre-computation scheme. Our pre-computation scheme requires $6\mathbf{M} + 6\mathbf{S}$, $18\mathbf{M} + 17\mathbf{S}$, $44\mathbf{M} + 32\mathbf{S}$, and $88\mathbf{M} + 62\mathbf{S}$ ($a = 0$) and $6\mathbf{M} + 6\mathbf{S}$, $19\mathbf{M} + 17\mathbf{S}$, $46\mathbf{M} + 32\mathbf{S}$, and $90\mathbf{M} + 62\mathbf{S}$ ($a = 1$) for window τNAF with widths from 4 to 7 respectively. It is about two times faster, compared to the state-of-the-art technique of pre-computation in the literature. The impact of our new efficient pre-computation is also reflected by the significant improvement of scalar multiplication. Traditionally, window τNAF with width at most 6 is used to achieve the best scalar multiplication. Because of the dramatic cost reduction of the proposed pre-computation, we are able to increase the width for window τNAF to 7 for a better scalar multiplication. This indicates that the pre-computation part becomes more important in performing scalar multiplication. With our efficient pre-computation and the new window width, our scalar multiplication runs in at least 85.2% the time of Kohel's work (Eurocrypt'2017) combining the best previous pre-computation. Our results push the scalar multiplication of Koblitz curves, a very well-studied and long-standing research area, to a significant new stage.

Keywords: Elliptic curve cryptography · Koblitz curve · Scalar multiplication · Window τNAF · Pre-computation

1 Introduction

Elliptic curve cryptography has drawn extensive attention from the literature [24,29]. The family of Koblitz curves, proposed by Koblitz in [12], are non-

A. Canteaut and F.-X. Standaert (Eds.): EUROCRYPT 2021, LNCS 12697, pp. 187–218, 2021.
https://doi.org/10.1007/978-3-030-77886-6_7

supersingular curves defined over $\mathbb{F}_2$. The arithmetic of Koblitz curves has been of theoretical and practical significance since the start of elliptic curve cryptography. 4 Koblitz curves were recommended to be used in digital signature, key-establishment, and key management by National Institute of Standards and Technology (NIST) FIPS 186-5(draft) [20]–"digital signature standard" (October of 2019), NIST special publication 800-56A (revision 3)–"recommendation for pair-wise key-establishment schemes using discrete logarithm cryptography" [3] (April of 2018), and NIST special publication 800-57 Part 1 (revision 5)–"recommendation for key management, part 1: general" [2] (May of 2020) respectively. These indicate that Koblitz curves can still be useful in practice.

Koblitz curves has a computational advantage that a faster scalar multiplication can be achieved by replacing point doubling with the Frobenius map. For each bit $a \in \{0, 1\}$, the Koblitz curves are given as

$$E_a : y^2 + xy = x^3 + ax^2 + 1.$$

These curves can be considered over the binary extension $\mathbb{F}_{2^m}$ as m varies. Since $E_a(\mathbb{F}_2)$ is a subgroup of $E_a(\mathbb{F}_{2^m})$, one sees that $|E_a(\mathbb{F}_{2^m})| = |E_a(\mathbb{F}_2)| \cdot p$ for some positive integer p. It is of cryptographic interest to choose suitable m that makes p a prime. In the rest of our discussion, we just consider cases that p is a prime. In the range of $160 < m < 2000$, $\frac{|E_0(\mathbb{F}_{2^m})|}{|E_0(\mathbb{F}_2)|}$ is a prime when $m = 233, 239, 277, 283, 349, 409, 571, 1249$, and 1913, and $\frac{|E_1(\mathbb{F}_{2^m})|}{|E_1(\mathbb{F}_2)|}$ is a prime when $m = 163, 283, 311, 331, 347, 359, 701, 1153, 1597$, and 1621. Four Koblitz curves with $a = 0$ have been recommended by NIST [2,3,20]: K-233($a = 0$), K-283($a = 0$), K-409($a = 0$), and K-571($a = 0$). Koblitz curves with $a = 1$ over $\mathbb{F}_{2^{163}}$, $\mathbb{F}_{2^{283}}$, $\mathbb{F}_{2^{359}}$, and $\mathbb{F}_{2^{701}}$ denoted by K1-163(for legacy-use only), K1-283, K1-359, and K1-701 respectively are also investigated in this work.

The Frobenius map τ is an endomorphism of $E_a(\mathbb{F}_{2^m})$ defined by $\tau(x, y) = (x^2, y^2)$ and $\tau(\mathcal{O}) = \mathcal{O}$ where $\mathcal{O}$ is the point at infinity. Let $\mu = (-1)^{1-a}$, then for each point P in $E_a(\mathbb{F}_{2^m})$,

$$\tau^2(P) + 2P = \mu\tau(P).$$

This means that τ can be interpreted as a complex number satisfying $\tau^2 - \mu\tau + 2 = 0$. The Euclidean domain $\mathbb{Z}[\tau] = \mathbb{Z} + \tau\mathbb{Z}$ can be identified as a set of endomorphisms of E_a in the sense that $(g + h\tau)P = gP + h\tau(P)$.

Let M be the main subgroup of $E_a(F_{2^m})$, namely the subgroup of order p. M is an annihilating subgroup of $\delta = \frac{\tau^m - 1}{\tau - 1}$ in the sense that $\delta(P) = \mathcal{O}$ for every $P \in M$. We also note that $N(\delta) = p$ where N is the norm function on $\mathbb{Z}[\tau]$ defined as $N(g + h\tau) = |g + h\tau|^2 = g^2 + \mu gh + 2h^2$. It is easy to see that for an integer n and an element $\rho \in \mathbb{Z}[\tau]$, if $\rho \equiv n \pmod{\delta}$, then $\rho P = nP$ holds for all $P \in M$.

Koblitz [12] proposed a method of computing scalar multiplication nP with P from the main subgroup of a Koblitz curve by representing $n = \sum_{i=0}^{l-1} \epsilon_i \tau^i$ with $\epsilon_i \in \{0, 1\}$ and evaluating $\sum_{i=0}^{l-1} \epsilon_i \tau^i(P)$. In [26], Solinas further developed an extremely efficient window τNAF to compute nP. Refinements and extensions of Solinas' method were obtained by Blake, Murty and Xu [5,6].

The procedure of window τNAF can be described as four steps [5,27].

1. Reduction. Find a suitable $\rho \in \mathbb{Z}[\tau]$ satisfying $\rho \equiv n \pmod{\delta}$.
2. Window τNAF with width w. We shall just consider the nontrivial case of $w \geq 3$. Let $I_w = \{1, 3, \ldots, 2^{w-1} - 1\}$. For each $i \in I_w$, we choose an element c_i from the set $R_i = \{g + h\tau | g + h\tau \equiv i \pmod{\tau^w}, N(g + h\tau) < 2^w\}$, and construct the coefficient set $C = \{c_1, c_3, \ldots, c_{2^{w-1}-1}\}$. The window τNAF of n is the following sparse τ expansion of its reduction ρ:
$$\rho = \sum_{i=0}^{l-1} \epsilon_i u_i \tau^i,$$
where $\epsilon_i \in \{-1, 1\}$ and $u_i \in C \cup \{0\}$ with the property that any set $\{u_k, u_{k+1}, \ldots, u_{k+w-1}\}$ contains at most one nonzero element.
3. Pre-computation. Compute $Q_i = c_i P$ for each $i \in I_w$.
4. Computing nP. Employ Horner's algorithm to calculate nP using window τNAF and pre-computation.

Pre-computation plays a significant role in improving the efficiency of scalar multiplications using window τNAF. For window τ-NAF with widths w, $2^{w-2} - 1$ pre-computed points require to be stored in memory. Several ways of designing pre-computations have been proposed by Solinas [26], Blake, Murty and Xu [5], and Hankerson, Menezes, and Vanstone [10]. In fact, [5] established a framework under which pre-computations for window τNAF can be made more flexible. This framework also enables a rigorous proof of termination of window τNAF. In [6], the authors investigated fast scalar multiplications for larger family of elliptic curves by developing non-adjacent radix-τ expansions for integers in other Euclidean imaginary quadratic number fields. Later, Trost and Xu [27] introduced an optimal pre-computation of window τNAF that improves previous results. However, the main objective of the pre-computation in [27] is its mathematically natural and clean forms. The optimality is based on the fact that it requires $2^{w-2} - 1$ point additions and two evaluations of the Frobenius map τ. They employed λ-coordinates [23] to achieve an improvement on performance of scalar multiplication and provided a convenient structure for further work.

In 2017, Kohel introduced a twisted μ_4-normal form elliptic curve over a binary field for its efficiency in [15]. Kohel proved that twisted μ_4-normal form elliptic curves cover all the elliptic curves over binary fields recommended by NIST. A Koblitz curve using twisted μ_4-normal form is called a μ_4-Koblitz curve. Because of its promising computational advantage, it is of great interest to consider the use of μ_4-Koblitz curves in the window τNAF, especially for the pre-computation part.

Let us summarize the cost of existing pre-computation schemes for window τ-NAF with widths $w = 4$, 5, and 6 on μ_4-Koblitz curves (for $w = 3$, $P - \mu\tau P$ is the only pre-computation). We write **I**, **M**, and **S** for the costs of an inversion, a multiplication, and a squaring in $\mathbb{F}_{2^m}$ respectively. The pre-computation scheme in [26] covers $w = 4$ and 5 only. The corresponding costs are $15\mathbf{M} + 15\mathbf{S}$ and $38\mathbf{M} + 38\mathbf{S}$ with $a = 0$ and those are $18\mathbf{M} + 15\mathbf{S}$ and $45\mathbf{M} + 38\mathbf{S}$ with $a = 1$. In

[10], $w = 4$, 5, and 6 are considered. The corresponding costs are $15\mathbf{M}+15\mathbf{S}$, $40\mathbf{M}+35\mathbf{S}$, and $89\mathbf{M}+67\mathbf{S}$ with $a = 0$ and those are $18\mathbf{M}+15\mathbf{S}$, $47\mathbf{M}+35\mathbf{S}$, and $104\mathbf{M}+67\mathbf{S}$ with $a = 1$. The pre-computation scheme constructed in [27] has improved the above costs to $15\mathbf{M}+12\mathbf{S}$, $39\mathbf{M}+20\mathbf{S}$, and $87\mathbf{M}+36\mathbf{S}$ with $a = 0$ and $18\mathbf{M}+12\mathbf{S}$, $46\mathbf{M}+20\mathbf{S}$, and $102\mathbf{M}+36\mathbf{S}$ with $a = 1$ for $w = 4$, 5, and 6.

Our Contributions. The main purpose of this work is twofold. Firstly, we develop an efficient way of calculating pre-computation for the window τNAF on Koblitz curves; and secondly, we propose to use a bigger width in the window τNAF together with our pre-computation to achieve a significant speedup on scalar multiplication. By using a μ_4-Koblitz curve, our results show a great improvement over previous results. The main contributions are described as follows.

1. Let $\bar{\tau} = \mu - \tau$ be the complex conjugate of τ and P be a rational point on a Koblitz curve. Both Avanzi, Dimitrov, Doche, and Sica [1] and Doche, Kohel, and Sica [8] used complex multiplication $\bar{\tau}P$ in double-base representation to speed up scalar multiplication. Inspired by their elegant results, we introduce a new radix $\mu\bar{\tau}$. Under this radix, we design new formulas for $\mu\bar{\tau}P$ which only requires $2\mathbf{M}+2\mathbf{S}$. Trost and Xu proved that one point addition is necessary for computing each pre-computation point Q_i, $i \in \{3, 5, \ldots, 2^{w-1}-1\}$ [27]. We use $\mu\bar{\tau}$-operations to replace point additions or mixed additions in pre-computation scheme. As the cost of one full addition is $7\mathbf{M}+2\mathbf{S}$ and that of one mixed addition is $6\mathbf{M}+2\mathbf{S}$ for $a = 0$ and those are $8\mathbf{M}+2\mathbf{S}$ and $7\mathbf{M}+2\mathbf{S}$ respectively for $a = 1$, our formulas of $\mu\bar{\tau}P$ save quite a few field operations. Our formulas for $\mu\bar{\tau}P$ are part of doubling formulas, which may lead to a simplicity of the implementation.
2. We propose a plane search to generate R_i whose elements are with the form of $g + h\mu\tau$. To take full advantage of our $\mu\bar{\tau}$-operations, we choose one suitable $c_i \in R_i$ for each $i \in I_w$ generated by the plane search. A novel pre-computation scheme is developed to save more field operations. Our pre-computation scheme requires $6\mathbf{M}+6\mathbf{S}$, $18\mathbf{M}+17\mathbf{S}$, $44\mathbf{M}+32\mathbf{S}$, and $88\mathbf{M}+62\mathbf{S}$ ($a = 0$) and $6\mathbf{M}+6\mathbf{S}$, $19\mathbf{M}+17\mathbf{S}$, $46\mathbf{M}+32\mathbf{S}$, and $90\mathbf{M}+62\mathbf{S}$ ($a = 1$) for window τNAF with widths from 4 to 7 respectively. The cost of Solinas' pre-computation scheme, that of Hankerson, Menezes, and Vanstone's pre-computation scheme, that of Trost and Xu's pre-computation scheme, and that our pre-computation scheme on μ_4-Koblitz curves with $a = 0$ and $a = 1$ are shown in Table 1. The practical implementations show that our pre-computation is two times faster than Trost and Xu's pre-computation and are consistent with our theoretical analysis.
3. In window τNAF, a bigger window width corresponds to a sparser τ expansion for scalar multiplication. However, one should not make the width too big as it would increase the pre-computation cost and affect the overall performance. Currently, the state-of-the-art pre-computation scheme suggests

to use width at most 6 to achieve the best efficiency of scalar multiplication. Our pre-computation reduces the cost by half in most practical cases, namely, scheme with width 7 is about the same as the cost of existing pre-computation scheme with width 6. This allows us to use a bigger window width (e.g., 7) to get a faster scalar multiplication. The balance between the pre-computation part and the other part of scalar multiplication shows that the pre-computation takes a bigger ratio of scalar multiplication than before. This is useful especially for scalar multiplication with unfixed point. Constant-time scalar multiplication using our novel pre-computation on a μ_4-Koblitz curve saves up to 33.5% compared to that using Trost and Xu's pre-computation in López-Dahab (LD) coordinates [19], saves up to 28.6% compared to Trost and Xu's original work [27], and saves up to 14.8% compared to Kohel's work [15] combining Trost and Xu's pre-computation. It is about 4 times faster compared to the state-of-the-art non-pre-computation-based constant-time scalar multiplication in LD coordinates, about 4 times faster in λ-coordinates, and over 3 times faster on a μ_4-Koblitz curve.

Table 1. Cost of pre-computations on a μ_4-Koblitz curve

		$w = 4$	$w = 5$	$w = 6$
$a = 0$	Solinas [26]	15M + 15S	38M + 38S	–
	Hankerson, Menezes, Vanstone[10]	15M + 15S	40M + 35S	89M + 67S
	Trost, Xu [27]	15M + 12S	39M + 20S	87M + 36S
	Ours	6M + 6S	18M + 17S	44M + 32S
$a = 1$	Solinas [26]	18M + 15S	45M + 38S	–
	Hankerson, Menezes, Vanstone[10]	18M + 15S	47M + 35S	104M + 67S
	Trost, Xu [27]	18M + 12S	46M + 20S	102M + 36S
	Ours	6M + 6S	19M + 17S	47M + 32S

This paper is organized as follows. In Sect. 2, we present previous pre-computation schemes of window τNAF for Koblitz curves. In Sect. 3, we propose new formulas of $P \pm Q$ and $\mu\bar{\tau}$-operations. In Sect. 4, we design a novel pre-computation. In Sect. 5, scalar multiplications using different pre-computation schemes are analyzed. In Sect. 6, we compare our pre-computation scheme to other pre-computation schemes and compare scalar multiplications in experimental implementations. Finally, we discuss our pre-computation in Sect. 7.

2 Preliminary

We shall include some technical preparation and three existing designs of pre-computations in this section.

2.1 Determine $\tau^w|(g + h\tau)$

In the later discussion, we need a convenient criterion to determine whether $\tau^w|(g + h\tau)$ holds in $\mathbb{Z}[\tau]$. This can be done by Lucas sequence in [26] or by the approach suggested in [6] based on Hensel's lifting procedure [13].

Using Lucas sequence or Hensel's lifting algorithm, we get $s_2 = 2\mu$, $s_3 = 6\mu$, $s_4 = 6\mu$, $s_5 = 6\mu$, $s_6 = 38\mu$, $s_7 = 38\mu$, $s_8 = 166\mu$, $s_9 = 422\mu$, and $s_{10} = 934\mu$. When $w \geq 2$, $s_w \equiv 0 \pmod 2$ and $s_w/2$ is odd.

It has been proved in [6,26] that for each positive integer w,

$$\tau^w|(g + h\tau) \Leftrightarrow 2^w|(g + hs_w). \tag{1}$$

2.2 Costs of Point Operations on Koblitz Curves

We summarize the costs of point operations on Koblitz curves using LD coordinates [19], λ-coordinates [23], and those on a μ_4-Koblitz curve [15] shown as Table 2. We neglect the cost of a field addition since it involves only bitwise XORs.

Table 2. Costs of point operations on Koblitz curves

Coordinates	$\tau(P)$	τ-affine operation	Addition	Mixed addition*
LD coordinates [16,19]	3**S**	2**S**	13**M** + 4**S**	8**M** + 5**S**
λ-coordinates [23]	3**S**	2**S**	11**M** + 2**S**	8**M** + 2**S**
μ_4-Koblitz curve ($a = 0$) [14]	4**S**	3**S**	7**M** + 2**S**	6**M** + 2**S**
μ_4-Koblitz curve ($a = 1$) [15,17]	4**S**	3**S**	8**M** + 2**S**	7**M** + 2**S**

* Let P, Q be rational points in the main subgroup M. $\tau(P)$ is denoted by τ-affine operation or $P + Q$ is denoted by mixed addition when the Z-coordinate of P is 1 using LD coordinates, that is 1 using λ-coordinates, or X_2-coordinate of P is 1 on a μ_4-Koblitz curve.

Let $a \in \{0, 1\}$. A Koblitz curve $y^2 + xy = x^3 + ax^2 + 1$ can be translated into a μ_4-Koblitz curve $X_0^2 + X_2^2 = X_1X_3 + aX_0X_2$, $X_1^2 + X_3^2 = X_0X_2$ via the map $(x, y) \mapsto (x^2 : x^2 + y : 1 : x^2 + y + x)$ and the inverse is $(X_0 : X_1 : X_2 : X_3) \mapsto (X_1 + X_3 : X_0 + X_1 : X_2)$ [15]. The identity of a μ_4-Koblitz curve is $(1 : 1 : 0 : 1)$. The inverse morphism is $[-1](X_0 : X_1 : X_2 : X_3) = (X_0 : X_3 : X_2 : X_1)$. The projective point $(X_0 : X_1 : X_2 : X_3)$ on a μ_4-Koblitz curve can be translated into an affine point $(\frac{X_0}{X_2} : \frac{X_1}{X_2} : 1 : \frac{X_3}{X_2})$. $\tau(X_0 : X_1 : X_2 : X_3) = (X_0^2 : X_1^2 : X_2^2 : X_3^2)$ and $\tau^2(P) + 2P = \mu\tau(P)$ where $\mu = (-1)^{1-a}$. On a μ_4-Koblitz curve, a τ-operation requires 4**S** and a τ-affine operation requires 3**S**.

In particular, μ_4-Koblitz curve with $a = 0$ corresponds to the curve given in Theorem 4 of [14] with $c = 1$. In the case of $a = 0$, one full point addition requires 7**M** + 2**S**, one mixed addition requires 6**M** + 2**S**, and one point addition with both affine points (X_2-components of both summands can be set to 1) requires 5**M** + 2**S** [14]. In the case of $a = 1$, one full point addition requires

$8\mathbf{M} + 2\mathbf{S}$, one mixed addition requires $7\mathbf{M} + 2\mathbf{S}$, and one point addition with both affine points requires $6\mathbf{M} + 2\mathbf{S}$ [15,17].

The LD coordinates system and λ-coordinates system, proposed by López and Dahab [19] and by Oliveira, López, Aranha, and Rodríguez-Henríquez [23] respectively, are also efficient coordinate systems for binary elliptic curves. In Appendixes B and C, we will utilize our pre-computation scheme on Koblitz curves using LD coordinates and λ-coordinates.

2.3 Previous Pre-computation Schemes

We will consider the efficiency of pre-computation schemes on a μ_4-Koblitz curve.

Solinas' Pre-computation [26]**.** Solinas suggested an efficient design of the pre-computation and gave an example shown in Table 3. Computing $Q_3 = -P + \tau^2 P$ requires one point addition with both affine points and two τ-affine operations at the total cost of $(5\mathbf{M} + 2\mathbf{S}) + 6\mathbf{S}$. The other costs are similarly computed in Table 3 and in the following pre-computation schemes. The costs of Solinas' pre-computation are $15\mathbf{M} + 15\mathbf{S}$ and $38\mathbf{M} + 38\mathbf{S}$ with $a = 0$ and $18\mathbf{M} + 15\mathbf{S}$ and $45\mathbf{M} + 38\mathbf{S}$ with $a = 1$ for window τNAF with widths 4 and 5 respectively.

Table 3. Pre-computation scheme in [26]

	$a = 0$	$a = 1$	cost$(a = 0)$
$w = 4$			15M+15S
	$Q_3 = -P + \tau^2 P(c_3 = -\tau - 3)$	$Q_3 = -P + \tau^2 P(c_3 = \tau - 3)$	(5M+2S)+6S
	$Q_5 = P + \tau^2 P(c_5 = -\tau - 1)$	$Q_5 = P + \tau^2 P(c_5 = \tau - 1)$	5M+2S
	$Q_7 = -P + \tau^3 P(c_7 = -\tau + 1)$	$Q_7 = -P - \tau^3 P(c_7 = \tau + 1)$	(5M+2S)+3S
$w = 5$			38M+38S
	$Q_3 = -P + \tau^2 P(c_3 = -\tau - 3)$	$Q_3 = -P + \tau^2 P(c_3 = \tau - 3)$	(5M+2S)+6S
	$Q_5 = P + \tau^2 P(c_5 = -\tau - 1)$	$Q_5 = P + \tau^2 P(c_5 = \tau - 1)$	5M+2S
	$Q_7 = -P + \tau^3 P(c_7 = -\tau + 1)$	$Q_7 = -P - \tau^3 P(c_7 = \tau + 1)$	(5M+2S)+3S
	$Q_9 = P + \tau^3 Q_5(c_9 = -2\tau - 3)$	$Q_9 = P - \tau^3 Q_5(c_9 = 2\tau - 3)$	(6M+2S)+12S
	$Q_{11} = -\tau^2 Q_5 - P(c_{11} = -2\tau - 1)$	$Q_{11} = -\tau^2 Q_5 - P(c_{11} = 2\tau - 1)$	6M+2S
	$Q_{13} = -\tau^2 Q_5 + P(c_{13} = -2\tau + 1)$	$Q_{13} = -\tau^2 Q_5 + P(c_{13} = 2\tau + 1)$	6M+2S
	$Q_{15} = -P + \tau^4 P(c_{15} = 3\tau + 1)$	$Q_{15} = -P + \tau^4 P(c_{15} = -3\tau + 1)$	(5M+2S)+3S

Hankerson, Menezes, and Vanstone's Pre-computation [10]**.** Hankerson, Menezes, and Vanstone presented an improved design of pre-computation shown in Table 4. The costs of Hankerson, Menezes, and Vanstone's pre-computation are $15\mathbf{M}+15\mathbf{S}$, $40\mathbf{M}+35\mathbf{S}$, and $89\mathbf{M}+75\mathbf{S}$ with $a = 0$ and $18\mathbf{M}+15\mathbf{S}$, $47\mathbf{M}+35\mathbf{S}$, and $104\mathbf{M}+75\mathbf{S}$ with $a = 1$ for window τNAF with widths 4, 5, and 6 respectively.

Trost and Xu's Pre-computation [27]**.** Trost and Xu proposed a mathematically natural and clean form of pre-computation. The pre-computation requires

Table 4. Pre-computation scheme in [10]

	$a = 0$	$a = 1$	cost($a = 0$)
$w = 4$			15M+15S
	$Q_3 = -P + \tau^2 P(c_3 = -\tau - 3)$	$Q_3 = -P + \tau^2 P(c_3 = \tau - 3)$	(5M+2S)+6S
	$Q_5 = P + \tau^2 P(c_5 = -\tau - 1)$	$Q_5 = P + \tau^2 P(c_5 = \tau - 1)$	5M+2S
	$Q_7 = -P + \tau^3 P(c_7 = -\tau + 1)$	$Q_7 = -P - \tau^3 P(c_7 = \tau + 1)$	(5M+2S)+3S
$w = 5$			40M+35S
	$Q_3 = -P + \tau^2 P(c_3 = -\tau - 3)$	$Q_3 = -P + \tau^2 P(c_3 = \tau - 3)$	(5M+2S)+6S
	$Q_5 = P + \tau^2 P(c_5 = -\tau - 1)$	$Q_5 = P + \tau^2 P(c_5 = \tau - 1)$	5M+2S
	$Q_7 = -P + \tau^3 P(c_7 = -\tau + 1)$	$Q_7 = -P - \tau^3 P(c_7 = \tau + 1)$	(5M+2S)+3S
	$Q_9 = P + \tau^3 Q_5(c_9 = -2\tau - 3)$	$Q_9 = P - \tau^3 Q_5(c_9 = 2\tau - 3)$	(6M+2S)+12S
	$Q_{11} = -\tau^2 Q_5 - P(c_{11} = -2\tau - 1)$	$Q_{11} = -\tau^2 Q_5 - P(c_{11} = 2\tau - 1)$	6M+2S
	$Q_{13} = -\tau^2 Q_5 + P(c_{13} = -2\tau + 1)$	$Q_{13} = -\tau^2 Q_5 + P(c_{13} = 2\tau + 1)$	6M+2S
	$Q_{15} = -Q_5 + \tau^2 Q_5(c_{15} = 3\tau + 1)$	$Q_{15} = -Q_5 + \tau^2 Q_5(c_{15} = -3\tau + 1)$	7M+2S
$w = 6$			89M+75S
	$Q_{23} = -P - \tau^3 P(c_{23} = \tau - 3)$	$Q_{23} = -P + \tau^3 P(c_{23} = -\tau - 3)$	(5M+2S)+9S
	$Q_{25} = P - \tau^3 P(c_{25} = \tau - 1)$	$Q_{25} = P + \tau^3 P(c_{25} = -\tau - 1)$	5M+2S
	$Q_{27} = -P - \tau^2 P(c_{27} = \tau + 1)$	$Q_{27} = -P - \tau^2 P(c_{27} = -\tau + 1)$	5M+2S
	$Q_{29} = P - \tau^2 P(c_{29} = \tau + 3)$	$Q_{29} = P - \tau^2 P(c_{29} = -\tau + 3)$	5M+2S
	$Q_3 = \tau^2 Q_{25} - P(c_3 = 3)$	$Q_3 = \tau^2 Q_{25} - P(c_3 = 3)$	(6M+2S)+8S
	$Q_5 = \tau^2 Q_{25} + P(c_5 = 5)$	$Q_5 = \tau^2 Q_{25} + P(c_5 = 5)$	6M+2S
	$Q_7 = -\tau^3 Q_{27} - P(c_7 = -2\tau - 5)$	$Q_7 = \tau^3 Q_{27} - P(c_7 = 2\tau - 5)$	(6M+2S)+12S
	$Q_9 = -\tau^3 Q_{27} + P(c_9 = -2\tau - 3)$	$Q_9 = \tau^3 Q_{27} + P(c_9 = 2\tau - 3)$	6M+2S
	$Q_{11} = \tau^2 Q_{27} - P(c_{11} = -2\tau - 1)$	$Q_{11} = \tau^2 Q_{27} - P(c_{11} = 2\tau - 1)$	6M+2S
	$Q_{13} = \tau^2 Q_{27} + P(c_{13} = -2\tau + 1)$	$Q_{13} = \tau^2 Q_{27} + P(c_{13} = 2\tau + 1)$	6M+2S
	$Q_{15} = -\tau^2 Q_{27} + Q_{27}(c_{15} = 3\tau + 1)$	$Q_{15} = -\tau^2 Q_{27} + Q_{27}(c_{15} = -3\tau + 1)$	7M+2S
	$Q_{17} = -\tau^2 Q_{27} + Q_{29}(c_{17} = 3\tau + 3)$	$Q_{17} = -\tau^2 Q_{27} + Q_{29}(c_{17} = -3\tau + 3)$	7M+2S
	$Q_{19} = -\tau^2 Q_3 - P(c_{19} = 3\tau + 5)$	$Q_{19} = -\tau^2 Q_3 - P(c_{19} = -3\tau + 5)$	(6M+2S)+8S
	$Q_{21} = \tau^2 Q_{29} + P(c_{21} = -4\tau - 3)$	$Q_{21} = \tau^2 Q_{29} + P(c_{21} = 4\tau - 3)$	(6M+2S)+8S
	$Q_{31} = \tau^2 Q_{25} + Q_{27}(c_{31} = \tau + 5)$	$Q_{31} = \tau^2 Q_{25} + Q_{27}(c_{31} = -\tau + 5)$	7M+2S

the least number of point additions and τ evaluations. We include their pre-computation scheme for window τNAF with widths 4, 5, and 6 in Table 5. The costs are 15**M**+12**S**, 39**M**+20**S**, and 87**M**+36**S** with $a = 0$ and 18**M**+12**S**, 46**M**+20**S**, and 102**M**+36**S** with $a = 1$.

Trost and Xu did not get into field arithmetic details to speed up the pre-computation. Our main objective of this paper is to design a novel pre-computation and efficient formulas to achieve a great saving of scalar multiplication. To implement scalar multiplication, Montgomery trick may be useful.

2.4 Montgomery Trick

Montgomery trick [7] computes simultaneously the inversions of n elements. It requires one inversion and $3(n-1)$ multiplications. Montgomery trick is powerful to translate points in projective coordinates to those in affine coordinates shown as Algorithm 1. For n points $(X_{0i} : X_{1i} : X_{2i} : X_{3i}), 1 \le i \le n$, we use Montgomery trick to compute X_{2i}^{-1}, and then compute $(\frac{X_{0i}}{X_{2i}} : \frac{X_{1i}}{X_{2i}} : 1 : \frac{X_{3i}}{X_{2i}})$. This trick translates n projective points on a μ_4-Koblitz curve to those in affine coordinates on a μ_4-Koblitz curve. When projective points are converted to affine

Table 5. Pre-computation scheme in [27]

	$a = 0$	$a = 1$	cost($a = 0$)
$w = 4$			15M+12S
	$Q_5 = -P - \tau P(c_5 = -\tau - 1)$	$Q_5 = -P + \tau P(c_5 = \tau - 1)$	(5M+2S)+3S
	$Q_7 = P - \tau P(c_7 = -\tau + 1)$	$Q_7 = P + \tau P(c_7 = \tau + 1)$	5M+2S
	$Q_3 = -P + \tau^2 P(c_3 = -\tau - 3)$	$Q_3 = -P + \tau^2 P(c_3 = \tau - 3)$	(5M+2S)+3S
$w = 5$			39M+20S
	$Q_5 = -P - \tau P(c_5 = -\tau - 1)$	$Q_5 = -P + \tau P(c_5 = \tau - 1)$	(5M+2S)+3S
	$Q_7 = P - \tau P(c_7 = -\tau + 1)$	$Q_7 = P + \tau P(c_7 = \tau + 1)$	5M+2S
	$Q_3 = -P + \tau^2 P(c_3 = -\tau - 3)$	$Q_3 = -P + \tau^2 P(c_3 = \tau - 3)$	(5M+2S)+3S
	$Q_9 = Q_3 - \tau P(c_9 = -2\tau - 3)$	$Q_9 = Q_3 + \tau P(c_9 = 2\tau - 3)$	6M+2S
	$Q_{11} = Q_5 - \tau P(c_{11} = -2\tau - 1)$	$Q_{11} = Q_5 + \tau P(c_{11} = 2\tau - 1)$	6M+2S
	$Q_{13} = Q_7 - \tau P(c_{13} = -2\tau + 1)$	$Q_{13} = Q_7 + \tau P(c_{13} = 2\tau + 1)$	6M+2S
	$Q_{15} = -Q_{11} + \tau P(c_{15} = 3\tau + 1)$	$Q_{15} = -Q_{11} - \tau P(c_{15} = -3\tau + 1)$	6M+2S
$w = 6$			87M+36S
	$Q_{27} = P + \tau P(c_{27} = \tau + 1)$	$Q_{27} = P - \tau P(c_{27} = -\tau + 1)$	(5M+2S)+3S
	$Q_{25} = -P + \tau P(c_{25} = \tau - 1)$	$Q_{25} = -P - \tau P(c_{25} = -\tau - 1)$	5M+2S
	$Q_{29} = P - \tau^2 P(c_{29} = \tau + 3)$	$Q_{29} = P - \tau^2 P(c_{29} = -\tau + 3)$	(5M+2S)+3S
	$Q_3 = Q_{29} - \tau P(c_3 = 3)$	$Q_3 = Q_{29} + \tau P(c_3 = 3)$	6M+2S
	$Q_9 = -Q_{29} - \tau P(c_9 = -2\tau - 3)$	$Q_9 = -Q_{29} + \tau P(c_9 = 2\tau - 3)$	6M+2S
	$Q_{31} = Q_3 - \tau^2 P(c_{31} = \tau + 5)$	$Q_{31} = Q_3 - \tau^2 P(c_{31} = -\tau + 5)$	6M+2S
	$Q_5 = Q_{31} - \tau P(c_5 = 5)$	$Q_5 = Q_{31} + \tau P(c_5 = 5)$	6M+2S
	$Q_7 = -Q_{31} - \tau P(c_7 = -2\tau - 5)$	$Q_7 = -Q_{31} + \tau P(c_7 = 2\tau - 5)$	6M+2S
	$Q_{11} = -Q_{27} - \tau P(c_{11} = -2\tau - 1)$	$Q_{11} = -Q_{27} + \tau P(c_{11} = 2\tau - 1)$	6M+2S
	$Q_{13} = -Q_{25} - \tau P(c_{13} = -2\tau + 1)$	$Q_{13} = -Q_{25} + \tau P(c_{13} = 2\tau + 1)$	6M+2S
	$Q_{15} = -Q_{11} + \tau P(c_{15} = 3\tau + 1)$	$Q_{15} = -Q_{11} - \tau P(c_{15} = -3\tau + 1)$	6M+2S
	$Q_{17} = -Q_9 + \tau P(c_{17} = 3\tau + 3)$	$Q_{17} = -Q_9 - \tau P(c_{17} = -3\tau + 3)$	6M+2S
	$Q_{19} = -Q_7 + \tau P(c_{19} = 3\tau + 5)$	$Q_{19} = -Q_7 - \tau P(c_{19} = -3\tau + 5)$	6M+2S
	$Q_{21} = -Q_{17} - \tau P(c_{21} = -4\tau - 3)$	$Q_{21} = -Q_{17} + \tau P(c_{21} = 4\tau - 3)$	6M+2S
	$Q_{23} = -Q_3 + \tau P(c_{23} = \tau - 3)$	$Q_{23} = -Q_3 - \tau P(c_{23} = -\tau - 3)$	6M+2S

Algorithm 1. Montgomery trick [7]

Input: $a_1, a_2, \ldots, a_n$
Output: $b_1 = a_1{}^{-1}, b_2 = a_2{}^{-1}, \ldots, b_n = a_n{}^{-1}$
Computation

1. $c_1 \leftarrow a_1$
2. for i from 2 to n
   $c_i \leftarrow c_{i-1} \cdot a_i$
3. $d \leftarrow c_n^{-1}$
4. for i from n to 2
   $b_i \leftarrow c_{i-1} \cdot d$
   $d \leftarrow a_i \cdot d$
5. $b_1 \leftarrow d$
6. output b_i

points, we replace full point addition with mixed point addition to get a higher efficiency of scalar multiplication when the ratio of **I**/**M** is not too high.

In the next section, we will propose new formulas on a μ_4-Koblitz curve to design an efficient pre-computation scheme.

3 New Formulas on μ_4-Koblitz Curves

Let $P(X_0 : X_1 : X_2 : X_3)$ and $Q(Y_0 : Y_1 : Y_2 : Y_3)$ be rational points on a μ_4-Koblitz curve. Let $U_{ij} = X_iY_j$ in the following text. Point addition $P+Q$ on a μ_4-Koblitz curve can be calculated as

$$\left((U_{13}+U_{31})^2 : U_{02}U_{31}+U_{20}U_{13}+aF : (U_{02}+U_{20})^2 : U_{02}U_{13}+U_{20}U_{31}+aF\right)$$

where $F = (X_1+X_3)(Y_1+Y_3)(U_{02}+U_{20})$. It also can be calculated as

$$\left((U_{00}+U_{22})^2 : U_{00}U_{11}+U_{22}U_{33}+aG : (U_{11}+U_{33})^2 : U_{00}U_{33}+U_{11}U_{22}+aG\right)$$

where $G = (X_1+X_3)(Y_1+Y_3)(U_{00}+U_{22})$. This point addition requires 9**M**+2**S** and mixed addition requires 8**M**+2**S**. The point addition with $a = 0$ is shown in Lemma 1 and that with $a = 1$ is shown in Lemma 2.

Lemma 1 (Corollary 5 in [14]). *Let $P(X_0 : X_1 : X_2 : X_3)$ and $Q(Y_0 : Y_1 : Y_2 : Y_3)$ be rational points on a μ_4-Koblitz curve with $a = 0$. Point addition $P+Q$ can be computed at the cost of* 7**M**+2**S** *as*

$$\begin{aligned}&\left((U_{00}+U_{22})^2 : U_{00}U_{11}+U_{22}U_{33} : (U_{11}+U_{33})^2 :\right.\\&\left.(U_{00}+U_{22})(U_{11}+U_{33})+U_{00}U_{11}+U_{22}U_{33}\right).\end{aligned}$$

Mixed addition costs 6**M**+2**S**. *Point addition with both affine points costs* 5**M**+2**S**.

Lemma 2 (Theorem 1 in [17]). *Let $P(X_0 : X_1 : X_2 : X_3)$ and $Q(Y_0 : Y_1 : Y_2 : Y_3)$ be rational points on a μ_4-Koblitz curve with $a = 1$. Point addition $P+Q$ can be computed at the cost of* 8**M**+2**S** *as*

$$\begin{aligned}&\left((U_{00}+U_{22})^2 : U_{00}(U_{11}+H)+U_{22}(U_{33}+H) : (U_{11}+U_{33})^2 :\right.\\&\left.(U_{00}+U_{22})(U_{11}+U_{33})+U_{00}(U_{11}+H)+U_{22}(U_{33}+H)\right),\end{aligned}$$

where $H = (X_1+X_3)(Y_1+Y_3)$. Mixed addition costs 7**M**+2**S**. *Point addition with both affine points costs* 6**M**+2**S**.

Jarvinen, Forsten, and Skytta first proposed $P \pm Q$ to improve the efficiency of scalar multiplication on Koblitz curves in affine coordinates [11]. Longa and Gebotys used $P \pm Q$ to improve the efficiency of pre-computation on elliptic curves over a prime field [18]. To avoid the expensive inversion, we will show the formulas of $P \pm Q$ on μ_4-Koblitz curves in Theorem 1. Avanzi, Dimitrov, Doche, and Sica [1] first introduced $\bar{\tau}$ to improve the efficiency of scalar multiplication. They noticed that $2 = \tau\bar{\tau}$ and computed $\bar{\tau}P$ requiring a point doubling and three square roots. Doche, Kohel, and Sica [8] proposed a new way to compute $\bar{\tau}P$ which induces a speedup on the scalar multiplication using double-base representation over 15% in LD coordinates. Inspired by their works, we introduce a new radix $\mu\bar{\tau}$ to speed up the pre-computation stage of scalar multiplication using window τNAF shown in Theorem 1.

Theorem 1. *Let $P(X_0 : X_1 : X_2 : X_3)$ and $Q(Y_0 : Y_1 : Y_2 : Y_3)$ be rational points on a μ_4-Koblitz curve. The two operations of $P+Q$ and $P-Q$ ($(P \pm Q)$-operation) can be computed at the total cost of* 10**M**+3**S** ($a=0$) *and* 11**M**+3**S** ($a=1$) *when $X_2 = 1$, and $\mu\bar{\tau}P$ are calculated at the cost of* 2**M**+2**S**.

Proof. Let $P(X_0 : X_1 : X_2 : X_3)$, $Q(Y_0 : Y_1 : Y_2 : Y_3)$, and $-Q(Y_0 : Y_3 : Y_2 : Y_1)$.

When $a = 0$, $P+Q$ and $P-Q$ are computed as

$$\begin{aligned} P+Q &= \big((U_{00}+U_{22})^2 : U_{00}U_{11}+U_{22}U_{33} : (U_{11}+U_{33})^2 : \\ &\qquad (U_{00}+U_{22})(U_{11}+U_{33})+U_{00}U_{11}+U_{22}U_{33}\big)\,, \\ P-Q &= \big((U_{11}+U_{33})^2 : U_{02}U_{33}+U_{20}U_{11} : (U_{02}+U_{20})^2 : \\ &\qquad (U_{02}+U_{20})(U_{11}+U_{33})+U_{02}U_{33}+U_{20}U_{11}\big)\,. \end{aligned} \tag{2}$$

Notice that $U_{22} = Y_2$ and $U_{20} = Y_0$, the total cost of computing $P \pm Q$ is 10**M**+3**S**.

When $a = 1$, $P+Q$ and $P-Q$ are computed as

$$\begin{aligned} P+Q &= \big((U_{00}+U_{22})^2 : U_{00}(U_{11}+H)+U_{22}(U_{33}+H) : (U_{11}+U_{33})^2 : \\ &\qquad (U_{00}+U_{22})(U_{11}+U_{33})+U_{00}(U_{11}+H)+U_{22}(U_{33}+H)\big)\,, \\ P-Q &= \big((U_{11}+U_{33})^2 : U_{02}(U_{33}+H)+U_{20}(U_{11}+H) : (U_{02}+U_{20})^2 : \\ &\qquad (U_{02}+U_{20})(U_{11}+U_{33})+U_{02}(U_{33}+H)+U_{20}(U_{11}+H)\big)\,, \end{aligned} \tag{3}$$

where $H = (X_1+X_3)(Y_1+Y_3)$. Since $U_{22} = Y_2$ and $U_{20} = Y_0$, the total cost of computing $P \pm Q$ is 11**M**+3**S**.

Notice that $2 = \tau\bar{\tau}$. We have $2\mu P = \tau(\mu\bar{\tau}P)$.

It is pointed out that there is one typographical error in Sect. 6 of [15], the correct doubling formulas are in Kohel's slides [15] where $2\mu P$ is computed as

$$\big((X_0+X_2)^4 : (X_0X_3+X_1X_2)^2 : (X_1+X_3)^4 : (X_0X_1+X_2X_3)^2\big)\,.$$

Then

$$\mu\bar{\tau}P = \big((X_0+X_2)^2 : (X_0X_3+X_1X_2) : (X_1+X_3)^2 : (X_0X_1+X_2X_3)\big)\,. \tag{4}$$

When $a = 0$, since $(X_0X_3+X_1X_2) = (X_0+X_1)(X_2+X_3)+(X_0+X_2)^2+(X_1+X_3)^2$ and $(X_0X_1+X_2X_3) = (X_0+X_2)(X_1+X_3)+(X_0X_3+X_1X_2)$, the cost of $\mu\bar{\tau}P$ is 2**M**+2**S**.

When $a = 1$, since $(X_0X_3+X_1X_2) = (X_0+X_1)(X_2+X_3)+(X_0+X_2)^2$ and $(X_0X_1+X_2X_3) = (X_0+X_2)(X_1+X_3)+(X_0X_3+X_1X_2)$, the cost of $\mu\bar{\tau}P$ is 2**M**+2**S**. □

Since separate computations of $P+Q$ and $P-Q$ require 12**M**+4**S** ($a=0$) and 14**M**+4**S** ($a=1$), our formulas save 2**M**+**S** ($a=0$) and 3**M**+**S** ($a=1$). In the case of $a=0$, using our formulas of $P \pm Q$, Solinas' pre-computation scheme saves 2**M**+**S** for $w=4$ and 4**M**+2**S** for $w=5$; Hankerson, Menezes, and Vanstone's pre-computation scheme saves 2**M**+**S** for $w=4$, 4**M**+2**S** for $w=5$, and 10**M**+5**S** for $w = 6$; Trost and Xu's pre-computation scheme saves 4**M**+2**S** for $w = 6$.

Our formulas of $\mu\bar{\tau}$-operation save 4**M**($a = 0$) and 5**M**($a = 1$). The costs of point operations including $(P \pm Q)$-operation and $\mu\bar{\tau}P$ are summarized in Table 6. Notice that formulas of $(P \pm Q)$-operation are the two forms of the formulas of point addition and formulas of $\mu\bar{\tau}P$ are part of the formulas of point doubling. This leads to software and hardware implementations with simplicity. These new efficient point operations will be used to improve the arithmetics on a μ_4-Koblitz curve.

4 A Novel Pre-computation Scheme

Solinas' pre-computation in Section 7.4 of [26], Hankerson, Menezes, and Vanstone's pre-computation shown as Tables 3.9 and 3.10 in [10], and Trost and Xu's pre-computation shown as Tables 5 and 6 in [27] all have a pre-computation scheme on E_0 and another pre-computation scheme on E_1. In this section, we will introduce a unified pre-computation without treating $a = 0$ and $a = 1$ separately. Our method is to write pre-computations with variable curve coefficient hidden in μ. Let $c_i \in R_i$ and $c_i = g + h\mu\tau$ for $i \in I_w$. Then $Q_i = c_i P$ works on both E_0 and E_1. We call $Q_i = c_i P$ a unified pre-computation scheme when c_i has the form $g + h\mu\tau$ for all $i \in I_w$. Trost and Xu's pre-computation can be unified. Take $w = 4$ for example, we have $Q_5 = -P + \mu\tau P$, $Q_7 = P + \mu\tau P$, $Q_3 = -3P + \mu\tau P$. Also Solinas' pre-computation, and Hankerson, Menezes, and Vanstone's pre-computation can be unified.

Table 6. Costs of point operations on a μ_4-Koblitz curve

Point operation	Cost ($a = 0$)	Cost ($a = 1$)
$(P \pm Q)$-operation (this work)	10**M**+3**S** (Eq. (2))	11**M**+3**S** (Eq. (3))
$\mu\bar{\tau}P$ (this work)	2**M**+2**S** (Eq. (4))	2**M**+2**S** (Eq. (4))

To design an efficient pre-computation, some properties of R_i, $i \in I_w$ are useful.

4.1 Basic Lemmas

Recall that for $w \geq 3$, $I_w = \{1, 3, \cdots, 2^{w-1} - 1\}$ and R_i consists of the elements of the class i modulo τ^w whose norms are smaller than 2^w for each $i \in I_w$. Since elements of I_w are odd integers, we will work on the subset $(2\mathbb{Z}+1)+\mathbb{Z}\tau \subset \mathbb{Z}[\tau]$ as $R_i \subset (2\mathbb{Z}+1)+\mathbb{Z}\tau$.

Lemma 3. *We have the following facts:*

1. *If $g + h\tau \in R_i$ for some $i \in I_w$, then $g - h\tau \notin R_i$ for any $h \neq 0$.*

2. *If $g + h\tau \in R_i$ for some $i \in I_w$, then $g' + h\tau \notin R_i$ for any $g' \in \mathbb{Z} \setminus \{g\}$.*
3. *For any $g + h\tau \in (2\mathbb{Z}+1) + \mathbb{Z}\tau$, there exists an $i \in I_w$ such that $i \equiv g + h\tau \pmod{\tau^w}$ or $-i \equiv g + h\tau \pmod{\tau^w}$.*

Proof. From [27], we know that if $g + h\tau \in R_i$, then $|g| < \frac{2^{\frac{w+2}{2}}}{\sqrt{3}}$ and $|h| < 2^{\frac{w}{2}}$.

(1) Assume both $g + h\tau$ and $g - h\tau$ are in R_i, then $\tau^w | 2h\tau$. By Eq. (1), this implies that $2^w | 2hs_w$ and hence $2^{w-2}|h$ as $\frac{s_w}{2}$ is odd. On the other hand, since $N(g \pm h\tau) < 2^w$, we see that $h^2 < 2^{w-1}$. This reaches a contradiction.

(2) Assume both $g+h\tau$ and $g'+h\tau$ are in R_i for some $g' \neq g$, then $\tau^w|(g-g')$. We get $2^w|(g-g')$ by Eq. (1). Since $|g|, |g'| < \frac{2^{\frac{w+2}{2}}}{\sqrt{3}}$, then $|g-g'| < 2 \cdot \frac{2^{\frac{w+2}{2}}}{\sqrt{3}} \leq 2^w$. We get a contradiction again.

(3) Since $g + hs_w$ is odd, it must be in one of the congruence classes of $-2^{w-1}+1, -2^{w-1}+3, \ldots, -3, -1, 1, 3, \ldots, 2^{w-1}-3, 2^{w-1}-1$ modulo 2^w. □

We can show that the number of elements of R_i is well bounded.

Lemma 4. *Let $i \in I_w$, then $\#R_i \leq \left\lfloor 2^{\frac{w+2}{2}} \right\rfloor$.*

Proof. If $g + h\tau \in R_i$, then $|h| < 2^{\frac{w}{2}}$. So the cardinality of $T = \{h \in \mathbb{Z} | g + h\tau \in R_i \text{ for some odd number } g\}$ is less than $2 \cdot 2^{\frac{w}{2}}$. By Lemma 3, for each $h \in T$, there is only one g available such that $g + h\tau \in R_i$. Thus $\#R_i = \#T \leq \left\lfloor 2^{\frac{w+2}{2}} \right\rfloor$. □

If $g + h_1\tau \equiv g + h_2\tau \pmod{\tau^w}$, then $s_w(h_2 - h_1) \equiv 0 \pmod{2^w}$. Since s_w is even and $s_w/2$ is odd, $h_2 = h_1 + c \cdot 2^{w-1}$. Thus $g + h\tau, g + (h+1)\tau, \ldots, g + (h + 2^{w-1} - 1)\tau$ cover all congruence classes R_i and R_{-i}, $i \in I_w$ when g is odd. On average, $\#R_i$ is less than 4.62. We have calculated out that $\#R_i \leq 3$ for $i \in I_w$ and $3 \leq w \leq 10$.

4.2 Calculating R_i

We propose a plane search to generate R_i, $i \in I_w$, shown as Algorithm 2. For each $g + h\mu\tau \in (2\mathbb{Z}+1) + \mathbb{Z}\tau$ with $N(g + h\mu\tau) = g^2 + gh + 2h^2 < 2^w$, we treat it as the point (g, h) on the Euclidean plane. To determine whether $g + h\mu\tau$ is in the set R_i for some i satisfying $2^w | g - i + h\mu s_w$, we search all points (g, h) and append $g + h\mu\tau$ to the corresponding R_i where $-\left\lfloor \frac{2^{\frac{w+2}{2}}}{\sqrt{3}} \right\rfloor \leq g \leq \left\lfloor \frac{2^{\frac{w+2}{2}}}{\sqrt{3}} \right\rfloor$, $-\left\lfloor 2^{\frac{w}{2}} \right\rfloor \leq h \leq \left\lfloor 2^{\frac{w}{2}} \right\rfloor$, and g is odd. We collect all such elements and form a set $C = \{c_i | c_i \in R_i, \ i \in I_w\}$. Then $Q_i = c_iP$ with $c_i \in C$ for all $i \in I_w$ form a unified pre-computation. We set the trivial case $c_1 = 1$.

Algorithm 2. Plane search to generate R_i, $i \in I_w$

Computation

1. $R_i \leftarrow <>$
2. for g from $-\left\lfloor \frac{2^{\frac{w+2}{2}}}{\sqrt{3}} \right\rfloor$ to $\left\lfloor \frac{2^{\frac{w+2}{2}}}{\sqrt{3}} \right\rfloor$ and g is odd
   for h from $-\left\lfloor 2^{\frac{w}{2}} \right\rfloor$ to $\left\lfloor 2^{\frac{w}{2}} \right\rfloor$
   if $(2^w | g - i + h\mu s_w)$ and $(g^2 + gh + 2h^2 < 2^w)$
   then append $(g + h\mu\tau)$ to R_i
3. output R_i

4.3 Our Novel Pre-computation

We design a novel pre-computation for window τNAF with widths from 4 to 8.

Theorem 2. *Let* $P = (x_P, \lambda_P)$ *and* $Q_i = (X_i, \Lambda_i, Z_i)$ *with* $i \in I_w$. *There exists a unified pre-computation scheme shown in Tables 7, 14, and 15 requiring* 6**M**+6**S**, 18**M**+17**S**, 44**M**+32**S**, 88**M**+62**S**, *and* 186**M**+123**S** *on a* μ_4*-Koblitz curve with* $a = 0$ *and* 6**M**+6**S**, 19**M**+17**S**, 47**M**+32**S**, 93**M**+72**S**, *and* 198**M**+123**S** *with* $a = 1$ *for window* τ*NAF with widths from* 4 *to* 8 *respectively.*

Proof. The explicit design of calculating pre-computations for window τNAF with widths from 4 to 6 is shown as Table 7, for that with width 7 is shown as Table 14 in Appendix A.1, and for that with width 8 is shown as Table 15 in Appendix A.2. Let $c_i = g + h\mu\tau$ for each $i \in I_w$ in Tables 7, 14, and 15. Since $c_i = g + h\mu\tau$ for each $i \in I_w$, our pre-computation scheme for w from 4 to 8 is unified. Since $g + h\mu s_w \equiv i \pmod{2^w}$ and $N(c_i) < 2^w$ for all $i \in I_w$, this novel pre-computation is correct for window τNAF with widths from 4 to 8.

We show our novel pre-computation for window τNAF with widths 4, 5, and 6 as follows.

1. $w = 4$. $Q_5 = -(\mu\bar{\tau}P)$, $Q_7 = -(\mu\bar{\tau})^2P$, $Q_3 = (\mu\bar{\tau})^3P$ are shown as Table 7. Our pre-computation scheme for window τNAF with width 4 requires 6**M**+6**S**.
2. $w = 5$. Let $\tau P = (x_{\tau P}, \lambda_{\tau P}) = (x_P^2, \lambda_P^2)$. $Q_5 = -(\mu\bar{\tau}P)$, $Q_7 = -(\mu\bar{\tau})^2P$, $Q_3 = (\mu\bar{\tau})^3P$, $Q_{15} = -(\mu\bar{\tau})^4P$, $Q_{11} = \mu\tau P + Q_5$, $Q_9 = \mu\bar{\tau}Q_{11}$, $Q_{13} = -(\mu\bar{\tau})^2Q_{11}$ are shown as Table 7. This pre-computation scheme requires 18**M**+17**S** with $a = 0$ and 19**M**+17**S** with $a = 1$.
3. $w = 6$. Let $\tau P = (x_{\tau P}, \lambda_{\tau P}) = (x_P^2, \lambda_P^2)$. $Q_{27} = \mu\bar{\tau}P$, $Q_{25} = (\mu\bar{\tau})^2P$, $Q_{29} = -(\mu\bar{\tau})^3P$, $Q_{15} = -(\mu\bar{\tau})^4P$, $Q_{21} = -(\mu\bar{\tau})^5P$, $(Q_3, Q_9) = \mu\tau P \pm Q_{29}$ ($Q_3 = \mu\tau P + Q_{29}$, $Q_9 = \mu\tau P - Q_{29}$), $Q_{13} = -(\mu\bar{\tau})Q_9$, $Q_{31} = -(\mu\bar{\tau})^2Q_9$, $Q_{17} = \mu\bar{\tau}Q_3$, $Q_{11} = (\mu\bar{\tau})^2Q_3$, $Q_{23} = \mu\tau P - Q_{15}$, $Q_{19} = -\mu\bar{\tau}Q_{23}$, $Q_5 = -\mu\tau P - Q_{21}$, $Q_7 = \mu\bar{\tau}Q_5$ are shown as Table 7. This scheme requires 44**M**+32**S** with $a = 0$ and 47**M**+32**S** with $a = 1$.

Table 7. Novel pre-computation for widths from 4 to 6

	c_i		Q_i	$a = 0/a = 1$
$w = 4$				6M+6S
	$c_5 = -1 + \mu\tau$	$c_5 = -\mu\bar{\tau}$	$Q_5 = -\mu\bar{\tau}P$	2M+2S
	$c_7 = 1 + \mu\tau$	$c_7 = \mu\bar{\tau}c_5$	$Q_7 = -(\mu\bar{\tau})^2P$	2M+2S
	$c_3 = -3 + \mu\tau$	$c_3 = -\mu\bar{\tau}c_7$	$Q_3 = (\mu\bar{\tau})^3P$	2M+2S
$w = 5$				18M+17S/19M+17S
	$c_5 = -1 + \mu\tau$	$c_5 = -\mu\bar{\tau}$	$Q_5 = -\mu\bar{\tau}P$	2M+2S
	$c_7 = 1 + \mu\tau$	$c_7 = \mu\bar{\tau}c_5$	$Q_7 = -(\mu\bar{\tau})^2P$	2M+2S
	$c_3 = -3 + \mu\tau$	$c_3 = -\mu\bar{\tau}c_7$	$Q_3 = (\mu\bar{\tau})^3P$	2M+2S
	$c_{15} = 1 - 3\mu\tau$	$c_{15} = -\mu\bar{\tau}c_3$	$Q_{15} = -(\mu\bar{\tau})^4P$	2M+2S
	$c_{11} = -1 + 2\mu\tau$	$c_{11} = \mu\tau + c_5$	$Q_{11} = \mu\tau P + Q_5$	(6M+2S)+3S/(7M+2S) + 3S*
	$c_9 = 3 + \mu\tau$	$c_9 = \mu\bar{\tau}c_{11}$	$Q_9 = \mu\bar{\tau}Q_{11}$	2M+2S
	$c_{13} = -5 + 3\mu\tau$	$c_{13} = -\mu\bar{\tau}c_9$	$Q_{13} = -(\mu\bar{\tau})^2Q_{11}$	2M+2S
$w = 6$				44M+32S/47M+32S
	$c_{27} = 1 - \mu\tau$	$c_{27} = \mu\bar{\tau}$	$Q_{27} = \mu\bar{\tau}P$	2M+2S
	$c_{25} = -1 - \mu\tau$	$c_{25} = \mu\bar{\tau}c_{27}$	$Q_{25} = (\mu\bar{\tau})^2P$	2M+2S
	$c_{29} = 3 - \mu\tau$	$c_{29} = -\mu\bar{\tau}c_{25}$	$Q_{29} = -(\mu\bar{\tau})^3P$	2M+2S
	$c_{15} = 1 - 3\mu\tau$	$c_{15} = \mu\bar{\tau}c_{29}$	$Q_{15} = -(\mu\bar{\tau})^4P$	2M+2S
	$c_{21} = -5 - \mu\tau$	$c_{21} = \mu\bar{\tau}c_{15}$	$Q_{21} = -(\mu\bar{\tau})^5P$	2M+2S
	$c_3 = 3$	$c_3 = \mu\tau + c_{29}$	$Q_3 = \mu\tau P + Q_{29}$	
	$c_9 = -3 + 2\mu\tau$	$c_9 = \mu\tau - c_{29}$	$Q_9 = \mu\tau P - Q_{29}$	(10M+3S)+3S/(11M+3S)+3S*
	$c_{13} = -1 - 3\mu\tau$	$c_{13} = -\mu\bar{\tau}c_9$	$Q_{13} = -(\mu\bar{\tau})Q_9$	2M+2S
	$c_{31} = -7 + \mu\tau$	$c_{31} = \mu\bar{\tau}c_{13}$	$Q_{31} = -(\mu\bar{\tau})^2Q_9$	2M+2S
	$c_{17} = 3 - 3\mu\tau$	$c_{17} = \mu\bar{\tau}c_3$	$Q_{17} = \mu\bar{\tau}Q_3$	2M+2S
	$c_{11} = -3 - 3\mu\tau$	$c_{11} = \mu\bar{\tau}c_{17}$	$Q_{11} = (\mu\bar{\tau})^2Q_3$	2M+2S
	$c_{23} = -1 + 4\mu\tau$	$c_{23} = \mu\tau - c_{15}$	$Q_{23} = \mu\tau P - Q_{15}$	6M+2S/7M+2S
	$c_{19} = -7 - \mu\tau$	$c_{19} = -\mu\bar{\tau}c_{23}$	$Q_{19} = -\mu\bar{\tau}Q_{23}$	2M+2S
	$c_5 = 5$	$c_5 = -\mu\tau - c_{21}$	$Q_5 = -\mu\tau P - Q_{21}$	6M+2S/7M+2S
	$c_7 = 5 - 5\mu\tau$	$c_7 = \mu\bar{\tau}c_5$	$Q_7 = \mu\bar{\tau}Q_5$	2M+2S

* "+3S" is the cost of τP. For window width 6, Q_3 and Q_9 can be computed as one $(P \pm Q)$-operation.

The explicit computing process and the value of c_i for window τNAF with widths from 4 to 6 are shown as Table 7; those for window τNAF with width 7 are shown as Table 14; and those for window τNAF with width 8 are shown as Table 15. □

For each Q_i $(i = 3, 5, \ldots, 2^{w-1} - 1)$, one point addition is necessary. We employ $\mu\bar{\tau}(P)$ and $(P \pm Q)$-operations to replace point addition which leads to a speedup of our pre-computation algorithm. Next, we will compare our scheme with other pre-computation schemes.

4.4 Comparison of Pre-computation Schemes in M and S

The ratio of **I**/**M** and that of **S**/**M** both affect the cost of pre-computation schemes and that of scalar multiplications. Suppose that **I**/**M**=10, **S**/**M**=0; or **I**/**M**=10, **S**/**M**=0.2; or **I**/**M**=150, **S**/**M**=0.5. The first two cases are both suggested by Bernstein and Lange in their explicit-formulas database [4]. The third case suits for binary fields over desktop architectures embedded with the carry-less multiplication instruction [9]. The first two ratios are reasonable in the experiments of our environments shown as Sect. 6 where **I**/**M**=10 and 0.06<**S**/**M**<0.12.

The costs of Solinas' pre-computation scheme, Hankerson, Menezes, and Vanstone's pre-computation scheme, Trost and Xu's pre-computation scheme, and our pre-computation scheme on the μ_4-Koblitz curves with $a = 0$ and $a = 1$ for window τNAF are summarized in Table 1. Our pre-computation scheme is the fastest one among these four pre-computation schemes. Our novel pre-computation scheme is about two times faster than Trost and Xu's scheme for window τNAF with widths 4, 5, and 6 for all three cases.

5 Scalar Multiplications Using Window τNAF on μ_4-Koblitz Curves

Let the costs of pre-computation schemes for window τNAF with width w be denoted by Pre_w.

5.1 Expected Costs of Scalar Multiplications

Scalar multiplication using window τNAF has two situations.

1. Scalar multiplication uses pre-computations in projective coordinates. It requires m τ-operations, $\frac{m}{w+1} \cdot \frac{2^{w-2}-1}{2^{w-2}}$ point additions, $\frac{m}{w+1} \cdot \frac{1}{2^{w-2}}$ mixed additions, and the pre-computation. Scalar multiplication is expected to cost

$$4m\mathbf{S} + \frac{m}{w+1}\left((7+a)\mathbf{M} + 2\mathbf{S} - \frac{1}{2^{w-2}}\mathbf{M}\right) + \text{Pre}_w.$$

2. Scalar multiplication uses pre-computations in affine coordinates. This method fully uses mixed additions and requires Montgomery trick to translate the pre-computation points in projective coordinates to those in affine coordinates. It requires m τ-projective operations, $\frac{m}{w+1}$ mixed additions, Montgomery trick, and the pre-computation. Scalar multiplication is expected to cost

$$4m\mathbf{S} + \frac{m}{w+1}\left((6+a)\mathbf{M} + 2\mathbf{S}\right) + \mathbf{I} + (6 \cdot 2^{w-2} - 9)\mathbf{M} + \text{Pre}_w.$$

For window τNAF with width w, one should choose Case 1 or Case 2 to compute the scalar multiplication. The selection is not affected by the efficiency of the pre-computation. For the case of $a = 0$, the lowest costs of scalar multiplications on K-233, K-283, K-409, and K-571 using μ_4-Koblitz curves utilizing our pre-computation scheme and Trost and Xu's pre-computation scheme are summarized in Table 8. For the case of $a = 1$, the lowest costs of scalar multiplications on K1-163, K1-283, K1-359, and K1-701 utilizing our pre-computation scheme and Trost and Xu's pre-computation scheme are summarized in Table 9.

Table 8. The expected costs of scalar multiplications on K-233, K-283, K-409, and K-571 using μ_4-Koblitz curves in **M**

		K-233(w)	K-283(w)	K-409(w)	K-571(w)
S = 0M	τNAF	466	566	818	1142
	Trost, Xu	306.0(5)	363.3(5)	492.3(6)	652.9(6)
	Ours	274.9(6)	324.5(6)	444.3(7)	585.4(7)
S = 0.2M	regular τNAF	683.5	830.1	1199.7	1674.9
	Trost, Xu	511.9(5)	612.5(5)	850.1(6)	1149.5(6)
	Ours	481(6)	573.4(6)	804.3(7)	1083.1(7)
S = 0.5M	regular τNAF	1009.7	1226.3	1772.3	2474.3
	Trost, Xu	835.2(6)	991.9(6)	1386.8(6)	1894.5(6)
	Ours	790.2(6)	946.9(6)	1341.8(6)	1829.8(7)

Table 9. The expected costs of scalar multiplications on K1-163, K1-283, K1-359, and K1-701 using μ_4-Koblitz curves in **M**

		K1-163(w)	K1-283(w)	K1-359(w)	K1-701(w)
S = 0M	τNAF	380.3	660.3	837.7	1635.7
	Trost, Xu	259.9(5)	417.4(5)	509.1(6)	896.9(6)
	Ours	231.8(6)	367.9(6)	450.6(7)	791.3(7)
S = 0.2M	τNAF	532.5	924.5	1172.7	2289.9
	Trost, Xu	405.2(5)	666.7(5)	824(6)	1505(6)
	Ours	377.9(6)	616.9(6)	768.1(7)	1399.5(7)
S = 0.5M	τNAF	760.7	1320.7	1675.3	3271.3
	Trost, Xu	623.1(5)	1040.6(5)	1296.4(6)	2417.3(6)
	Ours	594.6(5)	990.3(6)	1239.4(6)	2311.9(7)

5.2 Expected Costs of Constant-Time Scalar Multiplications

When a constant running time is required, a regular window τNAF [22], the improved recoding of zero-free representation [21,28], is used to implement scalar multiplication. Scalar multiplication using pre-computations in projective coordinates requires

$$4m\mathbf{S} + \frac{m}{w-1}((7+a)\mathbf{M} + 2\mathbf{S}) + \text{Pre}_w.$$

Scalar multiplication using pre-computations in affine coordinates requires

$$4m\mathbf{S} + \frac{m}{w-1}((6+a)\mathbf{M} + 2\mathbf{S}) + \mathbf{I} + (6 \cdot 2^{w-2} - 9)\mathbf{M} + \text{Pre}_w.$$

We summarize the lowest costs of constant-time scalar multiplications using our pre-computation scheme and Trost and Xu's pre-computation scheme on curves with $a = 0$ in Table 10 and on curves with $a = 1$ in Table 11. Our pre-computation saves 9**M**+6**S** with $a = 0$ and 12**M**+6**S** with $a = 1$ for $w = 4$, 21**M**+3**S** with $a = 0$ and 27**M**+3**S** with $a = 1$ for $w = 5$, 43**M**+4**S** with $a = 0$ and 55**M**+4**S** with $a = 1$ for $w = 6$, compared to the state-of-the-art pre-computation. Our pre-computation scheme only requires 88**M**+62**S** with $a = 0$ and 93**M**+62**S** with $a = 1$ for $w = 7$, and 186**M**+123**S** with $a = 0$ and 198**M**+123**S** with $a = 1$ for $w = 8$. Since constant-time scalar multiplication usually uses window τNAF with a bigger window width, the ratios of the improvements of scalar multiplication become higher.

Table 10. The expected costs of constant-time scalar multiplications on K-233, K-283, K-409, and K-571 using μ_4-Koblitz curves in **M**

		K-233(w)	K-283(w)	K-409(w)	K-571(w)
S = 0M	regular τNAF	1398	1698	2454	3426
	Trost, Xu	413.2(6)	483.2(6)	659.6(6)	869.2(6,M)
	Ours	359.8(7)	418.2(7)	565.2(7)	754.2(7)
S = 0.2M	regular τNAF	1677.6	2037.6	2944.8	4111.2
	Trost, Xu	625.4(6)	739.4(6)	1026.7(6)	1378.9(6,M)
	Ours	574.2(7)	675.8(7)	932(7)	1261.4(7)
S = 0.5M	regular τNAF	2097	2547	3681	5139
	Trost, Xu	943.8(6)	1123.8(6)	1577.4(6)	2160.6(6)
	Ours	895.7(7)	1062.3(7)	1482.3(7)	2022.3(7)

If we use Montgomery trick, we denote it by M. This notation is also used in the following tables.

Table 11. The expected costs of constant-time scalar multiplications on K1-163, K1-283, K1-359, and K1-701 using μ_4-Koblitz curves in **M**

		K1-163(w)	K1-283(w)	K1-359(w)	K1-701(w)
S = 0M	regular τNAF	1141	1981	2513	4907
	Trost, Xu	362.8(6)	554.8(6)	676.4(6)	1180.4(6,M)
	Ours	307.8(6)	470.3(7)	571.7(7)	999.1(8)
S = 0.2M	regular τNAF	1336.6	2320.6	2943.8	5748.2
	Trost, Xu	513.4(6)	811(6)	999.5(6)	1804.5(6,M)
	Ours	457.6(6)	728(7)	895.2(7)	1624.6(8)
S = 0.5M	regular τNAF	1630	2830	3590	7010
	Trost, Xu	739.4(6)	1195.4(6)	1484.2(6)	2783.8(6)
	Ours	682.4(6)	1114.5(7)	1380.5(7)	2562.8(8)

6 Experiments

Miracl lib [25] is used to implement field arithmetics over $\mathbb{F}_{2^m}$. Our experiments are tested by C++ programs compiled by Microsoft visual studio 2015. The processor is Intel® Core™ i7-6567U 3.3 GHZ with Skylake architecture and the operating system is 64-bit Windows 10.

6.1 Pre-Computation Schemes on μ_4-Koblitz Curves

We run each pre-computation scheme 1000 times on six Koblitz curves. The time costs of pre-computation schemes on K1-163, K-233, K-283, K1-283, K-409, and K-571 using μ_4-Koblitz curves for window τNAF with widths from 4 to 6 are shown in Table 12.

Table 12. Time costs of pre-computations on K1-163, K-233, K-283, K1-283, K-409, and K-571 using μ_4-Koblitz curves in μs

		K1-163	K-233	K-283	K1-283	K-409	K-571
$w = 4$	Solinas	4.4	5.36	7.08	8.36	10.48	12.35
	Hankerson, Menezes, Vanstone	4.4	5.36	7.08	8.36	10.48	12.35
	Trost, Xu	4.36	5.28	6.52	7.64	10	11.76
	Ours	1.76	2.24	3.04	3.4	4.5	5.432
$w = 5$	Solinas	11.24	13.68	17.6	20.72	27.86	31.81
	Hankerson, Menezes, Vanstone	11.52	14.04	18.32	20.92	29.12	33.77
	Trost, Xu	10.88	13.28	17.56	20.36	27.47	31.75
	Ours	4.96	6.44	8.36	9.16	13.5	15.2
$w = 6$	Hankerson, Menezes, Vanstone	25.16	30.68	40.48	46.36	63.83	73.64
	Trost, Xu	24.88	30.36	39.24	45.28	62.96	71.89
	Ours	11.44	15.32	19.96	21.16	31.72	36.54

Our pre-computation scheme is about two times faster than Trost and Xu's scheme. Within the bounds of the error, the practical implementations are consistent with the theoretical analysis. The reason of some tiny differences is that a few field additions were ignored, that the number of temporary variables affects the performance, and that the ratio of $\mathbf{S}/\mathbf{M}$ is about 0.06 to 0.12 which depends on the size of the binary field.

6.2 Scalar Multiplications on μ_4-Koblitz Curves

The costs of constant-time scalar multiplications on K1-163, K-233, K-283, K1-283, K-409, and K-571 using μ_4-Koblitz curves are shown in Table 13. Our constant-time scalar multiplication is over 3 times faster, compared to the state-of-the-art non-pre-computation-based constant-time scalar multiplication. The constant-time scalar multiplication using our pre-computation on μ_4-Koblitz curves runs in 85.6%, 88.7%, 87.9%, 85.2%, 87.7%, and 87.9% the time of that using Trost and Xu's pre-computation on μ_4-Koblitz curves. The experimental results also show that the lowest constant-time scalar multiplication using our pre-computation usually employs width 7, and that using Trost and Xu's pre-computation usually employs width 6.

Table 13. Time cost of scalar multiplications using μ_4-Koblitz curves in μs

		K1-163(w)	K-233(w)	K-283(w)	K1-283(w)	K-409(w)	K-571(w)
	τNAF	70.42	98.6	171.9	167.3	384.2	424.6
	Trost, Xu	48.9(5)	70.23(5)	114.9(5)	132.1(5)	225(6)	268.4(6)
	Ours	44.75(6)	64.05(6)	104.3(6)	117.8(6)	207.4(7)	243.3(7)
constant-time	regular τNAF	173.7	265.6	432.4	491.8	860.1	1038.5
	Trost, Xu	63.95(6)	88.7(6)	143.6(6)	164.8(6)	283.6(6)	336.2(6,M)
	Ours	54.77(6)	78.67(7)	126.2(7)	140.5(7)	248.8(7)	294.7(7)

7 Conclusion

In the previous works of scalar multiplication using window τNAF [10,21,22,26–28], the authors employed a window τNAF with width at most 6. From Tables 8, 9, 10, 11, and 13, scalar multiplication using our pre-computation usually employs a bigger window width (e.g., 7) to achieve a lower cost of the total scalar multiplication.

In Appendix B, we employed our pre-computation scheme on Koblitz curves using LD coordinates. Our pre-computation scheme requires 5**M**+6**S**, 19**M**+19**S**, 51**M**+40**S**, 99**M**+76**S**, and 214**M**+158**S** when $a = 0$, and 5**M**+3**S**, 19**M**+13**S**, 51**M**+29**S**, 99**M**+53**S**, and 214**M**+113**S** when $a = 1$ using LD coordinates for window τNAF with widths from 4 to 8 respectively. Constant-time scalar multiplication using Trost and Xu's pre-computation requires 74.35, 109.4, 189.8, 357.9, and 433.1 μs on K1-163, K-233, K-283/K1-283, K-409, and K-571 respectively. Non-pre-computation-based constant-time scalar multiplication 216.3, 339.7, 547.8, 1078.3, and 1330.6 μs on these curves. These experimental results show that constant-time scalar multiplication using our pre-computation on μ_4-Koblitz curves runs in 73.7%, 71.9%, 66.5%, 74%, 69.5%, and 68% the time of Trost and Xu's work on K1-163, K-233, K-283, K1-283, K-409, and K-571 respectively where they used LD coordinates to perform scalar multiplication. Our scalar multiplication on μ_4-Koblitz curves is about 4 times faster than non-pre-computation-based constant-time scalar multiplication in LD coordinates and saves up to 33.5% on the scalar multiplication compared to scalar multiplication using Trost and Xu's pre-computation in LD coordinates.

In Appendix C, we employed our pre-computation scheme on Koblitz curves using λ-coordinates. The costs of our pre-computation scheme are 7**M**+5**S**, 26**M**+16**S**, 66**M**+36**S**, 135**M**+72**S**, and 282**M**+148**S** using λ-projective coordinates for window τNAF with widths from 4 to 8 respectively. Constant-time scalar multiplication using Trost and Xu's pre-computation requires 71.21, 102.2, 176.7, 335.9, and 402.5 μs on K1-163, K-233, K-283/K1-283, K-409, and K-571 respectively. Non-pre-computation-based constant-time scalar multiplication 211.7, 332.3, 540.8, 1065.2, and 1316.1 μs on these curves. These experimental results show that constant-time scalar multiplication using our pre-computation on μ_4-Koblitz curves runs in 76.9%, 77%, 71.4%, 79.5%, 74.1%, and 73.2% the time of Trost and Xu's work on K1-163, K-233, K-283, K1-283, K-409, and K-571 respectively where they used λ-coordinates to perform scalar multiplication. Based on our novel pre-computation, the efficient arithmetics on μ_4-Koblitz curves, and a bigger window width, our scalar multiplication on μ_4-Koblitz curves is about 4 times faster than non-pre-computation-based constant-time scalar multiplication in λ-coordinates and can save up to 28.6% on the scalar multiplication compared to [27].

It is noted that the arithmetic of Koblitz curves has been of theoretical and practical importance since the start of elliptic curve cryptography. Our results make a significant progress on the scalar multiplication for Koblitz curves which is a long-standing and well-studied area.

The idea of using $\mu\bar{\tau}$ to design an efficient pre-computation scheme and using a window τNAF with a bigger window width to improve the efficiency of scalar multiplication can be extended to Koblitz curves over $\mathbb{F}_{3^m}$ and $\mathbb{F}_{q^m}$ for some small primes $q \geq 5$. The efficient $\mu\bar{\tau}$-operations can also be used to speed up scalar multiplication utilizing double-base chain [29] and double-base number system [1], and to speed up multi-scalar multiplication utilizing double-base number system [8].

Acknowledgments. The authors would like to thank the anonymous reviewers for many helpful comments and thank Bao Li, Kunpeng Wang, Xianhui Lu, and Song Tian for their helpful suggestions. This work is supported by the National Natural Science Foundation of China (No. 61872442 and U1936209), by National Key Research and Development Program of China (No. 2018YFA0704702), and by Department of Science and Technology of Shandong Province of China (No. 2019JZZY010133). W. Yu is supported by Beijing Municipal Science & Technology Commission (No. Z191100007119006), by the National Cryptography Development Fund (No. MMJJ20180216), and by the National Natural Science Foundation of China (No. 61772515 and 61502487).

A Pre-computation for Window τNAF with Widths 7 and 8

A.1 Pre-computation for Window Width $w = 7$

Our pre-computation on a μ_4-Koblitz curve for window τNAF with width 7 is shown in Table 14. The cost of this pre-computation is 88**M**+62**S** with $a = 0$ and 93**M**+62**S** with $a = 1$.

Table 14. Novel pre-computation for $w = 7$

c_i		Q_i	$a = 0/a = 1$
			88M+62S/93M+62S
$c_{37} = -1 + \mu\tau$	$c_{37} = -\mu\bar{\tau}$	$Q_{37} = -\mu\bar{\tau}P$	2M+2S
$c_{39} = 1 + \mu\tau$	$c_{39} = \mu\bar{\tau}c_{37}$	$Q_{39} = -(\mu\bar{\tau})^2 P$	2M+2S
$c_{35} = -3 + \mu\tau$	$c_{35} = -\mu\bar{\tau}c_{39}$	$Q_{35} = (\mu\bar{\tau})^3 P$	2M+2S
$c_{15} = 1 - 3\mu\tau$	$c_{15} = -\mu\bar{\tau}c_{35}$	$Q_{15} = -(\mu\bar{\tau})^4 P$	2M+2S
$c_{43} = 5 + \mu\tau$	$c_{43} = -\mu\bar{\tau}c_{15}$	$Q_{43} = (\mu\bar{\tau})^5 P$	2M+2S
$c_{53} = 1 - 2\mu\tau$	$c_{53} = \mu\tau + c_{15}$	$Q_{53} = \mu\tau P + Q_{15}$	
$c_{23} = -1 + 4\mu\tau$	$c_{23} = \mu\tau - c_{15}$	$Q_{23} = \mu\tau P - Q_{15}$	(10M+3S) + 3S/(11M+3S) + 3S
$c_{41} = 3 + \mu\tau$	$c_{41} = -\mu\bar{\tau}c_{53}$	$Q_{41} = -\mu\bar{\tau}Q_{53}$	2M+2S
$c_{19} = 5 - 3\mu\tau$	$c_{19} = \mu\bar{\tau}c_{41}$	$Q_{19} = -(\mu\bar{\tau})^2 Q_{53}$	2M+2S
$c_{63} = 1 + 5\mu\tau$	$c_{63} = -\mu\bar{\tau}c_{19}$	$Q_{63} = (\mu\bar{\tau})^3 Q_{53}$	2M+2S
$c_{27} = -11 + \mu\tau$	$c_{27} = -\mu\bar{\tau}c_{63}$	$Q_{27} = -(\mu\bar{\tau})^4 Q_{53}$	2M+2S
$c_{45} = 7 + \mu\tau$	$c_{45} = \mu\bar{\tau}c_{23}$	$Q_{45} = \mu\bar{\tau}Q_{23}$	2M+2S
$c_3 = 3$	$c_3 = \mu\tau - c_{35}$	$Q_3 = \mu\tau P - Q_{35}$	
$c_{55} = 3 - 2\mu\tau$	$c_{55} = -\mu\tau - c_{35}$	$Q_{55} = -\mu\tau P - Q_{35}$	10M+3S/11M+3S
$c_{17} = 3 - 3\mu\tau$	$c_{17} = \mu\bar{\tau}c_3$	$Q_{17} = \mu\bar{\tau}Q_3$	2M+2S
$c_{11} = -3 - 3\mu\tau$	$c_{11} = \mu\bar{\tau}c_{17}$	$Q_{11} = (\mu\bar{\tau})^2 Q_3$	2M+2S
$c_{13} = -1 - 3\mu\tau$	$c_{13} = \mu\bar{\tau}c_{55}$	$Q_{13} = \mu\bar{\tau}Q_{55}$	2M+2S
$c_{31} = -7 + \mu\tau$	$c_{31} = \mu\bar{\tau}c_{13}$	$Q_{31} = (\mu\bar{\tau})^2 Q_{55}$	2M+2S
$c_5 = 5 + 7\mu\tau$	$c_5 = \mu\bar{\tau}c_{31}$	$Q_5 = (\mu\bar{\tau})^3 Q_{55}$	2M+2S
$c_{51} = -1 - 2\mu\tau$	$c_{51} = \mu\tau + c_{13}$	$Q_{51} = \mu\tau P + Q_{13}$	
$c_{25} = 1 + 4\mu\tau$	$c_{25} = \mu\tau - c_{13}$	$Q_{25} = \mu\tau P - Q_{13}$	10M+3S/11M+3S
$c_{33} = -5 + \mu\tau$	$c_{33} = \mu\bar{\tau}c_{51}$	$Q_{33} = \mu\bar{\tau}Q_{51}$	2M+2S
$c_{59} = -3 + 5\mu\tau$	$c_{59} = \mu\bar{\tau}c_{33}$	$Q_{59} = (\mu\bar{\tau})^2 Q_{51}$	2M+2S
$c_7 = -7 - 3\mu\tau$	$c_7 = -\mu\bar{\tau}c_{59}$	$Q_7 = -(\mu\bar{\tau})^3 Q_{51}$	2M+2S
$c_{29} = -9 + \mu\tau$	$c_{29} = -\mu\bar{\tau}c_{25}$	$Q_{29} = -\mu\bar{\tau}Q_{25}$	2M+2S
$c_{49} = -3 - 2\mu\tau$	$c_{49} = -\mu\tau - c_{41}$	$Q_{49} = -\mu\tau P - Q_{41}$	6M+2S/7M+2S
$c_{21} = 7 - 3\mu\tau$	$c_{21} = -\mu\bar{\tau}c_{49}$	$Q_{21} = -\mu\bar{\tau}Q_{49}$	2M+2S
$c_9 = -1 + 7\mu\tau$	$c_9 = -\mu\bar{\tau}c_{21}$	$Q_9 = (\mu\bar{\tau})^2 Q_{49}$	2M+2S
$c_{57} = 5 - 2\mu\tau$	$c_{57} = -\mu\tau - c_{33}$	$Q_{57} = -\mu\tau P - Q_{33}$	6M+2S/7M+2S
$c_{61} = -1 + 5\mu\tau$	$c_{61} = -\mu\bar{\tau}c_{57}$	$Q_{61} = -\mu\bar{\tau}Q_{57}$	2M+2S
$c_{47} = 9 + \mu\tau$	$c_{47} = \mu\bar{\tau}c_{61}$	$Q_{47} = -(\mu\bar{\tau})^2 Q_{57}$	2M+2S

A.2 Pre-computation for Window Width $w = 8$

Our pre-computation on a μ_4-Koblitz curve for window τNAF with width 8 is shown in Table 15. The cost of this pre-computation is 186**M**+123**S** with $a = 0$ and 198**M**+123**S** with $a = 1$.

B Our Pre-computation Scheme on Koblitz Curves Using LD Coordinates

A projective point $P = (X : Y : Z)$ in LD coordinates on an elliptic curve $E/\mathbb{F}_{2^m}$ can be converted to an affine point $(\frac{X}{Z}, \frac{Y}{Z^2})$ [19]. Let $P = (x_P, y_P)$.

Table 15. Novel pre-computation for $w = 8$

c_i		Q_i	$a = 0/a = 1$
			186M+123S/198M+123S
$c_{91} = 1 - \mu\tau$	$c_{91} = \mu\bar{\tau}$	$Q_{91} = \mu\bar{\tau}P$	2M+2S
$c_{89} = -1 - \mu\tau$	$c_{89} = \mu\bar{\tau}c_{91}$	$Q_{89} = (\mu\bar{\tau})^2 P$	2M+2S
$c_{93} = 3 - \mu\tau$	$c_{93} = -\mu\bar{\tau}c_{89}$	$Q_{93} = -(\mu\bar{\tau})^3 P$	2M+2S
$c_{15} = 1 - 3\mu\tau$	$c_{15} = \mu\bar{\tau}c_{93}$	$Q_{15} = -(\mu\bar{\tau})^4 P$	2M+2S
$c_{85} = -5 - \mu\tau$	$c_{85} = \mu\bar{\tau}c_{15}$	$Q_{85} = -(\mu\bar{\tau})^5 P$	2M+2S
$c_{55} = -7 + 5\mu\tau$	$c_{55} = \mu\bar{\tau}c_{85}$	$Q_{55} = -(\mu\bar{\tau})^6 P$	2M+2S
$c_{115} = -3 - 7\mu\tau$	$c_{115} = -\mu\bar{\tau}c_{55}$	$Q_{115} = (\mu\bar{\tau})^7 P$	2M+2S
$c_{75} = -1 + 2\mu\tau$	$c_{75} = -\mu\tau - c_{15}$	$Q_{75} = -\mu\tau P - Q_{15}$	
$c_{105} = 1 - 4\mu\tau$	$c_{105} = -\mu\tau + c_{15}$	$Q_{105} = -\mu\tau P + Q_{15}$	10M+3S+3S/11M+3S+3S
$c_{87} = -3 - \mu\tau$	$c_{87} = -\mu\bar{\tau}c_{75}$	$Q_{87} = -\mu\bar{\tau}Q_{75}$	2M+2S
$c_{19} = 5 - 3\mu\tau$	$c_{19} = -\mu\bar{\tau}c_{87}$	$Q_{19} = (\mu\bar{\tau})^2 Q_{75}$	2M+2S
$c_{63} = 1 + 5\mu\tau$	$c_{63} = -\mu\bar{\tau}c_{19}$	$Q_{63} = -(\mu\bar{\tau})^3 Q_{75}$	2M+2S
$c_{101} = 11 - \mu\tau$	$c_{101} = \mu\bar{\tau}c_{63}$	$Q_{101} = -(\mu\bar{\tau})^4 Q_{75}$	2M+2S
$c_{25} = -9 + 11\mu\tau$	$c_{25} = -\mu\bar{\tau}c_{101}$	$Q_{25} = (\mu\bar{\tau})^5 Q_{75}$	2M+2S
$c_{83} = -7 - \mu\tau$	$c_{83} = \mu\bar{\tau}c_{105}$	$Q_{83} = \mu\bar{\tau}Q_{105}$	2M+2S
$c_{127} = 9 - 7\mu\tau$	$c_{127} = -\mu\bar{\tau}c_{83}$	$Q_{127} = -(\mu\bar{\tau})^2 Q_{105}$	2M+2S
$c_{37} = -5 - 9\mu\tau$	$c_{37} = \mu\bar{\tau}c_{127}$	$Q_{37} = -(\mu\bar{\tau})^3 Q_{105}$	2M+2S
$c_3 = 3$	$c_3 = -\mu\tau - c_{87}$	$Q_3 = -\mu\tau P - Q_{87}$	
$c_{79} = 3 + 2\mu\tau$	$c_{79} = \mu\tau - c_{87}$	$Q_{79} = \mu\tau P - Q_{87}$	10M+3S/11M+3S
$c_{17} = 3 - 3\mu\tau$	$c_{17} = \mu\bar{\tau}c_3$	$Q_{17} = \mu\bar{\tau}Q_3$	2M+2S
$c_{11} = -3 - 3\mu\tau$	$c_{11} = \mu\bar{\tau}c_{17}$	$Q_{11} = (\mu\bar{\tau})^2 Q_3$	2M+2S
$c_{23} = 9 - 3\mu\tau$	$c_{23} = -\mu\bar{\tau}c_{11}$	$Q_{23} = -(\mu\bar{\tau})^3 Q_3$	2M+2S
$c_{45} = 3 - 9\mu\tau$	$c_{45} = \mu\bar{\tau}c_{23}$	$Q_{45} = -(\mu\bar{\tau})^4 Q_3$	2M+2S
$c_{21} = 7 - 3\mu\tau$	$c_{21} = \mu\bar{\tau}c_{49}$	$Q_{21} = \mu\bar{\tau}Q_{79}$	2M+2S
$c_{119} = 1 - 7\mu\tau$	$c_{119} = \mu\bar{\tau}c_{21}$	$Q_{119} = (\mu\bar{\tau})^2 Q_{79}$	2M+2S
$c_{73} = -3 + 2\mu\tau$	$c_{73} = -\mu\tau - c_{17}$	$Q_{73} = -\mu\tau P - Q_{17}$	
$c_{107} = 3 - 4\mu\tau$	$c_{107} = -\mu\tau + c_{17}$	$Q_{107} = -\mu\tau P + Q_{17}$	10M+3S/11M+3S
$c_{13} = -1 - 3\mu\tau$	$c_{13} = -\mu\bar{\tau}c_{73}$	$Q_{13} = -\mu\bar{\tau}Q_{73}$	2M+2S
$c_{97} = 7 - \mu\tau$	$c_{97} = -\mu\bar{\tau}c_{13}$	$Q_{97} = (\mu\bar{\tau})^2 Q_{73}$	2M+2S
$c_{123} = 5 - 7\mu\tau$	$c_{123} = \mu\bar{\tau}c_{97}$	$Q_{123} = (\mu\bar{\tau})^3 Q_{73}$	2M+2S
$c_9 = -5 - 3\mu\tau$	$c_9 = \mu\bar{\tau}c_{107}$	$Q_9 = \mu\bar{\tau}Q_{107}$	2M+2S
$c_{51} = -11 + 5\mu\tau$	$c_{51} = \mu\bar{\tau}c_9$	$Q_{51} = (\mu\bar{\tau})^2 Q_{107}$	2M+2S
$c_{33} = -1 + 11\mu\tau$	$c_{33} = \mu\bar{\tau}c_{51}$	$Q_{33} = (\mu\bar{\tau})^3 Q_{107}$	2M+2S
$c_{77} = 1 + 2\mu\tau$	$c_{77} = -\mu\tau - c_{13}$	$Q_{77} = -\mu\tau P - Q_{13}$	
$c_{103} = -1 - 4\mu\tau$	$c_{103} = -\mu\tau + c_{13}$	$Q_{103} = -\mu\tau P + Q_{13}$	10M+3S/11M+3S
$c_{95} = 5 - \mu\tau$	$c_{95} = \mu\bar{\tau}c_{77}$	$Q_{95} = \mu\bar{\tau}Q_{77}$	2M+2S
$c_{59} = -3 + 5\mu\tau$	$c_{59} = -\mu\bar{\tau}c_{95}$	$Q_{59} = -(\mu\bar{\tau})^2 Q_{77}$	2M+2S
$c_7 = -7 - 3\mu\tau$	$c_7 = -\mu\bar{\tau}c_{59}$	$Q_7 = (\mu\bar{\tau})^3 Q_{77}$	2M+2S
$c_{125} = -13 + 7\mu\tau$	$c_{125} = \mu\bar{\tau}c_7$	$Q_{125} = (\mu\bar{\tau})^4 Q_{77}$	2M+2S
$c_{99} = 9 - \mu\tau$	$c_{99} = -\mu\bar{\tau}c_{103}$	$Q_{99} = -\mu\bar{\tau}Q_{103}$	2M+2S
$c_{49} = 7 - 9\mu\tau$	$c_{49} = \mu\bar{\tau}c_{99}$	$Q_{49} = -(\mu\bar{\tau})^2 Q_{103}$	2M+2S
$c_5 = 5$	$c_5 = -\mu\tau - c_{85}$	$Q_5 = -\mu\tau P - Q_{85}$	6M+2S/7M+2S
$c_{57} = -5 + 5\mu\tau$	$c_{57} = -\mu\bar{\tau}c_5$	$Q_{57} = -\mu\bar{\tau}Q_5$	2M+2S
$c_{67} = 5 + 5\mu\tau$	$c_{67} = \mu\bar{\tau}c_{57}$	$Q_{67} = -(\mu\bar{\tau})^2 Q_5$	2M+2S
$c_{47} = -15 + 5\mu\tau$	$c_{47} = -\mu\bar{\tau}c_{67}$	$Q_{47} = (\mu\bar{\tau})^3 Q_5$	2M+2S
$c_{71} = -5 + 2\mu\tau$	$c_{71} = -\mu\tau - c_{19}$	$Q_{71} = -\mu\tau P - Q_{19}$	
$c_{61} = -1 + 5\mu\tau$	$c_{61} = \mu\bar{\tau}c_{71}$	$Q_{61} = \mu\bar{\tau}Q_{71}$	2M+2S
$c_{109} = 5 - 4\mu\tau$	$c_{109} = -\mu\tau + c_{19}$	$Q_{109} = -\mu\tau P + Q_{19}$	10M+3S/11M+3S
$c_{81} = -9 - \mu\tau$	$c_{81} = -\mu\bar{\tau}c_{61}$	$Q_{81} = -(\mu\bar{\tau})^2 Q_{71}$	2M+2S

(continued)

Table 15. (*continued*)

c_i		Q_i	$a = 0/a = 1$
$c_{53} = 11 - 9\mu\tau$	$c_{53} = -\mu\bar{\tau}c_{81}$	$Q_{53} = (\mu\bar{\tau})^3 Q_{71}$	2M+2S
$c_{65} = 3 + 5\mu\tau$	$c_{65} = -\mu\bar{\tau}c_{109}$	$Q_{65} = -\mu\bar{\tau}Q_{109}$	2M+2S
$c_{27} = 13 - 3\mu\tau$	$c_{27} = \mu\bar{\tau}c_{65}$	$Q_{27} = -(\mu\bar{\tau})^2 Q_{109}$	2M+2S
$c_{69} = -7 + 2\mu\tau$	$c_{69} = -\mu\tau - c_{21}$	$Q_{69} = -\mu\tau P - Q_{21}$	
$c_{111} = 7 - 4\mu\tau$	$c_{111} = -\mu\tau + c_{21}$	$Q_{111} = -\mu\tau P + Q_{21}$	10M+3S/11M+3S
$c_{121} = 3 - 7\mu\tau$	$c_{121} = -\mu\bar{\tau}c_{69}$	$Q_{121} = -\mu\bar{\tau}Q_{69}$	2M+2S
$c_{117} = -1 - 7\mu\tau$	$c_{117} = \mu\bar{\tau}c_{111}$	$Q_{117} = \mu\bar{\tau}Q_{111}$	2M+2S
$c_{113} = 9 - 4\mu\tau$	$c_{113} = -\mu\tau + c_{23}$	$Q_{113} = -\mu\tau P + Q_{23}$	6M+2S/7M+2S
$c_{43} = 1 - 9\mu\tau$	$c_{43} = \mu\bar{\tau}c_{113}$	$Q_{43} = \mu\bar{\tau}Q_{113}$	2M+2S
$c_{39} = 11 - 6\mu\tau$	$c_{39} = -\mu\tau - c_{51}$	$Q_{39} = -\mu\tau P - Q_{51}$	6M+2S/7M+2S
$c_{35} = 1 + 11\mu\tau$	$c_{35} = -\mu\bar{\tau}c_{39}$	$Q_{35} = -\mu\bar{\tau}Q_{39}$	2M+2S
$c_{29} = 1 - 6\mu\tau$	$c_{29} = -\mu\tau - c_{61}$	$Q_{29} = -\mu\tau P - Q_{61}$	6M+2S/7M+2S
$c_{31} = 3 - 6\mu\tau$	$c_{31} = -\mu\tau - c_{59}$	$Q_{31} = -\mu\tau P - Q_{59}$	6M+2S/7M+2S
$c_{41} = 13 - 6\mu\tau$	$c_{41} = \mu\tau - c_{125}$	$Q_{41} = \mu\tau P - Q_{125}$	6M+2S/7M+2S

The projective LD coordinates of P are (X_P, Y_P, Z_P) where $x_P = \frac{X_P}{Z_P}$ and $y_P = \frac{Y_P}{Z_P^2}$. We have $-(x_P, y_P) = (x_P, x_P + y_P)$, $-(X_P, Y_P, Z_P) = (X_P, X_P Z_P + Y_P, Z_P)$, $\tau(x_P, y_P) = (x_P^2, y_P^2)$, and $\tau(X_P, Y_P, Z_P) = (X_P^2, Y_P^2, Z_P^2)$. Let $P = (X_P, Y_P, Z_P)$ and $Q = (X_Q, Y_Q, Z_Q)$. Point addition $P + Q = (x_{P+Q}, \lambda_{P+Q})$ with $Z_P = 1$ was given in Sect. 3 of [16] as

$$
\begin{aligned}
A = Z_Q^2 Y_P + Y_Q, B &= Z_Q X_P + X_Q, C = Z_Q B,\\
Z_{P+Q} &= C^2, D = Z_{P+Q} X_P, E = X_P + Y_P,\\
X_{P+Q} &= A^2 + C(A + B^2 + aC),\\
Y_{P+Q} &= (D + X_{P+Q})(AC + Z_{P+Q}) + Z_{P+Q}^2 E.
\end{aligned}
$$

One full point addition costs 13**M**+4**S**, one mixed point addition costs 8**M**+5**S**, and one point addition with both affine points costs 5**M**+5**S**. Furthermore, evaluation of $-P$ costs 1**M**, evaluation of $\tau(P)$ costs 3**S**, and τ-affine operation requires 2**S**.

B.1 New Formulas Using LD Coordinates

New Formulas for $P \pm Q$. We introduce efficient formulas of $P \pm Q$ in LD coordinates by Theorem 5.

Theorem 3. *Let $P = (x_P, y_P)$ and $Q = (X_Q, Y_Q, Z_Q)$ where $P \neq \pm Q$. Notice that $-Q = (X_Q, X_Q Z_Q + Y_Q, Z_Q)$. The two operations of $P + Q$ and $P - Q$ ($(P \pm Q)$-operation) can be computed as Eq. (5) at the total cost of* 12**M**+6**S**.

$$\begin{aligned}
A =& Z_Q^2 Y_P + Y_Q, B = Z_Q X_P + X_Q, C = Z_Q B && \mathbf{3M+S} \\
Z_{P+Q} =& Z_{P-Q} = C^2 && \mathbf{S} \\
D =& Z_{P+Q} X_P, E = X_P + Y_P, F = AC && \mathbf{2M} \\
X_{P+Q} =& A^2 + C(A + B^2 + aC) && \mathbf{M+2S} \\
Y_{P+Q} =& (D + X_{P+Q})(F + Z_{P+Q}) + Z_{P+Q}^2 E && \mathbf{2M+S} \\
G =& X_Q Z_Q C, H = (X_Q Z_Q)^2 + G && \mathbf{2M+S} \\
X_{P-Q} =& X_{P+Q} + H && \\
Y_{P-Q} =& Y_{P+Q} + H(G + F + Z_{P+Q}) + (D + X_{P+Q})G && \mathbf{2M}
\end{aligned} \tag{5}$$

Theorem 4. ([8]) *Let $P = (X_P, Y_P, Z_P)$ in LD coordinates. $\mu\bar{\tau}P$ can be computed as*

$$\begin{aligned}
X_{\mu\bar{\tau}P} =& (X_P + Z_P)^2 \\
Z_{\mu\bar{\tau}P} =& X_P Z_P \\
Y_{\mu\bar{\tau}P} =& (Y_P + (1-a)X_{\mu\bar{\tau}P})(Y_P + aX_{\mu\bar{\tau}P} + Z_{\mu\bar{\tau}P}) + (1-a)Z_{\mu\bar{\tau}P}^2
\end{aligned}$$

at the cost of **2M+2S** *with $a = 0$ and* **2M+S** *with $a = 1$ when $Z_P \neq 1$ and at the cost of* **M+2S** *with $a = 0$ and* **M+S** *with $a = 1$ when $Z_P = 1$. The cost of $-\mu\bar{\tau}P$ is the same as that of $\mu\bar{\tau}P$.*

B.2 Pre-computation Schemes Using LD Coordinates

Our pre-computation scheme for window τNAF in LD coordinates is the same as that on a μ_4-Koblitz curve. Our pre-computation scheme requires **5M+6S**, **19M+19S**, **51M+40S**, **99M+76S**, and **214M+158S** when $a = 0$, and **5M+3S**, **19M+13S**, **51M+29S**, **99M+53S**, and **214M+113S** when $a = 1$ using LD coordinates for window τNAF with widths from 4 to 8 respectively.

The costs of different pre-computation schemes for window τNAF with widths from 4 to 6 are summarized in Table 16. Trost and Xu's pre-computation scheme requires **15M+19S**, **48M+39S**, and **120M+79S** for $w = 4$, 5, and 6. Both theoretical analysis and experimental results show that our pre-computation scheme is about 2.4 times faster than Trost and Xu's scheme using LD coordinates.

Table 16. Cost of pre-computations using LD coordinates with $a = 0/a = 1$

	$w = 4$	$w = 5$	$w = 6$
Solinas	15M+21S	45M+52S	–
Hankerson, Menezes, Vanstone	15M+21S	54M+49S	125M+105S
Trost, Xu	15M+19S	48M+39S	120M+79S
Ours	5M+6S/5M+3S	19M+19S/19M+13S	51M+40S/51M+29S

B.3 Scalar Multiplications Using Window τNAF in LD Coordinates

The Montgomery trick transferring n pre-computations in LD coordinates to affine coordinates costs $\mathbf{I}+(5n-3)\mathbf{M}+n\mathbf{S}$. Let the costs of pre-computation schemes for window τNAF with width w be denoted by PreLD_w.

Constant-time scalar multiplication using window τNAF has two situations.

1. Scalar multiplication uses pre-computations in LD coordinates. It requires m τ-operations, $\frac{m}{w-1}$ point additions, the pre-computation, and negative of the pre-computation. Scalar multiplication is expected to cost

$$3m\mathbf{S}+\frac{m}{w-1}(13\mathbf{M}+4\mathbf{S})+\text{PreLD}_w+(2^{w-2}-1)\mathbf{M}.$$

2. Scalar multiplication uses pre-computations in affine coordinates. It requires m τ-projective operations, $\frac{m}{w-1}$ mixed additions, Montgomery trick, and the pre-computation. Scalar multiplication is expected to cost

$$3m\mathbf{S}+\frac{m}{w-1}(8\mathbf{M}+5\mathbf{S})+\mathbf{I}+(5\cdot 2^{w-2}-8)\mathbf{M}+(2^{w-2}-1)\mathbf{S}+\text{PreLD}_w.$$

We summarize the lowest costs of constant-time scalar multiplications on K1-163, K-233, K-283, K1-283, K-409, and K-571 using our pre-computation scheme in Table 17. Our experimental results show that our constant-time scalar multiplication on Koblitz curves using LD coordinates saves up to 10% compared to Trost and Xu's work using LD coordinates.

Table 17. The expected costs of constant-time scalar multiplications using our pre-computation in LD coordinates on K1-163, K-233, K-283/K1-283, K-409, and K-571 in **M**

		K1-163(w)	K-233(w)	K-283(w)/K1-283(w)	K-409(w)	K-571(w)
S = 0M	regular τNAF	1304	1864	2264	3272	4568
	Trost, Xu	416(5,M)	556(5,M)	654.8(6,M)	856.4(6,M)	1115.6(6,M)
	Ours	387(5,M)	505.8(6,M)	585.8(6,M)	787.4(6,M)	1022.3(7,M)
S = 0.2M	regular τNAF	1564.8	2236.8	2716.8	3926.4	5481.6
	Trost, Xu	563.8(5,M)	763.3(5,M)	900(6,M)	1202.4(6,M)	1591.2(6,M)
	Ours	529.6(5,M)	703.2(6,M)	823.2(6,M)/821(6,M)	1125.6(6,M)	1481.5(7,M)
S = 0.5M	regular τNAF	1956	2796	3396	4908	6852
	Trost, Xu	908(6)	1214.1(5,M)	1407.8(6,M)	1861.4(6,M)	2444.6(6,M)
	Ours	808.5(6)	1100(7)	1300(7)/1288.5(7)	1772.9(6,M)	2310.3(7,M)

C Our Pre-computation Scheme on Koblitz Curves Using λ-Coordinates

Given an affine point $P=(x,y)$ on an elliptic curve $E/\mathbb{F}_{2^m}$, its lambda representation is (x,λ) with $\lambda=x+\frac{y}{x}$ [23]. Let $P=(x_P,\lambda_P)$ with $\lambda_P=x_P+\frac{y_P}{x_P}$.

The λ-coordinates of $-P$ are $(x_P, \lambda_P + 1)$. The λ-projective coordinates of P are (X_P, Λ_P, Z_P) where $x_P = \frac{X_P}{Z_P}$ and $\lambda_P = \frac{\Lambda_P}{Z_P}$. We have $\tau(x_P, \lambda_P) = (x_P^2, \lambda_P^2)$ and $\tau(X_P, \Lambda_P, Z_P) = (X_P^2, \Lambda_P^2, Z_P^2)$. Let $P = (x_P, \lambda_P)$ and $Q = (x_Q, \lambda_Q)$. Point addition $P + Q = (x_{P+Q}, \lambda_{P+Q})$ was given in Section 3.1 of [23] as

$$\begin{cases} x_{P+Q} = \frac{x_P x_Q}{(x_P+x_Q)^2}(\lambda_P + \lambda_Q), \\ \lambda_{P+Q} = \frac{x_Q(x_{P+Q}+x_P)^2}{x_{P+Q}x_P} + \lambda_P + 1. \end{cases}$$

One full point addition costs 11**M**+2**S**, one mixed point addition costs 8**M**+2**S** and one point addition with both affine points costs 5**M**+2**S**. Furthermore, evaluation of $\tau(P)$ costs 3**S** and τ-affine operation requires 2**S**.

C.1 New Formulas Using λ-Coordinates

New Formulas for $P \pm Q$. We introduce efficient formulas of $P \pm Q$ in λ-projective coordinates by Theorem 5.

Theorem 5. *Let $P = (x_P, \lambda_P)$ and $Q = (X_Q, \Lambda_Q, Z_Q)$ where $P \neq \pm Q$. Notice that $-Q = (X_Q, \Lambda_Q + Z_Q, Z_Q)$. The two operations of $P+Q$ and $P-Q$ ($(P \pm Q)$-operation) can be computed as Eq. (6) at the total cost of* 12**M**+5**S**.

$$\begin{aligned}
A =& \lambda_P Z_Q + \Lambda_Q && \mathbf{M} \\
B =& (x_P Z_Q + X_Q)^2 && \mathbf{M}+\mathbf{S} \\
C =& X_Q Z_Q && \mathbf{M} \\
D =& x_P C && \mathbf{M} \\
X_{P+Q} =& A^2 D && \mathbf{M}+\mathbf{S} \\
Z_{P+Q} =& BAZ_Q && 2\mathbf{M} \\
\Lambda_{P+Q} =& (AX_Q + B)^2 + Z_{P+Q}(\lambda_P + 1) && 2\mathbf{M}+\mathbf{S} \\
X_{P-Q} =& X_{P+Q} + DZ_Q^2 && \mathbf{M}+\mathbf{S} \\
Z_{P-Q} =& Z_{P+Q} + BZ_Q^2 && \mathbf{M} \\
\Lambda_{P-Q} =& \Lambda_{P+Q} + C^2 + BZ_Q^2(\lambda_P + 1) && \mathbf{M}+\mathbf{S}
\end{aligned} \tag{6}$$

Formulas for $\mu\bar{\tau}$-Operations. An efficient formula for $\mu\bar{\tau}P$ in λ-coordinates has been obtained in Sect. 4 of [27] under the form of $P - \mu\tau P$. We shall use their formula $\mu\bar{\tau}P = \left(\frac{x_P^2+1}{x_P}, \frac{x_P^2}{x_P^2+1} + \lambda_P\right)$ with $P = (x_P, \lambda_P)$. Formulas for $(\mu\bar{\tau})^2 P$ and $(\mu\bar{\tau})^3 P$ were also reported in Sect. 4 of [27] under the form of $P + \mu\tau P$ and $P - \tau^2 P$, however in [27], these formulas were not based on the one for $\mu\bar{\tau}P$. We can get a good improvement by designing efficient formulas of $(\mu\bar{\tau})^i P$ by utilizing $(\mu\bar{\tau})^{i-1} P$ if it is already computed.

Theorem 6. *Let $P = (X_P, \Lambda_P, Z_P)$. $\mu\bar{\tau}P$ and $(\mu\bar{\tau})^i P, i \geq 2$ can be computed at the cost of* 5**M**+3**S** *and* 3**M**+2**S** *respectively.*

Proof. 1. By $\mu\bar{\tau}P = \left(\frac{x_P^2+1}{x_P}, \frac{x_P^2}{x_P^2+1} + \lambda_P\right)$ in Sect. 4.1 of [27], we have

$$\mu\bar{\tau}P = \left(\frac{(\frac{X_P}{Z_P})^2+1}{\frac{X_P}{Z_P}}, \frac{(\frac{X_P}{Z_P})^2}{(\frac{X_P}{Z_P})^2+1} + \frac{\Lambda_P}{Z_P}\right).$$

Then $\mu\bar{\tau}P$ can be calculated as Eq. (7) at the cost of 5**M**+3**S**.

$$\begin{aligned} \alpha &= X_P Z_P && \mathbf{M} \\ A_1 &= X_P^2 + Z_P^2 && 2\mathbf{S} \\ X_{\mu\bar{\tau}P} &= A_1^2 && \mathbf{S} \\ \Lambda_{\mu\bar{\tau}P} &= \alpha X_P^2 + X_P \Lambda_P A_1 && 3\mathbf{M} \\ Z_{\mu\bar{\tau}P} &= A_1 \alpha && \mathbf{M} \end{aligned} \tag{7}$$

2. The values for computing previous point operations are utilized to compute a new point operation in [18,27]. Motivated by their trick, some values for computing $\mu\bar{\tau}P$ are used to compute $(\mu\bar{\tau})^2P$. Let $\mu\bar{\tau}P = (X_{\mu\bar{\tau}P}, \Lambda_{\mu\bar{\tau}P}, Z_{\mu\bar{\tau}P})$ be computed as Eq. (7) where $x_{\mu\bar{\tau}P} = \frac{A_1}{\alpha}$. Notice that $(\mu\bar{\tau})^2P = \mu\bar{\tau}(\mu\bar{\tau}P)$. We have

$$\begin{aligned} (\mu\bar{\tau})^2P &= \left(\frac{x_{\mu\bar{\tau}P}^2+1}{x_{\mu\bar{\tau}P}}, \frac{x_{\mu\bar{\tau}P}^2}{x_{\mu\bar{\tau}P}^2+1} + \lambda_{\mu\bar{\tau}P}\right) \\ &= \left(\frac{A_1^2+\alpha^2}{A_1\alpha}, \frac{A_1^2}{A_1^2+\alpha^2} + \frac{\Lambda_{\mu\bar{\tau}P}}{Z_{\mu\bar{\tau}P}}\right) \\ &= \left(\frac{X_{\mu\bar{\tau}P}+\alpha^2}{Z_{\mu\bar{\tau}P}}, \frac{X_{\mu\bar{\tau}P}}{X_{\mu\bar{\tau}P}+\alpha^2} + \frac{\Lambda_{\mu\bar{\tau}P}}{Z_{\mu\bar{\tau}P}}\right). \end{aligned}$$

Then $(\mu\bar{\tau})^2P$ can be computed as Eq. (8) at the cost of 3**M**+2**S**.

$$\begin{aligned} A_2 &= X_{\mu\bar{\tau}P} + \alpha^2 && \mathbf{S} \\ X_{(\mu\bar{\tau})^2P} &= A_2^2 && \mathbf{S} \\ \Lambda_{(\mu\bar{\tau})^2P} &= X_{\mu\bar{\tau}P} Z_{\mu\bar{\tau}P} + \Lambda_{\mu\bar{\tau}P} A_2 && 2\mathbf{M} \\ Z_{(\mu\bar{\tau})^2P} &= Z_{\mu\bar{\tau}P} A_2 && \mathbf{M} \end{aligned} \tag{8}$$

3. When $i \geq 3$, $(\mu\bar{\tau})^iP = \mu\bar{\tau}((\mu\bar{\tau})^{i-1}P)$. We have

$$(\mu\bar{\tau})^iP = \left(\frac{x_{(\mu\bar{\tau})^{i-1}P}^2+1}{x_{(\mu\bar{\tau})^{i-1}P}}, \frac{x_{(\mu\bar{\tau})^{i-1}P}^2}{x_{(\mu\bar{\tau})^{i-1}P}^2+1} + \lambda_{(\mu\bar{\tau})^{i-1}P}\right).$$

Some values of calculating $(\mu\bar{\tau})^{i-1}P$ are used to calculate $(\mu\bar{\tau})^iP$. When $i = 3$, $x_{(\mu\bar{\tau})^{i-1}P} = \frac{A_{i-1}}{Z_{(\mu\bar{\tau})^{i-2}P}}$ and $X_{(\mu\bar{\tau})^{i-1}P} = A_{i-1}^2$ are computed by Eq. (8); when $i > 3$, $x_{(\mu\bar{\tau})^{i-1}P} = \frac{A_{i-1}}{Z_{(\mu\bar{\tau})^{i-2}P}}$ and $X_{(\mu\bar{\tau})^{i-1}P} = A_{i-1}^2$ are computed by

Eq. (9). $(\mu\bar{\tau})^i P$ can be computed as

$$\left(\frac{(\frac{A_{i-1}}{Z_{(\mu\bar{\tau})^{i-2}P}})^2+1}{\frac{A_{i-1}}{Z_{(\mu\bar{\tau})^{i-2}P}}}, \frac{(\frac{A_{i-1}}{Z_{(\mu\bar{\tau})^{i-2}P}})^2}{(\frac{A_{i-1}}{Z_{(\mu\bar{\tau})^{i-2}P}})^2+1} + \frac{\Lambda_{(\mu\bar{\tau})^{i-1}P}}{Z_{(\mu\bar{\tau})^{i-1}P}} \right)$$
$$= \left(\frac{X_{(\mu\bar{\tau})^{i-1}P} + Z^2_{(\mu\bar{\tau})^{i-2}P}}{Z_{(\mu\bar{\tau})^{i-1}P}}, \frac{X_{(\mu\bar{\tau})^{i-1}P}}{X_{(\mu\bar{\tau})^{i-1}P} + Z^2_{(\mu\bar{\tau})^{i-2}P}} + \frac{\Lambda_{(\mu\bar{\tau})^{i-1}P}}{Z_{(\mu\bar{\tau})^{i-1}P}} \right).$$

Then $(\mu\bar{\tau})^i P$, $i \geq 3$ can be computed as Eq. (9) at the cost of 3**M**+2**S**.

$$\begin{aligned} A_i &= X_{(\mu\bar{\tau})^{i-1}P} + Z^2_{(\mu\bar{\tau})^{i-2}P} && \mathbf{S} \\ X_{(\mu\bar{\tau})^i P} &= A_i^2 && \mathbf{S} \\ \Lambda_{(\mu\bar{\tau})^i P} &= X_{(\mu\bar{\tau})^{i-1}P} Z_{(\mu\bar{\tau})^{i-1}P} + \Lambda_{(\mu\bar{\tau})^{i-1}P} A_i && 2\mathbf{M} \\ Z_{(\mu\bar{\tau})^i P} &= Z_{(\mu\bar{\tau})^{i-1}P} A_i && \mathbf{M} \end{aligned} \tag{9}$$

□

Notice that $\mu\bar{\tau}P = P - \mu\tau P$, $(\mu\bar{\tau})^2 P = -(P + \mu\tau P)$, and $(\mu\bar{\tau})^3 P = -(P - \tau^2 P)$. Trost and Xu showed that $P - \mu\tau P$, $P + \mu\tau P$, and $P - \tau^2 P$ cost 5**M**+3**S**, 7**M**+5**S**, and 5**M**+3**S** respectively. Their formula of $P - \mu\tau P$ is still the state-of-the-art. The costs of $(\mu\bar{\tau})^2 P$ and $(\mu\bar{\tau})^3 P$ are 3**M**+2**S** and 3**M**+2**S** which largely improves their costs of 7**M**+5**S** and 5**M**+3**S**.

When Z-coordinate of P is 1, by $\Lambda_{(\mu\bar{\tau})^2 P} = X_{\mu\bar{\tau}P} Z_{\mu\bar{\tau}P} + \Lambda_{\mu\bar{\tau}P} A_2 = A_2 Z_{\mu\bar{\tau}P} \lambda_P + x_P$ in Eq. (8), the formulas of $\mu\bar{\tau}P$ and $(\mu\bar{\tau})^2 P$ are shown as Eq. (10) at the total cost of 4**M**+3**S**.

$$\begin{aligned} \beta &= x_P^2 && \mathbf{S} \\ X_{\mu\bar{\tau}P} &= \beta^2 + 1 && \mathbf{S} \\ Z_{\mu\bar{\tau}P} &= x_P \beta + x_P && \mathbf{M} \\ \Lambda_{\mu\bar{\tau}P} &= (\lambda_P + 1) Z_{\mu\bar{\tau}P} + x_P && \mathbf{M} \\ A_2 &= X_{\mu\bar{\tau}P} + \beta && \\ X_{(\mu\bar{\tau})^2 P} &= A_2^2 && \mathbf{S} \\ Z_{(\mu\bar{\tau})^2 P} &= A_2 Z_{\mu\bar{\tau}P} && \mathbf{M} \\ \Lambda_{(\mu\bar{\tau})^2 P} &= Z_{(\mu\bar{\tau})^2 P} \lambda_P + x_P && \mathbf{M} \end{aligned} \tag{10}$$

C.2 Pre-computation Schemes Using λ-Coordinates

Our pre-computation scheme for window τNAF in λ-coordinates is the same as that on a μ_4-Koblitz curve except Q_5 and Q_7 for window width 6 in Table 7 and Q_{35} for window width 8 in Table 15. Q_5 and Q_7 are computed as $Q_5 = \mu\tau P + Q_{31}$ and $Q_7 = \mu\tau P - Q_{31}$ with $c_5 = -7 + 2\mu\tau$ and $c_7 = 7$ by one $(P \pm Q)$-operation. Q_{35} is computed as $\mu\tau P + Q_{125}$ with $c_{35} = -13 + 8\mu\tau$. Our

Table 18. Cost of pre-computations using λ-coordinates

	$w = 4$	$w = 5$	$w = 6$
Solinas	15**M**+12**S**	44**M**+31**S**	–
Hankerson, Menezes, Vanstone	15**M**+12**S**	50**M**+29**S**	117**M**+63**S**
Trost, Xu	12**M**+8**S**	44**M**+18**S**	108**M**+36**S**
Ours	7**M**+5**S**	26**M**+16**S**	66**M**+36**S**

pre-computation scheme requires 7**M**+5**S**, 26**M**+16**S**, 66**M**+36**S**, 135**M**+72**S**, and 282**M**+148**S** using λ-projective coordinates for window τNAF with widths from 4 to 8 respectively.

The costs of different pre-computation schemes for window τNAF with widths from 4 to 6 are summarized in Table 18. Trost and Xu's pre-computation scheme requires 12**M**+8**S**, 44**M**+18**S**, and 108**M**+36**S** for $w = 4$, 5, and 6 based on their efficient formulas for $P - \mu\tau(P)$, $P + \mu\tau(P)$ and $P - \tau^2(P)$. Both theoretical analysis and experimental results show that our pre-computation scheme is about 40% faster than Trost and Xu's scheme using λ-coordinates.

C.3 Scalar Multiplications Using Window τNAF in λ-Coordinates

The Montgomery trick transferring n pre-computations in λ-projective coordinates to λ-coordinates costs **I**+$(5n - 3)$**M**. Let the costs of pre-computation schemes for window τNAF with width w be denoted by $\mathrm{Pre}\lambda_w$.

Constant-time scalar multiplication using window τNAF has two situations.

1. Scalar multiplication uses pre-computations in λ-projective coordinates. It requires m τ-operations, $\frac{m}{w-1}$ point additions, and the pre-computation. Scalar multiplication is expected to cost
$$3m\mathbf{S} + \frac{m}{w-1}(11\mathbf{M} + 2\mathbf{S}) + \mathrm{Pre}\lambda_w.$$
2. Scalar multiplication uses pre-computations in λ-coordinates. It requires m τ-projective operations, $\frac{m}{w-1}$ mixed additions, Montgomery trick, and the pre-computation. Scalar multiplication is expected to cost
$$3m\mathbf{S} + \frac{m}{w-1}(8\mathbf{M} + 2\mathbf{S}) + \mathbf{I} + (5 \cdot 2^{w-2} - 8)\mathbf{M} + \mathrm{Pre}\lambda_w.$$

We summarize the lowest costs of constant-time scalar multiplications on K1-163, K-233, K-283, K1-283, K-409, and K-571 using our pre-computation scheme in Table 19. Our experimental results show that our constant-time scalar multiplication on Koblitz curves using λ-coordinates saves up to 6.5% compared to Trost and Xu's work using λ-coordinates.

Table 19. The expected costs of constant-time scalar multiplications using our pre-computation in λ-coordinates on K1-163, K-233, K-283/K1-283, K-409, and K-571 in **M**

		K1-163(w)	K-233(w)	K-283/K1-283(w)	K-409(w)	K-571(w)
S = 0M	regular τNAF	1304	1864	2264	3272	4568
	Trost, Xu	412(5,M)	552(5,M)	642.8(6,M)	844.4(6,M)	1103.6(6,M)
	Ours	394(5,M)	520.8(6,M)	600.8(6,M)	802.4(6,M)	1058.3(7,M)
S = 0.2M	regular τNAF	1467	2097	2547	3681	5139
	Trost, Xu	529.7(5,M)	718.7(5,M)	842.4(6,M)	1129.7(6,M)	1499.1(6,M)
	Ours	511.3(5,M)	686.4(6,M)	800.4 (6,M)	1087.7(6,M)	1453.4(7,M)
S = 0.5M	regular τNAF	1711.5	2446.5	2971.5	4294.5	5995.5
	Trost, Xu	755.6(6)	1026(6)	1219.1(6)	1697.7(6,M)	2232.3(6,M)
	Ours	713.6(6)	982.9(7)	1157.1(7)	1596.1(7)	2160.6(7)

References

1. Avanzi, R., Dimitrov, V., Doche, C., Sica, F.: Extending scalar multiplication using double bases. In: Lai, X., Chen, K. (eds.) ASIACRYPT 2006. LNCS, vol. 4284, pp. 130–144. Springer, Heidelberg (2006). https://doi.org/10.1007/11935230_9
2. Barker, E.: Draft NIST special publication 800–57 part 1 revision 5 - recommendation for key management, part 1: general, May 2020. https://doi.org/10.6028/NIST.SP.800-57pt1r5
3. Barker, E., Chen, L., Roginsky, A., Vassilev, A., Davis, R.: NIST special publication 800–56A revision 3 - recommendation for pair-wise key-establishment schemes using discrete logarithm cryptography, April 2018. https://doi.org/10.6028/NIST.SP.800-56Ar3
4. Bernstein, D.J., Lange, T.: Explicit-formulas database (2020). http://hyperelliptic.org/EFD/
5. Blake, I., Murty, V., Xu, G.: A note on window τ-NAF algorithm. Inf. Process. Lett. **95**(5), 496–502 (2005)
6. Blake, I., Murty, V., Xu, G.: Nonadjacent radix-τ expansions of integers in Euclidean imaginary quadratic number fields. Can. J. Math. **60**, 1267–1282 (2008)
7. Bos, J., Lenstra, A., Te Riele, H., Shumow, D.: Introduction. In: Bos, J., Lenstra, A. (eds.) Topics in Computational Number Theory Inspired by Peter L. Montgomery, pp. 1–9. Cambridge University Press, Cambridge, October 2017. https://doi.org/10.1017/9781316271575.002
8. Doche, C., Kohel, D.R., Sica, F.: Double-base number system for multi-scalar multiplications. In: Joux, A. (ed.) EUROCRYPT 2009. LNCS, vol. 5479, pp. 502–517. Springer, Heidelberg (2009). https://doi.org/10.1007/978-3-642-01001-9_29
9. Gueron, S., Kounavis, M.: Intel carry-less multiplication instruction and its usage for computing the GCM mode, Revision 2.02, Intel, April 2014. https://software.intel.com/sites/default/files/managed/72/cc/clmul-wp-rev-2.02-2014-04-20.pdf
10. Hankerson, D., Menezes, A., Vanstone, S.: Guide to Elliptic Curve Cryptography. SPC, 1st edn. Springer, New York (2004). https://doi.org/10.1007/b97644
11. Järvinen, K., Forsten, J., Skyttä, J.: FPGA design of self-certified signature verification on Koblitz curves. In: Paillier, P., Verbauwhede, I. (eds.) CHES 2007. LNCS, vol. 4727, pp. 256–271. Springer, Heidelberg (2007). https://doi.org/10.1007/978-3-540-74735-2_18
12. Koblitz, N.: CM-curves with good cryptographic properties. In: Feigenbaum, J. (ed.) CRYPTO 1991. LNCS, vol. 576, pp. 279–287. Springer, Heidelberg (1992). https://doi.org/10.1007/3-540-46766-1_22

13. Koblitz, N.: p-adic Numbers, p-adic Analysis, and Zeta-Functions. GTM, vol. 58, New York, Springer, Heidelberg (1984)
14. Kohel, D.: Efficient arithmetic on elliptic curves in characteristic, February 2016. https://arxiv.org/abs/1601.03669
15. Kohel, D.: Twisted μ_4-normal form for elliptic curves. In: Coron, J.-S., Nielsen, J.B. (eds.) EUROCRYPT 2017. LNCS, vol. 10210, pp. 659–678. Springer, Cham (2017). https://doi.org/10.1007/978-3-319-56620-7_23. https://eurocrypt.iacr.org/2017/slides/A03-twisted.pdf
16. Lange, T.: A note on Lez-Dahab coordinates. Cryptology ePrint Archive, Report 2004/323 (2004). https://eprint.iacr.org/2004/323.pdf
17. Li, W., Yu, W., Li, B., Fan, X.: Speeding up scalar multiplication on Koblitz curves using μ_4 coordinates. In: Jang-Jaccard, J., Guo, F. (eds.) ACISP 2019. LNCS, vol. 11547, pp. 620–629. Springer, Cham (2019). https://doi.org/10.1007/978-3-030-21548-4_34
18. Longa, P., Gebotys, C.: Novel precomputation schemes for elliptic curve cryptosystems. In: Abdalla, M., Pointcheval, D., Fouque, P.-A., Vergnaud, D. (eds.) ACNS 2009. LNCS, vol. 5536, pp. 71–88. Springer, Heidelberg (2009). https://doi.org/10.1007/978-3-642-01957-9_5
19. López, J., Dahab, R.: Improved algorithms for elliptic curve arithmetic in $GF(2^n)$. In: Tavares, S., Meijer, H. (eds.) SAC 1998. LNCS, vol. 1556, pp. 201–212. Springer, Heidelberg (1999). https://doi.org/10.1007/3-540-48892-8_16
20. National Institute of Standards and Technology(NIST).: Digital signature standard (DSS). FIPS PUB 186–5(Draft), October 2019. https://doi.org/10.6028/NIST.FIPS.186-5-draft
21. Okeya, K., Takagi, T., Vuillaume, C.: Efficient representations on Koblitz curves with resistance to side channel attacks. In: Boyd, C., González Nieto, J.M. (eds.) ACISP 2005. LNCS, vol. 3574, pp. 218–229. Springer, Heidelberg (2005). https://doi.org/10.1007/11506157_19
22. Oliveira, T., Aranha, D.F., López, J., Rodríguez-Henríquez, F.: Fast point multiplication algorithms for binary elliptic curves with and without precomputation. In: Joux, A., Youssef, A. (eds.) SAC 2014. LNCS, vol. 8781, pp. 324–344. Springer, Cham (2014). https://doi.org/10.1007/978-3-319-13051-4_20
23. Oliveira, T., López, J., Aranha, D.F., Rodríguez-Henríquez, F.: Two is the fastest prime: Lambda coordinates for binary elliptic curves. J. Cryptography Eng. **4**(1), 3–7 (2014). https://doi.org/10.1007/s13389-013-0069-z
24. Renes, J., Costello, C., Batina, L.: Complete addition formulas for prime order elliptic curves. In: Fischlin, M., Coron, J.-S. (eds.) EUROCRYPT 2016. LNCS, vol. 9665, pp. 403–428. Springer, Heidelberg (2016). https://doi.org/10.1007/978-3-662-49890-3_16
25. Scott, M.: MIRACL-Multiprecision integer and rational arithmetic cryptographic library, C/C++ Library. https://github.com/miracl/MIRACL
26. Solinas, J.: Efficient arithmetic on Koblitz curves. Des. Codes Cryptography **19**, 195–249 (2000). https://doi.org/10.1023/A:1008306223194
27. Trost, W., Xu, G.: On the optimal pre-computation of window τNAF for Koblitz curves. IEEE Trans. Comput. **65**(9), 2918–2924 (2016)
28. Vuillaume, C., Okeya, K., Takagi, T.: Defeating simple power analysis on Koblitz curves. IEICE Trans. Fundam. Electron. Commun. Comput. Sci. **E89–A**(5), 1362–1369 (2006)
29. Yu, W., Musa, S.A., Li, B.: Double-base chains for scalar multiplications on elliptic curves. In: Canteaut, A., Ishai, Y. (eds.) EUROCRYPT 2020. LNCS, vol. 12107, pp. 538–565. Springer, Cham (2020). https://doi.org/10.1007/978-3-030-45727-3_18

Dummy Shuffling Against Algebraic Attacks in White-Box Implementations

Alex Biryukov[1(✉)] and Aleksei Udovenko[2]

[1] DCS and SnT, University of Luxembourg, Luxembourg City, Luxembourg
alex.biryukov@uni.lu
[2] CryptoExperts, Paris, France
aleksei@affine.group

Abstract. At CHES 2016, Bos et al. showed that most of existing white-box implementations are easily broken by standard side-channel attacks. A natural idea to apply the well-developed side-channel countermeasure - linear masking schemes - leaves implementations vulnerable to linear algebraic attacks which exploit absence of noise in the white-box setting and are applicable for any order of linear masking. At ASIACRYPT 2018, Biryukov and Udovenko proposed a security model (BU-model for short) for protection against linear algebraic attacks and a new *quadratic* masking scheme which is provably secure in this model. However, countermeasures against higher-degree attacks were left as an open problem.

In this work, we study the effectiveness of another well-known side-channel countermeasure - shuffling - against linear and higher-degree algebraic attacks in the white-box setting. First, we extend the classic shuffling to include dummy computation slots and show that this is a crucial component for protecting against the algebraic attacks. We quantify and prove the security of dummy shuffling against the linear algebraic attack in the BU-model. We introduce a *refreshing* technique for dummy shuffling and show that it allows to achieve close to optimal protection in the model for arbitrary degrees of the attack, thus solving the open problem of protection against the algebraic attack in the BU-model. Furthermore, we describe an interesting proof-of-concept construction that makes the slot function public (while keeping the shuffling indexes private).

Keywords: White-box · Obfuscation · Provable security · Shuffling · Algebraic attack

1 Introduction

White-box model studies security of cryptographic implementations under full control of an adversary. In seminal works, Chow *et al.* [8,9] proposed first white-box implementations of the AES and DES block ciphers, which were later broken

This work was partly supported by the French FUI-AAP25 IDECYS+ project, by the French ANR-AAPG2019 SWITECH project and by the Luxembourg National Research Fund (FNR) project FinCrypt (C17/IS/11684537).

A. Canteaut and F.-X. Standaert (Eds.): EUROCRYPT 2021, LNCS 12697, pp. 219–248, 2021.
https://doi.org/10.1007/978-3-030-77886-6_8

with practical attacks [1,24]. Further attempts at fixing the implementations did not succeeded. The main idea behind these implementations is to implement the cipher as a network of lookup tables (LUTs) and obfuscate tables by composing them with random encodings. In 2016, Bos *et al.* [6] showed that most existing white-box implementations can be defeated with classic correlation attacks known from side-channel analysis. The adaptation of the attack to the white-box model was called *Differential Computation Analysis* (DCA). More recently, Rivain and Wang [20] showed that any table-based encoding of LUTs is always susceptible to the DCA attack, possibly applied to a later round.

The DCA attack can be fully automated and is easy to mount. Therefore, a natural question is how to protect white-box implementations against the DCA attack. A well-studied countermeasure against correlation attacks is *masking*. The idea is to split sensitive variables in the implementation into pseudorandom shares and perform computations without recombining the shares explicitly. The classic masking schemes are *linear*. While this is not a problem in the side-channel setting (*e.g.* analyzing power measurements) because of large amounts of noise in measurements, it becomes an issue in the white-box setting. Recently, Biryukov *et al.* [2] and Goubin *et al.* [13] showed that the linear masking countermeasure in the white-box setting can be easily and generically broken using elementary linear algebra. The attack was called *algebraic DCA* in the former and *linear decoding analysis (LDA)* in the latter and was used in a sophisticated multi-stage cryptanalysis of the winning challenge from the CHES 2017 CTF/WhibOx Contest 2017 [13,18]. Biryukov *et al.* further developed a security model and a *quadratic* masking scheme achieving provable security against the linear algebraic attack. Seker *et al.* [21] combined the nonlinear masking scheme with a linear scheme and extended it to a *cubic* masking scheme, offering protection against degree-2 algebraic attacks.

Another known side-channel countermeasure is *shuffling*, inspired by hardware randomization techniques and described by Herbst *et al.* [15] and later analyzed in [19,22,23]. The idea is to shuffle the evaluation of identical components (mainly S-boxes) to introduce more noise into measurements. It provides limited security against the correlation attacks by itself and is usually combined with the masking countermeasure. Security of shuffling against the correlation DCA attack in the white-box setting was recently studied by Bogdanov *et al.* [5]. In addition, Goubin *et al.* [14] developed *data-dependency higher-order DCA* and used it to cryptanalyze the winning challenges of the CHES 2019 CTF/WhibOx Contest 2019 [4]. One of the challenges included a shuffling countermeasure, which was defeated by a fault attack.

It can be expected that shuffling provides security against the algebraic attack due to its nonlinearity. However, the algebraic security of shuffling has not yet been evaluated. This work aims to fill this gap and analyzes shuffling rigorously and extensively.

Our Contribution

- We show that *classic shuffling* provides weak security against the linear algebraic attack, especially against chosen-plaintext attacks. We describe a simple

generalization of the attack called *differential algebraic attack*, which defeats the classic shuffling countermeasure by analyzing *pairs of executions* with well-chosen differences in the inputs. However, we show that the model of [2] guarantees protection against the new *differential* algebraic attack as well, highlighting rigidity of the model.
- We define *dummy shuffling*, which extends the classic shuffling by adding dummy "random" inputs. While the idea of adding dummy operations was already present in previous works, our new definition is the first to emphasise the importance of dummy slots. In addition, we distinguish *hidden* and *public* shuffling, the property which is relevant in the white-box model.
- We prove and quantify security of dummy shuffling against the degree-1 algebraic attack, in the model of [2]. We show that it depends on a particular property of the implementation being protected, however this property is hard to evaluate. To overcome this problem, we introduce a novel *refreshing* technique, that transforms any implementation into an equivalent one, but with the relevant property being known and optimal, leading to provable security against linear algebraic attacks.
- We prove that such "refreshed" implementations in fact provide protection against algebraic attacks of *any degree* up to the amount of dummy slots used. The degree bound is tight as shown by our generic higher-degree attack. As a result, we obtain the first provable method of protection against algebraic attacks of arbitrary (predetermined) degree. Our main result is stated in Theorem 3. Surprisingly, our new protection has quite low complexity, as illustrated in Table 1.
- We describe an interesting proof-of-concept construction of *uniform public dummy shuffling*. In this construction, shuffling is done implicitly by calling a single slot function with an extra "index" argument. This construction shows that a white-box designer needs only to obfuscate a single slot function, rather than the whole shuffling process and evaluation of all the slots.

To summarize, our work provides extensive analysis of the dummy shuffling as a countermeasure against algebraic attacks. This proves useful as it turns out to be a solid provably secure protection. We believe that it is a useful tool for protecting white-box implementations against generic attacks.

We remark that this work studies dummy shuffling strictly in the gray-box model of algebraic security of [2] and white-box related problems such as white-box-secure pseudorandomness generation, structure hiding, fault protection, etc. are out of scope for this paper.

2 The Framework

In this section, we fix the notation, recall necessary preliminaries and the framework of white-box algebraic attacks.

We write := to note that the equation holds by definition. For $a \le b$ integers, the sequence $(a, a+1, \ldots, b-1, b)$ is denoted by $[a \ldots b]$. The finite field of size 2 is denoted by $\mathbb{F}_2$, and the n-dimensional vector space over $\mathbb{F}_2$ is denoted by

Table 1. Estimation of gate complexity for protections against algebraic attacks per original AND/XOR gate. \$ stands for one random bit generation. The error bound τ is a security parameter (larger is more secure). Instances from [21] are created with minimal order of linear masking ($n = 1$). The parameter t is an arbitrary integer greater or equal than the protection degree.

Protection degree	XOR	AND	Error τ	Ref.
1	$33 + 6\$$	$43 + 6\$$	1/16	[2, Alg. 3]
1	7	$16 + 2\$$	1/16	[21]
1	2	$8 + 1\$$	1/8	Section 5
2	16	$46 + 3\$$	1/4096	[21]
2	3	$14 + 3\$$	1/48	Section 5
$d\ \ (t \geq d)$	$t + 1$	$(6t + 2) + t\$$	$\frac{t+1-d}{t+1} \cdot \frac{1}{2^{2d}}$	Section 5

$\mathbb{F}_2^n$. Vectors/sequences are written as $v = (v_1, v_2, \ldots, v_n)$. The symbol $||$ denotes concatenation of vectors/sequences. $|X|$ denotes the size of the vector/set X, or weight of the Boolean function X, or the number of computed functions in the implementation X. $\mathbf{0}, \mathbf{1}$ denote constant Boolean functions. The *bias* of a Boolean function $f : \mathbb{F}_2^n \to \mathbb{F}_2$ is given by $\mathcal{E}(f) := |f|/2^n - 1/2$, and the *error* of f is given by $\mathsf{err}(f) := \min(|f|, |f \oplus 1|)/2^n = 1/2 - |\mathcal{E}(f)|$. The Kronecker delta function $[x = y] : \mathbb{F}_2^n \times \mathbb{F}_2^n \to \mathbb{F}_2$ is a Boolean function that is equal to 1 if and only if $x = y$; its complement is denoted by $[x \neq y]$. For a Boolean function $f(x_1, \ldots, x_t)$ we denote its restriction to $x_i = c$ by $f|_{x_i=c}$. Every Boolean function $f : \mathbb{F}_2^n \to \mathbb{F}_2$ can be uniquely written in the algebraic normal form (ANF): $f(x) = \bigoplus_{u \in \mathbb{F}_2^n} a_u x^u$, where $a_u \in \mathbb{F}_2$ and x^u is a shorthand for $x_1^{u_1} \ldots x_n^{u_n}$. The *algebraic degree* (or simply *degree*) of f, denoted $\deg f$, is the maximum Hamming weight of all u with $a_u = 1$.

2.1 Implementations and Computational Traces

In this work, we do not restrict our *analysis* to any particular type of implementations (*e.g.* Boolean circuits or programs), even though our *constructions* are most naturally and generally expressed as Boolean circuits. The only requirement for analysis is that an implementation represents a finite sequence of Boolean functions, which can be efficiently evaluated on arbitrary inputs (resulting in a *computational trace*). Note that not all programs are easily expressed in this form due to possibly varying control flow paths on different inputs. However, various techniques for recording and processing (e.g. aligning) computational traces of (compiled) programs are described in the literature [6,7]. Our setting is formalized as follows.

Definition 1 (Implementation). *An* implementation *is a vectorial Boolean function $C : \mathbb{F}_2^n \to \mathbb{F}_2^m$ together with an associated sequence of efficiently computable Boolean functions*

$$\mathcal{F}(C) = (\mathcal{F}_i(C) : \mathbb{F}_2^n \to \mathbb{F}_2 \mid i \in [1 \ldots |C|]) .$$

The functions $x \mapsto x_i$ representing the input variables $x \in \mathbb{F}_2^n$ and the output coordinates of C are included in $\mathcal{F}(C)$.

Remark 1. For ease of understanding one can think of C as a Boolean circuit and $\mathcal{F}_i(C)$ as nodes of this circuit. Note that our definition omits data-dependency relations. While out of scope for this work, they can be used to aid higher-order correlation or algebraic attacks by selecting nearby nodes and thus reducing the combinatorial complexity, as was recently shown in [14].

In the context of white-box attacks, an adversary typically analyzes a part of the implementation, for example the first 10% of operations to target the first round of a block cipher. We call such part a *window*.

Definition 2 (Window). *Let C be an implementation. A* window *$\mathcal{W}$ is a subsequence of $\mathcal{F}(C)$.*

For the correlation/algebraic attacks, an adversary runs the analyzed implementation on a chosen input and records all intermediate computed values inside the chosen window, producing a so-called *computational trace.*

Definition 3 (Computational trace). *A* computational trace *of an implementation $C : \mathbb{F}_2^n \to \mathbb{F}_2^m$ on a window $\mathcal{W} \subseteq \mathcal{F}(C)$ and on input $x \in \mathbb{F}_2^n$ is the vector $\mathcal{W}(x) := (f(x) \mid f \in \mathcal{W}) \in \mathbb{F}_2^{|\mathcal{W}|}$.*

After recording a certain amount of computational traces, the adversary is trying to check whether a chosen *sensitive function* is computed in the implementation. This analysis can be done statistically (correlation attacks) or algebraically (algebraic attacks). A standard example of a *sensitive function* that we will use throughout the paper is an output bit of the S-box in the first round of AES. This function depends on one key byte and the adversary recovers the key byte by matching the correct sensitive function with the traces. More generally, one may also consider an obfuscation-related scenario, where an adversary's goal is to decide whether a given protected implementation computes internally a certain function or not. In order to develop generic protection against such adversaries, we will consider *every* function in the original unprotected implementation to be sensitive. The protection is then required to "hide" all original computations and anything related to them. This is also a standard requirement in the side-channel context of correlation attacks.

2.2 Algebraic Attack

We now recall and restate formally the notion of an algebraic attack. In the degree-1 (linear) algebraic attack, the idea is to find a linear combination of functions computed in the analyzed implementation that results in a sensitive function. For example, in an implementation protected by a linear masking scheme, the shares of a sensitive value describe such a linear combination. By utilizing elementary linear algebra, the shares can be located efficiently, given a sufficient amount of computational traces. This allows to avoid the step of *guessing* the locations of shares and thus avoid the combinatorial explosion in the complexity.

Note that it may be possible to find the shares by other methods, for example, by analyzing the implementation structure. Indeed, the attacks against winning challenges of the WhibOx 2017/2019 competitions included analysis of the data-dependency graphs of the implementations [13,14]. Nonetheless, the current state-of-the-art of white-box implementations struggles to provide security even against *generic, automated* attacks. Thus achieving security against the powerful algebraic attack is already an ambitious goal.

The linear algebraic attack can be naturally extended to higher degrees. The idea is to include products of 2, 3 or more computed functions in the allowed linear combinations. This extension can break *nonlinear* masking schemes, such as quadratic masking proposed in [2]. In addition, it can also defeat table-based encodings, since in that case a sensitive value can be computed as a higher-degree function of the exposed encoded value.

We first define the degree-d expansion of a vector, which captures the idea of including products of degree up to d.

Definition 4. (Degree-d expansion and closure). *Let x be an n-dimensional vector over a ring K. For an integer $d \geq 1$ define the* degree-d expansion *of x, denoted $\pi_d(x)$, as a concatenation of all products of* $0, 1, 2, \ldots, d$ *coordinates of x in a fixed order:*

$$\pi_d(x) := (1) \mid\mid x \mid\mid (x_{i_1}x_{i_2} \mid 1 \leq i_1 < i_2 \leq n) \mid\mid \ldots \\ \mid\mid (x_{i_1}x_{i_2}\ldots x_{i_d} \mid 1 \leq i_1 < i_2 < \ldots < i_d \leq n).$$

Let $\mathcal{V}$ be a sequence of Boolean functions with the same domain $\mathbb{F}_2^n$. The degree-d closure of $\mathcal{V}$ [2] is defined as:

$$\mathcal{V}^{(d)} := \operatorname{span} c(\pi_d(\mathcal{V})) = \operatorname{span}\left(\{\mathbf{1}\} \cup \{f_1 f_2 \cdots f_d \mid f_1, f_2, \ldots, f_d \in \mathcal{V}\}\right),$$

where c maps a vector to the set of its coordinates[1].

Example 1. Let $\mathcal{V} = (f_1, f_2, f_3)$ for some Boolean functions $f_1, f_2, f_3 : \mathbb{F}_2^n \to \mathbb{F}_2$. Then $\mathcal{V}^{(2)}$ is a vector space of Boolean functions spanned by $\mathbf{1}$, f_1, f_2, f_3, f_1f_2, f_1f_3, f_2f_3.

Example 2. We will usually consider $\mathcal{F}^{(d)}(C)$ for an implementation $C : \mathbb{F}_2^n \to \mathbb{F}_2^m$. This set consists of all degree-d combinations of intermediate functions computed in C. Elements of this set are Boolean functions f mapping $\mathbb{F}_2^n$ to $\mathbb{F}_2$.

Let $\binom{n}{\leq d} := \sum_{i=0}^{d}\binom{n}{i}$. It is easy to see that the length of $\pi_d(x)$ is equal to $\binom{|x|}{\leq d}$. When $n \gg d$, $\binom{n}{\leq d} = n^d/d! + \mathcal{O}(n^{d-1})$. We are now ready to formalize the algebraic attack.

[1] Products of degrees less than d are included by setting, for example, $f_1 = f_2$.

Definition 5 (Algebraic attack). *A* degree-d *algebraic attack against an implementation* $C : \mathbb{F}_2^n \rightarrow \mathbb{F}_2^m$ *targeting a sensitive function* $f : \mathbb{F}_2^n \rightarrow \mathbb{F}_2$ *consists of the following steps :*

1. *choose a* window $\mathcal{W} \subseteq \mathcal{F}(C)$;
2. *choose an input vector* $\mathbf{x} := (\mathbf{x}_1, \ldots, \mathbf{x}_t) \in (\mathbb{F}_2^n)^t$, *where* $t := \binom{|\mathcal{W}|}{\leq d} + \epsilon$ *for some small integer* ϵ;
3. *compute on these inputs the* t *traces* $\mathcal{W}(\mathbf{x}_i)$ *and their degree-*d *expansion;*
4. *compute on these inputs the sensitive function* $f(\mathbf{x}_i)$;
5. *solve the following linear system in* z:

$$\begin{pmatrix} \pi_d(\mathcal{W}(\mathbf{x}_1)) \\ \vdots \\ \pi_d(\mathcal{W}(\mathbf{x}_t)) \end{pmatrix} \times z = \begin{pmatrix} f(\mathbf{x}_1) \\ \vdots \\ f(\mathbf{x}_t) \end{pmatrix}. \tag{1}$$

The attack succeeds if at least one non-trivial solution is found. It is further required that $\mathbf{x}$ *is such that the right-hand side of the equation is non-zero.*

Example 3. Consider an AES implementation protected with a Boolean masking of an arbitrarily large order (for example, the ISW scheme [17]). An adversary may choose f as a coordinate of an S-box output in the first round. Then, the degree-1 algebraic attack succeeds, as f can be expressed as a linear combination of shares which are computed in the implementation. Note that in order to compute f (for the right part of the Eq. 1), the adversary has to guess a subkey byte.

The time complexity of the attack on a single window $\mathcal{W}$ with $|\mathcal{W}| \gg d$ is

$$\mathcal{O}\left(\binom{|\mathcal{W}|}{\leq d}^{2.8}\right) = \mathcal{O}\left(\frac{|\mathcal{W}|^{2.8d}}{d!^{2.8}}\right), \tag{2}$$

where 2.8 is the matrix multiplication exponent using the Strassen algorithm. We leave out the discussion about the choice of the window(s). For a relevant analysis we refer to [2,13].

2.3 Security Model

We now recall the security model introduced in [2] and reformulate it concisely. Biryukov *et al.* proposed a game-based notion of *prediction security*, which aimed to motivate the security goals. Furthermore, the authors defined *algebraically secure* circuits and encoding functions, which together implied a stronger notion [2, Def. 3] sufficient for achieving prediction security. In this work, we concentrate on this strongest combined notion, which we equivalently reformulate as an *algebraically secure scheme*.

The model is a variant of the gray box model allowing a particular type of leakage. Roughly speaking, the implementation may leak a degree-d function of intermediate inputs, whereas in t-probing security, the implementation may leak t intermediate wires. The model relies on the use of *randomness*, which in the white-box setting has to be derived pseudorandomly from the inputs. The model formally defines security of a *scheme*, containing an *encoding function*, an *implementation* and a *decoding function*.

Definition 6 (Scheme). *Let $f : \mathbb{F}_2^n \to \mathbb{F}_2^m$ be a function. A* scheme S *computing f consists of*

1. *an* encoding function $\mathsf{S.enc}(x, r_e) : \mathbb{F}_2^n \times \mathbb{F}_2^{|r_e|} \to \mathbb{F}_2^{n'}$;
2. *an* implementation $\mathsf{S.comp}(x', r_c) : \mathbb{F}_2^{n'} \times \mathbb{F}_2^{|r_c|} \to \mathbb{F}_2^{m'}$;
3. *a* decoding function $\mathsf{S.dec}(y') : \mathbb{F}_2^{m'} \to \mathbb{F}_2^m$.

It is required that for all $r_e \in \mathbb{F}_2^{|r_e|}, r_c \in \mathbb{F}_2^{|r_c|}$ $\quad \mathsf{S.dec}(\mathsf{S.comp}(\mathsf{S.enc}(x, r_e), r_c)) = f(x)$.

The encoding step is considered as a black-box and its implementation is not analyzed. However, it is important that it has access to the random bits r_e. The output of the encoding step $\mathsf{S.enc}$ is passed to the implementation $\mathsf{S.comp}$, which may access additional random bits r_c. The output of $\mathsf{S.comp}$ is then decoded by the black-box function $\mathsf{S.dec}$ to obtain the final output. Full computation process can be described as

$$x' \leftarrow \mathsf{S.enc}(x, r_e), \quad y' \leftarrow \mathsf{S.comp}(x', r_c), \quad y \leftarrow \mathsf{S.dec}(y').$$

Remark 2. The randomness r_c used in $\mathsf{S.comp}$ can always be generated in $\mathsf{S.enc}$ and included in the "encoded" input x'. The schemes that we propose in this work in fact do not use any randomness in $\mathsf{S.comp}$ *by construction*. A downside of this is that the intermediate state x' may become very large because of the included randomness, which otherwise could be computed "on the fly".

The algebraic security model requires that the implementation $\mathsf{S.comp}$ provides security against the algebraic attacks. In the attacks, the adversary controls the input $x \in \mathbb{F}_2^n$ to $\mathsf{S.enc}$ and is mounting the algebraic attack on $\mathsf{S.comp}$ as described in Definition 5. The security goal is to prevent the algebraic attack from succeeding on *any* function computed in $\mathsf{S.comp}$ and *any* set of inputs chosen by the adversary. This becomes possible due to the use of (pseudo)randomness.

Note that functions $\mathcal{F}(\mathsf{S.comp})$ computed in the implementation are functions of the "encoded" input (that is, of the output of $\mathsf{S.enc}$), which is not directly controlled by the adversary. This requirement can be captured by composing each function from $\mathcal{F}(\mathsf{S.comp})$ with $\mathsf{S.enc}$.

We are now ready to reformulate the main security definition given in [2]. Recall that $\mathcal{F}^{(d)}(\mathsf{S.comp})$ contains all degree-d combinations of intermediate functions from $\mathsf{S.comp}$. The idea is to require *every* non-trivial function from $\mathcal{F}^{(d)}(\mathsf{S.comp}(\mathsf{S.enc}))$ and *restricted to any fixed input* x to have a non-negligible error (as a function of random bits r_e, r_c)[2].

[2] In a real white-box implementation r_e, r_c would be constant for fixed x, but in our definitions we allow a more powerful adversary with ability to re-randomize for the same x.

Then, any such function would be hard to predict and target in the attack *even when the input is fully controlled.* Such security requirement guarantees hardness of launching an algebraic attack even when the adversary knows all the intermediate values computed in the original implementation (for example, knows the secret key if the scheme implements a white-box AES). While such an adversary would not need anymore to launch such an attack, this property highlights the universality of the protection.

We define the algebraic security in terms of the *error* (τ-error-d-AS scheme) instead of the *bias* as in [2] ($(1/2 - \tau)$-d-AS circuits and encoding functions), as it simplifies the notation. Indeed, the error in our cases is small, especially for the higher-degree case but sufficient to thwart an attacker. Furthermore, it highlights the link with the *Learning Parity with Noise* (LPN) problem, where a linear system with errors has to be solved. Indeed, if some equations in Eq. 1 from Definition 5 are erroneous, the attack might still succeed if the fraction of erroneous equations is small enough for LPN-solving algorithms to be applicable. For example, in the case of an extremely small error, the constructed linear system may be error-free and then even the basic algebraic attack succeeds.

Definition 7. (τ-error-d-AS scheme). *Let* S *be a scheme and let $d \geq 1$ be an integer. Let τ be the minimum error among all non-trivial functions from* $\mathcal{F}^{(d)}(\mathsf{S.comp})$ *composed with* S.enc *and with any* fixed $x = \tilde{x} \in \mathbb{F}_2^n$*:*

$$\tau := \min \left\{ \mathsf{err}\left(\ f(\mathsf{S.enc}(\tilde{x}, \cdot), \cdot)\ \right) \ \middle|\ f(x, r_c) \in \mathcal{F}^{(d)}(\mathsf{S.comp}) \setminus \{\mathbf{0}, \mathbf{1}\},\ \ \tilde{x} \in \mathbb{F}_2^n \right\},$$

where the error is computed over r_e, r_c. If $\tau > 0$, the scheme S *is said to be* degree-d *algebraically secure with error τ (τ-error-d-AS).*

Remark 3. The larger is the error bound τ, the more secure the scheme is against LPN attacks. As noted above, an extremely low error may even allow the basic algebraic attack to succeed.

Remark 4. The algebraic security definition does not cover the decoding function S.dec, which is defined for completeness and to restrict the analysis to *useful* schemes - schemes that indeed compute the desired function $C : \mathbb{F}_2^n \to \mathbb{F}_2^m$.

A major goal is to develop a method of embedding any given implementation into a τ-error-d-AS scheme with a *constant* $\tau > 0$ (i.e. independent of the circuit size) and with the encoding function independent of the circuit structure. Biryukov *et al.* proposed a quadratic masking scheme that achieves 1/16-error-1-AS (i.e. based on 7/16-1-AS circuit gadgets), but didn't provide schemes for degree $d > 1$. The aim of this work is to evaluate shuffling techniques as such a protection method.

What is the maximum value of τ that could possibly be achieved by a scheme? Consider a Boolean circuit-based scheme and consider d independent functions computed in the scheme. Their product has error 2^{-d} if the functions are balanced and less otherwise. As a linear computation would not be universal, we assume that d AND gates with independent balanced inputs are present. Since each computed function in such gate has error $1/4$, the degree-d product of these functions has error 2^{-2d}. We conclude that in Boolean circuit implementations the error lower bound close to 2^{-2d} would be optimal to achieve. In other implementation models, such as lookup table (LUT) networks, a larger error bound may be achievable.[3]

In a recent exposition of algorithms for solving LPN by Esser *et al.* [12], all time complexities are exponential in the number of unknowns k, with the base of the exponent close to 2^{τ} for small errors (excluding BKW [3] with complexity $2^{\frac{k}{\log k - \log \tau}}$). Since the number of unknowns $k = \binom{|\mathcal{W}|}{\le d}$ in the algebraic attack grows much faster than $\tau^{-1} \ge 2^{2d}$, the error bound close to 2^{-2d} provide a sound protection with roughly estimated attack complexity $2^{\tau k} \approx 2^{(|\mathcal{W}|/4)^d}$ or $2^{\frac{|\mathcal{W}|^d}{(d+1)! \log |\mathcal{W}|}}$ using the BKW algorithm. More precise analysis of the complexity of solving LPN instances with such errors is beyond the scope of this work.

3 Shuffling Definitions

We first briefly survey the literature on the shuffling countermeasure with a stress on the white-box model in Subsect. 3.1 and then proceed with our new definitions. High-level definition of dummy shuffling is given in Subsect. 3.2 and its variants in the white-box setting are discussed in Subsect. 3.3. Finally, we describe our formal model of dummy shuffling in the algebraic security framework in Subsect. 3.4.

3.1 Related Work

Shuffling is a side-channel countermeasure that often complements masking. The idea is to randomize the order of the operations to desynchronize sensitive leakage points. A comprehensive study from the side-channel point of view is given by Veyrat-Charvillon *et al.* [23]. More recently, two works analyzed shuffling in the white-box setting and described two classifications.

Bogdanov *et al.* [5] distinguished two *dimensions* of shuffling in white-box implementations: time and memory. *Time shuffle* randomizes the order of the computations. This is precisely what matters from the classic side-channel point of view, as it desynchronizes the leakage channel. In the white-box setting however, such shuffling can be defeated by synchronizing computational traces by memory addresses, rather than by time. Therefore, it is necessary to augment time shuffle with *memory shuffle*, which randomizes the addresses of stored intermediate values.

Goubin *et al.* [14] distinguished *horizontal* and *vertical* shuffling. In horizontal shuffling, the computations are performed at the same time, while the data being

[3] Absence of intermediate nodes in pure LUT-based implementation gives less variables to use for an attack. As an extreme case, consider one big LUT e.g. of a permutation. Since inputs and outputs are balanced, best error bound to get is 2^{-d}, which is better than 2^{-2d} for circuits.

processed is shuffled. In vertical shuffling, slots are processed sequentially, and the data is shuffled. Thus, both time and memory shuffle are performed. The authors further allowed dummy slots, which could be based on pseudorandom input or on an irrelevant dummy key.

3.2 Dummy Shuffling

In order to distinguish the time/memory and vertical/horizontal separation from the presence of dummy computations, we propose a definition that specifically focuses on the "dummy" part, while being independent of being serial/parallel. The main idea is to hide the real computation among several redundant but similarly looking computations. We start by defining a computational *slot*, which is the target of shuffling: an operation that is computed multiple times independently.

We remark that the definitions in this and the next subsection are informal and introduce only the terminology and broad implementation and hiding strategies.

Definition 8. (Slot (*informal*)). *A* slot *is a part of the implementation computing a particular sensitive function. In the context of shuffling, it is expected that the implementation contains multiple* slots *for each (sub)function being protected.*

Example 4. In a Boolean or arithmetic circuit, an example of a slot is a subcircuit reproduced multiple times, possibly with modifications or alternative circuit representations. In a program, an example of a slot is a function or a piece of code that is called multiple times, or simply multiple pieces of code each computing the same sensitive function.

We are now ready to provide informal definition of our main protection tool - *dummy shuffling.*

Definition 9. (Dummy Shuffling (*informal*)). Dummy shuffling *is an implementation strategy, in which a sensitive function is computed in multiple* slots, *such that during an execution:*

1. *at least one of the slots* (main slot(s)) *computes the function on the correct (*main*) input(s);*
2. *at least one of the slots* (dummy slot(s)) *computes the function on a (pseudo)randomly generated input(s);*
3. *the locations of the main slots are (pseudo)randomly generated on each execution or on each distinct input.*

Dummy shuffling is performed in three phases (see Fig. 1):

1. *in the* input-shuffling *phase, the dummy inputs are generated and shuffled together with the main inputs;*

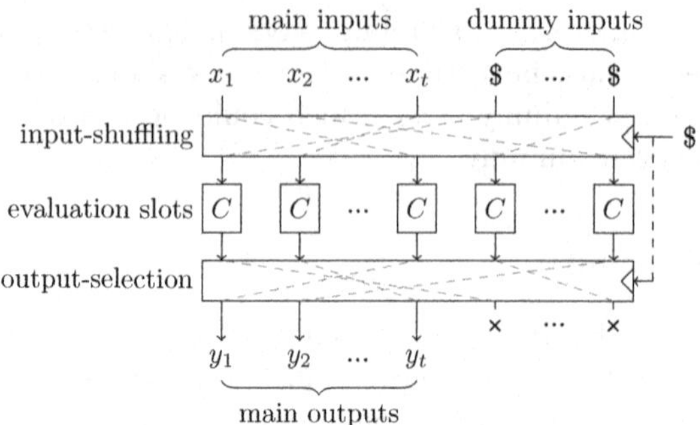

Fig. 1. Dummy Shuffling. The symbol $ denotes a uniform and independent source of randomness. Implementation of each application of C can be different or, for example, can be one shared procedure in software implementations.

2. *in the* evaluation *phase, the sensitive function is evaluated on each of the inputs, using slots;*
3. *in the* output-selection *phase, the main outputs are extracted and passed into further computations (by unshuffling or by any other means).*

Multiple main slots can be used for two reasons. First, multiple main slots may be running on the *same* main input, with the goal of error detection and/or correction. Second, multiple main slots may be running on *different* main inputs, when in the reference implementation the sensitive function is computed multiple times. The second case corresponds to the standard shuffling, for example, the 16 identical S-boxes (or 4 identical MixColumns operations) in the AES may constitute main slots.

3.3 Hidden and Public Dummy Shuffling

We now introduce a further classification of dummy shuffling techniques with respect to whether the slots are clearly isolated in the implementation or are intertwined with each other to hide the shuffling structure. Furthermore, another important factor is whether all slots have an identical implementation.

Definition 10 (informal). Hidden dummy shuffling *is an implementation of dummy shuffling for which it must be difficult for an adversary to isolate any single slot or a group of slots, no matter main or dummy.*

Public dummy shuffling *is an implementation of dummy shuffling in which all slots are clearly separated in the implementation and are easy to isolate. However, the locations of the main/dummy slots must still be difficult to predict for an adversary in any evaluation. Furthermore, if all slots' implementations are fully identical and an adversary is able to interchange them freely, then we say that the dummies are* uniform.

This definition captures the level at which an obfuscation is performed. In hidden dummy shuffling, the whole implementation is obfuscated and the slots are hard to locate and isolate. In public dummy shuffling, each slot may be obfuscated but is still easy to locate and isolate in the implementation.

In this work we analyze dummy shuffling as a countermeasure against the algebraic attack. In this context, the difference between hidden and public dummy shuffling mainly affects the size of the window that contains all nodes of the circuit used in the attack. Typically, two configurations of attacked nodes arise in the attacks: (1) all attacked nodes are contained in a single slot; (2) attacked nodes contain the same group of nodes in multiple/all slots. Case 2 is illustrated in Fig. 2, where the adversary tries to blindly select a window in the full implementation such that it contains the same target sensitive function computed in *each* of the slots; the red areas highlight the uncertainty for selecting such a window.

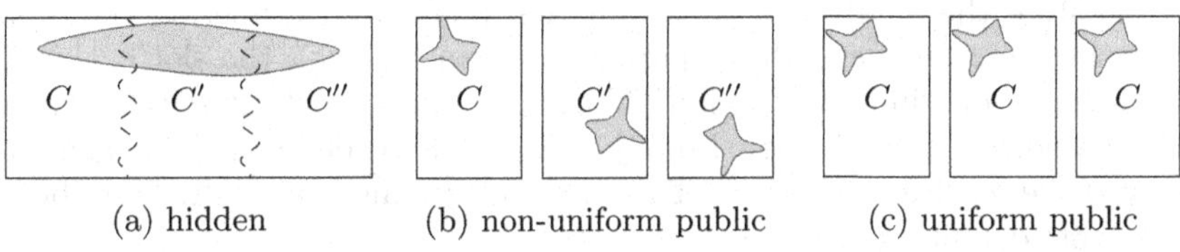

Fig. 2. Variants of dummy shuffling and window selection uncertainty. Red areas illustrate possible positions of a window relatively to the slots. (Color figure online)

1. In *hidden dummy shuffling*, the slots are not clearly separated and thus a window has to be selected from the *entire implementation* including all slots. Furthermore, in the case (2) the size of the window has to be much larger to be able to cover multiple slots.
2. In *non-uniform public shuffling* (for example, if each slot is obfuscated independently), the slots are easy to isolate. Therefore, a window in a single slot is selected from *that slot only*, reducing the combinatorial complexity and the required window size. A window covering the same group of nodes in multiple slots is still similar to the hidden dummy shuffling case, since it should be hard to find the parts of obfuscated circuits related to the target attacked group.
3. In *uniform public shuffling*, the slots are clearly isolated and are identical. Therefore, in both cases (1) and (2), the window can be selected *inside a single slot*, and extended to *the same area* in the other slots in the case (2). This case allows minimal combinatorial complexity of the attacks. However, from the designer's viewpoint, it removes the high-level obfuscation requirement and leads to a cleaner solution.

In Sect. 6, we describe a proof-of-concept construction for uniform public dummy shuffling. It shows that it is possible to implement dummy shuffling in a way that, even given a black-box access to the slot function, it is hard to distinguish main slots from dummy slots for any particular input. Therefore, a white-box designer aiming to use dummy shuffling does not have to obfuscate the whole implementation including the shuffling procedure and all slot evaluations; obfuscating a single slot function is sufficient.

3.4 Modeling Algebraic Security of Dummy Shuffling

In this work, we analyze security of the slot evaluation phase, which is the core of dummy shuffling. It is the most critical part where all the computations of the original implementation take place. This subsection defines a formal model for analyzing security of dummy shuffling in the framework of [2].

In the following, let s_{main} denote the number of main inputs, s_{dummy} the number of dummy inputs, and $s := s_{\text{main}} + s_{\text{dummy}}$. For simplicity, we assume that there are no always-duplicate main inputs and all main inputs are independent, i.e. an adversary can set each main input to any value independently.

We analyze the security of the evaluation phase by considering the input-shuffling phase as the "encoding" part of a scheme (S.enc), the slot evaluation phase as the main "implementation" (S.comp), and the output-selection phase as the "decoding" part (S.dec). Finally, the goal is to determine the algebraic security of the resulting scheme S. This gray-box setting is formally described in the following definition.

Definition 11 (Evaluation-Phase Model). *Let* $C(x) : \mathbb{F}_2^n \to \mathbb{F}_2^m$ *be an implementation. Let* s_{main}, s_{dummy} *be positive integers,* $s := s_{main} + s_{dummy}$. *In the* evaluation-phase model, *we analyze the algebraic security (in the sense of Definition 7) of the scheme* $\mathsf{EPM}(C, s_{main}, s_{dummy}) := \mathsf{S}$, *constructed as follows:*

Func.
$\mathsf{S.enc}(x, r_e) : (\mathbb{F}_2^n)^{s_{main}} \times \mathbb{F}_2^{|r_e|} \to (\mathbb{F}_2^n)^s$
  let $v \in (\mathbb{F}_2^n)^s$
  for $i \in [1 \ldots s_{main}]$ ***do***
    $v_i \leftarrow x_i$
  $(r'_e, r''_e) \leftarrow r_e$
  for $i \in [(s_{main}+1) \ldots s]$ ***do***
    $v_i \xleftarrow{r'_e} \mathbb{F}_2^n$
  return $x' \xleftarrow{r''_e} \mathsf{Shuffle}(v_1, \ldots, v_s)$

Impl. $\mathsf{S.comp}(x') : (\mathbb{F}_2^n)^s \to (\mathbb{F}_2^m)^s$
  let $y' \in (\mathbb{F}_2^m)^s$
  for $i \in [1 \ldots s]$ ***do***
    $y'_i \leftarrow C(x'_i)$
  return $y' \leftarrow (y'_1, \ldots, y'_s)$

Func. $\mathsf{S.dec}(y', r''_e) : (\mathbb{F}_2^m)^s \to (\mathbb{F}_2^m)^{s_{main}}$
  $y \xleftarrow{r''_e} \mathsf{Unshuffle}(y'_1, \ldots, y'_s)$
  return $(y_1, \ldots, y_{s_{main}})$

Here, by $\xleftarrow{r'_e}$ $(\xleftarrow{r''_e})$ *we mean that* r'_e (r''_e) *is used as randomness to generate the value (sample uniformly from* $\mathbb{F}_2^n$ *shuffle almost-uniformly).*

Remark 5. The EPM scheme does not use randomness in the implementation part, so the argument r_c in S.comp is omitted.

Remark 6. We define the decoding function by unshuffling the computed state y using saved randomness r''_e which was used to shuffle in S.enc. Formally, we could include r''_e in S.comp by encrypting it in S.enc so that it does not introduce algebraic leakage, and decrypting in S.dec. This just an example method of implementing the output-selection. As we focus on the evaluation phase, this process is out of scope of this model.

Remark 7. The shuffling permutation does not have to be perfectly uniform (in fact, it is not possible for $s \geq 3$). In addition, it is easy to show that it is enough to choose uniformly locations of s_{main} *main* slots and shuffle them; shuffling dummy slots does not change the output distribution of S.enc.

4 Algebraic Attacks on Dummy(less) Shuffling

In this section, we describe weaknesses in the algebraic security of dummy(less) shuffling. We start by exhibiting leakage of classic *dummyless* shuffling in the model in Subsect. 4.1, where we also sketch a standard linear algebraic attack to highlight the practical relevance. In Subsect. 4.2, we develop a *differential algebraic attack* which exploits the leakage more effectively. We show however in Subsect. 4.3 that the security model of [2] is strong enough to provide security against the differential attack technique out-of-the-box. We continue by generalizing the attack to a *higher-degree* algebraic attack against shuffling *with dummy slots* in Subsect. 4.4. This attack gives an upper-bound on the degree of algebraic security of dummy shuffling depending on the number of dummy slots.

4.1 Standard Algebraic Attack Against Dummyless Shuffling

Shuffling without dummy slots requires the implementation to have multiple main slots and thus is quite limited in its applications. Nonetheless, a typical application is a block cipher utilizing the Substitution-Permutation Network (SPN) structure and almost all such ciphers use the same S-box in each round, clearly exposing multiple main slots for the substitution layer. The linear layers however have a large variety of structures and the applicability of classic dummyless shuffling depends on each case. Since white-box implementations of SPN ciphers is a typical goal, we analyze this case.

We start by exhibiting a critical weakness of dummyless shuffling. Briefly speaking, shuffling leaks any symmetric function of the permuted values. For a degree one attack, the only such function is the sum of the value over all slots. For higher degrees, there are more possibilities.

Proposition 1. *Let* $C : \mathbb{F}_2^n \to \mathbb{F}_2^m$ *be an implementation and let* $\mathsf{S} := \mathsf{EPM}(C, s, 0)$ *for an integer* $s \geq 1$*. Then, for any* $f \in \mathcal{F}(C)$ *and any symmetric function* $g : \mathbb{F}_2^s \to \mathbb{F}_2$ *the following function* h *is leaked, i.e. there exists* $h' \in \mathcal{F}^{(\deg g)}(\mathsf{S.comp})$*, such that* $h'(\mathsf{S.enc}(x, r_e)) = h(x)$*, where*

$$h \; : \; (\mathbb{F}_2^n)^s \to \mathbb{F}_2 \; : \; (x_1, \ldots, x_s) \mapsto g(f(x_1), \ldots, f(x_s)).$$

Proof. Since $f(x_i)$ is computed in clear in each slot, a degree-d symmetric combination h' of these functions belongs to $\mathcal{F}^{(\deg g)}(\mathsf{S.comp})$. The effect of S.enc only permutes the inputs $x_1, \ldots, x_n$, which does not have an effect on h' since it is symmetric: $h(x) = h'(\mathsf{S.enc}(x, r_e)) = h'(x)$. □

Example 5. The most trivial example is the sum of a sensitive function f over all slots being vulnerable to the algebraic attack. Note that a related technique called *integration attack* was applied to differential power analysis (DPA) of randomized implementations in [10] in order to reduce the introduced noise and lower the required number of traces.

The proposition shows that classic dummyless shuffling does not achieve security in the evaluation-phase model. We now show a concrete practical attack on the example of the AES.

Consider an AES implementation where the 16 S-boxes are shuffled and possibly protected by a linear masking scheme. We target any single bit output of the S-box after the first round. However, as observed above, only the sum of these bits of all 16 S-boxes is leaked. Let $S_1 : \mathbb{F}_2^8 \to \mathbb{F}_2$ denote the first output bit of the AES S-box and define a function f as follows:

$$f : (\mathbb{F}_2^8)^{16} \to \mathbb{F}_2 : (x_1, \ldots, x_{16}) \mapsto S_1(x_1 \oplus k_1) \oplus \ldots \oplus S_1(x_{16} \oplus k_{16}),$$

where $k_1, \ldots, k_{16}$ is the first round subkey. Clearly, f can be computed via a linear combination of some intermediate variables in the analyzed implementation. The standard approach of guessing a portion of the key to compute f does not work, since it depends on the full key. We show that in the *chosen-plaintext* (CPA) setting an efficient attack is possible. Note that the algebraic security model assumes CPA and so such attack is covered by the model. The idea is to fix $x_2, \ldots, x_{16}$ to arbitrary constants and guess one bit

$$c := S_1(x_2 \oplus k_2) \oplus \ldots \oplus S_1(x_{16} \oplus k_{16}).$$

Then, after guessing k_1 the value of f can be computed for all 256 values of x_1, i.e. on inputs of the form $(\mathbb{F}_2^8, x_2, \ldots, x_{16})$. The limited number of inputs upper bounds the window size that can be used for the attack which can become a limitation for an attacker. While this is already a proof-of-concept attack, we can further overcome the limitation. Let us guess another bit, which is now a bit of difference

$$S_1(x'_2 \oplus k_2) \oplus S_1(x_2 \oplus k_2)$$

for some $x'_2 \neq x_2$. This allows to compute the value of f on 256 more inputs of the form $(\mathbb{F}_2^8, x'_2, x_3, \ldots, x_{16})$. More generally, we can guess $t \leq 15$ bits of difference (in addition to the 8 bits of k_1) to be able to compute f on $256 \cdot 2^t$ different inputs, which already allows a huge window. Further, more difference bits per each byte can be guessed to cover more inputs at a little cost.

We conclude that dummyless shuffling provides little security even against standard algebraic attack (with modified key guessing method) in the chosen plaintext setting.

4.2 Differential Algebraic Attack Against Dummyless Shuffling

In this section, we describe a generalization of the algebraic attack called *differential algebraic attack*. The idea follows rather naturally from the previously described attack, where bits of differences were guessed. Let us attack the difference of f on pairs of inputs (i.e. $f(x) \oplus f(x')$), instead of the function f itself (i.e. $f(x)$). Indeed, the difference is at least not harder to compute and, in particular cases, may be much easier.

This modification works very well for the dummyless shuffling setting described above. In fact, it works out-of-the-box with a standard key guessing procedure. First, an attacker chooses pairs (x, x') such that $(x_2, \ldots, x_{16}) = (x'_2, \ldots, x'_{16})$ and $x_1 \neq x'_1$. Then, she records computational traces $\mathcal{W}(x), \mathcal{W}(x')$ and computes a new *differential* trace

$$v(x) := (\mathcal{W}_i(x) \oplus \mathcal{W}_i(x') \mid 1 \leq i \leq |\mathcal{W}|),$$

which is used further as in the standard algebraic attack. Similarly, instead of computing $f(x)$ for a given key guess, the attacker computes $f(x) \oplus f(x')$. In the AES example, it requires only one key byte guess as

$$f(x) \oplus f(x') = S_1(x_1 \oplus k_1) \oplus S_1(x'_1 \oplus k_1),$$

while computing $f(x)$ requires 16 key bytes:

$$f(x) = S_1(x_1 \oplus k_1) \oplus \ldots \oplus S_1(x_{16} \oplus k_{16}).$$

The attack can be viewed as a standard algebraic attack with an extra preprocessing step of the collected traces and of the predicted sensitive function. A formal definition of a general degree-d differential attack, similar to Definition 5 (Algebraic attack), can be found in the full version of this paper.

4.3 Security Against Differential Algebraic Attack

We will show that the differential algebraic attack does not provide any advantage against algebraically secure schemes (τ-error-d-AS), in particular, against secure variants of dummy shuffling which we will identify later. To state it formally, we define an analogue of the security notion τ-error-d-AS and show that the new notion is implied by τ-error-d-AS.

Definition 12. *Let* S *be a scheme and let* $d \geq 1$ *be an integer. Let* τ *be defined as follows*[4]*:*

$$\tau := \min\left\{ \mathsf{err}\left(f(\mathsf{S.enc}(x, \cdot), \cdot) \oplus f(\mathsf{S.enc}(x', \cdot), \cdot) \right) \;\middle|\; f \in \mathcal{F}^{(d)}(\mathsf{S.comp}) \setminus \{\mathbf{0}, \mathbf{1}\}, x, x' \in \mathbb{F}_2^n \right\}.$$

If $\tau > 0$*, the scheme* S *is said to be* degree-d differentially algebraically secure with error τ (τ-error-d-DAS).

[4] The randomness variables r_e, r_c are independent in each application of f and $\mathsf{S.enc}$.

We now show that standard algebraic security implies differential algebraic security.

Proposition 2. *Let* S *be a scheme. If it is* τ*-error-d-AS for some* τ, d*, then it is* τ'*-error-d-DAS with* $\tau' = 2\tau(1-\tau) \geq \tau$.

Proof. Let $f \in \mathcal{F}^{(d)}(\mathsf{S.comp}) \setminus \{\mathbf{0}, \mathbf{1}\}$ and $x, x' \in \mathbb{F}_2^n$. Define

$$e := \mathsf{err}\left(f(\mathsf{S.enc}(x, \cdot), \cdot)\right) \geq \tau, \qquad e' := \mathsf{err}\left(f(\mathsf{S.enc}(x', \cdot), \cdot)\right) \geq \tau,$$
$$e'' := \mathsf{err}\left(f(\mathsf{S.enc}(x, \cdot), \cdot) \oplus f(\mathsf{S.enc}(x', \cdot), \cdot)\right).$$

Since $f(\mathsf{S.enc}(x, \cdot), \cdot)$ and $f(\mathsf{S.enc}(x', \cdot), \cdot)$ each use independent inputs r_c, r_e, it follows that

$$e'' = e(1-e') + (1-e)e' = e + e' - 2ee',$$

which is minimized when both e and e' are minimized, that is $e'' \geq 2\tau - 2\tau^2 = 2\tau(1-\tau)$. This is always not less than τ, since $\tau \leq 1/2$ and so $2(1-\tau) \geq 1$. □

The proof shows that, in fact, the error only increases when multiple traces are combined. It is trivial to prove a similar statement for the case of higher-order differentials or general integrals (i.e. adding values of f in more than 2 inputs). Therefore, the differential algebraic attack is not useful against algebraically secure schemes. Note that this was not a problem in the dummyless shuffling setting, because the attack targeted a function with error 0. We conclude that τ-error-d-AS is a strong security notion and automatically covers some extensions of the algebraic attack.

4.4 Generic Higher-Degree Attack

After (crypt)analyzing dummyless shuffling, we switch to dummy shuffling with at least one dummy slot. We consider higher-degree attacks in order to establish an upper bound on the *degree* of the algebraic security of dummy shuffling. We describe a generic degree-($s_{\text{dummy}} + 1$) attack in the evaluation-phase model (meaning that the attack is very generic), and further sketch how an actual attack would look like in practice. In a way, this attack generalizes the attack from Subsect. 4.1. Indeed, the former attack described a degree-1 attack on shuffling with $s_{\text{dummy}} = 0$.

Proposition 3. *Let* C *be an implementation, and let* $s_{main} \geq 1, s_{dummy} \geq 0$. *The evaluation-phase model scheme* $\mathsf{EPM}(C, s_{main}, s_{dummy})$ *is not* τ*-error-*$(s_{dummy} + 1)$*-AS for any* $\tau > 0$.

Proof. Let $d = s_{\text{dummy}} + 1$. The idea is to select the same sensitive variable $z \in \mathcal{F}^{(1)}(C)$ in arbitrary d slots (for the sake of the proof, any input bit function of $\mathsf{S.comp}$ suffices), and to multiply these linear functions. The resulting function, denoted $\mathbf{z} \in \mathcal{F}^{(d)}(\mathsf{S.comp})$, is always a product of some bits computed on dummy inputs and of the sensitive variable at one (or more) of the main slots.

Let p denote the probability of $z = 1$ when the input is sampled uniformly at random, i.e. $p = \Pr_{x \in \mathbb{F}_2^n}[z(x) = 1] > 0$. Let us consider all main inputs set to the same value, namely x_0 or x_1, such that $z(x_0) = 0, z(x_1) = 1$.

In the first case, the sensitive variable z is equal to 0 in at least one of the considered slots and the product is always equal to zero:

$$\Pr_{r_e}\left[\mathbf{z}(\mathsf{S.enc}(x_0, r_e)) = 0\right] = 1.$$

In the second case, the probability of the product being equal to 1 is p^t where t denotes the number of dummy slots among the chosen d slots. It is minimal when all $d-1$ dummy slots are selected. We conclude that the whole product is equal to 1 with probability at least p^{d-1}:

$$\Pr_{r_e}\left[\mathbf{z}(\mathsf{S.enc}(x_1, r_e)) = 1\right] \geq p^{d-1}.$$

This concludes the proof, since for the described non-constant function $\mathbf{z} \in \mathcal{F}^{(d)}(\mathsf{S.comp}) \setminus \{\mathbf{0}, \mathbf{1}\}$, the function $\mathbf{z}(\mathsf{S.enc}(x_0, \cdot), \cdot)$ is constant and thus has the error equal to 0. □

The proposition shows that dummy shuffling does not achieve τ-error-d-AS, but it does not prove that it is in fact insecure against the algebraic attack. We go further and sketch a concrete attack that is applicable to an implementation protected with dummy shuffling. Let $\mathcal{W} \subseteq \mathcal{F}(\mathsf{S.comp})$ denote the attacked window and let $w := |\mathcal{W}|$ denote its size, e.g. $w = |\mathsf{S.comp}| = s\,|C|$ for the whole circuit. We assume that there is a sensitive variable $z \in \mathcal{W}^{(1)}$ that defines a balanced or a close to balanced Boolean function.

Let X_0 (resp. X_1) denote the set of inputs for which the sensitive variable is equal to 0 (resp. 1). The adversary chooses $t := w^d/d! + \epsilon$ inputs from X_0 for which the sensitive variable is equal to 0 and computes traces on these inputs. Then, she chooses an input from X_1 for which the sensitive variable is equal to 1 and computes a single trace on it. She applies the degree-d algebraic attack to the $t+1$ traces together, searching for the vector $(0, \ldots, 0, 1)$ in the space $\mathcal{W}^{(d)}$ restricted to the traced inputs, which has size at most $\binom{w}{\leq d} < w^d/d!$. The sensitive function $\mathbf{z}$ constructed as in the proof above would match the first t zeroes with probability 1 and match the last one with probability at least $1/2^{d-1}$. We assume that the probability of other vectors matching (i.e. a false positive) is negligible since t is larger then the dimension of the vector space. With probability $1/2^{d-1}$ an attack trial succeeds. Therefore, $\mathcal{O}(2^d)$ traces with inputs from X_1 are enough to find the desired degree-d combination with high probability. The complexity of the attack is thus $\mathcal{O}(2^d \cdot (w^d/d!)^{2.8})$ (using the Strassen algorithm).

Example 6. Consider an AES implementation protected with dummy shuffling, $s_{\mathsf{main}} = 1$ and $s_{\mathsf{dummy}} \geq 1$, i.e. a slot computes the whole cipher. The sensitive variable z is as usual the output of a first-round S-box, and we target $\mathbf{z}$: the product of z taken over all $s = s_{\mathsf{dummy}} + 1$ slots. A guess of the respective subkey byte allows to split the input space into X_0 and X_1. A standard assumption is that the wrong subkey guess results in an incorrect split and leads to an unsuccessful attack. We conclude that the correct subkey can be identified by running the attack 256 times.

5 Provable Algebraic Security of Dummy Shuffling

After establishing the *limits* of the algebraic security of dummy shuffling in the previous section, we switch to quantifying and *proving* security of dummy shuffling. In Subsect. 5.1, we analyze the security of basic dummy shuffling against the linear attack. Next, we develop a refreshing technique which allows to achieve provable security in Subsect. 5.2. Finally, we use the same technique to prove security against *higher-degree* algebraic attack in the case of a single main slot in Subsect. 5.3.

5.1 Security Analysis (Linear Case)

After showing an upper-bound on the algebraic security degree provided by dummy shuffling, we now study the case of degree-1 attack, and analyze when dummy shuffling indeed provides a protection and evaluate the security parameter τ. We show that algebraic security of the EPM scheme depends on a particular property of the original circuit, which is defined formally in the following definition.

Definition 13. *Let C be an implementation. For an integer $d \geq 1$, denote by $\mathsf{err}_d(C)$ the minimum error of a nontrivial function from $\mathcal{F}^{(d)}(C)$:*

$$\mathsf{err}_d(C) := \min_{f \in \mathcal{F}^{(d)}(C) \setminus \{\mathbf{0},\mathbf{1}\}} \tau f.$$

We now give a bound on the 1-AS security of the EPM scheme, parameterized by the value err_1 and the number of main and dummy slots.

Theorem 1. *Let C be an implementation and let $s_{main} \geq 1, s_{dummy} \geq 0$ be integers, $s = s_{main} + s_{dummy}$. Then the evaluation-phase model scheme $S :=$ $\mathsf{EPM}(C, s_{main}, s_{dummy})$ is τ-error-1-AS, where*

$$\tau \geq \frac{s_{dummy}}{s} \cdot \mathsf{err}_1(C).$$

Proof. Consider a function $f \in \mathcal{F}^{(1)}(\mathsf{S.comp}) \setminus \{\mathbf{0},\mathbf{1}\}$ and an arbitrary input x. Since f is nontrivial, it can be expressed *w.l.o.g.* as $f(x') = g(x'_1) + h(x'_2, \cdots, x'_s)$, where $g \in \mathcal{F}^{(1)}(C) \setminus \{\mathbf{0},\mathbf{1}\}$ is a function computed in one of the slots, and h is a function computed in the other slots. The slot of g is a dummy slot with probability $\frac{s_{dummy}}{s}$. In this case, g takes as input an independent uniformly random input (derived from r'_e in $\mathsf{S.enc}$), and its error is lower-bounded by

$\mathsf{err}_1(C)$. In the case it is a main slot, the value of g is constant and the error is equal to 0. It follows that

$$\mathsf{err}\left(g(\mathsf{S.enc}(x,\cdot)\right) \geq \frac{s_{\mathrm{dummy}}}{s} \cdot \mathsf{err}_1(C) + \frac{s_{\mathrm{main}}}{s} \cdot 0.$$

For any fixed shuffling order outcome (decided by r_e'' in $\mathsf{S.enc}$), g and h are independent, and so the error $\mathsf{err}\left(f(\mathsf{S.enc}(x,\cdot))\right)$ satisfies the same bound. □

Simply stating, the error bound is proportional to $\mathsf{err}_1(C)$ with coefficient equal to the fraction of dummy slots: when all slots are dummy slots, the bound is equal to $\mathsf{err}_1(C)$; when all slots are main slots, the bound is equal to 0.

According to this theorem, dummy shuffling provides security against the linear algebraic attack as soon as at least one dummy slot is used. However, the security parameter τ depends on the original circuit C and thus is not generally a constant. Furthermore, even determining or approximating the bound $\mathsf{err}_1(C)$ for an arbitrary implementation C is not an easy problem. We consider one special case when the bias can be upper bounded.

Corollary 1. *Let $C : \mathbb{F}_2^n \to \mathbb{F}_2^m$ be an implementation and let $r = \deg C := \max_{f \in \mathcal{F}(C)} \deg f$. Then the scheme $\mathsf{EPM}(C, s_{main}, s_{dummy})$ is τ-error-1-AS with*

$$\tau \geq \frac{1}{2^r} \cdot \frac{s_{dummy}}{s}.$$

Proof. We use the well-known facts that the minimum weight of a nonzero Boolean function of degree r is 2^{n-r}, i.e. the minimum error satisfies $\mathsf{err}_1(C) \geq 1/2^r$, and that a linear combination of such functions can not increase the degree. □

In the following subsection, we propose a solution to obtain concrete security guarantees for arbitrary circuits.

5.2 Provable Security via Refreshing (Linear Case)

In this solution, we first transform the original implementation C before applying the shuffling countermeasure. For simplicity, we assume that the implementation is based on a Boolean circuit.

First, we add extra inputs to the circuit. After embedding the extended circuit in the EPM scheme, the extra bits would be set to zero on main inputs, while on dummy inputs they would be uniformly random (by the definition of EPM). Then, we use these extra inputs to "refresh" each non-linear gate by an extra XOR. In a main slot, this will have no effect on the computation, since the extra bits are equal to zero. In a dummy slot, this will randomize all computations and maximize the value $\mathsf{err}_1(\tilde{C})$ of the new implementation $\tilde{C}$.

Definition 14 (Refreshed Circuit). *Let $C(x) : \mathbb{F}_2^n \to \mathbb{F}_2^m$ be a Boolean circuit implementation with l AND gates and an arbitrary amount of XOR and*

NOT gates. Define the refreshed circuit $\tilde{C}(x,r) : \mathbb{F}_2^n \times \mathbb{F}_2^l \to \mathbb{F}_2^m$ *as follows. Replace each AND gate* $a_k = z_i \wedge z_j$ *in* C, $1 \le k \le l$ *by the circuit* $a'_k = r_k \oplus a_k = r_k \oplus (z_i \wedge z_j)$, *where* r_k *is the k-th extra bit; each wire using* a_k *is rewired to use* a'_k.

Refreshing has a useful effect on the computed functions: up to a bijective modification of the input, a refreshed circuit computes only quadratic functions of the input. This immediately implies $\mathsf{err}_1(\tilde{C}) \ge 1/4$ for any circuit C and will also be useful for proving higher-degree security in Subsect. 5.3.

Lemma 1. *Let* $C : \mathbb{F}_2^n \to \mathbb{F}_2^m$ *be an implementation in a form of a Boolean circuit in the {AND,XOR,NOT} basis using* l *AND gates and let* $\tilde{C}$ *be its refreshed version. Then, there exists a bijection* h *mapping* $\mathbb{F}_2^n \times \mathbb{F}_2^l$ *to itself, such that* $\deg f \circ h^{-1} \le 2$ *for all* $f(x,r) \in \mathcal{F}(\tilde{C})$.

Proof. We use the notation from Defintion 14. For all $1 \le k \le l$, let

$$g_k \ : \ \mathbb{F}_2^n \times \mathbb{F}_2^l \to \mathbb{F}_2^n \times \mathbb{F}_2^l \ : \ (x,r) \mapsto (x,r'), \text{ where}$$

$$r'_i = \begin{cases} r_i \oplus a_k(x,(r_1,\ldots,r_{k-1})), & \text{if } i = k \\ r_i & \text{if } i \ne k. \end{cases}$$

That is, g_k replaces r_k by $r_k + a_k = a'_k$ in the full state (x,r). Note that a_k is a function of x and $r_1,\ldots,r_{k-1}$ and so g_k is a bijection.

Define $h := g_l \circ \ldots \circ g_1$ and let $(x,r') := h(x,r)$. Then, we have $r'_k = a'_k(x,r)$ for all k. Let $f \in \mathcal{F}(\tilde{C})$ be the function computed in an arbitrary AND gate of $\tilde{C}$. Note that outputs of AND gates are used only to compute a'_k in $\tilde{C}$ and the inputs of AND gates can only be affine functions of x and all refreshed AND gates a'_k. That is,

$$f(x,r) = p(x,a'(x,r))q(x,a'(x,r))$$

for some affine functions p,q. Since $(x,a') = (x,r')$ is the output of $h(x,r)$, it follows that

$$f(x,r) = p(h(x,r))q(h(x,r)).$$

The right-hand side defines (at most) quadratic function $o(z) := p(z)q(z)$ such that $f = o \circ h$. We conclude that $f \circ h^{-1} = o$ has degree at most 2. □

Remark 8. From the proof it can be observed that the last topologically independent AND gates (i.e. those, output of which does not affect any other AND) do not have to be refreshed for the lemma to hold.

The linear algebraic security of dummy shuffling with refreshing follows naturally from the lemma and Corollary 1.

Theorem 2. *Let* $C(x) : \mathbb{F}_2^n \to \mathbb{F}_2^m$ *be an implementation in a form of a Boolean circuit in the {AND,XOR,NOT} basis. Then,* $\mathsf{EPM}(\tilde{C}, s_{main}, s_{dummy})$ *is* τ*-error-1-AS, where*

$$\tau \ \ge \ \frac{1}{4} \cdot \frac{s_{dummy}}{s}.$$

In particular, $\mathsf{EPM}(\tilde{C},1,1)$ *is a 1/8-error-1-AS scheme.*

Proof. The weight/error of any function $f \in \mathcal{F}^{(1)}(\tilde{C}) \setminus \{\mathbf{0}, \mathbf{1}\}$ is unchanged when the function is composed with a bijection (in this case, the bijection h^{-1} from Lemma 1): $\mathsf{err}(f) = \mathsf{err}(f \circ h^{-1}) \geq 1/4$. Therefore, any considered function f is weight-equivalent to a (non-zero) quadratic function, which has error at least 1/4, and so $\mathsf{err}_1(\tilde{C}) \geq 1/4$. The result follows from Theorem 1. □

5.3 Provable Security via Refreshing (Higher-Degree)

We now switch to higher-degree algebraic security. In this subsection we show that the refreshing technique allows to achieve algebraic security of degree matching the upper-bound given by the generic attack given in Subsect. 4.4, namely the degree equal to the number of dummy slots.

We will use the following lemma. Intuitively, consider s parallel applications of an implementation $C : \mathbb{F}_2^n \to \mathbb{F}_2^m$ and assume $f : (\mathbb{F}_2^n)^s \to \mathbb{F}_2$ be a non-constant function of the s inputs obtained by applying a degree-d function to intermediate functions inside all copies of C. Assume that we can set one of the inputs to any constant $c \in \mathbb{F}_2^n$, making all intermediate computations in that C constant as well. However, which one out of s copies is set to the constant is chosen uniformly at random. The lemma says that f can be constant in at most d such choices out of s.

The motivation for the lemma comes from a simple choice of such f and c (coming from the generic attack from Subsect. 4.4) set $c = 0$ and f be (for example) a product of the first input bit of the first d copies of C: $f(x_1, \ldots, x_s) = x_{1,1}x_{2,1}\ldots x_{d,1}$. Clearly, $f = 0$ when $x_1 = c = 0$, or $x_2 = c = 0$, ..., or $x_d = c = 0$. However, it is non-constant in all other $s - d$ choices, namely $x_{d+1} = c = 0$, ..., or $x_s = c = 0$. The lemma thus states that such a choice of f, c is the best an adversary (aiming to find f that is constant as often as possible) can achieve.

Lemma 2. *Let $C : \mathbb{F}_2^n \to \mathbb{F}_2^m$ be an implementation. For an integer $s \geq 1$ denote s parallel applications of C by $C^{\otimes s}$ (as an implementation):*

$$C^{\otimes s} : (\mathbb{F}_2^n)^s \to (\mathbb{F}_2^m)^s : (x_1, \ldots, x_s) \mapsto (C(x_1), \ldots, C(x_s)).$$

Let $f \in \mathcal{F}^{(d)}(C^{\otimes s}) \setminus \{\mathbf{0}, \mathbf{1}\}$ for an integer d, $1 \leq d \leq s$. Then, for any $c \in \mathbb{F}_2^n$ the number of positions i, $1 \leq i \leq s$ such that $f|_{x_i=c}$ is constant is at most d:

$$\left|\left\{f|_{x_i=c} \in \{\mathbf{0}, \mathbf{1}\} \;\middle|\; i \in [1 \ldots s]\right\}\right| \leq d.$$

Proof. The proof is by contradiction. Let g denote the degree-d function associated to f, that is the function applied to $(\mathcal{F}(C))^s$ to obtain f:

$$g : \left(\mathbb{F}_2^{|\mathcal{F}(C)|}\right)^s \to \mathbb{F}_2, \text{ such that}$$
$$g(\mathcal{F}(C)(x_1), \ldots, \mathcal{F}(C)(x_s)) = f(x_1, \ldots, x_s) \text{ for all } x_1, \ldots, x_s \in \mathbb{F}_2^n.$$

Here $\mathcal{F}(C)(x_i)$ is the computational trace of C on input x_i (the bit-vector of all intermediate values computed in C on input x_i).

Assume that there exist (at least) $d+1$ positions $j_1, \ldots, j_{d+1}$ such that for all $j \in \{j_1, \ldots, j_{d+1}\}$, $f|_{x_j=c}$ is constant. Note that it is the same constant for all such positions, since these restrictions intersect at $x_{j_1} = c, \ldots, x_{j_{d+1}} = c$. We can assume *w.l.o.g.* that the constant is 0. Since f is not constant, there exist $a = (a_1, \ldots, a_s) \in (\mathbb{F}_2^n)^s$ such that $f(a) = 1$. Consider the affine subspace $V = V_1 \times \ldots \times V_s$, where

$$V_i = \begin{cases} \{\mathcal{F}(C)(a_i), \mathcal{F}(C)(c)\}, & \text{if } i \in \{j_1, \ldots, j_{d+1}\}, \\ \{\mathcal{F}(C)(a_i)\}, & \text{otherwise.} \end{cases}$$

Observe that $\bigoplus_{v \in V} g(v) = 1$. Indeed, $g(v) = 0$ for all $v \in V$ except $v = (\mathcal{F}(C)(a_1), \ldots, \mathcal{F}(C)(a_s))$. Since V is a $(d+1)$-dimensional affine subspace, it follows that $\deg g \geq d+1$, which is a contradiction. □

We can now prove our main result. At its core, it relies on the above lemma to bound the number of (bad) shuffling outcomes when f is constant, and on Lemma 1 (stating that a refreshed circuit is equivalent to a quadratic circuit) to lower-bound the error in good shuffling outcomes.

Theorem 3 (Main). *Let C be an implementation and $s \geq 2$ an integer. The evaluation-phase model scheme* $\mathsf{S} := \mathsf{EPM}(\tilde{C}, 1, s-1)$ *is τ-error-d-AS for any $1 \leq d \leq s-1$, with*

$$\tau \geq \frac{1}{2^{2d}} \cdot \frac{s-d}{s}.$$

Proof. Consider arbitrary $f \in \mathcal{F}^{(d)}(\mathsf{S.comp}) \setminus \{\mathbf{0}, \mathbf{1}\}$. We need to prove that when the input x of $\mathsf{S.enc}(x, r_e)$ is fixed, the error of $f(\mathsf{S.enc}(x, \cdot))$ is at least τ. Recall that $\mathsf{S.enc}$ uses r''_e (part of r_e) to shuffle the sequence $(x, r'_{e,1}, \ldots, r'_{e,s-1})$ (r'_e being another part of r_e), which is then passed to the input to f. By Lemma 2, in at most d/s fraction of the shuffling outcomes (i.e. positions i with $x'_i = x$) the function $f(\mathsf{S.enc}(x, \cdot)) = f|_{x_i=x}$ can be constant. Consider the remaining $(s-d)/s$ fraction of the outcomes. By Lemma 1, we can see $\mathcal{F}^{(1)}(\mathsf{S.comp})$ as spanned by at most quadratic functions of the input (it has the structure of a refreshed circuit), and so $\mathcal{F}^{(d)}(\mathsf{S.comp}) = (\mathcal{F}^{(1)}(\mathsf{S.comp}))^{(d)}$ spanned by functions of degree at most $2d$ (when composed with h^{-1} from Lemma 1). Since in the considered case f is non-constant, we can use the bound $\mathsf{err}(f) \geq 1/2^{2d}$. By combining the two different shuffling outcomes we obtain

$$\mathsf{err}(f(\mathsf{S.enc}(x, \cdot))) \geq \frac{d}{s} \cdot 0 + \frac{s-d}{s} \cdot \frac{1}{2^{2d}} = \frac{1}{2^{2d}} \cdot \frac{s-d}{s}.$$ □

This result shows that dummy shuffling together with the refreshing technique provides algebraic security for degrees up to the number of dummy slots. Furthermore, the error bound τ can be seen as close to the maximal $1/2^{2d}$ in e.g. Boolean circuit implementations, as was discussed in Subsect. 2.3. We conclude that dummy shuffling with refreshing solves the problem of algebraic security, at least in the gray-box model of [2].

5.4 Implementation Cost Estimation

Dummy shuffling with refreshing allows cheap provably secure protection against algebraic attacks of any predetermined degree $d \geq 1$ using a single main slot and d dummy slots ($s_{\mathsf{dummy}} = d$). We estimate roughly the number of gates required for implementing dummy shuffling.

Let l_{A} (resp. l_{X}) denote the number of AND gates (resp. the number of XOR gates) in the original implementation. In the input-shuffling phase, the cost is to generate $|x| + s_{\mathsf{dummy}} l_{\mathsf{A}}$ bits of randomness and shuffle s vectors of size $|x| + l_{\mathsf{A}}$ bits. For typical complex circuits C, the number of AND gates is much larger than the input size: $l_{\mathsf{A}} \gg |x|$, so we ignore the latter for our estimation. We utilize the controlled swap construction, which can be implemented in Boolean circuits as

$$(x_i, y_i) \mapsto \big((c \wedge (x_i \oplus y_i)) \oplus x_i,\ (c \wedge (x_i \oplus y_i)) \oplus y_i\big)$$

for each index i, where c is the control (random) bit. For $d = 1$, one controlled swap of l-bit state is sufficient for perfectly uniform shuffling. For $d > 1$, we only have to place the single main slot in a random position. This can be implemented in circuits using s_{dummy} conditional swaps of l_{A}-bit states, assuming a random bitstring with a single one is generated, which would be negligible for the final cost. The output-selection phase can be for example implemented as the inverse of the input-shuffling and has the same cost, excluding random bits. The total cost of such implementation of input-shuffling is $4 s_{\mathsf{dummy}} l_{\mathsf{A}} = 4 d l_{\mathsf{A}}$ gates for swaps and generation of $s_{\mathsf{dummy}} l_{\mathsf{A}}$ random bits for dummy slots. The cost of the evaluation phase is $s(|C| + l_{\mathsf{A}}) = 2 s l_{\mathsf{A}} + s l_{\mathsf{X}} = (2d + 2) l_{\mathsf{A}} + (d + 1) l_{\mathsf{X}}$ gates. We conclude with the total cost estimation of $(6d + 2) l_{\mathsf{A}} + (d + 1) l_{\mathsf{X}}$ gates and $d \cdot l_{\mathsf{A}}$ random bits.

6 Public Dummy Shuffling Construction

In this section, we describe a construction of *public* dummy shuffling. This proof-of-concept shows that a white-box designer willing to implement dummy shuffling does not have to obfuscate the whole implementation but rather a single slot function.

The goal of the construction is to have a clear slot separation without any interaction between slots except the final merging step, which in our case is simply XOR of outputs of all the slots. The input-shuffling phase is also implicit and is performed inside the slot, using an extra *index* input, specifying the slot index. The high-level description of the scheme is as follows:

$$\mathit{output} = \bigoplus_{0 \leq \mathit{index} < s} \mathrm{slot}(\mathit{input}, \mathit{index}).$$

The construction implements dummy shuffling with a single main slot and multiple dummy slots. The location of main slot depends pseudorandomly on the input. More precisely, for any fixed input there exists a unique value of the index i that corresponds to the main slot computation, and this value should be hard to predict for an adversary, even after observing the outputs of slots. For this purpose, the output of each slot is "masked" by a pseudorandom mask, with the property that all masks XOR to zero. Note that the output of the main slot is masked too, since otherwise it would match the final output and thus would be trivial to locate.

When the slot function is implemented as a Boolean circuit, the construction can be implemented in a bit-slice style by performing bitwise operations on 32- or 64-bit registers. This allows to compute up to 32 or 64 slots in parallel without any significant overhead, leading to very efficient implementations.

The construction requires two standard pseudorandom functions (PRFs) and a special primitive called *tweakable zero-sum PRF*, which we formally define in the following.

Definition 15 (TZS-PRF). *A function with the signature* $F_k[t](x) : \mathbb{F}_2^{|k|} \times \mathbb{F}_2^{|t|} \times \mathbb{F}_2^n \to \mathbb{F}_2^m$ *is called a* tweakable zero-sum PRF *if*

1. *for all* k, t *the function* $F_k[t]$ *sums to zero over* $\mathbb{F}_2^n$*:* $\bigoplus_{x \in \mathbb{F}_2^n} F_k[t](x) = 0$;
2. *for a uniformly sampled* $k \in \mathbb{F}_2^{|k|}$*, the family* F_k *is computationally indistinguishable from a uniformly sampled function family* $(f_t : \mathbb{F}_2^n \to \mathbb{F}_2^m)_{t \in \mathbb{F}_2^{|t|}}$ *with the constraint* $\bigoplus_{x \in \mathbb{F}_2^n} f_t(x) = 0$ *for all* $t \in \mathbb{F}_2^{|t|}$.

We describe a simple TZS-PRF construction from a PRF in the full version of this paper, with the TZS-PRF security reduced to the PRF security. It is based on the following simple observation: the zero-sum property is equivalent to requiring each $F_k[t]$ have algebraic degree at most $n - 1$. The general idea follows: multiply each monomial of degree at most $n - 1$ by a pseudorandom bit derived from the tweak using another PRF, and sum all monomials to get one output coordinate. This construction is tailored to our application, where the TZS-PRF input has size logarithmic in the number of slots and so the number of considered monomials is linear in the number of slots.

We are now ready to describe our proof-of-concept public dummy shuffling construction. The high-level pseudocode is given in Algorithm 1. We now describe each step of the algorithm in details.

Line 1–4 First, the input x is used to determine the index $i \in \mathbb{F}_2^h$ of the main slot. For this purpose, the PRF G_{k_1} (with a hardcoded key) is used. If $G_{k_1}(x)$ is not equal to the value of i passed into the current slot, then the dummy input is generated by applying the PRF H_{k_2} to the full input (x, i). Otherwise, the original input is used and padded with zeroes.

Line 5 Main computation is done by using the refreshed circuit (as in Definition 14). By Line 1–4 of the algorithm, the input in the main slot is the original input x padded with zeroes, and the input in a dummy slot is fully pseudorandom. Note that x, i are passed through the slot evaluation phase. This does not introduce algebraic leakage, since otherwise an algebraic attack would serve as a distinguisher for the PRF G_{k_1} or H_{k_2}.

Algorithm 1. Public Dummy Shuffling Construction

Input: an implementation $C : \mathbb{F}_2^n \to \mathbb{F}_2^m$ with l AND gates;
an integer $h \geq 1$;
$G_{k_1}(x) : \mathbb{F}_2^n \to \mathbb{F}_2^h$: a PRF instance (impl.);
$H_{k_2}(x) : \mathbb{F}_2^{n+h} \to \mathbb{F}_2^{n+l}$: a PRF instance (impl.);
$F_{k_3}[t](x) : \mathbb{F}_2^n \times \mathbb{F}_2^h \to \mathbb{F}_2^m$: a tweakable zero-sum PRF instance (impl.);
Output: slot implementation $S(x, i) : \mathbb{F}_2^n \times \mathbb{F}_2^h \to \mathbb{F}_2^m$, such that $\bigoplus_{i \in \mathbb{F}_2^h} S(x, i) = C(x)$.

Input-Shuffling:
1: **if** $G_{k_1}(x) = i$ **then** ▷ $G_{k_1}(x)$ determines the main slot index
2: $x' \leftarrow (x \mid\mid 0^l)$
3: **else**
4: $x' \leftarrow H_{k_2}(x \mid\mid i)$

Slot Evaluation:
5: $y' \leftarrow \tilde{C}(x')$ ▷ x, i are passed through

Output-Selection:
6: $mask \leftarrow F_{k_3}[x](i)$
7: **if** $G_{k_1}(x) = i$ **then** ▷ determine the main output
8: **return** $y \oplus mask$
9: **else**
10: **return** $mask$

Line 6 The output mask is generated using the tweakable zero-sum PRF F_{k_3} tweaked by x. The necessary property is that the generated masks XOR to zero for any fixed input x.

Lines 7–10 The PRF G_{k_1} is again used to identify the main slot. In the main slot, the generated mask is XOR-ed with the output y' (which is equal to the main output) and returned. In dummy slots, the generated mask is returned unmodified. As a result, the output of the main slot is the correct output XOR-ed with an output mask, and the output of a dummy slot is simply an output mask. Since all output masks sum to zero, the sum of all slots outputs results in the desired output $C(x)$.

The slot evaluation phase can be proven to provide algebraic security, under the assumption of the pseudorandomness of H. More precisely, by Theorem 3, the scheme S with S.enc defined by Lines 1–4, S.comp defined by Line 5, and S.dec defined by lines 6–10, is τ-error-d-AS for any $1 \leq d \leq s - 1$, with

$$\tau \geq \frac{1}{2^{2d}} \cdot \frac{s-d}{s}.$$

This proves that algebraically secure *computations* are possible for any fixed degree and any target circuit. However, the whole construction can be still susceptible to algebraic attacks of degree 2, if the sensitive terms are computed in clear, namely $[G_{k_1}(x) = i]$, which identifies the main slot. Provably secure implementation of these functions is left as future work: it would first require a meaningful extension of the algebraic security model to include encoding and decoding phases[5].

Note that the output masks used in the construction are used not for achieving the algebraic security, but to prevent black-box slot identification attacks. Indeed, without the masks, all the dummy slots will have the all-zero output and thus, the main slot at each execution would be trivially identifiable. Any obfuscation of the slot procedure would not prevent the attack, since only outputs of the slots are used. Therefore, the outputs should not reveal the location of the main slot. In particular, the output of the main slot should be indistinguishable from an output of any dummy slot, even with the knowledge of the main output. This is naturally guaranteed by the tweakable zero-sum PRF security. Indeed, in our scheme the adversary is given access to the TZS-PRF modified by XORing a constant (the main output of the scheme) to a single output of the TZS-PRF per each tweak. Note that for an ideal TZS-PRF this modification produces the same distribution of random function families independently of which output is modified (and of the constant, which can be chosen adversarially). Therefore, the adversary can not gain any advantage in guessing which output is modified, or, equivalently, what is the index of the main slot.

7 Conclusions

In this work, we analyzed algebraic security of dummyless and dummy shuffling in the gray-box model of [2]. Dummy shuffling allows to achieve close to optimal security for arbitrary degrees of the attack with reasonable overhead. This is a rather surprising development, since the minimalist quadratic masking scheme of [2] was already rather heavy. We conclude that this work solves the open problem of higher-order algebraic security and provides useful tools for white-box implementations. Nonetheless, there are still many open questions around the topic.

Towards White-Box Model. The current BU-model covers only the main computation part. A natural question is how to extend this model to cover both encoding and decoding steps, including pseudorandomness generation. Steps were made towards such a solution in the context of probing security [11,16]. Finally, dummy shuffling requires to generate a lot of random bits *in the encoding* step. This leads to large intermediate state and may incur a large overhead for further obfuscation. Therefore, a masking-style solution to higher-degree algebraic security is still a desirable tool.

Public Dummy Shuffling. We proposed a proof-of-concept construction of public dummy shuffling. An interesting task is to develop an efficient instantiation using existing PRFs or develop new white-box-friendly PRFs.

[5] Direct extension is not possible, since input and output are sensitive functions by definition and will be leaked in the encoding/decoding phases.

Fault Attacks. Fault attacks pose a dangerous threat to dummy shuffling. Most importantly, faults can be used to distinguish main slots from dummy slots in public dummy shuffling (as was done in [14]), and aid algebraic attacks in hidden dummy shuffling. For example, the attacker can filter the inputs for which chosen intermediate values lead to a difference in the output when faulted. In a basic dummy shuffling, this would identify the inputs for which those intermediate values belong to a main slot.

We conclude that the topic of algebraic security and, in general, provable countermeasures for white-box implementations still has many interesting open problems and research directions.

Acknowledgements. We thank the anonymous reviewers for their insightful comments. The work of Aleksei Udovenko was partly supported by the French FUI-AAP25 IDECYS+ project and by the French ANR-AAPG2019 SWITECH project; part of his work was performed while he was at the University of Luxembourg and supported by the Luxembourg National Research Fund (FNR) project FinCrypt (C17/IS/11684537).

References

1. Billet, O., Gilbert, H., Ech-Chatbi, C.: Cryptanalysis of a white box AES implementation. In: Handschuh, H., Hasan, M.A. (eds.) SAC 2004. LNCS, vol. 3357, pp. 227–240. Springer, Heidelberg (2004). https://doi.org/10.1007/978-3-540-30564-4_16
2. Biryukov, A., Udovenko, A.: Attacks and countermeasures for white-box designs. In: Peyrin, T., Galbraith, S. (eds.) ASIACRYPT 2018. LNCS, vol. 11273, pp. 373–402. Springer, Cham (2018). https://doi.org/10.1007/978-3-030-03329-3_13
3. Blum, A., Kalai, A., Wasserman, H.: Noise-tolerant learning, the parity problem, and the statistical query model. In: 32nd ACM STOC, pp. 435–440. ACM Press (2000)
4. Bogdanov, A., et al.: CHES 2019 Capture The Flag Challenge. The WhibOx Contest, 2nd edn. (2019). https://whibox-contest.github.io/2019/
5. Bogdanov, A., Rivain, M., Vejre, P.S., Wang, J.: Higher-order DCA against standard side-channel countermeasures. In: Polian, I., Stöttinger, M. (eds.) COSADE 2019. LNCS, vol. 11421, pp. 118–141. Springer, Cham (2019). https://doi.org/10.1007/978-3-030-16350-1_8
6. Bos, J.W., Hubain, C., Michiels, W., Teuwen, P.: Differential computation analysis: hiding your white-box designs is not enough. In: Gierlichs, B., Poschmann, A.Y. (eds.) CHES 2016. LNCS, vol. 9813, pp. 215–236. Springer, Heidelberg (2016). https://doi.org/10.1007/978-3-662-53140-2_11
7. Breunesse, C.B., Kizhvatov, I., Muijrers, R., Spruyt, A.: Towards fully automated analysis of whiteboxes: perfect dimensionality reduction for perfect leakage. Cryptology ePrint Archive, Report 2018/095 (2018)
8. Chow, S., Eisen, P., Johnson, H., van Oorschot, P.C.: A white-box DES implementation for DRM applications. In: Feigenbaum, J. (ed.) DRM 2002. LNCS, vol. 2696, pp. 1–15. Springer, Heidelberg (2003). https://doi.org/10.1007/978-3-540-44993-5_1
9. Chow, S., Eisen, P., Johnson, H., Van Oorschot, P.C.: White-box cryptography and an AES implementation. In: Nyberg, K., Heys, H. (eds.) SAC 2002. LNCS, vol. 2595, pp. 250–270. Springer, Heidelberg (2003). https://doi.org/10.1007/3-540-36492-7_17

10. Clavier, C., Coron, J.-S., Dabbous, N.: Differential power analysis in the presence of hardware countermeasures. In: Koç, Ç.K., Paar, C. (eds.) CHES 2000. LNCS, vol. 1965, pp. 252–263. Springer, Heidelberg (2000). https://doi.org/10.1007/3-540-44499-8_20
11. Coron, J.-S., Greuet, A., Zeitoun, R.: Side-channel masking with pseudo-random generator. In: Canteaut, A., Ishai, Y. (eds.) EUROCRYPT 2020. LNCS, vol. 12107, pp. 342–375. Springer, Cham (2020). https://doi.org/10.1007/978-3-030-45727-3_12
12. Esser, A., Kübler, R., May, A.: LPN decoded. In: Katz, J., Shacham, H. (eds.) CRYPTO 2017. LNCS, vol. 10402, pp. 486–514. Springer, Cham (2017). https://doi.org/10.1007/978-3-319-63715-0_17
13. Goubin, L., Paillier, P., Rivain, M., Wang, J.: How to reveal the secrets of an obscure white-box implementation. J. Cryptogr. Eng. **10**(1), 49–66 (2019). https://doi.org/10.1007/s13389-019-00207-5
14. Goubin, L., Rivain, M., Wang, J.: Defeating state-of-the-art white-box countermeasures. IACR TCHES **2020**(3), 454–482 (2020)
15. Herbst, C., Oswald, E., Mangard, S.: An AES smart card implementation resistant to power analysis attacks. In: Zhou, J., Yung, M., Bao, F. (eds.) ACNS 2006. LNCS, vol. 3989, pp. 239–252. Springer, Heidelberg (2006). https://doi.org/10.1007/11767480_16
16. Ishai, Y., et al.: Robust pseudorandom generators. In: Fomin, F.V., Freivalds, R., Kwiatkowska, M., Peleg, D. (eds.) ICALP 2013. LNCS, vol. 7965, pp. 576–588. Springer, Heidelberg (2013). https://doi.org/10.1007/978-3-642-39206-1_49
17. Ishai, Y., Sahai, A., Wagner, D.: Private circuits: securing hardware against probing attacks. In: Boneh, D. (ed.) CRYPTO 2003. LNCS, vol. 2729, pp. 463–481. Springer, Heidelberg (2003). https://doi.org/10.1007/978-3-540-45146-4_27
18. Prouff, E., et al.: CHES 2017 Capture The Flag Challenge. The WhibOx Contest (2017). https://whibox-contest.github.io/2017/
19. Rivain, M., Prouff, E., Doget, J.: Higher-order masking and shuffling for software implementations of block ciphers. In: Clavier, C., Gaj, K. (eds.) CHES 2009. LNCS, vol. 5747, pp. 171–188. Springer, Heidelberg (2009). https://doi.org/10.1007/978-3-642-04138-9_13
20. Rivain, M., Wang, J.: Analysis and improvement of differential computation attacks against internally-encoded white-box implementations. IACR TCHES **2019**(2), 225–255 (2019)
21. Seker, O., Eisenbarth, T., Liskiewicz, M.: A white-box masking scheme resisting computational and algebraic attacks. IACR TCHES **2021**(2), 61–105 (2021). https://tches.iacr.org/index.php/TCHES/article/view/8788
22. Tillich, S., Herbst, C., Mangard, S.: Protecting AES software implementations on 32-bit processors against power analysis. In: Katz, J., Yung, M. (eds.) ACNS 2007. LNCS, vol. 4521, pp. 141–157. Springer, Heidelberg (2007). https://doi.org/10.1007/978-3-540-72738-5_10
23. Veyrat-Charvillon, N., Medwed, M., Kerckhof, S., Standaert, F.-X.: Shuffling against side-channel attacks: a comprehensive study with cautionary note. In: Wang, X., Sako, K. (eds.) ASIACRYPT 2012. LNCS, vol. 7658, pp. 740–757. Springer, Heidelberg (2012). https://doi.org/10.1007/978-3-642-34961-4_44
24. Wyseur, B., Michiels, W., Gorissen, P., Preneel, B.: Cryptanalysis of white-box DES implementations with arbitrary external encodings. In: Adams, C., Miri, A., Wiener, M. (eds.) SAC 2007. LNCS, vol. 4876, pp. 264–277. Springer, Heidelberg (2007). https://doi.org/10.1007/978-3-540-77360-3_17

Advanced Lattice Sieving on GPUs, with Tensor Cores

Léo Ducas(✉), Marc Stevens, and Wessel van Woerden

CWI, Amsterdam, The Netherlands
{L.Ducas, Wessel.van.Woerden}@cwi.nl

Abstract. In this work, we study GPU implementations of various state-of-the-art sieving algorithms for lattices (Becker-Gama-Joux 2015, Becker-Ducas-Gama-Laarhoven 2016, Herold-Kirshanova 2017) inside the General Sieve Kernel (G6K, Albrecht *et al.* 2019). In particular, we extensively exploit the recently introduced Tensor Cores – originally designed for raytracing and machine learning – and demonstrate their fitness for the cryptanalytic task at hand. We also propose a new *dual-hash* technique for efficient detection of 'lift-worthy' pairs to accelerate a key ingredient of G6K: finding short lifted vectors.

We obtain new computational records, reaching dimension 180 for the SVP Darmstadt Challenge improving upon the previous record for dimension 155. This computation ran for 51.6 days on a server with 4 NVIDIA Turing GPUs and 1.5TB of RAM. This corresponds to a gain of about two orders of magnitude over previous records both in terms of wall-clock time and of energy efficiency.

Keywords: Lattice sieving · Shortest vector · G6K · Cryptanalysis · Challenges

1 Introduction

Lattice reduction is a key tool in cryptanalysis at large, and is of course a central interest for the cryptanalysis of lattice-based cryptography. With the expected standardisation of lattice-based cryptosystems, the question of the precise performance of lattice reduction algorithms is becoming a critical one. The crux of the matter is the cost of solving the Shortest Vector Problem (SVP) with sieving algorithms. While even in the RAM model numerous questions remain regarding the precise cost of the fastest algorithms, one may also expect a significant gap between this model and practice, due to their high-memory requirements.

Lattice sieving algorithms [AKS01,NV08,MV10] are asymptotically superior to enumeration techniques [FP85,Kan83,SE94,GNR10], but this has only recently been shown in practice. Recent progress on sieving, both on its theoretical [Laa15,BGJ15,BDGL16,HKL18] and practical performances [FBB+14, Duc18,LM18,ADH+19], brought the cross-over point with enumeration as low as dimension 80. The work of Albrecht *et al.* at Eurocrypt 2019, named the General Sieve Kernel (G6K), set new TU Darmstadt SVP-records [SG10] on a single

A. Canteaut and F.-X. Standaert (Eds.): EUROCRYPT 2021, LNCS 12697, pp. 249–279, 2021.
https://doi.org/10.1007/978-3-030-77886-6_9

machine up to dimension 155, while before the highest record was at 152 using a cluster with multiple orders of magnitude more core-hours of computation.

Before scaling up to a cluster of computers, a natural step is to port cryptanalytic algorithms to Graphical Processing Units (GPUs); not only are GPUs far more efficient for certain parallel tasks, but their bandwidth/computation capacity ratio are already more representative of the difficulties to expect when scaling up beyond a single computational server. This step can therefore already teach us a great deal about how a cryptanalytic algorithm should scale in practice. The only GPU implementation of sieving so far [YKYC17] did not make use of advanced algorithmic techniques (such as the Nearest Neighbour Search techniques, Progressive Sieving or the Dimensions for Free technique [Laa15,LM18,Duc18]), and is therefore not very representative of the current state of the art.

An important consideration for assessing practical cryptanalysis is the direction of computation technologies, and one should in particular note the advent of *Tensor* architectures [JYP+17], offering extreme performance for low-precision matrix multiplication. While this development has been mostly motivated by machine learning applications, the potential application for cryptanalytic algorithms must also be considered. Interestingly, such architectures are now also available on commodity GPUs (partly motivated by ray-tracing applications), and therefore accessible even with modest resources.

1.1 Contributions

The main contribution of this work is to show that lattice sieving, including the more complex and recent algorithmic improvements, can effectively be accelerated by GPUs. In particular, we show that the NVIDIA Tensor cores, only supporting specific low-precision computations, can be used efficiently for lattice sieving. We exhibit how the most computationally intensive parts of complex sieving algorithms can be executed in low-precision even in large dimensions.

We show and demonstrate by an implementation that the use of Tensor cores results in large efficiency gains for cryptanalytic attacks, both in hardware and energy costs. We present several new computational records, reaching dimension 180 for the TU Darmstadt SVP challenge record with a single high-end machine with 4 GPUs and 1.5TB RAM in 51.6 days. Not only did we break SVP-records significant faster, but also with <4% of the energy cost compared to a CPU only attack. For instance, we solved dimension 176 using less time and with less than 2 times the overall energy cost compared to the previous record of dimension 155. Furthermore by re-computing data at appropriate points in our algorithms we reduced the memory usage per vector by 60% compared to the base G6K implementation with minimal computational overhead.

Our work also includes the first implementation of asymptotically best sieve (BDGL) from [BDGL16] inside the G6K framework, both for CPU-only (multi-threaded and `AVX2`-optimized) and with GPU acceleration. We use this to shed some light on the practicality of this algorithm. In particular we show that our CPU-only BDGL-sieve already improves over the previous record-holding sieve in dimensions as low as 95, but that this cross-over point lies much higher for our GPU accelerated sieve due to memory-bottleneck constraints.

One key feature of G6K is to also consider lifts of pairs even if such a pair is not necessarily reducible, so as to check whether such lifts are short; the more such pairs are lifted, the more dimensions for free one can hope for [Duc18, ADH+19]. Yet, Babai lifting of a vector has quadratic running time which makes it too expensive to apply to each pair. We introduce a filter based on dual vectors that detects whether pairs are worth lifting. With adequate pre-computation on each vector, filtering a pair for lifting can be made linear-time, fully parallelizable, and very suitable to implement on GPUs.

Open Source Code. Since the writing of this report, our CPU implementation of `bdgl` has been integrated in G6K, with further improvements, and we aim for long term maintenance.[1] The GPU implementations has also been made public, but with lower expectation of quality, documentation and maintenance.[2]

2 Preliminaries

2.1 Lattices and the Shortest Vector Problem

Notation. Given a matrix $\mathbf{B} = (\mathbf{b}_0, \ldots, \mathbf{b}_{d-1}) \subset \mathbb{R}^d$ with linearly independent columns, we define the lattice generated by the basis $\mathbf{B}$ as $\mathcal{L}(\mathbf{B}) := \{\sum_i^d x_i \mathbf{b}_i : x_i \in \mathbb{Z}\}$. We denote the volume of the fundamental area $\mathbf{B} \cdot [0,1]^d$ by $\det(\mathcal{L}) := |\det(\mathbf{B})|$. Given a basis $\mathbf{B}$ we define π_i as the projections orthogonal to the span of $(\mathbf{b}_0, \ldots, \mathbf{b}_{i-1})$ and the Gram-Schmidt orthogonalisation as $\mathbf{B}^* = (\mathbf{b}_0^*, \ldots, \mathbf{b}_{d-1}^*)$ where $\mathbf{b}_i^* := \pi_i(\mathbf{b}_i)$. The projected sublattice $\mathcal{L}_{[l:r]}$ where $0 \leq l < r \leq d$ is defined as the lattice with basis $\mathbf{B}_{[l:r]} := (\pi_l(\mathbf{b}_l), \ldots, \pi_l(\mathbf{b}_{r-1}))$. Note that the Gram-Schmidt orthogonalisation of $\mathbf{B}_{[l:r]}$ is induced by $\mathbf{B}^*$ and equals $(\mathbf{b}_l^*, \ldots, \mathbf{b}_{r-1}^*)$; consequently $\det(\mathcal{L}_{[l:r]}) = \prod_{i=l}^{r-1} \|\mathbf{b}_i^*\|$. When working with the projected sublattice $\mathcal{L}_{[l:r]}$ and the associated basis $\mathbf{B}_{[l:r]}$ we say that we work in the *context* $[l : r]$.

The Shortest Vector Problem. The computationally hard problem on which lattice-based cryptography is based relates to the Shortest Vector Problem (SVP), which given a basis asks for a non-zero lattice vector of minimal length. More specifically, security depends on approximate versions of SVP, where we only try to find a non-zero lattice vector at most a factor poly(d) longer than the minimal length. However, via block reduction techniques like (D)BKZ [SE94, MW16] or slide reduction [GN08, ALNSD20], the approximate version can be reduced to a polynomial number of exact SVP instances in a lower dimension.

Definition 1 (Shortest Vector Problem (SVP)). *Given a basis* $\mathbf{B}$ *of a lattice* $\mathcal{L}$*, find a non-zero lattice vector* $\mathbf{v} \in \mathcal{L}$ *of minimal length* $\lambda_1(\mathcal{L}) := \min_{0 \neq \mathbf{w} \in \mathcal{L}} \|\mathbf{w}\|$.

[1] https://github.com/fplll/g6k/pull/61.
[2] https://github.com/WvanWoerden/G6K-GPU-Tensor.

For the purpose of cryptanalysis, SVP instances are typically assumed to be random, in the sense that they are distributed close to the Haar measure [GM03]. While the exact distribution is irrelevant, it is assumed for analysis that these instances follow the Gaussian Heuristic for 'nice' volumes K; which is widely verified to be true for lattices following the Haar measure.

Heuristic 1 (The Gaussian Heuristic (GH)). *Let $K \subset \mathbb{R}^d$ be a measurable body, then the number $|K \cap \mathcal{L}|$ of lattice points in K is approximately equal to $Vol(K)/\det(\mathcal{L})$.*

Note that the number of lattice points the Gaussian Heuristic indicates is exactly the expected number of lattice points in a random translation of K. When applying the Gaussian Heuristic to a d-dimensional ball of volume $\det(\mathcal{L})$ we obtain that the minimal length $\lambda_1(\mathcal{L})$ is approximately the radius of this ball, which asymptotically means that $\lambda_1(\mathcal{L}) \approx \sqrt{d/(2\pi e)} \cdot \det(\mathcal{L})^{1/d}$. For a lattice $\mathcal{L} \subset \mathbb{R}^d$ we denote this radius by $\mathrm{gh}(\mathcal{L})$, and to shorten notation we denote $\mathrm{gh}(l : r) := \mathrm{gh}(\mathcal{L}_{[l:r]})$. In practice for random lattices the minimal length deviates at most 5% from the predicted value starting around dimension 50, and even less in larger dimensions [GNR10, Che13]. Note that a ball of radius $\delta \cdot \mathrm{gh}(\mathcal{L})$ contains an exponential number of δ^d lattice vectors not much longer than the minimal length. We say that a list of lattice vectors *saturates* a volume K if it contains some significant ratio (say 50%) of the lattice vectors in $\mathcal{L} \cap K$ as predicted by the Gaussian Heuristic.

Lifting and Dimensions for Free. We discuss how to change context without increasing the length of vectors too much. Extending the context to the right (from $[l : r]$ to $[l : r + k]$) is merely following the inclusion $\mathcal{L}_{[l:r]} \subset \mathcal{L}_{[l:r+k]}$. Extending the context on the left is more involved. To *lift* a vector $\mathbf{v}$ from $\mathcal{L}_{[l:r]}$ to $\mathcal{L}_{[l-k:r]}$ for $0 \leq k \leq l$ we have to undo the projections away from $\mathbf{b}^*_{l-k}, \ldots, \mathbf{b}^*_{l-1}$. Such a lift is not unique, e.g., if $\mathbf{w} \in \mathcal{L}_{[l-k:r]}$ projects to $\mathbf{v}$, then so would the infinite number of lattice vectors $\mathbf{w} - \mathbf{c}$ with $\mathbf{c} \in \mathcal{L}_{[l-k:l]}$, and our goal is to find a rather short one.

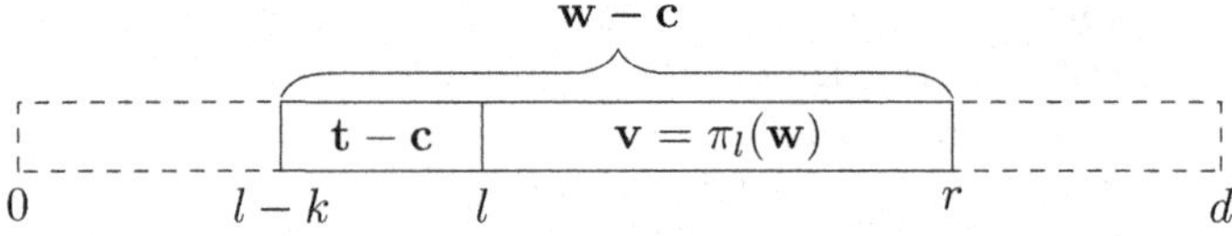

Note that we can orthogonally decompose any lift as $\mathbf{w} - \mathbf{c} = (\mathbf{t} - \mathbf{c}) + \mathbf{v}$ with $\mathbf{t} \in \mathrm{span}(\mathcal{L}_{[l-k:l]}), \mathbf{c} \in \mathcal{L}_{[l-k:l]}$ and $\mathbf{v} \in \mathcal{L}_{[l:r]}$. So each lift has squared length $\|\mathbf{t} - \mathbf{c}\|^2 + \|\mathbf{v}\|^2$ and to minimize this we need to find a lattice vector $\mathbf{c} \in \mathcal{L}_{[l-k:l]}$ that lies close to $\mathbf{t}$. Note that even if we find a closest lattice point the added squared length $\|\mathbf{t} - \mathbf{c}\|^2$ is lower bounded by $\mathrm{dist}^2(\mathbf{t}, \mathcal{L}_{[l-k:l]})$. Instances for which this distance is very small are better known as δ-BDD (Bounded Distance Decoding) instances, where δ indicates the maximum distance of the target to the lattice.

Finding a close lattice point is at least as hard as finding a short vector, so for optimal lifts one would need the dimension k to stay small. E.g., for a 1-dimensional lattice the problem is equivalent to integer rounding. A famous polynomial time algorithm to find a somewhat close lattice point is Babai's nearest plane algorithm: lift in 1-dimensional steps $[l : r] \to [l-1 : r] \to \cdots \to [l-k : r]$, greedily finding the closest lattice point in the 1-dimensional lattices $\mathbf{b}^*_{l-1}\mathbb{Z}, \ldots, \mathbf{b}^*_{l-k}\mathbb{Z}$. Babai's nearest plane algorithm finds a lattice point at squared distance at most $\frac{1}{4}\sum_{i=l-k}^{l-1} \|\mathbf{b}^*_i\|^2$, and always returns the closest lattice point for δ-BDD instances with $\delta \leq \frac{1}{2}\min_{l-k\leq i<l} \|\mathbf{b}^*_i\|$.

Lifting vectors to a larger context on the left increases their length. However under reasonable assumptions one can think of $\|\mathbf{b}^*_0\|, \ldots, \|\mathbf{b}^*_{d-1}\|$ as a decreasing sequence, which means that the minimal length over the extended context can be much larger than that of the original under the Gaussian Heuristic. So even though a vector becomes larger from lifting in the absolute sense, it can actually become shorter relatively to the context. Consequently lifting many short lattice vectors from $\mathcal{L}_{[l:d]}$ can result in finding a shortest vector in the full lattice $\mathcal{L}_{[0:d]} = \mathcal{L}$. Note that such a successful lift corresponds exactly to BDD instances, as the added length cannot be too large. When lifting a single-exponential number of short vectors, then l can be as large as $O(d/\log(d))$ [Duc18]. So for SVP algorithms that happen to find an exponential number of short vectors (instead of just a shortest), it suffices to run in a lower dimension; luckily lattice sieving algorithms do precisely that, essentially getting $O(d/\log(d))$ dimensions for free.

Lattice Sieving. Lattice sieving algorithms are among the current best asymptotic algorithms to solve SVP, running in single exponential time and memory. Sieving algorithms start with an exponentially large database of lattice vectors and try to find sums and differences of these vectors that are relatively short. These shorter combinations, which we call *reductions*, are inserted back into the database, possibly replacing longer vectors. The search for reductions is repeated until the database contains many short vectors, among which (hopefully) one of minimal length. As we do not know the exact length of the shortest vector a priori we need to fall back to alternative stopping conditions. In line with the dimensions for free technique explained before it makes sense to stop when the database saturates a ball with some *saturation radius* R, i.e., when the database contains a significant ratio of the short lattice vectors of length at most R. A simple sieving algorithm is summarized in Algorithm 1.

Provably solving SVP with lattice sieving leads to many technical problems like showing that we can actually find enough short combinations and in particular that they are new, i.e., they are not present in our database yet; unfortunately side-stepping these technicalities leads to high time and memory complexities [AKS01, MV10, PS09]. In contrast there are also sieving algorithms based mainly on the Gaussian and similar heuristics and these do fall in the practical regime. The first and simplest of these practical sieving algorithms by Nguyen and Vidick uses a database of $N = (4/3)^{d/2+o(d)} = 2^{0.2075d+o(d)}$ vectors and runs in time $N^{2+o(1)} = 2^{0.415d+o(d)}$ by repeatedly checking all pairs $\mathbf{v} \pm \mathbf{w}$ [NV08]. The database size of $(4/3)^{d/2+o(d)}$ is the minimal number of vectors that is needed in order to keep finding enough shorter pairs, and eventually saturate the ball of radius of $\sqrt{4/3} \cdot \mathrm{gh}(\mathcal{L})$. In a line of works [Laa15,BGJ15,BL16,BDGL16] the time complexity was gradually improved to $2^{0.292d+o(d)}$ by nearest neighbour searching techniques to find close pairs more efficiently. Instead of checking all pairs they first apply some bucketing strategy in which close vectors are more likely to fall into the same bucket. By only considering the somewhat-close pairs inside each bucket, the total number of checked pairs can be decreased. In order to lower the memory requirement of $2^{0.2075d+o(d)}$ one can also look at triplets of vectors in addition to pairs. This leads to a time-memory trade-off; lowering the memory cost while increasing the computational cost. The current best triple sieve with minimal memory $2^{0.1887d+o(d)}$ takes time $2^{0.3588d+o(d)}$ [HKL18].

2.2 The General Sieve Kernel

The General Sieve Kernel (G6K) [ADH+19] is a lattice reduction framework based on sieving algorithms that is designed to be 'stateful' instead of treating sieving as a black-box SVP oracle. This encompasses recent algorithmic progress like progressive sieving and dimensions for free. Besides an abstract state machine that allows to easily describe many reduction strategies, it also includes an open-source implementation that broke several new TU Darmstadt SVP Challenges [SG10] up to dimension 155. This implementation is multi-threaded and low-level optimized and includes many of the implementation tricks from the lattice sieving literature and some more. In this section we recall the state and instructions of G6K.

Algorithm 1: Lattice sieving algorithm.

Input : A basis $\mathbf{B}$ of a lattice $\mathcal{L}$, list size N and a saturation radius R.
Output: A list L of short vectors saturating the ball of radius R.

Sample a list $L \subset \mathcal{L}$ of size N.
while *L does not saturate the ball of radius R* **do**
  for *every pair* $\mathbf{v}, \mathbf{w} \in L$ **do**
    if $\mathbf{v} - \mathbf{w} \notin L$ ***and*** $\|\mathbf{v} - \mathbf{w}\| < \max_{\mathbf{u} \in L} \|\mathbf{u}\|$ **then**
      Replace a longest element of L by $\mathbf{v} - \mathbf{w}$.
return L

State. Naturally, the state includes a lattice basis $\mathbf{B} \in \mathbb{Z}^{d \times d}$ and its corresponding Gram-Schmidt basis $\tilde{\mathbf{B}}$. The current state keeps track of a *sieving context* $[l : r]$ and a *lifting context* $[\kappa : r]$. In the remainder of this work the sieving dimension will be denoted by $n := r - l$. There is a database L containing N lattice vectors from the sieving context. To conclude G6K also keeps track of good insertion candidates $\mathbf{i}_\kappa, \ldots, \mathbf{i}_l$ for the corresponding positions in the current lattice basis.

Instructions. In order to move between several contexts there are several instructions like EXTEND RIGHT, SHRINK LEFT and EXTEND LEFT. To avoid invalidating the database the vectors are lifted to the new context as explained in Sect. 2.1, keeping the lifted vectors somewhat short. The INSERTION instruction inserts one of the insertion candidates back into the basis $\mathbf{B}$, replacing another basis vector, and the Gram-Schmidt basis $\tilde{\mathbf{B}}$ is updated correspondingly. By some carefully chosen transformations and by moving to the slightly smaller sieving context $[l+1:r]$ we can recycle most of the database after an insertion. We can also SHRINK the database by throwing away the longest vectors or GROW it by sampling new (long) vectors. The SIEVE instruction reduces vectors in the database until saturation of a ball of a given radius. G6K also allows for well-chosen vectors that are encountered during sieving to be lifted from the sieving context $[l:r]$ to hopefully short vectors in the lifting context $[\kappa:r]$, and storing the best insertion candidates. The SIEVE instruction is agnostic about the sieving algorithm used, which allows to relatively easily implement and then compare sieving algorithms with each other, while letting G6K take care of global strategies.

Global Strategies. The implementation of G6K consists of a high level `Python` layer and a low-level `C++` layer. The earlier mentioned instructions can be called and parametrized from the `Python` layer, while the core implementation consists of highly optimized `C++` code. This allows one to quickly experiment with different global strategies. An important global strategy is known as the *pump up*: start in a small context of say $[d-40:d]$ and alternate the EXTEND LEFT, GROW and SIEVE instructions until the context reaches a certain dimension (passed as a parameter). Note that the sieve in each dimension already starts with a database consisting of many relatively short vectors, thus taking significantly less iterations to complete. This technique is also known as *progressive sieving* [Duc18, LM18] and gives a significant practical speed-up. A full *pump* consists of a pump up followed by a *pump down*: repeat the INSERTION instruction to improve the basis while making the context smaller again, and optionally combine this with the SIEVE instruction to find better insertion candidates. To solve SVP-instances among other things G6K combines such pumps in a *workout*, which is a sequence of longer and longer pumps, until a short enough vector is found in the full context by lifting. Each pump improves the quality of the basis, which as a result lowers the expected length increase from lifting, making consequent pumps faster and simultaneously improving the probability to find a short vector in the full context.

G6K Sieve Implementations. The current open-source implementation of G6K contains multiple sieving algorithms that implement the SIEVE instruction. There are single-threaded implementations of the Nguyen–Vidick sieve (`nv`) [NV08] and Gauss sieve (`gauss`) [MV10], mostly for testing purposes. Furthermore G6K includes a fully multi-threaded and low-level optimized version of the Becker–Gama–Joux (BGJ) sieve with a single bucketing layer (`bgj1`) [BGJ15].

The filtering techniques from `bgj1` were also extended and used in a triple sieve implementation (`triple`) [BLS16,HK17]. This implementation considers both pairs and triples and its behaviour automatically adjusts based on the database size, allowing for a continuous time-memory trade-off between the (pair) sieve `bgj1` and a full triple sieve with minimal memory. Note that the asymptotically best sieve algorithm, which we will refer to as BDGL, has been implemented before [BDGL16,MLB17], but not inside of G6K.

Data Representation. Given that lattice sieving uses an exponential number of vectors, it is of practical importance how much data is stored per vector in the database. G6K stores for each lattice vector $\mathbf{v} = \mathbf{B}\mathbf{x} \in \mathbb{R}^n$ the (16-bit integer) coordinates $\mathbf{x} \in \mathbb{Z}^n$ as well as the (32-bit floating-point) Gram-Schmidt representation $\mathbf{y} = (\langle \mathbf{v}, \mathbf{b}_i^* \rangle / \|\mathbf{b}_i^*\|)_i \in \mathbb{R}^n$ normalized by the Gaussian Heuristic of the current sieving context. The latter representation is used to quickly compute inner products between any two lattice vectors in the database. On top of that other preprocessed information is stored for each vector, like the corresponding lift target $\mathbf{t}$ in $\mathrm{span}(\mathcal{L}_{[\kappa:l]})$, the squared length, a 256-bit SimHash (see [Cha02,FBB+14,Duc18]) and a 64-bit hash as identifier. In order to sort the database on length, without having to move the entries around, there is also a lightweight database that only stores for each vector the length, a SimHash and the corresponding database index. A hash table keeps track of all hash identifiers, which are derived from the $\mathbf{x}$-coordinates, in order to quickly check for duplicates. All of this quickly adds up to a total of $\approx 2^{10}$ bytes per vector in a sieving dimension of $n = 128$.

3 Architecture

3.1 GPU Device Architecture

In this section we give a short summary of the NVIDIA Turing GPU architecture on which our implementations and experiments are based. During the write-up of this paper a new generation named Ampere was launched, doubling many of the performance metrics mentioned here.

CUDA Cores and Memory. A NVIDIA GPU can have up to thousands of so-called *CUDA cores* organized into several execution units called Streaming Multiprocessors (*SM*). These SM use their many CUDA cores (e.g. 64) to service many more resident *threads* (e.g. 1024), in order to hide latencies of computation and memory operations. Threads are bundled per 32 in a *warp*, that follow the single-instruction multiple-data paradigm.

The execution of a GPU program, also called a *kernel*, consists out of multiple *blocks*, each consisting of some warps. Each individual block is executed on any available single SM. The GPU RAM, also called *global memory*, can be accessed by all cores. Global memory operations always pass through a GPU-wide L2

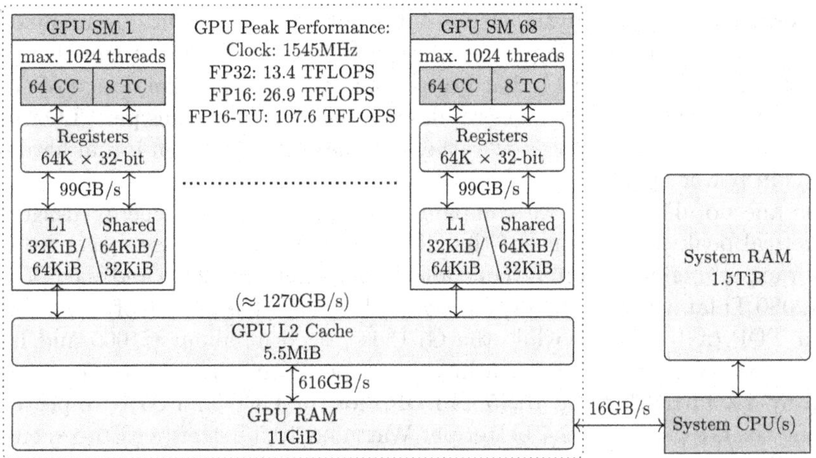

Fig. 1. Device architecture of the NVIDIA RTX 2080 Ti used in this work.

cache. In addition, each SM benefits from a individual L1 cache and offers an addressable *shared memory* that can only be used by threads in that block.

In this work we focus on the NVIDIA RTX2080 Ti that we used, whose architecture is depicted in Fig. 1. While a high-end CPU with many cores can reach a performance in the order of a few tera floating point operations per second (TFLOPS), the RTX2080 Ti can achieve 13 TFLOPS for 32-bit floating point operations on its regular CUDA cores.

To implement GPU kernel functions for a NVIDIA GPU one can use CUDA [NBGS08,NVF20] which is an extension of the `C/C++` and `FORTRAN` programming languages. A kernel is executed by a specified number of threads grouped into blocks, all with the same code and input parameters. During execution each thread learns that it is thread t inside block b and one needs to use this information to distribute the work. For example when loading data from global memory we can let thread t read the t-th integer at an offset computed from b, because the requested memory inside each block is contiguous such a memory request can be executed very efficiently; such memory request are known as *coalescing* reads or writes and they are extremely important to obtain an efficient kernel.

Tensor Cores. Driven by the machine learning domain there have been tremendous efforts in the past few years to speed up low-precision matrix multiplications. This lead to the so-called Tensor cores, that are now standard in high-end NVIDIA GPUs. Tensor cores are optimized for 4×4 matrix multiplication and also allow a trade-off between performance and precision. In particular we are interested in the 16-bit floating point format `fp16` with a 5-bit exponent and a 10-bit mantissa, for which the tensor cores obtain an $8\times$ speed-up over regular 32-bit operations on CUDA cores.

Efficiency. For cryptanalytic purposes it is not only important how many operations are needed to solve a problem instance, but also how cost effective these operations can be executed in hardware. The massively-parallel design of GPUs with many relatively simple cores results in large efficiency gains per FLOP compared to CPU designs with a few rather complex cores; both in initial hardware cost as in power efficiency.

As anecdotal evidence we compare the acquisition cost, energy usage and theoretical peak performance of the CPU and GPU in the new server we used for our experiments: the Intel Xeon Gold 6248 launched in 2019 and the NVIDIA RTX2080 Ti launched in 2018 respectively. The CPU has a price of about €2500 and a TDP of 150 Watt, while the GPU is priced at about €1000 and has a TDP of 260 Watt. For 32-bit floating point operations the peak performance is given by 3.2 TFLOPS[3] and 13.45 TFLOPS for the CPU and GPU respectively, making the GPU a factor 2.4 better per Watt and 10.5 better per Euro spend on acquisition. For general 16-bit floating point operations these number double for the GPU, while the CPU obtains no extra speed-up (one actually has to convert the data back to 32-bit). When considering the specialized Tensor cores with 16-bit precision the GPU has a theoretical peak performance of 107.6 TFLOPS, improving by a factor 19.4 per Watt and a factor 84 per Euro spend on acquisition compared to the CPU.

3.2 Sieve Design

The great efficiency of the GPU is only of use if the state-of-the-art algorithms are compatible with the massively-parallel architecture and the specific low-precision operations of the Tensor cores. To show this we extended the lattice sieving implementation of G6K. We will focus our main discussion on the sieving part, as the other G6K instructions are asymptotically irrelevant and relatively straightforward to accelerate on a GPU (which we also did).

All of our CPU multi-threaded and GPU-powered sieve implementations follow a similar design (cf. Fig. 2) consisting out of three sequential phases: bucketing, reducing and result insertion. We call the execution of this triplet an *iteration* and these iterations are repeated until the desired saturation is achieved. Note that our sieves are not 'queued' sieves such as the Gauss-Sieve of [MV10] and the previous record setting `triple_sieve`; this relaxation aligns with the batched nature of GPU processing and allows to implement an asymptotically optimal BDGL-like sieve [BDGL16], without major memory overhead.

Bucketing. During the bucketing phase, the database is subdivided in several buckets $B_1, \ldots, B_m \subset L$, each containing relatively close vectors. We do not necessarily bucket our full database, as some vectors might be too large to be interesting for the reduction phase in the first few iterations. For each bucket we collect the database indices of the included vectors. For the sieves we consider,

[3] With 64 FLOP per core per cycle using two `AVX-512` FMA units and a maximal clock frequency of 2500 MHz when using `AVX-512` on all 20 cores.

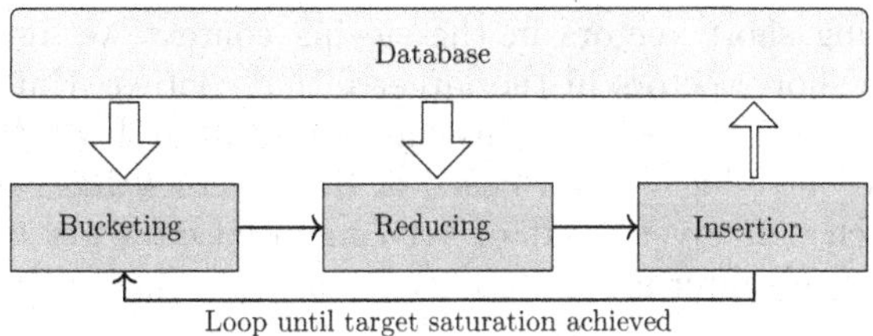

Fig. 2. High level diagram of the implemented Sieving process.

these buckets can geometrically be interpreted as spherical caps or cones with for each bucket B_k an explicit or implicit *bucket center* $\mathbf{c}_k \in \mathbb{R}^n$ indicating its direction. For each included vector $\mathbf{v} \in B_k$, we also store the inner product $\langle \mathbf{c}_k, \mathbf{v} \rangle$ with the bucket center, which is obtained freely from the bucketing process. Note that a vector may be included in several buckets, something which we tightly control by the *multi-bucket* parameter, whose value we will denote by M. The optimal amount of buckets m and the expected number of vectors in a bucket differs for each of our bucketing implementations. In Sect. 4, we further exhibit our different bucketing implementations and compare their performance and quality.

Reducing. During the reduction phase, we try to find all close pairs of lattice vectors inside each bucket, i.e., at distance at most some *length bound* ℓ. Using negation, we orient the vectors inside a bucket into the direction of the bucket center based on the earlier computed inner product $\langle \mathbf{c}_k, \mathbf{v}_i \rangle$. In case the bucketing center $\mathbf{c}_k$ is itself a lattice vector (as can be the case for BGJ-like sieves, but not for BDGL), it is also interesting to check if $\mathbf{c}_k - \mathbf{v}_i - \mathbf{v}_j$ is a short lattice vector, leading to a triple reduction [HK17].

For each bucket B_k, we compute all pairwise inner products $\langle \mathbf{v}_i, \mathbf{v}_j \rangle$ for $\mathbf{v}_i, \mathbf{v}_j \in B_k$. Together with the already computed lengths $\|\mathbf{v}_i\|, \|\mathbf{v}_j\|, \|\mathbf{c}_k\|$ and inner products $\langle \mathbf{c}_k, \mathbf{v}_i \rangle, \langle \mathbf{c}_k, \mathbf{b}_j \rangle$ we can then efficiently decide if $\mathbf{v}_i - \mathbf{v}_j$ or $\mathbf{c}_k - \mathbf{v}_i - \mathbf{v}_j$ is short. Note that we compute the length of both the pair and the triple essentially from a single inner product computation. We return the indices of pairs and triplets that result in a vector of length at most the length bound ℓ, together with the length of the new vector. In Sect. 5 we further discuss the reduction phase, and in Appendix B and exhibit implementation details of our reduction kernel on the GPU using low-precision Tensor cores.

The number of inner products we have to compute per bucket grows quadratically in the bucket size $|B_k|$, while the number of buckets only decreases linearly in the bucket size. Therefore, one would in principle want many buckets that are rather small and of high quality, improving the probability that a checked pair actually gives a reduction. For a fixed bucketing algorithm more buckets generally increase the cost of the bucketing phase, while decreasing the cost of the reduction phase due to smaller bucket sizes. We try to balance the cost of these phases to obtain optimal performance.

Next to finding short vectors in the sieving context we also want to find pairs that lift to short vectors in the larger lifting context. Unfortunately it is too costly to just lift all pairs as this has a cost of at least $\Theta((l-\kappa)^2)$ per pair. In Sect. 6 we introduce a filter based on dual vectors that can be computed efficiently for each pair given a bit of pre-computed data per vector. The few pairs that survive this filter are more likely to lift to a short vector and we only lift those pairs.

Result Insertion. After the sieving part we have a list of tuples with indices and the corresponding length of the new vector they represent. The hash identifier of the new vector can efficiently be recomputed by linearity of the hash function and we check for duplicates in our current database. For all non-duplicate vectors we then compute their $\mathbf{x}$-representation. After all new entries are created they are inserted back in the database, replacing entries of greater length.

3.3 Data Storage and Movement

Recall from Sect. 2.2 that G6K stores quite some data per vector such as the coefficients $\mathbf{x}$ in terms of the basis, a Gram-Schmidt representation $\mathbf{y}$, the lift target $\mathbf{t}$, a SimHash, and more. Theoretically we could remove all data except the $\mathbf{x}$-representation and compute all other information on-the-fly. However, as most of this other information has a cost of $\Theta(n^2)$ to compute from the $\mathbf{x}$-representation this would mean a significant computational overhead, for example increasing the cost of an inner product from $\Theta(n)$ to $\Theta(n^2)$. Also given the limited amount of performance a CPU has compared to a GPU we certainly want to minimize the amount of such overhead for the CPU. By recomputing at some well chosen points on the GPU, our accelerated sieves minimize this overhead, while only storing the $\mathbf{x}$-representation, length and a hash identifier per vector, leading to an approximately 60% reduction in storage compared to the base G6K implementation. As a result we can sieve in significantly larger dimensions with the same amount of system RAM.

While GPUs have an enormous amount of computational power, the memory bandwidth between the database in system RAM and the GPU's RAM is severely limited. These are so imbalanced that one can only reach theoretical peak performance with Tensor cores if every byte that is transferred to the GPU is used in at least 2^{13} computations. A direct result is that reducing in small buckets is (up to some threshold) bandwidth limited. Growing the bucket size in this regime would not increase the wall-clock time of the reduction phase, while at the same time considering more pairs. So larger buckets are preferred, in our hardware for a single active GPU the threshold seems to be around a bucket size of 2^{14}, matching the 2^{13} computations per byte ratio. Because in our hardware each pair of GPUs share their connection to the CPU, halving the bandwidth for each, the threshold grows to around 2^{15} when using all GPUs simultaneously. The added benefit of large buckets is that the conversion from the $\mathbf{x}$-representation to the $\mathbf{y}$-representation, which can be done directly on the

GPU, is negligible compared to computing the many pairwise inner products. To further limit the movement of data we only return indices instead of a full vector; if we find a short pair $\mathbf{v}_i - \mathbf{v}_j$ on the GPU we only return i, j and $\|\mathbf{v}_i - \mathbf{v}_j\|^2$. The new $\mathbf{x}$-representation and hash identifier can efficiently (in $O(n)$) be computed on the CPU directly from the database.

4 Bucketing

The difference between different lattice sieve algorithms mainly lies in their bucketing method. These methods differ in their time complexity and their performance in catching close pairs. In this section we exhibit a Tensor-GPU accelerated bucketing implementation `triple_gpu` similar to `bgj1` and `triple` inspired by [BGJ15,HK17], and two optimized implementations of the asymptotically best known bucketing algorithm [BDGL16], one for CPU making use of `AVX2` (`bdgl`) and one for GPU (`bdgl_gpu`). After this we show the practical performance difference between these bucketing methods.

4.1 BGJ-like Bucketing (`triple_gpu`)

The bucketing method used in `bgj1` and `triple` is based on spherical caps directed by explicit bucket centers that are also lattice points. To start the bucketing phase we first choose some bucket centers $\mathbf{b}_1, \dots, \mathbf{b}_m$ from the database; preferably the directions of these vectors are somewhat uniformly distributed over the sphere. Then each vector $\mathbf{v} \in L$ in our database is associated to bucket $B_{k_\mathbf{v}}$ with

$$k_\mathbf{v} = \arg\max_{1 \le k' \le m} \left| \left\langle \frac{\mathbf{b}_{k'}}{\|\mathbf{b}_{k'}\|}, \mathbf{v} \right\rangle \right| .$$

We relax this condition somewhat by the multi bucket parameter M, to associate a vector to the best M buckets. In this we differ from the original versions of `bgj1` and `triple` [BGJ15,HK17,ADH+19] in that they use a fixed filtering threshold on the angle $|\langle \mathbf{b}_k / \|\mathbf{b}_k\|, \mathbf{v} / \|\mathbf{v}\| \rangle|$. As a result our buckets do not exactly match spherical caps, but they should still resemble them; in particular such a change does not affect the asymptotic analysis. We chose for this alternation as this fixes the amount of buckets per vector, which reduced some communication overhead in our highly parallel GPU implementations.

In each iteration the new bucket centers are chosen, normalized and stored once on each GPU. Then we stream our whole database $\mathbf{v}_1, \dots, \mathbf{v}_N$ through the GPUs and try to return for each vector the indices of the M closest normalized bucket vectors and their corresponding inner products $\langle \mathbf{v}_i, \mathbf{b}_k \rangle$. For efficiency reasons the bucket centers are distributed over 16 threads and each thread stores only the best encountered bucket for each vector. Then we return the buckets from the best $M \le 16$ threads, which are not necessarily the best M buckets overall. The main computational part of computing the pairwise inner products is similar to the Tensor-GPU implementation for reducing, and we refer to Appendix B for further implementation details.

The cost of bucketing is $O(N \cdot n)$ per bucket. Assuming that the buckets are of similar size $|B_k| \approx M \cdot N/m$ the cost to reduce is $O(\frac{M \cdot N}{m} \cdot n)$ per bucket. To balance these costs for an optimal runtime one should choose $m \sim M \cdot \sqrt{N}$ buckets per iteration. For the regular 2-sieve strategy with an asymptotic memory usage of $N = (4/3)^{n/2+o(n)} = 2^{0.208n+o(n)}$ this leads to a total complexity of $2^{0.349n+o(n)}$ using as little as $2^{0.037n+o(n)}$ iterations. Note that in low dimensions we might prefer a lower number of buckets to achieve the minimum required bucket size to reach peak efficiency during the reduction phase.

4.2 BDGL-Like Bucketing (bdgl and bdgl_gpu)

The asymptotically optimal bucketing method from [BDGL16] is similar to bgj1 as in that it is based on spherical caps. The difference is that in contrast to bgj1 the bucket centers are not arbitrary but structured, allowing to find the best bucket without having to compute the inner product with each individual bucket center.

Following [BDGL16], such a bucketing strategy would look as follows. First we split the dimension n into k smaller blocks (say, $k = 2, 3$ or 4 in practice) of similar dimensions $n_1, \ldots, n_k$ that sum up to n. In order to randomize this splitting over different iterations one first applies a random orthonormal transformation $\mathbf{Q}$ to each input vector. Then the set C of bucket centers is constructed as a direct product of random local bucket centers, i.e., $C = C_1 \times \pm C_2 \cdots \times \pm C_k$ with $C_b \subset \mathbb{R}^{n_b}$. Note that for a vector $\mathbf{v}$ we only have to pick the closest local bucket centers to find the closest global bucket center, implicitly considering $m = 2^{k-1} \prod_b |C_b|$ bucket centers at the cost of only $\sum_b |C_b| \approx O(m^{1/k})$ inner products. By sorting the local inner products we can also efficiently find all bucket centers within a certain angle or say the closest M bucket centers. With similar reasons as for triple_gpu we always return the closest M bucket centers for each vector instead of a fixed threshold based on the angle. While for a fixed number of buckets m we can expect some performance loss compared to bgj1 as the bucket centers are not perfectly random, this does not influence the asymptotics.[4]

To optimize the parameters we again balance the cost of bucketing and reducing. Note that for $k = 1$ we essentially obtain bgj1 with buckets of size $O(N^{1/2})$ and a time complexity of $2^{0.349n+o(n)}$. For $k = 2$ or $k = 3$ the buckets become smaller of size $O(N^{1/3})$ and $O(N^{1/4})$ respectively and of higher quality, leading to a time complexity of $2^{0.3294n+o(n)}$ and $2^{0.3198n+o(n)}$ respectively. By letting k slowly grow, e.g., $k = O(\log(n))$ there will only be a sub-exponential $2^{o(n)}$ number of vectors in each bucket, leading to the best known time complexity of $2^{0.292n+o(n)}$. Note however that a lot of sub-exponential factors might be hidden inside this $o(n)$, and thus for practical dimensions a rather small value of k might give best results.

We will take several liberties with the above strategy to address practical efficiency consideration and fine-tune the algorithm. For example, for a pure CPU

[4] The analysis of [BDGL16, Theorem 5.1] shows this is up to a sub-exponential loss.

implementation we may prefer to make the average bucket size somewhat larger than the $\approx N^{1/(k+1)}$ vectors that the theory prescribes; this will improve cache re-use when searching for reducible pairs inside buckets. In our GPU implementation, we make this average bucket size even larger, to prevent memory bottlenecks in the reduction phase.

Furthermore, we optimize the construction of the local bucket centers $\mathbf{c} \in C_i$ to allow for a fast computation of the local inner products $\langle \mathbf{c}, \mathbf{v} \rangle$. While [BDGL16] choose the local bucket centers C_i uniformly at random, we apply some extra structure to compute each inner product with a vector $\mathbf{v}$ in time $O(\log(n_i))$ instead of $O(n_i)$. The main idea is to use the (Fast) Hadamard Transform $\mathcal{H}$ on say $32 \leq n_i$ coefficients of $\mathbf{v}$. Note that this computes the inner product between $\mathbf{v}$ and 32 orthogonal ternary vectors, which implicitly form the bucket centers, using only $32 \log_2(32)$ additions or subtractions. To obtain more than 32 different buckets we permute and negate coefficients of $\mathbf{v}$ in a pseudo-random way before applying $\mathcal{H}$ again. This strategy can be heavily optimized both for CPU using the vectorized `AVX2` instruction set (`bdgl`) and for GPU by using special warp-wide instructions (`bdgl_gpu`). In particular this allows a CPU core to compute an inner product every 1.3 to 1.6 cycles for $17 \leq n_i \leq 128$. For further implementation details we refer to Appendix A.

Since the writing of this report, our CPU implementation of `bdgl` has been integrated in G6K, with further improvements.[5] As it may be of independant interest, the `AVX2` bucketer is also provided as a standalone program.[6]

4.3 Quality Comparison

In this section we compare the practical bucketing quality of the BGJ- and BDGL-like bucketing methods we implemented. More specifically, we consider `triple_gpu`, `1-bdgl_gpu` and `2-bdgl_gpu` where the latter two are instances of `bdgl_gpu` with $k = 1$ and $k = 2$ blocks respectively. Their quality is compared to the idealized theoretical performance of `bgj1` with uniformly distributed bucket centers.[7] For `triple_gpu`, we follow the Gaussian Heuristic and sample bucket centers whose directions are uniformly distributed. As a result the quality difference between `triple_gpu` and the idealized version highlights the quality loss resulting from our implementation decisions. Recall that compared to `bgj1` the main difference is that for every vector we return the M closest bucket centers instead of using a fixed threshold for each bucket. Also these are not exactly the M closest bucket centers, as we first distribute the buckets over 16 threads and only store a single close bucket per thread. For our `bdgl_gpu` implementation the buckets are distributed over 32 threads and we add to this that the bucket centers are not random but somewhat structured by the Hadamard construction.

[5] https://github.com/fplll/g6k/pull/61.

[6] https://github.com/lducas/AVX2-BDGL-bucketer.

[7] Volumes of caps and wedges for predicting the idealized behavior where extracted from [AGPS19], and more specifically https://github.com/jschanck/eprint-2019-1161/blob/main/probabilities.py.

To compare the geometric quality of bucketing implementations, we measure how uniform vectors are distributed over the buckets and how many close pairs end up in at least one common bucket. The first measure is important as the reduction cost does not depend on the square of the average bucket size $\left(\frac{1}{m}\sum_{k=1}^{m}|B_k|\right)^2$, which is fixed, but on the average of the squared bucket size $\frac{1}{m}\sum_{k=1}^{m}|B_k|^2$, which is only minimal if the vectors are equally distributed over the buckets. For all our experiments we observed at most an overhead of 0.2% compared to perfectly equal bucket sizes and thus we will further ignore this part of the quality assessment. To measure the second part efficiently we sample 2^{20} close unit pairs $(\mathbf{x}, \mathbf{y}) \in \mathcal{S}^n \times \mathcal{S}^n$ uniformly at random such that $\langle \mathbf{x}, \mathbf{y} \rangle = \pm\frac{1}{2}$. Then we count the number of pairs that have at least 1 bucket in common, possibly over multiple iterations. We run these experiments with parameters that are representative for practical runs. In particular we consider (sieving) dimensions up to $n = 144$ and a database size of $N = 3.2 \cdot 2^{0.2075n}$ to compute the number of buckets given the desired average bucket size and the multi-bucket parameter M. Note that we specifically consider the geometric quality of these bucketing implementations for equivalent parameters and not the cost of the bucketing itself.

To compare the bucketing quality between the different methods and the idealized case we first consider the experimental results in graphs **a.** and **b.** of Fig. 3. Note that the bucketing methods `triple_gpu` and `1-bdgl_gpu` obtain extremely similar results overall, showing that the structured Hadamard construction is competitive with fully random bucket centers. We see a slight degradation of 5% to 20% for `triple_gpu` with respect to the idealized case as a result of not using a fixed threshold. We do however see this gap decreasing when M grows to 4 or 8, indicating that these two methods of assigning the buckets become more similar for a larger multi-bucket parameter. At $M = 16$ we see a sudden degradation for `triple_gpu` which exactly coincides with the fact that the buckets are distributed over 16 threads and we only store the closest bucket per thread. The quality loss of `2-bdgl_gpu` seems to be between 15% and 36% in the relevant dimensions, which is quite significant but reasonable given a loss potentially as large as sub-exponential [BDGL16, Theorem 5.1].

Now we focus our attention on graph **c.** of Fig. 3 to consider the influence of the average bucket size on the quality. We observe that increasing the average bucket size reduces the bucketing quality; many small buckets have a better quality than a few large ones. This is unsurprising as the asymptotically optimal BDGL sieve aims for high quality buckets of small size. Although our `k-bdgl_gpu` bucketing method has no problem with efficiently generating many small buckets, the reduction phase cannot efficiently process small buckets due to memory bottlenecks. This is the main trade-off of (our implementation of) GPU acceleration, requiring a bucket size of 2^{15} versus e.g. 2^{10} leads to a potential loss factor of 7 to 8 as shown by this graph. For `triple_gpu` this gives no major problems as for the relevant dimensions $n \geq 130$ the optimal bucket sizes are large enough. However `2-bdgl_gpu` should become faster than `bgj1` exactly by considering many smaller buckets of size $N^{1/3}$ instead of $N^{1/2}$, and a minimum

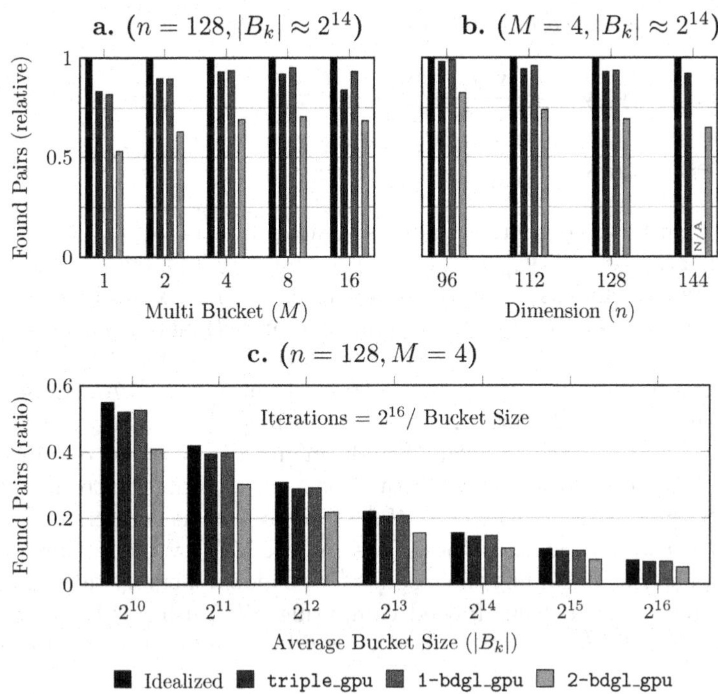

Fig. 3. Bucketing Quality Comparison. We sampled 2^{20} pairs $\mathbf{v}, \mathbf{w}$ of unit vectors such that $|\langle \mathbf{v}, \mathbf{w} \rangle| = 0.5$ and we measured how many fell into at least 1 common bucket. The number of buckets is computed based on the desired average bucket size $|B_k|$, the multi-bucket parameter M, and a representative database size of $N = 3.2 \cdot 2^{0.2075n}$. The found pairs in **a.** and **b.** are normalized w.r.t. idealized theoretical performance of `bgj1` (perfectly random spherical caps). For **c.** the number of applied iterations is varied such that the total reduction cost is fixed.

bucket size of 2^{15} shifts the practical cross-over point above dimension 130, and potentially much higher.

5 Reducing with Tensor Cores

Together with bucketing, the most computationally intensive part of sieving algorithms is that of finding reducing pairs or triples inside a bucket. We consider a bucket of s vectors $\mathbf{v}_1, \ldots, \mathbf{v}_s \in \mathbb{R}^n$ with bucket center $\mathbf{c}$. Only the $\mathbf{x}$-representations are send to the GPU and there they are converted to the 16-bit Gram-Schmidt representations $\mathbf{y}_1, \ldots, \mathbf{y}_s$ and $\mathbf{y_c}$ that are necessary to quickly compute inner products. Together with the pre-computed squared lengths $\|\mathbf{y}_1\|^2$, $\ldots$, $\|\mathbf{y}_s\|^2$ and inner products $\langle \mathbf{y_c}, \mathbf{y}_1 \rangle, \ldots, \langle \mathbf{y_c}, \mathbf{y}_s \rangle$, the goal is to find all pairs $\mathbf{y}_i - \mathbf{y}_j$ or triples $\mathbf{y_c} - \mathbf{y}_i - \mathbf{y}_j$ of length at most some bound ℓ. A simple derivation shows that this is the case if and only if

$$\text{for } \textbf{pairs:} \quad \langle \mathbf{y}_i, \mathbf{y}_j \rangle \geq \frac{\|\mathbf{y}_i\|^2 + \|\mathbf{y}_j\|^2 - \ell^2}{2}, \text{ or}$$

$$\text{for } \textbf{triples:} \quad \langle \mathbf{y}_i, \mathbf{y}_j \rangle \leq -\frac{\|\mathbf{y}_\mathbf{c}\|^2 + \|\mathbf{y}_i\|^2 + \|\mathbf{y}_j\|^2 - \ell^2 - 2\langle \mathbf{y}_\mathbf{c}, \mathbf{y}_i \rangle - 2\langle \mathbf{c}, \mathbf{y}_j \rangle}{2}.$$

And thus we need to compute all pairwise inner products $\langle \mathbf{y}_i, \mathbf{y}_j \rangle$. If we consider the matrix $\mathbf{Y} := [\mathbf{y}_1, \ldots, \mathbf{y}_s] \in \mathbb{R}^{n \times s}$ then computing all pairwise inner products is essentially the same as computing one half of the matrix product $\mathbf{Y}^t\mathbf{Y}$.

Many decades have been spend optimizing (parallel) matrix multiplication for CPUs, and this has also been a prime optimization target for GPUs. As a result we now have heavily parallelized and low-level optimized BLAS (Basic Linear Algebra Subprograms) libraries for matrix multiplication (among other things). For NVIDIA GPUs close to optimal performance can often be obtained using the proprietary cuBLAS library, or the open-source, but slightly less optimal CUTLASS library. Nevertheless the BLAS functionality is not perfectly adapted to our goal. Computing and storing the matrix $\mathbf{Y}^t\mathbf{Y}$ would require multiple gigabytes of space. Streaming the result $\mathbf{Y}^t\mathbf{Y}$ to global memory takes more time than the computation itself. Indeed computing $\mathbf{Y}^t\mathbf{Y}$ using cuBLAS does not exceed 47 TFLOPS for $n \leq 160$, and this will be even lower when also filtering the results.

For high performance, in our implementation we combined the matrix multiplication with result filtering. We made sure to only return the few indices of pairs that give an actual reduction to global memory; filtering the results locally while the computed inner products are still in registers. Nevertheless the data-movement design, e.g. how we efficiently stream the vectors $\mathbf{y}_i$ into the registers of the SMs, is heavily inspired by CUTLASS and cuBLAS. To maximize memory read throughput, we had to go around the dedicated CUDA tensor API and reverse engineer the internal representation to obtain double the read throughput. Further implementation details are discussed in Appendix A.

Efficiency. To measure the efficiency of our Tensor-accelerated GPU kernel we did two experiments: the first experiment runs only the kernel with all (converted) data already present in global memory on the GPU, while the second experiment emulates the practical efficiency by including all overhead. This overhead consists of obtaining the vectors from the database, sending them to the GPU, converting them to the appropriate representation, running the reduction kernel, recomputing the length of the resulting close pairs, and retrieving the results from the GPU. Each experiment processed a total of 2^{28} vectors of dimension 160 in a pipelined manner on a single NVIDIA RTX 2080 Ti GPU and with a representative number of 10 CPU threads. We only counted the $2n$ 16-bit floating point operations per inner product and not any of the operations necessary to transfer data or to filter and process the results. The theoretical limit for this GPU when only using Tensor cores and continuously running at boost clock speeds is 107 TFLOPS, something which is unrealistic in practice.

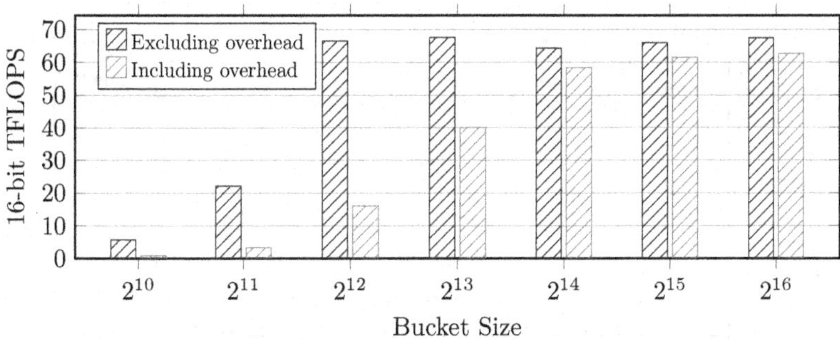

Fig. 4. Efficiency of the reduction GPU kernel for different bucket sizes on a RTX 2080 Ti, only counting the $2n$ FLOPS per inner product. The overhead includes obtaining the vectors from the database, sending them to the GPU, conversions, recomputing length at higher precision, and retrieving the results from the GPU in a pipelined manner.

The results of these experiments are displayed in Fig. 4. We see that the kernel itself reaches around 65 TFLOPS starting at a bucket size of at least 2^{12}. When including the overhead we see that the performance is significantly limited below a bucket size of 2^{13} which can fully be explained by CPU-GPU memory-bottlenecks. For bucket sizes of at least 2^{14} we see that the overhead becomes reasonably small. We observed that this threshold moves to 2^{15} when using multiple GPUs, because in our hardware the CPU-GPU bandwidth is shared per pair of GPUs.

Precision. The main drawback of the high performance of the tensor cores is that the operations are at low precision. Because the runtime of sieving algorithms is dominated by computing pairwise inner products to find reductions or for bucketing (in case of `triple_gpu`) we focus our attention on this part. Other operations like converting between representations are computationally insignificant and can easily be executed by regular CUDA cores at higher precisions. As the GPU is used as a filter to find (extremely) likely candidates for reduction, we can tolerate some relative error, say up to 2^{-7} in the computed inner product, at the loss of more false positives or missed candidates. Furthermore it is acceptable for our purposes if say 1% of the close vectors are missed because of even larger errors. In Appendix C we show under a reasonable randomized error model that problems due to precision are insignificant up to dimensions as large as $n = 2048$. This is also confirmed by practical experiments as shown in Fig. 5.

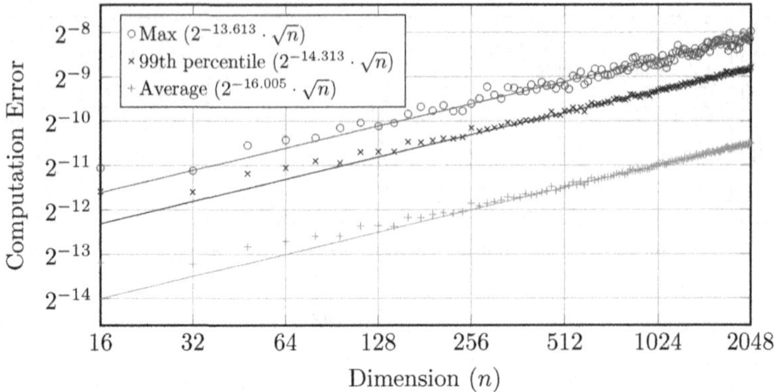

Fig. 5. Computation error $|S - \hat{S}|$ observed in dimension n over 16384 sampled pairs of unit vectors $\mathbf{y}, \mathbf{y}'$ that satisfy $S := \langle \mathbf{y}, \mathbf{y}' \rangle \approx 0.5$.

6 Filtering Lifts with Dual Hash

Let us recall the principle of the 'dimensions for free' trick [Duc18]; by lifting many short vectors in the sieving context $[l : r]$ we can recover a short(est) vector in some larger context $[l - k : r]$ for $k > 0$. The sieving implementation G6K [ADH+19] puts extra emphasis on this by lifting any short pair it encounters while reducing a bucket, even when this vector is not short enough to be added to the database. Note that G6K first filters on the length in the sieving context because lifting has a significant cost of $O(n \cdot k + k^2)$ per pair. The $O(n \cdot k)$ part to compute the corresponding target $\mathbf{t}_i - \mathbf{t}_j \in \mathbb{R}^k$ in the context $[l - k : l]$ can be amortized to $O(k)$ over all pairs by pre-computing $\mathbf{t}_1, \ldots, \mathbf{t}_s$, leaving a cost of $O(k^2)$ for the Babai nearest plane algorithm.

We went for a stronger filter with an emphasis on the extra length added by the lifting. Most short vectors will lift to rather large vectors, as by the Gaussian Heuristic we can expect an extra length of $\mathrm{gh}(l - k : l) \gg \mathrm{gh}(l - k : r)$. For the few lifts that we are actually interested in we expect an extra length of only $\delta \cdot \mathrm{gh}(l - k : l)$, for some $0 < \delta < 1$ (say $\delta \in [0.1, 0.5]$ in practice). This means that we need to catch those pairs $\mathbf{t}_i - \mathbf{t}_j$ that lie exceptionally close to the lattice $[l - k : l]$, also known as BDD instances.

More abstractly we need a filter that quickly checks if pairs are (exceptionally) close over the *torus* $\mathbb{R}^k/\mathcal{L}$. Constructing such a filter directly for this rather complex torus and our practical parameters seems to require at least quadratic time like Babai's nearest plane algorithm. Instead we introduce a *dual hash* to move the problem to the much simpler but possibly higher dimensional torus $\mathbb{R}^h/\mathbb{Z}^h$. More specifically, we will use inner products with short dual vectors to build a BDD distinguisher in the spirit of the so-called dual attack on LWE given in [MR09] (the general idea can be traced back at least to [AR05]). This is however done in a different regime, where the shortest dual vectors are very easy to find (given the small dimension of the considered lattice); we will also carefully select a subset of those dual vectors to optimize the fidelity of our filter. Recall that the dual of a lattice $\mathcal{L}$ is defined as $\mathcal{L}^* := \{\mathbf{w} \in \text{span}(\mathcal{L}) : \langle \mathbf{w}, \mathbf{v} \rangle \in \mathbb{Z} \text{ for all } \mathbf{v} \in \mathcal{L}\}$.

Definition 1 (Dual hash). For a lattice $\mathcal{L} \subset \mathbb{R}^k$, $h \geq k$ and a full (row-rank) matrix $\mathbf{D} \in \mathbb{R}^{h \times k}$ with rows in the dual $\mathcal{L}^*$, we define the dual hash

$$\mathcal{H}_{\mathbf{D}} : \mathbb{R}^k/\mathcal{L} \to \mathbb{R}^h/\mathbb{Z}^h,$$
$$\mathbf{t} \mapsto \mathbf{D}\mathbf{t}.$$

The dual hash relates distances in $\mathbb{R}^k/\mathcal{L}$ to those in $\mathbb{R}^h/\mathbb{Z}^h$.

Lemma 2. *Let $\mathcal{L} \subset \mathbb{R}^k$ be a lattice with some dual hash $\mathcal{H}_{\mathbf{D}}$. Then for any $\mathbf{t} \in \mathbb{R}^k$ we have*

$$\text{dist}(\mathcal{H}_{\mathbf{D}}(\mathbf{t}), \mathbb{Z}^h) \leq \sigma_1(\mathbf{D}) \cdot \text{dist}(\mathbf{t}, \mathcal{L}),$$

where $\sigma_1(\mathbf{D})$ denotes the largest singular value of $\mathbf{D}$.

Proof. Let $\mathbf{x} \in \mathcal{L}$ such that $\|\mathbf{x} - \mathbf{t}\| = \text{dist}(\mathbf{t}, \mathcal{L})$. By definition we have $\mathbf{D}\mathbf{x} \in \mathbb{Z}^h$ and thus $\mathcal{H}_{\mathbf{D}}(\mathbf{t}-\mathbf{x}) \equiv \mathcal{H}_{\mathbf{D}}(\mathbf{t})$. We conclude by noting that $\text{dist}(\mathcal{H}_{\mathbf{D}}(\mathbf{t}-\mathbf{x}), \mathbb{Z}^h) \leq \|\mathbf{D}(\mathbf{t} - \mathbf{x})\| \leq \sigma_1(\mathbf{D}) \|\mathbf{t} - \mathbf{x}\|$.

So if a target $\mathbf{t}$ lies very close to the lattice then $\mathcal{H}_{\mathbf{D}}(\mathbf{t})$ lies very close to $\mathbb{Z}^h$. We can use this to define a filter that passes through BDD instances.

Definition 3 (Filter). Let $\mathcal{L} \subset \mathbb{R}^k$ be a lattice with some dual hash $\mathcal{H}_{\mathbf{D}}$. For a hash bound H we define the filter function

$$\mathcal{F}_{D,H} : \mathbf{t} \mapsto \begin{cases} 1, \text{ if } \text{dist}(\mathcal{H}_{\mathbf{D}}(\mathbf{t}), \mathbb{Z}^h) \leq H, \\ 0, \text{ else.} \end{cases}$$

Note that computing the filter has a cost of $O(h \cdot k)$ for computing $\mathbf{D}\mathbf{t}$ for $\mathbf{D} \in \mathbb{R}^{h \times k}$ followed by a cost of $O(h)$ for computing $\text{dist}(\mathbf{D}\mathbf{t}, \mathbb{Z}^h)$ using simple coordinate-wise rounding. Given that $h \geq k$, computing the filter is certainly not cheaper than ordinary lifting, which is the opposite of our goal. However this changes when applying the filter to all pairs $\mathbf{t}_i - \mathbf{t}_j$ with $1 \leq i < j \leq h$. We can pre-compute $\mathbf{D}\mathbf{t}_1, \ldots, \mathbf{D}\mathbf{t}_s$ once, which gives a negligible overhead for large buckets, and then compute $\mathbf{D}(\mathbf{t}_i - \mathbf{t}_j)$ by linearity, lowering the total cost to $O(h)$ per pair.

6.1 Dual Hash Analysis

We further analyse the dual hash filter and try to understand the correlation between the distance $\text{dist}(\mathbf{t}, \mathcal{L})$ and the dual hash $\mathcal{H}_{\mathbf{D}}(\mathbf{t})$. In fact we consider two regimes, the preserved and unpreserved regime. Consider a target $\mathbf{t} \in \mathbb{R}^k$ and let $\mathbf{x}$ be a closest vector in $\mathcal{L}$ to $\mathbf{t}$. We will say that we are in the preserved regime whenever $\mathbf{D}(\mathbf{t} - \mathbf{x}) \in [-\frac{1}{2}, \frac{1}{2}]^h$ (i.e., $\mathbf{D}\mathbf{x}$ remains a closest vector of $\mathbf{D}\mathbf{t}$ among $\mathbb{Z}^h$), in which case it holds that $\|\mathbf{D}(\mathbf{t} - \mathbf{x})\|_2 = \text{dist}(\mathcal{H}_{\mathbf{D}}(\mathbf{t}), \mathbb{Z}^h)$. In the general case, we only have the inequality $\|\mathbf{D}(\mathbf{t} - \mathbf{x})\|_2 \geq \text{dist}(\mathcal{H}_{\mathbf{D}}(\mathbf{t}), \mathbb{Z}^h)$. For the relevant parameters, the BDD instances we are interested in will fall almost surely in the preserved regime, while most of the instances we wish to discard quickly will fall in the unpreserved regime.

Preserved Regime. We have that $\|\mathbf{D}(\mathbf{t}-\mathbf{x})\|_2 = \text{dist}(\mathcal{H}_{\mathbf{D}}(\mathbf{t}), \mathbb{Z}^h)$, and therefore Lemma 2 can be complemented with a lower bound as follows:

$$\sigma_k(\mathbf{D}) \cdot \text{dist}(\mathbf{t}, \mathcal{L}) \leq \text{dist}(\mathcal{H}_{\mathbf{D}}(\mathbf{t}), \mathbb{Z}^h) \leq \sigma_1(\mathbf{D}) \cdot \text{dist}(\mathbf{t}, \mathcal{L}).$$

Setting a conservative hash bound based on the above upper bound leads to false positives of distance at most $\sigma_1(\mathbf{D})/\sigma_k(\mathbf{D})$ further away than the targeted BDD distance. This is a worst-case view, however, and we are more interested in the average behavior. We will assume without loss of generality that $\mathbf{x} = 0$, such that $\text{dist}(\mathbf{t}, \mathcal{L}) = \|\mathbf{t}\|$. To analyse what properties play a role in this correlation we assume that $\mathbf{t}$ is spherically distributed for some fixed length $\|\mathbf{t}\|$. Suppose that $\mathbf{D}^t\mathbf{D}$ has eigenvalues $\sigma_1^2, \ldots, \sigma_k^2$ with corresponding normalized (orthogonal) eigenvectors $\mathbf{v}_1, \ldots, \mathbf{v}_k$. We can equivalently assume that $\mathbf{t} = \sum_{i=1}^k t_i \mathbf{v}_i$ with $(t_1, \ldots, t_k)/\|\mathbf{t}\|$ uniformly distributed over the sphere. Computing the expectation and variation we see

$$\mathbb{E}[\|\mathbf{D}\mathbf{t}\|^2] = \mathbb{E}\left[\sum_{i=1}^k t_i^2 \cdot \sigma_i^2\right] = \sum_{i=1}^k \sigma_i^2 \cdot \mathbb{E}[t_i^2] = \|t\|^2 \cdot \frac{1}{k}\sum_{i=1}^k \sigma_i^2$$

$$\text{Var}\left[\|\mathbf{D}\mathbf{t}\|^2\right] = \frac{\|t\|^4}{(k/2+1)}\left(\frac{1}{k} \cdot \sum_{i=1}^k \sigma_i^4 - \left(\frac{1}{k}\sum_{i=1}^k \sigma_i^2\right)^2\right).$$

So instead of the worst case bounds from Lemma 2, $\text{dist}(\mathcal{H}_{\mathbf{D}}(\mathbf{t}), \mathbb{Z}^h)$ is more or less close to $\sqrt{\frac{1}{k}\sum_{i=1}^k \sigma_i^2} \cdot \|\mathbf{t}\|$.

Unpreserved Regime. In this regime $\text{dist}(\mathcal{H}_{\mathbf{D}}(\mathbf{t}), \mathbb{Z}^h)$ is not really a useful metric, as there will seemingly be no relation with $\|\mathbf{D}(\mathbf{t}-\mathbf{x})\|_2$. Note that we can expect this regime to mostly contain targets that lie rather far from the lattice, i.e., these are targets we want to not pass our filter. Therefore it is interesting to analyse how many (false) positives we can expect from this regime.

Inspired by practical observations, we analyse these positives from the heuristic assumption in this regime that every $\mathbf{D}\mathbf{t}$ is just uniformly distributed over $[-\frac{1}{2}, \frac{1}{2}]^h$ modulo $\mathbb{Z}^h$. Then we can ask the question how probable it is that $\|\mathbf{D}\mathbf{t}\|_2 = \text{dist}(\mathbf{D}\mathbf{t}, \mathbb{Z}^h) \leq H$; i.e., that the target passes the filter. This is equivalent to the volume of the intersection of an h-dimensional ball with radius H and the hypercube $[-\frac{1}{2}, \frac{1}{2}]^h$. We can bound this by just the volume of the ball, which is quite tight if H is not too large. Therefore we would expect in this regime a false positive rate bounded by $H^h \cdot \frac{\pi^{h/2}}{\Gamma(h/2+1)}$. Note that this only depends on the filter threshold H and the number of dual vectors h and not on the specific matrix $\mathbf{D}$.

Choosing a Dual Hash. We will shortly discuss how to pick the dual hash matrix $\mathbf{D} \in \mathbb{R}^{h \times k}$. The goal is to obtain a filter with a good correlation, i.e., a good trade-off between the positive-rate and the number of false negatives.

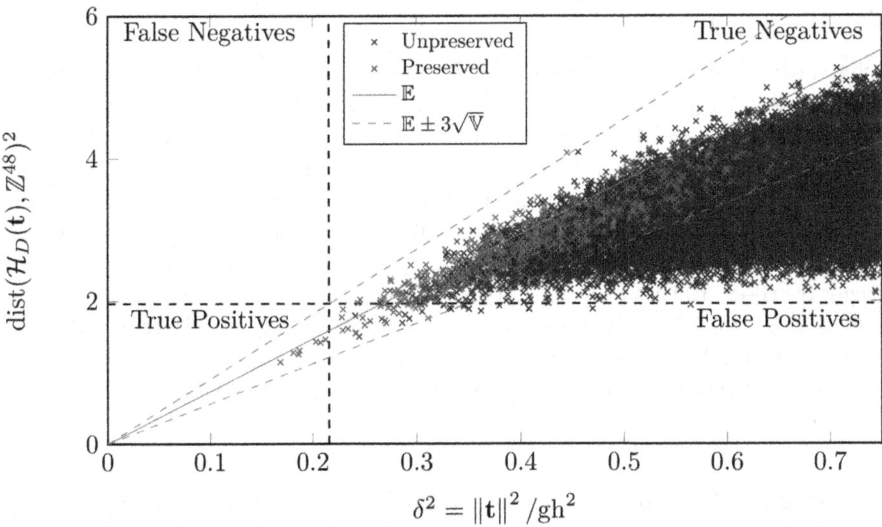

Fig. 6. Dual hash filter correlation on the context [14 : 30] for a reduced 160-dimensional lattice using 48 dual vectors. The BDD-bound was computed with a representative squared length bound of 1.44 and the 2^{20} targets are uniformly sampled over the Voronoi cell around 0.

As the computational cost mostly depends on the number of dual vectors h we will try to optimize $\mathbf{D}$ for a fixed h.

In the preserved regime we see that the variation is minimized if all singular values are equal, so we want $\mathbf{D}$ to be well conditioned in the sense that all singular values are somewhat the same. For the unpreserved regime we want the filter bound H to be small, which means we want $\sum_{i=1}^{k} \sigma_i(D)^2$ to be small (together with the variance); this can be achieved by working with short dual vectors.

To summarize we want to find a set of short dual vectors to form the dual hash such that $\mathbf{D}$ is well conditioned. One initial method is to just pick the h shortest dual vectors (modulo sign). This definitely satisfies the needs of the unpreserved regime, but the conditioning of the resulting matrix is often not that great. Given a list of short dual vectors we can greedily try to improve the conditioning of $\mathbf{D}$ by replacing some of the (row) vectors from the list. A good continuous metric to measure if all singular values are somewhat the same is $\mathrm{Tr}(\mathbf{D}^t\mathbf{D}) / \det(\mathbf{D}^t\mathbf{D})^{1/k}$. From experiments we can conclude that this greedy method to improve the filter works really well. For example with the parameters as in Fig. 6, picking the 48 shortest dual vectors leads to a positive rate of $1.3 \cdot 10^{-4}$ for a false negative rate of 1%; using the greedy construction improves the positive rate down to $1.4 \cdot 10^{-5}$ for the same false negative rate. The additional overhead of the greedy method is negligible and easily won back from allowing a lower number of dual vectors h.

6.2 Implementation

Given a list of pre-computed $\mathbf{Dt}_1, \ldots, \mathbf{Dt}_m$ we want to use the GPU to efficiently compute $\operatorname{dist}(\mathbf{D}(\mathbf{t}_i - \mathbf{t}_j), \mathbb{Z}^h)$ for all $i < j$. As usual the actual implementation requires some trade-offs to significantly improve performance. Given that the dimension of the dual hash seems to have more impact than the precision of the values we choose for an 8-bit integer representation for the dual hash coordinates in $[-1/2, 1/2)$ by dividing it in 256 equally sized intervals. The added benefit of this representation is that the $\bmod \mathbb{Z}$ operations are implicitly handled by integer overflow. Both CUDA and Tensor cores have special instructions and very good performance for 8-bit arithmetic, even when using 32 bits to accumulate inner products. We refer to Appendix D for more implementation details on computing all pairwise dual hash filters using CUDA cores; we also discuss how one could adapt it for Tensor cores.

Choosing the Parameters. To use the dual hash in practice as a filter we need to decide on what context to use it and what the threshold should be. Applying the dual hash to the full lift context $[\kappa : l]$ would fail to return short vectors for positions $l' > \kappa$, which are also needed to improve the quality of the basis. Therefore we apply the dual hash to a subcontext $[f : l]$ (the lift-filter context) of the lift context $[\kappa : l]$. If a vector is short in the context $[l' : r]$ for some $l' < f$ then we can also expect it to be short in the filter context, and therefore to be catched by our filter.

We also need to decide on a distance threshold. Let $\mathbf{v}$ be a lattice vector in the sieving context $[l : r]$ of length R. We can assume that $R \geq \ell$ as otherwise the vector would already be inserted (and always lifted) in the sieving database. Suppose that $\mathbf{v}$ lifts to a short vector with length at most $\ell_{l'}$ in some context $[l' : r]$ for $\kappa \leq l' \leq f$. This corresponds to a target $\mathbf{t}$ at distance at most

$$\operatorname{dist}(\mathbf{t}, \mathcal{L}_{[l':l]}))^2 \leq \ell_{l'}^2 - \ell^2.$$

in the context $[l' : l]$. Although we cannot know what the length of $\mathbf{t}$ would be in the filter context we can expect this to be close to $\sqrt{\frac{l-f}{l-l'}}\,\|\mathbf{t}\|$ by the Gaussian Heuristic. Therefore setting the filter length bound to

$$F_{l'} := \sqrt{\frac{l-f}{l-l'}\left(\ell_{l'}^2 - \ell^2\right)}$$

allows a significant part of the short lifts in the context $[l' : r]$ through the filter. Note that most of the pairs we lift are much larger on the sieving part, and thus have to be even shorter in the filter context; definitely passing the above filter length bound. We conclude by setting the filter to aim for a length of at most $F := \max_{\kappa \leq l' \leq f}\{F_{l'}\}$.

Given the filter length bound we could immediately apply Lemma 2 to obtain a threshold for the dual hash that guarantees that our filter has no false negatives. However as usual there is a trade-off between the number of false negatives and the positive rate of the filter. For our purposes we set the bound at the expectation plus 3 standard deviations in the preserved regime to prevent most false negatives. For a more precise bound under a fixed false negative ratio one could fall back to Monte-Carlo sampling methods as we do not know of a closed form formula for the distribution. Figure 6 shows the effectiveness of the dual hash filter based on realistic parameters as encountered during a 130-dimensional pump on a 160-dimensional lattice. The pre-processing of the basis consisted of a workout with pumps up to dimension 128.

7 Sieving in Practice

7.1 Comparison

We compare several of our sieve implementations. Although our BDGL-like implementations `bdgl` and `bdgl_gpu` will eventually be faster than the BGJ-like implementations `triple` by G6K and `triple_gpu` by us, the cross-over point could be outside of practical dimensions. For the comparison we run a pump up to dimension 120 and 140 for CPU and GPU respectively in a lattice of dimension 160 that has been pre-processed by a workout up to dimension 118 and 138. In Fig. 7 we display the wall-clock time taken for each Sieve during the pump up. All our GPU implementations use a multi-bucket parameter of 4, which should give a balanced comparison based on Fig. 3. Any on-the-fly lifting or dual hash techniques are disabled. For the remaining parameters we refer to the next Sect. 7.2. The cross-over point between our `3-bdgl` and record-holding `triple` sieve from [AGPS19] is already in a sieving dimension of 94, and our speed-up grows to a speed-up of 2.7 in dimension 120. This shows that for CPU implementations BDGL is already extremely practical. For `2-bdgl_gpu` and `triple_gpu` the cross-over point lies above dimension 140, and given the extrapolations we expect them to cross in dimension $n \approx 149$. The large minimum bucket size shifts the cross-over point by more than 50 dimensions. In this light, it did not appear pertinent to implement `3-bdgl_gpu`, which, while being asymptotically faster, would cross-over even later.

7.2 SVP Parameter Tuning

There are many parameters in our implementation that can be tuned for optimal performance with respect to memory and time complexity. We will focus on `triple_gpu` as we have shown it to be the fastest implementation in practical sieving dimensions $n \leq 150$. As low level parameters, such as minimum bucket sizes for GPUs, are discussed earlier, here we discuss the higher level parameters to solve 1.05-approxSVP for a lattice of dimension d.

Given the large amount of computational power available with the 4 GPUs, we can potentially solve lattice 1.05-approxSVP up to dimension 180 in reasonable time on a single machine. The main limiting factor at that point is the available memory, in our case 1.5 TiB RAM. We have spent significant efforts

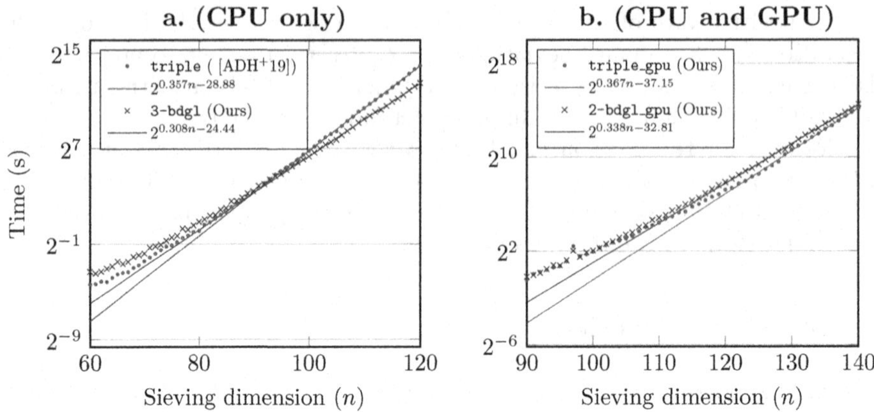

Fig. 7. Comparison of different sieve implementations from [ADH+19] and from this work. We ran a single pump up in a 160-dimensional lattice to a sieving dimension of 120 and 140 for CPU only and GPU accelerated respectively. The timings give the amount of time spend in each sieving dimension before reaching a saturation of 37.5% with a database size of $2.77 \cdot 2^{0.2075n}$. The fitting is obtained by a linear least-squares regression on the last 20 dimensions in log-space.

aiming to reduce the memory footprint of our G6K-GPU implementation, such as maintaining only basis coordinates, length and a hash of each vector in our database. Many parameters can be safely tweaked in certain regions without significantly affecting time complexity, hence we focus more on suitable values that limit memory usage.

To increase dimensions-for-free, and thus decrease memory usage, we enabled DownSieve for all workouts for a stronger preprocessing. We found that with DownSieve on, a larger PreferLeftInsert is more benificiary. I.e., prefer to insert even a slightly improved b'_i into the basis over a more significantly improved b'_{i+1}.

Another main parameter affecting memory use is the constant factor in database size, normally chosen as 3.2 in G6K [ADH+19]. We opted to reduce this to 2.77, resulting in $\mathsf{DBSize}(d) = 2.77 \times (4/3)^{(d/2)}$ for sieve dimension d, and compensate by also reducing SaturationRatio from .5 to .375.

Additionally, we introduced a database size limit by setting an experimentally-verified target dimensions-for-free $\mathsf{TD4F}(n) = \lfloor n/\log(n) \rfloor$, and limiting the database size to $\mathsf{DBSizeLimit}(n) = \mathsf{DBSize}(n - \mathsf{T4DF}(n))$. This means that the database size limit does not affect sieving up to the target dimensions-for-free. However, for unlucky cases, we allow G6K workouts of up to 4 dimensions larger without further increasing the database size. Because `triple_gpu` also considers triples we can be certain that saturation will still be reached.

As discussed before, we use DualHash lifting: starting from a sieving dimension of 106 in the filter context $[l - 24, l]$ using 32 dual vectors. To reduce memory overhead from storing buckets and results (before insertion), we set

Table 1. Darmstadt Lattice 1.05-approxSVP Challenge results

(T)D4F = target/actual dimensions for free
MSD = actual maximum sieving dimension
FLOP = # bucketing + reduction core floating point operations

dim	TD4F	D4F	MSD	Norm	Norm/GH	FLOP	Walltime	Mem GiB
158	31	29	129	3303	1.04329	$2^{62.1}$	9h 16m	89
160	31	33	127	3261	1.02302	$2^{61.8}$	8h 24m	88
162	31	31	131	3341	1.04220	$2^{63.2}$	18h 32m	156
164	32	28	136	3362	1.04368	$2^{64,8}$	2d 01h	179
166	32	30	136	3375	1.03969	$2^{64.8}$	2d 01h	234
168	32	31	137	3424	1.04946	$2^{65.3}$	2d 18h	318
170	33	31	139	3435	1.04594	$2^{66.3}$	5d 11h	364
172	33	35	137	3455	1.04582	$2^{65.0}$	2d 09h	364
174	33	35	139	3482	1.04913	$2^{66.3}$	5d 06h	518
176	34	33	143	3487	1.04412	$2^{67.5}$	12d 11h	806
178	34	32	146	3447	1.02725	$2^{68.6}$	22d 18h	1060
180	34	30	150	3509	1.04003	$2^{69.9}$	51d 14h	1443

Machine specification:
2× Intel Xeon Gold 6248 (20C/40T @ 2.5-3.9GHz)
4× Gigabyte RTX 2080 TI (4352C @ 1.5-1.8GHz)
1.5 TiB RAM (2666 MHz)
Average load: 40 CPU threads @ 93%, 4 GPUs @ 79%/1530MHz/242Watt

$\mathsf{MultiBucket} = 2$. Thus, our main parameters are:

$\mathsf{TD4F}(n) = \lfloor n/\log(n) \rfloor$, $\mathsf{MaxSieveDim}(n) = n - \mathsf{TD4F}(n) + 4$,
$\mathsf{DBSize}(d) = 2.77 \times (4/3)^{(d/2)}$, $\mathsf{DBSizeLimit}(n) = \mathsf{DBSize}(n - \mathsf{T4DF}(n))$,
$\mathsf{SaturationRadius} = 4/3$, $\mathsf{SaturationRatio} = .375$,
$\mathsf{DualHashMinDim} = 106$, $\mathsf{DualHashDim} = 24$, $\mathsf{DualHashVecs} = 32$,
$\mathsf{PreferLeftInsert} = 1.2$, $\mathsf{DownSieve} = \mathsf{True}$,
$\mathsf{MultiBucket} = 2$ $\mathsf{Sieve} = \texttt{triple\_gpu}$,

7.3 New SVP Records

With the parameters tuned as discussed above, we have solved several Darmstadt Lattice 1.05-approxSVP Challenges for lattices with dimension in the range of 158 till 180 (all with seed=0). Details about the effort and results for each challenge are presented in Table 1.

With a new top record of the 1.05-approxSVP challenges with dimension 180, we improve significantly upon the last record of dimension 155 by [ADH+19]. Note that this last record was achieved on a single large machine with 72 CPU cores in 14 days and 16 h, where we were able to find an even shorter vector of length $0.9842 \cdot \mathrm{gh}$ in about 5 hours (68× faster). Also we can improve this record from 155 by no less than 21 dimensions by solving lattice 1.05-approxSVP for dimension 176 on our 4-GPU machine in less wall-clock time: 12 days and 11 h.

Table 2. Power use comparison for records of dimension 155 (G6K) and 176 (ours).

dim	time	CPU+GPU only	system	CPU+GPU only	system
155	352 h	560 W	720 W	197 kWh	254 kWh
176	229 h	1268 W	1428 W	379 kWh	427 kWh

As proof we present our short vector for Darmstadt Lattice 1.05-approxSVP Challenge dimension 180 with seed 0:

(68, 33, -261, 11, 101, 354, -48, -398, 196, -84, 217, 319, -137, -157, -29, 304, -14, 312, 28,
-240, -347, -6, -153, -35, -214, 67, -565, 91, 365, 382, -168, 152, 30, 42, -12, -14, -230, 54,
304, 51, 398, 380, 76, -111, 437, 374, -554, -171, -90, -92, 564, 32, 217, 60, -107, 475,
-290, -326, -224, -218, 27, -271, 12, 200, 463, -365, 119, -431, 92, 450, 58, 183, 342, 82,
-144, 77, -95, -62, -245, 171, 169, -106, -330, 236, 194, 41, -84, -297, 567, 58, 553, 279,
260, 140, -141, -30, -183, -448, -112, 45, 135, -260, -261, 1, -105, 507, 105, -414, -161,
-9, -337, -287, 431, 92, -91, 350, -376, -75, 11, -249, 119, -172, -351, 410, 97, -320, -270,
223, -287, 97, 235, 242, 279, -222, 384, -95, 501, 317, 167, -130, -103, 441, 424, 25, 187,
-128, -9, -90, 328, -107, -132, -81, 2, 94, -326, -109, 465, 49, -30, 345, 125, -114, 909, 180,
-5, -112, 190, 182, -65, -291, -83, 445, -68, -318, -18, -732, -241, 246, -34, 299)

7.4 Remarks

Power Use. To compare power efficiency of our new record computation for dimension 176 with the previous record computation for dimension 155 regarding power usage, we estimated power use as shown in Table 2 as follows. Their dimension 155 computation ran for 352 h on 4 CPUs (Intel Xeon E7-8860V4) that have a TDP of 140 W each. Our dimension 176 computation ran for 299 h on 2 CPUs (Intel Xeon Gold 6248) with a TDP of 150 W each, and 4 GPUs that typically used 242 W as measured through the `nvidia-smi` tool. For both systems we approximate other system power usage covering motherboard, RAM and disk as about 160W.

Note in Table 2 that while solving the challenge for dimension 176 is about two orders of magnitude harder compared to dimension 155, we spent less than a factor 2 more in electricity.

Memory Use. From these, we estimate that our implementation requires about 416 Bytes per vector for dimensions higher than 137. Hence, sieving up to dimension 146 could still fit within our 1.5 TiB of available RAM, which allowed us to solve the lattice challenge of dimension 180.

Appendix. The Appendix can be found in the full version.[8]

Acknowledgments. The authors would like to express their gratitude to Joe Rowell for his precious feedback and support on parts of our code.

[8] https://eprint.iacr.org/2021/141.

The research of L. Ducas was supported by the European Union's H2020 Programme under PROMETHEUS project (grant 780701) and the ERC-StG-ARTICULATE project (no. 947821). W. van Woerden is funded by the ERC-ADG-ALGSTRONGCRYPTO project (no. 740972). The computational hardware enabling this research was acquired thanks to a Veni Innovational Research Grant from NWO under project number 639.021.645 and to the Google Security and Privacy Research Award awarded to M. Stevens.

References

[ADH+19] Albrecht, M.R., Ducas, L., Herold, G., Kirshanova, E., Postlethwaite, E.W., Stevens, M.: The general sieve kernel and new records in lattice reduction. In: Ishai, Y., Rijmen, V. (eds.) EUROCRYPT 2019. LNCS, vol. 11477, pp. 717–746. Springer, Cham (2019). https://doi.org/10.1007/978-3-030-17656-3_25

[AGPS19] Albrecht, M.R., Gheorghiu, V., Postlethwaite, E.W., Schanck, J.M.: Estimating quantum speedups for lattice sieves. In: Moriai, S., Wang, H. (eds.) Advances in Cryptology - ASIACRYPT 2020. ASIACRYPT 2020. LNCS, vol. 12492, pp. 583–613. Springer, Cham (2020). https://doi.org/10.1007/978-3-030-64834-3_20

[AKS01] Ajtai, M., Kumar, R., Sivakumar, D.: A sieve algorithm for the shortest lattice vector problem. In: Proceedings of the Thirty-Third Annual ACM Symposium on Theory of Computing. pp. 601–610 (2001)

[ALNSD20] Aggarwal, D., Li, J., Nguyen, P.Q., Stephens-Davidowitz, N.: Slide reduction, revisited—filling the gaps in SVP approximation. In: Micciancio, D., Ristenpart, T. (eds.) CRYPTO 2020. LNCS, vol. 12171, pp. 274–295. Springer, Cham (2020). https://doi.org/10.1007/978-3-030-56880-1_10

[AR05] Aharonov, D., Regev, O.: Lattice problems in NP $\cap$ coNP. J. ACM (JACM) **52**(5), 749–765 (2005)

[BDGL16] Becker, A., Ducas, L., Gama, N., Laarhoven, T.: New directions in nearest neighbor searching with applications to lattice sieving. In: Proceedings of the Twenty-Seventh Annual ACM-SIAM Symposium on Discrete Algorithms, SIAM, pp. 10–24 (2016)

[BGJ15] Becker, A., Gama, N., Joux, A.: Speeding-up lattice sieving without increasing the memory, using sub-quadratic nearest neighbor search. IACR Cryptology ePrint Archive 2015/522 (2015)

[BL16] Becker, A., Laarhoven, T.: Efficient (ideal) lattice sieving using cross-polytope LSH. In: Pointcheval, D., Nitaj, A., Rachidi, T. (eds.) AFRICACRYPT 2016. LNCS, vol. 9646, pp. 3–23. Springer, Cham (2016). https://doi.org/10.1007/978-3-319-31517-1_1

[BLS16] Bai, S., Laarhoven, T., Stehlé, D.: Tuple lattice sieving. LMS J. Comput. Math. **19**(A), 146–162 (2016)

[Cha02] Charikar, M.S.: Similarity estimation techniques from rounding algorithms. In: Proceedings of the Thiry-Fourth Annual ACM Symposium on Theory of Computing, pp. 380–388 (2002)

[Che13] Chen, Y.: Réduction de réseau et sécurité concrete du chiffrement complètement homomorphe. Ph.D. thesis, Paris 7 (2013)

[Duc18] Ducas, L.: Shortest vector from lattice sieving: a few dimensions for free. In: Nielsen, J.B., Rijmen, V. (eds.) EUROCRYPT 2018. LNCS, vol. 10820, pp. 125–145. Springer, Cham (2018). https://doi.org/10.1007/978-3-319-78381-9_5

[FBB+14] Fitzpatrick, R., et al.: Tuning GaussSieve for speed. In: Aranha, D.F., Menezes, A. (eds.) LATINCRYPT 2014. LNCS, vol. 8895, pp. 288–305. Springer, Cham (2015). https://doi.org/10.1007/978-3-319-16295-9_16

[FP85] Fincke, U., Pohst, M.: Improved methods for calculating vectors of short length in a lattice, including a complexity analysis. Math. Comput. **44**(170), 463–471 (1985)

[GM03] Goldstein, D., Mayer, A.: On the equidistribution of hecke points. Forum Mathematicum **15**, 165–189 (2003)

[GN08] Gama, N. Nguyen, P.Q.: Finding short lattice vectors within Mordell's inequality. In: Proceedings of the Fortieth Annual ACM Symposium on Theory of Computing, pp. 207–216 (2008)

[GNR10] Gama, N., Nguyen, P.Q., Regev, O.: Lattice enumeration using extreme pruning. In: Gilbert, H. (ed.) EUROCRYPT 2010. LNCS, vol. 6110, pp. 257–278. Springer, Heidelberg (2010). https://doi.org/10.1007/978-3-642-13190-5_13

[HK17] Herold, G., Kirshanova, E.: Improved algorithms for the approximate k-list problem in Euclidean norm. In: Fehr, S. (ed.) PKC 2017. LNCS, vol. 10174, pp. 16–40. Springer, Heidelberg (2017). https://doi.org/10.1007/978-3-662-54365-8_2

[HKL18] Herold, G., Kirshanova, E., Laarhoven, T.: Speed-ups and time–memory trade-offs for tuple lattice sieving. In: Abdalla, M., Dahab, R. (eds.) PKC 2018. LNCS, vol. 10769, pp. 407–436. Springer, Cham (2018). https://doi.org/10.1007/978-3-319-76578-5_14

[JYP+17] Jouppi, N.P., et al.: In-datacenter performance analysis of a tensor processing unit. In: Proceedings of the 44th Annual International Symposium on Computer Architecture, pp. 1–12 (2017)

[Kan83] Kannan, R.: Improved algorithms for integer programming and related lattice problems. In: Proceedings of the Fifteenth Annual ACM Symposium on Theory of Computing, pp. 193–206 (1983)

[Laa15] Laarhoven, T.: Sieving for shortest vectors in lattices using angular locality-sensitive hashing. In: Gennaro, R., Robshaw, M. (eds.) CRYPTO 2015. LNCS, vol. 9215, pp. 3–22. Springer, Heidelberg (2015). https://doi.org/10.1007/978-3-662-47989-6_1

[LM18] Laarhoven, T., Mariano, A.: Progressive lattice sieving. In: Lange, T., Steinwandt, R. (eds.) PQCrypto 2018. LNCS, vol. 10786, pp. 292–311. Springer, Cham (2018). https://doi.org/10.1007/978-3-319-79063-3_14

[MLB17] Mariano, A., Laarhoven, T., Bischof, C.: A parallel variant of LDSieve for the SVP on lattices. In: 2017 25th Euromicro International Conference on Parallel, Distributed and Network-Based Processing (PDP), pp. 23–30. IEEE (2017)

[MR09] Micciancio, D., Regev, O.: Lattice-based cryptography. In: Bernstein, D.J., Buchmann, J., Dahmen, E. (eds.) Post-Quantum Cryptography. Springer, Heidelberg (2009). https://doi.org/10.1007/978-3-540-88702-7_5

[MV10] Micciancio, D., Voulgaris, P.: Faster exponential time algorithms for the shortest vector problem. In: Proceedings of the Twenty-First Annual ACM-SIAM Symposium on Discrete Algorithms, SIAM, pp. 1468–1480 (2010)

[MW16] Micciancio, D., Walter, M.: Practical, predictable lattice basis reduction. In: Fischlin, M., Coron, J.-S. (eds.) EUROCRYPT 2016. LNCS, vol. 9665, pp. 820–849. Springer, Heidelberg (2016). https://doi.org/10.1007/978-3-662-49890-3_31

[NBGS08] Nickolls, J., Buck, I., Garland, M., Skadron, K.: Scalable parallel programming with CUDA. Queue **6**(2), 40–53 (2008)

[NV08] Nguyen, P.Q., Vidick, T.: Sieve algorithms for the shortest vector problem are practical. J. Math. Cryptol. **2**(2), 181–207 (2008)

[NVF20] NVIDIA, Vingelmann, P., Fitzek, F.H.P.: CUDA, release: 10.2.89 (2020)

[PS09] Pujol, X., Stehlé, D.: Solving the shortest lattice vector problem in time 22.465 n. IACR Cryptology ePrint Archive 2009/605 (2009)

[SE94] Schnorr, C.-P., Euchner, M.: Lattice basis reduction: improved practical algorithms and solving subset sum problems. Math. Program. **66**(1–3), 181–199 (1994)

[SG10] Schneider, M., Gama, N.: Darmstadt SVP Challenges (2010). https://www.latticechallenge.org/svp-challenge/index.php. Accessed 06 Oct 2020

[YKYC17] Yang, S.-Y., Kuo, P.-C., Yang, B.-Y., Cheng, C.-M.: Gauss sieve algorithm on GPUs. In: Handschuh, H. (ed.) CT-RSA 2017. LNCS, vol. 10159, pp. 39–57. Springer, Cham (2017). https://doi.org/10.1007/978-3-319-52153-4_3

Masking and Secret-Sharing

Fast Verification of Masking Schemes in Characteristic Two

Nicolas Bordes(✉) and Pierre Karpman

Univ. Grenoble Alpes, CNRS, Grenoble INP, Institute of Engineering Univ. Grenoble Alpes, LJK, 38000 Grenoble, France
{nicolas.bordes,pierre.karpman}@univ-grenoble-alpes.fr

Abstract. We revisit the matrix model for non-interference (NI) probing security of masking gadgets introduced by Belaïd *et al.* at CRYPTO 2017. This leads to two main results.

1) We generalise the theorems on which this model is based, so as to be able to apply them to masking schemes over any finite field—in particular $\mathbb{F}_2$—and to be able to analyse the *strong* non-interference (SNI) security notion. We also follow Faust *et al.* (TCHES 2018) to additionally consider a *robust* probing model that takes hardware defects such as glitches into account.

2) We exploit this improved model to implement a very efficient verification algorithm that improves the performance of state-of-the-art software by three orders of magnitude. We show applications to variants of NI and SNI multiplication gadgets from Barthe *et al.* (EUROCRYPT 2017) which we verify to be secure up to order 11 after a significant parallel computation effort, whereas the previous largest proven order was 7; SNI refreshing gadgets (*ibid.*); and NI multiplication gadgets from Groß *et al.* (TIS@CCS 2016) secure in presence of glitches. We also reduce the randomness cost of some existing gadgets, notably for the implementation-friendly case of 8 shares, improving here the previous best results by 17% (resp. 19%) for SNI multiplication (resp. refreshing).

Keywords: High-order masking · Probing model · Multiplication gadget · Refreshing gadget · Linear code

1 Introduction

Since their introduction in the late last century, side-channel attacks and in particular *Differential Power Analysis* (DPA) [KJJ99] have developed into one of the most efficient attack techniques on implementations of cryptographic primitives. The importance of this new threat and its practical relevance soon lead to the design of appropriate counter-measures, one of the most influential to date being the "ISW" private multiplication circuit of Ishai, Sahai and Wagner [ISW03]. This is a foremost example of a *masking scheme*, where sensitive data are split into several shares using a secret sharing scheme; the crux of the

A. Canteaut and F.-X. Standaert (Eds.): EUROCRYPT 2021, LNCS 12697, pp. 283–312, 2021.
https://doi.org/10.1007/978-3-030-77886-6_10

design is then to devise a way to perform field arithmetic over the shares without leaking too much information to the adversary in the process.

A major characteristic of a masking scheme is the *order* at which it is secure: in a probing model such as the one introduced by Ishai, Sahai and Wagner, a circuit secure at order d is such that no adversary can learn information about its input and output even when being given d intermediate values of its computation. The usefulness of increasing the security order is then justified by the fact that under reasonable assumptions, the number of measurements needed for a successful attack increases exponentially in d [DFS15].

Unfortunately, high-order schemes also come with a significant overhead, since the cost of ISW multiplication is quadratic in d for three relevant metrics: to secure one field multiplication, one needs $2d(d+1)$ sums, $(d+1)^2$ products and $d(d+1)/2$ fresh random masks. This lead to several attempts to find more efficient multiplication circuits, especially with respect to the last two metrics.

A number of new schemes for private multiplication were introduced in the past few years by Belaïd *et al.* [BBP+16,BBP+17]. At EUROCRYPT 2016, they design a new high-order scheme whose randomness cost is decreased to $\approx d^2/4+d$, and which can be easily instantiated over any finite field of characteristic two (they also give specific schemes with even lower cost up to order 4). The security of this multiplication is analysed in the composable model of *non interference* (NI) from Barthe *et al.* [BBD+16]. This is slightly weaker than the *strong non-interference* (SNI) security achieved by ISW multiplication but remains of high practical relevance: for instance, one can replace half of the multiplications in a masked AES S-box computation by the ones of [BBP+16] while maintaining the overall strong SNI security for the entire S-box. At CRYPTO 2017, the same authors propose two new schemes, one with linear *bilinear multiplication* cost, and the other with linear randomness cost. However, those are complex to securely instantiate and cannot be done so over $\mathbb{F}_2$. As an example, over $\mathbb{F}_{2^8}$, Belaïd *et al.* only manage to instantiate their algorithms at order 2 and 3 respectively; this was later slightly improved to 4 in both cases by Karpman and Roche [KR18]. In this second paper, Belaïd *et al.* also analyse the security of their schemes thanks to a powerful matrix-based model that they introduce. This model is however not complete for schemes defined over small fields such as $\mathbb{F}_2$; while this was not a limitation in their case, it precludes its full application to this common setting. Finally, Barthe *et al.* introduced some of the most efficient known NI and SNI multiplication and refreshing schemes at EUROCRYPT 2017 [BDF+17], selected instances of which were then later improved by Grégoire *et al.* [GPSS18] and Barthe *et al.* [BBD+18]. Complementary approaches to decrease the overhead of masking implementations consist in batching multiplications in order to amortise their cost (for instance by sharing some of the shares across several multiplications [CGPZ16] or by using a "packing" strategy [WGS+20]) or in carrying a global analysis of the primitive to be masked, so that one may for instance use fewer refreshing gadgets [BGR18,BDM+20]. Both of these are quite orthogonal to the design and analysis of individual gadgets.

On the implementation side, several recent work have investigated the efficiency of high-order masking in practice [GR17,JS17,GJRS18,GPSS18]; they show in particular the increasing feasibility of masking block ciphers at quite high order such as 7, and the possibility of masking at very high order such as 31. Such high-order masking may be useful to secure implementations running on devices with low noise level. This was recently highlighted by a practical attack of Bronchain and Standaert on a protected AES implementation where the low noise and masking order were found to be contributing factors to its feasibility [BS19]. From a technical point-of-view, high-order implementations share the common approach of exploiting bitslicing or vectorisation to amortise the overhead brought by the use of many shares; since bitslicing works with operations at the bit level, this strategy typically requires the masking to be performed over $\mathbb{F}_2$. These implementations also confirm the high cost of randomness generation; for instance, depending on the random number generator performance and the block cipher under consideration Journault and Standaert report that 68–92% of the time is spent generating fresh masks in their 32-share implementations [JS17]. All in all, concrete implementations of high-order masking confirm the importance of schemes defined over $\mathbb{F}_2$ with low randomness cost.

All of the above work are chiefly concerned with software-oriented countermeasures and are designed with respect to a high-level computation model. While this abstraction is beneficial to the formal analysis of the schemes and their implementation, it comes with the inherent downside of ignoring some of the micro-architectural phenomena that may enable side-channel attacks in the first place. It was for instance recently noted by Gao *et al.* that some independence assumptions made in bitsliced implementations do not seem to hold in practice, and that in-register bit interaction leakage may in fact significantly decrease the actual resistance of a scheme from what could be theoretically expected [GMPO20]. In the case of hardware circuits, it is also well-known that their protection additionally requires to take into account the possibility of physical defects such as glitches. From a formalisation perspective this can for instance be done by generalising probing security to a *robust* variant proposed by Faust *et al.* [FGP+18], or by following the more physical approach of Bloem *et al.* [BGI+18]. As was recently noted by Moos *et al.* [MMSS19], the analysis of masking schemes in this harder model is currently quite less mature than in the software case.

Finally although some schemes such as the original ISW multiplication benefit from analytical proofs of security at an arbitrary order, the security of many gadgets from the literature is checked using some verification software. This is true in particular for most of the improvements over ISW from recent work [BBP+16,BBP+17,BDF+17,GPSS18,BBD+18]. One of the main verification software is the maskVerif tool from Barthe *et al.* [BBC+19], which allows to verify the security of a scheme described with a high-level language with respect to a range of models such as (S)NI in the (robust) probing model. A recent alternative is the SILVER software from Knichel, Sasdrich and Moradi [KSM20], whose notable features are that it proves gadgets described at the gate level from an actual hardware synthesis file rather than from a high-level description, and that it is complete (*i.e.* does not produce false negatives, as maskVerif may). While those are clear advantages in the case of hardware implementations, the somewhat slower verification time compared to maskVerif makes SILVER less competitive in the software case, where one may wish to prove a scheme at a higher order and where a high-level description is not limiting.

1.1 Our Contribution

Our work brings two main contributions. On the theoretical side, we extend the matrix model of [BBP+17] to make it complete over any finite field and thus for instance usable to prove the security of schemes defined over $\mathbb{F}_2$; we also extend it to analyse SNI security, whereas it was only formulated in the NI case by Belaïd *et al.*, and incorporate the robust probing model of Faust *et al.* [FGP+18] to offer some support for verification in presence of glitches. The extension to $\mathbb{F}_2$ is particularly relevant to concrete masking schemes since up to a few exceptions such as the one of [BBP+17], most schemes are intrinsically defined over this field. A corollary of our new theorems is also a simple proof that a scheme proven secure over $\mathbb{F}_2$ remains so when used over any extension, which is a common practice.

On the practical side, we use this extended model to derive a very efficient implementation of a verification algorithm whose performance beats the state-of-the-art maskVerif tool of Barthe *et al.* [BBC+19] by three orders of magnitude in the case of software multiplication gadgets; we illustrate this on software and hardware multiplication and refreshing schemes from the literature. We then take advantage of our improved verification performance and spend significant computation effort into proving the security of (variants of) the software multiplication gadgets of Barthe *et al.* [BDF+17] at mid-to-high order. This is all the more relevant since those do not have known generic proof of security at any order and are used in concrete implementations [JS17, GPSS18]. We verify NI and SNI gadgets up to order 11 at a total combined cost of close to 2^{55} basic operations, whereas the previously largest proven order was 7. We justify on the way the necessity of performing this kind of verification for schemes that do not have generic proofs by disproving a conjecture of Barthe *et al.* on the security of a natural transformation of NI schemes into SNI ones. Finally, we propose various improvements to decrease the randomness cost of several software gadgets. This results for instance in a decrease of 17% (resp. 19%) over the state-of-the-art for 8-share SNI multiplication (resp. refreshing) schemes, which could then for instance be used as stand-in replacements in the vectorised implementation of Grégoire *et al.* [GPSS18].

1.2 Roadmap

We present the security models and extend the matrix approach from CRYPTO 2017 in Sect. 2. We then introduce our verification algorithm and discuss its implementation in Sects. 3 and 4. We conclude with experimental results and the description of new gadgets in Sect. 5.

1.3 Notation

We use $\mathbb{K}^{n\times m}$ to denote the ring of matrices of n rows and m columns over the field $\mathbb{K}$. We write $[\![a, a+t]\!]$ for the set of integers $\{a, a+1, \ldots, a+t\}$. Matrices and vectors are named with bold upper- and lower-case variables respectively; $\boldsymbol{I}_n$, $\boldsymbol{0}_{n\times m}$, $\boldsymbol{1}_{n\times m}$ always denote the n-dimensional identity matrix and all-zero and all-one $n \times m$ matrices respectively, over any field $\mathbb{K}$.

2 Security Models for Masking Schemes

2.1 Simulatability and Non-interference

We start by recalling the definitions of the models of non-interference (NI), tight non-interference (TNI) and strong non-interference (SNI), introduced by Barthe *et al.* at CCS 2016 [BBD+16]. Our presentation closely follows the one of Belaïd *et al.* [BBP+17].

Definition 1 (Gadgets). *Let $f : \mathbb{K}^n \to \mathbb{K}^m$, u, $v \in \mathbb{N}$; a (u, v)-*gadget *for the function f is a randomised circuit C such that for every tuple $(\boldsymbol{x}_1, \ldots, \boldsymbol{x}_n) \in (\mathbb{K}^u)^n$ and every set of random coins $\mathcal{R}$, $(\boldsymbol{y}_1, \ldots, \boldsymbol{y}_m) \leftarrow C(\boldsymbol{x}_1, \ldots, \boldsymbol{x}_n; \mathcal{R})$ satisfies:*

$$\left(\sum_{j=1}^{v} \boldsymbol{y}_{1,j}, \ldots, \sum_{j=1}^{v} \boldsymbol{y}_{m,j}\right) = f\left(\sum_{j=1}^{u} \boldsymbol{x}_{1,j}, \ldots, \sum_{j=1}^{u} \boldsymbol{x}_{m,j}\right).$$

We then use x_i to denote $\sum_{j=1}^{u} \boldsymbol{x}_{i,j}$, and similarly for y_i; $\boldsymbol{x}_{i,j}$ is called the jth share *of x_i.*

In this definition, a randomised circuit C is a directed acyclic graph whose vertices represent arithmetic operation *gates* (addition and multiplication) over $\mathbb{K}$ of arity two, or random gates of arity zero whose outputs are uniform over $\mathbb{K}$ and pairwise independent for every execution of the circuit, and recorded in the variable $\mathcal{R}$; the edges of the graph are *wires* that connect the input and output of the gates together so as to describe the full computation of a given function.

A *probe* on a circuit C is a map that for every execution $C(\boldsymbol{x}_1, \ldots, \boldsymbol{x}_n; \mathcal{R})$ returns the value propagated on one of the wires of C. One may further distinguish between *external* probes on the output wires or output shares $\boldsymbol{y}_{i,j}$'s of C, and the remaining *internal* probes.

Definition 2 (t-Simulatability). *Let C be a (u, v)-gadget for $f : \mathbb{K}^n \to \mathbb{K}^n$, and ℓ, $t \in \mathbb{N}$. A set $\mathcal{P} = \{p_1, \ldots, p_\ell\}$ of probes of C is said to be* t-simulatable *if $\exists I_1, \ldots, I_n \subseteq [\![1, u]\!]$; $\#I_i \leq t$ and a randomised function $\pi : (\mathbb{K}^t)^n \to \mathbb{K}^\ell$ such that for any fixed $(\boldsymbol{x}_1, \ldots, \boldsymbol{x}_n) \in (\mathbb{K}^u)^n$, $\{p_1, \ldots, p_\ell\} \sim \{\pi(\{\boldsymbol{x}_{1,i}, i \in I_1\}, \ldots, \{\boldsymbol{x}_{n,i}, i \in I_n\})\}$.*

Less formally, a set $\mathcal{P}$ of probes on C is t-simulatable if there exists a randomised function that perfectly simulates the distribution of $\{p_1, \ldots, p_\ell\}$ while requiring at most t shares of every input to C to do so. It is important to remark here that the simulation is done w.r.t. a *fixed* input $(\boldsymbol{x}_1, \ldots, \boldsymbol{x}_n)$, regardless of the fact that one may randomise these inputs across many executions of C.

Thanks to Definition 2, we may now define the following.

Definition 3 (d-Non-interference). *A (u, v)-gadget C for a function over $\mathbb{K}^n$ is* d-non-interfering *(d-NI) if and only if for any set $\mathcal{P}$ of at most d probes on C $\exists t \leq d$ s.t. $\mathcal{P}$ is t-simulatable.*

Definition 4 (d-Tight non-interference). *A (u, v)-gadget C for a function over $\mathbb{K}^n$ is* d-tight-non-interfering *(d-TNI) if and only if any set of $t \leq d$ probes on C is t-simulatable.*

Definition 5 (d-Strong non-interference). *A (u, v)-gadget C for a function over $\mathbb{K}^n$ is* d-strong non-interfering *(d-SNI) if and only if for every set $\mathcal{P}_1$ of d_1 internal probes and every set $\mathcal{P}_2$ of d_2 external probes such that $d_1 + d_2 \leq d$, then $\mathcal{P}_1 \cup \mathcal{P}_2$ is d_1-simulatable.*

It is clear that strong non-interference implies tight non-interference at the same order, which itself implies non-interference. Barthe *et al.* [BBD+16] showed that tight non-interference did not imply strong non-interference, but that the composition of a d-NI gadget with a d-SNI one is d-SNI, while the composition of two d-NI gadgets was not necessarily d-NI. On the other hand they also showed that non-interference and tight non-interference are in fact equivalent, which in proofs allows to select the most convenient notion.

2.2 Matrix Model for Non-interference

We now recall Theorem 3.5 from Belaïd *et al.* [BBP+17], which defines a powerful matrix model to analyze the (T)NI property of a gadget over a sufficiently large field $\mathbb{K}$ for which all probes are *bilinear*. We then generalise it as Theorem 12 to work with schemes over any finite field (and $\mathbb{F}_2$ in particular), and to also analyse SNI security in Theorem 20.

In all of the following, we restrict our interest to gadgets for binary functions[1] $f : \mathbb{K}^2 \to \mathbb{K}$, and the inputs to f (resp. their sharings in a gadget C) will be denoted a and b (resp. $\boldsymbol{a} = (\boldsymbol{a}_0, \ldots, \boldsymbol{a}_{u-1})^t$, $\boldsymbol{b} = (\boldsymbol{b}_0, \ldots, \boldsymbol{b}_{u-1})^t$). We also write the elements of $\mathcal{R}$ as a vector $\boldsymbol{r} = (\boldsymbol{r}_1, \ldots, \boldsymbol{r}_R)^t$

Definition 6 (Bilinear probe). *A probe p on a $(d+1, v)$-gadget C for a function $f : \mathbb{K}^2 \to \mathbb{K}$ is called* bilinear *iff. it is an affine function in $\boldsymbol{a}_i$, $\boldsymbol{b}_j$, $\boldsymbol{a}_i\boldsymbol{b}_j$, $\boldsymbol{r}_k$; $0 \leq i, j \leq d$, $1 \leq k \leq R$. Equivalently, p is bilinear iff. $\exists\, \boldsymbol{M} \in \mathbb{K}^{(d+1)\times(d+1)}$, $\boldsymbol{\mu}$, $\boldsymbol{\nu} \in \mathbb{K}^{d+1}$, $\boldsymbol{\sigma} \in \mathbb{K}^R$ and $\tau \in \mathbb{K}$ s.t. $p = \boldsymbol{a}^t\boldsymbol{M}\boldsymbol{b} + \boldsymbol{a}^t\boldsymbol{\mu} + \boldsymbol{b}^t\boldsymbol{\nu} + \boldsymbol{r}^t\boldsymbol{\sigma} + \tau$.*

[1] Results for unary functions can then easily be obtained by *e.g.* fixing one input.

Definition 7 (Functional dependence). *An expression $E(x_1, \ldots, x_n)$ is said to* functionally depend *on x_n iff. $\exists c_1, \ldots, c_{n-1}$ s.t. the mapping $x_n \mapsto E(c_1, \ldots, c_{n-1}, x_n)$ is not constant.*

We now introduce the following condition.

Condition 8 ([BBP+17, Condition 3.2]). *A set of bilinear probes $\mathcal{P} = \{p_1, \ldots, p_\ell\}$ on a $(d+1, v)$-gadget C for a function $f : \mathbb{K}^2 \to \mathbb{K}$ satisfies Condition 8 iff. $\exists \boldsymbol{\lambda} \in \mathbb{K}^\ell$, $\boldsymbol{M} \in \mathbb{K}^{(d+1)\times(d+1)}$, $\boldsymbol{\mu}$, $\boldsymbol{\nu} \in \mathbb{K}^{d+1}$, and $\tau \in \mathbb{K}$ s.t. $\sum_{i=1}^{\ell} \boldsymbol{\lambda}_i p_i = \boldsymbol{a}^t \boldsymbol{M} \boldsymbol{b} + \boldsymbol{a}^t \boldsymbol{\mu} + \boldsymbol{b}^t \boldsymbol{\nu} + \tau$ and all the rows of the block matrix $\begin{pmatrix} \boldsymbol{M} & \boldsymbol{\mu} \end{pmatrix}$ or all the columns of the block matrix $\begin{pmatrix} \boldsymbol{M} \\ \boldsymbol{\nu}^t \end{pmatrix}$ are non-zero.*

In other words, this condition states that there exists a linear combination of probes of $\mathcal{P}$ that does not functionally depend on any random scalar and that functionally depends on either all of the shares for a or all of the shares for b.

We are now ready to state the following theorem.

Theorem 9 ([BBP+17, Theorem 3.5]). *Let $\mathcal{P}$ be a set of bilinear probes on a $(d+1, v)$-gadget C for a function $f : \mathbb{K}^2 \to \mathbb{K}$. If $\mathcal{P}$ satisfies Condition 8, then it is not d-simulatable. Furthermore, if $\mathcal{P}$ is not d-simulatable and $\#\mathbb{K} > d+1$, then it satisfies Condition 8.*

The next immediate corollary is more useful in practice.

Corollary 10 ([BBP+17, Corollary 3.7]). *Let C be a $(d+1, v)$-gadget for a function $f : \mathbb{K}^2 \to \mathbb{K}$ for which all probes are bilinear. If C is d-NI, then there is no set of d probes on C satisfying Condition 8. Furthermore, if $\#\mathbb{K} > d+1$ and there is no set of d probes on C satisfying Condition 8, then C is d-NI.*

For the masking schemes of CRYPTO 2017 [BBP+17] the restriction $\#\mathbb{K} > d+1$ is never an issue, as they are defined over large fields; however, this condition means that one cannot directly apply Corollary 10 to prove the security of a scheme over a small field such as $\mathbb{F}_2$.

We now sketch a proof of the second statement of Theorem 9 as a preparation to extending it to any field.

Proof (Theorem 9 right to left, sketch). Let $\mathcal{P} = \{p_1, \ldots, p_\ell\}$ be a set of bilinear probes that is not d-simulatable. We call $\boldsymbol{R}$ the block matrix $\begin{pmatrix} \boldsymbol{\sigma}_1 \cdots \boldsymbol{\sigma}_\ell \end{pmatrix}$, where $\boldsymbol{\sigma}_i$ denotes as in Definition 6 the vector of random scalars on which p_i depends. Up to a permutation of its rows and columns, the reduced column echelon form $\boldsymbol{R}'$ of $\boldsymbol{R}$ is of the shape $\begin{pmatrix} \boldsymbol{I}_t & \boldsymbol{0}_{t,\ell-t} \\ \boldsymbol{N} & \boldsymbol{0}_t \end{pmatrix}$, where $t < \ell$ is the rank of $\boldsymbol{R}$ and $\boldsymbol{N}$ is arbitrary. If we now consider the formal matrix $\boldsymbol{P} = \begin{pmatrix} p_1 \cdots p_\ell \end{pmatrix}^t$ and multiply it by the change-of-basis matrix from $\boldsymbol{R}$ to $\boldsymbol{R}'$, we obtain the matrix $\boldsymbol{P}' = \begin{pmatrix} \boldsymbol{P}'_r \ \boldsymbol{P}'_d \end{pmatrix}$ where $\boldsymbol{P}'_r$ represents t linear combinations $\{p'_1, \ldots, p'_t\}$ of probes that each depend on at least one random scalar which does not appear across any of the other linear combinations, and $\boldsymbol{P}'_d$ represents $\ell - t$ linearly independent linear combinations

$\mathcal{P}' = \{p'_{t+1}, \ldots, p'_\ell\}$ of probes that do not depend on any random scalar. All of the $\{p'_1, \ldots, p'_t\}$ can then be simulated by independent uniform distributions without requiring the knowledge of any share, and as $\mathcal{P}$ is not d-simulatable, $\mathcal{P}'$ cannot be d-simulatable either. W.l.o.g., this means that for every share $\boldsymbol{a}_i$, there is at least one linear combination of probes in $\mathcal{P}'$ that depends on it. In other words, the matrix $\boldsymbol{D} = \left(\boldsymbol{M}'_{t+1}\, \boldsymbol{\mu}_{t+1} \cdots \boldsymbol{M}'_\ell\, \boldsymbol{\mu}_\ell\right)$ that records this dependence has no zero row. We now finally want to show that there is a linear combination $\left(\boldsymbol{\lambda}_{t+1} \cdots \boldsymbol{\lambda}_\ell\right)^t$ of elements of $\mathcal{P}'$ that satisfies Condition 8. This can be done by showing that $\exists\, \boldsymbol{\Lambda} = \left(\boldsymbol{\Lambda}_{t+1} \cdots \boldsymbol{\Lambda}_\ell\right)^t$ s.t. $\boldsymbol{D\Lambda}$ has no zero row, where the $\boldsymbol{\Lambda}_i$'s are the $(d+2) \times (d+2)$ scalar matrices of multiplication by the $\boldsymbol{\lambda}_i$'s. By the Schwartz-Zippel-DeMillo-Lipton lemma this is always the case as soon as $\#\mathbb{K} > d+1$ [Sch80], and this last step is the only one that depends on $\mathbb{K}$. □

We now wish to extend Theorem 9 and its corollary to any finite field $\mathbb{K}$. We do this using the TNI notion rather than NI, and so first state an appropriate straightforward adaptation of Condition 8:

Condition 11. *A set of bilinear probes $\mathcal{P} = \{p_1, \ldots, p_\ell\}$ on a $(d+1, v)$-gadget C for a function $f : \mathbb{K}^2 \to \mathbb{K}$ satisfies Condition 11 iff. $\exists \boldsymbol{\lambda} \in \mathbb{K}^\ell$, $\boldsymbol{M} \in \mathbb{K}^{(d+1)\times(d+1)}$, $\boldsymbol{\mu}$, $\boldsymbol{\nu} \in \mathbb{K}^{d+1}$, and $\tau \in \mathbb{K}$ s.t. $\sum_{i=1}^{\ell} \boldsymbol{\lambda}_i p_i = \boldsymbol{a}^t \boldsymbol{M} \boldsymbol{b} + \boldsymbol{a}^t \boldsymbol{\mu} + \boldsymbol{b}^t \boldsymbol{\nu} + \tau$ and the block matrix $\left(\boldsymbol{M}\ \boldsymbol{\mu}\right)$ (resp. the block matrix $\begin{pmatrix}\boldsymbol{M} \\ \boldsymbol{\nu}^t\end{pmatrix}$) has at least $\ell+1$ non-zero rows (resp. columns).*

In other words, Condition 11 states that the expression $\sum_{i=1}^{\ell} \boldsymbol{\lambda}_i p_i$, which involves ℓ probes, functionally depends on no random scalar and on at least $\ell+1$ shares of a or $\ell+1$ shares of b, and hence is a TNI attack. We will then show the following:

Theorem 12. *Let $\mathcal{P}$ be a set of at most d bilinear probes on a $(d+1, v)$-gadget C for a function $f : \mathbb{K}^2 \to \mathbb{K}$. If $\mathcal{P}$, is not d-simulatable then $\exists \mathcal{P}' \subseteq \mathcal{P}$ s.t. $\mathcal{P}'$ satisfies Condition 11.*

Corollary 13 (Corollary of Theorems 9 and 12). *Let C be a $(d+1, v)$-gadget C for a function $f : \mathbb{K}^2 \to \mathbb{K}$ for which all probes are bilinear. If C is d-NI, then there is no set of d probes on C satisfying Condition 8. Furthermore, if there is no set of $t \leq d$ probes on C satisfying Condition 11, then C is d-NI.*[2]

The proof of Theorem 12 essentially relies on the following lemmas, conveniently formulated with linear codes[3]:

Lemma 14. *Let $\mathcal{C}_1$ (resp. $\mathcal{C}_2$) be an $[n_1, k]$ (resp. $[n_2, k]$, $n_2 > n_1$) linear code over a finite field $\mathbb{K}$. Let $\boldsymbol{G}_1 \in \mathbb{K}^{k \times n_1}$ and $\boldsymbol{G}_2 \in \mathbb{K}^{k \times n_2}$ be two generator matrices*

[2] As Condition 11 directly implies an attack, one could also formulate this corollary solely in terms of this condition.

[3] Recall that an $[n, k]$ linear code over a field $\mathbb{K}$ is a k-dimensional linear subspace of $\mathbb{K}^n$.

for $\mathcal{C}_1$ and $\mathcal{C}_2$ that have no zero column. Then the concatenated code $\mathcal{C}_{1,2}$ of $\mathcal{C}_1$ and $\mathcal{C}_2$ generated by $\boldsymbol{G}_{1,2} := \begin{pmatrix}\boldsymbol{G}_1 & \boldsymbol{G}_2\end{pmatrix}$ has the following property: $\exists\, \boldsymbol{c} \in \mathcal{C}_{1,2}$ s.t. $\mathrm{wt}_1(\mathrm{c}) < \mathrm{wt}_2(\mathrm{c})$, where $\mathrm{wt}_1(\cdot)$ (resp. $\mathrm{wt}_2(\cdot)$) denotes the Hamming weight function restricted to the first n_1 (resp. last n_2) coordinates of $\mathcal{C}_{1,2}$.

One may remark that if $\#\mathbb{K}$ is sufficiently large w.r.t. the parameters of the codes, then by the Schwartz-Zippel-DeMillo-Lipton lemma there exists a word in $\mathcal{C}_{1,2}$ of maximal wt_2 weight, and the conclusion immediately follows; yet this argument does not hold over any field.

Lemma 15. *The statement of Lemma 14 still holds if $\mathbb{K}$ is replaced by a matrix ring $\mathbb{K}'^{d\times d}$ and if $\boldsymbol{G}_1$ is defined over the subfield of the scalar matrices of $\mathbb{K}'^{d\times d}$.*

We first recall the following:

Definition 16 (Shortening of a linear code). *Let $\mathcal{C}$ be an $[n,k]$ linear code over $\mathbb{K}$ generated by $\boldsymbol{G} \in \mathbb{K}^{k\times n}$. The* shortened code *$\mathcal{C}'$ w.r.t. coordinate $i \in [\![1,n]\!]$ is the subcode made of all codewords of $\mathcal{C}$ that are zero at coordinate i, with this coordinate then being deleted.*

We also give:

Definition 17 (Isolated coordinate). *Let $\boldsymbol{M} \in \mathbb{K}^{m\times n}$. A coordinate $i \in [\![1,n]\!]$ is called* isolated *for the row $\boldsymbol{M}_j$ of $\boldsymbol{M}$, $j \in [\![1,m]\!]$, iff. $\boldsymbol{M}_{j,i} \neq 0$ and $\forall j' \neq j \in [\![1,m]\!]$, $\boldsymbol{M}_{j',i} = 0$.*

And:

Procedure 18. *We reuse the notation of the statement of Lemma 14. We* apply Procedure *18 on a row of $\boldsymbol{G}_{1,2}$ by doing the following: denote $\mathcal{I}_1$ (resp. $\mathcal{I}_2$) the (possibly empty) set of isolated coordinates on its first n_1 (resp. last n_2) columns; then if $\#\mathcal{I}_1 \geq \#\mathcal{I}_2$, shorten $\mathcal{C}_{1,2}$ w.r.t. all the coordinates in $\mathcal{I}_1 \cup \mathcal{I}_2$. Practically, this means deleting from $\boldsymbol{G}_{1,2}$ the row being processed and all the columns in $\mathcal{I}_1 \cup \mathcal{I}_2$. This results in a code $\mathcal{C}'_{1,2}$ generated by $\begin{pmatrix}\boldsymbol{G}'_1 & \boldsymbol{G}'_2\end{pmatrix}$ where $\boldsymbol{G}'_1 \in \mathbb{K}^{(k-1)\times n'_1}$ (resp. $\boldsymbol{G}'_2 \in \mathbb{K}^{(k-1)\times n'_2}$) is a submatrix of $\boldsymbol{G}_1$ (resp. $\boldsymbol{G}_2$) and $n'_1 < n_1$, $n'_2 < n_2$, $n'_1 < n'_2$, and none of the columns of $\boldsymbol{G}'_{1,2}$ is zero. One may also remark that since $\boldsymbol{G}'_1$ is of rank $k-1$, we have $k-1 \leq n'_1$.*

We are now ready to prove Lemmas 14 and 15.

Proof (Lemma 14*).* We prove this lemma by induction using Procedure 18.

In a first step one applies Procedure 18 to every row of $\boldsymbol{G}_{1,2}$ one at a time and repeats this process again until either there is no row for which applying the procedure results in a shortening, or the dimension of the shortened code reaches 1.

In the latter case, this means that the only non-zero codeword in $\boldsymbol{G}'_{1,2} \in \mathbb{K}^{1\times(n'_1+n'_2)}$ is of full weight $n'_1+n'_2$ with $n'_1 < n'_2$ (since $\boldsymbol{G}'_{1,2}$ only has a single row and none of its columns is zero). This induces a codeword c of $\mathcal{C}$ s.t. $\mathrm{wt}_1(\mathrm{c}) = \mathrm{n}'_1$ and $\mathrm{wt}_2(\mathrm{c}) = \mathrm{n}'_2$, so we are done.

In the former case, one is left with a matrix $\boldsymbol{G}'_{1,2} \in \mathbb{K}^{k' \times (n'_1+n'_2)}$, $k' > 1$. One then computes the reduced row echelon form of $\boldsymbol{G}'_{1,2}$ (this does not introduce any zero column since the elementary row operations are invertible) and again iteratively applies Procedure 18 on the resulting matrix as done in the first step. Now either the application of Procedure 18 leads to a shortened code of dimension 1 and then we are done as above, or we are left with a matrix $\boldsymbol{G}''_{1,2} \in \mathbb{K}^{k'' \times (n''_1+n''_2)}$ which can be of two forms:

1. $k'' = n''_1$. Up to permutation of its columns, $\boldsymbol{G}''_{1,2}$ can be written as:
$$\left(\boldsymbol{I}_{n''_1} \,\middle|\, \boldsymbol{I}_{n''_1}\ \boldsymbol{I}_{n''_1}\ *\right),$$
where $*$ is arbitrary. The left $k'' \times n''_1$ block is justified from $\boldsymbol{G}''_{1,2}$ being in reduced row echelon form and having full rank. The right $k'' \times n''_2$ block is justified from the fact that every row of the left block has exactly one isolated coordinate; since no simplification can be done anymore to $\boldsymbol{G}''_{1,2}$ by applying Procedure 18, this means that those rows have at least two isolated coordinates on the right block. This is enough to conclude on the existence of a codeword of $\mathcal{C}$ satisfying the desired property.
Recall that it is not possible to have $k'' > n''_1$ from the last remark in Procedure 18. The only remaining case is then:
2. $k'' < n''_1$. Up to a permutation of its columns, the rank-k'' matrix $\boldsymbol{G}''_{1,2}$ can be written as:
$$\left(\boldsymbol{I}_{k''}\ *_L \,\middle|\, \boldsymbol{I}_{k''}\ \boldsymbol{I}_{k''}\ *_R\right),$$
and it has no zero column. One then applies Lemma 14 inductively on the code generated by the submatrix $\boldsymbol{G}'''_{1,2} := \left(*_L \,\middle|\, \boldsymbol{I}_{k''}\ *_R\right)$ which is of strictly smaller length. Let $c''' = \boldsymbol{\lambda}\boldsymbol{G}'''_{1,2}$ be a codeword of this latter code that satisfies the desired property, then $\boldsymbol{\lambda}\boldsymbol{G}''_{1,2}$ also satisfies it for $\mathcal{C}_{1,2}$, which concludes the proof.

□

Proof (Lemma 15). The proof simply consists in remarking that all the steps of the proof of Lemma 14 can be carried out in the modified setting of Lemma 15. Mainly:

- Definitions 16 and 17 and Procedure 18 naturally generalise to matrices over rings, and the application of Procedure 18 is unchanged.
- Recall that by induction the left $k' \times n'_1$ submatrix is always of full rank k', which is also the rank of $\boldsymbol{G}'_{1,2}$. Since $\boldsymbol{G}_1$ is defined over scalar matrices, Gauß-Jordan elimination can be computed as if over a field.

□

The proof of Theorem 12 then follows.

Proof (Theorem 12). We start similarly from the proof of Theorem 9, and use the same notation: let $\mathcal{P}'$ be a set of $\ell - t$ linearly independent linear combinations of probes of $\mathcal{P}$ that do not depend on any random scalar, and let

$\boldsymbol{D} = (\boldsymbol{M}'_{t+1}\ \boldsymbol{\mu}_{t+1} \cdots \boldsymbol{M}'_{\ell}\ \boldsymbol{\mu}_{\ell})$ be the matrix that records the dependence of these probes on every share $\boldsymbol{a}_i$. We will show that $\exists \mathcal{P}'' \subseteq \mathcal{P}$ that satisfies Condition 11. To do this, we introduce two new indicator matrices:

- Let $\boldsymbol{\Pi} \in \mathbb{K}^{(d+2)\times(d+2)^{(\ell-t)\times\ell}}$ be s.t. for every $p' \in \mathcal{P}'$ it records in its rows its dependence on the probes of $\mathcal{P}$ as scalar matrices;[4] that is, $\boldsymbol{\Pi}$ is s.t. $p'_i = \sum_{j=1}^{\ell} \pi_{i,j} p_j$ where $\pi_{i,j}$ is the scalar on the diagonal of the scalar matrix $\boldsymbol{\Pi}_{i,j}$. W.l.o.g., we may assume that every probe of $\mathcal{P}$ appears at least once in a linear combination of $\mathcal{P}'$, otherwise it is simply discarded, so $\boldsymbol{\Pi}$ has no zero column.
- Let $\boldsymbol{\Delta} \in \mathbb{K}^{(d+2)\times(d+2)^{(\ell-t)\times(d+1)}}$ be the matrix that for every $p' \in \mathcal{P}'$ records in its rows its dependence on the shares $\boldsymbol{a}_i$s; that is if the bilinear probe p'_i can be written as $p'_i = \boldsymbol{a}^t\boldsymbol{M}'\boldsymbol{b} + \boldsymbol{a}^t\boldsymbol{\mu}' + \boldsymbol{b}^t\boldsymbol{\nu}' + \tau'$, then $\boldsymbol{\Delta}_{i,j}$ is set to the diagonal matrix of the jth row of $(\boldsymbol{M}'\ \boldsymbol{\mu}')$.[5] Note that since by assumption $\boldsymbol{D}$ has no zero row, $\boldsymbol{\Delta}$ has no zero *column*.

Now we invoke Lemma 15 with $\boldsymbol{\Pi}$ as $\boldsymbol{G}_1$ and $\boldsymbol{\Delta}$ as $\boldsymbol{G}_2$ the generator matrices for the concatenated code $\mathcal{C}_{1,2}$. Let $\boldsymbol{c} \in \mathcal{C}_{1,2}$ be a codeword that satisfies $\mathrm{wt}_1(\mathrm{c}) < \mathrm{wt}_2(\mathrm{c})$; this translates to a linear combination of $\ell'' := \mathrm{wt}_1(\mathrm{c})$ probes of $\mathcal{P}'' \subseteq \mathcal{P}$ that (as linear combinations of elements of $\mathcal{P}'$) does not depend on any randomness and s.t. the associated matrix $(\boldsymbol{M}''\ \boldsymbol{\mu}'')$ has $\mathrm{wt}_2(\mathrm{c}) \geq \ell'' + 1$ non-zero rows (by applying the inverse transformation from $\boldsymbol{\Delta}$ to $\boldsymbol{D}$), hence $\mathcal{P}''$ satisfies Condition 11. □

Finally, the proof of Corollary 13 is immediate from Theorems 9 and 12.

2.3 Matrix Model for Strong Non-interference

We now wish to adapt the approach of Theorems 9 and 12 to be able to prove that a scheme is SNI. This is in fact quite straightforward, and it mostly consists in defining a suitable variant of Condition 11 and in applying Lemma 15 to well-chosen matrices, to show again that there is a subset of probes that satisfies the condition whenever there is an attack.

Condition 19. *A set of* $\ell = \ell_1 + \ell_2$ *bilinear probes* $\mathcal{P} = \{p_1, \ldots, p_\ell\}$ *on a* $(d+1, v)$*-gadget* C *for a function* $f : \mathbb{K}^2 \to \mathbb{K}$*, of which* ℓ_1 *are internal, satisfies*

[4] This use of scalar matrices is only so that $\boldsymbol{\Pi}$ is defined on the same base structure as $\boldsymbol{\Delta}$ below. As an example, taking $\ell = d = 2$ and considering two probes in $\mathcal{P}'$ as $p'_1 = p_1 + p_2$; $p'_2 = p_2$, then $\boldsymbol{\Pi} = \begin{pmatrix} \boldsymbol{I}_4 & \boldsymbol{I}_4 \\ \boldsymbol{0}_4 & \boldsymbol{I}_4 \end{pmatrix}$.

[5] This use of diagonal matrices allows to keep track of (the lack of) simplifications when combining several probes; for instance, if two probes depend on the same $\boldsymbol{a}_i$ as $\boldsymbol{a}_i\boldsymbol{b}_j$ and $\boldsymbol{a}_i\boldsymbol{b}_{j'}$ with $j \neq j'$, then the sum of those probes still depends on $\boldsymbol{a}_i$. Continuing the previous example and taking $p'_1 = \boldsymbol{a}_0\boldsymbol{b}_0 + \boldsymbol{a}_0\boldsymbol{b}_1 + \boldsymbol{a}_1\boldsymbol{b}_2 + \boldsymbol{a}_2$, then the first row of $\boldsymbol{\Delta}$ (whose entries are 4×4 matrices) is $\begin{pmatrix} 1 & & & & 0 & & & & 0 & & & \\ & 1 & & & & 0 & & & & 0 & & \\ & & 0 & & & & 1 & & & & 0 & \\ & & & 0 & & & & 0 & & & & 1 \end{pmatrix}$.

Condition 19 iff. $\exists \boldsymbol{\lambda} \in \mathbb{K}^{\ell}$, $\boldsymbol{M} \in \mathbb{K}^{(d+1)\times(d+1)}$, $\boldsymbol{\mu}$, $\boldsymbol{\nu} \in \mathbb{K}^{d+1}$, *and* $\tau \in \mathbb{K}$ *s.t.* $\sum_{i=1}^{\ell} \boldsymbol{\lambda}_i p_i = \boldsymbol{a}^t \boldsymbol{M} \boldsymbol{b} + \boldsymbol{a}^t \boldsymbol{\mu} + \boldsymbol{b}^t \boldsymbol{\nu} + \tau$ *and the block matrix* $(\boldsymbol{M}\ \boldsymbol{\mu})$ *(resp. the block matrix* $\begin{pmatrix}\boldsymbol{M}\\ \boldsymbol{\nu}^t\end{pmatrix}$*) has at least* $\ell_1 + 1$ *non-zero rows (resp. columns).*

Theorem 20. *Let* $\mathcal{P}$ *be a set of at most* d *bilinear probes on a* $(d+1, v)$*-gadget* C *for a function* $f : \mathbb{K}^2 \to \mathbb{K}$*, of which* ℓ_1 *are internal. If* $\mathcal{P}$ *is not* ℓ_1*-simulatable then* $\exists \mathcal{P}' \subseteq \mathcal{P}$ *s.t.* $\mathcal{P}'$ *satisfies Condition 19.*

Proof. In the full version [BK19].

And we then have the immediate corollary:

Corollary 21. *Let* C *be a* $(d+1, v)$*-gadget for a function* $f : \mathbb{K}^2 \to \mathbb{K}$ *for which all probes are bilinear, then* C *is d-SNI iff. there is not set of* $t \leq d$ *probes on* C *that satisfies Condition 19.*

2.4 Security of Binary Schemes over Finite Fields of Characteristic Two

Let C be a d-NI or SNI gadget for a function defined over $\mathbb{F}_2$; a natural question is whether its security is preserved if it is lifted to an extension $\mathbb{F}_{2^n}$. Indeed, the probes available to the adversary are the same in the two cases, but the latter offers more possible linear combinations $\sum_{i=1}^{\ell} \boldsymbol{\lambda}_i p_i$, since the $\boldsymbol{\lambda}_i$s are no longer restricted to $\{0, 1\}$. We answer this question positively, and give a simple proof based on Theorems 12 and 20.

Theorem 22. *Let* C *be a d-NI (resp. d-SNI) gadget for a function* $f : \mathbb{F}_2^2 \to \mathbb{F}_2$*, then for any* n*, the natural lifting* $\widehat{C}$ *of* C *to* $\widehat{f} : \mathbb{F}_{2^n}^2 \to \mathbb{F}_{2^n}$ *is also d-NI (resp. d-SNI).*

Proof. We only prove the d-NI case, the d-SNI one being similar. From Corollary 13, it is sufficient to show that if $\nexists \mathcal{P}$ for C that satisfies Condition 11, then the same holds for $\widehat{C}$. We do this by showing the following contrapositive: if a set of probes $\mathcal{P}$ is not d-simulatable for $\widehat{C}$, then it is not d-simulatable either for C.

From the proofs of Theorems 9 and 12, if $\mathcal{P}$ is not d-simulatable for $\widehat{C}$, then there is a matrix $\widehat{\boldsymbol{D}}$ that leads to the existence of $\mathcal{P}'$ s.t. Condition 11 is satisfied. All we need to do is showing that a similar matrix $\boldsymbol{D}$ can also be found for C. Since C is defined over $\mathbb{F}_2$, the matrices $\boldsymbol{R}$ and $\boldsymbol{P}$, and thence $\widehat{\boldsymbol{R}}$ and $\widehat{\boldsymbol{P}}$ have all their coefficients in $\{0, 1\}$. As 1 is its own inverse, the change-of-basis matrix from $\widehat{\boldsymbol{R}}$ to $\widehat{\boldsymbol{R}}'$ is also binary; equivalently, this means that the Gauß-Jordan elimination of $\widehat{\boldsymbol{R}}$ can be done in the subfield $\mathbb{F}_2$. Thus one only has to take $\boldsymbol{D} = \widehat{\boldsymbol{D}}$ to satisfy Condition 11 on C. □

This result is quite useful as it means that the security of a binary scheme only needs to be proven once in $\mathbb{F}_2$, even if it is eventually used in one or several extension fields. Proceeding thusly is in particular beneficial in terms of verification performance, since working over $\mathbb{F}_2$ limits the number of linear combinations to consider and may lead to some specific optimisations (cf. *e.g.* Sects. 3 and 4).

REMARK. This result was in fact already implicitly used (in a slight variant) by Barthe *et al.* in their masking compiler [BBD+15] and in maskVerif [BBC+19], since they use gadgets defined over an arbitrary structure $(\mathbb{K}, 0, 1, \oplus, \ominus, \odot)$. However we could not find a proof, which actually seems necessary to justify the correctness of this approach and of our algorithms of the next section.

3 An Algorithm for Checking Non-interference

In this section, we present a new efficient algorithm to check if a scheme is (strong) non-interfering. This algorithm is a modification of the one presented by Belaïd *et al.* at EUROCRYPT 2016 [BBP+16, Section 8], and its correctness crucially relies on Theorems 12 and 20; it thus only applies to schemes for which all probes are bilinear, but this is not a hard restriction in practice.

In all of the following we assume that the field $\mathbb{K}$ over which the scheme is defined is equal to $\mathbb{F}_2$, which means that we will simultaneously assess its security in that field and all its extensions (cf. Sect. 2.4). Some discussion of implementation in the NI case for schemes natively defined over larger fields (meaning that shares or random masks may be multiplied by constants not in $\{0, 1\}$) for which the new Theorem 12 is not needed can be found in [KR18].

We start by introducing some vocabulary and by recalling the algorithm from Belaïd *et al.*

Definition 23 (Elementary probes). *A probe p is called* elementary *if it is of the form $p = \boldsymbol{a}_i\boldsymbol{b}_j$ (elementary* deterministic *probe) or $p = \boldsymbol{r}_i$ (elementary* random *probe).*

Definition 24 (Shares indicator matrix). *Let p be a bilinear probe. We call* shares indicator matrix *and write $\boldsymbol{M}_p$ the matrix $\boldsymbol{M}$ from Definition 6.*

Definition 25 (Randomness indicator matrix). *Let p be a bilinear probe. We call* randomness indicator matrix *and write $\boldsymbol{\sigma}_p$ the column matrix $\boldsymbol{\sigma}$ from Definition 6.*

3.1 The Algorithm from EUROCRYPT 2016

At EUROCRYPT 2016, Belaïd *et al.* presented an efficient probabilistic algorithm to find potential attacks against the d-privacy notion[6] for masking schemes for the multiplication over $\mathbb{F}_2$. By running the algorithm many times and not detecting any attack, one can also establish the security of a scheme up to some probability, but deriving a deterministic counterpart is less trivial. This algorithm works as follows.

[6] It can also be trivially modified to check attacks against NI security.

Consider a scheme on which all possible probes $\mathcal{P}$ are bilinear, and let $\boldsymbol{H}_{\mathcal{P}} := (\boldsymbol{\sigma}_p), p \in \mathcal{P}$ be the block matrix constructed from all the corresponding randomness indicator matrices. The algorithm of [BBP+16, Sect. 8] starts by finding a set of fewer than d probes whose sum[7] does not depend on any randomness. That is to say, it is looking for a vector $\boldsymbol{x}$ such that $\boldsymbol{H}_{\mathcal{P}} \cdot \boldsymbol{x} = \boldsymbol{0}$ and $\mathrm{wt(x)} \leq \mathrm{d}$. This can be immediately reformulated as a coding problem, as one is in fact searching for a codeword of weight less than d in the dual code of $\boldsymbol{H}_{\mathcal{P}}$. This search can then be performed using any information set decoding algorithm, and Belaïd *et al.* used the original one of Prange [Pra62].[8] Once such a set has been found, it is tested against [BBP+16, Condition 2] (which is similar to Condition 8) to determine if it is a valid attack against the d-NI notion, and [BBP+16, Condition 1] to determine if it is an attack for d-privacy. This procedure is then repeated until an attack is found or one has gained sufficient confidence in the security of the scheme.

Removing elementary *deterministic* probes. To make the above procedure more efficient, an important observation made by Belaïd *et al.* is that if the sum of every probe of a given set does not functionally depend on some $\boldsymbol{a}_i$ or $\boldsymbol{b}_j$, it is always possible to make it so by adding a corresponding elementary probe $\boldsymbol{a}_i\boldsymbol{b}_j$. This can be used to check, say, d-NI security by simply comparing the number of missing $\boldsymbol{a}_i$ or $\boldsymbol{b}_j$ to $d - \mathrm{wt(x)}$. This allows to reduce the number of probes that one has to include in $\mathcal{P}$ (and thus the dimension of $\boldsymbol{H}_{\mathcal{P}}$), making the algorithm more efficient.

3.2 A New Algorithm Based on Enumeration

We now describe a new algorithm based on a partial enumeration of the power set $\wp(\mathcal{P})$ of $\mathcal{P}$. The idea is to simply consider every sum of fewer than d probes and check if it depends on all shares and no random masks, relying on Corollaries 13 and 21 for correctness. Since the cost of such an enumeration quickly grows with the size of $\mathcal{P}$, we then follow and extend the above observation by Belaïd *et al.* and only perform the enumeration on a reduced set. We first describe a simple extension of this "dimension reduction" strategy, before detailing the algorithms themselves. A more elaborate dimension reduction process is then described in Sect. 3.3, and we discuss implementation aspects in Sect. 4.

Removing elementary *random* probes. It is easy to adapt a deterministic enumeration so that one can completely remove elementary random probes; it suffices to remark that if the sum of every probe of a given set functionally depends on some $\boldsymbol{r}_i$, it is always possible to make it not so by adding the corresponding elementary probes.

[7] That is, the only non-trivial linear combination over $\mathbb{F}_2$ that depends on all the elements of the set.

[8] One may remark that since information set decoding relies on Gaussian elimination, the cost of one step of this algorithm increases more than linearly in the size of $\mathcal{P}$.

Combining the two above observations, we may remove every elementary probe from the set $\mathcal{P}$.[9] This can be summarized by saying that in the enumeration, one is not restricted anymore to finding exactly a combination of fewer than d probes that depends on all shares and no random masks, as it is enough to find a combination of $\ell \leq d$ probes that depends on u shares and v masks as long as $d - \ell \geq (d + 1 - u) + v$, since the missing shares and extra masks can be dealt with elementary probes in a predictable way. This is in fact exactly the check that is performed in our implementation in the case of NI security, as is detailed and justified below.

Checking a Scheme for Non-interference. We now state the following:

Proposition 26. *Let C be a $(d+1, v)$-gadget for a function $f : \mathbb{F}_2^2 \to \mathbb{F}_2$ for which all probes are bilinear, and $\mathcal{Q}_0$ be a set of n_0 non-elementary probes on C that functionally depends on n_a shares $\boldsymbol{a}_i$s, n_b shares $\boldsymbol{b}_j$s, and n_r random scalars $\boldsymbol{r}_i$s. Let $\mathcal{Q}_1$ be one of the smallest sets of elementary probes needed to complete $\mathcal{Q}_0$ such that $\mathcal{Q}_0 \cup \mathcal{Q}_1$ satisfies Condition 11 and functionally depends on all the $\boldsymbol{a}_i$s or all the $\boldsymbol{b}_i$s.[10] Then $n_1 := \#\mathcal{Q}_1 = n_r + (d + 1 - \max(n_a, n_b))$.*

Proof. In the full version [BK19].

This proposition can then be used in a straightforward way to check if a scheme is d-NI. To do so, one simply has to enumerate every set $\mathcal{Q}_0 \in \wp(\mathcal{P})$ of d non-elementary probes or fewer and check if $n_0 + n_1 \leq d$. By Corollary 13, if no such set $\mathcal{Q}_0$ can be completed as in Proposition 26 and still contain fewer than d probes, then the scheme is d-NI.

Checking a Scheme for Strong Non-interference. We only need to adapt Proposition 26 to distinguish between internal and external probes:

Proposition 27. *Let C be a $(d+1, v)$-gadget for a function $f : \mathbb{F}_2^2 \to \mathbb{F}_2$ for which all probes are bilinear, and $\mathcal{Q}_0$ be a set of n_0 non-elementary probes on C that functionally depends on n_a shares $\boldsymbol{a}_i$s, n_b shares $\boldsymbol{b}_j$s, and n_r random scalars $\boldsymbol{r}_i$s. Let n_I denote the number of internal probes in $\mathcal{Q}_0$. Then there is a set $\mathcal{Q}_1$ of n_r elementary random probes such that $\mathcal{Q}_0 \cup \mathcal{Q}_1$ satisfies Condition 19 iff.* $\max(n_a, n_b) > n_I + n_r$.

Proof. In the full version [BK19].

9 Note that this means that one would not detect the existence of an attack that would use *only* elementary probes. However, it is easy to see from their definitions that ℓ such probes functionally depend on at most ℓ shares, and so can never lead to a non-trivial attack.

10 This additional constraint is not in itself necessary, but it simplifies the overall algorithm.

This proposition can then be used in a straightforward way to check if a scheme is d-SNI. To do so, one simply has to enumerate every set $\mathcal{Q}_0 \in \wp(\mathcal{P})$ of d non-elementary probes or fewer and check if $\max(n_a, n_b) > n_I + n_r$ and $n_0 + n_r \leq d$. If no such set satisfying this condition is found, then the scheme is d-SNI by Corollary 21.

3.3 Dimension Reduction

To further reduce the size of the space to explore during the verification, it may be possible to filter additional non-elementary probes from the set $\mathcal{P}$, in the case where they can be replaced by "better" ones. To do so while preserving the correctness of our verification algorithm, we first define the following:

Definition 28 (Reduced sets). *Let $\mathcal{P} := \cup_{k=0}^{v} \mathcal{P}_k$ and $\mathcal{P}' := \cup_{k=0}^{v} \mathcal{P}'_k$ be two sets of probes on a $(d+1, v)$-gadget C for a function $f : \mathbb{F}_2^2 \to \mathbb{F}_2$ for which all probes are bilinear, where $\mathcal{P}_k$ (resp. $\mathcal{P}'_k$) denotes the probes on the wires of C that are connected to the output share $\boldsymbol{c}_k$. Then $\mathcal{P}'$ is said to be a* reduced set *for $\mathcal{P}$ iff.:*

- *$\#\mathcal{P}' \leq \#\mathcal{P}$*
- *For all output wires k, for every linear combination of probes of $\mathcal{P}_k$ there is a linear combination of equal or lower weight of probes of $\mathcal{P}'_k$ with: 1) exactly the same randomness dependence (reusing the notation of Definition 6 this means that both combinations have the same $\boldsymbol{\sigma}$ term); 2) the shares dependence of the combination from $\mathcal{P}'_k$ covers the one of the combination from $\mathcal{P}_k$ (*i.e. *the support of the $\boldsymbol{M}$, $\boldsymbol{\mu}$, $\boldsymbol{\nu}$ terms of the former include the ones of the same terms of the latter).*

We then have:

Lemma 29. *If two linear combinations of probes $\sum \boldsymbol{\lambda}_i p_i$ and $\sum \boldsymbol{\lambda}'_i p'_i$ functionally depend on disjoint sets of elementary probes and shares $\boldsymbol{a}_i\boldsymbol{b}_j$, $\boldsymbol{a}_i$ and $\boldsymbol{b}_j$, then their sum functionally depends on the union of those sets.*

Proof. Immediate, since using the notation of Definition 6, the supports of $\boldsymbol{M}$, $\boldsymbol{\mu}$, $\boldsymbol{\nu}$ are disjoint from the ones of $\boldsymbol{M}'$, $\boldsymbol{\mu}'$, $\boldsymbol{\nu}'$. □

Finally, we conclude with the following:

Proposition 30. *Let $\mathcal{P}'$ be a reduced set for a set of probes $\mathcal{P}$ on a $(d+1, v)$-gadget C for a function $f : \mathbb{F}_2^2 \to \mathbb{F}_2$ for which all probes are bilinear and for which all output shares functionally depend on pairwise disjoint sets of elementary probes and shares $\boldsymbol{a}_i\boldsymbol{b}_j$, $\boldsymbol{a}_i$ and $\boldsymbol{b}_j$. Then if $\mathcal{Q} \subseteq \mathcal{P}$ satisfies Condition 11, $\exists\, \mathcal{Q}' \subseteq \mathcal{P}'$, $\#\mathcal{Q}' \leq \#\mathcal{Q}$ that also satisfies Condition 11.*

Proof. In the full version [BK19].

EXAMPLES. Consider a set $\mathcal{P}$ of two probes $\boldsymbol{a}_0\boldsymbol{b}_0 + \boldsymbol{r}_0 + \boldsymbol{a}_0\boldsymbol{b}_1$ and $\boldsymbol{a}_0\boldsymbol{b}_0 + \boldsymbol{r}_0 + \boldsymbol{a}_0\boldsymbol{b}_1 + \boldsymbol{a}_1\boldsymbol{b}_0$ on the same output share. Then provided that none of the $\boldsymbol{a}_i\boldsymbol{b}_j$ appears in other output shares, this set can be simplified by keeping only the second probe, since it covers all the shares of the first one.

On the other hand, a set containing two probes $\boldsymbol{a}_0\boldsymbol{b}_0 + \boldsymbol{r}_0 + \boldsymbol{a}_0\boldsymbol{b}_1 + \boldsymbol{a}_1\boldsymbol{b}_0$ and $\boldsymbol{a}_0\boldsymbol{b}_0 + \boldsymbol{r}_0 + \boldsymbol{a}_0\boldsymbol{b}_1 + \boldsymbol{a}_1\boldsymbol{b}_0 + \boldsymbol{r}_1$ cannot be simplified since the two probes do not include exactly the same random masks.

We will see in Sect. 5 how Proposition 30 can be used in practice to significantly improve verification performance. The nature of the probes that can be removed of course depends on the scheme under consideration, and we will later detail how to do this for some concrete gadgets.

3.4 Adaptation to the Robust Probing Model

A limitation of the traditional probing model is that it does not capture interactions between intermediate values of a computation made possible by either physical or micro-architectural effects. For instance Gao *et al.* showed that some bitslicing implementation strategies of software masking schemes could exhibit unwanted bit-interactions, thereby violating typical independence assumptions from the probing model and resulting in unwanted leakage [GMPO20]. Similarly, Grégoire *et al.* had noticed that their 4-share vectorised implementation of a masked AES was subject to such an order reduction, without identifying the exact cause [GPSS18].

In the case of hardware implementations, additional violations to the probing model are typically witnessed and some of them are well-identified enough to be formally captured. For one such phenomenon known as *glitches*, a probe at an arithmetic gate (*i.e.* an addition or a multiplication) can leak more to the adversary than its sole output—something that is not taken into account in the basic model. In an effort to remedy this situation, Faust *et al.* recently proposed to extend probing security into a *robust probing model* [FGP+18], able to take several types of hardware defects into account. In the case of glitches, this is done by assuming that a probe at an arithmetic gate leaks the union of what is leaked by its two inputs. One consequence is that if two arithmetic gates are connected together, leakage at the first one also propagates to the second. To stop this propagation, one must then use a memory gate (a register), which only leaks its output value.

Concretely, the robust probing model defines a leakage set $\mathfrak{L}(p)$ of possibly more than one value for every probe p at an arbitrary gate. This is more complex than, and not directly compatible with the usual probing security model and how we exploit it in our algorithm, where a probe leaks a single expression and verification implies enumerating and summing all subsets of size up to some order d. Nevertheless, one can opt for the following simple two-step strategy: 1) iterate over all subsets $\mathcal{P}$ of d probes or fewer; 2) then compute and check every possible full-weight linear combination of values leaked by this set of probes. In a non-robust model and for schemes over $\mathbb{F}_2$, step 2) only involves a single expression (*viz.* the sum of all the single values leaked by each probe), but in a robust model there are in general $\prod_{p \in \mathcal{P}} \left(2^{\#\mathfrak{L}(p)} - 1\right)$ expressions to consider (since for each probe one must now consider all the non-trivial binary linear combinations of the values it leaked).

RELATED WORK. The maskVerif tool [BBC+19] also implements the robust probing model to check security in presence of glitches. More dedicated approaches are the ones of Bloem *et al.* [BGI+18] and of the SILVER tool [KSM20].

4 Implementation

We now describe an efficient `C` implementation of the algorithm of the previous section for $\mathbb{K} = \mathbb{F}_2$. Our software is publicly available at https://github.com/NicsTr/binary_masking.

4.1 Data Structures

To evaluate if a set of probes $\mathcal{P}$ may lead to an attack, it is convenient to define the following:

Definition 31 (Attack matrix). *The* attack matrix $\boldsymbol{A}_{\mathcal{P}}$ *of a set of probes* $\mathcal{P}$ *is defined as the sum of the share indicator matrices of the probes in* $\mathcal{P}$*:*

$$\boldsymbol{A}_{\mathcal{P}} = \sum_{p \in \mathcal{P}} \boldsymbol{M}_p.$$

Definition 32 (Noise matrix). *The* noise matrix $\boldsymbol{B}_{\mathcal{P}}$ *of a set of probes* $\mathcal{P}$ *is defined as the sum of the randomness indicator matrices of the probes in* $\mathcal{P}$*:*

$$\boldsymbol{B}_{\mathcal{P}} = \sum_{p \in \mathcal{P}} \boldsymbol{\sigma}_p.$$

One can then simply compute the quantities n_a, n_b and n_r needed in Propositions 26 and 27 as the number of non-zero rows or columns of these two matrices, which we do using an efficient vectorised Hamming weight routine. To analyse a given scheme, one then just has to provide a full description of $\boldsymbol{M}_p$ and $\boldsymbol{\sigma}_p$ for every non-elementary probe. Additionally, since Propositions 27 requires to compute the number of internal probes n_I in a set, those have to be labelled as such.

4.2 Amortised Enumeration and Parallelisation

Recall that to prove the security of a scheme at order d, the algorithm of Sect. 3 requires to enumerate all the $\sum_{i=1}^{d} \binom{n}{i}$ subsets of a (possibly filtered) set of probes $\mathcal{P}$ of size n. For a subset $\mathcal{P}' \subseteq \mathcal{P}$ of size ℓ, a naïve approach in computing $\boldsymbol{A}_{\mathcal{P}'}$ would use $\ell - 1$ additions, and this for every such $\mathcal{P}'$. However, a well-known optimisation for this kind of enumeration is instead to go through all the subsets of a fixed weight in a way that ensures that two consecutive sets $\mathcal{P}'$ and $\mathcal{P}''$ only differ by two elements. One can then compute, say, $\boldsymbol{A}_{\mathcal{P}''}$ efficiently by updating $\boldsymbol{A}_{\mathcal{P}'}$ with one addition and one subtraction. We do this in our implementation by using a so-called "revolving-door algorithm" (cf. *e.g.* [Knu11, Algorithm R]) for the Nijenhuis-Wilf-Liu-Tang "combination Gray code" [NW78,LT73].

In the robust probing model setting one may also need to enumerate more than one expression for a given set of probes; this can still be done efficiently using Gray codes. First one uses the same approach as described above to enumerate the sets of probes thanks to a combination Gray code. Then for each of these sets $\mathcal{P}$, checking if it leads to an attack or not requires one to go over the $\prod_{p\in\mathcal{P}}(2^{\#\mathfrak{L}(p)} - 1)$ linear combinations of the relevant leakage sets as explained in Sect. 3.4. This enumeration itself is done using two layers of Gray codes: an outer layer is composed of a mixed-radix Gray code of length $\#\mathcal{P}$, with the radix associated with probe p being equal to $2^{\#\mathfrak{L}(p)}$; this outer Gray code indicates at each step which probes needs to be "incremented" to obtain the next linear combination. Then this increment is itself implemented efficiently by using an inner ("standard") Gray code in dimension $\#\mathfrak{L}(p)$.

The enumeration can also be easily parallelised, and the main challenge is to couple this with the above amortised approach. This can in fact be done quite efficiently, as the combination Gray code that we use possesses an efficient *unranking* map from the integers to arbitrary configurations [Wal]. One can then easily divide a full enumeration of a total of n combinations into j jobs by starting each of them independently at one of the configurations given by the unranking of $i \times n/j$, $i \in [\![0, j[\![$.

4.3 From High-Level Representation to `C` description

We use a custom parser to convert a readable description of a masking scheme into a `C` description of its probes' indicator matrices.

Each line of the high-level description corresponds to an output share. The available symbols are:

- `sij` which represents a product $\boldsymbol{a}_i\boldsymbol{b}_j$;
- `ri` which represents a random mask $\boldsymbol{r}_i$;
- a space '␣', a binary operator which represents an addition (*i.e.* XOR) gate;
- parentheses, which allow explicit scheduling of the operations;
- `|`, a postfixed unary operator which represents the use of a register to store the expression that is *before* the symbol. This is only needed for an analysis in presence of glitches.

Additionally, the user needs to specify the order d of the scheme as well as the list of random masks used.

The scheduling of the operations needed to compute the output shares is important, as it determines the probes available to the adversary. In that respect, the parser uses by default an implicit left-to-right scheduling and addition gates have precedence over registers. As an example the scheme whose output shares are defined as:

$$c_0 = ((((a_0 b_0 \oplus r_0) \oplus a_0 b_1) \oplus a_1 b_0) \oplus r_1)$$
$$c_1 = ((((a_1 b_1 \oplus r_1) \oplus a_1 b_2) \oplus a_2 b_1) \oplus r_2)$$
$$c_2 = ((((a_2 b_2 \oplus r_2) \oplus a_2 b_0) \oplus a_0 b_2) \oplus r_0)$$

is described by the file:

```
ORDER = 2
MASKS = [r0, r1, r2]
s00 r0 s01 s10 r1
s11 r1 s12 s21 r2
s22 r2 s20 s02 r0
```

Another example is the following *DOM-indep* multiplication by Groß *et al.* [GMK16], which is NI at order two even in the presence of glitches:

```
ORDER = 2
MASKS = [r0, r1, r2]
 s00       (s01 r0|) (s02 r1|)
(s10 r0|)  s11       (s12 r2|)
(s20 r1|) (s21 r2|)  s22
```

5 Applications

In this section we apply our fast implementation of the verification algorithm of Sect. 3 to various state-of-the-art masking gadgets and also propose new improved instances in medium order, including better SNI multiplication and refreshing gadgets for the practically-relevant case of 8 shares.

We analyse:

- In Sect. 5.1: NI and SNI multiplication gadgets originally from [BDF+17, GPSS18].
- In Sect. 5.2: SNI refreshing gadgets originally from [BDF+17, BBD+18].
- In Sect. 5.3: Glitch-resistant NI multiplication from [GMK16].

5.1 NI and SNI Multiplication Gadgets

We first study a family of multiplication gadgets that were introduced by Barthe *et al.* at EUROCRYPT 2017 [BDF+17] and used in the efficient masked AES implementation of Grégoire *et al.* [GPSS18] (who also propose improvements in the 4-share setting) and in the very high order implementations of Journault and Standaert [JS17].

Our motivations in doing so are the following: since there is no known security proof at arbitrary order for these schemes, it is natural to try to prove them computationally at the highest possible order. Barthe *et al.* originally did this up to order 7,[11] and we manage to reach order 11 both for NI and SNI security,

[11] We ourselves used the latest version of maskVerif to do so up to order 8.

which represents a significant improvement.[12] A second motivation is that the verification of multiplication gadgets quickly becomes intractable with increasing order, and such a task allows us to clearly demonstrate our performance gain over maskVerif. Finally, this improved verification efficiency is exploited in trying to find *ad hoc* gadget variants with lower cost.

On the negative side our verification shows that a conjecture from Barthe *et al.* on the security of a natural strategy to convert NI multiplication into SNI fails at order 10. More positively, we were able to find *ad hoc* conversions tuned to every NI multiplication we considered, which sometimes also bring a significant improvement in randomness cost over Barthe *et al.*'s strategy. For instance we are able to gain 17% for an 8-share, 7-SNI gadget similar to the one used in [GPSS18]. Finally using a slight variant of Barthe *et al.*'s gadget generation algorithm, we occasionally obtain some improvements also in the NI case, notably at order 5.

We give details of our improvements in Table 1 and the descriptions of all the gadgets at https://github.com/NicsTr/binary_masking. Note however that Belaïd *et al.* also propose optimized gadgets in [BBP+16] up to order 4, that ISW is also better than [BDF+17] at order 3 and that Grégoire *et al.* already proposed improvements at this same order in [GPSS18]. The main range of interest of Table 1 is thus at order 5 and beyond.

The NI Multiplication Gadget Family of [BDF+17, **Algorithm 3**]. We give in Algorithm 1 a description of a slightly modified variant of [BDF+17, Algorithm 3], which occasionally gives better gadgets than the original. We also provide a small script to automatically generate a scheme at a given order at https://github.com/NicsTr/binary_masking.

This description relies on the following convenient definition:

Definition 33 (Pair of shares). *Let* $(\boldsymbol{a}_i\boldsymbol{b}_j)$, $i, j \in [\![0, d]\!]$ *be the input shares of a* $(d+1, v)$ *gadget. We define* $\hat{\boldsymbol{\alpha}}_{i,j}$ *as:*

$$\hat{\boldsymbol{\alpha}}_{i,j} = \begin{cases} \boldsymbol{a}_i\boldsymbol{b}_j & \textit{if } i = j \\ \boldsymbol{a}_i\boldsymbol{b}_j + \boldsymbol{a}_j\boldsymbol{b}_i & \textit{otherwise} \end{cases}$$

Extension to SNI Security. One can derive an SNI multiplication gadget from Algorithm 1 by doing the following: 1) proving NI security at some order d; 2) proving SNI security at the same order for a *refreshing gadget*; 3) composing the two gadgets.

This strategy can for instance be implemented with the refreshing gadgets also introduced in [BDF+17] that we discuss in the next Sect. 5.2, but Barthe *et al.* already remarked that it was in fact apparently not necessary to use full refreshing gadgets and that one could do better by using a degraded variant thereof: in a nutshell, one starts from a secure NI multiplication and simply

[12] This however still cannot theoretically justify the use of this masked multiplication at order 31 as is done in [JS17].

Table 1. Explicit randomness cost of multiplication gadgets

Order d		Defined *and* verified in [BDF+17]		Defined *or* verified in §5	
		Random masks	XOR gates	Random masks	XOR gates
2	SNI	3	12	=	=
3	NI	4	20	=	=
	SNI	8	28	5	24
4	NI	5	30	=	=
	SNI	10	40	9	38
5	NI	12	54	10	50
	SNI	18	66	12	54
6	NI	14	70	=	=
	SNI	21	84	18	78
7	NI	—	—	16	88
	SNI	24	104	20	96
8	NI	—	—	18	108
	SNI	—	—	27	126
9	NI	—	—	26	142
	SNI	—	—	30	150
10	NI	—	—	33	176
	SNI	—	—	39	188
11	NI	—	—	36	204
	SNI	—	—	42	216

masks every output share with a fresh random mask and then again with the mask of the following share in a circular fashion.

Barthe *et al.* then conjecture in [BDF+17] that this transformation is always enough to convert an NI scheme into an SNI one. However we could check that this is not true for 11- and 12-share gadgets: the respective instantiations of Algorithm 1 are NI, but the transformation fails to provide SNI multiplications. Yet it is in fact still possible to derive an 11-share, 10-SNI multiplication gadget at no additional cost by simply rotating the last repeated masks by two positions instead of one, for a total cost of 44 random masks.

We explored several other transformation strategies, trying to exploit the special shape of the NI multiplication gadgets as much as possible. This almost always improved on the use of a new mask for every share (the current exception being the order-8 gadget), usually requiring only about half. For instance our best 11-share gadget in fact only requires 39 masks instead of the above 44 as shown in Fig. 1, and we found a 7-SNI multiplication with only 20 masks shown in Fig. 2, which is 4 less than [BDF+17]. While this latter improvement is somewhat moderate at about 17%, this 8-share case is quite relevant due

Algorithm 1: A conjectured d-NI $(d+1, d+1)$-gadget for multiplication over fields of characteristic two.

Input : $\mathcal{S} = \{\hat{\boldsymbol{\alpha}}_{i,j}, 0 \leq i \leq j \leq d\}$
Input : $\mathcal{R} = \{\boldsymbol{r}_i\}$, $i \in \mathbb{N}$
Output: $(\boldsymbol{c}_i)_{0 \leq i \leq d}$, such that $\sum_{i=0}^{d} \boldsymbol{c}_i = \sum_{i=0}^{d} \boldsymbol{a}_i \sum_{i=0}^{d} \boldsymbol{b}_i$

for $i \leftarrow 0$ **to** d **do**
  $\boldsymbol{c}_i \leftarrow \hat{\boldsymbol{\alpha}}_{i,i}$
  $\mathcal{S} \leftarrow \mathcal{S} \setminus \{\hat{\boldsymbol{\alpha}}_{i,i}\}$
end
$\mathcal{R}' \leftarrow \{\}$
$j \leftarrow 1$
while $\mathcal{S} \neq \emptyset$ **do**
  for $i \leftarrow 0$ **to** d **do**
    if $j \equiv 1 \mod 2$ **then**
      $\boldsymbol{c}_i \leftarrow \boldsymbol{c}_i + \boldsymbol{r}_{\frac{(j-1)}{2}.(d+1)+i}$
      $\mathcal{R}' \leftarrow \mathcal{R}' \cup \left\{\boldsymbol{r}_{\frac{(j-1)}{2}.(d+1)+i}\right\}$
    else
      $\boldsymbol{c}_i \leftarrow \boldsymbol{c}_i + \boldsymbol{r}_{\frac{(j-2)}{2}.(d+1)+(i+1 \mod (d+1))}$
      $\mathcal{R}' \leftarrow \mathcal{R}' \setminus \left\{\boldsymbol{r}_{\frac{(j-2)}{2}.(d+1)+(i+1 \mod (d+1))}\right\}$
    end
    if $\mathcal{S} \neq \emptyset$ **then**
      $\boldsymbol{c}_i \leftarrow \boldsymbol{c}_i + \hat{\boldsymbol{\alpha}}_{i,((i+j) \mod (d+1))}$
      $\mathcal{S} \leftarrow \mathcal{S} \setminus \{\hat{\boldsymbol{\alpha}}_{i,((i+j) \mod (d+1))}\}$
    else
      break
    end
  end
  $j \leftarrow j+1$
end
$k \leftarrow \#\mathcal{R}'$
for $i \leftarrow 0$ **to** d **do**
  $\boldsymbol{c}_i \leftarrow \boldsymbol{c}_i + \boldsymbol{r}_{\frac{(j-1)}{2}(d+1)+(i+1 \mod k)}$
end

to its use in the efficient vectorised masked AES implementation of Grégoire *et al.* [GPSS18]; using our new variant should then result in a noticeable decrease in randomness usage.

We provide a summary of the cost of the multiplication gadgets that we have verified and their improvement over the previously best known ones in Table 1, and we give their full description at https://github.com/NicsTr/binary_masking.

```
s00 r00 s01 s10 r01 s02 s20 r11 s03 s30 r12 s04 s40 r22 s05 s50 r23 r40
s11 r01 s12 s21 r02 s13 s31 r12 s14 s41 r13 s15 s51 r23 s16 s61 r24 r41
s22 r02 s23 s32 r03 s24 s42 r13 s25 s52 r14 s26 s62 r24 s27 s72 r25 r42
s33 r03 s34 s43 r04 s35 s53 r14 s36 s63 r15 s37 s73 r25 s38 s83 r26 r43
s44 r04 s45 s54 r05 s46 s64 r15 s47 s74 r16 s48 s84 r26 s49 s94 r27 r44
s55 r05 s56 s65 r06 s57 s75 r16 s58 s85 r17 s59 s95 r27 s5a sa5 r28 r45
s66 r06 s67 s76 r07 s68 s86 r17 s69 s96 r18 s6a sa6 r28 s60 s06 r29 r40
s77 r07 s78 s87 r08 s79 s97 r18 s7a sa7 r19 s70 s07 r29 s71 s17 r30 r41
s88 r08 s89 s98 r09 s8a sa8 r19 s80 s08 r20 s81 s18 r30 s82 s28 r31 r42
s99 r09 s9a sa9 r10 s90 s09 r20 s91 s19 r21 s92 s29 r31 s93 s39 r32 r43
saa r45 sa0 s0a r00 sa1 s1a r21 sa2 s2a r11 sa3 s3a r32 sa4 s4a r22 r44 r10
```

Fig. 1. 10-SNI gadget for multiplication, using 39 random masks.

```
s00 r00 s01 s10 r01 s02 s20 r08 s03 s30 r09 s04 r20
s11 r01 s12 s21 r02 s13 s31 r09 s14 s41 r10 s15 r21
s22 r02 s23 s32 r03 s24 s42 r10 s25 s52 r11 s26 r22
s33 r03 s34 s43 r04 s35 s53 r11 s36 s63 r12 s37 r23
s44 r04 s45 s54 r05 s46 s64 r12 s47 s74 r13 s40 r20
s55 r05 s56 s65 r06 s57 s75 r13 s50 s05 r14 s51 r21
s66 r06 s67 s76 r07 s60 s06 r14 s61 s16 r15 s62 r22
s77 r07 s70 s07 r00 s71 s17 r15 s72 s27 r08 s73 r23
```

Fig. 2. 7-SNI gadget for multiplication, using 20 random masks.

Verification Performance. We now analyse the performance of our verification software on these multiplication schemes, and compare it with the one of the latest version of maskVerif [BBC+19].[13]

PROBES FILTERING. Following the results of Sect. 3.3, we use a filtering process to reduce the initial set of probes that one has to enumerate to prove security. For the gadgets of Algorithm 1 and their SNI counterparts, this means removing probes of the form: $\hat{\boldsymbol{\alpha}}_{*,*}+\sum(\boldsymbol{r}_*+\hat{\boldsymbol{\alpha}}_{*,*})+\boldsymbol{r}_*+\boldsymbol{a}_*\boldsymbol{b}_*$,[14] and the fact that the filtered set really is a reduced set in the sense of Definition 28 is verified by an exhaustive check on the subsets corresponding to every output share; this filtering process was only partially automated since an initial human intervention was necessary to identify the probes that could be removed. Intuitively, the idea is that one can always replace in an attack a probe of the above form with one that includes one extra $\boldsymbol{a}_j\boldsymbol{b}_i$ term, *i.e.* one of the form $\hat{\boldsymbol{\alpha}}_{*,*}+\sum(\boldsymbol{r}_*+\hat{\boldsymbol{\alpha}}_{*,*})+\boldsymbol{r}_*+\hat{\boldsymbol{\alpha}}_{*,*}$, since the latter only adds an additional functional dependence on the input shares "for free".

The concrete impact of filtering on the verification performance of our schemes can be seen in Table 2, where we give the size of the attack sets to enumerate before and after this filtering.

PERFORMANCE. For order $d \leq 10$ (except the 10-SNI case) we have run our software on a single core of the `retourdest` server, which features a single Intel Xeon Gold 6126 at 2.60 GHz. The corresponding timings are given in Table 2. At peak performance, we are able to enumerate $\approx 2^{27.5}$ candidate attack sets per second for NI verification, while SNI performance is slightly worse.

[13] Available at https://gitlab.com/benjgregoire/maskverif.

[14] This corresponds exactly to the probes made of an even number of $\boldsymbol{a}_*\boldsymbol{b}_*$ terms.

Using filtered sets significantly improves verification time, especially at high order. For instance, the running times of 2 and 6 h for NI and SNI multiplication at order 9 are an order of magnitude faster than the 3 and 6 d initially spent before we implemented filtering. This optimisation was also essential in allowing to check the security of 10-NI multiplication in less than one calendar day on a single machine (using parallelisation); it would otherwise have taken a rather costly 1 core-year.

We also tested a multi-threaded implementation of our software on schemes at order 8–10, using all 12 physical cores of the same Xeon Gold 6126; the results are shown in the right column of Table 2. While we do not have many data points, the speed-up offered by the parallelisation seems to be close to linear, albeit slightly less for NI verification: the 9-SNI multi-threaded wall time is $\approx$11.7 times less than the single-threaded one, and multi-threading for 9- and 10-NI saves a factor $\approx$9.7.

The largest schemes that we verified are NI (resp. SNI) multiplication at order $d = 11$. We relied heavily on parallelisation to enumerate the $\approx 2^{52.72}$ (resp. $\approx 2^{54.48}$) possible attack sets,[15] using up to 40 nodes of the *Dahu* cluster.[16] Each node has two 16-core Intel Xeon Gold 6130 at 2.10 GHz, and when using hyperthreading allows to enumerate $\approx 2^{31.38}$ sets per second. This cluster was also used to verify the best version of our 10-SNI gadget.[17]

Comparison with maskVerif. We used the maskVerif tool from Barthe *et al.* [BBC+19] to check the security of the gadgets at order 6 to 8. Due to system constraints, we could not run the verification on `retourdest`, and instead defaulted to the older `hpac`, which features an Intel Xeon E5-4620 at 2.20 GHz. We compare this to our software on this machine using 4 threads—the same amount of parallelisation that maskVerif is able to exploit.

The running times are summarised in Table 3. Even though we cannot benefit from vectorisation due to the absence of AVX2 instructions on `hpac`, it is notable that our own software is faster by three orders of magnitude, for instance taking slightly more than two minutes to check 8-NI multiplication *versus* two days for maskVerif. Note that this comparison is done after filtering in our case, which saves us up to a factor $\approx$30 (*cf.* for instance the 8-NI case) as can be computed from Table 2.

5.2 SNI Refreshing Gadgets

We used our software to verify the SNI security of some (variations of) refreshing gadgets introduced in [BDF+17], and subsequently improved in [GPSS18, BBD+18]. Such schemes are useful when designing large circuits based on gadgets satisfying composable security notions since they help in providing strong

[15] This is after filtering of the initial $\approx 2^{59}$ (resp. $\approx 2^{59.76}$) sets.

[16] https://ciment.univ-grenoble-alpes.fr/wiki-pub/index.php/Hardware:Dahu.

[17] This is somewhat slow compared to performance on the similar '6126. The reason is currently unclear, but might involve the different build environment and overall setup.

Table 2. Running time of our verification software on `retourdest`.

Order d		$\log_2$(number of sets)	Wall time (1 thread)	Wall time (12 threads)
		Before/After filtering	Best (after filtering)	Best (after filtering)
1	NI	2.6/2.6	< 0.01 s	—
	SNI	2.6/2.6	< 0.01 s	—
2	NI	6.3/5.5	< 0.01 s	—
	SNI	6.3/5.5	< 0.01 s	—
3	NI	10.4/8.9	< 0.01 s	—
	SNI	11.2/9.96	< 0.01 s	—
4	NI	15.0/12.6	< 0.01 s	—
	SNI	16.4/14.6	< 0.01 s	—
5	NI	21.2/18.6	< 0.01 s	—
	SNI	21.7/19.3	< 0.01 s	—
6	NI	27.1/23.9	0.09 s	—
	SNI	28.0/25.3	0.28 s	—
7	NI	32.7/28.7	2.43 s	—
	SNI	33.6/30.6	11.70 s	—
8	NI	38.5/33.7	1 min. 17 s	7.43 s
	SNI	40.3/36.3	9 min. 28 s	47.0 s
9	NI	45.6/40.5	2 h. 18 min	14 min 20 s
	SNI	46.3/41.6	6 h. 30 min	33 min. 20 s
10	NI	52.6/47.1	9 d 3h	22 h. 30 min
	SNI	53.5/48.4	—	—

Table 3. Comparison with maskVerif [BBC+19] on `hpac`.

Order d		Wall time	Wall time
		maskVerif (4 threads)	Our software (4 threads, filtered)
6	NI	2 min 44 s	0.57 s
	SNI	8 min. 11 s	1.48 s
7	NI	1 h. 39 min	4.13 s
	SNI	5 h. 54 min	15.60 s
8	NI	2 d 10h	2 min 15 s
	SNI	13 d 6h	14 min 35 s

security for the overall design. However, refreshing also comes with a significant cost in terms of randomness while not performing any sort of useful computation, leading several prior work to try finding new low-cost gadgets.

The best current results come from [BBD+18] who prove the SNI security at any order of a "block" refreshing gadget introduced in [BDF+17], when iterated enough times. Yet together with [GPSS18], they also remark that it is possible to make significant improvements in practice at the cost of losing generic proofs, and they give cheaper alternatives verified secure up to order 16.

Our contribution here is an 8-share, 7-SNI refreshing gadget shown in Fig. 3 that only needs 13 masks, which improves slightly on the best gadget from [BBD+18], which requires 16. Since such gadgets are used in the implementation of [GPSS18], it could again lead to actual practical gains.

We also compared the verification time of our tool with the one of maskVerif on the largest "RefreshZero" instances of [BBD+18], and actually have worse performance. For instance, even using 24 threads on the 12-core `retourdest`, verifying $\mathsf{RefreshZero}^{14}_{[1,3]}$ took us about 3 h 40 min, while [BBD+18] reports an "Order of Magnitude" of 1 h 30 min. We suspect this to be caused by the fact that there is no obvious probe filtering to be done on this sort of gadget, whereas maskVerif is likely able to successfully exploit their structure to reduce the number of attack sets to consider.

```
s00 r00 r01 r10 r20
s11 r01 r02 r11 r20
s22 r02 r03 r12 r20
s33 r03 r04 r13 r20
s44 r04 r05 r10
s55 r05 r06 r11
s66 r06 r07 r12
s77 r07 r00 r13
```

Fig. 3. 7-SNI refreshing gadget, using 13 random masks..

5.3 Glitch-Resistant NI Multiplication

We conclude with a brief application to the *DOM-indep* family of multiplication gadgets introduced by Groß *et al.* [GMK16]. While those schemes are not more efficient than the state-of-the-art in terms of randomness cost, their main advantage is their resistance to glitches. A description of an instantiation at order 2 can be found in Fig. 4.3, and at any order less than 5 at https://github.com/NicsTr/binary_masking.

These gadgets can be instantiated at an arbitrary order d but do not come with a generic security proof guaranteeing the security of the result. We then have used our implementation to verify that instantiations up to order 5 are NI in the robust probing model. The running times on `retourdest` are summarised in Table 4.

Table 4. Running time of our verification software on `retourdest` for the *DOM-indep* schemes.

Order d	Wall time (1 thread)
1	< 0.01 s
2	< 0.01 s
3	< 0.01 s
4	0.12 s
5	2 min. 22 s

Acknowledgments. We thank Clément Pernet for his contribution to the proof of Lemma 14, Yann Rotella for an early discussion on the possibility of further filtering, the authors of [BBC+19] for providing us access to an up-to-date version of maskVerif, and finally all the reviewers for their constructive comments.

This work is partially supported by the French National Research Agency in the framework of the *Investissements d'avenir* programme (ANR-15-IDEX-02).

Some of the computations presented in this paper were performed using the GRICAD infrastructure (https://gricad.univ-grenoble-alpes.fr), which is partially supported by the Equip@Meso project (ANR-10-EQPX-29-01) of the *Investissements d'Avenir* programme.

References

[BBC+19] Barthe, G., Belaïd, S., Cassiers, G., Fouque, P.-A., Grégoire, B., Standaert, F.-X.: maskVerif: automated verification of higher-order masking in presence of physical defaults. In: Sako, K., Schneider, S., Ryan, P.Y.A. (eds.) ESORICS 2019. LNCS, vol. 11735, pp. 300–318. Springer, Cham (2019). https://doi.org/10.1007/978-3-030-29959-0_15

[BBD+15] Barthe, G., Belaïd, S., Dupressoir, F., Fouque, P.-A., Grégoire, B.: Compositional verification of higher-order masking: application to a verifying masking compiler. IACR Cryptology ePrint Archive **2015**, 506 (2015)

[BBD+16] Barthe, G., et al.: Strong non-interference and type-directed higher-order masking. In: Weippl, E.R., Katzenbeisser, S., Kruegel, C., Myers, A.C., Halevi, S. (eds.) ACM CCS 2016, pp. 116–129. ACM (2016)

[BBD+18] Barthe, G., et al.: Improved parallel mask refreshing algorithms: generic solutions with parametrized non-interference & automated optimizations. IACR Cryptology ePrint Archive **2018**, 505 (2018)

[BBP+16] Belaïd, S., Benhamouda, F., Passelègue, A., Prouff, E., Thillard, A., Vergnaud, D.: Randomness complexity of private circuits for multiplication. In: Fischlin, M., Coron, J.-S. (eds.) EUROCRYPT 2016. LNCS, vol. 9666, pp. 616–648. Springer, Heidelberg (2016). https://doi.org/10.1007/978-3-662-49896-5_22

[BBP+17] Belaïd, S., Benhamouda, F., Passelègue, A., Prouff, E., Thillard, A., Vergnaud, D.: Private multiplication over finite fields. In: Katz, J., Shacham, H. (eds.) CRYPTO 2017. LNCS, vol. 10403, pp. 397–426. Springer, Cham (2017). https://doi.org/10.1007/978-3-319-63697-9_14

[BDF+17] Barthe, G., et al.: Parallel implementations of masking schemes and the bounded moment leakage model. In: Coron and Nielsen [CN17], pp. 535–566 (2017)

[BDM+20] Belaïd, S., Dagand, P.É., Mercadier, D., Rivain, M., Wintersdorff, R.: Tornado: automatic generation of probing-secure masked bitsliced implementations. In: Canteaut, A., Ishai, Y. (eds.) EUROCRYPT 2020. LNCS, vol. 12107, pp. 311–341. Springer, Cham (2020). https://doi.org/10.1007/978-3-030-45727-3_11

[BGI+18] Bloem, R., Gross, H., Iusupov, R., Könighofer, B., Mangard, S., Winter, J.: Formal verification of masked hardware implementations in the presence of glitches. In: Nielsen, J.B., Rijmen, V. (eds.) EUROCRYPT 2018. LNCS, vol. 10821, pp. 321–353. Springer, Cham (2018). https://doi.org/10.1007/978-3-319-78375-8_11

[BGR18] Belaïd, S., Goudarzi, D., Rivain, M.: Tight private circuits: achieving probing security with the least refreshing. In: Peyrin and Galbraith [PG18], pp. 343–372

[BK19] Bordes, N., Karpman, P.: Fast verification of masking schemes in characteristic two. IACR Cryptol. ePrint Arch. **2019**, 1165 (2019)

[BS19] Bronchain, O., Standaert, F.-X.: Side-channel countermeasures' dissection and the limits of closed source security evaluations. IACR Cryptology ePrint Archive **2019**, 1008 (2019)

[CGPZ16] Coron, J.-S., Greuet, A., Prouff, E., Zeitoun, R.: Faster evaluation of SBoxes via common shares. In: Gierlichs, B., Poschmann, A.Y. (eds.) CHES 2016. LNCS, vol. 9813, pp. 498–514. Springer, Heidelberg (2016). https://doi.org/10.1007/978-3-662-53140-2_24

[CN17] Coron, J.-S., Nielsen, J.B. (eds.): EUROCRYPT 2017. LNCS, vol. 10210. Springer, Cham (2017). https://doi.org/10.1007/978-3-319-56620-7

[DFS15] Duc, A., Faust, S., Standaert, F.-X.: Making masking security proofs concrete. In: Oswald, E., Fischlin, M. (eds.) EUROCRYPT 2015. LNCS, vol. 9056, pp. 401–429. Springer, Heidelberg (2015). https://doi.org/10.1007/978-3-662-46800-5_16

[FG18] Fan, J., Gierlichs, B. (eds.): COSADE 2018. LNCS, vol. 10815. Springer, Cham (2018). https://doi.org/10.1007/978-3-319-89641-0

[FGP+18] Faust, S., Grosso, V., Pozo, S.M.D., Paglialonga, C., Standaert, F.-X.: Composable masking schemes in the presence of physical defaults & the robust probing model. IACR Trans. Cryptogr. Hardw. Embed. Syst. **2018**(3), 89–120 (2018)

[GJRS18] Goudarzi, D., Journault, A., Rivain, M., Standaert, F.-X.: Secure multiplication for bitslice higher-order masking: optimisation and comparison. In: Fan and Gierlichs [FG18], pp. 3–22

[GMK16] Groß, H., Mangard, S., Korak, T.: Domain-oriented masking: compact masked hardware implementations with arbitrary protection order. In: Bilgin, B., Nikova, S., Rijmen, V. (eds.) ACM TIS@CCS 2016, p. 3. ACM (2016)

[GMPO20] Gao, S., Marshall, B., Page, D., Oswald, E.: Share-slicing: friend or foe? IACR Trans. Cryptogr. Hardw. Embed. Syst. **2020**(1), 152–174 (2020)

[GPSS18] Grégoire, B., Papagiannopoulos, K., Schwabe, P., Stoffelen, K.: Vectorizing higher-order masking. In: Fan and Gierlichs [FG18], pp. 23–43

[GR17] Goudarzi, D., Rivain, M.: How fast can higher-order masking be in software? In: Coron and Nielsen [CN17], pp. 567–597

[ISW03] Ishai, Y., Sahai, A., Wagner, D.: Private circuits: securing hardware against probing attacks. In: Boneh, D. (ed.) CRYPTO 2003. LNCS, vol. 2729, pp. 463–481. Springer, Heidelberg (2003). https://doi.org/10.1007/978-3-540-45146-4_27

[JS17] Journault, A., Standaert, F.-X.: Very high order masking: efficient implementation and security evaluation. In: Fischer, W., Homma, N. (eds.) CHES 2017. LNCS, vol. 10529, pp. 623–643. Springer, Cham (2017). https://doi.org/10.1007/978-3-319-66787-4_30

[KJJ99] Kocher, P., Jaffe, J., Jun, B.: Differential power analysis. In: Wiener, M. (ed.) CRYPTO 1999. LNCS, vol. 1666, pp. 388–397. Springer, Heidelberg (1999). https://doi.org/10.1007/3-540-48405-1_25

[Knu11] Knuth, D.E.: Combinatorial Algorithms, Part 1, volume 4A of The Art of Computer Programming. Addison Wesley (2011)

[KR18] Karpman, P., Roche, D.S.: New instantiations of the CRYPTO 2017 masking schemes. In: Peyrin and Galbraith [PG18], pp. 285–314

[KSM20] Knichel, D., Sasdrich, P., Moradi, A.: SILVER – statistical independence and leakage verification. In: Moriai, S., Wang, H. (eds.) ASIACRYPT 2020. LNCS, vol. 12491, pp. 787–816. Springer, Cham (2020). https://doi.org/10.1007/978-3-030-64837-4_26

[LT73] Liu, C.N., Tang, D.T.: Enumerating combinations of m out of n objects [G6] (algorithm 452). Commun. ACM **16**(8), 485 (1973)

[MMSS19] Moos, T., Moradi, A., Schneider, T., Standaert, F.-X.: Glitch-resistant masking revisited or why proofs in the robust probing model are needed. IACR Trans. Cryptogr. Hardw. Embed. Syst. **2019**(2), 256–292 (2019)

[NW78] Nijenhuis, A., Wilf, H.S.: Combinatorial Algorithms for Computers and Calculators, 2nd edn. Academic Press, New York (1978)

[PG18] Peyrin, T., Galbraith, S. (eds.): ASIACRYPT 2018. LNCS, vol. 11273. Springer, Cham (2018). https://doi.org/10.1007/978-3-030-03329-3

[Pra62] Prange, E.: The use of information sets in decoding cyclic codes. IRE Trans. Inf. Theory **8**(5), 5–9 (1962)

[Sch80] Schwartz, J.T.: Fast probabilistic algorithms for verification of polynomial identities. J. ACM **27**(4), 701–717 (1980)

[Wal] Walsh, T.R.: A simple sequencing and ranking method that works on almost all gray codes. Unpublished research report. https://www.labunix.uqam.ca/~walsh_t/papers/sequencing_and_ranking.pdf

[WGS+20] Wang, W., Guo, C., François-Xavier Standaert, Y.Y., Cassiers, G.: Packed multiplication: how to amortize the cost of side-channel masking? IACR Cryptol. ePrint Arch. **2020**, 1103 (2020)

On the Power of Expansion: More Efficient Constructions in the Random Probing Model

Sonia Belaïd[1(✉)], Matthieu Rivain[1], and Abdul Rahman Taleb[1,2]

[1] CryptoExperts, Paris, France
{sonia.belaid,matthieu.rivain,abdul.taleb}@cryptoexperts.com
[2] Sorbonne Université, CNRS, LIP6, 75005 Paris, France

Abstract. The random probing model is a leakage model in which each wire of a circuit leaks with a given probability p. This model enjoys practical relevance thanks to a reduction to the noisy leakage model, which is admitted as the right formalization for power and electromagnetic side-channel attacks. In addition, the random probing model is much more convenient than the noisy leakage model to prove the security of masking schemes. In a recent work, Ananth, Ishai, and Sahai (CRYPTO 2018) introduce a nice expansion strategy to construct random probing secure circuits. Their construction tolerates a leakage probability of 2^{-26}, which is the first quantified achievable leakage probability in the random probing model. In a follow-up work, Belaïd, Coron, Prouff, Rivain, and Taleb (CRYPTO 2020) generalize their idea and put forward a complete and practical framework to generate random probing secure circuits. The so-called expanding compiler can bootstrap simple base gadgets as long as they satisfy a new security notion called *random probing expandability* (RPE). They further provide an instantiation of the framework which tolerates a 2^{-8} leakage probability in complexity $\mathcal{O}(\kappa^{7.5})$ where κ denotes the security parameter.

In this paper, we provide an in-depth analysis of the RPE security notion. We exhibit the first upper bounds for the main parameter of a RPE gadget, which is known as the *amplification order*. We further show that the RPE notion can be made tighter and we exhibit strong connections between RPE and the *strong non-interference* (SNI) composition notion. We then introduce the first generic constructions of gadgets achieving RPE for any number of shares and with nearly optimal amplification orders and provide an asymptotic analysis of such constructions. Last but not least, we introduce new concrete constructions of small gadgets achieving maximal amplification orders. This allows us to obtain much more efficient instantiations of the expanding compiler: we obtain a complexity of $\mathcal{O}(\kappa^{3.9})$ for a slightly better leakage probability, as well as $\mathcal{O}(\kappa^{3.2})$ for a slightly lower leakage probability.

Keywords: Random probing model · Masking · Side-channel security

A. Canteaut and F.-X. Standaert (Eds.): EUROCRYPT 2021, LNCS 12697, pp. 313–343, 2021.
https://doi.org/10.1007/978-3-030-77886-6_11

1 Introduction

Most commonly used cryptographic algorithms are assumed to be secure against *black-box* attacks, when the adversary is limited to the knowledge of some inputs and outputs. However, as revealed in the late nineties [18], their implementation on physical devices can be vulnerable to the more powerful *side-channel attacks*. The latter additionally exploit the physical emanations of the underlying device such as the execution time or the device temperature, power consumption, or electromagnetic radiations during the algorithm execution.

To counteract side-channel attacks which often only require cheap equipment and can be easily mounted in a short time interval, the cryptographic community has searched for efficient countermeasures. Among the different approaches, one of the most widely used is known as *masking*. Simultaneously introduced by Chari, Jutla, Rao and Rohatgi [10], and by Goubin and Patarin [16] in 1999, it happens to be strongly related to techniques usually applied in secure multi-party computation. In a nutshell, the idea is to split each sensitive variable of the implementation into n shares such that $n-1$ of them are generated uniformly at random whereas the last one is computed as a combination of the original value and the random shares. Doing so, one aims to ensure that an adversary cannot recover the secret without knowledge of all the shares. When the shares are combined by bitwise addition, the masking is said to be *Boolean*, and it enjoys simple implementation for linear operations which can be simply applied on each share separately. However, things are trickier for non-linear operations for which it is impossible to compute the result without combining shares.

In order to reason about the security of these countermeasures, the community has introduced a variety of models. Among them, the *probing model* introduced by Ishai, Sahai, and Wagner in 2003 [17] is well suited to analyze the security of masked implementations. Basically, it assumes that an adversary is able to get the exact values of a certain number t of intermediate variables in an implementation. This way, it captures the increasing difficulty of combining noisy leakage to recover secrets. Despite its wide use by the community [8,11–13,20], the probing model raised a number of concerns regarding its relevance in practice. Therefore, in 2013, Prouff and Rivain introduced a general and practical model, known as the *noisy leakage model* [19]. This model well captures the reality of embedded devices by assuming that all the manipulated data leak together with some noise. Unfortunately, proving the security of a masking scheme in this model is rather tedious, which is why Duc, Dziembowski, and Faust provided in 2014 a reduction showing that a scheme secure in the probing model is also secure in the noisy leakage model [14].

This reduction is based on an intermediate leakage model, known as *random probing model*, to which the security in the noisy leakage model tightly reduces. In this model, every wire of a circuit is assumed to leak with some constant leakage probability. Then, a circuit is secure if there is a negligible probability that these leaking wires actually reveal information on the secrets. Compared to the probing model, the random probing model is closer to the noisy leakage model and, in particular, captures *horizontal attacks* which exploit the repeated manipulations of variables throughout the implementation. Classical probing secure schemes are also secure in the random probing model but the tolerated leakage probability (a.k.a. leakage rate) might not be constant which is not satisfactory from a practical viewpoint. Indeed, in practice, the leakage probability translates to some side-channel noise amount which might not be customizable by the implementer.

So far, only a few constructions [1–3, 9] tolerate a constant leakage probability. The two former ones [1, 3] are based on expander graphs and the tolerated probability is not made explicit. The third construction [2] is based on multi-party computation protocols and an expansion strategy. It reaches a tolerated leakage probability of around 2^{-26} for a complexity of $\mathcal{O}(\kappa^{8.2})$ for some security parameter κ, as computed by the authors of [9]. Finally, the more recent construction [9] relies on masking gadgets and a similar expansion strategy and reaches a tolerated leakage probability of 2^{-8} for a complexity of $\mathcal{O}(\kappa^{7.5})$. While obtaining such quantified tolerated leakage probability is of great practical interest, the obtained complexity is high which makes this construction hardly practical.

Besides their explicit construction, the authors of [9] provide a complete and practical framework to generate random probing secure implementations. Namely, they formalize the *expanding compiler* which produces a random probing secure version of any circuit from three base gadgets (for addition, copy, and multiplication) achieving a *random probing expandability* (RPE) property. The advantage of this approach is that it enables to bootstrap small gadgets (defined for a small number of shares) into a circuit achieving arbitrary security in the random probing model while tolerating a constant and quantified leakage probability. Although the concrete results of [9] in terms of complexity and tolerated leakage probability are promising, the authors left open the analysis of this RPE property and the design of better gadgets in this paradigm.

Our Contributions. In this paper, we provide an in-depth analysis of the random probing expandability security notion. We first provide some upper bounds for the *amplification order* of an RPE gadget, which is the crucial parameter in view of a low-complexity instantiation of the expanding compiler. We further show that the RPE notion can be made tighter and we exhibit strong relations between RPE and the *strong non-interference* (SNI) composition notion for probing-secure gadgets.

From these results, we introduce the first generic constructions of gadgets achieving RPE for any number of shares and with nearly optimal amplification orders. These generic gadgets are derived from the widely known Ishai-Sahai-Wagner (ISW) construction. We show that the obtained expanding compiler can approach a quadratic complexity depending on the leakage probability that must be tolerated: the smaller the leakage probability, the closer the complexity to $\mathcal{O}(\kappa^2)$. We further introduce a new multiplication gadget achieving the optimal amplification order, which allows us to improve the convergence to a quadratic complexity.

Finally, we provide new concrete constructions of copy, addition, and multiplication gadgets achieving maximal amplification orders for small numbers of shares. These gadgets yield much more efficient instantiations than all the previous schemes (including the analysed ISW-based constructions). While slightly improving the tolerated leakage probability to $p = 2^{-7.5}$, our 3-share instantiation achieves a complexity of $\mathcal{O}(\kappa^{3.9})$. For a slightly lower leakage probability, our 5-share instantiation drops the complexity to $\mathcal{O}(\kappa^{3.2})$.

We thus achieve a significant step forward in the quest for efficient random probing secure schemes that tolerate a quantified leakage probability. Besides our concrete instantiations, our work introduces several tools (new bounds, relations, and generic gadgets) that shall be instrumental for future constructions.

2 Preliminaries

Along the paper, we shall use similar notations and formalism as [9]. In particular, $\mathbb{K}$ shall denote a finite field. For any $n \in \mathbb{N}$, we shall denote $[n]$ the integer set $[n] = [1, n] \cap \mathbb{Z}$. For any tuple $\boldsymbol{x} = (x_1, \dots, x_n) \in \mathbb{K}^n$ and any set $I \subseteq [n]$, we shall denote $\boldsymbol{x}|_I = (x_i)_{i \in I}$.

2.1 Linear Sharing, Circuits, and Gadgets

In the following, the *n-linear decoding* mapping, denoted LinDec, refers to the function $\mathbb{K}^n \to \mathbb{K}$ defined as

$$\mathsf{LinDec} : (x_1, \dots, x_n) \mapsto x_1 + \cdots + x_n \ ,$$

for every $n \in \mathbb{N}$ and $(x_1, \dots, x_n) \in \mathbb{K}^n$. We shall further consider that, for every $n, \ell \in \mathbb{N}$, on input $(\widehat{x}_1, \dots, \widehat{x}_\ell) \in (\mathbb{K}^n)^\ell$ the n-linear decoding mapping acts as

$$\mathsf{LinDec} : (\widehat{x}_1, \dots, \widehat{x}_\ell) \mapsto (\mathsf{LinDec}(\widehat{x}_1), \dots, \mathsf{LinDec}(\widehat{x}_\ell)).$$

Definition 1 (Linear Sharing). *Let $n, \ell \in \mathbb{N}$. For any $x \in \mathbb{K}$, an* n-linear sharing *of x is a random vector $\widehat{x} \in \mathbb{K}^n$ such that* $\mathsf{LinDec}(\widehat{x}) = x$. *It is said to be* uniform *if for any set $I \subseteq [n]$ with $|I| < n$ the tuple $\widehat{x}|_I$ is uniformly distributed over $\mathbb{K}^{|I|}$. A* n-linear encoding *is a probabilistic algorithm* LinEnc *which on input a tuple $\boldsymbol{x} = (x_1, \dots, x_\ell) \in \mathbb{K}^\ell$ outputs a tuple $\widehat{\boldsymbol{x}} = (\widehat{x}_1, \dots, \widehat{x}_\ell) \in (\mathbb{K}^n)^\ell$ such that $\widehat{x}_i$ is a uniform n-sharing of x_i for every $i \in [\ell]$.*

An *arithmetic circuit* on a field $\mathbb{K}$ is a labeled directed acyclic graph whose edges are *wires* and vertices are *arithmetic gates* processing operations on $\mathbb{K}$. We consider circuits composed of addition gates, $(x_1, x_2) \mapsto x_1 + x_2$, multiplication gates, $(x_1, x_2) \mapsto x_1 \cdot x_2$, and copy gates, $x \mapsto (x, x)$. A *randomized arithmetic circuit* is equipped with an additional random gate which outputs a fresh uniform random value of $\mathbb{K}$.

In the following, we shall call an *(n-share, ℓ-to-m) gadget*, a randomized arithmetic circuit that maps an input $\widehat{\boldsymbol{x}} \in (\mathbb{K}^n)^\ell$ to an output $\widehat{\boldsymbol{y}} \in (\mathbb{K}^n)^m$ such that $\boldsymbol{x} = \mathsf{LinDec}(\widehat{\boldsymbol{x}}) \in \mathbb{K}^\ell$ and $\boldsymbol{y} = \mathsf{LinDec}(\widehat{\boldsymbol{y}}) \in \mathbb{K}^m$ satisfy $\boldsymbol{y} = g(\boldsymbol{x})$ for some function g. In this paper, we shall consider gadgets for three types of functions (corresponding to the three types of gates): the addition $g : (x_1, x_2) \mapsto x_1 + x_2$, the multiplication $g : (x_1, x_2) \mapsto x_1 \cdot x_2$ and the copy $g : x \mapsto (x, x)$. We shall generally denote such gadgets G_{add}, G_{mult} and G_{copy} respectively.

2.2 Random Probing Security

Let $p \in [0, 1]$ be some constant leakage probability parameter, a.k.a. the *leakage rate*. In the p-random probing model, an evaluation of a circuit C leaks the value carried by each wire with a probability p (and leaks nothing otherwise), all the wire leakage events being mutually independent.

As in [9], we formally define the random-probing leakage of a circuit from the two following probabilistic algorithms:

- The *leaking-wires sampler* takes as input a randomized arithmetic circuit C and a probability $p \in [0, 1]$, and outputs a set $\mathcal{W}$, denoted as

$$\mathcal{W} \leftarrow \mathsf{LeakingWires}(C, p),$$

where $\mathcal{W}$ is constructed by including each wire label from the circuit C with probability p to $\mathcal{W}$ (where all the probabilities are mutually independent).
- The *assign-wires sampler* takes as input a randomized arithmetic circuit C, a set of wire labels $\mathcal{W}$ (subset of the wire labels of C), and an input $\boldsymbol{x}$, and it outputs a $|\mathcal{W}|$-tuple $\boldsymbol{w} \in (\mathbb{K} \cup \{\perp\})^{|\mathcal{W}|}$, denoted as

$$\boldsymbol{w} \leftarrow \mathsf{AssignWires}(C, \mathcal{W}, \boldsymbol{x}),$$

where $\boldsymbol{w}$ corresponds to the assignments of the wires of C with label in $\mathcal{W}$ for an evaluation on input $\boldsymbol{x}$.

Definition 2 (Random Probing Leakage). *The* p-random probing leakage *of a randomized arithmetic circuit C on input $\boldsymbol{x}$ is the distribution $\mathcal{L}_p(C, \boldsymbol{x})$ obtained by composing the leaking-wires and assign-wires samplers as*

$$\mathcal{L}_p(C, \boldsymbol{x}) \stackrel{id}{=} \mathsf{AssignWires}(C, \mathsf{LeakingWires}(C, p), \boldsymbol{x}).$$

Definition 3 (Random Probing Security). *A randomized arithmetic circuit C with $\ell \cdot n \in \mathbb{N}$ input gates is* (p, ε)-random probing secure *with respect to encoding* Enc *if there exists a simulator* Sim *such that for every $\boldsymbol{x} \in \mathbb{K}^\ell$:*

$$\mathsf{Sim}(C) \approx_\varepsilon \mathcal{L}_p(C, \mathsf{Enc}(\boldsymbol{x})). \tag{1}$$

2.3 Expanding Compiler

In [2], Ananth, Ishai and Sahai propose an *expansion* approach to build a random-probing-secure circuit compiler from a secure multiparty protocol. This approach was later revisited by Belaïd, Coron, Prouff, Rivain, and Taleb who formalize the notion of *expanding compiler* [9].

The principle of the expanding compiler is to recursively apply a base compiler, denoted CC, and which simply consists in replacing each gate in the input circuit by the corresponding gadget. More specifically, assume we have three n-share gadgets G_{add}, G_{mult}, G_{copy}, for the addition, the multiplication, and the copy on $\mathbb{K}$. The base compiler CC simply consists in replacing each addition gate in the original gadget by G_{add}, each multiplication gate by G_{mult}, and each copy gate by G_{copy}, and by replacing each wire by n wires carrying a sharing of the original wire. One can derive three new n^2-share gadgets by simply applying CC to each gadget: $G^{(2)}_{\text{add}} = \mathsf{CC}(G_{\text{add}})$, $G^{(2)}_{\text{mult}} = \mathsf{CC}(G_{\text{mult}})$, and $G^{(2)}_{\text{copy}} = \mathsf{CC}(G_{\text{copy}})$. Doing so, we obtain n^2-share gadgets for the addition, multiplication, and copy on $\mathbb{K}$. This process can be iterated an arbitrary number of times, say k, to an input circuit C:

$$C \xrightarrow{\mathsf{CC}} \widehat{C}_1 \xrightarrow{\mathsf{CC}} \cdots \xrightarrow{\mathsf{CC}} \widehat{C}_k .$$

The first output circuit $\widehat{C}_1$ is the original circuit in which each gate is replaced by a base gadget G_{add}, G_{mult}, or G_{copy}. The second output circuit $\widehat{C}_2$ is the original circuit C in which each gate is replaced by an n^2-share gadget $G^{(2)}_{\text{add}}$, $G^{(2)}_{\text{mult}}$, or $G^{(2)}_{\text{copy}}$ as defined above. Equivalently, $\widehat{C}_2$ is the circuit $\widehat{C}_1$ in which each gate is replaced by a base gadget. In the end, the output circuit $\widehat{C}_k$ is hence the original circuit C in which each gate has been replaced by a k-expanded gadget and each wire has been replaced by n^k wires carrying an (n^k)-linear sharing of the original wire.

This expanding compiler achieves random probing security if the base gadgets verify a property called *random probing expandability* [9].

2.4 Random Probing Expandability

We recall hereafter the original definition of the random probing expandability (RPE) property for 2-input 1-output gadgets.

Definition 4 (Random Probing Expandability [9]**).** *Let $f : \mathbb{R} \to \mathbb{R}$. An n-share gadget $G : \mathbb{K}^n \times \mathbb{K}^n \to \mathbb{K}^n$ is (t, f)-*random probing expandable (RPE) *if there exists a deterministic algorithm Sim_1^G and a probabilistic algorithm Sim_2^G such that for every input $(\widehat{x}, \widehat{y}) \in \mathbb{K}^n \times \mathbb{K}^n$, for every set $J \subseteq [n]$ and for every $p \in [0, 1]$, the random experiment*

$$\begin{aligned} &\mathcal{W} \leftarrow \mathsf{LeakingWires}(G, p) \\ &(I_1, I_2, J') \leftarrow \mathsf{Sim}_1^G(\mathcal{W}, J) \\ &out \leftarrow \mathsf{Sim}_2^G(\mathcal{W}, J', \widehat{x}|_{I_1}, \widehat{y}|_{I_2}) \end{aligned}$$

ensures that

1. the failure events $\mathcal{F}_1 \equiv \big(|I_1| > t\big)$ and $\mathcal{F}_2 \equiv \big(|I_2| > t\big)$ verify

$$\Pr(\mathcal{F}_1) = \Pr(\mathcal{F}_2) = \varepsilon \quad and \quad \Pr(\mathcal{F}_1 \wedge \mathcal{F}_2) = \varepsilon^2 \tag{2}$$

with $\varepsilon = f(p)$ *(in particular* $\mathcal{F}_1$ *and* $\mathcal{F}_2$ *are mutually independent),*

2. J' *is such that* $J' = J$ *if* $|J| \leq t$ *and* $J' \subseteq [n]$ *with* $|J'| = n - 1$ *otherwise,*
3. *the output distribution satisfies*

$$out \stackrel{id}{=} \left(\mathsf{AssignWires}(G, \mathcal{W}, (\widehat{x}, \widehat{y}))\ ,\ \widehat{z}|_{J'}\right) \tag{3}$$

where $\widehat{z} = G(\widehat{x}, \widehat{y})$.

The RPE notion can be simply extended to gadgets with 2 outputs: the Sim_1^G simulator takes two sets $J_1 \subseteq [n]$ and $J_2 \subseteq [n]$ as input and produces two sets J_1' and J_2' satisfying the same property as J' in the above definition (w.r.t. J_1 and J_2). The Sim_2^G simulator must then produce an output including $\widehat{z}_1|_{J_1'}$ and $\widehat{z}_2|_{J_1'}$ where $\widehat{z}_1$ and $\widehat{z}_2$ are the output sharings. The RPE notion can also be simply extended to gadgets with a single input: the Sim_1^G simulator produces a single set I so that the failure event $(|I| > t)$ occurs with probability ε (and the Sim_2^G simulator is then simply given $\widehat{x}|_I$ where $\widehat{x}$ is the single input sharing). We refer the reader to [9] for the formal definitions of these variants. Eventually, the RPE notion can also be extended to gadgets with an arbitrary number ℓ of inputs. The Sim_1^G simulator then produces ℓ sets $I_1, \ldots, I_\ell$ so that the corresponding failures $(|I_1| > t), \ldots (|I_\ell| > t)$ occur with probability ε and are additionally mutually independent. The Sim_2^G simulator then simply gets use of the shares of each input as designated respectively by the corresponding sets $I_1, \ldots, I_\ell$.

Note that as explained in [9], the requirement of the RPE notion on the mutual independence of the failure events might seem too strong. We can actually use the proposed relaxation referred to as *weak random probing expandability*. Namely, the equalities (Eq. (2)) are replaced by inequalities as upper bounds are sufficient in our context. We refer the reader to [9] for the concrete reduction, which does not impact the amplification orders.

2.5 Complexity of the Expanding Compiler

We start by recalling the definition of the *amplification order* of a function and of a gadget.

Definition 5 (Amplification Order).

- *Let* $f : \mathbb{R} \to \mathbb{R}$ *which satisfies*

$$f(p) = c_d\, p^d + \mathcal{O}(p^{d+\varepsilon})$$

as p *tends to* 0*, for some* $c_d > 0$ *and* $\varepsilon > 0$*. Then* d *is called the amplification order of* f.
- *Let* $t > 0$ *and* G *a gadget. Let* d *be the maximal integer such that* G *achieves* (t, f)*-RPE for* $f : \mathbb{R} \to \mathbb{R}$ *of amplification order* d*. Then* d *is called the amplification order of* G *(with respect to* t*).*

We stress that the amplification order of a gadget G is defined with respect to the RPE threshold t. Namely, different RPE thresholds t are likely to yield different amplification orders d for G (or equivalently d can be thought of as a function of t).

As shown in [9], the complexity of the expanding compiler relates to the (minimum) amplification order of the three gadgets used in the base compiler CC. If the latter achieves (t, f)-RPE with an amplification order d, the expanding compiler achieves $(p, 2^{-\kappa})$-random probing security with a complexity blowup of $\mathcal{O}(\kappa^e)$ for an exponent e satisfying

$$e = \frac{\log N_{\max}}{\log d} \tag{4}$$

with

$$N_{\max} = \max\left(N_{\mathrm{m,m}}\ ,\ \mathsf{eigenvalues}\left(\begin{pmatrix} N_{\mathrm{a,a}} & N_{\mathrm{c,a}} \\ N_{\mathrm{a,c}} & N_{\mathrm{c,c}} \end{pmatrix}\right)\right) \tag{5}$$

where $N_{\mathrm{x,y}}$ denotes the number of gates "x" in a gadget "y", with "m" meaning multiplication, "a" meaning addition, and "c" meaning copy. As an illustration, the instantiation proposed in [9] satisfies $N_{\max} = 21$ and $d = \frac{3}{2}$ which yields an asymptotic complexity of $\mathcal{O}(\kappa^{7.5})$.

Finally, we recall the notion of maximum *tolerated leakage probability* which corresponds to the maximum value p for which we have $f(p) < p$. This happens to be a necessary and sufficient condition for the expansion strategy to apply with (t, f)-RPE gadgets. The instantiation proposed in [9] tolerates a leakage probability up to $2^{-7.80}$.

3 Bounding the Amplification Order

As recalled above, the amplification order of a gadget is a crucial parameter of its random probing expandability. The higher the amplification order, the lower the asymptotic complexity of the expanding compiler, *ceteris paribus*. A natural question which was left open in [9] is to determine the best amplification order that can be hoped for given the different parameters of a gadget. In this section, we exhibit concrete upper bounds on the amplification order that can be achieved by a gadget depending on its input-output dimensions (ℓ, m), its number of shares n, and its RPE threshold t.

Before giving the bounds let us make a key observation on the amplification order of a gadget. Let G be a 2-to-1 n-share gadget achieving (t, f)-RPE. A subset $\mathcal{W}$ of the wires of G is said to be a *failure set* with respect to the first input (resp. the second input) if there exists a set $J \subseteq [n]$ such that $(I_1, I_2, J') \leftarrow \mathsf{Sim}_1^G(\mathcal{W}, J)$ implies $|I_1| > t$ (resp. $|I_2| > t$), namely if a leaking set $\mathcal{W}$ implies the failure event $\mathcal{F}_1$ (resp. $\mathcal{F}_2$) in the definition of RPE. One can check that G has amplification order $d \leq d_{up}$ if one of the two following events occurs:

1. there exists a failure set $\mathcal{W}$ w.r.t. the first input *or* the second input such that $|\mathcal{W}| = d_{up}$,

2. there exists a failure set $\mathcal{W}$ w.r.t. the first input *and* the second input such that $|\mathcal{W}| = 2d_{up}$.

In the former case, the existence of the failure set implies that the function $f(p)$ has a non-zero coefficient in $p^{d_{up}}$ and hence $d \leq d_{up}$. In the latter case, the existence of the double failure set implies that the function $f^2(p)$ has a non-zero coefficient in $p^{2d_{up}}$ and hence $d \leq d_{up}$. The case of a single-input gadget is simpler: it has amplification order $d \leq d_{up}$ if there exists a failure set $\mathcal{W}$ (w.r.t. its single input) such that $|\mathcal{W}| = d_{up}$.

We start by exhibiting a generic upper bound for the amplification order and then look at the particular case of what we shall call a *standard* multiplication gadget.

3.1 Generic Upper Bound

In the following we will say that a function $g : \mathbb{K}^\ell \to \mathbb{K}^m$ is *complete* if at least one of its m outputs is functionally dependent on the ℓ inputs. Similarly, we say that a gadget G is complete if its underlying function g is complete.

The following lemma gives our generic upper bound on the amplification order.

Lemma 1. *Let $f : \mathbb{R} \to \mathbb{R}$, $n \in \mathbb{N}$ and $\ell, m \in \{1, 2\}$. Let $G : (\mathbb{K}^n)^\ell \to (\mathbb{K}^n)^m$ be an ℓ-to-m n-share complete gadget achieving (t, f)-RPE. Then its amplification order d is upper bounded by*

$$\min((t+1), (3-\ell) \cdot (n-t)).$$

Proof. The first part of the bound on the amplification order $d \leq (t+1)$ is immediate since by probing $t+1$ shares of any input, the considered set will be a failure set of cardinality $t+1$. We then consider two cases depending on the number of inputs:

1. *1-input gadgets ($\ell = 1$):* We show that we can exhibit a failure set of size $2(n-t)$. Let us denote the output shares $z_1, \ldots, z_n$ (for two-output gadgets, *i.e.* $m = 2$, $z_1, \ldots, z_n$ can be any of the output sharings). In the evaluation of the (t, f)-RPE property, t shares among the z_i's (corresponding to the set J) must be simulated. Without loss of generality, let $z_1, \ldots, z_t$ be those shares (*i.e.* $J = [t]$). By including both input gates of each of the remaining output shares $z_{t+1}, \ldots, z_n$ in the set $\mathcal{W}$, the distribution to be simulated requires the knowledge of the full input (by completeness of the gadget). The set $\mathcal{W}$ is thus a failure set with $2(n-t)$ elements.
2. *2-input gadgets ($\ell = 2$):* Considering the same failure set as in the above case, the simulation of *out* requires the full two input sharings. Hence $\mathcal{W}$ is a failure set of size $2(n-t)$ with respect to the two inputs, and so the amplification order satisfies $d \leq (n-t)$.

We hence conclude that $d \leq \min((t+1), 2(n-t))$ for one-input gadgets, and $d \leq \min((t+1), (n-t))$ for two-input gadgets. □

Corollary 1 (One-input gadget). *The amplification order d of a one-input gadget achieving (t, f)-RPE is upper bounded by*

$$d \leq \frac{2(n+1)}{3}.$$

The above corollary directly holds from Lemma 1 for a RPE threshold $t = \frac{2n-1}{3}$ (which balances the two sides of the min).

Corollary 2 (Two-input gadget). *The amplification order d of a two-input gadget achieving (t, f)-RPE is upper bounded by*

$$d \leq \frac{n+1}{2}.$$

The above corollary directly holds from Lemma 1 for a RPE threshold $t = \frac{n-1}{2}$ (which balances the two sides of the min).

We deduce from the two above corollaries that for a circuit composed of addition, multiplication and copy gadgets, the amplification order is upper bounded

$$d \leq \min\left(\frac{2(n+1)}{3}, \frac{n+1}{2}\right) = \frac{n+1}{2},$$

which can only be achieved for an odd number of shares by taking $t = \frac{n-1}{2}$ as RPE threshold.

3.2 Upper Bound for Standard Multiplication Gadgets

The generic bound exhibited above is not tight in the special case of a standard multiplication gadget which computes cross products between the input shares, such as the ISW multiplication gadget [17]. We exhibit hereafter a tighter bound for such gadgets.

Formally, a n-share multiplication gadget G is a *standard multiplication gadget*, if on input $(\boldsymbol{x}, \boldsymbol{y}) \in (\mathbb{K}^n)^2$, G computes the cross products $x_i \cdot y_j$ for $1 \leq i, j \leq n$. Our upper bound on the amplification order for such gadgets is given in the following lemma.

Lemma 2. *Let $f : \mathbb{R} \to \mathbb{R}$ and $n \in \mathbb{N}$. Let G be an n-share standard multiplication gadget achieving (t, f)-RPE. Then its amplification order d is upper bounded by*

$$d \leq \min\left(\frac{t+1}{2}, (n-t)\right).$$

Proof. The second part of the bound $(n - t)$ holds directly from Lemma 1. We now prove the bound $(t + 1)/2$ by exhibiting a failure set of size $t + 1$ with t output shares, which will be a failure on both inputs. Let $\{m_{ij}\}_{0 \leq i,j \leq n}$ denote the cross products such that $m_{ij} = x_i \cdot y_j$. Consider a set $\mathcal{W}$ made of $t + 1$ such variables $\{m_{ij}\}$ for which the indexes i and j are all distinct. Specifically,

$\mathcal{W} = \{x_{i_1} \cdot y_{j_1}, \ldots, x_{i_{t+1}} \cdot y_{j_{t+1}}\}$ such that $\{i_\ell\}_{1 \le \ell \le t+1}$ and $\{j_\ell\}_{1 \le \ell \le t+1}$ are both sets of $(t+1)$ distinct indexes. Clearly, such a set is a failure set for both inputs $\boldsymbol{x}$ and $\boldsymbol{y}$ since it requires $t+1$ shares of each of them to be perfectly simulated (even without considering the output shares to be also simulated). We hence have a double failure set of cardinality $t+1$ which implies the $(t+1)/2$ upper bound on the amplification order. □

The above lemma implies that the highest amplification order for standard multiplication gadgets might be achieved for a RPE threshold $t = \frac{2n-1}{3}$ which yields the following maximal upper bound:

$$d \le \frac{n+1}{3},$$

which is lower than the generic upper bound for 2-to-1 gadgets exhibited in Corollary 2. This loss suggests that better amplification orders could be achieved for multiplication gadgets that do not compute direct cross products of the input shares. We actually provide new constructions of multiplication gadgets avoiding this loss in Sect. 5.

4 A Closer Look at Random Probing Expandability

In this section, we give a closer look at the RPE notion. We first show that it naturally splits into two different notions, that we shall call RPE1 and RPE2, and further introduce a tighter variant which will be useful for our purpose. We then study the relations between (tight) RPE and the *Strong Non-Interference* (SNI) notion used for probing security. We exhibit strong connections between (tight) RPE1 and SNI, which will be very useful for our constructive results depicted in Sect. 5.

4.1 Splitting RPE

From Definition 4, we can define two sub-properties which are jointly equivalent to RPE. In the first one, designated by RPE1, the set J is constrained to satisfy $|J| \le t$ and $J' = J$ (the simulator does not choose J'). In the second one, designated by RPE2, J' is chosen by the simulator such that $J' \subseteq [n]$ with $|J'| = n - 1$ (and J does not matter anymore). For the sake of completeness, these two notions are formally defined in the full version of this paper.

This split is somehow a partition of the RPE notion since we have:

$$G \text{ is } (t,f)\text{-RPE} \iff G \text{ is } (t,f)\text{-RPE1 } \textit{and } G \text{ is } (t,f)\text{-RPE2}$$

for any gadget G. As a result of the above equivalence, we can show that a gadget achieves RPE1 and RPE2 independently in order to obtain RPE for this gadget. Formally, we use the following lemma.

Lemma 3. *An n-share gadget $G : \mathbb{K}^n \times \mathbb{K}^n \to \mathbb{K}^n$ which is (t, f_1)-RPE1 and (t, f_2)-RPE2 is also (t, f)-RPE with $f(p) \ge \max(f_1(p), f_2(p))$ for every $p \in [0,1]$.*

We can refine the upper bounds introduced in Sect. 3 with respect to this split. In Lemma 1, the bound $d \leq t+1$ applies to both RPE1 and RPE2, while the bound $d \leq (3-\ell) \cdot (n-t)$ only applies to RPE1. Similarly, in Lemma 2, the bound $d \leq (t+1)/2$ applies to both RPE1 and RPE2, while the bound $d \leq (n-t)$ only applies to RPE1.

4.2 Tightening RPE

We introduce a tighter version of the RPE security property. The so-called *tight random probing expandability* (TRPE) is such that a failure occurs when the simulation requires more than t input shares (as in the original RPE notion) but also whenever this number of shares is greater than the size of the leaking set $\mathcal{W}$. Formally, the failure event $\mathcal{F}_j$ is defined as

$$\mathcal{F}_j \equiv \big(|I_j| > \min(t, |\mathcal{W}|)\big)$$

for every $j \in [\ell]$.

This tighter security property will be instrumental in the following to obtain generic RPE constructions. Similarly to the original RPE property, the TRPE property can be split into two intermediate properties, namely TRPE1 and TRPE2 and Lemma 3 also applies to the case of TRPE. Moreover the upper bounds on the amplification order for RPE in Lemmas 1 and 2 further apply to the amplification order for TRPE (which holds by definition). The formal TRPE, TRPE1, and TRPE2 definitions are given in the full version of this paper for the sake of completeness.

We show hereafter that the TRPE notion is actually equivalent to the RPE notion if and only if the function f is of maximal amplification order $t+1$.

Lemma 4. *Let $t \in \mathbb{N}$, let $f : \mathbb{R} \to \mathbb{R}$ of amplification order d. Let G be a gadget.*

1. *If G achieves (t, f)-TRPE, then it achieves (t, f')-RPE for some $f' : \mathbb{R} \to \mathbb{R}$ of amplification order $d' \geq d$.*
2. *If G is of amplification order d with respect to t (i.e. d is the max amplification order of a function f for which G is (t, f)-RPE), then for all $f' : \mathbb{R} \to \mathbb{R}$ for which G achieves (t, f')-TRPE, f' is of amplification order $d' \leq d$.*
3. *If $d = t+1$, then G achieves (t, f)-TRPE if and only if G achieves (t, f)-RPE.*

Proof. The proof for the first two points is easy. In particular, for the first point, if G achieves TRPE with an amplification order of d, then G achieves RPE with amplification order at least d, since a failure in the TRPE setting *i.e.* $|I_j| > \min(t, |\mathcal{W}|)$ does not necessarily imply a failure in the RPE setting *i.e.* $|I_j| > t$, meanwhile if there is no failure for TRPE for a leaking set of wires $\mathcal{W}$, then this implies that $|I_j| \leq \min(t, |\mathcal{W}|) \leq t$ so there is no failure in the RPE setting either.

As for the second point, the proof is similar: if G achieves an amplification of d in the RPE setting, then it achieves an amplification order of at most d in the TRPE setting, since a failure in the RPE setting *i.e.* $|I_j| > t$ immediately implies a failure in the TRPE setting $|I_j| > \min(t, |\mathcal{W}|)$. But also, even if there is no failure for a leaking set of wires $\mathcal{W}$ in the RPE setting we might still have a failure in the TRPE setting for the same set $\mathcal{W}$. This is mainly the case where $\mathcal{W}$ can be simulated with sets of input shares I_j such that $|\mathcal{W}| < |I_j| \leq t$, so we have $|I_j| \leq t$ (*i.e.* no failure for RPE) and $|I_j| > \min(t, |\mathcal{W}|) = |\mathcal{W}|$ (*i.e.* failure on TRPE). This concludes the proof for the second point.

We will now prove the third point. Let $d = t+1$. We will show that for every set $J' \subseteq [n]$ of output shares and every leaking set of wires $\mathcal{W}$, a failure occurs in the TRPE setting if and only if a failure also occurs in the RPE setting. If $|\mathcal{W}| \geq t$, then the two settings are equivalent since $\min(t, |\mathcal{W}|) = t$. We will thus only focus on the case $|\mathcal{W}| < t$. Clearly, a failure in the RPE setting, *i.e.* $|I_j| > t$, implies a failure in the TRPE setting, *i.e.* $|I_j| > \min(t, |\mathcal{W}|)$. Let us now show that the converse is also true.

We assume by contradiction that there exists J' and $\mathcal{W}$ implying a TRPE failure which is not an RPE failure, that is a set I_j satisfying $|\mathcal{W}| < |I_j| \leq t$. We then show that there exists a leaking set $\mathcal{W}'$ of size $|\mathcal{W}'| < t+1$ for which an RPE failure always occurs, which implies an amplification order strictly lower than $t+1$ and hence contradicts the lemma hypothesis. This set $\mathcal{W}'$ is constructed as $\mathcal{W}' = \mathcal{W} \cup I'_j$ for some set $I'_j \subset [n] \setminus I_j$ such that $|I'_j| = t+1-|I_j|$. The simulation of $\mathcal{W}'$ and J' then requires the input shares from $I_j \cup I'_j$. However, we have

$$|I_j \cup I'_j| = |I_j| + |I'_j| = t + 1$$

implying an RPE failure, and

$$|\mathcal{W}'| = |\mathcal{W} \cup I'_j| \leq |\mathcal{W}| + |I'_j| = |\mathcal{W}| + t + 1 - |I_j| < |\mathcal{W}| + t + 1 - |\mathcal{W}| = t + 1.$$

Thus, we have built a failure set $\mathcal{W}'$ of size strictly less than the amplification order $t + 1$, which contradicts the hypothesis and hence concludes the proof. □

The above proof also applies to the case of the split notions, specifically for ((t, f)-RPE1, (t, f)-TRPE1) and for ((t, f)-RPE2, (t, f)-TRPE2).

4.3 Unifying (Tight) RPE and SNI

Strong non-interference (SNI) is a widely used notion to compose probing-secure gadgets [5]. In [9], the authors exhibit a relation between the SNI and the *random probing composability* (RPC) property in their Proposition 1. We go one step further and study the relation between SNI and (T)RPE.

We state hereafter some equivalence results between the (T)RPE1 and SNI notions, up to some constraints on the parameters. Let us first recall the definition of the SNI notion.

Definition 6 (Strong Non-Interference (SNI)). *Let n, ℓ and τ be positive integers. An n-share gadget $G : (\mathbb{K}^n)^\ell \to \mathbb{K}^n$ is τ-SNI if there exists a deterministic algorithm Sim_1^G and a probabilistic algorithm Sim_2^G such that for every* *set $J \subseteq [n]$ and subset $\mathcal{W}$ of wire labels from G satisfying $|\mathcal{W}| + |J| \leqslant \tau$, the following random experiment with any $\widehat{\boldsymbol{x}} \in (\mathbb{K}^n)^\ell$*

$$\boldsymbol{I} \leftarrow \mathsf{Sim}_1^G(\mathcal{W}, J)$$
$$out \leftarrow \mathsf{Sim}_2^G(\widehat{\boldsymbol{x}}|_{\boldsymbol{I}})$$

yields

$$|I_1| \leqslant |\mathcal{W}|, \ldots, |I_\ell| \leqslant |\mathcal{W}| \tag{6}$$

and

$$out \stackrel{id}{=} (\mathsf{AssignWires}(G, \mathcal{W}, \widehat{\boldsymbol{x}}) \ , \ \widehat{\boldsymbol{y}}|_J) \tag{7}$$

where $\boldsymbol{I} = (I_1, \ldots, I_\ell)$ and $\widehat{\boldsymbol{y}} = G(\widehat{\boldsymbol{x}})$.

We first formally show that (T)RPE1 implies SNI.

Lemma 5. *Let $t \in \mathbb{N}$ and $f : \mathbb{R} \to \mathbb{R}$ of amplification order $t+1$. Let G be a gadget which achieves (t, f)-TRPE1. Then G is also t-SNI.*

Proof. By definition of TRPE1 and by hypothesis on the amplification order, there exist input sets $I_1, \ldots, I_\ell$ which can perfectly simulate any leaking wires set $\mathcal{W}$ such that $|\mathcal{W}| \leq t$ and any set of output shares J such that $|J| \leq t$, satisfying $|I_1|, \ldots, |I_\ell| \leq |\mathcal{W}|$. Consequently, there exist input sets $I_1, \ldots, I_\ell$ which can perfectly simulate any leaking wires set $\mathcal{W}$ such that $|\mathcal{W}| = t_i \leq t$ and any set of output shares J such that $|\mathcal{W}| + |J| \leq t$ with $|I_1|, \ldots, |I_\ell| \leq t_i$. G is thus t-SNI. □

We now show that SNI implies TRPE1 up to some constraints on the parameters t and τ.

Lemma 6. *Let $\tau, \ell \in \mathbb{N}$. Let G be an ℓ-to-1 gadget which achieves τ-SNI. Then G satisfies (t, f)-TRPE1 for some $f : \mathbb{R} \to \mathbb{R}$ with an amplification order of*

$$d \geq \frac{1}{\ell} \min(t+1, \tau - t + 1) \ .$$

Proof. Since G is τ-SNI, then for any set of leaking wires $\mathcal{W}$ and output shares J such that $|\mathcal{W}| + |J| \leq \tau$, the wires indexed by $\mathcal{W}$ and the output shares indexed by J can be perfectly simulated from input shares indexed by $I_1, \ldots, I_\ell$ such that $|I_j| \leq |\mathcal{W}|$ for every $1 \leq j \leq \ell$. In the TRPE1 property, the set J of output shares can be any set of size $|J| \leq t$ so we can assume $|J| = t$ without loss of generality.

For a leaking set $\mathcal{W}$ of size $|\mathcal{W}| < \min(t+1, \tau - t + 1)$ no failure event occurs. Indeed τ-SNI and $|\mathcal{W}| < \tau - t + 1$ implies $|\mathcal{W}| + |J| \leq \tau$ and hence the existence of the sets $I_1, \ldots, I_\ell$ allowing the simulation with $|I_j| \leq |\mathcal{W}|$. And $|\mathcal{W}| < t + 1$ implies $|I_j| \leq \min(t, |\mathcal{W}|)$ for every j which implies the absence of failure. Then for a leaking set $\mathcal{W}$ of size $|\mathcal{W}| \geq \min(t+1, \tau - t + 1)$, no condition remains to rule out simulation failures and one could actually get a failure for every input. In the latter case, the amplification order would equal $\frac{1}{\ell} \min(t+1, n-t)$, but in all generality it could be higher (*i.e.* this value is a lower bound). □

An illustrative summary of the relations between RPE1, TRPE1 and SNI is depicted in Fig. 1 (d denotes the amplification order of the function f). We hence observe an equivalence between the three notions up to some constraints on the parameters t, d, τ and ℓ.

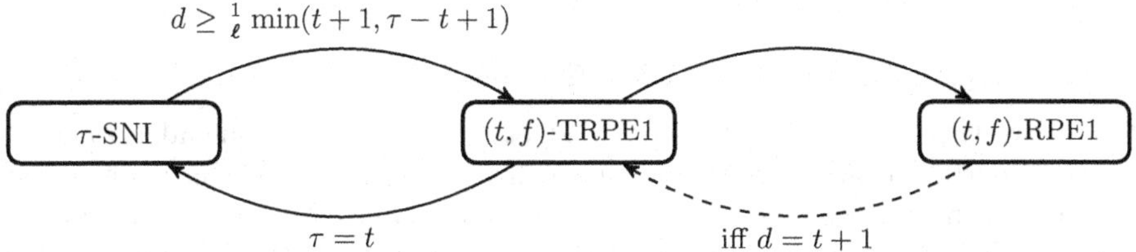

Fig. 1. Summary of relations between the different notions.

Relation and Separation Between (T)RPE2 and SNI. For a given n-share gadget G, the (T)RPE2 notion exclusively focuses on the simulation of a set of leaking intermediate variables together with a chosen set of $(n-1)$ output shares. If G is τ-SNI for $\tau < n-1$, then nothing can be claimed on the simulation of the latter sets. But if G is $(n-1)$-SNI, then any set of $(n-1)$ output shares can be perfectly simulated without the knowledge of any input share. Concretely, it implies that G is (t, f)-(T)RPE2 of amplification order at least 1 as a chosen output set of $(n-1)$ shares alone can be perfectly simulated without any additional knowledge on the input shares. Namely, we have

$$(n-1)\text{-SNI} \Rightarrow (t, f)\text{-(T)RPE2 of amplification order at least 1.}$$

Nevertheless, there is no relation from τ-SNI to (t, f)-(T)RPE2 for amplification orders strictly greater than 1 as (T)RPE2 would then consider leaking sets of size larger than or equal to n (for n-share gadgets, $\tau < n$). On the other side, there is no direct implication either from (t, f)-(T)RPE2 to τ-SNI since the former property does not consider all possible output sets of size $(n-1)$, but only a chosen one.

5 Generic Constructions

To the best of our knowledge, the only RPE gadgets in the literature are the ones designed in [9] which are restricted to a small number of shares, specifically $n \in \{2, 3\}$. A natural open question is the definition of RPE gadgets with good amplification orders, typically achieving or approaching the upper bounds exhibited in Sect. 3, for *any* number of shares n. In this section, we exhibit copy, addition, and multiplication gadgets derived from the widely known Ishai-Sahai-Wagner (ISW) construction [17]. Based on the results demonstrated in Sect. 4, we are able to show that these gadgets achieve RPE for any number of shares n with amplification orders close to the upper bounds (up to a small constant factor). We further provide an asymptotic analysis of the expanding compiler using these gadgets as well as a new multiplication gadget reaching the optimal amplification order hence improving the convergence to a better asymptotic complexity.

5.1 Generic Copy and Addition Gadgets

As intuitively proposed in [9] for small gadgets, copy and addition gadgets can be naturally derived from a refresh gadget. Such a gadget takes one sharing as input and outputs a new refreshed sharing of the same value. We formally introduce these natural constructions hereafter and show that their RPE security can be reduced to that of the underlying refresh gadget.

Generic Copy Gadget. Algorithm 1 displays the generic construction for the copy gadget from a refresh gadget. It simply consists in refreshing the input sharing twice to obtain two fresh copies.

Algorithm 1: Copy gadget G_{copy}

Input : $(a_1, \ldots, a_n)$ input sharing
Output: $(e_1, \ldots, e_n)$, $(f_1, \ldots, f_n)$ fresh copies of $(a_1, \ldots, a_n)$
$(e_1, \ldots, e_n) \leftarrow G_{\text{refresh}}(a_1, \ldots, a_n)$;
$(f_1, \ldots, f_n) \leftarrow G_{\text{refresh}}(a_1, \ldots, a_n)$;

We have the following lemma (see the proof in the full version of this paper).

Lemma 7. *Let $G_{refresh}$ be an n-share (t, f)-TRPE refresh gadget of amplification order d. Then, the copy gadget G_{copy} displayed in Algorithm 1 is (t, f')-TRPE also of amplification order d.*

As a consequence of this result, a TRPE refresh gadget directly yields a TRPE copy gadget achieving the same amplification order. Both gadgets can then reach the upper bound for 1-input gadgets whenever $t + 1 = 2(n - t)$ implying an amplification order $d = \frac{2(n+1)}{3}$.

Generic Addition Gadget. Algorithm 2 displays the generic construction for the addition gadget from a refresh gadget. It simply consists in refreshing both input sharings before adding them.

Algorithm 2: Addition Gadget G_{add}

Input : $(a_1, \ldots, a_n), (b_1, \ldots, b_n)$ input sharings
Output: $(c_1, \ldots, c_n)$ sharing of $a + b$
$(e_1, \ldots, e_n) \leftarrow G_{\text{refresh}}(a_1, \ldots, a_n)$;
$(f_1, \ldots, f_n) \leftarrow G_{\text{refresh}}(b_1, \ldots, b_n)$;
$(c_1, \ldots, c_n) \leftarrow (e_1 + f_1, \ldots, e_n + f_n)$;

We have the following lemma (see the proof in the full version of this paper).

Lemma 8. *Let $G_{refresh}$ be an n-share refresh gadget and let G_{add} be the corresponding addition gadget displayed in Algorithm 2. Then if $G_{refresh}$ is (t, f)-RPE (resp. (t, f)-TRPE) of amplification order d, then G_{add} is (t, f')-RPE (resp. (t, f')-TRPE) for some f' of amplification order $d' \geq \lfloor \frac{d}{2} \rfloor$.*

The above lemma shows that a (T)RPE refresh gadget of amplification order d directly yields a (T)RPE addition gadget of amplification order at least $\lfloor \frac{d}{2} \rfloor$. If the refresh gadget achieves the optimal $d = \frac{2(n+1)}{3}$, then the generic addition gadget has an amplification order at least $\lfloor \frac{n}{3} \rfloor$ which is not far from the upper bound for two-input gadgets of $\frac{n+1}{2}$.

We stress that the results of Lemma 7 and Lemma 8 are general and apply for any refresh gadget satisfying the (T)RPE property. In the rest of the section, we shall focus on a particular refresh gadget, namely the ISW-based refresh gadget. We show that this gadget achieves (T)RPE from which we obtain (T)RPE copy and addition gadgets for any number of shares n and with amplification orders close to the upper bound (up to a small constant factor).

5.2 ISW-Based Copy and Addition Gadgets

As a basis of further constructions, we focus our analysis on the most deployed refresh gadget, which is based on the ISW construction [17].

ISW Refresh Gadget. This refresh can be seen as an ISW multiplication between the input sharing and the n-tuple $(1, 0, \ldots, 0)$. This is formally depicted in Algorithm 3.

Algorithm 3: ISW Refresh

```
Input  : (a_1, ..., a_n) input sharing, {r_ij}_{1≤i<j≤n} random values
Output: (c_1, ..., c_n) such that c_1 + ··· + c_n = a_1 + ··· + a_n
for i ← 1 to n do
  | c_i ← a_i;
end
for i ← 1 to n do
  | for j ← 1 to i − 1 do
  |   | c_i ← c_i + r_ji;
  | end
  | for j ← i + 1 to n do
  |   | c_i ← c_i + r_ij;
  | end
end
return (c_1, ..., c_n);
```

We demonstrate through Lemma 9 that the ISW refresh gadget satisfies TRPE with an amplification order close to the optimal one. The proof is given in the full version of this paper.

Lemma 9. *Let $n \in \mathbb{N}$. For every $t \leq n-2$, the n-share ISW refresh gadget is (t, f_1)-TRPE1 and (t, f_2)-TRPE2 for some functions $f_1, f_2 : \mathbb{R} \to \mathbb{R}$ of amplification orders d_1, d_2 which satisfy:*

- $d_1 = \min(t+1, n-t)$ *for* f_1,
- $d_2 = t+1$ *for* f_2.

Corollary 3 then directly follows from Lemma 3 applied to TRPE and Lemma 9.

Corollary 3. *Let $n \in \mathbb{N}$. For every $t \leq n-2$, the n-share ISW refresh gadget is (t, f)-TRPE of amplification order*

$$d = \min(t+1, n-t).$$

According to Lemma 1, the upper bound on the amplification order of 1-input gadgets is $d \leq \min(t+1, 2(n-t))$ which gives $d \leq \frac{2n+2}{3}$ for $t = \frac{2n-1}{3}$. In contrast, the ISW refresh gadget reaches $d = \lfloor \frac{n+1}{2} \rfloor$ by taking $t = \lceil \frac{n-1}{2} \rceil$. While applying this result to the generic constructions of addition and copy gadgets introduced above, we obtain:

- a copy gadget of amplification order $d_c = \lfloor \frac{n+1}{2} \rfloor$ (Lemma 7),
- an addition gadget of amplification order at least $d_a = \lfloor \frac{n+1}{4} \rfloor$ (Lemma 8).

In the following, we demonstrate a tighter result than Lemma 8 for the ISW-based addition gadget (namely which does not imply the loss of a factor 2).

ISW-Based Copy Gadget. The copy gadget G_{copy} that uses the n-share ISW refresh gadget as a building block in Algorithm 1 achieves the same amplification order as the ISW refresh for the TRPE setting, *i.e.* $d = \min(t+1, n-t)$. This is a direct implication from Lemma 7. Then, from Lemma 4, we have that ISW-based G_{copy} also achieves (t, f')-RPE with amplification order $d' \geq d$. We can actually prove that ISW-based G_{copy} achieves (t, f')-RPE with amplification order d' exactly equal to the amplification order in the TRPE setting, *i.e.* $d' = d = \min(t+1, n-t)$. This is stated in the following lemma which proof is given in the full version of this paper.

Lemma 10. *Let G_{copy} be the n-share copy gadget displayed in Algorithm 1 and instantiated with the ISW refresh gadget. Then for every $t \leq n-2$, G_{copy} achieves (t, f)-RPE with amplification order $d = \min(t+1, n-t)$.*

ISW-Based Addition Gadget. The addition gadget G_{add} that uses the n-share ISW refresh gadget as a building block in Algorithm 2 achieves the same amplification order as the ISW refresh gadget, which is tighter than the bound from Lemma 8. This is stated in the following Lemma, which follows from Lemma 9, and from the fact that ISW refresh is $(n-1)$-SNI. The proof is given in the full version of this paper.

Lemma 11. *Let G_{add} be the n-share addition gadget displayed in Algorithm 2 and instantiated with the ISW refresh gadget. Then for every $t \leq n-2$, G_{add} achieves (t, f_1)-TRPE1 and (t, f_2)-TRPE2 for some functions $f_1, f_2 : \mathbb{R} \to \mathbb{R}$ of amplification orders d_1, d_2 which satisfy:*

- $d_1 = \min(t+1, n-t)$,
- $d_2 = t+1$.

Corollary 4 then directly follows from Lemma 11 by applying Lemma 3 (TRPE1 ∩ TRPE2 ⇒ TRPE) and Lemma 4 (TRPE ⇒ RPE).

Corollary 4. *Let $n \in \mathbb{N}$. For every $t \leq n-2$, the n-share gadget G_{add} displayed in Algorithm 2 and instantiated with the ISW refresh gadget is (t, f)-RPE of amplification order $d = \min(t+1, n-t)$.*

5.3 ISW Multiplication Gadget

In contrast to the copy and addition gadgets that are built from generic schemes with a refresh gadget as a building block, the multiplication gadget can be directly defined as the standard ISW multiplication, which is recalled in Algorithm 4.

Algorithm 4: ISW Multiplication

```
Input  : (a_1, ..., a_n),(b_1, ..., b_n) input sharings, {r_ij}_{1≤i<j≤n} random
         values
Output: (c_1, ..., c_n) sharing of a · b
for i ← 1 to n do
  | c_i ← a_i · b_i;
end
for i ← 1 to n do
  | for j ← i + 1 to n do
  |   | c_i ← c_i + r_ij;
  |   | r_ji ← (a_i · b_j + r_ij) + a_j · b_i;
  |   | c_j ← c_j + r_ji;
  | end
end
return (c_1, ..., c_n);
```

We have the following lemma (see the proof in the full version of this paper).

Lemma 12. *Let $n \in \mathbb{N}$. For every $t \leq n-2$, the n-share ISW multiplication gadget displayed in Algorithm 4 is (t, f_1)-RPE1 and (t, f_2)-RPE2 for some functions $f_1, f_2 : \mathbb{R} \rightarrow \mathbb{R}$ of amplification orders d_1, d_2 which satisfy:*

- $d_1 = \dfrac{\min(t+1, n-t)}{2}$,
- $d_2 = \dfrac{t+1}{2}$.

Corollary 5 then directly follows from Lemma 12 by applying Lemma 3 (RPE1 $\cap$ RPE2 $\Rightarrow$ RPE).

Corollary 5. *Let $n \in \mathbb{N}$. For every $t \leq n-2$, the n-share ISW multiplication gadget displayed in Algorithm 4 is (t, f)-RPE of amplification order*

$$d = \frac{\min(t+1, n-t)}{2} .$$

According to Lemma 2, the upper bound on the amplification order of a standard multiplication gadget (*i.e.* which starts with the cross-products of the input shares) is $d \leq \min((t+1)/2, (n-t))$ which gives $d \leq (n+1)/3$ for $t = (2n-1)/3$. In contrast, the ISW multiplication gadget reaches $d = \lfloor \frac{n+1}{4} \rfloor$ by taking $t = \lceil \frac{n-1}{2} \rceil$.

5.4 Application to the Expanding Compiler

As recalled in Sect. 2.5, instantiating the expanding compiler with three RPE base gadgets gives a $(p, 2^{-\kappa})$-random probing secure compiler (*i.e.* achieving κ bits of security against a leakage probability p) with a complexity blowup of $\mathcal{O}(\kappa^e)$ for an exponent e satisfying

$$e = \frac{\log N_{\max}}{\log d}$$

where $N_{\max}$ satisfies (5) and where d is the minimum amplification order of the three base gadgets.

We can instantiate the expanding compiler using the above ISW-based gadgets. Specifically, we use the ISW multiplication for the multiplication gadget G_{mult}, and the generic constructions of addition and copy gadgets based on the ISW refresh. From Lemmas 10, 11, and 12, the maximum amplification order achievable by the compiler is the minimum of the three gadgets, which is the order of the ISW multiplication gadget:

$$d = \frac{\min(t+1, n-t)}{2}.$$

Hence, for a given number of shares n, the maximum amplification order achievable is

$$d_{\max} = \left\lfloor \frac{n+1}{4} \right\rfloor$$

which is obtained for $t = \lceil \frac{n-1}{2} \rceil$. On the other hand, the value of $N_{\max}$ can be characterized in terms of the number of shares n from the ISW algorithm. Recall from Sect. 2.5 that

$$N_{\max} = \max\left(N_{\mathrm{m,m}} \text{ , } \mathsf{eigenvalues}\left(\begin{pmatrix} N_{\mathrm{a,a}} & N_{\mathrm{c,a}} \\ N_{\mathrm{a,c}} & N_{\mathrm{c,c}} \end{pmatrix} \right) \right).$$

In the case of the ISW-based gadgets, we have $N_{\mathrm{m,m}} = n^2$ and

$$\begin{pmatrix} N_{\mathrm{a,a}} & N_{\mathrm{c,a}} \\ N_{\mathrm{a,c}} & N_{\mathrm{c,c}} \end{pmatrix} = \begin{pmatrix} n(2n-1) & 2n(n-1) \\ n(n-1) & n^2 \end{pmatrix}.$$

The eigenvalues of the above matrix are $\lambda_1 = n$ and $\lambda_2 = 3n^2 - 2n$, implying $N_{\max} = 3n^2 - 2n$. Thus, the expanding compiler instantiated by our ISW-based gadgets has a complexity blowup $\mathcal{O}(\kappa^e)$ with exponent

$$e = \frac{\log(3n^2 - 2n)}{\log(\lfloor (n+1)/4 \rfloor)}.$$

Figure 2 (blue curve) shows the evolution of the value of this exponent with respect to the number of shares n (where we assume an odd n). The value of e clearly decreases as the number of shares grows, and this decrease is faster for a small number of shares ($5 \leq n \leq 10$). The exponent value reaches $e \approx 4$ for a number of shares around 25 and then slowly converges towards $e = 2$ as n grows. This is to be compared with the $\mathcal{O}(\kappa^{7.5})$ complexity achieved by the instantiation from [2,9].

Towards a Better Complexity. Choosing gadgets which attain the upper bound $\min(t+1, n-t)$ on the amplification order from Lemma 1 allows the compiler to have the maximum amplification order $d = (n+1)/2$ and thus have the lowest complexity blowup. Our ISW-based copy and addition gadgets achieve this bound while the ISW multiplication gadget is limited to $(n+1)/4$ (Lemma 12). To reach the optimal amplification order, one would need a different multiplication gadget and in particular a multiplication gadget which does not perform a direct product of shares (because of the bound from Lemma 2). We introduce such a multiplication gadget hereafter (see Sect. 5.5). Specifically, our new multiplication gadget achieves the upper bound on the amplification order $\min(t+1, n-t)$ by avoiding a direct product of shares using a prior refresh on the input sharings. The orange curve in Fig. 2 shows the evolution of the value of the exponent when instantiating the expanding compiler with our previous addition and copy gadgets and this new multiplication gadget. For such an instantiation, the complexity exponent still slowly converges towards $e = 2$ but, as we can see

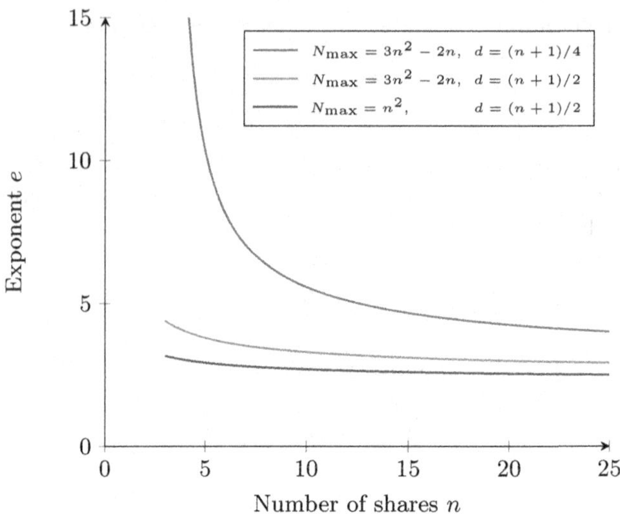

Fig. 2. Evolution of the complexity exponent $e = \log(N_{\max})/\log(d)$ with respect to the number of shares n. The blue curve matches the instantiation with the ISW-based gadgets; the orange curve assumes the optimal amplification order (*i.e.* an improvement of the multiplication gadget); the pink curve assumes a better complexity for addition and copy gadgets (so that $N_{\max}$ matches $N_{\mathrm{m,m}} = n^2$). (Color figure online)

from Fig. 2, the exponent value is much better for small values of n. For example, we obtain $e \approx 3$ for $n = 20$.

Another possible direction for improvement would be to lower the complexity of the addition and copy gadgets, which is mainly dominated by the refreshing. Assume that we can design a (T)RPE refresh gadget in sub-quadratic complexity, *e.g.* as the refresh gadgets proposed in [7,15,20], then the eigenvalues of the matrix in (5) would also be sub-quadratic and the value of $N_{\max}$ from Eq. (5) would drop to $N_{\mathrm{m,m}} = n^2$ (if the multiplication gadget still requires n^2 multiplication gates). The pink curve in Fig. 2 depicts the evolution of the exponent value under this assumption. We still have a slow convergence towards $e = 2$ but the exponent value is yet better for small values of n. For example, a complexity blowup of $\mathcal{O}(\kappa^{2.5})$ is obtained with 20 shares. We leave the task of finding such a sub-quadratic (T)RPE refresh gadget as an open question for further research.

The above analysis shows that the expanding compiler can theoretically approach a quadratic complexity at the cost of increasing the number of shares in the base gadgets. The downside of it is that the tolerated leakage probability is likely to decrease as the number of shares grow. For instance, the ISW construction is known to only tolerate a leakage probability $p = \mathcal{O}(1/n)$ [14]. The number of shares hence offers multiple trade-offs between the tolerated probability and the asymptotic complexity of the compiler. Starting from a target leakage probability p, one could determine the highest number of shares admissible from a generic construction (such as the ISW-based instantiation exhibited above) and thus deduce the best complexity exponent achievable. In Sect. 6, we exhibit concrete trade-offs that can be reached for small values of n.

5.5 Multiplication Gadget with Maximal Amplification Order

Constructing a multiplication gadget which achieves the upper bound on the amplification order from Lemma 1 is tricky. First, as a standard multiplication gadget (*i.e.* which computes the cross products of the input shares), the ISW multiplication cannot achieve the maximal amplification order (see Lemma 2). In order to reach the upper bound for two-input gadgets (see Corollary 2), we need a non-standard multiplication gadget, *i.e.* which does not perform a direct product between the input shares. As an additional observation, the addition, copy, and random gates are *virtually free* in a multiplication gadget since they do not impact the final complexity of the expanding compiler (see Sect. 2.5). This suggests that we can be greedy in terms of randomness to reach the maximal amplification order.

In the following, we will describe the construction of a new multiplication gadget which achieves the maximum amplification order $\min(t+1, n-t)$. We first describe our standard n-share multiplication gadget and then explain how we avoid the initial cross products of shares. First, the gadget constructs the matrix of the cross product of input shares:

$$M = \begin{pmatrix} a_1 \cdot b_1 & a_1 \cdot b_2 & \cdots & a_1 \cdot b_n \\ a_2 \cdot b_1 & a_2 \cdot b_2 & \cdots & a_2 \cdot b_n \\ \vdots & \vdots & \ddots & \vdots \\ a_n \cdot b_1 & a_n \cdot b_2 & \cdots & a_n \cdot b_n \end{pmatrix}$$

Then, it picks n^2 random values which define the following matrix:

$$R = \begin{pmatrix} r_{1,1} & r_{1,2} & \cdots & r_{1,n} \\ r_{2,1} & r_{2,2} & \cdots & r_{2,n} \\ \vdots & \vdots & \ddots & \vdots \\ r_{n,1} & r_{n,2} & \cdots & r_{n,n} \end{pmatrix}$$

It then performs an element-wise addition between the matrices M and R:

$$P = M + R = \begin{pmatrix} p_{1,1} & p_{1,2} & \cdots & p_{1,n} \\ p_{2,1} & p_{2,2} & \cdots & p_{2,n} \\ \vdots & \vdots & \ddots & \vdots \\ p_{n,1} & p_{n,2} & \cdots & p_{n,n} \end{pmatrix}$$

At this point, the gadget randomizes each product of input shares from the matrix M with a single random value from R. In order to generate the correct output, the gadget adds all the columns of P into a single column V of n elements, and adds all the columns of the transpose matrix $R^\intercal$ into a single column X of n elements:

$$V = \begin{pmatrix} p_{1,1} + \cdots + p_{1,n} \\ p_{2,1} + \cdots + p_{2,n} \\ \vdots \\ p_{n,1} + \cdots + p_{n,n} \end{pmatrix}, \qquad X = \begin{pmatrix} r_{1,1} + \cdots + r_{n,1} \\ r_{1,2} + \cdots + r_{n,2} \\ \vdots \\ r_{1,n} + \cdots + r_{n,n} \end{pmatrix}$$

The n-share output is finally defined as $(c_1, \ldots, c_n) = V + X$.

In order to further increase the maximum amplification order attainable by the gadget, we need to avoid performing a direct product of shares (because of the bound proved in Lemma 2). For this, we add a pre-processing phase to the gadget using a refresh gadget G_{refresh}. Specifically, we refresh the input $(b_1, \ldots, b_n)$ each time it is used. In other terms, each row of the matrix M uses a fresh copy of $(b_1, \ldots, b_n)$ produced using the considered refresh gadget. This amounts to performing n independent refreshes of the input $(b_1, \ldots, b_n)$. The matrix M is thus defined as

$$M = \begin{pmatrix} a_1 \cdot b_1^{(1)} & a_1 \cdot b_2^{(1)} & \cdots & a_1 \cdot b_n^{(1)} \\ a_2 \cdot b_1^{(2)} & a_2 \cdot b_2^{(2)} & \cdots & a_2 \cdot b_n^{(2)} \\ \vdots & \vdots & \ddots & \vdots \\ a_n \cdot b_1^{(n)} & a_n \cdot b_2^{(n)} & \cdots & a_n \cdot b_n^{(n)} \end{pmatrix}$$

where $(b_1^{(j)}, \ldots, b_n^{(j)})$, $j \in [n]$, are the n independent refreshings of the input $(b_1, \ldots, b_n)$.

With this refreshing scheme, we avoid using the same share more than once for one of the two input sharings. As a consequence, the double failure set of size $t + 1$ which is the reason behind the bound $(t + 1)/2$ in Lemma 2, becomes a simple failure set (*i.e.* provoking a failure on a single input sharing). In addition, the computational overhead of these additional n refreshes is negligible compared to the joint contribution of the copy and addition gadgets to the complexity of the expanding compiler.

For the sake of completeness, we present the full algorithm for this multiplication gadget in Algorithm 5.

Algorithm 5: Our multiplication gadget

```
Input  : (a_1, ..., a_n),(b_1, ..., b_n) input sharings, {r_ij}_{1≤i≤n,1≤j≤n}
         random values, refresh gadget G_refresh
Output: (c_1, ..., c_n) sharing of a · b
for i ← 1 to n do
|  (b_1^(i), ..., b_n^(i)) ← G_refresh(b_1, ..., b_n);
end
for i ← 1 to n do
|  for j ← 1 to n do
|  |  p_{i,j} ← a_i × b_j^(i) + r_{i,j};
|  end
end
(v_1, ..., v_n) ← (0, ..., 0);
(x_1, ..., x_n) ← (0, ..., 0);
for i ← 1 to n do
|  for j ← 1 to n do
|  |  v_i ← v_i + p_{i,j};
|  |  x_i ← x_i + r_{i,j};
|  end
end
for i ← 1 to n do
|  c_i ← v_i + x_i;
end
return (c_1, ..., c_n);
```

In the following lemma, we show that if the refresh gadget G_{refresh} achieves the TRPE1 property with the amplification order at least $d = \min(t+1, n-t)$ for any t, then the multiplication gadget depicted in Algorithm 5 achieves TRPE with the maximum amplification orders. The proof is given in the full version of this paper.

Lemma 13. *Let $t \leq n-1$. Let $G_{refresh}$ be a (t, f')-TRPE1 refresh gadget for some function $f' : \mathbb{R} \to \mathbb{R}$, and G_{mult} the n-share multiplication gadget from Algorithm 5. If f' is of amplification order $d' \geq d = \min(t+1, n-t)$, then G_{mult} achieves (t, f)-TRPE for some function $f : \mathbb{R} \to \mathbb{R}$ of amplification order $d = \min(t+1, n-t)$.*

Corollary 6 then directly follows from Lemma 13 by applying Lemma 4 (TRPE $\Rightarrow$ RPE).

Corollary 6. *Let $t \leq n-1$. Let $G_{refresh}$ be a (t, f')-TRPE1 refresh gadget for some function $f' : \mathbb{R} \to \mathbb{R}$, and G_{mult} the n-share multiplication gadget from Algorithm 5. If f' is of amplification order $d' \geq d = \min(t+1, n-t)$, then G_{mult} achieves (t, f)-RPE for some function $f : \mathbb{R} \to \mathbb{R}$ of amplification order $d = \min(t+1, n-t)$.*

6 Efficient Small Gadgets

This section displays our new constructions of small gadgets for copy, addition, and multiplication operations with a low number of shares. As explained in [9], we cannot achieve RPE security with relevant amplification orders for gadgets of less than 3 shares. Then, as explained in Sect. 3.1, the highest amplification orders can only be achieved for gadgets with an odd number of shares. We therefore omit 4-share gadgets and display our best trade-offs in terms of RPE security and complexity for 3-share and 5-share gadgets. Each one of these gadgets is experimentally verified using the VRAPS verification tool from [9].

Addition and Copy Gadgets. For the construction of small 3-share and 5-share addition and copy gadgets, we use the generic constructions depicted in Algorithms 1 and 2 (in Sect. 5) which naturally use a refresh gadget as a building block. We hence start by looking for refresh gadgets that have a good complexity in terms of gates count, and achieve the upper bound on the amplification order for the specific case of 3-share and 5-share constructions (but not necessarily for a higher number of shares).

Multiplication Gadget. For the construction of small 3-share and 5-share multiplication gadgets, we use the generic construction depicted in Algorithm 5 from Sect. 5.5 which, to the best of our knowledge, is the only multiplication gadget which achieves the maximum amplification order for any number of shares, and specifically for 3-share and 5-share constructions. As for the refresh gadget G_{refresh} which is used to perform n refreshes on the second input, we use the same scheme as for the construction of small addition and copy gadgets (and which shall satisfy the necessary condition on G_{refresh} from Corollary 6).

While the multiplication gadget from Sect. 5.5 achieves the desired amplification order, we add another pre-processing phase to the gadget in order to further improve the tolerated leakage probability. In addition to the n refreshes performed on the second input b (see Algorithm 5), we add another single refresh of the input $(a_1, \ldots, a_n)$ before computing the cross-products, using the same refresh gadget G_{refresh}. Refreshing the input $(a_1, \ldots, a_n)$ before usage experimentally shows a further increase in the maximum tolerated leakage probability, by adding more randomness to the input shares before computing the cross-product matrix M in Algorithm 5. And since the refresh gadget G_{refresh} achieves the maximum amplification order, the amplification order achieved by G_{mult} is not affected by adding another refresh to the first input a.

The above construction achieves the maximum amplification order for 3-share ($d = 2$) and 5-share ($d = 3$) gadgets based on natural refresh gadgets detailed hereafter.

6.1 3-Share Gadgets

We start with the construction of 3-share gadgets for our three base operations.

Copy and Addition Gadgets. We build our copy and addition gadgets from the instantiation of the generic constructions of Sect. 5 (Algorithms 1 and 2) with 3 shares. However, we do not use the ISW refresh gadget but the following more efficient construction with only two random values (instead of three):

$$\begin{aligned} G_{\text{refresh}} : c_1 &\leftarrow r_1 + a_1 \\ c_2 &\leftarrow r_2 + a_2 \\ c_3 &\leftarrow (r_1 + r_2) + a_3. \end{aligned}$$

This refresh is sufficient to reach the upper bounds on the amplification orders (from Lemma 1). From this basis, we obtain the following 3-share addition gadget with four random values:

$$\begin{aligned} G_{\text{add}} : c_1 &\leftarrow (r_1 + a_1) + (r_3 + b_1) \\ c_2 &\leftarrow (r_2 + a_2) + (r_4 + b_2) \\ c_3 &\leftarrow \big((r_1 + r_2) + a_3\big) + \big((r_3 + r_4) + b_3\big) \end{aligned}$$

and the following 3-share copy gadget with also four random values:

$$\begin{aligned} G_{\text{copy}} : c_1 &\leftarrow r_1 + a_1; & d_1 &\leftarrow r_3 + a_1 \\ c_2 &\leftarrow r_2 + a_2; & d_2 &\leftarrow r_4 + a_2 \\ c_3 &\leftarrow (r_1 + r_2) + a_3; & d_3 &\leftarrow (r_3 + r_4) + a_3. \end{aligned}$$

Multiplication Gadget. The following construction is a 3-share instantiation of the multiplication gadget described in Sect. 5.5. For the input refreshing, we use the 3-share refresh gadget described above with two uniformly random values. The construction achieves the bound on the amplification order from Lemma 1 with 17 random values:

$$\begin{aligned} G_{\text{mult}} : i_{1,1} &\leftarrow r_1 + b_1; & i_{1,2} &\leftarrow r_2 + b_2; & i_{1,3} &\leftarrow (r_1 + r_2) + b_3 \\ i_{2,1} &\leftarrow r_3 + b_1; & i_{2,2} &\leftarrow r_4 + b_2; & i_{2,3} &\leftarrow (r_3 + r_4) + b_3 \\ i_{3,1} &\leftarrow r_5 + b_1; & i_{3,2} &\leftarrow r_6 + b_2; & i_{3,3} &\leftarrow (r_5 + r_6) + b_3 \\ a'_1 &\leftarrow r_7 + a_1; & a'_2 &\leftarrow r_8 + a_2; & a'_3 &\leftarrow (r_7 + r_8) + a_3 \end{aligned}$$

$$\begin{aligned} c_1 &\leftarrow (a'_1 \cdot i_{1,1} + r_{1,1}) + (a'_1 \cdot i_{1,2} + r_{1,2}) + (a'_1 \cdot i_{1,3} + r_{1,3}) + (r_{1,1} + r_{2,1} + r_{3,1}) \\ c_2 &\leftarrow (a'_2 \cdot i_{2,1} + r_{2,1}) + (a'_2 \cdot i_{2,2} + r_{2,2}) + (a'_2 \cdot i_{2,3} + r_{2,3}) + (r_{1,2} + r_{2,2} + r_{3,2}) \\ c_3 &\leftarrow (a'_3 \cdot i_{3,1} + r_{3,1}) + (a'_3 \cdot i_{3,2} + r_{3,2}) + (a'_3 \cdot i_{3,3} + r_{3,3}) + (r_{1,3} + r_{2,3} + r_{3,3}). \end{aligned}$$

Table 1. Results for the 3-share gadgets for $(t = 1, f)$-RPE, achieving the bound on the amplification order.

Gadget	Complexity (N_a, N_c, N_m, N_r)	Amplification order	$\log_2$ of maximum tolerated proba
G_{refresh}	$(4, 2, 0, 2)$	2	−5.14
G_{add}	$(11, 4, 0, 4)$	2	−4.75
G_{copy}	$(8, 7, 0, 4)$	2	−7.50
G_{mult}	$(40, 29, 9, 17)$	2	−7.41
Compiler	$\mathcal{O}(\lvert C\rvert \cdot \kappa^{\mathbf{3.9}})$	**2**	**−7.50**

Results. Table 1 displays the results for the above gadgets obtained through the `VRAPS` tool. The second column gives the complexity, where N_a, N_c, N_m, N_r stand for the number of addition gates, copy gates, multiplication gates and random gates respectively. The third column provides the amplification order of the gadget. And the last column gives the maximum tolerated leakage probability. The last row gives the global complexity, amplification order, and maximum tolerated leakage probability for the expanding compiler using these three gadgets from the results provided in [9].

6.2 5-Share Gadgets

We now present our 5-share gadgets for our three base operations, which reach the optimal amplification order from Lemma 1.

Copy and Addition Gadgets. As for the 3-share case, we use the generic constructions from Sect. 5. Instead of using the ISW refresh gadget which would require 10 uniformly random values for a 5-share construction, we use the *circular refresh gadget* described in [4,6] (a.k.a. *block refresh gadget*):

$$\begin{aligned} G_{\text{refresh}} : c_1 &\leftarrow (r_1 + r_2) + a_1 \\ c_2 &\leftarrow (r_2 + r_3) + a_2 \\ c_3 &\leftarrow (r_3 + r_4) + a_3 \\ c_4 &\leftarrow (r_4 + r_5) + a_4 \\ c_5 &\leftarrow (r_5 + r_1) + a_5. \end{aligned}$$

This gadget only uses n randoms for an n-share construction, and while it does not achieve enough security in the generic case (unless the refresh block is iterated on the input a certain number of times [4,6]), it proves to be more than enough to achieve the necessary amplification order for our 5-share constructions. We use a variant of the original version (also suggested in [4]): we choose to sum the random values first (thus obtaining a sharing of 0) before adding them to the input shares. The idea is to avoid using the input shares in any of the intermediate variables, so that input shares only appear in the input variables $\{a_i\}_{1 \leq i \leq n}$ and the final output variables $\{c_i\}_{1 \leq i \leq n}$. Intuitively, this trick allows to have less failure tuples in the gadget because there are less variables that could leak information about the input. This is validated experimentally where we obtain better results in terms of amplification order and tolerated leakage probability for small gadgets.

From this circular refresh, we obtain an addition gadget and a copy gadget that both reach the upper bound on the amplification order while making use of ten random values. The description of those 5-share gadgets is given in the full version of the paper.

Multiplication Gadget. We use the 5-share instantiation of the multiplication gadget described in Sect. 5.5. For the input refreshing, we use the 5-share circular refresh gadget described above. The gadget advantageously achieves the optimal amplification order (given by Lemma 1) with 55 random values. The description of this 5-share multiplication gadget is given in the full version of the paper.

Results. Table 2 gives the results for the above gadgets obtained through the VRAPS tool.

Table 2. Results for the 5-share gadgets for $(t = 2, f)$-RPE, achieving the bound on the amplification order.

Gadget	Complexity	Amplification order	$\log_2$ of maximum tolerated proba
G_{refresh}	$(10, 5, 0, 5)$	3	-4.83
G_{add}	$(25, 10, 0, 10)$	3	$[-6.43, -3.79]$
G_{copy}	$(20, 15, 0, 10)$	3	$[-6.43, -5.78]$
G_{mult}	$(130, 95, 25, 55)$	3	$[-12.00, -6.03]$
Compiler	$\mathcal{O}(\lvert C\rvert \cdot \kappa^{\mathbf{3.23}})$	**3**	$[\mathbf{-12.00}, \mathbf{-6.03}]$

From Tables 1 and 2, we observe that the asymptotic complexity is better for the instantiation based on 5-share gadgets as they provide a better amplification order with limited overhead. While this result can seem to be counterintuitive, it actually comes from the fact that each gadget will be expended less in the second scenario. We stress that we could only obtain an interval $[2^{-12}, 2^{-6}]$ for the tolerated leakage probability because it was computationally too expensive to obtain a tighter interval from the VRAPS tool, but this could probably be improved in the future. Meanwhile, we can consider that our best complexity $\mathcal{O}(|C| \cdot \kappa^{3.2})$ comes at the price of a lower tolerated leakage probability of 2^{-12} (5-share gadget) compared to the $\mathcal{O}(|C| \cdot \kappa^{3.9})$ complexity and $2^{-7.5}$ tolerated leakage probability obtained for our 3-share instantiation.

In comparison, the previous instantiation of the expanding compiler [9] could only achieve a complexity of $\mathcal{O}(|C| \cdot \kappa^{7.5})$ for maximum tolerated probabilities of 2^{-8}, and the instantiation of the expanding approach with a multi-party computation protocol [2], could only achieve a complexity of $\mathcal{O}(|C| \cdot \kappa^{8.2})$ for maximum tolerated probabilities of 2^{-26}.

Acknowledgments. This work is partly supported by the French FUI-AAP25 VeriSiCC project.

References

1. Ajtai, M.: Secure computation with information leaking to an adversary. In: Fortnow, L., Vadhan, S.P., (eds.) 43rd ACM STOC, pp. 715–724. ACM Press, June 2011
2. Ananth, P., Ishai, Y., Sahai, A.: Private circuits: a modular approach. In: Shacham, H., Boldyreva, A. (eds.) CRYPTO 2018. LNCS, vol. 10993, pp. 427–455. Springer, Cham (2018). https://doi.org/10.1007/978-3-319-96878-0_15
3. Andrychowicz, M., Dziembowski, S., Faust, S.: Circuit compilers with $O(1/\log(n))$ Leakage Rate. In: Fischlin, M., Coron, J.-S. (eds.) EUROCRYPT 2016. LNCS, vol. 9666, pp. 586–615. Springer, Heidelberg (2016). https://doi.org/10.1007/978-3-662-49896-5_21
4. Barthe, G., et al.: Improved parallel mask refreshing algorithms: generic solutions with parametrized non-interference and automated optimizations. J. Cryptogr. Eng. **10**(1), 17–26 (2019). https://doi.org/10.1007/s13389-018-00202-2
5. Barthe, G., et al.: Strong non-interference and type-directed higher-order masking. In: Weippl, E.R., Katzenbeisser, S., Kruegel, C., Myers, A.C., Halevi, S. (eds.) ACM CCS 2016, pp. 116–129. ACM Press, October 2016
6. Barthe, G., Dupressoir, F., Faust, S., Grégoire, B., Standaert, F.-X., Strub, P.-Y.: Parallel implementations of masking schemes and the bounded moment leakage model. In: Coron, J.-S., Nielsen, J.B. (eds.) EUROCRYPT 2017. LNCS, vol. 10210, pp. 535–566. Springer, Cham (2017). https://doi.org/10.1007/978-3-319-56620-7_19
7. Battistello, A., Coron, J.-S., Prouff, E., Zeitoun, R.: Horizontal side-channel attacks and countermeasures on the ISW masking scheme. Cryptology ePrint Archive, Report 2016/540 (2016). http://eprint.iacr.org/2016/540
8. Belaïd, S., Benhamouda, F., Passelègue, A., Prouff, E., Thillard, A., Vergnaud, D.: Randomness complexity of private circuits for multiplication. In: Fischlin, M., Coron, J.-S. (eds.) EUROCRYPT 2016. LNCS, vol. 9666, pp. 616–648. Springer, Heidelberg (2016). https://doi.org/10.1007/978-3-662-49896-5_22
9. Belaïd, S., Coron, J.-S., Prouff, E., Rivain, M., Taleb, A.R.: Random probing security: verification, composition, expansion and new constructions. In: Micciancio, D., Ristenpart, T. (eds.) CRYPTO 2020. LNCS, vol. 12170, pp. 339–368. Springer, Cham (2020). https://doi.org/10.1007/978-3-030-56784-2_12
10. Chari, S., Jutla, C.S., Rao, J.R., Rohatgi, P.: Towards sound approaches to counteract power-analysis attacks. In: Wiener, M. (ed.) CRYPTO 1999. LNCS, vol. 1666, pp. 398–412. Springer, Heidelberg (1999). https://doi.org/10.1007/3-540-48405-1_26

11. Coron, J.-S.: Higher order masking of look-up tables. In: Nguyen, P.Q., Oswald, E. (eds.) EUROCRYPT 2014. LNCS, vol. 8441, pp. 441–458. Springer, Heidelberg (2014). https://doi.org/10.1007/978-3-642-55220-5_25
12. Coron, J.-S., Greuet, A., Zeitoun, R.: Side-channel masking with pseudo-random generator. In: Canteaut, A., Ishai, Y. (eds.) EUROCRYPT 2020. LNCS, vol. 12107, pp. 342–375. Springer, Cham (2020). https://doi.org/10.1007/978-3-030-45727-3_12
13. Coron, J.-S., Prouff, E., Rivain, M., Roche, T.: Higher-order side channel security and mask refreshing. In: Moriai, S. (ed.) FSE 2013. LNCS, vol. 8424, pp. 410–424. Springer, Heidelberg (2014). https://doi.org/10.1007/978-3-662-43933-3_21
14. Duc, A., Dziembowski, S., Faust, S.: Unifying leakage models: from probing attacks to noisy leakage. In: Nguyen, P.Q., Oswald, E. (eds.) EUROCRYPT 2014. LNCS, vol. 8441, pp. 423–440. Springer, Heidelberg (2014). https://doi.org/10.1007/978-3-642-55220-5_24
15. Dziembowski, S., Faust, S., Zebrowski, K.: Simple refreshing in the noisy leakage model. In: Galbraith, S.D., Moriai, S. (eds.) ASIACRYPT 2019. Part III, volume 11923 of LNCS, pp. 315–344. Springer, Heidelberg (2019)
16. Goubin, L., Patarin, J.: DES and differential power analysis the "duplication" method. In: Koç, Ç.K., Paar, C. (eds.) CHES 1999. LNCS, vol. 1717, pp. 158–172. Springer, Heidelberg (1999). https://doi.org/10.1007/3-540-48059-5_15
17. Ishai, Y., Sahai, A., Wagner, D.: Private Circuits: Securing Hardware against Probing Attacks. In: Boneh, D. (ed.) CRYPTO 2003. LNCS, vol. 2729, pp. 463–481. Springer, Heidelberg (2003). https://doi.org/10.1007/978-3-540-45146-4_27
18. Kocher, P.C.: Timing attacks on implementations of Diffie-Hellman, RSA, DSS, and other systems. In: Koblitz, N. (ed.) CRYPTO 1996. LNCS, vol. 1109, pp. 104–113. Springer, Heidelberg (1996). https://doi.org/10.1007/3-540-68697-5_9
19. Prouff, E., Rivain, M.: Masking against side-channel attacks: a formal security proof. In: Johansson, T., Nguyen, P.Q. (eds.) EUROCRYPT 2013. LNCS, vol. 7881, pp. 142–159. Springer, Heidelberg (2013). https://doi.org/10.1007/978-3-642-38348-9_9
20. Rivain, M., Prouff, E.: Provably secure higher-order masking of AES. In: Mangard, S., Standaert, F.-X. (eds.) CHES 2010. LNCS, vol. 6225, pp. 413–427. Springer, Heidelberg (2010)

Leakage-Resilience of the Shamir Secret-Sharing Scheme Against Physical-Bit Leakages

Hemanta K. Maji[1](✉), Hai H. Nguyen[1], Anat Paskin-Cherniavsky[2], Tom Suad[2], and Mingyuan Wang[1]

[1] Department of Computer Science, Purdue University, West Lafayette, USA
{hmaji,nguye245,wang1929}@purdue.edu

[2] Department of Computer Science, Ariel University, Ariel, Israel
anatpc@ariel.ac.il, tom.suad@msmail.ariel.ac.il

Abstract. Efficient Reed-Solomon code reconstruction algorithms, for example, by Guruswami and Wootters (STOC–2016), translate into local leakage attacks on Shamir secret-sharing schemes over characteristic-2 fields. However, Benhamouda, Degwekar, Ishai, and Rabin (CRYPTO–2018) showed that the Shamir secret sharing scheme over prime-fields is leakage resilient to one-bit local leakage if the reconstruction threshold is roughly 0.87 times the total number of parties. In several application scenarios, like secure multi-party multiplication, the reconstruction threshold must be at most half the number of parties. Furthermore, the number of leakage bits that the Shamir secret sharing scheme is resilient to is also unclear.

Towards this objective, we study the Shamir secret-sharing scheme's leakage-resilience over a prime-field F. The parties' secret-shares, which are elements in the finite field F, are naturally represented as λ-bit binary strings representing the elements $\{0, 1, \ldots, p-1\}$. In our leakage model, the adversary can independently probe m bit-locations from each secret share. The inspiration for considering this leakage model stems from the impact that the study of oblivious transfer combiners had on general correlation extraction algorithms, and the significant influence of protecting circuits from probing attacks has on leakage-resilient secure computation.

Consider arbitrary reconstruction threshold $k \geqslant 2$, physical bit-leakage parameter $m \geqslant 1$, and the number of parties $n \geqslant 1$. We prove that Shamir's secret-sharing scheme with random evaluation places is leakage-resilient with high probability when the order of the field F is

H. K. Maji, H. H. Nguyen and M. Wang—The research effort is supported in part by an NSF CRII Award CNS–1566499, an NSF SMALL Award CNS–1618822, the IARPA HECTOR project, MITRE Innovation Program Academic Cybersecurity Research Awards (2019–2020, 2020–2021), a Purdue Research Foundation (PRF) Award, and The Center for Science of Information, an NSF Science and Technology Center, Cooperative Agreement CCF–0939370.

A. Paskin-Cherniavsky and T. Suad—Research supported by the Ariel Cyber Innovation Center in conjunction with the Israel National Cyber directorate in the Prime Minister's Office.

A. Canteaut and F.-X. Standaert (Eds.): EUROCRYPT 2021, LNCS 12697, pp. 344–374, 2021.
https://doi.org/10.1007/978-3-030-77886-6_12

sufficiently large; ignoring polylogarithmic factors, one needs to ensure that $\log|F| \geqslant n/k$. Our result, excluding polylogarithmic factors, states that Shamir's scheme is secure as long as the total amount of leakage $m \cdot n$ is less than the entropy $k \cdot \lambda$ introduced by the Shamir secret-sharing scheme. Note that our result holds even for small constant values of the reconstruction threshold k, which is essential to several application scenarios.

To complement this positive result, we present a physical-bit leakage attack for $m = 1$ physical bit-leakage from $n = k$ secret shares and any prime-field F satisfying $|F| = 1 \mod k$. In particular, there are (roughly) $|F|^{n-k+1}$ such vulnerable choices for the n-tuple of evaluation places. We lower-bound the advantage of this attack for small values of the reconstruction threshold, like $k = 2$ and $k = 3$, and any $|F| = 1 \mod k$. In general, we present a formula calculating our attack's advantage for every k as $|F| \to \infty$.

Technically, our positive result relies on Fourier analysis, analytic properties of proper rank-r generalized arithmetic progressions, and Bézout's theorem to bound the number of solutions to an equation over finite fields. The analysis of our attack relies on determining the "discrepancy" of the Irwin-Hall distribution. A probability distribution's discrepancy is a new property of distributions that our work introduces, which is of potential independent interest.

Keywords: Random punctured Reed-Solomon codes · Physical-bit leakage · Local leakage resilience · Discrete Fourier analysis · Exponential sums · Rank-r generalized arithmetic progression · Bézout's theorem · Irwin-Hall distribution

1 Introduction

In the presence of an increasing number of side-channel attacks on cryptographic protocols, theoretical cryptography research has been revisiting its implicit assumptions in modeling secure cryptographic protocols. For example, results in reconstructing Reed-Solomon codes [11,15,16] imply that leaking even $(m = 1)$ bit from the secret shares of Shamir's secret-sharing scheme over characteristic-2 finite field F renders this secret sharing scheme insecure. That is, there exist two secrets $s^{(0)}, s^{(1)} \in F$ that an adversary can distinguish by leaking only $(m = 1)$-bit local leakage from every secret share. We emphasize that in locally leakage-resilient secret-sharing schemes,[1] the entire secret's reconstruction is not necessary to qualify as a successful attack. It suffices to achieve a non-negligible advantage in distinguishing any two secrets $s^{(0)}, s^{(1)} \in F$ of adversary's choice. Since secret-sharing schemes (typically, packed [13] Massey secret-sharing schemes [35] corresponding to linear error-correcting codes with "good" properties) are fundamental cryptographic primitives underlying nearly all of conceivable

[1] The term "*local*" in local leakage-resilience refers to the fact that the adversary performs arbitrary leakage on each secret-share *independently*.

cryptography, such innovative side-channel attacks threaten the security of most cryptographic protocols.

The recent ground-breaking work of Benhamouda, Degwekar, Ishai, and Rabin [3] identified several scenarios where Shamir's secret-sharing scheme and the additive secret-sharing scheme are resilient to such local leakage attacks;[2] thus, laying to rest the devastating possibility of side-channel attacks breaking all secret-sharing schemes. Recently, [37] propose even more sophisticated local leakage attacks on secret-sharing schemes. Since the work of Benhamouda et al. [3], several works [1,2,6,9,22,29,34,41] have introduced transformations to convert existing secret-sharing schemes into leakage-resilient versions. It seems insurmountable to replace every deployed secret-sharing scheme with its leakage-resilient version. Furthermore, the leakage-resilient versions of these secret-sharing schemes introduce encoding overheads that noticeably reduce these secret-sharing schemes' information-rate,[3] adversely affecting the applications' efficiency. Towards the objective of retaining the efficiency of existing secret-sharing schemes with minimal changes, other works [7,21,30,33] analyze the resilience of existing secret-sharing schemes or ensembles of secret-sharing schemes with good properties (for example, packed Massey secret-sharing schemes corresponding to (nearly) *maximum distance separable* linear error-correcting codes) that are already locally leakage-resilient. Currently, our understanding of the local leakage-resilience of existing secret-sharing schemes typically used in cryptography is still in a nascent state. The exact loss in the achievable parameters and information-rate to additionally ensure local leakage-resilience is even less clear. These losses in the feasible parameter regions and information-rate even render secret-sharing schemes unusable for various application scenarios.

For example, Benhamouda et al. [3] proved that if Shamir's secret-sharing scheme, one of the most widely used secret-sharing schemes, has a reconstruction threshold $k \geqslant 0.867n$, where n is the total number of parties, then it is leakage-resilient to $(m = 1)$-bit local leakage. Observe that using a large reconstruction threshold k introduces inefficiencies, which may not be necessary for various applications. Additionally, an even more concerning fact is that some cryptographic constructions crucially rely on the reconstruction threshold being low. For example, the secure computation of the multiplication of two (already secret-shared) secrets requires the reconstruction threshold $k < n/2$ even against honest-but-curious parties.

Summary of Our Work: Problem Statement and Results. Our work contributes to this research thrust on characterizing the local leakage-resilience of secret-sharing schemes. As a stepping-stone, our work considers the scenario where each party stores their secret-share in its natural λ-bit binary representation, and the adversary may (independently) probe arbitrary m physical-bits

[2] Leakage-resilient secret-sharing was also, independently, introduced by [14] as an intermediate primitive.

[3] The information-rate of a secret-sharing scheme is the ratio on the size of the secret to the largest size of the secret-share that a party receives.

from each secret-share. The particular choice of the physical-bit leakage draws inspiration from, for instance, the crucial role of the studies on oblivious transfer combiners [8,19,20,25,36] in furthering the state-of-the-art of general correlation extractors [4,5,24], and the techniques in protecting circuits against probing attacks [12,26,27] impacting the study of leakage-resilient secure computation (refer to the excellent recent survey [28]).

We present both feasibility and hardness of computation results. Roughly, our results prove that Shamir's secret-sharing scheme with n random evaluation places, for any reconstruction threshold $k \geqslant 2$, is locally leakage-resilient. The adversary can leak m physical-bits from each secret-share if the total amount of leakage $m \cdot n$ is less than the total entropy $k \cdot \lambda$ in the secret-sharing scheme, except with an exponentially small probability in λ. To complement this result, we also present new local physical-bit leakage attacks demonstrating several sets of *bad evaluation places* where Shamir's secret-sharing scheme is not leakage-resilient even when $m = 1$ and $n = k$. Technically, our positive result's analysis proceeds by discrete Fourier analysis relying on the analytical properties of exponential sums involving rank-r generalized arithmetic progressions, and Bézout's theorem to upper-bound the number of solutions to a system of equations over finite fields. On the other hand, our attack's analysis is equivalent to the "discrepancy" of the Irwin-Hall distribution [18,23], a new mathematical property of probability distributions that we introduce.

1.1 Our Contribution

This section, first, introduces some informal notations to facilitate the introduction of our results and discussion on them. Let λ represent the security parameter. Consider a prime-field F of order p such that $2^{\lambda-1} \leqslant p < 2^{\lambda}$. That is, every element in the finite field (when equivalently interpreted as elements of the set $\{0, 1, \ldots, p-1\}$) has a λ-bit binary representation. The parameter $k \in \mathbb{N}$ represents the reconstruction threshold, and $n \in \mathbb{N}$ represents the total number of parties.

Shamir Secret-Sharing Scheme. Suppose the secret is $s \in F$, and the tuple of distinct evaluation places is $\vec{X} := (X_1, X_2, \ldots, X_n) \in (F^*)^n$, such that $i \neq j$ implies $X_i \neq X_j$.[4] Shamir's secret-sharing scheme with threshold $k \in \mathbb{N}$, represented by $\mathsf{ShamirSS}(n, k, \vec{X})$, picks a random secret-sharing polynomial $P(X) \in F[X]/X^k$ conditioned on the fact that $P(0) = s$. The secret-shares for parties $1, 2, \ldots, n$

[4] We assume this for the ease of presentation for now, while our results do not require such restrictions. When there are two identical evaluation places, leaking one bit from each share is equivalent to leaking two bits from one of those shares. Since our results naturally extend to leaking multiple bits from each share, we do not need the restriction that all the evaluation places are distinct. Furthermore, when all the evaluation places are chosen independently randomly (at most a polynomial in the security parameter), the probability that there are two identical evaluation places are exponentially small (by the birthday bound) since the field size is exponentially large in the security parameter.

are $s_1 = P(X_1), s_2 = P(X_2), \ldots, s_n = P(X_n)$, respectively. Observe that, in a Shamir secret-sharing scheme, it is implicit that the number of parties satisfies $n < p$.

Physical Bit-Leakage. Our work represents all the secret shares $s_1, \ldots, s_n \in F$ with the parties as λ-bit binary representation. An m-bit local physical-bit leakage function specifies probing locations $\{\ell_{i,j}\}_{\substack{1 \leqslant i \leqslant n \\ 1 \leqslant j \leqslant m}}$ such that $\ell_{i,j} \in \{1, 2, \ldots, \lambda\}$ for each of the n secret shares. The output of the leakage function provides the $\ell_{i,j}$-th bit[5] in the i-th secret-share s_i, for all $1 \leqslant i \leqslant n$ and $1 \leqslant j \leqslant m$. For a fixed secret $s \in F$, the output of the leakage function is a distribution over the sample space $\{0,1\}^{mn}$ induced by the random choice of the secret-sharing polynomial $P(X)$ above.

Local Leakage-Resilience Against Physical Bit-Leakage. $\mathsf{ShamirSS}(n, k, \vec{X})$ is $(1-\varepsilon)$-secure against local physical-bit leakages if, for any two secrets $s^{(0)}, s^{(1)} \in F$ and an m-bit local physical-bit leakage function, the statistical distance between the leakage distributions is at most ε.[6]

Result I: Feasibility. Suppose we are given as input the number of parties $n \in \mathbb{N}$, the reconstruction threshold $2 \leqslant k \in \mathbb{N}$, the length of the binary representations $\lambda \in \mathbb{N}$, the insecurity tolerance $\varepsilon = 2^{-t}$, and the number of leakage bits m from each secret-share. Our experiment picks distinct evaluation places $\vec{X}$ uniformly at random from the set F^*. Given a fixed tuple of distinct evaluation places $\vec{X}$, one tests whether $\mathsf{ShamirSS}(n, k, \vec{X})$ is resilient to m-bit local physical-bit leakage resilient or not.

We prove that the $\mathsf{ShamirSS}(n, k, \vec{X})$ scheme is $(1 - \varepsilon)$-secure (except with an exponentially small probability in $(k-1) \cdot \lambda$ over the random choices of the evaluation places $\vec{X}$), if the following conditions are satisfied.

1. The number of bits λ satisfies $\lambda / \log^2 \lambda \geqslant \Theta(t/k)$, and
2. The total leakage mn satisfies $mn \leqslant k\lambda / \log^2 \lambda$.

This result is the summarized in Theorem 4 and Corollary 4.

The constants in the asymptotic notations are all universal positive constants. Given n, k, F parameters, note that one can choose the random evaluation places once (using a trusted setup, e.g., common random string) for all future instantiations of Shamir secret-sharing scheme. The probability that the instantiation is not $(1-\varepsilon)$-secure is exponentially small. We emphasize that the

[5] For instance, let $\lambda = 5$ and $p = 19$. The element $5 \in F = \{0, 1, \ldots, 18\}$ is represented as 00101. The first bit is 1, second bit is 0, third bit is 1, and the fourth and the fifth bits are both 0.

[6] One can simulate the leakage joint distribution as follows. The simulator shall fix an arbitrary secret (say, 0), generate its secret shares, and output the evaluation of the leakage function on the respective secret shares. The simulation error for this strategy is a two-approximation of the indistinguishability advantage by the triangle inequality.

result above holds for any $k \geqslant 2$, which is the best possible result. Therefore, for every n, k, m, ε, our result proves that Shamir secret-sharing scheme for all large-enough prime fields F is leakage-resilient.

A Concrete Example. As a representative example, consider the following scenario. Suppose the reconstruction threshold is $k = 2$, the number of bits leaked is $m = 1$, and the number of parties $n = 10, 100$, and 1000. Assume we wish to achieve insecurity $\varepsilon = 2^{-50}$ and succeed in picking a set of good evaluation places with probability (at least) $1 - 2^{-50}$. Our Theorem 3 states that picking a prime number p with more than 430, 4800, and 62000 bits, respectively, in its binary representation suffices. Intuitively, it scales (roughly) linearly with n. As k increases, even smaller primes suffice. The estimates above correspond to the most difficult case for security.

Reinterpretation: Randomly Punctured Reed-Solomon Code. Given a Reed-Solomon code of dimension k over a prime-field F, one punctures $(p-1)-n$ columns among the columns numbered $\{1, 2, \ldots, p-1\}$. Suppose the columns numbered $(0, X_1, \ldots, X_n)$ survive the puncturing operations. The Massey secret-sharing scheme [35] corresponding to this resulting $[n+1, k]_F$ linear error-correcting code is identical to the $\mathsf{ShamirSS}(n, k, \vec{X})$ secret-sharing scheme mentioned above. Consequently, our result proves that all puncturing operations (except an exponentially small fraction of them) result in an $(1-\varepsilon)$-secure leakage-resilient scheme.

Result II: Hardness of Computation. We present an attack strategy for any $k \geqslant 2$, $n \geqslant k$, $m \geqslant 1$, and $p = 1 \mod k$. For a fixed $k \geqslant 2$, there are infinitely many primes satisfying $p = 1 \mod k$ due to Dirichlet's theorem [39]. Our attack leaks only the least-significant bit of the secret-shares, and has a constant advantage in distinguishing two secrets based on this leakage. For given values of k, n, p satisfying the conditions above, there are (roughly) $n^k p^{n-k} \cdot (p-1)/k$ vulnerable tuples of evaluation places where our attack succeeds.

For $k = 2, 3$ (and any p), we calculate the exact advantage of our attack. Next, for any $k \geqslant 2$, as $p \to \infty$, we show that the quality of our attack is lower-bounded by the "discrepancy" of the Irwin-Hall distribution [18,23] (with parameter $(k-1)$, represented by I_{k-1}). The "discrepancy" of a distribution (see Definition 9) is a new property of probability distributions that we introduce, which is of potential independent interest. We explicitly calculate the discrepancy of the Irwin-Hall distribution for $(k-1) \in \{2, 3, \ldots, 24\}$, and Fig. 2 provides the details. If the discrepancy of the Irwin-Hall distribution I_{k-1} is non-zero, then the discrepancy is at least $1/k!$. However, based on our numerical experiments, we conjecture that the discrepancy of Irwin-Hall distribution (with parameter k) behaves as $\geqslant \exp(-\Theta(k))$, which is not negligible for $k = \mathcal{O}(\log \lambda)$. We emphasize that, given a fixed k, the conjectured distinguishing advantage of this attack depends only on k, independent of the security parameter. Intuitively, increasing the size of the prime should only make the scheme more secure, and the conjecture above considers $p \to \infty$.

Reinterpretation: Attack on Additive Secret-Sharing Scheme. Our physical bit leakage attack on the Shamir secret-sharing scheme directly translates into physical bit leakage attacks on the additive secret-sharing scheme. If the number of shares in the additive secret sharing scheme is $\mathcal{O}(\log \lambda)$ then, our conjecture above, states that the advantage of our attack is $1/\mathsf{poly}(\lambda)$.

Benhamouda et al. [3] proposed a general leakage attack on additive secret-sharing scheme. Their attack tests whether each share is smaller than $p/2k$ and has an advantage of (roughly) $1/k^k$. In comparison, our attack employs a simpler leakage function, i.e., physical-bit leakage, and will achieve similar advantage if our conjecture holds. Since the leakage function is simpler, the threat it poses is even more significant.

1.2 Technical Overview

Let λ be the security parameter. Let F be a prime field of order p such that p needs λ bits in its binary representation. That is, we have $p \in \{2^{\lambda-1}, 2^{\lambda-1}+1, \dots, 2^\lambda - 1\}$.

For a secret $s \in F$, assume that Shamir's secret sharing scheme uses a random polynomial $P(X)$ of degree $< k = \mathsf{poly}(\lambda)$ conditioned on $P(0) = s$ to share a secret among $n = \mathsf{poly}(\lambda)$ parties. Let the evaluation places be $\vec{X} = (X_1, X_2, \dots, X_n) \in (F^*)^n$ such that $i \neq j \implies X_i \neq X_j$ (i.e., all evaluation places are distinct). The share of party i is the evaluation of the polynomial $P(X)$ at the evaluation place X_i. $\mathsf{ShamirSS}(n, k, \vec{X})$ represents this secret-sharing scheme.

Fix the local leakage function $\vec{\tau}$ that leaks m physical-bits from the binary representation of the secret-shares of the n parties. Furthermore, $\vec{\tau}\left(\mathsf{Share}^{\vec{X}}(s)\right)$ represents the joint distribution of the leakage conditioned on the fact that the secret is $s \in F$. If this joint distribution of the leakage is independent of the secret, then the secret-sharing scheme is *locally leakage-resilient* to physical bit leakages.

Our objective is to prove that Shamir secret-sharing scheme is locally leakage-resilient for most evaluation places $\vec{X}$, when $\vec{X}$ is chosen uniformly at random from the set $(F^*)^n$ under the constraint that $i \neq j \implies X_i \neq X_j$. Theorem 3 formally states this result. To simplify the presentation of key technical ideas, it is instructive to use $m = 1$. The analysis for larger m is analogous.

Reduction 1. Fix any two secrets $s^{(0)}, s^{(1)} \in F$. We prove the following two bounds. First, by standard Fourier techniques, we prove

$$\mathsf{SD}\left(\vec{\tau}\left(\mathsf{Share}^{\vec{X}}(s^{(0)})\right), \vec{\tau}\left(\mathsf{Share}^{\vec{X}}(s^{(1)})\right)\right) \leqslant \sum_{\vec{\ell} \in \{0,1\}^n} \sum_{\vec{\alpha} \in C_{\vec{X}}^{\perp} \setminus \{0\}} \left(\prod_{i=1}^{n} \left|\widehat{\mathbb{1}_{\ell_i}}(\alpha_i)\right|\right).$$

Here, $\mathbb{1}_{\ell_i}$ is the indicator function of the set $\{x \colon L_i(x) = \ell_i\}$; $C_{\vec{X}}$ is the (punctured) Reed-Solomon code that corresponds to Shamir's secret-sharing with evaluation places $\vec{X}$; $C_{\vec{X}}^{\perp}$ is the dual code of $C_{\vec{X}}$.

Next, we show that it suffices to prove that, over randomly chosen evaluation places $\vec{X} \in (F^*)^n$ (under the constraint that $i \neq j \implies X_i \neq X_j$), this upper bound is small. That is,

$$\mathop{\mathrm{E}}_{\vec{X}}\left[\sum_{\vec{\ell}\in\{0,1\}^n}\ \sum_{\vec{\alpha}\in C_{\vec{X}}^{\perp}\setminus\{0\}} \left(\prod_{i=1}^{n}\left|\widehat{\mathbb{1}_{\ell_i}}(\alpha_i)\right|\right)\right] \leqslant \exp(-\Theta(\lambda)).$$

This bound above is sufficient for our objective. One could use a union bound on the leakage function to conclude that most evaluation places yield a locally leakage-resilient Shamir secret-sharing scheme. After that, a Markov inequality yields random evaluation places, except an exponentially small fraction of the evaluation places, result in a locally leakage-resilient Shamir secret-sharing scheme. Note that we avoid the union bound over secrets since the upper bound is insensitive to the secret. The above argument can be found in Sect. 5.2.

Reduction 2. We employ Fourier analysis to estimate the following bound

$$\mathop{\mathrm{E}}_{\vec{X}}\left[\sum_{\vec{\ell}\in\{0,1\}^n}\ \sum_{\vec{\alpha}\in C_{\vec{X}}^{\perp}\setminus\{0\}} \left(\prod_{i=1}^{n}\left|\widehat{\mathbb{1}_{\ell_i}}(\alpha_i)\right|\right)\right].$$

The analysis in Sect. 5.4 reduces this estimation to two problems, Problems A and B below.

Problem A. For simplicity of presenting the main technical ideas, assume that the parties' secret-shares are elements from the set $\{0,1\}^\lambda$. The Fourier analysis above relies on bounding certain exponential sums over the subset of elements that agree with an apriori fixed m-bit leakage. In particular, these elements will have m bits identical to the leakage, and all remaining $(\lambda - m)$ bits may either be zero or one. The abstraction of *generalized arithmetic progressions* (refer to Sect. 3.1) is adequate to capture the analytic properties of such subsets.

We import an estimate of the exponential sum mentioned in Imported Theorem 1. For the particular case of $m = 1$, we present a tight estimate of the constant in the above imported theorem (refer to Theorem 2). This tight estimate of the constant translates into near-optimal bounds on the local leakage-resilience of Shamir secret-sharing scheme.

A subtlety in the argument above is that the set of binary representations of a party's secret-share is *not* the set $\{0,1\}^\lambda$. It is, in fact, the set of the binary representations of $\{0,1,\ldots,p-1\}$. However, this subset can be partitioned into (at most) λ subsets such that each set is an *MSB-fixing set*, a set whose most significant bits are fixed and the least significant bits are uniformly random (for formal definition and examples, refer to Sect. 4). This notion of MSB-fixing sets introduced by us helps perform the simplified analysis mentioned above in the context of our problem.

Problem B. Once problem A is solved, the Fourier analysis requires another bound. Fix any $\vec{\alpha} \in F^n$. Next, consider the following equation.

$$\begin{pmatrix} X_1 & X_2 & \cdots & X_n \\ X_1^2 & X_2^2 & \cdots & X_n^2 \\ \vdots & \vdots & \ddots & \vdots \\ X_1^{k-1} & X_2^{k-1} & \cdots & X_n^{k-1} \end{pmatrix} \cdot \begin{pmatrix} \alpha_1 \\ \alpha_2 \\ \vdots \\ \alpha_n \end{pmatrix} = \begin{pmatrix} 0 \\ 0 \\ \vdots \\ 0 \end{pmatrix}.$$

How many solutions $\vec{X} \in (F^*)^n$ exist of the equation above, such that $i \neq j \implies X_i \neq X_j$?

Consider the simplification when $\vec{\alpha} = \vec{1}$. Fix any distinct values of $X_{k+1}, \ldots, X_n \in F^*$. If a solution $X_1, \ldots, X_k$ exists (where each $X_1, \ldots, X_n$ are distinct as well) then every permutation of $X_1, \ldots, X_k$ is also a solution. Consequently, the number of solutions of the equation above is at least $\min\{0, k!\}$.

We rely on Bézout's theorem (in particular, a form that has an easy-to-verify analytic test, refer to Imported Theorem 2) to claim that the number of solutions is, in fact, at most $k!$. Consequently, overall, the number of solutions $\vec{X} \in (F^*)^n$ is $\mathcal{O}\left(k! \cdot p^{n-k}\right)$. This bound holds for any $\vec{\alpha}$, in general, and not just for $\vec{\alpha} = \vec{1}$.

Resolving the problems A and B completes the proof of Theorem 3. Corollary 2 is an easy-to-use corollary of this theorem demonstrating that when $n = \mathsf{poly}(\lambda)$, $k = \mathcal{O}\left(\frac{t}{\lambda} + \frac{\log \lambda}{\lambda} \cdot n\right)$ suffices to ensure that $1 - \exp(-\Theta(\lambda))$ fraction of the evaluation places yield a Shamir secret-sharing scheme that is locally leakage-resilient to $m = 1$ physical-bit leakage with insecurity $\leqslant 2^{-t}$.

Generalization to m-Bit Leakage from Each Share. Observe that one can directly consider the leaking m-bit leakage from the secret-shares of the Shamir secret-sharing scheme. Towards this objective, one needs to consider MSB-fixing sets that are consistent with an apriori fixed leakage, which are proper rank-$(m+1)$ generalized arithmetic progressions. However, the constant in Imported Theorem 1 for rank-$(m+1)$ generalized arithmetic progressions is not explicit. Moreover, without an explicit constant, one can not provide concrete bound on the insecurity of the secret-sharing scheme. Consequently, our work relies on a different approach.

We consider secret-sharing scheme where each share of the Shamir secret-sharing scheme is duplicated m-times, and the adversary leaks one physical bit from each secret share. This technique allows using our Theorem 2 that has an explicit and tight constant, which is specifically tailored for our problem. The remainder of the technical analysis proceeds similar to the presentation above. The general result is summarized as Theorem 4.

New Physical-Bit Attack. For reconstruction threshold k, consider the number of parties $n = k$, and the prime $p = 1 \mod k$. Let F be the finite field of order p. Let $\left\{\alpha, \alpha^2, \ldots, \alpha^k = 1\right\} \subseteq F^*$ be the set of all solutions to the equation $Z^k - 1 = 0$. Consider $n = k$ evaluation places $X_1 = \alpha$, $X_2 = \alpha^2, \ldots,$ and $X_k = \alpha^k$. Let $f(X) \in F[X]/X^k$ be an arbitrary polynomial with $f(0) = s$, for some secret $s \in F$. Observe that $f(X_1) + f(X_2) + \cdots + f(X_k) = ks$.

To present the primary technical ideas, consider $k = 3$. Let s_1 be the secret share of party one. Over the random choice of the polynomial $f(X)$, the secret share s_1 is uniformly random over F. Similarly, the choice of s_2, the secret share of party two, is independent and uniformly random over F. However, the secret share of the k-th party satisfies the constraint $s_k = ks - \sum_{i=1}^{k-1} s_i$, i.e., $s_3 = 3s - (s_1 + s_2)$.

Our leakage functions shall leak the least significant digit of the shares s_1, s_2, and s_3 to construct a test that predicts the least significant digit of ks with constant advantage, for an appropriate $s \in F$. For a random secret, our test has (statistically close to) zero advantage. So, our test distinguishes, by an averaging argument, two secrets with a constant advantage.

Our New Test. Let $S_1, S_2, S_3 \in \{0, 1, \ldots, p-1\} \subseteq \mathbb{N}_0 := \{0, 1, 2, \ldots\}$ represent the whole numbers corresponding to the secret shares s_1, s_2, s_3. Our test predicts the least significant digit of ks as the parity of the least significant digits of S_1, S_2, S_3. Observe that (the addition in the equation below is over the set of whole numbers $\mathbb{N}_0$, and $(ks) \in F$ is interpreted as an element of $\{0, 1, \ldots, p-1\}$)

$$S_1 + S_2 + S_3 = p\mathbb{Z} + (ks).$$

Therefore, if $S_1 + S_2 + S_3 = ip + ks$, for an even integer i, then the parity of the least significant digits of S_1, S_2, S_3 correctly predicts the least significant digit of ks. On the other hand, if $S_1 + S_2 + S_3 = ip + ks$, for an odd integer i, then the parity of the least significant digits of S_1, S_2, S_3 incorrectly predicts the least significant digit of ks. Our objective is to prove that there exists $s \in F$ such that the absolute value of the difference between the correct and incorrect prediction probabilities is a constant. Equivalently, the objective is to prove that there exists $s \in F$ such that the probability of correct prediction probability is a constant larger than $1/2$ or a constant smaller than $1/2$.

So, for independent and uniformly random $S_1, S_2 \in \{0, 1, \ldots, p-1\}$, our objective is to compute the probability that

$$S_1 + S_2 + S_3 = ip + (ks),$$

where i is even and $S_3 \in \{0, 1, \ldots, p-1\}$. Equivalently, for independent and uniformly random $S_1, S_2 \in \{0, 1, \ldots, p-1\}$, our objective is to compute the probability that

$$S_1 + S_2 \in 2p\mathbb{Z} + (ks) - \{0, 1, \ldots, p-1\} = \mathbb{N}_0 \cap \bigcup_{\substack{i \in \mathbb{Z} \\ i \text{ odd}}} [ip + (ks) + 1, (i+1)p + (ks)].$$

For $k = 3$, we can show that this probability is <0.25 by choosing $ks = (p-1)/2$.

Extensions. Note that our attack naturally extends to that the evaluation places form an arbitrary coset in $F^*/\{\alpha, \ldots, \alpha^k = 1\}$. For $n > k$, one can choose the remainder of the evaluation places arbitrarily. Consequently, there are a total of $\sim n^k \cdot p^{n-k} \cdot (p-1)/k$ evaluation places where our attack works.

For a fixed k, and prime $p \to \infty$, Sect. 6.1 shows that the advantage of our test tends to $\mathsf{disc}(I_{k-1})$, where I_{k-1} is the Irwin-Hall distribution for parameter $(k-1)$, and Definition 9 defines the discrepancy of a probability distribution $\mathsf{disc}(\cdot)$. Figure 1 shows this discrepancy for $(k-1) = 4$ and $(k-1) = 5$. Figure 2 shows the conjectured bound for discrepancy for $(k-1) \in \{2, 3, \dots, 24\}$.

2 Preliminaries

In this work, λ represents the security parameter. Let p be a prime whose binary representation has λ bits. Or, equivalently, the prime satisfies $2^{\lambda-1} \leqslant p < 2^{\lambda}$. For any positive integer a and $i \geqslant 1$, $[a]_i$ denotes the ith least significant bit in the binary representation of a. For example, let $\lambda = 5$ and $p = 19$, the field element $5 \in F = \{0, 1, ..., 18\}$ is binary represented as 00101. Its least significant bit is $[5]_1 = 1$, second least significant bit is $[5]_2 = 0$, and so on. Using our notations, the binary representation of p is $[p]_\lambda [p]_{\lambda-1} \cdots [p]_1$.

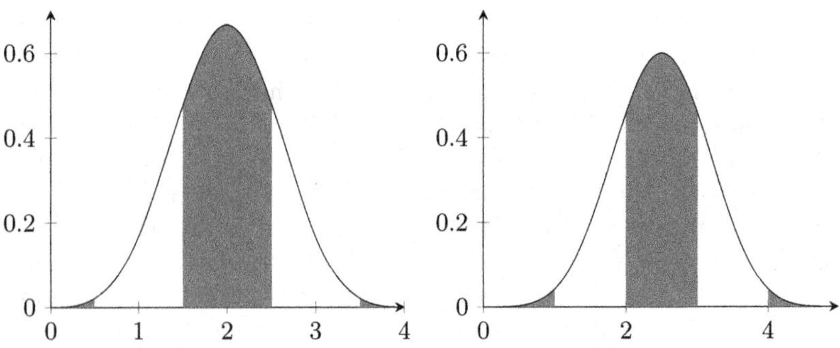

Fig. 1. Plot of the Irwin-Hall distribution for parameters $(k-1) = 4$ and $(k-1) = 5$. The black intervals have width 1, each black interval is separated from the next nearest black interval by distance 1, and the central mass of probability distribution is captured by a black interval. The discrepancy of the respective distributions is the difference between the probability mass inside the black bands and the total probability mass outside the black bands. For $(k-1) = 4$ and $(k-1) = 5$, the discrepancies are $5/24$ and $2/15$, respectively.

For any set S, $\mathbb{1}_S$ denotes its indicator function. That is, $\mathbb{1}_S(x) = 1$ if $x \in S$, and $\mathbb{1}_S(x) = 0$, otherwise.

For any two distributions A and B (over a countable sample space), the statistical distance between two distributions, represented by $\mathsf{SD}(A, B)$, is defined as $\frac{1}{2}\sum_x |\Pr[A = x] - \Pr[B = x]|$.

We shall use $f(\lambda) \sim g(\lambda)$ if $f(\lambda) = (1 + o(1))\, g(\lambda)$. Additionally, we write $f(\lambda) \lesssim g(\lambda)$ if $f(\lambda) \leqslant (1 + o(1))\, g(\lambda)$.

2.1 Secret Sharing Schemes

Definition 1 (**$(n,k)_F$-Secret Sharing Scheme**). *For any two positive integer $k < n$, an $(n,k)_F$-secret-sharing scheme over a finite field F consists of two functions* Share *and* Rec. Share *is a randomized function that takes a secret $s \in F$ and outputs* $\mathsf{Share}(s) = (\mathsf{Share}(s)_1, \dots, \mathsf{Share}(s)_n) \in F^n$. *The pair of function* (Share, Rec) *satisfies the following requirements.*

- ***Correctness.*** *For any secret $s \in F$ and a set of parties $\{i_1, i_2, \dots, i_t\} \subseteq \{1, 2, \dots, n\}$ such that $t \geqslant k$, we have*

$$Pr\left[\mathsf{Rec}(\mathsf{Share}(s)_{i_1}, \dots, \mathsf{Share}(s)_{i_t}) = s\right] = 1.$$

- ***Privacy.***[7] *For any two secret $s_0, s_1 \in F$ and a set of parties $\{i_1, i_2, \dots, i_t\} \subseteq \{1, 2, \dots, n\}$ such that $t < k$, we have*

$$\mathsf{SD}\left(\left(\mathsf{Share}(s_0)_{i_1}, \dots, \mathsf{Share}(s_0)_{i_t}\right), \left(\mathsf{Share}(s_1)_{i_1}, \dots, \mathsf{Share}(s_1)_{i_t}\right)\right) = 0.$$

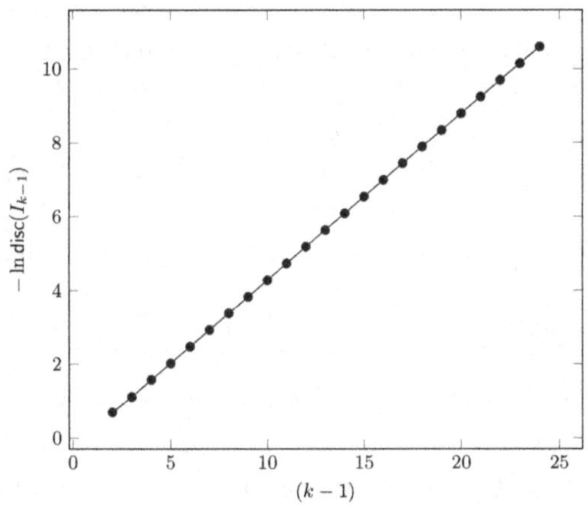

Fig. 2. Plot of $-\ln \mathsf{disc}(I_{k-1})$ versus $(k-1)$ for $(k-1) \in \{2, 3, \dots, 24\}$.

Definition 2 (**$(n,k,\vec{X})_F$-Shamir Secret-sharing**). *Let F be a prime field. For any positive integer $k \leqslant n$ and* evaluation places $\vec{X} = (X_1, \dots, X_n)$ *the following conditions are satisfied. (1) For all $1 \leqslant i \leqslant n$, $X_i \in F^*$, and (2) for all $1 \leqslant i < j \leqslant n$, $X_i \neq X_j$. The corresponding $(n,k,\vec{X})_F$-Shamir secret sharing is defined as follows.*

[7] The definition considers *perfect* privacy. For secret-sharing schemes based on Massey's construction [35] from linear error-correcting codes, the shares of any set of parties either witness perfect privacy, or the set of shares suffices to reconstruct the secret. A statistical notion of privacy is relevant when using non-linear codes instead. However, in our work we shall primarily study secret-sharing schemes based on Massey's construction from linear error-correcting codes. Consequently, we define perfect privacy only.

- *Given secret* $s \in F$, $\mathsf{Share}^{\vec{X}}(s)$ *independently samples a random* $a_i \in F$, *for all* $1 \leqslant i < k$. *The* i^{th} *share of* $\mathsf{Share}^{\vec{X}}(s)$ *is*

$$\mathsf{Share}^{\vec{X}}(s)_i := s + a_1 X_i + a_2 X_i^2 + \cdots + a_{k-1} X_i^{k-1}.$$

- *Given shares* $\left(\mathsf{Share}^{\vec{X}}(s)_{i_1}, \ldots, \mathsf{Share}^{\vec{X}}(s)_{i_t}\right)$, $\mathsf{Rec}^{\vec{X}}$ *interpolates to obtain the unique polynomial* $f \in F[X]/X^k$ *such that* $f(X_{i_j}) = \mathsf{Share}^{\vec{X}}(s)_{i_j}$ *for all* $1 \leqslant j \leqslant t$, *and outputs* $f(0)$ *to be the reconstructred secret.*

2.2 Physical-Bit Leakage Function

In this paper, we study the physical-bit leakage. Let F be the prime field of order p. Recall that $2^{\lambda-1} \leqslant p < 2^{\lambda}$. For every element $a \in F$, we let a be an element in the set $\{0, 1, \ldots, p-1\}$. We shall use λ bits for the binary representation of a, i.e., $[a]_\lambda [a]_{\lambda-1} \cdots [a]_1$. In particular, we pad with a sufficient number of 0s if $a < 2^{\lambda-1}$. For example, when $\lambda = 5$ the binary representation of $a = 6$ is 00110.

Definition 3. *An* m*-bit physical-bit leakage function* $\vec{\tau} = (\tau_1, \ldots, \tau_n)$ *on* $(n,k)_F$*-secret sharing, leaks* m *bits from every share locally. This leakage function is specified by indices* $u_1^{(i)}, \ldots, u_m^{(i)}$, *for all* $1 \leqslant i \leqslant n$. *Given the indices* $u_1^{(i)}, \ldots, u_m^{(i)}$, *the leakage on the* i^{th} *share is the joint distribution*

$$\tau_i(\mathsf{Share}(s)_i) := \left([\mathsf{Share}(s)_i]_{u_1^{(i)}}, [\mathsf{Share}(s)_i]_{u_2^{(i)}}, \ldots, [\mathsf{Share}(s)_i]_{u_m^{(i)}}\right).$$

Furthermore, $\vec{\tau}(\mathsf{Share}(s))$ *denotes the collection of leakage from every share*

$$(\tau_1(\mathsf{Share}(s)_1), \tau_2(\mathsf{Share}(s)_2), \ldots, \tau_n(\mathsf{Share}(s)_n)).$$

2.3 Local Leakage-Resilient Secret Sharing Scheme Against Physical-Bit Leakage

Definition 4 (**$[\![n,k,m,\varepsilon]\!]_F$-LLRSS**)**.** *An* $(n,k)_F$*-secret sharing scheme* (Share, Rec) *is an* $[\![n,k,m,\varepsilon]\!]_F$-local leakage-resilient secret sharing scheme against m physical-bit leakage *(tersely represented as* $[\![n,k,m,\varepsilon]\!]_F$*-LLRSS), if it provides the following guarantee. For any two secrets* $s_0, s_1 \in F$ *and any physical-bit leakage function* $\vec{\tau}$ *that leaks* m *physical bits from every share locally, we have*

$$\mathsf{SD}\left(\vec{\tau}(\mathsf{Share}(s_0)),\ \vec{\tau}(\mathsf{Share}(s_1))\right) \leqslant \varepsilon.$$

2.4 Generalized Reed-Solomon Code

Definition 5 (**$(n,k,\vec{X},\vec{\alpha})_F$-GRS**)**.** *A* generalized Reed-Solomon code *over prime field* F *with message length* k *and block length* n *consists of an encoding function* $\mathsf{Enc}\colon F^k \to F^n$ *and decoding function* $\mathsf{Dec}\colon F^n \to F^k$. *It is specified by the* evaluation places $\vec{X} = (X_1, \ldots, X_n)$, *such that for all* $1 \leqslant i \leqslant j \leqslant n$,

$X_i \neq X_j$, *and a* scaling vector $\vec{\alpha} = (\alpha_1, \ldots, \alpha_n)$ *such that for all* $1 \leqslant i \leqslant n$, $\alpha_i \in F^*$. *Given* $\vec{X}$ *and* $\vec{\alpha}$, *the* encoding function *is*

$$\mathsf{Enc}(m_1, \ldots, m_k) := (\alpha_1 \cdot f(X_1), \ldots, \alpha_n \cdot f(X_n)),$$

where $f(X) := m_1 + m_2 X + \cdots + m_k X^{k-1}$.

In particular, the generator matrix of the linear $(n, k, \vec{X}, \vec{\alpha})_F$*-GRS code is the matrix*

$$\begin{pmatrix} \alpha_1 \cdot 1 & \alpha_2 \cdot 1 & \cdots & \alpha_n \cdot 1 \\ \alpha_1 \cdot X_1 & \alpha_2 \cdot X_2 & \cdots & \alpha_n \cdot X_n \\ \vdots & \vdots & \ddots & \vdots \\ \alpha_1 \cdot X_1^{k-1} & \alpha_2 \cdot X_2^{k-1} & \cdots & \alpha_n \cdot X_n^{k-1} \end{pmatrix}.$$

Observation 1. *The joint distribution of the secret-shares of an* $(n, k, \vec{X})_F$*-Shamir secret sharing with secret* $s = 0$ *is identical to the uniform distribution over the codewords in the* $(n, k-1, \vec{X}, \vec{X})_F$*-GRS code.*

The following standard properties of generalized Reed-Solomon codes shall be helpful.

Theorem 1 (Properties of GRS).

1. *The distance of the* $(n, k, \vec{X}, \vec{\alpha})_F$*-GRS is* $(n - k + 1)$ *(i.e., the linear code is maximum distance separable [32]).*
2. *The dual code of* $(n, k, \vec{X}, \vec{\alpha})_F$*-GRS is identical to the* $(n, n-k, \vec{X}, \vec{\beta})_F$*-GRS, where for all* $1 \leqslant i \leqslant n$,

$$\beta_i := \left(\alpha_i \prod_{\substack{j=1 \\ j \neq i}}^{n} (X_i - X_j) \right)^{-1}.$$

The β_i's are the scalars from Lagrange interpolation. A proof for this theorem can be found in, for example, [17,31].

2.5 Fourier Analysis Basics

In this paper, we shall use Fourier analysis on prime field F of order p. We follow the notation of [38]. Define $\omega := \exp(2\pi\imath/p)$. For any functions $f, g \colon F \to \mathbb{C}$, define

$$\langle f, g \rangle := \frac{1}{p} \sum_{x \in F} f(x) \cdot \overline{g(x)},$$

where $\overline{z}$ is the complex conjugate of $z \in \mathbb{C}$. For $z \in \mathbb{C}$, $|z| := \sqrt{z\overline{z}}$. For any $\alpha \in F$, define the function $\widehat{f} \colon F \to \mathbb{C}$ as follows.

$$\widehat{f}(\alpha) := \frac{1}{p} \sum_{x \in F} f(x) \cdot \omega^{-\alpha x}.$$

The Fourier transform maps the function f to the function $\widehat{f}$. This transformation is a full-rank linear mapping, i.e., only the zero function has zero Fourier. In particular, it satisfies the following identities.

Lemma 1 (Fourier Inversion Formula). $f(x) = \sum_{\alpha \in F} \widehat{f}(\alpha) \cdot \omega^{\alpha x}$.

Lemma 2 (Parseval's Identity). $\frac{1}{p} \sum_{x \in F} |f(x)|^2 = \sum_{\alpha \in F} \left|\widehat{f}(\alpha)\right|^2$.

3 Imported Theorems

3.1 Generalized Arithmetic Progressions

Our first imported theorem is on the ℓ_1-norm of the Fourier-coefficients of the indicator function of a generalized arithmetic progression.

Definition 6 (r-GAP). *Let F be a finite field. A subset $S \subseteq F$ is a* generalized arithmetic progression of rank r *(i.e., an r-GAP) if*

$$S = \{a_0 + a_1 h_1 + a_2 h_2 + \cdots + a_r h_r \,:\, 0 \leqslant h_i < H_i \text{ for every } 1 \leqslant i \leqslant r\},$$

where $a_0, \ldots, a_r \in F$ and $2 \leqslant H_1, \ldots, H_r \leqslant |F|$.

Furthermore, the set S is proper *if $|S| = H_1 H_2 \cdots H_r$.*

Intuitively, in a proper GAP every element in the set has a unique decomposition.

Shao [40] proved that for any proper r-GAP S, the ℓ_1-norm of the Fourier-coefficients of its indicator function $\mathbb{1}_S$ is small.

Imported Theorem 1 (Theorem 3.1 of [40]).[8] *For every natural number r, there exists a constant $C_r > 0$ such that the following bounds holds for any proper r-GAP $S \subseteq F$.*

$$\sum_{\alpha \in F} \left|\widehat{\mathbb{1}_S}(\alpha)\right| \leqslant C_r \cdot \log(H_1) \cdots \log(H_r).$$

Shao [40] proved this result for vector spaces over F as well. However, we are importing the minimum result sufficient for our derivations.

In our setting, we are interested in a special type of proper 2-GAPs satisfying $a_1 = 1$ and $a_2 = 2H_1$. We carefully calculate the constant D_2 for this special case because a tight estimate itranslates into tight bounds on the insecurity of the cryptographic constructions. Our results are summarized in Theorem 2.

3.2 Number of Isolated Solutions of a Square Polynomial System

Our next imported theorem is regarding the number of the solutions of a square polynomial system. The specific version of Bézout's theorem that we are using

[8] Note that, in the definition of [40], the Fourier coefficients are scaled by the field size compared to our definition.

is due to Wooley [42]. Before we present Wooley's theorem, let us introduce the minimal necessary definitions. For this part of the presentation, we follow the notations introduced by [10].

Definition 7 (Degree, Formal Derivative, Determinant, and Jacobian).

1. *Let F be a prime field. The* degree *of a monomial $X_1^{i_1}X_2^{i_2}\cdots X_n^{i_n}$ is $\sum_{\ell=1}^{n} i_\ell$. For a polynomial $f \in F[X_1, X_2, \ldots, X_n]$, the degree of f is the largest degree of its monomial.*
2. *Suppose*
$$f = g_t X_i^t + g_{t-1} X_i^{t-1} + \cdots + g_1 X_i + g_0,$$
where $g_0, \ldots, g_t \in F[X_1, \ldots, X_{i-1}, X_{i+1}, \ldots, X_n]$. Then, the formal derivative of f with respect to X_i *is the polynomial in $F[X_1, X_2, \ldots, X_n]$ defined below.*
$$\frac{\partial f}{\partial X_i} := (t \cdot g_t) X_i^{t-1} + ((t-1) \cdot g_{t-1}) X_i^{t-2} + \cdots + (2 \cdot g_2) X_i + g_1.$$
3. *For a square matrix $M \in \left(F[X_1, X_2, \ldots, X_n]\right)^{k\times k}$,* $\det(M)$ *denotes the* determinant *of M defined as follows.*
$$\det(M) := \sum_{\substack{\sigma\colon \{1,2,\ldots,k\}\to\{1,2,\ldots,k\} \\ \sigma \text{ is a permutation}}} \operatorname{sgn}(\sigma) \cdot \prod_{i=1}^{k} M_{i,\sigma(i)},$$
where $\operatorname{sgn}(\sigma)$ *represents the $\{+1, -1\}$ sign of the permutation σ.*[9] *Note that* $\det(M) \in F[X_1, X_2, \ldots, X_n]$.
4. *For polynomials $f_1, \ldots, f_k \in F[X_1, X_2, \ldots, X_n]$, their* Jacobian *is*
$$\mathbf{J}(f_1, \ldots, f_k) := \begin{pmatrix} \frac{\partial f_1}{\partial X_1} & \frac{\partial f_2}{\partial X_1} & \cdots & \frac{\partial f_k}{\partial X_1} \\ \frac{\partial f_1}{\partial X_2} & \frac{\partial f_2}{\partial X_2} & \cdots & \frac{\partial f_k}{\partial X_2} \\ \vdots & \vdots & \ddots & \vdots \\ \frac{\partial f_1}{\partial X_n} & \frac{\partial f_2}{\partial X_n} & \cdots & \frac{\partial f_k}{\partial X_n} \end{pmatrix}.$$

Intuitively, the Jacobian encodes information pertinent to the independence of a system of polynomials.

A *square polynomial system* has equal number of polynomials and the number of variables. That is, in the presentation above, we have $n = k$. The following theorem bounds the number of isolated solutions of a square polynomial system.

[9] The sign of a permutation is +1 is an even number of swaps transform the permutation into the identity-permutation. Otherwise, the sign is −1.

Imported Theorem 2 (Consequence of [42]). *Let F be a prime order field. Let $f_1, \dots, f_k \in F[X_1, \dots, X_k]$ such that the degree of f_i is d_i. The number of $(x_1, \dots, x_k) \in F^k$ satisfying*

$$\forall 1 \leqslant i \leqslant k, \quad f_i(x_1, \dots, x_k) = 0 \qquad \text{and}$$
$$\det\Big(\mathbf{J}(f_1, \dots, f_k)\Big)(x_1, \dots, x_k) \neq 0.$$

is at most $(d_1 d_2 \cdots d_k)$.

Wooley's theorem covers the case of polynomial congruence equations $\mod p^s$, where $s \geqslant 1$. However, we import the result that suffices for our derivations.

Intuitively, a root with high multiplicity also occurs as a root of the Jacobian. On the other hand, the isolated roots occur only in the polynomials but *not* in the Jacobian. This theorem presented above, provides an easy-to-verify test to count the isolated roots of a square polynomial system.

4 Physical-Bit Witness Set as a Small Number of 2-GAPs

Let $1 \leqslant u \leqslant \lambda$ be an arbitrary index. Let $b \in \{0, 1\}$ be an arbitrary bit. We are interested in

$$A_{u,b} := \{a \in F \mid [a]_u = b\}.$$

We shall prove that for any u and b, $A_{u,b}$ is the disjoint union of (at most) λ number of 2-GAPs.

We first show that the prime field F can be partitioned as λ number of most-significant-bit-fixing sets, which is defined as follows.

Definition 8 (Most-significant-bit-fixing Set). *A set $S \subseteq F$ is called* most-significant-bit-fixing set *(MSB-fixing set) if there exists an index $1 \leqslant i^* \leqslant \lambda$ and a fixing $a_\lambda, a_{\lambda-1}, \dots, a_{i^*}$ such that S is identical to the following set.*

$$\left\{b \in \{0,1\}^\lambda \;\middle|\; \forall i^* \leqslant i \leqslant \lambda,\ [b]_i = a_i\right\}.$$

For example, when $\lambda = 5$, the set $S = 01\{0, 1\}^3$ (i.e., the bit-strings corresponding to the elements in the set $\{8, 9, 10, \dots, 15\}$) is an MSB-fixing set.

Given a prime field F, Fig. 3 demonstrates how to partition it as most significant bit-fixing sets. Easily, one can verify that $F_\lambda, F_{\lambda-1}, \dots, F_1$ are all MSB-fixing sets. For example, when $\lambda = 5$ and $p = 29$, the binary representations of the elements in $\{0, 1, \dots, 28\}$ partitions into subsets $0\{0, 1\}^4$, $10\{0, 1\}^3$, $110\{0, 1\}^2$, and $\{11100\}$.

Now, given $A_{u,b}$, for $0 \leqslant i \leqslant \lambda$, define

$$A_i := A_{u,b} \cap F_i.$$

One can verify that A_i consists of all bit-strings such that the following conditions hold simutaneously. (1) Some of most significant bits are fixed, (2) the uth

```
procedure PARTITION(F)
    Let index = λ.
    ∀i ∈ {1, 2, ..., λ}, let a_i = ⊥.
    while index > 1 do
        if ∃b ∈ F such that (1) ∀index + 1 ⩽ j ⩽ λ, [b]_j = a_j AND (2) [b]_index = 1 then
            F_index := { b | ∀index + 1 ⩽ j ⩽ λ, [b]_j = a_j and [b]_index = 0 }
            a_index = 1
        else
            F_index := ∅
            a_index = 0
        end if
        index = index − 1
    end while
    Until this point, a_λ, a_{λ−1}, ..., a_2 are fixed. a_1 is still undetermined.
    Let a^(0) be the integer whose binary representation is a_λ, a_{λ−1}, ..., a_2, 0.
    Let a^(1) be the integer whose binary representation is a_λ, a_{λ−1}, ..., a_2, 1.
    if a^(1) ⩽ p − 1 then
        F_1 := {a^(0), a^(1)}
    else
        F_1 := {a^(0)}
    end if
    return F_λ, F_{λ−1}, ..., F_1
end procedure
```

Fig. 3. Given a finite field F, this procedure partitions F into MSB-fixing sets $F_\lambda, F_{\lambda-1}, \ldots, F_1$.

least significant bit is fixed to b, and (3) finally, all the remaining positions are uniformly random. Continuing with the example above, the set $S_{2,0}$ is the subset of elements in S with their 2-nd LSB fixed to 0. That is, $S_{2,0} = 01\{0,1\}0\{0,1\}$, the binary representation of elements in the set $\{8, 9, 12, 13\}$. Therefore, one can write A_i as

$$A_i = \{a_0 + h_1 + a_2 h_2 \,:\, 0 \leqslant h_i < H_i \text{ for } i = 1, 2\ \},$$

for some a_0, a_2, H_1, and H_2 such that $a_2 = 2H_1$ and $a_2 H_2 < p$. For example, the elements whose binary representation are in the set $S_{2,0}$ above can be expressed as the proper 2-GAP $8+\{0,1\}+\{0,4\}$. We have the following theorem regarding the ℓ_1-norm of the Fourier coefficient of such special type of 2-GAP sets.

Theorem 2. *Let p be a prime and*

$$S = \{a_0 + h_1 + a_2 h_2 \,:\, 0 \leqslant h_i < H_i \text{ for } i = 1, 2\},$$

for some a_0, a_2, H_1, and H_2 such that $a_2 = 2H_1$ and $a_2 H_2 < p$. Then

$$\sum_{\alpha \in F} \left| \widehat{\mathbb{1}_S}(\alpha) \right| \leqslant (1 + o(1)) \cdot \left(\frac{2}{\pi}\right)^2 \cdot \log(H_1) \log(H_2).$$

We defer the proof of this theorem to the full version. This theorem immediately implies the following corollary.

Corollary 1. *For any index* $1 \leqslant u \leqslant \lambda$ *and bit* $b \in \{0,1\}$,

$$\sum_{\alpha \in F} \left| \widehat{\mathbb{1}_{A_{u,b}}}(\alpha) \right| \leqslant (1+o(1)) \cdot \frac{1}{\pi^2} \cdot (\log p)^2 \cdot \lambda.$$

Proof. We have

$$\begin{aligned}
\sum_{\alpha \in F} \left| \widehat{\mathbb{1}_{A_{u,b}}} \right| &\leqslant \sum_{\alpha \in F} \sum_{i=1}^{\lambda} \left| \widehat{\mathbb{1}_{A_i}} \right| && \text{(Triangle inequality)} \\
&= \sum_{i=1}^{\lambda} \sum_{\alpha \in F} \left| \widehat{\mathbb{1}_{A_i}} \right| \\
&\leqslant \sum_{i=1}^{\lambda} (1+\mathrm{o}(1)) \cdot \left(\frac{2}{\pi}\right)^2 \cdot \log(H_1)\log(H_2) && \text{(Theorem 2)} \\
&= (1+\mathrm{o}(1)) \cdot \left(\frac{2}{\pi}\right)^2 \cdot \log(H_1)\log(H_2) \cdot \lambda \\
&\leqslant (1+\mathrm{o}(1)) \cdot \left(\frac{2}{\pi}\right)^2 \cdot \left(\frac{\log(H_1)+\log(H_2)}{2}\right)^2 \cdot \lambda \\
& && \text{(AM-GM inequality)} \\
&< (1+\mathrm{o}(1)) \cdot \frac{1}{\pi^2} \cdot (\log p)^2 \cdot \lambda
\end{aligned}$$

The last inequality uses the fact that $H_1 \cdot H_2 < p$.

5 Physical-Bit Leakage on Shamir Secret Sharing

In this section, we prove the following theorems.

Theorem 3. *For any* $\varepsilon > 0$, *the following bound holds.*

$$\Pr_{\vec{X}}\left[\mathsf{ShamirSS}(n,k,\vec{X}) \text{ is not an } [\![n,k,1,\varepsilon]\!]_F\text{-}LLRSS\right] \lesssim \frac{1}{\varepsilon} \cdot \frac{2^n \cdot (\log p)^{3n} \cdot \lambda^n \cdot (k-1)!}{\pi^{2n} \cdot (p-n)^{k-1}}.$$

We emphasize that $\vec{X}$ is the uniform distribution over the set of all n-tuple of unique evaluation places in F^*.

Before we present the proof of this theorem, let us first interpret it through various parameter settings.

Corollary 2. *Let* $0 < d < \ln 2$ *be an arbitrary constant. There exists a (slightly) super-linear function* $P(\cdot,\cdot)$ *such that the following holds. For any number of parties* $n \in \mathbb{N}$, *reconstruction threshold* $2 \leqslant k \in \mathbb{N}$, *and insecurity tolerance* $\varepsilon = 2^{-t}$, *if the number of bits* λ *needed to represent the order of the prime-field*

F satisfies $\lambda > P(n/k, t/k)$, then $\mathsf{ShamirSS}(n, k, \vec{X})$ *is an* $[\![n, k, 1, \varepsilon]\!]_F$*-LLRSS with probability (at least)* $1 - \exp(-d \cdot (k-1)\lambda)$.

In particular, the (slightly super-linear) function $P(n/k, t/k) = d' \cdot \left(\frac{n}{k} + \frac{t}{k}\right) \cdot \log^2\left(\frac{n}{k} + \frac{t}{k}\right)$ *suffices, for an appropriate universal positive constant* d'.

In fact, our result can be generalized to multiple-bit physical leakage, which is summarized as follows.

Theorem 4. *For any $\varepsilon > 0$, for any positive integer m, the following bound holds.*

$$\Pr_{\vec{X}}\left[\mathsf{ShamirSS}(n, k, \vec{X}) \textit{ is not an } [\![n, k, m, \varepsilon]\!]_F\textit{-LLRSS}\right]$$
$$\lesssim \frac{1}{\varepsilon} \cdot \binom{\log p}{m}^n \cdot \frac{2^{mn} \cdot (\log p)^{2mn} \cdot \lambda^{mn} \cdot (k-1)!}{\pi^{2n} \cdot (p-n)^{k-1}}.$$

We remark that this result extends to the setting that m_i bits are leaked from the ith share for $i \in \{1, 2, \ldots, n\}$. In this case, the probability that $\mathsf{ShamirSS}(n, k, \vec{X})$ is not leakage resilient is bounded by

$$\frac{1}{\varepsilon} \cdot \binom{\log p}{m_1}\binom{\log p}{m_2} \cdots \binom{\log p}{m_n} \cdot \frac{2^M \cdot (\log p)^{2M} \cdot \lambda^M \cdot (k-1)!}{\pi^{2n} \cdot (p-n)^{k-1}},$$

where $M = \sum_{i=1}^{n} m_i$.

The proof of Theorem 4 is analogous to the proof of Theorem 3. Hence, we omit the proof of Theorem 4 and refer the reader to the full version for details.

Similarly, we interpret Theorem 4 as follows.

Corollary 3. *Let $0 < d < \ln 2$ be an arbitrary constant. There exists a (slightly) super-linear function $P(\cdot, \cdot)$ such that the following holds. For any number of parties $n \in \mathbb{N}$, reconstruction threshold $2 \leqslant k \in \mathbb{N}$, number of bits leaked from each share $m \in \mathbb{N}$, and insecurity tolerance $\varepsilon = 2^{-t}$, there exists $\lambda_0 = P(mn/k, t/k)$ such that if the number of bits λ needed to represent the order of the prime-field F satisfies $\lambda > \lambda_0$, then* $\mathsf{ShamirSS}(n, k, \vec{X})$ *is an* $[\![n, k, m, \varepsilon]\!]_F$*-LLRSS with probability (at least)* $1 - \exp(-d \cdot (k-1)\lambda)$.

In particular, function $P(mn/k, t/k) = d' \cdot \left(\frac{mn}{k} + \frac{t}{k}\right) \cdot \log^2\left(\frac{mn}{k} + \frac{t}{k}\right)$, *for an appropriate universal positive constant d', suffices.*

On the other hand, one can also interpret Theorem 4 as follows.

Corollary 4. *Let $0 < d < \ln 2$ be an arbitrary constant. For any number of parties $n \in \mathbb{N}$, reconstruction threshold $2 \leqslant k \in \mathbb{N}$, and insecurity tolerance $\varepsilon = 2^{-t}$, there exists $\lambda_0 = (t/k) \cdot \log(t/k)$ such that if the number of bits λ needed to represent the order of the prime-field F satisfies $\lambda > \lambda_0$, then for all m such that*

$$m \leqslant \frac{k\lambda}{n \log^2 \lambda},$$

it holds that $\mathsf{ShamirSS}(n, k, \vec{X})$ *is an* $[\![n, k, m, \varepsilon]\!]_F$*-LLRSS with probability (at least)* $1 - \exp(-d \cdot (k-1)\lambda)$.

5.1 Claims Needed to Prove Theorem 3

We prove Theorem 3 by proving the following claims.

In the first claim, we prove an upper bound on the statistical distance between the leakage of secrets s_0 and s_1. We emphasize that this upper bound is *not sensitive* to the actually secrets, but only sensitive to the leakage function $\vec{\tau}$ and evaluation places $\vec{X}$.

Claim 1. *Let* $(\mathsf{Share}^{\vec{X}}, \mathsf{Rec}^{\vec{X}})$ *be an* $(n, k, \vec{X})$ *Shamir secret sharing. Let* $C_{\vec{X}}$ *be the set of all possible secret shares of the secret* 0.[10] *Let* $C_{\vec{X}}^{\perp}$ *be the dual code of* $C_{\vec{X}}$. *For every* 1*-bit physical leakage function family* $\vec{\tau} = (\tau_1, \tau_2, \ldots, \tau_n)$, *for every leakage* $\vec{\ell} \in \{0,1\}^n$, *and for every pair of secrets* s_0 *and* s_1, *the following inequality holds.*

$$\mathsf{SD}\left(\vec{\tau}\left(\mathsf{Share}^{\vec{X}}(s_0)\right), \vec{\tau}\left(\mathsf{Share}^{\vec{X}}(s_1)\right)\right) \leqslant \sum_{\vec{\ell}\in\{0,1\}^n} \sum_{\vec{\alpha}\in C_{\vec{X}}^{\perp}\setminus\{0\}} \left(\prod_{i=1}^{n} \left|\widehat{\mathbb{1}_{\ell_i}}(\alpha_i)\right|\right).$$

Here, we abuse the notation and use $\mathbb{1}_{\ell_i}$ to stand for the indicator function $\mathbb{1}_{\tau_i^{-1}(\ell_i)}$. That is, $\mathbb{1}_{\ell_i}(s_i) = 1$ if $\tau_i(s_i) = \ell_i$ and $\mathbb{1}_{\ell_i}(s_i) = 0$ otherwise.

Our next claim states that the average of the upper bound proven in Claim 1 over all evaluation places $\vec{X}$ is sufficiently small.

Claim 2. *Let* $(\mathsf{Share}^{\vec{X}}, \mathsf{Rec}^{\vec{X}})$ *be an* $(n, k, \vec{X})$ *Shamir secret sharing. For every* 1*-bit physical leakage function family* $\vec{\tau} = (\tau_1, \tau_2, \ldots, \tau_n)$, *the following inequality holds.*

$$\mathop{\mathbb{E}}_{\vec{X}}\left[\sum_{\vec{\ell}\in\{0,1\}^n} \sum_{\vec{\alpha}\in C_{\vec{X}}^{\perp}\setminus\{0\}} \left(\prod_{i=1}^{n} \left|\widehat{\mathbb{1}_{\ell_i}}(\alpha_i)\right|\right)\right] \lesssim \frac{2^n \cdot (\log p)^{2n} \cdot \lambda^n \cdot (k-1)!}{\pi^{2n} \cdot (p-n)^{k-1}}.$$

We defer the proofs to Sect. 5.3 and Sect. 5.4. We shall first present why these claims imply Theorem 3.

[10] By Observation 1, $C_{\vec{X}}$ is an $(n, k-1, \vec{X}, \vec{X})$-GRS with generator matrix

$$\begin{pmatrix} X_1 & X_2 & \cdots & X_n \\ X_1^2 & X_2^2 & \cdots & X_n^2 \\ \vdots & \vdots & \ddots & \vdots \\ X_1^{k-1} & X_2^{k-1} & \cdots & X_n^{k-1} \end{pmatrix}.$$

5.2 Proof of Theorem 3 Using Claim 1 and Claim 2

By definition, we have[11]

$$
\begin{aligned}
&\Pr_{\vec{X}}\left[\mathsf{ShamirSS}(n,k,\vec{X}) \text{ is } \textit{not} \text{ an } [\![n,k,1,\varepsilon]\!]_F\text{-LLRSS}\right] \\
&= \Pr_{\vec{X}}\left[\exists s_0, s_1, \vec{\tau} \text{ s.t. } \mathsf{SD}\left(\vec{\tau}(\mathsf{Share}^{\vec{X}}(s_0))\ ,\ \vec{\tau}(\mathsf{Share}^{\vec{X}}(s_1)\right) \geqslant \varepsilon\right] \\
&\leqslant \Pr_{\vec{X}}\left[\exists s_0, s_1, \vec{\tau} \text{ s.t. } \sum_{\vec{\ell}\in\{0,1\}^n}\ \sum_{\vec{\alpha}\in C_{\vec{X}}^{\perp}\setminus\{0\}} \left(\prod_{i=1}^{n}\left|\widehat{\mathbb{1}_{\ell_i}}(\alpha_i)\right|\right) \geqslant \varepsilon\right] && \text{(Claim 1)} \\
&= \Pr_{\vec{X}}\left[\exists \vec{\tau} \text{ s.t. } \sum_{\vec{\ell}\in\{0,1\}^n}\ \sum_{\vec{\alpha}\in C_{\vec{X}}^{\perp}\setminus\{0\}} \left(\prod_{i=1}^{n}\left|\widehat{\mathbb{1}_{\ell_i}}(\alpha_i)\right|\right) \geqslant \varepsilon\right] \\
&\leqslant \sum_{\vec{\tau}} \Pr_{\vec{X}}\left[\sum_{\vec{\ell}\in\{0,1\}^n}\ \sum_{\vec{\alpha}\in C_{\vec{X}}^{\perp}\setminus\{0\}} \left(\prod_{i=1}^{n}\left|\widehat{\mathbb{1}_{\ell_i}}(\alpha_i)\right|\right) \geqslant \varepsilon\right] && \text{(Union bound)} \\
&\lesssim \sum_{\vec{\tau}} \frac{1}{\varepsilon}\cdot\frac{2^n\cdot(\log p)^{2n}\cdot\lambda^n\cdot(k-1)!}{\pi^{2n}\cdot(p-n)^{k-1}} && \text{(Markov's Inequality and Claim 2)} \\
&= (\log p)^n\cdot\frac{1}{\varepsilon}\cdot\frac{2^n\cdot(\log p)^{2n}\cdot\lambda^n\cdot(k-1)!}{\pi^{2n}\cdot(p-n)^{k-1}} \\
&\lesssim (\log p)^n\cdot\frac{1}{\varepsilon}\cdot\frac{2^n\cdot(\log p)^{2n}\cdot\lambda^n\cdot k!}{\pi^{2n}\cdot p^{k-1}} \\
&\sim \frac{k!}{\varepsilon}\cdot\left(\frac{2\lambda(\log p)^3}{\pi^2}\right)^n\cdot\frac{1}{2^{\lambda(k-1)}}.
\end{aligned}
$$

This completes the proof of Theorem 3.

5.3 Proof of Claim 1

We start with the following calculation, which can be proven using standard techniques in Fourier analysis. We refer the readers to the full version for a proof.

Claim 3. *For any leakage $\vec{\ell}\in\{0,1\}^n$, we have*

$$\Pr_{\vec{s}\leftarrow\mathsf{Share}^{\vec{X}}(s)}\left[\vec{\tau}(\vec{s})=\vec{\ell}\right] = \sum_{\vec{\alpha}\in C_{\vec{X}}^{\perp}} \left(\prod_{i=1}^{n}\widehat{\mathbb{1}_{\ell_i}}(\alpha_i)\right)\omega^{s(\alpha_1+\cdots+\alpha_n)}.$$

[11] We note that the $\lambda = \log_2 p$. However, in Theorem 2, the logrithm is natural log. Hence, we did not merge λ with $\log p$.

Now, given Claim 3, Claim 1 can be proven as follows.

$$\begin{aligned}
&\mathsf{SD}\left(\vec{\tau}\left(\mathsf{Share}^{\vec{X}}(s_0)\right), \vec{\tau}\left(\mathsf{Share}^{\vec{X}}(s_1)\right)\right)\\
&= \frac{1}{2}\sum_{\vec{\ell}\in\{0,1\}^n}\left|\Pr_{\vec{s}\leftarrow\mathsf{Share}^{\vec{X}}(s_0)}\left[\vec{\tau}(\vec{s})=\vec{\ell}\right] - \Pr_{\vec{s}\leftarrow\mathsf{Share}^{\vec{X}}(s_1)}\left[\vec{\tau}(\vec{s})=\vec{\ell}\right]\right|\\
&= \frac{1}{2}\sum_{\vec{\ell}\in\{0,1\}^n}\left|\sum_{\vec{\alpha}\in C_{\vec{X}}^{\perp}\setminus\{0\}}\left(\prod_{i=1}^{n}\widehat{\mathbb{1}_{\ell_i}}(\alpha_i)\right)\left(\omega^{s_0(\alpha_1+\cdots+\alpha_n)} - \omega^{s_1(\alpha_1+\cdots+\alpha_n)}\right)\right| && \text{(Claim 3)}\\
&\leqslant \frac{1}{2}\sum_{\vec{\ell}\in\{0,1\}^n}\sum_{\vec{\alpha}\in C_{\vec{X}}^{\perp}\setminus\{0\}}\left(\prod_{i=1}^{n}\left|\widehat{\mathbb{1}_{\ell_i}}(\alpha_i)\right|\right)\left|\omega^{s_0(\alpha_1+\cdots+\alpha_n)} - \omega^{s_1(\alpha_1+\cdots+\alpha_n)}\right| && \text{(Triangle inequality)}\\
&\leqslant \frac{1}{2}\sum_{\vec{\ell}\in\{0,1\}^n}\sum_{\vec{\alpha}\in C_{\vec{X}}^{\perp}\setminus\{0\}}\left(\prod_{i=1}^{n}\left|\widehat{\mathbb{1}_{\ell_i}}(\alpha_i)\right|\right)\cdot 2\\
&= \sum_{\vec{\ell}\in\{0,1\}^n}\sum_{\vec{\alpha}\in C_{\vec{X}}^{\perp}\setminus\{0\}}\left(\prod_{i=1}^{n}\left|\widehat{\mathbb{1}_{\ell_i}}(\alpha_i)\right|\right)
\end{aligned}$$

5.4 Proof of Claim 2

The proof of Claim 2 crucially relies on the following claim, which bounds the number of solutions to a polynomial system. We state and prove this claim first.

Claim 4. *Let $\vec{\alpha} = (\alpha_1, \alpha_2, \ldots, \alpha_n)$ be a non-zero vector in F^n. Then the number of solutions $\vec{X} = (X_1, X_2, \ldots, X_n) \in (F^*)^n$ of the equation $G_{\vec{X}} \cdot \vec{\alpha}^T = \vec{0}$ such that $X_i \neq X_j$ for every $1 \leqslant i < j \leqslant n$ is at most $(p-1)(p-2)\cdots(p-(n-k+1))\cdot(k-1)!$. Here, $G_{\vec{X}}$ stands for the generator matrix of $C_{\vec{X}}$, which is*

$$G_{\vec{X}} = \begin{pmatrix} X_1 & X_2 & \cdots & X_n \\ X_1^2 & X_2^2 & \cdots & X_n^2 \\ \vdots & \vdots & \ddots & \vdots \\ X_1^{k-1} & X_2^{k-1} & \cdots & X_n^{k-1} \end{pmatrix}.$$

Proof. Note that $G_{\vec{X}} \cdot \vec{\alpha}^T = \vec{0}$ implies that $\vec{\alpha} \in C_{\vec{X}}^{\perp}$. By Theorem 1, we know $C_{\vec{X}}^{\perp}$ has distance k, which implies that there are at least k non-zero coordinates in $\vec{\alpha}$. Therefore, without loss of generality, assume $\alpha_i \neq 0$ for every $1 \leqslant i \leqslant k-1$. Now, for $i = k, \ldots, n$, we fix X_i to be arbitrary distinct non-zero values . Note that there are $(p-1)(p-2)\ldots(p-(n-k+1))$ possible ways of doing this fixing.

Let $c_i := \sum_{j=k+1}^{n} \alpha_j X_j^i$ for $i = 1, 2, \ldots, k-1$. We can rewrite the equation $G_{\vec{X}} \cdot \vec{\alpha}^T = \vec{0}$ as a system of polynomial equations as follows.

$$\begin{aligned}
f_1(X_1, X_2, \ldots, X_{k-1}) &:= \alpha_1 X_1 + \alpha_2 X_2 + \ldots + \alpha_{k-1} X_{k-1} + c_1 = 0\\
f_2(X_1, X_2, \ldots, X_{k-1}) &:= \alpha_1 X_1^2 + \alpha_2 X_2^2 + \ldots + \alpha_{k-1} X_{k-1}^2 + c_2 = 0\\
&\vdots\\
f_{k-1}(X_1, X_2, \ldots, X_{k-1}) &:= \alpha_1 X_1^{k-1} + \alpha_2 X_2^{k-1} + \ldots + \alpha_{k-1} X_{k-1}^{k-1} + c_{k-1} = 0
\end{aligned}$$

Since $\alpha_i \neq 0$, it is a square polynomials system with $\deg(f_i) = i$, for every $1 \leqslant i \leqslant k-1$. Next, to apply Imported Theorem 2, we shall show that

$$\det\Big(\mathbf{J}(f_1, f_2, \ldots, f_{k-1})\Big)(X_1, X_2, \ldots, X_{k-1}) \neq 0 \text{ if } X_i \neq X_j \text{ for every } i \neq j.$$

We have

$$\mathbf{J}\Big(f_1, f_2, \ldots, f_{k-1}\Big)(X_1, X_2, \ldots, X_{k-1}) = \begin{pmatrix} \alpha_1 & 2\alpha_1 X_1 & \cdots & (k-1)\alpha_1 X_1^{k-2} \\ \alpha_2 & 2\alpha_2 X_2 & \cdots & (k-1)\alpha_2 X_2^{k-2} \\ \vdots & \vdots & \ddots & \vdots \\ \alpha_{k-1} & 2\alpha_{k-1} X_{k-1} & \cdots & (k-1)\alpha_{k-1} X_{k-1}^{k-2} \end{pmatrix}$$

By the properties of determinant,

$$\begin{aligned}
&\det\Big(\mathbf{J}\left(f_1, f_2, \ldots, f_{k-1}\right)\Big)(X_1, X_2, \ldots, X_{k-1})\\
&= \left(\prod_{i=1}^{k-1} \alpha_i\right) \cdot \det \begin{pmatrix} 1 & 2X_1 & \cdots & (k-1)X_1^{k-2} \\ 1 & 2X_2 & \cdots & (k-1)X_2^{k-2} \\ \vdots & \vdots & \ddots & \vdots \\ 1 & 2X_{k-1} & \cdots & (k-1)X_{k-1}^{k-2} \end{pmatrix}\\
&= \left(\prod_{i=1}^{k-1} \alpha_i\right) (k-1)! \cdot \det \begin{pmatrix} 1 & X_1 & \cdots & X_1^{k-1} \\ 1 & X_2 & \cdots & X_2^{k-1} \\ \vdots & \vdots & \ddots & \vdots \\ 1 & X_{k-1} & \cdots & X_{k-1}^{k-1} \end{pmatrix}\\
&\neq 0,
\end{aligned}$$

since α_i are non-zeros and the Vandermonde matrix is full-rank. By Imported Theorem 2, there are at most $(k-1)!$ solutions for the above square polynomial system. Since there are total $(p-1)(p-2)\ldots(p-(n-k+1))$ possible ways of fixing $X_k, X_{k+1}, \ldots, X_n$, the number of solutions of the equation $G_{\vec{X}} \cdot \vec{\alpha}^T = \vec{0}$ is at most $(p-1)(p-2)\ldots(p-(n-k+1)) \cdot (k-1)!$, which completes the proof of Claim 4.

Given Claim 4, we are ready to prove Claim 2 as follows.

$$\begin{aligned}
&\mathop{\mathrm{E}}_{\vec{X}}\left[\sum_{\vec{\ell}\in\{0,1\}^n}\sum_{\vec{\alpha}\in C_{\vec{X}}^{\perp}\setminus\{0\}}\left(\prod_{i=1}^{n}\left|\widehat{\mathbb{1}_{\ell_i}}(\alpha_i)\right|\right)\right]\\
&=\sum_{\vec{\ell}\in\{0,1\}^n}\mathop{\mathrm{E}}_{\vec{X}}\left[\sum_{\vec{\alpha}\in C_{\vec{X}}^{\perp}\setminus\{0\}}\left(\prod_{i=1}^{n}\left|\widehat{\mathbb{1}_{\ell_i}}(\alpha_i)\right|\right)\right]\\
&=\sum_{\vec{\ell}\in\{0,1\}^n}\sum_{\vec{\alpha}\in F^n\setminus\{0\}}\left(\prod_{i=1}^{n}\left|\widehat{\mathbb{1}_{\ell_i}}(\alpha_i)\right|\right)\cdot\Pr_{\vec{X}}\left[\vec{\alpha}\in C_{\vec{X}}^{\perp}\right] && \text{(Linearity of expectation)}\\
&\leqslant\sum_{\vec{\ell}\in\{0,1\}^n}\sum_{\vec{\alpha}\in F^n\setminus\{0\}}\left(\prod_{i=1}^{n}\left|\widehat{\mathbb{1}_{\ell_i}}(\alpha_i)\right|\right)\cdot\frac{(p-1)(p-2)\cdots(p-(n-k+1))\cdot(k-1)!}{(p-1)(p-2)\cdots(p-n)} && \text{(Claim 4)}\\
&\leqslant\sum_{\vec{\ell}\in\{0,1\}^n}\prod_{i=1}^{n}\left(\sum_{\alpha_i\in F}\left|\widehat{\mathbb{1}_{\ell_i}}(\alpha_i)\right|\right)\cdot\frac{(k-1)!}{(p-(n-k+2))\cdots(p-n)}\\
&\leqslant\sum_{\vec{\ell}\in\{0,1\}^n}\left((1+o(1))\cdot\frac{1}{\pi^2}\cdot(\log p)^2\cdot\lambda\right)^n\cdot\frac{(k-1)!}{(p-(n-k+2))\cdots(p-n)} && \text{(Corollary 1)}\\
&\lesssim 2^n\cdot\frac{(\log p)^{2n}\cdot\lambda^n\cdot(k-1)!}{\pi^{2n}\cdot(p-n)^{k-1}}.
\end{aligned}$$

This gives us the desired upper bound.

6 Physical-Bit Leakage Attack on Shamir Secret-Sharing Scheme

Consider the Shamir secret-sharing scheme with $<k$ degree polynomials, where $k \in \{2,3\}$, for n parties over a prime field F of order $p > 2$. Fix a secret $s \in F$. Suppose the random polynomial used for secret-sharing is $f(X) \in F[X]/X^k$ such that $P(0) = s$.

Suppose $p = 1 \bmod k$, that is there exists a solution of the equation $Z^k - 1 = 0$ in the multiplicative group F^*. Let $\alpha \in F$ be such that $E := \{\alpha, \alpha^2, \ldots, \alpha^{k-1}, \alpha^k = 1\} \subseteq F^*$ be the multiplicative sub-group of order k containing all k solutions of the equation $Z^k - 1 = 0$.

Suppose $n \geqslant k$, and the evaluation places for the first k parties be $\{1, \alpha, \alpha^2, \ldots, \alpha^{k-1}\} \subseteq F^*$, respectively. Remaining evaluation places are inconsequential as we shall leak only one bit from the shares of only the first k parties.

Define $s_i := f(\alpha^i)$, for $1 \leqslant i \leqslant k$, to be the secret-share of party i. Observe that we have the following properties

1. The secret shares $s_1, \ldots, s_{k-1}$ are independently and uniformly random over the set F, and
2. The secret share $s_k = ks - (s_1 + \cdots + s_{k-1})$.

Let $0 \leqslant S_1, S_2, \ldots, S_k \leqslant p-1$ be the whole numbers (i.e., the set $\mathbb{N}_0 := \{0, 1, 2, \ldots\}$) corresponding to the elements $s_1, s_2, \ldots, s_k \in F$. Note that

$$E\left[S_1 + S_2 + \cdots + S_{k-1}\right] = \mu := (k-1)(p-1)/2 \in \mathbb{N}.$$

Define $I_{k,\Delta} := \{\Delta+1, \Delta+2, \ldots, \Delta+p\}$, where $\Delta := \mu - (p-1)/2 - 1$. For $k \in \{2, 3\}$, we note that[12]

$$\Pr\left[\sum_{i=1}^{k-1} S_i \in I_{k,\Delta}\right] \geqslant 0.75.$$

Express $\Delta = u \cdot p + \delta$, where $u \in \mathbb{N}_0$ (the set of all whole numbers), and $\delta \in \{0, 1, \ldots, p-1\}$. Define the secret $s := k^{-1}\delta \in F$.

Following technical claim, which holds for any secret $s \in F$, is key to our attack strategy.

Claim. (Parity of the "Parity of Shares"). Let $P \in \{0, 1\}$ represent the LSB (or, equivalently, the parity) of ks when expressed as a whole number. For $1 \leqslant i \leqslant k$, let $P_i \in \{0, 1\}$ represent the LSB (or, equivalently, the parity) of the secret share S_i. Define the following subsets of whole numbers

$$S_{\mathsf{same}} := \mathbb{N}_0 \cap \bigcup_{\substack{i \in \mathbb{Z} \\ i \text{ odd}}} [ip + ks + 1, (i+1)p + ks]$$

$$S_{\mathsf{diff}} := \mathbb{N}_0 \cap \bigcup_{\substack{i \in \mathbb{Z} \\ i \text{ even}}} [ip + ks + 1, (i+1)p + ks].$$

If $S_1 + S_2 + \cdots + S_{k-1} \in S_{\mathsf{same}}$, then $P_1 \oplus P_2 \oplus \cdots \oplus P_k = P$. Otherwise, if $S_1 + S_2 + \cdots + S_{k-1} \in S_{\mathsf{diff}}$, then $P_1 \oplus P_2 \oplus \cdots \oplus P_k = 1 \oplus P$.

Proof. Since $s_1 + s_2 + \cdots + s_k = ks$, we have

$$S_1 + S_2 + \cdots + S_k = ks + ip,$$

for some $i \in \mathbb{N}_0$.

Observe that $P_1 \oplus P_2 \oplus \cdots \oplus P_k$ is the parity of $S_1 + S_2 + \cdots + S_k$, which is identical to the parity of ks (i.e., P) if and only if i is even.

Finally, since $S_k \in \{0, 1, \ldots, p-1\}$, the constraint "$S_1+S_2+\cdots+S_k = ks+ip$ for some even i" is equivalent to

$$S_1 + S_2 + \cdots + S_{k-1} \in S_{\mathsf{same}}.$$

[12] One can explicit calculate the probability. When $k=2$, $\Pr\left[S_1 \in I_{2,\Delta}\right] = 1$. When $k=3$, $\Pr\left[S_1 + S_2 \in I_{3,\Delta}\right] = \frac{3}{4}\left(1 + \frac{1}{p} - \frac{1}{p^2}\right)$.

The above claim gives us an attack for the case $k = 3$ because of the following argument.

Fix $k = 3$, the parity of ks is exactly the parity (LSB) of secret s. Observe that if u is odd, then $I_{k,\Delta} \subseteq S_{\mathsf{same}}$. In this case, the parity $P_1 \oplus P_2 \oplus \cdots \oplus P_k$ is identical to the LSB of the secret with probability >0.75. Otherwise, if u is even then $I_{k,\Delta} \subseteq S_{\mathsf{diff}}$. In this case, the parity $P_1 \oplus P_2 \oplus \cdots \oplus P_k$ is the opposite to the LSB of the secret with probability >0.75. In any case, since the adversary knows u, she can predict the LSB of the secret with probability >0.75.

For a randomly chosen secret, on the other hand, one can predict the LSB (using the strategy above) only with probability (statistically close to) 0.5.

Remark 1. Let $\rho \in F$ be the primitive root of the equation $Z^p - 1 = 0$. That is, ρ is a generator for of the multiplicative group F^*. The discussion above holds for all evaluation places of the form

$$\left\{\rho^i \cdot \alpha, \rho^i \cdot \alpha^2, \ldots, \rho^i \cdot \alpha^k\right\},$$

where $i \in \{0, 1, \ldots, (p-1)/3\}$. More generally, let $G \subseteq F^*$ be the multiplicative subgroup formed by the roots of the equation $Z^k - 1 = 0$. Any coset F^*/G suffices for our purposes.

Consequently, there is not just one k-tuple of evaluation places that witnesses our attack. There are, in fact, $k! \cdot (p-1)/k$ such tuples that witness our attack.

Therefore, the following result holds.

Theorem 5. *Let F be a prime field of order $p > 2$. Consider any natural number n such that $p > n \geqslant k = 3$ and $p = 1 \mod k$. There exist distinct secrets $s^{(0)}, s^{(1)} \in F$, distinct evaluation places $X_1, \ldots, X_n \in F^*$, and one physical-bit local leakage function $\vec{\tau}$ such that, based on the leakage, an adversary can efficiently distinguish the secret being $s^{(0)}$ or $s^{(1)}$ with advantage $> 2 \cdot (0.75 - 0.5) = 0.5$.*

Remark 2. We emphasize that our attacker leaks one bit from the first k shares and tries to predict the secret based solely on this. In particular, we do not rely on the information regarding the remaining $n - k$ shares. Asymptotically, this approach is doomed to fail as k grows. As Benhamouda et al. [3] prove that, Shamir secret sharing is resilient to arbitrary one-bit leakage from each share, as long as $k \geqslant n - n^c$ for some small constant $c > 0$. Therefore, to find more devastating attacks, one has to utilize the fact that n is larger than k and we are leaking from every share.

6.1 Our Attack and Discrepancy of Irwin-Hall Distribution

Consider any $2 \leqslant k \in \mathbb{N}$ and prime $p = 1 \mod k$. The following analysis is for the case when $p \to \infty$.

Observe that S_i is uniformly random over the set $\{0, 1, \ldots, p-1\}$. Instead of S_i, we normalize this random variable and consider $\widehat{S}_i$ that is uniformly random over the set $[0,1) \subset \mathbb{R}$. Now, the random variable $S_1 + \cdots + S_{k-1}$ over whole numbers corresponds to the normalized distribution $\widehat{S}_1 + \cdots + \widehat{S}_{k-1}$ over the set $[0, k-1) \subset \mathbb{R}$. It is well-known that the sum of $(k-1)$ independent and uniform distributions over the unit interval $[0,1)$ is the Irwin-Hall distribution [18,23] with parameter $(k-1)$, represented by I_{k-1}.

Let $\delta \in [0,1)$ be an offset. Define the intervals (as a function of δ)

$$\widehat{S}_{\mathsf{same}} = (1+\delta, 2+\delta] \cup (3+\delta, 4+\delta] \cup (5+\delta, 6+\delta] \cup \cdots, \text{ and}$$
$$\widehat{S}_{\mathsf{diff}} = (\delta, 1+\delta] \cup (2+\delta, 3+\delta] \cup (4+\delta, 5+\delta] \cup \cdots.$$

Intuitively, these two sets correspond to the normalized S_{same} and S_{diff} sets defined above. The attack above corresponds to finding the offset

$$\delta^* := \operatorname*{argmax}_{\delta \in [0,1)} \left| \Pr\left[I_{k-1} \in \widehat{S}_{\mathsf{same}}\right] - \Pr\left[I_{k-1} \in \widehat{S}_{\mathsf{diff}}\right] \right|,$$

and the advantage corresponding to that attack is

$$\varepsilon^* := \max_{\delta \in [0,1)} \left| \Pr\left[I_{k-1} \in \widehat{S}_{\mathsf{same}}\right] - \Pr\left[I_{k-1} \in \widehat{S}_{\mathsf{diff}}\right] \right|.$$

Intuitively, this offset δ^* witnesses the largest discrepancy and, in turn, determines the most vulnerable secret.

Definition 9 (Discrepancy of a Probability Distribution). *Let X be a real-valued random variable. The* discrepancy *of the random variable X, represented by* $\mathsf{disc}(X)$*, is*

$$\mathsf{disc}(X) := \max_{\delta \in [0,1)} |2 \cdot Pr[X \in I(\delta)] - 1|,$$

where $I(\delta)$ is the set $\delta + 2\mathbb{Z} + (0,1]$.

Then, $\mathsf{disc}(I_{k-1})$ represents the advantage of our attack presented above, as $p \to \infty$.

References

1. Aggarwal, D., et al.: Stronger leakage-resilient and non-malleable secret sharing schemes for general access structures. In: Boldyreva, A., Micciancio, D. (eds.) CRYPTO 2019. LNCS, vol. 11693, pp. 510–539. Springer, Cham (2019). https://doi.org/10.1007/978-3-030-26951-7_18
2. Badrinarayanan, S., Srinivasan, A.: Revisiting non-malleable secret sharing. In: Ishai, Y., Rijmen, V. (eds.) EUROCRYPT 2019. LNCS, vol. 11476, pp. 593–622. Springer, Cham (2019). https://doi.org/10.1007/978-3-030-17653-2_20
3. Benhamouda, F., Degwekar, A., Ishai, Y., Rabin, T.: On the local leakage resilience of linear secret sharing schemes. In: Shacham, H., Boldyreva, A. (eds.) CRYPTO 2018. LNCS, vol. 10991, pp. 531–561. Springer, Cham (2018). https://doi.org/10.1007/978-3-319-96884-1_18

4. Block, A.R., Gupta, D., Maji, H.K., Nguyen, H.H.: Secure computation using leaky correlations (asymptotically optimal constructions). In: Beimel, A., Dziembowski, S. (eds.) TCC 2018. LNCS, vol. 11240, pp. 36–65. Springer, Cham (2018). https://doi.org/10.1007/978-3-030-03810-6_2
5. Block, A.R., Maji, H.K., Nguyen, H.H.: Secure computation based on leaky correlations: high resilience setting. In: Katz, J., Shacham, H. (eds.) CRYPTO 2017. LNCS, vol. 10402, pp. 3–32. Springer, Cham (2017). https://doi.org/10.1007/978-3-319-63715-0_1
6. Bogdanov, A., Ishai, Y., Srinivasan, A.: Unconditionally secure computation against low-complexity leakage. In: Boldyreva, A., Micciancio, D. (eds.) CRYPTO 2019. LNCS, vol. 11693, pp. 387–416. Springer, Cham (2019). https://doi.org/10.1007/978-3-030-26951-7_14
7. Candel, G., Géraud-Stewart, R., Naccache, D.: How to compartment secrets. In: Laurent, M., Giannetsos, T. (eds.) WISTP 2019. LNCS, vol. 12024, pp. 3–11. Springer, Cham (2020). https://doi.org/10.1007/978-3-030-41702-4_1
8. Cascudo, I., Damgård, I., Farràs, O., Ranellucci, S.: Resource-efficient OT combiners with active security. In: Kalai, Y., Reyzin, L. (eds.) TCC 2017. LNCS, vol. 10678, pp. 461–486. Springer, Cham (2017). https://doi.org/10.1007/978-3-319-70503-3_15
9. Chattopadhyay, E., et al.: Extractors and secret sharing against bounded collusion protocols. In: 61st FOCS, pp. 1226–1242. IEEE Computer Society Press, November 2020
10. Chen, X., Kayal, N., Wigderson, A.: Partial derivatives in arithmetic complexity and beyond. Found. Trends Theor. Comput. Sci. **6**(1–2), 1–138 (2011). https://doi.org/10.1561/0400000043
11. Dau, H., Duursma, I.M., Kiah, H.M., Milenkovic, O.: Repairing Reed-Solomon codes with multiple erasures. IEEE Trans. Inf. Theory **64**(10), 6567–6582 (2018)
12. Duc, A., Dziembowski, S., Faust, S.: Unifying leakage models: from probing attacks to noisy leakage. In: Nguyen, P.Q., Oswald, E. (eds.) EUROCRYPT 2014. LNCS, vol. 8441, pp. 423–440. Springer, Heidelberg (2014). https://doi.org/10.1007/978-3-642-55220-5_24
13. Franklin, M.K., Yung, M.: Communication complexity of secure computation (extended abstract). In: 24th ACM STOC, pp. 699–710. ACM Press, May 1992
14. Goyal, V., Kumar, A.: Non-malleable secret sharing. In: Diakonikolas, I., Kempe, D., Henzinger, M. (eds.) 50th ACM STOC, pp. 685–698. ACM Press, June 2018
15. Guruswami, V., Wootters, M.: Repairing Reed-Solomon codes. In: Wichs, D., Mansour, Y. (eds.) 48th ACM STOC, pp. 216–226. ACM Press, June 2016
16. Guruswami, V., Wootters, M.: Repairing Reed-Solomon codes. IEEE Trans. Inf. Theory **63**(9), 5684–5698 (2017)
17. Hall, J.I.: Notes on Coding Theory (2015). https://users.math.msu.edu/users/halljo/classes/codenotes/coding-notes.html
18. Hall, P.: The distribution of means for samples of size n drawn from a population in which the variate takes values between 0 and 1, all such values being equally probable. Biometrika **19**, 240–245 (1927)
19. Harnik, D., Ishai, Y., Kushilevitz, E., Nielsen, J.B.: OT-combiners via secure computation. In: Canetti, R. (ed.) TCC 2008. LNCS, vol. 4948, pp. 393–411. Springer, Heidelberg (2008). https://doi.org/10.1007/978-3-540-78524-8_22
20. Harnik, D., Kilian, J., Naor, M., Reingold, O., Rosen, A.: On robust combiners for oblivious transfer and other primitives. In: Cramer, R. (ed.) EUROCRYPT 2005. LNCS, vol. 3494, pp. 96–113. Springer, Heidelberg (2005). https://doi.org/10.1007/11426639_6

21. Hazay, C. Ishai, Y., Marcedone, A. Venkitasubramaniam, M.: LevioSA: lightweight secure arithmetic computation. In: Cavallaro, L. Kinder, J., Wang, X., Katz, J. (eds.) ACM CCS 2019, pp. 327–344. ACM Press, November 2019
22. Hazay, C., Venkitasubramaniam, M., Weiss, M.: The price of active security in cryptographic protocols. In: Canteaut, A., Ishai, Y. (eds.) EUROCRYPT 2020. LNCS, vol. 12106, pp. 184–215. Springer, Cham (2020). https://doi.org/10.1007/978-3-030-45724-2_7
23. Irwin, J.O.: On the frequency distribution of the means of samples from a population having any law of frequency with finite moments, with special reference to Pearson's type II. Biometrika **19**, 225–239 (1927)
24. Ishai, Y., Kushilevitz, E., Ostrovsky, R., Sahai, A.: Extracting correlations. In: 50th FOCS, pp. 261–270. IEEE Computer Society Press, October 2009
25. Ishai, Y., Maji, H.K., Sahai, A., Wullschleger, J.: Single-use ot combiners with near-optimal resilience. In: 2014 IEEE International Symposium on Information Theory, Honolulu, HI, USA, 29 June–4 July 2014, pp. 1544–1548. IEEE (2014)
26. Ishai, Y., Prabhakaran, M., Sahai, A., Wagner, D.: Private circuits II: keeping secrets in tamperable circuits. In: Vaudenay, S. (ed.) EUROCRYPT 2006. LNCS, vol. 4004, pp. 308–327. Springer, Heidelberg (2006). https://doi.org/10.1007/11761679_19
27. Ishai, Y., Sahai, A., Wagner, D.: Private circuits: securing hardware against probing attacks. In: Boneh, D. (ed.) CRYPTO 2003. LNCS, vol. 2729, pp. 463–481. Springer, Heidelberg (2003). https://doi.org/10.1007/978-3-540-45146-4_27
28. Kalai, Y.T., Reyzin, L.: A survey of leakage-resilient cryptography. In: Goldreich, O. (ed.) Providing Sound Foundations for Cryptography: On the Work of Shafi Goldwasser and Silvio Micali, pp 727–794. ACM (2019)
29. Kumar, A., Meka, R., Sahai, A.: Leakage-resilient secret sharing against colluding parties. In: Zuckerman, D. (ed.) 60th FOCS, pp. 636–660. IEEE Computer Society Press, November 2019
30. Lin, F., Cheraghchi, M., Guruswami, V., Safavi-Naini, R., Wang, H.: Leakage-resilient secret sharing in non-compartmentalized models. In: Kalai, Y.T., Smith, A.D., Wichs, D. (eds.) 1st Conference on Information-Theoretic Cryptography, ITC 2020, Boston, MA, USA, 17–19 June 2020. LIPIcs, vol. 163, pp. 7:1–7:24. Schloss Dagstuhl - Leibniz-Zentrum für Informatik (2020)
31. Lindell, Y.: Introduction to coding theory lecture notes (2010)
32. MacWilliams, F.J., Sloane, N.J.A.: The Theory of Error Correcting Codes, vol. 16. Elsevier, Amsterdam (1977)
33. Maji, H.K. Paskin-Cherniavsky, A., Suad, T., Wang, M.: On leakage resilient secret sharing (2020)
34. Manurangsi, P., Srinivasan, A., Vasudevan, P.N.: Nearly optimal robust secret sharing against rushing adversaries. In: Micciancio, D., Ristenpart, T. (eds.) CRYPTO 2020. LNCS, vol. 12172, pp. 156–185. Springer, Cham (2020). https://doi.org/10.1007/978-3-030-56877-1_6
35. Massey, J.L.: Some applications of code duality in cryptography. In: Mat. Contemp, vol. 21, pp. 187–209:16th (2001)
36. Meier, R., Przydatek, B., Wullschleger, J.: Robuster combiners for oblivious transfer. In: Vadhan, S.P. (ed.) TCC 2007. LNCS, vol. 4392, pp. 404–418. Springer, Heidelberg (2007). https://doi.org/10.1007/978-3-540-70936-7_22
37. Nielsen, J.B., Simkin, M.: Lower bounds for leakage-resilient secret sharing. In: Canteaut, A., Ishai, Y. (eds.) EUROCRYPT 2020. LNCS, vol. 12105, pp. 556–577. Springer, Cham (2020). https://doi.org/10.1007/978-3-030-45721-1_20

38. Rao, A.: An exposition of Bourgain's 2-source extractor (2007)
39. Selberg, A.: An elementary proof of Dirichlet's theorem about primes in an arithmetic progression. Ann. Math. **50**, 297–304 (1949)
40. Shao, X.: On character sums and exponential sums over generalized arithmetic progressions. Bull. Lond. Math. Soc. **45**(3), 541–550 (2013)
41. Srinivasan, A., Vasudevan, P.N.: Leakage resilient secret sharing and applications. In: Boldyreva, A., Micciancio, D. (eds.) CRYPTO 2019. LNCS, vol. 11693, pp. 480–509. Springer, Cham (2019). https://doi.org/10.1007/978-3-030-26951-7_17
42. Wooley, T.D.: A note on simultaneous congruences. J. Number Theory **58**(2), 288–297 (1996)

Leakage, Faults and Tampering

Leakage Resilient Value Comparison with Application to Message Authentication

Christoph Dobraunig[1,2](✉) and Bart Mennink[3](✉)

[1] Lamarr Security Research, Graz, Austria
christoph.dobraunig@lamarr.at
[2] Graz University of Technology, Graz, Austria
[3] Radboud University, Nijmegen, The Netherlands
b.mennink@cs.ru.nl

Abstract. Side-channel attacks are a threat to secrets stored on a device, especially if an adversary has physical access to the device. As an effect of this, countermeasures against such attacks for cryptographic algorithms are a well-researched topic. In this work, we deviate from the study of cryptographic algorithms and instead focus on the side-channel protection of a much more basic operation, the comparison of a known attacker-controlled value with a secret one. Comparisons sensitive to side-channel leakage occur in tag comparisons during the verification of message authentication codes (MACs) or authenticated encryption, but are typically omitted in security analyses. Besides, also comparisons performed as part of fault countermeasures might be sensitive to side-channel attacks. In this work, we present a formal analysis on comparing values in a leakage resilient manner by utilizing cryptographic building blocks that are typically part of an implementation anyway. Our results indicate that there is no need to invest additional resources into implementing a protected comparison operation itself if a sufficiently protected implementation of a public cryptographic permutation, or a (tweakable) block cipher, is already available. We complement our contribution by applying our findings to the SuKS message authentication code used by lightweight authenticated encryption scheme ISAP, and to the classical Hash-then-PRF construction.

Keywords: Leakage resilience · Value comparison · Tag verification

1 Introduction

Side-channel attacks have been introduced to the public in the late 1990s [38, 39]. Especially differential power analysis (DPA) [39] turned out to be a very potent threat to implementations of cryptographic algorithms. A practical and sound countermeasure against differential power analysis is masking [12,28], and hence, a lot of research has been conducted in this direction bringing forward a myriad of different masking schemes [13,14,30,35,46,47,51,55]. Since the cost of masking is tied to the cryptographic primitive it protects, many newly designed

A. Canteaut and F.-X. Standaert (Eds.): EUROCRYPT 2021, LNCS 12697, pp. 377–407, 2021.
https://doi.org/10.1007/978-3-030-77886-6_13

cryptographic primitives take protection against DPA into account and have been designed to reduce the cost of masking [3,10,15,17,21,27,29,31,52].

Later, a research direction called leakage resilient cryptography [7,22–26,32,50,54] emerged. In principle, leakage resilient cryptography leads to modes of operation that take side-channel attacks into account and, thus, ease the investment on side-channel countermeasures on the primitive level (e.g., the protection of the public cryptographic permutation or block cipher). For instance, research in this direction lead to modes of operation that protect against (higher-order) DPA without the need of applying (higher-order) masking [19,20,43,44], or restrict the use of masking to a fraction of the building blocks [5,8,33,49]. However, it is worth noting that leakage resilient modes can only solve part of the problem. Thus, the protection of primitives against potent and skillful attackers that can perform simple power analysis or template attacks is still crucial [37]. Nevertheless, leakage resilient schemes have been implemented on micro-controllers and practical evaluation shows that protection against side-channel attacks can be efficiently achieved in practice against a set of realistic adversaries [56].

An operation that is part of many cryptographic schemes, but also part of some fault countermeasures, is the comparison of two values for equality. In cases where this comparison is made between a value that an attacker should not know with a known and potentially chosen value, side-channel countermeasures for this comparison have to be in place.

Alternatively, one can perform the comparison using a cryptographic primitive. During the last years, many authenticated encryption schemes have been proposed that use a "perfectly" protected (tweakable) block cipher as the last step before the tag output [5,7,8,33]. The advertised advantage of these schemes is that in the case of verification, the inverse of the "perfectly" protected (tweakable) block cipher can be applied to the candidate tag T. Then, the comparison of equality does not have to be done on the tag T directly but rather on an intermediate value. Therefore, the correct value of the tag $T^{\star}$ is never computed and cannot leak via side-channel attacks. Hence, the comparison operation itself does not need any protection against side-channel attacks. An alternative avenue is to use a public cryptographic permutation as, e.g., suggested in the ISAP v2.0 [19] specification. This approach was believed to have comparable advantages, with the added benefit that no key material needs to be protected.

Although various articles on this very topic appeared recently, culminating at a CRYPTO 2020 article [6], these works typically see the leakage resilient value comparison as integral part of a scheme or abstract the actual leakage resilience of the final value comparison and assume that it is "sufficiently leakage resilient secure." A formal qualitative and quantitative analysis of leakage resilient value comparison as a general method suitable for a wide range of applications is, despite its practical relevance, lacking.

1.1 Formal View on Leakage Resilient Value Comparison

In this paper, we present a formal leakage resilience study of comparing a secret value with a value chosen by an attacker, as would, e.g., typically happen during verification of a tag. By considering the problem in isolation, it allows for a neater model and cleaner bound, that compose properly with broader schemes like authenticated encryption schemes or fault countermeasures.

In detail, the formal model considers a set of μ secretly computed target values $T_1, \ldots, T_\mu$, and an adversary that can guess values $T^\star$ for which value comparison succeeds. To resolve the fact that unprotected implementations of this comparison allow for DPA to recover any of the T_j's [6], we will incorporate a value processing function and consider comparison of *processed values.* This value processing function takes as additional input a salt S_j, tied to the target value T_j, and is based on a cryptographic primitive. The adversary wins the security game if it ever makes value comparison succeed, where it may be aided with side-channel leakage coming from the value processing and value comparison. This model captures the non-adaptive bounded leakage of the cryptographic functions and the leakage of the value comparison, a non-adaptive leakage model, and works in the standard model and ideal model dependent on the cryptographic function in use. It is described in Sect. 3.

1.2 Two Practical Solutions

In Sects. 4 and 5, we present two concrete solutions that tackle the protection of value comparison. The first construction, PVP ("permutation-based value processing") of Sect. 4, processes the tag T and user input $T^\star$ along with a salt S using a cryptographic permutation to obtain an intermediate value U and $U^\star$, upon which comparison is evaluated. The cryptographic permutation can be a public permutation like Keccak-f [10] or a block cipher instantiated with a secret key like AES_K [18]. The construction with a public permutation is inspired by the informal proposal of the designers of ISAP v2.0 [19] to perform secure comparison. However, for PVP also the instantiation with a secret permutation is relevant, noting that this variant is naturally of use in implementations of schemes based on block ciphers that have an implementation of a heavily protected block cipher anyway, such as [1,36,40–42]. The scheme achieves very strong leakage resilience under the model defined in Sect. 3.

The second construction, TPVP ("tweakable permutation-based value processing") of Sect. 5, resembles much of PVP but is instantiated with a cryptographic tweakable permutation, which could in turn be a tweakable block cipher instantiated with a secret key like SKINNY_K [2]. The construction is particularly inspired by the idea to use a strongly protected tweakable block cipher for value comparison, as suggested by Berti et al. [8]. This construction, although different in nature from PVP, achieves comparable security.

These results are under the assumption that all target values $T_1, \ldots, T_\mu$ come with a unique and distinct salt $S_1, \ldots, S_\mu$. In Sect. 6 we discuss how the results on PVP and TPVP extend if one takes random salts or no salts at all.

1.3 Application to Message Authentication

A particularly interesting application is message authentication and authenticated encryption, after all the cradle of the problem that we tackle. In Sect. 7 we take a close look at how to apply the results from Sects. 4 and 5 to message authentication.

The first construction that we present is StP ("SuKS then PVP"), a construction built as composition of the SuKS ("suffix keyed sponge") message authentication code [9,20,23] and the PVP value comparison function. In this construction, the SuKS function outputs a tag, and one also takes a salt from the internal computation of SuKS, and these values are fed to PVP for value comparison. We demonstrate that, in fact, leakage resilience of StP follows from the leakage resilient PRF security of SuKS and the leakage resilient value comparison security of PVP, provided that the two individual constructions are built on independent cryptographic primitives. In other words, the functions compose nicely and cheaply.

The second construction that we present is HaFuFu ("hash function function"), a hash-then-PRF message authentication code that uses the same PRF for value comparison. As the message authentication code and the value comparison function use the same cryptographic primitive, black-box composition is not an option. Instead, we prove direct security of HaFuFu, while still reusing many aspects of the security analysis of the schemes from Sects. 4 and 5.

1.4 Comparison of Proposed Solutions

Our solutions fall into two categories depending on whether or not the used (tweakable) permutation is public or secret. In the case of public primitives, real-world instances would typically be based on public cryptographic permutations like Keccak-f [10], whereas for secret (tweakable) primitives, one would typically resort to (tweakable) block ciphers like AES [18] or SKINNY [2].

The most significant difference between using a public cryptographic permutation versus a (tweakable) block cipher is that the latter uses a secret key. Hence, this key has to be protected against a side-channel adversary that can freely choose inputs to this (tweakable) block cipher. As typical in this scenario, we assume that the block cipher is then perfectly protected [5,7,8,33], meaning that the secret key cannot be extracted using a side-channel attack.

In contrast, basing the value comparison on public cryptographic permutations does not require to protect an additional secret value in addition to the candidate tag T. Hence, we *do not* require the assumption that the public cryptographic permutation is perfectly protected.

2 Preliminaries

Throughout the entire work, the parameters $k, m, n, c, r, s, t, u, p, q, \epsilon, \mu, \lambda, \lambda'$ are natural numbers. We denote by $\{0,1\}^n$ the set of n-bit strings. By $\mathsf{func}(m, n)$ we define the set of all functions from $\{0,1\}^m$ to $\{0,1\}^n$, by $\mathsf{perm}(n) \subseteq \mathsf{func}(n,n)$ the set of permutations on $\{0,1\}^n$, and by $\mathsf{perm}(k,n)$ the set of families of 2^k permutations on $\{0,1\}^n$. We will write $\mathsf{func}(*,n)$ for the set of all functions from $\{0,1\}^*$ to $\{0,1\}^n$.

For a finite set $\mathcal{S}$, $S \xleftarrow{\$} \mathcal{S}$ denotes the uniformly random drawing of an element S from $\mathcal{S}$. We will sometimes abuse the notation a bit for infinite sets, as long as uniformly random sampling is possible. An example set is the family of functions $\mathsf{func}(*,n)$, for which uniformly random sampling can be simulated by lazy sampling (for each new input to the function, a random string of length n bits is generated). We denote by $S \xleftarrow{€} \mathcal{S}$ the drawing of an element S from $\mathcal{S}$ according to such a distribution that $\mathbf{Pr}\left(S = s\right) \leq 2^{\epsilon}/|S|$ for any $s \in \mathcal{S}$. Here, ϵ is some fixed constant which is typically required to be $\ll \log_2(|S|)$. Slightly abusing notation, we denote by $(S_1,\ldots,S_\mu) \xleftarrow{€} (\mathcal{S})^\mu$ the independent drawing of μ values $S_1,\ldots,S_\mu$ such that $\mathbf{Pr}\left(S_j = s\right) \leq 2^{\epsilon}/|S|$ for all $j = 1,\ldots,\mu$.

For a string $S \in \{0,1\}^n$, if $m \leq n$, we denote by $\text{left}_m(S)$ (resp., $\text{right}_m(S)$) the m leftmost (resp., rightmost) bits of S. For a predicate A, $[\![A]\!]$ equals 1 if A is true and 0 otherwise.

2.1 Multicollision Limit Function

We will use the notion of a multicollision limit function of Daemen et al. [16]. Consider the experiment of throwing q balls uniformly at random in 2^m bins, and let μ denote the maximum number of balls in a single bin. We define the multicollision limit function $\mathsf{mlf}^q_{m,n}$ as the smallest $x \in \mathbb{N}$ that satisfies

$$\mathbf{Pr}\left(\mu > x\right) \leq \frac{x}{2^n}\,.$$

Daemen et al. [16] demonstrated that this function is of the following order of magnitude:

$$\mathsf{mlf}^q_{m,n} \lesssim \begin{cases} (m+n)/\log_2\left(\dfrac{2^m}{q}\right), & \text{for } q \lesssim 2^m\,, \\ (m+n)\cdot\dfrac{q}{2^m}\,, & \text{for } q \gtrsim 2^m\,. \end{cases}$$

In addition, if the balls are not thrown uniformly at random, but rather according to a distribution D that prescribes that the probability P that the i-th ball ends up in a certain bin satisfies

$$\frac{2^n - (i-1)}{2^{m+n} - (i-1)} \leq P \leq \frac{2^n}{2^{m+n} - (i-1)}\,, \tag{1}$$

the corresponding multicollision function, defined as $\mathsf{mlf}^{D,q}_{m,n}$, satisfies $\mathsf{mlf}^{D,q}_{m,n} \leq \mathsf{mlf}^{2q}_{m,n}$ [16, Lemma 6].

2.2 Block Ciphers and Tweakable Block Ciphers

A block cipher $\mathsf{E} : \{0,1\}^k \times \{0,1\}^n \to \{0,1\}^n$ is a family of n-bit permutations indexed by a key $K \in \{0,1\}^k$. Its security is typically measured by the PRP-advantage. In detail, an adversary is given query access to either E_K for random and secret key $K \xleftarrow{\$} \{0,1\}^k$, or to a random permutation $\mathsf{P} \xleftarrow{\$} \mathsf{perm}(n)$, and its goal is to distinguish both worlds:

$$\mathbf{Adv}_{\mathsf{E}}^{\mathrm{prp}}(\mathcal{A}) = \left|\mathbf{Pr}\left(K \xleftarrow{\$} \{0,1\}^k \ : \ \mathcal{A}^{\mathsf{E}_K} = 1\right) - \mathbf{Pr}\left(\mathsf{P} \xleftarrow{\$} \mathsf{perm}(n) \ : \ \mathcal{A}^{\mathsf{P}} = 1\right)\right| .$$

Denoting by $\mathbf{Adv}_{\mathsf{E}}^{\mathrm{prp}}(q, \tau)$ the maximum advantage over any adversary making q construction queries and operating in time τ, the block cipher E is called PRP-secure if $\mathbf{Adv}_{\mathsf{E}}^{\mathrm{prp}}(q, \tau)$ is small.

A tweakable block cipher $\mathsf{TE} : \{0,1\}^k \times \{0,1\}^r \times \{0,1\}^n \to \{0,1\}^n$ is a family of n-bit permutations indexed by a key $K \in \{0,1\}^k$ and a tweak $R \in \{0,1\}^r$. Its security is typically measured by the TPRP-advantage. In detail, an adversary is given query access to either TE_K for random and secret key $K \xleftarrow{\$} \{0,1\}^k$, or to a family of random permutations $\mathsf{TP} \xleftarrow{\$} \mathsf{perm}(r, n)$, and its goal is to distinguish both worlds:

$$\mathbf{Adv}_{\mathsf{TE}}^{\mathrm{tprp}}(\mathcal{A}) = \\ \left|\mathbf{Pr}\left(K \xleftarrow{\$} \{0,1\}^k \ : \ \mathcal{A}^{\mathsf{TE}_K} = 1\right) - \mathbf{Pr}\left(\mathsf{TP} \xleftarrow{\$} \mathsf{perm}(r, n) \ : \ \mathcal{A}^{\mathsf{TP}} = 1\right)\right| .$$

Denoting by $\mathbf{Adv}_{\mathsf{TE}}^{\mathrm{tprp}}(q, \tau)$ the maximum advantage over any adversary making q construction queries and operating in time τ, the block cipher TE is called TPRP-secure if $\mathbf{Adv}_{\mathsf{TE}}^{\mathrm{tprp}}(q, \tau)$ is small.

3 Security Model for Value Comparison

We will present a security model for leakage resilient value comparison. To do so, we first describe how, perhaps pedantically, value comparison in the black-box model can be modeled (Sect. 3.1). Then, we explain how value comparison in a leaky model can be described in Sect. 3.2. The model of leakage resilient value comparison is then given in Sect. 3.3.

3.1 Value Comparison in Black-Box Model

In a black-box setting, value comparison is trivial. If a tag $T^\star \in \{0,1\}^t$ must be tested against a target value $T \in \{0,1\}^t$, one simply performs a comparison, and outputs 1 if and only if the values are correct. We can capture this by the following, trivial, value comparison function $\mathsf{VC} : \{0,1\}^t \times \{0,1\}^t \to \{0,1\}$:

$$\mathsf{VC}(T, T^\star) = \left[\!\!\left[T \stackrel{?}{=} T^\star \right]\!\!\right] . \tag{2}$$

For the pure sake of understanding the model of leakage resilient value comparison in Sect. 3.3, it makes sense to formally define value comparison security in the black-box model. The model is entirely trivial, but we write it in a slightly more complex way to suit further discussion. This is done by considering an adversary $\mathcal{A}$ that engages in the following game. Prior to the game, a list of μ target values $\boldsymbol{T} = (T_1, \ldots, T_\mu) \xleftarrow{\$} (\{0,1\}^t)^\mu$ is randomly generated. The adversary has query access to a value comparison oracle

$$\mathcal{O}_{\boldsymbol{T}} : (j, T^\star) \mapsto \left[\!\left[T_j \stackrel{?}{=} T^\star \right]\!\right] .$$

It wins if $\mathcal{O}_{\boldsymbol{T}}$ ever outputs 1:

$$\mathbf{Adv}_{\mathcal{O}}^{\mathrm{vc}[\mu]}(\mathcal{A}) = \mathbf{Pr}\left(\boldsymbol{T} \xleftarrow{\$} (\{0,1\}^t)^\mu \ : \ \mathcal{A}^{\mathcal{O}_{\boldsymbol{T}}} \text{ wins} \right) . \tag{3}$$

For completeness, we can define by $\mathbf{Adv}_{\mathcal{O}}^{\mathrm{vc}[\mu]}(q)$ the maximum advantage over any adversary making q queries. To confirm that the model is entirely trivial: if $\mathcal{A}$ has q guessing attempts, its success probability is at most $q/2^t$. However, as mentioned, it makes sense to describe this model as starter for the model of leakage resilient value comparison in Sect. 3.3.

3.2 Value Comparison in Leaky Model

In a leaky setting, plain value comparison as in Sect. 3.1 is risky: performing the comparison may potentially leak data [6]. In detail, an adversary can repeatedly perform verification attempts against a single target value T_j, and each verification attempt might leak a certain number of bits of information about T_j. In addition, leakage obtained in a verification attempt against one target value T_j might be useful for a later verification against another target value $T_{j'}$. Besides securing (masking) the comparison itself, another method proposed to counter such side-channel attacks is to pre-process tags with a cryptographic value processing function, and *compare the processed tags.* This value processing function is, in turn, based on a cryptographic function.

Let $\Pi \in \mathsf{perm}(r, n)$ be a cryptographic primitive. A value processing function is a function $\mathsf{VP}^\Pi : \{0,1\}^s \times \{0,1\}^t \to \{0,1\}^u$ that gets as input a salt S, value T, and processes it using cryptographic primitive Π to obtain a value U. Now, the basic idea is to not perform value comparison on $(T, T^\star)$ directly (as in (2)), but rather on the subtags:

$$\mathsf{VC}(\mathsf{VP}^\Pi(S,T), \mathsf{VP}^\Pi(S,T^\star)) = \left[\!\left[\mathsf{VP}^\Pi(S,T) \stackrel{?}{=} \mathsf{VP}^\Pi(S,T^\star) \right]\!\right] . \tag{4}$$

Remark 1. Looking ahead, for $r = 0$, the cryptographic primitive Π might be a public permutation that can in practice then be instantiated with a strong permutation like Keccak-f [10], or it could be a secret permutation that could for instance be instantiated with AES_K [18] for a secret key. The difference is subtle. In the former case, an adversary knows the permutation and can make queries to it. In the latter case, the adversary cannot make primitive evaluations, but this instantiation comes at the cost of the PRP-security of AES. In addition, the implementation of AES_K must then be strongly protected to prevent the key from leaking. We will elaborate on this in Sects. 4.2 and 4.3.

Likewise, if $r > 0$, the cryptographic primitive Π might be a public tweakable permutation (like keyless SKINNY) or a secret tweakable permutation that could for instance be instantiated with SKINNY [2]. Also here, the same differences between the two cases surface. We will elaborate on these two cases in Sects. 5.2 and 5.3.

Remark 2. Although our focus is on value processing functions instantiated with a (public or secret) family of permutations, the definition and later security models readily extend to instantiations with a different type of primitive, such as an arbitrary function $\mathsf{F} \in \mathsf{func}(r, n)$.

3.3 Security Model for Leakage Resilient Value Comparison

A straightforward generalization of the security model of Sect. 3.1 would be to consider a random $\Pi \xleftarrow{\$} \mathsf{perm}(r, n)$, a list of μ distinct salts $\boldsymbol{S} = (S_1, \ldots, S_\mu) \subseteq \{0,1\}^s$ and a list of μ target values $\boldsymbol{T} = (T_1, \ldots, T_\mu) \xleftarrow{\epsilon} (\{0,1\}^t)^\mu$, where we recall that each of the μ values T_j has min-entropy of at least $t - \epsilon$. This allows us to model the information an attacker might get via side-channels during the generation of the values T_j outside of our observation that just focuses on the value comparison and the leakage occurring there. Furthermore, we consider an adversary that has query access to a value comparison oracle

$$\mathcal{O}_{\boldsymbol{S},\boldsymbol{T}}^{\mathsf{VP},\Pi} : (j, T^\star) \mapsto \left[\!\left[\mathsf{VP}^\Pi(S_j, T_j) \stackrel{?}{=} \mathsf{VP}^\Pi(S_j, T^\star) \right]\!\right] . \tag{5}$$

The adversary can learn the salts $\boldsymbol{S}$. It a priori has bi-directional access to Π (if Π is a secret permutation, the number of queries to Π is bounded to 0, below).

However, it is not as simple as that: we will consider value comparison security in case of leakage resilience. We will restrict our focus to non-adaptive $\mathcal{L}$-resilience of Dodis and Pietrzak [24], where the adversary receives leakage under any leakage $\mathsf{L} \in \mathcal{L}$ of the scheme under investigation. In our case, leakage of secret data can occur in two occasions: evaluation of Π within the two evaluations of VP^Π, and the value comparison. Therefore, $\mathcal{L}$ consists of a Cartesian product of two leakage sets.

Let $\mathcal{L}_\Pi = \{\mathsf{L}_\Pi \colon \{0,1\}^r \times \{0,1\}^n \times \{0,1\}^n \to \{0,1\}^\lambda\}$ be a fixed set of leakage functions on the primitive Π within the value processing function VP, and let $\mathcal{L}_\mathsf{C} = \{\mathsf{L}_\mathsf{C} \colon \{0,1\}^u \times \{0,1\}^u \to \{0,1\}^{\lambda'}\}$ be a fixed set of leakage functions on the value comparison function VC. All functions are independent of Π, i.e., they do not internally evaluate Π or Π^{-1}. Write $\mathcal{L} = \mathcal{L}_\Pi \times \mathcal{L}_\mathsf{C}$. For any leakage function $\mathsf{L} = (\mathsf{L}_\Pi, \mathsf{L}_\mathsf{C}) \in \mathcal{L}$, define by $\left[\mathcal{O}_{\boldsymbol{S},\boldsymbol{T}}^{\mathsf{VP},\Pi}\right]_\mathsf{L}$ an evaluation of $\mathcal{O}_{\boldsymbol{S},\boldsymbol{T}}^{\mathsf{VP},\Pi}$ of (5) that not only returns the response of this function, but also leaks the following values:

$$\mathsf{L}_{\Pi}(X,Y) \in \{0,1\}^{\lambda} \left(\forall\ \Pi\text{-evaluation } (X,Y) \text{ in } \mathsf{VP}^{\Pi}(S_j,T_j)\right),$$
$$\mathsf{L}_{\Pi}(X,Y) \in \{0,1\}^{\lambda} \left(\forall\ \Pi\text{-evaluation } (X,Y) \text{ in } \mathsf{VP}^{\Pi}(S_j,T^{\star})\right),$$
$$\mathsf{L}_{\mathsf{C}}\left(\mathsf{VP}^{\Pi}(S_j,T_j), \mathsf{VP}^{\Pi}(S_j,T^{\star})\right) \in \{0,1\}^{\lambda'}.$$

The security model of Sect. 3.2 now extends as suggested in the beginning of this section, but with $\mathcal{A}$ having access to the *leaky variant* of $\mathcal{O}^{\mathsf{VP},\Pi}_{\boldsymbol{S},\boldsymbol{T}}$. In detail, consider an adversary $\mathcal{A}$ that, for any given tuple of leakage functions $\mathsf{L} = (\mathsf{L}_{\Pi}, \mathsf{L}_{\mathsf{C}}) \in \mathcal{L}$ and any tuple of μ distinct salts $\boldsymbol{S} \subseteq \{0,1\}^s$, has query access to $\left[\mathcal{O}^{\mathsf{VP},\Pi}_{\boldsymbol{S},\boldsymbol{T}}\right]_{\mathsf{L}}$ and bi-directional access to Π (bounded to 0 queries if Π is a secret permutation). The adversary wins if $\left[\mathcal{O}^{\mathsf{VP},\Pi}_{\boldsymbol{S},\boldsymbol{T}}\right]_{\mathsf{L}}$ ever outputs 1:

$$\mathbf{Adv}^{\text{lr-vc}[\mu]}_{\mathcal{O}^{\mathsf{VP}}}(\mathcal{A}) = \max_{\mathsf{L}=(\mathsf{L}_{\Pi},\mathsf{L}_{\mathsf{C}})\in\mathcal{L}} \ \max_{\boldsymbol{S}\subseteq\{0,1\}^s} \mathbf{Pr}\left(\Pi \xleftarrow{\$} \mathsf{perm}(r,n)\,,\, \boldsymbol{T} \xleftarrow{\epsilon} (\{0,1\}^t)^{\mu} \ :\ \mathcal{A}^{[\mathcal{O}^{\mathsf{VP},\Pi}_{\boldsymbol{S},\boldsymbol{T}}]_{\mathsf{L}},\Pi^{\pm}}(\boldsymbol{S}) \text{ wins}\right). \quad (6)$$

For completeness, we can define by $\mathbf{Adv}^{\text{lr-vc}[\mu]}_{\mathcal{O}^{\mathsf{VP}}}(q,p)$ the maximum advantage over any adversary making q queries to $\left[\mathcal{O}^{\mathsf{VP},\Pi}_{\boldsymbol{S},\boldsymbol{T}}\right]_{\mathsf{L}}$ and p bi-directional queries to $\Pi^{\pm}$. In the bigger picture, q refers to the number of verification queries an adversary can make. In case the primitive Π is a secretly keyed primitive, one restricts to $p = 0$.

4 Value Comparison Based on Permutation

Let $\mathsf{P} \in \mathsf{perm}(n)$ be a permutation (for now, we will not yet limit ourselves to secret or public permutation). Assume that $\log_2(\mu) \leq s$ and $s+t, u \leq n$. Define the following, arguably most straightforward, permutation-based value processing function $\mathsf{PVP}^{\mathsf{P}} : \{0,1\}^s \times \{0,1\}^t \to \{0,1\}^u$:

$$\mathsf{PVP}^{\mathsf{P}}(S,T) = \text{left}_u(\mathsf{P}(S \parallel T \parallel 0^{n-s-t})). \quad (7)$$

Value verification then follows as in (4), using above value processing function PVP (see also Fig. 1):

$$\mathsf{PVC}(\mathsf{PVP}^{\mathsf{P}}(S,T), \mathsf{PVP}^{\mathsf{P}}(S,T^{\star})) = \left[\!\left[\mathsf{PVP}^{\mathsf{P}}(S,T) \stackrel{?}{=} \mathsf{PVP}^{\mathsf{P}}(S,T^{\star})\right]\!\right]. \quad (8)$$

A general security bound of value comparison using PVP is given in Sect. 4.1. Note that we did not put any stringent condition on s, t, u, and n yet: all we need is that $s+t, u \leq n$. Depending on whether P is a secret or public permutation, an additional condition is needed. Both cases are rather different in nature, in practical appearance, and in the security level that they achieve. We elaborate on the case of secret permutation in Sect. 4.2, and on the case of public permutation in Sect. 4.3.

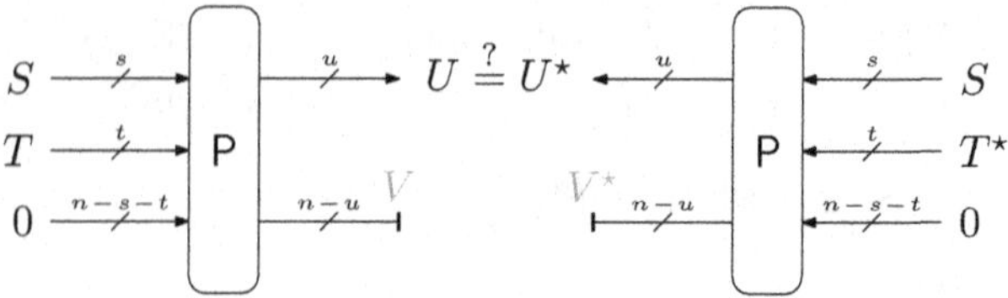

Fig. 1. Depiction of leakage resilient value comparison using permutation.

4.1 Leakage Resilience of Value Comparison with PVP

We derive a general bound on the leakage resilience of value comparison using PVP,

$$\mathcal{O}_{\boldsymbol{S},\boldsymbol{T}}^{\mathsf{PVP},\mathsf{P}} : (j, T^\star) \mapsto \left[\!\left[\mathsf{PVP}^{\mathsf{P}}(S_j, T_j) \stackrel{?}{=} \mathsf{PVP}^{\mathsf{P}}(S_j, T^\star) \right]\!\right] , \tag{9}$$

in the security definition of (6) against any adversary making q construction queries and p primitive queries. We note that the bound is meaningless for certain choices of n, s, t, u, q, p: in particular, if $p > 0$ (i.e., if we consider instantiation using a *public* permutation), one requires $t, u \ll n$. The bound is nevertheless derived in full generality, and will only be interpreted for the specific cases in Sects. 4.2 and 4.3.

Theorem 1. *Assume that* $\log_2(\mu) \leq s$ *and* $s + t, u \leq n$. *For any adversary* $\mathcal{A}$ *with construction complexity* q *and primitive complexity* p,

$$\mathbf{Adv}_{\mathcal{O}^{\mathsf{PVP}}}^{\text{lr-vc}[\mu]}(\mathcal{A}) \leq \frac{2(q+p)}{2^{\min\{t-\epsilon-\lambda,u\}} - (\mu+q+p)} + \frac{2\mathsf{mlf}_{u,n-u}^{2\mu} p}{2^{n-\max\{t,u+\lambda\}} - (\mu+q+p)} + \frac{\mathsf{mlf}_{u,n-u}^{2\mu}}{2^{n-u}} .$$

Proof. Let $\mathsf{L} = (\mathsf{L}_{\mathsf{P}}, \mathsf{L}_{\mathsf{C}}) \in \mathcal{L}$ be any two leakage functions and let $\boldsymbol{S} \subseteq \{0,1\}^s$ be a list of q distinct salts. Let $\mathsf{P} \xleftarrow{\$} \mathsf{perm}(n)$ be a random permutation, and let $\boldsymbol{T} \xleftarrow{\epsilon} (\{0,1\}^t)^\mu$ be a list of μ target values T_j, where each T_j has at least a min-entropy of at least $t - \epsilon$. For any $j \in \{1, \ldots, \mu\}$, define $\mathsf{P}(S_j \| T_j \| 0^{n-s-t}) = U_j \| V_j$, where $U_j \in \{0,1\}^u$ and $V_j \in \{0,1\}^{n-u}$. By definition, we have $U_j = \mathsf{PVP}^{\mathsf{P}}(S_j, T_j)$. Consider any adversary $\mathcal{A}$ that can make q queries $(j, T^\star)$ to $\mathcal{O}_{\boldsymbol{S},\boldsymbol{T}}^{\mathsf{PVP},\mathsf{P}}$ of (9), and p direct queries to $\mathsf{P}^{\pm}$. For each of the q construction queries, $\mathcal{A}$ also learns the following values:

$$\begin{aligned} \mathsf{L}_{\mathsf{P}}\left(S_j \| T_j \| 0^{n-s-t}, U_j \| V_j\right) &\in \{0,1\}^\lambda, \\ \mathsf{L}_{\mathsf{P}}\left(S_j \| T^\star \| 0^{n-s-t}, \mathsf{P}(S_j \| T^\star \| 0^{n-s-t})\right) &\in \{0,1\}^\lambda, \\ \mathsf{L}_{\mathsf{C}}\left(U_j, \mathsf{PVP}^{\mathsf{P}}(S_j, T^\star)\right) &\in \{0,1\}^{\lambda'}. \end{aligned}$$

Note that, as L_{P} and L_{C} are fixed, predetermined, functions, the adversary learns *at most* λ bits of leakage on T_j, λ bits of leakage on V_j, and $\lambda + q\lambda'$ bits of leakage on U_j, for any $j \in \{1, \ldots, \mu\}$.

The adversary wins if any of its q construction queries returns 1. However, the probability for this to occur depends on "lucky" primitive queries. In detail, if the adversary happens to make a primitive query of the form

$$(S_j \parallel *^t \parallel 0^{n-s-t}, U_j \parallel *^{n-u}),$$

for any $j \in \{1, \ldots, \mu\}$, it can use this to make the construction oracle output 1 with probability 1. Therefore, we *also* say that the adversary wins if any of its p primitive queries is of above form. Finally, it turns out that the adversary might have a significantly increased success probability if there exists a multicollision in $\{U_1, \ldots, U_\mu\}$. We will also count that as a win for the adversary.

More detailed, write $\mathsf{m} = \mathsf{mlf}^{2\mu}_{u,n-u}$ for brevity. We denote by bad the event that there exist $\mathsf{m}+1$ distinct indices $j_1, \ldots, j_{\mathsf{m}+1} \in \{1, \ldots, \mu\}$ such that $U_{j_1} = \cdots = U_{j_{\mathsf{m}+1}}$. In addition, for $i \in \{1, \ldots, q+p\}$, we denote by win_i the event that the i-th query is

- a construction query $(j, T^\star)$ that satisfies $\mathsf{PVP}^\mathsf{P}(S_j, T^\star) = U_j$, or
- a primitive query (X, Y) that satisfies $\text{left}_s(X) = S_j$, $\text{right}_{n-s-t}(X) = 0^{n-s-t}$, and $\text{left}_u(Y) = U_j$ for some $j \in \{1, \ldots, \mu\}$.

Write $\mathsf{win} = \bigvee_{i=1}^{q+p} \mathsf{win}_i$. Our goal is to bound

$$\begin{aligned}
\mathbf{Pr}(\mathsf{win}) &\le \mathbf{Pr}(\mathsf{win} \wedge \neg\mathsf{bad}) + \mathbf{Pr}(\mathsf{bad}) \\
&= \mathbf{Pr}\left(\bigvee_{i=1}^{q+p} \mathsf{win}_i \wedge \neg\mathsf{bad}\right) + \mathbf{Pr}(\mathsf{bad}) \\
&\le \sum_{i=1}^{q+p} \mathbf{Pr}(\mathsf{win}_i \wedge \neg\mathsf{win}_{1..i-1} \wedge \neg\mathsf{bad}) + \mathbf{Pr}(\mathsf{bad}) , \qquad (10)
\end{aligned}$$

where $\mathsf{win}_{1..0} = \mathsf{false}$ by definition.

Bound on $\mathbf{Pr}(\mathsf{win}_i \wedge \neg\mathsf{win}_{1..i-1} \wedge \neg\mathsf{bad})$. Consider any $i \in \{1, \ldots, q+p\}$, and consider the i-th query. We will make a distinction between a construction query, forward primitive query, and inverse primitive query.

- Construction query. Consider any construction query $(j, T^\star)$ to $\mathcal{O}^{\mathsf{PVP},\mathsf{P}}_{\boldsymbol{S},\boldsymbol{T}}$. If there were an earlier primitive query of the form $S_j \| T^\star \| 0^{n-s-t}$, then by $\neg\mathsf{win}_{1..i-1}$ its outcome is not of the form $U_j \| *^{n-u}$, and the oracle will not output 1. Therefore, we can assume that this query has not been made directly to P yet.
  The oracle outputs 1 if:
  - $T^\star = T_j$. As the values T_j are randomly generated with a min-entropy of at least $t - \epsilon$, and as the adversary has so far learned at most λ bits of leakage on T_j, this condition is set with probability at most $1/2^{t-\epsilon-\lambda}$;
  - $T^\star \ne T_j$ but $\mathsf{PVP}^\mathsf{P}(S_j, T^\star) = U_j$. As there was no earlier evaluation of $\mathsf{P}(S_j \| T^\star \| 0^{n-s-t})$, the result will be randomly drawn from a set of size at least $2^n - (\mu + i - 1) \ge 2^n - (\mu + q + p)$ values, and at most 2^{n-u} of these satisfy $\mathsf{PVP}^\mathsf{P}(S_j, T^\star) = U_j$. Thus, the condition is set with probability at most $2^{n-u}/(2^n - (\mu + q + p))$.

Adding both cases, we get

$$\mathbf{Pr}\left(\mathsf{win}_i \wedge \neg\mathsf{win}_{1..i-1} \wedge i\text{-th query to construction}\right) \leq \frac{2}{2^{\min\{t-\epsilon-\lambda,u\}} - (\mu+q+p)}; \quad (11)$$

– Forward primitive query. Consider any forward primitive query (X, Y) to P. Without loss of generality, $X = S_j\|T^\star\|0^{n-s-t}$ for some $j \in \{1,\ldots,\mu\}$ and $T^\star \in \{0,1\}^t$ (otherwise, the query cannot set win_i). Note that the value j is unique as $\boldsymbol{S}$ *is assumed to contain no collisions.* We can also assume that neither this query has been made to P yet, nor $(j, T^\star)$ has been queried to the construction oracle before.
Now, the forward primitive query sets win_i if $T^\star = T_j$ or if $Y = U_j\|*^{n-u}$, and the analysis is identical to that of construction queries. We thus obtain

$$\mathbf{Pr}\left(\mathsf{win}_i \wedge \neg\mathsf{win}_{1..i-1} \wedge i\text{-th query to forward primitive}\right) \leq \frac{2}{2^{\min\{t-\epsilon-\lambda,u\}} - (\mu+q+p)}; \quad (12)$$

– Inverse primitive query. Consider any inverse primitive query (X, Y) to P. We can assume that this query has not been made to P yet. At the point of making this primitive query, the adversary has learned at most $\lambda + q\lambda'$ bits of information about all U_j's. We will be more generous, and assume w.l.o.g. that any inverse query is of the form $U_j\|V^\star$ for some $j \in \{1,\ldots,\mu\}$ and $V^\star \in \{0,1\}^{n-u}$. Note that the value j might not be unique as there might be collisions in $\{U_1,\ldots,U_\mu\}$. However, due to $\neg\mathsf{bad}$, the largest size of a multicollision is at most $\mathsf{mlf}^{2\mu}_{u,n-u}$. Therefore, there are at most $\mathsf{mlf}^{2\mu}_{u,n-u}$ possible values j.
The inverse primitive query sets win_i if for any of these possible values j:
  - $V^\star = V_j$. As the adversary has so far learned at most λ bits of leakage on V_j, this condition is set with probability at most $1/2^{n-u-\lambda}$;
  - $V^\star \neq V_j$ but $X = S_j\|T^\star\|0^{n-s-t}$ for some $T^\star$. As there was no earlier evaluation of $\mathsf{P}^{-1}(U_j\|V^\star)$, the result will be randomly drawn from a set of size at least $2^n - (\mu + i - 1) \geq 2^n - (\mu + q + p)$ values, and at most 2^t of these satisfy $\mathrm{left}_s(X) = S_j$ and $\mathrm{right}_{n-s-t}(X) = 0^{n-s-t}$. Thus, the condition is set with probability at most $2^t/(2^n - (\mu + q + p))$.

Adding both cases, and summing over all $\leq \mathsf{mlf}^{2\mu}_{u,n-u}$ possible value j, we get

$$\mathbf{Pr}\left(\mathsf{win}_i \wedge \neg\mathsf{win}_{1..i-1} \wedge i\text{-th query to inverse primitive}\right) \leq \frac{2\mathsf{mlf}^{2\mu}_{u,n-u}}{2^{n-\max\{t,u+\lambda\}} - (\mu+q+p)}. \quad (13)$$

Bound on $\mathbf{Pr}(\mathsf{bad})$. The values U_j are all uniformly randomly drawn from a set of size $2^n - (j - 1)$ values, and they are truncated to take any value from a set of 2^u elements. The event is thus a balls-and-bins experiment in the notation of Sect. 2.1 with μ balls randomly thrown into 2^u bins, in such a way that any of the bins contains more than $\mathsf{mlf}^{2\mu}_{u,n-u}$ balls. The distribution satisfies the condition of (1). Therefore, we obtain that

$$\mathbf{Pr}\left(\mathsf{bad}\right) \leq \frac{\mathsf{mlf}^{2\mu}_{u,n-u}}{2^{n-u}}. \tag{14}$$

Conclusion. The adversary makes q construction queries, each of which succeeds with probability at most (11), and p primitive queries, each of which succeeds with probability the maximum of (12) and (13). For simplicity, we do not maximize, but rather take the sum. Finally, we have to add (14). We thus obtain from (10) that

$$\mathbf{Adv}^{\text{lr-vc}[\mu]}_{\mathcal{O}^{\mathsf{PVP}}}(\mathcal{A}) \leq \frac{2(q+p)}{2^{\min\{t-\epsilon-\lambda,u\}} - (\mu+q+p)} + \frac{2\mathsf{mlf}^{2\mu}_{u,n-u}p}{2^{n-\max\{t,u+\lambda\}} - (\mu+q+p)} + \frac{\mathsf{mlf}^{2\mu}_{u,n-u}}{2^{n-u}}.$$

The reasoning holds for any adversary making q construction queries and p primitive queries, and this completes the proof. □

4.2 PVP with Secret Permutation

Let $\mathsf{E} : \{0,1\}^k \times \{0,1\}^n \to \{0,1\}^n$ be a block cipher. If E is PRP-secure (see Sect. 2.2), one can instantiate the *secret* permutation P in the value processing function $\mathsf{PVP}^{\mathsf{P}}$ using the block cipher with a secret key, and de facto consider

$$\mathsf{EVP}^{\mathsf{E}_K}(S,T) = \text{left}_u(\mathsf{E}_K(S \parallel T \parallel 0^{n-s-t})). \tag{15}$$

A value comparison via an inverse block cipher call is part of the constructions proposed in [8].

The security bound of Theorem 1 carries over to EVP, with the following four changes:

- The term $\mathbf{Adv}^{\text{prp}}_{\mathsf{E}}(q,\tau)$ is added (where q is exactly the number of queries described in Theorem 1 and τ is an additional time complexity measure on $\mathcal{A}$);
- The function E_K must be strongly protected, so that the function leaks no information about its inputs and outputs;
- The number of primitive queries is bounded to $p = 0$;
- As the number of primitive queries is bounded to $p = 0$, the auxiliary bad event bad has become obsolete, and hence the term $\mathsf{mlf}^{2\mu}_{u,n-u}/2^{n-u}$ disappears.

More formally, we obtain the following corollary. Notably, the sole term with $2^{n-\max\{t,u\}}$ in the denominator disappeared, and we do not need to put any condition on $n - \max\{t, u\}$.

Corollary 1 (Value Comparison Using Block Cipher). *Assume that* $\log_2(\mu) \leq s$ *and* $s+t, u \leq n$*. Let* $\mathsf{E} : \{0,1\}^k \times \{0,1\}^n \to \{0,1\}^n$ *be a block cipher that is perfectly protected. For any adversary* $\mathcal{A}$ *with construction complexity* q *and operating in time* τ,

$$\mathbf{Adv}_{\mathcal{O}^{\mathsf{EVP}}}^{\text{lr-vc}[\mu]}(\mathcal{A}) \leq \frac{2q}{2^{\min\{t-\epsilon-\lambda,u\}} - (\mu+q)} + \mathbf{Adv}_{\mathsf{E}}^{\text{prp}}(q,\tau)\,.$$

4.3 PVP with Public Permutation

Assuming that P is a *public* permutation, the permutation-based value processing function PVP of (7) is similar to the one proposed by the designers of NIST Lightweight Cryptography candidate ISAP [19]. In this case, the adversary can evaluate the public primitive, or in terms of Theorem 1: $p > 0$. This also means that, for the last term of this theorem to be small, we require $t, u \ll n$. We obtain the following corollary:

Corollary 2 (Value Comparison Using Permutation). *Assume that* $\log_2(\mu) \leq s \leq n-t$ *and* $t, u \ll n$*. Let* $\mathsf{P} \in \mathsf{perm}(n)$ *be a permutation that is assumed to be perfectly random. For any adversary* $\mathcal{A}$ *with construction complexity* q *and primitive complexity* p,

$$\mathbf{Adv}_{\mathcal{O}^{\mathsf{PVP}}}^{\text{lr-vc}[\mu]}(\mathcal{A}) \leq \frac{2(q+p)}{2^{\min\{t-\epsilon-\lambda,u\}} - (\mu+q+p)} + \frac{2\mathsf{mlf}_{u,n-u}^{2\mu} p}{2^{n-\max\{t,u+\lambda\}} - (\mu+q+p)} + \frac{\mathsf{mlf}_{u,n-u}^{2\mu}}{2^{n-u}}\,.$$

5 Value Comparison Based on Tweakable Permutation

Let $\mathsf{TP} \in \mathsf{perm}(r,n)$ be a cryptographic family of permutations (for now, we will not yet limit ourselves to families of secret or public permutations). Assume that $s \leq r$ and $t, u \leq n$. Define the following tweakable permutation-based value processing function $\mathsf{TPVP}^{\mathsf{TP}} : \{0,1\}^s \times \{0,1\}^t \to \{0,1\}^u$:

$$\mathsf{TPVP}^{\mathsf{TP}}(S,T) = \text{left}_u(\mathsf{TP}(S \parallel 0^{r-s}, T \parallel 0^{n-t})). \tag{16}$$

Tag verification then follows as in (4), using above value processing function TPVP (see also Fig. 2):

$$\mathsf{TPVC}(\mathsf{TPVP}^{\mathsf{TP}}(S,T), \mathsf{TPVP}^{\mathsf{TP}}(S,T^\star)) = \left[\!\left[\mathsf{TPVP}^{\mathsf{TP}}(S,T) \stackrel{?}{=} \mathsf{TPVP}^{\mathsf{TP}}(S,T^\star)\right]\!\right]. \tag{17}$$

As before, we did not put any stringent condition on r, s, t, u, and n yet: all we need is that $s \leq r$ and $t, u \leq n$. Depending on whether TP is a family of secret or public permutations, an additional condition is needed. A general security bound of value comparison using TPVP is given in Sect. 5.1. We elaborate on the case of families of secret permutations in Sect. 5.2, and on the case of families of public permutations in Sect. 5.3.

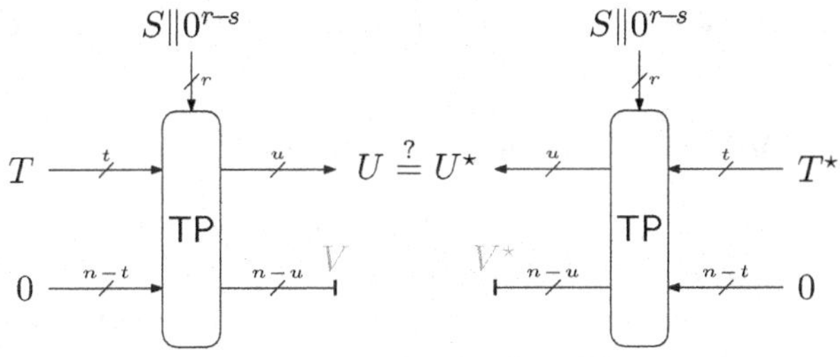

Fig. 2. Leakage resilient value comparison using a tweakable permutation.

5.1 Leakage Resilience of Value Comparison with TPVP

We derive a general bound on the leakage resilience of value comparison using TPVP,

$$\mathcal{O}_{\boldsymbol{S},\boldsymbol{T}}^{\mathsf{TPVP},\mathsf{TP}} : (j, T^\star) \mapsto \left[\!\!\left[\mathsf{TPVP}^{\mathsf{TP}}(S_j, T_j) \stackrel{?}{=} \mathsf{TPVP}^{\mathsf{TP}}(S_j, T^\star) \right]\!\!\right], \tag{18}$$

in the security definition of (6) against any adversary making q construction queries and p primitive queries. We note that the bound is meaningless for certain choices of n, r, s, t, u, q, p: in particular, if $p > 0$ (i.e., if we consider instantiation using a *public* permutation), one requires $t, u \ll n$. The bound is nevertheless derived in full generality, and will only be interpreted for the specific cases in Sects. 5.2 and 5.3.

Theorem 2. *Assume that* $\log_2(\mu) \leq s \leq r$ *and* $t, u \leq n$. *For any adversary* $\mathcal{A}$ *with construction complexity* q *and primitive complexity* p,

$$\mathbf{Adv}_{\mathcal{O}^{\mathsf{TPVP}}}^{\text{lr-vc}[\mu]}(\mathcal{A}) \leq \frac{2(q+p)}{2^{\min\{t-\epsilon-\lambda, u\}} - (\mu+q+p)} + \frac{2p}{2^{n-\max\{t, u+\lambda\}} - (\mu+q+p)}.$$

The proof is a direct simplification of the proof of Theorem 1. Most importantly, as the salt S_j is processed by TP as tweak input in both forward and inverse primitive queries, the adversary restricts itself to a unique choice of j (as salts are assumed not to collide) and hence there is no need to bother about multicollisions in $\{U_1, \ldots, U_\mu\}$. This means that event bad, as well as its analysis, drops out. A second change is in the analysis of the probability that an inverse primitive queries sets win_i: now we need that either "$V^\star = V_j$" or "$V^\star \neq V_j$ but $X = T^\star \| 0^{n-t}$". The resulting bound is identical to the one before, with the term $\mathsf{mlf}_{u,n-u}^{2\mu}$ removed. A formal proof is included in the full version of the paper.

5.2 TPVP with Secret Tweakable Permutation

Let $\mathsf{TE} : \{0,1\}^k \times \{0,1\}^r \times \{0,1\}^n \to \{0,1\}^n$ be a tweakable block cipher. If TE is TPRP-secure (see Sect. 2.2), one can instantiate the *secret* tweakable permutation TP in the value processing function $\mathsf{TPVP}^{\mathsf{TP}}$ using the block cipher with a secret key, and de facto consider

$$\mathsf{TEVP}^{\mathsf{TE}_K}(S,T) = \text{left}_u(\mathsf{TE}_K(S \parallel 0^{r-s}, T \parallel 0^{n-t})). \tag{19}$$

A variant of this using tweakable block ciphers is, in fact, proposed in NIST Lightweight Cryptography candidate Spook [5].

Identical to the analysis in Sect. 4.2, the security bound of Theorem 2 carries over to TEVP, with the following three changes:

- The term $\mathbf{Adv}_{\mathsf{TE}}^{\mathrm{tprp}}(q,\tau)$ is added (where q is exactly the number of queries described in Theorem 2 and τ is an additional time complexity measure on $\mathcal{A}$);
- The function TE_K must be strongly protected, so that the function leaks no information about its inputs and outputs;
- The number of primitive queries is bounded to $p = 0$.

More formally, we obtain the following corollary, in analogy with Corollary 1.

Corollary 3 (Value Comparison Using Tweakable Block Cipher). *Assume that* $\log_2(\mu) \leq s \leq r$ *and* $t, u \leq n$. *Let* $\mathsf{E} : \{0,1\}^k \times \{0,1\}^r \times \{0,1\}^n \to \{0,1\}^n$ *be a tweakable block cipher that is perfectly protected. For any adversary* $\mathcal{A}$ *with construction complexity* q *and operating in time* τ,

$$\mathbf{Adv}_{\mathcal{O}^{\mathsf{TEVP}}}^{\mathrm{lr\text{-}vc}[\mu]}(\mathcal{A}) \leq \frac{2q}{2^{\min\{t-\epsilon-\lambda,u\}} - (\mu+q)} + \mathbf{Adv}_{\mathsf{TE}}^{\mathrm{tprp}}(q,\tau).$$

5.3 TPVP with Public Tweakable Permutation

If one takes a block cipher $\mathsf{E} : \{0,1\}^r \times \{0,1\}^n \to \{0,1\}^n$ (see Sect. 4.2 for the definition) that does not only satisfy that its PRP-security is strong, but that does not even have any inherent weaknesses and that can be modeled as an ideal cipher, one can use this block cipher *as* tweakable permutation in the TPVP construction. Just like in Sect. 4.3, the adversary can evaluate the public primitive, or in terms of Theorem 2: $p > 0$. This also means that, for the last term of this theorem to be small, we require $t, u \ll n$. We obtain the following corollary:

Corollary 4 (Value Comparison Using Tweakable Permutation). *Assume that* $\log_2(\mu) \leq s \leq r$ *and* $t, u \ll n$. *Let* $\mathsf{TP} \in \mathsf{perm}(r,n)$ *be a family of permutations that is assumed to be perfectly random. For any adversary* $\mathcal{A}$ *with construction complexity* q *and primitive complexity* p,

$$\mathbf{Adv}_{\mathcal{O}^{\mathsf{TPVP}}}^{\mathrm{lr\text{-}vc}[\mu]}(\mathcal{A}) \leq \frac{2(q+p)}{2^{\min\{t-\epsilon-\lambda,u\}} - (\mu+q+p)} + \frac{2p}{2^{n-\max\{t,u+\lambda\}} - (\mu+q+p)}.$$

6 Freedom of Salts

In the security model of Sect. 3.3, the salts $\boldsymbol{S} \in (\{0,1\}^s)^\mu$ are unique and paired to the values in $\boldsymbol{T} \xleftarrow{\epsilon} (\{0,1\}^t)^\mu$. This might require state and/or another technique to obtain these salts. Nevertheless, it appears that this condition can be released at almost no efficiency or security cost. In this section, we consider various cases and inspect how the bounds of Theorems 1 and 2 deteriorate. First, in Sect. 6.1 we consider the case of randomly generated salts. Then, in Sect. 6.2, we discuss how the bounds change if the salts are omitted. Finally, we briefly elaborate on the theoretical benefit of *not* disclosing salts to the adversary in Sect. 6.3.

6.1 Random Salts

One can simply take uniformly random $\boldsymbol{S} \xleftarrow{\$} (\{0,1\}^s)^\mu$. This will induce an additional term to the proof of Theorem 1. In detail, for the probability that the i-th query is a forward primitive query and sets win_i, we rely on the uniqueness of the values S_j. (In fact, closer inspection shows that it suffices to rely on uniqueness of the values $S_j \| T_j$, but the distribution of the T_j's might be a bit odd and might not fit the modeling of multicollisions as per Sect. 2.1.) This means that we need to expand the bad event bad to cover multicollisions in $\boldsymbol{S} \xleftarrow{\$} (\{0,1\}^s)^\mu$, leading to an additional term $\mathsf{mlf}^\mu_{s,t}/2^t$. Subsequently the multiplication of p in the numerator of the first term of the bound of Theorem 1 by $\mathsf{mlf}^\mu_{s,t}$. Here, when defining the multicollision event, we had some freedom to choose the value of the denominator, which we set to t to match the denominator in the first term of the bound. In total, the complete bound becomes:

$$\frac{2(q+\mathsf{mlf}^\mu_{s,t}p)}{2^{\min\{t-\epsilon-\lambda,u\}}-(\mu+q+p)} + \frac{2\mathsf{mlf}^{2\mu}_{u,n-u}p}{2^{n-\max\{t,u+\lambda\}}-(\mu+q+p)} + \frac{\mathsf{mlf}^{2\mu}_{u,n-u}}{2^{n-u}} + \frac{\mathsf{mlf}^\mu_{s,t}}{2^t}. \quad (20)$$

We remark that the changes are obsolete if we consider a secret primitive, in which case $p = 0$, and also the two last terms of above equation disappear (see also the explanation before Corollary 1).

For the bound of TPVP, there was no bad event bad in the first place. However, we must consider multicollisions in $\{S_1\|T_1,\ldots,S_\mu\|T_\mu\}$ as well as in $\{S_1\|U_1,\ldots,S_\mu\|U_\mu\}$. As before, subtleties arise in the distribution of the T_j's as well as in the U_j's, and we will restrict our focus to multicollisions in $\boldsymbol{S} \xleftarrow{\$} (\{0,1\}^s)^\mu$. This can be bound by $\mathsf{mlf}^\mu_{s,t}/2^t$. The expanded bound becomes

$$\frac{2(q+\mathsf{mlf}^\mu_{s,t}p)}{2^{\min\{t-\epsilon-\lambda,u\}}-(\mu+q+p)} + \frac{2\mathsf{mlf}^\mu_{s,t}p}{2^{n-\max\{t,u+\lambda\}}-(\mu+q+p)} + \frac{\mathsf{mlf}^\mu_{s,t}}{2^t}.$$

6.2 Omission of Salt

In practice, it might not be that straightforward to pair salts with tags. However, an option that is always available is to just use the same salt for every tag.

Compared to the random selection of salts in Sect. 6.1, we do not have a strong bound on the largest multicollision on $\boldsymbol{S}$. Instead, in the worst case we have a single μ-collision. Hence, in contrast to Sect. 6.1, we do not need to introduce an additional term $\mathsf{mlf}^{\mu}_{s,t}/2^t$, since we cannot have more than a single μ-collision on μ-values. Akin to (20), the complete bound for the PVP scenario becomes:

$$\frac{2(q+\mu p)}{2^{\min\{t-\epsilon-\lambda,u\}}-(\mu+q+p)}+\frac{2\mathsf{mlf}^{2\mu}_{u,n-u}p}{2^{n-\max\{t,u+\lambda\}}-(\mu+q+p)}+\frac{\mathsf{mlf}^{2\mu}_{u,n-u}}{2^{n-u}}.$$

Since using a tweakable permutation with a single tweak/salt gives a single permutation scenario we omit to spell out the TPVP case.

Furthermore, we note that the term $\frac{2\mu p}{2^{\min\{t-\lambda,u\}}-(\mu+q+p)}$ that introduces a birthday-like trade-off in the bound between number of tags μ and primitive calls p stems from the ability of a side-channel adversary to recover all μ possible U_j's. In absence of a side-channel adversary, the bound in the black-box model omits this term. In particular, for fixed S and no leakage, we would allow the adversary access to a oracle similar to (9):

$$\mathcal{O}^{\mathsf{PVP},\mathsf{P}}_{\boldsymbol{T}} : (j, T^\star) \mapsto \left[\!\left[\mathsf{PVP}^{\mathsf{P}}(T_j) \stackrel{?}{=} \mathsf{PVP}^{\mathsf{P}}(T^\star)\right]\!\right],$$

and the adversary wins if $\mathcal{O}^{\mathsf{PVP},\mathsf{P}}_{\boldsymbol{T}}$ ever outputs 1:

$$\mathbf{Adv}^{\mathrm{pvc}[\mu]}_{\mathcal{O}^{\mathsf{PVP},\mathsf{P}}_{\boldsymbol{T}}}(\mathcal{A}) = \mathbf{Pr}\left(\mathsf{P} \xleftarrow{\$} \mathsf{perm}(n)\,,\, \boldsymbol{T} \xleftarrow{\$} (\{0,1\}^t)^\mu \ :\ \mathcal{A}^{\mathcal{O}^{\mathsf{PVP},\mathsf{P}}_{\boldsymbol{T}},\mathsf{P}^{\pm}} \text{ wins}\right).$$

For completeness, we can define by $\mathbf{Adv}^{\mathrm{pvc}[\mu]}_{\mathcal{O}^{\mathsf{PVP},\mathsf{P}}_{\boldsymbol{T}}}(q,p)$ the maximum advantage over any adversary making q queries to $\mathcal{O}^{\mathsf{PVP},\mathsf{P}}_{\boldsymbol{T}}$ and p bi-directional queries to $\mathsf{P}^{\pm}$.

Proposition 1 (Saltless Value Comparison using Permutation in the Black-Box Model). *Assume that $t, u \ll n$. Let $\mathsf{P} \in \mathsf{perm}(n)$ be a permutation that is assumed to be perfectly random. For any adversary $\mathcal{A}$ with construction complexity q and primitive complexity p,*

$$\mathbf{Adv}^{\mathrm{pvc}[\mu]}_{\mathcal{O}^{\mathsf{PVP},\mathsf{P}}_{\boldsymbol{T}}}(\mathcal{A}) \leq \frac{2q}{2^{\min\{t,u\}}-q}.$$

Proof. Since we work in the black-box model, the only thing an adversary learns from a failed verification query is that $T_j \neq T$. What an adversary learns from a successful verification query does not matter, since the adversary has won anyway. As a consequence, an adversary cannot detect matches of forward primitive queries $(*^t\|0^{n-t}, U^\star\|*^{n-u})$ with $U^\star = U_j$ only if it already won. The same counts for inverse primitive queries, hence the adversary does not profit from calls to P.

The possibilities for an adversary to win on a single query to the construction is to either guess the tag T_j correctly, or to be lucky that an incorrect guess still leads to the same U. Summing over q construction queries and considering that all U_j's are computed via a perfectly random permutation, we hence get:

$$\mathbf{Adv}^{\mathrm{pvc}[\mu]}_{\mathcal{O}_T^{\mathsf{PVP},\mathsf{P}}}(\mathcal{A}) \leq \frac{2q}{2^{\min\{t,u\}} - q}.$$

The reasoning holds for any adversary making q construction queries and p primitive queries, and this completes the proof. □

6.3 Note on Disclosing Salts

We remark that the security model of Sect. 3.3 prescribes that $\mathcal{A}$ actually obtains the salts. In practice, it might often be more practical to not disclose them. This will, clearly, only *improve* security.

7 Application to Message Authentication

Our leakage resilient solutions have many applications. We already mentioned some in Sect. 1. In this section, we will consider the application of our solutions to message authentication. In Sect. 7.2, we consider a composition of SuKS with PVP, dubbed StP. The composition is very powerful against leakage resilience, even though it requires that the building blocks (SuKS and PVP) are built from independent cryptographic permutations. The result has immediate application to the ISAP authenticated encryption scheme [19,20], that is currently in submission to the NIST Lightweight Cryptography competition. This function uses SuKS for message authentication.

In Sect. 7.3, we go one step further, and stretch the analysis to a MAC construction whose cryptographic primitive is related to that in value verification. In detail, we present HaFuFu, a hash-then-PRF message authentication code that uses the same PRF for value comparison, and prove that this construction is a leakage resilient MAC function. The result can be relevant for many other submissions to the NIST Lightweight Cryptography competition [48], given the prevalence of the hash-then-PRF construction.

Both results are derived in a model for leakage resilient message authentication plus value verification, that is described in Sect. 7.1. It is a slight extension of the model of Sect. 3.3.

7.1 Security Model for Leakage Resilient MAC Plus Value Comparison

We will describe the security model for leakage resilient message authentication with integrated value comparison in generality, so as it is applicable to both StP and HaFuFu.

Let $\Pi \in \mathsf{prims}$ be a cryptographic primitive or a set of cryptographic primitives, taken from a set of primitives prims from which uniform sampling is possible. A message authentication code $\mathsf{MAC}^{\Pi} : \{0,1\}^k \times \{0,1\}^* \rightarrow \{0,1\}^t$ takes as input a key K and an arbitrarily-long message M, and uses the cryptographic primitive Π to generate a tag T. Associated to MAC^{Π} is a verification function $\mathsf{VFY}^{\Pi} : \{0,1\}^k \times \{0,1\}^* \times \{0,1\}^t \to \{0,1\}$ that gets as input a key K, a message M, and a tag $T^\star$, and it outputs 1 if the tag belongs to the message and 0 otherwise. Whereas typical verification function do plain value comparison of $\mathsf{MAC}^{\Pi}_K(M)$ with $T^\star$, in our case verification will include leakage resilient value comparison. Before proceeding, we remark that the key input to MAC^{Π} may be optional: sometimes, Π is a secretly keyed primitive (like a secret permutation) and the key would be implicit.

As before, we consider non-adaptive $\mathcal{L}$-resilience [24], where the adversary receives leakage under any leakage $\mathsf{L} \in \mathcal{L}$ of the scheme under investigation. Any cryptographic evaluation of secret material may leak information, and a proper definition of $\mathcal{L}$ depends on the scheme and primitive under consideration. For StP and HaFuFu, the set will thus be formalized as soon as we go on to prove leakage resilience (in Sects. 7.2.3 and 7.3.2, respectively). For any leakage function $\mathsf{L} \in \mathcal{L}$, define by $\left[\mathsf{MAC}^{\Pi}_K\right]_{\mathsf{L}}$ an evaluation of MAC^{Π}_K of (25) that not only returns the response of this function, but also leaks secret material in consistency with the evaluation of L (details for the two specific schemes will follow in the corresponding sections). The function $\left[\mathsf{VFY}^{\Pi}_K\right]_{\mathsf{L}}$ is defined analogously.

Leakage resilience of the MAC function now extends from the conventional definition of unforgeability, but now with the adversary $\mathcal{A}$ having access to the leaky oracles. In detail, let $\mathsf{L} \in \mathcal{L}$ be any tuple of leakage functions. Consider an adversary $\mathcal{A}$ that has query access to $\left[\mathsf{MAC}^{\Pi}_K\right]_{\mathsf{L}}$ and $\left[\mathsf{VFY}^{\Pi}_K\right]_{\mathsf{L}}$. It wins if $\left[\mathsf{VFY}^{\Pi}_K\right]_{\mathsf{L}}$ ever outputs 1 on input of a message/tag tuple that was not the result of an earlier query to $\left[\mathsf{MAC}^{\Pi}_K\right]_{\mathsf{L}}$:

$$\mathbf{Adv}^{\text{lr-mac}}_{\mathsf{MAC}}(\mathcal{A}) = \max_{\mathsf{L}\in\mathcal{L}} \mathbf{Pr}\left(K \xleftarrow{\$} \{0,1\}^k\,,\, \Pi \xleftarrow{\$} \mathsf{prims} \;:\; \mathcal{A}^{[\mathsf{MAC}^{\Pi}_K]_{\mathsf{L}},[\mathsf{VFY}^{\Pi}_K]_{\mathsf{L}}} \text{ wins}\right). \tag{21}$$

For completeness, we can define by $\mathbf{Adv}^{\text{lr-mac}}_{\mathsf{MAC}}(q,v)$ the maximum advantage over any adversary making q authentication queries to $\left[\mathsf{MAC}^{\Pi}_K\right]_{\mathsf{L}}$ and v verification queries to $\left[\mathsf{VFY}^{\Pi}_K\right]_{\mathsf{L}}$.

7.2 StP: SuKS-then-PVP

7.2.1 Description of SuKS

Assume that $c + r = n$ and $k, s, t \le n$. Let $\mathsf{P} \in \mathsf{perm}(n)$ be a cryptographic permutation and $\mathsf{G} : \{0,1\}^k \times \{0,1\}^s \to \{0,1\}^s$ be a keyed function. The suffix keyed sponge $\mathsf{SuKS} : \{0,1\}^k \times \{0,1\}^* \to \{0,1\}^t$, formalized by Dobraunig and Mennink [23], is depicted in Fig. 3.

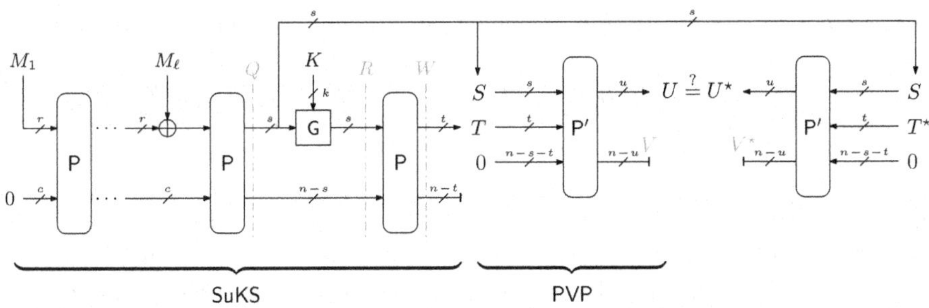

Fig. 3. The SuKS-then-PVP construction StP. The message M is first injectively padded into r-bit blocks $M_1 \dots M_\ell$.

Dobraunig and Mennink [23] proved that if P is a random permutation, G has good uniformity and universality,[1] then SuKS behaves like a random function. In addition, if G is strongly protected and any evaluation of P only leaks λ bits of data non-adaptively, SuKS still behaves like a random function.

The security model under consideration is PRF-security under non-adaptive leakage (as in Sect. 3.3). Let $\mathcal{L}_{\mathsf{P}} = \{\mathsf{L}_{\mathsf{P}} \colon \{0,1\}^n \times \{0,1\}^n \to \{0,1\}^\lambda\}$ be a fixed set of leakage functions on the primitive P, and let $\mathcal{L}_{\mathsf{G}} = \{\mathsf{L}_{\mathsf{G}} \colon \{0,1\}^k \times \{0,1\}^s \times \{0,1\}^s \to \{0,1\}^{\lambda'}\}$ be a fixed set of leakage functions on the function G. All functions are independent of P, i.e., they do not internally evaluate P or P^{-1}. Write $\mathcal{L} = \mathcal{L}_{\mathsf{P}} \times \mathcal{L}_{\mathsf{G}}$. For any leakage function $\mathsf{L} = (\mathsf{L}_{\mathsf{P}}, \mathsf{L}_{\mathsf{G}}) \in \mathcal{L}$, define by $\left[\mathsf{SuKS}_K^{\mathsf{P}}\right]_{\mathsf{L}}$ an evaluation of $\mathsf{SuKS}_K^{\mathsf{P}}$ of Fig. 3 that not only returns the response of this function, but also leaks the values $\mathsf{L}_{\mathsf{G}}(K, \mathrm{left}_s(Q), \mathrm{left}_s(R))$ and $\mathsf{L}_{\mathsf{P}}(R, W)$ (see Fig. 3 for the values Q, R, and W). Then, non-adaptive leakage resilient pseudorandom function (LR-PRF) security is defined as the maximum advantage of any distinguisher to distinguish the following two worlds:

$$\mathbf{Adv}_{\mathsf{SuKS}}^{\mathrm{lr\text{-}prf}}(\mathcal{A}) = \left|\mathbf{Pr}\left(K \xleftarrow{\$} \{0,1\}^k,\, \mathsf{P} \xleftarrow{\$} \mathsf{perm}(n) \;:\; \mathcal{A}^{\left[\mathsf{SuKS}_K^{\mathsf{P}}\right]_{\mathsf{L}}, \mathsf{SuKS}_K^{\mathsf{P}}, \mathsf{P}} = 1\right) - \right.$$
$$\left.\mathbf{Pr}\left(K \xleftarrow{\$} \{0,1\}^k,\, \mathsf{P} \xleftarrow{\$} \mathsf{perm}(n),\, \mathsf{F} \xleftarrow{\$} \mathsf{func}(*, t) \;:\; \mathcal{A}^{\left[\mathsf{SuKS}_K^{\mathsf{P}}\right]_{\mathsf{L}}, \mathsf{F}, \mathsf{P}} = 1\right)\right| .$$

Under this model, Dobraunig and Mennink proved the following result.

Proposition 2 (Leakage Resilience of SuKS [23, Theorem 3]). *Assume that $c + r = n$ and $k, s, t \leq n$. Consider the* SuKS *construction of Fig. 3 based on random permutation* $\mathsf{P} \xleftarrow{\$} \mathsf{perm}(n)$ *and a function* $\mathsf{G} : \{0,1\}^k \times \{0,1\}^s \to \{0,1\}^s$. *Assume that* G *is strongly protected $2^{-\delta}$-uniform and $2^{-\varepsilon}$-universal. For any*

[1] Uniformity means that the probability (over the drawing of K) that any fixed input X maps to any fixed output Y is at most $2^{-\delta}$. Universality means that the probability (over the drawing of K) that any fixed distinct inputs X, X' map to the same value is at most $2^{-\varepsilon}$.

adversary $\mathcal{A}$ *with construction complexity* $q \geq 2$ *and primitive complexity* $p \leq 2^{n-1}$,

$$\mathbf{Adv}_{\mathsf{SuKS}}^{\text{lr-prf}}(\mathcal{A}) \leq \frac{2p^2}{2^c} + \frac{\mathsf{mlf}_{s,n-s}^{2(p-q)}}{2^{n-s}} + \frac{\mathsf{mlf}_{n-s,s}^{2(p-q)} \cdot p}{2^{\min\{\delta,\varepsilon\}-\mathsf{mlf}_{s,n-s}^{2(p-q)}\lambda}} + \frac{\mathsf{mlf}_{t,n-t}^{2q} \cdot p}{2^{n-t-\lambda}}.$$

One term that is important in this bound is $\frac{\mathsf{mlf}_{s,n-s}^{2(p-q)}}{2^{n-s}}$. In the proof of SuKS, the authors upper bound the maximum size of a multicollision on $\text{left}_s(Q)$ by $\mathsf{mlf}_{s,n-s}^{2(p-q)}$. The fact that this bounding is already performed in the proof of SuKS itself will become useful when we consider composition of SuKS with PVP.

7.2.2 Description of StP

Let $\mathsf{P}, \mathsf{P}' \in \mathsf{perm}(n)$, and let $\mathsf{MAC}^{\mathsf{P},\mathsf{P}'}: \{0,1\}^k \times \{0,1\}^* \to \{0,1\}^t$ be the SuKS message authentication code:

$$\mathsf{MAC}_K^{\mathsf{P},\mathsf{P}'}(M) = \mathsf{SuKS}^{\mathsf{P}}(K, M) = T. \tag{22}$$

Verification $\mathsf{VFY}^{\mathsf{P},\mathsf{P}'}: \{0,1\}^k \times \{0,1\}^* \times \{0,1\}^t \to \{0,1\}$ now incorporates $\mathsf{PVP}^{\mathsf{P}'}$. It takes $S = \text{left}_s(Q)$ from the computation of $\mathsf{SuKS}^{\mathsf{P}}(K, M)$ (see Fig. 3) as salt, and is defined as follows:

$$\mathsf{VFY}_K^{\mathsf{P},\mathsf{P}'}(M, T^\star) = \left[\!\left[\text{left}_u(\mathsf{P}(S \parallel \mathsf{MAC}_K^{\mathsf{P},\mathsf{P}'}(M) \parallel 0^{n-s-t})) \stackrel{?}{=} \text{left}_u(\mathsf{P}(S \parallel T^\star \parallel 0^{n-s-t}))\right]\!\right], \tag{23}$$

where $S = \text{left}_s(Q)$ is a function of M as specified in Fig. 3.

7.2.3 Leakage Resilience of StP

We will prove security of StP, provided that $\mathsf{P}, \mathsf{P}' \stackrel{\$}{\leftarrow} \mathsf{perm}(n)$ are two random permutations.

In StP, leakage occurs on evaluations of P, G, P′, and in the value comparison. Let $\mathcal{L}_{\mathsf{P}} = \{\mathsf{L}_{\mathsf{P}}: \{0,1\}^n \times \{0,1\}^n \to \{0,1\}^\lambda\}$ be a fixed set of leakage functions on the primitive P, and let $\mathcal{L}_{\mathsf{G}} = \{\mathsf{L}_{\mathsf{G}}: \{0,1\}^k \times \{0,1\}^s \times \{0,1\}^s \to \{0,1\}^{\lambda'}\}$ be a fixed set of leakage functions on the function G. Let $\mathcal{L}_{\mathsf{P}'} = \{\mathsf{L}_{\mathsf{P}'}: \{0,1\}^n \times \{0,1\}^n \to \{0,1\}^\lambda\}$ be a fixed set of leakage functions on the value processing function P′, and let $\mathcal{L}_{\mathsf{C}} = \{\mathsf{L}_{\mathsf{C}}: \{0,1\}^u \times \{0,1\}^u \to \{0,1\}^{\lambda'}\}$ be a fixed set of leakage functions on the value comparison within VFY. All functions are independent of P and P′. Write $\mathcal{L} = \mathcal{L}_{\mathsf{P}} \times \mathcal{L}_{\mathsf{G}} \times \mathcal{L}_{\mathsf{P}'} \times \mathcal{L}_{\mathsf{C}}$. For any leakage function $\mathsf{L} = (\mathsf{L}_{\mathsf{P}}, \mathsf{L}_{\mathsf{G}}, \mathsf{L}_{\mathsf{P}'}, \mathsf{L}_{\mathsf{C}}) \in \mathcal{L}$, define by $\left[\mathsf{MAC}_K^{\mathsf{P},\mathsf{P}'}\right]_{\mathsf{L}}$ an evaluation of $\mathsf{MAC}_K^{\mathsf{P},\mathsf{P}'}$ of (22) that not only returns the response of this function, but also leaks the following values:

$$\begin{aligned} \mathsf{L}_{\mathsf{G}}(K, \text{left}_s(Q), \text{left}_s(R)) &\in \{0,1\}^\lambda, \\ \mathsf{L}_{\mathsf{P}}(R, W) &\in \{0,1\}^\lambda, \end{aligned}$$

where K, Q, R, and W are values related to the computation of $\mathsf{MAC}_K^{\mathsf{P},\mathsf{P}'}(K, M)$, as outlined in Fig. 3. Similarly, define by $\left[\mathsf{VFY}_K^{\mathsf{P},\mathsf{P}'}\right]_{\mathsf{L}}$ an evaluation of $\mathsf{VFY}_K^{\mathsf{P},\mathsf{P}'}$ of (23) that not only returns the response of this function, but also leaks the following values:

$$\begin{aligned}\mathsf{L_G}(K, \mathrm{left}_s(Q), \mathrm{left}_s(R)) &\in \{0,1\}^\lambda\,,\\ \mathsf{L_P}(R, W) &\in \{0,1\}^\lambda\,,\\ \mathsf{L_{P'}}\left(S\|T\|0^{n-s-t}, U\|V\right) &\in \{0,1\}^\lambda\,,\\ \mathsf{L_{P'}}\left(S\|T^\star\|0^{n-s-t}, U^\star\|V^\star\right) &\in \{0,1\}^\lambda\,,\\ \mathsf{L_C}\left(U, U^\star\right) &\in \{0,1\}^{\lambda'}\,,\end{aligned}$$

where $K, Q, R, W, S, T, U, U^\star, V$, and $V^\star$ are values related to the computation of $\mathsf{VFY}_K^{\mathsf{P},\mathsf{P}}(M, T^\star)$ as outlined in Fig. 3.

We can now prove leakage resilience of StP in the security model of Sect. 7.1.

Theorem 3. *Assume that $k, s{+}t, u \leq n$. Consider the StP construction based on two random permutations $\mathsf{P}, \mathsf{P}' \xleftarrow{\$} \mathsf{perm}(n)$ and a function $\mathsf{G} : \{0,1\}^k \times \{0,1\}^s \to \{0,1\}^s$. Assume that G is strongly protected $2^{-\delta}$-uniform and $2^{-\varepsilon}$-universal. For any adversary $\mathcal{A}$ with construction query q and verification complexity v, with $q + v \geq 2$, and primitive complexity $p \leq 2^{n-1}$,*

$$\begin{aligned}\mathbf{Adv}_{\mathsf{StP}}^{\text{lr-mac}}(\mathcal{A}) \leq\; & \frac{2p^2}{2^c} + \frac{\mathsf{mlf}_{s,n-s}^{2(p-q)}}{2^{n-s}} + \frac{\mathsf{mlf}_{n-s,s}^{2(p-q)} \cdot p}{2^{\min\{\delta,\varepsilon\} - \mathsf{mlf}_{s,n-s}^{2(p-q)}\lambda}} + \frac{\mathsf{mlf}_{t,n-t}^{2(q+v)} \cdot p}{2^{n-t-\lambda}} \\ & + \frac{2(v + \mathsf{mlf}_{s,n-s}^{2(p-q)} p)}{2^{\min\{t-2\lambda, u\}} - (2v+p)} + \frac{2\mathsf{mlf}_{u,n-u}^{2v} p}{2^{n-\max\{t,u+\lambda\}} - (2v+p)} + \frac{\mathsf{mlf}_{u,n-u}^{2v}}{2^{n-u}}\,.\end{aligned}$$

Proof. Let $\mathsf{L} = (\mathsf{L_P}, \mathsf{L_G}, \mathsf{L_{P'}}, \mathsf{L_C}) \in \mathcal{L}$ be any four leakage functions, let $K \xleftarrow{\$} \{0,1\}^k$ and $\mathsf{P}, \mathsf{P}' \xleftarrow{\$} \mathsf{perm}(n)$. Consider any adversary $\mathcal{A}$ that aims to mount a forgery against $\mathsf{StP}_K^{\mathsf{P},\mathsf{P}'}$. It can make q construction queries, v verification queries, and p primitive queries to both P and P'.

It is important to note that the functions $\mathsf{SuKS}_K^{\mathsf{P}}$ and $\mathsf{PVP}^{\mathsf{P}'}$ are independent primitives. In addition, $\mathsf{SuKS}_K^{\mathsf{P}}$ is a pseudorandom function under leakage. Concretely, up to the bound of Proposition 2, each new evaluation of $\mathsf{SuKS}_K^{\mathsf{P}}$ outputs a T that has min-entropy at least $t - \lambda$ and is independent of earlier evaluations of the construction, and associated with this value T is a value S that is not secret but that has the property that if the construction is evaluated q times, the maximum size of a multicollision is $\mathsf{mlf}_{s,n-s}^{2(p-q)}$.

In fact, within StP, $\mathsf{SuKS}_K^{\mathsf{P}}$ gets evaluated up to q times for different inputs and *at most* v additional times in new verification queries. Say that the number of unique messages under which $\mathcal{A}$ queries $\mathsf{SuKS}_K^{\mathsf{P}}$ is q'. Then, we can replace $\mathsf{SuKS}_K^{\mathsf{P}}$ by generating a list of random elements $\boldsymbol{T} = (T_1, \ldots, T_{q'}) \xleftarrow{\epsilon} (\{0,1\}^t)^{q'}$ with $\epsilon = \lambda$, and an arbitrary randomly generated list $\boldsymbol{S} = (S_1, \ldots, S_{q'})$ of which each element occurs at most $\mathsf{mlf}_{s,n-s}^{2(p-q')} \leq \mathsf{mlf}_{s,n-s}^{2(p-q)}$. This replacement comes at the cost of

$$\frac{2p^2}{2^c} + \frac{\mathsf{mlf}_{s,n-s}^{2(p-q')}}{2^{n-s}} + \frac{\mathsf{mlf}_{n-s,s}^{2(p-q')} \cdot p}{2^{\min\{\delta,\varepsilon\}-\mathsf{mlf}_{s,n-s}^{2(p-q')}\lambda}} + \frac{\mathsf{mlf}_{t,n-t}^{2q'} \cdot p}{2^{n-t-\lambda}}$$

$$\leq \frac{2p^2}{2^c} + \frac{\mathsf{mlf}_{s,n-s}^{2(p-q)}}{2^{n-s}} + \frac{\mathsf{mlf}_{n-s,s}^{2(p-q)} \cdot p}{2^{\min\{\delta,\varepsilon\}-\mathsf{mlf}_{s,n-s}^{2(p-q)}\lambda}} + \frac{\mathsf{mlf}_{t,n-t}^{2(q+v)} \cdot p}{2^{n-t-\lambda}}. \tag{24}$$

Having made this replacement, one can then see that, as evaluations of $\mathsf{SuKS}_K^{\mathsf{P}}$ are independent for different messages, only the elements in $\boldsymbol{T}$ and $\boldsymbol{S}$ that are considered in the evaluation of $\mathsf{PVP}^{\mathsf{P}}$ are useful. Therefore, the game of mounting a forgery against the resulting construction is equivalent to the game of mounting an attack against the value comparison function $\mathsf{PVP}^{\mathsf{P}'}$ in the model of Sect. 3.3, where $\mu = v$.

In summary, we have obtained that

$$\mathbf{Adv}_{\mathsf{StP}}^{\text{lr-mac}}(\mathcal{A}) \leq (24) + \mathbf{Adv}_{\mathcal{O}\mathsf{PVP}}^{\text{lr-vc}[v]}(\mathcal{A}),$$

for some adversary $\mathcal{A}'$ with construction complexity v and primitive complexity p, that operates in the game with salts that may repeat up to $\mathsf{mlf}_{s,n-s}^{2(p-q)}$ times. We can take the bound of Theorem 1 with the p in the numerator of the first term multiplied by $\mathsf{mlf}_{s,n-s}^{2(p-q)}$ (or, alternatively, take (20) with $\mathsf{mlf}_{s,t}^{v}$ replaced by $\mathsf{mlf}_{s,n-s}^{2(p-q)}$ and with the last term dropped as it is already accounted for in the bound of $\mathsf{SuKS}_K^{\mathsf{P}}$), for $\mu = v$, $\epsilon = \lambda$, and $q = v$. □

7.3 HaFuFu: MAC Plus Value Comparison with Same Primitive

7.3.1 Description of HaFuFu

We will describe the HaFuFu message authentication with dependent value comparison. Given the non-triviality of the problem, we consider a simpler scenario compared to the results of Sects. 4 and 5, namely one based on a random function (cf., Remark 2). In addition, for simplicity we assume that $s + t = n$ (the analysis easily extends to the case of $s + t \leq n$) and $t = u$. Let $\mathsf{H} \in \mathsf{func}(*, n)$ be a cryptographic hash function, and $\mathsf{F} \in \mathsf{func}(n, t)$ a (secret) cryptographic function. As F is a secret primitive, there is no key involved. Define the following message authentication code $\mathsf{MAC}^{\mathsf{H},\mathsf{F}} : \{0,1\}^* \to \{0,1\}^t$:

$$\mathsf{MAC}^{\mathsf{H},\mathsf{F}}(M) = \mathsf{F}(\mathsf{H}(M)) = T. \tag{25}$$

The corresponding verification function $\mathsf{VFY}^{\mathsf{H},\mathsf{F}} : \{0,1\}^* \times \{0,1\}^t \to \{0,1\}$ is defined as follows:

$$\mathsf{VFY}^{\mathsf{H},\mathsf{F}}(M, T^\star) = \left[\!\left[\mathsf{F}(\text{left}_s(\mathsf{H}(M)) \| \mathsf{MAC}^{\mathsf{H},\mathsf{F}}(M)) \stackrel{?}{=} \mathsf{F}(\text{left}_s(\mathsf{H}(M)) \| T^\star) \right]\!\right], \tag{26}$$

The function is depicted in Fig. 4. The picture also includes definitions of intermediate values R, S, T, U, and $U^\star$, that we will use when analyzing MAC and VFY. Note that the name HaFuFu is derived from the verification oracle, that operates in a Hash-then-Function-then-Function mode.

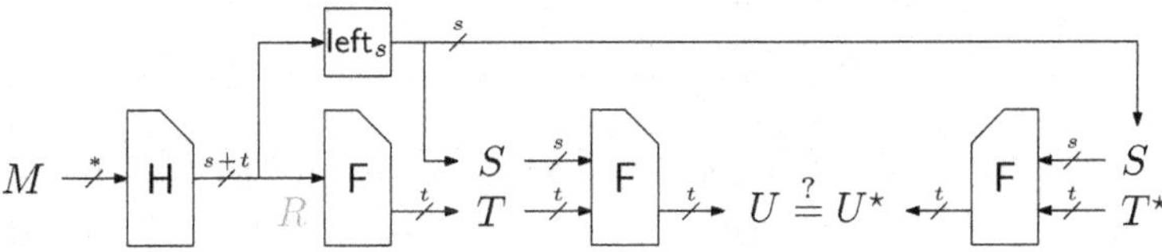

Fig. 4. HaFuFu algorithms MAC and VFY of (25) and (26), respectively. H is a cryptographic hash function and F a secret random permutation.

7.3.2 Leakage Resilience of HaFuFu

We will prove security of HaFuFu, provided that $\mathsf{H} \xleftarrow{\$} \mathsf{func}(*, n)$ is a random oracle, and $\mathsf{F} \xleftarrow{\$} \mathsf{func}(n, t)$ a secret random function. In practice, one might consider instantiating H with any good cryptographic hash function, and F by a strongly protected PRF, which can in turn be built from a (tweakable) block cipher with n-bit block size, followed by truncation [4,11,34,45,53].

In HaFuFu, leakage occurs on evaluations of F and in the value comparison. Let $\mathcal{L}_\mathsf{F} = \{\mathsf{L}_\mathsf{F} \colon \{0,1\}^n \times \{0,1\}^t \to \{0,1\}^\lambda\}$ be a fixed set of leakage functions on the value processing function F, and let $\mathcal{L}_\mathsf{C} = \{\mathsf{L}_\mathsf{C} \colon \{0,1\}^t \times \{0,1\}^t \to \{0,1\}^{\lambda'}\}$ be a fixed set of leakage functions on the value comparison within VFY. All functions are independent of F itself, i.e., they do not internally evaluate F. Write $\mathcal{L} = \mathcal{L}_\mathsf{F} \times \mathcal{L}_\mathsf{C}$. For any leakage function $\mathsf{L} = (\mathsf{L}_\mathsf{F}, \mathsf{L}_\mathsf{C}) \in \mathcal{L}$, define by $\left[\mathsf{MAC}^{\mathsf{H},\mathsf{F}}\right]_\mathsf{L}$ an evaluation of $\mathsf{MAC}^{\mathsf{H},\mathsf{F}}$ of (25) that not only returns the response of this function, but also leaks the following value:

$$\mathsf{L}_\mathsf{F}(R, T) \in \{0,1\}^\lambda,$$

where R and T are values related to the computation of $\mathsf{MAC}^{\mathsf{H},\mathsf{F}}(M)$, as outlined in Fig. 4. Similarly, define by $\left[\mathsf{VFY}^{\mathsf{H},\mathsf{F}}\right]_\mathsf{L}$ an evaluation of $\mathsf{VFY}^{\mathsf{H},\mathsf{F}}$ of (26) that not only returns the response of this function, but also leaks the following values:

$$\begin{aligned}\mathsf{L}_\mathsf{F}(R, T) &\in \{0,1\}^\lambda,\\ \mathsf{L}_\mathsf{F}(S\|T, U) &\in \{0,1\}^\lambda,\\ \mathsf{L}_\mathsf{F}(S\|T^\star, U^\star) &\in \{0,1\}^\lambda,\\ \mathsf{L}_\mathsf{C}(U, U^\star) &\in \{0,1\}^{\lambda'},\end{aligned}$$

where R, S, T, U, and $U^\star$ are values related to the computation of $\mathsf{VFY}^{\mathsf{H},\mathsf{F}}(M, T^\star)$ as outlined in Fig. 4.

We can now prove leakage resilience of HaFuFu in the security model of Sect. 7.1.

Theorem 4. *Assume that $s + t = n$. Consider the* HaFuFu *construction based on a random oracle* $\mathsf{H} \xleftarrow{\$} \mathsf{func}(*, n)$ *and a secret random function* $\mathsf{F} \xleftarrow{\$} \mathsf{func}(n, t)$. *For any adversary $\mathcal{A}$ with construction query q and verification complexity v,*

$$\mathbf{Adv}^{\text{lr-mac}}_{\mathsf{HaFuFu}}(\mathcal{A}) \le \frac{2q}{2^{t-2\lambda}} + \frac{2\binom{q+v}{2}}{2^n} .$$

Proof. Let $\mathsf{L} = (\mathsf{L_F}, \mathsf{L_C}) \in \mathcal{L}$ be any two leakage functions, let $\mathsf{H} \xleftarrow{\$} \mathsf{func}(*, n)$ be a random oracle and $\mathsf{F} \xleftarrow{\$} \mathsf{func}(n, t)$ a random function. Consider any adversary $\mathcal{A}$ that aims to mount a forgery against $\mathsf{HaFuFu}^{\mathsf{H,F}}$. It can make q construction queries and v verification queries. For each verification query $\mathsf{VFY}^{\mathsf{H,F}}(M, T^\star)$, $\mathcal{A}$ learns the following values:

$$\begin{aligned} \mathsf{L_F}(R, T) &\in \{0,1\}^\lambda , \\ \mathsf{L_F}(S\|T, U) &\in \{0,1\}^\lambda , \\ \mathsf{L_F}(S\|T^\star, U^\star) &\in \{0,1\}^\lambda , \\ \mathsf{L_C}(U, U^\star) &\in \{0,1\}^{\lambda'} . \end{aligned}$$

Here, R, S, T, U, and $U^\star$ are as described in Fig. 4. *Under the assumption that outputs of* H *never collide*, we can observe that these are the only functions that leak information about R, T, and U for this message M. In other words, under this assumption, leakages for different messages are independent. As $\mathsf{L_F}$ and $\mathsf{L_C}$ are fixed, predetermined, functions, they adversary learns *at most* 2λ bits of leakage on T and at most $\lambda + v\lambda'$ bits of leakage on U, for any message M.

The adversary wins if any of its q construction queries returns 1. However, as suggested above, we have to argue based on the non-existence of collisions in the output of H, labeled R. In fact, it turns out that the adversary also has a gain if there are collisions in the values $S\|U$. Therefore, we will count both types of collisions as a win for the adversary.

More detailed, we denote by bad the event that there exist two queries to $\mathsf{MAC}^{\mathsf{H,F}}$ and $\mathsf{VFY}^{\mathsf{H,F}}$ that satisfy $R = R'$ or $S\|U = S'\|U'$. For $i \in \{1, \ldots, v\}$, we denote by win_i the event that the i-th verification query succeeds. Write $\mathsf{win} = \bigvee_{i=1}^{v} \mathsf{win}_i$. Our goal is to bound

$$\begin{aligned} \mathbf{Pr}(\mathsf{win}) &\le \mathbf{Pr}(\mathsf{win} \wedge \neg\mathsf{bad}) + \mathbf{Pr}(\mathsf{bad}) \\ &= \mathbf{Pr}\left(\bigvee_{i=1}^{v} \mathsf{win}_i \wedge \neg\mathsf{bad}\right) + \mathbf{Pr}(\mathsf{bad}) \\ &\le \sum_{i=1}^{v} \mathbf{Pr}(\mathsf{win}_i \wedge \neg\mathsf{win}_{1..i-1} \wedge \neg\mathsf{bad}) + \mathbf{Pr}(\mathsf{bad}) , \end{aligned} \tag{27}$$

where $\mathsf{win}_{1..0} = \mathsf{false}$ by definition.

Bound on $\mathbf{Pr}(\mathsf{win}_i \wedge \neg\mathsf{win}_{1..i-1} \wedge \neg\mathsf{bad})$. Consider any $i \in \{1, \ldots, v\}$, and consider the i-th query $(M, T^\star)$. By $\neg\mathsf{bad}$, message M defines a unique R, so the construction query is independent of all other construction queries that were not made for the message M. The oracle outputs 1 if:

- $T^\star = T$. As the adversary has so far learned at most 2λ bits of leakage on T, this condition is set with probability at most $1/2^{t-2\lambda}$;

- $T^\star \neq T$ but $\mathsf{F}(S\|T^\star) = U$. Clearly, if there were an earlier message M' for which $S' = S$ and $T' = T^\star$, the equation $\mathsf{F}(S\|T^\star) = U$ would contradict with the assumption that there is no collision $S\|U = S'\|U'$. Therefore, necessarily, there was no earlier evaluation of $\mathsf{F}(S\|T^\star)$, and the result will be randomly drawn from a set of size at least 2^t values. Thus, the condition is set with probability at most $1/2^t$.

Adding both cases, we get

$$\mathbf{Pr}\left(\mathsf{win}_i \wedge \neg\mathsf{win}_{1..i-1}\right) \leq \frac{2}{2^{t-2\lambda}}. \tag{28}$$

Bound on $\mathbf{Pr}(\mathsf{bad})$. The hash function is invoked a total number of $q+v$ times, and any pair of invocations has colliding $R = R'$ with probability $1/2^n$ and colliding $S\|U = S'\|U'$ with probability $s+t$. As we assumed that $s+t = n$, we obtain that

$$\mathbf{Pr}\left(\mathsf{bad}\right) \leq \frac{2\binom{q+v}{2}}{2^n}. \tag{29}$$

Conclusion. The adversary makes q construction queries, each of which succeeds with probability at most (28). Next, we have to add (29). We thus obtain from (27) that

$$\mathbf{Adv}^{\text{lr-mac}}_{\mathsf{HaFuFu}}(\mathcal{A}) \leq \frac{2q}{2^{t-2\lambda}} + \frac{2\binom{q+v}{2}}{2^n}.$$

The reasoning holds for any adversary making q construction queries and v verification queries, and this completes the proof. □

8 Conclusion

In this paper, we examined leakage resilient value comparison via cryptographic building blocks. In short, we showed that is possible to perform value comparison via cryptographic building blocks in a sound and leakage resilient way without the need to protect the comparison operation at all. Hence, there is no strict need in putting resources into the additional protection of the comparison operation. Instead, implementers could choose an area/speed trade-off by just saving the area needed to implement a protected verification operation in exchange for two additional primitive executions during verification.

The probability that an adversary guesses the right value in q attempts for just a plain tag comparison in the black box setting is $q/2^t$. When comparing this with the security bounds we get for value comparison via cryptographic functions, we see that doing the comparison cryptographic functions give the adversary a slightly bigger advantage in succeeding. The main reason for this is that U and $U^\star$ can have the same value although T and $T^\star$ might differ. We consider this advantage to be negligible in most practical cases and value the benefits in resistance against side-channel attacks more. However, in case this additional advantage over a plain comparison is a concern, it is possible to lessen it by increasing the size of U and $U^\star$.

Acknowledgements. This work has been supported in part by the Austrian Science Fund (FWF): J 4277-N38, and the European Research Council (ERC) under the European Union's Horizon 2020 research and innovation programme (grant agreement No 681402).

References

1. Andreeva, E., et al.: COLM v1. CAESAR, second choice for defense in depth (2016)
2. Beierle, C., et al.: The SKINNY family of block ciphers and its low-latency variant MANTIS. In: Robshaw, M., Katz, J. (eds.) CRYPTO 2016. LNCS, vol. 9815, pp. 123–153. Springer, Heidelberg (2016). https://doi.org/10.1007/978-3-662-53008-5_5
3. Beierle, C., Leander, G., Moradi, A., Rasoolzadeh, S.: CRAFT: lightweight tweakable block cipher with efficient protection against DFA attacks. IACR Trans. Symmetric Cryptol. **2019**(1), 5–45 (2019)
4. Bellare, M., Impagliazzo, R.: A tool for obtaining tighter security analyses of pseudorandom function based constructions, with applications to PRP to PRF conversion. Cryptology ePrint Archive, Report 1999/024 (1999)
5. Bellizia, D., et al.: Spook: sponge-based leakage-resistant authenticated encryption with a masked tweakable block cipher. IACR Trans. Symmetric Cryptol. **2020**, 295–349 (2020)
6. Bellizia, D., et al.: Mode-Level vs. implementation-level physical security in symmetric cryptography. In: Micciancio, D., Ristenpart, T. (eds.) 12170. LNCS, vol. 12170, pp. 369–400. Springer, Cham (2020). https://doi.org/10.1007/978-3-030-56784-2_13
7. Berti, F., Guo, C., Pereira, O., Peters, T., Standaert, F.X.: Tedt, a leakage-resist AEAD mode for high physical security applications. IACR Trans. Cryptogr. Hardw. Embed. Syst. **2020**(1), 256–320 (2020)
8. Berti, F., Pereira, O., Peters, T., Standaert, F.X.: On leakage-resilient authenticated encryption with decryption leakages. IACR Trans. Symmetric Cryptol. **2017**(3), 271–293 (2017)
9. Bertoni, G., Daemen, J., Peeters, M., Van Assche, G.: Cryptographic sponge functions, January 2011
10. Bertoni, G., Daemen, J., Peeters, M., Van Assche, G.: The Keccak reference. Submission to NIST (Round 3) (2011)
11. Bhattacharya, S., Nandi, M.: A note on the chi-square method: A tool for proving cryptographic security. Cryptogr. Commun. **10**(5), 935–957 (2018)
12. Chari, S., Jutla, C.S., Rao, J.R., Rohatgi, P.: Towards sound approaches to counteract power-analysis attacks. In: Wiener, M. (ed.) CRYPTO 1999. LNCS, vol. 1666, pp. 398–412. Springer, Heidelberg (1999). https://doi.org/10.1007/3-540-48405-1_26
13. Daemen, J.: Changing of the guards: a simple and efficient method for achieving uniformity in threshold sharing. In: Fischer, W., Homma, N. (eds.) CHES 2017. LNCS, vol. 10529, pp. 137–153. Springer, Cham (2017). https://doi.org/10.1007/978-3-319-66787-4_7
14. Daemen, J., Dobraunig, C., Eichlseder, M., Groß, H., Mendel, F., Primas, R.: Protecting against statistical ineffective fault attacks. IACR Trans. Cryptogr. Hardw. Embed. Syst. **2020**(3), 508–543 (2020)
15. Daemen, J., Hoffert, S., Van Assche, G., Van Keer, R.: The design of xoodoo and xoofff. IACR Trans. Symmetric Cryptol. **2018**(4), 1–38 (2018)

16. Daemen, J., Mennink, B., Van Assche, G.: Full-state keyed duplex with built-in multi-user support. In: Takagi, T., Peyrin, T. (eds.) ASIACRYPT 2017. LNCS, vol. 10625, pp. 606–637. Springer, Cham (2017). https://doi.org/10.1007/978-3-319-70697-9_21
17. Daemen, J., Peeters, M., Van Assche, G., Rijmen, V.: The NOEKEON block cipher (2000), nessie Proposal
18. Daemen, J., Rijmen, V.: The Design of Rijndael - The Advanced Encryption Standard (AES). Springer, Information Security and Cryptography (2002)
19. Dobraunig, C., et al.: Isap v2.0. IACR Trans. Symmetric Cryptol. **2020**(S1), 390–416 (2020)
20. Dobraunig, C., Eichlseder, M., Mangard, S., Mendel, F., Unterluggauer, T.: ISAP - towards side-channel secure authenticated encryption. IACR Trans. Symmetric Cryptol. **2017**(1), 80–105 (2017)
21. Dobraunig, C., Eichlseder, M., Mendel, F., Schläffer, M.: Ascon v1.2. Submission to NIST Lightweight Cryptography (2019)
22. Dobraunig, C., Mennink, B.: Leakage resilience of the duplex construction. In: Galbraith, S.D., Moriai, S. (eds.) ASIACRYPT 2019. LNCS, vol. 11923, pp. 225–255. Springer, Cham (2019). https://doi.org/10.1007/978-3-030-34618-8_8
23. Dobraunig, C., Mennink, B.: Security of the suffix keyed sponge. IACR Trans. Symmetric Cryptol. **2019**(4), 223–248 (2019)
24. Dodis, Y., Pietrzak, K.: Leakage-resilient pseudorandom functions and side-channel attacks on feistel networks. In: Rabin, T. (ed.) CRYPTO 2010. LNCS, vol. 6223, pp. 21–40. Springer, Heidelberg (2010). https://doi.org/10.1007/978-3-642-14623-7_2
25. Dziembowski, S., Pietrzak, K.: Leakage-resilient cryptography. In: FOCS, pp. 293–302. IEEE Computer Society (2008)
26. Faust, S., Pietrzak, K., Schipper, J.: Practical leakage-resilient symmetric cryptography. In: Prouff, E., Schaumont, P. (eds.) CHES 2012. LNCS, vol. 7428, pp. 213–232. Springer, Heidelberg (2012). https://doi.org/10.1007/978-3-642-33027-8_13
27. Gérard, B., Grosso, V., Naya-Plasencia, M., Standaert, F.-X.: Block ciphers that are easier to mask: how far can we go? In: Bertoni, G., Coron, J.-S. (eds.) CHES 2013. LNCS, vol. 8086, pp. 383–399. Springer, Heidelberg (2013). https://doi.org/10.1007/978-3-642-40349-1_22
28. Goubin, L., Patarin, J.: DES and differential power analysis the "Duplication" method. In: Koç, Ç.K., Paar, C. (eds.) CHES 1999. LNCS, vol. 1717, pp. 158–172. Springer, Heidelberg (1999). https://doi.org/10.1007/3-540-48059-5_15
29. Goudarzi, D., et al.: Pyjamask: Block cipher and authenticated encryption with highly efficient masked implementation. IACR Trans. Symmetric Cryptol. **2020**(S1), 31–59 (2020)
30. Gross, H., Mangard, S.: Reconciling $d + 1$ masking in hardware and software. In: Fischer, W., Homma, N. (eds.) CHES 2017. LNCS, vol. 10529, pp. 115–136. Springer, Cham (2017). https://doi.org/10.1007/978-3-319-66787-4_6
31. Grosso, V., Leurent, G., Standaert, F.-X., Varıcı, K.: LS-designs: bitslice encryption for efficient masked software implementations. In: Cid, C., Rechberger, C. (eds.) FSE 2014. LNCS, vol. 8540, pp. 18–37. Springer, Heidelberg (2015). https://doi.org/10.1007/978-3-662-46706-0_2
32. Guo, C., Pereira, O., Peters, T., Standaert, F.X.: Towards low-energy leakage-resistant authenticated encryption from the duplex sponge construction. IACR Trans. Symmetric Cryptol. **2020**(1), 6–42 (2020)

33. Guo, C., Standaert, F.X., Wang, W., Yu, Y.: Efficient side-channel secure message authentication with better bounds. IACR Trans. Symmetric Cryptol. **2019**(4), 23–53 (2019)
34. Hall, C., Wagner, D., Kelsey, J., Schneier, B.: Building PRFs from PRPs. In: Krawczyk, H. (ed.) CRYPTO 1998. LNCS, vol. 1462, pp. 370–389. Springer, Heidelberg (1998). https://doi.org/10.1007/BFb0055742
35. Ishai, Y., Sahai, A., Wagner, D.: Private circuits: securing hardware against probing attacks. In: Boneh, D. (ed.) CRYPTO 2003. LNCS, vol. 2729, pp. 463–481. Springer, Heidelberg (2003). https://doi.org/10.1007/978-3-540-45146-4_27
36. Jean, J., Nikolić, I., Peyrin, T., Seurin, Y.: Deoxys v1.41. CAESAR, first choice for defense in depth (2016)
37. Kannwischer, M.J., Pessl, P., Primas, R.: Single-trace attacks on keccak. IACR Trans. Cryptogr. Hardw. Embed. Syst. **2020**(3), 243–268 (2020)
38. Kocher, P.C.: Timing Attacks on Implementations of Diffie-Hellman, RSA, DSS, and Other Systems. In: Koblitz, N. (ed.) CRYPTO 1996. LNCS, vol. 1109, pp. 104–113. Springer, Heidelberg (1996). https://doi.org/10.1007/3-540-68697-5_9
39. Kocher, P., Jaffe, J., Jun, B.: Differential power analysis. In: Wiener, M. (ed.) CRYPTO 1999. LNCS, vol. 1666, pp. 388–397. Springer, Heidelberg (1999). https://doi.org/10.1007/3-540-48405-1_25
40. Krovetz, T., Rogaway, P.: The software performance of authenticated-encryption modes. In: Joux, A. (ed.) FSE 2011. LNCS, vol. 6733, pp. 306–327. Springer, Heidelberg (2011). https://doi.org/10.1007/978-3-642-21702-9_18
41. Krovetz, T., Rogaway, P.: The OCB authenticated-encryption algorithm. RFC **7253**, 1–19 (2014)
42. McGrew, D.A., Viega, J.: The security and performance of the Galois/Counter Mode (GCM) of operation. In: Canteaut, A., Viswanathan, K. (eds.) INDOCRYPT 2004. LNCS, vol. 3348, pp. 343–355. Springer, Heidelberg (2004). https://doi.org/10.1007/978-3-540-30556-9_27
43. Medwed, M., Standaert, F.-X., Joux, A.: Towards super-exponential side-channel security with efficient leakage-resilient PRFs. In: Prouff, E., Schaumont, P. (eds.) CHES 2012. LNCS, vol. 7428, pp. 193–212. Springer, Heidelberg (2012). https://doi.org/10.1007/978-3-642-33027-8_12
44. Medwed, M., Standaert, F.-X., Nikov, V., Feldhofer, M.: Unknown-input attacks in the parallel setting: improving the security of the CHES 2012 leakage-resilient PRF. In: Cheon, J.H., Takagi, T. (eds.) ASIACRYPT 2016. LNCS, vol. 10031, pp. 602–623. Springer, Heidelberg (2016). https://doi.org/10.1007/978-3-662-53887-6_22
45. Mennink, B.: Linking stam's bounds with generalized truncation. In: Matsui, M. (ed.) CT-RSA 2019. LNCS, vol. 11405, pp. 313–329. Springer, Cham (2019). https://doi.org/10.1007/978-3-030-12612-4_16
46. Nikova, S., Rechberger, C., Rijmen, V.: Threshold implementations against side-channel attacks and glitches. In: Ning, P., Qing, S., Li, N. (eds.) ICICS 2006. LNCS, vol. 4307, pp. 529–545. Springer, Heidelberg (2006). https://doi.org/10.1007/11935308_38
47. Nikova, S., Rijmen, V., Schläffer, M.: Secure hardware implementation of nonlinear functions in the presence of glitches. J. Cryptology **24**(2), 292–321 (2011)
48. NIST: Lightweight Cryptography, February 2019
49. Pereira, O., Standaert, F.X., Vivek, S.: Leakage-resilient authentication and encryption from symmetric cryptographic primitives. In: ACM CCS, pp. 96–108. ACM (2015)

50. Pietrzak, K.: A leakage-resilient mode of operation. In: Joux, A. (ed.) EUROCRYPT 2009. LNCS, vol. 5479, pp. 462–482. Springer, Heidelberg (2009). https://doi.org/10.1007/978-3-642-01001-9_27
51. Rivain, M., Prouff, E.: Provably secure higher-order masking of AES. In: Mangard, S., Standaert, F.-X. (eds.) CHES 2010. LNCS, vol. 6225, pp. 413–427. Springer, Heidelberg (2010). https://doi.org/10.1007/978-3-642-15031-9_28
52. Simon, T., Batina, L., Daemen, J., Grosso, V., Massolino, P.M.C., Papagiannopoulos, K., Regazzoni, F., Samwel, N.: Friet: an authenticated encryption scheme with built-in fault detection. In: Canteaut, A., Ishai, Y. (eds.) EUROCRYPT 2020. LNCS, vol. 12105, pp. 581–611. Springer, Cham (2020). https://doi.org/10.1007/978-3-030-45721-1_21
53. Stam, A.J.: Distance between sampling with and without replacement. Statistica Neerlandica **32**(2), 81–91 (1978)
54. Standaert, F.-X., Pereira, O., Yu, Yu.: Leakage-resilient symmetric cryptography under empirically verifiable assumptions. In: Canetti, R., Garay, J.A. (eds.) CRYPTO 2013. LNCS, vol. 8042, pp. 335–352. Springer, Heidelberg (2013). https://doi.org/10.1007/978-3-642-40041-4_19
55. Trichina, E.: Combinational logic design for AES subbyte transformation on masked data. Cryptology ePrint Archive, Report 2003/236 (2003)
56. Unterstein, F., Schink, M., Schamberger, T., Tebelmann, L., Ilg, M., Heyszl, J.: Retrofitting leakage resilient authenticated encryption to microcontrollers. IACR Trans. Cryptogr. Hardw. Embed. Syst. **2020**(4), 365–388 (2020)

The Mother of All Leakages: How to Simulate Noisy Leakages via Bounded Leakage (Almost) for Free

Gianluca Brian[1(✉)], Antonio Faonio[2], Maciej Obremski[3], João Ribeiro[4], Mark Simkin[5], Maciej Skórski[6], and Daniele Venturi[1]

[1] Sapienza University of Rome, Rome, Italy
{brian,venturi}@di.uniroma1.it
[2] EURECOM, Sophia-Antipolis, France
antonio.faonio@eurecom.fr
[3] National University of Singapore, Singapore, Singapore
[4] Imperial College London, London, UK
j.lourenco-ribeiro17@imperial.ac.uk
[5] Aarhus University, Aarhus, Denmark
simkin@cs.au.dk
[6] University of Luxembourg, Luxembourg, Luxembourg
maciej.skorski@uni.lu

Abstract. We show that the most common flavors of noisy leakage can be simulated in the information-theoretic setting using a single query of bounded leakage, up to a small statistical simulation error and a slight loss in the leakage parameter. The latter holds true in particular for one of the most used noisy-leakage models, where the noisiness is measured using the conditional average min-entropy (Naor and Segev, CRYPTO'09 and SICOMP'12).

Our reductions between noisy and bounded leakage are achieved in two steps. First, we put forward a new leakage model (dubbed the *dense leakage* model) and prove that dense leakage can be simulated in the information-theoretic setting using a single query of bounded leakage, up to small statistical distance. Second, we show that the most common noisy-leakage models fall within the class of dense leakage, with good parameters. Third, we prove lower bounds on the amount of bounded leakage required for simulation with sub-constant error, showing that our reductions are nearly optimal. In particular, our results imply that useful general simulation of noisy leakage based on statistical distance and mutual information is impossible. We also provide a complete picture of the relationships between different noisy-leakage models.

Our result finds applications to leakage-resilient cryptography, where we are often able to lift security in the presence of bounded leakage to security in the presence of noisy leakage, both in the information-theoretic and in the computational setting. Additionally, we show how to use lower bounds in communication complexity to prove that bounded-collusion protocols (Kumar, Meka, and Sahai, FOCS'19) for certain functions do not only require long transcripts, but also necessarily need to reveal enough information about the inputs.

A. Canteaut and F.-X. Standaert (Eds.): EUROCRYPT 2021, LNCS 12697, pp. 408–437, 2021.
https://doi.org/10.1007/978-3-030-77886-6_14

1 Introduction

1.1 Background

The security analysis of cryptographic primitives typically relies on the assumption that the underlying secrets (including, e.g., secret keys and internal randomness) are uniformly random to the eyes of the attacker. In reality, however, this assumption may simply be false due to the presence of so-called side-channel attacks [4,36,37], where an adversary can obtain partial information (also known as leakage) on the secret state of an implementation of a cryptographic scheme, by exploiting physical phenomena.

Leakage-resilient cryptography [28,34,43] aims at bridging this gap by allowing the adversary to launch leakage attacks in theoretical models too. The last decade has seen an impressive amount of work in this area, thanks to which we now dispose of a large number of leakage-resilient cryptographic primitives in different leakage models. We refer the reader to the recent survey by Kalai and Reyzin [35] for an overview of these results.

From an abstract viewpoint, we can think of the leakage on a random variable X (corresponding, say, to the secret key of an encryption scheme) as a correlated random variable $Z = f(X)$ for some leakage function f that can be chosen by the adversary. Depending on the restriction[1] we put on f, we obtain different leakage models. The first such restriction, introduced for the first time by Dziembowski and Pietrzak [28], is to simply assume that the length $\ell \in \mathbb{N}$ of the leakage Z is small enough. This yields the so-called *Bounded Leakage Model.* Thanks to its simplicity and versatility, this model has been used to construct many cryptographic primitives that remain secure in the presence of bounded leakage.

A considerable limitation of the Bounded Leakage Model is the fact that, in real-world side-channel attacks, the leakage obtained by the attacker is rarely bounded in length. For instance, the power trace on a physical implementation of AES typically consists of several Megabytes of information, which is much larger than the length of the secret key.

This motivates a more general notion of *noisy leakage*, where there is no upper bound on the length of Z but instead we assume the leakage is somewhat noisy, in the sense that it does not reveal too much information about X. It turns out that the level of noisiness of the leakage can be measured in several ways, each yielding a different leakage model. The first such model, proposed for the first time by Naor and Segev [44] in the setting of leakage-resilient public-key encryption, assumes that the uncertainty of X given Z drops at most by some parameter $\ell \in \mathbb{R}_{>0}$. The latter can be formalized by means of conditional[2] average min-entropy [22], i.e. by requiring that $\widetilde{\mathbb{H}}_\infty(X|Z) \geq \mathbb{H}_\infty(X) - \ell$. In this work, we will refer to this model as the *Min-Entropy-Noisy (ME-Noisy) Leakage Model.* Dodis,

[1] Clearly, there must be some restriction as otherwise $f(X) = X$ and there is no hope for security.

[2] Intuitively, the conditional average min-entropy of a random variable X given Z measures how hard it is to predict X given Z on average (by an unbounded predictor).

Haralambiev, López-Alt, and Wichs [20] considered a similar model, which we refer to as the *Uniform-Noisy (U-Noisy) Leakage Model*, where the condition about the min-entropy drop is defined w.r.t. the uniform distribution U (rather than on X which may not[3] be uniform).

Another variant of noisy leakage was pioneered by Prouff and Rivain [47] (building on previous work by Chari, Jutla, Rao, and Rohatgi [16]), who suggested to measure the noisiness of the leakage by bounding the Euclidean norm between the joint distribution P_{XZ} and the product distribution $P_X \otimes P_Z$ with some parameter $\eta \in (0, 1)$. Follow-up works by Duc, Dziembowski, and Faust [24] and by Prest, Goudarzi, Martinelli, and Passelègue [46] replaced the Euclidean norm, respectively, with the statistical distance and the mutual information, yielding what we refer to as the *SD-Noisy Leakage* and the *MI-Noisy Leakage Models*. More precisely,[4] Duc, Dziembowski, and Faust considered a strict subset of SD-noisy leakage—hereafter dubbed *DDF-noisy leakage*—for the special case where $X = (X_1, \ldots, X_n)$, for some fixed parameter $n \in \mathbb{N}$, and the function f has a type $f = (f_1, \ldots, f_n)$ such that $\Delta(P_{X_i} \otimes P_{Z_i}, P_{X_i Z_i}) \leq \eta$ for each X_i and $Z_i = f_i(X_i)$. All of these works studied noisy leakage in the setting of leakage-resilient circuit compilers (see Sect. 1.4).

The different flavors of noisy leakage discussed above capture either a more general class of leakage functions than bounded leakage (as in the case of ME-noisy and U-noisy leakage), or an orthogonal class of leakage functions (as in the case of SD-noisy and MI-noisy leakage). On the other hand, it is usually easiest (and most common) to prove security of a cryptographic primitive against bounded leakage, whereas extending the analysis to other types of noisy leakage requires non-trivial specialized proofs for each primitive. Motivated by this situation, we consider the following question: *Can we reduce noisy-leakage resilience to bounded-leakage resilience in a general way?*

1.2 Our Results

In this work, we answer the above question to the positive in the information-theoretic setting. In a nutshell, we achieve this by proving that a novel and very general leakage model, which we refer to as the *Dense Leakage Model* and that encompasses all the aforementioned noisy-leakage models, can be simulated almost for free (albeit possibly inefficiently) using a single query of bounded leakage. Our result allows us to show in a streamlined way that many cryptographic primitives which have only been proved to be resilient against bounded leakage are also secure against noisy leakage, with only a small loss in parameters. Importantly, the latter does not only hold for cryptographic schemes with information-theoretic security, but also for ones with computational security

[3] For instance, in the setting of public-key encryption [44], the random variable X corresponds to the distribution of the secret key SK given the public key PK, which may not be uniform.

[4] The work by Prest, Goudarzi, Martinelli, and Passelègue considered a similar restriction for MI-noisy leakage.

only. We elaborate on our contributions in more details in the paragraphs below, and refer the reader to Sect. 1.3 for a more technical overview.

Simulating Dense Leakage with Bounded Leakage. As the starting point for our work, in Sect. 3, we introduce a meaningful simulation paradigm between leakage models. Informally, given some random variable X and two families of leakage functions $\mathcal{F}$ and $\mathcal{G}$ on X, we say $\mathcal{F}$ is ε-simulatable from $\mathcal{G}$ if for every $f \in \mathcal{F}$ we can simulate $(X, f(X))$ to within statistical distance ε using a *single* query of the form $g(X)$ for some $g \in \mathcal{G}$.

Taking into account the above simulation paradigm, the question we tackle is whether we can have simulation theorems stating that different noisy-leakage families $\mathcal{F}$ are ε-simulatable from the family $\mathcal{G}$ of ℓ-bounded leakage (for some small ε). We prove such a simulation theorem for a new leakage model that we call *dense leakage.*

In order to define the Dense Leakage Model, we begin with the concept of *δ-density*: Given two distributions P and P' over a discrete set $\mathcal{X}$, we say P is δ-dense in P' if $P(x) \leq \frac{P'(x)}{\delta}$ for all $x \in \mathcal{X}$. In particular, δ-density implies that $P(x) = 0$ whenever $P'(x) = 0$, and thus this concept is connected to the notion of absolute continuity of one measure with respect to another. Given this notion, it is simple to describe the Dense Leakage Model. If $Z = f(X)$ denotes some leakage from X, then Z is (p, γ, δ)-dense leakage from X if, with probability $1-p$ over the choice of $X = x$, we have $P_{Z|X=x}(z) \leq \frac{P_Z(z)}{\delta}$ with probability $1 - \gamma$ over the choice of $Z = z$. Intuitively, Z being a dense leakage of X essentially corresponds to the distributions $P_{Z|X=x}$ being "approximately" dense in the marginal distribution P_Z for most choices of $x \in \mathcal{X}$.

Our first result is a simulation theorem for dense leakage with respect to bounded leakage, which we state in simplified form below.

Theorem 1 (Informal). *For any random variable X, and every parameter $\varepsilon \in (0, 1)$, the family of (p, γ, δ)-dense leakage functions on X is $(\varepsilon + \varepsilon^{1/4\delta} + \gamma + p)$-simulatable from the family of ℓ-bounded leakage functions on X, so long as*

$$\ell \geq \log(1/\delta) + \log\log(1/\varepsilon) + 2\log\left(\frac{1}{1-\gamma}\right) + 2.$$

On the Power of Dense Leakage. Second, we show that dense leakage captures all of the noisy-leakage models considered above. In particular, we obtain the following informal result.

Theorem 2 (Informal). *The families of ME-noisy, U-noisy, and DDF-noisy leakages fall within the family of dense leakage with good[5] parameters.*

By combining Theorem 1 and Theorem 2, we obtain non-trivial simulation theorems for the families of ME-noisy, U-noisy, and DDF-noisy leakage from bounded

[5] In particular, small enough in order to be combined with Theorem 1 yielding interesting applications.

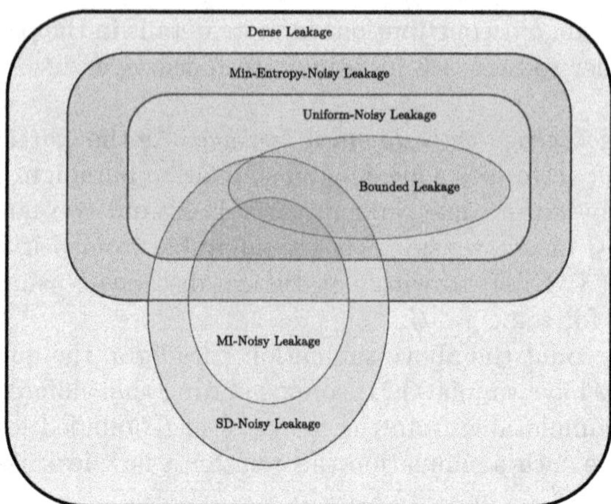

Fig. 1. Containment of the different leakage models considered in this paper. Our main result is that a single query of bounded leakage is enough to simulate dense leakage to within small statistical distance.

leakage, with small simulation error and small bounded leakage parameter. It is worth mentioning that, for the specific case of ME-noisy leakage, Theorem 2 only holds for distributions X that are almost flat. As we shall prove, this restriction is nearly optimal in the sense that there exist "non-flat" distributions X for which we cannot simulate ME-noisy leakage on X from bounded leakage on X with good parameters, *even when the drop in min-entropy is minimal.*

Fundamental Limitations of SD-noisy and MI-noisy Leakages. Turning to the families of SD-noisy and MI-noisy leakage, one can show that they fall within the family of dense leakage too. However, the parameters we obtain in this case are not good enough to be combined with Theorem 1 in order to yield interesting applications. In fact, we prove that the families of η-SD-noisy and η-MI-noisy leakage are trivially simulatable with statistical error roughly η even from the degenerate family of 0-bounded leakage. Unfortunately, this is inherent for the general form of SD-noisy and MI-noisy leakage we consider: we prove that no simulator can achieve simulation error significantly smaller than η even when leaking almost all of the input. In contrast, Duc, Dziembowski, and Faust [23, 24] gave a non-trivial[6] simulation theorem for the family of DDF-noisy leakage (which is a strict subset of SD-noisy leakage) from a special type of bounded leakage called *threshold probing leakage.* Consistently, Theorem 2 establishes that DDF-noisy leakage is dense leakage with good parameters which in combination with Theorem 1 gives an alternative (non-trivial) simulation theorem for DDF-noisy leakage from bounded leakage. While this result is not new, we believe it showcases the generality of our techniques.

[6] In particular, with negligible simulation error and small bounded leakage parameter even for constant η.

A Complete Picture, and Near-Optimality of our Simulation Theorems. We also provide a complete picture of inclusions and separations between the different leakage models, as depicted in Fig. 1. Some of these relationships were already known (e.g., the fact that the family of U-noisy leakage is a strict subset of the family of ME-noisy leakage), and some are new (e.g., the separations between the family of SD-noisy leakage and the families of ME-noisy and MI-noisy leakage).

Moreover, we prove a series of results showing that the amount of bounded leakage we use in our simulation theorems is nearly optimal with respect to the desired simulation error.

Applications in Brief. Next, we explore applications of our results to leakage-resilient cryptography. Intuitively, the reason why the simulation paradigm is useful is that it may allow us to reduce leakage resilience of a cryptographic scheme against $\mathcal{F}$ to leakage resilience against $\mathcal{G}$. In particular, when $\mathcal{G}$ is taken to be the family of bounded-leakage functions, we obtain that many primitives which were already known to be secure against bounded leakage are also secure against dense (and thus noisy) leakage. Examples include forward-secure storage [26], leakage-resilient one-way functions and public-key encryption [5], cylinder-intersection extractors [38], symmetric non-interactive key exchange [40], leakage-resilient secret sharing [1,9,38,41,48] and two-party computation [32].

1.3 Technical Overview

Due to space constraints, most proofs have been deferred to the full version of this paper [13].

Simulation via Rejection Sampling. We begin by giving an overview of the approach we use to simulate dense leakage from bounded leakage. As discussed before, our goal is to show that, for a random variable X and some associated dense leakage function f (where f may be randomized), there is a (possibly inefficient) simulator that makes *at most one* black-box query $g(X)$ for some ℓ-bounded leakage function $g : \mathcal{X} \to \{0,1\}^\ell$ and outputs $\widetilde{Z}$ such that

$$(X, f(X)) \approx_\varepsilon (X, \widetilde{Z}), \tag{1}$$

where $\approx_\varepsilon$ denotes statistical distance at most ε. For simplicity, we focus here on the setting where f is "exactly" δ-dense leakage from X, meaning that, if $Z = f(X)$, we have $P_{Z|X=x}(z) \leq \frac{P_Z(z)}{\delta}$ for all x and z. This setting is already appropriate to showcase our main ideas.

The key observation that enables the design of our simulator, as we formalize in Sect. 2, is that if a distribution P is δ-dense in P', then it is possible to sample $\widetilde{P}$ satisfying $\widetilde{P} \approx_\varepsilon P$ with access only to $s = \frac{\log(1/\varepsilon)}{\delta}$ independent and identically distributed (i.i.d.) samples from P', say $z_1, z_2, \ldots, z_s$, and knowledge of the distribution P, via *rejection sampling*: For $i = 1, 2, \ldots, s$, either output

z_i with probability $\delta P(z_i)/P'(z_i) \leq 1$, or move to $i+1$ otherwise (if $i = s+1$, abort).

This suggests the following simulator for f exploiting δ-density: The simulator generates s i.i.d. samples $\mathbf{z} = (z_1, z_2, \ldots, z_s)$ from P_Z. Then, it queries the bounded-leakage oracle with the randomized function $g_{\mathbf{z}}$ which, with full knowledge of x, performs rejection sampling of $P_{Z|X=x}$ from P_Z using $\mathbf{z}$. If rejection sampling outputs z_i, then $g_{\mathbf{z}}(x) = i$, and if rejection sampling aborts we may set $g_{\mathbf{z}}(x) = \perp$. In particular, $g_{\mathbf{z}}$ has $1+s$ possible outputs, and so it is ℓ-bounded-leakage from X with $\ell = \log(1+s) \leq \log(1/\delta) + \log\log(1/\varepsilon) + 1$. The behavior of the simulator is now clear: Since it knows $\mathbf{z}$, it can simply output $\widetilde{Z} = z_i$ (or $\widetilde{Z} = \perp$ if rejection sampling aborted). The discussion above guarantees that the output of the simulator is ε-close in statistical distance to $f(x)$, which yields Eq. (1).

As previously discussed, in the actual proof (which appears in Sect. 4.1) we must deal with an approximate variant of δ-density. However, we show that the above approach still works in the setting of approximate density at the price of some additional small terms in the simulation error and in the bounded leakage length.

Noisy Leakage is Dense Leakage. As an example of how we manage to frame many types of noisy leakage as dense leakage with good parameters, we discuss how this can be accomplished for ME-noisy leakage assuming X satisfies a property we call *α-semi-flatness*. The full proof appears in Sect. 4.2. The property states that X satisfies $P_X(x) \leq 2^{\alpha} \cdot P_X(x')$ for all $x, x' \in \mathrm{supp}(X)$, and, as we shall see, it is usually satisfied in applications with small α (or even $\alpha = 0$, which corresponds to a flat distribution). We stress that for the case of U-noisy, DDF-noisy, SD-noisy, and MI-noisy leakages, *no* assumption is required on X to place these types of leakage inside the set of dense leakages. More details can be found in Sect. 4.3 and Sect. 4.4.

Consider some α-semi-flat X and leakage function f such that $Z = f(X)$ satisfies

$$\mathbb{H}_{\infty}(X|Z=z) \geq \mathbb{H}_{\infty}(X) - \ell \tag{2}$$

for some $\ell > 0$ and all z. Note that this is a special case of ME-noisy leakage, but it suffices to present the main ideas of our approach. Our goal is to show that f is $(0,0,\delta)$-dense leakage of X for an appropriate parameter δ, meaning that we wish to prove that $P_{Z|X=x}(z) \leq \frac{P_Z(z)}{\delta}$ for all x and z. Observe that, by Eq. (2), we have $P_{X|Z=z}(x) \leq 2^{\ell} \max_{x'} P_X(x') \leq 2^{\ell+\alpha} P_X(x)$ for all x and z, where the rightmost inequality makes use of the fact that X is α-semi-flat. Rewriting the inequality above using Bayes' theorem yields $P_{Z|X=x}(z) \leq 2^{\ell+\alpha} P_Z(z)$, meaning that f is $(p = 0, \gamma = 0, \delta = 2^{-\ell-\alpha})$-dense leakage of X. By Theorem 1, we then have that $f(X)$ can be simulated with statistical error 2ε using $\ell' = \ell + \alpha + \log\log(1/\varepsilon) + 2$ bits of bounded leakage from X. This statement allows for significant flexibility in the choice of parameters. For example, setting $\varepsilon = 2^{-\lambda}$ for some security parameter λ yields negligible simulation error from $\ell + \alpha + \log(\lambda) + 2$ bits of bounded leakage. Since α is usually very small in applications (often we have $\alpha = 0$), in practice we can achieve negligible simulation error using $\ell + \log(\lambda) + O(1)$ bits of bounded leakage, i.e., by paying only an extra $\log(\lambda)+O(1)$ bits of leakage. Extending the argument above to general ME-noisy leakage from X requires the addition of small error terms p and γ, but setting parameters similarly to the above still allows us to simulate general ℓ-ME-noisy leakage from X using only, say, $\ell + O(\log^2(\lambda))$ bits of bounded leakage from X.

Trivial Simulation of SD-noisy and MI-noisy Leakages. Consider the trivial simulator that given the function f simply samples $\widetilde{X}$ according to the distribution of X and then outputs $\widetilde{Z} = f(\widetilde{X})$. Assuming f belongs to the family of η-SD-noisy leakage, the above gives a simulation theorem for SD-noisy leakage with simulation error η (and without requiring any leakage from X). By Pinsker inequality, the above also implies a simulation theorem for η-MI-noisy leakage with simulation error $\sqrt{2\eta}$ (again without leaking anything from X).

Unfortunately, it turns out that one cannot do much better than the trivial simulator (even when using large bounded leakage) for our general definition of SD-noisy leakage. More specifically, there exists some X such that any simulator for a function f that is η-SD-noisy leakage for X must incur a simulation error of at least $\eta/2$ even when leaking all but one bit from X. In the case of MI-noisy leakage, we prove a similar result: There exists an X such that any simulator must have simulation error at least $\frac{\eta}{2n}$ when simulating η-MI-noisy leakage from X, even when leaking all but one bit of X. Notably, this means that negligible simulation error is impossible to achieve when η is non-negligible, and thus one cannot do significantly better than the trivial simulator for MI-noisy leakage either.

It is instructive to compare the above trivial simulation theorem for SD-noisy leakage with the result by Duc, Dziembowski, and Faust [24], who gave a non-trivial simulation theorem for DDF-noisy leakage from a special case of bounded leakage known as threshold probing leakage. Notice that by the triangle inequality, the trivial simulation theorem for η-SD-noisy leakage implies a trivial simulation theorem for η-DDF-noisy leakage with large simulation error $n \cdot \eta$, which in particular becomes uninteresting as soon as η is non-negligible.

Nevertheless, in [13], we show that the family of η-DDF-noisy leakage falls within the family of U-noisy (and thus dense) leakage with good parameters, which in turn gives a non-trivial simulation theorem for η-DDF-noisy leakage from ℓ-bounded leakage with negligible simulation error and for small bounded leakage parameter ℓ, even when $\eta \in (0, 1)$ is constant.

Separations Between Leakage Families, and Tradeoffs Between Simulation Error and Bounded Leakage Parameter. We complement our positive results in several ways. First, we present missing separations between the different types of leakages we consider in [13], leading to a complete picture of their relationships (as depicted in Fig. 1). Second, we study the minimum amount of bounded leakage required to simulate different types of noisy leakage with a given simulation error, and show that our simulation theorems are close to optimal. For example, in the case of ME-noisy leakage, for a large range of ℓ and α we show that

$\ell+\alpha-O(1)$ bits of bounded leakage are required to simulate ℓ-ME-noisy leakage from some α semi-flat X. In contrast, as discussed above, our simulation theorem states that approximately $\ell+\alpha$ bits of bounded leakage are sufficient to achieve negligible simulation error.

To showcase our approach towards obtaining tradeoffs between simulation error and the bounded leakage parameter, we discuss here one particularly insightful implication of a more general theorem we obtain, which states that enforcing α-semi-flatness of X is necessary to obtain a non-trivial simulation theorem for ME-noisy leakage with sub-constant simulation error. More precisely, there exists X with support in $\{0,1\}^n$ with an associated 0-noisy leakage function f (meaning that $\widetilde{\mathbb{H}}_\infty(X|f(X)) = \mathbb{H}_\infty(X)$) with the property that simulating $Z = f(X)$ with simulation error less than $1/4$ requires one ℓ'-bounded-leakage query for $\ell' \geq n-2$. In other words, to achieve small simulation error without semi-flatness, we must leak almost all of the input X. The statement above is proved as follows. Consider $X \in \{0,1\}^n$ satisfying $P_X(0^n) = 1/2$ and $P_X(x) = \frac{1}{2(2^n-1)}$ for $x \neq 0^n$. Moreover, set $Z = f(X)$ for a leakage function f such that $f(0^n)$ is uniformly distributed over $\{0,1\}^n \setminus \{0^n\}$ and $f(x) = x$ with probability 1 for $x \neq 0^n$. Routine calculations show that $\mathbb{H}_\infty(X) = 1$ and $\mathbb{H}_\infty(X|Z=z) = 1$ for all z, meaning that $\widetilde{\mathbb{H}}_\infty(X|Z=z) = 1 = \mathbb{H}_\infty(X)$, as desired. Finally, every simulator for (X, Z) above with access to one query of ℓ'-bounded-leakage for $\ell' \leq n-2$ must have simulation error $1/4$ because, conditioned on $X \neq 0^n$ (which holds with probability $1/2$), we have $f(X) = X$ and X uniform over $\{0,1\}^n \setminus \{0^n\}$. Therefore, under this conditioning, we can only correctly guess $f(X)$ with probability at most $1/2$ from any one $(n-2)$-bounded-leakage query of X.

Sample Application: Leakage-Resilient Secret Sharing. We now explain how to use our result in order to lift bounded-leakage resilience to noisy-leakage resilience (almost) for free in cryptographic applications. In fact, in the information-theoretic setting, the latter is an almost immediate consequence of our result.

For the purpose of this overview, let us focus on the concrete setting of secret sharing schemes with local leakage resilience [9]. Briefly, a t-out-of-n secret sharing scheme allows to share a message y into n shares $(x_1, \ldots, x_n)$ in such a way that y can be efficiently recovered using any subset of t shares. Local leakage resilience intuitively says that no unbounded attacker obtaining in full all of the shares $x_{\mathcal{U}}$ within an unauthorized subset $\mathcal{U} \subset [n]$ of size $u < t$, and further leaking at most ℓ bits of information z_i from each of the shares x_i independently, should be able to tell apart a secret sharing of message y_0 from a secret sharing of message y_1. Benhamouda, Degwekar, Ishai and Rabin [9] recently proved that both Shamir secret sharing and additive secret sharing satisfy local leakage resilience for certain ranges of parameters.

Thanks to Theorem 1, in Sect. 5.1, we show that any secret sharing scheme meeting the above property continues to be secure even if the attacker obtains dense (rather than bounded) leakage on each of the shares x_i independently.

The proof of this fact is simple. We move to a mental experiment in which leakages $(z_1, \ldots, z_n)$ corresponding to dense-leakage functions $(f_1, \ldots, f_n)$ are replaced by $(\tilde{z}_1, \ldots, \tilde{z}_n)$ obtained as follows: For each $i \in [n]$, first run the simulator guaranteed by Theorem 1 in order to obtain an ℓ'-bounded leakage function f'_i and compute $z'_i = f'_i(x_i)$; then, run the simulator upon input z'_i in order to obtain a simulated leakage $\tilde{z}_i$.

By a hybrid argument, the above experiment is statistically close to the original experiment. Furthermore, we can reduce a successful attacker in the mental experiment to an attacker breaking local bounded-leakage resilience. The proofs follows. Finally, thanks to Theorem 2, we can use the abstraction of dense leakage in order to obtain security also in the presence of ME-noisy and U-noisy leakage as well. Note that in the case of ME-noisy leakage, for the second step to work, we need that the distribution X_i of each share outside $\mathcal{U}$ given the shares $x_{\mathcal{U}}$ is almost flat, which is the case for Shamir and additive secret sharing.

Applications in the Computational Setting. The above proof technique can be essentially applied to any cryptographic primitive with bounded leakage resilience in the information-theoretic setting. Further examples include, e.g., forward-secure storage [26], leakage-resilient storage [19], leakage-resilient non-malleable codes [2], non-malleable secret sharing [14,38] and algebraic manipulation detection codes [3,6,42]. (We work out the details for some of these primitives in [13].) However, we cannot apply the same trick in the computational setting or when in the proof of security we need to define an efficient simulator (e.g., for leakage-resilient non-interactive zero knowledge [7] and leakage-resilient multi party computation [9,32]), as the simulation of dense leakage with bounded leakage guaranteed by Theorem 1 may not be efficient.

Nevertheless, we show that our results are still useful for lifting bounded-leakage to noisy-leakage resilience in the computational setting too. In particular, in [13], we exemplify how to do that for the concrete construction of leakage-resilient one-way functions in the floppy model proposed by Agrawal, Dodis, Vaikuntananthan, and Wichs [5], and in the setting of multi-party computation.

We give an overview of the former application, and refer to [13] for the latter. Let $\mathbb{G}$ be a cyclic group with generator g and prime order q, and define $g_i = g^{\tau_i}$ for each $i \in [n]$. Upon input a vector $\boldsymbol{x} = (x_1, \ldots, x_n)$, the one-way function outputs $y = \prod_{i=1}^{n} g_i^{x_i}$; moreover, there is a refreshing procedure that given y and $\boldsymbol{\tau} = (\tau_1, \ldots, \tau_n)$ can generate a fresh pre-image $\boldsymbol{x}'$ of y by simply letting $\boldsymbol{x}' = \boldsymbol{x} + \boldsymbol{\sigma}$ for randomly chosen $\boldsymbol{\sigma}$ orthogonal to $\boldsymbol{\tau}$. Here, one should think of $\boldsymbol{\tau}$ as a sort of master secret key to be stored in some secure hardware (i.e., the floppy). Agrawal, Dodis, Vaikuntananthan, and Wichs proved that, under the discrete logarithm assumption in $\mathbb{G}$, no efficient attacker can successfully invert y even when given ℓ-bounded leakage on $\boldsymbol{x}$, so long as $\ell \approx (n-3)\log(q)$ and assuming that after each leakage query the value $\boldsymbol{x}$ is refreshed using the floppy. The proof of this fact follows in two steps. First, we move to a mental experiment where each of the leakage queries is answered using a random $(n-2)$-dimensional subspace $\mathcal{S} \subseteq \ker(\boldsymbol{\tau})$. By the subspace hiding lemma [12], this experiment is *statistically close* to the original experiment. Thus, we can use Theorem 1 and

Theorem 2 to show that the above still holds in the case of ME-noisy and U-noisy leakage.[7] Second, one finally reduces a successful attacker in the mental experiment to an efficient breaker for the discrete logarithm problem; in this last step, however, the reduction can trivially answer leakage queries by using $\mathcal{S}$, and thus it does not matter whether the leakage is bounded or noisy. We believe the above blueprint can be applied to analyze other cryptographic primitives whose leakage resilience is derived through the subspace hiding lemma; we mention a few natural candidates in [13].

Bounded-Collusion Protocols. Finally, motivated by additional applications to leakage-resilient cryptography and by exploring new lower bounds in communication complexity [49], in Sect. 5.2, we investigate the setting of bounded-collusion protocols (BCPs) as proposed by Kumar, Meka, and Sahai [38]. Here, a set of n parties each holding an input x_i wishes to evaluate a Boolean function ϕ of their inputs by means of an interactive protocol π. At the j-th round, a subset of k parties (where $k < n$ is called the collusion bound) is selected, and appends to the protocol transcript τ an arbitrary (possibly unbounded) function f_j of their joint inputs. The goal is to minimize the size ℓ of the transcript, which leads to what we call an ℓ-bounded communication k-bounded collusion protocol (BC-BCP). BC-BCPs interpolate nicely between the well-studied number-in-hand (NIH) [45] (which corresponds to $k = 1$) and number-on-forehead (NOF) [15] (which corresponds to $k = n - 1$) models.

We put forward two natural generalizations of BC-BCPs, dubbed *dense* (resp. *noisy*) communication k-bounded collusion protocols (DC-BCPs, resp. NC-BCP), in which there is no restriction on the length of the final transcript τ but the round functions are either dense or U-noisy leakage functions. It is easy to see that any BC-BCP is also a NC-BCP as well as a DC-BCP. By Theorem 1 and Theorem 2, we are able to show that the converse is also true: namely, we can simulate[8] the transcript τ of any DC-BCP or NC-BCP π using the transcript τ' of a related BC-BCP π' up to a small statistical distance. Protocol π' roughly runs π and uses the simulation paradigm in order to translate the functions used within π into functions to be used within π'. The proof requires a hybrid argument, and thus the final simulation error grows linearly with the number of rounds of the underlying BC-BCP.

The above fact has two consequences. The first consequence is that we can translate communication complexity lower bounds for BC-BCPs into lower bounds on the noisiness of NC-BCPs. A communication complexity lower bound for a Boolean function ϕ says that any BC-BCP computing ϕ with good probability must have long transcripts (i.e., large ℓ). Concrete examples of such functions ϕ include those based on the generalized inner product and on quadratic

[7] The former requires the distribution of $\boldsymbol{x}$ given y and $(\mathbb{G}, g, g_1, \ldots, g_n, q)$ to be almost flat which is easily seen to be the case.

[8] The reason for not considering NC-BCPs where the round functions are ME-noisy (instead of U-noisy) leakage functions is that simulating ME-noisy leakage with bounded leakage inherently requires semi-flatness, but we cannot ensure this condition is maintained throughout the entire execution of a leakage protocol.

residues in the NOF model with logarithmic (in the input length) number of parties [8,18], and more recently a new function (based on the Bourgain extractor [11]) for more general values of k and even for super-logarithmic number of parties [39]. Note that the above lower bounds do not necessarily say how much information a transcript must reveal about the inputs. Thanks to our results, we can show that any NC-BCP (i.e., where there is no upper bound on the transcript length) computing the above functions with good probability must also in some sense reveal enough information about the inputs. However, for technical reasons, the latter holds true only so long as the number of rounds is not too large. We refer the reader to Sect. 5.2 for further details.

The second consequence is that we can lift the security of cryptographic primitives whose leakage resilience is modeled as a BC-BCP (which intuitively corresponds to security against adaptive bounded joint leakage) to the more general setting where leakage resilience is modeled as a NC-BCP or DC-BCP (which intuitively corresponds to security against adaptive noisy joint leakage). Examples include secret sharing with security against adaptive joint leakage [17,38,39] (see Sect. 5.2), extractors for cylinder-intersection sources [17,38–40] (see [13]), and leakage-resilient non-interactive key exchange [40] (see [13]). Interestingly, the security of these applications in the bounded-leakage setting has been derived exploiting communication complexity lower bounds for BC-BCPs. We can instead directly lift security to the dense and U-noisy leakage setting in a fully black-box way, and thus without re-doing the analysis.

1.4 Related Work

Naor and Segev [44] conjectured that ME-noisy leakage may be compressed to small leakage in the information-theoretic setting. In this light, our results prove this conjecture to be false for arbitrary distributions and establish the exact conditions under which the above statement holds true not only in the case of ME-noisy leakage, but also for U-noisy leakage.

Most relevant to our work is the line of research on leakage-resilient circuit compilers (see, e.g., [29,30,34]), where the equivalence of different leakage models has also been explored. For instance, the beautiful work by Duc, Dziembowski, and Faust [23,24] shows that DDF-noisy leakage on masking schemes used to protect the internal values within a cryptographic circuit can be simulated by probing a limited number of wires (which can be thought of as bounded leakage in the circuit setting). The notion of DDF-noisy leakage was studied further, both experimentally and theoretically, by Duc, Faust, and Standaert [25]. Follow-up work by Dziembowski, Faust, and Skórski [27] and by Prest, Goudarzi, Martinelli, and Passelègue [46] further improved the parameters of such a reduction and extended it to other noisy-leakage models as well. The difference between the above results and our work is that we prove simulation theorems between very abstract and general leakage models, which ultimately allows us to obtain a broad range of applications which goes beyond the setting of leakage-resilient circuits. In a complementary direction, Fuller and Hamlin [31] studied the relationship between different types of computational leakage.

Harsha, Ishai, Kilian, Nissim, and Venkatesh [33] investigate tradeoffs between communication complexity and time complexity in non-cryptographic settings, including deterministic two-party protocols, query complexity and property testing. Our simulation theorems can be thought of as similar tradeoffs in the cryptographic setting.

1.5 Notation

We denote by $[n]$ the set $\{1,\ldots,n\}$. For a string $x \in \{0,1\}^*$, we denote its length by $|x|$; if $\mathcal{X}$ is a set, $|\mathcal{X}|$ represents the number of elements in $\mathcal{X}$. When x is chosen randomly in $\mathcal{X}$, we write $x \leftarrow\!\!\$\ \mathcal{X}$. When A is a randomized algorithm, we write $y \leftarrow\!\!\$\ \mathsf{A}(x)$ to denote a run of A on input x (and implicit random coins r) and output y; the value y is a random variable and $\mathsf{A}(x;r)$ denotes a run of A on input x and randomness r. An algorithm A is *probabilistic polynomial-time* (PPT for short) if A is randomized and for any input $x, r \in \{0,1\}^*$, the computation of $\mathsf{A}(x;r)$ terminates in a polynomial number of steps (in the size of the input). For a random variable X, we write $\mathbb{P}[X = x]$ for the probability that X takes on a particular value $x \in \mathcal{X}$, with $\mathcal{X}$ being the set where X is defined. The probability mass function of X is denoted P_X, *i.e.*, $P_X(x) = \mathbb{P}[X = x]$ for all $x \in \mathcal{X}$; we sometimes omit X and just write P when X is clear from the context. For a set (or event) $\mathcal{S} \subseteq \mathcal{X}$, we write $P(\mathcal{S})$ for the probability of event $\mathcal{S}$, i.e., $P(\mathcal{S}) = \sum_{x\in\mathcal{S}} P(x)$. We denote the statistical distance between two distributions P and P' by $\Delta(P;P')$. The min-entropy of a random variable X is denoted by $\mathbb{H}_\infty(X)$, and the average conditional min-entropy of X given Y is denoted by $\widetilde{\mathbb{H}}_\infty(X|Y)$.

We denote with $\lambda \in \mathbb{N}$ the security parameter. A function p is *polynomial* (in the security parameter), denoted $p \in \mathrm{poly}(\lambda)$, if $p(\lambda) \in O(\lambda^c)$ for some constant $c > 0$. A function $\nu : \mathbb{N} \to [0,1]$ is *negligible* (in the security parameter) if it vanishes faster than the inverse of any polynomial in λ, i.e. $\nu(\lambda) \in O(1/p(\lambda))$ for all positive polynomials $p(\lambda)$. We sometimes write $\mathrm{negl}(\lambda)$ to denote an unspecified negligible function. Unless stated otherwise, throughout the paper, we implicitly assume that the security parameter is given as input (in unary) to all algorithms.

Basic definitions and lemmas in cryptography used throughout the paper are discussed in [13].

2 Rejection Sampling for Approximate Density

The problem that we consider in this section is the following: How can we sample from a distribution P with statistical error at most ε, given only *black-box* access to i.i.d. samples from another distribution P'?

It turns out that the problem above can be solved via rejection sampling, assuming that P is approximately dense in P' as defined below.

Definition 1 (δ-density). *Given distributions P and P' over a set $\mathcal{Z}$ and $\delta \in (0,1]$, we say P is δ-*dense *in P' if for every $z \in \mathcal{Z}$ it holds that $P(z) \le \frac{P'(z)}{\delta}$.*

Definition 2 (**(γ, δ)-density**). *Given distributions P and P' over a set $\mathcal{Z}$ and $\gamma \in [0,1]$, $\delta \in (0,1]$, we say P is* γ-approximate δ-dense in P', *or simply* (γ, δ)-dense in P', *if there exists a set $\mathcal{S} \subseteq \mathcal{Z}$ such that $P(\mathcal{S}), P'(\mathcal{S}) \geq 1 - \gamma$, and for all $z \in \mathcal{S}$ it holds that $P(z) \leq \frac{P'(z)}{\delta}$.*

2.1 The Case of Exact Density

First, we consider the special case where P is δ-dense in P'.

Lemma 1. *Suppose P is δ-dense in P'. Then, for any $\varepsilon \in (0,1]$, it is possible to sample $\widetilde{P}$ such that $\widetilde{P} \approx_\varepsilon P$ given access to $s = \frac{\log(1/\varepsilon)}{\delta}$ i.i.d. samples from P'.*

Proof. Consider the following rejection sampling algorithm:

1. Sample $z_1, \ldots, z_s$ i.i.d. according to the distribution P', and set $y := \perp$;
2. For $i = 1, \ldots, s$ do the following: Set $B_i := 1$ with probability $p_i = \frac{\delta P(z_i)}{P'(z_i)}$ and $B_i := 0$ otherwise. If $B_i := 1$, set $y := z_i$ and stop the cycle;
3. Output y.

Observe that $\frac{\delta P(z_i)}{P'(z_i)} \leq 1$ for all z_i (hence the algorithm above is valid), and that the probability that the algorithm outputs some z in the i-th round is

$$\mathbb{P}[B_i = 1] = \sum_z P'(z) \cdot \frac{\delta P(z)}{P'(z)} = \delta. \tag{3}$$

Let $\widetilde{P}$ denote the distribution of the output of the algorithm above and let Y be the corresponding output. Observe that $(Y|Y \neq \perp)$ is distributed exactly like P. This holds because, in view of Eq. (3), the probability that the algorithm outputs z in the i-th round given that it stops in the i-th round is

$$\mathbb{P}[Y = z | B_i = 1, \forall j < i : B_j = 0] = \frac{(1-\delta)^{i-1} \cdot P'(z) \cdot \frac{\delta P(z)}{P'(z)}}{(1-\delta)^{i-1} \cdot \delta} = P(z).$$

Moreover, we have

$$\mathbb{P}[Y = \perp] = (1-\delta)^s \leq \exp(-\delta \cdot s) = \varepsilon.$$

From these observations, we conclude that $\Delta(\widetilde{P}; P) \leq \Pr[Y = \perp] \leq \varepsilon$.

2.2 The Case of Approximate Density

The analogous result for approximate density follows by a similar proof.

Lemma 2. *Suppose P is (γ, δ)-dense in P'. Then, for any $\varepsilon \in (0,1]$, it is possible to sample $\widetilde{P}$ such that $\widetilde{P} \approx_{\varepsilon + \varepsilon^{\frac{1}{4\delta}} + \gamma} P$ given access to $\frac{2\log(1/\varepsilon)}{\delta(1-\gamma)^2}$ i.i.d. samples from P'.*

3 Leakage Models

In this section, we review several leakage models from the literature, and introduce the simulation paradigm which will later allow us to draw connections between different leakage models. Our take is very general, in that we think as the leakage as a randomized function f on a random variable X, over a set $\mathcal{X}$, which yields a correlated random variable $Z = f(X)$. Different leakage models are then obtained by putting restrictions on the joint distribution (X, Z). We refer the reader to Sect. 5 for concrete examples of what the distribution X is in applications.

3.1 Bounded Leakage

A first natural restriction is to simply assume an upper bound $\ell \in \mathbb{N}$ on the total length of the leakage. This yields the so-called Bounded Leakage Model, which was formalized for the first time by Dziembowski and Pietrzak [28].

Definition 3 (Bounded leakage). *Given a random variable X over $\mathcal{X}$, we say a randomized function $f : \mathcal{X} \to \mathcal{Z}$ is an ℓ-*bounded leakage function for X *if $\mathcal{Z} \subseteq \{0,1\}^\ell$. For fixed X, we denote the set of all its ℓ-bounded leakage functions by* $\mathsf{Bounded}_\ell(X)$.

3.2 Noisy Leakage

A considerable drawback of the Bounded Leakage Model is that physical leakage is rarely of bounded length. The Noisy Leakage Model overcomes this limitation by assuming that the length of the leakage is unbounded but somewhat *noisy.*

There are different ways from the literature how to measure the noisiness of the leakage. A first way, considered for the first time by Naor and Segev [44], is to assume that the leakage drops the min-entropy of X by at most $\ell \in \mathbb{R}_{>0}$ bits. We will refer to this model as the ME-Noisy Leakage Model.

Definition 4 (ME-noisy leakage). *Given a random variable X over $\mathcal{X}$, we say a randomized function $f : \mathcal{X} \to \mathcal{Z}$ is an ℓ-*ME-noisy leakage function for X *if, denoting $Z = f(X)$, we have $\widetilde{\mathbb{H}}_\infty(X|Z) \geq \mathbb{H}_\infty(X) - \ell$. For fixed X, we denote the set of all its ℓ-ME-noisy leakage functions by* $\mathsf{Noisy}_{\infty,\ell}(X)$.

Dodis *et al.* [20] considered a slight variant of the above definition where the min-entropy drop is measured w.r.t. the uniform distribution U over $\mathcal{X}$ (rather than X itself). We will refer to this model as the U-Noisy Leakage Model.

Definition 5 (U-noisy leakage). *Given a random variable X over $\mathcal{X}$, we say a randomized function $f : \mathcal{X} \to \mathcal{Z}$ is an ℓ-*U-noisy leakage function for X *if it holds that $\widetilde{\mathbb{H}}_\infty(U|f(U)) \geq \mathbb{H}_\infty(U) - \ell$, where U denotes the uniform distribution over $\mathcal{X}$. For fixed X, we denote the set of all its ℓ-U-noisy leakage functions by* $\mathsf{UNoisy}_{\infty,\ell}(X)$.

A second way to measure noisiness is to assume that the leakage only implies a bounded bias in the distribution X, which is formally defined as distributions P_{XZ} and $P_X \otimes P_Z$ being close according to some distance when seen as real-valued vectors. Prouff and Rivain [47] were the first to consider this restriction using the Euclidean norm (i.e., the ℓ_2-norm), whereas Duc, Dziembowski and Faust [24] used the statistical distance (i.e., the ℓ_1-norm). We recall the latter definition below, which we will refer to as the SD-Noisy Leakage Model.

Definition 6 (SD-noisy leakage). *Given a random variable X over $\mathcal{X}$, we say a randomized function $f : \mathcal{X} \to \mathcal{Z}$ is an η-*SD-noisy leakage function for X *if, denoting $Z = f(X)$, it holds that $\Delta(P_{XZ}; P_X \otimes P_Z) \leq \eta$, where $P_X \otimes P_Z$ denotes the product distribution of X and Z. For fixed X, we denote the set of all its η-SD-noisy leakage functions by* $\mathsf{Noisy}_{\Delta,\eta}(X)$.

Duc, Dziembowski, and Faust [24] considered only a restricted subset of SD-noisy leakage, which we call *DDF-noisy leakage.* We discuss it in [13], placing it with respect to other leakage models and deriving an associated simulation theorem.

Alternatively, as suggested by Prest *et al.* [46], we can measure the noisiness of the leakage by looking at the mutual information between X and Z. We can define the mutual information between X and Z as $I(X;Z) = D_{\mathsf{KL}}(P_{XZ} \| P_X \otimes P_Z)$, where $D_{\mathsf{KL}}(P \| P') = \sum_{x \in \mathcal{X}} P(x) \log\left(\frac{P(x)}{P'(x)}\right)$ is the Kullback-Leibler divergence between P and P'.

Definition 7 (MI-noisy leakage). *Given a random variable X over $\mathcal{X}$, we say a randomized function $f : \mathcal{X} \to \mathcal{Z}$ is an η-*MI-noisy leakage function for X *if, denoting $Z = f(X)$, it holds that $I(X;Z) \leq \eta$. For fixed X, we denote the set of all its η-MI-noisy leakage functions by* $\mathsf{MINoisy}_\eta(X)$.

The well-known Pinsker inequality allows us to relate MI-noisy leakage to SD-noisy leakage.

Lemma 3 (Pinsker inequality). *For arbitrary distributions P and P' over a set $\mathcal{X}$ it holds that $\Delta(P; P') \leq \sqrt{2 \cdot D_{\mathsf{KL}}(P \| P')}$.*

As an immediate corollary of Lemma 3, we obtain the following result (which was observed also in [46]).

Corollary 1. *For any $\eta > 0$ and X we have* $\mathsf{MINoisy}_\eta(X) \subseteq \mathsf{Noisy}_{\Delta,\sqrt{2\eta}}(X)$.

3.3 Dense Leakage

Next, we introduce a new leakage model which we dub the Dense Leakage Model. This model intuitively says that the distribution of $Z|X = x$ is approximately dense in the distribution of Z for a large fraction of x's. Looking ahead, dense leakage will serve as a powerful abstraction to relate different leakage models.

Definition 8 (Dense leakage). *Given a random variable X over $\mathcal{X}$, we say a randomized function $f : \mathcal{X} \to \mathcal{Z}$ is a (p, γ, δ)*-dense leakage function *for X if, denoting $Z = f(X)$, there exists a set $\mathcal{T} \subseteq \mathcal{X}$ with $P_X(\mathcal{T}) \geq 1 - p$ such that $P_{Z|X=x}$ is (γ, δ)-dense in P_Z for all $x \in \mathcal{T}$. For fixed X, we denote the set of all its (p, γ, δ)-dense leakage functions by $\mathsf{Dense}_{p,\gamma,\delta}(X)$.*

3.4 The Simulation Paradigm

Finally, we define the simulation paradigm which allows to draw connections between different leakage models. Intuitively, for any random variable X, we will say that a leakage family $\mathcal{F}(X)$ is simulatable from another leakage family $\mathcal{G}(X)$ if for all functions $f \in \mathcal{F}(X)$ there exists a simulator Sim_f which can generate $\widetilde{Z}$ such that (X, Z) and $(X, \widetilde{Z})$ are statistically close, using a single sample $g(X)$ for some function $g \in \mathcal{G}(X)$.

Definition 9 (Leakage simulation). *Given a random variable X and two leakage families $\mathcal{F}(X)$ and $\mathcal{G}(X)$, we say $\mathcal{F}(X)$ is* ε-simulatable from $\mathcal{G}(X)$ *if for all $f \in \mathcal{F}(X)$ there is a (possibly inefficient) randomized algorithm Sim_f such that $(X, Z) \approx_\varepsilon (X, \mathsf{Sim}_f^{\mathsf{Leak}(X,\cdot)})$, where $Z = f(X)$ and the oracle $\mathsf{Leak}(X, \cdot)$ accepts a single query $g \in \mathcal{G}(X)$ and outputs $g(X)$.*

Remark 1 (On the simulator). Note that since the simulator Sim_f knows the distribution P_X of X and the leakage function f, it also knows the joint distribution $P_{X,Z}$ where $Z = f(X)$. We will use this fact to design our leakage simulators. We will also sometimes think of the simulator Sim_f as two machines with a shared random tape, where the first machine outputs the description of a leakage function $g \in \mathcal{G}(X)$, while the second machine outputs the simulated leakage $\widetilde{Z}$ given the value $g(X)$.

4 Relating Different Leakage Models

In this section, we show both implications and separations between the leakage models defined in Sect. 3. In a nutshell, our implications show that all the noisy-leakage models from Sect. 3 can be simulated by bounded leakage with good parameters. We achieve this in two main steps: First, we prove that dense leakage can be simulated by bounded leakage with good parameters. Second, we show that dense leakage contains the other leakage models we have previously defined. Combining the two steps above, we conclude that many different leakage models can be simulated by bounded leakage with good parameters. To complement these results, our separations show that the containment of the different leakage models in dense leakage are essentially the best we can hope for in general.

The simulation theorem for the case of ME-noisy leakage only holds for certain distributions X, which are nevertheless the most relevant in applications. In particular, we will require to assume that the random variable X is semi-flat, as formally defined below.

Definition 10 (Semi-flat distribution). *We say that X is* α-semi-flat *if for all $x, x' \in \text{supp}(X)$ we have $P_X(x) \leq 2^\alpha \cdot P_X(x')$.*

4.1 Simulating Dense Leakage with Bounded Leakage

The following theorem states that one dense leakage query can be simulated with one bounded leakage query to within small statistical error. The efficiency of the simulator and the bounded leakage function is essentially governed by the density parameter δ.

Theorem 3. *For arbitrary X, and for any $\varepsilon \in (0,1]$, the set of dense leakages $\mathsf{Dense}_{p,\gamma,\delta}(X)$ is $(\varepsilon + \varepsilon^{1/4\delta} + \gamma + p)$-simulatable from $\mathsf{Bounded}_\ell(X)$ with*

$$\ell = 1 + \log\left(\frac{2\log(1/\varepsilon)}{(1-\gamma)^2\delta}\right) = \log(1/\delta) + \log\log(1/\varepsilon) + 2\log\left(\frac{1}{1-\gamma}\right) + 2.$$

Proof. Fix any $f \in \mathsf{Dense}_{p,\gamma,\delta}(X)$. By hypothesis, there is a set $\mathcal{T} \subseteq \mathcal{X}$ such that $P_X(\mathcal{T}) \geq 1 - p$ and $P_{Z|X=x}$ is (γ,δ)-dense in P_Z for all $x \in \mathcal{T}$. Thus, we may assume that $X \in \mathcal{T}$ by adding p to the simulation error.

We consider the simulator Sim_f which, given the distribution P_{XZ}, samples $s^* = \frac{2\log(1/\varepsilon)}{(1-\gamma)\delta}$ i.i.d. samples $\mathbf{z} = (z_1, z_2, \ldots, z_{s^*})$ from P_Z. Then, Sim_f makes a query to $Z' = g_{\mathbf{z}}(X) \in \mathsf{Bounded}_\ell(X)$, where $\ell = 1 + \log s^*$ and $g_{\mathbf{z}} : \mathcal{X} \to \{0,1\}^\ell$ on input $x \in \mathcal{T}$ runs the rejection sampling algorithm from the proof of Lemma 2 to sample from $P_{Z|X=x}$ to within statistical error $\varepsilon + \varepsilon^{1/4\delta} + \gamma$ using the s^* i.i.d. samples $(z_1, \ldots, z_{s^*})$ from P_Z, and outputs the index $i \leq s^*$ such that z_i is output by the rejection sampling algorithm, or s^*+1 if this algorithm outputs $\perp$. Finally, if $I = g_{\mathbf{z}}(X) \leq s^*$, then Sim_f outputs z_I, and otherwise it outputs $\perp$. Let $\widetilde{Z}$ the random variable corresponding to the output of the simulator. Summing up all simulation errors, Lemma 2 guarantees that $(X,Z) \approx_{\varepsilon+\varepsilon^{1/4\delta}+\gamma+p} (X,\widetilde{Z})$, which completes the proof. □

Remark 2 (On useful parameters). The statement of Theorem 3 is most useful when ε, γ, and p are negligible in the security parameter, so as to obtain negligible simulation error. The parameter δ essentially dictates the number of bits of bounded leakage required to simulate a given class of dense leakages. Indeed, it is usually the case that $\log\log(1/\varepsilon) + 2\log\left(\frac{1}{1-\gamma}\right)$ *is much smaller than* $\log(1/\delta)$.

Remark 3 (On efficiency of the simulation). The complexity of the simulator from Theorem 3 is dominated by the complexity of computing the distributions P_Z (possible with knowledge of P_X and f) and $P_{Z|X=x}$ (possible with knowledge of X and f), and of sampling both the z_i according to P_Z and the decision in each step of rejection sampling. If these steps can be implemented in polynomial time with respect to some parameter of interest, then the simulator is efficient.

4.2 Min-Entropy-Noisy Leakage Is Dense Leakage

The following theorem states that all ME-noisy leakage is also dense leakage for semi-flat distributions. Looking ahead, we will later establish that the semi-flatness condition is necessary.

Theorem 4. *Suppose X is α-semi-flat. Then, for every $\beta > 0$ and $\ell > 0$, and for $p = 2^{-\beta/2}$, $\gamma = 2^{-\beta/2}$ and $\delta = 2^{-(\ell+\beta+\alpha)}$, we have $\mathsf{Noisy}_{\infty,\ell}(X) \subseteq \mathsf{Dense}_{p,\gamma,\delta}(X)$.*

Combining Theorem 3 and Theorem 4, we immediately obtain the following corollary.

Corollary 2. *If X is α-semi-flat, then, for any $\beta > 0$ and $\varepsilon > 0$, the set of leakages $\mathsf{Noisy}_{\infty,\ell}(X)$ is $(\varepsilon + \varepsilon^{2^{\ell+\beta+\alpha-2}} + 2^{-\beta/2+1})$-simulatable from $\mathsf{Bounded}_{\ell'}(X)$ with $\ell' = \ell + \beta + \alpha + \log\log(1/\varepsilon) + 2\log\left(\frac{1}{1-2^{-\beta/2}}\right) + 2$.*

The remark below says that there is a natural tradeoff between the simulation error in the above corollary and the leakage bound.

Remark 4 (Trading simulation error with ME-noisy leakage). By choosing $\varepsilon = 2^{-\lambda}$ and $\beta = 2 + \log^2(\lambda)$ in Corollary 2, we can obtain negligible simulation error $\varepsilon' = \lambda^{-\omega(1)}$ with leakage[9] $\ell' = \ell + O(\log^2(\lambda) + \alpha)$. By choosing $\beta = \lambda$, we can instead obtain a much smaller simulation error of $\varepsilon' = 2^{-\Omega(\lambda)}$ with larger leakage $\ell' = \ell + O(\lambda + \alpha)$.

Near-optimality of simulation theorem for ME-noisy leakage. We now show that our simulation result for ME-noisy leakage (Corollary 2) is essentially optimal. More precisely, we obtain the following result.

Theorem 5. *For every n and $\alpha, \ell > 0$ such that $\ell + \alpha < n - 2$ there exists an $(\alpha+1)$-semi-flat random variable X and $f \in \mathsf{Noisy}_{\infty,\ell+2}(X)$ such that simulating $f(X)$ with error less than $1/4$ requires one ℓ'-bounded leakage query for $\ell' \geq \ell + \alpha - 1$.*

Essentially, Theorem 5 states that $\ell + \alpha - O(1)$ bits of bounded leakage are required to simulate ℓ-ME-noisy leakage from an α-semi-flat random variable X with useful simulation error. Our simulation theorem from Corollary 2 complements this negative result, showing that $\ell' \approx \ell + \alpha$ bits of bounded leakage are enough even with *negligible* simulation error.

Necessity of the semi-flatness assumption in Corollary 2. Theorem 5 implies that assuming α-semi-flatness of X is necessary to obtain a non-trivial simulation theorem for ME-noisy leakage, even when we are attempting to simulate only 0-ME-noisy leakage functions. Indeed, setting $\ell = 0$ and $\alpha = n - 3$ in Theorem 5, we conclude that there exists a random variable X along with an associated 0-ME-noisy-leakage function $f \in \mathsf{Noisy}_{\infty,0}(X)$ that requires $n - O(1)$ bits of bounded leakage from X in order to be simulated with error less than $1/4$.

Note also that the proof of Theorem 5 shows the impossibility of non-trivial simulation theorems for ME-noisy leakage even for a restricted subset of semi-flat distributions X for which there exists x^* such that $P_X(x^*)$ may be large but $(X|X \neq x^*)$ is flat.

[9] In fact, we can push the leakage bound down to $\ell' = \ell + O(\log\log(\lambda)\log(\lambda) + \alpha)$ or even $\ell' = \ell + O(\log^*(\lambda)\log(\lambda) + \alpha)$, while still obtaining negligible simulation error.

4.3 Uniform-Noisy Leakage Is Also Dense Leakage

There is a known connection between U-noisy and ME-noisy leakage, i.e., every U-noisy leakage function is also a ME-noisy leakage function by itself.

Lemma 4. ([20]). *Given any randomized function $f : \mathcal{X} \to \mathcal{Z}$, if it holds that $\widetilde{\mathbb{H}}_\infty(U|f(U)) \geq \mathbb{H}_\infty(U) - \ell$, then for any X over $\mathcal{X}$ it is the case that $\widetilde{\mathbb{H}}_\infty(X|f(X)) \geq \mathbb{H}_\infty(X) - \ell$. In particular, this implies that $\mathsf{UNoisy}_{\infty,\ell}(X) \subseteq \mathsf{Noisy}_{\infty,\ell}(X)$.*

We remark that there also exist some X and a leakage function f such that $f \in \mathsf{Noisy}_{\infty,\ell}(X)$ but $f \notin \mathsf{UNoisy}_{\infty,\ell}(X)$ (such an example is provided in [20]). This shows that the containment of U-noisy leakage in ME-noisy leakage may be strict for some X.

Although Lemma 4 immediately yields an analogue of Corollary 2 for U-noisy leakage, we can obtain a better result by arguing directly that every U-noisy leakage function is also a dense leakage function *for arbitrary* X, i.e., without requiring that X be semi-flat. Our result is stated formally in the next theorem.

Theorem 6. *For every $\beta > 0$ and X, we have $\mathsf{UNoisy}_{\infty,\ell}(X) \subseteq \mathsf{Dense}_{p,\gamma,\delta}(X)$, where $p = 2^{-\beta/2}$, $\gamma = 2^{-\beta/2}$ and $\delta = 2^{-(\ell+\beta)}$.*

Combining Theorem 3 and Theorem 6 immediately yields the following result.

Corollary 3. *For every X and every $\beta > 0$ and $\varepsilon > 0$, the set of leakages $\mathsf{UNoisy}_{\infty,\ell}(X)$ is $(\varepsilon + \varepsilon^{2^{\ell+\beta-2}} + 2^{-\beta/2+1})$-simulatable from $\mathsf{Bounded}_{\ell'}(X)$ with $\ell' = \ell + \beta + \log\log(1/\varepsilon) + 2\log\left(\frac{1}{1-2^{-\beta/2}}\right) + 2$.*

The remark below says that there is a natural tradeoff between the simulation error in the above corollary and the leakage bound.

Remark 5 (Trading simulation error with U-noisy leakage). By choosing $\varepsilon = 2^{-\lambda}$ and $\beta = 2 + \log^2(\lambda)$ in Corollary 3, we can obtain negligible simulation error $\varepsilon' = \lambda^{-\omega(1)}$ with leakage $\ell' = \ell + O(\log^2(\lambda))$. By choosing $\beta = \lambda$, we can instead obtain a much smaller simulation error of $\varepsilon' = 2^{-\Omega(\lambda)}$ with larger leakage $\ell' = \ell + O(\lambda)$.

Near-optimality of simulation theorem for U-noisy leakage. We now show that in order to simulate arbitrary ℓ-U-noisy leakage from X uniformly distributed over $\{0,1\}^n$ with simulation error less than $1/2$, we need access to one query of ℓ'-bounded leakage from X for $\ell' \geq \ell - 1$. As we shall see, this result implies that our simulation theorem from Corollary 3 is nearly optimal.

Theorem 7. *For X uniform over $\{0,1\}^n$ and every $\ell \geq 1$ there exists $f \in \mathsf{UNoisy}_{\infty,\ell}(X) \subseteq \mathsf{Noisy}_{\infty,\ell}(X)$ such that $f(X)$ cannot be simulated with error less than $1/2$ by one $(\ell - 1)$-bounded leakage query to X. Moreover, it also holds that $f \in \mathsf{Dense}_{p=0,\gamma=0,\delta=2^{-\ell}}(X)$.*

Comparing Theorem 7 with Corollary 3, we see that our simulation theorem for U-noisy leakage is nearly optimal with respect to the bounded leakage parameter, since we only require approximately ℓ bits of bounded leakage to simulate U-noisy leakage for uniform X. Furthermore, we can achieve this result with negligible simulation error.

4.4 SD-Noisy and MI-Noisy Leakage Are Also Dense Leakage

We now proceed to relate SD-noisy leakage and dense leakage.

Theorem 8. *For every $\gamma > 0$ and X, we have $\mathsf{Noisy}_{\Delta,\eta}(X) \subseteq \mathsf{Dense}_{p,\gamma,\delta}(X)$ with $p = 2\eta/\gamma$ and $\delta = 1/2$.*

By combining Corollary 1 and Theorem 8, we immediately obtain an analogous result for MI-noisy leakage.

Theorem 9. *For every $\gamma > 0$ and X, we have $\mathsf{MINoisy}_{\eta}(X) \subseteq \mathsf{Dense}_{p,\gamma,\delta}(X)$ with $p = \sqrt{8\eta}/\gamma$ and $\delta = 1/2$.*

Near-Optimality of Trivial Simulator for SD-Noisy and MI-Noisy Leakages. While one can combine Theorem 8 and Theorem 9 with Theorem 3 in order to obtain simulation theorems for SD-noisy and MI-noisy leakage from bounded leakage, it turns out that these simulation theorems do not perform better than the trivial simulator that makes no bounded leakage queries to X: Sample $\widetilde{X}$ according to P_X, and output $\widetilde{Z} = f(\widetilde{X})$. In [13], we show that this is inherent, since the trivial simulator is nearly optimal for SD-noisy and MI-noisy leakages.

5 Applications

In this section we show that our results have interesting implications for so-called leakage-resilient cryptography. In particular, we will show that many cryptographic primitives that have been shown to be resilient to bounded leakage are also resilient to different forms of noisy leakage, with only a small loss in parameters.

5.1 Secret Sharing with Local Leakage Resilience

In this section, we consider the following kind of local leakage attack on a threshold secret sharing scheme: after seeing an unauthorized subset of shares, the adversary performs one query of leakage from all the shares independently.

Definition 11 (Local leakage-resilient secret sharing). *Let $t, n, u \in \mathbb{N}$ be parameters such that $u < t \leq n$, and let $\Sigma = (\mathsf{Share}, \mathsf{Rec})$ be a t-out-of-n secret sharing scheme. We say that Σ is a (p, γ, δ)-dense u-local ε-leakage-resilient secret sharing scheme (or $(u, p, \gamma, \delta, \varepsilon)$-DLLR-SS for short) if for all messages $y_0, y_1 \in \{0,1\}^m$, all unauthorized subsets $\mathcal{U} \subseteq [n]$ such that $|\mathcal{U}| \leq u$, and every tuple of leakage functions $(f_1, \ldots, f_n)$ such that f_i is (p, γ, δ)-dense for all $i \in [n]$, we have $\Delta\big((X^0_{\mathcal{U}}, (f_i(X^0_{\mathcal{U}}, X^0_i))_{i\in[n]}), (X^1_{\mathcal{U}}, (f_i(X^1_{\mathcal{U}}, X^1_i))_{i\in[n]})\big) \leq \varepsilon$, where $(X^b_1, \ldots, X^b_n) = \mathsf{Share}(y_b)$ for all $b \in \{0,1\}$.*

Moreover, in case the functions f_i in the above definition are:

- ℓ-bounded leakage functions, we say that Σ is ℓ-bounded u-local ε-leakage-resilient (or (u,ℓ,ε)-BLLR-SS);
- ℓ-ME-noisy leakage functions, we say that Σ is ℓ-min-entropy-noisy u-local ε-leakage-resilient (or (u,ℓ,ε)-ME-NLLR-SS);
- ℓ-U-noisy leakage functions, we say that Σ is ℓ-uniform-noisy u-local ε-leakage-resilient (or (u,ℓ,ε)-U-NLLR-SS).

The theorem below says that any bounded leakage-resilient secret sharing scheme is also secure in the presence of dense leakage.

Theorem 10. *Any (u,ℓ,ε)-BLLR-SS is also a $(u,p,\gamma,\delta,\varepsilon')$-DLLR-SS so long as*

$$\ell = \log(1/\delta) + \log\log(1/\varepsilon) + 2\log\left(\tfrac{1}{1-\gamma}\right) + 2$$
$$\varepsilon' = (2n+1)\varepsilon + 2n\varepsilon^{1/4\delta} + 2n\gamma + 2np.$$

Next, using the connection between ME-noisy and U-noisy leakage with dense leakage established in Sect. 4, we obtain the following corollary.

Corollary 4. *Any (u,ℓ',ε')-BLLR-SS is also an:*

(i) (u,ℓ,ε)-ME-NLLR-SS so long as $\ell = \ell' - 2\log(1/\varepsilon') - \alpha - \log\log(1/\varepsilon') - 1$ and $\varepsilon = (6n+1)\varepsilon'$, and assuming that $(X_1,\ldots,X_n) = \mathsf{Share}(y)$ is such that X_i is α-semi-flat for all $i \in [n]$.
(ii) (u,ℓ,ε)-U-NLLR-SS so long as $\ell = \ell' - 2\log(1/\varepsilon') - \log\log(1/\varepsilon') - 1$ and $\varepsilon = (6n+1)\varepsilon'$.

Proof. The statement follows by choosing $\beta = 2 + 2\log(1/\varepsilon')$ and $\varepsilon = \varepsilon'$ in Corollary 2 and Corollary 3. □

We present concrete instantiations of Corollary 4 in [13].

5.2 Bounded-Collusion Protocols

In this section, we deal with applications related to so-called bounded-collusion protocols (BCPs). These are interactive protocols between n parties where at each round a subset of $k < n$ parties are selected, and the output of a leakage function applied to the input of such parties is appended to the protocol's transcript.

Definition 12 (Bounded-communication BCPs). *An interactive (possibly randomized) protocol π is called an n-party r-round ℓ-bounded communication k-bounded-collusion protocol ((n,r,ℓ,k)-BC-BCP, for short) if:*

(i) the n parties start the protocol with input $x_1,\ldots,x_n \in \mathcal{X}$, and the transcript τ is empty at the beginning of the protocol;

(ii) there is a function $\mathsf{Next} : \{0,1\}^* \to \binom{[n]}{k}$ *taking as input a (partial) transcript* τ *and outputting a set* $\mathcal{S} \subset [n]$ *with* $|\mathcal{S}| = k$ *along with a function* $f : \mathcal{X}^k \to \{0,1\}^*$*;*

(iii) at each round $j \in [r]$ *with current transcript* τ*, the protocol runs* $\mathsf{Next}(\tau)$ *obtaining* $(\mathcal{S}_j, f_j)$ *and appends the message* $f_j(X_{\mathcal{S}_j})$ *to the current transcript* τ*;*

(iv) the final transcript τ *consists of at most* $\ell \in \mathbb{N}$ *bits.*

The above notion, which was introduced by Kumar, Meka, and Sahai [38], interpolates nicely between the well-known *number-in-hand* (NIH) and *number-on-forehead* (NOF) models, which correspond respectively to the extreme cases $k = 1$ and $k = n - 1$. Note that the number of rounds in a BC-BCP is at most $r \le \ell$.

Below, we generalize the definition of BCPs to settings where the round functions correspond to noisy-leakage (in particular, dense and uniform-noisy leakage) functions on the parties' inputs, and thus there is no restriction on the size of the final transcript.

Definition 13 (Dense-communication BCPs). *An interactive (possibly randomized) protocol* π *is called an* n*-party* r*-round* (p, γ, δ)*-dense communication* k*-bounded-collusion protocol (*$(n, r, p, \gamma, \delta, k)$*-DC-BCP, for short) if it satisfies the same properties as in Definition 12, except that property (iv) is replaced by*

> *(iv') for each* $j \in [r]$*, the function* $f_j : \mathcal{X}^k \to \{0,1\}^*$ *is* (p, γ, δ_j)*-dense leakage for* $X_{\mathcal{S}_j} | \tau_{j-1}$*, where* τ_j *denotes the transcript up to the* j*-th round and* $0 < \delta_j \le 1$*, and where additionally* $\prod_{j=1}^{r} \delta_j \ge \delta$*.*

Definition 14 (Noisy-communication BCPs). *An interactive (possibly randomized) protocol* π *is called an* n*-party* r*-round* ℓ*-noisy communication* k*-bounded-collusion protocol (*(n, r, ℓ, k)*-NC-BCP, for short) if it satisfies the same properties as in Definition 12, except that property (iv) is replaced by*

> *(iv") for each* $j \in [r]$*, the function* $f_j : \mathcal{X}^k \to \{0,1\}^*$ *is* ℓ_j*-U-noisy leakage for* $X_{\mathcal{S}_j}$*, where* $\ell_j \ge 0$ *and additionally* $\left\lceil \sum_{j=1}^{r} \ell_j \right\rceil \le \ell$*.*

Observe that the number of rounds in a DC-BCP or NC-BCP is unbounded. Also, note that property (iv") in Definition 14 implicitly implies that the overall leakage drops the min-entropy of the uniform distribution over any subset of k inputs by at most ℓ. More formally, the final transcript τ is such that[10] for all subsets $\mathcal{S} \in \binom{[n]}{k}$ we have

$$\widetilde{\mathbb{H}}_\infty(U_{\mathcal{S}} | \pi(U_1, \ldots, U_n)) \ge \mathbb{H}_\infty(U_{\mathcal{S}}) - \ell, \tag{4}$$

[10] This is because, by [20, Lemma L.3], any sequence of (adaptively chosen) functions $f_1, \ldots, f_r$ on a random variable X, such that each function f_j is ℓ_j-ME-noisy leakage for some $\ell_j \ge 0$ and where $\sum_{j=1}^{r} \ell_j \le \ell$, satisfies $\widetilde{\mathbb{H}}_\infty(X | f_1(X), \ldots, f_r(X)) \ge \mathbb{H}_\infty(X) - \ell$. Furthermore, for the case of NC-BCPs, in the worst case all the leakage happens on the same subset $\mathcal{S}$ of inputs.

where $U = (U_1, \ldots, U_n)$ is uniform over $\mathcal{X}^n$ and $\pi(U_1, \ldots, U_n)$ denotes the distribution of the transcript τ at the end of the protocol.

Clearly, any BC-BCP is also a NC-BCP with the same leakage parameter. Below, we show that the converse is also true, in the sense that the transcript of any NC-BCP π can be simulated using the transcript of a related BC-BCP π', up to a small statistical distance. In fact, the latter statement holds true for the more general case of DC-BCPs.

Theorem 11. *Let π be an $(n, r, p, \gamma, \delta, k)$-DC-BCP. There exists an (n, r, ℓ', k)-BC-BCP π' such that, for any $\varepsilon > 0$, a transcript of π can be simulated within statistical distance $r \cdot (\varepsilon + \varepsilon^{1/4} + \gamma + p)$ given a transcript of π' with length $\ell' = \log(1/\delta) + r \cdot (\log\log(1/\varepsilon) + 2\log(1/(1-\gamma)) + 2)$.*

Proof. We start by describing protocol π' acting on a random variable $X = (X_1, \ldots, X_n)$. Consider the simulator Sim_f guaranteed by Theorem 3.

- Let τ' be initially empty, and sample r independent random tapes $\rho_1, \ldots, \rho_r$ for Sim.
- At each round $j \in [r]$, the function Next' takes as input the current transcript $\tau' = z'_1 || \ldots || z'_{j-1}$ and runs $\mathsf{Next}(\tilde{\tau})$, where
$$\tilde{\tau} = \mathsf{Sim}_{f_1}(z'_1; \rho_1) || \ldots || \mathsf{Sim}_{f_{j-1}}(z'_{j-1}; \rho_{j-1}).$$
- Let $(f_j, \mathcal{S}_j)$ be the j-th output of Next. Then, Next' runs Sim_{f_j} on $X_{\mathcal{S}_j} | \tilde{\tau}$ (with fixed random tape ρ_j), obtaining a leakage function $f'_j : \mathcal{X}^k \to \{0,1\}^{\ell'_j}$, and outputs $(f'_j, \mathcal{S}_j)$.

Next, we claim that protocol π' has ℓ'-bounded communication for ℓ' as in the statement of the theorem. Recall that, for each $j \in [r]$, the function f_j output by Next is (p, γ, δ_j)-dense leakage for $X_{\mathcal{S}_j} | \tilde{\tau}$, with $0 < \delta_j \le 1$. Then, by applying Theorem 3, for any $\varepsilon > 0$ we get that $\ell'_j = \log(1/\delta_j) + \log\log(1/\varepsilon) + 2\log(1/(1-\gamma)) + 2$. Hence, the final transcript τ' has size at most $\ell' = \sum_{j=1}^{r} \ell'_j = \log(1/\delta) + r \cdot (\log\log(1/\varepsilon) + 2\log(1/(1-\gamma)) + 2)$, which is the bound in the statement of the theorem.

It remains to prove that we can simulate a transcript of π given a transcript of π'. Consider the simulator that, after running π' with random tapes $\rho_1, \ldots, \rho_r$, obtains the transcript $\tau' = z'_1 || \ldots || z'_r$ and simply outputs the simulated transcript $\tilde{\tau} = \mathsf{Sim}_{f_1}(z'_1; \rho_1) || \ldots || \mathsf{Sim}_{f_r}(z'_r; \rho_r)$. By a hybrid argument, Theorem 3 implies that the transcript $\tilde{\tau}$ is within statistical distance at most $r \cdot (\varepsilon + \gamma + p) + \sum_{j=1}^{r} \varepsilon^{1/4\delta_j} \le r \cdot (\varepsilon + \varepsilon^{1/4} + \gamma + \delta)$ from the transcript τ obtained by running π. This finishes the proof. □

Theorem 12. *Let π be an (n, r, ℓ, k)-NC-BCP. There exists an (n, r, ℓ', k)-BC-BCP π' such that, for any $0 < \delta < 1$, a transcript of π can be simulated within statistical distance $r \cdot 3\delta$ given a transcript of π' with length $\ell' \le \ell + r \cdot (6 + 2\log(1/\delta) + \log\log(1/\delta))$.*

Next, we show that Theorem 11 and Theorem 12 have applications to communication complexity lower bounds, and to constructing cryptographic primitives with adaptive noisy-leakage resilience (i.e., where leakage resilience is modeled either as a NC-BCP or as a DC-BCP).

Communication Complexity Lower Bounds. We say that an (n, r, ℓ, k)-BCP π (with either bounded or noisy communication) ε-computes a (deterministic) Boolean function $\phi : \mathcal{X}^n \to \{0, 1\}$, if there exists an unbounded predictor P that, after running a BCP protocol π on the parties' inputs yielding a final transcript τ, outputs $\phi(X_1, \ldots, X_n)$ with probability at least $1/2 + \varepsilon$ (over the randomness of $(X_i)_{i \in [n]}$, π and P). The theorem below says that for any NC-BCP π that computes a Boolean function ϕ there is a BC-BCP π' that computes the same function with roughly the same probability, where the size ℓ' of a transcript of π' is related to the leakage parameter ℓ of π.

Corollary 5. *Let π be any (n, r, ℓ, k)-NC-BCP that ε-computes a Boolean function ϕ. Then, there exists an (n, r, ℓ', k)-BC-BCP π' that ε'-computes ϕ so long as $\ell' \le \ell + r \cdot (6 + 2\log(6r/\varepsilon) + \log\log(6r/\varepsilon))$ and $\varepsilon' = \varepsilon/2$.*

The above corollary can be used to translate known lower bounds in communication complexity for BC-BCPs to the more general setting of NC-BCPs.[11] Note that a lower bound on the communication complexity of BC-BCPs does not necessarily imply a lower bound on the noisiness of NC-BCPs, as the fact that the transcript must consist of *at least* ℓ bits does not say anything about how each round function reveals on the players' inputs. We argue how the result from Corollary 5 can be used to lift lower bounds on bounded communication needed to compute certain functions ϕ to more general lower bounds on *noisy* communication in [13].

Remark 6 (On lower bounds on the leakage parameters of NC-BCPs). It may seem that a lower bound on the parameter ℓ of NC-BCPs does not necessarily mean that any protocol must reveal a lot of information on the parties' inputs, as the actual min-entropy drop in Eq. (4) *could be much smaller*[12] *than ℓ. Nevertheless, we observe that the definition of NC-BCP implies that there must exist an index $j^* \in [r]$ such that, say, $\ell_{j^*} \ge \frac{\ell-1}{r}$. This is because, if $\ell_j < \frac{\ell-1}{r}$ for all $j \in [r]$, then $\lceil \sum_{j=1}^{r} \ell_j \rceil \le \ell - 1$. In this light, the corollaries below still say that, for certain Boolean functions, a transcript must necessarily reveal enough information about the inputs so long as the number of rounds is not too large.*

BCP Leakage Resilience. Finally, we show how to lift bounded-leakage resilience to dense-leakage and uniform-noisy-leakage resilience in applications

---

[11] In fact, using Theorem 11, we could also derive lower bounds on DC-BCPs. However, we stick to the setting of NC-BCPs for simplicity.

[12] For instance, take $k = 1$ and consider the functions $f_1, \ldots, f_n$ that always reveal the first bit of X_1. Then, $\ell = \sum_{j=1}^{n} \ell_j = n$, but $\widetilde{\mathbb{H}}_\infty(U_1 | \pi(U_1, \ldots, U_n)) = \mathbb{H}_\infty(U_1) - 1$.

where the leakage itself is modelled as a BCP protocol. For concreteness, we focus again on secret sharing schemes and refer the reader to [13] for additional examples.

Let $\Sigma = (\mathsf{Share}, \mathsf{Rec})$ be a secret sharing scheme. The definition below captures security of Σ in the presence of an adversary leaking information jointly from subsets of the shares of size $k < n$, where both the leakage functions and the subsets of shares are chosen adaptively. For simplicity, we focus on threshold secret sharing but our treatment can be generalized to arbitrary access structures.

Definition 15 (Secret sharing with BCP leakage resilience). *Let $t, n, \ell \in \mathbb{N}, \varepsilon \in [0,1]$ be parameters. A t-out-of-n secret sharing scheme* $(\mathsf{Share}, \mathsf{Rec})$ *is a k-joint r-adaptive (p, γ, δ)-dense ε-leakage-resilient secret sharing scheme, $(k, r, p, \gamma, \delta, \varepsilon)$-JA-DLR-SS for short, if for all messages $y_0, y_1 \in \{0,1\}^m$ and all $(n, r, p, \gamma, \delta, k)$-DC-BCP π we have $\pi(X_1^{(0)}, \ldots, X_n^{(0)}) \approx_\varepsilon \pi(X_1^{(1)}, \ldots, X_n^{(1)})$, where $(X_1^{(b)}, \ldots, X_n^{(b)}) = \mathsf{Share}(y_b)$ is the distribution of the shares of message $y_b \in \{0,1\}^m$ for all $b \in \{0,1\}$.*

Moreover, in case the protocol π in the above definition is an:

- (n, r, ℓ, k)-NC-BCP, we say that Σ is k-joint r-adaptive ℓ-noisy ε-leakage-resilient (or $(k, r, \ell, \varepsilon)$-JA-NLR-SS);
- (n, r, ℓ, k)-BC-BCP, we say that Σ is k-joint r-adaptive ℓ-bounded ε-leakage-resilient (or $(k, r, \ell, \varepsilon)$-JA-BLR-SS).

Corollary 6. *Every $(k, r, \ell, \varepsilon)$-JA-BLR-SS scheme Σ is also a $(k, r, p, \gamma, \delta, \varepsilon')$-JA-DLR-SS so long as $\ell = \log(1/\delta) + r \cdot (\log\log(1/\varepsilon) + 2\log(1/(1-\gamma)) + 2)$ and $\varepsilon' = \varepsilon + 2r \cdot (\varepsilon + \varepsilon^{1/4} + \gamma + p)$.*

Corollary 7. *Every $(k, r, \ell', \varepsilon')$-JA-BLR-SS scheme Σ is also a $(k, r, \ell, \varepsilon)$-JA-NLR-SS scheme so long as $\ell' = \ell + r \cdot O(\log(r/\varepsilon))$ and $\varepsilon = 3\varepsilon'$.*

Explicit constructions of secret sharing schemes with BCP leakage resilience in the bounded leakage setting can be built for any leakage bound ℓ and any $\varepsilon > 0$ from n-party functions with large NOF complexity with collusion bound $k = O(\log(n))$ [38] (for arbitrary access structures) and $k = O(t/\log(t))$ [39] (for threshold access structures). By the above corollaries, these schemes are also directly secure in the settings of dense and U-noisy leakage.

6 Conclusions and Open Problems

We have shown that a single query of *noisy* leakage can be simulated in the information-theoretic setting using a single query of *bounded* leakage, up to a small statistical distance and at the price of a slight loss in the leakage parameter. The latter holds true for a fairly general class of noisy leakage (which we introduce) dubbed *dense* leakage. Importantly, dense leakage captures many already existing noisy-leakage models including those where the noisiness of the leakage is measured using the conditional average min-entropy [20,44], the statistical distance [24], or the mutual information [46]. For some of these models, our simulation theorems require additional assumptions on the input distribution or only hold for certain range of parameters, but in each case we show this is the best one can hope for.

The above result has applications to leakage-resilient cryptography, where we can reduce noisy-leakage resilience to bounded-leakage resilience in a black-box way. Interestingly, for some applications, the latter holds true even in the *computational* setting. Additionally, we have shown that our simulation theorems yield new lower bounds in communication complexity.

Several interesting open questions remain. We list some of them below:

- Can we prove that other families of noisy leakage (e.g., hard-to-invert leakage [21]) fall within the class of dense leakage (or directly admit simulation theorems with good parameters from bounded leakage)?
- Can we make the simulator efficient for certain families of noisy leakage? The latter would allow to lift bounded-leakage resilience to noisy-leakage resilience for *all* computationally-secure applications, and for statistically-secure applications with simulation-based security in which the running time of the simulator needs to be polynomial in the running time of the adversary (such as leakage-tolerant MPC [10]).
- Can we generalize Theorem 12 to a more general setting where the leakage parameter ℓ of NC-BCPs measures the worst-case average min-entropy drop w.r.t. the final transcript of the protocol (instead of being the summation over the worst-case min-entropy drops of each round function in isolation)? The latter would allow to strengthen the lower bounds in Sect. 5.2, as well as the security of the applications in Sect. 5.2 and [13].

Acknowledgments. We thank François-Xavier Standaert for bringing [25,31] to our attention. Maciej Obremski was funded by the Singapore Ministry of Education and the National Research Foundation under grant R-710-000-012-135. Daniele Venturi was partially supported by the research project SPECTRA funded by Sapienza University of Rome.

References

1. Aggarwal, D., et al.: Stronger leakage-resilient and non-malleable secret sharing schemes for general access structures. In: Boldyreva, A., Micciancio, D. (eds.) CRYPTO 2019. LNCS, vol. 11693, pp. 510–539. Springer, Cham (2019). https://doi.org/10.1007/978-3-030-26951-7_18
2. Aggarwal, D., Dziembowski, S., Kazana, T., Obremski, M.: Leakage-resilient non-malleable codes. In: Dodis, Y., Nielsen, J.B. (eds.) TCC 2015. LNCS, vol. 9014, pp. 398–426. Springer, Heidelberg (2015). https://doi.org/10.1007/978-3-662-46494-6_17
3. Aggarwal, D., Kazana, T., Obremski, M.: Leakage-resilient algebraic manipulation detection codes with optimal parameters. In: IEEE International Symposium on Information Theory, pp. 1131–1135 (2018)

4. Agrawal, D., Archambeault, B., Rao, J.R., Rohatgi, P.: The EM side—channel(s). In: Kaliski, B.S., Koç, K., Paar, C. (eds.) CHES 2002. LNCS, vol. 2523, pp. 29–45. Springer, Heidelberg (2003). https://doi.org/10.1007/3-540-36400-5_4
5. Agrawal, S., Dodis, Y., Vaikuntanathan, V., Wichs, D.: On continual leakage of discrete log representations. In: Sako, K., Sarkar, P. (eds.) ASIACRYPT 2013. LNCS, vol. 8270, pp. 401–420. Springer, Heidelberg (2013). https://doi.org/10.1007/978-3-642-42045-0_21
6. Ahmadi, H., Safavi-Naini, R.: Detection of algebraic manipulation in the presence of leakage. In: Padró, C. (ed.) ICITS 2013. LNCS, vol. 8317, pp. 238–258. Springer, Cham (2014). https://doi.org/10.1007/978-3-319-04268-8_14
7. Ananth, P., Jain, A., Sahai, A.: Indistinguishability obfuscation for turing machines: constant overhead and amortization. In: Katz, J., Shacham, H. (eds.) CRYPTO 2017. LNCS, vol. 10402, pp. 252–279. Springer, Cham (2017). https://doi.org/10.1007/978-3-319-63715-0_9
8. Babai, L., Nisan, N., Szegedy, M.: Multiparty protocols, pseudorandom generators for logspace, and time-space trade-offs. J. Comput. Syst. Sci. **45**(2), 204–232 (1992)
9. Benhamouda, F., Degwekar, A., Ishai, Y., Rabin, T.: On the local leakage resilience of linear secret sharing schemes. In: Shacham, H., Boldyreva, A. (eds.) CRYPTO 2018. LNCS, vol. 10991, pp. 531–561. Springer, Cham (2018). https://doi.org/10.1007/978-3-319-96884-1_18
10. Bitansky, N., Canetti, R., Halevi, S.: Leakage-tolerant interactive protocols. In: Cramer, R. (ed.) TCC 2012. LNCS, vol. 7194, pp. 266–284. Springer, Heidelberg (2012). https://doi.org/10.1007/978-3-642-28914-9_15
11. Bourgain, J.: More on the sum-product phenomenon in prime fields and its applications. Int. J. Number Theor. **1**(1), 1–32 (2005)
12. Brakerski, Z., Kalai, Y.T., Katz, J., Vaikuntanathan, V.: Overcoming the hole in the bucket: Public-key cryptography resilient to continual memory leakage. In: 51st FOCS, pp. 501–510. IEEE Computer Society Press (October 2010). https://doi.org/10.1109/FOCS.2010.55
13. Brian, G., et al.: The mother of all leakages: How to simulate noisy leakages via bounded leakage (almost) for free. Cryptology ePrint Archive, Report 2020/1246 (2020). https://eprint.iacr.org/2020/1246
14. Brian, G., Faonio, A., Obremski, M., Simkin, M., Venturi, D.: Non-malleable secret sharing against bounded joint-tampering attacks in the plain model. Cryptology ePrint Archive, Report 2020/725 (2020). https://eprint.iacr.org/2020/725
15. Chandra, A.K., Furst, M.L., Lipton, R.J.: Multi-party protocols. In: 15th ACM STOC, pp. 94–99. ACM Press (April 1983). https://doi.org/10.1145/800061.808737
16. Chari, S., Jutla, C.S., Rao, J.R., Rohatgi, P.: Towards sound approaches to counteract power-analysis attacks. In: Wiener, M. (ed.) CRYPTO 1999. LNCS, vol. 1666, pp. 398–412. Springer, Heidelberg (1999). https://doi.org/10.1007/3-540-48405-1_26
17. Chattopadhyay, E., Goodman, J., Goyal, V., Li, X.: Leakage-resilient extractors and secret-sharing against bounded collusion protocols. Cryptology ePrint Archive, Report 2020/478 (2020). https://eprint.iacr.org/2020/478
18. Chung, F.R.K.: Quasi-random classes of hypergraphs. Random Struct. Algorithms **1**(4), 363–382 (1990)
19. Davì, F., Dziembowski, S., Venturi, D.: Leakage-resilient storage. In: Garay, J.A., De Prisco, R. (eds.) SCN 2010. LNCS, vol. 6280, pp. 121–137. Springer, Heidelberg (2010). https://doi.org/10.1007/978-3-642-15317-4_9

20. Dodis, Y., Haralambiev, K., López-Alt, A., Wichs, D.: Cryptography against continuous memory attacks. In: 51st FOCS, pp. 511–520. IEEE Computer Society Press (October 2010). https://doi.org/10.1109/FOCS.2010.56
21. Dodis, Y., Kalai, Y.T., Lovett, S.: On cryptography with auxiliary input. In: Mitzenmacher, M. (ed.) 41st ACM STOC, pp. 621–630. ACM Press (May/June 2009). https://doi.org/10.1145/1536414.1536498
22. Dodis, Y., Ostrovsky, R., Reyzin, L., Smith, A.D.: Fuzzy extractors: How to generate strong keys from biometrics and other noisy data. SIAM J. Comput. **38**(1), 97–139 (2008)
23. Duc, A., Dziembowski, S., Faust, S.: Unifying leakage models: from probing attacks to noisy leakage. In: Nguyen, P.Q., Oswald, E. (eds.) EUROCRYPT 2014. LNCS, vol. 8441, pp. 423–440. Springer, Heidelberg (2014). https://doi.org/10.1007/978-3-642-55220-5_24
24. Duc, A., Dziembowski, S., Faust, S.: Unifying leakage models: From probing attacks to noisy leakage. J. Cryptology **32**(1), 151–177 (2019). https://doi.org/10.1007/s00145-018-9284-1
25. Duc, A., Faust, S., Standaert, F.X.: Making masking security proofs concrete (or how to evaluate the security of any leaking device), extended version. J. Cryptology **32**(4), 1263–1297 (2019). https://doi.org/10.1007/s00145-018-9277-0
26. Dziembowski, S.: Intrusion-resilience via the bounded-storage model. In: Halevi, S., Rabin, T. (eds.) TCC 2006. LNCS, vol. 3876, pp. 207–224. Springer, Heidelberg (2006). https://doi.org/10.1007/11681878_11
27. Dziembowski, S., Faust, S., Skorski, M.: Noisy leakage revisited. In: Oswald, E., Fischlin, M. (eds.) EUROCRYPT 2015. LNCS, vol. 9057, pp. 159–188. Springer, Heidelberg (2015). https://doi.org/10.1007/978-3-662-46803-6_6
28. Dziembowski, S., Pietrzak, K.: Leakage-resilient cryptography. In: 49th FOCS, pp. 293–302. IEEE Computer Society Press (October 2008). https://doi.org/10.1109/FOCS.2008.56
29. Faust, S., Rabin, T., Reyzin, L., Tromer, E., Vaikuntanathan, V.: Protecting circuits from leakage: the computationally-bounded and noisy cases. In: Gilbert, H. (ed.) EUROCRYPT 2010. LNCS, vol. 6110, pp. 135–156. Springer, Heidelberg (2010). https://doi.org/10.1007/978-3-642-13190-5_7
30. Faust, S., Rabin, T., Reyzin, L., Tromer, E., Vaikuntanathan, V.: Protecting circuits from computationally bounded and noisy leakage. SIAM J. Comput. **43**(5), 1564–1614 (2014)
31. Fuller, B., Hamlin, A.: Unifying leakage classes: simulatable leakage and pseudoentropy. In: Lehmann, A., Wolf, S. (eds.) ICITS 2015. LNCS, vol. 9063, pp. 69–86. Springer, Cham (2015). https://doi.org/10.1007/978-3-319-17470-9_5
32. Goyal, V., Ishai, Y., Maji, H.K., Sahai, A., Sherstov, A.A.: Bounded-communication leakage resilience via parity-resilient circuits. In: Dinur, I. (ed.) 57th FOCS, pp. 1–10. IEEE Computer Society Press (October 2016). https://doi.org/10.1109/FOCS.2016.10
33. Harsha, P., Ishai, Y., Kilian, J., Nissim, K., Venkatesh, S.: Communication versus computation. In: Díaz, J., Karhumäki, J., Lepistö, A., Sannella, D. (eds.) ICALP 2004. LNCS, vol. 3142, pp. 745–756. Springer, Heidelberg (2004). https://doi.org/10.1007/978-3-540-27836-8_63
34. Ishai, Y., Sahai, A., Wagner, D.: Private circuits: securing hardware against probing attacks. In: Boneh, D. (ed.) CRYPTO 2003. LNCS, vol. 2729, pp. 463–481. Springer, Heidelberg (2003). https://doi.org/10.1007/978-3-540-45146-4_27

35. Kalai, Y.T., Reyzin, L.: A survey of leakage-resilient cryptography. In: Providing Sound Foundations for Cryptography: On the Work of Shafi Goldwasser and Silvio Micali, pp. 727–794. ACM (2019)
36. Kocher, P.C.: Timing attacks on implementations of Diffie-Hellman, RSA, DSS, and other systems. In: Koblitz, N. (ed.) CRYPTO 1996. LNCS, vol. 1109, pp. 104–113. Springer, Heidelberg (1996). https://doi.org/10.1007/3-540-68697-5_9
37. Kocher, P., Jaffe, J., Jun, B.: Differential power analysis. In: Wiener, M. (ed.) CRYPTO 1999. LNCS, vol. 1666, pp. 388–397. Springer, Heidelberg (1999). https://doi.org/10.1007/3-540-48405-1_25
38. Kumar, A., Meka, R., Sahai, A.: Leakage-resilient secret sharing against colluding parties. In: Zuckerman, D. (ed.) 60th FOCS, pp. 636–660. IEEE Computer Society Press (November 2019). https://doi.org/10.1109/FOCS.2019.00045
39. Kumar, A., Meka, R., Zuckerman, D.: Bounded collusion protocols, cylinder-intersection extractors and leakage-resilient secret sharing. Cryptology ePrint Archive, Report 2020/473 (2020). https://eprint.iacr.org/2020/473
40. Li, X., Ma, F., Quach, W., Wichs, D.: Leakage-resilient key exchange and two-seed extractors. Cryptology ePrint Archive, Report 2020/771 (2020). https://eprint.iacr.org/2020/771
41. Lin, F., Cheraghchi, M., Guruswami, V., Safavi-Naini, R., Wang, H.: Leakage-resilient secret sharing in non-compartmentalized models. In: Kalai, Y.T., Smith, A.D., Wichs, D. (eds.) 1st Conference on Information-Theoretic Cryptography (ITC 2020). Leibniz International Proceedings in Informatics (LIPIcs), vol. 163, pp. 7:1–7:24. Schloss Dagstuhl-Leibniz-Zentrum für Informatik, Dagstuhl, Germany (2020). https://doi.org/10.4230/LIPIcs.ITC.2020.7
42. Lin, F., Safavi-Naini, R., Wang, P.: Detecting algebraic manipulation in leaky storage systems. In: Nascimento, A.C.A., Barreto, P. (eds.) ICITS 2016. LNCS, vol. 10015, pp. 129–150. Springer, Cham (2016). https://doi.org/10.1007/978-3-319-49175-2_7
43. Micali, S., Reyzin, L.: Physically observable cryptography. In: Naor, M. (ed.) TCC 2004. LNCS, vol. 2951, pp. 278–296. Springer, Heidelberg (2004). https://doi.org/10.1007/978-3-540-24638-1_16
44. Naor, M., Segev, G.: Public-key cryptosystems resilient to key leakage. SIAM J. Comput. **41**(4), 772–814 (2012)
45. Phillips, J.M., Verbin, E., Zhang, Q.: Lower bounds for number-in-hand multi-party communication complexity, made easy. In: Proceedings of the Twenty-Third Annual ACM-SIAM Symposium on Discrete Algorithms, SODA 2012, Kyoto, Japan, 17–19 January 2012, pp. 486–501 (2012)
46. Prest, T., Goudarzi, D., Martinelli, A., Passelègue, A.: Unifying leakage models on a Rényi day. In: Boldyreva, A., Micciancio, D. (eds.) CRYPTO 2019. LNCS, vol. 11692, pp. 683–712. Springer, Cham (2019). https://doi.org/10.1007/978-3-030-26948-7_24
47. Prouff, E., Rivain, M.: Masking against side-channel attacks: a formal security proof. In: Johansson, T., Nguyen, P.Q. (eds.) EUROCRYPT 2013. LNCS, vol. 7881, pp. 142–159. Springer, Heidelberg (2013). https://doi.org/10.1007/978-3-642-38348-9_9
48. Srinivasan, A., Vasudevan, P.N.: Leakage resilient secret sharing and applications. In: Boldyreva, A., Micciancio, D. (eds.) CRYPTO 2019. LNCS, vol. 11693, pp. 480–509. Springer, Cham (2019). https://doi.org/10.1007/978-3-030-26951-7_17
49. Yao, A.C.: Some complexity questions related to distributive computing (preliminary report). In: Proceedings of the 11h Annual ACM Symposium on Theory of Computing, April 30–May 2, 1979, Atlanta, Georgia, USA. pp. 209–213 (1979)

Message-Recovery Laser Fault Injection Attack on the *Classic McEliece* Cryptosystem

Pierre-Louis Cayrel[1], Brice Colombier[2], Vlad-Florin Drăgoi[3,4](✉), Alexandre Menu[5], and Lilian Bossuet[1]

[1] Univ Lyon, UJM-Saint-Etienne, CNRS, Laboratoire Hubert Curien UMR 5516, 42023 Saint-Etienne, France

[2] Univ Grenoble Alpes, CNRS, Grenoble INP, TIMA, 38000 Grenoble, France

[3] Faculty of Exact Sciences, Aurel Vlaicu University, Arad, Romania
vlad.dragoi@uav.ro

[4] LITIS, University of Rouen Normandie, Mont-Saint-Aignan, France

[5] IMT, Mines Saint-Etienne, Centre CMP, Equipe Commune CEA Tech-Mines Saint-Etienne, 13541 Gardanne, France

Abstract. Code-based public-key cryptosystems are promising candidates for standardization as quantum-resistant public-key cryptographic algorithms. Their security is based on the hardness of the syndrome decoding problem. Computing the syndrome in a finite field, usually $\mathbb{F}_2$, guarantees the security of the constructions. We show in this article that the problem becomes considerably easier to solve if the syndrome is computed in $\mathbb{N}$ instead. By means of laser fault injection, we illustrate how to compute the matrix-vector product in $\mathbb{N}$ by corrupting specific instructions, and validate it experimentally. To solve the syndrome decoding problem in $\mathbb{N}$, we propose a reduction to an integer linear programming problem. We leverage the computational efficiency of linear programming solvers to obtain real-time message recovery attacks against the code-based proposal to the NIST Post-Quantum Cryptography standardization challenge. We perform our attacks in the worst-case scenario, *i.e.* considering random binary codes, and retrieve the initial message within minutes on a desktop computer.

Our attack targets the reference implementation of the Niederreiter cryptosystem in the NIST PQC competition finalist *Classic McEliece* and is practically feasible for all proposed parameters sets of this submission. For example, for the 256-bit security parameters sets, we successfully recover the message in a couple of seconds on a desktop computer Finally, we highlight the fact that the attack is still possible if only a fraction of the syndrome entries are faulty. This makes the attack feasible even though the fault injection does not have perfect repeatability and reduces the computational complexity of the attack, making it even more practical overall.

Keywords: Code-based cryptography · Classic McEliece · Syndrome decoding problem · Laser fault injection · Integer linear programming

A. Canteaut and F.-X. Standaert (Eds.): EUROCRYPT 2021, LNCS 12697, pp. 438–467, 2021.
https://doi.org/10.1007/978-3-030-77886-6_15

1 Introduction

For the last three decades, public key cryptography has been an essential component of digital communications. Communication protocols rely on three core cryptographic functionalities: public key encryption (PKE), digital signatures, and key exchange. These are implemented using Diffie-Hellman key exchange [16], the RSA cryptosystem [44], and elliptic curve cryptosystems [26,39]. Their security relies on the difficulty of number theoretic problems such as the Integer Factorization Problem or the Discrete Logarithm Problem. Shor proved that quantum computers can efficiently solve each of these problems [47], potentially making all public-key cryptosystems (PKC) based on such assumptions impotent.

Since then, cryptographers proposed alternative solutions which remain safe in the quantum era. These schemes are called *post-quantum secure* [9]. In 2016, the National Institute of Standards and Technology (NIST) made a call to the community to propose post-quantum secure solutions for standardization. Multiple candidates were submitted, that are based on various hard problems (lattices, error-correcting codes, multivariate systems of equations and hash functions). In this work, we analyze one of the four finalists, the only one that uses error-correcting codes, *Classic McEliece*[1] [1].

1.1 General Decoding and Integer Linear Programming

The hardness of general decoding for a linear code is an $\mathcal{NP}$-complete problem in coding theory [8], which makes it an appealing candidate for code-based post-quantum cryptography. From the original scheme proposed by McEliece [36] to the latest variants submitted to the NIST PQC competition [1,3–5], the majority of these PKCs base their security on the syndrome decoding problem (SDP). Informally, for a binary linear code $\mathcal{C}$ of length n and dimension k, having a parity-check matrix $\boldsymbol{H}$, the SDP is defined as follows: given $\boldsymbol{s} \in \mathbb{F}_2^{n-k}$, find a binary vector $\boldsymbol{x}$ having less than t values equal to one, such that $\boldsymbol{Hx} = \boldsymbol{s}$.

A recent possible solution to solve the general decoding problem is to use Integer Linear Programming (ILP). The idea was first proposed by Feldman [19] and later improved by Feldman *et al.* [20]. Since the initial problem is nonlinear, some relaxation was proposed in order to decrease the complexity. For more details on these aspects, we refer the reader to the excellent review of Helmling *et al.* [22]. One of the latest proposals [50] introduces a new method for transforming the initial decoding problem into an ILP, formalism that fits perfectly the ideas that we will put forward in this article. Let us briefly explain the idea of Tanatmis *et al.* [50]. The general decoding problem can be tackled using the well-known maximum-likelihood decoder. Let $\mathcal{C}$ be a binary linear code of length n and dimension k, with parity-check matrix $\boldsymbol{H}$. The integer linear programming formulation of maximum-likelihood decoding is given in Eq. (1).

$$\min\{\boldsymbol{v}\boldsymbol{x}^T \mid \boldsymbol{Hx} = 0\,, \boldsymbol{x} \in \{0,1\}^n\}, \tag{1}$$

[1] https://classic.mceliece.org/nist.html.

where $\boldsymbol{v}$ is the log-likelihood ratio (see [20,33]). Tanatmis *et al.* proposed to introduce an auxiliary positive variable $\boldsymbol{z} \in \mathbb{N}^{n-k}$, and define a new problem:

$$\min\{\boldsymbol{v}\boldsymbol{x}^T \mid \boldsymbol{H}\boldsymbol{x} = 2\boldsymbol{z} \ , \boldsymbol{x} \in \{0,1\}^n, \boldsymbol{z} \in \mathbb{N}^{n-k}\}. \quad (2)$$

The advantage of (2) compared to (1) is that $\boldsymbol{z}$ introduces real/integer constraints, which are much easier to handle for solvers than binary constraints. Also, there are as many constraints as rows in $\boldsymbol{H}$. Finding an appropriate variable $\boldsymbol{z}$ is not trivial and algorithms such as [50] are constantly modifying the values of $\boldsymbol{z}$ in order to find the correct solution.

Inspired by the ideas of Tanatmis *et al.*, we define the SDP as an ILP. Then, we propose to determine a valid constraints integer vector $\boldsymbol{z}$ so that the problem becomes easier to solve. Such an approach was recently proposed as a proof of concept in [17]. Simulations for small to medium sized random codes ($n < 1500$ and $k < 750$) using the simplex algorithm were performed in [17]. However, cryptographic parameters were out of reach. Hence, in order to achieve our goal we will propose several improvements compared to [17] (detailed in Sect. 3.4), among which we count the following:

- Instead of solving the integer constrains problem using the simplex we will solve a relaxed version (with real constrains) using the interior point method.
- An optimization scheme, where only a small proportion of the parity-check rows are required, is proposed. This amount of information required to retrieve a valid solution points out to an information theoretical threshold of the integer-SDP.
- Simulations show that the overall complexity empirically decreases from $\mathcal{O}(n^3)$ for the initial algorithm to $\mathcal{O}(n^2)$ for the optimized algorithm.
- In a practical implementation, real cryptographic instances are solved within minutes, proving the efficiency of the algorithm.

Before that, we need to put forward a recent result in laser fault injection [14].

1.2 Related Works

Understanding how fault attacks allow to corrupt the instructions executed by a microcontroller has been a vivid topic of research in recent years. While electromagnetic fault injection is probably the most commonly used technique, certainly because of its relatively low cost, it has several drawbacks. Indeed, while the "instruction skip" or "instruction replay" fault models were clearly identified [45], most of the time going down to the instruction set level leaves a lot of questions open [40]. As such, only a handful of the observed faults can be tracked down and explained by a modification of the bits in the instruction [31]. Last, but not least, electromagnetic fault injection usually exhibits poor repeatability [13], as low as a few percents in some cases.

Conversely, another actively studied technique is laser fault injection, which offers several advantages when it comes to interpreting the observed faults. For example, the instruction skip fault model has been experimentally validated by laser fault injection, with perfect repeatability and the ability to skip one or multiple instructions [18]. On a deeper level of understanding, it has been shown in [14] that it was possible to perform a bit-set on any of the bits of an instruction while it is fetched from the Flash memory of the microcontroller. This modification is temporary since it is performed during the fetch process. As such, the instruction stored in the Flash memory remains untouched. We place ourselves in this framework here. We reproduce the fault injection setup to show how this powerful fault model gives the possibility to actively corrupt the instructions and allows to mount a fault attack on code-based cryptosystems.

In a recent article [27], the authors present a physical attack on the code-based finalist *Classic McEliece*. The idea is to combine side-channel information and the use of the information set decoding algorithm to recover the message from a *Classic McEliece* hardware reference implementation. In this paper, we will focus on the same candidate. Our approach of combining techniques coming from laser fault attacks and algorithms for general decoding problem fits well in this new trend in cryptanalysis.

Moreover, implementations of the Classic McEliece on memory-constrained is an active research topic [46]. These implementations are typically subject to physical attacks, such as the one described in this article.

1.3 Contributions

This article makes the following contributions.

- First, we propose a new attack on code-based cryptosystems which security relies on the SDP. We show by simulations that, if the syndrome is computed in $\mathbb{N}$ instead of $\mathbb{F}_2$, then the SDP can be solved in polynomial time by linear programming.
- Second, we experimentally demonstrate that such a change of set is feasible by corrupting the instructions executed during the syndrome computation. To this end, we rely on backside laser fault injection in Flash memory in order to transform an addition over $\mathbb{F}_2$ into an addition over $\mathbb{N}$. We perform this by corrupting the instruction when it is fetched from Flash memory, thereby replacing the exclusive-OR operation with an add-with-carry operation.
- Third, we then show, starting with the faulty syndrome, that the secret error-vector can be recovered very efficiently by linear programming. By means of software simulations we show that, in particular, this attack scales to cryptographically strong parameters for the considered cryptosystems.
- Finally, we highlight a very practical feature of the attack, which is that only a fraction of the syndrome entries need to be faulty in order for the attack to be successful. On top of that, this fraction decreases when the cryptographic parameters grow. This has important practical consequences, since the attack can be carried out even if the fault injection is not perfectly repeatable. Moreover, this also drastically reduces the number of inequalities to be considered in the linear programming problem, thereby making the problem much easier to solve.

The proposed attack fits in the following framework. We perform a message recovery attack against code-based cryptosystems based on Niederreiter's model. Specifically, we recover the message from one faulty syndrome and the public key. The attacker must have physical access to the device, where the laser fault injection is performed during encryption, *i.e.*, the matrix-vector multiplication. The total number of faults the attacker must inject is upper-bounded by the code dimension.

Our attack was performed on a real microcontroller, embedding an ARM Cortex-M3 core, where we corrupted the XOR operation and obtained the faulty outputs. As in our case, one needs to perform single-bit and double-bit faults, in a repeatable and controlled manner. This method strongly relies on the work of Colombier *et al.* [14] and thus can be verified and repeated experimentally. We stress out that constant-time implementations are of great help for this attack setting, since they allow to easily synchronize the laser shots with the execution of the algorithm.

We chose to attack here two multiplication methods: the schoolbook and the packed version. The former is general, and is considered for example in the NTL library[2]. The later is the reference implementation of the *Classic McEliece* cryptosystem and makes optimum use of the computer words.

The article is organized as follows. In Sect. 2, we focus on code-based cryptosystems,and in particular the NIST PQC competition finalist *Classic McEliece.* Section 3 defines the SDP in $\mathbb{N}$ and shows how it relates to linear programming. In Sect. 4, we show how the corruption of instructions by laser fault injection allows to switch from $\mathbb{F}_2$ to $\mathbb{N}$ during the syndrome computation. Section 5 presents experimental results following the attack path, from laser fault injection to the exploitation of the faulty syndrome by linear programming. Finally, we conclude this article in Sect. 6.

2 Code-Based Cryptosystems

2.1 Coding Theory – Preliminaries

Notations. The following conventions and notations are used. A finite field is denoted by $\mathbb{F}$, and the ring of integers by $\mathbb{N}$. Vectors (column vectors) and matrices are written in bold, *e.g.*, a binary vector of length n is $\boldsymbol{x} \in \{0,1\}^n$, an $m \times n$ integer matrix is $\boldsymbol{A} = (a_{i,j})_{\substack{0 \le i \le m-1 \\ 0 \le j \le n-1}} \in \mathcal{M}_{m,n}(\mathbb{N})$. A row sub-matrix of $\boldsymbol{A}$ indexed by a set $I \subseteq \{0, \ldots, m-1\}$ is denoted by $\boldsymbol{A}_{I,} = (a_{i,j})_{\substack{i \in I \\ 0 \le j \le n-1}}$. The same applies to column vectors, *i.e.*, $\boldsymbol{x}_I$ is the sub-vector induced by the set I on $\boldsymbol{x}$.

Error Correcting Codes. We say that $\mathcal{C}$ is an $[n, k]$ linear error-correcting code, or simply a linear code, over a finite field $\mathbb{F}$ if $\mathcal{C}$ is a linear subspace of

[2] https://www.shoup.net/ntl/.

dimension k of the vector space $\mathbb{F}^n$, where k, n are positive integers with $k < n$. The elements of $\mathcal{C}$ are called codewords. The support of a codeword $\mathsf{Supp}(\boldsymbol{c})$ is the set of non-zero positions of $\boldsymbol{c}$. We will represent a code either by its generator matrix, $\boldsymbol{G} \in \mathcal{M}_{k,n}(\mathbb{F})$ ($\mathtt{rank}(\boldsymbol{G}) = k$), or by its parity-check matrix, $\boldsymbol{H} \in \mathcal{M}_{n-k,n}(\mathbb{F})$, ($\mathtt{rank}(\boldsymbol{H}) = n - k$), where $\boldsymbol{H}\boldsymbol{G}^T = \boldsymbol{0}$ holds. One of the key ingredients for decoding is the usage of a metric. The Hamming weight of a vector $\mathsf{wt}(\boldsymbol{x})$ is the number of non-zero components of $\boldsymbol{x}$. Now, we can define a well-known strategy used for general decoding, *i.e.*, syndrome decoding.

Definition 1 (Binary-SDP).

Input: $\boldsymbol{H} \in \mathcal{M}_{n-k,n}(\mathbb{F}_2)$ *of rank* $n - k$, *a vector* $\boldsymbol{s} \in \mathbb{F}_2^{n-k}$ *and* $t \in \mathbb{N}^*$.
Output: $\boldsymbol{x} \in \mathbb{F}_2^n$, *with* $\mathsf{wt}(\boldsymbol{x}) \leq t$, *such that* $\boldsymbol{H}\boldsymbol{x} = \boldsymbol{s}$.

2.2 NIST PQC Competition

The main goal of the process started by NIST is to replace three standards that are considered the most vulnerable to quantum attacks, *i.e.*, FIPS 186-4[3] (for digital signatures), NIST SP 800-56A[4] and NIST SP 800-56B[5](both for keys establishment in public-key cryptography). For the first round of this competition, 69 candidates met the minimum criteria and the requirements imposed by NIST. 26 out of 69 were announced on January 30, 2019 for moving to the second round. From these, 17 are public-key encryption and/or key-establishment schemes and 9 are digital signature schemes. Since July 2020, NIST started the third round of this process where only seven finalists were admitted (four PKE/KEM and three signature schemes). In addition to the finalists, eight alternate candidates were selected.

In this article, we focus on one of the finalists, *Classic McEliece*, which is a merger of the former *Classic McEliece* submission and NTS-KEM. In Table 1 the design rationale of the McEliece [36] and Niederreiter [42] schemes is illustrated. The private key is a structured code, and the public key its masked variant. We would like to stress out that our method applies to any code-based cryptosystem that bases its security on the binary SDP.

2.3 Security and Practical Parameters

Basically, all the code-based schemes support their security on the hardness of the SDP. Hence, state-of-the-art algorithms for solving the SDP are used to set up the security level of any such proposals. The best strategy in this direction is the class of so-called Information Set Decoding (ISD) algorithms. The original algorithm was proposed by Prange [43] and has been significantly improved since then [7,28,30,34,35,48]. Under the assumption that the public code is indistinguishable from a random code, the ISD techniques are considered the

[3] https://nvlpubs.nist.gov/nistpubs/FIPS/NIST.FIPS.186-4.pdf.
[4] https://nvlpubs.nist.gov/nistpubs/SpecialPublications/NIST.SP.800-56Ar2.pdf.
[5] https://nvlpubs.nist.gov/nistpubs/SpecialPublications/NIST.SP.800-56Br1.pdf.

Table 1. McEliece and Niederreiter PKE schemes

McEliece PKE	Niederreiter PKE
$\mathsf{KeyGen}(n, k, t) = (\mathsf{pk}, \mathsf{sk})$	
$\boldsymbol{G}$-generator matrix matrix of $\mathcal{C}$	$\boldsymbol{H}$-parity-check of $\mathcal{C}$
\\\\ $\mathcal{C}$ an $[n, k]$ that corrects t errors	
An $n \times n$ permutation matrix $\boldsymbol{P}$	
A $k \times k$ invertible matrix $\boldsymbol{S}$	An $(n-k) \times (n-k)$ invertible Matrix $\boldsymbol{S}$
Compute $\boldsymbol{G}_{\text{pub}} = \boldsymbol{SGP}$	Compute $\boldsymbol{H}_{\text{pub}} = \boldsymbol{SHP}$
$\mathsf{pk} = (\boldsymbol{G}_{\text{pub}}, t)$ $\mathsf{sk} = (\boldsymbol{S}, \boldsymbol{G}, \boldsymbol{P})$	$\mathsf{pk} = (\boldsymbol{H}_{\text{pub}}, t)$ $\mathsf{sk} = (\boldsymbol{S}, \boldsymbol{H}, \boldsymbol{P})$
$\mathsf{Encrypt}(\boldsymbol{m}, \mathsf{pk}) = \boldsymbol{z}$	
Encode $\boldsymbol{m} \rightarrow \boldsymbol{c} = \boldsymbol{m}\boldsymbol{G}_{\text{pub}}$ Choose $\boldsymbol{e}$	Encode $\boldsymbol{m} \rightarrow \boldsymbol{e}$
\\\\ $\boldsymbol{e}$ a vector of weight t	
$\boldsymbol{z} = \boldsymbol{c} + \boldsymbol{e}$	$\boldsymbol{z} = \boldsymbol{H}_{\text{pub}}\boldsymbol{e}$
$\mathsf{Decrypt}(\boldsymbol{z}, \mathsf{sk}) = \boldsymbol{m}$	
Compute $\boldsymbol{z}^* = \boldsymbol{z}\boldsymbol{P}^{-1}$ $\boldsymbol{z}^* = \boldsymbol{mSG} + \boldsymbol{eP}^{-1}$ $\boldsymbol{m}^* = \mathcal{D}ecode(\boldsymbol{z}^*, \boldsymbol{G})$ Retrieve $\boldsymbol{m}$ from $\boldsymbol{m}^*\boldsymbol{S}^{-1}$	Compute $\boldsymbol{z}^* = \boldsymbol{S}^{-1}\boldsymbol{z}$ $\boldsymbol{z}^* = \boldsymbol{HPe}$ $\boldsymbol{e}^* = \mathcal{D}ecode(\boldsymbol{z}^*, \boldsymbol{H})$ Retrieve $\boldsymbol{m}$ from $\boldsymbol{P}^{-1}\boldsymbol{e}^*$

best strategy for message recovery. For *Classic McEliece*, the error weight t is of order $o(n)$, when $n \rightarrow \infty$, to be more precise is of order $\frac{(n-k)}{\log_2(n)}$. In this case, the time complexity of the ISD variants is $2^{ct(1-o(1))}$, where c is a constant given by the code rate. Table 2 gives the list of parameters for the *Classic McEliece* proposal.

Table 2. IND-CCA2 KEM McEliece parameters.

Parameters set	348864	460896	6688128	6960119	8192128
n	3488	4608	6688	6960	8192
k	2720	3360	5024	5413	6528
t	64	96	128	119	128
Equivalent bit-level security	128	196	256	256	256

3 Syndrome Decoding over $\mathbb{N}$

3.1 Description of the Problem

Definition 2 ($\mathbb{N}$-SDP).

Input: $\boldsymbol{H} \in \mathcal{M}_{n-k,n}(\mathbb{N})$ *with* $h_{i,j} \in \{0,1\}$ *for all* i, j,
$\boldsymbol{s} \in \mathbb{N}^{n-k}$ *and* $t \in \mathbb{N}^*$ *with* $t \neq 0$.
Output: $\boldsymbol{x} \in \mathbb{N}^n$ *with* $x_i \in \{0,1\}$ *and* $\mathsf{wt}(\boldsymbol{x}) \leq t$, *such that* $\boldsymbol{Hx} = \boldsymbol{s}$.

Notice that $\boldsymbol{H}$ and $\boldsymbol{x}$ are binary, as in the SDP, whereas $\boldsymbol{s}$ is integer. Basically, $\boldsymbol{H}$ and $\boldsymbol{x}$ are sampled exactly as for the SDP, it is only the operation, *i.e.*, matrix-vector multiplication, that changes, and thus its result.

Possible Solutions. Based on the similarities with SDP, one might try to solve $\mathbb{N}$-SDP using techniques from coding theory. We briefly enumerate three possible solutions.

1. The simplest solution is to solve it as a linear system. If we consider the system $\boldsymbol{Hx} = \boldsymbol{s}$, it has $n - k$ equations and n unknowns, and hence, can be solved efficiently. However, there are k free variables, and 2^k possible solutions, since $\boldsymbol{x} \in \{0,1\}$. For each instance, compute the Hamming weight, and stop when the value is smaller than or equal to t. This procedure is not feasible in practice for cryptographic parameters, due to the values of k.
2. Another possible solution is combinatorial (emulating an exhaustive search). One can choose subsets of s_i elements from $\mathsf{Supp}(\boldsymbol{H}_{i,})$ for increasing values of i, until it finds the correct combinations. This solution can be further optimised by choosing subsets from a smaller set at each iteration, where previously selected positions are rejected from the updated set. Even so, the time complexity will be dominated by a product of binomial coefficients that is asymptotically exponential in t.
3. A modified ISD to the integer requirements. Let us choose the original algorithm of Prange [43], that is randomly permuting the matrix $\boldsymbol{H}$ (denote $\boldsymbol{P}$ such a permutation) until the support of the permuted $\boldsymbol{x}$ is included in the set $\{0, \ldots, n-k-1\}$, *i.e.*, the set where the $\boldsymbol{HP}$ is in upper triangular form. To put an integer matrix in the upper triangular form, one has to use the equivalent of the Gaussian elimination for the integers, *i.e.*, the Hermite normal form. So, by computing an integer matrix $\boldsymbol{A}$ and $\boldsymbol{H}^*$, so that $\boldsymbol{H}^*$ is upper triangular on its first $n-k$ positions we obtain:
$$\boldsymbol{AHP}\left(\boldsymbol{P}^T\boldsymbol{x}\right) = \boldsymbol{AH}'\boldsymbol{x}' = \boldsymbol{H}^*\boldsymbol{x}' = \boldsymbol{As}. \quad (3)$$
If $\mathsf{Supp}(\boldsymbol{x}') \subseteq \{0, \ldots, n-k-1\}$ then the new syndrome $\boldsymbol{s}^* = \boldsymbol{As}$ has rather small integer entries, that directly allow the computation of $\boldsymbol{x}'$. This algorithm has time complexity similar to the classic ISD, and hence, remains exponential in t.

Since all these methods are not feasible in practice for cryptographic parameters, we propose another solution. For that, let us notice the following fact.

Remark 1. As for the maximum-likelihood decoding problem, we can reformulate ℕ-SDP as an optimization problem:

$$\min\{\mathsf{wt}(\boldsymbol{x}) \mid \boldsymbol{H}\boldsymbol{x} = \boldsymbol{s}, \boldsymbol{x} \in \{0,1\}^n\}, \tag{4}$$

where $\boldsymbol{H}$ and $\boldsymbol{s}$ are given as in Definition 2.

This fact leads us to searching for mathematical optimization techniques, such as integer linear programming.

3.2 Integer Linear Programming

ILP was already used in a cryptographic context, mainly for studying stream ciphers [11,12,41]. The authors of [41] implemented ILP-based methods that gave practical results for Enocoro-128v2, as well as for calculating the number of active S-boxes for AES. In [11,12] ILP was used for studying the Trivium stream cipher and the lightweight block cipher Ktantan. In all of these, the technique was to reformulate the original cryptographic problems by means of ILP, and use some well-known solvers in order to obtain practical evidence of their security. Typically, in [12] the authors used the CPLEX solver. There are mainly three big solvers for LP and ILP problems: lpSolve[6], IBM CPLEX[7] and Gurobi[8], recently tested for various types of practical problems [32].

We point here some necessary facts about ILP, as we will use ILP as a tool only. Interested readers might check [10,23] for more details.

Definition 3 (ILP problem). *Let* $n, m \in \mathbb{N}^+, \boldsymbol{b} \in \mathbb{N}^n, \boldsymbol{s} \in \mathbb{N}^m$ *and* $\boldsymbol{A} \in \mathcal{M}_{m,n}(\mathbb{N})$. *The ILP problem is defined as the optimization problem*

$$\min\{\boldsymbol{b}^T\boldsymbol{x} | \boldsymbol{A}\boldsymbol{x} = \boldsymbol{c}, \boldsymbol{x} \in \mathbb{N}^n, \boldsymbol{x} \geq 0\}. \tag{5}$$

Any vector $\boldsymbol{x}$ satisfying $\boldsymbol{A}\boldsymbol{x} = \boldsymbol{s}$ is called a feasible solution. If a feasible solution $\boldsymbol{x}^*$ satisfies the minimum condition in (5) then $\boldsymbol{x}^*$ is optimal. In order to redefine our initial problem, *i.e.*, (4) into an ILP problem, we need to redefine the Hamming weight of a vector as a linear operation.

3.3 Solving ℕ-SDP Using ILP

Theorem 1 **([17]).** *Let us suppose that there exists a unique vector* $\boldsymbol{x}^* \in \{0,1\}^n$ *with* $\mathsf{wt}(\boldsymbol{x}^*) = t$*, solution to the* ℕ*-SDP. Then* $\boldsymbol{x}^*$ *is the optimum solution of an ILP problem.*

[6] http://lpsolve.sourceforge.net/5.5/.

[7] https://www.ibm.com/products/ilog-cplex-optimization-studio.

[8] https://www.gurobi.com.

Proof. Suppose that such an $\boldsymbol{x}^*$ exists and is unique, *i.e.*, $\boldsymbol{H}\boldsymbol{x}^* = \boldsymbol{s}$ with $\boldsymbol{s} \in \mathbb{N}^{n-k}$ and $\mathsf{wt}(\boldsymbol{x}^*) = t$. We will construct an ILP problem for which $\boldsymbol{x}^*$ is the optimum solution. For that, we simply set $\boldsymbol{A} = \boldsymbol{H}, \boldsymbol{c} = \boldsymbol{s}$, and $\boldsymbol{b}^T = (1, \ldots, 1)$ in (5). Since $\boldsymbol{x} \in \{0,1\}^n$ $\mathsf{wt}(\boldsymbol{x}) = \sum_{i=1}^{n} x_i = (1, \ldots, 1) \cdot \boldsymbol{x}$, but this is equal to $\boldsymbol{b}^T\boldsymbol{x}^*$. The ILP problem we need to solve can now be defined as:

$$\min\{\boldsymbol{b}^T\boldsymbol{x} | \boldsymbol{H}\boldsymbol{x} = \boldsymbol{s}, \boldsymbol{x} \in \{0,1\}^n\}, \tag{6}$$

which is exactly (4). This implies that $\boldsymbol{x}^*$ is a feasible solution to (6), and as $\boldsymbol{x}^*$ is the unique vector satisfying $\boldsymbol{H}\boldsymbol{x}^* = \boldsymbol{s}$ with $\mathsf{wt}(\boldsymbol{x}^*) \leq t$, $\boldsymbol{x}^*$ is optimum for the minimum weight condition.

ILP problems are defined as LP problems with integer constraints, hence any algorithm for solving an LP problem could potentially be used as a subroutine for solving the corresponding ILP problem. Usually, these are formalised in a sequential process, where the solution to one LP problem is close to the solution to the next LP problem, and so on, until eventually the ILP problem is solved. One of the most efficient method for solving ILP problems is the *branch and cut* method. In a branch and cut algorithm, an ILP problem is relaxed into an LP problem that is solved using an algorithm for LP problems. If the optimal solution is integral then it gives the solution to the ILP problem. There are mainly two famous methods for solving the linear problem: the simplex and the interior point method.

The simplex algorithm, introduced by Dantzig in [15], is one of the most popular methods for solving LP problems. The idea of this algorithm is to move from one vertex to another on the underlying polytope, as long as the solution is improved. The algorithm stops when no more neighbours of the current vertex improve the objective function. It is known to be really efficient in practice, by solving a large class of problems in polynomial time. However, it was proved in [25] that there are instances where the simplex falls into the exponential time complexity class.

Interior point algorithms represent a class of alternative algorithms to the simplex method, and were first proposed by [24]. Several variants improved the initial method, also by providing polynomial time complexity [29,51]. As the name suggests, this method starts by choosing a point in the interior of the feasible set. Moving inside the polyhedron, this point is improved, until the optimal solution is found.

Efficient solutions using interior point methods were proposed for the problem of maximum-likelihood decoding of binary codes [49,53,54]. These have running times dominated by low-degree polynomial functions in the length of the code. Also, they are in particular very efficient for large scale codes [49,53]. For these particular interesting arguments, we choose the interior point method for solving the $\mathbb{N}$-SDP.

Solving the $\mathbb{N}$*-SDP.* The algorithm we propose here to solve the $\mathbb{N}$-SDP can be described as follows. Initiate the parameters from (6), solve a relaxation of the

N-SDP (using the interior point methods), round the solution to binary entries (using the method from [37]) and finally verify if the binary solution satisfies the parity-check equations and the weight condition. The relaxation of the ILP problem to an LP problem is a common method, more exactly, the LP problem that we have to solve is:

$$\min\{\boldsymbol{b}^T\boldsymbol{x} \mid \boldsymbol{H}\boldsymbol{x} = \boldsymbol{s}, \boldsymbol{0} \preceq \boldsymbol{x} \preceq \boldsymbol{1}, \boldsymbol{x} \in \mathbb{R}^n\}, \tag{7}$$

where $\preceq$ is defined by $\boldsymbol{x} \preceq \boldsymbol{y}$ if and only if $x_i \leq y_i$ for all $0 \leq i \leq n-1$.

Algorithm 1. ILP solver for N-SDP

Input: $\boldsymbol{H}, \boldsymbol{s}, t$
Output: $\boldsymbol{x}$ solution to N-SDP or ERROR

```
Set b = (1, ..., 1)^T
Solve equation (7)                                ▷ Using the interior-point method
round the solution x* to x* ∈ {0,1}^n             ▷ as done in [37]
if Hx* = s and wt(x) ≤ t then
    return x*
else
    return ERROR
end if
```

3.4 Optimization

In this paragraph we propose an optimization to Algorithm 1. Let us first define the following sets :

Definition 4. *Let* $0 < \ell < n-k$ *and* $\emptyset \subset I_0 \subset \cdots \subset I_\ell \subseteq \{0, \ldots, n-k-1\}$. *For* $0 \leq i \leq \ell$ *we define* $\mathcal{H}_{I_j} = \{\boldsymbol{x} \in \{0,1\}^n \mid \boldsymbol{H}_{I_j,}\boldsymbol{x} = \boldsymbol{s}_{I_j}\}$, *and* $\mathcal{H} = \{\boldsymbol{x} \in \{0,1\}^n \mid \boldsymbol{H}\boldsymbol{x} = \boldsymbol{s}\}$.

Now, let us prove how to reduce the number of constraints to our initial problem. First, notice that N-SDP can be written as $\min\{\boldsymbol{b}^T\boldsymbol{x} \mid \boldsymbol{x} \in \mathcal{H}\}$. Secondly, we prove that:

Proposition 1. *Let* $0 < \ell < n-k$ *and* $\emptyset \subset I_0 \subset \cdots \subset I_\ell \subseteq \{0, \ldots, n-k-1\}$ *and* $\boldsymbol{x}^*_{I_j} = \min\{\boldsymbol{b}^T\boldsymbol{x} \mid \boldsymbol{x} \in \mathcal{H}_{I_j}\}$, *for any* $0 \leq j \leq \ell$. *Then* $\mathsf{wt}(\boldsymbol{x}^*) \geq \mathsf{wt}(\boldsymbol{x}^*_{I_\ell}) \geq \cdots \geq \mathsf{wt}(\boldsymbol{x}^*_{I_0})$.

Proof. From Definition 4 we deduce

$$\mathcal{H} \subseteq \mathcal{H}_{I_\ell} \cdots \subseteq \mathcal{H}_{I_0}. \tag{8}$$

Since the sets $\mathcal{H}_{I_j}$ are finite, we can take the minimum and use the inclusion from (8) to deduce the result.

Hence, the sequence $\mathsf{wt}(x_{I_0^*}), \ldots, \mathsf{wt}(x_{I_\ell^*})$ is non-decreasing. If the initial set is $I_0 = \{s_{i_0}\}$ then the sequence of Hamming weight of the solutions starts from $\mathsf{wt}(x_{I_0^*}) = s_{i_0}$.

We will thus use Proposition 1 as a reduction of our initial problem to a shorter one, in terms of constraints or equivalently in the dimension of the system. Two algorithms exploiting the result of Proposition 1, are presented here. Both are based on the same rationale:

1. Choose I_0 and call the ILP solver for $\mathbb{N}$-SDP (Algorithm 1);
2. if the output is an optimum solution for the full problem then stop;
3. if not add an extra row to I_0 to create I_1 and continue until a solution is found.

This procedure allows us to solve an easier instance and reduce the overall time complexity of our algorithm. The way rows are sampled for building $I_0, I_1, \ldots, I_\ell$ has a significant impact on the length of the chain ℓ. Two natural methods for creating the sets are described. The first one, uses uniform random sampling (each row has a probability $1/(n-k)$ of being selected), and as we shall see in Sect. 5.2 it allows to solve the $\mathbb{N}$-SDP for all the *Classic McEliece* parameters only by using less than 40% of the rows. Reducing the parameter ℓ might be achievable by starting in a more clever way. More exactly, by including rows in an ordered manner, where the ordering corresponds to the decreasing order on the entries of the syndrome. By doing so, we start at $\mathsf{wt}(x_{I_0^*}) = \max\{s_i, 0 \leq i \leq n-k\}$. For the parameters used in the *Classic McEliece* proposal, the improvement of this method compared with the random sampling, reduces the number of required rows for solving the $\mathbb{N}$-SDP by a multiplicative factor close to 2. As we shall see in Sect. 5.2, considering only a fraction of the syndrome entries decreases the empirically observed time complexity of the $\mathbb{N}$-SDP from $\mathcal{O}(n^3)$ to $\mathcal{O}(n^2)$.

4 Fault Injection

As shown in the previous section, computing the syndrome in $\mathbb{N}$ instead of $\mathbb{F}_2$ makes the SDP considerably easier to solve. In order to perform this change, we must have the processor perform the additions in $\mathbb{N}$ instead of $\mathbb{F}_2$ during the syndrome computation. This is done by replacing the exclusive-OR instruction with an add-with-carry instruction. Since both these arithmetic instructions are performed by the arithmetic logic unit of the processor, their associated opcodes are close, in the sense that the Hamming distance between them is small. Therefore, only few bits must be modified to switch from one to the other.

We focus on the Thumb instruction set here since it is widely used in embedded systems. The fact that, in the Thumb instruction set, the exclusive-OR instruction can be transformed into an add-with-carry instruction by a single bit-set can be considered pure luck. This is at least partially true but this is not as surprising as it seems. Indeed, both these instructions are "data processing" instructions. As such, they are handled by the arithmetic logic unit. Therefore, the opcode bits are used to generate similar control signals, and it is not surprising that they differ by only a few bits. A few examples of corruptions in other instruction sets are given in Appendix A, showing that this attack could be easily ported to other targets.

4.1 Previous Work

The single-bit fault model is a very powerful one and allows an attacker to mount efficient attacks [21]. However, performing a single-bit fault in practice is far from trivial. While these can be performed by global fault injection techniques, such as under-powering [6], further analysis is necessary to filter the exploitable faults. Indeed, while performing a single-bit fault at a non-chosen position is feasible, targeting one bit specifically is much more complicated.

To this end, a more precise fault injection technique is required. In this regard, laser fault injection is a well-suited method. Indeed, as shown in [14], it is possible to perform a single-bit bit-set fault on data fetched from the Flash memory. This makes it possible to alter the instruction while it is fetched, before it is executed by the processor. We insist here on the fact that, as detailed in [14], the corruption is temporary, and only performed on the fetched instruction. The content of the Flash memory is left untouched. Therefore, if the instruction is fetched again from the Flash memory while no laser fault injection is performed then it is executed normally.

Colombier *et al.* showed that targeting a single bit in a precise manner is relatively easy, since it only requires to position the laser spot at the right location on the y-axis in the Flash memory [14], aiming at different word lines. Indeed, moving along the x-axis does not change the affected bit, since the same word line is covered by the laser spot. Therefore, targeting a single bit of the fetched instruction is possible. This observation was experimentally confirmed on two different hardware targets in [38], further proving the validity of this fault model. Moreover, they also showed that two adjacent bits can also be set by shooting with sufficient power between two word lines. This single-bit or dual-bit bit-set fault model is the one we use as a framework for the rest of the article.

4.2 Bit-Set Fault on an Exclusive-OR Instruction

Using the fault injection technique described above, we now show how to apply it to replace an exclusive-OR instruction with an add-with-carry instruction. Figure 1 shows the Thumb encoding of both instructions, given in the ARMv7-M Architecture Reference Manual[9]. When comparing both instructions, we observe that only one single-bit bit-set fault, on the bit of index 8, is required to replace the exclusive-OR instruction with an add-with-carry instruction. This is highlighted in red in Fig. 1.

[9] https://static.docs.arm.com/ddi0403/e/DDI0403E_B_armv7m_arm.pdf.

15	14	13	12	11	10	9	8	7	6	5	4	3	2	1	0
Generic EORS: R_d = R_m ^ R_n															
0	1	0	0	0	0	0	0	0	1	R_m			R_{dn}		
Generic ADCS: R_d = R_m + R_n															
0	1	0	0	0	0	0	1	0	1	R_m			R_{dn}		

Fig. 1. Thumb encoding of the exclusive-OR (EORS) and add-with-carry (ADCS) instructions. The bit set by laser fault injection is highlighted in red. (Color figure online)

Algorithm 2. Matrix-vector multiplication.

```
function MAT_VEC_MULT(matrix, error_vector)
  for r ← 0 to n − k − 1 do
    syndrome[r] = 0                                   ▷ Initialisation
  for r ← 0 to n − k − 1 do
    for c ← 0 to n − 1 do
      syndrome[r] ^= matrix[r][c] & error_vector[c]
                                                      ▷ Multiplication and addition
  return syndrome
```

4.3 Bit-Set Fault on Schoolbook Matrix-Vector Multiplication

Now that we have shown that a single-bit fault can replace an exclusive-OR instruction with an add-with-carry instruction, we will extend it to a matrix-vector multiplication, used to compute the syndrome in code-based cryptosystems. The syndrome computation is typically implemented as shown in Algorithm 2. This is how it is done in the NTL library for instance, which is widely used by NIST PQC competition candidates.

When performing laser fault injection in this setting, an attacker has essentially three delays to tune. According to this implementation, an exclusive-OR instruction will be executed at each run of the inner *for* loop. The delay between the execution of these instructions is constant. We refer to it as t_{inner}. The second delay of interest is between the last and the first exclusive-OR instruction of the inner *for* loop, when one iteration of the outer *for* loop is performed. This delay is constant too. We refer to it as t_{outer}. Finally, the last delay to tune is the initial delay, before the matrix-vector multiplication starts. We refer to it as $t_{initial}$. Figure 2 shows these three delays on an example execution.

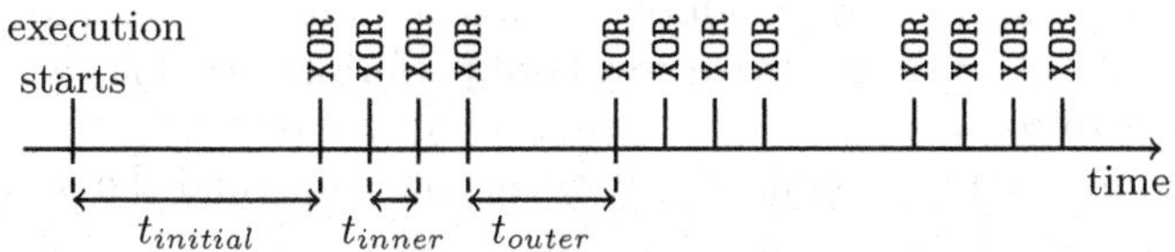

Fig. 2. Laser fault injection delays to tune

These delays can be tuned one after the other. The first delay to tune is $t_{initial}$, then t_{inner} and finally t_{outer}. Therefore, performing laser fault injection on the schoolbook matrix-vector multiplication does not induce much additional practical complexity compared with the exclusive-OR instruction alone because of the regularity of the computation. Overall, $(n-k) \times n$ faults are necessary to obtain the full faulty syndrome in $\mathbb{N}$.

4.4 Bit-Set Fault on a Packed Matrix-Vector Multiplication

The matrix-vector multiplication method described in Algorithm 2 makes poor use of the capacity of the computer words when matrix entries are in $\mathbb{F}_2$. Indeed, even if both the matrix and the error-vector are binary, their elements are stored in a full computer word. Although the smallest type available can be used, it still takes a byte to store only one bit of information.

To overcome this, consecutive bits in the rows of the parity-check matrix can be packed together in a single computer word. Typically, eight bits are packed in a byte. In this setting, the dimensions of the matrix, error-vector and syndrome are changed. The parity-check matrix now has $n-k$ rows and $n/8$ columns. The error-vector now has $n/8$ entries. The syndrome now has $(n-k)/8$ entries..

Algorithm 3. Matrix-vector multiplication with packed bits[10].

```
1: function MAT_VEC_MULT_PACKED(matrix, error_vector)
2:   for r ← 0 to n − k − 1 do
3:     syndrome[r/8] = 0                                   ▷ Initialisation
4:   for r ← 0 to n − k − 1 do
5:     b = 0
6:     for c ← 0 to n/8 − 1 do
7:       b ^= matrix[r][c] & error_vector[c]     ▷ Multiplication and addition
8:     b ^= b >> 4;                              ▷
9:     b ^= b >> 2;                              ▷ Exclusive-OR folding
10:    b ^= b >> 1;                              ▷
11:    b &= 1;                                             ▷ LSB extraction
12:    syndrome[r/8] |= b << (r%8)                         ▷ Bits packing
13:  return syndrome
```

Compared to the schoolbook method shown in Algorithm 2, a variable `b` is used to store the intermediate result of the multiplication and addition (see line 7 of Algorithm 3). Next, a few extra steps are performed on this variable. First, it is necessary to compute the exclusive-OR of all the bits of this variable. This is done by computing the exclusive-OR of the lower half and the upper half, by shifting by four positions (see line 8 of Algorithm 3). This is repeated again by

[10] As implemented by the `syndrome` function in the `encrypt.c` source file of the software submission of *Classic McEliece*: https://classic.mceliece.org/nist.html.

shifting by two and finally one position (see lines 9 and 10 of Algorithm 3). We refer to this technique as exclusive-OR folding. The least-significant bit is then extracted (see line 11 of Algorithm 3). Finally, it is packed into the syndrome byte at the correct position (see line 12 of Algorithm 3).

Compared to the schoolbook matrix-vector multiplication shown in Algorithm 2, several different faults are required here. They are detailed below.

Fault on the Multiplication and Addition *for* Loop. The first specific fault to perform on the packed matrix-vector multiplication is on the inner *for* loop found on line 6 of Algorithm 3. Indeed, since the bits of the parity-check matrix are now packed, we cannot perform the sum over $\mathbb{N}$ and expect the final value to be the sum of all individual bits. This is because, when bits are stored in a word, performing the addition in $\mathbb{N}$ will incur carries which will propagate and make the final byte useless, since individual contributions of the rows of the parity check matrix are mixed.

To overcome this issue, we propose to prematurely exit this *for* loop. Before explaining how this can be achieved in practice by laser fault injection, we detail the consequences it has on the packed matrix-vector multiplication.

Consequence of a Premature Exit of the Inner for Loop of the Packed Matrix-Vector Multiplication. If we are able to prematurely exit the inner for loop, then the value of the intermediate variable `b`, which holds the temporary result of the multiplication and addition, is changed. We shall identify the possible values of `b` by induction. Let us refer to the value of `b` after the i-th execution of the *for* loop as $\mathtt{b_i}$.

Let us first identify the base case, that is, exiting after only one execution. We have:

$$\mathtt{b_0} = \mathtt{matrix[r][0]} \mathbin{\&} \mathtt{error\_vector[0]} \tag{9}$$

We can now identify the induction step, which corresponds to the subsequent executions of the for loop. We then have:

$$\mathtt{b_i} = \mathtt{b_{i-1}} \;\hat{}\; (\mathtt{matrix[r][i]} \mathbin{\&} \mathtt{error\_vector[i]}) \tag{10}$$

Therefore, we now have the values of `b` from $\mathtt{b_0}$ to $\mathtt{b_{n/8-1}}$. The value $\mathtt{b_i}$ is obtained by executing the *for* loop i times and prematurely exiting it only then. As mentioned in Subsect. 4.1, this is feasible since instructions are corrupted "on the fly", only when they are fetched from the Flash memory.

In order to obtain the faulty syndrome entry, that is, the sum over $\mathbb{N}$, we must compute the sum given in Eq. (11). We use the Hamming weight (`wt`) to obtain the sum of the individual bits.

$$\mathtt{wt}(\mathtt{b_0}) + \sum_{i=1}^{n/8-1} \mathtt{wt}(\mathtt{b_i} \;\hat{}\; \mathtt{b_{i-1}}) \tag{11}$$

We then obtain a faulty syndrome entry just like the one we got after performing fault injection on the schoolbook matrix-vector multiplication. The next paragraph describes how to perform it practically by laser fault injection.

```
mov r1, #0
inner:
...
...
...
add r1, #1
cmp r1, #N/8
ble @inner
```

(a) Typical assembly code of a *for* loop.

15	14	13	12	11	10	9	8	7	6	5	4	3	2	1	0
Generic ADD: R_{dn} += imm8															
0	0	1	1	0	R_{dn}			imm8							
ADD r1 #1															
0	0	1	1	0	0	0	1	0	0	0	0	0	0	0	1
ADD r1 #193															
0	0	1	1	0	0	0	1	1	1	0	0	0	0	0	1

(b) Thumb encoding of the ADD instruction and two examples with different immediate values. The bits which must be set by laser fault injection are highlighted in red.

Fig. 3. Assembly code of a *for* loop and a way to exit it prematurely by corrupting the loop variable increment.

Premature Exit of a for Loop by Laser Fault Injection. As discussed in [14], prematurely exiting a *for* loop is feasible by corrupting the loop variable increment. Instead of incrementing the loop variable by only 1, we can try to make this increment as large as possible. As shown in Fig. 3, the increment of the loop variable at the end of the *for* loop is performed by a 16-bit ADD instruction. It has been demonstrated in [14] that it is possible to perform a bit-set fault on two adjacent bits of the instruction. Here, we can thus make the increment step as large as 193 by setting the bits of index 6 and 7 of the ADD instruction.

As shown in Algorithm 3, the body of the inner *for* loop normally executes $n/8$ times. By performing the previously described fault, we can make the loop variable increment step as large as 193. Therefore, the loop is executed $\lceil \frac{n}{8\times 193} \rceil = \lceil \frac{n}{1544} \rceil$ times. Our objective is to exit the *for* loop prematurely. In this regard, for large values of n, executing the loop $\lceil \frac{n}{1544} \rceil$ times can lead to execute the *for* loop for a few more iterations.

For instance, if $n = 3488$, then the loop should be executed $\frac{n}{8} = 436$ times. If we want to exit after 5 iterations to obtain $\texttt{b}_5$, then we will in fact obtain:

$$\begin{aligned} \texttt{b}_5 = \texttt{b}_4 \ \hat{}\ & \texttt{matrix[r][5] \& error\_vector[5]} \ \hat{} \\ & \texttt{matrix[r][198] \& error\_vector[198]} \ \hat{} \\ & \texttt{matrix[r][391] \& error\_vector[391]} \end{aligned} \tag{12}$$

instead of:

$$\texttt{b}_5 = \texttt{b}_4 \ \hat{}\ \texttt{matrix[r][5] \& error\_vector[5]} \tag{13}$$

since $391 \equiv 198 \equiv 5 \bmod 193$.

Therefore, we have a few parasitic extra elements in the $\texttt{b}_\texttt{i}$ value. However, since the error-vector has low weight, we can expect the associated bytes, `error_vector[198]` and `error_vector[391]` in Eq. 12, to be all zeros and therefore not change the $\texttt{b}_\texttt{i}$ value.

Another approach would be to obtain multiple values for every $\texttt{b}_\texttt{i}$, by exploring several increment steps. The correct one could then potentially be extracted as the common pattern of all these values. This will not be investigated further in this article but could be the subject of future research.

Fault on the Exclusive-OR Folding. Now that we obtained a temporary faulty syndrome entry stored in the intermediate variable `b`, we must deal with the exclusive-OR folding (see lines 8 to 10 of Algorithm 3) in order to keep this value intact.

There are two ways to address the exclusive-OR folding. The first possibility is to corrupt the destination register in the instruction. Depending on the level of optimisation used for the compilation, the exclusive-OR folding can be either decomposed into three consecutive shift-exclusive-OR pairs or be performed directly by three consecutive "wide" exclusive-OR operations. Indeed, as specified in the ARM reference manual, the exclusive-OR instruction can be made "wide" to include an optional shift of one of the operands (see ARMv7-M Reference Manual). In both cases, corrupting the destination register is easy and consists only in performing a bit-set on the $\mathtt{R_d}$ part of the instruction.

The second possibility, which is the one we consider more practical, is to notice that the sequence of three operations that make up the exclusive-OR folding constitute a permutation over $\mathbb{F}_2^8$. We verified it exhaustively for the 256 possible values. Therefore, rather than performing the destination register corruption described previously, one can simply inverse the permutation.

Fault on the Least-Significant Bit Extraction. The next operation to address is the least-significant bit (LSB) extraction (see line 11 of Algorithm 3).

Again here, there are two possible faults. Similarly to what was presented before for the exclusive-OR folding, it is also possible to corrupt the destination register. This would leave the source register untouched and preserve the full value of $\mathtt{b_i}$, not only its LSB. The second option is to corrupt the "immediate" operand of the `AND` instruction that performs the masking to extract the LSB. To extract the LSB, this immediate value is `0x01`. The objective here is to set as many bits as possible to 1 in the immediate value, in order for the `AND` masking to reset as few bits as possible. Depending on the level of optimisation used for the compilation, the LSB extraction can be performed in one or two instructions. For the sake of readability, we consider only the case where two 16-bit instructions are used instead of a condensed 32-bit one. However, the idea to apply is exactly the same.

Figure 4a shows the two assembly instructions that perform the LSB extraction. First, the mask value is loaded. It is then used as a mask in the subsequent `AND` instruction. Ideally, we would like to load 255 as a mask instead, so that no bits are reset by the AND masking. However, this requires to perform a bit-set on seven adjacent bits, which is out of reach with a single-spot laser that can at most fault two adjacent bits [14]. This could be done with a multi-spot laser setup though. Therefore, here, four intermediate faults are necessary. For each of them, two bits of the mask are set, as shown in Fig. 4b, giving the following mask values: `0x03`, `0x0D`, `0x31` and `0xC1`. We refer to the four consecutive faulty

```
mov r1, #1
and r1, r2
```

(a) Assembly code of the LSB extraction.

15	14	13	12	11	10	9	8	7	6	5	4	3	2	1	0
Generic MOV: R_d = imm8															
0	1	0	0	0	R_d			imm8							
MOV r1 #1															
0	1	0	0	0	0	0	1	0	0	0	0	0	0	0	1
MOV r1 #3															
0	1	0	0	0	0	0	1	0	0	0	0	0	0	1	1
MOV r1 #13															
0	1	0	0	0	0	0	1	0	0	0	0	1	1	0	1
MOV r1 #49															
0	1	0	0	0	0	0	1	0	0	1	1	0	0	0	1
MOV r1 #193															
0	1	0	0	0	0	0	1	1	1	0	0	0	0	0	1

(b) Thumb encoding of the MOV instruction and the set of four corruptions required to get the full byte value. The bits which must be set by laser fault injection are highlighted in red.

Fig. 4. Assembly code of the LSB extraction and the four necessary corruptions required to prevent it and obtain the full byte value.

byte values as $\mathtt{b}_{\#3}$, $\mathtt{b}_{\#13}$, $\mathtt{b}_{\#49}$ and $\mathtt{b}_{\#193}$. Then the correct b value, without LSB extraction, is given in Eq. (14).

$$\mathtt{b} = \mathtt{b}_{\#3} \mid \mathtt{b}_{\#13} \mid \mathtt{b}_{\#49} \mid \mathtt{b}_{\#193} \tag{14}$$

Fault on the Bits Packing Operation. The previous sections showed how it is possible to keep the b value intact. Finally, the last operation to address is the bits packing operation (see line 12 of Algorithm 3). There are two issues to address here. First, we must deal with the left shift that will cause the most significant bits of b to be dropped. Second, we must address the eight successive OR operations performed for each syndrome entry.

We will actually start without dealing with the shift. The objective here is to have the b stored in the syndrome vector directly, to make them available to the attacker. To this end, we will apply again the idea of modifying the loop increment (as shown in Fig. 3 but this time for the outer *for* loop). The pattern to observe is the following. If we increase the loop increment after the first execution of the outer *for* loop, then we have: $\mathtt{s}[0] = \mathtt{b}$, with b not being shifted. All other syndrome entries are altered and unusable. If we increase the loop increment after the ninth execution of the outer *for* loop, then we have: $\mathtt{s}[0] = \mathtt{b}$, with b not being shifted. Again, all other syndrome entries are altered and unusable. We then repeat this process and exit the outer *for* loop after the i-th execution, $i \in \{8m+1 \mid m \in \mathbb{N},\ m < k/8\}$.

This fault leaves us with a syndrome vector which entries contain every eighth faulty syndrome value, those for which the row index r verifies $r \equiv 0 \bmod 8$. Therefore, we only have 12.5 % of the faulty syndrome entries to feed to the linear programming solver. We briefly examine some possibilities to obtain a higher percentage.

The issue here is with the left shift operation, which discards the most significant bits of the byte `b`. This shift is implemented with the `LSL` instruction. As it turns out, performing a one-bit bit-set at different positions of this instruction leads quite a few corrupted instructions. They are listed in Fig. 5. The most interesting corruption is probably to turn the `LSL` instruction into a `CMP` instruction, which compares the values stored in the registers and updates the processor flags but does not modify the content of the registers. Therefore, this is the corruption that we pick. Alternatively, other corruptions such as `LSR` (logical shift right) or `SBC` (subtract with carry) could also be exploited, but would require more analysis.

15	14	13	12	11	10	9	8	7	6	5	4	3	2	1	0
Generic LSL: R_{dn} <<= R_m															
0	1	0	0	0	0	0	0	1	0	R_m			R_{dn}		
Generic LSR: R_{dn} >>= R_m															
0	1	0	0	0	0	0	0	1	**1**	R_m			R_{dn}		
Generic SBC: R_{dn} -= R_m															
0	1	0	0	0	0	0	**1**	1	0	R_m			R_{dn}		
Generic CMP: Compare(R_m, R_n)															
0	1	0	0	0	0	**1**	0	1	0	R_m			R_n		

Fig. 5. Possible corruptions of the `LSL` instruction with a one-bit bit-set fault

At last, the final operation to deal with is the OR operation which packs the bits together without affecting the ones which have already been packed. This must be addressed by premature exit of the outer *for* loop again.

After the row of index $r \equiv 0 \bmod 8$ has been processed, the syndrome entry holds the correct value, as mentioned before, making 12.5% of the faulty entries readily available. However, if we run the outer *for* loop for one more iteration, the row of index $r \equiv 1 \bmod 8$ is processed. The syndrome entry value is then: $\mathtt{b}_{\mathtt{r}\equiv 0} \mid (\mathtt{b}_{\mathtt{r}\equiv 1} << 1)$. If the value $\mathtt{b}_{\mathtt{r}\equiv 0}$ had many zeroes and the most significant bit of $\mathtt{b}_{\mathtt{r}\equiv 1}$ is not 1, then the value of $\mathtt{b}_{\mathtt{r}\equiv 1}$ can be deduced. However, this might not be correct, but considering the low error weight t for the *Classic McEliece* parameter sets, this might be possible. A trial-and-error process could then be followed, trying to include those new faulty syndrome entries into the problem fed to the solver.

Summary and Feasibility of Faulting the Packed Matrix-Vector Multiplication. Figure 6 summarizes the steps performed in the packed matrix-vector multiplication and the associated faults required to compute the multiplication in $\mathbb{N}$ instead of $\mathbb{F}_2$. Essentially, a lot of required faults involve prematurely exiting the inner and outer *for* loops.

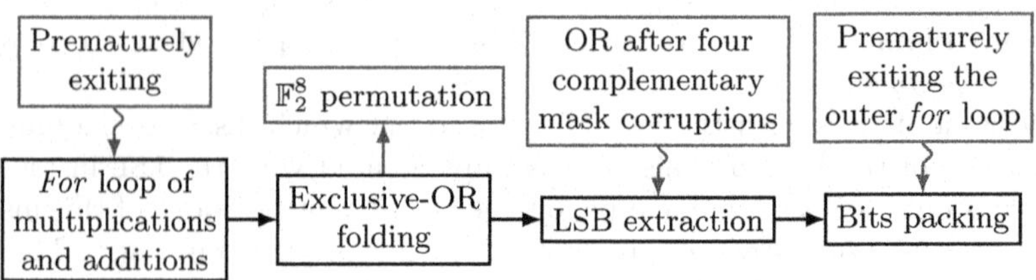

Fig. 6. Summary of the operations found in the packed matrix-vector multiplication and the required associated faults.

For practical reasons, it is worth noting which bits of the instructions must be set. Indeed, this determines the position of the laser spot in the Flash memory. The timing of the laser fault injection can be tuned very precisely, allowing to selectively target one instruction only. However, given the linear speed at which a typical XYZ stage travels and the operating frequency of the device, it is foolish to try to fault consecutive instructions at different bit positions. Premature exit of a *for* loop requires to set the bits of index 7 and 6. Corrupting the `MOV` instruction to avoid LSB extraction, as depicted in Fig. 4b, requires to set the bits 7 and 6, then 5 and 4, then 3 and 2, and finally 1. This is thus not feasible with a single-spot laser injection station, but would be possible with a multi-spot station.

5 Experimental Results

5.1 Fault Injection

We did perform the fault described above by laser fault injection. This allowed us to replace the exclusive-OR instruction by an add-with-carry instruction. We use an infrared laser, at a wavelength of 1064 nm and perform backside injection on the target. We reused the laser fault injection parameters given in [14]. The injection power is 1 W. The laser spot has a diameter of 5 µm. The duration of the laser pulse is 135 ns. This is roughly equal to the clock period of the microcontroller, which runs at 7.4 MHz. Laser synchronisation is becoming more precise and circuit with faster clocks are definitely within reach, with laser pulses as short as a few nanoseconds. Then, the fault is achieved by placing the laser spot in the Flash memory of the 32-bit microcontroller. This device embeds an ARM Cortex-M3 core, which is a very common processor core found in many embedded systems. We validated that the fault injection was indeed correctly performed by comparing input/output pairs with and without fault injection. This confirmed that the exclusive-OR instruction can indeed be replaced with an add-with-carry instruction.

Figure 7 shows a detailed example of instruction corruption performed by laser fault injection. The example code simply loads an identical constant value into two registers and performs the exclusive-OR of them. The value is then read out from the destination register.

Fault	Assembly code	Binary machine code	Readout

No	`mov r3, #90`
	`mov r4, #90`
	`eors r3, r4`
		0010 0011 0101 1010
		0010 0100 0101 1010
		0010 0000 0110 0011
			r3 = 0x00

Yes	`mov r3, #90`
	`mov r4, #90`
	`adcs r3, r4`
		0010 0011 0101 1010
		0010 0100 0101 1010
		0010 0001 0110 0011
			r3 = 0xB4

Fig. 7. Detailed example of instruction corruption by laser fault injection. The effects of the fault are highlighted in red (Color figure online)

On the first line, no fault injection is performed. Since the value loaded into the registers is the same, the exclusive-OR leads to a byte where all bits are zero, as shown in the readout value of the destination register.

On the second line, a fault is injected. This allows to perform a bit-set on the bit of index 8, as shown in red in the "Binary machine code" column. This in turns changes the exclusive-OR operation into an add-with-carry operation. This is visible in the "Assembly code" column, where the `eors` instruction is replaced with an `adcs` instruction. As a consequence, the value stored in the destination register is different from zero and equal to the sum of both registers instead. Since we observe precisely this value in our experimentation, it confirms that the instruction has been successfully corrupted.

Following the fault injection strategies detailed in Sect. 4, we are able to obtain a syndrome with values in $\mathbb{N}$. The following section describes the actual exploitation of this syndrome to recover the binary error-vector.

5.2 Syndrome Decoding over $\mathbb{N}$ with Integer Linear Programming

After obtaining a faulty syndrome with entries in $\mathbb{N}$, we feed it and the parity-check matrix to the linear programming solver. We used the `linprog` function of the `scipy.optimize` [52] Python module. It implements the interior point method as described in [2]. As mentioned in Sect. 3, we chose the interior point method over the simplex, for several already known arguments. We still performed a comparison between these two methods for our specific problem, and indeed, the interior point method turned out to be much faster.

In order to remain as general as possible, we consider parity-check matrices of random binary codes. Since no efficient decoding algorithm exists for these, they can be considered the worst-case scenario. Also, all the code-based proposals to the NIST competition state that the public codes are indistinguishable from random codes. Parity-check matrices which are associated with structured codes thus cannot be harder to handle than the ones of random binary codes. All experiments are conducted on a desktop computer, embedding a 6-core CPU clocked at 2.8 GHz and 32 GB of RAM.

In Table 3 the precise timings (in seconds) to solve the modified SDP for all the proposed parameters of the *Classic McEliece* submission are given. Notice that even for the 256 bit security level parameters, using ILP, we retrieve the secret message in less than three seconds.

Table 3. Execution time for solving the modified SDP using the optimal number of rows in the ILP (optimized version) for *Classic McEliece* parameters.

Parameters set	348864	460896	6688128	6960119	8192128
n	3488	4608	6688	6960	8192
k	2720	3360	5024	5413	6528
t	64	96	128	119	128
Equivalent bit-level security	128	192	256	256	256
Required number of rows	340	470	625	597	658
Execution time [s]	0.6925	1.2045	2.3865	2.1295	2.7625

As highlighted in Sect. 3.4, only a fraction of the parity-check matrix rows and syndrome entries are required to solve the linear programming problem. This fraction depends on at least three parameters: the length of the code n, the weight of the solution t, and the method used for adding extra rows to the system. Here, we will limit our discussion to the case where the algorithm randomly selects rows until a valid solution to the initial problem is found. Hence, there is a threshold, a minimum number of rows required to solve the $\mathbb{N}$-SDP.

In order to realize how efficient the ILP is at solving the $\mathbb{N}$-SDP, and to sustain our method for other potential sets of parameters, we simulate our attack on a wider range of parameters. For that, we choose values of t of order $\sqrt{n}$ and $\sqrt{n\log(n)}$. One might argue that in the case of the *Classic McEliece* cryptosystem, the value of t equals $\frac{n-k}{\log(n)}$, which is different from what we propose here. Notice that in the *Classic McEliece* cryptosystem, the order of k is about $\frac{2n}{3}$, which makes t approximately $\frac{n}{3\log(n)}$. At these orders, for any $n \in \{854, \ldots, 29\,448\}$ we have that $\sqrt{n} \leq \frac{n}{3\log(n)} \leq \sqrt{n\log(n)}$. Hence, the two cases considered here represent lower and upper bounds for any potential set of parameters of the *Classic McEliece* cryptosystem. As we will detail in the next paragraph, for any parameters within this range of values, the ILP solver will retrieve the secret message from the faulty syndrome within minutes.

Required Percentage of Faulty Syndrome Entries for Random Sampling. Figure 8 shows how the percentage of required syndrome entries changes for different values of n. The value of k equals as in the case of the *Classic McEliece* $n/3$. This depends not only on n but also on the weight of the error-vector. Figure 8a shows the required percentage of syndrome entries for $t = \sqrt{n}$. Figure 8b shows the required percentage of syndrome entries for $t = \sqrt{n\log(n)}$.

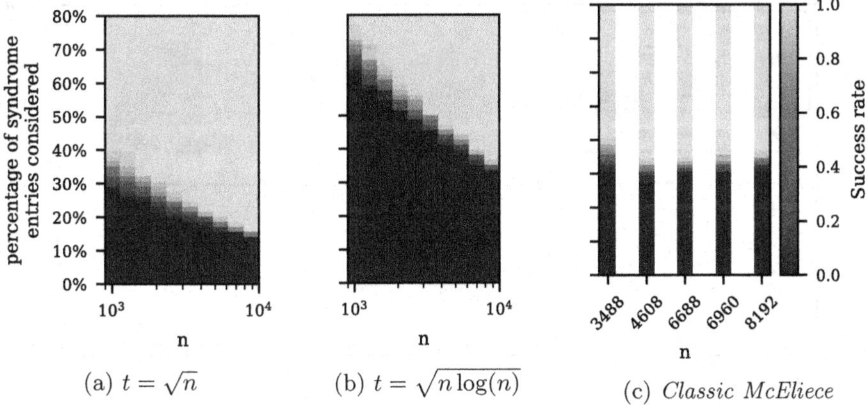

(a) $t = \sqrt{n}$

(b) $t = \sqrt{n \log(n)}$

(c) *Classic McEliece*

Fig. 8. Success rate of solving the linear programming problem for different values of n and percentage of syndrome entries considered.

As stated before when the exact parameters or the McEliece are considered (see Fig. 8c) the percentage of required rows is in between $t = \sqrt{n}$ and $t = \sqrt{n \log(n)}$, being closer to the former for small security levels, an closer to the later for high security levels. For each value of n and every percentage we estimate the success rate by solving the linear programming problem 20 times.

For $t = \sqrt{n \log(n)}$, as shown in Fig. 8b, the required percentage of syndrome entries does not drop as fast. Moreover, this leads to an issue related to large values of t. For example, $n = 10\,000$ leads to $t = \sqrt{n \log(n)} = 303$. This is already higher than the biggest value of t in *Classic McEliece* (see Table 2). At this number of errors, since n is not so large, the linear programming problem to solve is better satisfied by non-binary vectors. Therefore, it is necessary to add bounds on the variables of the problem to make sure that they remain in the $[0, 1]$ interval. This dramatically increases the memory requirements of the solver, thereby limiting the largest value of n to 2×10^4 approximately. Note that this is only dictated by the RAM available on the desktop computer we used and is not an algorithmic limit.

When the precise parameters of the *Classic McEliece* are considered, about $n/10$ rows were sufficient to solve the $\mathbb{N}$-SDP when random sampling is used in the optimizations (see Table 3). Further simulations show that this number could be reduced to $n/20$ when the second optimization algorithm is used. Hence, considering high-rate Goppa codes with $k/n \leq 0.90$ leads to practical attacks on the corresponding $\mathbb{N}$-SDP.

It is worth mentioning that, for any $t < \sqrt{n \log(n)}$, the ILP solver finds the binary solution directly, which makes it really efficient. However, for larger values of t, we need to bound the solution to the $[0, 1]$ interval in order to be able to practically solve the ILP. In addition, when parameters grow, the

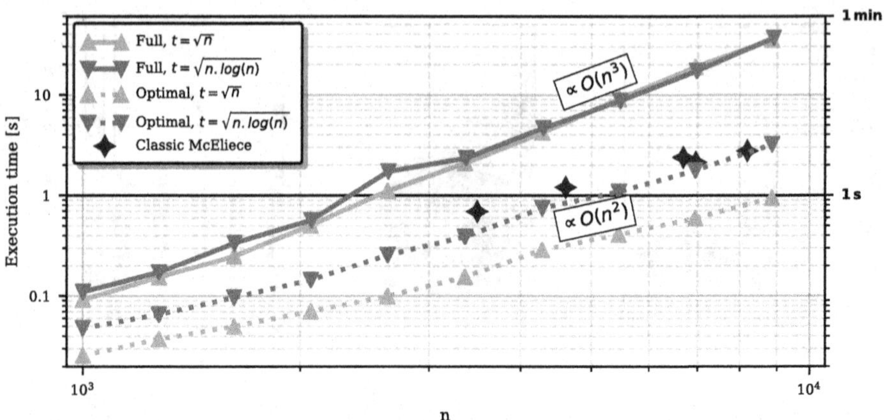

Fig. 9. Execution time of the linear programming solver for different values of n. In the "Full" case, all syndrome entries are considered. In the "Optimal" case, only the required percentage of syndrome entries are considered.

required percentage is reduced. This contradicts the common sense that larger cryptographic parameters offer better security.

Execution Time. Figure 9 shows how the execution time of the linear programming solver changes for different values of n. Two cases are displayed. In the "Full" case, the whole faulty syndrome is fed to the solver. In the "Optimal" case, only the required percentage of syndrome entries are used.

We can observe that considering only the required percentage of syndrome entries drastically reduces the computation time. For $n = 9000$, and $t = \sqrt{n}$, more than one order of magnitude of computation time is saved. For the *Classic McEliece* parameters, less than three seconds of computation are necessary in the 256-bit security case. For 128 bits of security, the problem is solved in one second approximately.

We can empirically observe on Fig. 9 that the slope is different for the "Full" and the "Optimal" cases, having respectively $\mathcal{O}(n^3)$ and $\mathcal{O}(n^2)$ time complexities. We do not have an explanation for this behaviour at the moment. This could be the subject of future works.

6 Conclusion

We have shown in this paper that, using laser fault injection, we are able to modify one of the building blocks of code-based cryptosystems, *i.e.*, the well-known syndrome decoding problem. We modeled the modified instance by means of an integer linear programming problem, and further solve it experimentally in polynomial time. We have provided real-time attacks against all the parameters of the *Classic McEliece* proposal.

Furthermore, we have shown that the number of fault injected can be drastically reduced if we focus on only a few percent of the number of rows of the matrices involved. Combining laser fault injection to obtain an easier problem such as the syndrome decoding problem over $\mathbb{N}$ instead of $\mathbb{F}_2$ and then using linear programming to solve this problem is an interesting combination that potentially could be applied to other interesting problems, such as the Shortest Integer Problem or the Shortest Vector Problem.

We can identify several research perspectives to continue this work. First, finding a better attack path for the packed version would be an advantage. This would make the attack more practical. Hardware implementations of *Classic McEliece* could also be targeted. On a more theoretical side, studying the complexity of the problem discussed here would also be interesting. In particular, the drop from cubic to quadratic complexity when considering only the optimal number of syndrome entries is particularly intriguing.

Acknowledgments. This work was carried out in the framework of the FUIAAP22-Project PILAS supported by Bpifrance. V-F. Drăgoi was supported by a grant of the Romanian Ministry of Education and Research, CNCS - UEFISCDI, project number PN-III-P1-1.1-PD-2019-0285, within PNCDI III.

A Other Instruction Sets

Here are a few examples of possible corruptions of the exclusive-OR instruction in other instruction sets than the one we considered in the article.

ARMv7 In the ARMv7[11] instruction set, the exclusive-OR instruction (`EORS.W`) can be corrupted into a saturated addition instruction (`QADD`) as shown in Fig. 10.

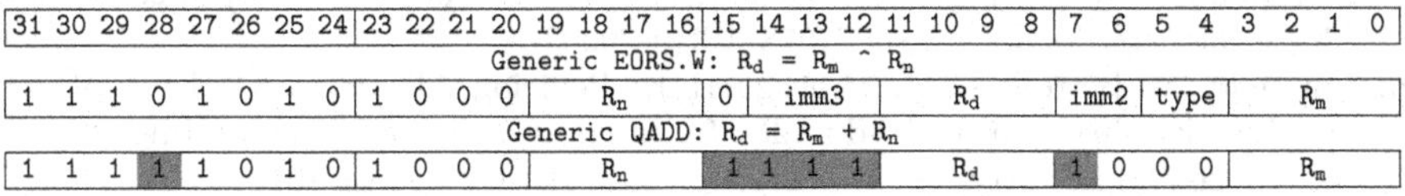

31	30	29	28	27	26	25	24	23	22	21	20	19	18	17	16	15	14	13	12	11	10	9	8	7	6	5	4	3	2	1	0
Generic EORS.W: $R_d = R_m$ ^ R_n																															
1	1	1	0	1	0	1	0	1	0	0	0	R_n				0	imm3			R_d				imm2		type		R_m			
Generic QADD: $R_d = R_m + R_n$																															
1	1	1	1	1	0	1	0	1	0	0	0	R_n				1	1	1	1	R_d				1	0	0	0	R_m			

Fig. 10. Fault by bit-sets on the ARMv7 exclusive-OR instruction

PIC. In the PIC[12] instruction set, the exclusive-OR instruction (`XORWF`) can be corrupted into an addition instruction (`ADDWF`) as shown in Fig. 11.

RISC-V Compressed. In the RISC-V compressed[13] instruction set, the exclusive-OR instruction (`C.XOR`) can be corrupted into an addition instruction (`C.ADDW`) as shown in Fig. 12.

[11] https://static.docs.arm.com/ddi0403/e/DDI0403E_B_armv7m_arm.pdf.

[12] http://ww1.microchip.com/downloads/en/devicedoc/31029a.pdf.

[13] https://riscv.org/specifications/isa-spec-pdf/.

13	12	11	10	9	8	7	6	5	4	3	2	1	0
Generic XORWF: W = W ^ R_f													
0	0	0	1	1	0	d	R_f						
Generic ADDWF: W = W + R_f													
0	0	0	1	1	**1**	d	R_f						

Fig. 11. Fault by bit-set on the PIC exclusive-OR instruction

15	14	13	12	11	10	9	8	7	6	5	4	3	2	1	0
Generic C.XOR: R_d = R_{s1} ^ R_{s2}															
1	0	0	0	1	1	$R_{s1/d}$			0	1	R_{s2}			0	1
Generic C.ADDW: R_d = R_{s1} + R_{s2}															
1	0	0	**1**	1	1	$R_{s1/d}$			0	1	R_{s2}			0	1

Fig. 12. RISC-V encoding of the exclusive-OR instruction and a possible fault feasible by bit-set

References

1. Albrecht, M.R., et al.: Classic McEliece, submission to the NIST post quantum standardization process (November 2017)
2. Andersen, E.D., Andersen, K.D.: The MOSEK interior point optimizer for linear programming: an implementation of the homogeneous algorithm. In: Frenk, H., Roos, K., Terlaky, T., Zhang, S. (eds.) High performance optimization, vol. 33, pp. 197–232. Springer, Boston (2000) https://doi.org/10.1007/978-1-4757-3216-0_8
3. Aragon, N., et al.: BIKE: Bit Flipping Key Encapsulation, submission to the NIST post quantum standardization process (December 2017)
4. Aragon, N., et al.: Rollo (merger of Rank-Ouroboros, LAKE and LOCKER). Second round submission to the NIST post-quantum cryptography call (2020)
5. Baldi, M., Barenghi, A., Chiaraluce, F., Pelosi, G., Santini, P.: LEDAkem: a post-quantum key encapsulation mechanism based on QC-LDPC codes. In: Lange, T., Steinwandt, R. (eds.) PQCrypto 2018. LNCS, vol. 10786, pp. 3–24. Springer, Cham (2018). https://doi.org/10.1007/978-3-319-79063-3_1
6. Barenghi, A., Bertoni, G.M., Breveglieri, L., Pellicioli, M., Pelosi, G.: Fault attack on AES with single-bit induced faults. In: International Conference on Information Assurance and Security, pp. 167–172. Atlanta, IEEE (August 2010)
7. Becker, A., Joux, A., May, A., Meurer, A.: Decoding random binary linear codes in $2^{n/20}$: how 1+1=0 improves information set decoding. In: Pointcheval, D., Johansson, T. (eds.) EUROCRYPT 2012. LNCS, vol. 7237, pp. 520–536. Springer, Heidelberg (2012). https://doi.org/10.1007/978-3-642-29011-4_31
8. Berlekamp, E.R., McEliece, R.J., van Tilborg, H.C.A.: On the inherent intractability of certain coding problems (corresp.). IEEE Trans. Inf. Theor. **24**(3), 384–386 (1978)
9. Bernstein, D.J.: Post-quantum cryptography. In: van Tilborg, H.C.A., Jajodia, S. (eds.) Encyclopedia of Cryptography and Security, 2nd edn., pp. 949–950. Springer, New York (2011). https://doi.org/10.1007/978-1-4419-5906-5_386
10. Bertsimas, D., Tsitsiklis, J.N.: Introduction to Linear Organisation, Athena Scientific Optimization and Computation Series, vol. 6. Athena Scientific, Belmont (1997)

11. Borghoff, J.: Mixed-integer linear programming in the analysis of trivium and ktantan. IACR Cryptology ePrint Archive 2012, 676 (2012). http://eprint.iacr.org/2012/676
12. Borghoff, J., Knudsen, L.R., Stolpe, M.: Bivium as a mixed-integer linear programming problem. In: Parker, M.G. (ed.) IMACC 2009. LNCS, vol. 5921, pp. 133–152. Springer, Heidelberg (2009). https://doi.org/10.1007/978-3-642-10868-6_9
13. Bukasa, S.K., Lashermes, R., Lanet, J., Legay, A.: Let's shock our IoT's heart: ARMv7-M under (fault) attacks. In: Doerr, S., Fischer, M., Schrittwieser, S., Herrmann, D. (eds.) International Conference on Availability, Reliability and Security, pp. 33:1–33:6. ACM, Hamburg, Germany (August 2018)
14. Colombier, B., Menu, A., Dutertre, J.M., Moëllic, P.A., Rigaud, J.B., Danger, J.L.: Laser-induced single-bit faults in flash memory: Instructions corruption on a 32-bit microcontroller. In: IEEE International Symposium on Hardware Oriented Security and Trust, pp. 1–10. McLean, VA, USA (May 2019)
15. Dantzig, G.B.: Maximization of a linear function of variables subject to linear inequalities. Activity Anal. Prod. Allocation **13**, 339–347 (1951)
16. Diffie, W., Hellman, M.E.: New directions in cryptography. IEEE Trans. Inf. Theory **22**(6), 644–654 (1976)
17. Dragoi, V.F., Cayrel, P.L., Colombier, B., Bucerzan, D., Hoara, S.: Solving a modified syndrome decoding problem using integer programming. Int. J. Comput. Commun. Control **15**(5), 1–9 (2020)
18. Dutertre, J.-M., Riom, T., Potin, O., Rigaud, J.-B.: Experimental analysis of the laser-induced instruction skip fault model. In: Askarov, A., Hansen, R.R., Rafnsson, W. (eds.) NordSec 2019. LNCS, vol. 11875, pp. 221–237. Springer, Cham (2019). https://doi.org/10.1007/978-3-030-35055-0_14
19. Feldman, J.: Decoding error-correcting codes via linear programming. Ph.D. thesis, Massachusetts Institute of Technology, Cambridge, MA, USA (2003)
20. Feldman, J., Wainwright, M.J., Karger, D.R.: Using linear programming to decode binary linear codes. IEEE Trans. Inf. Theory **51**(3), 954–972 (2005)
21. Giraud, C.: DFA on AES. In: Dobbertin, H., Rijmen, V., Sowa, A. (eds.) AES 2004. LNCS, vol. 3373, pp. 27–41. Springer, Heidelberg (2005). https://doi.org/10.1007/11506447_4
22. Helmling, M., Ruzika, S., Tanatmis, A.: Mathematical programming decoding of binary linear codes: theory and algorithms. IEEE Trans. Inf. Theory **58**(7), 4753–4769 (2012)
23. Johnson, E.L., Nemhauser, G.L., Savelsbergh, M.W.P.: Progress in linear programming-based algorithms for integer programming: an exposition. INFORMS J. Comput. **12**(1), 2–23 (2000)
24. Karmarkar, N.: A new polynomial-time algorithm for linear programming. Combinatorica **4**(4), 373–396 (1984)
25. Klee, V., Minty, G.J.: How good is the simplex algorithm. Inequalities **3**(3), 159–175 (1972)
26. Koblitz, N.: Elliptic curve cryptosystems. Math. Comput. **48**(177), 203–209 (1987)
27. Lahr, N., Niederhagen, R., Petri, R., Samardjiska, S.: Side channel information set decoding using iterative chunking. In: Moriai, S., Wang, H. (eds.) ASIACRYPT 2020. LNCS, vol. 12491, pp. 881–910. Springer, Cham (2020). https://doi.org/10.1007/978-3-030-64837-4_29
28. Lee, P.J., Brickell, E.F.: An observation on the security of McEliece's public-key cryptosystem. In: Barstow, D., Barstow, D., et al. (eds.) EUROCRYPT 1988. LNCS, vol. 330, pp. 275–280. Springer, Heidelberg (1988). https://doi.org/10.1007/3-540-45961-8_25

29. Lee, Y.T., Sidford, A.: Efficient inverse maintenance and faster algorithms for linear programming. In: Guruswami, V. (ed.) IEEE Annual Symposium on Foundations of Computer Science, pp. 230–249. IEEE Computer Society, Berkeley, CA, USA (October 2015)
30. Leon, J.S.: A probabilistic algorithm for computing minimum weights of large error-correcting codes. IEEE Trans. Inf. Theory **34**(5), 1354–1359 (1988)
31. Liao, H., Gebotys, C.H.: Methodology for EM fault injection: charge-based fault model. In: Teich, J., Fummi, F. (eds.) Design, Automation & Test in Europe Conference & Exhibition, pp. 256–259. IEEE, Florence, Italy (March 2019)
32. Luppold, A., Oehlert, D., Falk, H.: Evaluating the performance of solvers for integer-linear programming. Technical Report, Hamburg University of Technology (2018). https://doi.org/10.15480/882.1839, https://tore.tuhh.de/handle/11420/1842
33. MacWilliams, F.J., Sloane, N.J.A.: The Theory of Error Correcting Codes, vol. 16. Elsevier, New York (1977)
34. May, A., Meurer, A., Thomae, E.: Decoding random linear codes in $\tilde{\mathcal{O}}(2^{0.054n})$. In: Lee, D.H., Wang, X. (eds.) ASIACRYPT 2011. LNCS, vol. 7073, pp. 107–124. Springer, Heidelberg (2011). https://doi.org/10.1007/978-3-642-25385-0_6
35. May, A., Ozerov, I.: On computing nearest neighbors with applications to decoding of binary linear codes. In: Oswald, E., Fischlin, M. (eds.) EUROCRYPT 2015. LNCS, vol. 9056, pp. 203–228. Springer, Heidelberg (2015). https://doi.org/10.1007/978-3-662-46800-5_9
36. McEliece, R.J.: A public-key system based on algebraic. Coding Theory **4244**, 114–116 (1978)
37. Megiddo, N.: On finding primal- and dual-optimal bases. INFORMS J. Comput. **3**(1), 63–65 (1991)
38. Menu, A., Dutertre, J., Rigaud, J., Colombier, B., Moëllic, P., Danger, J.: Single-bit laser fault model in NOR flash memories: analysis and exploitation. In: Workshop on Fault Detection and Tolerance in Cryptography, pp. 41–48. IEEE, Milan, Italy (September 2020)
39. Miller, V.S.: Use of elliptic curves in cryptography. In: Williams, H.C. (ed.) CRYPTO 1985. LNCS, vol. 218, pp. 417–426. Springer, Heidelberg (1986). https://doi.org/10.1007/3-540-39799-X_31
40. Moro, N., Dehbaoui, A., Heydemann, K., Robisson, B., Encrenaz, E.: Electromagnetic fault injection: Towards a fault model on a 32-bit microcontroller. In: Fischer, W., Schmidt, J. (eds.) Workshop on Fault Diagnosis and Tolerance in Cryptography, pp. 77–88. IEEE Computer Society, Los Alamitos, CA, USA (August 2013)
41. Mouha, N., Wang, Q., Gu, D., Preneel, B.: Differential and linear cryptanalysis using mixed-integer linear programming. In: Wu, C.-K., Yung, M., Lin, D. (eds.) Inscrypt 2011. LNCS, vol. 7537, pp. 57–76. Springer, Heidelberg (2012). https://doi.org/10.1007/978-3-642-34704-7_5
42. Niederreiter, H.: Knapsack-type cryptosystems and algebraic coding theory. Prob. Control Inf. Theory **15**(2), 159–166 (1986)
43. Prange, E.: The use of information sets in decoding cyclic codes. IRE Trans. Inf. Theory **8**(5), 5–9 (1962)
44. Rivest, R.L., Shamir, A., Adleman, L.M.: A method for obtaining digital signatures and public-key cryptosystems. Commun. ACM **21**(2), 120–126 (1978)
45. Rivière, L., Najm, Z., Rauzy, P., Danger, J., Bringer, J., Sauvage, L.: High precision fault injections on the instruction cache of armv7-m architectures. In: IEEE International Symposium on Hardware Oriented Security and Trust. pp. 62–67. IEEE Computer Society, Washington, DC, USA (May 2015)

46. Roth, J., Karatsiolis, E., Krämer, J.: Classic McEliece implementation with low memory footprint. In: Liardet, P.-Y., Mentens, N. (eds.) CARDIS 2020. LNCS, vol. 12609, pp. 34–49. Springer, Cham (2021). https://doi.org/10.1007/978-3-030-68487-7_3
47. Shor, P.W.: Polynomial-time algorithms for prime factorization and discrete logarithms on a quantum computer. SIAM J. Comput. **26**(5), 1484–1509 (1997)
48. Stern, J.: A method for finding codewords of small weight. In: Cohen, G., Wolfmann, J. (eds.) Coding Theory 1988. LNCS, vol. 388, pp. 106–113. Springer, Heidelberg (1989). https://doi.org/10.1007/BFb0019850
49. Taghavi, M.H., Shokrollahi, A., Siegel, P.H.: Efficient implementation of linear programming decoding. IEEE Trans. Inf. Theory **57**(9), 5960–5982 (2011)
50. Tanatmis, A., Ruzika, S., Hamacher, H.W., Punekar, M., Kienle, F., Wehn, N.: A separation algorithm for improved lp-decoding of linear block codes. IEEE Trans. Inf. Theory **56**(7), 3277–3289 (2010)
51. Vaidya, P.M.: Speeding-up linear programming using fast matrix multiplication (extended abstract). In: Annual Symposium on Foundations of Computer Science, pp. 332–337. IEEE Computer Society, Research Triangle Park, North Carolina, USA (October 1989)
52. Virtanen, P., et al.: SciPy 1.0: fundamental algorithms for scientific computing in python. Nature Methods **17**(3), 261–272 (2020)
53. Vontobel, P.O.: Interior-point algorithms for linear-programming decoding. In: Information Theory and Applications Workshop, pp. 433–437. IEEE, San Diego, CA, USA (January 2008)
54. Wadayama, T.: An LP decoding algorithm based on primal path-following interior point method. In: International Symposium on Information Theory, pp. 389–393. IEEE, Seoul, Korea (June 2009)

Multi-source Non-malleable Extractors and Applications

Vipul Goyal[1(✉)], Akshayaram Srinivasan[2], and Chenzhi Zhu[3]

[1] CMU and NTT Research, Pittsburgh, USA
vipul@cmu.edu
[2] Tata Institute of Fundamental Research, Mumbai, India
akshayaram.srinivasan@tifr.res.in
[3] Tsinghua University, Beijing, China

Abstract. We introduce a natural generalization of two-source non-malleable extractors (Cheragachi and Guruswami, TCC 2014) called as *multi-source non-malleable extractors.* Multi-source non-malleable extractors are special independent source extractors which satisfy an additional non-malleability property. This property requires that the output of the extractor remains close to uniform even conditioned on its output generated by tampering *several sources together.* We formally define this primitive, give a construction that is secure against a wide class of tampering functions, and provide applications. More specifically, we obtain the following results:

- For any $s \geq 2$, we give an explicit construction of a s-source non-malleable extractor for min-entropy $\Omega(n)$ and error $2^{-n^{\Omega(1)}}$ in the *overlapping joint tampering model.* This means that each tampered source could depend on any strict subset of all the sources and the sets corresponding to each tampered source could be overlapping in a way that we define. Prior to our work, there were no known explicit constructions that were secure even against disjoint tampering (where the sets are required to be disjoint without any overlap).
- We adapt the techniques used in the above construction to give a t-out-of-n non-malleable secret sharing scheme (Goyal and Kumar, STOC 2018) for any $t \leq n$ in the *disjoint tampering model.* This is the first general construction of a threshold non-malleable secret sharing (NMSS) scheme in the disjoint tampering model. All prior constructions had a restriction that the size of the tampered subsets could not be equal.
- We further adapt the techniques used in the above construction to give a t-out-of-n non-malleable secret sharing scheme (Goyal and Kumar, STOC 2018) for any $t \leq n$ in the *overlapping joint tampering model.* This is the first construction of a threshold NMSS in the overlapping joint tampering model.
- We show that a stronger notion of s-source non-malleable extractor that is multi-tamperable against disjoint tampering functions gives a single round network extractor protocol (Kalai et al., FOCS 2008) with attractive features. Plugging in with a new construction of multi-tamperable, 2-source non-malleable extractors provided in

A. Canteaut and F.-X. Standaert (Eds.): EUROCRYPT 2021, LNCS 12697, pp. 468–497, 2021.
https://doi.org/10.1007/978-3-030-77886-6_16

our work, we get a network extractor protocol for min-entropy $\Omega(n)$ that tolerates an *optimum* number ($t = p - 2$) of faulty processors and extracts random bits for *every* honest processor. The prior network extractor protocols could only tolerate $t = \Omega(p)$ faulty processors and failed to extract uniform random bits for a fraction of the honest processors.

1 Introduction

Non-malleable Extractors. Randomness extractors are fundamental objects in the study of computer science and combinatorics. They allow to extract uniform random bits from a source that has "some" randomness which may not necessarily be uniform. The amount of randomness in a source X is captured by the notion of min-entropy defined as $H_\infty(X) = \min_{s \in \mathsf{sup}(X)}\{\log \frac{1}{\Pr[X=s]}\}$. It is well-known that if we only have a single source with min-entropy less than full, then it is impossible to extract uniform random bits out of this source. One way to get around this impossibility result is to assume that we have two or more sources that are independent and the goal is to extract uniform random bits from these independent sources. Such extractors are called as multi-source (or independent source) extractors. A long line of work starting from the seminal work of Chor and Goldreich [CG88] have focused on constructing multi-source extractors for lower min-entropy. This recently resulted in a breakthrough work of Chattopadhyay and Zuckerman showing explicit constructions of two-source extractors for poly logarithmic min-entropy [CZ16]. See also the follow-up works of [Li16,Li17a,BDT17,GKK19].

A natural strengthening of multi-source extractors (that have also been used as a key tool in the recent breakthroughs) is the notion of a non-malleable extractor [CG14]. Roughly speaking, non-malleable extractors require that the output of the extractor (when run on independent sources) to be statistically close to uniform even conditioned on the output of the extractor generated by tampered version of the sources. Formally, we say that a s-source extractor is non-malleable against a tampering function family $\mathcal{F}$ if for any set of s independent sources $X_1, \ldots, X_s$ with sufficient min-entropy and for any tampering function $f \in \mathcal{F}$, there exists a distribution D_f with support in $\{0,1\}^m \cup \{\mathsf{same}^*\}$ that is independent of $X_1, \ldots, X_s$ such that:

$$|\mathsf{MNMExt}(X_1, \ldots, X_s) \circ \mathsf{MNMExt}(f(X_1, \ldots, X_s)) - U_m \circ \mathsf{copy}(D_f, U_m)| \le \epsilon$$

Here, $\mathsf{copy}(x, y) = x$ if $x \neq \mathsf{same}^*$; else, it is equal to y and $|X - Y|$ denotes the statistical distance between the random variables X and Y. Such extractors have wide applications in computer science and specifically, in cryptography; in particular, they can be used to construct two-source extractors [CZ16], non-malleable codes [DPW18,CG14,CGL16], non-malleable secret sharing [GK18a], round-optimal non-malleable commitments [GPR16,GKP+18] and cryptography with correlated random tapes [GS19].

Almost all of the prior work in constructing non-malleable multi-source extractors have focused on protecting against tampering functions that tamper each of the sources independently (aka individual tampering family). In this work, we are interested in constructing multi-source extractors that are secure against richer classes of tampering functions that could tamper several sources together. For the case of two sources (that has been the focus of the majority of the prior work), any tampering function that can tamper with both the sources can easily break the non-malleability property and hence, the individual tampering is the best that one could hope for. However, this is not the case for more than two sources.

Non-malleable Secret Sharing. Non-malleable secret sharing introduced in the work of Goyal-Kumar [GK18a] strengthens the traditional secret sharing with an additional non-malleability property. Specifically, in addition to the standard correctness and privacy properties, a non-malleable secret sharing scheme requires that any tampering attack from a family of allowable tampering functions either preserves the original secret that was shared or completely destroys it. Most of the works in this area [BS19, SV19, ADN+19, KMS18, FV19] focused on constructing non-malleable secret sharing against the individual tampering setting. Specifically, these constructions become insecure even if a tampering function can tamper with two shares together. The work of Goyal and Kumar [GK18a] gave a construction of t-out-of-n non-malleable secret sharing in a restricted version of the disjoint tampering model. Here, the tampering function first chooses a set of t shares, then partitions this share into two sets of unequal sizes and then tampers each partition independently. *It was crucial to their security analysis that the partitions are of unequal size and this construction does not work for equal size partitions.* In [GK18b], this assumption was removed for the specific case of $t = n$ and a construction that was secure in the overlapping joint tampering model with cover-free subsets (the exact description of this model can be found in Sect. 1.1) was given. However, the construction and the analysis crucially rely on the fact that $t = n$ and does not work for any $t < n$. Despite a number of follow up works, overcoming this restriction for threshold NMSS has remained an open problem. This brings us to the following questions.

Can we construct a threshold non-malleable secret sharing scheme secure in the disjoint tampering model (without restriction on the size of tampering sets)?

Can we construct a threshold non-malleable secret sharing scheme in the overlapping joint tampering model?

Network Extractor Protocols. Network extractor [DO03, GSV05, KLRZ08, KLR09] is a protocol between p processors, each starting with an independent source X_i of length n with min-entropy k. The processors exchange some messages during the protocol and these messages are sent over public channels. At the end of the protocol, we require each (honest) processor to end up with an independent (statistically close to) uniform string. We require this guarantee to hold even in the face of a centralized adversary who can corrupt a set of processors and instruct these processors to arbitrarily deviate from the protocol specification (byzantine corruptions). Such network extractor protocols can be run prior to any secure multiparty computation protocol or distributed computation protocols where the honest parties necessarily require private uniform random bits but they only start with independent sources with some min-entropy.

Formally, if B is the random variable denoting all the messages exchanged during the protocol and Z_i is the random variable denoting the output of the i-th processor, then the definition of a network extractor protocol is as follows.

Definition 1 (Network Extractor Protocol [KLRZ08]**).** *A protocol for p processors is a (t, g, ϵ) network extractor for min-entropy k if for any (n, k) independent sources $X_1, \ldots, X_p$ and any choice T of t faulty processors, after running the protocol, there exists a set $G \in [p] \setminus T$ of size at least g such that*

$$|B, \{X_i\}_{i \notin G}, \{Z_i\}_{i \in G} - B, \{X_i\}_{i \notin G}, U_{gm}| < \epsilon$$

Here U_{gm} is the uniform distribution on gm bits, independent of B, and $\{X_i\}_{i \notin G}$.

It is easy to see that if we allow the adversary to corrupt $p - 1$ processors then this task is impossible as it amounts to extracting random bits from a single source. Kalai et al. [KLRZ08] gave a $(t = \Omega(p), p - (1 + O(1))t, 2^{-n^{\Omega(1)}})$-network extractor protocol for min-entropy $k = (1/2 + O(1))n$. This protocol required a single round of interaction. They also showed another multi-round protocol for lower min-entropy (specifically, $k = 2^{\log^{\beta} n}$ for some $\beta < 1$) but in this protocol, a smaller number of honest processors end up with a uniform string. Li [Li13] further improved this result and gave a 2-round network extractor protocol for $k \geq \log^c n$. However, all these protocols only allow an adversary to corrupt $\Omega(p)$ processors and additionally, there exists a fraction of the honest processors whose output is not statistically close to uniform. This brings us to the next question.

Can we construct a network extractor protocol where the adversary can corrupt upto $p - 2$ processors and the protocol ensures that every honest processor ends up with a uniform output?

We note that in the computational setting, the work of Kalai et al. [KLR09] gave a protocol satisfying both the properties assuming sub-exponential hardness of one-way permutations.

Our Work. In this work, we provide positive answers to the question on non-malleable secret sharing as well as the network extractor protocols by viewing them through the lens of multi-source non-malleable extractors. The details follow.

1.1 Our Results

In this work, we initiate the systematic study of multi-source non-malleable extractors and give constructions that are secure against a wide class of tampering function families. We also show applications of this primitive in constructing non-malleable codes [DPW18], non-malleable secret sharing [GK18a], and network extractor protocols [DO03, GSV05, KLRZ08, KLR09]. Before we state the formal theorem statements, we first describe the tampering functions of interest.

Overlapping Joint Tampering. For any $s \in \mathbb{N}$, the overlapping joint tampering family is given by a sequence of sets $(T_1, \ldots, T_s)$ where $T_s \subset [s]$ and the associated tampering functions $(f_{T_1}, \ldots, f_{T_s})$. The i-th tampered source $\widetilde{X}_i$ is generated by applying f_{T_i} on the sources $\{X_j\}_{j \in T_i}$. In other words, the tampered source $\widetilde{X}_i$ is generated by tampering all the sources indexed by the set T_i using the function f_{T_i}.

We say that $(T_1, \ldots, T_s)$ are *cover-free*, if for every $i \in [s]$, the union of all T_j such that $i \in T_j$ has size at most $s - 1$. Some examples of cover-free subsets are:

- **Individual Tampering:** This is the setting where $T_i = \{i\}$.
- **Disjoint Tampering:** Here, $(T_1, \ldots, T_s)$ are such that for each $i, j \in [s]$, either $T_i = T_j$ or $T_i \cap T_j = \emptyset$.
- **Cycles of size at most** $\lfloor s/2 \rfloor$**:** Here, $T_i = \{i, i+1 \mod s, \ldots, i + \lfloor s/2 \rfloor - 1 \mod s\}$.

Cover-free subsets include a rich class of joint tampering functions and it strictly generalizes the individual tampering functions considered in the previous works. In this work, we focus on constructing multi-source non-malleable extractors in the overlapping joint tampering model with cover-free subsets (cover-free tampering, in short). We note that prior to our work, no construction of non-malleable extractors was known even in the disjoint tampering model.

Multi-source Non-malleable Extractors. Our first result in this paper is a construction of multi-source non-malleable extractors that are secure against cover-free tampering. The formal theorem statement appears below.

Theorem 1. *For any $s \geq 2$, there exists a constants $\gamma > 0$ and n_0 such that for any $n > n_0$, there exists an efficient construction of a s-source, non-malleable extractor* $\mathsf{MNMExt} : (\{0,1\}^n)^s \to \{0,1\}^m$ *against cover-free tampering at min-entropy $n(1-\gamma)$ and error $2^{-n^{\Omega(1)}}$ with output length $m = n^{\Omega(1)}$.*

We note that extending the class of tampering functions beyond cover-free tampering requires a new set of tools as there are sources which are tampered together with every other source. We leave open the fascinating problem of constructing explicit extractors that are secure against a generalization of cover-free tampering.

Split-State Non-malleable Codes. We show that (a variant of) our multi-source extractor is efficiently pre-image sampleable, meaning that there exists an efficient algorithm such that given any string of length m, the algorithm outputs (except with negligible probability) an uniform pre-image of this string. This feature combined with a straightforward generalization of the result of Cheraghchi and Guruswami [CG14] gives the following theorem.

Theorem 2. *For any $s \geq 2$ and $m \in \mathbb{N}$, there exists an efficient construction of s-split-state non-malleable code for messages of length m that is secure against cover-free tampering with error $2^{-m^{\Omega(1)}}$.*

This result is a conceptual contribution as we already know constructions of s-split state non-malleable codes against cover-free tampering from the work of [GK18b]. However, as we will see below this construction leads to a t-out-of-n non-malleable secret sharing in the overlapping joint tampering model.

Non-malleable Secret Sharing. An interesting aspect of our construction of multi-source non-malleable extractor is that a minor modification to this construction gives a t-out-of-n non-malleable secret sharing against t-cover-free tampering. t-cover free tampering is the same as cover-free tampering defined above except that we require that for every i, the union of all T_j's such that $i \in T_j$ has size at most $t-1$. As before, t-cover-free tampering includes disjoint tampering where each partition is of size at most $t-1$. We note if any set of t or more shares are tampered together, then the tampering function can trivially reconstruct the secret and hence, obtaining non-malleability is impossible. The formal statement about our construction is given below.

Theorem 3. *For every $t \geq 2$, $n \geq t$ and $m \in \mathbb{N}$, there exists an efficient construction of t-out-of-n non-malleable secret sharing for secrets of length m against t-cover-free tampering with error $2^{-m^{\Omega(1)}}$.*

As a corollary, we get a construction of t-out-of-n non-malleable secret sharing in the disjoint tampering model.

Corollary 1. *For every $t \geq 2$, $n \geq t$ and $m \in \mathbb{N}$, there exists an efficient construction of t-out-of-n non-malleable secret sharing for secrets of length m in the disjoint tampering model with error $2^{-m^{\Omega(1)}}$.*

As mentioned before, this is the first construction of threshold NMSS in the disjoint tampering model without restriction on the size of the tampering sets. This answers an explicit open problem from the work of Goyal and Kumar [GK18a]. In addition, ours is also the first construction of threshold NMSS in the overlapping joint tampering model. The only previous construction of NMSS in the overlapping joint tampering model was for n-of-n secret sharing [GK18b].

Network Extractor Protocols. For any $s \geq 2$, we show that a stronger notion of s-source non-malleable extractor that is multi-tamperable and whose non-malleability property holds even conditioned on all but one of the sources implies a single round network extractor protocol with at least s honest processors. It is sufficient for such multi-source non-malleable extractors to be resilient against a weaker form of disjoint tampering. For the case of 2 sources, we give a compiler that transforms a single tamperable non-malleable extractor to a multi-tamperable non-malleable extractor by building on the ideas of Cohen [Coh16a] who gave such a compiler for seeded non-malleable extractors. This result might be of independent interest. We show that the resultant extractor is sufficient to instantiate the network extractor protocol. This leads to a single round network extractor protocol that is resilient against an optimum number of byzantine corruptions of $p-2$ (where p is the total number of processors) and ensures that all the honest processors end up with a string that is statistically close to uniform. Specifcially, we show the following result.

Theorem 4. *For any $p \geq 2$, there exists constants $\gamma > 0$ and n_0 such that for all $n > n_0$ and for any $t \leq p-2$, there exists a single-round, $(t, p-t, 2^{-n^{\Omega(1)}})$-network extractor protocol for p processors and $(n, n(1-\gamma))$ sources.*

We note that all the prior information-theoretic network extractor protocols could only tolerate $\Omega(p)$ number of byzantine corruptions and furthermore, these protocols could not extract uniform randomness for a $\Omega(t)$ number of honest processors. Our protocol tolerates an optimum number of corruptions and ensures that every honest processor outputs a string that is statistically close to uniform. This matches the best protocols known in the computational setting [KLR09] that relied on sub-exponential hardness assumptions but has weaker min-entropy requirements.

2 Technical Overview

In this section, we give a high-level overview of the techniques used in obtaining our main results. We start our overview with the construction of multi-source non-malleable extractors. Then, we will extend this result to obtain a non-malleable secret sharing. Finally, we give the description of our network extractor protocol.

2.1 Multi-source Non-malleable Extractor

An s-source non-malleable extractor $\mathsf{MNMExt} : (\{0,1\}^n)^s \rightarrow \{0,1\}^m$ is just like any other independent source extractor with an additional non-malleability property. Recall that an s-source extractor is said to be non-malleable against the tampering function family $\mathcal{F}$ if for any set of s independent sources $X_1, \ldots, X_s$ with sufficient min-entropy and for any tampering function $f \in \mathcal{F}$, there exists a distribution D_f with support in $\{0,1\}^m \cup \{\mathsf{same}^*\}$ that is independent of $X_1, \ldots, X_s$ such that:

$$|\mathsf{MNMExt}(X_1, \ldots, X_s) \circ \mathsf{MNMExt}(f(X_1, \ldots, X_s)) - U_m \circ \mathsf{copy}(D_f, U_m)| \leq \epsilon$$

Here, $\mathsf{copy}(x, y) = x$ if $x \neq \mathsf{same}^*$; else, it is equal to y. A standard two-source non-malleable extractor is a special case of a multi-source extractor that is secure against the independent tampering family. Furthermore, it can be shown that any two-source non-malleable extractor implies an s-source non-malleable extractor for any $s \geq 2$ where each of the s-sources are tampered independently. However, in this work, we are interested in designing multi-source non-malleable extractors that are secure against richer forms of tampering where several sources can potentially be tampered together. In such a scenario, the trivial construction of extending any two-source extractor to an s-source extractor is insecure.

To explain the key ideas behind our construction without getting bogged down with the details, let us make the following simplifying assumptions. We stress that our actual construction does not make any of the following assumptions.

- Let us assume that there are only 3 sources X_1, X_2 and X_3 and each of the sources have full min-entropy. Even when the sources have full entropy, non-malleable extractors are known to imply non-malleable codes [CG14].
- We are interested in protecting against tampering functions that tamper two sources together and tampers the other source independently. The identity of the two sources that are tampered together is not fixed apriori. Specifically, we assume that the tampering functions are given by (f_{ij}, g_k) for distinct $i, j, k \in [3]$ where f_{ij} takes in sources X_i, X_j and outputs $\widetilde{X}_i, \widetilde{X}_j$. Similarly, g_k takes in X_k and outputs $\widetilde{X}_k$.

A Simple Construction. A natural attempt at constructing a multi-source non-malleable extractor is to take any 2 source non-malleable extractor $\mathsf{2NMExt}$ and output $\mathsf{2NMExt}(X_1 \circ 1, X_2 \circ 2) \oplus \mathsf{2NMExt}(X_2 \circ 2, X_3 \circ 3) \oplus \mathsf{2NMExt}(X_3 \circ 3, X_1 \circ 1)$ where $\circ$ denotes concatenation. Recall that our tampering functions satisfy the property that for every source there exists at least one other source that is not tampered together with this source. Since the above construction applies a non-malleable extractor for every pair of sources, we can hope to reduce the security of this construction to the security of the underlying non-malleable extractor. However, proving this is not straightforward as the tampering function may not modify these two sources and thus, proving independence between the tampered output and the untampered output is tricky. Nevertheless, with some non-trivial work, we can show using the techniques developed in [CGGL19] (for completeness, we provide a detailed proof in the full version of the paper) that this construction is indeed secure against cover-free tampering if the underlying non-malleable extractor is multi-tamperable[1] and is symmetric (meaning that $\mathsf{2NMExt}(x, y) = \mathsf{2NMExt}(y, x)$ for every x, y). However, a major problem with this simple construction is that it is *not efficiently* pre-image sampleable. Recall that for a non-malleable extractor to be efficiently pre-image sampleable, we need

[1] A multi-tamperable non-malleable extractor introduced in [CGL16] considers several sets of split-state tampering functions and requires the output of the extractor to be random even conditioned on all the tampered outputs generated by each split-state tampering function. An equivalent way to view the multi tamperable (or, t tamperable) non-malleable extractor is to allow the split-state tampering functions to have t sets of outputs and we require the real output to be close to random even conditioned on joint distribution of the t tampered outputs.

an efficient algorithm that given any output of the non-malleable extractor, samples an uniform pre-image of this output. This property is crucially needed to construct a s-split state non-malleable code from non-malleable extractors using the approach of Cheraghchi and Guruswami [CG14]. To see why this construction is not efficiently pre-image sampleable, consider any output $s \in \{0,1\}^m$ of the extractor. Now, we need to sample three sources, X_1, X_2, X_3 such that $\mathsf{2NMExt}(X_1 \circ 1, X_2 \circ 2) \oplus \mathsf{2NMExt}(X_2 \circ 2, X_3 \circ 3) \oplus \mathsf{2NMExt}(X_3 \circ 3, X_1 \circ 1) = s$. Even if we assume that 2NMExt is efficiently pre-image sampleable, fixing any two sources, say X_1, X_2, requires the third source to satisfy the equation $\mathsf{2NMExt}(X_2 \circ 2, X_3 \circ 3) \oplus \mathsf{2NMExt}(X_3 \circ 3, X_1 \circ 1) = s \oplus \mathsf{2NMExt}(X_1 \circ 1, X_2 \circ 2)$. Efficiently sampling from the set of such X_3's seems highly non-trivial. This seems to be a major roadblock with this simple construction (and is crucial to obtain our main application in constructing non-malleable secret sharing) and hence, it calls for a more sophisticated construction that is efficiently pre-image sampleable.

A Starting Point. In order to construct a multi-source non-malleable extractor with efficient pre-image sampling, we could try to make the following generalization. We can parse the sources X_1 as $(X^{(1)}, Y^{(3)})$, X_2 as $(X^{(2)}, Y^{(1)})$, X_3 as $(X^{(3)}, Y^{(2)})$ and output $\oplus_i \mathsf{2NMExt}(X^{(i)}, Y^{(i)})$. This construction is efficiently pre-image sampleable since the inputs to each invocation of the underlying 2NMExt is "non-overlapping". Specifically, given any output $s \in \{0,1\}^m$, we can sample $X^{(1)}, Y^{(1)}, X^{(2)}, Y^{(2)}$ uniformly at random and sample $X^{(3)}, Y^{(3)}$ such that $\mathsf{2NMExt}(X^{(3)}, Y^{(3)}) = s \oplus \mathsf{2NMExt}(X^{(2)}, Y^{(2)}) \oplus \mathsf{2NMExt}(X^{(2)}, Y^{(2)})$. This process is efficient if the underlying 2NMExt has efficient pre-image sampling. This seems like progress but unfortunately, we prove this construction is insecure. In particular, consider any tampering function that tampers X_1, X_2 together. Such a tampering function takes as input $(X^{(1)}, Y^{(3)})$ and $(X^{(2)}, Y^{(1)})$, leaves $X^{(2)}, Y^{(3)}$ untampered, but tampers $X^{(1)}, Y^{(1)}$ to $\widetilde{X}^{(1)}, \widetilde{Y}^{(1)}$ such that $\mathsf{2NMExt}(\widetilde{X}^{(1)}, \widetilde{Y}^{(1)}) = \overline{\mathsf{2NMExt}(X^{(1)}, Y^{(1)})}$ (where $\overline{z}$ denotes flipping each bit of z). If the tampering function against X_3 is the identity function, then we infer that the real output XORed with the tampered output will be the all 1s string.

Our Construction. If we look a little bit closely into the analysis of the above construction, we realize that the main reason for the attack is that $X^{(1)}, Y^{(1)}$ was available in the clear to one of the tampering functions. However, this attack could have been avoided if every tampering function does not get hold of both $X^{(i)}, Y^{(i)}$ together. With this intuition, we are ready to describe our extractor with efficient pre-image sampleability.

1. Parse X_i as $(X_i^{(1)}, X_i^{(2)}, X_i^{(3)}, Y^{(i)})$.
2. Compute $X^{(i)} = X_1^{(i)} \oplus X_2^{(i)} \oplus X_3^{(i)}$ for each $i \in [3]$.
3. Output $\mathsf{2NMExt}(X^{(1)}, Y^{(1)}) \oplus \mathsf{2NMExt}(X^{(2)}, Y^{(2)}) \oplus \mathsf{2NMExt}(X^{(3)}, Y^{(3)})$.

Notice that any tampering function that looks at any two sources X_i, X_j cannot determine $X^{(i)}$ and $X^{(j)}$ since these are "secret shared" between all the three sources. Furthermore, we observe that this construction has efficient pre-image sampling if the underlying 2NMExt is efficiently pre-image sampleable. This is because for any image $s \in \{0,1\}^m$, we can sample $X^{(2)}, Y^{(2)}$ and $X^{(3)}, Y^{(3)}$ uniformly at random and we sample $X^{(1)}, Y^{(1)}$ conditioned on its output being equal to $\mathsf{2NMExt}(X^{(2)}, Y^{(2)}) \oplus \mathsf{2NMExt}(X^{(3)}, Y^{(3)}) \oplus s$. Then, for every $i \in [3]$, we sample $X_1^{(1)}, X_2^{(i)}, X_3^{(i)}$ uniformly at random conditioned on its XOR being equal to $X^{(i)}$. This allows to efficiently find the sources X_1, X_2, X_3 such that applying the extractor on these sources yields s. Below, we give the main ideas behind proving the non-malleability of this construction.

Proof Idea. The key technical component of our security proof is a way to reduce the tampering of our extractor to a multi-tampering of the underlying non-malleable extractor 2NMExt. However, unlike the simple construction, this reduction is highly non-trivial and it requires the underlying extractor to satisfy a strong leakage-resilience property. The details follow.

Recall that in the tampering functions of our interest, for every source j, there exists at least one other source j^* that is not tampered together with this source. The main trick in the reduction is that we view $X_i^{(j)}$ for every i as a *secret share* of the source $X^{(j)}$. Viewing $X_i^{(j)}$ as a secret share of $X^{(j)}$ allows us to fix all the shares except $X_{j^*}^{(j)}$. Hence, $X_{j^*}^{(j)}$ is completely determined by the source $X^{(j)}$ and the fixed shares. Now, since j and j^* are not tampered together, we infer that $Y^{(j)}$ and $X^{(j)}$ are tampered independently! This allows us to reduce any tampering attack on our extractor to a split-state tampering attack on 2NMExt. Thus, relying on this reduction, we can hope to make the tampered output of our extractor to be "independent" of $\mathsf{2NMExt}(X^{(j)}, Y^{(j)})$ and thus, conclude that the real output is independent of the tampered output. However, arguing independence is not as straightforward as it seems. Notice that nothing prevents a tampering function from leaving $X^{(j)}, Y^{(j)}$ untampered. In this case, $\mathsf{2NMExt}(\widetilde{X}^{(j)}, \widetilde{Y}^{(j)}) = \mathsf{2NMExt}(X^{(j)}, Y^{(j)})$ and hence, it is impossible to argue that the tampered output is independent of $\mathsf{2NMExt}(X^{(j)}, Y^{(j)})$.

To get around this problem, we prove a *weaker property* about our reduction to split-state multi-tampering of 2NMExt. Specifically, we show that for every $i, j \in [3]$, the tampered output $\mathsf{2NMExt}(\widetilde{X}^{(i)}, \widetilde{Y}^{(i)})$ is either independent of $\mathsf{2NMExt}(X^{(j)}, Y^{(j)})$ (meaning that a non-trivial tampering attack has taken place) or is the same as $\mathsf{2NMExt}(X^{(j)}, Y^{(j)})$ (meaning that the tampering function has just copied). This in fact allows us to argue (via a hybrid argument going over every $j \in [\lambda]$)[2] that the tampered tuple $(\mathsf{2NMExt}(\widetilde{X}^{(1)}, \widetilde{Y}^{(1)}), \mathsf{2NMExt}(\widetilde{X}^{(2)}, \widetilde{Y}^{(2)}), \mathsf{2NMExt}(\widetilde{X}^{(3)}, \widetilde{Y}^{(3)}))$ is either a permutation of $(\mathsf{2NMExt}(X^{(1)}, Y^{(1)}), \mathsf{2NMExt}(X^{(2)}, Y^{(2)}), \mathsf{2NMExt}(X^{(3)}, Y^{(3)}))$ in which case the adversarial tampering functions have not changed the output of the extractor or there exists at least one j such that the tampered tuple is independent of $\mathsf{2NMExt}(X^{(j)}, Y^{(j)})$. This allows us to argue that the real output

[2] This is where we need the stronger property that for every source j there exists at least one other source that is not tampered together with this source.

is independent of the tampered output and it is in fact, close to uniform since $\mathsf{2NMExt}(X^{(j)}, Y^{(j)})$ is close to uniform.

Below, we show a sketch of a proof of this property. This is shown via a reduction to the multi-tampering of the underlying 2-source non-malleable extractor. As mentioned before, for this reduction to go through, we need the underlying non-malleable extractor to satisfy an additional strong leakage resilience property.

The Main Reduction. Let us try to sketch the above reduction for $j = 1$ by considering specific tampering functions f_{12}, g_3. Recall that f_{12} takes X_1, X_2 as input and outputs $\widetilde{X}_1, \widetilde{X}_2$ and g_3 takes X_3 as input and outputs $\widetilde{X}_3$. The goal here is to show that each entry of the tampered tuple $(\mathsf{2NMExt}(\widetilde{X}^{(1)}, \widetilde{Y}^{(1)}), \mathsf{2NMExt}(\widetilde{X}^{(2)}, \widetilde{Y}^{(2)}), \mathsf{2NMExt}(\widetilde{X}^{(3)}, \widetilde{Y}^{(3)}))$ is either equal to $\mathsf{2NMExt}(X^{(1)}, Y^{(1)})$ or independent of this value. As mentioned before, we prove this via a reduction from any tampering attack against our extractor to a split-state tampering attack (f', g') against $X^{(1)}, Y^{(1)}$.

Towards this goal, we will fix $X^{(2)}, Y^{(2)}, X^{(3)}, Y^{(3)}$ and all the shares of $X^{(2)}$ and $X^{(3)}$. In addition to this, we will fix the shares $X_1^{(1)}$ and $X_2^{(1)}$. Notice that by the choice of our tampering functions, X_1 and X_3 are tampered independently and thus, by fixing $X_1^{(1)}, X_2^{(1)}$, we have ensured that $X^{(1)}$ and $Y^{(1)}$ are tampered independently. Let us additionally assume that there exists a special string Y^* such that for every $s \in \{0,1\}^m$, there exists an $x \in \{0,1\}^m$ such that $\mathsf{2NMExt}(x, Y^*) = s$ (it will be clear on why this property is needed when we explain our reduction). We show that for any non-malleable extractor with sufficiently low-error, there exists such an Y^*.

Given the fixed values and the string Y^*, designing the multi-tampering function g' against $Y^{(1)}$ is straightforward. On input $Y^{(1)}$, g' uses the fixed values and the input $Y^{(1)}$ to reconstruct the sources X_1, X_2. It then applies f_{12} on these two sources and obtains $\widetilde{X}_1, \widetilde{X}_2$. It now outputs $(\widetilde{Y}^{(1)}, \widetilde{Y}^{(2)}, Y^*)$ (where $\widetilde{Y}^{(1)}, \widetilde{Y}^{(2)}$ are obtained from $\widetilde{X}_1, \widetilde{X}_2$) as the three tampered outputs. However, constructing a tampering function against $X^{(1)}$ is not as straightforward. Notice that the tampering function against $X^{(1)}$ must somehow get $\{\widetilde{X}_1^{(i)}, \widetilde{X}_2^{(i)}, \widetilde{X}_3^{(i)}\}_{i \in [3]}$, XOR them together and finally output the XORed value as the tampered source $\widetilde{X}^{(i)}$. However, $\{\widetilde{X}_1^{(i)}, \widetilde{X}_2^{(i)}\}_{i \in [3]}$ are generated by the tampering function f_{12} that depends on $Y^{(1)}$. Hence, we cannot directly invoke the security of $\mathsf{2NMExt}$ since the tampering against $X^{(1)}$ and $Y^{(1)}$ are not independent of each other. To solve this issue, we rely on a "strong leakage-resilience" property of $\mathsf{2NMExt}$. Under this stronger property, one of the tampering functions can get a leakage about the other source such that the amount of leakage is an arbitrary polynomial in the length of the tampered source. If we have such an extractor, we can view $\{\widetilde{X}_1^{(i)}, \widetilde{X}_2^{(i)}\}_{i \in [3]}$ as leakage from the source $Y^{(1)}$ given to the tampering function f' against $X^{(1)}$. Given this leakage and the input $X^{(3)}$, f' reconstructs the source X_3 from the fixed values and the input $X^{(3)}$ and applies $g_3(X_3)$ to obtain $\widetilde{X}_3$. Now, it can use the leakage $\{\widetilde{X}_1^{(i)}, \widetilde{X}_2^{(i)}\}_{i \in [3]}$

and $\{\widetilde{X}_3^{(i)}\}_{i\in[3]}$ (obtained from $\widetilde{X}_3$) to obtain $\widetilde{X}^{(i)}$ for every $i \in [3]$. Furthermore, f' also has $\widetilde{Y}^{(3)}$. It computes $\mathsf{2NMExt}(\widetilde{X}^{(3)}, \widetilde{Y}^{(3)})$ and samples a string x such that $\mathsf{2NMExt}(x, Y^*) = \mathsf{2NMExt}(\widetilde{X}^{(3)}, \widetilde{Y}^{(3)})$. It outputs $(\widetilde{X}^{(1)}, \widetilde{X}^{(2)}, x)$ as the tampered sources. Notice that applying 2NMExt on the outputs of f', g' precisely yields $(\mathsf{2NMExt}(\widetilde{X}^{(1)}, \widetilde{Y}^{(1)}), \mathsf{2NMExt}(\widetilde{X}^{(2)}, \widetilde{Y}^{(2)}), \mathsf{2NMExt}(\widetilde{X}^{(3)}, \widetilde{Y}^{(3)}))$. Further, it now follows from the split-state non-malleability of 2NMExt that each of these outputs is either independent of $\mathsf{2NMExt}(X^{(1)}, Y^{(1)})$ or is exactly the same as $\mathsf{2NMExt}(X^{(1)}, Y^{(1)})$. This shows the main claim of the proof.

In the next subsection, we show how to construct such a strong leakage-resilient non-malleable extractor.

2.2 Strong Leakage-Resilient Non-malleable Extractor

Recall that a $(2, t)$-non-malleable extractor $\mathsf{2NMExt} : \{0,1\}^n \times \{0,1\}^n \to \{0,1\}^m$ (introduced in [CG14, CGL16]) satisfies the following property: for any t split-state tampering functions $F = (f_1, g_1) \ldots, (f_t, g_t)$ and independent sources X, Y with sufficient min-entropy, there exists a distribution D_F with support on $\{0,1\}^m \cup \{\mathsf{same}^*\}$ that is independent of X, Y such that

$$|\mathsf{2NMExt}(X, Y), \{\mathsf{2NMExt}(f_i(X), g_i(Y))\}_{i\in[t]} - U_m, \mathsf{copy}^{(t)}(D_F, U_m)| < \epsilon \quad (1)$$

where both U_m's refer to the same uniform m-bit string. Here, $\mathsf{copy}^{(t)}((x_1, \ldots, x_t), y) = (z_1, \ldots, z_t)$ where $z_i = \begin{cases} x_i & \text{if } x_i \neq \mathsf{same}^* \\ y & \text{if } x_i = \mathsf{same}^* \end{cases}$.

A leakage-resilient variant of such an extractor requires that even when one half of these tampering functions, say $\{f_i\}_{i\in[t]}$ gets some bounded leakage on the other source Y, the non-malleability property still holds. Specifically, for any leakage function $h : \{0,1\}^n \to \{0,1\}^\mu$, we require that

$$|\mathsf{2NMExt}(X, Y), \{\mathsf{2NMExt}(f_i(X, h(Y)), g_i(Y))\}_{i\in[t]} - U_m, \mathsf{copy}^{(t)}(D_{F,h}, U_m)| < \epsilon \quad (2)$$

It is not hard to see that if the underlying non-malleable extractor tolerates a min-entropy loss of roughly μ, then such a non-malleable extractor can be shown to be leakage-resilient. Notice that for this approach to work, the length of the source must be far greater than the amount of leakage tolerated. However, for our application to constructing multi-source non-malleable extractor, we require the amount of leakage from one of the sources to be an arbitrary polynomial in the length of the other source. Of course, if we insist on both the sources to be of same length then it is easy to see that such a primitive does not exist. Hence, this primitive necessarily requires uneven length sources. We call such a non-malleable extractor as $(2, t)$-strong leakage-resilient non-malleable extractor where we require the output length of h in Eq. 2 to be an arbitrary polynomial in the length of X.

A similar primitive for the case of non-malleable codes was studied in the work of Goyal and Kumar [GK18a]. They showed that the CGL construction [CGL16] of non-malleable code satisfies this property. Unfortunately, they neither give a construction of a non-malleable extractor for sufficiently low min-entropy nor do they give a multi-tamperable version of the result. Both of these properties are crucial in obtaining our main results.

In this work, we show that any $(2, t)$-leakage-resilient non-malleable extractor (where the leakage tolerated is only a fraction of the source length) can be bootstrapped to a $(2, t)$-strong leakage-resilient non-malleable extractors (where the leakage tolerated is an arbitrary polynomial in the length of the other source). This gives a modular approach of constructing such primitives and additionally, simplifies the construction of strong leakage resilient non-malleable codes in the work of [GK18a].

Our Compiler. To illustrate the main ideas behind our compiler, let us simplify the problem and assume that X and Y are independent full entropy sources with length n_1 and n_2 respectively. Further, assume that $n_2 >> p(n_1)$ where $p(\cdot)$ is a polynomial denoting the amount of leakage tolerated.

Our compiler under these assumptions is extremely simple. We view the source X as (S, X') where S is the seed of a strong extractor Ext. We apply $\mathsf{Ext}(Y, S)$ to obtain Y' where the length of Y' is equal to the length of X'. We finally apply $\mathsf{2NMExt}(X', Y')$ and output the result. The main intuition behind the compiler is that conditioned on the output of the leakage function, it can be shown (via standard approaches [MW97, DORS08]) that Y has sufficient min-entropy. Hence, if we apply a seeded extractor on this Y, the output is close to uniform.

While the main intuition is relatively straightforward, proving the non-malleability of this construction requires new tricks. Notice that to prove the non-malleability of the compiled construction, we need to invoke the non-malleability of the underlying $\mathsf{2NMExt}$. However, if we closely notice the compiler, we see that the tampered version of the source $\widetilde{Y}'$ that is fed as the second input to $\mathsf{2NMExt}$ is not only a function of Y but also a function of the other source X' via the tampered seed $\widetilde{S}$. In particular, $\widetilde{S}$ could be a function of the source X' and hence, $\widetilde{Y}'$ is a function of both X' and Y. This means that the tampering of the second source is not independent of the first source and hence, we cannot directly invoke the security of $\mathsf{2NMExt}$. To solve this issue, we recall that $\mathsf{2NMExt}$ is in fact, a leakage-resilient non-malleable extractor. In particular, we can fix the length of the seed S to be small enough so that it is only a fraction of the length of X'. We now view the tampered seed $\widetilde{S}$ as leakage from the source X' to the tampering function of Y. This allows us to reduce the non-malleability of the compiled construction to the leakage-resilient, non-malleability of $\mathsf{2NMExt}$.

Lower Min-Entropy Case. Recall that the above construction crucially relied on the fact that X is a full entropy source to make sure that the seed S has full-entropy. This compiler completely breaks down if X didn't have full entropy as otherwise, we cannot rely on the pseudorandomness of Ext. Thus, we require a new approach to deal with the case where the entropy of the sources are not full. In this setting, we modify our compiler as follows. We view X as (X', X_1)

and Y as (Y_1, Y_2). We first apply a strong two-source extractor $\mathsf{2Ext}(X_1, Y_1)$ to get a short seed S. We later apply a strong seeded extractor $\mathsf{Ext}(Y_2, S)$ to obtain Y'. Finally, we output $\mathsf{2NMExt}(X', Y')$.

As in the previous construction, we can show that conditioned on the leakage $h(Y)$, the source Y has sufficient min-entropy. Now, since X_1, Y_1 are independent sources, it follows from the pseudorandomness of $\mathsf{2Ext}$ that the output S is close to uniform. Now, we can rely on the pseudorandomness of Ext to show that Y' is close to uniform. Again, as in the previous case, we can rely on the leakage-resilience property of the underlying $\mathsf{2NMExt}$ extractor to leak the tampered version $\widetilde{X}_1$ to the tampering function of Y and this allows us to argue non-malleability of the compiled construction. However, one subtlety that arises here is that we necessarily require the length of Y_1 to be much larger than the length of the other source X_1 that is fed as input to the strong two-source extractor. This is because we require Y_1 to have sufficient min-entropy even conditioned on the output of the leakage function h and the output of the leakage function is a polynomial in the length of the other source. This means that the length of X_1 is much smaller than the length of Y_1 and hence, we have to rely on the uneven length two-source extractor given by Raz [Raz05].

2.3 Non-malleable Secret Sharing

A significant advantage of our construction of multi-source non-malleable extractor is its generality to give other primitives. In particular, we show that a minor modification to our construction gives a t-out-of-n non-malleable secret sharing scheme for every t and n against a family of t-cover-free tampering functions. Roughly speaking, t-cover-free family requires that every share is tampered with at most $t-2$ other shares. This family includes disjoint tampering (as defined in [GK18a]) as a special case and gives the first construction of threshold non-malleable secret sharing scheme that is secure against a strict super class of disjoint tampering[3].

Our Construction. The construction we give for t-out-of-n non-malleable secret closely resembles the construction of our n-source non-malleable extractor. Specifically, the i-th share of our non-malleable secret sharing scheme is viewed as $(X_i^{(1)}, X_i^{(2)}, \ldots, X_i^{(n)}, Y^{(i)})$. The only difference in the semantics is that instead of viewing $(X_1^{(i)}, \ldots, X_n^{(i)})$ as an XOR (or equivalently, n-out-of-n) secret sharing of the value $X^{(i)}$, we consider them to be a t-out-of-n secret sharing of $X^{(i)}$. Now, given any t-shares, say corresponding to $i_1, \ldots, i_t$, we would be able to reconstruct $X^{(1)}, \ldots, X^{(n)}$ and compute $\mathsf{2NMExt}(X^{(i_j)}, Y^{(i_j)})$ for every $j \in [t]$. We now interpret $\mathsf{2NMExt}(X^{(i_j)}, Y^{(i_j)})$ as the i_j-th Shamir share of a secret message $s \in \{0,1\}^m$ and these t Shamir shares can be put together to reconstruct the secret s. Recall that in the case of multi-source non-malleable extractors, we interpreted $\mathsf{2NMExt}(X^{(i_j)}, Y^{(i_j)})$ as an n-out-of-n secret sharing of the output.

[3] We note that even for the case of disjoint tampering, the work of Goyal and Kumar [GK18a] assumes that the partitioned subsets must be of unequal length.

Below, we give the description of our sharing algorithm assuming that $\mathsf{2NMExt}$ is efficiently pre-image sampleable. Here, we use a t-out-of-n secret sharing scheme Share with perfect privacy.

To share a secret $s \in \{0,1\}^m$, we do the following:

1. $(\mathsf{Sh}_1, \ldots, \mathsf{Sh}_n) \leftarrow \mathsf{Share}(s)$.
2. For each $i \in [n]$, compute $(X^{(i)}, Y^{(i)}) \leftarrow \mathsf{2NMExt}^{-1}(\mathsf{Sh}_i)$.
3. For each $i \in [n]$, $(X_1^{(i)}, \ldots, X_n^{(i)}) \leftarrow \mathsf{Share}(X^{(i)})$.
4. Set $\mathsf{share}_i = (X_i^{(1)}, \ldots, X_i^{(n)}, Y^{(i)})$.
5. Output $(\mathsf{share}_1, \ldots, \mathsf{share}_n)$.

We show via a similar argument to the proof of our multi-source non-malleable extractor that if the underlying $\mathsf{2NMExt}$ is strong leakage-resilient then the above non-malleable secret sharing is secure against t-cover-free tampering. The complete analysis of the construction appears in Sect. 8.

2.4 Network Extractor Protocol

Another application of our multi-source non-malleable extractors is to get improved results for network extractor protocols [DO03, GSV05, KLRZ08, KLR09]. In the setting of network extractors, there are p processors, each with an independent source X_i having some min-entropy. The processors exchange some messages and at the end of the protocol, we require that every honest processor end up with an uniform random string independent of outputs of the other processors and the transcript of the protocol. This property must hold even if a subset of the processors are corrupted by a centralized adversary who can instruct the corrupted processors to deviate arbitrarily from the protocol. It is easy to see that if the adversary controls $p-1$ processors then this task is impossible as it amounts to extracting random bits from a single source with min-entropy less than full. However, if the adversary corrupts at most $p-s$ processors, we show that a s-source non-malleable extractor that is multi-tamperable can give a one-round protocol for this task. Additionally, unlike the other prior works (except in the computational setting), this approach allows every honest party to extract uniform random bits.

For simplicity, let us show a variant of our protocol from a multi-tamperable 2-source non-malleable extractor $\mathsf{2NMExt}$. This allows us to obtain optimal results for the case of $p-2$ corruptions. We give the description of the protocol below.

1. Each processor parses X_i as $X_1^{(i)}, \ldots, X_p^{(i)}$.
2. It broadcast $\{X_j^{(i)}\}_{j \neq i}$.
3. It receive $\{X_i^{(j)}\}_{j \neq i}$ from all the processors. If some processor j does not send any message, it replaces $X_i^{(j)}$ with a default value.
4. For every $j \subseteq [p] \setminus \{i\}$, processor P_i
   (a) Computes $y_j = \mathsf{2NMExt}(X_i^{(i)}, X_i^{(j)})$.
5. It removes the duplicates from the sequence $(y_j)_{j \neq i}$ to get $y'_1, \ldots, y'_k$.
6. It outputs $z_i = y'_1 \oplus \ldots \oplus y'_k$.

The main intuition behind the proof of this network extractor protocol is that for every honest processor i, the message $X_i^{(j)}$ sent by every adversarial processor j can be viewed as a tampering of the message $X_i^{(i^*)}$ of one another honest processor i^*. Thus, it now follows from the multi-tamperability of 2NMExt that the tampered output $\mathsf{2NMExt}(X_i^{(i)}, X_i^{(j)})$ is independent of the real output $\mathsf{2NMExt}(X_i^{(i)}, X_i^{(i^*)})$ which in turn is close to uniform. However, for this argument to hold, we require the non-malleability property to hold even conditioned on $X_i^{(i^*)}$, in other words, we require 2NMExt to be a strong non-malleable extractor. Fortunately, Li [Li17a] showed that every non-malleable extractor with sufficiently low min-entropy is also a strong non-malleable extractor and this allows us to complete the proof.

The new constructions of multi-source extractors for $s \geq 3$ given in this paper have the same min-entropy requirement as that of the two source extractors and hence, do not provide any further improvements over the above result. We leave open the fascinating problem of constructing multi-source extractors for $s \geq 3$ for lower min-entropy requirements.

3 Preliminaries

Notation. We use capital letters to denote distributions and their support, and the corresponding lowercase letters to denote a sample from the same. $x \sim X$ is used to denote a sample x from a distribution X. We will slightly abuse the notation and use X to denote a random variable as well as a distribution. Let $[n]$ denote the set $\{1, 2, \ldots, n\}$, and U_r denote the uniform distribution over $\{0,1\}^r$. For any finite set S, we use $s \leftarrow S$ to denote the process of sampling s uniformly at random from S. For any $i \in [n]$, let x_i denote the symbol at the i-th co-ordinate of x, and for any $T \subseteq [n]$, let $x_T \in \{0,1\}^{|T|}$ denote the projection of x to the co-ordinates indexed by T. We write $\circ$ to denote concatenation.

We give the standard definitions and results about min-entropy, seeded and seedless extractors and non-malleable codes in the full version of this paper.

3.1 Seedless Non-malleable Extractors

We now give the definition of 2-source, non-malleable extractors that are tamperable t times [CGL16]. Such an extractor is called as $(2,t)$-non-malleable extractors.

Definition 2 ((2,t)-Non-malleable Extractor). *A function* $\mathsf{2NMExt} : \{0,1\}^n \times \{0,1\}^n \to \{0,1\}^m$ *is a* $(2,t)$*-non-malleable extractor at min-entropy* k *and error* ϵ *if it satisfies the following property: if* X *and* Y *are independent* (n,k)*-sources and* $\mathcal{A}_1 = (f_1, g_1), \ldots, \mathcal{A}_t = (f_t, g_t)$ *are* t *arbitrary 2-split-state tampering functions, then there exists a random variable* $D_{\vec{f},\vec{g}}$ *on* $(\{0,1\}^m \cup \{\mathsf{same}^*\})^t$ *which is independent of the random variables* X *and* Y*, such that*

$$|\mathsf{2NMExt}(X,Y), \{\mathsf{2NMExt}(f_i(X), g_i(Y))\}_{i\in[t]} - U_m, \mathsf{copy}^{(t)}(D_{\vec{f},\vec{g}}, U_m)| < \epsilon$$

where both U_m's refer to the same uniform m-bit string. Here, $\mathsf{copy}^{(t)}((x_1,\ldots,x_t),y) = (z_1,\ldots,z_t)$ *where* $z_i = \begin{cases} x_i & \text{if } x_i \neq \mathsf{same}^* \\ y & \text{if } x_i = \mathsf{same}^* \end{cases}$.

For $t = 1$, *we call* 2NMExt *a non-malleable 2-source extractor.*

Theorem 5 ([CGL16]). *There exists a constant* $\gamma > 0$ *such that for all* $n > 0$ *and* $t < n^\gamma$, *there exists a* $(2,t)$*-non-malleable extractor* $\mathsf{2NMExt} : \{0,1\}^n \times \{0,1\}^n \to \{0,1\}^{n^{\Omega(1)}}$ *at min-entropy* $n - n^\gamma$ *with error* 2^{-n^γ}.

Theorem 6 ([Li17b]). *For any* $n > 0$, *there exists a constant* γ *such that there exists a non-malleable 2-source extractor* $\mathsf{NMExt} : \{0,1\}^n \times \{0,1\}^n \to \{0,1\}^m$ *with min-entropy* $(1-\gamma)n$, $m = \Omega(k)$ *and error* $\epsilon = 2^{-\Omega(n/\log(n))}$.

4 $(2,t)$-Non-malleable Randomness Extractors

In this section, we give a construction of $(2,t)$-Non-malleable extractors for min-entropy $\Omega(n)$. We achieve this by giving a generic transformation from $(2,1)$-non-malleable extractor to $(2,t)$-non-malleable randomness extractor. This follows a similar approach given in [Coh16b] for the case of seeded non-malleable extractors.

One of the main tools used in this transformation is a correlation breaker with advice and we start by recalling this definition.

Definition 3 (t**-Correlation-breaker with advice** [Coh16a]). *For an integer* $t \geq 1$ *a t-correlation-breaker with advice for min-entropy k and error* ϵ *is a function* $\mathsf{AdvBC} : \{0,1\}^w \times \{0,1\}^l \times \{0,1\}^a \to \{0,1\}^m$ *with the following property. Let* $X, X^{(1)}, \ldots, X^{(t)}$ *be random variables distributed over* $\{0,1\}^w$ *such that X has min-entropy k. Let* $Y, Y^{(1)}, \ldots, Y^{(t)}$ *be random variables distributed over* $\{0,1\}^l$ *that are jointly independent of* $(X, X^{(1)}, \ldots, X^{(t)})$ *such that Y is uniform. Then, for any string* $s, s^{(1)}, \ldots, s^{(t)} \in \{0,1\}^a$ *such that* $s \notin \{s^{(1)}, \ldots, s^{(t)}\}$, *it holds that*

$$|\mathsf{AdvBC}(X,Y,s), \{\mathsf{AdvBC}(X^{(i)},Y^{(i)},s^{(i)})\}_{i\in[t]} - U_m, \{\mathsf{AdvBC}(X^{(i)},Y^{(i)},s^{(i)})\}_{i\in[t]}| \leq \epsilon.$$

Theorem 7 ([CGL16]). *For all integers* ℓ, w, a, t *and for any* $\epsilon \in (0,1)$ *such that*

$$\ell = \Omega(at \cdot \log(aw/\epsilon)),$$

there exists a poly(ℓ, w)*-time computable t-correlation-breaker with advice* $\mathsf{AdvBC} : \{0,1\}^w \times \{0,1\}^\ell \times \{0,1\}^a \to \{0,1\}^m$, *for entropy*

$$k = \Omega(at \cdot \log(a\ell/\epsilon)),$$

with error ϵ *and* $m = \Omega(\ell/(at))$ *output bits.*

4.1 Transformation

Building blocks and parameters

1. Let $\mathsf{NMExt} : \{0,1\}^{d_1} \times \{0,1\}^{d_1} \to \{0,1\}^{l_1}$ be a non-malleable 2-source extractor with min-entropy $d_1 - \Delta$ and error ϵ, where $l_1 = \Omega(\log(1/\epsilon))$.
2. Let $\mathsf{ECC} : \{0,1\}^{d_2} \to \{0,1\}^{D_2}$ be an error correcting code with $D_2 = O(d_2)$ and relative distance 1/4.
3. Let $\mathsf{IP} : \{0,1\}^{d_1} \times \{0,1\}^{d_1} \to \{0,1\}^{l'_2}$ be a strong 2-source extractor with error ϵ and min-entropy $d_1 - \Delta$, where $l'_2 = l_2 \log(D_2)$ and $l_2 = \Omega(\log(1/\epsilon))$.
4. Let $\mathsf{Raz} : \{0,1\}^n \times \{0,1\}^{d_2} \to \{0,1\}^{l_3}$ be a strong 2-source extractor with error ϵ, where the min-entropy requirement for the first source is $n - \Delta - (1+t)(d_1 + l_2) - \log(1/\epsilon)$ and that for the second source is $d_2 - \Delta - (1+t)(d_1 + l_2) - \log(1/\epsilon)$.
5. Let $\mathsf{AdvBC} : \{0,1\}^{d_3} \times \{0,1\}^{l_3} \times \{0,1\}^a \to \{0,1\}^m$ be an efficient t-correlation-breaker with advice for error ϵ and min-entropy $d_3 - \Delta - (1+t)(d_1 + l_2 + d_2) - \log(1/\epsilon)$, where $a = l_1 + 2l_2$

Construction. On the input sources X, Y, NMExt' is computed as follows.

1. Let $X = X_1 \circ X_2$, $Y = Y_1 \circ Y_2$, where $|X_1| = |Y_1| = d_1$.
2. Let $\mathsf{AdvGen}(X,Y) = \mathsf{NMExt}(X_1,Y_1) \circ \mathsf{ECC}(X_2)_{\mathsf{IP}(X_1,Y_1)} \circ \mathsf{ECC}(Y_2)_{\mathsf{IP}(X_1,Y_1)}$, where $S_{\mathsf{IP}(X_1,Y_1)}$ means to take the bits from S with indexes represented by $\mathsf{IP}(X_1,Y_1)$.
3. Let $Y_2 = Y_3 \circ Y_4$, where $|Y_3| = d_2$ and $|Y_4| = d_3$.
4. Return $\mathsf{AdvBC}(Y_4, \mathsf{Raz}(X, Y_3), \mathsf{AdvGen}(X,Y))$.

Theorem 8. *In the above construction,* NMExt' *is a* t*-non-malleable 2-source extractor with min-entropy* $n - \Delta$ *and error* $O(t\sqrt{\epsilon})$.

With the proper instantiation, we get the following corollary. The proof of the above theorem and the instantiation are presented in the full version of this paper.

Corollary 2. *For any* $t \geq 1$, *there exists constant* $n'_0, \gamma' > 0$ *such that for any* $n > n'_0$ *there exists a* t*-non-malleable 2-source extractor* $\mathsf{2NMExt} : \{0,1\}^n \times \{0,1\}^n \to \{0,1\}^m$ *satisfying Definition 2 with error* $2^{-n^{\Omega(1)}}$, *min-entropy* $(1-\gamma')n$ *and output length* $m = n^{\Omega(1)}$.

5 Strong Leakage-Resilient Non-malleable Extractor

In this section, we give a construction of a $(2,t)$-non-malleable extractor where one of the tampering functions, say g, that is tampering the source Y, can get leakage about the other source X. The crucial property we will need is that the amount of leakage can be an arbitrary polynomial in the length of the source Y. We call such non-malleable extractors as *strong leakage-resilient non-malleable extractors*. This, in particular would require that the length of the source X to be much larger than the length of the other source Y.

Definition. We now define a strong leakage-resilient non-malleable extractor.

Definition 4 (Strong Leakage-Resilient Non-malleable Extractor). *For any polynomial $p(\cdot)$, a $(2,t)$ non-malleable extractor $\mathsf{2SLNMExt} : \{0,1\}^{n_1} \times \{0,1\}^{n_2} \rightarrow \{0,1\}^m$ is said to be p-strong leakage resilient if it satisfies the following property: if X and Y are independent (n_1,k_1) and (n_2,k_2) sources, $\mathcal{A}_1 = (f_1,g_1),\ldots,\mathcal{A}_t = (f_t,g_t)$ are t arbitrary 2-split-state tampering functions and $h : \{0,1\}^{n_1} \rightarrow \{0,1\}^{p(n_2)}$ is an arbitrary leakage function, then there exists a random variable $D_{\overrightarrow{f},\overrightarrow{g},h}$ on $(\{0,1\}^m \cup \{\mathsf{same}^*\})^t$ which is independent of the random variables X and Y, such that*

$$|\mathsf{2SLNMExt}(X,Y), \{\mathsf{2SLNMExt}(f_i(X), g_i(h(X),Y))\}_{i\in[t]} \\ -U_m, \mathsf{copy}^{(t)}(D_{\overrightarrow{f},\overrightarrow{g},h}, U_m)| < \epsilon$$

where both U_m's refer to the same uniform m-bit string.

Organization. This section is organized as follows. In Sect. 5.1, we define a weaker variant called as leakage resilient non-malleable extractor. The main difference between this variant and our strong leakage-resilience is that here, the sources are of same length but one of the tampering functions can get some fractional leakage about the other source. We show that any non-malleable extractors that works for sufficiently small min-entropy already satisfies this property. Next, in Sect. 5.2, we show how to bootstrap leakage-resilience to strong leakage-resilience with the help of a strong seeded extractor and strong two-source extractors. In Sect. 5.3, we give a variant of our extractor that is additionally preimage sampleable.

5.1 Leakage-Resilient Non-malleable Extractors

We now give the definition of a $(2,t)$-leakage resilient non-malleable extractor.

Definition 5 (Leakage-Resilient Non-malleable Extractor). *For some $\mu \in \mathbb{N}$, a $(2,t)$ non-malleable extractor $\mathsf{2NMExt} : \{0,1\}^n \times \{0,1\}^n \rightarrow \{0,1\}^m$ is said to be μ-leakage resilient if it satisfies the following property: if X and Y are independent (n,k)-sources, $\mathcal{A}_1 = (f_1,g_1),\ldots,\mathcal{A}_t = (f_t,g_t)$ are t arbitrary 2-split-state tampering functions and $h : \{0,1\}^n \rightarrow \{0,1\}^\mu$ is an arbitrary leakage function, then there exists a random variable $D_{\overrightarrow{f},\overrightarrow{g},h}$ on $(\{0,1\}^m \cup \{\mathsf{same}^*\})^t$ which is independent of the random variables X and Y, such that*

$$|\mathsf{2NMExt}(X,Y), \{\mathsf{2NMExt}(f_i(X,h(Y)), g_i(Y))\}_{i\in[t]} \\ -U_m, \mathsf{copy}^{(t)}(D_{\overrightarrow{f},\overrightarrow{g},h}, U_m)| < \epsilon$$

where both U_m's refer to the same uniform m-bit string.

We now prove the following lemma which states that any $(2,t)$-non-malleable extractor is also a leakage-resilient non-malleable extractor. A similar result was also shown in [GKP+18] and we include it here for the sake of completeness.

Lemma 1 ([GKP+18]). *Let* $\mathsf{2NMExt} : \{0,1\}^n \times \{0,1\}^n \to \{0,1\}^m$ *be a* $(2,t)$*-non-malleable extractor at min-entropy* k *and error* ϵ. *For any function* $h : \{0,1\}^n \to \{0,1\}^\mu$, $\mathsf{2NMExt}$ *is* μ*-leakage resilient at min-entropy* k' *and error* 2ϵ *for any* $n \geq k' \geq k + \mu + \log 1/\epsilon$.

5.2 Bootstrapping

We will now show how to bootstrap a leakage-resilient non-malleable extractor to a strong leakage-resilient non-malleable extractor.

Building Blocks and Parameters. Let $n_1, n_2 \in \mathbb{N}$ and let Δ be another parameter that will denote the entropy loss. Let ϵ denote the error parameter and $p(\cdot)$ be any polynomial. In our construction, we will use the following building blocks and set the parameters as shown below.

- Let $\mathsf{2Ext} : \{0,1\}^{n_1'} \times \{0,1\}^{n_2'} \to \{0,1\}^d$ be a a strong two sources extractor at min-entropy $(n_1' - \Delta - p(n_2) - \log(1/\epsilon), n_2' - \Delta - \log(1/\epsilon))$ and error ϵ.
- Let $\mathsf{Ext} : \{0,1\}^{n_1 - n_1'} \times \{0,1\}^d \to \{0,1\}^{n_2 - n_2'}$ be a strong seeded extractor at min-entropy $n_1 - n_1' - \Delta - p(n_2) - \log(1/\epsilon)$ and error ϵ.
- Fix $\mu = n_2't$. Let $\mathsf{2NMExt} : \{0,1\}^{n_2 - n_2'} \times \{0,1\}^{n_2 - n_2'} \to \{0,1\}^m$ be a $(2,t)$-non-malleable extractor at min-entropy $n_2 - n_2' - \Delta - \mu - 2\log(1/\epsilon)$ and error ϵ. By Lemma 1, we infer that $\mathsf{2NMExt}$ is μ-leakage-resilient for min-entropy $n_2 - n_2' - \Delta - \log(1/\epsilon)$ and error 2ϵ.
- We set $n_1' = n_2 + p(n_2)$, $n_2' = 3\Delta$, and $n_1 \geq 4n_2 + 2p(n_2)$.

Construction 1. On input $((x_1, x_2), (y_1, y))$ where $x_1 \in \{0,1\}^{n_1'}, y_1 \in \{0,1\}^{n_2'}$, $x_2 \in \{0,1\}^{n_1 - n_1'}$, and $y \in \{0,1\}^{n_2 - n_2'}$, the function $\mathsf{2SLNMExt}$ is computed as follows:

1. Compute $s = \mathsf{2Ext}(x_1, y_1)$.
2. Compute $x = \mathsf{Ext}(x_2, s)$.
3. Output $\mathsf{2NMExt}(x, y)$.

Theorem 9. *For any polynomial* $p(\cdot)$, $\mathsf{2SLNMExt}$ *described in Construction 1 is a* p*-strong leakage-resilient,* $(2,t)$*-non-malleable extractor at min-entropy* $(n_1 - \Delta, n_2 - \Delta)$ *with error* 8ϵ.

With the proper instantiation, we get the following corollary. The proof of the above theorem and the instantiation are presented in the full version of this paper.

Corollary 3. *For any polynomial* p *and constant* t, *there exists constants* $\gamma, n_0 > 0$ *such that for any* $n_2 > n_0$, *there exists an* p*-strong leakage-resilient* $(2,t)$*-non-malleable extractor* $\mathsf{2SLNMExt} : \{0,1\}^{n_1} \times \{0,1\}^{n_2} \to \{0,1\}^m$ *with min-entropy* $(n_1 - \gamma n_2, n_2 - \gamma n_2)$ *and error* $2^{-n_2^{\Omega(1)}}$, *where* $n_1 = 4n_2 + 2p(n_2)$.

5.3 Efficient Pre-image Sampleability

We also get a construction of strong leakage-resilient non-malleable extractor with *efficient pre-image sampleability* and we obtain the following corollary. See the full version of this paper for more details.

Corollary 4. *For any polynomial p and n_2, there exists an efficiently pre-image sampleable p-strong leakage-resilient $(2, n_2^{\Omega(1)})$-non-malleable extractor* $\mathsf{2SLNMExt} : \{0,1\}^{n_1} \times \{0,1\}^{n_2} \to \{0,1\}^m$ *with min-entropy (n_1, n_2) and error* $2^{-n_2^{\Omega(1)}}$*, where $n_1 = 4n_2 + p(n_2)$ and $m = n_2^{\Omega(1)}$.*

6 Multi-source Non-malleable Extractors

In this section, we will define and construct multi-source non-malleable extractors against a wide class of tampering function families.

6.1 Definition

Definition 6 (Multi-source Non-malleable Extractors). *A function* $\mathsf{MNMExt} : \{0,1\}^n \times \{0,1\}^n \ldots \times \{0,1\}^n \to \{0,1\}^m$ *is a s-source non-malleable extractor against a tampering family $\mathcal{F}$ at min-entropy k and error ϵ if it satisfies the following property: If $X_1, \ldots, X_s$ are independent (n,k)-sources and for any $f \in \mathcal{F}$, there exists a random variable D_f with support on $\{0,1\}^m \cup \{\mathsf{same}^*\}$ that is independent of $(X_1, \ldots, X_s)$ such that*

$$|\mathsf{MNMExt}(X_1, \ldots, X_s) \circ \mathsf{MNMExt}(f(X_1, \ldots, X_s)) - U_m \circ \mathsf{copy}(D_f, U_m)| \leq \epsilon$$

where both U_m's refer to the same uniform m-bit string and

$$\mathsf{copy}(x, y) = \begin{cases} x & \textit{if } x \neq \mathsf{same}^* \\ y & \textit{if } x = \mathsf{same}^* \end{cases}.$$

Tampering Function Family. We are interested in constructing multi-source non-malleable extractors that are secure against the tampering function families of the following form. Let $T_1, \ldots, T_s \subset [s]$. The tampering family $\mathcal{F}_{T_1,\ldots,T_s}$ consists of the set of all functions $f = (f_{T_1}, \ldots, f_{T_s})$ such that on input $(X_1, \ldots, X_s)$, f outputs $(\widetilde{X}_1, \ldots, \widetilde{X}_s)$ where for every $i \in [s]$, $f_{T_i}(\{X_j\}_{j \in T_i}) = \widetilde{X}_i$. In other words, $\widetilde{X}_i$ is generated by applying f_{T_i} on the set of sources $\{X_j\}_{j \in T_i}$. Depending on the properties required from the sets $\{T_1, \ldots, T_s\}$, we get two interesting classes of tampering functions.

- **Disjoint Tampering Family.** The disjoint tampering family $\mathcal{F}_{\mathsf{dis}}$ is the set of all $\mathcal{F}_{T_1,\ldots,T_s}$ for every possible $T_1, \ldots, T_s$ such that each T_i is non-empty, $|T_i| \leq s-1$, and if $x \in T_i, T_j$ then $T_i = T_j$.

- **Cover-free Tampering Family.** For every $i \in [s]$, let us define $\mathsf{Cover}(i)$ w.r.t. $T_1, \ldots, T_s$ to be the union of all the sets T_j where $i \in T_j$. The cover-free tampering family $\mathcal{F}_{\mathsf{cover-free}}$ is the set of all $\mathcal{F}_{T_1,\ldots,T_s}$ for all possible $T_1, \ldots, T_s \subset [s]$ such that for every $i \in [s]$, the size of $\mathsf{Cover}(i)$ w.r.t. $T_1, \ldots, T_s$ is at most $s-1$.

Observe that $\mathcal{F}_{\mathsf{dis}} \subset \mathcal{F}_{\mathsf{cover-free}}$ and hence in the rest of the section, we will focus on constructing non-malleable extractors that are secure against $\mathcal{F}_{\mathsf{cover-free}}$.

6.2 Construction

In this subsection, we will give a construction of s-source non-malleable extractor that is secure against $\mathcal{F}_{\mathsf{cover-free}}$.

Building Blocks and Parameters. In our construction, we will use the following building blocks and set the parameters as shown below. Let $n_1, n_2 \in \mathbb{N}$ and let ϵ denote the error and Δ denote the entropy loss parameter.

- Define the polynomial $p(\cdot)$ as $p(x) = xs^2$. Let $\mathsf{2SLNMExt} : \{0,1\}^{n_1} \times \{0,1\}^{n_2} \rightarrow \{0,1\}^m$ be a p-strong leakage-resilient, $(2,s)$-non-malleable extractor (see Definition 4). Let the min-entropy requirement of the extractor be $(n_1 - \Delta, n_2 - \Delta)$ and error be ϵ.
- We set $n = n_1 + sn_2$.
- We set $\epsilon < 1/2^m$.

Construction 2. On input strings $(x_1, \ldots, x_s)$ where each $x_i \in \{0,1\}^n$, the function MNMExt is computed as follows:

1. For each $i \in [s]$, partition x_i into $(s+1)$ blocks $(x^{(i)}, y_i^{(1)}, \ldots, y_i^{(s)})$ where $x^{(i)}$ has length n_1 and each $y_i^{(j)}$ has length n_2.
2. For each $i \in [s]$, compute $y^{(i)} = y_1^{(i)} \oplus y_2^{(i)} \ldots \oplus y_s^{(i)}$
3. Output $\mathsf{2SLNMExt}(x^{(1)}, y^{(1)}) \oplus \mathsf{2SLNMExt}(x^{(2)}, y^{(2)}) \ldots \oplus \mathsf{2SLNMExt}(x^{(s)}, y^{(s)})$.

Theorem 10. *Assume that* $\mathsf{2SLNMExt}$ *is a p-strong leakage resilient* $(2,s)$-*non-malleable extractor with error* ϵ. *Then, construction 2 is a s-source, non-malleable extractor against* $\mathcal{F}_{\mathsf{cover-free}}$ *at min-entropy* $n - \Delta + \log(1/\epsilon)$ *and error* $O(s(\epsilon + s2^{-m}))$.

The proof of the above theorem is given in the full version of this paper.

6.3 Instantiation

We now instantiate construction 3 with the strong leakage-resilient non-malleable extractors from Sect. 4.1.

From Corollary 3, by setting $p(n_2) = s^2 n_2$, there exists n_0 such that for any $n_2 > n_0$, we get could a p-strong leakage-resilient $(2,s)$-non-malleable extractor $\mathsf{2NMExt} : \{0,1\}^{n_1} \times \{0,1\}^{n_2} \rightarrow \{0,1\}^m$ with min-entropy $(n_1 - \Delta, n_2 - \Delta)$ and error ϵ, where $n_1 = 4n_2 + 2p(n_2)$, $m = n_2^{\Omega(1)}$, $\Delta = \gamma n_2$, $\epsilon = 2^{-n_2^{\Omega(1)}}$ for some constant γ. We can assume $m < \log 1/\epsilon$ since we can cut any number of bits from the output of 2SLNMExt while the error bound ϵ still holds. We can also let $\Delta > 2\log 1/\epsilon$ by enlarging ϵ.

Let $n = (2s^2+s+4)n_2$ and $\gamma' = \gamma/(2s^2+s+4)$. From Theorem 10, we get a s-source, non-malleable extractor against $\mathcal{F}_{\mathsf{cover-free}}$ at min-entropy $(1-\gamma')n$ and error $2^{-n^{\Omega(1)}}$ with output length $n^{\Omega(1)}$. We summarize the instantiation with the following corollary.

Corollary 5. *For any $s \geq 2$, there exists a constant n_0 and γ such that for any $n > n_0$, there exists a s-source, non-malleable extractor against $\mathcal{F}_{\mathsf{cover-free}}$ at min-entropy $(1-\gamma)n$ and error $2^{-n^{\Omega(1)}}$ with output length $n^{\Omega(1)}$.*

6.4 Efficient Pre-image Sampleability

We now show that if the underlying 2SLNMExt is efficiently pre-image sampeable, then our construction of multi-source non-malleable extractor is also efficiently pre-image sampleable.

Pre-image Sampling Procedure. Given any $\mathsf{msg} \in \{0,1\}^m$, the pre-image sampling procedure does the following:

1. Sample $\mathsf{msg}_1, \ldots, \mathsf{msg}_{s-1}$ uniformly from $\{0,1\}^m$.
2. Set $\mathsf{msg}_s = \mathsf{msg} \oplus \mathsf{msg}_1 \oplus \mathsf{msg}_2 \ldots \oplus \mathsf{msg}_{s-1}$.
3. Sample $(x^{(i)}, y^{(i)}) \leftarrow \mathsf{2SLNMExt}^{-1}(\mathsf{msg}_i)$ for all $1 \leq i \leq s$.
4. Sample $y_1^{(i)}, \ldots, y_{s-1}^{(i)}$ from $\{0,1\}^{n_2}$ for all $1 \leq i \leq s$.
5. Set $y_s^{(i)} = y^{(i)} \oplus y_1^{(i)} \oplus y_2^{(i)} \ldots \oplus y_{s-1}^{(i)}$ for all $1 \leq i \leq s$.
6. Output $(x_1, y_1^{(1)}, \ldots, y_1^{(s)}) \circ (x_2, y_2^{(1)}, \ldots, y_2^{(s)}) \ldots \circ (x_s, y_s^{(1)}, \ldots, y_s^{(s)})$.

It is clear that the above procedure give an uniform sample from $\mathsf{MNMExt}^{-1}(\mathsf{msg})$, and if the step 3 can be done efficiently, which means the underlying 2SLNMExt is efficiently pre-image sampleable, then the whole sampling procedure is also efficient.

Instantiation. We now instantiate 2SLNMExt from Sect. 5.3. Recall that this extractor has efficient pre-image sampleability.

From Corollary 4, by setting $p(n_2) = s^2 n_2$, we get could a p-strong leakage-resilient $(2,s)$-non-malleable extractor $\mathsf{2SLNMExt} : \{0,1\}^{n_1} \times \{0,1\}^{n_2} \rightarrow \{0,1\}^m$ with min-entropy (n_1, n_2) and error ϵ, where $n_1 = 4n_2 + p(n_2)$, $m = n_2^{\Omega(1)}$, $\epsilon = 2^{-n_2^{\Omega(1)}}$ and $s < n_2^{\gamma}$ for some constant γ. We assume $m < \log 1/\epsilon$ as above.

Let $n = (s^2+s+4)n_2$, which implies $n_2 = n^{\Omega(1)}$. Let $\gamma' > 0$ be constant such that $\gamma' < \frac{\gamma}{2\gamma+1}$. From Theorem 10, for any $s \leq n^{\gamma'}$, we get a s-source, non-malleable extractor against $\mathcal{F}_{\mathsf{cover-free}}$ at min-entropy n and error $2^{-n^{\Omega(1)}}$ with output length $n^{\Omega(1)}$, which is also efficiently pre-image sampleable.

Corollary 6. *For any $s \geq 2$ and $n \geq s^{1/\gamma'}$, there exists an efficiently pre-image sampleable s-source, non-malleable extractor against $\mathcal{F}_{\mathsf{cover-free}}$ at min-entropy n and error $2^{-n^{\Omega(1)}}$ with output length $n^{\Omega(1)}$.*

7 Multi-Split-State Non-malleable Codes

In this section, we will define multi-split-state non-malleable codes and show how to construct the multi-split-state non-malleable codes against a certain tampering function families, such as $\mathcal{F}_{\mathsf{dis}}$ or $\mathcal{F}_{\mathsf{cover-free}}$, from a multi-source non-malleable extractor against the same tampering function families. The construction follows the same paradigm as in [CG14].

7.1 Definition

In this subsection, we define multi-split-state non-malleable codes, which is similar to multi-source non-malleable extractor. The codeword is split into s states, where the tampering function for each state takes some but not all states as input and outputs the tampered version of that state.

Definition 7 (Multi-Split-State Non-malleable Codes). *A coding scheme* $\mathsf{MNMEnc} : \{0,1\}^m \rightarrow \{0,1\}^n \times \{0,1\}^n \ldots \times \{0,1\}^n$, $\mathsf{MNMDec} : \{0,1\}^n \times \{0,1\}^n \ldots \times \{0,1\}^n \rightarrow \{0,1\}^m$ *is a s-split-state non-malleable code with error ϵ against a family of tampering functions $\mathcal{F}$ if for every $f \in \mathcal{F}$, there exists a random variable D_f on $\{0,1\}^m \cup \{\mathsf{same}\}t$ such that for all messages $\mathsf{msg} \in \{0,1\}^m$, it holds that*

$$|\mathsf{MNMDec}(f(X_1, \ldots, X_s)) - \mathsf{copy}(D_f, \mathsf{msg})| \leq \epsilon$$

where $X_1, \ldots, X_t = \mathsf{MNMEnc}(\mathsf{msg})$.

Note the tampering function families $\mathcal{F}_{\mathsf{dis}}$ and $\mathcal{F}_{\mathsf{cover-free}}$ defined in 6.1 are also the tampering function families for multi-split-state codes. Therefore, we could use them to define s-split-state non-malleable codes against $\mathcal{F}_{\mathsf{dis}}$ or $\mathcal{F}_{\mathsf{cover-free}}$.

7.2 Construction

We now recall the result of [CG14] and generalize it to s-independent sources.

Theorem 11 ([CG14]). *Let* $\mathsf{MNMExt} : \{0,1\}^n \times \{0,1\}^n \cdots \times \{0,1\}^n \rightarrow \{0,1\}^m$ *be a s-source non-malleable extractor against a tampering function family $\mathcal{F}$ with error ϵ. Construct* $(\mathsf{MNMEnc}, \mathsf{MNMDec})$ *as following:*

- $\mathsf{MNMEnc} : \{0,1\}^m \rightarrow \{0,1\}^n \times \{0,1\}^n \ldots \times \{0,1\}^n$ *such that* $\mathsf{MNMEnc}(\mathsf{msg})$ *outputs a uniform sample from* $\mathsf{MNMExt}^{-1}(\mathsf{msg})$.
- $\mathsf{MNMDec} : \{0,1\}^n \times \{0,1\}^n \ldots \times \{0,1\}^n \rightarrow \{0,1\}^m$ *such that* $\mathsf{MNMDec}(x_1, \ldots, x_s)$ *outputs* $\mathsf{MNMExt}(x_1, \ldots, x_s)$.

Then, the above construction is a s-split-state non-malleable against $\mathcal{F}$ with error $\epsilon(2^{(m+1)}+1)$.

The proof of the above theorem and the instantiation are presented in the full version of this paper. With the instantiation, we get the following corollary.

Corollary 7. *For any $s \geq 2$ and for all $m \in \mathbb{N}$, there exists an efficient construction of s-split-state non-malleable code for messages of length m that is secure against cover-free tampering with error $2^{-m^{\Omega(1)}}$ and codeword length $(m+s)^{O(1)}$.*

8 Non-malleable Secret Sharing

In this section, we give a construction of threshold non-malleable secret sharing schemes with security against t-cover-free tampering. We give the definition of NMSS and t-cover-free tampering in the full version of this paper.

8.1 Construction

In this subsection, we will give a construction of t-out-of-n non-malleable secret sharing scheme that is secure against $\mathcal{F}_{t-\mathsf{cover-free}}$.

Building Blocks. In our construction, we will use the following building blocks.

- Let $(\mathsf{Share}, \mathsf{Rec})$ be a t-out-of-n Shamir secret sharing scheme. The length of each share is same as the length of the message.
- Define the polynomial $p(\cdot)$ as $p(x) = xn^2$. Let $\mathsf{2SLNMExt} : \{0,1\}^{n_1} \times \{0,1\}^{n_2} \rightarrow \{0,1\}^{3m}$ be a p-strong leakage-resilient, $(2,t)$-non-malleable extractor with efficient pre-image sampleability and error ϵ.
- We set $\epsilon < 1/2^{3m}$[4].

Construction 3. We give the description of $(\mathsf{NMShare}, \mathsf{NMRec})$.

- $\mathsf{NMShare}(s)$: On input a message $s \in \{0,1\}^m$, do:
  1. $(\mathsf{Sh}_1, \ldots, \mathsf{Sh}_n) \leftarrow \mathsf{Share}(s)$.
  2. For each $i \in [n]$, compute $(\mathsf{L}^{(i)}, \mathsf{R}^{(i)}) \leftarrow \mathsf{2SLNMExt}^{-1}(\mathsf{Sh}_i \circ U_{2m})$.
  3. For each $i \in [n]$, $(\mathsf{R}_1^{(i)}, \ldots, \mathsf{R}_n^{(i)}) \leftarrow \mathsf{Share}(\mathsf{R}^{(i)})$.
  4. Set $\mathsf{share}_i = (\mathsf{L}^{(i)}, \mathsf{R}_i^{(1)}, \ldots, \mathsf{R}_i^{(n)})$.
  5. Output $(\mathsf{share}_1, \ldots, \mathsf{share}_n)$.
- $\mathsf{NMRec}(\mathsf{share}_{i_1}, \ldots, \mathsf{share}_{i_\ell})$: On input $(\mathsf{share}_{i_1}, \ldots, \mathsf{share}_{i_t})$ for distinct $i_1, \ldots, i_t$:
  1. For each $i \in \{i_1, \ldots, i_t\}$,
     (a) Parse share_i as $(\mathsf{L}^{(i)}, \mathsf{R}_i^{(1)}, \ldots, \mathsf{R}_i^{(n)})$.

[4] Similar to the construction of multi-source non-malleable extractor in Sect. 6.2, we need this condition since in proof, we need the fact that there exists L^* such that for every $s \in \{0,1\}^{3m}$ there exists an R_s such that $\mathsf{2SLNMExt}(L^*, R_s) = s$.

   (b) Compute $\mathsf{R}^{(i)} := \mathsf{Rec}(\mathsf{R}^{(i)}_{i_1}, \ldots, \mathsf{R}^{(i)}_{i_t})$.
   (c) Set $\mathsf{Sh}_i := \mathsf{2SLNMExt}(\mathsf{L}^{(i)}, \mathsf{R}^{(i)})_{[m]}$.
2. Output $s := \mathsf{Rec}(\mathsf{Sh}_{i_1}, \ldots, \mathsf{Sh}_{i_t})$.

Theorem 12. *For any $t \geq 2$, $(\mathsf{NMShare}, \mathsf{NMRec})$ described above is a $(t, n, 0, 0)$ secret sharing scheme that is $O(n(\epsilon \cdot 2^{3m} + t2^{-m}))$-non-malleable against $\mathcal{F}_{t-\mathsf{cover-free}}$.*

The proof of the above theorem and the instantiation of the protocol are presented in the full version of this paper. With the instantiation, we get the following corollary.

Corollary 8. *For every $t \geq 2$, $n \geq t$ and any $m \in \mathbb{N}$, there exists an efficient construction of t-out-of-n non-malleable secret sharing for secrets of length m against t-cover-free tampering with error $2^{-m^{\Omega(1)}}$.*

9 Network Extractor Protocol

In this section, we show that a strong version of s-source non-malleable extractors give rise to a network extractor protocol. We start with the definition of a network extractor protocol from [KLRZ08].

Notation. We follow the same notation that was used in [KLRZ08]. Processor i begins with a sample from a weak source $x_i \in \{0,1\}^n$ and ends in possession of a hopefully uniform sample $z_i \in \{0,1\}^m$. Let b be the concatenation of all the messages that were sent during the protocol. Capital letters such as X_i, Z_i and B denote these strings viewed as random variables.

Definition 8 (Network Extractor Protocol [KLRZ08]). *A protocol for p processors is a (t, g, ϵ) network extractor for min-entropy k if for any (n, k) independent sources $X_1, \ldots, X_p$ and any choice T of t faulty processors, after running the protocol, there exists a set $G \in [p] \setminus T$ of size at least g such that*

$$|B, \{X_i\}_{i \notin G}, \{Z_i\}_{i \in G} - B, \{X_i\}_{i \notin G}, U_{gm}| < \epsilon$$

Here U_{gm} is the uniform distribution on gm bits, independent of B, and $\{X_i\}_{i \notin G}$.

9.1 Building Block

In this subsection, we give a building block that will be used in the construction of network extractor protocols.

Weak Disjoint Tampering function family. The weak disjoint tampering function family $\mathcal{F}_{\mathsf{wDis}}$ is the set of all functions given by $f = (i, g)$. Given $(x_1, \ldots, x_s)$, f outputs $\widetilde{x}_1, \ldots, \widetilde{x}_s$ where $\widetilde{x}_i = x_i$ and $g(x_{[s]\setminus\{i\}}) = \widetilde{x}_{[s]\setminus\{i\}}$. In other words, the tampering function leaves the i-th source as it is, and for the rest of the sources, it applies the tampering function g to generate their tampered version.

Below, we give an useful definition.

Definition 9. *The function* Deduplicate *takes in* $a_1, \ldots, a_t$ *and removes all the duplicates in the input. That is, if for any* $i \in [s]$, $a_i = a_{i_1} = \ldots = a_{i_\ell}$ *where* $i < i_1 < \ldots < i_\ell$, *then* Deduplicate *removes* $a_{i_1}, \ldots, a_{i_\ell}$.

We are now ready to give the definition of the building block.

Definition 10 ((s, t)-Strong Multi-source Non-malleable Extractors). *A function* $\mathsf{MNMExt} : \{0,1\}^n \times \{0,1\}^n \ldots \times \{0,1\}^n \rightarrow \{0,1\}^m$ *is a* (s,t)*-strong non-malleable extractor against the tampering family* $\mathcal{F}_{\mathsf{wDis}}$ *at min-entropy* k *and error* ϵ *if it satisfies the following property: If* $X_1, \ldots, X_s$ *are independent* (n, k)*-sources and for any* $f_1 = (i, g_1), \ldots, f_t = (i, g_t) \in \mathcal{F}_{\mathsf{wDis}}$, *there exists a random variable* $D_{\vec{f}}$ *with support on* $(\{0,1\}^m)^t$ *which is independent of the random variables* $X_1, \ldots, X_s$, *such that*

$$|X_{[s]\setminus\{i\}}, \mathsf{Deduplicate}(\mathsf{MNMExt}(X), \mathsf{MNMExt}(f_1(X)), \ldots, \mathsf{MNMExt}(f_t(X))) \\ - X'_{[s]\setminus\{i\}}, U_m, Z| < \epsilon$$

where $X = (X_1, \ldots, X_s)$, U_m *refers to an uniform* m*-bit string and* $(X'_{[s]\setminus\{i\}}, Z) \sim D_{\vec{f}}$.

We show in the full version of this paperthat the construction from Sect. 4 satisfies this definition for $s = 2$.

9.2 The Protocol

In this subsection, we give the description of our network extractor protocol. Let p be the number of processors and Δ denote the entropy loss parameter. We use a $(s, \binom{p}{s-1})$-strong non-malleable extractor $\mathsf{MNMExt} : (\{0,1\}^{n/p})^s \rightarrow \{0,1\}^m$ for min-entropy $n/p - \Delta$ and error ϵ against tampering family $\mathcal{F}_{\mathsf{wDis}}$.

Protocol 1. On input $x_i \in \{0,1\}^n$, processor i does the following.

1. Parse x_i as $x_1^{(i)}, \ldots, x_p^{(i)}$.
2. Broadcast $\{x_j^{(i)}\}_{j \neq i}$.
3. Receive $\{x_i^{(j)}\}_{j \neq i}$ from all the processors. If some processor j does not send any message, replace $x_i^{(j)}$ with a default value.
4. For every set $\{i_1, \ldots, i_{s-1}\} \subseteq [p]$ of size $s - 1$,
   (a) Compute $y_{i_1,\ldots,i_{s-1}} = \mathsf{MNMExt}(x_i^{(i)}, x_i^{(i_1)}, \ldots, x_i^{(i_{s-1})})$.
5. Remove the duplicates from the sequence $(y_{i_1,\ldots,i_{s-1}})_{i_1,\ldots,i_{s-1}}$ to get $y'_1, \ldots, y'_k$.
6. Output $z_i = y'_1 \oplus \ldots \oplus y'_k$.

Theorem 13. *For any* $p, s, n \in \mathbb{N}$*, assume* $(s, \binom{p}{s-1})$*-strong non-malleable extractor* $\mathsf{MNMExt} : (\{0,1\}^{n/p})^s \to \{0,1\}^m$ *for min-entropy* $n/p - \Delta$ *and error* ϵ *against tampering family* $\mathcal{F}_{\mathsf{wDis}}$*. Then, for any* $t \leq p - s$ *and* $g = p - t$*, protocol 1 is a* $(t, g, 2g \cdot \epsilon)$ *network extractor protocol for min-entropy* $n - \Delta + \log(1/\epsilon)$*. When* $s = O(1)$*, the running time of the protocol is* $\text{poly}(n, p)$*.*

The proof of the above theorem and the instantiation are presented in the full version of this paper. With the instantiation, we get the following corollary.

Corollary 9. *For any* $p \geq 2$*, there exists constants* $\gamma, n_0 > 0$ *and* γ *such that for all* $n > n_0$ *and for any* $t \leq p-2$*, there exists a single-round,* $(t, p-t, 2^{-n^{\Omega(1)}})$*-network extractor protocol for* p *processors and* $(n, n(1-\gamma))$ *sources.*

Acknowledgements. We thank the anonymous reviewers of Eurocrypt 2021 for useful comments on our manuscript. The first author was supported in part by NSF grant 1916939, a gift from Ripple, a JP Morgan Faculty Fellowship, and a Cylab seed funding award. Work partially done while the second author was at UC Berkeley and supported in part from AFOSR Award FA9550-19-1-0200, AFOSR YIP Award, NSF CNS Award 1936826, DARPA and SPAWAR under contract N66001-15-C-4065, a Hellman Award and research grants by the Okawa Foundation, Visa Inc., and Center for Long-Term Cybersecurity (CLTC, UC Berkeley). The work was partially done while the second and third authors were visiting CMU. The views expressed are those of the authors and do not reflect the official policy or position of the funding agencies.

References

[ADN+19] Aggarwal, D., et al.: Stronger leakage-resilient and non-malleable secret sharing schemesfor general access structures. In: Advances in Cryptology - CRYPTO 2019 - 39th Annual International Cryptology Conference, Santa Barbara, CA, USA, 18–22 August 2019, Proceedings, Part II, pp. 510–539 (2019)

[BDT17] Ben-Aroya, A., Doron, D., Ta-Shma, A.: An efficient reduction from two-source to non-malleable extractors: achieving near-logarithmic min-entropy. In: Proceedings of the 49th Annual ACM SIGACT Symposium on Theory of Computing, STOC 2017, Montreal, QC, Canada, 19–23 June 2017, pp. 1185–1194 (2017)

[BS19] Badrinarayanan, S., Srinivasan, A.: Revisiting non-malleable secret sharing. In: Ishai, Y., Rijmen, V. (eds.) EUROCRYPT 2019. LNCS, vol. 11476, pp. 593–622. Springer, Cham (2019). https://doi.org/10.1007/978-3-030-17653-2_20

[CG88] Chor, B., Goldreich, O.: Unbiased bits from sources of weak randomness and probabilistic communication complexity. SIAM J. Comput. **17**(2), 230–261 (1988)

[CG14] Cheraghchi, M., Guruswami, V.: Non-malleable coding against bit-wise and split-state tampering. In: Lindell, Y. (ed.) TCC 2014. LNCS, vol. 8349, pp. 440–464. Springer, Heidelberg (2014). https://doi.org/10.1007/978-3-642-54242-8_19

[CGGL19] Chattopadhyay, E., Goodman, J., Goyal, V., Li, X.: Extractors for adversarial sources via extremal hypergraphs. Manuscript (2019)

[CGL16] Chattopadhyay, E., Goyal, V., Li, X.: Non-malleable extractors and codes, with their many tampered extensions. In: Wichs, D., Mansour, Y. (eds.) 48th Annual ACM Symposium on Theory of Computing, pp. 285–298. ACM Press (2016)

[Coh16a] Cohen, G.: Making the most of advice: new correlation breakers and their applications. In: IEEE 57th Annual Symposium on Foundations of Computer Science, FOCS 2016, Hyatt Regency, New Brunswick, New Jersey, USA, 9–11 October 2016, pp. 188–196 (2016)

[Coh16b] Cohen, G.: Two-source dispersers for polylogarithmic entropy and improved ramsey graphs. In: Wichs, D., Mansour, Y. (eds.) 48th Annual ACM Symposium on Theory of Computing, pp. 278–284. ACM Press (2016)

[CZ16] Chattopadhyay, E., Zuckerman, D.: Explicit two-source extractors and resilient functions. In: Wichs, D., Mansour, Y. (eds.) 48th Annual ACM Symposium on Theory of Computing, pp. 670–683. ACM Press (2016)

[DO03] Dodis, Y., Oliveira, R.: On extracting private randomness over a public channel. In: Arora, S., Jansen, K., Rolim, J.D.P., Sahai, A. (eds.) APPROX/RANDOM -2003. LNCS, vol. 2764, pp. 252–263. Springer, Heidelberg (2003). https://doi.org/10.1007/978-3-540-45198-3_22

[DORS08] Dodis, Y., Ostrovsky, R., Reyzin, L., Smith, A.: Fuzzy extractors: how to generate strong keys from biometrics and other noisy data. SIAM J. Comput. **38**, 97–139 (2008)

[DPW18] Dziembowski, S., Pietrzak, K., Wichs, D.: Non-malleable codes. J. ACM **65**(4), 20:1–20:32 (2018)

[FV19] Faonio, A., Venturi, D.: Non-malleable secret sharing in the computational setting: adaptive tampering, noisy-leakage resilience, and improved rate. In: Boldyreva, A., Micciancio, D. (eds.) CRYPTO 2019. LNCS, vol. 11693, pp. 448–479. Springer, Cham (2019). https://doi.org/10.1007/978-3-030-26951-7_16

[GK18a] Goyal, V., Kumar, A.: Non-malleable secret sharing. In: Diakonikolas, I., Kempe, D., Henzinger, M. (eds.) 50th Annual ACM Symposium on Theory of Computing, pp. 685–698. ACM Press (2018)

[GK18b] Goyal, V., Kumar, A.: Non-malleable secret sharing for general access structures. In: Shacham, H., Boldyreva, A. (eds.) CRYPTO 2018. LNCS, vol. 10991, pp. 501–530. Springer, Cham (2018). https://doi.org/10.1007/978-3-319-96884-1_17

[GKK19] Garg, A., Kalai, Y.T., Khurana, D.: Computational extractors with negligible error in the crs model. Cryptology ePrint Archive, Report 2019/1116 (2019). https://eprint.iacr.org/2019/1116

[GKP+18] Goyal, V., Kumar, A., Park, S., Richelson, S., Srinivasan, A.: Non-malleable commitments from non-malleable extractors. Manuscript, accessed via personal communication (2018)

[GPR16] Goyal, V., Pandey, O., Richelson, S.: Textbook non-malleable commitments. In: Wichs, D., Mansour, Y. (eds.) 48th Annual ACM Symposium on Theory of Computing, pp. 1128–1141. ACM Press (2016)

[GS19] Goyal, V., Song, Y.: Correlated-source extractors and cryptography with correlated-random tapes. In: Ishai, Y., Rijmen, V. (eds.) EUROCRYPT 2019. LNCS, vol. 11476, pp. 562–592. Springer, Cham (2019). https://doi.org/10.1007/978-3-030-17653-2_19

[GSV05] Goldwasser, S., Sudan, M., Vaikuntanathan, V.: Distributed computing with imperfect randomness. In: Fraigniaud, P. (ed.) DISC 2005. LNCS, vol. 3724, pp. 288–302. Springer, Heidelberg (2005). https://doi.org/10.1007/11561927_22

[KLR09] Kalai, Y.T., Li, X., Rao, A.: 2-source extractors under computational assumptions and cryptography with defective randomness. In: 50th Annual Symposium on Foundations of Computer Science, pp. 617–626. IEEE Computer Society Press (2009)

[KLRZ08] Kalai, Y.T., Li, X., Rao, A., Zuckerman, D.: Network extractor protocols. In: 49th Annual Symposium on Foundations of Computer Science, pp. 654–663. IEEE Computer Society Press (2008)

[KMS18] Kumar, A., Meka, R., Sahai, A.: Leakage-resilient secret sharing. Electron. Colloquium Comput. Complex. (ECCC) **25**, 200 (2018)

[Li13] Li, X.: New independent source extractors with exponential improvement. In: Boneh, D., Roughgarden, T., Feigenbaum, J. (eds.) 45th Annual ACM Symposium on Theory of Computing, pp. 783–792. ACM Press (2013)

[Li16] Li, X.: Improved two-source extractors, and affine extractors for polylogarithmic entropy. In: Dinur, I. (ed.) 57th Annual Symposium on Foundations of Computer Science, pages 168–177. IEEE Computer Society Press (2016)

[Li17a] Li, X.: Improved non-malleable extractors, non-malleable codes and independent source extractors. In: STOC (2017)

[Li17b] Li, X.: Improved non-malleable extractors, non-malleable codes and independent source extractors. In: Hatami, H., McKenzie, P., King, V. (eds.) 49th Annual ACM Symposium on Theory of Computing, pp. 1144–1156. ACM Press (2017)

[MW97] Maurer, U., Wolf, S.: Privacy amplification secure against active adversaries. In: Kaliski, B.S. (ed.) CRYPTO 1997. LNCS, vol. 1294, pp. 307–321. Springer, Heidelberg (1997). https://doi.org/10.1007/BFb0052244

[Raz05] Raz, R.: Extractors with weak random seeds. In: Gabow, H.N., Fagin, R. (eds.) 37th Annual ACM Symposium on Theory of Computing, pp. 11–20. ACM Press (2005)

[SV19] Srinivasan, A., Vasudevan, P.N.: Leakage resilient secret sharing and applications. In: Boldyreva, A., Micciancio, D. (eds.) CRYPTO 2019. LNCS, vol. 11693, pp. 480–509. Springer, Cham (2019). https://doi.org/10.1007/978-3-030-26951-7_17

Quantum Constructions and Proofs

Secure Software Leasing

Prabhanjan Ananth[1(✉)] and Rolando L. La Placa[2]

[1] UC Santa Barbara, Santa Barbara, USA
prabhanjan@cs.ucsb.edu
[2] MIT, Santa Barbara, USA
rlaplaca@mit.edu

Abstract. Formulating cryptographic definitions to protect against software piracy is an important research direction that has not received much attention. Since natural definitions using classical cryptography are impossible to achieve (as classical programs can always be copied), this directs us towards using techniques from quantum computing. The seminal work of Aaronson [CCC'09] introduced the notion of quantum copy-protection precisely to address the problem of software anti-piracy. However, despite being one of the most important problems in quantum cryptography, there are no provably secure solutions of quantum copy-protection known for *any* class of functions.

We formulate an alternative definition for tackling software piracy, called secure software leasing (SSL). While weaker than quantum copy-protection, SSL is still meaningful and has interesting applications in software anti-piracy.

We present a construction of SSL for a subclass of evasive circuits (that includes natural implementations of point functions, conjunctions with wild cards, and affine testers) based on concrete cryptographic assumptions. Our construction is the first provably secure solution, based on concrete cryptographic assumptions, for software anti-piracy. To complement our positive result, we show, based on cryptographic assumptions, that there is a class of quantum unlearnable functions for which SSL does not exist. In particular, our impossibility result also rules out quantum copy-protection [Aaronson CCC'09] for an arbitrary class of quantum unlearnable functions; resolving an important open problem on the possibility of constructing copy-protection for arbitrary quantum unlearnable circuits.

1 Introduction

Almost all proprietary software requires a legal document, called software license, that governs the use against illegal distribution of software, also referred to as pirating. The main security requirement from such a license is that any malicious user no longer has access to the functionality of the software after the lease associated with the software license expires. While ad hoc solutions existed in the real world, for a long time, no theoretical treatment of this problem was known.

A. Canteaut and F.-X. Standaert (Eds.): EUROCRYPT 2021, LNCS 12697, pp. 501–530, 2021.
https://doi.org/10.1007/978-3-030-77886-6_17

This was until Aaronson, who in his seminal work [3] introduced and formalized the notion of quantum software copy-protection, a quantum cryptographic primitive that uses quantum no-cloning techniques to prevent pirating of software by modeling software as boolean functions. Roughly speaking, quantum copy-protection says[1] that given a quantum state computing a function f, the adversary cannot produce two quantum states (possibly entangled) such that each of the states individually computes f. This prevents a pirate from being able to create a new software from his own copy and re-distribute it; of course it can circulate its own copy to others but it will lose access to its own copy.

Need for Alternate Notions. While quantum copy-protection does provide a solution for software piracy, constructing quantum copy-protection has been notoriously difficult. Despite being introduced more than a decade ago, not much is known on the existence of quantum copy-protection. There are no known provably secure constructions of quantum copy-protection for *any* class of circuits. All the existing constructions of quantum copy-protection are either proven in an oracle model [3,5] or are heuristic[2] candidates for very simple functions such as point functions [3]. In a recent blog post, Aaronson [2] even mentioned constructing quantum copy-protection from cryptographic assumptions as one of the five big questions he wishes to solve.

This not only prompted us to explore the possibility of copy-protection but also look for alternate notions to protect against software piracy. Specifically, we look for application scenarios where the full power of quantum copy-protection is not needed and it suffices to settle for weaker notions. Let us consider one such example.

Example: Anti-Piracy Solutions for Microsoft Office. Microsoft Office is one of the most popular software tools used worldwide. Since Microsoft makes a sizeable portion of their revenue from this tool [1], it is natural to protect Microsoft Office from falling prey to software piracy. A desirable requirement is that pirated copies cannot be sold to other users such that these copies can run successfully on other Microsoft Windows systems. Importantly, it does not even matter if the pirated copies can be created as long as they cannot be executed on other Windows systems; this is because, only the pirated copies that run on Windows systems are the ones that bite into the revenue of Microsoft. Indeed, there are open source versions of Office publicly available but our aim is to prevent these open source versions from being sold off as authentic versions of Microsoft Office software.

This suggests that instead of quantum copy-protection – which prevents the adversary from creating *any* pirated copy of the copy-protected software – we can consider a weaker variant that only prevents the adversary from being able to create *authenticated* pirated copies (for instance, that runs only on specific

[1] More generally, Aaronson considers the setting where the adversary gets multiple copies computing f and not just one.

[2] That is, there is no known reduction to concrete cryptographic assumptions.

operating systems). To capture this, we present a new definition called secure software leasing.

Our Work: Secure Software Leasing (SSL). Roughly speaking, a secure leasing scheme allows for an authority (the lessor[3]) to lease a classical circuit C to a user (the lessee[4]) by providing a corresponding quantum state ρ_C. The user can execute ρ_C to compute C on any input it desires. Leases can expired, requiring ρ_C to be returned at a later point in time, specified by the lease agreement. After it returns the state, we require the security property that the lessee can no longer compute C.

In more detail, a secure software leasing scheme (SSL) for a family of circuits $\mathcal{C}$ is a collection, $(\mathsf{Gen}, \mathsf{Lessor}, \mathsf{Run}, \mathsf{Check})$, of quantum polynomial-time algorithms (QPT) satisfying the following conditions. $\mathsf{Gen}(1^\lambda)$, on input a security parameter λ, outputs a secret key sk that will be used by a lessor to validate the states being returned after the expiration of the lease. For any circuit $C : \{0,1\}^n \rightarrow \{0,1\}^m$ in $\mathcal{C}$, $\mathsf{Lessor}(\mathsf{sk}, C)$ outputs a quantum state ρ_C, where ρ_C allows Run to evaluate C. Specifically, for any $x \in \{0,1\}^n$, we want that $\mathsf{Run}(\rho_C, x) = C(x)$; this algorithm is executed by the lessee. Finally, $\mathsf{Check}(\mathsf{sk}, \rho_C)$ checks if ρ_C is a valid leased state. Any state produced by the lessor is a valid state and will pass the verification check.

A SSL scheme can have two different security guarantees depending on whether the leased state is supposed to be returned or not.

- *Infinite-Term Lessor Security*: In this setting, there is no time duration associated with the leased state and hence, the user can keep this leased state forever[5]. Informally, we require the guarantee that the lessee, using the leased state, cannot produce two *authenticated* copies of the leased state. Formally speaking, any (malicious) QPT user $\mathcal{A}$ holding a leased state $\mathcal{A}(\rho_C)$ (produced using classical circuit C) cannot output a (possibly entangled) bipartite state σ^* such that both $\sigma_1^* = \mathrm{Tr}_2[\sigma^*]$ and $\sigma_2^* = \mathrm{Tr}_1[\sigma^*]$ can be used to compute C with Run.
- *Finite-Term Lessor Security*: On the other hand, we could also consider a weaker setting where the leased state is associated with a fixed term. In this setting, the lessee is obligated to return back the leased state after the term expires. We require the property that after the lessee returns back the state, it can no longer produce another *authenticated* state having the same functionality as the leased state.

  Formally speaking, we require that any (malicious) QPT user $\mathcal{A}$ holding a leased state ρ_C (produced using C) cannot output a (possibly entangled) bipartite states σ^* such that $\sigma_1^* := \mathrm{Tr}_2[\sigma^*]$[6] passes the lessor's verification $(\mathsf{Check}(\mathsf{sk}, \sigma_1^*) = 1)$ and such that the resulting state, after the first register

[3] The person who leases the software to another.
[4] The person to whom the software is being leased to.
[5] Although the lessor will technically be the owner of the leased state.
[6] This denotes tracing out the second register.

has been verified by the lessor, on the second register, σ_2^*, can also be used to evaluate C with the Run algorithm, $\mathsf{Run}(\sigma_2^*, x) = C(x)$.

A SSL scheme satisfying infinite-term security would potentially be useful to tackle the problem of developing anti-piracy solutions for Microsoft Office. However, there are scenarios where finite-term security suffices. We mention two examples below.

Trial Versions. Before releasing the full version of a program C, a software vendor might want to allow a selected group of people[7] to run a beta version of it, C_β, in order to test it and get user feedback. Naturally, the vendor would not want the beta versions to be pirated and distributed more widely. Again, they can lease the beta version C_β, expecting the users to return it back when the beta test is over. At this point, they would know if a user did not return their beta version and they can penalize such a user according to their lease agreement.

Subscription Models. Another example where finite-term SSL would be useful is for companies that use a subscription model for their revenue. For example, Microsoft has a large library of video games for their console, the Xbox, which anyone can have access to for a monthly subscription fee. A malicious user could subscribe in order to have access to the collection of games, then make copies of the games intending to keep them after cancelling the subscription. The same user will not be able to make another copy of a game that also runs on Xbox.

1.1 Our Results

We present a construction of SSL for a restricted class of unlearnable circuits; in particular, our construction is defined for a subclass of evasive circuits. This demonstrates the first provably secure construction for the problem of software anti-piracy in the standard model (i.e., without using any oracles).

Our construction does not address the possibility of constructing SSL for an arbitrary class of unlearnable circuits. Indeed, given the long history of unclonable quantum cryptographic primitives (see Section A) along with the recent boom in quantum cryptographic techniques [8,13,20,22–25,35,36,41], one might hope that existing techniques could lead us to achieve a general result. We show, rather surprisingly, assuming cryptographic assumptions, there exists a class of unlearnable circuits such that no SSL exists for this class. This also rules out the existence of quantum copy-protection for arbitrary unlearnable functions[8]; *thus resolving an important open problem in quantum cryptography.*

---

[7] For instance, they could be engineers assigned to test whether the beta version contains bugs.

[8] Both the notions (quantum copy-protection and secure software leasing) are only meaningful for unlearnable functions: if a function is learnable, then one could learn the function from the quantum state and create another authenticated quantum state computing the same function.

We explain our results in more detail. We first start with the negative result before moving on to the positive result.

Impossibility Result. To demonstrate our impossibility result, we identify a class of classical circuits $\mathcal{C}$ that we call a *de-quantumizable* circuit class. This class has the nice property that given *any* efficient quantum implementation of $C \in \mathcal{C}$, we can efficiently 'de-quantumize' it to obtain a classical circuit $C' \in \mathcal{C}$ that has the same functionality as C. If $\mathcal{C}$ is learnable then, from the definition of learnability, there could be a QPT algorithm that finds C'. To make the notion interesting and non-trivial, we add the additional requirement that this class of circuits is quantum unlearnable. A circuit class $\mathcal{C}$ is quantum unlearnable if given black-box access to $C \in \mathcal{C}$, any QPT algorithm cannot find a quantum implementation of C.

We show the existence of a de-quantumizable circuit class from cryptographic assumptions.

Proposition 1 (Informal). *Assuming the quantum hardness of learning with errors (QLWE), and asssuming the existence of quantum fully homomorphic encryption*[9] *(QFHE), there exists a de-quantumizable class of circuits.*

We show how non-black-box techniques introduced in seemingly different contexts – proving impossibility of obfuscation [7,12,19] and constructing zero-knowledge protocols [9,14,16] – are relevant to proving the above proposition. We give an overview, followed by a formal construction, in Sect. 3.

We then show that for certain de-quantumizable class of circuis, there does not exist a SSL scheme (with either finite or infinite-term security) for this class. Combining this with the above proposition, we have the following:

Theorem 1 (Informal). *Assuming the quantum hardness of learning with errors (QLWE), and asssuming the existence of quantum fully homomorphic encryption (QFHE), there exists a class of quantum unlearnable circuits $\mathcal{C}$ such that there is no SSL for $\mathcal{C}$.*

On the Assumption of QFHE: There are lattice-based constructions of QFHE proposed by [17,35] although we currently don't know how to base them solely on the assumption of LWE secure against QPT adversaries (QLWE). Brakerski [17] shows that the security of QFHE can be based on QLWE and a circular security assumption.

Impossibility of Quantum Copy-Protection. Since copy-protection implies SSL, we have the following result.

[9] We need additional properties from the quantum fully homomorphic encryption scheme but these properties are natural and satisfied by existing schemes [17,35]. Please refer to full version for a precise description of these properties.

Corollary 1 (Informal). *Assuming the quantum hardness of learning with errors (QLWE), and asssuming the existence of quantum fully homomorphic encryption (QFHE), there exists a class of quantum unlearnable circuits $\mathcal{C}$ that cannot be quantumly copy-protected.*

Main Construction. Our impossibility result does not rule out the possibility of constructing SSL schemes for specific circuit classes. For instance, it does not rule out the feasibility of SSL for *evasive functions*; this is a class of functions with the property that given black-box access, an efficient algorithm cannot find an accepting input (an input on which the output of the function is 1).

We identify a subclass of evasive circuits for which we can construct SSL. infinite

Searchable Compute-and-Compare Circuits. We consider the following circuit class $\mathcal{C}$: every circuit in $\mathcal{C}$, associated with a circuit C and a lock α, takes as input x and outputs 1 iff $C(x) = \alpha$. This circuit class has been studied in the cryptography literature in the context of constructing program obfuscation [32, 39]. We require this circuit class to additionally satisfy a *searchability* condition: there is an efficient (classical) algorithm, denoted by $\mathcal{S}$, such that given any $C \in \mathcal{C}$, $\mathcal{S}(C)$ outputs x such that $C(x) = 1$.

There are natural and interesting sub-classes of compute-and-compare circuits:

- Point circuits $C(\alpha, \cdot)$: the circuit $C(\alpha, \cdot)$ is a point circuit if it takes as input x and outputs $C(\alpha, x) = 1$ iff $x = \alpha$. If we define the class of point circuits suitably, we can find α directly from the description of $C(\alpha, \cdot)$; for instance, α is the value assigned to the input wires of C.
- Conjunctions with wild cards $C(S, \alpha, \cdot)$: the circuit $C(S, \alpha, \cdot)$ is a conjunction with wild card if it takes as input x and outputs $C(S, \alpha, x) = 1$ iff $y = \alpha$, where y is such that $y_i = x_i$ for all $i \in S$ and $y_i = 0$ for all $i \notin S$. Again, if we define this class of circuits suitably, we can find S and α directly from the description of $C(S, \alpha, \cdot)$.

On Searchability: We note that the searchability requirement in our result statement is natural and is implicit in the description of the existing constructions of copy-protection by Aaronson [3]. Another point to note is that this notion is associated with circuit classes rather than a function family.

We prove the following result. Our construction is in the common reference string (CRS) model. In this model, we assume that both the lessor and the lessee will have access to the CRS produced by a trusted setup. We note that our impossibility result also holds in the CRS model.

Theorem 2. *Assuming the existence of: (a) quantum-secure subspace obfuscators [41] and, (b) learning with errors secure against sub-exponential quantum algorithms, there exists an infinite-term secure SSL scheme in the common reference string model for searchable compute-and-compare circuits.*

Notice that for applications in which the lessor is the creator of software, the lessor can dictate how the circuit class is defined and thus would choose an implementation of the circuit class that is searchable.

On the Assumptions in Theorem 2. A discussion about the primitives described in the above theorem statement is in order. A subspace obfuscator takes as input a subspace A and outputs a circuit that tests membership of A while hiding A even against quantum adversaries. This was recently constructed by [41] based on the quantum-security of indistinguishability obfuscation [28]. Moreover, recently, there has been exciting progress in constructing quantum-secure indistinguishability obfuscation schemes [18,30,38] from cryptographic assumptions that hold against quatum adversaries.

With regards to the assumption of learning with errors against sub-exponential quantum algorithms, we firstly note that classical sub-exponential security of learning with errors has been used in the construction of many cryptographic primitives and secondly, there are no known significant quantum speedups known to solving this problem.

In the technical sections, we prove a more general theorem.

Theorem 3 (SSL for General Evasive Circuits; Informal). *Let $\mathcal{C}$ be a searchable class of circuits. Assuming the existence of: (a) quantum-secure input-hiding obfuscators [11] for $\mathcal{C}$, (b) quantum-secure subspace obfuscators [41] and, (c) learning with errors secure against sub-exponential quantum algorithms, there exists an infinite-term secure SSL scheme in the setup model for $\mathcal{C}$.*

An input-hiding obfuscator is a compiler that converts a circuit C into another functionally equivalent circuit $\widetilde{C}$ such that given $\widetilde{C}$ it is computationally hard to find an accepting point. To achieve Theorem 2, we instantiate searchable input-hiding obfuscators for compute-and-compare circuits from quantum hardness of learning with errors. However, we can envision quantum-secure instantiations of input-hiding obfuscators for more general class of searchable evasive circuits; we leave this problem open.

We admittedly use heavy cryptographic hammers to prove our result, but as will be clear in the overview given in the next section, each of these hammers will be necessary to solve the different technical challenges we face.

Concurrent Work on qVBB. Our impossibility result also rules out the existence of quantum VBB for classical circuits assuming quantum FHE and quantum learning of errors; this was stated as an open problem by Alagic and Fefferman [7]. Concurrently, [6] also rule out quantum virtual black-box obfuscation under the assumption of quantum hardness of learning with errors; unlike our work they don't additionally assume the existence of quantum FHE.

In hindsight, it shouldn't be surprising that non-black box techniques developed in the context of quantum zero-knowledge [9,16] are relevant to proving the impossibility of quantum obfuscation; the breakthrough work of Bitansky and Paneth [15] show how to construct (classical) zero-knowledge protocols with non-black box simulation using techniques developed in the context of (classical) obfuscation.

1.2 Overview of Construction of SSL

For this overview, we only focus on constructing a SSL sscheme satisfying finite-term lessor security. Our ideas can be easily adapted to the infinite-term lessor security.

To construct a SSL scheme in the setup model $(\mathsf{Setup}, \mathsf{Gen}, \mathsf{Lessor}, \mathsf{Run}, \mathsf{Check})$ against arbitrary quantum poly-time (QPT) pirates, we first focus on two weaker class of adversaries, namely, *duplicators* and *maulers*. Duplicators are adversaries who, given ρ_C generated by the lessor for a circuit C sampled from a distribution $\mathcal{D}_C$, produce $\rho_C^{\otimes 2}$; that is, all they do is replicate the state. Maulers, who given ρ_C, output $\rho_C \otimes \rho_C^*$, where ρ_C^* is far from ρ_C in trace distance and ρ_C is the copy returned by the mauler back to the lessor; that is the second copy it produces is a modified version of the original copy.

While our construction is secure against arbitrary pirates, it will be helpful to first focus on these restricted type of adversaries. We propose two schemes: the first scheme is secure against QPT maulers and the second scheme against QPT duplicators. Once we discuss these schemes, we will then show how to combine the techniques from these two schemes to obtain a construction secure against arbitrary pirates.

SSL Against Maulers. To protect SSL against a mauler, we attempt to construct a scheme using only classical cryptographic techniques. The reason why it could be possible to construct such a scheme is because maulers never produce a pirated copy ρ_C^* that is the same as the original copy ρ_C.

A natural attempt to construct a SSL scheme is to use virtual black-box obfuscation [12] (VBB): this is a compiler that transforms a circuit C into another functionally equivalent circuit $\widetilde{C}$ such that $\widetilde{C}$ only leaks the input-output behavior of C and nothing more. This is a powerful notion and implies almost all known cryptographic primitives. We generate the leased state ρ_C to be the VBB obfuscation of C, namely $\widetilde{C}$. The hope is that a mauler will not output another leased state ρ_C^* that is different from $\widetilde{C}$.

Unfortunately, this scheme is insecure. A mauler on input $\widetilde{C}$, obfuscates $\widetilde{C}$ once more to obtain $\widetilde{\widetilde{C}}$ and outputs this re-obfsuscated circuit. Moreover, note that the resulting re-obfuscated circuit still computes C. This suggests that program obfuscation is insufficient for our purpose. In hindsight, this should be unsurprising: VBB guarantees that given an obfuscated circuit, an efficient adversary should not learn anything about the implementation of the circuit, but this doesn't prevent the adversary from being able to re-produce modified copies of the obfuscated circuit.

To rectify this issue, we devise the following strategy:

- Instead of VBB, we start with a different obfuscation scheme that has the following property: given an obfuscated circuit $\widetilde{C}$, where C corresponds to an evasive function, it is computationally infeasible to determine an accepting input for C.
- We then combine this with a special proof system that guarantees the property: suppose an adversary, upon receiving $\widetilde{C}$ and a proof, outputs a *different* but functionally equivalent obfuscated circuit $\widetilde{C}^*$ along with a new proof. Then we can extract an accepting input for $\widetilde{C}$ from the adversary's proof. But this would contradict the above bullet and hence, it follows that its computationally infeasible for the adversary to output a different circuit $\widetilde{C}^*$.

To realize the above strategy, we need two separate cryptographic tools, that we define below.

Input-Hiding Obfuscators [11]: We recall the notion of input-hiding obfuscators [11]. An input-hiding obfuscator guarantees that given an obfuscated circuit $\widetilde{C}$, any efficient adversary cannot find an accepting input x, i.e., an input x such that $\widetilde{C}(x) = 1$. Of course this notion is only meaningful for an evasive class of functions: a function is evasive if given oracle access to this function, any efficient adversary cannot output an accepting point. The work of Barak et al. [11] proposed candidates for input-hiding obfuscators.

Simulation-Extractable NIZKs [26,37]: Another primitive we consider is simulation-extractable non-interactive zero-knowledge [26,37] (seNIZKs). A seNIZK system is a non-interactive protocol between a prover and a verifier with the prover trying to convince the verifier that a statement belongs to the NP language. By non-interactive we mean that the prover only sends one message to the verifier and the verifier is supposed to output the decision bit: accept or reject. Moreover, this primitive is defined in the common reference string model. In this model, there is a trusted setup that produces a common reference string and both the prover and the verifier have access to this common reference string.

As in a traditional interactive protocol, we require a seNIZK to satisfy the completeness property. Another property we require is simulation-extractability. Simulation-extractability, a property that implies both zero-knowledge and soundness, guarantees that if there exists an efficient adversary $\mathcal{A}$ who upon receiving a *simulated* proof[10] for an instance x, produces an accepting proof for a different instance x', i.e., $x' \neq x$, then there also exists an adversary $\mathcal{B}$ that given the same simulated proof produces an accepting proof for x' along with simultaneously producing a valid witness for x'.

---

[10] A simulated proof is one that is generated by an efficient algorithm, called a simulator, who has access to some private coins that was used to generate the common reference string. Moreover, a simulated proof is indistinguishable from an honestly generated proof. A simulator has the capability to generate simulated proofs for YES instances even without knowing the corresponding witness for these instances.

Combining Simulation-Extractable NIZKs and Input-Hiding Obfuscators: We now combine the two tools we introduced above to obtain a SSL scheme secure against maulers. Our SSL scheme will be associated with searchable circuits; given a description of a searchable circuit C, an input x can be determined efficiently such that $C(x) = 1$.

To lease a circuit C, do the following:

- Compute an input-hiding obfuscation of C, denoted by $\widetilde{C}$,
- Produce a seNIZK proof π that proves knowledge of an input x such that $C(x) = 1$. Note that we can find this input using the searchability property.

Output $(\widetilde{C}, \pi)$ as the leased circuit. To evaluate on any input x, we first check if π is a valid proof and if so, we compute $\widetilde{C}$ on x to obtain $C(x)$.

To see why this scheme is secure against maulers, suppose an adversary $\mathcal{A}$ given $(\widetilde{C}, \pi)$ produces $(\widetilde{C}^*, \pi^*)$, where $\widetilde{C}^* \neq \widetilde{C}$. Since $\mathcal{A}$ is a valid mauler we are guaranteed that $\widetilde{C}^*$ is functionally equivalent to C. We first run the seNIZK simulator to simulate π and once this is done, we no longer need x to generate π. Now, we invoke the simulation-extractability property to convert $\mathcal{A}$ into one who not only produces $(\widetilde{C}^*, \pi^*)$ but also simultaneously produces x such that $\widetilde{C}^*(x) = 1$. Since $\widetilde{C}^*$ is functionally equivalent to C, it follows that $C(x) = 1$ as well. But this violates the input-hiding property which says that no efficient adversary given $\widetilde{C}$ can produce an accepting input.

Issue: Checking Functional Equivalence. There is a subtlety we skipped in the proof above. The maulers that we consider have multi-bit output which is atypical in the cryptographic setting where the focus is mainly on boolean adversaries. This causes an issue when we switch from the honestly generated proof to a simulated proof. Upon receiving the honestly generated proof, $\mathcal{A}$ outputs $(\widetilde{C}^*, \pi^*)$ such that $\widetilde{C}^*$ is functionally equivalent to C but upon receiving the simulated proof, the adversary outputs $(\widetilde{C}^*, \pi^*)$ where $\widetilde{C}^*$ differs from C on one point. From $\mathcal{A}$, we need to extract one bit that would help distinguish the real and simulated proofs. To extract this bit, we rely upon sub-exponential security. Given $\widetilde{C}^*$, we run in time 2^n, where n is the input length, and check if $\widetilde{C}^*$ is still functionally equivalent to C; if indeed $\widetilde{C}^*$ is not functionally equivalent to C then we know for a fact that the adversary was given a simulated proof, otherwise it received an honestly generated proof. We set the security parameter in the seNIZK system to be sufficiently large (for eg, $\text{poly}(n)$) such that the seNIZK is still secure against adversaries running in time 2^n.

SSL Against Duplicators. Next we focus on constructing SSL secure against duplicators. If our only goal was to protect against duplicators, we could achieve this with a simple scheme. The lessor, in order to lease C, will output $(|\psi\rangle, C)$ where $|\psi\rangle$ is a random quantum state generated by applying a random polynomial sized quantum circuit U on input $|0^{\otimes\lambda}\rangle$. Run on input $(|\psi\rangle, C, x)$ ignores the quantum state $|\psi\rangle$, and outputs $C(x)$. By quantum no-cloning, an attacker cannot output two copies of $(|\psi\rangle, C)$, which means that this scheme is already secure against duplicators.

Recall that we focused on designing SSL for duplicators in the hope that it will be later helpful for designing SSL for arbitrary pirates. But any SSL scheme in which Run ignores the quantum part would not be useful for obtaining SSL secure against arbitrary pirates; an attacker can simply replace the quantum state as part of the leased state with its own quantum state and copy the classical part. To overcome this insufficiency, we need to design SSL schemes where the Run algorithm only computes correctly when the input leased state belongs to a sparse set of quantum states. This suggests that the Run algorithm implicitly satisfies a verifiability property; it should be able to verify that the input quantum state lies in this sparse set.

Publicly Verifiable Unclonable States. We wish to construct a family of efficiently preparable states $\{|\psi_s\rangle\}_s$ with the following verifiability property. For any state $|\psi_s\rangle$ in the family, there is a way to sample a classical description d_s for $|\psi_s\rangle$ in such a way that it can be verified that d_s is a corresponding description of $|\psi_s\rangle$. To be more precise, there should be a verification algorithm $\mathsf{Ver}(|\psi_s\rangle, d)$ that accepts if d is a valid description for $|\psi_s\rangle$. Furthermore, we want the guarantee that given a valid pair $(|\psi_s\rangle, d_s)$, no QPT adversary can produce $|\psi_s\rangle^{\otimes 2}$.

Our requirement has the same flavor as public-key quantum money, but a key difference is that we do not require any secret parameters associated with the scheme. Moreover, we allow anyone to be able to generate such tuples $(|\psi_s\rangle, d_s)$ and not just the minting authority (bank).

Given such verifiable family, we can define the Run algorithm as follows,

$\mathsf{Run}(C, (|\psi_s\rangle, d), x)$:

- If $\mathsf{Ver}(|\psi_s\rangle, d) = 0$, output $\perp$.
- Otherwise, output $C(x)$.

Any lessor can now lease a state $(|\psi_s\rangle, d_s, C)$, which would allow anyone to compute C using Run. Of course, any pirate that is given $(|\psi_s\rangle, d_s, C)$ can prepare their own $(|\psi_{s'}\rangle, d_{s'})$ and then input $(|\psi_{s'}\rangle, d_{s'}, C)$ into Run. But recall that we are only interested in ruling out *duplicators*. From the public verifiable property of the quantum states, we have the fact that no QPT pirate could prepare $|\psi_s\rangle^{\otimes 2}$ from $(|\psi_s\rangle, d_s)$ and thus, it is computationally infeasible to duplicate the leased state.

Publicly Verifiable Unclonable States from Subspace Hiding Obfuscation. The notion of publicly verifiable unclonable states was first realized by Zhandry [41]. The main tool used in Zhandry's construction is yet another notion of obfuscation, called subspace hiding obfuscation. Roughly speaking, a subspace hiding obfuscator (shO) takes as input a description of a linear subspace A, and outputs a circuit that computes the membership function for A, i.e. $\mathsf{shO}(A)(x) = 1$ iff $x \in A$. Zhandry shows that for a uniformly random $\frac{\lambda}{2}$-dimensional subspace $A \subset \mathbb{Z}_q^\lambda$, given $|A\rangle := \frac{1}{\sqrt{q^{\lambda/2}}} \sum_{a \in A} |a\rangle$ along with $\widetilde{g} \leftarrow \mathsf{shO}(A), \widetilde{g_\perp} \leftarrow \mathsf{shO}(A^\perp)$, no QPT algorithm can prepare $|A\rangle^{\otimes 2}$ with non-negligible probability. Nevertheless, because $\widetilde{g}$ and $\widetilde{g_\perp}$ compute membership for A and $A^\perp$ respectively, it is possible to project onto $|A\rangle\langle A|$ using $(\widetilde{g},\widetilde{g_\perp})$. This lets anyone check the tuple $(|\psi\rangle,(\widetilde{g},\widetilde{g_\perp}))$ by measuring $|\psi\rangle$ with the projectors $\{|A\rangle\langle A|, I-|A\rangle\langle A|\}$.

Main Template: SSL Against Pirates. Our goal is to construct SSL against arbitrary QPT pirates and not just duplicators or maulers. To achieve this goal, we combine the techniques we have developed so far.

To lease a circuit C, do the following:

1. First prepare the state the state $|A\rangle = \frac{1}{\sqrt{q^{\lambda/2}}}\sum_{a\in A}|a\rangle$, along with $\tilde{g}\leftarrow \mathsf{shO}(A)$ and $\widetilde{g_\perp}\leftarrow \mathsf{shO}(A^\perp)$.
2. Compute an input-hiding obfuscation of C, namely $\widetilde{C}$.
3. Let x be an accepting point of C. This can be determined using the searchability condition.
4. Compute a seNIZK proof π such that: (1) the obfuscations $(\widetilde{g},\widetilde{g_\perp},\widetilde{C})$ were computed correctly, as a function of $(A, A^\perp, C)$, and, (2) $C(x)=1$.
5. Output $|\psi_C\rangle = (|A\rangle,\widetilde{g},\widetilde{g_\perp},\widetilde{C},\pi)$.

The Run algorithm on input $(|\psi_C\rangle,\widetilde{g},\widetilde{g_\perp},\widetilde{C},\pi)$ and x, first checks the proof π, and outputs $\perp$ if it does not accept the proof. If it accepts the proof, it knows that $\widetilde{g}$ and $\widetilde{g_\perp}$ are subspace obfuscators for some subspaces A and $A^\perp$ respectively; it can use them to project $|\psi_C\rangle$ onto $|A\rangle\langle A|$. This checks whether $|\psi_C\rangle$ is the same as $|A\rangle$ or not. If it is not, then it outputs $\perp$. If it has not output $\perp$ so far, then it computes $\widetilde{C}$ on x to obtain $C(x)$.

Proof Intuition: To prove the lessor security of the above scheme, we consider two cases depending on the behavior of the pirate:

- *Duplicator*: in this case, the pirate produces a new copy that is of the form $(\sigma^*,\widetilde{g},\widetilde{g_\perp},\widetilde{C},\pi)$; that is, it has the same classical part as before. If σ^* is close to $|A\rangle\langle A|$, it would violate the no-cloning theorem. On the other hand, if σ^* is far from $|A\rangle\langle A|$, we can argue that the execution of Run on the copy produced by the pirate will not compute C. The reason being that at least one of the two subspace obfuscators $\widetilde{g},\widetilde{g_\perp}$ will output $\perp$ on the state σ^*.
- *Mauler*: suppose the pirate produces a new copy that is of the form $(\sigma^*,\widetilde{g}^*,\widetilde{g_\perp}^*,\widetilde{C}^*,\pi^*)$ such that $(\widetilde{g}^*,\widetilde{g_\perp}^*,\widetilde{C}^*)\neq(\widetilde{g},\widetilde{g_\perp},\widetilde{C})$. We invoke the simulation-extractability property to find an input x such that $\widetilde{C}^*(x)=1$. Since $\widetilde{C}^*$ is assumed to have the same functionality as C, this means that $C(x)=1$. This would contradict the security of input-hiding obfuscation, since any QPT adversary even given $\widetilde{C}$ should not be able to find an accepting input x such that $C(x)=1$.

Organization. We provide the related works and preliminary background in the full version. We present the formal definition of secure software leasing in Sect. 2. The impossibility result is presented in Sect. 3. Finally, we present the positive result in Sect. 4.

2 Secure Software Leasing (SSL)

We present the definition of secure software leasing schemes. A secure software leasing (SSL) scheme for a class of circuits $\mathcal{C} = \{\mathcal{C}_\lambda\}_{\lambda \in \mathbb{N}}$ consists of the following QPT algorithms.

- **Private-key Generation,** $\mathsf{Gen}(1^\lambda)$: On input security parameter λ, outputs a private key sk.
- **Software Lessor,** $\mathsf{Lessor}(\mathrm{sk}, C)$: On input the private key sk and a poly(n)-sized classical circuit $C \in \mathcal{C}_\lambda$, with input length n and output length m, outputs a quantum state ρ_C.
- **Evaluation,** $\mathsf{Run}(\rho_C, x)$: On input the quantum state ρ_C and an input $x \in \{0,1\}^n$, outputs y, and some state $\rho'_{C,x}$.
- **Check of Returned Software,** $\mathsf{Check}(\mathrm{sk}, \rho^*_C)$: On input the private key sk and the state ρ^*_C, it checks if ρ^*_C is a valid leased state and if so it outputs 1, else it outputs 0.

Setup. In this work, we only consider SSL schemes in the setup model. In this model, all the lessors in the world have access to a common reference string generated using a PPT algorithm Setup. The difference between Setup and Gen is that Setup is run by a trusted third party whose output is used by all the lessors while Gen is executed by each lessor separately. We note that our impossibility result rules out SSL schemes for all quantum unlearnable class of circuits even in the setup model.

We define this notion below.

Definition 1 (SSL with Setup). *A secure software leasing scheme* (Gen, Lessor, Run, Check) *is said to be in the common reference string (CRS) model if additionally, it has an algorithm* Setup *that on input* 1^λ *outputs a string* crs.

Moreover, the algorithm Gen *now takes as input* crs *instead of* 1^λ *and* Run *additionally takes as input* crs.

We require that a SSL scheme, in the setup model, satisfies the following properties.

Definition 2 (Correctness). *A SSL scheme* (Setup, Gen, Lessor, Run, Check) *for* $\mathcal{C} = \{\mathcal{C}_\lambda\}_{\lambda \in \mathbb{N}}$ *is* ε*-correct if for all* $C \in \mathcal{C}_\lambda$*, with input length* n*, the following two properties holds for some negligible function* ε*:*

- *Correctness of Run:*

$$\Pr\left[\forall x \in \{0,1\}^n,\ y = C(x)\ :\ \begin{array}{c} \mathsf{crs} \leftarrow \mathsf{Setup}(1^\lambda), \\ \mathsf{sk} \leftarrow \mathsf{Gen}(\mathsf{crs}), \\ \rho_C \leftarrow \mathsf{Lessor}(\mathsf{sk}, C) \\ (\rho'_{C,x}, y) \leftarrow \mathsf{Run}(\mathsf{crs}, \rho_C, x) \end{array}\right] \geq 1 - \varepsilon$$

- *Correctness of Check:*

$$\Pr\left[\mathsf{Check}(\mathrm{sk}, \rho_C) = 1\ :\ \begin{array}{c} \mathsf{crs} \leftarrow \mathsf{Setup}(1^\lambda), \\ \mathsf{sk} \leftarrow \mathsf{Gen}(\mathsf{crs}) \\ \rho_C \leftarrow \mathsf{Lessor}(\mathsf{sk}, C) \end{array}\right] \geq 1 - \varepsilon$$

Reusability. A desirable property of a SSL scheme is reusability: the lessee should be able to repeatedly execute Run on multiple inputs. A SSL scheme does not necessarily guarantee reusability; for instance, Run could destroy the state after executing it just once. But fortunately, we can transform this scheme into another scheme that satisfies reusability.

We define reusability formally.

Definition 3. *(Reusability) A SSL scheme* (Setup, Gen, Lessor, Run, Check) *for* $\mathcal{C} = \{\mathcal{C}_\lambda\}_{\lambda \in \mathbb{N}}$ *is said to be reusable if for all* $C \in \mathcal{C}$ *and for all* $x \in \{0,1\}^n$,

$$\left\|\rho'_{C,x} - \rho_C\right\|_{tr} \leq negl(\lambda).$$

Note that the above requirement $\left\|\rho'_{C,x} - \rho_C\right\|_{\text{tr}} \leq \text{negl}(\lambda)$ would guarantee that an evaluator can evaluate the leased state on multiple inputs; on each input, the original leased state is only disturbed a little which means that the resulting state can be reused for evaluation on other inputs.

The following proposition states that any SSL scheme can be converted into one that is reusable.

Proposition 2. *Let* (Setup, Gen, Lessor, Run, Check) *be any SSL scheme (not necessarily satisfying the reusability condition). Then, there is a QPT algorithm* Run′ *such that* (Setup, Gen, Lessor, Run′, Check) *is a reusable SSL scheme.*

Proof. For any $C \in \mathcal{C}$ and for any $x \in \{0,1\}^n$, we have that $\mathsf{Run}(\mathsf{crs}, \rho_C, x)$ outputs $C(x)$ with probability $1 - \varepsilon$. By the Almost As Good As New Lemma (see full version), there is a way to implement Run such that it is possible to obtain $C(x)$, and then recover a state $\widetilde{\rho_C}$ satisfying $\|\widetilde{\rho_C} - \rho_C\|_{\text{tr}} \leq \sqrt{\varepsilon}$. We let Run′ be this operation.

Thus, it suffices to just focus on the correctness property when constructing a SSL scheme.

2.1 Security

Our notion intends to capture the different scenarios discussed in the introduction. In particular, we want to capture the security guarantee that given an authorized (valid) copy ρ_C, no pirate can output two authorized copies. We will assume that these valid copies contain a quantum state and a classical string. The Run algorithm expects valid copies to have this form; without loss of generality, the classical part can always be measured before executing Run.

Finite-Term Lessor Security. We require the following security guarantee: suppose a QPT adversary (pirate) receives a leased copy of C generated using Lessor; denote this by ρ_C. We require that the pirate cannot produce a bipartite state σ^* on registers R_1 and R_2, such that $\sigma_1^* := \text{Tr}_2[\sigma^*]$ passes the verification by Check, and the resulting *post-measurement* state on R_2, which we denote by $P_2(\sigma^*)$, still computes C by $\mathsf{Run}(P_2(\sigma^*), x) = C(x)$.

Before formally stating the definition, let us fix some notation. We will use the following notation for the state that the pirate keeps after the initial copy has been returned and verified. If the pirate outputs the bipartite state σ^*, then we will write

$$P_2(\mathsf{sk}, \sigma^*) \propto \mathrm{Tr}_1 \left[\Pi_1[\mathsf{Check}(\mathsf{sk}, \cdot)_1 \otimes I_2 (\sigma^*)]\right]$$

for the state that the pirate keeps *after* the first register has been returned and verified. Here, Π_1 denotes projecting the output of Check onto 1, and where $\mathsf{Check}(\mathsf{sk}, \cdot)_1 \otimes I_2(\sigma^*)$ denotes applying the Check QPT onto the first register, and the identity on the second register of σ^*. In other words, $P_2(\mathsf{sk}, \sigma^*)$ is used to denote the post-measurement state on R_2 conditioned on $\mathsf{Check}(\mathsf{sk}, \cdot)$ accepting on R_1.

Definition 4 (Finite-Term Perfect Lessor Security). *We say that a SSL scheme* (Setup, Gen, Lessor, Run, Check) *for a class of circuits* $\mathcal{C} = \{\mathcal{C}_\lambda\}_{\lambda \in \mathbb{N}}$ *is said to satisfy* $(\beta, \gamma, \mathcal{D}_{\mathcal{C}})$-**perfect finite-term lessor security**, *with respect to a distribution* $\mathcal{D}_{\mathcal{C}}$ *on* $\mathcal{C}$, *if for every QPT adversary* $\mathcal{A}$ *(pirate) that outputs a bipartite (possibly entangled) quantum state on two registers,* R_1 *and* R_2*, the following holds:*

$$\Pr\left[\begin{array}{c} \mathsf{Check}(\mathsf{sk},\sigma_1^*)=1 \\ \bigwedge \\ \forall x,\ \Pr[\mathsf{Run}(\mathsf{crs},P_2(\mathsf{sk},\sigma^*),x)=C(x)]\geq\beta \end{array} : \begin{array}{c} \mathsf{crs}\leftarrow\mathsf{Setup}(1^\lambda), \\ C\leftarrow\mathcal{D}_{\mathcal{C}}(\lambda), \\ \mathsf{sk}\leftarrow\mathsf{Gen}(\mathsf{crs}), \\ \rho_C\leftarrow\mathsf{Lessor}(\mathsf{sk},C), \\ \sigma^*\leftarrow\mathcal{A}(\mathsf{crs},\rho_C) \\ \sigma_1^*=Tr_2[\sigma^*] \end{array}\right] \leq \gamma$$

Remark 1. The reason why we use the word perfect here is because we require $\mathsf{Run}(P_2(\sigma^*), x) = C(x)$ to hold with probability at least β on *every* input x. Note that Run is not necessarily deterministic (for instance, it could perform measurements) and thus we allow it to output the incorrect value with some probability.

2.2 Infinite-Term Lessor Security

In the infinite-term lease case, we want the following security notion: given (σ_1^*, σ_2^*) generated by a pirate $\mathcal{A}(\rho_C)$, guarantees that if one copy satisfies the correctness,

$$\forall x \Pr[\mathsf{Run}(\mathsf{crs}, \sigma_1^*, x) = C(x)] \geq \beta$$

for some non-negligible β, then after successfully evaluating $C(x)$ using σ_1^* on any input x^*, it should be the case that the resulting state on the second register, which we will denote by $\mathcal{E}_{x^*}^{(2)}(\sigma^*)$, cannot also satisfy

$$\forall x \Pr[\mathsf{Run}(\mathsf{crs}, \mathcal{E}_{x^*}^{(2)}(\sigma^*), x) = C(x)] \geq \beta.$$

In other words, if one of the copies has already been succesful in computing C in Run, then there will be inputs in which the second copy cannot evaluate C with better than negligible probability.

This security notion would rule out the following scenario. Eve gets a copy of ρ_C and gives σ_1^* to Alice and σ_2^* to Bob. Alice now chooses an input x_A, and Bob an input x_B. It cannot be the case that for all inputs (x_A, x_B) they choose, they will compute $(C(x_A), C(x_B))$ with non-negligible probability.

Definition 5 (Infinite-term Perfect Lessor Security). *We say that a SSL scheme* (Setup, Gen, Lessor, Run, Check) *for a class of circuits* $\mathcal{C} = \{\mathcal{C}_\lambda\}_{\lambda \in \mathbb{N}}$ *is said to be* $(\gamma, \beta, \mathcal{D}_\mathcal{C})$*-**infinite-term perfect lessor secure**, with respect to a distribution* $\mathcal{D}_\mathcal{C}$*, if for every QPT adversary* $\mathcal{A}$ *(pirate) that outputs a bipartite (possibly entangled) quantum state on two registers,* R_1 *and* R_2*, the following holds:*

$$\Pr\left[\forall x, \begin{pmatrix} \Pr[(\mathsf{Run}(\mathsf{crs},x,\sigma_1^*)=C(x)]\geq\beta \\ \wedge \\ \forall x', \Pr\left[\mathsf{Run}(\mathsf{crs},x',\mathcal{E}_x^{(2)}(\sigma^*))=C(x')\right]\geq\beta \end{pmatrix} : \begin{array}{c} \mathsf{crs}\leftarrow\mathsf{Setup}(1^\lambda), \\ C\leftarrow\mathcal{D}_\mathcal{C}(\lambda), \\ \mathsf{sk}\leftarrow\mathsf{Gen}(\mathsf{crs}), \\ \rho_C\leftarrow\mathsf{Lessor}(\mathsf{sk},C), \\ \sigma^*\leftarrow\mathcal{A}(\mathsf{crs},\rho_C) \\ \sigma_1^*=Tr_2[\sigma^*] \end{array}\right] \leq \gamma.$$

Remark 2. Both finite and infinite-term security can be extended to the case where the pirate is given multiple copies, $\rho_C^{\otimes m}$, where ρ_C is the output of Lessor on C. In the finite-term case, we require the following: if a pirate outputs $m+1$ copies and moreover, the m initial copies are returned and succesfully checked, computing Run on the remaining copy (that the pirate did not return) will not be functionally equivalent to the circuit C. In the infinite-term case, the pirate cannot output $m+1$ copies where Run on each of the $m+1$ copies can be used to successfully compute C.

3 Impossibility of SSL

To prove the impossibility of SSL, we first construct *de-quantumizable* class of circuits.

3.1 De-Quantumizable Circuits: Definition

A de-quantumizable class of circuits $\mathcal{C}$ is a class of circuits for which there is a QPT algorithm that given any quantum circuit with the same functionality as $C \in \mathcal{C}$, it finds a (possibly different) classical circuit $C' \in \mathcal{C}$ with the same functionality as C. Of course if $\mathcal{C}$ is learnable, then it could be possible to just observe the input-output behavior of the quantum circuit to find such a C'. To make this notion meaningful, we additionally impose the requirement that $\mathcal{C}$ needs to be quantum unlearnable; given only oracle access to C, any quantum algorithm can find a circuit (possibly a quantum circuit and an auxiliary input state ρ) with the same functionality as C with only negligible probability.

Definition 6. *We say that a collection of QPT algorithms, $\{U_C, \rho_C\}_{C\in\mathcal{C}}$, computes $\mathcal{C}$ if for any $C \in \mathcal{C}$, with input length n and output length m, ρ_C is a* poly(n)*-qubits auxiliary state, and U_C a QPT algorithm satisfying that for all $x \in \{0,1\}^n$,*

$$\Pr[U_C(\rho_C, x) = C(x)] \geq 1 - negl(\lambda),$$

where the probability is over the measurement outcomes of U_C. We also refer to (U_C, ρ_C) as an efficient quantum implementation of C. A class of classical circuits $\mathcal{C}$, associated with a distribution $\mathcal{D}_\mathcal{C}$, is said to be de-quantumizable *if the following holds:*

- **Efficient de-quantumization***: There is a QPT algorithm $\mathcal{B}$ such that, for any $\{U_C, \rho_C\}_{C\in\mathcal{C}}$ that computes $\mathcal{C}$, the following holds:*

$$\Pr\left[\bigwedge_{\forall x\in\{0,1\}^n, C(x)=C'(x)}^{C'\in\mathcal{C}} \ : \ {}^{C\leftarrow\mathcal{D}_\mathcal{C}}_{C'(x)\leftarrow\mathcal{B}(U_C,\rho_C)}\right] \geq 1 - negl(\lambda)$$

- **ν-Quantum Unlearnability:** *For any QPT adversary $\mathcal{A}$, the following holds:*

$$\Pr\left[\forall x, \Pr[U^*(\rho^*, x) = C(x)] \geq \nu \ : \ {}^{C\leftarrow\mathcal{D}_\mathcal{C}}_{(U^*,\rho^*)\leftarrow\mathcal{A}^{C(\cdot)}(1^\lambda)}\right] \leq negl(\lambda)$$

Remark 3. By the Almost As Good As New Lemma (we present the lemma in the full version), we can assume that the QPT algorithm U_C also output a state $\rho'_{C,x}$ that is negligibly close in trace distance to ρ_C, i.e. for all $C \in \mathcal{C}$ and $x \in \{0,1\}^n$ it holds that

$$\Pr[U_C(\rho_C, x) = (\rho'_{C,x}, C(x))] \geq 1 - \text{negl}(\lambda)$$

and $\left\|\rho'_{C,x} - \rho_C\right\|_{\text{tr}} \leq \text{negl}(\lambda)$.

Remark 4. We emphasize that the efficient de-quantumization property requires that the circuit C' output by the adversary should be in the same circuit class $\mathcal{C}$.

Remark 5. We can relax the unlearnability condition in the above definition to instead have a distribution over the inputs and have the guarantee that the adversary has to output a circuit (U^*, ρ^*) such that it agrees with C only on inputs drawn from this distribution. Our impossibility result will also rule out this relaxed unlearnability condition; however, for simplicity of exposition, we consider the unlearnability condition stated in the above definition.

From the above definition, we can see why a de-quantumizable class $\mathcal{C}$ cannot be copy-protected, as there is a QPT $\mathcal{B}$ that takes any (U_C, ρ_C) efficiently computing C, and outputs a functionally equivalent *classical* circuit C', which can be copied. In the following theorem we will show that if every circuit $C \in \mathcal{C}$ have a unique representation in $\mathcal{C}$, then it is also not possible to have SSL for this circuit class. To see why we need an additional condition, lets consider a QPT pirate $\mathcal{A}$ that wants to break SSL given (Run, ρ_C) computing $C \in \mathcal{C}$. Then, $\mathcal{A}$ can run $\mathcal{B}$ to obtain a circuit $C' \in \mathcal{C}$, but in the proccess it could have destroyed ρ_C, hence it wouldn't be able to return the initial copy. If $\mathcal{B}$ takes as input (Run, ρ_C) and outputs a *fixed* C' with probability neglibly close to 1, then by the Almost As Good As New Lemma, it could uncompute and recover ρ_C. The definition of de-quantumizable class does not guarantee that $\mathcal{B}$ will output a fixed circuit C', unless each circuit in the family has a unique representation in $\mathcal{C}$. If each circuit has a unique representation, the pirate would obtain $C' = C$ with probability neglibly close to 1, and uncompute to recover ρ_C. At this point, the pirate can generate its own leasing keys sk', and run $\mathsf{Lessor}(\mathsf{sk}', C')$ to obtain a valid leased state $\rho'_{C'}$. The pirate was able to generate a new valid leased state for C, while preserving the initial copy ρ_C, which it can later return to the lessor.

Theorem 4. *Let $(\mathcal{C}, \mathcal{D}_\mathcal{C})$ be a de-quantumizable class of circuits in which every circuit in the support of $\mathcal{D}_\mathcal{C}$ has a unique representation in $\mathcal{C}$. Then there is no SSL scheme* $(\mathsf{Setup}, \mathsf{Gen}, \mathsf{Lessor}, \mathsf{Run}, \mathsf{Check})$ *(in CRS model) for $\mathcal{C}$ satisfying ε-correctness and $(\beta, \gamma, \mathcal{D}_\mathcal{C})$-perfect finite-term lessor security for any negligible γ, and any $\beta \leq (1 - \varepsilon)$.*

Proof. Consider the QPT algorithm $\mathcal{A}$ (pirate) that is given $\rho_C \leftarrow \mathsf{Lessor}(\mathsf{sk}, C)$ for some $C \leftarrow \mathcal{D}_\mathcal{C}$. The pirate will run $\mathcal{B}$, the QPT that de-quantumizes $(\mathcal{C}, \mathcal{D}_\mathcal{C})$, on input (Run, ρ_C) to obtain a functionally equivalent circuit $C' \in \mathcal{C}$. Because C has a unique representation in $\mathcal{C}$, we have $C' = C$. Since this succeeds with probability neglibly close to 1, by the Almost As Good As New Lemma, it can all be done in a way such that it is possible to obtain C and to recover a state $\widetilde{\rho_C}$ satisfying $\|\widetilde{\rho_C} - \rho_C\|_{\mathrm{tr}} \leq \mathrm{negl}(\lambda)$. At this point, the pirate generates its own key $\mathrm{sk}' \leftarrow \mathsf{Gen}(\mathsf{crs})$, and prepares $\rho'_C \leftarrow \mathsf{Lessor}(\mathsf{sk}', C)$. It outputs $\widetilde{\rho_C} \otimes \rho'_C$.

This means that ρ'_C is a valid leased state and by correctness of the SSL scheme,

$$\Pr\left[\forall x \in \{0,1\}^n,\ \mathsf{Run}(\mathsf{crs}, \rho'_C, x) = C(x)\ :\ \begin{array}{c}\mathsf{crs} \leftarrow \mathsf{Setup}(1^\lambda),\\ \mathsf{sk}' \leftarrow \mathsf{Gen}(\mathsf{crs}),\\ \rho'_C \leftarrow \mathsf{Lessor}(\mathsf{sk}', C)\end{array}\right] \geq 1 - \varepsilon$$

Furthermore, since $\|\widetilde{\rho_C} - \rho_C\|_{\mathrm{tr}} \leq \mathrm{negl}(\lambda)$, the probability that $\widetilde{\rho_C}$ passes the return check is neglibly close to 1. Putting these together, we have

$$\Pr\left[\begin{array}{c}\mathsf{Check}(\mathsf{sk}, \widetilde{\rho_C}) = 1\\ \wedge\\ \forall x,\ \Pr\left[\mathsf{Run}(\mathsf{crs}, \rho'_C, x) = C(x)\right] \geq 1 - \varepsilon\end{array}\ :\ \begin{array}{c}\mathsf{crs} \leftarrow \mathsf{Setup}(1^\lambda),\\ C \leftarrow \mathcal{D}_\mathcal{C}(\lambda),\\ \mathsf{sk} \leftarrow \mathsf{Gen}(\mathsf{crs}),\\ \rho_C \leftarrow \mathsf{Lessor}(\mathsf{sk}, C),\\ \widetilde{\rho_C} \otimes \rho'_C \leftarrow \mathcal{A}(\mathsf{crs}, \rho_C)\end{array}\right] \geq 1 - \mathrm{negl}(\lambda)$$

3.2 De-Quantumizable Circuit Class: Construction

All that remains in the proof of impossibility of SSL is the construction of a de-quantumizable circuits class $(\mathcal{C}, \mathcal{D}_\mathcal{C})$ in which every circuit in the support of $\mathcal{D}_\mathcal{C}$ has a unique representation in $\mathcal{C}$. We begin with an overview of the construction.

Constructing de-quantumizable Circuits: Challenges. The starting point is the seminal work of Barak et al. [12], who demonstrated a class of functions, where each function is associated with a secret key k, such that: (a) *Non-black-box secret extraction*: given non-black-box access to any classical circuit implementation of this function, the key can be efficiently recovered, (b) *Classical Unlearnability of secrets*: but given black-box access to this circuit, any classical adversary who can only make polynomially many queries to the oracle cannot recover the key.

While the result of Barak et al. has the ingredients suitable for us, it falls short in many respects:

- The proof of non-black-box secret extraction crucially relies upon the fact that we are only given a classical obfuscated circuit. In fact there are inherent difficulties that we face in adapting Barak et al. to the quantum setting; see [7].
- As is the case with many black-box extraction techniques, the proof of Barak et al. involves evaluating the obfuscated circuit multiple times in order to recover the secret. As is typically the case with quantum settings, evaluating the same circuit again and again is not always easy – the reason being that evaluating a circuit once could potentially destroy the state thus rendering it impossible to run it again.
- Barak et al. only guarantees extraction of secrets given black-box access to the classical circuit implementation of the function. However, our requirement is qualitatively different: given a quantum implementation of the classical circuit, we need to find a (possible different) classical circuit with the same functionality.
- Barak et al.'s unlearnability result only ruled out adversaries who make classical queries to the oracle. On the other hand, we need to argue unlearnability against QPT adversaries who can perform superposition queries to the oracle.

Nonetheless, we show that the techniques introduced in a simplified version of Barak[11] can be suitably adapted for our purpose by using two tools: quantum fully homomorphic encryption (QFHE) and lockable obfuscation. Combining QFHE and lockable obfuscation for the purpose of secret extraction has been recently used in a completely different context, that of building zero-knowledge protocols [9,16] (and in classical setting was first studied by [14]).

Construction. We present the construction of de-quantumizable circuits.

Theorem 5. *Assuming the quantum hardness of learning with errors (QLWE), and assuming that there is a* QFHE *that supports evaluation of arbitrary polynomial-sized quantum circuits, and has the following two properties: (a) ciphertexts have classical plaintexts have classical descriptions and, (b) classical ciphertexts can be decrypted using a classical circuit,*

there exists a de-quantumizable class of circuits $(\mathcal{C}, \mathcal{D}_{\mathcal{C}})$.

[11] See [15] for a description of this simplified version.

Proof. We define a de-quantumizable class of circuits $\mathcal{C} = \{\mathcal{C}_\lambda\}_{\lambda\in\mathbb{N}}$, where every circuit in $\mathcal{C}_\lambda$ is defined as follows:

$\underline{C_{a,b,r,\mathsf{pk},\mathcal{O}}(x)}$:

1. If $x = 0\cdots0$, output $\mathsf{QFHE.Enc}(\mathsf{pk}, a; r)\,|\mathcal{O}|\mathsf{pk}$.
2. Else if $x = a$, output b.
3. Otherwise, output $0\cdots0$

We will suitably pad with zeroes such that all the inputs (resp., outputs) are of the same length n (resp., of the same length m).

Let $\mathcal{D}_{\mathcal{C}}(\lambda)$ be the distribution that outputs a circuit from $\mathcal{C}_\lambda$ by sampling $a, b, r \xleftarrow{\$} \{0,1\}^\lambda$, then computing $(\mathsf{pk}, \mathsf{sk}) \leftarrow \mathsf{QFHE.Gen}(1^\lambda)$, and finally computing an obfuscation $\mathcal{O} \leftarrow \mathsf{LO.Obf}(\mathbf{C}[\mathsf{QFHE.Dec}(\mathsf{sk}, \cdot), b, (\mathsf{sk}|r)])$, where $\mathbf{C}$ is a compute-and-compare circuit.

We show that with respect to this distribution: (a) $\mathcal{C}$ is quantum unlearnable (Proposition 3) and, (b) $\mathcal{C}$ is efficiently de-quantumizable (Proposition 4).

Proposition 3. *For any non-negligible ν, the circuit class $\mathcal{C}$ is ν-quantum unlearnable with respect to $\mathcal{D}_{\mathcal{C}}$.*

We provide a proof of the above proposition in the full version.

Proposition 4. *$(\mathcal{C}, \mathcal{D}_{\mathcal{C}})$ is efficiently de-quantumizable.*

Proof. We will start with an overview of the proof.

Overview: Given a quantum circuit (U_C, ρ_C) that computes $C_{a,b,r,\mathsf{pk},\mathcal{O}}(\cdot)$, first compute on the input $x = 0\cdots0$ to obtain $\mathsf{QFHE.Enc}(\mathsf{pk}, a; r)|\mathcal{O}|\mathsf{pk}$. We then homomorphically evaluate the quantum circuit on $\mathsf{QFHE.Enc}(\mathsf{pk}, a; r)$ to obtain $\mathsf{QFHE.Enc}(\mathsf{pk}, b')$, where b' is the output of the quantum circuit on input a; this is part where we crucially use the fact that we are given (U_C, ρ_C) and not just black-box access to the functionality computing (U_C, ρ_C). But b' is nothing but b! Given QFHE encryption of b, we can then use the lockable obfuscation to recover sk; since the lockable obfuscation on input a valid encryption of b outputs sk. Using sk we can then recover the original circuit $C_{a,b,r,\mathsf{pk},\mathcal{O}}(\cdot)$. Formal details follow.

For any $C \in \mathcal{C}$, let (U_C, ρ_C) be any QPT algorithm (with auxiliary state ρ_C) satisfying that for all $x \in \{0,1\}^n$,

$$\mathsf{Pr}\left[U_C(\rho_C, x) = \left(\rho'_{C,x}, C(x)\right)\right] \geq 1 - \mathrm{negl}(\lambda),$$

where the probability is over the measurement outcomes of U_C, and $\rho'_{C,x}$ is neglibly close in trace distance to ρ_C (see Remark 3). We will show how to constuct a QPT $\mathcal{B}$ to de-quantumize $(\mathcal{C}, \mathcal{D}_{\mathcal{C}})$.

$\mathcal{B}$ will perform a QFHE evaluation, which we describe here. Given $\mathsf{QFHE.Enc}(\mathsf{pk}, x)$, we want to homomorphically evaluate $C(x)$ to obtain

$\mathsf{QFHE.Enc}(\mathsf{pk}, C(x))$. To do this, first prepare $\mathsf{QFHE.Enc}(\mathsf{pk}, \rho_C, x)$, then evaluate U_C homomorphically to obtain the following:

$$\mathsf{QFHE.Enc}(\mathsf{pk}, \rho'_{C,x}, C(x)) = \mathsf{QFHE.Enc}(\mathsf{pk}, \rho'_{C,x})|\mathsf{QFHE.Enc}(\mathsf{pk}, C(x))$$

Consider the following QPT algorithm $\mathcal{B}$ that is given (U_C, ρ_C) for any $C \in \mathcal{C}$. $\mathcal{B}(U_C, \rho_C)$:

1. Compute $(\rho', \mathsf{ct}_1|\mathcal{O}'|\mathsf{pk}') \leftarrow U_C(\rho_C, 0\cdots 0)$.
2. Compute $\sigma|\mathsf{ct}_2 \leftarrow \mathsf{QFHE.Eval}(U_C(\rho', \cdot), \mathsf{ct}_1)$
3. Compute $\mathsf{sk}'|r' \leftarrow \mathcal{O}(\mathsf{ct}_2)$
4. Compute $a' \leftarrow \mathsf{QFHE.Dec}(\mathsf{sk}', \mathsf{ct}_1)$, $b' \leftarrow \mathsf{QFHE.Dec}(\mathsf{sk}', \mathsf{ct}_2)$.
5. Output $C_{a',b',r',\mathsf{pk}',\mathcal{O}'}$.

We claim that with probability negligibly close to 1, $(a', b', r', \mathsf{pk}', \mathcal{O}') = (a, b, r, \mathsf{pk}, \mathcal{O})$ when $C := C_{a,b,r,\mathsf{pk},\mathcal{O}} \leftarrow \mathcal{D}_\mathcal{C}$. This would finish our proof.

Lets analyze the outputs of $\mathcal{B}$ step-by-step.

- After Step (1), with probability neglibibly close to 1, we have that $\mathsf{ct}_1 = \mathsf{QFHE.Enc}(\mathsf{pk}, a; r)$, $\mathsf{pk}' = \mathsf{pk}$, and $\mathcal{O}' = \mathcal{O} \leftarrow \mathsf{LO.Obf}(\mathbf{C}[\mathsf{QFHE.Dec}(\mathsf{sk}, \cdot), b, (\mathsf{sk}|r)])$. Furthermore, we have that ρ' is negligibly close in trace distance to ρ_C.
- Conditioned on Step (1) computing $C(0\cdots 0)$ correctly, we have that $\mathsf{QFHE.Eval}(U_C(\rho', .), \mathsf{ct}_1)$ computes correctly with probability negligibly close to 1. This is because $\|\rho' - \rho_C\|_{\mathrm{tr}} \leq \mathrm{negl}(\lambda)$, and by correctness of both QFHE and (U_C, ρ_C). Conditioned on $\mathsf{ct}_1 = \mathsf{QFHE.Enc}(\mathsf{pk}, a; r)$, when Step (2) evaluates correctly, we have $\mathsf{ct}_2 = \mathsf{QFHE.Enc}(\mathsf{pk}, C(a)) = \mathsf{QFHE.Enc}(\mathsf{pk}, b)$
- Conditioned on $\mathsf{ct}_2 = \mathsf{QFHE.Enc}(\mathsf{pk}, b)$, by correctness of lockable obfuscation, we have that $\mathcal{O}(\mathsf{ct}_2)$ outputs $\mathsf{sk}|r$. Furthermore, by correctness of QFHE, decryption is correct: $\mathsf{QFHE.Dec}(\mathsf{sk}, \mathsf{ct}_1)$ outputs a with probability neglibly close to 1, and $\mathsf{QFHE.Dec}(\mathsf{sk}, \mathsf{ct}_2)$ outputs b with probability neglibly close to 1.

With probability negligibly close to 1, we have shown that $(a', b', r', \mathsf{pk}', \mathcal{O}') = (a, b, r, \mathsf{pk}, \mathcal{O})$.

Note that it is also possible to recover ρ'' that is neglibly close in trace distance to ρ_C. This is because $\sigma = \mathsf{QFHE.Enc}(\mathsf{pk}, \rho'')$ for some ρ'' satisfying $\|\rho'' - \rho_C\|_{\mathrm{tr}}$. Once $\mathsf{sk}' = \mathsf{sk}$ has been recovered, it is possible to also decrypt σ and obtain ρ''. To summarize, we have shown a QPT $\mathcal{B}$ satisfying

$$\mathsf{Pr}[\mathcal{B}(U_C, \rho_C) = (\rho'', C) \ : \ C \leftarrow \mathcal{D}_\mathcal{C}] \geq 1 - \mathrm{negl}(\lambda)$$

where $\|\rho'' - \rho_C\|_{\mathrm{tr}} \leq \mathrm{negl}(\lambda)$.

Implications to Copy-Protection. We have constructed a class $\mathcal{C}$ and an associated distribution $\mathcal{D}_\mathcal{C}$ that is efficient de-quantumizable. In particular, this means that there is no copy-protection for $\mathcal{C}$. If for all inputs x, there is a QPT (U_C, ρ_C) to compute $U_C(\rho_C, x) = C(x)$ with probability $1 - \varepsilon$ for some negligible ε, then it is possible to find, with probability close to 1, a circuit C' that computes the same functionality as C. We also proved that $(\mathcal{C}, \mathcal{D}_\mathcal{C})$ is quantum unlearnable. We summarize the result in the following corollary,

Corollary 2. *There is $(\mathcal{C}, \mathcal{D}_\mathcal{C})$ that is quantum unlearnable, but $\mathcal{C}$ cannot be copy-protected against $\mathcal{D}_\mathcal{C}$. Specifically, for any $C \leftarrow \mathcal{D}_\mathcal{C}$ with input length n, and for any QPT algorithm (U_C, ρ_C) satisfying that for all $x \in \{0,1\}^n$,*

$$\mathsf{Pr}[U_C(\rho_C, x) = C(x)] \geq 1 - \varepsilon$$

for some negligible ε, there is a QPT algorithm (pirate) that outputs a circuit C', satisfying $C'(x) = C(x)$ for all $x \in \{0,1\}^n$, with probability negligibly close to 1.

Further Discussion. Notice that in our proof that $\mathcal{C}$ is efficient de-quantumizable, we just need to compute $U_C(\rho_C, x)$ at two different points $x_1 = 0 \cdots 0$ and $x_2 = a$, where the evaluation at x_2 is done homomorphically. This means that any scheme that lets a user evaluate a circuit C at least 2 times (for 2 possibly different inputs) with non-negligible probability cannot be copy-protected. Such a user would be able to find all the parameters of the circuit, $(a, b, r, \mathsf{pk}, \mathcal{O})$, succesfully with non-negligible probability, hence it can prepare as many copies of a functionally equivalent circuit C'.

In our proof, we make use of the fact that (U_C, ρ_C) evaluates correctly with probability close to 1. This is in order to ensure that the pirate can indeed evaluate at 2 points by uncomputing after it computes $C(0 \cdots 0)$. Since any copy-protection scheme can be amplified to have correctness neglibly close to 1 by providing multiple copies of the copy-protected states, our result also rules out copy-protection for non-negligible correctness parameter ε, as long as the correctness of (U_C, ρ_C) can be amplified to neglibily close to 1 by providing $\rho_C^{\otimes k}$ for some $k = \text{poly}(\lambda)$.

Impossibility of Quantum VBB with Single Uncloneable State. Our techniques also rule out the possibility of quantum VBB for classical circuits. In particular, this rules the possibility of quantum VBB for classical circuits with the obfucated circuit being a single uncloneable state, thus resolving an open problem by Alagic and Fefferman [7].

Proposition 5. *Assuming the quantum hardness of learning with errors and assuming that there is a QFHE satisfying the properties described in Theorem 5, there exists a circuit class $\mathcal{C}$ such that any quantum VBB for $\mathcal{C}$ is insecure.*

Proof. We construct a circuit class $\mathcal{C} = \{\mathcal{C}_\lambda\}_{\lambda \in \mathbb{N}}$, where every circuit in $\mathcal{C}_\lambda$ is of the form $C_{a,b,r,\mathsf{pk},\mathcal{O}}$ defined in the proof of Theorem 5.

Given any quantum VBB of $C_{a,b,r,\mathsf{pk},\mathcal{O}}$, there exists an adversary $\mathcal{A}$ that recovers b and outputs the first bit of b. The adversary $\mathcal{A}$ follows steps 1–4 of $\mathcal{B}$ defined in the proof of Proposition 4 and then outputs the first bit of b'. In the same proof, we showed that the probability that $b' = b$ is negligibly close to 1 and thus, the probability it outputs the first bit of b is negligibly close to 1.

On the other hand, any QPT simulator Sim with superposition access to $C_{a,b,r,\mathsf{pk},\mathcal{O}}$ can recover b with probability negligibly close to 1/2. To prove this, we rely upon the proof of Proposition 3 (see full version for details). Suppose T is the number of superposition queries made by Sim to $C_{a,b,r,\mathsf{pk},\mathcal{O}}$. Let $|\psi^0\rangle$ is the initial state of Sim and more generally, let $|\psi^t\rangle$ be the state of Sim after t queries, for $t \leq T$.

We define an alternate QPT simulator Sim' which predicts the first bit of b with probability negligibly close to Sim. Before we describe Sim', we give the necessary preliminary background. Define $|\phi^t\rangle = U_t U_{t-1} \cdots U_1 |\psi^0\rangle$. We proved the following claim.

Claim. $|\langle \phi^t | \psi^t \rangle| = 1 - \delta_t$ for every $t \in [T]$.

Sim' starts with the initial state $|\psi^0\rangle$. It then computes $|\phi^T\rangle$. If U is a unitary matrix Sim applies on $|\psi^T\rangle$ followed by a measurement of a register $\mathbf{D}$ then Sim' also performs U on $|\phi^T\rangle$ followed by a measurement of $\mathbf{D}$. By the above claim, it then follows that the probability that Sim' outputs 1 is negligibly close to the probability that Sim outputs 1. But the probability that Sim' predicts the first bit of b is 1/2. Thus, the probability that Sim predicts the first bit of b is negligibly close to 1/2.

4 Main Construction

In this section, we present the main construction of SSL satisfying infinite-term perfect lessor security. We first start by describing the class of circuits of interest.

4.1 Circuit Class of Interest: Evasive Circuits

The circuit class we consider in our construction of SSL is a subclass of evasive circuits. We recall the definition of evasive circuits below.

Evasive Circuits. Informally, a class of circuits is said to be evasive if a circuit drawn from a suitable distribution outputs 1 on a fixed point with negligible probability.

Definition 7 (Evasive Circuits). *A class of circuits $\mathcal{C} = \{\mathcal{C}_\lambda\}_{\lambda \in \mathbb{N}}$, associated with a distribution $\mathcal{D}_\mathcal{C}$, is said to be* **evasive** *if the following holds: for every $\lambda \in \mathbb{N}$, every $x \in \{0,1\}^{\mathrm{poly}(\lambda)}$,*

$$\Pr_{C \leftarrow \mathcal{D}_\mathcal{C}} [C(x) = 1] \leq negl(\lambda),$$

Compute-and-Compare Circuits. The subclass of circuits that we are interested in is called compute-and-compare circuits, denoted by $\mathcal{C}_{\mathsf{cnc}}$. A compute-and-compare circuit is of the following form: $\mathbf{C}[C, \alpha]$, where α is called a lock and C has output length $|\alpha|$, is defined as follows:

$$\mathbf{C}[C,\alpha](x) = \begin{cases} 1, & \text{if } C(x)=\alpha, \\ 0, & \text{otherwise} \end{cases}$$

Multi-bit Compute-and-Compare Circuits. We can correspondingly define the notion of multi-bit compute-and-compare circuits. A multi-bit compute-and-compare circuit is of the following form:

$$\mathbf{C}[C, \alpha, \mathsf{msg}](x) = \begin{cases} \mathsf{msg}, & \text{if } C(x)=\alpha, \\ 0, & \text{otherwise} \end{cases},$$

where msg is a binary string.

We consider two types of distributions as defined by [39].

Definition 8 (Distributions for Compute-and-Compare Circuits). *We consider the following distributions on* $\mathcal{C}_{\mathsf{cnc}}$*:*

- $\mathcal{D}_{\mathsf{unpred}}(\lambda)$*: For any* $(\mathbf{C}[C, \alpha])$ *along with* aux *sampled from this unpredictable distribution, it holds that* α *is computationally unpredictable given* (C, aux)*.*
- $\mathcal{D}_{\mathsf{pseud}}(\lambda)$*: For any* $\mathbf{C}[C, \alpha]$ *along with* aux *sampled from this distribution, it holds that* $\mathbf{H}_{\mathsf{HILL}}(\alpha | (C, \mathsf{aux})) \geq \lambda^{\varepsilon}$*, for some constant* $\epsilon > 0$*, where* $\mathbf{H}_{\mathsf{HILL}}(\cdot)$ *is the HILL entropy [33].*

Note that with respect to the above distributions, the compute-and-compare class of circuits $\mathcal{C}_{\mathsf{cnc}}$ is evasive.

Searchability. For our construction of SSL for $\mathcal{C}$, we crucially use the fact that given a circuit $C \in \mathcal{C}$, we can read off an input x from the description of C such that $C(x) = 1$. We formalize this by defining a search algorithm $\mathcal{S}$ that on input a circuit C outputs an accepting input for C. For many interesting class of functions, there do exist a corresponding efficiently implementable class of circuits associated with a search algorithm $\mathcal{S}$.

Definition 9 (Searchability). *A class of circuits* $\mathcal{C} = \{\mathcal{C}_\lambda\}_{\lambda \in \mathbb{N}}$ *is said to be* $\mathcal{S}$*-searchable, with respect to a PPT algorithm* $\mathcal{S}$*, if the following holds: on input* C*,* $\mathcal{S}(C)$ *outputs* x *such that* $C(x) = 1$*.*

Searchable Compute-and-Compare Circuits: Examples. As mentioned in the introduction, there are natural and interesting classes of searchable compute-and-compare circuits. For completeness, we state them again below with additional examples [39].

- Point circuits $C(\alpha, \cdot)$: the circuit $C(\alpha, \cdot)$ is a point circuit if it takes as input x and outputs $C(\alpha, x) = 1$ iff $x = \alpha$. If we define the class of point circuits suitably, we can find α directly from C_α; for instance, α can be the value assigned to the input wires of C.
- Conjunctions with wild cards $C(S, \alpha, \cdot)$: the circuit $C(S, \alpha, \cdot)$ is a conjunction with wild cards if it takes as input x and outputs $C(S, \alpha, x) = 1$ iff $y = \alpha$, where y is such that $y_i = x_i$ for all $i \in S$. Again, if we define this class of circuits suitably, we can find S and α directly from the description of $C(S, \alpha, \cdot)$. Once we find S and α, we can find the accepting input.

- Affine Tester: the circuit $C(\mathbf{A}, \alpha, \cdot)$ is an affine tester, with $\mathbf{A}, \mathbf{y}$ where $\mathbf{A}$ has a non-trivial kernel space, if it takes as input $\mathbf{x}$ and outputs $C(\mathbf{A}, \alpha, \mathbf{x}) = 1$ iff $\mathbf{A} \cdot \mathbf{x} = \alpha$. By reading off $\mathbf{A}$ and α and using Gaussian elimination we can find $\mathbf{x}$ such that $\mathbf{A} \cdot \mathbf{x} = \alpha$.
- Plaintext equality checker $C(\mathsf{sk}, \alpha, \cdot)$: the circuit $C(\mathsf{sk}, \alpha, \cdot)$, with hardwired values decryption key sk associated with a private key encryption scheme, message α, is a plaintext equality checker if it takes as input a ciphertext ct and outputs $C(\mathsf{sk}, \alpha, \mathsf{ct}) = 1$ iff the decryption of ct with respect to sk is α. By reading off α and sk, we can find a ciphertext such that ct is an encryption of α.

Remark 6. We note that both the candidate constructions of copy-protection for point functions by Aaronson [3] use the fact that the accepting point of the point function is known by whoever is generating the copy-protected circuit.

4.2 Ingredients

We describe the main ingredients used in our construction.

Let $\mathcal{C} = \{\mathcal{C}_\lambda\}$ be the class of $\mathcal{S}$-searchable circuits associated with SSL. We denote $s(\lambda) = \mathrm{poly}(\lambda)$ to be the maximum size of all circuits in $\mathcal{C}_\lambda$. And let $\mathcal{D}_\mathcal{C}$ be the distribution associated with $\mathcal{C}$. All the notions below are described in detail in the full version.

Q-Input-Hiding Obfuscators. The notion of q-input-hiding obfuscators states that given an obfuscated circuit, it should be infeasible for a QPT adversary to find an accepting input; that is, an input on which the circuit outputs 1. We denote the q-input-hiding obfuscator scheme to be $\mathsf{qIHO} = (\mathsf{qIHO.Obf}, \mathsf{qIHO.Eval})$ and the class of circuits associated with this scheme is $\mathcal{C}$.

Subspace Hiding Obfuscation. This notion allows for obfuscating a circuit, associated with subspace A, that checks if an input vector belongs to this subspace A or not. In terms of security, we require that the obfuscation of this circuit is indistinguishable from obfuscation of another circuit that tests membership of a larger random (and hidden) subspace containing A. We denote the scheme to be $\mathsf{shO} = (\mathsf{shO.Obf}, \mathsf{shO.Eval})$. The field associated with shO is $\mathbb{Z}_q$ and the dimensions will be clear in the construction.

Q-Simulation-Extractable Non-Interactive Zero-Knowledge (seNIZK) System. This notion is a strengthening of a non-interactive zero-knowledge (NIZK) system. It guarantees the following property: suppose a malicious adversary, after receiving a simulated NIZK proof, produces another proof. Then, there exists an extractor that can extract the underlying witness associated with this proof with probability negligibly close to the probability of acceptance of the proof. We denote the seNIZK proof system to be $\mathsf{qseNIZK} = (\mathsf{CRSGen}, \mathcal{P}, \mathcal{V})$ and we describe the NP relation associated with this system in the construction. We require this scheme to satisfy sub-exponential security. We refer to the full version for an appropriate instantiation.

4.3 Construction

We describe the scheme of SSL below. We encourage the reader to look at the overview of the construction presented in Sect. 1.2 before reading the formal details below.

- $\mathsf{Setup}(1^\lambda)$: Compute $\mathsf{crs} \leftarrow \mathsf{CRSGen}\left(1^{\lambda_1}\right)$, where $\lambda_1 = \lambda + n$ and n is the input length of the circuit. Output crs.

- $\mathsf{Gen}(\mathsf{crs})$: On input common reference string crs, choose a random $\frac{\lambda}{2}$-dimensional subspace $A \subset \mathbb{Z}_q^\lambda$. Set $\mathrm{sk} = A$.

- $\mathsf{Lessor}(\mathrm{sk} = A, C)$: On input secret key sk, circuit $C \in \mathcal{C}_\lambda$, with input length n,
  1. Prepare the state $|A\rangle = \frac{1}{\sqrt{q^{\lambda/2}}} \sum_{a \in A} |a\rangle$.
  2. Compute $\widetilde{C} \leftarrow \mathsf{qIHO.Obf}(C; r_o)$
  3. Compute $\widetilde{g} \leftarrow \mathsf{shO}(A; r_A)$.
  4. Compute $\widetilde{g_\perp} \leftarrow \mathsf{shO}(A^\perp; r_{A^\perp})$.
  5. Let $x = \mathcal{S}(C)$; that is, x is an accepting point of C.
  6. Let L be the NP language defined by the following NP relation.

$$\mathcal{R}_L := \left\{ \left(\left(\widetilde{g}, \widetilde{g_\perp}, \widetilde{C} \right),\ (A, r_o, r_A, r_{A^\perp}, C, x) \right) \middle| \begin{array}{c} \widetilde{g} = \mathsf{shO}(A; r_A) \\ \widetilde{g_\perp} = \mathsf{shO}(A^\perp; r_{A^\perp}) \\ \widetilde{C} = \mathsf{qIHO.Obf}(C; r_o), \\ C(x) = 1 \end{array} \right\}.$$

  Compute $\pi \leftarrow \mathcal{P}\left(\mathsf{crs}, \left(\widetilde{g}, \widetilde{g_\perp}, \widetilde{C}\right), (A, r_o, r_A, r_{A^\perp}, C, x)\right)$
  7. Output $\rho_C = |\Phi_C\rangle\langle\Phi_C| = \left(|A\rangle\langle A|, \widetilde{g}, \widetilde{g_\perp}, \widetilde{C}, \pi\right)$.

- $\mathsf{Run}(\mathsf{crs}, \rho_C, x)$:
  1. Parse ρ_C as $\left(\rho, \widetilde{g}, \widetilde{g_\perp}, \widetilde{C}, \pi\right)$. In particular, measure the last 4 registers. *Note: This lets us assume that the input to those registers is just classical, since anyone about to perform* Run *might as well measure those registers themselves.*
  2. We denote the operation $\mathsf{shO.Eval}(\widetilde{g}, |x\rangle|y\rangle) = |x\rangle|y \oplus \mathbb{1}_A(x)\rangle$ by $\widetilde{g}[|x\rangle|y\rangle]$, where $\mathbb{1}_A(x)$ is an indicator function that checks membership in A. Compute $\widetilde{g}[\rho \otimes |0\rangle\langle 0|]$ and measure the second register. Let a denote the outcome bit, and let ρ' be the post-measurement state.
  3. As above, we denote the operation $\mathsf{shO.Eval}(\widetilde{g_\perp}, |x\rangle|y\rangle) = |x\rangle|y \oplus \mathbb{1}_A(x)\rangle$ by $\widetilde{g_\perp}[|x\rangle|y\rangle]$. Compute $\widetilde{g_\perp}[\mathsf{FT}\rho'\mathsf{FT}^\dagger \otimes |0\rangle\langle 0|]$ and measure the second register. Let b denote the outcome bit. *Note: in Step 2 and 3,* Run *is projecting* ρ *onto* $|A\rangle\langle A|$ *if* $a = 1$ *and* $b = 1$.
  4. Afterwards, perform the Fourier Transform again on the first register of the post-measurement state, let ρ'' be the resulting state.
  5. Compute $c \leftarrow \mathcal{V}\left(\mathsf{crs}, \left(\widetilde{g}, \widetilde{g_\perp}, \widetilde{C}\right), \pi\right)$

6. If either $a = 0$ or $b = 0$ or $c = 0$, reject and output $\perp$.
7. Compute $y \leftarrow \mathsf{qIHO.Eval}\left(\widetilde{C}, x\right)$.
8. Output $\left(\rho'', \widetilde{g}, \widetilde{g_\perp}, \widetilde{C}, \pi\right)$ and y.

– $\mathsf{Check}(\mathsf{sk} = A, \rho_C)$:
  1. Parse ρ_C as $\left(\rho, \widetilde{g}, \widetilde{g_\perp}, \widetilde{C}, \pi\right)$.
  2. Perform the measurement $\{|A\rangle\langle A|, I - |A\rangle\langle A|\}$ on ρ. If the measurement outcome corresponds to $|A\rangle\langle A|$, output 1. Otherwise, output 0.

Lemma 1 (Overwhelming probability of perfect correctness). *The above scheme satisfies $\epsilon = negl(\lambda)$ correctness.*

Proof. We first argue that the correctness of Run holds. Since qIHO is perfectly correct, it suffices to show that Run will not output $\perp$. For this to happen, we need to show that $a, b, c = 1$. Since $\widetilde{g} = \mathsf{shO}(A)$, $\widetilde{g_\perp} = \mathsf{shO}(A^\perp)$, and the input state is $|A\rangle\langle A|$, then $a = 1$ and $b = 1$ with probability negligibly close to 1 by correctness of shO. If π is a correct proof, then by perfect correctness of $\mathsf{qseNIZK}$, we have that $\Pr[c = 1] = 1$.

To see that the correctness of Check also holds, note that the leased state is $\rho = |A\rangle\langle A|$, which will pass the check with probability 1.

Lemma 2. *Fix $\beta = \mu(\lambda)$, where $\mu(\lambda)$ is any non-negligible function. Assuming the security of $\mathsf{qIHO}, \mathsf{qseNIZK}$ and shO, the above scheme satisfies $(\beta, \gamma, \mathcal{D}_C)$-infinite-term perfect lessor security, where γ is a negligible function.*

The proof of the above lemma is presented in the full version.

Acknowledgements. We thank Alex Dalzell and Aram Harrow for helpful discussions. During this work, RL was funded by NSF grant CCF-1729369 MIT-CTP/5204.

A Related Work

Quantum Money and Quantum Lightning. Using quantum mechanics to achieve unforgeability has a history that predates quantum computing itself. Wiesner [40] informally introduced the notion of unforgeable quantum money – unclonable quantum states that can also be (either publicly or privately) verified to be valid states. A few constructions [3,4,27,29,34] achieved quantum money with various features and very recently, in a breakthrough work, Zhandry [41] shows how to construct publicly-verifiable quantum money from cryptographic assumptions.

Certifiable Deletion and Unclonable Encryption. Unclonability has also been studied in the context of encryption schemes. The work of Gottesman [31] studies the problem of quantum tamper detection. Alice can use a quantum state to send Bob an encryption of a classical message m with the guarantee that any eavsdropper could not have cloned the ciphertext. In a recent work, Broadbent and Lord [23] introduced the notion of unclonable encryption. Roughly speaking, an unclonable encryption allows Alice to give Bob and Charlie an encryption of a classical message m, in the form of a quantum state $\sigma(m)$, such that Bob and Charlie cannot 'split' the state among them.

In a follow-up work, Broadbent and Islam [22], construct a one-time use encryption scheme with certifiable deletion. An encryption scheme has certifiable deletion property, if there is an algorithm to check that a ciphertext was deleted.

Quantum Obfuscation. Our proof of the impossibility of SSL is inspired by the proof of Barak et al. [10] on the impossibility of VBB for arbitrary functions. Alagic and Fefferman [7] formalized the notion of program obfuscation via quantum tools, defining quantum virtual black-box obfuscation (qVBB) and quantum indistinguishability obfuscation (qiO), as the natural quantum analogues to the respective classical notions (VBB and iO). They also proved quantum analogues of some of the previous impossibility results from [10], as well as provided quantum cryptographic applications from qVBB and qiO.

Quantum One-Time Programs and One-Time Tokens. Another related primitive is quantum one-time programs. This primitive wasn shown to be impossible by [21]. This rules out the possibility of having a copy-protection scheme where a single copy of the software is consumed by the evaluation procedure. Despite the lack of quantum one-time programs, there are constructions of secure 'one-time' signature tokens in the oracle models [8,13]. A quantum token for signatures is a quantum state that would let anyone in possession of it to sign an arbitrary document, but only once. The token is destroyed in the signing process.

Recent Work on Copy-Protection. While finishing this manuscript, we became aware of very recent work on copy-protection. Aaronson et al. [5] constructed copy-protection for unlearnable functions relative to a classical oracle. Our work complements their results, since we show that obtaining copy-protection in the standard model (i.e., without oracles) is not possible.

References

1. How microsoft corporation makes most of its money. https://www.fool.com/investing/2017/06/29/how-microsoft-corporation-makes-most-of-its-money.aspx
2. Scott Aaronson. Shtetl-Optimized. Ask Me Anything: Apocalypse Edition. https://www.scottaaronson.com/blog/?p=4684#comment-1834174. Comment #283, Posted: 03–24-2020. Accessed 25 Mar 2020
3. Aaronson, S.: Quantum copy-protection and quantum money. In: 2009 24th Annual IEEE Conference on Computational Complexity, pp. 229–242. IEEE (2009)
4. Aaronson, S., Christiano, P.: Quantum money from hidden subspaces. In: Proceedings of the Forty-Fourth Annual ACM Symposium on Theory of Computing, pp. 41–60 (2012)
5. Aaronson, S., Liu, J., Zhang, R.: Quantum copy-protection from hidden subspaces. arXiv preprint arXiv:2004.09674 (2020)

6. Alagic, G., Brakerski, Z., Dulek, Y., Schaffner, C.: Impossibility of quantum virtual black-box obfuscation of classical circuits. arXiv preprint arXiv:2005.06432 (2020)
7. Alagic, G., Fefferman, B.: On quantum obfuscation. arXiv preprint arXiv:1602.01771 (2016)
8. Amos, R., Georgiou, M., Kiayias, A., Zhandry, M.: One-shot signatures and applications to hybrid quantum/classical authentication. Cryptology ePrint Archive, Report 2020/107 (2020)
9. Ananth, P., La Placa, R.L.: Secure quantum extraction protocols. Cryptology ePrint Archive, Report 2019/1323 (2019)
10. Barak, B.: How to go beyond the black-box simulation barrier. In: Proceedings 42nd IEEE Symposium on Foundations of Computer Science, pp. 106–115. IEEE (2001)
11. Barak, B., Bitansky, N., Canetti, R., Kalai, Y.T., Paneth, O., Sahai, A.: Obfuscation for evasive functions. In: Lindell, Yehuda (ed.) TCC 2014. LNCS, vol. 8349, pp. 26–51. Springer, Heidelberg (2014). https://doi.org/10.1007/978-3-642-54242-8_2
12. Barak, B., et al.: On the (Im)possibility of obfuscating programs. In: Kilian, Joe (ed.) CRYPTO 2001. LNCS, vol. 2139, pp. 1–18. Springer, Heidelberg (2001). https://doi.org/10.1007/3-540-44647-8_1
13. Ben-David, S., Sattath, O.: Quantum tokens for digital signatures. arXiv preprint arXiv:1609.09047 (2016)
14. Bitansky, N., Khurana, D., Paneth, O.: Weak zero-knowledge beyond the black-box barrier. In: Proceedings of the 51st Annual ACM SIGACT Symposium on Theory of Computing, pp. 1091–1102. ACM (2019)
15. Bitansky, N., Paneth, O.: On the impossibility of approximate obfuscation and applications to resettable cryptography. In: Proceedings of the Forty-Fifth Annual ACM Symposium on Theory of Computing, pp. 241–250 (2013)
16. Bitansky, N., Shmueli, O.: Post-quantum zero knowledge in constant rounds. In: STOC (2020)
17. Brakerski, Z.: Quantum FHE (Almost) as secure as classical. In: Shacham, H., Boldyreva, A. (eds.) CRYPTO 2018. LNCS, vol. 10993, pp. 67–95. Springer, Cham (2018). https://doi.org/10.1007/978-3-319-96878-0_3
18. Brakerski, Z., Döttling, N., Garg, S.: and Giulio Malavolta. Circular-secure lwe suffices, Factoring and pairings are not necessary for io (2020)
19. Brakerski, Z., Perlman, R.: Lattice-based fully dynamic multi-key FHE with short ciphertexts. In: Robshaw, M., Katz, J. (eds.) CRYPTO 2016. LNCS, vol. 9814, pp. 190–213. Springer, Heidelberg (2016). https://doi.org/10.1007/978-3-662-53018-4_8
20. Broadbent, A., Grilo, A.B.: Zero-knowledge for qma from locally simulatable proofs. arXiv preprint arXiv:1911.07782 (2019)
21. Broadbent, A., Gutoski, G., Stebila, D.: Quantum one-time programs. In: Canetti, R., Garay, J.A. (eds.) CRYPTO 2013. LNCS, vol. 8043, pp. 344–360. Springer, Heidelberg (2013). https://doi.org/10.1007/978-3-642-40084-1_20
22. Broadbent, A., Islam, R.: Quantum encryption with certified deletion. arXiv preprint arXiv:1910.03551 (2019)
23. Broadbent, A., Lord, S.: Uncloneable quantum encryption via random oracles. arXiv preprint arXiv:1903.00130 (2019)
24. Coladangelo, A.: Smart contracts meet quantum cryptography. arXiv preprint arXiv:1902.05214 (2019)
25. Coladangelo, A., Vidick, T., Zhang, T.: Non-interactive zero-knowledge arguments for qma, with preprocessing. arXiv preprint arXiv:1911.07546 (2019)

26. De Santis, A., Di Crescenzo, G., Ostrovsky, R., Persiano, G., Sahai, A.: Robust non-interactive zero knowledge. In: Kilian, J. (ed.) CRYPTO 2001. LNCS, vol. 2139, pp. 566–598. Springer, Heidelberg (2001). https://doi.org/10.1007/3-540-44647-8_33
27. Farhi, E., Gosset, D., Hassidim, A., Lutomirski, A., Shor, P.: Quantum money from knots. In: Proceedings of the 3rd Innovations in Theoretical Computer Science Conference, pp. 276–289 (2012)
28. Garg, S., Gentry, C., Halevi, S., Raykova, M., Sahai, A., Waters, B.: Candidate indistinguishability obfuscation and functional encryption for all circuits. In: FOCS (2013)
29. Gavinsky, D.: Quantum money with classical verification. In: 2012 IEEE 27th Conference on Computational Complexity, pp. 42–52. IEEE (2012)
30. Gay, R., Pass, R.: Indistinguishability obfuscation from circular security. Technical report, Cryptology ePrint Archive, Report 2020/1010 (2020)
31. Gottesman, D.: Uncloneable encryption. Quant. Inf. Comput. **3**(6), 581–602 (2003)
32. Goyal, R., Koppula, V., Waters, B.: Lockable obfuscation. In: FOCS (2017)
33. Håstad, J., Impagliazzo, R., Levin, L.A., Luby, M.: A pseudorandom generator from any one-way function. SIAM J. Comput. **28**(4), 1364–1396 (1999)
34. Lutomirski, A., et al.: Breaking and making quantum money: toward a new quantum cryptographic protocol. arXiv preprint arXiv:0912.3825 (2009)
35. Mahadev, U.: Classical homomorphic encryption for quantum circuits. In: 2018 IEEE 59th Annual Symposium on Foundations of Computer Science (FOCS), pp. 332–338. IEEE (2018)
36. Mahadev, U.: Classical verification of quantum computations. In: 2018 IEEE 59th Annual Symposium on Foundations of Computer Science (FOCS), pp. 259–267. IEEE (2018)
37. Sahai, A.: Non-malleable non-interactive zero knowledge and adaptive chosen-ciphertext security. In: 40th Annual Symposium on Foundations of Computer Science (Cat. No. 99CB37039), pp. 543–553. IEEE (1999)
38. Wee, H., Wichs, D.: Candidate obfuscation via oblivious LWE sampling (2020)
39. Wichs, D., Zirdelis, G.: Obfuscating compute-and-compare programs under LWE. In: 2017 IEEE 58th Annual Symposium on Foundations of Computer Science (FOCS), pp. 600–611. IEEE (2017)
40. Wiesner, S.: Conjugate coding. ACM Sigact News **15**(1), 78–88 (1983)
41. Zhandry, M.: Quantum lightning never strikes the same state twice. In: Ishai, Y., Rijmen, V. (eds.) EUROCRYPT 2019. LNCS, vol. 11478, pp. 408–438. Springer, Cham (2019). https://doi.org/10.1007/978-3-030-17659-4_14

Oblivious Transfer Is in MiniQCrypt

Alex B. Grilo[1(✉)], Huijia Lin[2(✉)], Fang Song[3(✉)], and Vinod Vaikuntanathan[4(✉)]

[1] CNRS, LIP6, Sorbonne Université, Paris, France
Alex.Bredariol-Grilo@lip6.fr
[2] University of Washington, Seattle, WA, USA
rachel@cs.washington.edu
[3] Portland State University, Portland, OR, USA
fsong@pdx.edu
[4] MIT, Cambridge, MA, USA
vinodv@csail.mit.edu

Abstract. MiniQCrypt is a world where quantum-secure one-way functions exist, and quantum communication is possible. We construct an oblivious transfer (OT) protocol in MiniQCrypt that achieves simulation-security in the plain model against malicious quantum polynomial-time adversaries, building on the foundational work of Crépeau and Kilian (FOCS 1988) and Bennett, Brassard, Crépeau and Skubiszewska (CRYPTO 1991). Combining the OT protocol with prior works, we obtain secure two-party and multi-party computation protocols also in MiniQCrypt. This is in contrast to the classical world, where it is widely believed that one-way functions alone do not give us OT.

In the common random string model, we achieve a *constant-round* universally composable (UC) OT protocol.

1 Introduction

Quantum computing and modern cryptography have enjoyed a highly productive relationship for many decades ever since the conception of both fields. On the one hand, (large-scale) quantum computers can be used to break many widely used cryptosystems based on the hardness of factoring and discrete logarithms, thanks to Shor's algorithm [60]. On the other hand, quantum information and computation have helped us realize cryptographic tasks that are otherwise impossible, for example quantum money [65] and generating certifiable randomness [13,17,63].

Yet another crown jewel in quantum cryptography is the discovery, by Bennett and Brassard [8], of a key exchange protocol whose security is unconditional. That is, they achieve information-theoretic security for a cryptographic task that classically necessarily has to rely on unproven computational assumptions. In a nutshell, they accomplish this using the uncloneability of quantum states, a bedrock principle of quantum mechanics. What's even more remarkable is the

A full version of this paper appears on ePrint Archive Report 2020/1500 [35].

A. Canteaut and F.-X. Standaert (Eds.): EUROCRYPT 2021, LNCS 12697, pp. 531–561, 2021.
https://doi.org/10.1007/978-3-030-77886-6_18

fact that their protocol makes minimalistic use of quantum resources, and consequently, has been implemented in practice over very large distances [23,45]. This should be seen in contrast to large scale quantum *computation* whose possibility is still being actively debated.

Bennett and Brassard's groundbreaking work raised a *tantalizing* possibility for the field of cryptography:

Could every *cryptographic primitive*
be realized unconditionally using quantum information?

A natural next target is oblivious transfer (OT), a versatile cryptographic primitive which, curiously, had its origins in Wiesner's work in the 1970s on quantum information [65] before being rediscovered in cryptography by Rabin [56] in the 1980s. Oblivious transfer (more specifically, 1-out-of-2 OT) is a two-party functionality where a receiver Bob wishes to obtain one out of two bits that the sender Alice owns. The OT protocol must ensure that Alice does not learn which of the two bits Bob received, and that Bob learns only one of Alice's bits and no information about the other. Oblivious transfer lies at the foundation of secure computation, allowing us to construct protocols for the secure multiparty computation (MPC) of any polynomial-time computable function [33,42,43].

Crépeau and Killian [19] and Bennett, Brassard, Crépeau and Skubiszewska [9] constructed an OT protocol given an *ideal* bit commitment protocol and quantum communication. In fact, the only quantum communication in their protocol consisted of Alice sending several so-called "BB84 states" to Bob. Unfortunately, *unconditionally secure* commitment [49,53] and *unconditionally secure* OT [16,48] were soon shown to be impossible even with quantum resources.

However, given that bit commitment can be constructed from one-way functions (OWF) [37,54], the hope remains that OT, and therefore a large swathe of cryptography, can be based on only *OWF* together with (practically feasible) quantum communication. Drawing our inspiration from Impagliazzo's five worlds in cryptography [39], we call such a world, where post-quantum secure one-way functions (pqOWF) exist and quantum computation and communication are possible, Mini**Q**Crypt. The question that motivates this paper is:

Do OT and MPC exist in MiniQCrypt?

Without the quantum power, this is widely believed to be impossible. That is, given only OWFs, there are no *black-box* constructions of OT or even key exchange protocols [40,57]. The fact that [8] overcome this barrier and construct a key exchange protocol with quantum communication (even without the help of OWFs) reinvigorates our hope to do the same for OT.

Aren't We Done Already? At this point, the reader may wonder why we do not have an affirmative answer to this question already, by combining the OT protocol of [9,19] based on bit commitments, with a construction of bit commitments from pqOWF [37,54]. Although this possibility was mentioned already in [9], where they note that "...computational complexity based quantum cryptography is interesting since it allows to build oblivious transfer around one-way functions.", attaining this goal remains elusive as we explain below.

First, proving the security of the [9,19] OT protocol (regardless of the assumptions) turns out to be a marathon. After early proofs against limited adversaries [52,66], it is relatively recently that we have a clear picture with formal proofs against arbitrary quantum polynomial-time adversaries [12,20,21,61]. Based on these results, we can summarize the state of the art as follows.

- *Using Ideal Commitments:* If we assume an *ideal* commitment protocol, formalized as universally composable (UC) commitment, then the quantum OT protocol can be proven secure in strong simulation-based models, in particular the quantum UC model that admits sequential composition or even concurrent composition in a network setting [12,20,30,61]. However, UC commitments, in contrast to vanilla computationally-hiding and statistically-binding commitments, are powerful objects that do not live in Minicrypt. In particular, UC commitments give us key exchange protocols and are therefore black-box separated from Minicrypt.[1]
- *Using Vanilla Commitments:* If in the [9,19] quantum OT protocol we use a *vanilla* statistically-binding and computationally hiding commitment scheme, which exists assuming a pqOWF, the existing proofs, for example [12], fall short in two respects.
  First, for a malicious receiver, the proof of [12] constructs only an *in*efficient simulator. Roughly speaking, this is because the OT receiver in [9,19] acts as a committer, and vanilla commitments are not extractable. Hence, we need an inefficient simulator to extract the committed value by brute force. Inefficient simulation makes it hard, if not impossible, to use the OT protocol to build other protocols (even if we are willing to let the resulting protocol have inefficient simulation). Our work will focus on achieving the standard ideal/real notion of security [32] with efficient simulators.
  Secondly, it is unclear how to construct a simulator (even ignoring efficiency) for a malicious sender. Roughly speaking, the issue is that simulation seems to require that the commitment scheme used in [9,19] be secure against selective opening attacks, which vanilla commitments do not guarantee [6].
- *Using Extractable Commitments:* It turns out that the first difficulty above can be addressed if we assume a commitment protocol that allows *efficient extraction* of the committed value – called extractable commitments. Constructing extractable commitments is surprisingly challenging in the quantum world because of the hardness of rewinding. Moreover, to plug into the quantum OT protocol, we need a strong version of extractable commitments from which the committed values can be extracted efficiently *without destroying or*

[1] The key exchange protocol between Alice and Bob works as follows. Bob, playing the simulator for a malicious sender in the UC commitment protocol, chooses a common reference string (CRS) with a trapdoor TD and sends the CRS to Alice. Alice, playing the sender in the commitment scheme, chooses a random K and runs the committer algorithm. Bob runs the straight-line simulator-extractor (guaranteed by UC simulation) using the TD to get K, thus ensuring that Alice and Bob have a common key. An eavesdropper Eve should not learn K since the above simulated execution is indistinguishable from an honest execution, where K is hidden.

even disturbing the quantum states of the malicious committer,[2] a property that is at odds with quantum unclonability and rules out several extraction techniques used for achieving arguments of knowledge such as in [62]. In particular, we are not aware of a construction of such extractable commitments without resorting to strong assumptions such as (unleveled) quantum FHE and LWE [2,10], which takes us out of minicrypt. Another standard way to construct extractable commitments is using public-key encryption in the CRS model, which unfortunately again takes us out of minicrypt.

To summarize, we would like to stress that before our work, the claims that quantum OT protocols can be constructed from pqOWFs [9,28] were rooted in misconceptions.

Why MiniQCrypt. Minicrypt is one of five Impagliazzo's worlds [39] where OWFs exist, but public-key encryption schemes do not. In Cryptomania, on the other hand, public-key encryption schemes do exist.

Minicrypt is robust *and* efficient. It is robust because there is an abundance of candidates for OWFs that draw from a variety of sources of hardness, and most do not fall to quantum attacks. Two examples are (OWFs that can be constructed from) the advanced encryption standard (AES) and the secure hash standard (SHA). They are "structureless" and hence typically do not have any subexponential attacks either. In contrast, cryptomania seems fragile and, to some skeptics, even endangered due to the abundance of subexponential and quantum attacks, except for a handful of candidates. It is efficient because the operations are combinatorial in nature and amenable to very fast implementations; and the key lengths are relatively small owing to OWFs against which the best known attacks are essentially brute-force key search. We refer the reader to a survey by Barak [3] for a deeper perspective.

Consequently, much research in (applied) cryptography has been devoted to minimizing the use of public-key primitives in advanced cryptographic protocols [5,41]. However, complete elimination seems hard. In the classical world, in the absence of quantum communication, we can construct pseudorandom generators and digital signatures in Minicrypt, but not key exchange, public-key encryption, oblivious transfer or secure computation protocols. With quantum *communication* becoming a reality not just academically [23,38,55] but also commercially [45], we have the ability to reap the benefits of robustness and efficiency that Minicrypt affords us, *and* construct powerful primitives such as oblivious transfer and secure computation that were so far out of reach.

Our Results. In this paper, we finally show that the longstanding (but previously unproved) claim is true.

Theorem 1.1 (Informal). *Oblivious transfer protocols in the plain model that are simulation-secure against malicious quantum polynomial-time adversaries*

---

[2] This is because when using extractable commitment in a bigger protocol, the proof needs to extract the committed value and continue the execution with the adversary.

exist assuming that post-quantum one-way functions exist and that quantum communication is possible.

Our main technical contribution consists of showing a construction of an extractable commitment scheme based solely on pqOWFs and using quantum communication. Our construction involves three ingredients. The first is vanilla post-quantum commitment schemes which exist assuming that pqOWFs exist [54]. The second is post-quantum zero-knowledge protocols which also exist assuming that pqOWFs exist [64]. The third and final ingredient is a special multiparty computation protocol called conditional disclosure of secrets (CDS) constructing which in turns requires OT. This might seem circular as this whole effort was to construct an OT protocol to begin with! Our key observation is that the CDS protocol is only required to have a mild type of security, namely *unbounded simulation*, which *can* be achieved with a slight variant of the [9,19] protocol. Numerous difficulties arise in our construction, and in particular proving consistency of a protocol execution involving quantum communication appears difficult: how do we even write down an statement (e.g., NP or QMA) that encodes consistency? Overcoming these difficulties constitutes the bulk of our technical work. We provide a more detailed discussion on the technical contribution of our work in Sect. 1.1.

We remark that understanding our protocol requires only limited knowledge of quantum computation. Thanks to the composition theorems for (stand-alone) simulation-secure quantum protocols [36], much of our protocol can be viewed as a *classical* protocol in the (unbounded simulation) OT-hybrid model. The only quantumness resides in the instantiation of the OT hybrid with [9,19].

We notice that just as in [8,9,19], the honest execution of our protocols does not need strong quantum computational power, since one only needs to create, send and measure "BB84" states, which can be performed with current quantum technology.[3] Most notably, creating the states does not involve creating or maintaining long-range correlations between qubits.

In turn, plugging our OT protocol into the protocols of [24,27,42,61] (and using the sequential composition theorem [36]) gives us secure two-party computation and multi-party computation (with a dishonest majority) protocols, even for quantum channels.

Theorem 1.2 (Informal). *Assuming that post-quantum one-way functions exist and quantum communication is possible, for every classical two-party and multi-party functionality $\mathcal{F}$, there is a quantum protocol in the plain model that is simulation-secure against malicious quantum polynomial-time adversaries. Under the same assumptions, there is a quantum two-party and multi-party protocol for any quantum circuit Q.*

Finally, we note that our OT protocol runs in $\mathsf{poly}(\lambda)$ number of rounds, where λ is a security parameter, and that is only because of the zero-knowledge

[3] A BB84 state is a single-qubit state that is chosen uniformly at random from $\{|0\rangle, |1\rangle, |+\rangle, |-\rangle\}$. Alternatively, it can be prepared by computing $H^h X^x |0\rangle$ where X is the bit-flip gate, H is the Hadamard gate, and $h, x \in \{0,1\}$ are random bits.

proof. Watrous' ZK proof system [64] involves repeating a classical ZK proof (such as that graph coloring ZK proof [34] or the Hamiltonicity proof [11]) *sequentially*. A recent work of Bitansky and Shmueli [10] for the first time constructs a *constant-round* quantum ZK protocol (using only classical resources) but they rely on a strong assumption, namely (unleveled) quantum FHE and quantum hardness of LWE, which does not live in minicrypt. Nevertheless, in the common random string (CRS) model, we can instantiate the zero-knowledge protocol using a WI protocol and a Pseudo-Random Generator (PRG) with additive λ bit stretch as follows: To prove a statement x, the prover proves using the WI protocol that either x is in the language or the common random string is in the image of the PRG. To simulate a proof, the simulator samples the CRS as a random image of the PRG, and proves using the WI protocol that it belongs to the image in a straight-line. Moreover, this modification allows us to achieve *straight-line simulators*, leading to *universally-composable* (UC) security [15]. Therefore, this modification would give us the following statement.

Theorem 1.3 (Informal). *Constant-round oblivious transfer protocols in the common random string (CRS) model that are UC-simulation-secure against malicious quantum poly-time adversaries exist assuming that post-quantum one-way functions exist and that quantum communication is possible.*

Plugging the above UC-simulation-secure OT into the protocol of [42] gives constant-round multi-party computation protocols for classical computation in the common random string model that are UC-simulation-secure against malicious quantum poly-time adversaries.

Going Below MiniQCrypt? We notice that all of the primitives that we implement in our work *cannot* be implemented unconditionally, even in the quantum setting [16,48,49,53]. Basing their construction on pqOWFs seems to be the next best thing, but it does leave with the intriguing question if they could be based on weaker assumptions. More concretely, assume a world with quantum communication as we do in this paper. Does the existence of quantum OT protocols imply the existence of pqOWFs? Or, does a weaker *quantum* notion of one-way functions suffice? We leave the exploration of other possible cryptographic worlds below MiniQCrypt to future work.

Other Related Work. Inspired by the quantum OT protocol [9,19], a family of primitives, named *k-bit cut-and-choose*, has been shown to be sufficient to realize OT statistically by quantum protocols [25,29] which is provably impossible by classical protocols alone [51]. These offer further examples demonstrating the power of quantum cryptographic protocols.

There has also been extensive effort on designing quantum protocols OT and the closely related primitive of *one-time-memories* under *physical* rather than *computational* assumptions, such as the bounded-storage model, noisy-storage model, and isolated-qubit model, which restrict the quantum memory or admissible operations of the adversary [21,22,44,46,47,58]. They provide important alternatives, but the composability of these protocols are not well understood.

Meanwhile, there is strengthening on the impossibility for quantum protocols to realize secure computation statistically from scratch [14,59].

We note that there exist classical protocols for two-party and multi-party computation that are quantum-secure assuming strong assumptions such as post-quantum dense encryption and superpolynomial quantum hardness of the learning-with-errors problem [1,36,50]. And prior to the result in [24], there is a long line of work on secure multi-party *quantum* computation (Cf. [7,18,26,27]).

We remark that the idea to use OT and ZK for obtaining extractable commitment was also used (at least implicitly) in [10,36,50].

Finally, we notice that [4] have independently and concurrently proposed a quantum protocol for extractable and equivocal commitments, which can be used in the protocol of [9,19] to achieve OT (and secure multi-party computation) in MiniQCrypt. In comparison, their extractable and equivocal commitment scheme is statistically hiding, which leads to one-sided statistical security in their OT protocols. Furthermore, their commitment and OT protocols make black-box use of the underlying one-way function. Our protocols do not have these properties. On the other hand, our commitment scheme is statistically binding, and we give constant-round UC-secure protocols in the *reusable* CRS model. We also believe that our notion of verifiable CDS is of independent interest.

1.1 Technical Overview

We give an overview of our construction of post-quantum OT protocol in the plain model from post-quantum one-way functions. In this overview, we assume some familiarity with post-quantum MPC in the stand-alone, sequential composition, and UC models, and basic functionalities such as $\mathcal{F}_{\texttt{ot}}$ and $\mathcal{F}_{\texttt{com}}$. We will also consider *parallel versions* of them, denoted as $\mathcal{F}_{\texttt{p-ot}}$ and $\mathcal{F}_{\texttt{so-com}}$. The parallel OT functionality $\mathcal{F}_{\texttt{p-ot}}$ enables the sender to send some polynomial number of pairs of strings $\{s_0^i, s_1^i\}_i$ and the receiver to choose one per pair to obtain $s_{c_i}^i$ in parallel. The commitment with selective opening functionality $\mathcal{F}_{\texttt{so-com}}$ enables a sender to commit to a string m while hiding it, and a receiver to request opening of a subset of bits at locations $T \subseteq [|m|]$ and obtain $m_T = (m_i)_{i \in T}$. We refer the reader to Sect. 2 for formal definitions of these functionalities.

BBCS OT in the $\mathcal{F}_{\texttt{so-com}}$-Hybrid Model. We start by describing the quantum OT protocol of [9] in the $\mathcal{F}_{\texttt{so-com}}$ hybrid model.

BBCS OT protocol: The sender ot.S has strings $s_0, s_1 \in \{0,1\}^\ell$, the receiver ot.R has a choice bit $c \in \{0,1\}$.

1. **Preamble.** ot.S sends $n \gg \ell$ BB94 qubits $|x^A\rangle_{\theta^A}$ prepared using random bits $x^A \in_R \{0,1\}^n$ and random basis $\theta^A \in_R \{+,\times\}^n$.
   ot.R measures these qubits in randomly chosen bases $\theta^B \in_R \{+,\times\}^n$ and commits to the measured bits together with the choice of the bases, that is $\{\theta_i^B, x_i^B\}_i$, using $\mathcal{F}_{\texttt{so-com}}$.
2. **Cut and Choose.** ot.S requests to open a random subset T of locations, of size say $n/2$, and gets $\{\theta_i^B, x_i^B\}_{i \in T}$ from $\mathcal{F}_{\texttt{so-com}}$.
   Importantly, it aborts if for any i $\theta_i^B = \theta_i^A$ but $x_i^B \neq x_i^A$. Roughly speaking, this is because it's an indication that the receiver has not reported honest measurement outcomes.

3. **Partition Index Set.** ot.S reveals $\theta^A_{\bar{T}}$ for the unchecked locations $\bar{T}$. ot.R partitions $\bar{T}$ into a subset of locations where it measured in the same bases as the sender $I_c := \{i \in \bar{T} : \theta^A_i = \theta^B_i\}$ and the rest $I_{1-c} := \bar{T} - I_c$, and sends (I_0, I_1) to the sender.
4. **Secret Transferring.** ot.S hides the two strings s_i for $i = 0, 1$ using randomness extracted from $x^A_{I_i}$ via a universal hash function f and sends $m_i := s_i \oplus f(x^A_{I_i})$, from which ot.R recovers $s := m_c \oplus f(x^B_{I_c})$.

Correctness follows from that for every $i \in I_c$, $\theta^A_i = \theta^B_i$ and $x^A_{I_c} = x^B_{I_c}$, hence the receiver decodes s_c correctly.

The security of the BBCS OT protocol relies crucially on two important properties of the $\mathcal{F}_{\texttt{so-com}}$ commitments, namely extractability and equivocability, which any protocol implementing the $\mathcal{F}_{\texttt{so-com}}$ functionality must satisfy.

Equivocability: To show the receiver's privacy, we need to efficiently simulate the execution with a malicious sender ot.S* without knowing the choice bit c and extract both sender's strings s_0, s_1. To do so, the simulator ot.SimS would like to measure at these unchecked locations $\bar{T}$ using exactly the same bases $\theta^A_{\bar{T}}$ as ot.S* sends in Step 3. In an honest execution, this is impossible as the receiver must commit to its bases θ^B and pass the checking step. However, in simulation, this can be done by invoking the equivocability of $\mathcal{F}_{\texttt{so-com}}$. In particular, ot.SimS can *simulate* the receiver's commitments in the preamble phase without committing to any value. When it is challenged to open locations at T, it measures qubits at T in random bases, and *equivocates* commitments at T to the measured outcomes and bases. Only after ot.S* reveals its bases $\theta^A_{\bar{T}}$ for the unchecked locations, does ot.SimS measure qubits at $\bar{T}$ in exactly these bases. This ensures that it learns both $x^A_{I_0}$ and $x^A_{I_1}$ and hence can recover both s_0 and s_1.

Extractability: To show the sender's privacy, we need to efficiently extract the choice bit c from a malicious receiver ot.R* and simulate the sender's messages using only s_c. To do so, the simulator ot.SimR needs to extract efficiently from the $\mathcal{F}_{\texttt{so-com}}$ commitments all the bases θ^B, so that, later given I_0, I_1 it can figure out which subset I_c contains more locations i where the bases match $\theta^B_i = \theta^A_i$, and use the index of that set as the extracted choice bit. Observe that it is important that extraction does not "disturb" the quantum state of ot.R* at all, so that ot.SimR can continue simulation with ot.R*. This is easily achieved using $\mathcal{F}_{\texttt{so-com}}$ as extraction is done in a straight-line fashion, but challenging to achieve in the plain model as rewinding a quantum adversary is tricky. Indeed, the argument of knowledge protocol of [62] can extract a witness but disturbs the state of the quantum adversary due to measurement. Such strong extractable commitment is only known in the plain model under stronger assumptions [2,10,36] or assuming public key encryption in the CRS model.

It turns out that equivocability *can* be achieved using zero-knowledge protocols, which gives a post-quantum OT protocol with an inefficient simulator ot.SimR against malicious receivers (and efficient ot.SimS). Our main technical contribution lies in achieving efficient extractability while assuming only post-quantum one-way functions. In particular, we will use the OT with unbounded simulation as a tool for this. We proceed to describing these steps in more detail.

Achieving Equivocability Using Zero-Knowledge. The idea is to let the committer commit $c = \texttt{com}(\mu; \rho)$ to a string $\mu \in \{0,1\}^n$ using any statistically binding computationally hiding commitment scheme com whose decommitment can be verified classically, for instance, Naor's commitment scheme [54] from post-quantum one-way functions. For now in this overview, think of com as non-interactive. (Jumping ahead, later we will also instantiate this commitment with a multi-round extractable commitment scheme that we construct.)

Any computationally hiding commitment can be simulated by simply committing to zero, $\widetilde{c} = \texttt{com}(0; \rho)$. The question is how to equivocate $\widetilde{c}$ to any string μ' later in the decommitment phase. With a post-quantum ZK protocol, instead of asking the committer to reveal its randomness ρ which would statistically bind $\widetilde{c}$ to the zero string, we can ask the committer to send μ' and give a zero-knowledge proof that $\widetilde{c}$ indeed commits to μ'. As such, the simulator can cheat and successfully open to any value μ' by simulating the zero-knowledge argument to the receiver.

Equivocable Commitment: The sender com.S has a string $\mu \in \{0,1\}^n$, the receiver com.R has a subset $T \subseteq [n]$.

1. **Commit Phase.** com.S commits to μ using a statistically binding commitment scheme com using randomness ρ. Let c be the produced commitment. NOTE: *Simulation against malicious receivers commits to* 0^n. *Simulation against malicious senders is inefficient to extract* μ *by brute force.*
2. **Decommit Phase.** Upon com.R requesting to open a subset T of locations, com.S sends μ' and gives a single zero knowledge argument that c commits to μ such that $\mu' = \mu_T$. NOTE: *To equivocate to* $\mu' \neq \mu_T$*, the simulator sends* μ' *and simulates the zero-knowledge argument (of the false statement).*

The above commitment protocol implements $\mathcal{F}_{\texttt{so-com}}$ with efficient simulation against malicious receivers, but inefficient simulation against malicious senders. Plugging it into BBCS OT protocol, we obtain the following corollary:

Corollary 1.1 (Informal). *Assume post-quantum one-way functions. In the plain model, there is:*

- *a protocol that securely implements the OT functionality* $\mathcal{F}_{\texttt{ot}}$*, and*
- *a protocol that securely implements the parallel OT functionality* $\mathcal{F}_{\texttt{p-ot}}$*,*

in the sequential composition setting, and with efficient simulation against malicious senders but inefficient simulation against malicious receivers.

The second bullet requires some additional steps, as parallel composition does not automatically apply in the stand-alone (as opposed to UC) setting (e.g., the ZK protocol of [64] is not simulatable in parallel due to rewinding). Instead, we first observe that the BBCS OT UC-implements $\mathcal{F}_{\texttt{ot}}$ in the $\mathcal{F}_{\texttt{so-com}}$ hybrid model, and hence parallel invocation of BBCS OT UC-implements $\mathcal{F}_{\texttt{p-ot}}$ in the $\mathcal{F}_{\texttt{so-com}}$ hybrid model. Note that parallel invocation of BBCS OT invokes $\mathcal{F}_{\texttt{so-com}}$ in parallel, which in fact can be merged into a single invocation to $\mathcal{F}_{\texttt{so-com}}$. Therefore, plugging in the above commitment protocol gives an OT protocol that implements $\mathcal{F}_{\text{p-ot}}$. In particular, digging deeper into the protocol, this ensures that we are invoking a *single* ZK protocol for all the parallel copies of the parallel OT, binding the executions together.

Achieving Extractability Using OT with Unbounded Simulation. Interestingly, we show that OT with (even 2-sided) unbounded simulation plus zero-knowledge is sufficient for constructing extractable commitments, which when combined with zero-knowlege again as above gives an implementation of $\mathcal{F}_{\texttt{so-com}}$ in the sequential composition setting in the plain model.

The initial idea is to convert the power of simulation into the power of extraction via two-party computation, and sketched below.

Initial Idea for Extractable Commitment: The sender com.S has $\mu \in \{0,1\}^n$.

1. **Trapdoor setup:** The receiver com.R sends a commitment c of a statistically binding commitment scheme $\texttt{com}$, and gives a zero-knowledge proof that c commits to 0.
2. **Conditional Disclosure of Secret (CDS):** com.S and com.R run a two-party computation protocol implementing the CDS functionality $\mathcal{F}_{\mathsf{cds}}$ for the language $\mathcal{L}_{\mathsf{com}} = \{(c', b') : \exists r' \text{ s.t. } c' = \texttt{com}(b'; r')\}$, where the CDS functionality $\mathcal{F}_{\mathsf{cds}}$ for $\mathcal{L}_{\mathsf{com}}$ is defined as below:

   $\mathcal{F}_{\mathsf{cds}}$: Sender input (x, μ), Receiver input w

   $$\text{Sender has no output, Receiver outputs } x \text{ and } \mu' = \begin{cases} \mu & \text{if } \mathcal{R}_{\mathcal{L}_{\mathsf{com}}}(x, w) = 1 \\ \bot & \text{otherwise} \end{cases}$$

   com.S acts as the CDS sender using input $(x = (c, 1), \mu)$ while com.R acts as the CDS receiver using witness $w = 0$.

It may seem paradoxical that we try to implement commitments using the much more powerful tool of two-party computation. The *key observation* is that the hiding and extractability of the above commitment protocol only relies on the *input-indistinguishability property* of the CDS protocol, which is *implied by unbounded simulation.*

- *Hiding:* A commitment to μ can be simulated by simply commiting to 0^n honestly, that is, using $(x = (c, 1), 0^n)$ as the input to the CDS. The simulation is indistinguishable as the soundness of ZK argument guarantees that c must be a commitment to 0 and hence the CDS statement $(c, 1)$ is false and should always produce $\mu' = \bot$. Therefore, the unbounded-simulation security of the CDS protocol implies that it is indistinguishable to switch the sender's input from μ to 0^n.
- *Extraction:* To efficiently extract from a malicious sender com.S*, the idea (which however suffers from a problem described below) is to let the simulator-extractor com.SimS set up a trapdoor by committing to 1 (instead of 0) and simulate the ZK argument; it can then use the decommitment (call it r) to 1 as a valid witness to obtain the committed value from the output of the CDS protocol. Here, the unbounded-simulation security of CDS again implies that

interaction with an honest receiver who uses $w = 0$ is indistinguishable from that with com.SimS who uses $w = r$ as com.S* receives no output via CDS.

The advantage of CDS with unbounded simulation is that it can be implemented using OT with unbounded simulation: Following the work of [42,43,61], post-quantum MPC protocols exist in the $\mathcal{F}_{\mathsf{ot}}$-hybrid model, and instantiating them with the unbounded-simulation OT yields unbounded simulation MPC and therefore CDS.

NP-VERIFIABILITY AND THE LACK OF IT. Unfortunately, the above attempt has several problems: how do we show that the commitment is binding? how to decommit? and how to guarantee that the extracted value agrees with the value that can be decommitted to? We can achieve binding by having the sender additionally commit to μ using a statistically binding commitment scheme com, and send the corresponding decommitment in the decommitment phase. However, to guarantee that the extractor would extract the same string μ from CDS, we need a way to verify that the same μ is indeed used by the CDS sender. Towards this, we formalize a verifiability property of a CDS protocol:

A CDS protocol is verifiable if

- The honest CDS sender cds.S additionally outputs (x, μ) and a "proof" π (on a special output tape) at the end of the execution.
- There is an efficient *classical* verification algorithm $\mathsf{Ver}(\tau, x, \mu, \pi)$ that verifies the proof, w.r.t. the transcript τ of the *classical* messages exchanged in the CDS protocol.
- *Binding:* No malicious sender cds.S* after interacting with an honest receiver cds.R(w) can output (x, μ, π), such that the following holds simultaneously: (a) $\mathsf{Ver}(\tau, x, \mu, \pi) = 1$, (b) cds.R did not abort, and (c) cds.R outputs μ' inconsistent with the inputs (x, μ) and w, that is, $\mu' \neq \begin{cases} \mu & \text{if } \mathcal{R}_{\mathcal{L}}(x, w) = 1 \\ \bot & \text{otherwise} \end{cases}$

We observe first that classical protocols with perfect correctness have verifiability for free: The proof π is simply the sender's random coins r, and the verification checks if the honest sender algorithm with input (x, μ) and random coins r produces the same messages as in the transcript τ. If so, perfect correctness guarantees that the output of the receiver must be consistent with x, μ. However, verifiability cannot be taken for granted in the $\mathcal{F}_{\mathsf{ot}}$ hybrid model or in the quantum setting. In the $\mathcal{F}_{\mathsf{ot}}$ hybrid model, it is difficult to write down an NP-statement that captures consistency as the OT input is *not* contained in the protocol transcript and is unconstrained by it. In the quantum setting, protocols use quantum communication, and consistency cannot be expressed as an NP-statement. Take the BBCS protocol as an example, the OT receiver receives from the sender ℓ qubits and measures them locally; there is no way to "verify" this step in NP.

Implementing Verifiable CDS. To overcome the above challenge, we implement a verifiable CDS protocol in the $\mathcal{F}_{\mathsf{p\text{-}ot}}$ hybrid model assuming only post-quantum one-way functions. We develop this protocol in a few steps below.

Let's start by understanding why the standard two-party comptuation protocol is not verifiable. The protocol proceeds as follows: First, the sender cds.S locally garbles a circuit computing the following function into $\widehat{G}$ with labels $\{\ell_b^j\}_{j\in[m],b\in\{0,1\}}$ where $m = |w|$:

$$G_{x,\mu}(w) = \mu' = \begin{cases} \mu & \text{if } \mathcal{R}_{\mathcal{L}}(x,w) = 1 \\ \bot & \text{otherwise} \end{cases} \tag{1}$$

Second, cds.S sends the pairs of labels $\{\ell_0^j, \ell_1^j\}_j$ via $\mathcal{F}_{\texttt{p-ot}}$. The receiver cds.R on the other hand chooses $\{w_j\}_j$ to obtain $\{\widetilde{\ell_{w_j}^j}\}_j$, and evaluates $\widehat{G}$ with these labels to obtain μ'. This protocol is not NP-verifiable because consistency between the labels of the garbled circuit and the sender's inputs to $\mathcal{F}_{\texttt{p-ot}}$ cannot be expressed as a NP statement.

To fix the problem, we devise a way for the receiver to verify the OT sender's strings. Let cds.S additionally commit to all the labels $\{c_b^j = \texttt{com}(\ell_b^j; r_b^j)\}_{j,b}$ and the message $c = \texttt{com}(\mu; r)$ and prove in ZK that $\widehat{G}$ is consistent with the labels and message committed in the commitments, as well as the statement x. Moreover, the sender sends both the labels and decommitments $\{(\ell_0^j, r_0^j), (\ell_1^j, r_1^j)\}_j$ via $\mathcal{F}_{\texttt{p-ot}}$. The receiver after receiving $\{\widetilde{\ell_{w_j}^j}, \widetilde{r_{w_j}^j}\}_j$ can now verify their correctness by verifying the decommitment w.r.t. $c_{w_j}^j$, and aborts if verification fails. This gives the following new protocol:

A Verifiable but Insecure CDS Protocol: The sender cds.S has (x, μ) and the receiver cds.R has w.

1. **Sender's Local Preparation:** cds.S generate a garbled circuits $\widehat{G}$ for the circuit computing $G_{x,\mu}$ (Equation (1)), with labels $\{\ell_b^{i,j}\}_{j,b}$. Moreover, it generates commitments $c = \texttt{com}(\mu, r)$ and $c_b^j = \texttt{com}(\ell_b^j; r_b^j)$ for every j, b.
2. **OT:** cds.S and cds.R invoke $\mathcal{F}_{\texttt{p-ot}}$. For every j, the sender sends $(\ell_0^j, r_0^j), (\ell_1^j, r_1^j)$, and the receiver chooses w_j and obtains $(\widetilde{\ell_{w_j}^j}, \widetilde{r_{w_j}^j})$.
3. **Send Garbled Circuit and Commitments:** cds.S sends $\widehat{G}$, c, and $\{c_b^j\}_{j,b}$ and proves via a ZK protocol that they are all generated consistently w.r.t. each other and x.
4. **Receiver's Checks:** cds.R aborts if ZK is not accepting, or if for some j, $c_{w_j}^j \neq \texttt{com}(\widetilde{\ell_{w_j}^j}, \widetilde{r_{w_j}^j})$. Otherwise, it evaluates $\widehat{G}$ with the labels and obtain $\mu' = G_{x,\mu}(w)$.

We argue that this protocol is NP-verifiable. The sender's proof is simply the decommitment r of c, and $\mathsf{Ver}(\tau, (x, \mu), r) = 1$ iff r is a valid decommitment to μ of the commitment c contained in the transcript τ. To show the binding property, consider an interaction between a cheating sender cds.S* and cds.R(w). Suppose cds.R does not abort, it means that 1) the ZK argument is accepting and hence $\widehat{G}$ must be consistent with $x, \{c_b^j\}, c$, and 2) the receiver obtains the labels committed in $c_{w_j}^j$'s. Therefore, evaluating the garbled circuit with these labels must produce $\mu' = G_{x,\mu}(w)$ for the μ committed to in c.

Unfortunately, the checks that the receiver performs render the protocol insecure. A malicious sender com.S* can launch the so-called selective abort attack to learn information of w. For instance, to test if $w_1 = 0$ or not, it replaces ℓ_0^1 with zeros. If $w_1 = 0$ the honest receiver would abort; otherwise, it proceeds normally.

THE FINAL PROTOCOL. To circumvent the selective abort attack, we need a way to check the validity of sender's strings that is independent of w. Our idea is to use a variant of cut-and-choose. Let cds.S create 2λ copies of garbled circuits and commitments to their labels, $\{\widehat{G}^i\}_{i\in[2\lambda]}$ and $\{c_b^{i,j} = \mathtt{com}(\ell_b^{i,j}; r_b^{i,j})\}_{i,j,b}$ and prove via a ZK protocol that they are all correctly generated w.r.t. the same c and x. Again, cds.S sends the labels and decommitment via $\mathcal{F}_{\mathsf{p\text{-}ot}}$, but cds.R does not choose w universally in all copies. Instead, it secretly samples a random subset $\Lambda \in [2\lambda]$ by including each i with probability $1/2$; for copy $i \in \Lambda$, it chooses random string $s^i \leftarrow \{0,1\}^m$ and obtains $\{\widetilde{\ell}^{i,j}_{s^i_j}, \widetilde{r}^{i,j}_{s^i_j}\}_j$, whereas for copy $i \notin \Lambda$, it choose w and obtains $\{\widetilde{\ell}^{i,j}_{w_j}, \widetilde{r}^{i,j}_{w_j}\}_j$. Now, in the checking step, cds.R only verifies the validity of $\{\widetilde{\ell}^{i,j}_{s^i_j}, \widetilde{r}^{i,j}_{s^i_j}\}_{i\in\Lambda,j}$ received in copies in Λ. Since the check is now completely independent of w, it circumvents the selective abort attack.

Furthermore, NP-verifiability still holds. The key point is that if the decommitments cds.R receives in copies in Λ are all valid, with overwhelming probability, the number of *bad copies* where the OT sender's strings are not completely valid is bounded by $\lambda/4$. Hence, there must exist a copy $i \notin \Lambda$ where cds.R receives the right labels $\ell^{i,j}_{w_j}$ committed to in $c^{i,j}_{w_j}$. cds.R can then evaluate $\widehat{G}^i$ to obtain μ'. By the same argument as above, μ' must be consistent with the (x, μ) and w, for μ committed in c, and NP-verifiability follows. The final protocol is described in Fig. 3.

Organization of the Paper. We review the quantum stand-alone security model introduced by [36] in Sect. 2. In section Sect. 3, we construct a quantum parallel-OT protocol with one-sided, unbounded simulation. In more detail, we review in Sect. 3.1 the quantum OT protocol from [9] based on ideal commitments with selective opening security. Then in Sect. 3.2, we show how to boost it to construct a *parallel* OT protocol from the same assumptions. And finally, we provide a classical implementation of the commitment scheme with selective opening security in Sect. 3.3 which gives us ideal/real security except with unbounded receiver simulation. This result will be fed into our main technical contribution in Sect. 4 where we show how to construct extractable commitments from unbounded-simulation parallel-OT. In Sect. 4.2, we show how to construct (the intermediate primitive of) CDS from parallel-OT and one-way functions, and then in Sect. 4.3 we construct extractable commitments from CDS. Finally, in Sect. 5 we lift our results to achieve quantum protocols for multi-party (quantum) computation from one-way functions.

2 Quantum Stand-Alone Security Model

We adopt the quantum stand-alone security model from the work of Hallgren, Smith and Song [36], tailored to the two-party setting.

Let $\mathcal{F}$ denote a *functionality*, which is a classical interactive machine specifying the instructions to realize a cryptographic task. A two-party protocol Π consists of a pair of quantum interactive machines (A, B). We call a protocol *efficient* if A and B are both quantum poly-time machines. If we want to emphasize that a protocol is classical, i.e., all computation and all messages exchanged are classical, we then use lower-case letters (e.g., π). Finally, an adversary $\mathcal{A}$ is another quantum interactive machine that intends to attack a protocol.

When a protocol $\Pi = (A, B)$ is executed under the presence of an adversary $\mathcal{A}$, the state registers are initialized by a security parameter 1^λ and a joint quantum state σ_λ. Adversary $\mathcal{A}$ gets activated first, and may either **deliver** a message, i.e., instructing some party to read the proper segment of the network register, or **corrupt** a party. We assume all registers are authenticated so that $\mathcal{A}$ cannot modify them, but otherwise $\mathcal{A}$ can schedule the messages to be delivered in any arbitrary way. If $\mathcal{A}$ corrupts a party, the party passes all of its internal state to $\mathcal{A}$ and follows the instructions of $\mathcal{A}$. Any other party, once receiving a message from $\mathcal{A}$, gets activated and runs its machine. At the end of one round, some message is generated on the network register. Adversary $\mathcal{A}$ is activated again and controls message delivery. At some round, the party generates some output and terminates.

We view Π and $\mathcal{A}$ as a whole and model the composed system as another QIM, call it $M_{\Pi,\mathcal{A}}$. Then executing Π in the presence of $\mathcal{A}$ is just running $M_{\Pi,\mathcal{A}}$ on some input state, which may be entangled with a reference system available to a distighuisher.

Protocol emulation and secure realization of a functionality. A secure protocol is supposed to "emulate" an idealized protocol. Consider two protocols Π and Γ, and let $M_{\Pi,\mathcal{A}}$ be the composed machine of Π and an adversary $\mathcal{A}$, and $M_{\Gamma,\mathcal{S}}$ be that of Γ and another adversary $\mathcal{S}$. Informally, Π emulates Γ if the two machines $M_{\Pi,\mathcal{A}}$ and $M_{\Gamma,\mathcal{S}}$ are indistinguishable.

It is of particular interest to emulate an *ideal-world* protocol $\widetilde{\Pi}_{\mathcal{F}}$ for a functionality $\mathcal{F}$ which captures the security properties we desire. In this protocol, two (dummy) parties $\widetilde{A}$ and $\widetilde{B}$ have access to an additional "trusted" party that implements $\mathcal{F}$. We abuse notation and call the trusted party $\mathcal{F}$ too. Basically $\widetilde{A}$ and $\widetilde{B}$ invoke $\mathcal{F}$ with their inputs, and then $\mathcal{F}$ runs on the inputs and sends the respective outputs back to $\widetilde{A}$ and $\widetilde{B}$. An execution of $\widetilde{\Pi}$ with an adversary $\mathcal{S}$ is as before, except that $\mathcal{F}$ cannot be corrupted. We denote the composed machine of $\mathcal{F}$ and $\widetilde{\Pi}_{\mathcal{F}}$ as $M_{\mathcal{F},\mathcal{S}}$.

Definition 2.1 (Computationally Quantum-Stand-Alone Emulation). *Let Π and Γ be two poly-time protocols. We say Π* computationally quantum-stand-alone *(*`C-QSA`*) emulates Γ, if for any poly-time QIM $\mathcal{A}$ there exists a poly-time QIM $\mathcal{S}$ such that $M_{\Pi,\mathcal{A}} \approx_{qc} M_{\Gamma,\mathcal{S}}$.*

Definition 2.2 (`C-QSA`** Realization of a Functionality).** *Let $\mathcal{F}$ be a poly-time two-party functionality and Π be a poly-time two-party protocol. We say Π* computationally quantum-stand-alone *realizes $\mathcal{F}$, if Π* `C-QSA` *emulates $\widetilde{\Pi}_{\mathcal{F}}$.*

Namely, for any poly-time $\mathcal{A}$, there is a poly-time $\mathcal{S}$ such that $M_{\Pi,\mathcal{A}} \approx_{qc} M_{\mathcal{F},\mathcal{S}}$.

Definition 2.3 (Statistically Quantum-Stand-Alone Emulation). *Let Π and Γ be two poly-time protocols. We say Π* statistically quantum-stand-alone *(*`S-QSA`*) emulates Γ, if for any QIM $\mathcal{A}$ there exists an QIM $\mathcal{S}$ that runs in poly-time of that of $\mathcal{A}$, such that $M_{\Pi,\mathcal{A}} \approx_{\diamond} M_{\Gamma,\mathcal{S}}$.*

We assume *static* corruption only in this work, where the identities of corrupted parties are determined before protocol starts. The definitions above consider computationally bounded (poly-time) adversaries, including simulators. Occasionally, we will work with *inefficient* simulators, which we formulate as unbounded simulation of corrupted party P.

Definition 2.4 (Unbounded Simulation of Corrupted P). *Let Π and Γ be two poly-time protocols. For any poly-time QIM $\mathcal{A}$ corrupting party P, we say that Π* `C-QSA`*-emulates Γ against corrupted P with unbounded simulation, if there exists a QIM $\mathcal{S}$ possibly unbounded such that $M_{\Pi,\mathcal{A}} \approx_{qc} M_{\Gamma,\mathcal{S}}$.*

2.1 Modular Composition Theorem

It's shown that protocols satisfying the definitions of stand-alone emulation admit a modular composition [36]. Specifically, let Π be a protocol that uses another protocol Γ as a subroutine, and let Γ' be a protocol that QSA emulates Γ. We define the *composed* protocol, denoted $\Pi^{\Gamma/\Gamma'}$, to be the protocol in which each invocation of Γ is replaced by an invocation of Γ'. We allow multiple calls to a subroutine and also using multiple subroutines in a protocol Π. **However, quite importantly, we require that at any point, only one subroutine call be in progress.** This is more restrictive than the "network" setting, where many instances and subroutines may be executed *concurrently*.

In a *hybrid* model, parties can make calls to an ideal-world protocol $\widetilde{\Pi}_{\mathcal{G}}$ of some functionality $\mathcal{G}$[4]. We call such a protocol a *$\mathcal{G}$-hybrid* protocol, and denote it $\Pi^{\mathcal{G}}$. The execution of a hybrid-protocol in the presence of an adversary $\mathcal{A}$ proceeds in the usual way. Assume that we have a protocol Γ that realizes $\mathcal{G}$ and we have designed a $\mathcal{G}$-hybrid protocol $\Pi^{\mathcal{G}}$ realizing another functionality $\mathcal{F}$. Then the composition theorem allows us to treat sub-protocols as equivalent to their ideal versions.

If the secure emulation involves unbounded simulation against a party, the proof in [36] can be extended to show that the composed protocol also emulates with unbounded simulation against the corresponding corrupted party.

Theorem 2.1 (Modular Composition). *All of the following holds.*

- *Let Π, Γ and Γ' be two-party protocols such that Γ'* `C-QSA`*-emulates Γ, then $\Pi^{\Gamma/\Gamma'}$* `C-QSA` *emulates Π. If Γ'* `C-QSA` *emulates Γ against corrupted P with unbounded simulation, then $\Pi^{\Gamma/\Gamma'}$* `C-QSA` *emulates against corrupted P with unbounded simulation.*

[4] In contrast, we call it the *plain model* if no such trusted set-ups are available.

– *Let $\mathcal{F}$ and $\mathcal{G}$ be poly-time functionalities. Let $\Pi^{\mathcal{G}}$ be a $\mathcal{G}$-hybrid protocol that* C-QSA *realizes $\mathcal{F}$, and Γ be a protocol that* C-QSA *realizes $\mathcal{G}$, then $\Pi^{\mathcal{G}/\Gamma}$* C-QSA *realizes $\mathcal{F}$. If Γ* C-QSA *realizes $\mathcal{G}$ against corrupted P with unbounded simulation then $\Pi^{\mathcal{G}/\Gamma}$* C-QSA *realizes $\mathcal{F}$ against corrupted P with unbounded simulation.*

3 Parallel OT with Unbounded Simulation from OWF

The goal of this section is to prove the following theorem.

Theorem 3.1. *Assuming the existence of pqOWF, there exists a protocol $\Pi_{\texttt{p-ot}}$ that* C-QSA*-emulates $\mathcal{F}_{\texttt{p-ot}}$ with unbounded simulation against a malicious receiver.*

We prove this theorem as follows. In Sect. 3.1, we review the protocol of [9] that implies stand-alone-secure OT in $\mathcal{F}_{\texttt{so-com}}$-hybrid model. Then, in Sect. 3.2, we show how to build $\mathcal{F}_{\texttt{p-ot}}$ from $\mathcal{F}_{\texttt{so-com}}$. Finally in Sect. 3.3, we construct $\mathcal{F}_{\texttt{so-com}}$ with unbounded simulation against malicious sender.

3.1 Stand-Alone-Secure OT in $\mathcal{F}_{\texttt{so-com}}$-hybrid Model

In this section we present the quantum OT protocol assuming a selective opening-secure commitment scheme, that is, in the $\mathcal{F}_{\texttt{so-com}}$ hybrid model. We would like to stress that the results in this section are not novel; they consist of a straightforward adaptation of previous results [9,20,61] to our setting/language, and our goal in this presentation is to to provide a self-contained proof of its security. We describe the protocol $\Pi_{\texttt{QOT}}$ in Sect. 1.1 and we have the following.

Theorem 3.2. *$\Pi_{\texttt{QOT}}$* C-QSA*-realizes $\mathcal{F}_{ot}$ in the $\mathcal{F}_{so\text{-}com}$ hybrid model.*

3.2 Parallel Repetition for Protocols with Straight-Line Simulation

We show now that if π implements $\mathcal{F}$ in the $\mathcal{G}$-hybrid model with an (efficient/unbounded) *straight-line* simulator, then a parallel repetition of π, denoted $\pi^{||}$ implements $\mathcal{F}^{||}$ in the $\mathcal{G}^{||}$-hybrid model with an (efficient/unbounded) simulator. As a corollary, we get that a parallel repetition of the $\mathcal{F}_{ot}$ protocol from the previous section is a secure implementation of parallel OT in the $\mathcal{F}_{\texttt{so-com}}$ hybrid model.

Theorem 3.3 (Parallel Repetition). *Let $\mathcal{F}$ and $\mathcal{G}$ be two-party functionalities and let π be a secure implementation of $\mathcal{F}$ in the $\mathcal{G}$-hybrid model with a* straight-line *simulator. Then, $\pi^{||}$ is a secure implementation of $\mathcal{F}^{||}$ in the $\mathcal{G}^{||}$-hybrid model with straight-line simulation as well.*

Corollary 3.1. *The parallel repetition of any protocol that* C-QSA*-realizes $\mathcal{F}_{ot}$ in the $\mathcal{F}_{so\text{-}com}$-hybrid model with a straight-line simulator achieves $\mathcal{F}_{p\text{-}ot}$ in the $\mathcal{F}_{so\text{-}com}$-hybrid model.*

3.3 Implementing $\mathcal{F}_{\texttt{so-com}}$ with Unbounded Simulation

In this section we provide an implementation of $\mathcal{F}_{\texttt{so-com}}$ from Naor's commitment scheme and ZK protocols. Our protocol $\Pi_{\texttt{so-com}}$ is described in Fig. 1 and we prove the following result.

Theorem 3.4. *Assuming the existence of pqOWF, $\Pi_{so\text{-}com}$ C-QSA-realizes $\mathcal{F}_{so\text{-}com}$. with unbounded simulation against malicious committer.*

We prove Theorem 3.4 by showing security against malicious committer with unbounded simulator in Lemma 3.1 and security against malicious receiver in Lemma 3.2.

Parties: The committer C and the receiver R.
Inputs: C gets k ℓ-bit strings $m_1,...m_k$ and R gets a subset $I \subseteq [k]$ of messages to be decommited

Commitment Phase

1. R sends ρ for Naor's commitment scheme
2. For $i \in [k]$, C generates the commitments $c_i = \texttt{com}_\rho(m_i, r_i)$, where r_i is some private randomness.
3. C sends $c_1, ..., c_k$ to R

Decommitment Phase

1. R sends I to C
2. C sends $(m_i)_{i\in I}$ to R and they run a ZK protocol to prove that there exists $((\widetilde{m}_i)_{i\notin I}, (r_i)_{i\in[k]}))$ such that $c_i = \texttt{com}_\rho(\widetilde{m}_i, r_i)$

Fig. 1. Protocol for selective-opening commitment scheme $\Pi_{\texttt{so-com}}$.

Lemma 3.1. *Assuming the existence of pqOWF, $\Pi_{so\text{-}com}$ C-QSA-emulates $\mathcal{F}_{so\text{-}com}$ against corrupted committer $\mathcal{A}$ with unbounded simulation.*

Proof. The unbounded simulator $\mathcal{S}$ works as follows:

1. In the commitment phase, $\mathcal{S}$ runs the honest protocol with $\mathcal{A}$ and when receives the commitments $\widehat{c}_1, ..., \widehat{c}_k$ from $\mathcal{A}$ and $\mathcal{S}$ finds the messages $\widehat{m}_1, ..., \widehat{m}_k$ by brute force. If there is a $\widehat{c}_i$ that does not decommit to any message or decommits to more than one message $\mathcal{S}$ aborts. Finally, $\mathcal{S}$ inputs $\widehat{m}_1, ..., \widehat{m}_k$ to $\mathcal{F}_{\texttt{so-com}}$
2. In the Decommitment phase, $\mathcal{S}$ receives I from $\mathcal{F}_{\texttt{so-com}}$, forwards it to $\mathcal{A}$. $\mathcal{S}$ receives $(\widetilde{m}_i)_{i\in I}$ from $\mathcal{A}$ runs the honest verifier in the ZK protocol with $\mathcal{A}$, and rejects iff the ZK rejects or if for any $i \in I$, $\widehat{m}_i \neq \widetilde{m}_i$.

The proof follows the statistically-binding property of Naor's commitment scheme, so we can ignore commitments that open to more than one message, and by the ZK soundness property, which ensures that, up to negligible probability, if the commitments are not well-formed or if the sender tries to open then to a different value, both the simulator and the original receiver abort.

Due to space restrictions, we leave the details to the full version of our paper.

We now show security against malicious receiver.

Lemma 3.2. *Assuming the existence of pqOWF, $\Pi_{\texttt{so-com}}$ C-QSA-realizes $\mathcal{F}_{\texttt{so-com}}$ against corrupted receiver $\mathcal{A}$.*

Proof. The simulator $\mathcal{S}$ works as follows:

1. In the commitment phase, $\mathcal{S}$ sends $c_i = \texttt{com}_\rho(0, r_i)$ to $\mathcal{A}$
2. In the decommitment phase, $\mathcal{S}$ receives I from $\mathcal{A}$, uses it as input of $\mathcal{F}_{\texttt{so-com}}$. $\mathcal{S}$ receives back the messages $(m_i)_{i \in I}$, sends them to $\mathcal{A}$ and runs the ZK simulator of the proof that $(c_i)_{i \in I}$ open to $(m_i)_{i \in I}$ and that $(c_i)_{i \notin I}$ are valid commitments.

The fact that $M_{\Pi_{\texttt{so-com}}, \mathcal{A}} \approx_{qc} M_{\mathcal{F}_{\texttt{so-com}}, \mathcal{S}}$ follows from the computational zero-knowledge of the protocol and the computatinally-hiding property of Naor's commitment scheme.

4 Extractable Commitment from Unbounded Simulation OT

In this section, we construct an extractable commitment scheme using the unbounded simulation OT from Sect. 3. We do this in two steps. First, we define a new primitive, namely *verifiable* conditional disclosure of secrets (vCDS) in Sect. 4.1, and we construct a (unbounded simulation) vCDS protocol in Sect. 4.2 from the unbounded simulation OT. We then show how to use vCDS to construct an extractable commitment protocol that implements $\mathcal{F}_{\texttt{so-com}}$ with efficient simulators in Sect. 4.3.

4.1 Verifiable Conditional Disclosure of Secrets (vCDS)

We define the primitive of (verifiable) conditional disclosure of secrets. Conditional disclosure of secrets [31] (CDS) for an NP-language $\mathcal{L}$ is a two-party protocol where a sender (denoted cds.S) and a receiver (denoted cds.R) have a common input x, the sender has a message μ, and the receiver (purportedly) has a witness w for the NP-relation $R_{\mathcal{L}}$. At the end of the protocol, cds.R gets μ if $R_{\mathcal{L}}(x, w) = 1$ and $\perp$ otherwise, and the sender gets nothing. In a sense, this can be viewed as a *conditional* version of oblivious transfer, or as an interactive version of witness encryption.

The CDS functionality is defined in Fig. 2. We will construct a protocol $\Pi = \langle \text{cds.S}, \text{cds.R} \rangle$ that securely realizes the CDS functionality in the quantum

The Conditional Disclosure of Secret (CDS) Functionality $\mathcal{F}_{CDS}$ for an NP language $\mathcal{L}$.

Security Parameter: λ.
Parties: Sender S and Receiver R, adversary $\mathcal{A}$.

Sender Query: $\mathcal{F}_{CDS}$ receives $(\text{Send}, sid, (x, \mu))$ from S, where $x \in \mathcal{L} \cap \{0,1\}^{n_1(\lambda)}$ and $m \in \{0,1\}^{n_2(\lambda)}$ for polynomials n_1 and n_2, records $(sid, (x, \mu))$ and sends (Input, sid, x) to R and $\mathcal{A}$.
$\mathcal{F}_{CDS}$ ignores further send messages from S with sid.

Receiver Query: $\mathcal{F}_{CDS}$ receives $(\text{Witness}, sid, w)$ from party R, where $w \in \{0,1\}^{m(\lambda)}$ for a polynomial m. $\mathcal{F}_{CDS}$ ignores the message if no $(sid, \star)$ was recorded. Otherwise $\mathcal{F}_{CDS}$ sends $(\text{Open}, sid, x, \mu')$ to R where

$$\mu' = \begin{cases} \mu \text{ if } \mathcal{R}_{\mathcal{L}}(x, w) = 1 \\ \bot \text{ if } \mathcal{R}_{\mathcal{L}}(x, w) = 0 \end{cases}$$

$\mathcal{F}_{CDS}$ sends (Open, sid, x) to $\mathcal{A}$ and ignores further messages from R with sid.

Fig. 2. The Conditional Disclosure of Secrets (CDS) functionality

stand-alone model. We will consider protocols with either efficient or unbounded simulators.

Verifiability. We will, in addition, also require the CDS protocol to be *verifiable.* Downstream, when constructing our extractable commitment protocol in Sect. 4.3, we want to be able to prove consistency of the transcript of a CDS sub-protocol. It is not a-priori clear how to do this since the CDS protocol we construct will either live in the OT-hybrid model, in which case the OT input is *not* contained in the protocol transcript and is unconstrained by it; or it uses quantum communication, in which case, again consistency cannot be expressed as an NP-statement.

Definition 4.1 (Verifiability). *Let $\mathcal{L}$ be an* NP *language, and $\Pi = \langle \mathsf{cds.S}, \mathsf{cds.R} \rangle$ be a CDS protocol between a sender* cds.S *and a receiver* cds.R. *Π is* verifiable *(w.r.t.* cds.S*) if there is a polynomial time classical algorithm* Ver*, such that, the following properties are true:*

Correctness: *For every (x, μ) and every w, $\mathsf{cds.S}(x, \mu)$ after interacting with $\mathsf{cds.R}(w)$, outputs on a special output tape a proof π, such that, $\mathsf{Ver}(\tau, x, \mu, \pi) = 1$ where τ is the transcript of classical messages exchanged in the interaction.*

Binding: *For every $\lambda \in \mathbb{N}$, every (potentially unbounded) adversary $\mathcal{A} = \{\mathcal{A}_\lambda\}_{\lambda \in \mathbb{N}}$, every sequence of witnesses $\{w_\lambda\}_\lambda$, the probability that $\mathcal{A}_\lambda$ wins in the following experiment is negligible.*

- *$\mathcal{A}_\lambda$ after interacting with $\mathsf{cds.R}(1^\lambda, w)$, outputs (x, μ, π). Let τ be the transcript of classical messages exchanged in the interaction.*

- $\mathcal{A}_\lambda$ *wins if (a)* $\mathsf{Ver}(\tau, x, \mu, \pi) = 1$*, (b)* cds.R *did not abort, and (c)* cds.R *outputs* μ' *inconsistent with inputs* (x, μ) *and* w*, that is,*

$$\mu' \neq \begin{cases} \mu & \text{if } \mathcal{R}_\mathcal{L}(x, w) = 1 \\ \bot & \text{otherwise} \end{cases}$$

Definition 4.2 (Verifiable CDS). *Let* $\mathcal{L}$ *be an* NP *language, and* $\Pi = \langle \mathsf{cds.S}, \mathsf{cds.R} \rangle$ *be a protocol between a sender* cds.S *and a receiver* cds.R. Π *is a* verifiable CDS *protocol if (a) it* C-QSA*-emulates* $\mathcal{F}_{\mathsf{cds}}$ *with an efficient simulator; and (b) it is verifiable according to Definition 4.1.*

4.2 CDS Protocol from Unbounded Simulation OT

Theorem 4.1. *Assume the existence of pqOWF. For every* NP *language* $\mathcal{L}$*, there is a verifiable CDS protocol* $\Pi = \langle \mathsf{cds.S}, \mathsf{cds.R} \rangle$ *that* C-QSA*-emulates* $\mathcal{F}_{\mathsf{cds}}$ *for* $\mathcal{L}$ *in the* $\mathcal{F}_{\texttt{p-ot}}$ *hybrid model.*

Corollary 4.1. *Assume the existence of pqOWF, and a protocol that* C-QSA*-emulates* $\mathcal{F}_{\texttt{p-ot}}$ *with unbounded simulation. Then, for every* NP *language* $\mathcal{L}$*, there is a verifiable CDS protocol* $\Pi = \langle \mathsf{cds.S}, \mathsf{cds.R} \rangle$ *that* C-QSA*-emulates* $\mathcal{F}_{\mathsf{cds}}$ *for* $\mathcal{L}$ *with unbounded simulation.*

Proof of Theorem 4.1. The verifiable CDS protocol is described in Fig. 3. The protocol uses Naor's classical statistically binding commitment protocol, Yao's garbled circuits, and post-quantum zero knowledge proofs, all of which can be implemented from pqOWF. For a more detailed description of these ingredients, see the full version of our paper.

In Lemma 4.1, we show that the protocol has an efficient simulator for a corrupted receiver, and in Lemma 4.2, an efficient simulator for a corrupted sender (both in the OT hybrid model). Lemma 4.3 shows that the protocol is verifiable. □

Lemma 4.1. *There is an efficient simulator against a malicious receiver.*

Proof. The simulator $\mathcal{S}$ interacts with $\mathsf{cds.R}^*$, receives a string ρ from $\mathsf{cds.R}^*$ in Step 1, and intercepts the OT queries $(\sigma^1, \ldots, \sigma^{2\lambda})$ in Step 4.

- **Case** 1. $R_\mathcal{L}(x, \sigma^i) = 1$ **for some** i. Send (Witness, sid, σ^i) to the CDS functionality and receive μ. Simulate the rest of the protocol honestly using the CDS sender input (x, μ).
- **Case** 2. $R_\mathcal{L}(x, \sigma^i) = 0$ **for all** i. Simulate the rest of the protocol honestly using the CDS sender input $(x, 0)$.

We now show, through a sequence of hybrids, that this simulator produces a view that is computationally indistinguishable from that in the real execution of $\mathsf{cds.S}(x, \mu)$ with $\mathsf{cds.R}^*$.

Parties: The sender cds.S and the receiver cds.R. Inputs: cds.S has input (x, μ) and cds.R has input $w \in \{0,1\}^m$.

1. **Preamble:** cds.R sends a random string ρ as the first message of Naor's commitment scheme to cds.S and cds.S sends x to cds.R
2. **Compute Garbled Circuits:** cds.S generates 2λ garbled circuits, for the circuit computing $G_{x,\mu}(w) = \mu' = \begin{cases} \mu & \text{if } \mathcal{R}_{\mathcal{L}}(x,w) = 1 \\ \bot & \text{otherwise} \end{cases}$.
   That is, for every $i \in [2\lambda]$, $(\widehat{G}^i, \{\ell_b^{i,j}\}_{j\in[m],b\in\{0,1\}}) = \mathsf{Garb}(G_{x,\mu}; \gamma_i)$, where $\widehat{G}^i$ are the garbled circuits, and ℓ's are its associated labels.
3. **Cut-and-Choose:** cds.R samples a random subset $\Lambda \subseteq [2\lambda]$, by including each $i \in [2\lambda]$ with probability 1/2. For every $i \in [2\lambda]$, set
   $\sigma^i = \begin{cases} s^i \leftarrow \{0,1\}^m & i \in \Lambda \\ w & i \notin \Lambda \end{cases}$
4. **OT:** For every $i \in [2\lambda], j \in [m], b \in \{0,1\}$, cds.S samples $r_b^{i,j}$, the random coins for committing to the labels $\ell_b^{i,j}$ via Naor's commitment scheme.
   cds.S and cds.R invokes $\mathcal{F}_{\text{p-ot}}$ for $2\lambda \times m$ parallel OT, where the (i,j)'th OT for $i \in [2\lambda], j \in [m]$ has sender's input strings $(\ell_0^{i,j}, r_0^{i,j})$ and $(\ell_1^{i,j}, r_1^{i,j})$, and receiver's choice bit $\sigma^{i,j}$ (which is the j-th bit of σ^i) and cds.R receives $(\widetilde{\ell}^{i,j}, \widetilde{r}^{i,j})$.
   We refer to the OTs with index $(i, \star)$ as the i'th batch. as they transfer labels of the i'th garbled circuit $\widehat{G}_i$.
5. **Send Garbled Circuits and Commitments to the Labels and μ:** cds.S samples r^* and computes $c^* = \mathtt{com}_\rho(\mu; r^*)$ and $c_b^{i,j} = \mathtt{com}_\rho(\ell_b^{i,j}; r_b^{i,j})$.
   Send $\{\widehat{G}^i\}_{i\in[2\lambda]}$ and $(c^*, \{c_b^{i,j}\}_{i\in[2\lambda],j\in[m],b\in\{0,1\}})$ to the receiver cds.R.
6. **Proof of Consistency:** cds.S proves via ZK protocol that (a) c^* is a valid commitment to μ, (b) every $\widehat{G}^i$ is a valid garbling of $G_{x,\mu}$ with labels $\{\ell_b^{i,j}\}_{j\in[m],b\in\{0,1\}}$, and (c) $c_b^{i,j}$ is a valid commitment to $\ell_b^{i,j}$.
7. **Checks:** cds.R performs the following checks:
   - If the ZK proof in the previous step is not accepting, cds.R aborts.
   - **Λ-checks.** If there is $i \in \Lambda$ and $j \in [m]$, such that, $c_{\sigma^{i,j}}^{i,j} \neq \mathtt{com}_\rho(\widetilde{\ell}^{i,j}, \widetilde{r}^{i,j})$, cds.R aborts and outputs $\bot$.
   - **$\overline{\Lambda}$-check.** If for every $i \notin \Lambda$, there exists $j \in [m]$, such that, $c_{\sigma^{i,j}}^{i,j} \neq \mathtt{com}_\rho(\widetilde{\ell}^{i,j}, \widetilde{r}^{i,j})$, cds.R aborts and outputs $\bot$.
8. **Output:** If cds.R does not abort, there must exist $i \notin \Lambda$ such that, for all $j \in [m]$, $c_{\sigma^{i,j}}^{i,j} = \mathtt{com}_\rho(\widetilde{\ell}^{i,j}, \widetilde{r}^{i,j})$. Evaluate the i'th garbled circuit $\widehat{G}^i$ to get $\mu' = \mathsf{GEval}(\widehat{G}^i, \{\widetilde{\ell}^{i,j}\}_{j\in[m]})$, and output x', μ'.

Fig. 3. The verifiable CDS Scheme in $\mathcal{F}_{\text{p-ot}}$-hybrid model. The steps in color involve communication while the others only involve local computation.

Hybrid 0. This corresponds to the real execution of the protocol where the sender has input (x, m). The view of cds.R* consists of

$$\left[\rho, \{\widehat{G}^i, \widetilde{\ell}^{i,j}, \widetilde{r}^{i,j}, c_b^{i,j}\}_{i\in[2\lambda], j\in[m], b\in\{0,1\}}, c^*, \tau_{\mathsf{ZK}}\right]$$

where ρ is the message sent by $\mathsf{cds.R}^*$ in Step 1, the strings $\widetilde{\ell}^{i,j}$ and $\widetilde{r}^{i,j}$ are received by $\mathsf{cds.R}^*$ from the OT functionality in Step 4, the garbled circuits $\widehat{G}^i$ and the commitments $c_b^{i,j}$ and c^* in Step 5, and τ_{ZK} is the transcript of the ZK protocol between $\mathsf{cds.S}$ and $\mathsf{cds.R}^*$ in Step 6. (See the protocol in Fig. 3).

Hybrid 1. This is identical to hybrid 0 except that we run the simulator to intercept the OT queries $(\sigma^1, \ldots, \sigma^{2\lambda})$ of $\mathsf{cds.R}^*$. The rest of the execution remains the same. Of course, the transcript produced is identical to that in hybrid 0.

Hybrid 2. In this hybrid, we replace the transcript τ_{ZK} of the zero-knowledge protocol with a simulated transcript. This is indistinguishable from hybrid 1 by (post-quantum) computational zero-knowledge. Note that generating this hybrid does not require us to use the randomness underlying the commitments $c_{1-\sigma^{i,j}}^{i,j}$ and c^*. (The randomness underlying $c_{\sigma^{i,j}}^{i,j}$ *are* revealed as part of the OT responses to $\mathsf{cds.R}^*$.)

Hybrid 3. In this hybrid, we replace half the commitments, namely $c_{1-\sigma^{i,j}}^{i,j}$, as well as c^* with commitments of 0. This is indistinguishable from hybrid 2 by (post-quantum) computational hiding of Naor commitments.

Hybrid 4. In this hybrid, we proceed as follows. If the simulator is in case 1, that is $R_{\mathcal{L}}(x, \sigma^i) = 1$ for some i, proceed as in hybrid 3 with no change. On the other hand, if the simulator is in case 2, that is $R_{\mathcal{L}}(x, \sigma^i) = 0$ for all i, replace the garbled circuits with simulated garbled circuits that always output $\perp$ and let the commitments $c_{\sigma^{i,j}}^{i,j}$ be commitments of the simulated labels. This is indistinguishable from hybrid 3 where the garbled circuits are an honest garbling of $G_{x,\mu}$ because of the fact that all the garbled evaluations output $\perp$ in hybrid 3, and because of the post-quantum security of the garbling scheme.

Hybrids 5–7 undo the effects of hybrids 2–4 in reverse.

Hybrid 5. In this hybrid, we replace the simulated garbled circuit with the real garbled circuit for the circuit $G_{x,0}$. This is indistinguishable from hybrid 4 because of the fact that all the garbled evaluations output $\perp$ in this hybrid, and because of the post-quantum security of the garbling scheme.

Hybrid 6. In this hybrid, we let all commitments be to the correct labels and messages. This is indistinguishable from hybrid 5 by (post-quantum) computational hiding of Naor commitments.

Hybrid 7. In this hybrid, we replace the simulated ZK transcript with the real ZK protocol transcript. This is indistinguishable from hybrid 7 by (post-quantum) computational zero-knowledge.

This final hybrid matches exactly the simulator. This finishes the proof.

Lemma 4.2. *There is an inefficient statistical simulator against a malicious sender.*

Proof. The simulator $\mathcal{S}$ interacts with $\mathsf{cds.S}^*$ as follows:

1. Send a string ρ to $\mathsf{cds.S}^*$ in Step 1, as in the protocol;
2. *Intercept* the OT messages $(\ell_0^{i,j}, r_0^{i,j})$ and $(\ell_1^{i,j}, r_1^{i,j})$ from $\mathsf{cds.S}^*$ in Step 4.
3. Run the rest of the protocol as an honest receiver $\mathsf{cds.R}$ would.
4. If the ZK proof rejects or if any Λ-check fails, $\mathcal{S}$ aborts and outputs $\perp$. (Note the simulator does not perform the $\overline{\Lambda}$-check).
5. Otherwise, extract μ from c^* using unbounded time, and send (x, μ) to the ideal functionality and halt.

The transcript generated by $\mathcal{S}$ is identical to the one generated in the real world where $\mathsf{cds.R}$ on input w interacts with $\mathsf{cds.S}^*$. It remains to analyze the output distribution of $\mathsf{cds.R}$ in the simulation vis-a-vis the real world.

1. Since the Λ-checks performed on the commitments of garbled instances in Λ by the simulator and the ones performed by the honest receiver in the real protocol are exactly the same, we have that the probability that the probability of abort is the same (for this step) in both scenarios.
2. The probability that the honest receiver in the real protocol aborts on the $\overline{\Lambda}$-check, conditioned on the fact that the Λ-checks passed, is negligible.

Thus, we have that the output distributions of the receiver are negligibly close between the simulation and the real world, finishing up the proof.

Lemma 4.3. *The protocol is verifiable.*

Proof. We first construct a verification algorithm Ver.

- The classical transcript τ consists of $\rho, x, \{\widehat{G}^i\}_{i\in[2\lambda]}, c^*, \{c_b^{i,j}\}_{i\in[2\lambda], j\in[m], b\in\{0,1\}}$.
- At the end of the protocol, $\mathsf{cds.S}$ outputs (x, μ, r^*) on its special output tape.
- The verification algorithm $\mathsf{Ver}(\tau, x, \mu', r') = 1$ iff $c^* = \mathtt{com}_\rho(\mu'; r')$.

We first claim that for honest $\mathsf{cds.S}$ and $\mathsf{cds.R}$ with $(x, w) \in \mathcal{R}_\mathcal{L}$, we have that $\mathsf{Ver}(\tau, x, \mu, r) = 1$. Since all parties in the protocol are honest the input x in τ is the same as the one output by $\mathsf{cds.S}$ and we have that c^* is the commitment to the honest message using the correct randomness, so Ver outputs 1.

To show binding, assume that the verification passes and the receiver does not abort. Then, we know that there is at least one $i \notin \Lambda$ such that the i-th garbled circuit+input pair is correct and the circuit is the garbling of $G_{x,\mu}$. The verifier will evaluate the circuit on input w and obtain either $\perp$ when $R_\mathcal{L}(x, w) = 0$ or μ when $R_\mathcal{L}(x, w) = 1$, exactly as required.

4.3 Extractable Commitment from CDS

Theorem 4.2. *Assume the existence of pqOWF. There is a commitment protocol* $\langle C, R\rangle$ *that* $\mathtt{C\text{-}QSA}$*-emulates* $\mathcal{F}_{\mathsf{so\text{-}com}}$ *with efficient simulators.*

Parties: The committer C and the receiver R.
Inputs: C gets a message vector $\vec{\mu} = (\mu_1, \ldots, \mu_{\ell(n)})$ and R gets 1^n.

Commitment Phase

1. **Preamble.** C sends a random string ρ to R, and R sends a random string ρ^* to C, as the first message of the Naor commitment scheme.
2. **Set up a Trapdoor Statement.**
   - R sends a Naor commitment $c = \mathtt{com}_\rho(0; r)$.
   - R proves to C using a ZK protocol that c is a commitment to 0, that is, $((c, \rho, 0), r) \in \mathcal{R}_{\mathcal{L}_{\mathsf{com}}}$. If the ZK verifier rejects, C aborts.
3. **CDS.** C and R run the CDS protocol $\langle \mathsf{cds.S}, \mathsf{cds.R} \rangle$ for the language $\mathcal{L}_{\mathtt{com}}$ where C acts as $\mathsf{cds.S}$ with input $x = (c, \rho, 1)$ and message $\vec{\mu}$, and R acts as $\mathsf{cds.R}$ with input 0.
   C aborts if $\mathsf{cds.S}$ aborts, else C obtains the protocol transcript τ and $\mathsf{cds.S}$'s proof π. R aborts if $\mathsf{cds.R}$ aborts, or if $\mathsf{cds.R}$ outputs $(x', \vec{\mu}')$ but $x' \neq (\rho, c, 1)$.
4. **Commit and Prove Consistency.**
   - C sends a Naor commitment $c^* = \mathtt{com}_{\rho^*}(\vec{\mu}; r^*)$.
   - C proves to R using a ZK protocol there exists a $\vec{\mu}$ such that $(x = (\rho, c, 1), \vec{\mu})$ is the input that C used in the CDS protocol and $\vec{\mu}$ is committed in c^*, that is:

$$\mathsf{Ver}(\tau, x, \vec{\mu}, \pi) = 1 \text{ and } c^* = \mathtt{com}_{\rho^*}(\vec{\mu}, r^*)$$

5. R accepts this commitment if the ZK proof is accepting.

Decommitment Phase

1. R sends $I \subseteq [\ell]$.
2. C sends $\vec{\mu}|_I$ and proves via a ZK protocol that $c^*|_I$ commits to $\vec{\mu}|_I$.
3. R accepts this decommitment if the ZK proof is accepting.

Fig. 4. Extractable Selective-Opening-Secure commitment scheme

Proof. The construction of our extractable commitment scheme is given in Fig. 4. The protocol uses Naor's classical statistically binding commitment protocol and a verifiable CDS protocol $\Pi = \langle \mathsf{cds.S}, \mathsf{cds.R} \rangle$ that $\mathtt{C\text{-}QSA}$-emulates $\mathcal{F}_{\mathsf{cds}}$ (with unbounded simulation) for $\mathcal{L}_{\mathtt{com}}$, the language consisting of all Naor's commtiments (ρ, c) to a bit b: $\mathcal{R}_{\mathcal{L}_{\mathtt{com}}}((\rho, c, b), r) = 1$ iff $c = \mathtt{com}_\rho(b; r)$.

We defer a detailed description of these tools to the full version of our paper.

In Lemma 4.4 (resp. Lemma 4.5), we show that the protocol has an efficient simulator for a corrupted sender (resp. receiver).

Lemma 4.4. *There is an efficient simulator against a malicious sender.*

Proof. The simulator $\mathcal{S}$ against a malicious committer C^* works as follows.

1. In step 1, proceed as an honest receiver would.

2. In step 2, send a Naor commitment $c = \mathtt{com}_\rho(1; r)$ (instead of 0) and simulate the ZK proof.
3. In step 3, run the honest CDS protocol with r as witness, gets $\boldsymbol{\mu}$ and sends it to the ideal functionality $\mathcal{F}_{\mathtt{so-com}}$.
4. Run the rest of the protocol as an honest receiver would.

We now show, through a sequence of hybrids, that this simulator produces a joint distribution of a view of C^* together with an output of R that is computationally indistinguishable from that in the real execution of C^* with R. In order to show this we consider the following sequence of hybrids.

Hybrid 0. This corresponds to the protocol $\Pi_{\mathtt{H}_0}^{\mathsf{ECom}}$, where $\mathcal{S}_0$ sits between C^* and the honest receiver in the real protocol and just forwards their messages. It follows trivially that $M_{\Pi_{\mathsf{ECom}}, C^*} \approx_{qc} M_{\Pi_{\mathtt{H}_0}^{\mathsf{ECom}}, \mathcal{S}_0}$.

Hybrid 1. $\mathcal{S}_1$ interacts with C^* following the protocol $\Pi_{\mathtt{H}_1}^{\mathsf{ECom}}$, which is the same as $\Pi_{\mathtt{H}_0}^{\mathsf{ECom}}$ except that $\mathcal{S}_1$ uses the ZK simulator instead of the proof that $((c, \rho, 0), r) \in \mathcal{R}_{\mathcal{L}_{\mathsf{com}}}$. From the computational zero-knowledge property of the protocol, we have that $M_{\Pi_{\mathtt{H}_0}^{\mathsf{ECom}}, \mathcal{S}_0} \approx_{qc} M_{\Pi_{\mathtt{H}_1}^{\mathsf{ECom}}, \mathcal{S}_1}$.

Hybrid 2. $\mathcal{S}_2$ interacts with C^* following the protocol $\Pi_{\mathtt{H}_2}^{\mathsf{ECom}}$, which is the same as $\Pi_{\mathtt{H}_1}^{\mathsf{ECom}}$ except that $\mathcal{S}_2$ sends $c' = \mathtt{com}_\rho(1; r)$ instead of the (honest) commitment of 0. When $\mathcal{S}_2$ simulates $\mathcal{F}_{\mathsf{zk}}$, she still sends a message that c' is a valid input. It follows from computationally hiding property of Naor's commitment scheme that $M_{\Pi_{\mathtt{H}_1}^{\mathsf{ECom}}, \mathcal{S}_1} \approx_{qc} M_{\Pi_{\mathtt{H}_2}^{\mathsf{ECom}}, \mathcal{S}_2}$.

Hybrid 3. $\mathcal{S}_3$ interacts with C^* following the protocol $\Pi_{\mathtt{H}_3}^{\mathsf{ECom}}$, which is the same as $\Pi_{\mathtt{H}_2}^{\mathsf{ECom}}$ except that $\mathcal{S}_3$ now uses the private randomness r as a witness that c' is a commitment of 1.

Since our protocol realizes $\mathcal{F}_{CDS}$, $\mathsf{cds.S}^*$ (controlled by C^*) does not behave differently depending on the input of $\mathsf{cds.R}$, so the probability of abort in step 3 does not change. Notice also that $\mathsf{Ver}(\tau, x, \boldsymbol{\mu}, \pi)$ is independent of $\mathsf{cds.R}$'s message, so the acceptance probability of the ZK proof does not change either.

Then, if the ZK proof leads to acceptance, by the soundness of the protocol, we know that $\mathsf{Ver}(\tau, x, \boldsymbol{\mu}, \pi) = 1$ and by the binding of the commitment c^*, such a $\boldsymbol{\mu}$ is uniquely determined.

Finally, by the verifiability of the CDS protocol, we know that the receiver either aborts or outputs the specified $\boldsymbol{\mu}$. Thus, the outputs of the receiver R in the simulated execution and the real execution must be the same in this case.

Lemma 4.5. *There is an efficient simulator against a malicious receiver.*

Proof. The simulator $\mathcal{S}$ against a malicious receiver R^* proceeds as follows.

- In steps 1 and 2, proceed as an honest sender would.
- In step 3, run the CDS protocol using a message vector $\boldsymbol{\mu} = \mathbf{0}$ of all zeroes.
- In step 4, commit to the all-0 vector and produce a simulated ZK proof.
- During decommitment, send $I \subseteq [\ell]$ to the ideal functionality and receive $\boldsymbol{\mu}|_I$. Send $\boldsymbol{\mu}|_I$ to R^*, and simulate the ZK proof.

We now show, through a sequence of hybrids, that this simulator is computationally indistinguishable from the real execution of $C(\boldsymbol{\mu})$ with R^*.

Hybrid 0. This corresponds to the protocol $\Pi_{\mathtt{H}_0}^{\mathsf{ECom}}$, where $\mathcal{S}_0$ sits between the honest commiter C and R^*, and it just forwards their messages. It follows trivially that $M_{\Pi_{\mathsf{ECom}},C^*} \approx_{qc} M_{\Pi_{\mathtt{H}_0}^{\mathsf{ECom}},\mathcal{S}_0}$.

Hybrid 1. $\mathcal{S}_1$ interacts with R^* following the protocol $\Pi_{\mathtt{H}_1}^{\mathsf{ECom}}$, which is the same as $\Pi_{\mathtt{H}_0}^{\mathsf{ECom}}$ except that $\mathcal{S}_1$ uses the ZK simulator in Step 4 and the decommitment phase. From the computational zero-knowledge property, we have that $M_{\Pi_{\mathtt{H}_0}^{\mathsf{ECom}},\mathcal{S}_0} \approx_{qc} M_{\Pi_{\mathtt{H}_1}^{\mathsf{ECom}},\mathcal{S}_1}$.

Hybrid 2. $\mathcal{S}_2$ interacts with R^* following the protocol $\Pi_{\mathtt{H}_2}^{\mathsf{ECom}}$, which is the same as $\Pi_{\mathtt{H}_1}^{\mathsf{ECom}}$ except that $\mathcal{S}_2$ sets c^* to be a commitment to 0. It follows from the computationally-hiding property of the commitment scheme that $M_{\Pi_{\mathtt{H}_1}^{\mathsf{ECom}},\mathcal{S}_1} \approx_{qc} M_{\Pi_{\mathtt{H}_2}^{\mathsf{ECom}},\mathcal{S}_2}$.

Hybrid 3. $\mathcal{S}_3$ interacts with R^* following the protocol $\Pi_{\mathtt{H}_3}^{\mathsf{ECom}}$, which is the same as $\Pi_{\mathtt{H}_2}^{\mathsf{ECom}}$ except that $\mathcal{S}_3$ uses $\boldsymbol{\mu} = 0^\ell$ as the cds.S message.

From the soundness of the ZK proof in Step 2, we have that c is not a commitment of 1. In this case, by the security of CDS, R^* does not receive $\boldsymbol{\mu}$, so the change of the message cannot be distinguished.

Notice that Hybrid 3 matches the description of the simulator $\mathcal{S}$, and therefore $M_{\Pi_{\mathtt{H}_2}^{\mathsf{ECom}},\mathcal{S}_2} \approx_{qc} M_{\mathcal{F}_{\mathtt{so-com}},\mathcal{S}}$.

5 Multiparty (Quantum) Computation in MiniQCrypt

Our quantum protocol realizing $\mathcal{F}_{\mathtt{so-com}}$ from quantum-secure OWF allows us to combine existing results and realize secure computation of any two-party or multi-party classical functionality as well as quantum circuit in MiniQCrypt.

Theorem 5.1. *Assuming that post-quantum secure one-way functions exist, for every classical two-party and multi-party functionality $\mathcal{F}$, there is a quantum protocol* C-QSA*-emulates $\mathcal{F}$.*

Proof. By Theorem 3.2, we readily realize $\mathcal{F}_{\mathtt{ot}}$ in MiniQCrypt. In the $\mathcal{F}_{\mathtt{ot}}$-hybrid model, any classical functionality $\mathcal{F}$ can be realized statistically by a classical protocol in the universal-composable model [42]. The security can be lifted to the quantum universal-composable model as shown by Unruh [61]. As a result, we also get a classical protocol in the $\mathcal{F}_{\mathtt{ot}}$-hybrid model that S-QSA emulates $\mathcal{F}$. Plugging in the quantum protocol for $\mathcal{F}_{\mathtt{ot}}$, we obtain a quantum protocol that C-QSA-emulates $\mathcal{F}$ assuming existence of quantum-secure one-way functions.

Now that we have a protocol that realizes any classical functionality in MiniQCrypt, we can instantiate $\mathcal{F}_{mpc}$ used in the work of [24] to achieve a protocol for secure multi-party quantum computation where parties can jointly evaluate an arbitrary quantum circuit on their private quantum input states. Specifically consider a quantum circuit Q with k input registers. Let $\mathcal{F}_Q$ be the ideal protocol where a trusted party receives private inputs from k parties, evaluate Q, and then send the outputs to respective parties. We obtain the following.

Theorem 5.2. *Assuming that post-quantum secure one-way functions exist, for any quantum circuit Q, there is a quantum protocol that* C-QSA*-emulates the $\mathcal{F}_Q$.*

Acknowledgements. We thank the Simons Institute for the Theory of Computing for providing a meeting place where the seeds of this work were planted. VV thanks Ran Canetti for patiently answering his questions regarding universally composable commitments.

Most of this work was done when AG was affiliated to CWI and QuSoft. HL was supported by NSF grants CNS-1528178, CNS-1929901, CNS-1936825 (CAREER), CNS-2026774, a Hellman Fellowship, a JP Morgan AI Research Award, the Defense Advanced Research Projects Agency (DARPA) and Army Research Office (ARO) under Contract No. W911NF-15-C-0236, and a subcontract No. 2017-002 through Galois. FS was supported by NSF grants CCF-2041841, CCF-2042414, and CCF-2054758 (CAREER). VV was supported by DARPA under Agreement No. HR00112020023, a grant from the MIT-IBM Watson AI, a grant from Analog Devices, a Microsoft Trustworthy AI grant, and a DARPA Young Faculty Award. The views expressed are those of the authors and do not reflect the official policy or position of the Department of Defense, DARPA, the National Science Foundation, or the U.S. Government.

References

1. Agarwal, A., Bartusek, J., Goyal, V., Khurana, D., Malavolta, G.: Post-quantum multi-party computation in constant rounds (2020). arXiv:2005.12904. https://arxiv.org/abs/2005.12904
2. Ananth, P., La Placa, R.L.: Secure quantum extraction protocols. CoRR, abs/1911.07672 (2019)
3. Barak, B.: The complexity of public-key cryptography. Cryptology ePrint Archive, Report 2017/365, 2017. https://eprint.iacr.org/2017/365
4. Bartusek, J., Coladangelo, A., Khurana, D., Ma, F.: One-way functions imply secure computation in a quantum world (2020)
5. Beaver, D.: Correlated pseudorandomness and the complexity of private computations. In: Miller, G.L. (ed.) Proceedings of the Twenty-Eighth Annual ACM Symposium on the Theory of Computing, pp. 479–488. ACM (1996)
6. Bellare, M., Hofheinz, D., Yilek, S.: Possibility and impossibility results for encryption and commitment secure under selective opening. In: Joux, A. (ed.) EUROCRYPT 2009. LNCS, vol. 5479, pp. 1–35. Springer, Heidelberg (2009). https://doi.org/10.1007/978-3-642-01001-9_1
7. Ben-Or, M., Crépeau, C., Gottesman, D., Hassidim, A., Smith, A.: Secure multi-party quantum computation with (only) a strict honest majority. In: 47th Annual IEEE Symposium on Foundations of Computer Science, pp. 249–260. IEEE (2006)
8. Bennett, C.H., Brassard, G.: Quantum cryptography: public key distribution and coin tossing. In: EEE International Conference on Computers, Systems and Signal Processing, vol. 175, p. 8 (1984)

9. Bennett, C.H., Brassard, G., Crépeau, C., Skubiszewska, M.-H.: Practical quantum oblivious transfer. In: Feigenbaum, J. (ed.) CRYPTO 1991. LNCS, vol. 576, pp. 351–366. Springer, Heidelberg (1992). https://doi.org/10.1007/3-540-46766-1_29 As references [10, 11] and [51, 52] are same, we have deleted the duplicate reference and renumbered accordingly. Please check and confirm
10. Bitansky, N., Shmueli, O.: Post-quantum zero knowledge in constant rounds. In: Makarychev, K., Makarychev, Y., Tulsiani, M., Kamath, G., Chuzhoy, J. (eds.) STOC 2020, pp. 269–279. ACM (2020)
11. Blum, M.: How to prove a theorem so no one else can claim it. In: Proceedings of the International Congress of Mathematicians (1986)
12. Bouman, N.J., Fehr, S.: Sampling in a quantum population, and applications. In: Rabin, T. (ed.) CRYPTO 2010. LNCS, vol. 6223, pp. 724–741. Springer, Heidelberg (2010). https://doi.org/10.1007/978-3-642-14623-7_39
13. Brakerski, Z., Christiano, P., Mahadev, U., Vazirani, U.V., Vidick, T.: A cryptographic test of quantumness and certifiable randomness from a single quantum device. In: FOCS 2018, pp. 320–331 (2018)
14. Buhrman, H., Christandl, M., Schaffner, C.: Complete insecurity of quantum protocols for classical two-party computation. Phys. Rev. Lett. **109**(16), 160501 (2012)
15. Canetti, R.: Universally composable security: a new paradigm for cryptographic protocols. In: FOCS, pp. 136–145. IEEE (2001)
16. Chailloux, A., Gutoski, G., Sikora, J.: Optimal bounds for semi-honest quantum oblivious transfer. Chic. J. Theor. Comput. Sci. **2016**, 1–17 (2016)
17. Colbeck, R.: Quantum and relativistic protocols for secure multi-party computation. Ph.D. Thesis, Trinity College, University of Cambridge (2009)
18. Crépeau, C., Gottesman, D., Smith, A.: Secure multi-party quantum computation. In: Proceedings of the Thiry-Fourth Annual ACM Symposium on Theory of Computing, pp. 643–652 (2002)
19. Crépeau, C., Kilian, J.: Achieving oblivious transfer using weakened security assumptions. In: 29th Annual Symposium on Foundations of Computer Science, pp. 42–52 (1988)
20. Damgård, I., Fehr, S., Lunemann, C., Salvail, L., Schaffner, C.: Improving the security of quantum protocols via commit-and-open. In: Halevi, S. (ed.) CRYPTO 2009. LNCS, vol. 5677, pp. 408–427. Springer, Heidelberg (2009). https://doi.org/10.1007/978-3-642-03356-8_24
21. Damgård, I.B., Fehr, S., Renner, R., Salvail, L., Schaffner, C.: A tight high-order entropic quantum uncertainty relation with applications. In: Menezes, A. (ed.) CRYPTO 2007. LNCS, vol. 4622, pp. 360–378. Springer, Heidelberg (2007). https://doi.org/10.1007/978-3-540-74143-5_20
22. Damgård, I.B., Fehr, S., Salvail, L., Schaffner, C.: Cryptography in the bounded-quantum-storage model. SIAM J. Comput. **37**(6), 1865–1890 (2008)
23. Dixon, A.R., Yuan, Z.L., Dynes, J.F., Sharpe, A.W., Shields, A.J.: Gigahertz decoy quantum key distribution with 1 mbit/s secure key rate. Opt. Express **16**(23), 18790 (2008)
24. Dulek, Y., Grilo, A.B., Jeffery, S., Majenz, C., Schaffner, C.: Secure multi-party quantum computation with a dishonest majority. In: Canteaut, A., Ishai, Y. (eds.) EUROCRYPT 2020, Part III. LNCS, vol. 12107, pp. 729–758. Springer, Cham (2020). https://doi.org/10.1007/978-3-030-45727-3_25
25. Dupuis, F., Fehr, S., Lamontagne, P., Salvail, L.: Adaptive versus non-adaptive strategies in the quantum setting with applications. In: Robshaw, M., Katz, J. (eds.) CRYPTO 2016, Part III. LNCS, vol. 9816, pp. 33–59. Springer, Heidelberg (2016). https://doi.org/10.1007/978-3-662-53015-3_2

26. Dupuis, F., Nielsen, J.B., Salvail, L.: Secure two-party quantum evaluation of unitaries against specious adversaries. In: Rabin, T. (ed.) CRYPTO 2010. LNCS, vol. 6223, pp. 685–706. Springer, Heidelberg (2010). https://doi.org/10.1007/978-3-642-14623-7_37
27. Dupuis, F., Nielsen, J.B., Salvail, L.: Actively secure two-party evaluation of any quantum operation. In: Safavi-Naini, R., Canetti, R. (eds.) CRYPTO 2012. LNCS, vol. 7417, pp. 794–811. Springer, Heidelberg (2012). https://doi.org/10.1007/978-3-642-32009-5_46
28. Fang, J., Unruh, D., Weng, J., Yan, J., Zhou, D.: How to base security on the perfect/statistical binding property of quantum bit commitment? IACR Cryptol. ePrint Arch. **2020**, 621 (2020)
29. Fehr, S., Katz, J., Song, F., Zhou, H.-S., Zikas, V.: Feasibility and completeness of cryptographic tasks in the quantum world. In: Sahai, A. (ed.) TCC 2013. LNCS, vol. 7785, pp. 281–296. Springer, Heidelberg (2013). https://doi.org/10.1007/978-3-642-36594-2_16
30. Fehr, S., Schaffner, C.: Composing quantum protocols in a classical environment. In: Reingold, O. (ed.) TCC 2009. LNCS, vol. 5444, pp. 350–367. Springer, Heidelberg (2009). https://doi.org/10.1007/978-3-642-00457-5_21
31. Gertner, Y., Ishai, Y., Kushilevitz, E., Malkin, T.: Protecting data privacy in private information retrieval schemes. In: Vitter, J.S. (ed.) STOC 1998, pp. 151–160. ACM (1998)
32. Goldreich, O.: Foundations of Cryptography: Volume 2 Basic Applications, 1st edn. Cambridge University Press, Cambridge (2009)
33. Goldreich, O., Micali, S., Wigderson, A.: How to play any mental game or a completeness theorem for protocols with honest majority. In: Aho, A. (ed.) 19th ACM STOC, pp. 218–229. ACM Press (May 1987)
34. Goldreich, O., Micali, S., Wigderson, A.: How to prove all NP statements in zero-knowledge and a methodology of cryptographic protocol design (extended abstract). In: Odlyzko, A.M. (ed.) CRYPTO 1986. LNCS, vol. 263, pp. 171–185. Springer, Heidelberg (1987). https://doi.org/10.1007/3-540-47721-7_11
35. Grilo, A.B., Lin, H., Song, F., Vaikuntanathan, V.: Oblivious transfer is in miniqcrypt. Cryptology ePrint Archive, Report 2020/1500 (2020). https://eprint.iacr.org/2020/1500
36. Hallgren, S., Smith, A., Song, F.: Classical cryptographic protocols in a quantum world. Int. J. Quant. Inf. **13**(04), 1550028 (2015). Preliminary version in Crypto 2011
37. Håstad, J., Impagliazzo, R., Levin, L.A., Luby, M.: A pseudorandom generator from any one-way function. SIAM J. Comput. **28**(4), 1364–1396 (1999)
38. Hiskett, P.A., et al.: Long-distance quantum key distribution in optical fibre. New J. Phys. **8**(9), 193 (2006)
39. Impagliazzo, R.: A personal view of average-case complexity. In: Structure in Complexity Theory Conference, Annual, p. 134, Los Alamitos, CA, USA. IEEE Computer Society (Jun 1995)
40. Impagliazzo, R., Rudich, S.: Limits on the provable consequences of one-way permutations. In: Johnson, D.S. (ed.) STOC 1989, pp. 44–61. ACM (1989)
41. Ishai, Y., Kilian, J., Nissim, K., Petrank, E.: Extending oblivious transfers efficiently. In: Boneh, D. (ed.) CRYPTO 2003. LNCS, vol. 2729, pp. 145–161. Springer, Heidelberg (2003). https://doi.org/10.1007/978-3-540-45146-4_9
42. Ishai, Y., Prabhakaran, M., Sahai, A.: Founding cryptography on oblivious transfer – efficiently. In: Wagner, D. (ed.) CRYPTO 2008. LNCS, vol. 5157, pp. 572–591. Springer, Heidelberg (2008). https://doi.org/10.1007/978-3-540-85174-5_32

43. Kilian, J.: Founding cryptography on oblivious transfer. In: 20th ACM STOC, pp. 20–31. ACM Press (May 1988)
44. Konig, R., Wehner, S., Wullschleger, J.: Unconditional security from noisy quantum storage. IEEE Trans. Inf. Theor. **58**(3), 1962–1984 (2012)
45. Liao, S.-K., et al.: Satellite-relayed intercontinental quantum network. Phys. Rev. Lett. **120**(3), 030501 (2018)
46. Liu, Y.K.: Building one-time memories from isolated qubits. In: 5th Conference on Innovations in Theoretical Computer Science, pp. 269–286 (2014)
47. Liu, Y.-K.: Single-shot security for one-time memories in the isolated qubits model. In: Garay, J.A., Gennaro, R. (eds.) CRYPTO 2014, Part II. LNCS, vol. 8617, pp. 19–36. Springer, Heidelberg (2014). https://doi.org/10.1007/978-3-662-44381-1_2
48. Lo, H.-K.: Insecurity of quantum secure computations. Phys. Rev. A **56**(2), 1154–1162 (1997)
49. Lo, H.K., Chau, H.F.: Is quantum bit commitment really possible? Phys. Rev. Lett. **78**(17), 3410–3413 (1997)
50. Lunemann, C., Nielsen, J.B.: Fully simulatable quantum-secure coin-flipping and applications. In: Nitaj, A., Pointcheval, D. (eds.) AFRICACRYPT 2011. LNCS, vol. 6737, pp. 21–40. Springer, Heidelberg (2011). https://doi.org/10.1007/978-3-642-21969-6_2
51. Maji, H.K., Prabhakaran, M., Rosulek, M.: A zero-one law for cryptographic complexity with respect to computational UC security. In: Rabin, T. (ed.) CRYPTO 2010. LNCS, vol. 6223, pp. 595–612. Springer, Heidelberg (2010). https://doi.org/10.1007/978-3-642-14623-7_32
52. Mayers, D., Salvail L.: Quantum oblivious transfer is secure against all individual measurements. In: Proceedings Workshop on Physics and Computation. PhysComp 1994, pp. 69–77 (1994)
53. Mayers, D.: Unconditionally secure quantum bit commitment is impossible. Phys. Rev. Lett. **78**(17), 3414 (1997)
54. Naor, M.: Bit commitment using pseudo-randomness. In: Brassard, G. (ed.) CRYPTO 1989. LNCS, vol. 435, pp. 128–136. Springer, New York (1990). https://doi.org/10.1007/0-387-34805-0_13
55. Pugh, C.J., et al.: Airborne demonstration of a quantum key distribution receiver payload. Quant. Sci. Technol. **2**(2), 024009 (2017)
56. Rabin, M.: How to exchange secrets by oblivious transfer. Technical Memo TR-81, Aiken Computation Laboratory, Harvard University (1981)
57. Rudich, S.: The use of interaction in public cryptosystems. In: Feigenbaum, J. (ed.) CRYPTO 1991. LNCS, vol. 576, pp. 242–251. Springer, Heidelberg (1992). https://doi.org/10.1007/3-540-46766-1_19
58. Salvail, L.: Quantum bit commitment from a physical assumption. In: Krawczyk, H. (ed.) CRYPTO 1998. LNCS, vol. 1462, pp. 338–353. Springer, Heidelberg (1998). https://doi.org/10.1007/BFb0055740
59. Salvail, L., Schaffner, C., Sotáková, M.: Quantifying the leakage of quantum protocols for classical two-party cryptography. Int. J. Quant. Inf. **13**(04), 1450041 (2015)
60. Shor, P.W.: Algorithms for quantum computation: discrete logarithms and factoring. In: FOCS 1994, pp. 124–134. IEEE Computer Society (1994)
61. Unruh, D.: Universally composable quantum multi-party computation. In: Gilbert, H. (ed.) EUROCRYPT 2010. LNCS, vol. 6110, pp. 486–505. Springer, Heidelberg (2010). https://doi.org/10.1007/978-3-642-13190-5_25

62. Unruh, D.: Quantum proofs of knowledge. In: Pointcheval, D., Johansson, T. (eds.) EUROCRYPT 2012. LNCS, vol. 7237, pp. 135–152. Springer, Heidelberg (2012). https://doi.org/10.1007/978-3-642-29011-4_10
63. Vazirani, U., Vidick, T.: Certifiable quantum dice: or, true random number generation secure against quantum adversaries. In: STOC 2012, pp. 61–76. Association for Computing Machinery (2012)
64. Watrous, J.: Zero-knowledge against quantum attacks. SIAM J. Comput. **39**(1), 25–58 (2009). Preliminary version in STOC 2006
65. Wiesner, S.: Conjugate coding. SIGACT News **15**(1), 78–88 (1983)
66. Yao, A.C.C.: Security of quantum protocols against coherent measurements. In: 27th ACM STOC, pp. 67–75. ACM Press (May/June 1995)

Security Analysis of Quantum Lightning

Bhaskar Roberts(✉)

UC Berkeley, Berkeley, USA
bhaskarr@eecs.berkeley.edu

Abstract. Quantum lightning is a new cryptographic object that gives a strong form of quantum money. Zhandry recently defined quantum lightning and proposed a construction of it based on superpositions of low-rank matrices. The scheme is unusual, so it is difficult to base the scheme's security on any widespread computational assumptions. Instead, Zhandry proposed a new hardness assumption that, if true, could be used to prove security.

In this work, we show that Zhandry's hardness assumption is in fact false, so the proof of security does not hold. However, we note that the proposal for quantum lightning has not been proven *insecure*. This work is the first step in analyzing the security of [3]'s proposal and moving toward a scheme that we can prove to be secure.

1 Introduction

A cryptographic protocol for money should satisfy two conditions:[1]

1. *Verification by untrusted users*: Any untrusted user, even an adversary seeking to counterfeit, can distinguish between valid and counterfeit banknotes.
2. *No counterfeiting*: Only the mint, a trusted administrator, can produce valid banknotes.

A classical bitstring can be easily duplicated, and will fail the *no counterfeiting* condition. However an arbitrary string of qubits cannot be duplicated, so quantum information is the first setting where *no counterfeiting* may hold. Therefore, there is interest in creating uncounterfeitable money from quantum states. This is known as public-key quantum money. However, we do not yet know how to construct public-key quantum money from widely used cryptographic assumptions, despite many attempts including [2] and [1].

More recently, [3] defined a new cryptographic object, called quantum lightning, that gives a strong form of public-key quantum money in which not even the mint can produce two copies of the same banknote. Zhandry also proposed a construction of quantum lightning, but it is unknown whether the scheme is secure. Instead, Zhandry proposed a plausible computational hardness assumption and

[1] There are several variations on the quantum money problem, each with slightly different conditions. These are adapted from ones presented in [2].

A. Canteaut and F.-X. Standaert (Eds.): EUROCRYPT 2021, LNCS 12697, pp. 562–567, 2021.
https://doi.org/10.1007/978-3-030-77886-6_19

proved that if it is true, then the scheme is secure. However, the assumption was untested.

Here, we show that the hardness assumption is false. Therefore the proof of security for [3]'s scheme does not hold. However, our work does not prove the scheme insecure, and it may be possible to fix the hardness assumption. Our work is the first step in determining whether [3]'s proposal is secure and whether a similar approach is viable.

The rest of the paper is organized as follows: first we summarize [3]'s proposed scheme for quantum lightning. Then we show that the hardness assumption that was used to prove security is false. Finally, we suggest where our work may lead: to a new plausible hardness assumption or to a stronger attack that proves the scheme insecure.

2 Proposed Construction of Quantum Lightning

For context, we summarize [3]'s proposed construction of quantum lightning in this section. The lightning bolt is a superposition that can be sampled efficiently, but not duplicated. Anyone can generate a random lightning bolt, and a verifier can check that the bolt was generated honestly. But it is supposedly hard to generate two states that appear to the verifier to be the same bolt.

Here is a simplified version of the construction. There is a collision-resistant hash function, $f_{\mathcal{A}}$, and the bolt is a superposition over the pre-image of some value output by $f_{\mathcal{A}}$. To generate a random bolt, we create a superposition over the domain of $f_{\mathcal{A}}$, apply $f_{\mathcal{A}}$ to the superposition, and write the output to a separate register. The output register is a superposition over the image of $f_{\mathcal{A}}$, and it is entangled with the first register. Finally, we measure the output register, which collapses to a single random eigenstate $|\mathbf{y}\rangle$, called the hash or the serial number. Since the two registers were entangled, the first register becomes a uniform superposition over the pre-image of $\mathbf{y}$. The first register's state is the bolt, and $\mathbf{y}$ is the classical serial number that identifies the bolt.

The bolt is unclonable if $f_{\mathcal{A}}$ is collision-resistant. If we can create two bolts that hash to the same serial number, then we can find a collision in $f_{\mathcal{A}}$ by simply measuring both bolts in the computational basis. Each measurement will give a random value in the pre-image of $\mathbf{y}$, and the two values are very likely to be distinct. These values represent a collision in $f_{\mathcal{A}}$, which contradicts the collision-resistance of $f_{\mathcal{A}}$.

More formally, the construction comprises three polynomial-time quantum algorithms: Setup, Gen, and Ver. Setup samples the hash function and the public verification key. This is performed by an honest administrator, called the mint. Gen generates a random bolt, and can be run by anyone, even the adversary. Finally, Ver verifies that a given state is an honestly generated bolt. Like Gen, Ver is also public-key. We describe the construction's variables, as well as the three algorithms, below.

Variables

- The scheme takes as parameters the positive integers m, q, d, e, k for which $m - d < e$ and $d < e$.
- Let $n = \binom{m+1}{2} - \binom{e+1}{2}$. n is the dimension of the image of $f_{\mathcal{A}}$.
- Let $\mathcal{D}$ be the set of $m \times m$ symmetric matrices over $\mathbb{Z}_q$ with rank $\leq d$. $\mathcal{D}$ is the domain of $f_{\mathcal{A}}$.
- Let $\mathcal{A} = \{\mathbf{A}_1, \mathbf{A}_2, \ldots, \mathbf{A}_n\}$ be some subset of the symmetric $m \times m$ matrices over $\mathbb{Z}_q$. $\mathcal{A}$ determines $f_{\mathcal{A}}$.
- Let $f_{\mathcal{A}} : \mathcal{D} \to \mathbb{Z}_q^n$ such that for an input $\mathbf{M} \in \mathcal{D}$ and each $i \in [n]$,

$$[f_{\mathcal{A}}(\mathbf{M})]_i = \sum_{j=1}^{m}\sum_{k=1}^{m}(\mathbf{A}_i)_{j,k} \cdot \mathbf{M}_{j,k} = \mathrm{Tr}(\mathbf{A}_i^T\mathbf{M}) \tag{1}$$

  $f_{\mathcal{A}}$ is the hash function used to sample the bolt. It maps matrices to vectors. $[f_{\mathcal{A}}(\mathbf{M})]_i$ is the dot product of $\mathbf{A}_i$'s entries with $\mathbf{M}$'s entries. To take the dot product of two matrices, we unfurl the entries of each matrix into a vector and dot the vectors together. This procedure is captured by (1).
- Let $|\text{↯}\rangle$ be the lightning bolt, which is an unclonable state.

Setup

Setup samples a verification trapdoor $\mathbf{R}$ and a hash function $f_{\mathcal{A}}$. $f_{\mathcal{A}}$ is chosen so that $\mathbf{R}^T\mathbf{R}$ is in the kernel of $f_{\mathcal{A}}$, a fact that will be useful in Ver.
<u>Setup</u>

1. Sample $\mathbf{R} \in_R \mathbb{Z}_q^{e\times m}$. $\mathbf{R}$ is the verification trapdoor.
2. Choose $\mathcal{A}$ such that $\mathbf{R}\cdot\mathbf{A}_i\cdot\mathbf{R}^T = \mathbf{0}$, $\forall i \in [n]$, and no $\mathbf{A}_i$ is a linear combination of the others. The purpose of this step is to ensure that $\mathbf{R}^T\mathbf{R}$ is in the kernel of $f_{\mathcal{A}}$.
3. Publish $\mathbf{R}$, $\mathcal{A}$, and the parameters n, m, q, d, e, k.

Note that the space of $m \times m$ symmetric matrices $\mathbf{A}$ for which $\mathbf{R} \cdot \mathbf{A} \cdot \mathbf{R}^T = \mathbf{0}$ has dimension $\binom{m+1}{2} - \binom{e+1}{2} = n$, so $\mathcal{A}$ is a basis for this space.

Gen

Gen generates a bolt. The bolt is statistically close to a tensor product of $k+1$ mini-bolts. A mini-bolt is a uniform superposition over the pre-image of $\mathbf{y}$, and all the mini-bolts that belong to a bolt have the same $\mathbf{y}$-value.
<u>Gen</u>

1. Create $|\phi^0\rangle$, a uniform superposition over all sets of $k+1$ rank-d matrices in $\mathcal{D}$ that are mapped to the same $\mathbf{y}$-value. Within a set of $k+1$ matrices, all matrices must map to the same value, but the various sets can map to any value in the image of $f_{\mathcal{A}}$. [3] explains how this step is accomplished.
2. Compute $f_{\mathcal{A}}(|\phi^0\rangle)$ in superposition, and measure the function's output, $\mathbf{y}$. After the measurement, $|\phi^0\rangle$ collapses to $|\phi^1\rangle$, a superposition over all sets of $k+1$ rank-d matrices in $\mathcal{D}$ that are pre-images of $\mathbf{y}$.
3. Let $|\text{↯}\rangle = |\phi^1\rangle$; then output $|\text{↯}\rangle$ and $\mathbf{y}$.

Ver

Ver verifies a purported bolt. It takes as input a serial number $\mathbf{y}$ and a purported bolt $|P\rangle$, which comprises the purported mini-bolts, $|P^{(1)}\rangle, \ldots, |P^{(k+1)}\rangle$. Ver checks each purported mini-bolt separately, and the bolt is accepted if all mini-bolts pass and have the same serial number $\mathbf{y}$.

Ver makes two measurements to verify the mini-bolt, one in the computational basis, the other in the Fourier basis. The computational basis test checks that the eigenstates of the mini-bolt are indeed in the pre-image of $\mathbf{y}$. The Fourier basis test checks that the mini-bolt is a superposition over many eigenstates, rather than a single eigenstate. See [3] for an explanation of why the test works.

<u>Ver</u>

1. For each purported mini-bolt, $|P^{(i)}\rangle$, let $|\mathbf{M}\rangle$ be a generic computational-basis eigenstate of $|P^{(i)}\rangle$. Compute and measure whether: $\mathbf{M} \in \mathcal{D}$ and $f_{\mathcal{A}}(\mathbf{M}) = \mathbf{y}$.
2. Take the quantum Fourier transform of the state. Let $|\mathbf{N}\rangle$ be a generic Fourier-basis eigenstate. Measure whether rank $(\mathbf{R} \cdot \mathbf{N} \cdot \mathbf{R}^T) \leq m - d$.
3. Take the inverse quantum Fourier transform, and output the resulting state. The mini-bolt passes if and only if our measurements in steps 1 and 2 passed.
4. The purported bolt passes if and only if all the mini-bolts passed relative to the same $\mathbf{y}$.

Crucially, the Fourier basis test uses the trapdoor $\mathbf{R}$ to check that the mini-bolt has the right structure, and Ver does not work without $\mathbf{R}$. However, $\mathbf{R}$ also gives information about the kernel of $f_{\mathcal{A}}$, which we will use to break the hardness assumption.

3 Analysis of the Security Proof

It is difficult to base the scheme's security on any widespread computational assumptions because superpositions of low-rank matrices are not well studied. Instead, Zhandry proposed a plausible new hardness Assumption (1) and showed that if Assumption 1 is true, then the proposed construction of quantum lightning is secure.

Essentially, Assumption 1 says that $f_{\mathcal{A}}$ is $(2k+2)$-multi-collision-resistant (MCR) *even when we publish the trapdoor* $\mathbf{R}$.

Assumption 1 ([3]). *For some functions d, e, k in m for which $n = \binom{m+1}{2} - \binom{e+1}{2} < dm - \binom{d}{2}$, $kn \leq dm - \binom{d}{2} < (2k+1)n$, and $e > d$, $f_{\mathcal{A}}$ is $(2k+2)$-multi-collision-resistant, even if* $\mathbf{R}$ *is public.*

Before this work, Assumption 1 was untested, but here we will show that it is false.

Breaking Assumption 1

We will show that $\mathbf{R}$ allows us to construct more than $2k+2$ low-rank matrices that are in the pre-image of $\mathbf{y}$. $\mathbf{R}^T\mathbf{R}$ is in the kernel of $f_{\mathcal{A}}$, so we use $\mathbf{R}^T\mathbf{R}$ to construct many low-rank matrices that are in the kernel of $f_{\mathcal{A}}$. All of these matrices hash to the same value: $\mathbf{y} = \mathbf{0}$.

First, observe that $\mathbf{R}^T\mathbf{R}$ is in the kernel of $f_{\mathcal{A}}$:

$$f_{\mathcal{A}}(\mathbf{R}^T\mathbf{R})_i = \text{Tr}(\mathbf{A}_i^T\mathbf{R}^T\mathbf{R}) = \text{Tr}(\mathbf{R}\mathbf{A}_i\mathbf{R}^T) = 0$$

Second, we will use the rows of $\mathbf{R}$ to construct a set of low-rank matrices in the kernel of $f_{\mathcal{A}}$. Let the rows of $\mathbf{R}$ be $\{\mathbf{r}_1, \ldots, \mathbf{r}_e\} \subset \mathbb{Z}_q^m$, expressed as column vectors. For any row $\mathbf{r}_j$, $\mathbf{r}_j\mathbf{r}_j^T$ is a symmetric matrix with rank $= 1$, so $\mathbf{r}_j\mathbf{r}_j^T \in \mathcal{D}$.

For any $i \in [n]$, $\mathbf{r}_j^T \cdot \mathbf{A}_i \cdot \mathbf{r}_j = 0$. This means that

$$f_{\mathcal{A}}(\mathbf{r}_j\mathbf{r}_j^T)_i = \text{Tr}(\mathbf{A}_i^T\mathbf{r}_j\mathbf{r}_j^T) = \text{Tr}(\mathbf{r}_j^T\mathbf{A}_i\mathbf{r}_j) = 0$$

Therefore, $\mathbf{r}_j\mathbf{r}_j^T$ is in the kernel of $f_{\mathcal{A}}$.

Third, let $K = \{\mathbf{r}_1\mathbf{r}_1^T, \ldots, \mathbf{r}_e\mathbf{r}_e^T\}$ be the e matrices that we constructed. Then take any linear combination of d of the matrices in K. The resulting matrix is also a symmetric matrix of rank $\leq d$ that maps to $\mathbf{0}$. This procedure can be easily modified to produce matrices in the pre-image of another output value.

Lastly, this procedure produces many more than $2k+2$ colliding inputs. Due to the restrictions on m, n, d, e, k, it is the case that $k < d < e$. It suffices to find $4e$ colliding inputs because $2k+2 < 2e+2 < 4e$. Since $\mathbf{R}$ is random, with overwhelming probability, $\mathbf{R}$ has rank e. Then the matrices in K are linearly independent, and the number of matrices we can construct from this procedure is on the order of $\binom{e}{d}q^d$ matrices, which is much more than $4e$.

In summary, we've given a procedure that uses $\mathbf{R}$ to construct many ($\geq 2k+2$) inputs to $f_{\mathcal{A}}$ that map to $\mathbf{0}$. Therefore Assumption 1 is false.

Implications and Future Work

The proof of security given in [3] was based on Assumption 1, and since Assumption 1 is false, the proof of security does not hold.

However we are optimistic that the construction can be patched (modified) to rule out the attack on Assumption 1 that we presented, and any similar attacks. We would need to find an $\mathbf{R}$ that is useful for verification but that does not give a matrix in the kernel of $f_{\mathcal{A}}$. Patching the construction is an open problem.

Additionally, we wonder whether [3]'s existing construction can be proven insecure with an attack similar to the one presented in this paper. After all, a similar attempt at constructing quantum lightning can be proven insecure with a similar attack. [3]'s scheme is similar to an attempted folklore construction of quantum lightning based on the SIS problem ([3], Sect. 1.1). Where [3]'s construction uses matrices of low rank, the SIS-based construction uses vectors of small norm. The SIS-based construction is insecure because the verification trapdoor can be used to construct a superposition over short vectors in the kernel of the hash function, and this state passes verification. Analogously, we hypothesize that **R** could be used to create a superposition of low-rank matrices in the kernel of $f_{\mathcal{A}}$ that passes verification.

Acknowledgements. I thank Mark Zhandry for useful discussions.

References

1. Aaronson, S., Christiano, P.: Quantum money from hidden subspaces. Theor. Comput. **9**(9), 349–401 (2013). https://doi.org/10.4086/toc.2013.v009a009
2. Farhi, E., Gosset, D., Hassidim, A., Lutomirski, A., Shor, P.: Quantum money from knots. In: Proceedings of the 3rd Innovations in Theoretical Computer Science Conference, pp. 276–289, ITCS 2012. ACM, New York (2012). https://doi.org/10.1145/2090236.2090260
3. Zhandry, M.: Quantum lightning never strikes the same state twice. In: Ishai, Y., Rijmen, V. (eds.) EUROCRYPT 2019, Part III. LNCS, vol. 11478, pp. 408–438. Springer, Cham (2019). https://doi.org/10.1007/978-3-030-17659-4_14

Classical vs Quantum Random Oracles

Takashi Yamakawa[1(✉)] and Mark Zhandry[2,3]

[1] NTT Secure Platform Laboratories, Tokyo, Japan
takashi.yamakawa.ga@hco.ntt.co.jp
[2] Princeton University, Princeton, USA
mzhandry@princeton.edu
[3] NTT Research, Palo Alto, USA

Abstract. In this paper, we study relationship between security of cryptographic schemes in the random oracle model (ROM) and quantum random oracle model (QROM). First, we introduce a notion of a *proof of quantum access to a random oracle* (PoQRO), which is a protocol to prove the capability to quantumly access a random oracle to a classical verifier. We observe that a proof of quantumness recently proposed by Brakerski et al. (TQC '20) can be seen as a PoQRO. We also give a construction of a publicly verifiable PoQRO relative to a classical oracle. Based on them, we construct digital signature and public key encryption schemes that are secure in the ROM but insecure in the QROM. In particular, we obtain the first examples of natural cryptographic schemes that separate the ROM and QROM under a standard cryptographic assumption.

On the other hand, we give lifting theorems from security in the ROM to that in the QROM for certain types of cryptographic schemes and security notions. For example, our lifting theorems are applicable to Fiat-Shamir non-interactive arguments, Fiat-Shamir signatures, and Full-Domain-Hash signatures etc. We also discuss applications of our lifting theorems to quantum query complexity.

1 Introduction

The random oracle model (ROM) [BR93] is a widely used heuristic in cryptography where a hash function is modeled as a random function that is only accessible as an oracle. The ROM was used for constructing practical cryptographic schemes including digital signatures [FS87, PS96, BR96], chosen-ciphertext attack (CCA) secure public key encryption (PKE) [BR95, FOPS01, FO13], identity-based encryption (IBE) [GPV08], etc.

In 2011, Boneh et al. [BDF+11] observed that the ROM may not be sufficient when considering post-quantum security, since a quantum adversary can quantumly evaluate hash functions on superpositions, while the ROM only gives a classically-accessible oracle to an adversary. Considering this observation, they

Takashi Yamakawa—This work was done while the author was visiting Princeton University.

A. Canteaut and F.-X. Standaert (Eds.): EUROCRYPT 2021, LNCS 12697, pp. 568–597, 2021.
https://doi.org/10.1007/978-3-030-77886-6_20

proposed the quantum random oracle model (QROM), which gives an adversary quantum access to an oracle that computes a random function.

Boneh et al. observe that many proof techniques in the ROM cannot be directly translated into one in the QROM, *even if the other building blocks of the system are quantum-resistant.* Therefore, new proof techniques are needed in order to justify the post-quantum security of random oracle model systems. Fortunately, recent advances of proof techniques have clarified that most important constructions that are originally proven secure in the ROM are also secure in the QROM. These include OAEP [TU16], Fujisaki-Okamoto transform [TU16,JZC+18,Zha19], Fiat-Shamir transform [LZ19,DFMS19,DFM20], Full-Domain Hash (FDH) signatures [Zha12], Gentry-Peikert-Vaikuntanathan (GPV) IBE [Zha12,KYY18], etc.

Given this situation, it is natural to ask if there may be a general theorem lifting *any* classical ROM proof into a proof in the QROM, provided that the other building blocks of the system remain quantum resistant. There are several known lifting theorems that ensure that certain types of security reductions in the ROM also work in the QROM [BDF+11,Son14,ZYF+19,KS20]. However, there is no known general lifting theorem that works regardless of form of security proofs in the ROM.

Such a general lifting theorem certainly seems like a challenging task. Nevertheless, demonstrating a separation—that is, a scheme using quantum-resistant building blocks that is secure in the ROM but insecure in the QROM—has also been elusive. Intuitively, the reason is that natural problems on random oracles (such as pre-image search, collision finding, etc.) only have *polynomial* gaps between classical and quantum query complexity.

We are aware of two works that consider the task of finding a separation. First, Boneh et al. [BDF+11] gave an example of an identification protocol that is secure in the ROM but insecure in the QROM, but is specific to a certain non-standard timing model. Concretely, the protocol leverages the polynomial gap in collision finding to allow an attacker with quantum oracle access to break the system somewhat faster than any classical-access algorithm. The verifier then rejects if the prover cannot respond to its challenges fast enough, thereby blocking classical attacks while allowing the quantum attack to go through. This unfortunately requires a synchronous model where the verifier keeps track of the time between messages; such a model is non-standard.

Second, a recent work of Zhang et al. [ZYF+19] showed that quantum random oracle is *differentiable* from classical random oracle, which roughly means that it is impossible to simulate quantum queries to a random oracle using only classical queries to the same function. Their result rules out a natural approach one may take to give a lifting theorem, but it fails to actually give a scheme separating classical from quantum access to a random oracle.[1]

[1] Subsequent to the posting of the initial version of this work online, Zhang et al. [ZYF+19] updated their paper to add a construction of a cryptographic scheme that separates the ROM and the QROM. See Sect. 1.3 for details.

In summary, there is no known classical cryptographic scheme (e.g., digital signatures or PKE) that can be proven secure in the ROM but insecure in the QROM. This leaves open the important question of whether or not a general lifting theorem for cryptographic schemes is possible.

1.1 Our Results

We give constructions of cryptographic schemes that separate the ROM and QROM, showing that a fully general lifting theorem is impossible. On the other hand, we also give lifting theorems from the ROM security to the QROM security for some constrained but still very general settings. Details are explained below:
Proof of Quantum Access to a Random Oracle. For showing separations between the ROM and QROM, we first introduce a primitive which we call a *proof of quantum access to random oracle* (PoQRO). Roughly speaking, a PoQRO is a protocol where a quantum prover proves his ability to quantumly access to a random oracle to a classical verifier who is only given classical access to the random oracle. This is closely related to the notion of a proof of quantumness [BCM+18], but the difference is that a proof of quantumness only requires soundness against completely classical adversaries whereas a PoQRO requires soundness against *quantum* adversaries with classical access to a random oracle.

First, we observe that a proof of quantumness recently proposed by Brakerski et al. [BKVV20] is actually also a PoQRO. As a result, we obtain a PoQRO under the assumed quantum hardness of the learning with errors (LWE) problem [Reg09] (which we call the QLWE assumption in the following). The construction is non-interactive in the sense that after a verifier generates a pair of a public and secret keys and publishes the public key, a prover can generate a proof without any interaction. However, the proof is not publicly verifiable since the verification relies on the secret key.

We also study the possibility of publicly verifiable PoQRO. We give a construction of a publicly verifiable PoQRO relative to a classical oracle (which can be queried in superposition) using the technique developed in the recent work by Amos et al. [AGKZ20]. Similarly to [AGKZ20], we can heuristically instantiate the protocol in the standard model by using candidate constructions of post-quantum obfuscation [Agr19, AP20, BDGM20, WW20, GP20].

Separation of ROM and QROM. A PoQRO itself is already an example of cryptographic task that can be done in the QROM but cannot be done in the ROM. By embedding a PoQRO into digital signatures and PKE, we obtain the following results:

- A digital signature scheme that is EUF-CMA secure in the ROM but completely broken by 1 signing query in the QROM, and
- A PKE scheme that is IND-CCA secure in the ROM but completely broken by 1 decryption query in the QROM.

Both these results rely on the QLWE assumption.

Moreover, by embedding a publicly verifiable PoQRO into them, we can show the existence of a classical oracle relative to which there exist the following schemes:

- A digital signature scheme that is EUF-CMA secure in the ROM but not even EUF-NMA secure[2] in the QROM, and
- A PKE scheme that is IND-CCA secure in the ROM but not even IND-CPA secure in the QROM.

These results can be understood as an evidence that a generic lifting theorem is unlikely to exist even for the weak security notions of EUF-NMA security of digital signatures and IND-CPA security of PKE. Specifically, the above results imply that there do not exist a relativizing lifting theorem for them that works relative to any classical oracle.

Lifting Theorem for Search-Type Games. We now turn to our positive results, giving lifting theorems for certain class of schemes and security notions. First, we give a lifting theorem for what we call *search-type games.* A search-type game is specified by a classical challenger that interacts with an adversary and finally outputs $\top$ indicating acceptance or $\bot$ indicating rejection. We say that the adversary wins if the verifier outputs $\top$. We say that the game is hard in the ROM (resp. QROM) if no efficient quantum adversary with classical (resp. quantum) access to the random oracle can win the game with non-negligible probability. For example, the soundness of PoQROs is captured by the hardness of a search-type game in the ROM (but not QROM!), and the EUF-CMA/NMA security of digital signatures in the ROM (resp. QROM) is captured by the hardness of a search-type game in the ROM (resp. QROM). We prove the following theorem:

Theorem 1 (Lifting Theorem for Search-Type Game, Informal). *For any search-type game where a challenger makes* constant *number of queries to the random oracle, if the game is hard in the ROM, then that is also hard in the QROM.*

As immediate corollaries of the theorem, we obtain lifting theorems for the following:

- EUF-NMA security of digital signatures whose key generation and verification algorithms make $O(1)$ random oracle queries, and
- Soundness of (non-)interactive arguments whose (setup algorithm and) verifier make at most $O(1)$ random oracle queries.

The latter lifting theorem is applicable to those obtained by the Fiat-Shamir transform to constant round interactive arguments. Though it is already proven that such arguments are sound in the QROM [LZ19,DFMS19,DFM20], we believe that the above general corollary would be still useful for the design

[2] The EUF-NMA security is an unforgeability against adversaries that do not make any signing query.

of non-interactive arguments in the QROM in the future without repeating a similar analyses to those works.

Theorem 1 also immediately implies the impossibility of PoQRO where the verifier makes $O(1)$ random oracle queries. We note that in our PoQRO protocols, the number of queries made by the verification algorithm is $\omega(\log \lambda)$. We leave it as an interesting open problem to study the (im)possibility of PoQRO with $O(\log \lambda)$-query verification.

Though the applicability of Theorem 1 is somewhat limited, to the best of our knowledge, this is the first general lifting theorem from ROM security to QROM security that does make any assumptions about the ROM security reduction.

Lifting Theorem for EUF-CMA Security of Digital Signatures. Unfortunately, Theorem 1 does not give a lifting theorem for the EUF-CMA security of digital signatures (except for a non-interesting case where the signing algorithm does not make random oracle query). On the other hand, we give a lifting theorem for the EUF-CMA security for digital signature shcmes that satisfy additional properties.

Theorem 2 (Lifting Theorem for Digital Signatures, Informal). *Suppose that a digital signature scheme satisfies the following:*

1. *EUF-NMA secure in the ROM,*
2. *The key generation algorithm does not make random oracle queries and the verification algorithm makes $O(1)$ random oracle queries,*
3. *Random oracle queries made by the signing and verification algorithms reveal the corresponding message, and*
4. *Signatures are simulatable without the signing key if one is allowed to non-adaptively program the random oracle.*

Then the scheme is EUF-CMA secure in the QROM.

This theorem is applicable to the FDH signatures and Fiat-Shamir signatures. To the best of our knowledge, this is the first lifting theorem that is simultaneously applicable to both of them.

Application to Quantum Query Complexity. Based on a slight variant of a quantitative version of Theorem 1, we obtain a general theorem about query complexity. We consider a class of oracle problems, where the adversary's goal is to find distinct inputs to H such that the corresponding outputs satisfy some relation. Our theorem can be seen as upper bounding the success probability of a q-query adversary in terms of the probability of an adversary that makes no queries at all. Slightly more formally:

Theorem 3 (Informal). *Let $H : \mathcal{X} \rightarrow \mathcal{Y}$ be a random oracle. For any relation $R \subseteq \mathcal{Y}^k$, the probability that a q-quantum-query adversary finds pair-wise distinct $x_1, ..., x_k$ such that $(H(x_1), ..., H(x_k)) \in R$ is at most*

$$(2q+1)^{2k} \Pr[\exists \pi \ s.t.\ (y_{\pi(1)}, ..., y_{\pi(k)}) \in R : (y_1, ..., y_k) \xleftarrow{\$} \mathcal{Y}^k] \qquad (1)$$

where π is a permutation over $\{1, ..., k\}$.

The probability in Eq. 1 is typically be very easy to analyze. Theorem 3 therefore yields very simple non-trivial query lower bounds for various problems including (multi-)preimage search and (multi- or generalized) collision finding. Though these bounds are already known and/or non-tight, an advantage of our proofs is its extreme simplicity once we have Theorem 3 in hand.

1.2 Technical Overview

PoQRO from LWE. We first observe that a proof of quantumness in [BKVV20] is also a PoQRO. Though the construction and security proof are essentially the same as theirs, we briefly review them for the reader's convenience. The protocol is based on a noisy trapdoor claw-free permutation constructed from the QLWE assumption [BCM+18,BKVV20]. In this overview, we assume that there is a clean trapdoor claw-free permutation for simplicity. A claw-free permutation is a function $f : \{0,1\} \times \{0,1\}^n \rightarrow \{0,1\}^n$ such that (1) $f(0,\cdot)$ and $f(1,\cdot)$ are injective, (2) it is difficult for an efficient quantum adversary given f to find a claw (x_0, x_1) such that $f(0, x_0) = f(1, x_1)$, but (3) there is a trapdoor that enables one to efficiently find both pre-images for any target value. Let H be a random oracle from $\{0,1\}^n$ to $\{0,1\}$. In the PoQRO, the verifier first generates f along with its trapdoor and only sends f to the prover as a public key. Then the prover generates a state $\frac{1}{2}(|0\rangle|x_0\rangle + |1\rangle|x_1\rangle)$ along with $y = f(0, x_0) = f(1, x_1)$ by using the technique of [BCM+18]. Then it applies the random oracle H into the phase to get $\frac{1}{2}((-1)^{H(x_0)}|0\rangle|x_0\rangle + (-1)^{H(x_1)}|1\rangle|x_1\rangle)$, applies the Hadamard transform, measures both registers to obtain (m, d), and sends (y, m, d) as a proof to the verifier. The verifier computes x_0 and x_1 from y by using the trapdoor and accepts if $m = d^T \cdot (x_0 \oplus x_1) \oplus H(x_0) \oplus H(x_1)$ holds. As shown in [BKVV20], the equation is satisfied if the prover honestly run the protocol. On the other hand, a cheating prover with classical access to H can pass the test with probability almost 1/2 since the only way to obtain an information of $H(x_0) \oplus H(x_1)$ is to query both x_0 and x_1; this happens with a negligible probability due to the claw-free property. This construction only gives a constant gap between completeness and soundness, so we amplify it to super-polynomial by $\omega(\log \lambda)$ parallel repetitions.

Publicly Verifiable PoQRO. We construct a publicly verifiable PoQRO based on a variant of an equivocal collision-resistant hash (ECRH) [AGKZ20]. An ECRH $f : \mathcal{X} \rightarrow \mathcal{Y}$ is a collision-resistant hash function with a special property called equivocality. The equivocality enables one to generate a pair of a classical string $y \in \mathcal{Y}$ and a quantum state $|\mathsf{sk}\rangle$ that can be used to find x such that $f(x) = y$ and $p(x) = b$ where $p : \mathcal{X} \rightarrow \{0,1\}$ is a pre-determined predicate and b is a bit chosen after $(y, |\mathsf{sk}\rangle)$ is generated. Amos et al. [AGKZ20] constructed an ECRH for a predicate p that returns the first bit of its input relative to a classical oracle. Here, we observe that their construction can be extended to support *any* predicate p. Specifically, we can define p as a predicate defined by a random oracle $H : \mathcal{X} \rightarrow \{0,1\}$. Based on such an ECRH, we can construct a 4-round publicly verifiable PoQRO as follows:

1. The verifier generates an ECRH f and sends f to the prover.
2. The prover generates y along with the corresponding $|\mathsf{sk}\rangle$ and sends y to the verifier
3. The verifier randomly chooses $b \xleftarrow{\$} \{0,1\}$ and sends b to the prover.
4. The prover finds x such that $f(x) = y$ and $H(x) = b$ by using $|sk\rangle$ and sends x to the verifier.
5. The verifier accepts if and only if $f(x) = y$ and $H(x) = b$.

By the functionality of ECRH, the verifier accepts with overwhelming probability if a prover with quantum access to H runs honestly. On the other hand, if a cheating prover is given only classical access to H, then the verifier will accept with probability almost $1/2$. To see this, consider the first query the prover makes to H on an x^* such that $f(x^*) = y$. If the prover ultimately sends an $x \neq x^*$ to the verifier that causes the verifier to accept, x and x^* will be a collision for f, contradicting the collision-resistance of f. On the other hand, if $x = x^*$, then $H(x) = H(x^*)$ has only a $1/2$ chance of being equal to b, regardless of whether the query on x^* happened before or after the prover learned b. The result is that, no matter what the prover does, the verifier rejects with probability essentially at least $1/2$.

This protocol only achieves a constant gap between completeness and soundness, but it can be amplified to super-polynomial by $\omega(\log \lambda)$ parallel repetitions. Moreover since the verifier's message in the third round is just a public coin, we can apply the Fiat-Shamir transform to the above protocol to make the protocol non-interactive considering the generation of f as a setup.

Separations for Digital Signatures and Public Key Encryption. Given a PoQRO, it is easy to construct digital signature and PKE schemes that are secure in the ROM but insecure in the QROM: Suppose that we have a EUF-CMA secure digital signature scheme in the ROM, consider a modified scheme in which the signing algorithm returns a secret key of the scheme if the queried message is a valid proof of the PoQRO. Clearly, this scheme is insecure in the QROM and completely broken by 1 signing query. On the other hand, security in the ROM is preserved since an adversary in the ROM cannot find a valid proof of the PoQRO. A separation for IND-CCA security of PKE can be obtained by embedding verification of PoQRO in a decryption algorithm in a similar manner.

Moreover, if the PoQRO is publicly verifiable, then we can embed the verification of the PoQRO into verification and encryption algorithms of digital signature and PKE schemes, respectively. As a result, we obtain separations even for EUF-NMA secure digital signatures and IND-CPA secure PKE schemes, assuming an equivocal collision-resistant hash function.

Lifting Theorem for Search-Type Games. Next, we give a brief overview of proofs of our lifting theorems. A starting point of our lifting theorem is the following *classical* lemma:

Lemma 1. *(Informal) For any search-type cryptographic game in which a challenger makes at most k classical random oracle queries, if there exists an efficient* *adversary $\mathcal{A}$ that makes at most q classical random oracle queries with winning probability ϵ, then there exists an efficient $\mathcal{B}$ that makes at most k classical random oracle queries with winning probability at least $\epsilon/(q+1)^k$.*

This lemma can be proven by considering $\mathcal{B}$ described as follows:

1. Let H be the "real" random oracle that is given to $\mathcal{B}$.
2. For each $j = 1, ..., k$, $\mathcal{B}$ randomly picks $i_j \stackrel{\$}{\leftarrow} [q+1]$. Intuitively, this is a guess of $\mathcal{A}$'s first query that is equal to the challenger's j-th query where $i_j = q+1$ is understood as a guess that "$\mathcal{A}$ does not make such a query".
3. $\mathcal{B}$ chooses a fresh "fake" random oracle H' by itself.[3]
4. $\mathcal{B}$ runs $\mathcal{A}$ by giving $\mathcal{A}$ a stateful oracle $\mathcal{O}$ simulated as follows: $\mathcal{B}$ initializes $\mathcal{O}$ to H'. Whenever $\mathcal{A}$ makes its i-th query x_i, $\mathcal{B}$ simulates the oracle $\mathcal{O}$ in one of the following ways:
   (a) If $i = i_j$ for some $j \in [k]$, then $\mathcal{B}$ queries x_i to the real random oracle H to obtain $H(x_i)$, returns $H(x_i)$, and reprograms $\mathcal{O}$ to output $H(x_i)$ on input x_i.
   (b) Otherwise, $\mathcal{B}$ just returns $\mathcal{O}(x_i)$.
   Whenever $\mathcal{A}$ sends some message to the challenger, $\mathcal{B}$ just forwards it to the external challenger, and whenever the challenger returns some message, $\mathcal{B}$ forwards it to $\mathcal{A}$.

Clearly, $\mathcal{B}$ makes at most k classical random oracle queries and is as efficient as $\mathcal{A}$. We can see that $\mathcal{B}$ perfectly simulates the game for $\mathcal{A}$ if the guess is correct (e.g., $\mathcal{A}$'s i_j-th query is its first query that is equal to the challenger's j-th query), which happens with probability $1/(q+1)^k$. Moreover, since the events that the guess is correct and the event that $\mathcal{A}$ wins are independent, we can conclude that $\mathcal{B}$'s winning probability is at least $1/(q+1)^k$ times $\mathcal{A}$'s winning probability.

Our idea is to apply a similar proof to $\mathcal{A}$ that may make quantum queries, with the goal of $\mathcal{B}$ still only needing classical queries. Then, an obvious problem is that $\mathcal{B}$ cannot forwards $\mathcal{A}$'s query in Step 4a since $\mathcal{A}$'s query may be quantum whereas $\mathcal{B}$ only has classical access to the real random oracle H. Here, our solution is to just let $\mathcal{B}$ measure $\mathcal{A}$'s query, query the measurement outcome to the real random oracle H, and then reprogram $\mathcal{O}$ according to this value. Of course, such a measurement can be noticed by $\mathcal{A}$ by a noticeable advantage. Nonetheless, we can rely on the techniques developed for Fiat-Shamir transform in the QROM [DFMS19,DFM20] to prove that this decreases the winning probability only by the factor of $(2q+1)^{2k}$. Therefore, as long as $k = O(1)$, the reduction works with a polynomial loss.

Application to Digital Signatures. Our lifting theorem for search-type games (Theorem 1) immediately implies a lifting theorem for EUF-NMA security for digital signature schemes where key generation and verification algorithms make

[3] More precisely, it simulates a fresh random oracle H' on the fly so that this can be done efficiently. Alternatively, it can choose H' from a family of q-wise independent functions.

constant number of random oracle queries. On the other hand, Kiltz et al. [KLS18] showed that the EUF-NMA security in the QROM implies EUF-CMA security in the QROM for Fiat-Shamir signatures. We generalize this result to a broader class of digital signature schemes that satisfy conditions given in Theorem 2. Roughly speaking, this can be proven based on the observation that if signatures are simulatable without the signing key by programming the random oracle, then the signing oracle is useless and thus the EUF-NMA and EUF-CMA security are equivalent. By combining this with Theorem 1, we obtain Theorem 2.

Application to Quantum Query Complexity. As one can see from the overview of the proof of Theorem 1, the security loss of the reduction from QROM adversary to ROM adversary is $(2q+1)^{2k}$. By applying a (slight variant of) this quantitative version of Theorem 1 to a search-type game to find a pair-wise distinct $(x_1, ..., x_k)$ such that $(H(x_1), ..., H(x_k)) \in R$, we obtain Theorem 3.

1.3 Related Works

P versus BQP Relative to a Random Oracle. As a related question to the topic of this paper, Fortnow and Rogers [FR99] asked if we can separate complexity classes **P** and **BQP** relative to a random oracle. Though Aaronson and Ambainis [AA14] gave an evidence that it is difficult to separate (an average case version of) **P** and **BQP** relative to a random oracle under a certain conjecture, an unconditional proof is still open. We note that our separations between ROM and QROM do not give any implication to the problem since we rely on computational assumptions and consider an interactive protocol, which cannot be captured as a decision problem.

Separation of ROM and QROM for Sampling. Aaronson [Aar10] showed that there is a sampling problem (called Fourier Sampling) that can be solved by 1 quantum query to a random oracle but requires exponential number of classical queries. We note that this does not give a separation of the ROM and QROM in a cryptographic setting since a classical verifier cannot efficiently check that the sample is taken according to the correct distribution.

Known Lifting Theorems. Though several works [BDF+11, Son14, ZYF+19, KS20] give lifting theorems from ROM security to QROM security, they assume certain conditions for security proofs in the ROM. On the other hand, our lifting theorem for search-type games only requires syntactic conditions of schemes and their security notions, and do not assume anything about security proofs in the ROM. Our lifting theorem for digital signatures requires slightly more involved conditions, but we believe that it is much easier to check them than to check that a security proof in the ROM relies on a certain type of reductions.

Quantum Query Complexity. Beals et al. [BBC+01] showed that quantum query complexity is polynomially related to classical query complexity for any total functions. Though this may seem closely related to our result on query complexity, there are two significant differences. First, they consider a problem to output a 1-bit predicate considering the oracle as an input, whereas we consider a problem to find k inputs whose oracle values are in a certain relation. Second, they consider the worst case complexity whereas we consider the average case complexity. Due to the above two differences, these two results are incomparable.

Zhandry [Zha19, Theorem 3] also gave a general theorem that gives average case quantum query lower bounds relative to a random oracle. Their theorem gives tighter lower bounds than ours for some problems (e.g., collision finding). On the other hand, we believe that ours is easier to apply and also more general than theirs. For example, their theorem does not (at least directly) give meaningful lower bounds for the generalized collision finding problems.

Concurrent Work. Subsequent to the posting of the initial version of this work online, Zhang et al. [ZYF+19] updated their paper to add a construction of (an interactive version of) PoQRO based on the QLWE assumption. Their construction is based on an ad hoc modification of Mahadev's classical verification of quantum computation protocol [Mah18], and completely different from ours.

2 Preliminaries

Notations. We use λ to mean the security parameter throughout the paper. For a set X, $|X|$ is the cardinality of X. We denote by $x \xleftarrow{\$} X$ to mean that we take x uniformly from X. For sets $\mathcal{X}$ and $\mathcal{Y}$, $\mathsf{Func}(\mathcal{X},\mathcal{Y})$ denotes the set of all functions from $\mathcal{X}$ to $\mathcal{Y}$. For a positive integer n, $[n]$ means a set $\{1,...,n\}$. We say that a quantum (resp. classical) algorithm is efficient if that runs in quantum (resp. classical) polynomial time. For a quantum or randomized classical algorithm $\mathcal{A}$, we denote $y \xleftarrow{\$} \mathcal{A}(x)$ to mean that $\mathcal{A}$ outputs y on input x, and denote $y \in \mathcal{A}(x)$ to mean that y is in the support of $\mathcal{A}(x)$.

Oracles. In this paper, we consider the following three types of oracles: quantum oracle, quantumly-accessible classical oracle, and classically-accessible classical oracle.

A *quantum oracle* is an oracle that applies a unitary U on a query register. A *quantumly-accessible classical oracle* is a special case of a quantum oracle where U computes a classical function, i.e., there exists a classical function f such that we have $U|x\rangle|y\rangle = |x\rangle|y \oplus f(x)\rangle$ for any x and y in the domain and range of f. By a standard technique, when f is a single-bit output function, we can implement an oracle that applies a unitary U' such that $U'|x\rangle = (-1)^{f(x)}|x\rangle$ for any x by a single call to an oracle that applies U as above. We call an oracle that applies U' a phase oracle of f. A *classically-accessible classical oracle* works similarly to a quantumly-accessible classical oracle except that it measures the first register (the register to store x) in standard basis in each query. When we just say that an oracle is a classical oracle, then that is quantumly-accessible for any quantum algorithm and classically-accessible for any classical algorithm. For an oracle-aided quantum algorithm $\mathcal{A}$ and a classical function f, we often denote by $\mathcal{A}^{|f\rangle}$ (resp. $\mathcal{A}^{f}$) to mean that $\mathcal{A}$ is given a quantumly-accessible (resp. classically-accessible) classical oracle that computes f.

Classical/Quantum Random Oracle Model. In the (classical) random oracle model (ROM) [BR93], a random function H (of a certain domain and range) is chosen at the beginning, and every party (including honest algorithms of a protocol whose security is analyzed and an adversary) can classically access H. In other words, they are given a classically-accessible classical oracle that computes H. The quantum random oracle model (QROM) [BDF+11] is defined similarly except that the access to H can be quantum. In other words, a quantumly-accessible classical oracle that computes H is available for the adversary.[4] We stress that the classical ROM can be considered even when we consider security against quantum adversaries. We say that an algorithm in the QROM (resp. ROM) is q-quantum-query (resp. q-classical-query) if it makes at most q queries to its oracle.

By the following lemma, we can efficiently simulate a quantum random oracle to a q-quantum-query algorithms by using $2q$-wise independent hash function.[5]

Lemma 2 ([Zha12]). *For any sets $\mathcal{X}$ and $\mathcal{Y}$ of classical strings and q-quantum-query algorithm $\mathcal{A}$, we have*

$$\Pr[\mathcal{A}^{|H\rangle} = 1 : H \xleftarrow{\$} \mathsf{Func}(\mathcal{X}, \mathcal{Y})] = \Pr[\mathcal{A}^{|H\rangle} = 1 : H \xleftarrow{\$} \mathcal{H}_{2q}]$$

where $\mathcal{H}_{2q}$ is a family of $2q$-wise independent hash functions from $\mathcal{X}$ to $\mathcal{Y}$.

Learning with Errors. Roughly speaking, a learning with errors (LWE) [Reg09] problem is a problem to solve a system of noisy linear equations. Regev [Reg09] gave a quantum reduction from hardness of LWE to hardness of worst-case lattice problems, and it has been conjectured that the LWE problem is hard to solve in quantum polynomial time. We call the assumption that no quantum polynomial time algorithm can solve the LWE problem QLWE assumption. We omit a detailed definition and a concrete parameter choice for the LWE problem since we use the QLWE assumption only as a building block for constructing general primitives such as noisy trapdoor claw-free functions [BCM+18, BKVV20], PKE [Reg09, PW08], and digital signatures [GPV08]. We refer to these works for concrete parameter choices.

Cryptographic Primitives. We give definitions of digital signatures and PKE and its security notions in the full version. They are mostly standard except that we use n-EUF-CMA (resp. n-IND-CCA) security to mean security of digital signatures (resp. PKE) against adversaries that make at most n signing (resp. decryption) queries.

---

[4] Since we consider the post-quantum setting where honest algorithms are classical, the only party who may quantumly access H is the adversary.

[5] Though Zhandry [Zha19] gives another method to simulate a quantum random oracle without upper bounding the number of queries, we use a simulation by $2q$-wise independent hash functions for simplicity.

3 Separation Between ROM and QROM

In this section, we show examples of cryptographic schemes that are secure in the ROM but insecure in the QROM.

3.1 Proof of Quantum Access to Random Oracle

First, we introduce a notion of proofs of quantum access to a random oracle (PoQRO).

Definition 1. *A (non-interactive) proof of quantum access to a random oracle (PoQRO) consists of algorithms* $(\mathsf{PoQRO.Setup}, \mathsf{PoQRO.Prove}, \mathsf{PoQRO.Verify})$.

$\mathsf{PoQRO.Setup}(1^\lambda)$: *This is a classical algorithm that takes the security parameter* 1^λ *as input and outputs a public key* pk *and a secret key* sk.

$\mathsf{PoQRO.Prove}^{|H\rangle}(\mathsf{pk})$: *This is a quantum oracle-aided algorithm that takes a public key* pk *as input and given a quantum access to a random oracle* H*, and outputs a proof* π.

$\mathsf{PoQRO.Verify}^{H}(\mathsf{sk}, \pi)$: *This is a classical algorithm that takes a secret key* sk *and a proof* π *as input and given a classical access to a random oracle* H*, and outputs* $\top$ *indicating acceptance or* $\bot$ *indicating rejection.*

We require PoQRO to satisfy the following properties.

Correctness. *We have*

$$\Pr\left[\mathsf{PoQRO.Verify}^{H}(\mathsf{sk}, \pi) = \bot : \begin{array}{l}(\mathsf{pk}, \mathsf{sk}) \xleftarrow{\$} \mathsf{PoQRO.Setup}(1^\lambda),\\ \pi \xleftarrow{\$} \mathsf{PoQRO.Prove}^{|H\rangle}(\mathsf{pk})\end{array}\right] \leq \mathsf{negl}(\lambda).$$

Soundness. *For any quantum polynomial-time adversary* $\mathcal{A}$ *that is given a classical oracle access to* H*, we have*

$$\Pr\left[\mathsf{PoQRO.Verify}^{H}(\mathsf{sk}, \pi) = \top : \begin{array}{l}(\mathsf{pk}, \mathsf{sk}) \xleftarrow{\$} \mathsf{PoQRO.Setup}(1^\lambda),\\ \pi \xleftarrow{\$} \mathcal{A}^{H}(\mathsf{pk})\end{array}\right] \leq \mathsf{negl}(\lambda).$$

Definition 2 (Public Verifiability). *We say that PoQRO is publicly verifiable if we have* $\mathsf{pk} = \mathsf{sk}$ *for any* $(\mathsf{pk}, \mathsf{sk})$ *in the support of* $\mathsf{PoQRO.Setup}$*. When we consider a publicly verifiable PoQRO, we omit* sk *from the output of the setup algorithm and gives* pk *instead of* sk *to the verification algorithm for notational simplicity.*

PoQRO from QLWE. We observe that proofs of quantumness recently proposed by Brakerski et al. [BKVV20] can also be seen as PoQRO. Specifically, by just replacing "classical prover" with "quantum prover with classical access to the random oracle", their security proof directly works as a security proof of PoQRO.

Theorem 4 (a variant of [BKVV20]). *If the QLWE assumption holds, then there exists a PoQRO.*

Since the proof is essentially identical to that in [BKVV20], we give the proof in the full version.

Publicly Verifiable PoQRO Relative to Classical Oracle. Next, we give a construction of a publicly verifiable PoQRO relative to a classical oracle based on a variant of equivocal collision-resistant hash functions recently introduced in [AGKZ20].

Theorem 5. *There exists a publicly verifiable PoQRO relative to a quantumly-accessible classical oracle that is independent of the random oracle.*

Remark 1. One may think that we can upgrade any PoQRO to publicly verifiable one by just relativizing to a classical oracle in which sk is hardwired that runs the verification algorithm. However, in such a construction, the classical oracle depends on the random oracle, which we believe is not desirable. Especially, such a construction cannot be instantiated in the standard model even assuming an ideal obfuscation since we do not know how to obfuscate a circuit with random oracle gates. On the other hand, we consider a construction relative to a classical oracle that does not depend on the random oracle, which enables us to heuristically instantiate the construction in the standard model by using an obfuscation.

For proving Theorem 5, we introduce a slightly stronger variant of equivocal collision-resistant hash functions [AGKZ20].

Definition 3 (Equivocal Collision-Resistant Hash Functions for General Predicates). *An equivocal collision-resistant hash function (ECRH) family for general predicates with a domain $\mathcal{X}$ and a range $\mathcal{Y}$ is a tuple* $(\mathsf{ECRH.Setup}, \mathsf{ECRH.Gen}, \mathsf{ECRH.Eval}, \mathsf{ECRH.Equiv})$ *of efficient algorithms with the following syntax:*

$\mathsf{ECRH.Setup}(1^\lambda)$: *This is a probabilistic classical algorithm that takes the security parameter 1^λ as input and outputs a classical common reference string* crs.

$\mathsf{ECRH.Eval}(\mathsf{crs}, x)$: *This is a deterministic classical algorithm that takes a common reference string* crs *and an input $x \in \mathcal{X}$ as input and outputs a hash value $y \in \mathcal{Y}$.*

$\mathsf{ECRH.Gen}(\mathsf{crs})$: *This is a quantum algorithm that takes a common reference string* crs *as input, and outputs a hash value $y \in \mathcal{Y}$ and a quantum secret key* $|\mathsf{sk}\rangle$.

$\mathsf{ECRH.Equiv}^{|p\rangle}(1^t, |\mathsf{sk}\rangle, b)$ *This is a quantum algorithm that is given a quantumly-accessible classical oracle that computes a function $p : \mathcal{X} \rightarrow \{0,1\}$ and an "iteration parameter" 1^t, a secret key $|sk\rangle$, and a bit $b \in \{0,1\}$ as input and outputs $x \in \mathcal{X}$.*

As correctness, we require that for any $p : \mathcal{X} \to \{0,1\}$ *and* $t \in \mathbb{N}$*, if we have*

$$\Pr_{x \xleftarrow{\$} \mathcal{X}} [\mathsf{ECRH.Eval}(\mathsf{crs}, x) = y \ \wedge \ p(x) = b \mid \mathsf{ECRH.Eval}(\mathsf{crs}, x) = y] \geq t^{-1},$$

for all $\mathsf{crs} \in \mathsf{ECRH.Setup}(1^\lambda)$*,* $y \in \mathcal{Y}$*, and* $b \in \{0,1\}$*, then we have*

$$\Pr\left[\begin{array}{l} \mathsf{ECRH.Eval}(\mathsf{crs}, x) = y \\ \wedge\ p(x) = b \end{array} : \begin{array}{l} \mathsf{crs} \xleftarrow{\$} \mathsf{ECRH.Setup}(1^\lambda), \\ (y, |\mathsf{sk}\rangle) \xleftarrow{\$} \mathsf{ECRH.Gen}(\mathsf{crs}), \\ x \xleftarrow{\$} \mathsf{ECRH.Equiv}^{|p\rangle}(1^t, |\mathsf{sk}\rangle, b) \end{array}\right] = 1 - \mathsf{negl}(\lambda).$$

As security, we require that $\mathsf{ECRH.Eval}(\mathsf{crs}, \cdot)$ *is collision-resistant, i.e., for any efficient quantum adversary* $\mathcal{A}$*, we have*

$$\Pr\left[\begin{array}{l} \mathsf{ECRH.Eval}(\mathsf{crs}, x) = \mathsf{ECRH.Eval}(\mathsf{crs}, x') \\ \wedge\ x \neq x' \end{array} : \begin{array}{l} \mathsf{crs} \xleftarrow{\$} \mathsf{ECRH.Setup}(1^\lambda), \\ (x, x') \xleftarrow{\$} \mathcal{A}(\mathsf{crs}) \end{array}\right] = \mathsf{negl}(\lambda).$$

The above definition is similar to that of a family of equivocal collision-resistant hash functions in [AGKZ20], but stronger than that. The difference is that the predicate p is specified by ECRH.Gen in the original definition (and ECRH.Equiv is not given oracle access to p and the iteration parameter 1^t since they can be hardwired into the algorithm) whereas we require the correctness for a general predicate p. They gave a construction of a family of equivocal collision resistant hash functions w.r.t. a predicate p that just returns the first bit of its input relative to a classical oracle. We observe that essentially the same construction actually works for general predicates. Thus, we obtain the following lemma.

Lemma 3. *There exists a family of equivocal collision resistant hash functions for general predicates with a domain* $\{0,1\}^{2\lambda}$ *and a range* $\{0,1\}^\lambda$ *relative to a classical oracle that is independent of the random oracle. In the construction, for any* crs *and* y*, we have*

$$\left| x \in \{0,1\}^{2\lambda} : \mathsf{ECRH.Eval}(\mathsf{crs}, x) = y \right| = 2^\lambda.$$

A proof of the above lemma can be found in the full version.

We construct a publicly verifiable PoQRO based on ECRH for the random oracle predicate.

Let (ECRH.Setup, ECRH.Gen, ECRH.Eval, ECRH.Equiv) be an ECRH for general predicates as in Lemma 3. Let $m = \omega(\log \lambda)$ be an integer. Let $H : \{0,1\}^{2\lambda} \to \{0,1\}$ and $H' : \{0,1\}^{2m\lambda} \to \{0,1\}^m$ be random oracles.[6] Then our publicly verifiable PoQRO is described as follows:

$\mathsf{PoQRO.Setup}(1^\lambda)$: It generates $\mathsf{crs} \xleftarrow{\$} \mathsf{ECRH.Setup}(1^\lambda)$ and outputs $\mathsf{pk} := \mathsf{crs}$.

[6] Two (quantum) random oracles can be implemented by a single (quantum) random oracle by considering the first bit of the input as an index that specifies which random oracle to access.

$\mathsf{PoQRO.Prove}^{|H\rangle,|H'\rangle}(\mathsf{pk})$: It parses $\mathsf{crs} \leftarrow \mathsf{pk}$, computes $(y_i, |\mathsf{sk}_i\rangle) \xleftarrow{\$} \mathsf{ECRH.Gen}(\mathsf{crs})$ for all $i \in [m]$, $c := H'(y_1||...||y_m)$, $x_i \xleftarrow{\$} \mathsf{ECRH.Equiv}^{|H\rangle}(1^3, |\mathsf{sk}_i\rangle, c_i)$ for all $i \in [m]$ where c_i denotes the i-th bit of c, and outputs $\pi := \{(x_i, y_i)\}_{i\in[m]}$.

$\mathsf{PoQRO.Verify}^{H,H'}(\mathsf{pk}, \pi)$: It parses $\mathsf{crs} \leftarrow \mathsf{pk}$ and $\{(x_i, y_i)\}_{i\in[m]} \leftarrow \pi$ and outputs $\top$ if and only if $\mathsf{ECRH.Eval}(\mathsf{crs}, x_i) = y_i$ and $H(x_i) = c_i$ hold for all $i \in [m]$.

Lemma 4. *The above PoQRO satisfies correctness and soundness as required in Definition 1. Moreover, the construction is relativizing, i.e., that works relative to any oracles.*

Proof. (sketch) For any crs and y, since we assume

$$\left|x \in \{0,1\}^{2\lambda} : \mathsf{ECRH.Eval}(\mathsf{crs}, x) = y\right| = 2^{\lambda},$$

by the Chernoff bound, for an overwhelming fraction of H, we have

$$\Pr_{x \xleftarrow{\$} \{0,1\}^{2\lambda}}[\mathsf{ECRH.Eval}(\mathsf{crs}, x) = y \wedge H(x) = b \mid \mathsf{ECRH.Eval}(\mathsf{crs}, x) = y] \geq 1/3.$$

Therefore, the correctness of the underlying ECRH immediately implies correctness of the above protocol.

Here, we only give a proof sketch for soundness. See the full version for a full proof. Roughly speaking, soundness can be proven as follows: First, we observe that the above protocol can be seen as a protocol obtained by applying Fiat-Shamir transform to a 4-round protocol where c is chosen by the verifier after receiving $\{y_i\}_{i\in[m]}$ from the prover. As shown in [LZ19, DFMS19, DFM20], Fiat-Shamir transform preserves soundness even in the quantum setting.[7] Therefore, it suffices to prove soundness of the 4-round protocol against a cheating prover with classical access to the random oracle H. This can be argued as follows: Let $\{y_i\}_{i\in[m]}$ be the adversary's second message. And $\{x_i\}_{i\in[m]}$ be the fourth message. Without loss of generality, we assume that the adversary queries x_i for all $i \in [m]$ to the random oracle H and does not make the same query twice. By the collision-resistance of ECRH, the only preimage of y_i that is contained in the adversary's random oracle query list is x_i for all $i \in [m]$ with overwhelming probability. Conditioned on this, the adversary can win only if $H(x_i) = c_i$ holds for all $i \in [m]$, which happens with probability 2^{-m}. Therefore, the adversary can win with probability at most $2^{-m} + \mathsf{negl}(\lambda) = \mathsf{negl}(\lambda)$.

Finally, we remark that the above reduction works relative to any oracles.

By combining Lemma 3 and 4, Theorem 5 follows.

[7] Actually, since we only consider quantum adversaries that are only given *classical* access to the random oracle, there is a simpler analysis than those in [LZ19, DFMS19, DFM20] as shown in the full version.

3.2 Separations for Digital Signatures

In this section, we construct digital signature schemes that are secure in the ROM but insecure in the QROM based on PoQRO.

Lemma 5. *If there exist a PoQRO and a digital signature scheme that is EUF-CMA secure against quantum adversaries in the ROM, then there exists a digital signature scheme that is EUF-CMA secure in the ROM but not* 1*-EUF-CMA secure in the QROM.*

Lemma 6. *If there exist a publicly verifiable PoQRO and a digital signature scheme that is EUF-CMA secure against quantum adversaries in the ROM, then there exists a digital signature scheme that is EUF-CMA secure in the ROM but not EUF-NMA secure in the QROM.*

These lemmas can be easily proven by embedding a PoQRO into digital signature schemes. See the full version for proofs.

By combining the above lemmas with Theorem 4 and 5 and the fact that there exists a digital signature scheme that is EUF-CMA secure against quantum adversaries in the ROM under the QLWE assumption [GPV08], we obtain the following corollaries.

Corollary 1. *If the QLWE assumption holds, then there exists a digital signature scheme that is EUF-CMA secure against quantum adversaries in the ROM but not* 1*-EUF-CMA secure against quantum adversaries in the QROM.*

Corollary 2. *There exists a classical oracle relative to which there exists digital signature scheme that is EUF-CMA secure against quantum adversaries in the ROM but not EUF-NMA secure against quantum adversaries in the QROM.*[8]

3.3 Separations for Public Key Encryption

In this section, we construct a PKE scheme schemes that are secure in the ROM but insecure in the QROM based on PoQRO.

Lemma 7. *If there exist a PoQRO and a PKE scheme that is IND-CCA secure against quantum adversaries in the ROM, then there exists a PKE scheme that is IND-CCA secure against quantum adversaries in the ROM but not* 1*-IND-CCA secure in the QROM.*

Lemma 8. *If there exist a publicly verifiable PoQRO and a PKE scheme that is IND-CCA secure against quantum adversaries in the ROM, then there exists a PKE scheme that is IND-CCA secure against quantum adversaries in the ROM but not IND-CPA secure in the QROM.*

[8] We do not need any computational assumption in this corollary since we can construct a EUF-CMA secure digital signature scheme relative to a classical oracle in a straightforward manner.

These lemmas can be easily proven by embedding a PoQRO into PKE schemes. See the full version for proofs.

By combining the above lemmas with Theorem 4 and 5 and the fact that there exists an IND-CCA secure PKE scheme in the standard model (and thus in the ROM) under the QLWE assumption [PW08], we obtain the following corollaries.

Corollary 3. *If the QLWE assumption holds, then there exists a PKE scheme that is IND-CCA secure against quantum adversaries in the ROM but not* 1*-IND-CCA secure in the QROM.*

Corollary 4. *There exists a classical oracle relative to which there exists a PKE scheme that is IND-CCA secure against quantum adversaries in the ROM but not IND-CPA secure in the QROM.*[9]

4 Lifting Theorem

In this section, we prove a lifting theorem from ROM security to QROM security for a certain type of security notions. Then we discuss applications of this theorem.

4.1 Statement of Lifting Theorem

First, we define a concept of classically verifiable games. The following formalization is based on the definition of falsifiable assumptions in [GW11].

Definition 4 (Classically verifiable games). *A classically verifiable game consists of an interactive classical challenger $\mathcal{C}^H$ that is given classical access to a random oracle H and a constant $c \in [0,1)$. In the ROM (resp. QROM), the challenger $\mathcal{C}^H(1^\lambda)$ interacts with an adversary $\mathcal{A}^H(1^\lambda)$ (resp. $\mathcal{A}^{|H\rangle}(1^\lambda)$) and finally outputs $\top$ indicating acceptance or $\bot$ indicating rejection. If the challenger returns $\top$, we say that $\mathcal{A}^H(1^\lambda)$ (resp. $\mathcal{A}^{|H\rangle}(1^\lambda)$) wins $\mathcal{C}^H(1^\lambda)$.*

We say that a classically verifiable game is hard in the ROM (resp. QROM) if for any efficient quantum[10] *adversary $\mathcal{A}^H$ (resp. $\mathcal{A}^{|H\rangle}$) that is given a classical (resp. quantum) access to the random oracle H, we have*

$$\Pr_H[\mathcal{A}^H(1^\lambda) \text{ wins } \mathcal{C}^H(1^\lambda)] \leq c + \mathsf{negl}(\lambda)$$
$$(\text{resp.} \Pr_H[\mathcal{A}^{|H\rangle}(1^\lambda) \text{ wins } \mathcal{C}^H(1^\lambda)] \leq c + \mathsf{negl}(\lambda))$$

[9] We do not need any computational assumption in this corollary since we can construct an IND-CCA secure PKE scheme relative to a classical oracle in a straightforward manner.

[10] Note that we consider quantum adversaries even in the classical ROM.

where the probability is over the choice of the random oracle H, the random coins of $\mathcal{A}$ and $\mathcal{C}$, and the randomness in measurements by $\mathcal{A}$.[11]

We say that a classically verifiable game is search-type if $c = 0$.

Remark 2. Though the above definition is based on the definition of falsifiable assumptions in [GW11], the hardness of a classically verifiable game may not be falsifiable since we allow the challenger to run in unbounded time.

Examples. Soundness of PoQRO can be seen as hardness of a search-type classically verifiable game in the ROM. On the other hand, completeness requires (at least) that the game is not hard in the QROM. Therefore, the existence of PoQRO implies 2-round search-type classically falsifiable cryptographic game that is hard in ROM but is not hard in QROM.

EUF-CMA and EUF-NMA security of digital signatures in the ROM (resp. QROM) require hardness of search-type classically falsifiable games in the ROM (resp. QROM).

CPA and CCA security of PKE in the ROM (resp. QROM) require hardness of classically falsifiable games in the ROM (resp. QROM), which are not search-type.

Our main lifting theorem is stated as follows.

Theorem 6 (Lifting Theorem for Search-Type Games). *Let $\mathcal{C}$ be an k-classical-query challenger of a search-type classically verifiable game and $\mathcal{A}$ be a q-quantum-query efficient adversary against the game in the QROM. Then there exists a k-classical-query efficient adversary $\mathcal{B}$ against the game in the ROM such that*

$$\Pr_H[\mathcal{B}^H(1^\lambda) \textit{ wins } \mathcal{C}^H(1^\lambda)] \geq \frac{1}{(2q+1)^{2k}} \Pr_H[\mathcal{A}^{|H\rangle}(1^\lambda) \textit{ wins } \mathcal{C}^H(1^\lambda)].$$

In particular, for any search-type classically verifiable game in which the challenger makes at most $O(1)$ queries, if the game is hard in the ROM, then that is also hard in the QROM.

We also give a variant of the above theorem, which gives a slightly stronger inequality assuming that $\mathcal{C}$'s queries are publicly computable. Looking ahead, this variant will be used in Sect. 4.5 where we give quantum query lower bounds.

Theorem 7 (Lifting Theorem for Public-Query Search-Type Games). *Let $\mathcal{C}$ and $\mathcal{A}$ be as in Theorem 6. Moreover, we assume that the game is public-query, i.e., the list of $\mathcal{C}$'s queries is determined by the transcript and com-*

[11] We only write H in the subscript of the probability since all the other randomness are always in the probability space whenever we write a probability throughout this section.

putable in quantum polynomial-time. Then there exists a k-classical-query efficient adversary $\mathcal{B}$ against the game in the ROM such that

$$\Pr_H[\mathcal{B}^H(1^\lambda) \text{ wins } \mathcal{C}^H(1^\lambda) \wedge L_\mathcal{B} = L_\mathcal{C}] \geq \frac{1}{(2q+1)^{2k}} \Pr_H[\mathcal{A}^{|H\rangle}(1^\lambda) \text{ wins } \mathcal{C}^H(1^\lambda)].$$

where $L_\mathcal{B}$ and $L_\mathcal{C}$ are the list of random oracle queries by $\mathcal{B}$ and $\mathcal{C}$, respectively.

4.2 Proof of Lifting Theorem

For proving Theorem 6 and 7, we introduce a lemma from [DFM20]. For stating the lemma, we introduce some notations. Before giving formal definitions, we give a rough explanations. For a quantumly-accessible classical oracle $\mathcal{O}$, we denote by $\mathcal{O} \leftarrow \mathsf{Reprogram}(\mathcal{O}, x, y)$ to mean that we reprogram $\mathcal{O}$ to output y on input x. For a q-quantum-query algorithm $\mathcal{A}$, function $H : \mathcal{X} \to \mathcal{Y}$, and $\mathbf{y} = (y_1, ..., y_k) \in \mathcal{Y}^k$, we denote by $\tilde{\mathcal{A}}[H, \mathbf{y}]$ to mean an algorithm that runs $\mathcal{A}$ w.r.t. an oracle that computes H except that randomly chosen k queries are measured and the oracle is reprogrammed to output y_j on j-th measured query. Formal definitions are given below:

Definition 5 (Reprogramming Oracle). *Let $\mathcal{A}$ be a quantum algorithm with quantumly-accessible oracle $\mathcal{O}$ that is initialized to be an oracle that computes some classical function from $\mathcal{X}$ to $\mathcal{Y}$. At some point in an execution of $\mathcal{A}^\mathcal{O}$, we say that we reprogram $\mathcal{O}$ to output $y \in \mathcal{Y}$ on $x \in \mathcal{X}$ if we update the oracle to compute the function $H_{x,y}$ defined by*

$$H_{x,y}(x') := \begin{cases} y & \text{if } x' = x \\ H(x') & \text{otherwise} \end{cases}$$

where H is a function computed by $\mathcal{O}$ before the update. This updated oracle is used in the rest of execution of $\mathcal{A}$. We denote $\mathcal{O} \leftarrow \mathsf{Reprogram}(\mathcal{O}, x, y)$ to mean the above reprogramming.

Definition 6 (Measure-and-Reprogram). *Let $\mathcal{X}$, $\mathcal{Y}$, and $\mathcal{Z}$ be sets of classical strings and k be a positive integer. Let $\mathcal{A}$ be a q-quantum-query algorithm that is given quantum oracle access to an oracle that computes a function from $\mathcal{X}$ to $\mathcal{Y}$ and a (possibly quantum) input inp and outputs $\mathbf{x} \in \mathcal{X}^k$ and $z \in \mathcal{Z}$. For a function $H : \mathcal{X} \to \mathcal{Y}$ and $\mathbf{y} = (y_1, ..., y_k) \in \mathcal{Y}^k$, we define a measure-and-reprogram algorithm $\tilde{\mathcal{A}}[H, \mathbf{y}]$ as follows:*

$\tilde{\mathcal{A}}[H, \mathbf{y}](\mathsf{inp})$: *Given a (possibly quantum) input inp, it works as follows:*

1. *For each $j \in [k]$, uniformly pick $(i_j, b_j) \in ([q] \times \{0, 1\}) \cup \{(\bot, \bot)\}$ such that there does not exist $j \neq j'$ such that $i_j = i_{j'} \neq \bot$.*
2. *Run $\mathcal{A}^\mathcal{O}(\mathsf{inp})$ where the oracle $\mathcal{O}$ is initialized to be a quantumly-accessible classical oracle that computes H, and when $\mathcal{A}$ makes its i-th query, the oracle is simulated as follows:*

   (a) *If* $i = i_j$ *for some* $j \in [k]$*, measure* $\mathcal{A}$*'s query register to obtain* x'_j*, and do either of the following.*
      i. *If* $b_j = 0$*, reprogram* $\mathcal{O} \leftarrow \mathsf{Reprogram}(\mathcal{O}, x'_j, y_j)$ *and answer* $\mathcal{A}$*'s* i_j*-th query by using the reprogrammed oracle.*
      ii. *If* $b_j = 1$*, answer* $\mathcal{A}$*'s* i_j*-th query by using the oracle before the reprogramming and then reprogram* $\mathcal{O} \leftarrow \mathsf{Reprogram}(\mathcal{O}, x'_j, y_j)$*.*
   (b) *Otherwise, answer* $\mathcal{A}$*'s* i*-th query by just using the oracle* $\mathcal{O}$ *without any measurement or reprogramming.*
3. *Let* $(\mathbf{x} = (x_1, ..., x_k), z)$ *be* $\mathcal{A}$*'s output.*
4. *For all* $j \in [k]$ *such that* $i_j = \bot$*, set* $x'_j := x_j$*.*
5. *Output* $\mathbf{x}' := ((x'_1, ..., x'_k), z)$*.*

Then we state [DFM20, Theorem 6] with alternative notations as defined above.

Lemma 9. *(Rephrasing of [DFM20, Theorem 6]) Let* $\mathcal{X}$*,* $\mathcal{Y}$*,* $\mathcal{Z}$*, and* $\mathcal{A}$ *be as in Definition 6. Then for any* inp*,* $H : \mathcal{X} \to \mathcal{Y}$*,* $\mathbf{x}^* = (x_1^*, ..., x_k^*) \in \mathcal{X}^k$ *such that* $x_j^* \neq x_{j'}^*$ *for all* $j \neq j'$*,* $\mathbf{y} = (y_1, ..., y_k) \in \mathcal{Y}^k$*, and a relation* $R \subseteq \mathcal{X}^k \times \mathcal{Y}^k \times \mathcal{Z}$*, we have*

$$\Pr[\mathbf{x}' = \mathbf{x}^* \wedge (\mathbf{x}', \mathbf{y}, z) \in R : (\mathbf{x}', z) \xleftarrow{\$} \tilde{A}[H, \mathbf{y}](\mathsf{inp})]$$
$$\geq \frac{1}{(2q+1)^{2k}} \Pr[\mathbf{x} = \mathbf{x}^* \wedge (\mathbf{x}, \mathbf{y}, z) \in R : (\mathbf{x}, z) \xleftarrow{\$} \mathcal{A}^{|H_{\mathbf{x}^*,\mathbf{y}}\rangle}(\mathsf{inp})].$$

where $\tilde{A}[H, \mathbf{y}]$ *is the measure-and-reprogram algorithm as defined in Definition 6 and* $H_{\mathbf{x}^*,\mathbf{y}}$ *is defined as*

$$H_{\mathbf{x}^*,\mathbf{y}}(x') := \begin{cases} y_j & \text{if } \exists j \in [k] \text{ s.t. } x' = x_j^* \\ H(x') & \text{otherwise} \end{cases}.$$

We prove Theorem 6 by using Lemma 9.

Proof. (of Theorem 6.) We prove a slightly stronger claim than Theorem 6, where we switch the order of the quantifiers of $\mathcal{B}$ and $\mathcal{C}$. Specifically, we prove that for any q-quantum-query efficient algorithm $\mathcal{A}$, there exists an k-classical-query efficient algorithm $\mathcal{B}$ such that for any k-classical-query challenger $\mathcal{C}$, we have

$$\Pr_H[\mathcal{B}^H(1^\lambda) \text{ wins } \mathcal{C}^H(1^\lambda)] \geq \frac{1}{(2q+1)^{2k}} \Pr_H[\mathcal{A}^{|H\rangle}(1^\lambda) \text{ wins } \mathcal{C}^H(1^\lambda)]. \quad (2)$$

For proving this claim, it suffices to prove it assuming $\mathcal{C}$ is deterministic since the claim for probabilistic $\mathcal{C}$ immediately follows from that for deterministic $\mathcal{C}$ by a simple averaging argument.[12] Therefore, in the following, we assume that $\mathcal{C}$ is deterministic. We also assume that $\mathcal{C}$ does not make the same query twice and makes exactly k queries (by introducing dummy queries if necessary) without loss of generality.

We construct $\mathcal{B}$ as follows:

[12] Here, it is important that $\mathcal{B}$ does not depend on $\mathcal{C}$ due to the switching of the order of quantifiers.

$\mathcal{B}^H(1^\lambda)$: This is an algorithm that interacts with a challenger as follows:

1. Chooses a function $H' : \mathcal{X} \to \mathcal{Y}$ from a family of $2q$-wise independent hash functions.
2. For each $j \in [k]$, uniformly pick $(i_j, b_j) \in ([q] \times \{0,1\}) \cup \{(\bot, \bot)\}$ so that there does not exist $j \neq j'$ such that $i_j = i_{j'} \neq \bot$.
3. Run $\mathcal{A}^{\mathcal{O}}(1^\lambda)$ by forwarding all messages supposed to be sent to the challenger to the external challenger and forwarding all messages sent back from the external challenger to $\mathcal{A}$ and simulating the oracle $\mathcal{O}$ as follows. Initialize $\mathcal{O}$ to be a quantumly-accessible classical oracle that computes H'. When $\mathcal{A}$ makes its i-th query, the oracle is simulated as follows:

   (a) If $i = i_j$ for some $j \in [k]$, measure $\mathcal{A}$'s query register to obtain x'_j, query x'_j to the random oracle H to obtain $H(x'_j)$, and do either of the following.

      i. If $b_j = 0$, reprogram $\mathcal{O} \leftarrow \mathsf{Reprogram}(\mathcal{O}, x'_j, H(x'_j))$ and answer $\mathcal{A}$'s i_j-th query by using the reprogrammed oracle.
      ii. If $b_j = 1$, answer $\mathcal{A}$'s i_j-th query by using the oracle before the reprogramming and then reprogram $\mathcal{O} \leftarrow \mathsf{Reprogram}(\mathcal{O}, x'_j, H(x'_j))$.

   (b) Otherwise, answer $\mathcal{A}$'s i-th query by just using the oracle $\mathcal{O}$ without any measurement or reprogramming.

It is clear that $\mathcal{B}$ only makes k classical queries to H and is efficient if $\mathcal{A}$ is efficient. We prove that $\mathcal{B}$ satisfies Eq. 2 for all k-classical-query challengers $\mathcal{C}$. Let $\mathcal{X}$ and $\mathcal{Y}$ be the domain and codomain of a random oracle that is used in the game, and $\mathcal{Z}$ be a set consisting of all possible transcripts between $\mathcal{A}$ and $\mathcal{C}$. Here, a transcript means a concatenation of all messages exchanged between $\mathcal{A}$ and $\mathcal{C}$ and does not contain query-response pairs of the oracle. We call the concatenation of all query-response pairs for $\mathcal{C}$ and the transcript a $\mathcal{C}$'s view. We denote $\mathcal{C}$'s view in the form of $(\mathbf{x} = (x_1, ..., x_k), \mathbf{y} = (y_1, ..., y_k), z) \in \mathcal{X}^k \times \mathcal{Y}^k \times \mathcal{Z}$ where (x_j, y_j) is the j-th query-response pair for $\mathcal{C}$ and z is the transcript. Since we assume that $\mathcal{C}$ is deterministic, a view determines if $\mathcal{C}$ accepts or rejects. Let $R_\lambda \subseteq \mathcal{X}^k \times \mathcal{Y}^k \times \mathcal{Z}$ be a relation consisting of accepting view with respect to the security parameter λ. More precisely, for $(\mathbf{x} = (x_1, ..., x_k), \mathbf{y} = (y_1, ..., y_k), z) \in \mathcal{X}^k \times \mathcal{Y}^k \times \mathcal{Z}$, $(\mathbf{x}, \mathbf{y}, z) \in R_\lambda$ if the following algorithm $\mathsf{VerView}$ returns $\top$ on input $(1^\lambda, \mathbf{x}, \mathbf{y}, z)$.

$\mathsf{VerView}(1^\lambda, \mathbf{x} = (x_1, ..., x_k), \mathbf{y} = (y_1, ..., y_k), z)$: Run $\mathcal{C}(1^\lambda)$ by simulating all messages supposed to be sent from $\mathcal{A}$ and random oracle's responses so that they are consistent with the view $(\mathbf{x}, \mathbf{y}, z)$. At some point in the simulation, if $\mathcal{C}$'s behavior is not consistent with the view (i.e., $\mathcal{C}$ sends a message that is not consistent with the transcript z or its j-th query is not equal to x_j), then $\mathsf{VerView}$ returns $\bot$. Otherwise, $\mathsf{VerView}$ outputs the final output of $\mathcal{C}$.

We remark that VerView is deterministic as we assume $\mathcal{C}$ is deterministic and thus the relation R_λ is well-defined.

For a function $H : \mathcal{X} \to \mathcal{Y}$, we consider a quantum algorithm $\mathcal{S}_H$, in which the function H is hardwired, that is given quantum access to an oracle that computes another function $H' : \mathcal{X} \to \mathcal{Y}$ described as follows:

$\mathcal{S}_H^{|H'\rangle}(1^\lambda)$: Simulate an interaction between $\mathcal{A}$ and $\mathcal{C}$ by simulating oracles for them as follows:

- $\mathcal{A}$'s queries are just forwarded to the oracle $|H'\rangle$ and responded as $|H'\rangle$ responds.
- For $\mathcal{C}$'s j-th query x_j for $j \in [k]$, the oracle returns $H(x_j)$.

Finally, it outputs $\mathcal{C}$'s queries $\mathbf{x} := (x_1, ..., x_k)$ and the transcript z between $\mathcal{A}$ and $\mathcal{C}$ in the above execution.

For any $\lambda \in \mathbb{N}$, $H, H' : \mathcal{X} \to \mathcal{Y}$, $\mathbf{x}^* = (x_1^*, ..., x_k^*) \in \mathcal{X}^k$ such that $x_j^* \neq x_{j'}^*$ for all $j \neq j'$, and $\mathbf{y} = (y_1, ..., y_k) \in \mathcal{Y}^k$, by applying Lemma 9 for $\mathcal{S}_H$, we have

$$\begin{aligned}&\Pr[\mathbf{x}' = \mathbf{x}^* \wedge (\mathbf{x}', \mathbf{y}, z) \in R_\lambda : (\mathbf{x}', z) \xleftarrow{\$} \tilde{\mathcal{S}}_H[H', \mathbf{y}](1^\lambda)] \\ &\geq \frac{1}{(2q+1)^{2k}} \Pr[\mathbf{x} = \mathbf{x}^* \wedge (\mathbf{x}, \mathbf{y}, z) \in R_\lambda : (\mathbf{x}, z) \xleftarrow{\$} \mathcal{S}_H^{|H'_{\mathbf{x}^*, \mathbf{y}}\rangle}(1^\lambda)].\end{aligned} \tag{3}$$

where $\tilde{\mathcal{S}}_H[H', \mathbf{y}]$ is to $\mathcal{S}_H$ as $\tilde{\mathcal{A}}[H', \mathbf{y}]$ is to $\mathcal{A}$ as defined in Definition 6 and $H'_{\mathbf{x}^*, \mathbf{y}}$ is as defined in Lemma 9.

Especially, since the above inequality holds for any $\mathbf{y}$, by setting $\mathbf{y} := H(\mathbf{x}^*) = (H(x_1^*), ..., H(x_k^*))$, we have

$$\begin{aligned}&\Pr[\mathbf{x}' = \mathbf{x}^* \wedge (\mathbf{x}', H(\mathbf{x}^*), z) \in R_\lambda : (\mathbf{x}', z) \xleftarrow{\$} \tilde{\mathcal{S}}_H[H', H(\mathbf{x}^*)](1^\lambda)] \\ &\geq \frac{1}{(2q+1)^{2k}} \Pr[\mathbf{x} = \mathbf{x}^* \wedge (\mathbf{x}, H(\mathbf{x}^*), z) \in R_\lambda : (\mathbf{x}, z) \xleftarrow{\$} \mathcal{S}_H^{|H'_{\mathbf{x}^*, H(\mathbf{x}^*)}\rangle}(1^\lambda)].\end{aligned} \tag{4}$$

Recall that $\mathcal{S}_H^{|H'_{\mathbf{x}^*, H(\mathbf{x}^*)}\rangle}(1^\lambda)$ is an algorithm that simulates an interaction between $\mathcal{A}$ and $\mathcal{C}$ where $\mathcal{A}$'s oracle and $\mathcal{C}$'s oracles are simulated by $|H'_{\mathbf{x}^*, H(\mathbf{x}^*)}\rangle$ and H, respectively, and outputs $\mathcal{C}$'s queries $\mathbf{x}$ and the transcript z. Thus, conditioned on that $\mathbf{x} = \mathbf{x}^*$, $\mathcal{S}_H^{|H'_{\mathbf{x}^*, H(\mathbf{x}^*)}\rangle}(1^\lambda)$ simulates an interaction between $\mathcal{A}$ and $\mathcal{C}$ where both oracles of $\mathcal{A}$ and $\mathcal{C}$ compute the same function $H'_{\mathbf{x}^*, H(\mathbf{x}^*)}$ since we have $H(\mathbf{x}^*) = H'_{\mathbf{x}^*, H(\mathbf{x}^*)}(\mathbf{x}^*)$ by definition. Moreover, conditioned on that $\mathbf{x} = \mathbf{x}^*$, $(\mathbf{x}, H(\mathbf{x}^*), z) \in R_\lambda$ is equivalent to that $\mathcal{A}^{|H'_{\mathbf{x}^*, H(\mathbf{x}^*)}\rangle}(1^\lambda)$ wins $\mathcal{C}^{H'_{\mathbf{x}^*, H(\mathbf{x}^*)}}(1^\lambda)$ in the execution simulated by $\mathcal{S}_H^{|H'_{\mathbf{x}^*, H(\mathbf{x}^*)}\rangle}(1^\lambda)$. Based on these observations, we have

$$\begin{aligned}&\Pr[\mathbf{x} = \mathbf{x}^* \wedge (\mathbf{x}, H(\mathbf{x}^*), z) \in R_\lambda : (\mathbf{x}, z) \xleftarrow{\$} \mathcal{S}_H^{|H'_{\mathbf{x}^*, H(\mathbf{x}^*)}\rangle}(1^\lambda)] \\ &= \Pr[\mathbf{x} = \mathbf{x}^* \wedge \mathcal{A}^{|H'_{\mathbf{x}^*, H(\mathbf{x}^*)}\rangle}(1^\lambda) \text{ wins } \mathcal{C}^{H'_{\mathbf{x}^*, H(\mathbf{x}^*)}}(1^\lambda)]\end{aligned} \tag{5}$$

where $\mathbf{x}$ in the RHS is the list of queries made by $\mathcal{C}$.

Moreover, if we uniformly choose $H, H' : \mathcal{X} \to \mathcal{Y}$, then the distribution of the function $H'_{\mathbf{x}^*, H(\mathbf{x}^*)}$ is uniform over all functions from $\mathcal{X}$ to $\mathcal{Y}$ for any fixed $\mathbf{x}^*$. Therefore, by substituting Eq. 5 for the RHS of Eq. 4, taking the average over the random choice of H and H', and summing up over all $\mathbf{x}^* \in \mathcal{X}^k$, we have

$$\begin{aligned}\sum_{\mathbf{x}^* \in \mathcal{X}^k} &\Pr_{H,H'}[\mathbf{x}' = \mathbf{x}^* \wedge (\mathbf{x}', H(\mathbf{x}^*), z) \in R_\lambda : (\mathbf{x}', z) \xleftarrow{\$} \tilde{\mathcal{S}}_H[H', H(\mathbf{x}^*)](1^\lambda)] \\ &\geq \frac{1}{(2q+1)^{2k}} \Pr_H[\mathcal{A}^{|H\rangle}(1^\lambda) \text{ wins } \mathcal{C}^H(1^\lambda)].\end{aligned} \tag{6}$$

For proving Eq. 2 and completing the proof, what is left is to prove that the LHS of Eq. 6 is smaller than or equal to the LHS of Eq. 2. For proving this, we spell out how $\tilde{\mathcal{S}}_H[H', H(\mathbf{x}^*)]$ works according to the definition:

$\tilde{\mathcal{S}}_H[H', H(\mathbf{x}^*)](1^\lambda)$**:** Given the security parameter 1^λ as input, it works as follows:

1. For each $j \in [k]$, uniformly pick $(i_j, b_j) \in ([q] \times \{0,1\}) \cup \{(\perp, \perp)\}$ so that there does not exist $j \neq j'$ such that $i_j = i_{j'} \neq \perp$.
2. Simulate the interaction between $\mathcal{A}$ and $\mathcal{C}$ by simulating oracles for them as follows:
   Initialize an oracle $\mathcal{O}$ to be a quantumly-accessible classical oracle that computes H'. When $\mathcal{A}$ makes its i-th query, the oracle is simulated as follows:

   (a) If $i = i_j$ for some $j \in [k]$, measure $\mathcal{A}$'s query register to obtain x'_j, and do either of the following.

      i. If $b_j = 0$, reprogram $\mathcal{O} \leftarrow \mathsf{Reprogram}(\mathcal{O}, x'_j, H(x^*_j))$ and answer $\mathcal{A}$'s i_j-th query by using the reprogrammed oracle.
      ii. If $b_j = 1$, answer $\mathcal{A}$'s i_j-th query by using the oracle before the reprogramming and then reprogram $\mathcal{O} \leftarrow \mathsf{Reprogram}(\mathcal{O}, x'_j, H(x^*_j))$.

   (b) Otherwise, answer $\mathcal{A}$'s i-th query by just using the oracle $\mathcal{O}$ without any measurement or reprogramming.

   When $\mathcal{C}$ makes its j-th query x_j, return $H(x_j)$ as a response by the random oracle for each $j \in [k]$.
   Let z be the transcript in the above simulated execution.
3. For all $j \in [k]$ such that $i_j = \perp$, set $x'_j := x_j$.
4. Output $\mathbf{x}' := ((x'_1, ..., x'_k), z)$.

One can see from the above description that an execution of the game simulated by $\tilde{\mathcal{S}}_H[H', H(\mathbf{x}^*)](1^\lambda)$ for a randomly chosen H' is very close to an interaction between $\mathcal{B}^H$ and $\mathcal{C}^H$. The only difference is that $\mathcal{B}^H$ reprograms $\mathcal{O}$ to output $H(x'_j)$ instead of $H(x^*_j)$ on input x'_j in Step 2a.[13] Therefore, conditioned on that

[13] Strictly speaking, there is another difference that we consider $\tilde{\mathcal{S}}_H[H', H(\mathbf{x}^*)](1^\lambda)$ for a uniformly chosen H' whereas $\mathcal{B}$ chooses H' from a family of $2q$-wise independent hash functions. However, by Lemma 2, this does not cause any difference.

$\mathbf{x}' = \mathbf{x}^*$, $\tilde{\mathcal{S}}_H[H', H(\mathbf{x}^*)](1^\lambda)$ for a randomly chosen H' perfectly simulates an interaction between $\mathcal{B}^H$ and $\mathcal{C}^H$. Moreover, if $\mathbf{x}' = \mathbf{x}^*$ and $(\mathbf{x}', H(\mathbf{x}^*), z) \in R_\lambda$, then we must have $\mathbf{x} = \mathbf{x}^*$ where $\mathbf{x}$ is the list of $\mathcal{C}$'s queries in the simulation since otherwise the view $(\mathbf{x}', H(\mathbf{x}^*), z)$ is not consistent with $\mathcal{C}$'s queries and cannot pass $\mathsf{VerfView}$. In this case, we have $(\mathbf{x}, H(\mathbf{x}), z) \in R_\lambda$, which means that $\mathcal{B}^H$ wins $\mathcal{C}^H$ in the simulated execution. Therefore, for any fixed H and $\mathbf{x}^*$, we have

$$\begin{aligned}&\Pr_{H'}[\mathbf{x}' = \mathbf{x}^* \wedge (\mathbf{x}', H'(\mathbf{x}^*), z) \in R_\lambda : (\mathbf{x}', z) \xleftarrow{\$} \tilde{\mathcal{S}}_H[H', H(\mathbf{x}^*)](1^\lambda)] \\ &\leq \Pr[\mathbf{x} = \mathbf{x}^* \wedge \mathcal{B}^H(1^\lambda) \text{ wins } \mathcal{C}^H(1^\lambda)]\end{aligned} \tag{7}$$

where $\mathbf{x}$ in the RHS is the list of queries by $\mathcal{C}^H$.

By substituting Eq. 7 for the LHS of Eq. 6, we obtain Eq. 2. This completes the proof of Theorem 6.

Theorem 7 can be proven by a slight modification to the proof of Theorem 6.

Proof. (of Theorem 7.) We consider an algorithm $\mathcal{B}$ that works similarly to that in the proof of Theorem 6 except that it does an additional step at the end:

$\mathcal{B}^H(1^\lambda)$: This is an algorithm that interacts with a challenger as follows:

1–3. Work similarly to $\mathcal{B}$ in the proof of Theorem 6.
4. After completing the interaction with $\mathcal{C}$, compute the list of $\mathcal{C}$'s query, and if any query in the list has not yet been queried in the previous steps, then query them to H.

We have Eq. 6 by exactly the same argument to that in the proof of Theorem 6 since we do not use anything about the construction of $\mathcal{B}$ until this point. By the modification of $\mathcal{B}$ as described above, in the simulation of an interaction between $\mathcal{B}$ and $\mathcal{C}$ by $\tilde{\mathcal{S}}_H[H', H(\mathbf{x}^*)](1^\lambda)$, $\mathcal{B}$'s query list exactly matches $\mathbf{x}'$ that appears in the description of $\tilde{\mathcal{S}}_H[H', H(\mathbf{x}^*)](1^\lambda)$. With this observation in mind, by a similar argument to that in the proof of Theorem 6, we can see that we have

$$\begin{aligned}&\Pr_{H'}[\mathbf{x}' = \mathbf{x}^* \wedge (\mathbf{x}', H'(\mathbf{x}^*), z) \in R_\lambda : (\mathbf{x}', z) \xleftarrow{\$} \tilde{\mathcal{S}}_H[H', H(\mathbf{x}^*)](1^\lambda)] \\ &\leq \Pr[L_{\mathcal{B}} = L_{\mathcal{C}} = \{x_1^*, ..., x_k^*\} \wedge \mathcal{B}^H(1^\lambda) \text{ wins } \mathcal{C}^H(1^\lambda)]\end{aligned}. \tag{8}$$

By substituting Eq. 8 for the LHS of Eq. 6, we obtain

$$\Pr_H[\mathcal{B}^H(1^\lambda) \text{ wins } \mathcal{C}^H(1^\lambda) \wedge L_{\mathcal{B}} = L_{\mathcal{C}}] \geq \frac{1}{(2q+1)^{2k}} \Pr_H[\mathcal{A}^{|H\rangle}(1^\lambda) \text{ wins } \mathcal{C}^H(1^\lambda)].$$

which completes the proof of Theorem 7.

4.3 Immediate Corollaries

Here, we list immediate corollaries of Theorem 6.

PoQRO. Soundness of PoQRO can be seen as hardness of a search-type classically verifiable game in the ROM. On the other hand, completeness requires (at least) that the game is not hard in the QROM. By Theorem 6, such a separation between ROM and QROM is impossible if the number of verifier's query is $O(1)$. Therefore, we obtain the following corollary:

Corollary 5. *There does not exist PoQRO where the verification algorithm makes a constant number of random oracle queries.*

We note that a similar statement holds even for an interactive version of PoQRO.

(Non-)Interactive Arguments. A post-quantum interactive argument for a language L is a protocol where an efficient classical prover given a statement x and some auxiliary information (e.g., witness in the case of L is an NP language) and a efficient classical verifier only given x interacts and the verifier finally returns $\top$ indicating acceptance or $\bot$ indicating rejection. As correctness, we require that the verifier returns $\top$ with overwhelming probability if both parties run honestly. As (post-quantum) soundness, we require that any efficient cheating prover cannot let the verifier accept on any $x \notin L$ with a non-negligible probability.

Here, we consider constructions of interactive arguments based on random oracles. Clearly, soundness requirement of interactive arguments is captured by a search-type classically verifiable game. Therefore, by Theorem 6, we obtain the following corollary:

Corollary 6. *If an interactive argument with constant-query verifier is sound in the ROM, then it is also sound in the QROM.*

Non-interactive arguments (in the common reference string model) is defined similarly except that a common reference string is generated by a trusted third party and distributed to both the prover and the verifier at the beginning of the protocol and then the protocol consists of only one-round communication, i.e., a prover just sends a proof to the verifier and verifies it. (Adaptive) soundness of non-interactive arguments is defined similarly to soundness of interactive arguments with the modification that the statement $x \notin L$ for which the cheating prover tries to generate a forged proof can be chosen after seeing the common reference string.

Similarly, by Theorem 6, we obtain the following corollary:[14]

[14] Note that the theorem is applicable even though the soundness game for non-interactive arguments is not falsifiable since the challenger in our definition of classically verifiable games is not computationally bounded.

Corollary 7. *If a non-interactive argument is sound in the ROM with constant-query verifier and constant-query common reference string generation algorithm is sound in the ROM, then it is also sound in the QROM.*

Digital Signatures. As already observed, EUF-CMA security can be seen as a hardness of a search-type classically verifiable game. Therefore, as an immediate corollary of Theorem 6, we obtain the following corollary.

Corollary 8. *If a digital signature scheme is n-EUF-CMA secure in the ROM for $n = O(1)$ and the key generation, signing, and verification algorithms make $O(1)$ random oracle queries, then the scheme is also n-EUF-CMA secure in the QROM. If $n = 0$ (i.e., if we consider EUF-NMA security), then a similar statement holds even if the signing algorithm makes arbitrarily many queries.*

Unfortunately, we cannot extend this result to the ordinary EUF-CMA security where the number of signing query is unbounded (except for a non-interesting case where the signing algorithm does not make a random oracle query) since the challenger in the EUF-CMA game may make as many random oracle queries as the adversary's signing queries, which is not bounded by a constant. In Sect. 4.4, we extend the above corollary to give a lifting theorem for EUF-CMA security (without restricting the number of signing queries) assuming a certain structure for the scheme.

4.4 Application to Digital Signatures

Here, we discuss implications of our lifting theorem for digital signatures.

Theorem 8. *Suppose that a digital signature scheme* $(\mathsf{Sig.KeyGen}, \mathsf{Sig.Sign}, \mathsf{Sig.Verify})$ *with a message space $\mathcal{M}$ relative to a random oracle $H : \mathcal{X} \to \mathcal{Y}$ is EUF-NMA secure against quantum adversaries in the ROM and satisfies the following properties:*

1. $\mathsf{Sig.KeyGen}$ *does not make a random oracle query and* $\mathsf{Sig.Verify}$ *makes $O(1)$ random oracle queries. (There is no restriction on the number of random oracle queries by* $\mathsf{Sig.Sign}$*.)*
2. *A random query made by* $\mathsf{Sig.Sign}$ *or* $\mathsf{Sig.Verify}$ *reveals the message given to them as input. More precisely, there exists a classically efficiently computable function* $\mathsf{XtoM} : \mathcal{X} \to \mathcal{M}$ *such that for any H, honestly generated* $(\mathsf{vk}, \mathsf{sigk})$*, m, and σ, if* $\mathsf{Sig.Sign}^H(\mathsf{sk}, m)$ *or* $\mathsf{Sig.Verify}^H(\mathsf{vk}, m, \sigma)$ *makes a random oracle query x, then we have* $\mathsf{XtoM}(x) = m$*.*
3. *A signature is simulatable without a signing key if we can (non-adaptively) program the random oracle. More precisely, there exist a classically efficiently computable function $F_{\mathsf{vk}} : \mathcal{R} \to \mathcal{Y}$ tagged by a verification key* vk *and an efficient classical algorithm $\mathcal{S}$ such that for any honestly generated* $(\mathsf{vk}, \mathsf{sigk})$ *and $m_1, ..., m_\ell$ for $\ell = \mathsf{poly}(\lambda)$, we have*

$$\left\{ (\{H(x)\}_{x\in\mathcal{X}}, \{\sigma_i\}_{i\in[\ell]}) : \begin{array}{l} H \xleftarrow{\$} \mathsf{Func}(\mathcal{X},\mathcal{Y}) \\ \sigma_i \xleftarrow{\$} \mathsf{Sig.Sign}^H(\mathsf{sigk}, m_i) \textit{ for all } i \in [\ell] \end{array} \right\}$$
$$\approx \left\{ \left(\{F_{\mathsf{vk}}(\widetilde{H}(x))\}_{x\in\mathcal{X}}, \{\sigma_i\}_{i\in[\ell]}\right) : \begin{array}{l} \widetilde{H} \xleftarrow{\$} \mathsf{Func}(\mathcal{X},\mathcal{R}) \\ \{\sigma_i\}_{i\in[\ell]} \xleftarrow{\$} \mathcal{S}^{\widetilde{H}}(\mathsf{vk}, m) \end{array} \right\}.$$

where $\approx$ means that two distributions are statistically indistinguishable.

Then the scheme is EUF-CMA secure against quantum adversaries in the QROM.

Examples. Though the requirements in the above theorem may seem quite restrictive, it captures at least two important constructions of digital signatures: FDH signatures (and its lattice-based variant by Gentry, Peikert, and Vaikuntanathan [GPV08]) and Fiat-Shamir signatures. See the full version for details.

Due to the lack of space, a proof of Theorem 8 is given in the full version.

4.5 Application to Quantum Query Lower Bounds

We use Theorem 7 to give a general theorem on quantum query lower bounds. Specifically, we prove the following theorem.

Theorem 9. *Let $\mathcal{X}$ and $\mathcal{Y}$ be sets, $H : \mathcal{X} \to \mathcal{Y}$ be a random function, k be a positive integer, and $R \subseteq \mathcal{Y}^k$ be a relation over $\mathcal{Y}^k$. Then for any q-quantum-query algorithm $\mathcal{A}$, we have*

$$\Pr_H[(H(x_1),...,H(x_k)) \in R \wedge x_j \neq x_{j'} \textit{ for } j \neq j' : (x_1,...,x_k) \xleftarrow{\$} \mathcal{A}^{|H\rangle}]$$
$$\leq (2q+1)^{2k} \Pr[\exists \pi \in \mathsf{Perm}([k]) \textit{ s.t. } (y_{\pi(1)},...,y_{\pi(k)}) \in R : (y_1,...,y_k) \xleftarrow{\$} \mathcal{Y}^k]$$

where $\mathsf{Perm}([k])$ denotes the set of all permutations over $[k]$.

Proof. We consider a (non-interactive) public-query search-type game where an adversary is given quantum access to a random oracle H and sends $(x_1,...,x_k) \in \mathcal{X}^k$ to the challenger and the challenger outputs $\top$ if and only if $(H(x_1),...,H(x_k)) \in R$ and $(x_1,...,x_k)$ is pair-wise distinct. The LHS of the inequality in Theorem 9 is the probability that $\mathcal{A}$ wins the game. By Theorem 7, there exists a k-classical-query adversary $\mathcal{B}$ that wins the game while making exactly the same queries as those made by the challenger with probability at least $\frac{1}{(2q+1)^{2k}}$ times the probability that $\mathcal{A}$ wins. We observe that $\mathcal{B}$ makes exactly the same queries as the challenger if and only if it just sends a permutation of its k queries as the message $(x_1,...,x_k)$. In this case, $\mathcal{B}$'s winning probability is at most $\Pr[\exists \pi \in \mathsf{Perm}([k])$ s.t. $(y_{\pi(1)},...,y_{\pi(k)}) \in R : (y_1,...,y_k) \xleftarrow{\$} \mathcal{Y}^k]$ since the random oracle values are uniformly and independently random over $\mathcal{Y}$. By combining the above, we obtain Theorem 9.

We can use Theorem 9 to give quantum query lower bounds for a variety of problems with very simple proofs. See the full version for details.

References

[AA14] Aaronson, S., Ambainis, A.: The need for structure in quantum speedups. Theor. Comput. **10**, 133–166 (2014)

[Aar10] Aaronson, S.: BQP and the polynomial hierarchy. In: Schulman, L.J. (ed.) 42nd ACM STOC, pp. 141–150. ACM Press (Jun 2010)

[AGKZ20] Amos, R., Georgiou, M., Kiayias, A., Zhandry, M.: One-shot signatures and applications to hybrid quantum/classical authentication. In: Makarychev, K., Makarychev, Y., Tulsiani, M., Kamath, G., Chuzhoy, J. (eds.) 52nd ACM STOC, pp. 255–268. ACM Press (Jun 2020)

[Agr19] Agrawal, S.: Indistinguishability obfuscation without multilinear maps: new methods for bootstrapping and instantiation. In: Ishai, Y., Rijmen, V. (eds.) EUROCRYPT 2019, Part I. LNCS, vol. 11476, pp. 191–225. Springer, Cham (2019). https://doi.org/10.1007/978-3-030-17653-2_7

[AP20] Agrawal, S., Pellet-Mary, A.: Indistinguishability obfuscation without maps: attacks and fixes for noisy linear FE. In: Canteaut, A., Ishai, Y. (eds.) EUROCRYPT 2020, Part I. LNCS, vol. 12105, pp. 110–140. Springer, Cham (2020). https://doi.org/10.1007/978-3-030-45721-1_5

[BBC+01] Beals, R., Buhrman, H., Cleve, R., Mosca, M., de Wolf, R.: Quantum lower bounds by polynomials. J. ACM **48**(4), 778–797 (2001)

[BCM+18] Brakerski, Z., Christiano, P., Mahadev, U., Vazirani, U.V., Vidick, T.: A cryptographic test of quantumness and certifiable randomness from a single quantum device. In: Thorup, M. (ed.) 59th FOCS, pp. 320–331. IEEE Computer Society Press (Oct 2018)

[BDF+11] Boneh, D., Dagdelen, Ö., Fischlin, M., Lehmann, A., Schaffner, C., Zhandry, M.: Random oracles in a quantum world. In: Lee, D.H., Wang, X. (eds.) ASIACRYPT 2011. LNCS, vol. 7073, pp. 41–69. Springer, Heidelberg (2011). https://doi.org/10.1007/978-3-642-25385-0_3

[BDGM20] Brakerski, Z., Döttling, N., Garg, S., Malavolta, G.: Factoring and pairings are not necessary for iO: circular-secure LWE suffices. IACR Cryptol. ePrint Arch. **2020**, 1024 (2020)

[BKVV20] Brakerski, Z., Koppula, V., Vazirani, U.V., Vidick, T.: Simpler proofs of quantumness. In: TQC 2020, volume 158 of LIPIcs, pp. 8:1–8:14 (2020)

[BR93] Bellare, M., Rogaway, P.: Random oracles are practical: a paradigm for designing efficient protocols. In: Denning, D.E., Pyle, R., Ganesan, R., Sandhu, R.S., Ashby, V. (eds.) ACM CCS 93, pp. 62–73. ACM Press (Nov 1993)

[BR95] Bellare, M., Rogaway, P.: Optimal asymmetric encryption. In: De Santis, A. (ed.) EUROCRYPT 1994. LNCS, vol. 950, pp. 92–111. Springer, Heidelberg (1995). https://doi.org/10.1007/BFb0053428

[BR96] Bellare, M., Rogaway, P.: The exact security of digital signatures-how to sign with RSA and rabin. In: Maurer, U. (ed.) EUROCRYPT 1996. LNCS, vol. 1070, pp. 399–416. Springer, Heidelberg (1996). https://doi.org/10.1007/3-540-68339-9_34

[DFM20] Don, J., Fehr, S., Majenz, C.: The measure-and-reprogram technique 2.0: multi-round fiat-shamir and more. In: Micciancio, D., Ristenpart, T. (eds.) CRYPTO 2020, Part III. LNCS, vol. 12172, pp. 602–631. Springer, Cham (2020). https://doi.org/10.1007/978-3-030-56877-1_21

[DFMS19] Don, J., Fehr, S., Majenz, C., Schaffner, C.: Security of the fiat-shamir transformation in the quantum random-oracle model. In: Boldyreva, A., Micciancio, D. (eds.) CRYPTO 2019, Part II. LNCS, vol. 11693, pp. 356–383. Springer, Cham (2019). https://doi.org/10.1007/978-3-030-26951-7_13

[FO13] Fujisaki, E., Okamoto, T.: Secure integration of asymmetric and symmetric encryption schemes. J. Cryptol. **26**(1), 80–101 (2013)

[FOPS01] Fujisaki, E., Okamoto, T., Pointcheval, D., Stern, J.: RSA-OAEP is secure under the RSA assumption. In: Kilian, J. (ed.) CRYPTO 2001. LNCS, vol. 2139, pp. 260–274. Springer, Heidelberg (2001). https://doi.org/10.1007/3-540-44647-8_16

[FR99] Fortnow, L., Rogers, J.D.: Complexity limitations on quantum computation. J. Comput. Syst. Sci. **59**(2), 240–252 (1999)

[FS87] Fiat, A., Shamir, A.: How to prove yourself: practical solutions to identification and signature problems. In: Odlyzko, A.M. (ed.) CRYPTO 1986. LNCS, vol. 263, pp. 186–194. Springer, Heidelberg (1987). https://doi.org/10.1007/3-540-47721-7_12

[GP20] Gay, R., Pass, R.: Indistinguishability obfuscation from circular security. Cryptology ePrint Archive, Report 2020/1010 (2020). https://eprint.iacr.org/2020/1010

[GPV08] Gentry, C., Peikert, C., Vaikuntanathan, V.: Trapdoors for hard lattices and new cryptographic constructions. In: Ladner, R.E., Dwork, C. (eds.) 40th ACM STOC, pp. 197–206. ACM Press (May 2008)

[GW11] Gentry, C., Wichs, D.: Separating succinct non-interactive arguments from all falsifiable assumptions. In: Fortnow, L., Vadhan, S.P. (eds.) 43rd ACM STOC, pp. 99–108. ACM Press (Jun 2011)

[JZC+18] Jiang, H., Zhang, Z., Chen, L., Wang, H., Ma, Z.: IND-CCA-secure key encapsulation mechanism in the quantum random oracle model, revisited. In: Shacham, H., Boldyreva, A. (eds.) CRYPTO 2018, Part III. LNCS, vol. 10993, pp. 96–125. Springer, Cham (2018). https://doi.org/10.1007/978-3-319-96878-0_4

[KLS18] Kiltz, E., Lyubashevsky, V., Schaffner, C.: A concrete treatment of fiat-shamir signatures in the quantum random-oracle model. In: Nielsen, J.B., Rijmen, V. (eds.) EUROCRYPT 2018, Part III. LNCS, vol. 10822, pp. 552–586. Springer, Cham (2018). https://doi.org/10.1007/978-3-319-78372-7_18

[KS20] Krämer, J., Struck, P.: Encryption schemes using random oracles: from classical to post-quantum security. In: Ding, J., Tillich, J.-P. (eds.) PQCrypto 2020. LNCS, vol. 12100, pp. 539–558. Springer, Cham (2020). https://doi.org/10.1007/978-3-030-44223-1_29

[KYY18] Katsumata, S., Yamada, S., Yamakawa, T.: Tighter security proofs for GPV-IBE in the quantum random oracle model. In: Peyrin, T., Galbraith, S. (eds.) ASIACRYPT 2018, Part II. LNCS, vol. 11273, pp. 253–282. Springer, Cham (2018). https://doi.org/10.1007/978-3-030-03329-3_9

[LZ19] Liu, Q., Zhandry, M.: Revisiting post-quantum fiat-shamir. In: Boldyreva, A., Micciancio, D. (eds.) CRYPTO 2019, Part II. LNCS, vol. 11693, pp. 326–355. Springer, Cham (2019). https://doi.org/10.1007/978-3-030-26951-7_12

[Mah18] Mahadev, U.: Classical homomorphic encryption for quantum circuits. In: Thorup, M. (ed.) 59th FOCS, pp. 332–338. IEEE Computer Society Press (Oct 2018)

[PS96] Pointcheval, D., Stern, J.: Security proofs for signature schemes. In: Maurer, U. (ed.) EUROCRYPT 1996. LNCS, vol. 1070, pp. 387–398. Springer, Heidelberg (1996). https://doi.org/10.1007/3-540-68339-9_33

[PW08] Peikert, C., Waters, B.: Lossy trapdoor functions and their applications. In: Ladner, R.E., Dwork, C. (eds.) 40th ACM STOC, pp. 187–196. ACM Press (May 2008)

[Reg09] Regev, O.: On lattices, learning with errors, random linear codes, and cryptography. J. ACM **56**(6), 34:1–34:40 (2009)

[Son14] Song, F.: A note on quantum security for post-quantum cryptography. In: Mosca, M. (ed.) PQCrypto 2014. LNCS, vol. 8772, pp. 246–265. Springer, Cham (2014). https://doi.org/10.1007/978-3-319-11659-4_15

[TU16] Targhi, E.E., Unruh, D.: Post-quantum security of the fujisaki-okamoto and OAEP transforms. In: Hirt, M., Smith, A. (eds.) TCC 2016, Part II. LNCS, vol. 9986, pp. 192–216. Springer, Heidelberg (2016). https://doi.org/10.1007/978-3-662-53644-5_8

[WW20] Wee, H., Wichs, D.: Candidate obfuscation via oblivious LWE sampling. IACR Cryptol. ePrint Arch. **2020**, 1042 (2020)

[Zha12] Zhandry, M.: Secure identity-based encryption in the quantum random oracle model. In: Safavi-Naini, R., Canetti, R. (eds.) CRYPTO 2012. LNCS, vol. 7417, pp. 758–775. Springer, Heidelberg (2012). https://doi.org/10.1007/978-3-642-32009-5_44

[Zha19] Zhandry, M.: How to record quantum queries, and applications to quantum indifferentiability. In: Boldyreva, A., Micciancio, D. (eds.) CRYPTO 2019, Part II. LNCS, vol. 11693, pp. 239–268. Springer, Cham (2019). https://doi.org/10.1007/978-3-030-26951-7_9

[ZYF+19] Zhang, J., Yu, Y., Feng, D., Fan, S., Zhang, Z.: On the (quantum) random oracle methodology: new separations and more. Cryptology ePrint Archive, Report 2019/1101 (2019). https://eprint.iacr.org/2019/1101

On the Compressed-Oracle Technique, and Post-Quantum Security of Proofs of Sequential Work

Kai-Min Chung[1(✉)], Serge Fehr[2,3], Yu-Hsuan Huang[4], and Tai-Ning Liao[5]

[1] Academia Sinica, Taipei City, Taiwan
kmchung@iis.sinica.edu.tw
[2] CWI, Amsterdam, Netherlands
serge.fehr@cwi.nl
[3] Mathematical Institute, Leiden University, Leiden, Netherlands
[4] National Chiao-Tung University, Hsinchu City, Taiwan
asd00012334.cs04@nctu.edu.tw
[5] National Taiwan University, Taipei City, Taiwan

Abstract. We revisit the so-called compressed oracle technique, introduced by Zhandry for analyzing quantum algorithms in the quantum random oracle model (QROM). To start off with, we offer a concise exposition of the technique, which easily extends to the parallel-query QROM, where in each query-round the considered algorithm may make several queries to the QROM in parallel. This variant of the QROM allows for a more fine-grained query-complexity analysis.

Our main technical contribution is a framework that simplifies the use of (the parallel-query generalization of) the compressed oracle technique for proving query complexity results. With our framework in place, whenever applicable, it is possible to prove quantum query complexity lower bounds by means of purely classical reasoning. More than that, for typical examples the crucial classical observations that give rise to the classical bounds are sufficient to conclude the corresponding quantum bounds.

We demonstrate this on a few examples, recovering known results but also obtaining new results. Our main target is the hardness of finding a q-chain with fewer than q parallel queries, i.e., a sequence $x_0, x_1, \ldots, x_q$ with $x_i = H(x_{i-1})$ for all $1 \leq i \leq q$.

The above problem of finding a hash chain is of fundamental importance in the context of proofs of sequential work. Indeed, as a concrete cryptographic application of our techniques, we prove quantum security of the "Simple Proofs of Sequential Work" by Cohen and Pietrzak.

This research is partially supported by Ministry of Science and Technology, Taiwan, under Grant no. MOST 109-2223-E-001 -001 -MY3, MOST QC project, under Grant no. MOST 109-2627-M-002-003 -, and Executive Yuan Data Safety and Talent Cultivation Project (AS-KPQ-110-DSTCP).

A. Canteaut and F.-X. Standaert (Eds.): EUROCRYPT 2021, LNCS 12697, pp. 598–629, 2021.
https://doi.org/10.1007/978-3-030-77886-6_21

1 Introduction

Background. The random oracle (RO) methodology [2], which treats a cryptographic hash function $H : \{0,1\}^n \to \{0,1\}^m$ as an external *oracle*, has proven to be a successful way to design very efficient cryptographic protocols and arguing them secure in a rigorous yet idealized manner. Even though it is known that in principle the methodology can break down [7] and a "proven secure" protocol may become insecure in the actual (non-idealized) setting, experience has shown that for natural protocols this does not seem to happen.

In case of a *quantum* adversary that may locally run a quantum computer, the RO needs to be modeled as a quantum operation that is capable of answering queries *in superposition*, in order to reasonably reflect the capabilities of an attacker in the non-idealized setting [5]. This is then referred to as the *quantum random oracle model* (QROM). Unfortunately, this change in the model renders typical RO-security proofs invalid. One reason is that in the ordinary RO model the security reduction can inspect the queries that the adversary makes to the RO, while this is not possible anymore in the quantum setting when the queries are quantum states in superposition — at least not without disturbing the query state significantly and, typically, uncontrollably.

The Compressed Oracle. A very powerful tool to deal with the QROM is the so-called *compressed oracle* technique, introduced by Zhandry [20]. On a conceptual level, the technique very much resembles the classical "lazy sampling" technique; on a technical level, the idea is to consider a *quantum purification* of the random choice of the function H, and to analyze the internal state of the RO then in the Fourier domain.

This idea has proven to be very powerful. On the one hand, it gave rise to new and shorter proofs for known lower bound results on the query complexity of quantum algorithms (like Grover [3,13]); on the other hand, it enabled to prove new cryptographic security results, like in the context of *indifferentiability* [11,20], or, more recently, the *Fiat-Shamir transformation* [17], when considering a quantum adversary. However, it still is quite cumbersome to actually employ the compressed oracle technique; proofs tend to be hard to read, and they require a good understanding of quantum information science.

Our Results. We first present a *concise* yet *mathematically rigorous* exposition of the compressed oracle technique. Our exposition differs from other descriptions (e.g. [8,11,14,15,20]) in that we adopt a more abstract view.

We also consider a generalization of the compressed-oracle technique to the *parallel-query* QROM. In this variation, the considered quantum oracle algorithm may make *several* queries to the QROM *in parallel* in each query-round. The main difference between parallel and sequential queries is of course that sequential queries may be *adaptive*, i.e., the queried value x may depend on the hash learned in a previous query, while parallel queries are limited to be *non-adaptive*. This variation of the QROM allows for a more fine-grained query-complexity analysis that distinguishes between the number q of query rounds, and the number k

of queries made *per round*; the *total* number of queries made is then obviously given by $Q = kq$. This way of studying the query complexity of quantum oracle algorithms is in particular suited for analyzing how well a computational task can or cannot be parallelized (some more on this below).

As our first main technical contribution, we propose an abstract framework that simplifies the use of (our generalized version of) the compressed oracle technique in certain cases. In particular, with our new framework in place and when applicable, it is possible to prove *quantum* query complexity lower bounds by means of purely *classical* reasoning: all the quantum aspects are abstracted away. This means that no knowledge about quantum information science is necessary in order to apply our framework. If applicable, the reasoning is purely by means of identifying some classical property of the problem at hand and applying our meta-theorems. More than that, the necessary classical property can typically be extracted from the — typically much simpler — proof for the classical bound.

We demonstrate the workings and the power of our framework on a few examples, recovering known and finding new bounds. For example, with q, k, m as above, we show that the success probability of finding a *preimage* is upper bounded by $O(kq^2/2^m)$, compared to the coarse-grained bound $O(Q^2/2^m)$ [3] that does not distinguish between sequential and parallel queries; this recovers the known fact that the naive way to parallelize a preimage search (by doing several executions of Grover [13] in parallel) is optimal [19]. We also show that the success probability of finding a *collision* is bounded by $O(k^2q^3/2^m)$, compared to the coarse-grained bound $O(Q^3/2^m)$ [1] that does not distinguish between sequential and parallel queries. Like for Grover, this shows optimality for the obvious parallelization of the BHT collision finding algorithm [6]. We are not aware of any prior optimality result on parallel collision search; [16] shows a corresponding bound for *element distinctness*, but that bound does not apply here when considering a hash function with many collisions. Finally, our main example application is to the problem of finding a *q-chain*, i.e., a sequence $x_0, x_1, \ldots, x_q$ with $x_i = H(x_{i-1})$ for all $1 \leq i \leq q$ (or, more generally, that $H(x_{i-1})$ satisfies some other relation with x_i). While classically it is well known and not too hard to show that q parallel queries are necessary to find a q-chain, there has been no proven bound in the quantum setting — at least not until very recently (see the recent-related-work paragraph below).[1] Here, we show that the success probability of finding a q-chain using *fewer* than q queries is upper bounded by $O(k^3q^3/2^m)$. The proof is by means of recycling an observation that is crucial to the classical proof and plugging it into the right theorem(s) of our framework.

The problem of producing a hash chain is of fundamental importance in the context of *proofs of sequential work* (PoSW); indeed, a crucial ingredient of a PoSW is a computational problem that is hard/impossible to parallelize. Following up on this, our second main technical contribution is to show that the "Simple Proofs of Sequential Work" proposed by Cohen and Pietrzak [10] remain secure against quantum attacks. One might hope that this is simply a matter of plugging in our bound on the chain problem; unfortunately, it is more

[1] The problem of finding a q-chain looks similar to the *iterated hashing* studied in [18]; however, a crucial difference is that the start of the chain, x_0, is freely chosen here.

complicated: the entire protocol needs to be analyzed in the light of a quantum attack, which requires substantial additional work. As a matter of fact, we enrich our framework with a "calculus" that facilitates the latter. In return, our proof of the quantum security of the PoSW scheme is purely classical, with no need to understand anything about quantum information science.

Related Work. Independently and concurrently to the preparation of our work, the hardness of finding a q-chain with fewer than q queries and the security of the Cohen and Pietrzak PoSW scheme [10] against quantum attacks have also been analyzed and tackled by Blocki, Lee and Zhou in [4]. Their bounds are comparable to ours, and both works are exploiting the compressed oracle idea; however, the actual derivations and the conceptual contributions are quite different. Indeed, Blocki *et al.*'s work is very specific to the q-chain problem and the PoSW scheme, while in our work we provide a *general* framework for proving *quantum* query complexity bounds by means of *classical* reasoning, opening the door to derive further quantum query complexity bounds.

In a similar spirit, Chiesa, Manohar and Spooner [8] also offer means to apply the compressed oracle technique using purely classical combinatorial reasoning. A major difference is that in our work we allow *parallel* queries (which is crucial for our PoSW application), which confronted us with the main technical challenges in our work. Our framework easily applies to the main application of the Chiesa *et al.* paper (post-quantum secure SNARGs), but not vice versa.

2 Warm-Up: Proving Classical Query Complexity Bounds

In this section, we discuss lower bounds on the *classical* query complexity in the classical ROM for a few example problems. This serves as a warm-up and allows us to point that, when it then comes to analyzing the *quantum* query complexity of these problems, it is simply a matter of recycling certain observations from the classical proofs and plugging them into our framework.

2.1 The Lazy-Sampling Technique

First, we briefly recall the *lazy sampling* technique for efficiently simulating the classical RO. Instead of choosing a uniformly random function $H : \mathcal{X} \to \mathcal{Y}$ and answering each query x to the RO as $y = H(x)$, one can build up the hash function H "on the fly". Introduce a special symbol $\perp$ and initiate D_0 to be the constant-$\perp$ function. Then, inductively for $i = 1, 2, \ldots$, on receiving the i-th query x_i, check if this query has been made before, i.e., if $\exists j < i : x_i = x_j$. If so then set $D_i := D_{i-1}$; else, choose a uniformly random $y_i \in \mathcal{Y}$ and set D_i to $D_i := D_{i-1}[x_i \mapsto y_i]$, where in general $D[x \mapsto y]$ is defined by $D[x \mapsto y](x) = y$ and $D[x \mapsto y](\bar{x}) = D(\bar{x})$ for $\bar{x} \neq x$.[2] In either case, answer the query then with $y_i = D_i(x_i)$. We refer to such a function $D_i : \mathcal{X} \to \mathcal{Y} \cup \{\perp\}$ as a *database*.

[2] We stress that we define $D[x \mapsto y]$ also for x with $D(x) \neq \perp$, which then means that D is redefined at point x; this will be useful later.

As it is easy to see, the lazy-sampling only affects the "internal workings" of the RO; any algorithm making queries to the standard RO (which samples H as a random function at the beginning of time), or to the lazy-sampled variant (which builds up $D_0, D_1, \ldots$ as explained above), cannot see any difference.

For below, it will be convenient to write D_i, the "update" of D_{i-1} in response to query x_i, as $D_i = D_{i-1}^{\circlearrowleft x_i}$. Note that since $D_i(x) = y_i$ is chosen in a randomized way, $D_{i-1}^{\circlearrowleft x_i}$ is a random variable, strictly speaking.

2.2 Proving Classical Lower Bounds

One important feature of the lazy-sampling technique is that it allows for an *efficient* simulation of the random oracle. In the work here, we are instead interested in the lazy sampling technique as a tool for proving query complexity lower bounds. Our goal here is to show that the well-understood classical reasoning is very close to the reasoning that our framework will admit for proving bounds in the quantum setting. In order to align the two, certain argumentation below may appear overkill given the simplicity of the classical case.

Finding a Preimage. We first consider the example of finding a preimage of H; say, without loss of generality, finding $x \in \mathcal{X}$ with $H(x) = 0$. Thus, let $\mathcal{A}$ be an algorithm making q queries to the random oracle and outputting some x at the end, with the goal of x being a zero-preimage. A first simple observation is the following: if in the lazy-sampling picture after q queries the built-up database $D_q : \mathcal{X} \to \mathcal{Y} \cup \{\perp\}$ does not map $\mathcal{A}$'s output x to 0, then $H(x)$ is unlikely to vanish, where $H(x)$ is understood to be obtained by making one more query to the oracle, i.e., $H(x) = D_{q+1}(x)$. More formally, if p is the probability that $H(x) = 0$ when $\mathcal{A}$ is interacting with the standard oracle, and p' is the probability that $D_q(x) = 0$ when $\mathcal{A}$ is interacting with the lazy-sampled oracle, then $p \leq p' + 1/|\mathcal{Y}|$. Looking ahead, this trivial observation is the classical counterpart of Corollary 1 (originally by Zhandry) that we encounter later.

By the above observation, it is sufficient to bound $P[\exists x : D_q(x) = 0]$. Furthermore, setting $\mathsf{PRMG} := \{D : \mathcal{X} \to \mathcal{Y} \cup \{\perp\} \mid \exists x : D(x) = 0\}$, we can write

$$P[\exists x : D_q(x) = 0] = P[D_q \in \mathsf{PRMG}] \leq \sum_i P[D_i \in \mathsf{PRMG} \mid D_{i-1} \notin \mathsf{PRMG}].$$

In order to align the reasoning here with our framework, we introduce the *classical transition capacity*

$$\big[\neg\mathsf{PRMG} \to \mathsf{PRMG}\big] := \max_{\substack{D \notin \mathsf{PRMG} \\ x \in \mathcal{X}}} P[D^{\circlearrowleft x} \in \mathsf{PRMG}]$$

as the maximal probability that a database $D : \mathcal{X} \to \mathcal{Y} \cup \{\perp\}$ with *no* zero-preimage will be turned into a database *with* a zero-preimage as a result of a query. Combining the above observations, we obtain that

$$p \leq q \cdot \big[\neg\mathsf{PRMG} \to \mathsf{PRMG}\big] + \frac{1}{|\mathcal{Y}|}. \tag{1}$$

Looking ahead, this is the classical counterpart to Theorem 1 (with P_s set to PRMG), which is in terms of the (appropriately defined) *quantum* transition capacity $[\![\cdot \to \cdot]\!]$.

The reader probably already sees that $\big[\neg\mathsf{PRMG} \to \mathsf{PRMG}\big] = 1/|\mathcal{Y}|$, leading to the (well-known) bound $p \leq (q+1)/|\mathcal{Y}|$. However, in order to better understand the general reasoning, we take a more careful look at bounding this transition capacity. For every $D \notin \mathsf{PRMG}$ and $x \in \mathcal{X}$, we identify a "*local*" property $\mathsf{L}^{D,x} \subseteq \mathcal{Y}$ that satisfies

$$D[x \mapsto y] \in \mathsf{PRMG} \iff y \in \mathsf{L}^{D,x} ;$$

therefore, $P[D^{\circlearrowleft x} \in \mathsf{PRMG}] \leq P\big[D[x \mapsto U] \in \mathsf{PRMG}\big] = P[U \in \mathsf{L}^{D,x}]$ where U is defined to be uniformly random in $\mathcal{Y}$. Here, we can simply set $\mathsf{L}^{D,x} := \{0\}$ and thus obtain $\big[\neg\mathsf{PRMG} \to \mathsf{PRMG}\big] = P[U=0] = 1/|\mathcal{Y}|$ as claimed.

The point of explicitly introducing $\mathsf{L}^{D,x}$ is that our framework will offer similar connections between the *quantum* transition capacity $[\![\cdot \to \cdot]\!]$ and the purely classically defined probability $P[U \in \mathsf{L}^{D,x}]$. Indeed, by means of the very same choice of local property $\mathsf{L}^{D,x}$, but then applying Theorem 2, we obtain

$$[\![\neg\mathsf{PRMG} \to \mathsf{PRMG}]\!] \leq \max_{D,x} \sqrt{10 P\big[U \in \mathsf{L}^{D,x}\big]} \leq \sqrt{\tfrac{10}{|\mathcal{Y}|}} \,.$$

By Theorem 1, this implies that the success probability p of a *quantum* algorithm to find a preimage is bounded by

$$p \leq \Big(q [\![\neg\mathsf{PRMG} \to \mathsf{PRMG}]\!] + \tfrac{1}{\sqrt{|\mathcal{Y}|}}\Big)^2 \leq \Big(q\sqrt{\tfrac{10}{|\mathcal{Y}|}} + \tfrac{1}{\sqrt{|\mathcal{Y}|}}\Big)^2 = O\big(\tfrac{q^2}{|\mathcal{Y}|}\big) \,,$$

confirming the optimality of the quadratic speed-up of Grover.

Finding a Preimage with Parallel Queries. The above (classical and quantum) reasoning can be extended to the parallel query model, where with each interaction with the RO, a query algorithm can make k queries in one go. The lazy-sampling technique then works in the obvious way, with the function update $D_i := D_{i-1}^{\circlearrowleft \mathbf{x}_i}$ now involving a query *vector* $\mathbf{x}_i \in \mathcal{X}^k$. This then gives rise to $\big[\neg\mathsf{PRMG} \xrightarrow{k} \mathsf{PRMG}\big]$, and (1) generalizes accordingly. For $D \notin \mathsf{PRMG}$ and $\mathbf{x} \in \mathcal{X}^k$, we then identify a *family* of local properties $\mathsf{L}_1^{D,\mathbf{x}}, \ldots, \mathsf{L}_k^{D,\mathbf{x}} \subseteq \mathcal{Y}$ so that

$$D[\mathbf{x} \mapsto \mathbf{y}] \in \mathsf{PRMG} \iff \exists i : y_i \in \mathsf{L}_i^{D,\mathbf{x}} \,, \tag{2}$$

and therefore, by the union bound, $P[D^{\circlearrowleft \mathbf{x}} \in \mathsf{PRMG}] \leq \sum_i P[U \in \mathsf{L}_i^{D,\mathbf{x}}]$. Setting $\mathsf{L}_1^{D,\mathbf{x}} = \ldots = \mathsf{L}_k^{D,\mathbf{x}} := \{0\}$, we now get $\big[\neg\mathsf{PRMG} \xrightarrow{k} \mathsf{PRMG}\big] = kP[U=0] = k/|\mathcal{Y}|$, showing a factor-$k$ increase in the bound as expected. More interesting is that Theorem 2 still applies, implying that for the quantum version we have

$$[\![\neg\mathsf{PRMG} \xrightarrow{k} \mathsf{PRMG}]\!] \leq \max_{D,\mathbf{x}} \sqrt{10 \sum_i P\big[U \in \mathsf{L}_i^{D,\mathbf{x}}\big]} \leq \sqrt{\tfrac{10k}{|\mathcal{Y}|}} \,.$$

Plugging this into Theorem 1, we then get the bound

$$p \le \Big(q\sqrt{\tfrac{10k}{|\mathcal{Y}|}} + \tfrac{1}{\sqrt{|\mathcal{Y}|}}\Big)^2 = O\big(\tfrac{q^2k}{|\mathcal{Y}|}\big),$$

showing optimality of running k parallel executions of Grover.

Finding a Chain (with Parallel Queries). Another example we want to discuss here, where we now stick to the parallel query model, is the problem of finding a $(q+1)$-chain, i.e., a sequence $x_0, x_1, \dots, x_{q+1}$ with $H(x_{i-1}) \lhd x_i$, with no more than q (parallel) queries. Here, $\lhd$ refers to an arbitrary relation among the elements of $\mathcal{X}$ and $\mathcal{Y}$; typical examples are: $y \lhd x$ if $x = y$, or if y is a prefix of y, or if y is an arbitrary continuous substring of x. Below, we set $\mathcal{Y}^{\lhd x} := \{y \in \mathcal{Y} \,|\, y \lhd x\}$ and $T := \max_x |\mathcal{Y}^{\lhd x}|$.

Using the same kind of reasoning as above, we can argue that

$$p \le \sum_{s=1}^{q} \big[\neg \mathsf{CHN}^s \xrightarrow{k} \mathsf{CHN}^{s+1}\big] + \frac{q+2}{|\mathcal{Y}|},$$

where $\mathsf{CHN}^s = \{D \,|\, \exists x_0, x_1, \dots, x_s \in \mathcal{X} : D(x_{i-1}) \lhd x_i \, \forall i\}$. Here, we will exploit that after s (parallel) queries, $D_s \in \mathsf{SZ}_{\le ks} := \{D \,|\, |\{x | D(x) \neq \bot\}| \le ks\}$. Thus, the above extends to

$$p \le \sum_{s=1}^{q} \big[\mathsf{SZ}_{\le k(s-1)} \backslash \mathsf{CHN}^s \xrightarrow{k} \mathsf{CHN}^{s+1}\big] + \frac{q+2}{|\mathcal{Y}|}, \tag{3}$$

with the (classical) transition capacity here given by $\max P[D^{\circlearrowleft \mathbf{x}} \in \mathsf{CHN}^{s+1}]$, maximized over all $D \in \mathsf{SZ}_{\le k(s-1)} \backslash \mathsf{CHN}^s$ and $\mathbf{x} \in \mathcal{X}^k$. To control the considered transition capacity, for any D and any $\mathbf{x} = (x_1, \dots, x_k) \in \mathcal{X}^k$, we introduce the following local properties $\mathsf{L}_i^{D,\mathbf{x}} \subseteq \mathcal{Y}$ with $i = 1, \dots, k$:

$$\mathsf{L}_i^{D,\mathbf{x}} = \bigcup_{\substack{x \in \mathcal{X} \\ D(x) \neq \bot}} \mathcal{Y}^{\lhd x} \cup \bigcup_{j=1}^{k} \mathcal{Y}^{\lhd x_j}, \tag{4}$$

so that $y_i \in \mathsf{L}_i^{D,\mathbf{x}}$ if $y_i \lhd x$ for some $x \in \mathcal{X}$ with $D(x) \neq \bot$ or $x \in \{x_1, \dots, x_k\}$. They satisfy the following condition, which is slightly weaker than (2) used above.

Lemma 1. $D[\mathbf{x} \mapsto \mathbf{r}] \notin \mathsf{CHN}^s \wedge D[\mathbf{x} \mapsto \mathbf{u}] \in \mathsf{CHN}^{s+1} \Rightarrow \exists i : r_i \neq u_i \wedge u_i \in \mathsf{L}_i^{D,\mathbf{x}}$.

Proof. Write $D_\circ$ for $D[\mathbf{x} \mapsto \mathbf{r}]$ and D' for $D[\mathbf{x} \mapsto \mathbf{u}]$. Assume that $D' \in \mathsf{CHN}^{s+1}$, and let $\hat{x}_0, \hat{x}_1, \dots, \hat{x}_{s+1} \in \mathcal{X}$ be such a chain, i.e., so that $D'(\hat{x}_j) \lhd \hat{x}_{j+1}$ for $j = 0, \dots, s$. Let $s_\circ$ be the smallest j so that $D_\circ(\hat{x}_j) \neq D'(\hat{x}_j)$; if $s_\circ \ge s$ (or no such j exists) then $D_\circ(\hat{x}_j) = D'(\hat{x}_j) \lhd \hat{x}_{j+1}$ for $j = 0, \dots, s-1$, and thus $D_\circ \in \mathsf{CHN}^s$ and we are done. Therefore, we may assume $s_\circ < s$. Furthermore, since $D_\circ(\bar{x}) = D'(\bar{x})$ for $\bar{x} \notin \{x_1, \dots, x_k\}$, we must have that $\hat{x}_{s_\circ} = x_i$ for some $i \in \{1, \dots, k\}$, and therefore $r_i = D_\circ(x_i) = D_\circ(\hat{x}_{s_\circ}) \neq D'(\hat{x}_{s_\circ}) = D'(x_i) = u_i$. Also, we have that $u_i = D'(x_i) = D'(\hat{x}_{s_\circ}) \lhd \hat{x}_{s_\circ+1}$ where $\hat{x}_{s_\circ+1}$ is such that $D'(\hat{x}_{s_\circ+1}) \lhd \hat{x}_{s_\circ+2}$ and thus $\neq \bot$. The latter means that either $D(\hat{x}_{s_\circ+1}) \neq \bot$ or $\hat{x}_{s_\circ+1} \in \{x_1, \dots, x_k\}$ (or both). In either case we have that $u_i \in \mathsf{L}_i^{D,\mathbf{x}}$.

Applied to $\mathbf{r} := D(\mathbf{x})$ so that $D[\mathbf{x} \mapsto \mathbf{r}] = D$, we obtain $P[D^{\circlearrowleft\mathbf{x}} \in \mathsf{CHN}^{s+1}] \leq \sum_i P[U \in \mathsf{L}_i^{D,\mathbf{x}}]$. Given that, for $D \in \mathsf{SZ}_{\leq k(s-1)}$, the set $\{x|D(x) \neq \bot\}$ is bounded in size by $k(s-1)$, and $|\mathcal{Y}^{\lhd x}|, |\mathcal{Y}^{\lhd x_j}| \leq T$, we can bound the relevant probability $P[U \in \mathsf{L}_i^{D,x}] \leq ksT/|\mathcal{Y}|$. Hence, the considered classical transition capacity is bounded by $k^2 sT/|\mathcal{Y}|$. By (3), we thus have $p = O(k^2 q^2 T/|\mathcal{Y}|)$, which is in line with the bound given by Cohen-Pietrzak [10].

Also here, our framework allows us to lift the above reasoning to the quantum setting by plugging the core elements of the above reasoning for the classical case into our framework. Concretely, choosing the local properties $\mathsf{L}_i^{D,\mathbf{x}}$ as above whenever $D \in \mathsf{SZ}_{\leq k(s-1)}$, and to be constant-false otherwise, Lemma 1 ensures that we can apply Theorem 3 to bound the *quantum* transition capacity as

$$[\![\mathsf{SZ}_{\leq k(s-1)} \backslash \mathsf{CHN}^s \xrightarrow{k} \mathsf{CHN}^{s+1}]\!] \leq e \max_{\mathbf{x},D} \sum_i \sqrt{10 P[U \in \mathsf{L}_i^{D,\mathbf{x}}]} \leq ek\sqrt{\tfrac{10k(q+1)T}{|\mathcal{Y}|}},$$

where e is Euler's number. Plugging this into Theorem 1, we then get the bound

$$p \leq \left(qek\sqrt{\tfrac{10k(q+1)T}{|\mathcal{Y}|}} + \tfrac{q+2}{|\mathcal{Y}|}\right)^2 = O\big(\tfrac{q^3k^3\,T}{|\mathcal{Y}|}\big)$$

on the success probability of a quantum oracle algorithm in finding a $(q+1)$-chain with no more than q k-parallel queries. Recall, T depends on the considered relation $y \lhd x$; $T = 1$ if y is required to be equal to x, or a prefix of x, and $T = m - n$ if y and x are n- and m-bit strings, respectively, and y is required to be a continuous substring of x.

3 Notation

3.1 Operators and Their Norms

Let $\mathcal{H} = \mathbb{C}^d$ be a finite-dimensional complex Hilbert space. We use the standard bra-ket notation for covariant and contravariant vectors in $\mathcal{H}$, i.e., for column and row vectors $\mathbb{C}^d$. We write $\mathcal{L}(\mathcal{H}, \mathcal{H}')$ for the linear maps, i.e., operators (or matrices), $A : \mathcal{H} \to \mathcal{H}'$, and we use $\mathcal{L}(\mathcal{H})$ as a short hand for $\mathcal{L}(\mathcal{H}, \mathcal{H})$. We write I for the identity operator in $\mathcal{L}(\mathcal{H})$. It is understood that pure states are given by norm-1 ket vectors $|\psi\rangle \in \mathcal{H}$ and mixed states by density operators $\rho \in \mathcal{L}(\mathcal{H})$.

A (possibly) mixed state $\rho \in \mathcal{L}(\mathcal{H})$ is said to be *supported* by subspace $\mathcal{H}_\circ \subseteq \mathcal{H}$ if the support of the operator ρ lies in $\mathcal{H}_\circ$, or, equivalently, if any purification $|\Psi\rangle \in \mathcal{H} \otimes \mathcal{H}$ of ρ lies in $\mathcal{H}_\circ \otimes \mathcal{H}$. A state is said to be supported by a family of (orthonormal) vectors if it is supported by the span of these vectors.

We write $\|A\|$ for the *operator norm* of $A \in \mathcal{L}(\mathcal{H}, \mathcal{H}')$ and recall that it is upper bounded by the *Frobenius norm*. Special choices of operators in $\mathcal{L}(\mathcal{H})$ are *projections* and *unitaries*. We assume familiarity with these notions, as well as with the notion of an *isometry* in $\mathcal{L}(\mathcal{H}, \mathcal{H}')$.

If $\mathcal{H}_\circ$ is a subspace of $\mathcal{H}$ and $A \in \mathcal{L}(\mathcal{H}_\circ)$ then we can naturally understand A as a map $A \in \mathcal{L}(\mathcal{H})$ by letting A act as zero-map on any $|\psi\rangle \in \mathcal{H}$ that is orthogonal to $\mathcal{H}_\circ$. We point out that this does not cause any ambiguity in

$\|A\|$. Vice versa, for any $A \in \mathcal{L}(\mathcal{H})$ we can consider its restriction to $\mathcal{H}_\circ$. Here, we have the following. If $\mathcal{H} = \mathcal{H}_1 \oplus \ldots \oplus \mathcal{H}_m$ is a decomposition of $\mathcal{H}$ into orthogonal subspaces $\mathcal{H}_i \subseteq \mathcal{H}$, and $A \in \mathcal{L}(\mathcal{H})$ is such that its restriction to $\mathcal{H}_i$ is a map $\mathcal{H}_i \to \mathcal{H}_i$ and coincides with $B_i \in \mathcal{L}(\mathcal{H}_i)$ for any $i \in \{1, \ldots, m\}$, then $\|A\| = \max_i \|B_i\|$. This is a property we are exploiting multiple times, typically making a reference then to "basic properties" of the operator norm.

3.2 The Computational and the Fourier Basis

Let $\mathcal{Y}$ be a finite Abelian group of cardinality M, and let $\{|y\rangle\}_{y\in\mathcal{Y}}$ be an (orthonormal) basis of $\mathcal{H} = \mathbb{C}^M$, where the basis vectors are labeled by the elements of $\mathcal{Y}$. We refer to this basis as the *computational basis*, and we also write $\mathbb{C}[\mathcal{Y}]$ for $\mathcal{H} = \mathbb{C}^M$ to emphasize that the considered space is spanned by basis vectors that are labeled by the elements in $\mathcal{Y}$. Let $\hat{\mathcal{Y}}$ be the *dual group* of $\mathcal{Y}$, which is known to be isomorphic to $\mathcal{Y}$, and thus to have cardinality M as well. Up to some exceptions, we consider $\hat{\mathcal{Y}}$ to be an *additive* group; the neutral element is denoted $\hat{0}$. We stress that we treat $\mathcal{Y}$ and $\hat{\mathcal{Y}}$ as disjoint sets, even though in certain (common) cases they are *naturally* isomorphic and thus considered to be equal. The *Fourier basis* $\{|\hat{y}\rangle\}_{\hat{y}\in\hat{\mathcal{Y}}}$ of $\mathcal{H}$ is defined by the basis transformations

$$|\hat{y}\rangle = \frac{1}{\sqrt{M}}\sum_y \hat{y}(y)^*|y\rangle \qquad \text{and} \qquad |y\rangle = \frac{1}{\sqrt{M}}\sum_{\hat{y}} \hat{y}(y)|\hat{y}\rangle\,, \tag{5}$$

where $(\cdot)^*$ denotes complex conjugation. With the above convention on the notation, we have $\mathbb{C}[\mathcal{Y}] = \mathbb{C}[\hat{\mathcal{Y}}] = \mathcal{H}$.An elementary property of the Fourier basis is that the operator in $\mathcal{L}(\mathbb{C}[\mathcal{Y}] \otimes \mathbb{C}[\mathcal{Y}])$ defined by $|y\rangle|y'\rangle \mapsto |y+y'\rangle|y'\rangle$ for $y, y' \in \mathcal{Y}$ acts as $|\hat{y}\rangle|\hat{y}'\rangle \mapsto |y\rangle|\hat{y}-\hat{y}'\rangle$ for $\hat{y}, \hat{y}' \in \hat{\mathcal{Y}}$.

We will also consider extensions $\mathcal{Y} \cup \{\perp\}$ and $\hat{\mathcal{Y}} \cup \{\perp\}$ of the sets $\mathcal{Y}$ and $\hat{\mathcal{Y}}$ by including a special symbol $\perp$. We will then fix a norm-1 vector $|\perp\rangle \in \mathbb{C}^{M+1}$ that is orthogonal to $\mathbb{C}[\mathcal{Y}] = \mathbb{C}[\hat{\mathcal{Y}}]$, given a fixed embedding of $\mathbb{C}[\mathcal{Y}] = \mathbb{C}^M$ into $\mathbb{C}^{M+1}$. In line with our notation, $\mathbb{C}^{M+1}$ is then referred to as $\mathbb{C}[\mathcal{Y} \cup \{\perp\}] = \mathbb{C}[\hat{\mathcal{Y}} \cup \{\perp\}]$.

3.3 Functions and Their (Quantum) Representations

For an arbitrary but fixed non-empty finite set $\mathcal{X}$, we let $\mathfrak{H}$ be the set of functions $H : \mathcal{X} \to \mathcal{Y}$. Similarly, $\hat{\mathfrak{H}}$ denotes the set of functions $\hat{H} : \mathcal{X} \to \hat{\mathcal{Y}}$. Given that we can represent H by its function table $\{H(x)\}_{x\in\mathcal{X}}$, and $|y\rangle \in \mathbb{C}[\mathcal{Y}]$ is understood as a "quantum representation" of $y \in \mathcal{Y}$, we consider $|H\rangle = \bigotimes_x |H(x)\rangle$ to be the "quantum representation" of H, where in such a tensor product we implicitly consider the different registers to be *labeled* by $x \in \mathcal{X}$ in the obvious way. By our naming convention, the space $\bigotimes_x \mathbb{C}[\mathcal{Y}]$ spanned by all vectors $|H\rangle = \bigotimes_x |H(x)\rangle$ with $H \in \mathfrak{H}$ is denoted $\mathbb{C}[\mathfrak{H}]$. Similarly, for the "quantum representation" of $\hat{H} \in \hat{\mathfrak{H}}$ as$|\hat{H}\rangle = \bigotimes_x |\hat{H}(x)\rangle$. By applying (5) register-wise, any $|H\rangle$ is supported by vectors $|\hat{H}\rangle$ with $\hat{H} \in \hat{\mathfrak{H}}$, and vice versa. Thus, $\mathbb{C}[\mathfrak{H}] = \mathbb{C}[\hat{\mathfrak{H}}]$.

Extending $\mathcal{Y}$ to $\bar{\mathcal{Y}} := \mathcal{Y} \cup \{\perp\}$, we also consider the set $\mathfrak{D}$ of functions (referred to as *databases*) $D : \mathcal{X} \to \bar{\mathcal{Y}}$. In line with the above, we then obtain

$|D\rangle = \bigotimes_x |D(x)\rangle \in \bigotimes_x \mathbb{C}[\bar{\mathcal{Y}}] = \mathbb{C}[\mathfrak{D}]$. We also consider the set $\hat{\mathfrak{D}}$ of functions $\hat{D} : \mathcal{X} \to \hat{\mathcal{Y}} \cup \{\bot\}$ and have $\mathbb{C}[\mathfrak{D}] = \mathbb{C}[\hat{\mathfrak{D}}]$.

For $D \in \mathfrak{D}$ and $\mathbf{x} = (x_1, \ldots, x_k) \in \mathcal{X}^k$, we write $D(\mathbf{x})$ for $\big(D(x_1), \ldots, D(x_k)\big)$ in $\bar{\mathcal{Y}}^k$; similarly for $H \in \mathfrak{H}$. Furthermore, for $\mathbf{x}$ with pairwise distinct entries and $\mathbf{r} = (r_1, \ldots, r_k) \in \bar{\mathcal{Y}}^k$, we define $D[\mathbf{x} \mapsto \mathbf{r}] \in \mathfrak{D}$ to be the database with $D[\mathbf{x}\mapsto\mathbf{r}](x_i) = r_i$ and $D[\mathbf{x}\mapsto\mathbf{r}](\bar{x}) = D(\bar{x})\ \ \forall\, \bar{x} \notin \{x_1, \ldots, x_k\}$.

4 Zhandry's Compressed Oracle - Refurbished

4.1 The Compressed Oracle

The core ideas of Zhandry's compressed oracle are, first, to consider a *superposition* $\sum_H |H\rangle$ of all possible functions $H \in \mathfrak{H}$, rather than a uniformly random choice; this *purified* oracle is indistinguishable from the original random oracle. Second, to then analyze the behavior of this purified oracle in the *Fourier* basis. Indeed, the initial state of the oracle is given by

$$|\Pi_0\rangle = \sum_H |H\rangle = \bigotimes_x \Big(\sum_y |y\rangle\Big) = \bigotimes_x |\hat{0}\rangle = |\hat{\mathbf{0}}\rangle \in \mathbb{C}[\mathfrak{H}]\,, \tag{6}$$

with $\hat{\mathbf{0}} \in \hat{\mathfrak{H}}$ the constant-$\hat{0}$ function. Furthermore, an oracle query invokes the unitary map O, given by

$$\mathsf{O} : |x\rangle|y\rangle \otimes |H\rangle \mapsto |x\rangle|y + H(x)\rangle \otimes |H\rangle$$

in the computational basis; in the Fourier basis, this becomes

$$\mathsf{O} : |x\rangle|\hat{y}\rangle \otimes |\hat{H}\rangle \mapsto |x\rangle|\hat{y}\rangle \otimes \mathsf{O}_{x\hat{y}}|\hat{H}\rangle = \ |x\rangle|\hat{y}\rangle \otimes |\hat{H} - \hat{y}\cdot\delta_x\rangle\,, \tag{7}$$

where the equality is the definition of $\mathsf{O}_{x\hat{y}}$, and $\delta_x : \mathcal{X} \to \{0,1\}$ satisfies $\delta_x(x) = 1$ and $\delta_x(x') = 0$ for all $x' \neq x$. Note that $\mathsf{O}_{x\hat{y}}$ acts on register x only, and $\mathsf{O}_{x\hat{y}}\mathsf{O}_{x\hat{y}'} = \mathsf{O}_{x,\hat{y}+\hat{y}'}$; thus, $\mathsf{O}_{x\hat{y}}$ and $\mathsf{O}_{x'\hat{y}'}$ all commute. As an immediate consequence of (6) and (7) above, the internal state of the oracle after q queries is supported by state vectors of the form $|\hat{H}\rangle = |\hat{y}_1\delta_{x_1} + \cdots + \hat{y}_q\delta_{x_q}\rangle$.

The actual *compressed* oracle (respectively some version of it) is now obtained by applying the isometry

$$\mathsf{Comp}_x = |\bot\rangle\langle\hat{0}| + \sum_{\hat{z}\neq\hat{0}} |\hat{z}\rangle\langle\hat{z}| : \mathbb{C}[\mathcal{Y}] \to \mathbb{C}[\bar{\mathcal{Y}}],\ |\hat{y}\rangle \mapsto \begin{cases} |\bot\rangle \text{ if } \hat{y} = \hat{0} \\ |\hat{y}\rangle\ \text{ if } \hat{y} \neq \hat{0} \end{cases}$$

to all registers $x \in \mathcal{X}$ (and then viewing the result in the computational basis). This "compression" operator $\mathsf{Comp} := \bigotimes_x \mathsf{Comp}_x : \mathbb{C}[\mathfrak{H}] \to \mathbb{C}[\mathfrak{D}]$ maps $|\Pi_0\rangle$ to

$$|\Delta_0\rangle := \mathsf{Comp}\,|\Pi_0\rangle = \Big(\bigotimes_x \mathsf{Comp}_x\Big)\Big(\bigotimes_x |\hat{0}\rangle\Big) = \bigotimes_x \mathsf{Comp}_x|\hat{0}\rangle = \bigotimes_x |\bot\rangle = |\bot\rangle,$$

which is the quantum representation of the trivial database $\bot$ that maps any $x \in \mathcal{X}$ to $\bot$. More generally, for any $\hat{H} \in \hat{\mathfrak{H}}$, $\mathsf{Comp}\,|\hat{H}\rangle = |\hat{D}\rangle$ where $\hat{D} \in \hat{\mathfrak{D}}$ is such that $\hat{D}(x) = \hat{H}(x)$ whenever $\hat{H}(x) \neq 0$, and $\hat{D}(x) = \bot$ whenever $\hat{H}(x) = 0$. Thus, the internal state of the compressed oracle after q queries is supported by vectors $|D\rangle$ in the computational basis (respectively $|\hat{D}\rangle$ in the Fourier basis) for which $D(x) = \bot$ (respectively $\hat{D}(x) = \bot$) for all but at most q choices of x.

This representation of the internal state of the purified random oracle is referred to as the *compressed* oracle because, for a bounded number of queries, these state vectors $|D\rangle$ can be efficiently represented and the evolution of the oracle then efficiently computed (see the full version [9]). In this work, we are not concerned with such a computational efficiency aspect.

4.2 Linking the Compressed and the Original Oracle

The following result (originally by Zhandry [20]) links the compressed oracle with the original standard oracle. Recall that $M = |\mathcal{Y}|$.

Lemma 2. *Consider an arbitrary normalized* $|\Pi\rangle \in \mathbb{C}[\mathfrak{H}]$. *Let* $|\Delta\rangle = \mathsf{Comp}\,|\Pi\rangle$ *in* $\mathbb{C}[\mathfrak{D}]$ *be the corresponding "compressed database". Let* $\mathbf{x} = (x_1, \ldots, x_\ell)$ *consist of pairwise distinct* $x_i \in \mathcal{X}$, *let* $\mathbf{y} = (y_1, \ldots, y_\ell) \in \mathcal{Y}^\ell$, *and set* $P_\mathbf{x} := |y_1\rangle\langle y_1| \otimes \cdots \otimes |y_\ell\rangle\langle y_\ell|$ *with the understanding that* $|y_i\rangle\langle y_i|$ *acts on register* x_i. *Then*

$$\|P_\mathbf{x}|\Pi\rangle\| \le \|P_\mathbf{x}|\Delta\rangle\| + \sqrt{\frac{\ell}{M}}\,.$$

This translates to the following statement in terms of algorithmic language; rigorous proofs of both statements are given in the full version [9].

Corollary 1 (Zhandry). *Let* $R \subseteq \mathcal{X}^\ell \times \mathcal{Y}^\ell$ *be a relation. Let* $\mathcal{A}$ *be an oracle quantum algorithm that outputs* $\mathbf{x} \in \mathcal{X}^\ell$ *and* $\mathbf{y} \in \mathcal{X}^\ell$. *Let* p *be the probability that* $\mathbf{y} = H(\mathbf{x})$ *and* $(\mathbf{x}, \mathbf{y}) \in R$ *when* $\mathcal{A}$ *has interacted with the standard random oracle, initialized with a random function* H. *Similarly, let* p' *be the probability that* $\mathbf{y} = D(\mathbf{x})$ *and* $(\mathbf{x}, \mathbf{y}) \in R$ *when* $\mathcal{A}$ *has interacted with the compressed oracle instead and* D *is obtained by measuring its internal state. Then*

$$\sqrt{p} \le \sqrt{p'} + \sqrt{\frac{\ell}{M}}\,.$$

4.3 Working Out the Transition Matrix

Here, we work out the matrix (in the computational basis) that describes the evolution that the compressed oracle undergoes as a result of an oracle query. For this, it is necessary to extend the domain $\mathbb{C}[\mathcal{Y}]$ of Comp_x to $\mathbb{C}[\bar{\mathcal{Y}}]$ by declaring that $\mathsf{Comp}_x|\bot\rangle = |\hat{0}\rangle$. This turns Comp_x into a *unitary* on $\mathbb{C}[\bar{\mathcal{Y}}]$, and correspondingly then for Comp. Formally, we are then interested in the unitary

$$\mathsf{cO} := \mathsf{Comp} \circ \mathsf{O} \circ \mathsf{Comp}^\dagger \in \mathcal{L}(\mathbb{C}[\mathcal{X}] \otimes \mathbb{C}[\mathcal{Y}] \otimes \mathbb{C}[\mathfrak{D}])\,,$$

which maps $|x\rangle|\hat{y}\rangle \otimes |D\rangle$ to $|x\rangle|\hat{y}\rangle \otimes \mathsf{cO}_{x\hat{y}}|D\rangle$ for any $D \in \mathfrak{D}$, where the unitary $\mathsf{cO}_{x\hat{y}} := \mathsf{Comp}_x \circ \mathsf{O}_{x\hat{y}} \circ \mathsf{Comp}_x^\dagger \in \mathcal{L}(\mathbb{C}[\bar{\mathcal{Y}}])$ acts on the x-register only.

Lemma 3. *For all* $\hat{y} \neq 0$ *and all* $r, u \in \bar{\mathcal{Y}} := \mathcal{Y} \cup \{\perp\}$*:* $\langle u|\mathsf{cO}_{x\hat{y}}|r\rangle = \gamma^{\hat{y}}_{u,r}$. *Furthermore,* $\mathsf{cO}_{x,\hat{0}} = \mathsf{I}$.

The proof is a straightforward computation and is provided in the full version.

	$\perp$	$r \in \mathcal{Y}$
$\perp$	$\gamma^{\hat{y}}_{\perp,\perp} = 0$	$\gamma^{\hat{y}}_{\perp,r} = \dfrac{\hat{y}^*(r)}{\sqrt{M}}$
$u \in \mathcal{Y}$	$\dfrac{\hat{y}(u)}{\sqrt{M}}$	$\gamma^{\hat{y}}_{u,r} = \begin{cases} \left(1 - \frac{2}{M}\right)\hat{y}(u) + \frac{1}{M} & \text{if } u = r \in \mathcal{Y} \\ \frac{1 - \hat{y}(r) - \hat{y}(u)}{M} & \text{if } u \neq r, \text{ both in } \mathcal{Y} \end{cases}$

Fig. 1. The evolution of the compressed oracle in the computational basis.

Since, for any fixed $\hat{y}$, the matrix $\mathsf{cO}_{x\hat{y}}$ is unitary, the squares of the absolute values of each column add to 1. Thus, for any $\hat{y}, r$ we can consider the probability distribution defined by $\tilde{P}[U = u|r, \hat{y}] := |\gamma^{\hat{y}}_{u,r}|^2$. This offers us a convenient notation, like $\tilde{P}[U \in \mathcal{S}|r, \hat{y}]$ for $\sum_{u \in \mathcal{S}} |\gamma^{\hat{y}}_{u,r}|^2$ or $\tilde{P}[U \neq r|r, \hat{y}]$ for $\sum_{u \neq r} |\gamma^{\hat{y}}_{u,r}|^2$. For later purposes, it is useful to observe that, for any $\mathsf{L} \subseteq \mathcal{Y}$ (i.e., $\perp \notin \mathsf{L}$),

$$\begin{aligned} \sum_r \tilde{P}[r \neq U \in \mathsf{L}|r, \hat{y}] &\leq \tilde{P}[U \in \mathsf{L}|\perp, \hat{y}] + \sum_{r \neq \perp} \tilde{P}[r \neq U \in \mathsf{L}|r, \hat{y}] \\ &\leq |\mathsf{L}|\frac{1}{M} + M|\mathsf{L}|\frac{9}{M^2} = 10P[U \in \mathsf{L}] \, , \end{aligned} \tag{8}$$

where $P[U \in \mathsf{L}] = \frac{|\mathsf{L}|}{M}$ is the probability for a random U in $\mathcal{Y}$ to be in L.

4.4 The Parallel-Query (Compressed) Oracle

Here, we extend the above compressed-oracle technique to the setting where a quantum algorithm may make *several* queries to the random oracle *in parallel.* Formally, for any positive integer k, a *k-parallel query* is given by k parallel applications of O, with the understanding that each application acts on a different input/output register pair. More explicitly, but slightly abusing notation of writing a k-th power, a k-parallel query is given by

$$\mathsf{O}^k : |\mathbf{x}\rangle|\mathbf{y}\rangle \otimes |H\rangle \mapsto |\mathbf{x}\rangle|\mathbf{y} + H(\mathbf{x})\rangle \otimes |H\rangle$$

for any $\mathbf{x} = (x_1, \ldots, x_k) \in \mathcal{X}^k$ and $\mathbf{y} = (y_1, \ldots, y_k) \in \mathcal{Y}^k$. The operator unitary $\mathsf{cO}^k := \mathsf{Comp} \circ \mathsf{O}^k \circ \mathsf{Comp}^\dagger$, which described the evolution of the compressed oracle under such a k-parallel query, then acts as

$$\mathsf{cO}^k : |\mathbf{x}\rangle|\hat{\mathbf{y}}\rangle \otimes |\Delta\rangle \mapsto |\mathbf{x}\rangle|\hat{\mathbf{y}}\rangle \otimes \mathsf{cO}_{\mathbf{x}\hat{\mathbf{y}}}|\Delta\rangle$$

for any $|\Delta\rangle \in \mathbb{C}[\mathfrak{D}]$, where $\mathsf{cO}_{\mathbf{x}\hat{\mathbf{y}}}$ is the product $\mathsf{cO}_{x_1\hat{y}_1} \cdots \mathsf{cO}_{x_k\hat{y}_k}$. We recall that $\mathsf{cO}_{x_i\hat{y}_i}$ acts on register x_i (only), and $\mathsf{cO}_{x_i\hat{y}_i}$ and $\mathsf{cO}_{x_j\hat{y}_j}$ commute.

5 A Framework for Proving Quantum Query Bounds

In this section we set up a framework for proving lower-bounds on the query complexity (actually, equivalently, upper bounds on the success probability) of *quantum* algorithms in the (quantum) random oracle model. Our framework closely mimics the reasoning for classical algorithms and allows to easily "lift" the typical kind of reasoning to the quantum setting.

5.1 Setting up the Framework

Definition 1. *A* database property *on $\mathfrak{D}$ is a subset* $\mathsf{P} \subseteq \mathfrak{D}$.

Remark 1. We think of P as a property that is either *true* or *false* for any $D \in \mathfrak{D}$. Furthermore, by convention, for any database property $\mathsf{P} \in \mathfrak{D}$, we overload notation and use P also to refer to the projection $\sum_{D \in \mathsf{P}} |D\rangle\langle D| \in \mathcal{L}(\mathbb{C}[\mathfrak{D}])$.

Three examples that we will later consider are

$$\mathsf{PRMG} := \{D \,|\, \exists x : D(x) = 0\}\,, \quad \mathsf{CL} := \{D \,|\, \exists x, x' : D(x) = D(x') \neq \bot\} \quad \text{and}$$
$$\mathsf{CHN}^q := \{D \,|\, \exists x_0, x_1, \ldots, x_q \in \mathcal{X} : D(x_{i-1}) \lhd x_i \; \forall i\}\,,$$

where $\lhd$ denotes an arbitrary relation, e.g., $y \lhd x$ if y is a prefix of x.

We introduce the following notation. For any tuple $\mathbf{x} = (x_1, \ldots, x_k)$ of pairwise distinct $x_i \in \mathcal{X}$ and for any $D : \mathcal{X} \to \bar{\mathcal{Y}}$ we let

$$D|^{\mathbf{x}} := \{D[\mathbf{x} \mapsto \mathbf{r}] \,|\, \mathbf{r} \in \bar{\mathcal{Y}}^k\} \subseteq \mathfrak{D}$$

be the set of databases that coincide with D outside of $\mathbf{x}$. Furthermore, for any database property $\mathsf{P} \subseteq \mathfrak{D}$, we then let

$$\mathsf{P}|_{D|^{\mathbf{x}}} := \mathsf{P} \cap D|^{\mathbf{x}}$$

be the restriction of P to the databases in $D|^{\mathbf{x}}$. We then typically think of $\mathsf{P}|_{D|^{\mathbf{x}}}$ as a property of functions $D' \in D|^{\mathbf{x}}$.

Remark 2. For fixed choices of $\mathbf{x}$ and D, we will often identify $D|^{\mathbf{x}}$ with $\bar{\mathcal{Y}}^k$ by means of the obvious map $\mathbf{r} \mapsto D[\mathbf{x} \mapsto \mathbf{r}]$. The property $\mathsf{P}|_{D|^{\mathbf{x}}}$ can then be considered to be a property/subset of $\bar{\mathcal{Y}}^k$, namely $\{\mathbf{r} \in \bar{\mathcal{Y}}^k \,|\, D[\mathbf{x} \mapsto \mathbf{r}] \in \mathsf{P}\}$. Accordingly, we do not distinguish between the projections

$$\sum_{D' \in \mathsf{P}|_{D|^{\mathbf{x}}}} |D'\rangle\langle D'| \in \mathcal{L}(\mathbb{C}[D|^{\mathbf{x}}]) \subseteq \mathcal{L}(\mathbb{C}[\mathfrak{D}]) \quad \text{and} \quad \sum_{\substack{\mathbf{r} \in \bar{\mathcal{Y}}^k \\ D[\mathbf{x} \mapsto \mathbf{r}] \in \mathsf{P}}} |\mathbf{r}\rangle\langle \mathbf{r}| \in \mathcal{L}(\mathbb{C}[\bar{\mathcal{Y}}^k])$$

but refer to both as $\mathsf{P}|_{D|^{\mathbf{x}}}$, using our convention to use the same variable for a property and the corresponding projection. This is justified by the fact that on the space spanned by $|D[\mathbf{x} \mapsto \mathbf{r}]\rangle$ with $\mathbf{r} \in \bar{\mathcal{Y}}^k$, both act identically (with the understanding that the latter acts on the registers labeled by $\mathbf{x}$.). In particular, they have the same operator norm.

Example 1. For a given $\mathbf{x}$ and D, as a subset of $\bar{\mathcal{Y}}^k$, we have

$$\mathsf{PRMG}|_{D|^{\mathbf{x}}} = \begin{cases} \bar{\mathcal{Y}}^k & \text{if } D(\bar{x}) = 0 \text{ for some } \bar{x} \notin \{x_1, \ldots, x_k\} \\ \{\mathbf{r} \mid \exists i : r_i = 0\} & \text{else} \end{cases}$$

In words: if D has a zero outside of $\mathbf{x}$ then $D[\mathbf{x} \mapsto \mathbf{r}]$ has a zero for any $\mathbf{r} \in \bar{\mathcal{Y}}^k$; otherwise, $D[\mathbf{x} \mapsto \mathbf{r}]$ has a zero if and only if one of the coordinates of $\mathbf{r}$ is zero.

The following definition is the first main ingredient of our framework. The upcoming theorem, which relates the success probability of a quantum algorithm to the quantum transition capacity, then forms the second main ingredient.

Definition 2 (Quantum transition capacity). *Let* P, P' *be two database properties. Then, the* quantum transition capacity *(of order* k*) is defined as*

$$[\![\mathsf{P} \xrightarrow{k} \mathsf{P}']\!] := \max_{\mathbf{x},\hat{\mathbf{y}},D} \|\mathsf{P}'|_{D|^{\mathbf{x}}}\, \mathsf{cO}_{\mathbf{x}\mathbf{y}}\, \mathsf{P}|_{D|^{\mathbf{x}}}\| \,.$$

Furthermore, we define

$$[\![\mathsf{P} \overset{k,q}{\Longrightarrow} \mathsf{P}']\!] := \sup_{U_2,\ldots,U_q} \|\mathsf{P}'\mathsf{cO}^k\, U_q\, \mathsf{cO} \cdots \mathsf{cO}^k\, U_2\, \mathsf{cO}^k\, \mathsf{P}\| \,.$$

where the supremum is over all positive $d \in \mathbb{Z}$ *and all unitaries* $U_2, \ldots, U_q$ *acting on* $\mathbb{C}[\mathcal{X}] \otimes \mathbb{C}[\mathcal{Y}] \otimes \mathbb{C}^d$.

By definition, the notion $[\![\mathsf{P} \overset{k,q}{\Longrightarrow} \mathsf{P}']\!]$ equals the square-root of the maximal probability that the internal state of the compressed oracle, when supported by databases $D \in \mathsf{P}$, turns into a database $D' \in \mathsf{P}'$ by means of a quantum query algorithm that performs q k-parallel queries, and when we then measure the internal state. In particular, for p' as in Corollary 1 and P^R as below in Theorem 1, it holds that $[\![\bot \overset{k,q}{\Longrightarrow} \mathsf{P}^R]\!] = \sqrt{p'}$.

Similarly, but on a more intuitive level so far, $[\![\mathsf{P} \xrightarrow{k} \mathsf{P}']\!]$ represents a measure of how likely it is that, as a result of *one* k-parallel query, a database $D \in \mathfrak{D}$ that satisfies P turns into a database D' that satisfies P'. In the context of these two notations, $\bot$ is understood to be the database property that is satisfied by $\bot \in \mathfrak{D}$ only, and $\neg\mathsf{P}$ is the complement of P, i.e., $\neg\mathsf{P} = \mathsf{I} - \mathsf{P}$ (as projections). We also write $\mathsf{P} \to \mathsf{P}'$ and refer to this as a *database transition* when considering two database properties P and P' in the context of the above two notions. Formally, they are related as follows.

Lemma 4. *For any sequence of database properties* $\mathsf{P}_0, \mathsf{P}_1, \ldots, \mathsf{P}_q$*,*

$$[\![\neg\mathsf{P}_0 \overset{k,q}{\Longrightarrow} \mathsf{P}_q]\!] \leq \sum_{s=1}^{q} [\![\neg\mathsf{P}_{s-1} \xrightarrow{k} \mathsf{P}_s]\!] \,.$$

Proof. By means of inserting $\mathsf{I} = \mathsf{P}_q + (\mathsf{I} - \mathsf{P}_q)$ before U_q and using properties of the norm, we obtain

$$\|\mathsf{P}_q\, \mathsf{cO}^k\, U_q\, \mathsf{cO}^k \cdots \mathsf{cO}^k\, (\mathsf{I} - \mathsf{P}_0)\| \le \|\mathsf{P}_{q-1}\, \mathsf{cO}^k \cdots \mathsf{cO}^k\, (\mathsf{I} - \mathsf{P}_0)\| + \|\mathsf{P}_q\, \mathsf{cO}^k\, U_q\, (\mathsf{I} - \mathsf{P}_{q-1})\|\,.$$

To the first term, we apply induction; so it remains to bound the second term by $[\![\neg \mathsf{P}_{q-1} \xrightarrow{k} \mathsf{P}_q]\!]$. Using that U_q and P_{q-1} commute (as they act on different subsystems) and setting $\mathsf{P} = \neg \mathsf{P}_{q-1}$ and $\mathsf{P}' = \mathsf{P}_q$, this follows from[3]

$$\|\mathsf{P}'\mathsf{cO}^k\, \mathsf{P}\| \le \max_{\mathbf{x},\hat{\mathbf{y}}} \|\mathsf{P}'\mathsf{cO}_{\mathbf{x}\hat{\mathbf{y}}}\, \mathsf{P}\| \le \max_{\mathbf{x},\hat{\mathbf{y}},D} \|\mathsf{P}'|_{D|^{\mathbf{x}}}\, \mathsf{cO}_{\mathbf{x}\mathbf{y}}\, (\mathsf{I} - \mathsf{P}|_{D|^{\mathbf{x}}})\|\,,$$

where for the first inequality we observe that $\mathsf{P}'\mathsf{cO}^k\mathsf{P}$ maps $|\mathbf{x}\rangle|\hat{\mathbf{y}}\rangle\otimes|\Gamma\rangle$ to $|\mathbf{x}\rangle|\hat{\mathbf{y}}\rangle\otimes \mathsf{P}'\mathsf{cO}_{\mathbf{x}\hat{\mathbf{y}}}\mathsf{P}|\Gamma\rangle$, and so the first inequality holds by basic properties of the operator norm. Similarly for the second inequality: For any fixed D, consider the subspace of $\mathbb{C}[\mathfrak{D}]$ spanned by $|D[\mathbf{x} \mapsto \mathbf{r}]\rangle$ with $\mathbf{r} \in \bar{\mathcal{Y}}^k$. On this subspace, P and $\mathsf{P}|_{D|^{\mathbf{x}}}$ are identical projections (and similarly for P'). Also, $\mathsf{cO}_{\mathbf{x}\mathbf{y}}$ is a unitary on this subspace. The claim then again follows again by basic properties of the operator norm.

The following is now a direct consequence of Corollary 1, the definition of $[\![\bot \overset{k,q}{\Longrightarrow} \mathsf{P}^R]\!]$, and the above lemma.

Theorem 1. *Let R be a relation, and let $\mathcal{A}$ be a k-parallel q-query quantum oracle algorithm with success probability p, as considered in Corollary 1. Consider the database property induced by R, given as*

$$\mathsf{P}^R = \big\{D \in \mathfrak{D} \,|\, \exists\, \mathbf{x} \in \mathcal{X}^\ell : \big(\mathbf{x}, D(\mathbf{x})\big) \in R\big\}\,.$$

Then, for any database properties $\mathsf{P}_0, \ldots, \mathsf{P}_q$ with $\mathsf{P}_0 = \neg\bot$ and $\mathsf{P}_q = \mathsf{P}^R$:

$$\sqrt{p} \le [\![\bot \overset{k,q}{\Longrightarrow} \mathsf{P}^R]\!] + \sqrt{\frac{\ell}{M}} \le \sum_{s=1}^{q} [\![\neg \mathsf{P}_{s-1} \xrightarrow{k} \mathsf{P}_s]\!] + \sqrt{\frac{\ell}{M}}\,.$$

Remark 3. This result implies that in order to bound p, it is sufficient to find a sequence $\bot \notin \mathsf{P}_0, \ldots, \mathsf{P}_q = \mathsf{P}^R$ of properties for which all quantum transition capacities $[\![\neg \mathsf{P}_{s-1} \to \mathsf{P}_s]\!]$ are small. Often, it is good to keep track of the (growing but bounded) size of the database and instead bound the capacities

$$[\![\mathsf{SZ}_{\le k(s-1)} \backslash \mathsf{P}_{s-1} \to \mathsf{P}_s]\!] = [\![\mathsf{SZ}_{\le k(s-1)} \backslash \mathsf{P}_{s-1} \to \mathsf{P}_s \cup \neg \mathsf{SZ}_{\le ks}]\!]\,,$$

where the equality is due to the fact that the size of a database cannot grow by more than k with one k-parallel query. Formally, we would then consider the database properties $\mathsf{P}'_s = \neg(\mathsf{SZ}_{\le ks} \setminus \mathsf{P}_s) = \mathsf{P}_s \cup \neg \mathsf{SZ}_{\le ks}$.

In the following section, we offer techniques to bound the quantum transition capacities (in certain cases) using *purely classical* reasoning. In connection with Theorem 1, this then provides means to prove lower bounds on the quantum query complexity (for certain computational problems in the random oracle model) using purely classical reasoning.

[3] In line with Remark 2, we consider $\mathsf{P}|_{D|^{\mathbf{x}}}$ to be a projection acting on $\mathbb{C}[\bar{\mathcal{Y}}^k]$, and thus I in the last term is the identity in $\mathcal{L}(\mathbb{C}[\bar{\mathcal{Y}}^k])$.

5.2 Bounding Transition Capacities Using Classical Reasoning only

The idea is to "recognize" a database transition $\neg\mathsf{P} \to \mathsf{P}$ in terms of *local* properties L, for which the truth value of $D \in^? \mathsf{L}$, i.e. whether $D \in \mathsf{L}$ or not, only depends on the function value $D(x)$ at *one single point* x (or at few points), and to use that the behavior of the compressed oracle at a single point x is explicitly given by Lemma 3. In the following two sections, we consider two possible ways to do this, but first, we provide the formal definition for local properties.

Definition 3. *A database property* $\mathsf{L} \subseteq \mathfrak{D}$ *is* ℓ-local *if* $\exists\, \mathbf{x} = (x_1, \dots, x_\ell) \in \mathcal{X}^\ell$ *so that*

1. *the truth value of* $D \in^? \mathsf{L}$ *is uniquely determined by* $D(\mathbf{x})$, *and*
2. *if* $D \in \mathsf{L} \wedge (\exists\, i \in \{1, \dots, \ell\} : D(x_i) = \bot)$ *then* $D[x_i \mapsto r_i] \in \mathsf{L}\; \forall\, r_i \in \mathcal{Y}$.

The set $\{x_1, \dots, x_\ell\}$ *is then called the* support *of* L, *and denoted by* $\mathsf{Supp}(\mathsf{L})$.

Remark 4. We observe that, as defined above, the support of an ℓ-local property is not necessarily uniquely defined: if ℓ is not minimal with the required property then there are different choices. A natural way to have a unique definition for $\mathsf{Supp}(\mathsf{L})$ is to require it to have minimal size. For us, it will be more convenient to instead consider the choice of the support to be part of the specification of L. Furthermore, we then declare that $\mathsf{Supp}(\mathsf{L} \cup \mathsf{M}) = \mathsf{Supp}(L) \cup \mathsf{Supp}(\mathsf{M})$, and $\mathsf{Supp}(\mathsf{L}|_{D|^{\mathbf{x}}}) = \mathsf{Supp}(\mathsf{L}) \cap \{x_1, \dots, x_k\}$ for any $D \in \mathfrak{D}$ and $\mathbf{x} = (x_1, \dots, x_k)$.

Remark 5. Condition 2 captures that $\bot$ is a special dummy symbol with no more "value" than any other $r \in \mathcal{Y}$.

For example, for any database property P, any $\mathbf{x} = (x_1, \dots, x_\ell)$ and D, the property $\mathsf{P}|_{D|^{\mathbf{x}}}$ satisfies requirement 1. of Definition 3. In line with this, Remark 2 applies here as well: we may identify an ℓ-local property L with a subset of $\bar{\mathcal{Y}}^\ell$.

Reasoning via Strong Recognizability

Definition 4. *A database transition* $\neg\mathsf{P} \to \mathsf{P}'$ *is* (uniformly) strongly recognizable *by* ℓ*-local properties if there exists a family of* ℓ*-local properties* $\{\mathsf{L}_i\}_i$ *with*

$$\mathsf{P}' \subseteq \bigcup_i \mathsf{L}_i \subseteq \mathsf{P}\,. \tag{9}$$

We also consider the following weaker but somewhat more intricate version.

Definition 5. *A database transition* $\neg\mathsf{P} \to \mathsf{P}'$ *is said be* k-non-uniformly strongly recognizable *by* ℓ*-local properties if for every* $\mathbf{x} = (x_1, \dots, x_k) \in \mathcal{X}^k$ *with disjoint entries, and for every* $D \in \mathfrak{D}$, *there exist a family* $\{\mathsf{L}_i^{\mathbf{x},D}\}_i$ *of* ℓ*-local properties* $\mathsf{L}_i^{\mathbf{x},D}$ *with supports in* $\{x_1, \dots, x_k\}$ *so that*

$$\mathsf{P}'|_{D|^{\mathbf{x}}} \subseteq \bigcup_i \mathsf{L}_i^{\mathbf{x},D} \subseteq \mathsf{P}|_{D|^{\mathbf{x}}}\,. \tag{10}$$

It is easiest to think about these definitions for the case $\mathsf{P} = \mathsf{P}'$, where (9) and (10) become equalities. Requirement (9) then means that for D to satisfy P it is *necessary* and *sufficient* that D satisfies one of the local properties.

Remark 6. In the above definitions, as long as the support-size remains bounded by ℓ, one can always replace two properties by their union without affecting (9), respectively (10). Thus, we may—and by default do—assume the L_i's to have *distinct* (though not necessarily disjoint) supports in Definition 4, and the same we may assume for the $\mathsf{L}_i^{\mathbf{x},D}$'s for every $\mathbf{x}$ and D in Definition 5.

Remark 7. Definition 4 implies Definition 5 with $\mathsf{L}_i^{\mathbf{x},D} := \mathsf{L}_i|_{D|^{\mathbf{x}}}$.

Theorem 2. *Let $\neg\mathsf{P} \to \mathsf{P}'$ be k-non-uniformly strongly recognizable by 1-local properties $\{\mathsf{L}_1^{\mathbf{x},D}, \ldots, \mathsf{L}_k^{\mathbf{x},D}\}$, where, w.l.o.g., the support of $\mathsf{L}_i^{\mathbf{x},D}$ is $\{x_i\}$. Then*

$$[\![\neg\mathsf{P} \xrightarrow{k} \mathsf{P}']\!] \leq \max_{\mathbf{x},D} \sqrt{10 \sum_i P\big[U \in \mathsf{L}_i^{\mathbf{x},D}\big]}$$

with the convention that $P\big[U \in \mathsf{L}_i^{\mathbf{x},D}\big] = 0$ if $\mathsf{L}_i^{\mathbf{x},D}$ is constant true or false.

Before doing the proof, let us look at one of the considered examples.

Example 2. $\mathsf{P}' = \mathsf{P} = \mathsf{PRMG}$ is uniformly strongly recognized by the 1-local properties $\mathsf{L}_x = \{D | D(x) = 0\}$. Also, as a subset of $\bar{\mathcal{Y}}$, the property $\mathsf{L}_x^{\mathbf{x},D} := \mathsf{L}_x|_{D|^{\mathbf{x}}}$ is either $\{0\}$ or constant true or false.[4] In the non-constant case, we obviously have $P\big[U \in \mathsf{L}_i^{\mathbf{x},D}\big] = P[U = 0] = 1/M$. It then follows from Theorem 2 that we can bound the transition capacity as $[\![\neg\mathsf{PRMG} \xrightarrow{k} \mathsf{PRMG}]\!] \leq \sqrt{10k/M}$ and thus from Theorem 1, setting $\mathsf{P}_i = \mathsf{PRMG}$ for all i, that the probability p of any k-parallel q-query algorithm outputting a 0-preimage x is bounded by

$$p \leq \Big(q\sqrt{\tfrac{10k}{M}} + \tfrac{1}{\sqrt{M}}\Big)^2 = O\big(\tfrac{kq^2}{M}\big)\,.$$

Proof. (of Theorem 2). Consider arbitrary $\mathbf{x}$ and D. To simplify notation, we then write L_i for $\mathsf{L}_i^{\mathbf{x},D}$. We introduce the properties $\mathsf{M}_i := \mathsf{L}_i \setminus (\bigcup_{j<i} \mathsf{L}_j)$ for $1 \leq i \leq k$. By assumption (10), as projectors they satisfy the operator inequalities $\mathsf{P}'|_{D|^{\mathbf{x}}} \leq \sum_i \mathsf{M}_i \leq \sum_i \mathsf{L}_i$ and $\mathsf{M}_i \leq \mathsf{L}_i \leq \mathsf{P}|_{D|^{\mathbf{x}}}$ $\forall i$, where, on top, the M_i's are mutually orthogonal. Then, exploiting the various properties, for any $\hat{\mathbf{y}}$ we have

$$\begin{aligned} &\|\mathsf{P}'|_{D,\mathbf{x}}\, \mathsf{cO}_{\mathbf{x}\hat{\mathbf{y}}}\, (\mathsf{I} - \mathsf{P}|_{D,\mathbf{x}})\|^2 \leq \Big\| \sum_i \mathsf{M}_i\, \mathsf{cO}_{\mathbf{x}\hat{\mathbf{y}}}\, (\mathsf{I} - \mathsf{P}|_{D|^{\mathbf{x}}}) \Big\|^2 \\ &= \sum_i \|\mathsf{M}_i\, \mathsf{cO}_{\hat{\mathbf{y}}}\, (\mathsf{I} - P|_{D|^{\mathbf{x}}})\|^2 \leq \sum_i \|\mathsf{L}_i\, \mathsf{cO}_{\mathbf{x}\hat{\mathbf{y}}}\, (\mathsf{I} - \mathsf{L}_i)\|^2 = \sum_i \|\mathsf{L}_i\, \mathsf{cO}_{x_i\hat{y}_i}\, (\mathsf{I} - \mathsf{L}_i)\|^2\,, \end{aligned}$$

[4] In more detail, $\mathsf{L}_x|_{D|^{\mathbf{x}}} = \{0\}$ whenever $x \in \{x_1, \ldots, x_k\}$, and otherwise it is constant true if $D(x) = 0$ and constant false if $D(x) \neq 0$.

where, by considering the map as a map on $\mathbb{C}[\bar{\mathcal{Y}}]$ and bounding the operator norm by the Frobenius norm,

$$\|\mathsf{L}_i\,\mathsf{cO}_{x_i\hat{y}_i}\,(\mathsf{I}-\mathsf{L}_i)\|^2 \leq \sum_{r_i,u_i\in\bar{\mathcal{Y}}} |\langle u_i|\mathsf{L}_i\,\mathsf{cO}_{x_i\hat{y}_i}\,(\mathsf{I}-\mathsf{L}_i)|r_i\rangle|^2$$
$$= \sum_{\substack{r_i\notin\mathsf{L}_i\\ u_i\in\mathsf{L}_i}} |\langle u_i|\mathsf{cO}_{x_i\hat{y}_i}|r_i\rangle|^2 = \sum_{r_i\notin\mathsf{L}_i} \tilde{P}[U\in\mathsf{L}_i|r_i,\hat{y}_i]\,.$$

The claim now follows from (8), with the additional observations that if $\perp\in\mathsf{L}_i$ (in which case (8) does not apply) then L_i is constant-true (by property 2 of Definition 3), and that the sum is empty if L_i is constant-true. □

Reasoning via Weak Recognizability Here, we consider a weaker notion of recognizability, which is wider applicable but results in a slightly worse bound. Note that it will be more natural here to speak of a transition $\mathsf{P}\to\mathsf{P}'$ instead of $\neg\mathsf{P}\to\mathsf{P}'$, i.e., we now write P for what previously was its complement.

Definition 6. *A database transition* $\mathsf{P}\to\mathsf{P}'$ *is* (uniformly) weakly recognizable *by* ℓ*-local properties if there exists a family of* ℓ*-local properties* $\{\mathsf{L}_i\}_i$ *so that*

$$D\in\mathsf{P}\ \wedge\ D'\in\mathsf{P}' \implies \exists i: D'\in\mathsf{L}_i\ \wedge\ \big(\exists x\in\mathsf{Supp}(\mathsf{L}_i): D(x)\neq D'(x)\big)\,.$$

Also here, we have a non-uniform version (see below). Furthermore, Remarks 6 and 7 apply correspondingly; in particular, we may assume the supports in the considered families of local properties to be distinct.

Definition 7. *A database transition* $\mathsf{P}\to\mathsf{P}'$ *is said be* k-non-uniformly weakly recognizable *by* ℓ*-local properties if for every* $\mathbf{x}=(x_1,\ldots,x_k)\in\mathcal{X}^k$ *with disjoint entries, and for every* $D\in\mathfrak{D}$*, there exist a family of* ℓ*-local properties* $\{\mathsf{L}_i^{\mathbf{x},D}\}_i$ *with supports in* $\{x_1,\ldots,x_k\}$ *so that*

$$\begin{aligned}&D_\circ\in\mathsf{P}|_{D|^{\mathbf{x}}}\ \wedge\ D'\in\mathsf{P}'|_{D|^{\mathbf{x}}}\\ &\qquad\implies \exists i: D'\in\mathsf{L}_i^{\mathbf{x},D}\ \wedge\ \big(\exists x\in\mathsf{Supp}(\mathsf{L}_i^{\mathbf{x},D}): D_\circ(x)\neq D'(x)\big)\,.\end{aligned}\tag{11}$$

Remark 8. Viewing $\mathsf{L}_i^{\mathbf{x},D}$ as subset of $\bar{\mathcal{Y}}^k$, and its support $\mathsf{L}_i^{\mathbf{x},D}=\{x_{i_1},\ldots,x_{i_\ell}\}$ then as subset $\{i_1,\ldots,i_\ell\}$ of $\{1,\ldots,k\}$, (11) can equivalently be written as follows, which is in line with Lemma 1 (where $\mathsf{Supp}(\mathsf{L}_i^{\mathbf{x},D})=\{i\}$):

$$D[\mathbf{x}\mapsto\mathbf{r}]\in\mathsf{P}\wedge D[\mathbf{x}\mapsto\mathbf{u}]\in\mathsf{P}' \implies \exists i:\mathbf{u}\in\mathsf{L}_i^{\mathbf{x},D}\wedge\big(\exists j\in\mathsf{Supp}(\mathsf{L}_i^{\mathbf{x},D}):\mathbf{r}_j\neq\mathbf{u}_j\big).$$

Example 3. Consider $\mathsf{CHN}^q=\{D\,|\,\exists x_0,x_1,\ldots,x_q\in\mathcal{X}: D(x_{i-1})\lhd x_i\ \forall i\}$ for an arbitrary positive integer q. For any $\mathbf{x}$ and D, we let $\mathsf{L}_i=\mathsf{L}_i^{\mathbf{x},D}$ be the 1-local property that has support $\{x_i\}$ and, as a subset of $\bar{\mathcal{Y}}$, is defined as (4), i.e., so that $u\in\mathsf{L}_i$ if and only if $u\lhd x$ for some x with $D(x)\neq\perp$ or $x\in\{x_1,\ldots,x_k\}$. Lemma 1 from the classical analysis shows that condition (11) is satisfied for the database transition $\neg\mathsf{CHN}^q\to\mathsf{CHN}^{q+1}$. This in particular implies that (11) is satisfied for the database transition $\mathsf{SZ}_{\leq k(q-1)}\setminus\mathsf{CHN}^q\to\mathsf{CHN}^{q+1}$.

Theorem 3. *Let $\mathsf{P} \to \mathsf{P}'$ be k-non-uniformly weakly recognizable by 1-local properties $\mathsf{L}_i^{\mathbf{x},D}$, where the support of $\mathsf{L}_i^{\mathbf{x},D}$ is $\{x_i\}$ or empty. Then*

$$[\![\mathsf{P} \xrightarrow{k} \mathsf{P}']\!] \leq \max_{\mathbf{x},D} e \sum_i \sqrt{10 P[U \in \mathsf{L}_i^{\mathbf{x},D}]}\,,$$

where e is Euler's number.

Example 4. In the above example regarding CHN^q with the considered $\mathsf{L}_i^{\mathbf{x},D}$'s for $D \in \mathsf{SZ}_{\leq kq}$, as in the derivation of the classical bound in Sect. 2.2, it holds that $P[U \in \mathsf{L}_i^{\mathbf{x},D}] \leq kqT/M$, where T denotes the maximal number of $y \in \mathcal{Y}$ with $y \lhd x$ (for any x). For $D \notin \mathsf{SZ}_{\leq kq}$ we may then choose $\mathsf{L}_i^{\mathbf{x},D} := \emptyset$. Thus,

$$[\![\mathsf{SZ}_{\leq k(q-1)} \backslash \mathsf{CHN}^q \xrightarrow{k} \mathsf{CHN}^{q+1}]\!] \leq ek\sqrt{\frac{10kqT}{M}}\,,$$

and applying Theorem 1 (and the subsequent remark) to the database transitions $\mathsf{SZ}_{\leq k(s-1)} \setminus \mathsf{CHN}^s \to \mathsf{CHN}^{s+1}$ for $s = 1, \ldots, q$, we obtain the following bound, which we state as a theorem here given that this is a new bound.

Theorem 4. *Let $\lhd$ be a relation over $\mathcal{Y}$ and $\mathcal{X}$. The probability p of any k-parallel q-query oracle algorithm $\mathcal{A}$ outputting $x_0, x_1, \ldots, x_{q+1} \in \mathcal{X}$ with the property that $H(x_i) \lhd x_{i+1}$ for all $i \in \{0, \ldots, q\}$ is bounded by*

$$p \leq \left(qk\sqrt{\frac{10qkT}{M}}e + \sqrt{\frac{q+2}{M}}\right)^2 = O\left(\frac{q^3k^3\,T}{M}\right),$$

where $T := \max_x |\{y \in \mathcal{Y} \,|\, y \lhd x\}|$ and $M := |\mathcal{Y}|$.

Proof. (of Theorem 3). We consider fixed choices of $\mathbf{x}$ and D, and we then write L_i for $\mathsf{L}_i^{\mathbf{x},D}$. For arbitrary but fixed $\hat{\mathbf{y}}$, we introduce

$$A_i := \sum_{\substack{u_i, r_i \text{ s.t.} \\ u_i \in \mathsf{L}_i \wedge r_i \neq u_i}} |u_i\rangle\langle u_i|\, \mathsf{cO}_{x_i \hat{y}_i} |r_i\rangle\langle r_i| \qquad \text{and}$$

$$B_i := \mathsf{cO}_{x_i \hat{y}_i} - A_i = \sum_{\substack{u_i, r_i \text{ s.t.} \\ u_i \notin \mathsf{L}_i \vee r_i = u_i}} |u_i\rangle\langle u_i|\, \mathsf{cO}_{x_i y_i} |r_i\rangle\langle r_i|$$

and observe that, taking it as understood that the operators $\mathsf{cO}_{x_1 \hat{y}_1}, \ldots, \mathsf{cO}_{x_k \hat{y}_k}$ act on different subsystems,

$$\begin{aligned}
\mathsf{cO}_{\mathbf{x}\hat{\mathbf{y}}} = \prod_{j=1}^{k} \mathsf{cO}_{x_j \hat{y}_j} &= \prod_{j=1}^{k-1} \mathsf{cO}_{x_j \hat{y}_j} A_k + \prod_{j=1}^{k-1} \mathsf{cO}_{x_j \hat{y}_j} B_k \\
&= \prod_{j=1}^{k-1} \mathsf{cO}_{x_j \hat{y}_j} A_k + \prod_{j=1}^{k-2} \mathsf{cO}_{x_j \hat{y}_j} A_{k-1} B_k + \prod_{j=1}^{k-2} \mathsf{cO}_{x_j \hat{y}_j} B_{k-1} B_k \\
&= \cdots = \sum_{i=0}^{k} \Big(\prod_{j<k-i} \mathsf{cO}_{x_j \hat{y}_j} \Big) A_{k-i} \Big(\prod_{j>k-i} B_j \Big)
\end{aligned}$$

with the convention that $A_0 = \mathsf{I}$. Furthermore, by assumption on the L_i's, it follows that

$$Q := \mathsf{P}'|_{D|^{\mathbf{x}}}\Big(\prod_{j>0} B_j\Big)\mathsf{P}|_{D|^{\mathbf{x}}} = 0\,.$$

Indeed, by definition of $\mathsf{P}'|_{D|^{\mathbf{x}}}$ and $\mathsf{P}|_{D|^{\mathbf{x}}}$ (considering them as subsets of $\bar{\mathcal{Y}}^k$ now), for $\langle\mathbf{u}|Q|\mathbf{r}\rangle$ *not* to vanish, it is necessary that $\mathbf{r} \in \mathsf{P}|_{D|^{\mathbf{x}}}$ and $\mathbf{u} \in \mathsf{P}'|_{D|^{\mathbf{x}}}$. But then, by assumption, for such $\mathbf{r}$ and $\mathbf{u}$ there exists i so that $u_i \in \mathsf{L}_i$ and $r_i \neq u_i$, and thus for which $\langle u_i|B_i|r_i\rangle = 0$. Therefore, $\langle\mathbf{u}|Q|\mathbf{r}\rangle = \langle\mathbf{u}|\prod_j B_j|\mathbf{r}\rangle = \prod_j\langle u_j|B_j|r_j\rangle$ still vanishes. As a consequence, we obtain

$$\begin{aligned}\|\mathsf{P}'|_{D|^{\mathbf{x}}}\,\mathsf{cO}_{\mathbf{x}\hat{\mathbf{y}}}\,\mathsf{P}|_{D|^{\mathbf{x}}}\| &\le \Big\|\sum_{i=0}^{k-1}\Big(\prod_{j<k-i}\mathsf{cO}_{x_j\hat{y}_j}\Big)A_{k-i}\Big(\prod_{j>k-i}B_j\Big)\Big\| \\ &\le \sum_{i=0}^{k-1}\Big(\|A_{k-i}\|\prod_{j>k-i}\|B_j\|\Big)\,.\end{aligned}$$

Using that $\|B_i\| = \|\mathsf{cO}_{x_i\hat{y}_i} - A_i\| \le 1 + \|A_i\|$, this is bounded by

$$\le \sum_{i=1}^{k}\|A_i\|\prod_{j=1}^{k}(1+\|A_j\|) \le \sum_i \|A_i\|\,e^{\sum_j \ln(1+\|A_j\|)} \le \sum_i \|A_i\|\,e$$

where the last inequality uses that $\ln(1+\|A_j\| \le \|A_j\|$, and so the last inequality holds if $\sum_j \|A_j\| \le 1$, while the final term is trivially an upper bound on the figure of merit otherwise. Using the fact that the operator norm is upper bounded by the Frobenius norm, we observe that

$$\|A_i\|^2 \le \sum_{r_i,u_i}|\langle u_i|A_i|r_i\rangle|^2 = \sum_{\substack{u_i,r_i \text{ s.t.}\\ u_i\in L_i\wedge r_i\neq u_i}}|\langle u_i|\mathsf{cO}_{x_iy_i}|r_i\rangle|^2 = \sum_{r_i}\tilde{P}[r_i\neq U\in L_i|r_i,y_i]\,,$$

and the final term is bounded by $10P[U\in\mathsf{L}_i]$ due to (8), here with the additional observation that if $\perp\,\in \mathsf{L}_i$ (and so (8) does not apply) then, by condition 2 of Definition 3, $\mathsf{L}_i = \bar{\mathcal{Y}}$, and hence the bound holds trivially. □

General ℓ-Locality and Collision Finding. We now remove the limitation on the locality being $\ell = 1$. The bound then becomes a bit more intricate, and we only have a version for *strong* recognizability.

Theorem 5. *Let $\mathsf{P} \to \mathsf{P}'$ be a database transition that is k-non-uniformly strongly recognizable by ℓ-local properties L_t, where we leave the dependency of $\mathsf{L}_t = \mathsf{L}_t^{\mathbf{x},D}$ on $\mathbf{x}$ and D implicit. Then*

$$[\![\mathsf{P}\xrightarrow{k}\mathsf{P}']\!] \le \max_{\mathbf{x},D}\, e\ell\sqrt{10\sum_t\max_{x\in\mathsf{Supp}(\mathsf{L}_t)}\max_{D'\in D|^{\mathsf{Supp}(\mathsf{L}_t)}}P\big[U\in\mathsf{L}_t|_{D'|^x}\big]}\,.$$

with the convention that $P\big[U\in\mathsf{L}_t|_{D'|^x}\big]$ vanishes if $\mathsf{L}_t|_{D'|^x}$ is trivial.

The proof is given in the full version [9]; it combines techniques from the proofs of Theorem 2 and Theorem 3.

Example 5. Consider $\mathsf{CL} = \{D \,|\, \exists x, x' : D(x) = D(x') \neq \bot\}$. For any $D \in \mathfrak{D}$ and $\mathbf{x} = (x_1, \ldots, x_k)$, consider the family of 2-local properties consisting of

$$\mathsf{CL}_{i,j} := \{D_\circ \in D|^{\mathbf{x}} \,|\, D_\circ(x_i) = D_\circ(x_j) \neq \bot\} \qquad \text{and}$$
$$\mathsf{CL}_i := \{D_\circ \in D|^{\mathbf{x}} \,|\, \exists \bar{x} \notin \{x_1, \ldots, x_k\} : D_\circ(x_i) = D(\bar{x}) \neq \bot\}$$

for $i \neq j \in \{1, \ldots, k\}$, with respective supports $\{x_i, x_j\}$ and $\{x_i\}$.

It is easy to see that this family of 2-local properties satisfies (10) for the database transition $\neg\mathsf{CL} \to \mathsf{CL}$. Indeed, if D and D' are identical outside of $\mathbf{x}$, and D has no collision while D' has one, then D''s collision must be for x_i, x_j inside $\mathbf{x}$, or for one x_i inside and one $\bar{x}$ outside. As an immediate consequence, the family also satisfies (10) for the database transition $(\mathsf{SZ}_{\leq ks} \setminus \mathsf{CL}) \to \mathsf{CL}$. In this case though, whenever $D \notin \mathsf{SZ}_{\leq k(s+1)}$ the left hand side of (10) is never satisfied and so we may replace the family of local properties to consist of (only) the constant-false property.

Consider $\mathbf{x} = (x_1, \ldots, x_k)$ and $D \in \mathsf{SZ}_{\leq k(s+1)}$ with $s \leq q$. Then, for $i \neq j$, as subsets of $\bar{\mathcal{Y}}$ we have that

$$\mathsf{CL}_{i,j}|_{D'|^{x_i}} = \{D'(x_j)\} \quad \text{and} \quad \mathsf{CL}_i|_{D'|^{x_i}} = \{D'(\bar{x}) \,|\, \bar{x} \notin \{x_1, \ldots, x_k\} : D'(\bar{x}) \neq \bot\}$$

for any $D' \in D|^{(x_i, x_j)}$ and $D' \in D|^{x_i}$, respectively, and therefore

$$P\big[U \in \mathsf{CL}_{i,j}|_{D'|^{x_i}}\big] = \frac{1}{M} \qquad \text{and} \qquad P\big[U \in \mathsf{CL}_i|_{D'|^{x_i}}\big] \leq \frac{kq}{M}.$$

So, by Theorem 5,

$$[\![\mathsf{SZ}_{\leq ks} \backslash \mathsf{CL} \xrightarrow{k} \mathsf{CL}]\!] \leq 2e\sqrt{10\left(\tfrac{k^2}{M} + \tfrac{k^2 q}{M}\right)} = 2ek\sqrt{10\,\tfrac{q+1}{M}}$$

and hence, by Theorem 1, we obtain the following bound.

Theorem 6. *The probability p of any k-parallel q-query algorithm outputting a collision is bounded by*

$$p \leq \left(2qek\sqrt{10\,\frac{q+1}{M}} + \frac{2}{\sqrt{M}}\right)^2 = O\left(\frac{k^2 q^3}{M}\right).$$

5.3 Some Rules for the Quantum Transition Capacity

As we have seen, certain "simple" lower bounds on the query complexity (respectively upper bounds on the success probability) can be obtained rather directly by bounding the quantum transition capacity by the means discussed above. In more complex scenarios, as we will encounter in the next section, it will be convenient to first *manipulate* the quantum transition capacity, e.g., to decompose it into different cases that can then be analyzed individually. We thus collect some useful manipulation rules here; all the proofs can be found in the full version [9].

To start with, since $\mathsf{cO}^\dagger_{\mathbf{x}\hat{\mathbf{y}}} = \mathsf{cO}_{\mathbf{x}\hat{\mathbf{y}}^*}$, we note that the quantum transition capacity is symmetric:

$$[\![\mathsf{P} \xrightarrow{k} \mathsf{P}']\!] = [\![\mathsf{P}' \xrightarrow{k} \mathsf{P}]\!] .$$

Therefore, the following bounds hold correspondingly also for $[\![\mathsf{P} \xrightarrow{k} \mathsf{P}' \cap \mathsf{Q}]\!]$ etc.

Lemma 5. *For any database properties* P, P' *and* Q,

$$[\![\mathsf{P} \cap \mathsf{Q} \xrightarrow{k} \mathsf{P}']\!] \le \min\{ [\![\mathsf{P} \xrightarrow{k} \mathsf{P}']\!], [\![\mathsf{Q} \xrightarrow{k} \mathsf{P}']\!] \} \qquad \textit{and}$$

$$\max\{ [\![\mathsf{P} \xrightarrow{k} \mathsf{P}']\!], [\![\mathsf{Q} \xrightarrow{k} \mathsf{P}']\!] \} \le [\![\mathsf{P} \cup \mathsf{Q} \xrightarrow{k} \mathsf{P}']\!] \le [\![\mathsf{P} \xrightarrow{k} \mathsf{P}']\!] + [\![\mathsf{Q} \xrightarrow{k} \mathsf{P}']\!] .$$

Corollary 2. *If* $\mathsf{P} \subseteq \mathsf{Q}$ *then* $[\![\mathsf{P} \xrightarrow{k} \mathsf{P}']\!] \le [\![\mathsf{Q} \xrightarrow{k} \mathsf{P}']\!]$ *and* $[\![\mathsf{P}' \xrightarrow{k} \mathsf{P}]\!] \le [\![\mathsf{P}' \xrightarrow{k} \mathsf{Q}]\!]$.

In the following, we extend the definition of the quantum transition capacity as follows, which captures a restriction of the query vector $\mathbf{x} = (x_1, \dots, x_k)$ to entries x_i in $X \subseteq \mathcal{X}$.

$$[\![\mathsf{P} \xrightarrow{k} \mathsf{P}' | X]\!] := \max_{\substack{\mathbf{x} \in X^k \\ \hat{\mathbf{y}}, D}} \| \mathsf{P}'|_{D|^{\mathbf{x}}} \, \mathsf{cO}_{\mathbf{x}\hat{\mathbf{y}}} \, \mathsf{P}|_{D|^{\mathbf{x}}} \| . \tag{12}$$

where the max is restricted to $\mathbf{x} \in X^k$. Obviously, $[\![\mathsf{P} \xrightarrow{k} \mathsf{P}']\!] = [\![\mathsf{P} \xrightarrow{k} \mathsf{P}' | \mathcal{X}]\!]$.

Lemma 6. *Let* $X = X' \cup X'' \subseteq \mathcal{X}$ *and* $k = k' + k''$. *Furthermore, let* $\mathsf{P}, \mathsf{P}', \mathsf{P}''$ *and* Q *be database properties. Then*

$$[\![\mathsf{P} \xrightarrow{k} \mathsf{P}'' | X]\!] \le [\![\mathsf{P} \xrightarrow{k} \mathsf{P}'' \backslash \mathsf{Q} | X]\!] + [\![\mathsf{P} \xrightarrow{k} \mathsf{Q} \cap \mathsf{P}'' | X]\!] ,$$

where furthermore

$$[\![\mathsf{P} \xrightarrow{k} \mathsf{Q} \cap \mathsf{P}'' | X]\!] \le [\![\mathsf{P} \xrightarrow{k'} \neg \mathsf{Q} | X]\!] + [\![\mathsf{P} \xrightarrow{k'} \mathsf{Q} \cap \mathsf{P}' | X]\!] + [\![\mathsf{Q} \backslash \mathsf{P}' \xrightarrow{k''} \mathsf{Q} \cap \mathsf{P}'' | X]\!]$$

as well as

$$[\![\mathsf{P} \xrightarrow{k} \mathsf{Q} \cap \mathsf{P}'' | X]\!] \le [\![\mathsf{P} \xrightarrow{k} \neg \mathsf{Q} | X']\!] + [\![\mathsf{P} \xrightarrow{k} \mathsf{Q} \cap \mathsf{P}' | X']\!] + [\![\mathsf{Q} \backslash \mathsf{P}' \xrightarrow{k} \mathsf{Q} \cap \mathsf{P}'' | X'']\!].$$

By recursive application of Lemma 6, we obtain the following.

Corollary 3 (Parallel Conditioning). *Let* $X = X_1 \cup \ldots \cup X_h \subseteq \mathcal{X}$ *and* $k = k_1 + \cdots + k_h$, *and let* $\mathsf{P}_0, \mathsf{P}_1, \dots, \mathsf{P}_h$ *and* $\neg \mathsf{P}_0 \subseteq \mathsf{Q}$ *be database properties. Then*

$$[\![\neg \mathsf{P}_0 \xrightarrow{k} \mathsf{P}_h | X]\!] \le \sum_{i=1}^{h} [\![\neg \mathsf{P}_0 \xrightarrow{\bar{k}_i} \neg \mathsf{Q} | X]\!] + \sum_{i=1}^{h} [\![\mathsf{Q} \backslash \mathsf{P}_{i-1} \xrightarrow{k_i} \mathsf{Q} \cap \mathsf{P}_i | X]\!] \qquad \textit{and}$$

$$[\![\neg \mathsf{P}_0 \xrightarrow{k} \mathsf{P}_h | X]\!] \le \sum_{i=1}^{h} [\![\neg \mathsf{P}_0 \xrightarrow{k} \neg \mathsf{Q} | \bar{X}_i]\!] + \sum_{i=1}^{h} [\![\mathsf{Q} \backslash \mathsf{P}_{i-1} \xrightarrow{k} \mathsf{Q} \cap \mathsf{P}_i | X_i]\!] ,$$

where $\bar{k}_i = k_1 + \cdots + k_i$ *and* $\bar{X}_i = X_1 \cup \ldots \cup X_i$.

The quantum transition capacity *with restricted input*, defined in (12), is just the original definition of the quantum transition capacity (Definition 2) but with the considered set $\mathcal{X}$ replaced by X. As a consequence, properties for $[\![\mathsf{P} \to \mathsf{P}']\!]$ carry over to $[\![\mathsf{P} \to \mathsf{P}' | X]\!]$. For instance, it is still symmetric, and Lemma 5 carries over to

$$[\![\mathsf{P} \cap \mathsf{Q} \xrightarrow{k} \mathsf{P}' | X]\!] \leq \min\{ [\![\mathsf{P} \xrightarrow{k} \mathsf{P}' | X]\!], [\![\mathsf{Q} \xrightarrow{k} \mathsf{P}' | X]\!] \}$$

etc. For completeness, we spell out here the definition of non-uniform recognizability as well as Theorem 3 for such input-restricted database transitions $\mathsf{P} \to \mathsf{P}' \,|\, X$ (the other types of recognizability can be generalized similarly).

Definition 8. *A database transition* $\mathsf{P} \to \mathsf{P}'$ *with input restricted in* $X \subseteq \mathcal{X}$ *is said to be* k-non-uniformly weakly recognizable *by* ℓ*-local properties if for every* $\mathbf{x} = (x_1, \ldots, x_k) \in X^k$ *with disjoint entries, and for every* $D \in \mathfrak{D}$*, there exist a family of* ℓ*-local properties* $\{\mathsf{L}_i^{\mathbf{x},D}\}_i$ *with supports in* $\{x_1, \ldots, x_k\}$ *so that*

$$D_\circ \in \mathsf{P}|_{D|^{\mathbf{x}}} \wedge D' \in \mathsf{P}'|_{D|^{\mathbf{x}}} \implies \exists\, i: D' \in \mathsf{L}_i^{\mathbf{x},D} \wedge \left(\exists\, x \in \mathsf{Supp}(\mathsf{L}_i^{\mathbf{x},D}) : D_\circ(x) \neq D'(x)\right).$$

Theorem 7. *Let* $\mathsf{P} \to \mathsf{P}'$ *with input restricted in* X *be* k*-non-uniformly weakly recognizable by* 1*-local properties* $\mathsf{L}_i^{\mathbf{x},D}$*, where the support of* $\mathsf{L}_i^{\mathbf{x},D}$ *is* $\{x_i\}$ *or empty. Then*

$$[\![\mathsf{P} \xrightarrow{k} \mathsf{P}' | X]\!] \leq \max_{\mathbf{x},D} e \sum_i \sqrt{10 P[U \in \mathsf{L}_i^{\mathbf{x},D}]}\,,$$

where the max *now is over all* $\mathbf{x} = (x_1, \ldots, x_k) \in X^k$.

6 Post-Quantum Proof of Sequential Works

In this section, we prove post-quantum security of the proof of sequential work (PoSW) construction by Cohen and Pietrzak [10] (referred to as Simple PoSW) using our framework developed in the last section. As a matter of fact, we directly analyze the non-interactive variant of their construction after applying the Fiat-Shamir transformation [12]. As we shall see, the proof is by means of purely classical reasoning, recycling observations that are relevant for arguing classical security and combining them with results provided by our framework.

6.1 Simple Proof of Sequential Works

For readers not familiar with PoSW, we review the definition in the full version [9]. Typically, underlying the construction of a PoSW is a directed acyclic graph (DAG) G with certain "depth-robust" properties, and a graph labeling that the prover $\mathcal{P}$ is required to compute using a hash function H. We proceed to describe the DAG used in Simple PoSW and the graph labeling.

Simple PoSW DAG and Graph Labeling. Let $n \in \mathbb{N}$ and $N = 2^{n+1} - 1$. Consider the (directed) complete binary tree $B_n = (V_n, E'_n)$ of depth n, where $V_n := \{0,1\}^{\leq n}$ and E'_n consists of the edges directed towards the root (black edges in Fig. 2). The Simple PoSW DAG, denoted by G_n^{PoSW}, is obtained by adding some additional edges to B_n (red edges in Fig. 2). Before giving the formal definition of G_n^{PoSW} (Definition 10), we recall some basic terminology and notation in the context of the complete binary tree B_n, which we will then also use in the context of G_n^{PoSW}.

Definition 9. *We write* $\mathsf{rt} := \epsilon$ *for the* root *and* $\mathsf{leaves}(V_n) := \{0,1\}^n$ *for the* leaves *in* V_n*. For* $T \subseteq V_n$*, we set* $\mathsf{leaves}(T) := T \cap \{0,1\}^n$*. For* $v \notin \mathsf{leaves}(V_n)$*, we set* $\mathsf{left}(v) := v\|0$ *and* $\mathsf{right}(v) := v\|1$*. For* $b \in \{0,1\}$ *and* $v \in \{0,1\}^{<n}$*, let* $\mathsf{par}(v\|b) := v$ *and* $\mathsf{sib}(v\|b) := v\|\neg b$ *(see Fig. 2, right).*

Finally, for a leaf $v \in \mathsf{leaves}(V_n)$*, we define the* ancestors *of* v *as* $\mathsf{anc}(v) = \{\mathsf{par}^i(v) \,|\, 0 \leq i \leq n\}$ *and the* authentication path *of* v *(as in the Merkle tree) as* $\mathsf{ap}(v) = (\mathsf{anc}(v)\backslash\{\mathsf{rt}\}) \cup \{\mathsf{sib}(u) \,|\, \mathsf{rt} \neq u \in \mathsf{anc}(v)\}$.

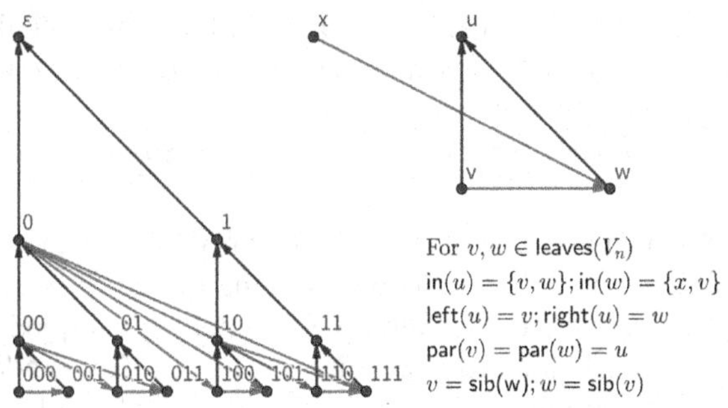

Fig. 2. Illustration of the Simple PoSW DAG G_n^{PoSW} for $n = 3$.

Definition 10. *Define the Simple PoSW DAG* $G_n^{\mathsf{PoSW}} := (V_n, E'_n \cup E''_n)$ *with*

$$E'_n := \{(\mathsf{left}(v), v), (\mathsf{right}(v), v) \,|\, v \in V_n \setminus \mathsf{leaves}(V_n)\} \quad \textit{and}$$
$$E''_n := \{(\mathsf{sib}(u), v) \,|\, v \in V_n, u \in \mathsf{anc}(v) \;\; s.t. \;\; u = \mathsf{right}(\mathsf{par}(u))\}.$$

For $v \in V_n$, we write $\mathsf{in}(v) := \{u \in V_n \,|\, (u,v) \in E'_n \cup E''_n\}$ to denote the inward neighborhood of v. We consider a fixed ordering of the vertices (e.g. lexicographic), so that for any set $\{v_1, \ldots, v_d\} \in V_n$ of vertices, the corresponding ordered list $(v_1, \ldots, v_d)$ is well defined.

We proceed to define the graph labeling for G_n^{PoSW} with respect to a hash function $H : \{0,1\}^{\leq B} \to \{0,1\}^w$, were w is a security parameter, and B is arbitrary large (and sufficiently large for everything below to be well defined).

Definition 11 (Graph Labeling). *A function* $\ell : V_n \to \{0,1\}^w$, $v \mapsto \ell_v$ *is a* labeling *of* G_n^{PoSW} *with respect to* H *if*

$$\ell_v = H(v, \ell_{\mathsf{in}(v)}) \tag{13}$$

for all $v \in V_n$*, were* $\ell_{\mathsf{in}(v)}$ *is shorthand for* $(\ell_{v_1}, \ldots, \ell_{v_d})$ *with* $\{v_1, \ldots, v_d\} = \mathsf{in}(v)$*. Similarly, for a subtree*[5] T *of* G_n^{PoSW}*, a function* $\ell : T \to \{0,1\}^w$, $v \mapsto \ell_v$ *is a called a* labeling *of* T *with respect to* H *if* $\ell_v = H(v, \ell_{\mathsf{in}(v)})$ *for all* $v \in V_n$ *for which* $\mathsf{in}(v) \subseteq T$*.*

By its structure, G_n^{PoSW} admits a unique labeling, which can be computed by making $N = 2^{n+1} - 1$ sequential queries to H, starting with the leftmost leaf. We speak of a *consistent* labeling (of G_n^{PoSW} or T) when we want to emphasize the distinction from an arbitrary function ℓ. The definition also applies when replacing the function H by a database $D : \{0,1\}^{\leq B} \to \{0,1\}^w \cup \{\perp\}$, where the requirement (13) then in particular means that $H(v, \ell_{\mathsf{in}(v)}) \neq \perp$.

We also make the following important remark.

Remark 9. Let T be a subtree of G_n^{PoSW} with a consistent labeling ℓ. Then, any path $P = (v_0, \ldots, v_r)$ of length $|P| = r$ in T induces an r-chain $(x_0, \ldots, x_r)$, where $x_i = (v_i, \ell_{v'_1}, \ldots, \ell_{v'_d})$ with $\{v'_1, \ldots, v'_d\} = \mathsf{in}(v_i)$, and where the relation $\lhd$ is defined as follows. $y \lhd x$ if and only if x is of form $(v, \ell_1, \ell_2, \ldots, \ell_d)$ with $v \in V_n, \ell_j \in \{0,1\}^w$, $|d| = |\mathsf{in}(v)| \leq n$, and $y = \ell_j$ for some j.

Simple PoSW Construction. In the Simple PoSW scheme, the prover $\mathcal{P}$ must provide the root label ℓ_{rt} of the consistent labeling of G_n^{PoSW} with respect to H_χ defined by $H_\chi(\cdot) := H(\chi, \cdot)$ for a random $\chi \in \{0,1\}^w$, sampled by the verifier $\mathcal{V}$, and open the labels of the authentication paths of a few random leaves.

Specifically, given parameters w, t and $N = 2^{n+1} - 1$, and a random oracel $H : \{0,1\}^{\leq B} \to \{0,1\}^w$, the Simple PoSW protocol is defined as follows.

- $(\phi, \phi_{\mathcal{P}}) := \mathsf{PoSW}^H(\chi, N)$: $\mathcal{P}$ computes the unique consistent labeling ℓ of G_n^{PoSW} with respect to hash function H_χ defined by $H_\chi(\cdot) := H(\chi, \cdot)$, and stores it in $\phi_{\mathcal{P}}$. $\mathcal{P}$ sets $\phi = \ell_{\mathsf{rt}}$ as the root label.
- The opening challenge: $\gamma := H_\chi^{\mathsf{ChQ}}(\phi) := \big(H_\chi(\phi, 1), \ldots, H_\chi(\phi, d)\big) \in \{0,1\}^{dw}$ for sufficiently large d, parsed as t leaves $\{v_1, \ldots, v_t\} \subseteq \mathsf{leaves}(V_n)$.
- $\tau := \mathsf{open}^H(\chi, N, \phi_{\mathcal{P}}, \gamma)$: For challenge $\gamma = \{v_1, \ldots, v_t\}$, the opening τ consists of the labels of the vertices in the authentication path $\mathsf{ap}(v_i)$ of v_i for $i \in [t]$, i.e., $\tau = \{\ell_{\mathsf{ap}(v_i)}\}_{i \in [t]}$.
- $\mathsf{verify}^H(\chi, N, \phi, \gamma, \tau)$: $\mathcal{V}$ verifies if the ancestors of every v_i are consistently labeled by τ. Specifically, for each $i \in [t]$, $\mathcal{V}$ checks if $\ell_u = H_\chi(u, \ell_{\mathsf{in}(u)})$ for all $u \in \mathsf{anc}(v_i)$. $\mathcal{V}$ outputs accept iff all the consistency checks pass.

---

[5] By a *subtree* of G_n^{PoSW} we mean a sub*graph* of G_n^{PoSW} that is a sub*tree* of the complete binary tree B_n when restricted to edges in E'_n. We are also a bit sloppy with not distinguishing between the graph T and the vertices of T.

Note that since we consider the non-interactive version of Simple PoSW after applying the Fair-Shamir transformation, the random oracle H is used to compute both the labels (as $H_{\mathcal{X}}(v, \ell_{\mathsf{in}(v)})$) and the challenge (as $H_{\mathcal{X}}^{\mathsf{ChQ}}(\phi)$). We silently assume that the respective inputs are specially formatted so as to distinguish a *label query* from a *challenge query*. E.g., a label query comes with a prefix 0 and a challenge query with prefix 1. We then denote the set of inputs for label and challenge queries by LbQ and $\mathsf{ChQ} \subseteq \{0,1\}^{\leq B}$, respectively. Also, for simplicity, we will treat $H_{\mathcal{X}}^{\mathsf{ChQ}}(\phi)$ as *one* oracle query, i.e., "charge" only one query for a challenge query; however, we keep the superscript ChQ to remind that the query response is (understood as) a set of leaves.

Classical Security Analysis of Simple PoSW. We first review the classical security analysis of [10]. For simplicity, here we consider the original (interactive) variant (i.e., $\mathcal{P}$ first sends ϕ, receives random γ from $\mathcal{V}$, and then sends τ to $\mathcal{V}$). Also, to start with, we assume that $\mathcal{P}$ does not make further oracle queries after sending ϕ. We review the argument of [10] for bounding the probability that a k-parallel q-query classical oracle algorithm $\mathcal{A}$ with $q < N$ makes $\mathcal{V}$ accept, using the terminology we introduced in Sect. 2.

Let $D : \{0,1\}^{\leq B} \to \{0,1\}^w \cup \{\bot\}$ be the database at the point that $\mathcal{A}$ sends ϕ to $\mathcal{V}$. Following the argument in Sect. 2, we can bound the success probability of $\mathcal{A}$ by the probability that a random challenge $\gamma = \{v_i\}_{i\in[t]}$ can be opened based on the information in the database D.

First, since the probability is small for the database D to contain a collision or a $(q+1)$-chain with respect to the relation defined in Remark 9, we can assume that D contains no collisions nor $(q+1)$-chains.

Next, given the database D and the "commitment" ϕ, claimed to be the root label ℓ_{rt}, we need to analyze the set of leaves v that $\mathcal{A}$ can open. One of the key observations in [10] is that, for a database D with no collisions, there exists a maximal subtree T of G_n^{PoSW} that contains rt and admits a consistent labeling ℓ with $\ell_{\mathsf{rt}} = \phi$. As observed in [10], this subtree T then contains all leaves that one can open given D. Thus, $\mathcal{A}$ can correctly answer a challenge $\gamma = \{v_1, \dots, v_t\}$ if $\gamma \subseteq \mathsf{leaves}(T)$, while otherwise it is unlikely that he succeeds.

The subtree T, together with the labeling ℓ of T, can be extracted using an algorithm $\mathsf{Extract}_n^D(\phi)$, described in the full version [9]. Roughly speaking, starting with $T := \{\mathsf{rt}\}$, consider $v := \mathsf{rt}$ and $\ell_{\mathsf{rt}} := \phi$, and add $\mathsf{left}(v)$ and $\mathsf{right}(v)$ to T if (and only if) there exist $\ell_{\mathsf{left}(v)}$ and $\ell_{\mathsf{right}(v)}$ such that $\ell_v = D\big(v, \ell_{\mathsf{left}(v)}, \ell_{\mathsf{right}(v)}\big)$, and repeat inductively with the newly added elements in T. In the end, for the leaves $v \in T$ check if $\ell_v = D(v, \ell_{\mathsf{in}(v)})$ and remove v from T if this is not the case; we note here that $v \in \mathsf{leaves}(T) \Rightarrow \mathsf{in}(v) \subseteq T$.

Lemma 7. *Let $D : \{0,1\}^{\leq B} \to \{0,1\}^w \cup \{\bot\}$ be a database with no collisions (beyond $\bot$). Then, for any $\phi \in \{0,1\}^w$, the subtree T and the labeling ℓ produced by $\mathsf{Extract}_n^D(\phi)$ are such that ℓ is a consistent labeling of T with respect to D, having root label $\ell_{\mathsf{rt}} = \phi$. Furthermore, for any leave v of V_n, if $v \in T$ then $\ell_u = D(u, \ell_{\mathsf{in}(u)})$ for all $u \in \mathsf{anc}(v_i)$, and if $v \notin T$ then there exists no labeling ℓ' with $\ell'_{\mathsf{rt}} = \phi$ and $\ell'_u = D(u, \ell'_{\mathsf{in}(u)})$ for all $u \in \mathsf{anc}(v_i)$.*

Another key argument in [10] uses a certain "depth-robust" property of G_n^{PoSW} to show that for any subtree $T \subseteq V_n$ with $\mathsf{rt} \in T$, there exists a path P in T with length $|P| \geq 2 \cdot |\mathsf{leaves}(T)| - 2$. Furthermore, Remark 9 applies here as well: a labeling of P with respect to D induces a $|P|$-chain in D. Combining these with the assumption that D contains no $q+1$-chain, we have $|\mathsf{leaves}(T)| \leq (q+2)/2$. Thus, the probability that $\mathcal{A}$ can open labels for a random challenge $\gamma = \{v_i\}_{i \in [t]}$ is at most

$$\left(\frac{|\mathsf{leaves}(T)|}{2^n}\right)^t \leq \left(\frac{q+2}{2^{n+1}}\right)^t .$$

Lemma 8. *Let $D : \{0,1\}^{\leq B} \to \{0,1\}^w \cup \{\bot\}$ be a database with no $(q+1)$-chain. Let T be a subtree of G_n^{PoSW} admitting a consistent labeling with respect to D. Then, $|\mathsf{leaves}(T)| \leq (q+2)/2$.*

Finally, we briefly discuss here how to deal with $\mathcal{A}$ making additional queries after sending ϕ. Recall that T contains all leaves v that admit consistently labeled ancestors. Thus, for the additional queries to be helpful, they must enlarge the extracted subtree T. More precisely, let D' be the database after the additional queries and let T' and ℓ' be extracted by $\mathsf{Extract}_n^{D'}(\phi)$. It must be that $T \subsetneq T'$ and $\ell'|_T = \ell$, and there must exist x with $D(x) = \bot$ while $D'(x) = \ell_v$ for some $v \in T$. This happens with probability at most $O(qk/2^w)$ for each query since ℓ has support size at most $O(qk)$. We capture the above crucial observation by means of the following formal statement, which, in this form, will then be recycled in the security proof against quantum attacks.

Lemma 9. *Let $D : \{0,1\}^{\leq B} \to \{0,1\}^w \cup \{\bot\}$ be a database with no collisions (beyond $\bot$). Let $\phi \in \{0,1\}^w$ and $(T, \ell) = \mathsf{Extract}_n^D(\phi)$. Furthermore, let $D' = D[\mathbf{x} \mapsto \mathbf{u}]$ and $(T', \ell') = \mathsf{Extract}_n^{D'}(\phi)$, and let v be a leave of V_n. If $v \in T' \setminus T$ then there exist $j \in \{1, \ldots, k\}$ and $z \in \mathsf{anc}(v)$ so that $D(x_j) \neq D'(x_j) = \ell'_z$.*

Proof. Given that $v \in T'$, the labeling ℓ' labels the ancestors of v consistently with respect to D', i.e., $\ell'_z = D'(z, \ell'_{\mathsf{in}(z)})$ for all $z \in \mathsf{anc}(v)$. On the other hand, as $v \notin T$, ℓ' does *not* label the ancestors of v consistently with respect to D, i.e., there must exist $z \in \mathsf{anc}(v)$ such that $D(z, \ell'_{\mathsf{in}(z)}) \neq \ell'_z = D'(z, \ell'_{\mathsf{in}(z)})$. Since D and D' differ only within $\mathbf{x}$, there exists $j \in \{1, \ldots, k\}$ with $x_j = (z, \ell'_{\mathsf{in}(z)})$. □

6.2 Post-Quantum Security of Simple PoSW

In this section, we prove post-quantum security of the (non-interactive) Simple PoSW protocol. As we shall see, relying on the framework we developed in Sect. 5, the proof uses *purely classical reasoning* only, and somewhat resembles the arguments in the classical analysis.

Theorem 8 (Post-Quantum Simple PoSW Security). *Consider the Simple PoSW protocol with parameters w, t and $N = 2^{n+1} - 1$ with $w \geq tn$. Let $\tilde{\mathcal{P}}$ be* *a k-parallel q-query quantum oracle algorithm acting as a prover. The probability p that $\tilde{\mathcal{P}}$ can make the verifier $\mathcal{V}$ accept is at most*

$$p = O\left(k^2 q^2 \left(\frac{q+2}{2^{n+1}}\right)^t + \frac{k^3 q^3 n}{2^w} + \frac{tn}{2^w}\right).$$

The first step towards the proof is to invoke Corollary 1 (using the notation from Theorem 1), which, in the case here, bounds the success probability p of a dishonest prover $\tilde{\mathcal{P}}$ by

$$\sqrt{p} \le [\![\bot \overset{k,q}{\Longrightarrow} \mathsf{P}^R]\!] + \sqrt{\frac{t \cdot (n+1) + 1}{2^w}},$$

where R is the relation that checks correctness of $\tilde{\mathcal{P}}$'s output according to the scheme. In the following, we write $\mathsf{Suc} := \mathsf{P}^R$ and $\mathsf{Fail} = \neg\mathsf{Suc}$. Also, recall the database properties CL, $\mathsf{SZ}_{\le s}$ and CHN^s defined previously, where the latter is with respect to the hash chain relation $\lhd$ considered in Remark 9. By the properties of (the subtree extracted with) $\mathsf{Extract}_n^D(\cdot)$, we have

$$\mathsf{Suc} \setminus \mathsf{CL} = \left\{D \in \neg\mathsf{CL} \,\middle|\, \exists \ell_{\mathsf{rt}} \in \{0,1\}^w \text{ s.t. } D^{\mathsf{ChQ}}(\ell_{\mathsf{rt}}) \subseteq \mathsf{Extract}_n^D(\ell_{\mathsf{rt}})\right\}. \quad (14)$$

To bound $[\![\bot \overset{k,q}{\Longrightarrow} \mathsf{P}^R]\!] = [\![\bot \overset{k,q}{\Longrightarrow} \mathsf{Suc}]\!]$, we consider database properties $\mathsf{P}_0, \ldots, \mathsf{P}_q$ with $\mathsf{P}_0 = \bot$ and $\mathsf{P}_s = \mathsf{Suc} \cup \mathsf{CL} \cup \mathsf{CHN}^{s+1}$ for $1 \le s \le q$. Using Lemma 4, Remark 3 and Corollary 2,

$$[\![\bot \overset{k,q}{\Longrightarrow} \mathsf{Suc}]\!] \le \sum_{1 \le s \le q} [\![\mathsf{SZ}_{\le k(s-1)} \backslash \mathsf{P}_{s-1} \overset{k}{\rightarrow} \mathsf{P}_s]\!].$$

Thus, the proof of Theorem 8 follows immediately from the following bound.

Proposition 1. *For integers $0 \le s \le q$, and for the database properties $\mathsf{P}_0, \ldots, \mathsf{P}_q$ as defined above*

$$[\![\mathsf{SZ}_{\le k(s-1)} \backslash \mathsf{P}_{s-1} \overset{k}{\rightarrow} \mathsf{P}_s]\!] \le 4ek\sqrt{10\frac{q+1}{2^w}} + 3ek\sqrt{\frac{10kqn}{2^w}} + ek\sqrt{10\left(\frac{q+2}{2^{n+1}}\right)^t}.$$

Proof. By applying Corollary 3 with $h := 2$, $X_1 := \mathsf{LbQ}$ and $X_2 := \mathsf{ChQ}$, and with $\mathsf{P}_0, \mathsf{P}_1, \mathsf{P}_2$ and Q suitably chosen (we have to refer to the full version [9] for the details here), we obtain

$$\begin{aligned}[\![\mathsf{SZ}_{\le k(s-1)} \backslash \mathsf{P}_{s-1} \overset{k}{\rightarrow} \mathsf{P}_s]\!] &\le 2[\![\mathsf{SZ}_{\le k(s-1)} \backslash \mathsf{P}_{s-1} \overset{k}{\rightarrow} \mathsf{CL} \cup \mathsf{CHN}^{s+1}]\!] \\ &\quad + [\![\mathsf{SZ}_{\le k(s-1)} \backslash \mathsf{P}_{s-1} \overset{k}{\rightarrow} \mathsf{Suc} \backslash \mathsf{CL} \,|\, \mathsf{LbQ}]\!] + [\![\neg\mathsf{P}_s \overset{k}{\rightarrow} \mathsf{Suc} \backslash \mathsf{CL} \,|\, \mathsf{ChQ}]\!].\end{aligned}$$

By Lemma 5 (and Corollary 2), and recalling that $\mathsf{P}_{s-1} = \mathsf{Suc} \cup \mathsf{CL} \cup \mathsf{CHN}^s$, the first capacity in the term can be controlled as

$$\begin{aligned}
&[\![\mathsf{SZ}_{\leq k(s-1)} \backslash \mathsf{P}_{s-1} \xrightarrow{k} \mathsf{CL} \cup \mathsf{CHN}^{s+1}]\!] \\
&\quad \leq [\![\mathsf{SZ}_{\leq k(s-1)} \backslash \mathsf{P}_{s-1} \xrightarrow{k} \mathsf{CL}]\!] + [\![\mathsf{SZ}_{\leq k(s-1)} \backslash \mathsf{P}_{s-1} \xrightarrow{k} \mathsf{CHN}^{s+1}]\!] \\
&\quad \leq [\![\mathsf{SZ}_{\leq k(s-1)} \backslash \mathsf{CL} \xrightarrow{k} \mathsf{CL}]\!] + [\![\mathsf{SZ}_{\leq k(s-1)} \backslash \mathsf{CHN}^s \xrightarrow{k} \mathsf{CHN}^{s+1}]\!] \\
&\quad \leq 2ek\sqrt{10\frac{q+1}{2^w}} + ek\sqrt{\frac{10kqn}{2^w}}
\end{aligned}$$

using earlier derived bounds. It remains to bound the remaining two capacities appropriately, which we do below. □

Lemma 10. *For any* $0 < q \in \mathbb{Z}$: $[\![\neg\mathsf{P}_q \xrightarrow{k} \mathsf{Suc} \backslash \mathsf{CL} | \mathsf{ChQ}]\!] \leq ek \cdot \sqrt{10\left(\frac{q+2}{2^{n+1}}\right)^t}$.

Proof. For convenience, we will denote $D[\mathbf{x} \mapsto \mathbf{y}]$ by $D_{\mathbf{x},\mathbf{y}}$. In order to bound the above capacity, we define 1-local properties $\mathsf{L}_j^{\mathbf{x},D}$ and show that $\mathsf{L}_j^{\mathbf{x},D}$ (weakly) recognize the considered transition (with input restricted to ChQ).

For any D and $\mathbf{x} = (\ell_{\mathsf{rt}}^1, \ldots, \ell_{\mathsf{rt}}^k) \in \mathsf{ChQ}^k$, we set

$$\mathsf{L}_j^{\mathbf{x},D} := \left\{ D_\circ \in D|^{\mathbf{x}} \;\middle|\; D_\circ^{\mathsf{ChQ}}(x_j) \subseteq \mathsf{leaves}\left(\mathsf{Extract}_n^{D_{\mathbf{x},\perp}}(\ell_{\mathsf{rt}}^j)\right) \right\}$$

Suppose $D_{\mathbf{x},\mathbf{r}} \in \neg\mathsf{P}_q = \mathsf{Fail} \setminus \mathsf{CL} \setminus \mathsf{CHN}^{q+1}$ but $D_{\mathbf{x},\mathbf{u}} \in \mathsf{Suc} \setminus \mathsf{CL}$. Thus, by (14), there exists $\ell_{\mathsf{rt}} \in \{0,1\}^w$ with

$$D_{\mathbf{x},\mathbf{u}}^{\mathsf{ChQ}}(\ell_{\mathsf{rt}}) \subseteq \mathsf{leaves}\left(\mathsf{Extract}_n^{D_{\mathbf{x},\mathbf{u}}}(\ell_{\mathsf{rt}})\right), \tag{15}$$

while

$$D_{\mathbf{x},\mathbf{r}}^{\mathsf{ChQ}}(\ell_{\mathsf{rt}}) \not\subseteq \mathsf{leaves}\left(\mathsf{Extract}_n^{D_{\mathbf{x},\mathbf{r}}}(\ell_{\mathsf{rt}})\right). \tag{16}$$

Since the output of the extraction procedure $\mathsf{Extract}_n^D(\cdot)$ only depends on those function values of D that correspond to *label* queries ($\mathbf{x}$ here consists of challenge queries), we have

$$\mathsf{Extract}_n^{D_{\mathbf{x},\mathbf{r}}}(\ell_{\mathsf{rt}}) = \mathsf{Extract}_n^{D_{\mathbf{x},\perp}}(\ell_{\mathsf{rt}}) = \mathsf{Extract}_n^{D_{\mathbf{x},\mathbf{u}}}(\ell_{\mathsf{rt}}).$$

If ℓ_{rt} is different from all ℓ_{rt}^j, then Eqs. (15) and (16) contradict. So there is some j such that $\ell_{\mathsf{rt}}^j = \ell_{\mathsf{rt}}$. Equations (15) and (16) thus become

$$u_j \subseteq \mathsf{leaves}\left(\mathsf{Extract}_n^{D_{\mathbf{x},\perp}}(\ell_{\mathsf{rt}})\right) \qquad \text{and} \qquad r_j \not\subseteq \mathsf{leaves}\left(\mathsf{Extract}_n^{D_{\mathbf{x},\perp}}(\ell_{\mathsf{rt}})\right),$$

understanding that u_j and r_j represent lists/sets of t (challenge) leaves. Hence $r_j \neq u_j$. This concludes that $\mathsf{L}_j^{\mathbf{x},D}$ indeed weakly recognizes the considered database transition.

We note that, for each $\mathbf{x} \in \mathsf{ChQ}^k$ and $D \in \mathsf{Fail} \backslash \mathsf{CL} \backslash \mathsf{CHN}^{q+1}$, since the longest hash chain in D is of length no more than q and $T := \mathsf{Extract}_n^{D_{\mathbf{x},\perp}}(\ell_{\mathsf{rt}}^j)$ admits a consistent labeling (Lemma 7), it follows from Lemma 8 that the number of leaves in T is bounded by $(q+2)/2$. Therefore,

$$P[U \in \mathsf{L}_j^{\mathbf{x},D}] \leq \left(\frac{\mathsf{leaves}(\mathsf{Extract}_n^{D_{\mathbf{x},\perp}}(\ell_{\mathsf{rt}}^j))}{2^n}\right)^t \leq \left(\frac{q+2}{2^{n+1}}\right)^t,$$

and so the claimed bound follows by applying Theorem 7. □

Lemma 11. *For any* $0 < q \in \mathbb{Z}$*:* $[\![\mathsf{SZ}_{\leq k(q-1)} \backslash \mathsf{P}_{q-1} \xrightarrow{k} \mathsf{Suc} \backslash \mathsf{CL} | \mathsf{LbQ}]\!] \leq ek\sqrt{\frac{10nkq}{2^w}}$.

Proof. Define the notion of labeling support $\mathrm{LSupp}(D)$ of a database $D \in \mathfrak{D}$ as follows.

$$\mathrm{LSupp}(D) := \left\{\lambda \in \{0,1\}^w \,\middle|\, \begin{array}{l}\exists 0 \leq i \leq d \leq n, v \in V_n, \ell_1, \ldots, \ell_d \in \{0,1\}^w \\ \text{s.t. } D(v, \ell_1, \ldots, \ell_{i-1}, \lambda, \ell_{i+1}, \ldots \ell_d) \neq \perp\end{array}\right\}$$
$$\cup \left\{\ell_{\mathsf{rt}} \in \{0,1\}^w \,\middle|\, D^{\mathsf{ChQ}}(\ell_{\mathsf{rt}}) \neq \perp\right\}.$$

We note that since LSupp is defined only in terms of where D is defined, but does not depend on the actual function values (beyond being non-$\perp$), $\mathrm{LSupp}(D) \subseteq \mathrm{LSupp}(D_{\mathbf{x},\mathbf{0}})$ for any $\mathbf{x} \in \mathcal{X}^k$, where $\mathbf{0} \in \{0,1\}^k$ is the all-0 string.

In order to bound above capacity, we define 1-local properties and show that they (weakly) recognize the considered transition (with input restricted to LbQ). For any D and $\mathbf{x} \in \mathsf{LbQ}^k$, consider the local properties

$$\mathsf{L}_j^{\mathbf{x},D} := \left\{D_\circ \in D|^{\mathbf{x}} \,\middle|\, D_\circ(x_j) \in \mathrm{LSupp}(D_{\mathbf{x},\mathbf{0}})\right\}.$$

Let $D_{\mathbf{x},\mathbf{r}} \in \neg\mathsf{P}_{q-1} = \mathsf{Fail} \setminus \mathsf{CL} \setminus \mathsf{CHN}^q$ yet $D_{\mathbf{x},\mathbf{u}} \in \mathsf{Suc} \setminus \mathsf{CL}$. By (14), there exists ℓ_{rt} so that $D^{\mathsf{ChQ}}_{\mathbf{x},\mathbf{u}}(\ell_{\mathsf{rt}}) \subseteq \mathsf{Extract}_n^{D_{\mathbf{x},\mathbf{u}}}(\ell_{\mathsf{rt}})$, while, on the other hand, there exists some $v \in D^{\mathsf{ChQ}}_{\mathbf{x},\mathbf{r}}(\ell_{\mathsf{rt}}) \setminus \mathsf{leaves}(\mathsf{Extract}_n^{D_{\mathbf{x},\mathbf{r}}}(\ell_{\mathsf{rt}}))$. Given that here $\mathbf{x} \in \mathsf{LbQ}^k$, we have $D_{\mathbf{x},\mathbf{r}}(\ell_{\mathsf{rt}}) = D_{\mathbf{x},\mathbf{u}}(\ell_{\mathsf{rt}})$, and thus, by (15), we have

$$v \in \mathsf{leaves}\Big(\mathsf{Extract}_n^{D_{\mathbf{x},\mathbf{u}}}(\ell_{\mathsf{rt}})\Big) \setminus \mathsf{leaves}\Big(\mathsf{Extract}_n^{D_{\mathbf{x},\mathbf{r}}}(\ell_{\mathsf{rt}})\Big).$$

Writing ℓ' for the labeling extracted by $\mathsf{Extract}_n^{D_{\mathbf{x},\mathbf{u}}}(\ell_{\mathsf{rt}})$, it then follows from Lemma 9 that there exist $j \in \{1, \ldots, k\}$ and $z \in \mathsf{anc}(v)$ such that $u_j = D_{\mathbf{x},\mathbf{u}}(x_j) = \ell'_z \neq D_{\mathbf{x},\mathbf{r}}(x_j) = r_j$. Furthermore, since $D^{\mathsf{ChQ}}_{\mathbf{x},\mathbf{u}}(\ell'_z) = D^{\mathsf{ChQ}}_{\mathbf{x},\mathbf{u}}(\ell_{\mathsf{rt}}) \neq \perp$ in case $z = \mathsf{rt}$, and ℓ'_z is part of the input that is mapped to $\ell'_{\mathsf{par}(z)}$ under $D_{\mathbf{x},\mathbf{u}}$ in all other cases, we also have $u_j = \ell'_z \in \mathrm{LSupp}(D_{\mathbf{x},\mathbf{u}}) \subseteq \mathrm{LSupp}(D_{\mathbf{x},\mathbf{0}})$. Therefore, the local properties $\mathsf{L}_j^{\mathbf{x},D}$ do indeed weakly recognize the considered transition for input restricted to LbQ.

For $D \in \mathsf{SZ}_{\leq k(q-1)} \setminus \mathsf{P}_{q-1}$, since there are only $k(q-1)$ entries in D, we have

$$P[U \in \mathsf{L}_j^{\mathbf{x},D}] \leq \frac{|\mathrm{LSupp}(D_{\mathbf{x},\mathbf{0}})|}{2^w} \leq \frac{nkq}{2^w}.,$$

and thus the claimed bound follows from applying Theorem 7. □

Acknowledgements. We thank Jeremiah Blocki, Seunghoon Lee, and Samson Zhou for the open discussion regarding their work [4], which achieves comparable results for the hash-chain problem and the Simple PoSW scheme.

References

1. Ambainis, A.: Polynomial degree and lower bounds in quantum complexity: collision and element distinctness with small range. Theor. Comput. **1**(1), 37–46 (2005)
2. Bellare, M., Rogaway, P.: Random oracles are practical: a paradigm for designing efficient protocols. In: First ACM Conference on Computer and Communications Security, pp. 62–73. ACM (1993)
3. Bennett, C.H., Bernstein, E., Brassard, G., Vazirani, U.: Strengths and weaknesses of quantum computing. SIAM J. Comput. **26**(5), 1510–1523 (1997)
4. Blocki, J., Lee, S., Zhou, S.: On the security of proofs of sequential work in a post-quantum world. arXiv/cs.CR, Report 2006.10972 (2020). https://arxiv.org/abs/2006.10972
5. Boneh, D., Dagdelen, Ö., Fischlin, M., Lehmann, A., Schaffner, C., Zhandry, M.: Random oracles in a quantum world. In: Lee, D.H., Wang, X. (eds.) ASIACRYPT 2011. LNCS, vol. 7073, pp. 41–69. Springer, Heidelberg (2011). https://doi.org/10.1007/978-3-642-25385-0_3
6. Brassard, G., Hoyer, P., Tapp, A.: Quantum algorithm for the collision problem. arXiv/quant-ph, Report 9705002 (1997). https://arxiv.org/abs/quant-ph/9705002
7. Canetti, R., Goldreich, O., Halevi, S.: The random oracle methodology, revisited. J. ACM (JACM) **51**(4), 557–594 (2004)
8. Chiesa, A., Manohar, P., Spooner, N.: Succinct arguments in the quantum random oracle model. In: Hofheinz, D., Rosen, A. (eds.) TCC 2019, Part II. LNCS, vol. 11892, pp. 1–29. Springer, Cham (2019). https://doi.org/10.1007/978-3-030-36033-7_1
9. Chung, K.M., Fehr, S., Huang, Y.H., Liao, T.N.: On the compressed-oracle technique, and post-quantum security of proofs of sequential work. Cryptology ePrint Archive, Report 2020/1305 (2020). https://eprint.iacr.org/2020/1305
10. Cohen, B., Pietrzak, K.: Simple proofs of sequential work. In: Nielsen, J.B., Rijmen, V. (eds.) EUROCRYPT 2018, Part II. LNCS, vol. 10821, pp. 451–467. Springer, Cham (2018). https://doi.org/10.1007/978-3-319-78375-8_15
11. Czajkowski, J., Majenz, C., Schaffner, C., Zur, S.: Quantum lazy sampling and game-playing proofs for quantum indifferentiability. arXiv/quant-ph, Report 1904.11477 (2019). https://arxiv.org/abs/1904.11477
12. Fiat, A., Shamir, A.: How to prove yourself: practical solutions to identification and signature problems. In: Odlyzko, A.M. (ed.) CRYPTO 1986. LNCS, vol. 263, pp. 186–194. Springer, Heidelberg (1987). https://doi.org/10.1007/3-540-47721-7_12
13. Grover, L.K.: A fast quantum mechanical algorithm for database search. In: Proceedings of the Twenty-Eighth Annual ACM Symposium on Theory of Computing, pp. 212–219 (1996)
14. Hamoudi, Y., Magniez, F.: Quantum time-space tradeoffs by recording queries. arXiv/quant-ph, Report 2002.08944 (2020). https://arxiv.org/abs/2002.08944
15. Hosoyamada, A., Iwata, T.: 4-round luby-rackoff construction is a qPRP. In: Galbraith, S.D., Moriai, S. (eds.) ASIACRYPT 2019, Part I. LNCS, vol. 11921, pp. 145–174. Springer, Cham (2019). https://doi.org/10.1007/978-3-030-34578-5_6
16. Jeffery, S., Magniez, F., de Wolf, R.: Optimal parallel quantum query algorithms. Algorithmica **79**(2), 509–529 (2017)

17. Liu, Q., Zhandry, M.: Revisiting post-quantum fiat-shamir. In: Boldyreva, A., Micciancio, D. (eds.) CRYPTO 2019, Part II. LNCS, vol. 11693, pp. 326–355. Springer, Cham (2019). https://doi.org/10.1007/978-3-030-26951-7_12
18. Unruh, D.: Revocable quantum timed-release encryption. In: Nguyen, P.Q., Oswald, E. (eds.) EUROCRYPT 2014. LNCS, vol. 8441, pp. 129–146. Springer, Heidelberg (2014). https://doi.org/10.1007/978-3-642-55220-5_8
19. Zalka, C.: Grover's quantum searching algorithm is optimal. Phys. Rev. A **60**, 2746–2751 (1999). https://doi.org/10.1103/PhysRevA.60.2746
20. Zhandry, M.: How to record quantum queries, and applications to quantum indifferentiability. In: Boldyreva, A., Micciancio, D. (eds.) CRYPTO 2019, Part II. LNCS, vol. 11693, pp. 239–268. Springer, Cham (2019). https://doi.org/10.1007/978-3-030-26951-7_9

Classical Proofs of Quantum Knowledge

Thomas Vidick[1(✉)] and Tina Zhang[2]

[1] Department of Computing and Mathematical Sciences, California Institute of Technology, Pasadena, USA
vidick@caltech.edu
[2] Division of Physics, Mathematics and Astronomy, California Institute of Technology, Pasadena, USA
tinazhang@caltech.edu

Abstract. We define the notion of a *proof of knowledge* in the setting where the verifier is classical, but the prover is quantum, and where the witness that the prover holds is in general a quantum state. We establish simple properties of our definition, including that, if a *non-destructive* classical proof of quantum knowledge exists for some state, then that state can be cloned by an unbounded adversary, and that, under certain conditions on the parameters in our definition, a proof of knowledge protocol for a hard-to-clone state can be used as a (destructive) quantum money verification protocol. In addition, we provide two examples of protocols (both inspired by private-key classical verification protocols for quantum money schemes) which we can show to be proofs of quantum knowledge under our definition. In so doing, we introduce techniques for the analysis of such protocols which build on results from the literature on nonlocal games. Finally, we show that, under our definition, the verification protocol introduced by Mahadev (FOCS 2018) is a classical *argument* of quantum knowledge for QMA relations. In all cases, we construct an explicit quantum extractor that is able to produce a quantum witness given black-box quantum (rewinding) access to the prover, the latter of which includes the ability to coherently execute the prover's black-box circuit controlled on a superposition of messages from the verifier.

1 Introduction

The notion of a *proof of knowledge* was first considered in the classical setting in [GMR89] and subsequently formalized in [TW87,FFS88] and [BG92].[1] Intuitively, a proof of knowledge protocol allows a prover to convince a verifier that it 'knows' or 'possesses' some piece of secret information (a 'witness', w) which satisfies a certain relation R relative to a publicly known piece of information x. (Symbolically, we might say that the prover wants to convince its verifier that, for a particular x, it knows w such that $R(x, w) = 1$.) For example, the witness

[1] These three works give inequivalent definitions, but the differences are not important for the purpose of this introduction.

A. Canteaut and F.-X. Standaert (Eds.): EUROCRYPT 2021, LNCS 12697, pp. 630–660, 2021.
https://doi.org/10.1007/978-3-030-77886-6_22

w might be a private password corresponding to a particular public username x, and a proof of knowledge protocol in this setting could allow the prover to demonstrate that it possesses the credentials to access sensitive information.

The formal definition of a classical proof of knowledge for NP relations R was settled in a series of works (see [BG92] for a summary) in the 1990s. The standard definition is as follows: the prover P is said to 'know' a witness w if there is an extractor E which, given black-box access to P (including the ability to rewind P and run it again on different messages from the verifier), can efficiently compute w. The applications of classical proofs of knowledge include identification protocols [FFS88], signature schemes [CL06], and encryption schemes secure against chosen-ciphertext attack [SJ00].

In this work, we consider a particular generalisation of the classical concept of a proof of knowledge to the quantum setting. We imagine a situation where the *verifier* remains classical, but the *prover* is quantum, and where the witness w is in general a quantum state; and we ask the prover to 'convince' the verifier that it knows that state. We call this type of protocol a *classical proof of quantum knowledge.* Recently, there have been works which show how a fully classical verifier can, under cryptographic assumptions, delegate a quantum computation on encrypted data to a quantum server [Mah18a], verify that such a server performed the computation correctly [Mah18b], delegate the preparation of single-qubitstates to the server in a composable fashion [GV19], and test classically that the server prepared an EPR pair in its own registers [MV20]. In short, as long as classical computational resources and classical communication channels remain less expensive than their quantum counterparts, it will be natural to wish to use classical devices to test quantum functionality. Although we focus here on information-theoretic rather than computational security, the current paper can be considered part of the preceding line of work.

Quantum proofs of quantum knowledge (i.e. proof of knowledge protocols for quantum witnesses in which quantum interaction is allowed) have recently been explored by [BG19] and [CVZ19]; these two papers give a definition for quantum proofs of quantum knowledge, and exhibit several examples which meaningfully instantiate the definition. Here, we consider the more challenging question of defining and constructing proofs of knowledge for quantum witnesses in which the verifier and the interaction are *classical.* In this setting there is an interesting difficulty involved in constructing an extractor: how does one argue that a quantum prover 'knows' a certain quantum state if the only information which the prover 'reveals' is classical? A first approach, following the classical definition, would only allow the extractor to access classical transcripts from the protocol. Under such a restriction, the problem the extractor faces becomes one of reconstructing a witness ρ based entirely on classical measurement outcomes. It is not hard to convince ourselves that this problem probably has no solution for any non-trivial class of quantum states, as indeed it may be as hard as quantum state tomography [HHJ+17]. This observation makes it clear that we must allow the extractor to engage in some sort of quantum interaction with the prover.

Our first contribution in this paper is to provide an adequate definition of a proof of quantum knowledge for the setting where the communication between verifier and prover is classical. In order to circumvent the difficulty described in the preceding paragraph, we adopt a definition of 'black-box access to the prover' which is naturally suited to the quantum setting. Informally speaking, we model the prover as a unitary map U that acts on two quantum registers, one which is private (and which is used for storing its internal state) and one which is public (used for sending and receiving messages). In each round of the real protocol, the verifier places a classical message in the public 'message register', and the prover then runs the unitary U, before the message register is measured in the computational basis; the measurement result is the message that the prover sends to the verifier for that round. We define 'black-box access to the prover' as follows: we allow the extractor to place any quantum state in the public 'message register', as well as run the prover's unitary U, which acts on both registers, or its inverse $U^\dagger$; we do not allow the extractor to access the prover's private register except through U or $U^\dagger$. We do, however, allow it to place a coherent superposition of messages in the message register, even though the verifier (in a real protocol) would only ever put one classical message there. We make use of this latter possibility in our instantiations of this definition.

This definition matches the definition of 'black-box access to a quantum machine' used in previous works [Unr12]. We emphasise that, even though we consider protocols with purely classical communication, the extractor according to this definition of 'black-box access' is allowed to coherently manipulate a unitary implementation of the prover, and the message registers are not necessarily measured after each round of interaction. This possibility was allowed in [Unr12], but not used; here we make essential use of it when we construct our extractors. We note also that this definition of 'black-box access' matches the definition given in prior works (e.g. [Wat09]) of the 'black-box access' to a malicious verifier which a zero-knowledge simulator for a post-quantumly zero-knowledge proof of knowledge is allowed to have.

Having formalised what 'black-box access to the prover' means in our context, we move to the task of defining a 'proof of quantum knowledge' for our setting. We have two main applications in mind for a 'proof of quantum knowledge': one of them (proofs of knowledge for QMA witnesses) is natural given the standard formulation of classical proofs of knowledge for NP witnesses, but the other (proofs of knowledge for *quantum money states* [AFG+12]) is both natural and unique to the quantum setting. The quantum money application does not fit well into the standard formalism which is used for NP and QMA verification. Therefore, in order to formulate our definition of a 'proof of quantum knowledge' generally enough that we can capture both applications, we introduce a broader framework that mirrors frameworks recently introduced for similar purposes in the classical literature. Formally, we base our definition of a 'proof of quantum knowledge' on the notion of an 'agree-and-prove scheme' introduced recently in [BJM19]. The main innovation in this framework is that it allows the instance x and the proof relation R to be determined dynamically through interactions between the prover, the verifier, and possibly a trusted setup entity (such as the provider of a common random string or a random oracle). This framework lends itself remarkably well to our applications. Since we do not need all the possibilities that it allows, we introduce a somewhat simplified version which is sufficient for our purposes; details are given in Sect. 3.

In Sect. 4 we show two elementary but potentially interesting properties of our definition of a 'proof of quantum knowledge'. The first property is that, if a classical proof of quantum knowledge leaves the witness state intact, then the witness state can be cloned by an unbounded adversary. This is a simple no-go result which precludes certain types of proofs of quantum knowledge in the scenarios which we consider. The second property is that, under certain conditions on the parameters in the definition, a proof of knowledge protocol for a hard-to-clone witness state can also be used as a quantum money verification protocol. This result formalises the intuition that the property of being a 'proof of quantum knowledge' is stronger than the property of being a quantum money verification protocol: the latter implies that no adversary can pass verification twice given access to only one money bill, and the former formalises the notion that no adversary can pass even once unless it is possible to efficiently compute the money bill by interacting with said adversary.

Our second main contribution is to provide several examples of protocols which can be shown to be proofs of knowledge under our definition, and in so doing introduce some techniques that may possibly find use in the analysis of such protocols. As we have mentioned, instantiating a secure quantum money scheme is a natural application for a proof of quantum knowledge protocol. Conversely, quantum money verification protocols are natural candidates for examples of proofs of quantum knowledge: in a quantum money protocol, there is a prover who holds a purported money state, and who wishes to demonstrate to the verifier (who might be the bank or an independent citizen) that it does indeed 'hold' or 'possess' the quantum money state. The first person to describe quantum money was Wiesner [Wie83], who proposed money states that are tensor products of n qubits, each qubit of which is chosen uniformly at random from the set $\{|0\rangle, |1\rangle, |+\rangle, |-\rangle\}$. Wiesner's states can be described classically by $2n$ classical bits, and in a quantum money scheme this classical description is kept secret by the bank; a typical classical description is the pair of strings (x, θ), where the money state can be described (denoting by H_i a Hadamard gate on the ith qubit of the state and identities on all other qubits) as $|\$\rangle_{x,\theta} = \prod_i H_i^{\theta_i} |x\rangle$. We choose to analyse as our first example of a proof of knowledge a *private-key*, destructive classical money verification protocol between a prover and the bank for Wiesner's quantum money states which has been described previously in [MVW12]. The protocol is as follows: the verifier issues a uniformly random challenge string c to the prover, which encodes the bases (standard or Hadamard) in which the prover should measure the money state; the prover measures the ith qubit of the state in the standard basis if $c_i = 0$, or in the Hadamard basis if $c_i = 1$, and sends all the measurement outcomes as a string m to the verifier; and the verifier checks that, whenever $c_i = \theta_i$, $m_i = x_i$. The property which makes this protocol and these states interesting is that no prover who is given only one copy of the money state can pass verification twice.

Perhaps surprisingly, showing even that this simple protocol is a proof of knowledge according to our definition turns out to be a non-trivial task. We may examine the following illustration of the difficulty. Consider, firstly, the following naïve approach to designing an extractor for the protocol described in the preceding paragraph. Recall that, according to our model of 'black-box access', the prover can be considered a unitary process; we denote by U_c the unitary that the prover applies to its private register and the message register in response to challenge c. The extractor could pick a challenge c at random, apply U_c, and then attempt to apply some unitary to the message register to 'correct' for the challenge bases in order to recover the original money state. (For example, if $n = 4$, and $c = 0110$, the extractor could apply the unitary U_{0110}, and then apply $H_2 H_3$ to the message register in hopes of recovering the original money state. This strategy would work on the honest prover, who simply measures the real money state in the bases indicated by c in order to obtain its message to the verifier; we may imagine that few meaningful deviations from this pattern are possible.) However, the prover (upon receipt of the challenge) may take its honest money state and decide to apply Pauli X (bit-flip) gates to some arbitrary subset of the qubits of the money state which it was told to measure in the Hadamard basis, and Pauli Z (phase-flip) gates to a subset of the qubits which it was told to measure in the standard basis. If the prover now measures the result in the bases indicated by c, it will pass with probability 1—but the state that it measures in the c basis in this scenario is almost certainly not the correct money state. (The exception is when $c = \theta$.)

A little thought will show that this is a fairly general obstacle to the extractor's constructing the money state from the state residing in the prover's message registers immediately before it performs the measurement whose outcomes it will send to the verifier. Since we know very little about what the prover might be doing to the money state at any other stage in its execution, meanwhile, it is difficult to reason about finding the money state in the prover's registers at other points in its operation. This simple argument shows that, in order to design an effective extractor, it is crucial to consider the prover's responses to all challenges c at once—the question, of course, is one of how.

Our way of overcoming these difficulties builds on results from the literature on nonlocal games. The key idea of our security proof for the Wiesner money verification protocol is as follows. Let the party which chooses and prepares the money state $|\$\rangle_{x,\theta} = \prod_i H_i^{\theta_i} |x\rangle$ that the prover receives be known as Alice, and let the prover be known as Bob. Consider the following thought experiment: instead of preparing $|\$\rangle_{x,\theta}$, Alice could prepare n EPR pairs and send half of each one to Bob. Let $E(\theta) = \{|\$\rangle\langle\$|_{x,\theta} \mid x \in \{0,1\}^n\}$ be a general measurement (POVM). Then, if Alice measures $E(\theta)$ on her side of the state, and obtains the outcome x, Alice's and Bob's joint state will collapse to two copies of $|\$\rangle_{x,\theta}$. Note that, from Bob's perspective, the protocol is the same regardless of whether Alice sent EPR pairs and then measured $E(\theta)$, or whether she chose x and θ uniformly at random and sent him $|\$\rangle_{x,\theta}$ to begin with. However, if Bob succeeds with high probability in the money verification protocol, then he also succeeds with high probability at recovering a subset of the string x which represents Alice's measurement outcomes after she measures the POVM $E(\theta)$, and which also forms part of the classical description of the money state $|\$\rangle_{x,\theta}$. This observation makes it possible to apply a theorem from [NV16] which states that, if two noncommunicating parties exhibit correlations like those which Alice and Bob exhibit in this thought experiment, then they must once have shared EPR pairs, up to local isometry. Since Alice is honest and did nothing to her shares of the EPR pairs, the local isometry on her side is the identity map. Then, in order to recover the original money state, the proof-of-knowledge extractor simply has to execute the correct isometry on Bob's side. This isometry can be implemented efficiently using only black-box access to the prover; this step, however, crucially makes use of the fact that the extractor can implement controlled versions of the prover's unitaries on a superposition of messages of its choice. A detailed analysis is given in Sect. 5.1.

Although the efficacy of this technique for showing that a protocol is a proof of knowledge depends strongly on the structure of the Wiesner verification protocol, we are also able to apply it to one other example. Wiesner states were the earliest and are the best-known kind of quantum money states, but there are other kinds, and one sort which has received some recent attention is the class of *subspace states* introduced in a quantum money context by [AC12]. Subspace states are states of the form $\frac{1}{\sqrt{|A|}}\sum_{x\in A}|x\rangle$ for some $n/2$-dimensional subspace $A \in \mathbb{Z}_2^n$, and they have similar no-cloning properties to those of Wiesner states; they are also of additional interest because they have been used in several schemes which make steps toward the goal of public-key quantum money [AC12], [Zha19], and in constructions of other quantum-cryptographic primitives such as quantum signing tokens [BDS16]. We were not able to find a simple classical verification protocol for subspace states that we could show to be a proof of quantum knowledge. Nonetheless, in Sect. 5.2, we propose a classical (private-key) verification protocol for what we call *one-time-padded subspace states* (that is, subspace states which have had random Pauli one-time-pads applied to them by the bank), and we are able to show under our new definition, using similar techniques to those which we applied to Wiesner states, that this simple verification protocol is a proof of knowledge for one-time-padded subspace states. This verification protocol is remarkable for having a challenge from the verifier that is only one bit long.

Our final contribution is to show that, under our definition, a classical *argument* of quantum knowledge exists for any relation in the class QMA.[2] The notion of a *QMA relation* was formalised jointly by [BG19] and [CVZ19], as a quantum analogue to the idea of an *NP relation* which was described in

[2] Argument systems differ from proof systems only in that the honest prover must be efficient, and that soundness is required to hold only against efficient provers. In this case, 'efficient' means quantum polynomial-time.

the first paragraphs of this introduction. [BG19] and [CVZ19] show that any QMA relation has a *quantum* proof of quantum knowledge. The protocol that we show to be a *classical* argument of quantum knowledge for QMA relations, meanwhile, is the classical verification protocol introduced recently by [Mah18b]. Mahadev [Mah18b] shows, under cryptographic assumptions, that quantum properties (in her case, any language in BQP) can be decided by a classical polynomial-time verifier through classical interaction alone with a quantum polynomial-time prover. We note that the proofs of the main results in [Mah18b] include statements which can be used to make the verification protocol which [Mah18b] introduces into a classical argument of quantum knowledge in the sense in which we have defined the latter. The main work that needs to be done in order to show this is to establish that the quantum witness, which as shown in [Mah18b] always *exists* for the case of a successful prover, can be *extracted* from the prover in a black-box manner. While all the required technical components for establishing this are already present in [Mah18b], we make the statement explicit. (In comparison, our proofs that specific quantum money schemes satisfy our definition of a proof of quantum knowledge do not use any cryptographic assumptions, and the protocols which we consider are very simple compared with the [Mah18b] protocol.) The [Mah18b] verification protocol can be shown to be an argument of quantum knowledge for any QMA relation; the only caveat, which was also a caveat for the *quantum* proofs of quantum knowledge for QMA exhibited by [BG19] and [CVZ19], is that an honest prover in the protocol may require multiple copies of a witness in order that the extractor can succeed in extracting *one* copy. We refer the reader to Sect. 6 for details.

2 Preliminaries

2.1 Terminology and Notation

Due to space constraints, we refer the reader to the full version [VZ21] for basic notation and terminology.

2.2 Black-Box Quantum Provers

Due to space constraints, we refer the reader to the full version [VZ21] for a discussion of the definitions we will now present relating to the notion of 'black-box access'. Formally, we use a similar framework to that which is described in [Unr12, Sect. 2.1] in order to capture black-box access to quantum provers. The following definitions of *interactive quantum machines* and *oracle access* to an interactive quantum machine are taken (with some modifications) from [Unr12]; a similar formulation of these definitions of [Unr12] appears in [CVZ19]. The modifications which we introduce are primarily for convenience in dealing with the situation where the verifier is known to be classical, instead of (potentially) quantum as it is in [Unr12].

Remark 1. Even though the possibility is not used in [Unr12], the framework presented there explicitly allows the extractor to coherently implement controlled versions of the prover's unitaries on a superposition of messages from the verifier. As we argued in the introduction, it is necessary to give this power to the extractor in our context (see e.g. [BCC+20] for impossibility results in related settings).

Interactive quantum machines. An *interactive quantum machine* is a machine M with two quantum registers: a register S for its internal state, and a register N for sending and receiving messages (the network register). Upon activation, M expects in N a message, and in S the state at the end of the previous activation. At the end of the current activation, N contains the outgoing message of M, and S contains the new internal state of M. A machine M gets as input: a security parameter $\lambda \in \mathbb{N}$, a classical input $x \in \{0,1\}^*$, and a quantum input $|\Phi\rangle$, which is stored in S. Formally, machine M is specified by a family of unitary circuits $\{M_{\lambda x}\}_{\lambda \in \mathbb{N}, x \in \{0,1\}^*}$ and a family of integers $\{r^M_{\lambda x}\}_{\lambda \in \mathbb{N}, x \in \{0,1\}^*}$. $M_{\lambda x}$ is the quantum circuit that M performs on the registers S and N upon invocation. $r_{\lambda x}$ determines the total number of messages/invocations. We might omit writing the security parameter and/or the classical input x when they are clear from the context. We say that M is *quantum-polynomial-time* (QPT for short) if the circuit $M_{\lambda x}$ has size polynomial in $\lambda + |x|$, the description of the circuit is computable in deterministic polynomial time in $\lambda + |x|$ given λ and x, and $r_{\lambda,x}$ is polynomially bounded in λ and x.

Oracle access to an interactive quantum machine. We say that a quantum algorithm A has oracle access to an interactive quantum machine M (with internal register S and network register N) *running on* $|\Phi\rangle$ to mean the following. We initialise S to $|\Phi\rangle$ and N to $|0\rangle$, we give A the security parameter λ and its own classical input x, and we allow A to execute (a controlled version of) the quantum circuit $M_{\lambda x'}$ (for any x') specifying M, and (a controlled version of) its inverse (recall that these act on the internal register S and on the network register N of M). Moreover, we allow A to provide and read messages from M (formally, we allow A to act freely on the network register N). We do not allow A to act on the internal register S of M, except via $M_{\lambda x'}$ or its inverse.

Interactive classical machines. An *interactive classical machine* is a machine C with two classical registers: a register T for its internal state, and a register N for sending and receiving messages (the network register). Upon activation, C expects in N a message, and in T the state at the end of the previous activation. At the end of the current activation, N contains the outgoing message of C, and T contains the new internal state of M. A machine C gets as input: a security parameter $\lambda \in \mathbb{N}$, a classical input $x \in \{0,1\}^*$, a random input $u \in \{0,1\}^{p(\lambda+|x|)}$ for some function $p \in \mathbb{N}$, and a classical auxiliary input $t \in \{0,1\}^{|\mathsf{T}|}$, which is stored in T. Formally, machine C is specified by a function $p \in \mathbb{N}$, a family of classical circuits $\{C_{\lambda x u}\}_{\lambda \in \mathbb{N}, x \in \{0,1\}^*, u \in \{0,1\}^{p(\lambda+|x|)}}$ and a family of integers $\{r^C_{\lambda x}\}_{\lambda \in \mathbb{N}, x \in \{0,1\}^*}$. $C_{\lambda x u}$ is the classical circuit that C performs on the registers T and N upon invocation. Without loss of generality, for convenience's sake, we assume that $C_{\lambda x u}$ is reversible. $r^C_{\lambda x}$ determines the total number of messages/invocations. We might omit writing the security parameter and/or the input when they are clear from the context. We say that C is *probabilistic-polynomial-time* (PPT for short) if p is a polynomial, the circuit $C_{\lambda x u}$ has size polynomial in $\lambda+|x|$, the description of the circuit is computable in deterministic polynomial time in $\lambda + |x|$ given λ, x and u, and $r^C_{\lambda x}$ is polynomially bounded in λ and x.

Oracle access to an interactive classical machine. We say that a quantum algorithm A has oracle access to an interactive classical machine C *running on string* t to mean the following. We initialise C's internal register T to t and the network register N to the all-zero string. We give A the security parameter and its own classical input x. Each time A wishes to run C (or its inverse), it must submit an input x' on which to run C (or its inverse). Upon receiving A's choice of x', we choose u uniformly at random, and then we run the classical circuit $C_{\lambda x' u}$ (or its inverse); recall that these act on the internal register T and on the network register N of C. Moreover, we allow A to provide and read messages from C (formally, we allow A to act freely on the network register N). We do not allow A to act on the internal register T of C, except via $C_{\lambda x' u}$ or its inverse.

Definition 1. We use the terminology *interactive Turing machine* (ITM) to refer to either an interactive classical machine or an interactive quantum machine. If the ITM is bounded-time, we may refer to a PPT ITM or a QPT ITM to clarify which model is used. An interactive oracle machine is an ITM that in addition has query access to an oracle.

Interaction between an interactive quantum machine and an interactive classical machine. Let $M = (\{M_{\lambda x}\}, \{r^M_{\lambda x}\})$ be an interactive quantum machine with internal register S and network register N. Let $C = (\{p, C_{\lambda x' u}\}, \{r^C_{\lambda x'}\})$ be an interactive classical machine with internal register T and network register N. For a given CQ state $\rho_{\mathsf{TS}} \in \mathrm{D}(\mathcal{H}_{\mathsf{T}} \otimes \mathcal{H}_{\mathsf{S}})$, we define the interaction $(C(x'), M(x))_{\rho_{\mathsf{TS}}}$ as the following quantum process: initialize register N to $|0\rangle$; initialise registers S and T to the CQ state ρ_{TS}; alternately apply $M_{\lambda x}$ to registers S and N and $C_{\lambda x' u}$ (for a uniformly chosen $u \in \{0,1\}^{p(\lambda+|x'|)}$ each time) to registers T and N, measuring N in the computational basis after each application of either $M_{\lambda x}$ or $C_{\lambda x' u}$; stop applying $M_{\lambda x}$ after $r^M_{\lambda x}$ times and $C_{\lambda x' u}$ after $r^C_{\lambda x'}$ times, and finally output the output of the circuit $C_{\lambda x' u}$. We denote the random variable representing this output by $\langle C(x'), M(x)\rangle_{\rho_{\mathsf{TS}}}$. We call the $r^M_{\lambda x} + r^C_{\lambda x'}$ measurement outcomes which are obtained after performing as many standard basis measurements of N during a single execution of the interaction $(C(x'), M(x))_{\rho_{\mathsf{TS}}}$ the *transcript* for this execution.

2.3 Implementing Oracles

Some of our formal definitions rely on 'oracles', which we generally visualise as functions $\mathcal{O} : \{0,1\}^* \to \{0,1\}^*$ to which query access is given. We refer the reader to the full version [VZ21] for some brief remarks on how query access to these oracles (which, expressed as functions, may take an exponential number of bits to specify) can be implemented efficiently in the number of queries made to the oracle, and also on our assumption that any query submitted to an oracle is measured in the standard basis before being answered.

3 Quantum Agree-and-Prove Schemes

To define the intuitive notion of a 'proof of quantum knowledge' in sufficient generality so that we can capture both quantum money verification and QMA verification we introduce a quantum variant of the 'agree-and-prove' framework from [BJM19], extending their formalism to our setting in which the prover and the witness are quantum, and simplifying some aspects of the formalism that are less important for the applications we have in mind. For convenience, we preserve much of the notation from [BJM19]. The reader might wish to consult the full version of this paper [VZ20] for a discussion of the intuition behind this agree-and-prove framework; the reader can also refer to [BJM19] for additional motivation and explanations relating to the framework.

In the next subsection we formalise the notion of a scenario. The following section discusses input generation algorithms; the one after that formalises protocols, and the one after that lays down the security conditions for agree-and-prove schemes.

3.1 Scenario

Definition 2 (Agree-and-Prove Scenario for quantum relations). An agree-and-prove (AaP for short) scenario for quantum relations is a triple $(\mathcal{F}, \mathcal{R}, \mathcal{C})$ of interactive oracle machines satisfying the following conditions:

- The *setup functionality* $\mathcal{F}$ is a QPT ITM taking a unary encoding of a security parameter λ as input. The ITM $\mathcal{F}$ runs an initialization procedure $\boldsymbol{init}$, and in addition returns the specification of an oracle (which we also model as an ITM) $\mathcal{O}_{\mathcal{F}}(i, q, arg)$. The oracle function takes three arguments: $i \in \{I, P, V\}$ denotes a 'role', q denotes a keyword specifying a query type, and arg denotes the argument for the query.[3]
  There are three different options for the 'role' parameter, which exists to allow $\mathcal{F}$ to release information selectively depending on the party asking for it. The roles I, P and V correspond respectively to the *input generator* (Definition 3), the prover, and the verifier.

[3] In [BJM19], $\mathcal{O}_{\mathcal{F}}$ has an additional function: when it is called with the argument `QUERIES`, $\mathcal{O}_{\mathcal{F}}$(`QUERIES`) returns a list of tuples representing all of the queries made to $\mathcal{O}_{\mathcal{F}}$ by the prover P and the replies that were given. This functionality is available only to the extractor, not to the parties I, P and V, and it is necessary in order to permit the design of an efficient extractor for some protocols, particularly those in the random oracle model (see, for example, the discussion at the bottom of page 10 in [BJM19]). Since we do not need to use this functionality in our protocols, we omit it here.

- The *agreement relation* $\mathcal{C}$ is a QPT oracle machine taking a unary encoding of the security parameter λ and a statement as inputs, and producing a decision bit as output.[4]
- The *proof relation* $\mathcal{R}$ is a QPT oracle machine taking a unary encoding of the security parameter λ, a (classical) statement x and a (quantum) witness ρ_{W} as inputs, and outputting a decision bit.

3.2 Input Generation

Before we formalise the notion of an agree-and-prove protocol, we introduce the notion of an *input generation algorithm*, which is an algorithm that produces the auxiliary inputs that the prover and the verifier receive before they begin interacting. The input generation algorithm models 'prior knowledge' which the prover and the verifier may possess. For a fuller discussion of the motivation for the input generation algorithm, please see the full version [VZ21].

Definition 3 (Input Generation Algorithm). An input generation algorithm I for an agree-and-prove scenario $\mathcal{S}$ is a machine I taking a unary encoding of the security parameter λ as input and producing a CQ state $\rho_{\mathsf{AUX}_V \mathsf{AUX}_P}$ specifying the auxiliary inputs for the verifier (in the classical register AUX_V) and prover (in the quantum register AUX_P) respectively as output. We may use the shorthand $\rho_{\mathsf{AUX}_P} \equiv \mathrm{Tr}_{\mathsf{AUX}_V}(\rho_{\mathsf{AUX}_V \mathsf{AUX}_P})$ and $\rho_{\mathsf{AUX}_V} \equiv \mathrm{Tr}_{\mathsf{AUX}_P}(\rho_{\mathsf{AUX}_V \mathsf{AUX}_P})$.

3.3 Protocol

Once a scenario has been fixed we can define a *protocol* for that scenario. Informally, the protocol specifies the actions of the honest parties. Each party, prover and verifier, is decomposed into two entities that correspond to the two phases, "agree" and "prove", of the protocol.

Definition 4 (Agree-and-prove Protocol). An agree-and-prove protocol is a tuple $(\mathcal{I}, P_1, P_2, V_1, V_2)$ consisting of a set $\mathcal{I}$ of input generation algorithms together with the following four interactive oracle machines (P_1, P_2, V_1, V_2):

- A (honest) first phase QPT prover P_1 taking a unary encoding of the security parameter λ and a (quantum) auxiliary input ρ_{AUX_P} as inputs. It produces a (classical) statement x_P or $\perp$ as output, as well as a (quantum) state ρ_{st_P}.
- A (honest) first phase PPT verifier V_1 taking a unary encoding of the security parameter λ and a (classical) auxiliary input AUX_V as inputs. It produces a (classical) statement x_V or $\perp$ as output, as well as a (classical) state st_V.
- A (honest) second phase QPT prover P_2 taking a classical instance x and a quantum state ρ_{st_P} as input, as well as a unary encoding of the security parameter λ, and producing as output a bit that indicates whether the proof has been accepted.

4 In [BJM19] the agreement relation also takes two auxiliary inputs. We will not need this.

- A (honest) second phase PPT verifier V_2 taking a classical instance x and a state string st_V as input, as well as a unary encoding of the security parameter λ, and producing as output a bit that indicates whether it accepts or rejects.

Note that in this definition the verifier is required to be a classical probabilistic polynomial time ITM. In general one may extend the definition to allow for quantum polynomial time verifiers; since our focus is on classical protocols we restrict our attention to classical verifiers. We also restrict the honest prover to run in quantum polynomial time; for soundness, this restriction will be lifted for the case of proofs of knowledge and maintained for the case of arguments of knowledge.

3.4 Security Conditions

We now specify the correctness and soundness conditions associated with an agree-and-prove scenario $\mathcal{S}$.

Definition 5 (Completeness Experiment). We define the following *completeness experiment* for an agree-and-prove protocol $\mathcal{K} = (\mathcal{I}, P_1, P_2, V_1, V_2)$ in the context of a scenario $\mathcal{S} = (\mathcal{F}, \mathcal{C}, \mathcal{R})$:

1. An input generation algorithm $I \in \mathcal{I}$ is executed. It is allowed to query $\mathcal{O}_\mathcal{F}(I, \cdot, \cdot)$. It produces the CQ state $\rho_{\mathsf{AUX}_V \mathsf{AUX}_P}$, and passes input ρ_{AUX_P} to P_1 and ρ_{AUX_V} to V_1.
2. The interaction $(V_1, P_1)_{\rho_{\mathsf{AUX}_V \mathsf{AUX}_P}}$ is executed (during which V_1 and P_1 are allowed to query $\mathcal{O}_\mathcal{F}(V, \cdot, \cdot)$ and $\mathcal{O}_\mathcal{F}(P, \cdot, \cdot)$, respectively), and if either V_1 or P_1 returns $\perp$, or if $x_V \neq x_P$, the agree phase returns 0. Otherwise, the outputs of V_1 and P_1 are passed to V_2 and P_2, respectively, and the agree phase returns 1. If the agree phase returns 1, let the CQ state representing the joint distribution of st_V and ρ_{st_P} be denoted by $\rho_{st_V\, st_P}$, and let $x = x_P = x_V$ be the instance that V_1 and P_1 have agreed on.
3. The interaction $(V_2(x), P_2(x))_{\rho_{st_V\, st_P}}$ is executed (during which V_2 and P_2 are allowed to query $\mathcal{O}_\mathcal{F}(V, \cdot, \cdot)$ and $\mathcal{O}_\mathcal{F}(P, \cdot, \cdot)$, respectively), and the outcome of the proof phase is set to the value which V_2 returns at the end of the protocol.

The completeness experiment returns 1 if the agree phase and the proof phase both return 1.

Definition 6 (Soundness experiment). We define the following *soundness experiment* for an agree-and-prove protocol $\mathcal{K} = (\mathcal{I}, P_1, P_2, V_1, V_2)$ and an extractor E, in the context of a scenario $\mathcal{S} = (\mathcal{F}, \mathcal{C}, \mathcal{R})$:

1. An input generation algorithm $\hat{I}$ is executed. It is allowed to query $\mathcal{O}_\mathcal{F}(I, \cdot, \cdot)$. It produces the CQ state $\rho_{\mathsf{AUX}_V \mathsf{AUX}_P}$, and passes input ρ_{AUX_P} to $\hat{P}_1$ and ρ_{AUX_V} to V_1.
2. The interaction $(V_1, \hat{P}_1)_{\rho_{\mathsf{AUX}_V \mathsf{AUX}_P}}$ is executed (during which V_1 and $\hat{P}_1$ are allowed to query $\mathcal{O}_\mathcal{F}(V, \cdot, \cdot)$ and $\mathcal{O}_\mathcal{F}(P, \cdot, \cdot)$, respectively), and if either V_1 or P_1 returns $\perp$, or if $x_V \neq x_P$, the agree phase returns 0. Otherwise, the

outputs of V_1 and $\hat{P}_1$ are passed to V_2 and $\hat{P}_2$, respectively, and the agree phase returns 1. If the agree phase returns 1, let the CQ state representing the joint distribution of st_V and ρ_{st_P} be denoted by $\rho_{st_V\, st_P}$, and let $x = x_P = x_V$ be the instance that V_1 and $\hat{P}_1$ have agreed on.

3. If the agree phase returns 1 in step 2, the extractor E is provided with the transcript of the interaction $(V_1, \hat{P}_1)_{\rho_{\mathsf{AUX}_V \mathsf{AUX}_P}}$ and the instance x resulting from the agree phase, along with oracle access to $\hat{P}_2$ running on input ρ_{st_P} (where ρ_{st_P} is the prover's half of the joint CQ state $\rho_{st_V\, st_P}$). In addition the extractor can access the oracle $\mathcal{O}_{\mathcal{F}}$ using any of the roles in $\{I, P\}$. It outputs a state ρ.

We are now ready to give the formal definition of security.

Definition 7 (Security of Protocol for Quantum Agree-and-Prove Scenario). Let λ be a security parameter. Let $c, \kappa, \delta : \mathbb{N} \to [0,1]$. A protocol $\mathcal{K} = (\mathcal{I}, P_1, V_1, P_2, V_2)$ for a scenario $(\mathcal{F}, \mathcal{C}, \mathcal{R})$ is secure with completeness c, up to knowledge error κ, and with extraction distance parameter δ if the following conditions hold:

- *Correctness:* The completeness experiment (Definition 5) returns 1 with probability at least c, and in addition the statement $x = x_V = x_P$ that is agreed on during the completeness experiment is such that $\mathcal{C}(1^\lambda, x) = 1$, whenever the honest parties P and V are provided with their inputs by some input generation algorithm $I \in \mathcal{I}$.[5]
- *Soundness:* There exists a QPT ITM E (called the "extractor") such that the following holds. Let $\hat{P} = (\hat{P}_1, \hat{P}_2)$ be a potentially dishonest prover for $\mathcal{K}$ and $\hat{I}$ an arbitrary input generation algorithm. Let x be an instance such that, conditioned on the agree phase of $\mathcal{K}$ returning 1 and the instance x being agreed upon, the prover $\hat{P}_2$ succeeds with probability $p > \kappa$ in the proof phase of $\mathcal{K}$. Then the state ρ returned by the extractor in the soundness experiment (Definition 6), conditioned on the agree phase of the soundness experiment returning 1 and x being agreed on, is such that $\Pr[\mathcal{R}(1^\lambda, x, \rho) = 1] > 1 - \delta(p)$, where δ, which may depend on λ, is such that $\delta(p) < 1$ for all $p > \kappa$. The expected number of steps of extractor E is required to be bounded by a polynomial in $\lambda/(p - \kappa)$, if executing the prover's unitary on any input counts as a unit-time procedure.

When the soundness condition only holds under the restriction that $\hat{P}$ must be implemented by a QPT ITM we say that the protocol is *computationally secure*, or that it is an *argument system* (as opposed to a *proof system*, which is sound against all possible provers).

[5] Note that, for completeness, we require that the input generation algorithm is chosen from a set $\mathcal{I}$ of 'honest' algorithms. Here we depart from [BJM19], where input generation is always unrestricted (even when the verifier and the prover are honest). We refer the reader to the full version [VZ21] for a fuller discussion of this subject.

Remark 2. When we wish to emphasize the connection between secure agree-and-prove protocols and the more usual notion of a 'proof of knowledge', we sometimes refer to an AaP scenario that satisfies Definition 7 as a 'classical proof (or argument) of quantum knowledge'. (Formally, proofs and arguments of knowledge can be formulated as protocols for AaP scenarios which have trivial agreement phases and which have as a proof relation an NP or a QMA relation; see Sect. 6.) When we use this terminology, it will be clear from context what the 'knowledge' is that we are referring to.

3.5 Agree-and-Prove Scenario for Quantum Money

As an example of a concrete agree-and-prove scenario, we define an agree-and-prove scenario that captures the scenario which arises in the problem of verifying quantum money. We firstly lay down the 'standard' security definitions for a quantum money scheme, and in so doing introduce some notation and some objects that will be useful in formulating quantum money in the agree-and-prove framework.

Definition 8. A "quantum money scheme" is specified by the following objects, each of which is parametrized by a security parameter λ:

- A algorithm Bank taking a string r as a parameter which initialises a database of valid *money bills* in the form of a table of tuples $(\mathsf{id}, \mathsf{public}, \mathsf{secret}, |\$\rangle_{\mathsf{id}})$. id represents a unique identifier for a particular money bill; public and secret represent, respectively, public and secret information that may be necessary to run the verification procedure for the bill labeled by id; and $|\$\rangle_{\mathsf{id}}$ is the quantum money state associated with the identifier id. The string r should determine a classical map H_r such that $H_r(\mathsf{id}) = (\mathsf{public}, \mathsf{secret})$.[6]
- A verification procedure $\mathit{Ver}(x, \mathsf{public}, \mathsf{secret}, \rho_W)$ that is a QPT algorithm which decides when a bill is valid.

In addition the scheme should satisfy the following conditions:

1. Completeness: for any valid money bill $(\mathsf{id}, \mathsf{public}, \mathsf{secret}, |\$\rangle_{\mathsf{id}})$ in the database created by Bank,

$$\Pr\big(\mathit{Ver}(\mathsf{id}, \mathsf{public}, \mathsf{secret}, |\$\rangle\langle\$|_{\mathsf{id}})\big) \geq c_M(\lambda) ,$$

   for some function $c_M(\cdot)$. We refer to c_M as the *completeness parameter* of the money scheme.
2. No-cloning: Consider the following game played between a challenger and an adversary: the challenger selects a valid money bill $(\mathsf{id}, \mathsf{public}, \mathsf{secret}, |\$\rangle_{\mathsf{id}})$ and

[6] The string r represents any random choices that Bank might make while generating valid bills; we make this string explicit for later convenience.

sends $(\mathsf{id}, \mathsf{public}, |\$\rangle_{\mathsf{id}})$ to the adversary; the adversary produces a state σ_{AB}. Then for any adversary in this game,[7]

$$\Pr_r\big(\mathit{Ver}(\mathsf{id}, \mathsf{public}, \mathsf{secret}, \mathrm{Tr}_B(\sigma_{AB})) = 1 \\ \text{and} \quad \mathit{Ver}(\mathsf{id}, \mathsf{public}, \mathsf{secret}, \mathrm{Tr}_A(\sigma_{AB})) = 1\big) \leq \mu_M(\lambda) ,$$

for some function $\mu_M(\cdot)$. We refer to μ_M as the *cloning parameter* of the money scheme. Note that the probability of the adversary's success is calculated assuming that the string r which ***Bank*** takes is chosen uniformly at random.

Fix a quantum money scheme according to Definition 8, with completeness parameter c_M and cloning parameter μ_M. We call an agree-and-prove scenario $(\mathcal{F}_M, \mathcal{C}_M, \mathcal{R}_M)$ that takes the form below a 'quantum money scenario with completeness parameter c_M and cloning parameter μ_M'.

- Setup functionality $\mathcal{F}_M(1^\lambda)$: The setup should run an initialization procedure init_M that instantiates[8] a database B_M whose records are of the form (and the distribution) that ***Bank*** would have produced running on a uniformly random input r. The setup should also return a specification of how the following oracles should be implemented:
  - $\mathcal{O}_{\mathcal{F}_M}(I, \mathit{id})$: returns an identifier id such that the bill $(\mathsf{id}, \mathsf{public}, \mathsf{secret}, |\$\rangle_{\mathsf{id}})$ is in B_M.[9]
  - $\mathcal{O}_{\mathcal{F}_M}(\cdot, \mathit{public}, \mathsf{id})$: Returns the public string associated with id. Returns $\perp$ if no record in B_M with the identifier id exists.
  - $\mathcal{O}_{\mathcal{F}_M}(I, \mathit{getMoney}, \mathsf{id})$: If no record in B_M with identifier id exists, returns $\perp$. Otherwise, returns $|\$\rangle_{\mathsf{id}}$ the first time it is called. If called again with the same id argument, returns $\perp$.
  - $\mathcal{O}_{\mathcal{F}_M}(V, \mathit{secret}, \mathsf{id})$: accesses B_M and returns the secret string associated with id. Returns $\perp$ if no record in B_M with the identifier id exists.
- Agreement relation $\mathcal{C}^{\mathcal{O}_{\mathcal{F}_M}}(1^\lambda, \mathsf{id})$: outputs 1 if and only if a record in B_M with identifier id exists.
- Proof relation $\mathcal{R}^{\mathcal{O}_{\mathcal{F}_M}}(1^\lambda, x, \rho_W)$: interprets x as an id (outputting $\perp$ if this fails), sets $\mathsf{public} \leftarrow \mathcal{O}_{\mathcal{F}_M}(V, \mathit{public}, x)$ and $\mathsf{secret} \leftarrow \mathcal{O}_{\mathcal{F}_M}(V, \mathit{secret}, x)$, and executes $\mathit{Ver}(x, \mathsf{public}, \mathsf{secret}, \rho_W)$.

---

[7] Many quantum money schemes are information-theoretically secure; however, it is also possible to consider computationally secure schemes by replacing 'any' with 'any QPT'.

[8] init_M doesn't necessarily need to actually allocate memory for the database; since the database will only ever be accessed through the oracle $\mathcal{O}_{\mathcal{F}_M}$, it is possible to 'instantiate' the database using the method described in Sect. 2.3.

[9] Which identifier is returned is at the discretion of any particular instantiation of this function. Intuitively, this oracle is used to represent identifiers of bills that have been generated in the past and are thus available in an "environment" that I may have access to.

4 Simple Properties

4.1 Nondestructive Proofs of Quantum Knowledge Imply Cloning

In this section we formalize the intuitive claim that a non-destructive proof of quantum knowledge implies the ability to clone the underlying witness state. To formalize this statement we make a number of assumptions that help simplify the presentation. More general statements can be proven depending on one's needs; see the end of the section for further discussion.

We use definitions and notation from Sect. 2.2 and Sect. 3.

Definition 9 (Nondestructive Interaction). Let $P = (\{P_{\lambda x}\}, \{r^P_{\lambda x}\})$ be an interactive quantum machine, and let $V = (p, \{V_{\lambda x u}\}, \{r^V_{\lambda x}\})$ be an interactive classical machine. Fix a security parameter λ. A *nondestructive interaction* $(V(x), P(x'))_{\rho_{\mathsf{TS}}}$ between V and P for some CQ state ρ_{TS} is an interaction in which the execution of $(V(x), P(x'))_{\rho_{\mathsf{TS}}}$ is unitary (including the standard-basis measurements of the network register that take place during the execution) for all possible random inputs u to V. More formally, for any choice of $r^V_{\lambda x}$ random strings $u_1, \ldots, u_{r^V_{\lambda x}}$ used during the interaction $(V(x), P(x'))_{\rho_{\mathsf{TS}}}$, there exists a unitary U acting on registers N, T and S such that the joint state of the registers N, T and S is identical after U has been applied to them (assuming they are initialised as described in Sect. 2.2) to their joint state after the execution of $(V(x), P(x'))_{\rho_{\mathsf{TS}}}$ using the random strings $u_1, \ldots, u_{r^V_{\lambda x}}$.

Definition 10 (Oracle Access to an Interactive Quantum Machine with Power of Initialisation). Recall the definition of oracle access to an interactive quantum machine given in Sect. 2.2. In that section, the initial state $|\Phi\rangle$ on which the quantum machine is run is fixed. We say that a quantum algorithm A has *oracle access to an interactive quantum machine M with power of initialisation* if A can do all the things described in Sect. 2.2, and in addition can initialise M's internal register S to a state of its choosing (but cannot read S, only write to it).

Proposition 1. *Let λ be a security parameter, let $(\mathcal{F}, \mathcal{C}, \mathcal{R})$ be an agree-and-prove scenario, and let $\mathcal{K} = (\mathcal{I}, P_1, P_2, V_1, V_2)$ be a protocol for $(\mathcal{F}, \mathcal{C}, \mathcal{R})$ with a classical honest verifier $V = (V_1, V_2)$, knowledge error κ and extraction distance δ. Let $\hat{P} = (\hat{P}_1, \hat{P}_2)$ be a prover for $\mathcal{K}$.*

Let $\hat{I}$ be any input generation algorithm, and x and ρ_{TS} an instance and a CQ state respectively such that the agree phase of $\mathcal{K}$, executed with $\hat{I}$, V_1 and $\hat{P}_1$, has positive probability of ending with x being agreed on, and such that the joint state of st_V and st_P conditioned on x being agreed on is ρ_{TS}.

Suppose further that (i) the interaction $\left(V_2(x), \hat{P}_2(x)\right)_{\rho_{\mathsf{TS}}}$ is nondestructive, (ii) the oracle $\mathcal{O}_{\mathcal{F}}$ does not keep state during the second phase of the protocol, i.e. any query to it by V_2 or $\hat{P}_2$ can be repeated with the same input-output behavior, *and (iii) the success probability of* $\hat{P}_2$ *conditioned on instance* x *being agreed on is at least* κ*. Then there exists a procedure* A[10] *such that the following holds.*

Let $\mathcal{R}_{\lambda x}^{\mathcal{O}_\mathcal{F}}(\cdot)$ *be the function such that* $\mathcal{R}_{\lambda x}^{\mathcal{O}_\mathcal{F}}(\rho) = \mathcal{R}^{\mathcal{O}_\mathcal{F}}(1^\lambda, x, \rho)$*, and let the single-bit-valued function* $(\mathcal{R}_{\lambda x}^{\mathcal{O}_\mathcal{F}})^{\otimes 2}(\cdot)$ *be the function whose output is the* AND *of the outcomes obtained by executing the tensor product of two copies of* $\mathcal{R}_{\lambda x}^{\mathcal{O}_\mathcal{F}}(\cdot)$ *on the state that is given as argument. Then the procedure* A*, given as input* x*, a copy of a communication transcript from the agree phase that led to* x*, and black-box access to* V_2 *and* $\hat{P}_2$ *as interactive machines (including any calls they might make to* $\mathcal{O}_\mathcal{F}$*) running on* ρ_{TS}*, with power of initialisation for* $\hat{P}_2$*, can produce a state* σ *such that*

$$\Pr[(\mathcal{R}_{\lambda x}^{\mathcal{O}_\mathcal{F}})^{\otimes 2}(\sigma) = 1] > 1 - 2\delta - \mathsf{negl}(\lambda). \tag{1}$$

Proof. Due to space constraints, we refer the reader to the full version [VZ21] for the proof.

Discussion. Due to space constraints, we refer the reader to the full version [VZ21] for a discussion of potential extensions of Proposition 1, including to the case where the protocol is not perfectly nondestructive but only 'slightly destructive', and to the case where computationally efficient cloning might be desirable.

4.2 Proofs of Quantum Knowledge Are Also Quantum Money Verification Protocols

The other simple property which we prove is that, under certain assumptions on the parameters in Definition 7, any protocol satisfying Definition 7 can be used as a quantum money verification protocol. Proposition 2 formalises the intuition that the property of being a 'proof of quantum knowledge' is stronger than the property of being a quantum money verification protocol: the latter implies that no adversary can pass verification twice given access to only one money bill, and the former formalises the notion that no adversary can pass even once unless it is possible to efficiently compute the money bill by interacting with said adversary.

Formalising interactive quantum money verification. Before we state Proposition 2, we must formalise what it means to 'be a quantum money verification protocol'. The standard definition of quantum money security (Definition 8) indicates what this means for a *passive* verification procedure, in which the verification procedure `Ver` is just an isometric map, but we need to formalise what it means for an *interactive* protocol. Due to space constraints, we refer the reader to the full version [VZ21] for a fuller motivation of the definition that we state below, and in particular of the no-communication assumption between provers $\hat{P}_A$ and $\hat{P}_B$.

[10] A is in general not efficient. It is also allowed slightly more invasive access to $\hat{P}_2$ than a typical extractor. This is acceptable because A is not an extractor, but a cloning procedure. We refer the reader to the full version [VZ21] for a fuller discussion of this topic.

Definition 11 (Interactive Quantum Money Verification Procedure). Let λ be a security parameter, and let $(\mathcal{F}_M, \mathcal{C}_M, \mathcal{R}_M)$ be a quantum money scenario (as defined in Sect. 3.5). A protocol $\mathcal{K} = (I, P_1, P_2, V_1, V_2)$ for $(\mathcal{F}_M, \mathcal{C}_M, \mathcal{R}_M)$ (see Definition 7) is an *interactive verification procedure* with completeness c and cloning error s for the quantum money scenario $(\mathcal{F}_M, \mathcal{C}_M, \mathcal{R}_M)$ if the following two conditions hold.[11] (Probabilities in these conditions are calculated assuming that r, the randomness that *Bank* takes as input, is drawn from the uniform distribution. See Definition 8 for a definition of Bank.)

1. Completeness: The protocol $\mathcal{K}$ has completeness c according to Definition 7.
2. Soundness: let $\hat{P}_A = (\hat{P}_{A,1}, \hat{P}_{A,2})$ and $\hat{P}_B = (\hat{P}_{B,1}, \hat{P}_{B,2})$ be two provers for $\mathcal{K}$, and let $\hat{I}$ be an algorithm that generates inputs for both of them. We define a no-cloning game as follows:
   (a) $\hat{I}$ prepares a (potentially entangled) joint state ρ_{AB}. During this phase, $\hat{I}$ is allowed to call the oracle $\mathcal{O}_{\mathcal{F}_M}$ using the role I. At the end of this phase, $\hat{I}$ gives $\rho_A = \mathrm{Tr}_B(\rho_{AB})$ to $\hat{P}_A$, and $\rho_B = \mathrm{Tr}_A(\rho_{AB})$ to $\hat{P}_B$.
   (b) Holding ρ_A, $\hat{P}_A$ executes $\mathcal{K}$ with a copy of the honest verifier of $\mathcal{K}$, the latter of which we denote by $V_A = (V_{A,1}, V_{A,2})$. Likewise, holding ρ_B, $\hat{P}_B$ also executes $\mathcal{K}$ with a copy of the honest verifier of $\mathcal{K}$, which we denote by $V_B = (V_{B,1}, V_{B,2})$. During the protocol executions, $\hat{P}_A$ and $\hat{P}_B$ are not allowed to communicate, but they are allowed to call the oracle $\mathcal{O}_{\mathcal{F}}$ using the role P.
   (c) $\hat{P}_A$ and $\hat{P}_B$ win the game if and only if the same instance x is agreed upon in the agree phases of both copies of $\mathcal{K}$ played in step 2, and in addition both V_A and V_B output 1 at the end of the game.

   We say that the protocol $\mathcal{K}$ for the quantum money scenario $(\mathcal{F}_M, \mathcal{C}_M, \mathcal{R}_M)$ is *secure against cloning* with cloning error s if any pair of provers $(\hat{P}_A, \hat{P}_B)$ with any input generation algorithm $\hat{I}$ wins the no-cloning game with probability less than s.

We are now ready to formally present our lemma which captures the fact that a secure agree-and-prove protocol can be used as a quantum money verification procedure. We refer the reader to the full version [VZ21] for an exposition of the parameters that appear in Proposition 2.

Proposition 2. *Let λ be a security parameter, and let $(\mathcal{F}_M, \mathcal{C}_M, \mathcal{R}_M)$ be a quantum money scenario (as defined in Sect. 3.5). Let $\mathcal{K} = (I, P_1, P_2, V_1, V_2)$ be a protocol for a quantum money agree-and-prove scenario $(\mathcal{F}_M, \mathcal{C}_M, \mathcal{R}_M)$. Let μ_M be the cloning parameter for the quantum money scenario $(\mathcal{F}_M, \mathcal{C}_M, \mathcal{R}_M)$.*

[11] This definition is distinct from the definition of security of a protocol $\mathcal{K}$ described in Definition 7. The latter is a security definition that can apply to any AaP scenario, and the present definition is a new definition tailored to quantum money that is a natural extension of the standard "no-cloning"-based definition recalled in Sect. 8. Our aim in this section, in fact, is to show that (qualitatively speaking) Definition 7 implies Definition 11.

Define $\delta_0 \equiv \frac{2-\sqrt{3}}{2}$. *Suppose there is a function* $\kappa(\cdot)$ *such that* $\mathcal{K}$ *is a* $(c = 1-\mathsf{negl}(\lambda), \delta)$*-secure protocol with knowledge error* $\kappa(\lambda)$ *and extraction distance* δ *(the latter of which we assume is a function of the prover's success probability* p *as well as the security parameter* λ*) such that* $\delta_0 - \delta(p(\lambda), \lambda) > \frac{1}{2}\frac{\mu_M(\lambda)}{\epsilon \cdot \kappa(\lambda)}$ *for arbitrary* $\epsilon > 0$ *and sufficiently large* λ *whenever* p *is a function such that* $p(\lambda) > \kappa(\lambda)$ *for sufficiently large* λ.

Then $\mathcal{K}$ *is an interactive quantum money verification protocol for the money scenario* $(\mathcal{F}_M, \mathcal{C}_M, \mathcal{R}_M)$ *(in the sense defined in Definition 11) with completeness* $1 - \mathsf{negl}(\lambda)$ *and cloning error* $(1+\epsilon)\kappa$.

Proof. Due to space constraints, we refer the reader to the full version [VZ21] for the proof.

Amplification. The bound on the maximum success probability of a cloning adversary which comes out of Proposition 2 is linear in the knowledge error of the agree-and-prove protocol which is being used as a money verification protocol. A typical expectation in a quantum money scenario is that any cloning adversary will only succeed with negligible probability (see Definition 11 of [AC12], for example), but in our analyses of quantum money verification protocols in Sects. 5.1 and 5.2, we only get constant (and not negligible) knowledge error. Therefore, in the full version [VZ21], we present a sequential amplification lemma which shows that a money scheme equipped with a classical agree-and-prove protocol that has constant knowledge error (and other parameters similar to those which we obtain in Sects. 5.1 and 5.2) can be modified into a money scheme which admits only cloning adversaries that pass with negligible probability.

5 Proofs of Quantum Knowledge for Quantum Money States

In this section we apply our notion of proofs of quantum knowledge to the problem of certifying quantum money. We give two examples for two protocols from the literature, Wiesner's quantum money in Sect. 5.1 and Aaronson and Christiano's public-key quantum money based on hidden subspaces in Sect. 5.2.

5.1 PoQK for Wiesner Money States

Our first concrete example of an Agree-and-Prove scheme for a quantum property is a verification protocol for Wiesner's quantum money states. Any Wiesner state can be described by 2λ classical bits; a typical classical description is the pair of strings $\$ = (v, \theta) \in \{0,1\}^{2\lambda}$, where the associated money state is

$$|\$\rangle_{v,\theta} = \Big(\prod_i H_i^{\theta_i}\Big)|v\rangle \;, \tag{2}$$

in which $|v\rangle = \otimes_i |v_i\rangle$ and H_i denotes a Hadamard on the ith qubit and identities on all other qubits. In the notation of Definition 8, valid bills in this scheme are quadruples $(\mathsf{id}, \mathsf{public}, \mathsf{secret}, |\$\rangle_{\mathsf{id}})$ such that id is an arbitrary string, public is empty, $\mathsf{secret} = (v, \theta) \in \{0,1\}^\lambda \times \{0,1\}^\lambda$ and $|\$\rangle_{\mathsf{id}} = |\$\rangle_{v,\theta}$. The verification procedure $\mathit{Ver}(x, \mathsf{public}, \mathsf{secret}, \rho_W)$ parses $\mathsf{secret} = (v, \theta)$ and measures each qubit of ρ_W in the basis indicated by θ. It accepts if and only if the outcomes obtained match v. This scheme clearly has completeness parameter 1, and it was shown in [MVW12] that its cloning parameter is $\mu_W(\lambda) = (3/4)^\lambda$.

Scenario 12. *We instantiate the generic AaP scenario for quantum money described in Sect. 3.5 as follows:*

- *Setup functionality $\mathcal{F}_W(1^\lambda)$:*
  - init_W *initializes a random oracle H taking strings of length 2λ to strings of length 2λ.*[12] *In addition, it initializes an empty database B_W that is destined to contain a record of all quantum money bills in circulation.*
  - $\mathcal{O}_{\mathcal{F}_W}(I, \mathit{getId})$*: generates* $\mathsf{id} \in \{0,1\}^{2\lambda}$ *uniformly at random. Sets* $(v, \theta) = H(\mathsf{id})$, $\mathsf{secret} = (v, \theta)$ *and* $|\$\rangle = |\$\rangle_{v,\theta}$. *If* id *already appears in B_W, then returns $\perp$. Otherwise, add* $(\mathsf{id}, \mathsf{public}, \mathsf{secret}, |\$\rangle_{v,\theta})$ *to B_W. Return* id.
  - $\mathcal{O}_{\mathcal{F}_W}(\cdot, \mathit{public}, \mathsf{id})$, $\mathcal{O}_{\mathcal{F}_W}(I, \mathit{getMoney}, \mathsf{id})$, *and* $\mathcal{O}_{\mathcal{F}_W}(V, \mathit{secret}, \mathsf{id})$*: as described in Sect. 3.5.*
- *Agreement relation $\mathcal{C}_W^{\mathcal{O}_{\mathcal{F}_W}}(1^\lambda, \mathsf{id})$: The agreement relation is the same as it is in Sect. 3.5.*
- *Proof relation $\mathcal{R}_W^{\mathcal{O}_{\mathcal{F}_W}}(1^\lambda, x, \rho_W)$: The proof relation firstly queries $\mathcal{O}_{\mathcal{F}_W}(V, \mathit{secret}, x)$ in order to get a tuple (v, θ). (If $\mathcal{O}_{\mathcal{F}}(V, \mathit{secret}, x)$ returns $\perp$, then $\mathcal{R}$ rejects.) Then it implements the Wiesner money verification procedure: it applies $\prod_i H_i^{\theta_i}$ to its quantum input ρ_W, measures all qubits in the computational basis, and accepts if and only if the outcome is v.*

Protocol 13. *We define our proof of knowledge protocol $\mathcal{K}_W = (\mathcal{I}_W, P_1, P_2, V_1, V_2)$ for the scenario $(\mathcal{F}_W, \mathcal{C}_W, \mathcal{R}_W)$. An honest input generation algorithm $I \in \mathcal{I}_W$ calls $\mathcal{O}_{\mathcal{F}_W}(I, \mathit{getId})$ repeatedly until it obtains a string* $\mathsf{id} \in \{0,1\}^{2\lambda}$ *such that* $\mathsf{id} \neq \perp$. *It then queries* $\mathcal{O}_{\mathcal{F}}(I, \mathit{getMoney}, \mathsf{id})$, *obtains a quantum state ρ_W, and gives* (id, ρ_W) *to the prover (it gives nothing to the verifier). In the agreement phase, the prover P_1 parses the auxiliary input ρ_{AUX_P} which it gets from I as a classical string* $\mathsf{id} \in \{0,1\}^{2\lambda}$ *in addition to a quantum state ρ_W. (If this fails, the prover halts.) Then the prover sends* id *to V_1 and outputs the statement* $x_P = \mathsf{id}$ *and the quantum state $\rho_{st_P} = \rho_W$. V_1, upon receiving* id *from P_1, queries* $\mathcal{O}_{\mathcal{F}_W}(V, \mathit{public}, \mathsf{id})$. *If this returns $\perp$ the verifier aborts. Otherwise, V_1 outputs* $x_V = \mathsf{id}$ *and $st_V = \perp$.*

This completes the description of the (honest) prover and verifier in the first (agree) phase. We now describe the interaction between the (honest) prover and verifier, P_2 and V_2, in the second (proof) phase:

1. *V_2 queries* $\mathcal{O}_{\mathcal{F}_W}(V, \mathit{secret}, \mathsf{id})$. *If it obtains $\perp$, V_2 aborts. Otherwise, let $\$ = (v, \theta)$ be the classical description obtained.*

---

[12] Formally the oracle is implemented in the standard way, recalled in Sect. 2.3.

2. *V_2 sends a uniformly random $c \in \{0,1\}^\lambda$ to the prover.*
3. *For each $i \in \{1,\ldots,n\}$ if the ith bit of c is 0, P_2 measures the ith qubit of ρ_{st_P} in the standard basis; and if it is 1, it measures the ith qubit in the Hadamard basis. Let $\beta \in \{0,1\}^\lambda$ denote the outcomes obtained. P_2 sends β to V_2.*
4. *Let $s = c \cdot \theta + \bar{c} \cdot \bar{\theta}$, where $\cdot$ denotes componentwise multiplication. In other words, $s_i = 1$ if and only if $c_i = \theta_i$. V_2 checks that, whenever $s_i = 1$, it holds that $v_i = \beta_i$. If not, then it returns 0.*

Lemma 1. *There is a constant $\kappa < 1$ such that Protocol $\mathcal{K}_W$ (Protocol 13) is a secure agree-and-prove protocol for $(\mathcal{F}_W, \mathcal{C}_W, \mathcal{R}_W)$ (Scenario 12) with completeness 1, knowledge error κ, and extraction distance $\delta = O(\mu^{1/4})$, where $\mu = 1-p$ and p is the prover's success probability.*

Proof. Due to space constraints, we refer the reader to the full version [VZ21] for the full proof. For intuition, we provide below a sketch of the main step, the design of the extraction procedure.

Our first step is to argue that we can replace $\mathcal{F}_W$ from Scenario 12 with a new setup functionality $\mathcal{F}'_W$ such that the prover is (perfectly) unable to distinguish the two. $\mathcal{F}_W$ and $\mathcal{F}'_W$ differ mainly in their implementations of $\mathcal{O}_{\mathcal{F}}(I, \textit{\textbf{getMoney}}, \mathsf{id})$: while $\mathcal{F}_W$ chooses v and θ uniformly and returns a money state $|\$\rangle_{v,\theta}$ to the prover when ***getMoney*** is called, $\mathcal{F}'_W$ returns *half EPR pairs* to the prover. (The number of such half-pairs is λ, the length of the money state.) $\mathcal{F}'_W$ keeps the halves of the EPR pairs that it does not give to the prover in a register A. Then, when the verifier calls $\mathcal{O}_{\mathcal{F}'_W}(V, \textit{\textbf{secret}}, \mathsf{id})$ in step 1 of Protocol 13, $\mathcal{F}'_W$ chooses a basis string $\theta \in \{0,1\}^\lambda$ uniformly and *measures* the state in A in the bases determined by θ. This action collapses the state in A to the state $|\$\rangle_{v,\theta}$ for some uniformly random $v \in \{0,1\}^\lambda$. For convenience, we will refer to a version of Scenario 12 with $\mathcal{F}_W$ replaced with $\mathcal{F}'_W$ as 'the purified Scenario 12'.

We then use the prover's unitary ($M_{\lambda x'}$ in Sect. 2.2, which the extractor has black-box access to) in order to define a set of $2 \cdot 2^\lambda$ measurement operators $X^B(s), Z^B(s)$ for $s \in \{0,1\}^\lambda$ that act on the prover's private space P as well as the message register M. We design $X^B(s), Z^B(s)$ so that, for any $c, \theta \in \{0,1\}^\lambda$, the outcome of measuring $Z^B(c \cdot \theta)$ is equal to the single bit $\oplus_{i:c_i=\theta_i=0}\beta_i$, and likewise the outcome of measuring $X^B(\bar{c} \cdot \bar{\theta})$ is equal to $\oplus_{i:c_i=\theta_i=1}\beta_i$ (given that the prover's private state is initialised the way that it is at the start of the prove stage of Protocol 13 in the purified Scenario 12).[13]

We define corresponding measurement operators $X^A(s), Z^A(s)$ which act on the register A, and which simply act as $\sigma_X(s), \sigma_Z(s)$ on the A register (where $\sigma_Z(s) \equiv \bigotimes_i \sigma_{Z,i}^{s_i}$, with $\sigma_{Z,i}$ representing σ_Z on the ith qubit, and $\sigma_X(s)$ is defined analogously). Recall the verifier's check in step 4 of Protocol 13. We argue that, if the verifier's check passes, the outcomes of measuring $Z^A(c \cdot \theta)$ and $Z^B(c \cdot \theta)$

[13] Formally, we mean that $Z^B(c \cdot \theta)$ and $X^B(\bar{c} \cdot \bar{\theta})$ both commute with the measurement that produces β when $\mathcal{F}'_W$'s choice of basis string is θ and when the verifier's choice of challenge is c, and that performing the measurement which produces β and computing $\oplus_{i:c_i=\theta_i=0}\beta_i$ (resp. $\oplus_{i:c_i=\theta_i=1}\beta_i$) always gives the same outcome as measuring $Z^B(c \cdot \theta)$ (resp. $X^B(\bar{c} \cdot \bar{\theta})$).

(on the registers on which they are respectively defined) are equal, and likewise the outcomes of measuring $X^A(\bar{c}\cdot\bar{\theta})$ and $X^B(\bar{c}\cdot\bar{\theta})$ are equal.[14]

We then apply a theorem similar to [NV16, Theorem 14] which states that, if we can define operators $X^A(s), Z^A(s), X^B(s), Z^B(s)$ for all $s \in \{0,1\}^\lambda$ satisfying certain conditions (which we satisfy), and if we can show that, for some state $|\psi\rangle_{AB}$, $\langle\psi|_{AB} Z^A(c\cdot\theta) \otimes Z^B(c\cdot\theta)|\psi\rangle_{AB} = 1$ and $\langle\psi|_{AB} X^A(\bar{c}\cdot\bar{\theta}) \otimes X^B(\bar{c}\cdot\bar{\theta})|\psi\rangle_{AB} = 1$ with high probability over uniformly chosen c, θ (in the previous paragraph we argued that these relations hold when $|\psi\rangle_{AB}$ is the joint state of registers $\mathsf{A}, \mathsf{M}, \mathsf{P}$ at the start of the prove phase of Protocol 13 in the purified Scenario 12, with $A = \mathsf{A}$ and $B = \mathsf{MP}$), then there is a local isometry of the form $\Phi^A \otimes \Phi^B$ which, applied to $|\psi\rangle_{AB}$, transforms $|\psi\rangle_{AB}$ (approximately) into shared EPR pairs between A and B. In our case, this means that we can recover the shared entanglement which initially existed between registers A and PM due to the EPR pairs which $\mathcal{F}'_W$ created and shared with the prover. In our case, it is also true that Φ^A is the identity map. We show in the full version of this proof that this conclusion about the purified Scenario 12 implies that we can recover the money state up to some error in the real Scenario 12 by applying Φ^B to the registers P and M, and also that the extractor can apply Φ^B efficiently using black-box access to the prover. (This step uses the fact that the extractor can execute the prover's unitary coherently on a message register which has been initialized in a quantum superposition.)

5.2 PoQK for Subspace Money States

Our second example of a proof of quantum knowledge protocol is a verification protocol for a modification of Aaronson and Christiano's *subspace states* [AC12]. Aaronson and Christiano present a quantum money scheme in which a λ-qubit money state, with $\lambda \in \mathbb{N}$ a security parameter, is specified by a (secret) $(\lambda/2)$-dimensional subspace $A \subseteq \mathbb{Z}_2^\lambda$, and defined as $|A\rangle = \frac{1}{\sqrt{|A|}}\sum_{x\in A}|x\rangle$. In the notation of Definition 8, valid bills in this scheme are quadruples $(\mathsf{id}, \mathsf{public}, \mathsf{secret}, |\$\rangle_{\mathsf{id}})$ such that id is an arbitrary string, public is empty[15], $\mathsf{secret} = \mathcal{Z} = \{z_1, \ldots, z_{\lambda/2}\}$ is a basis for a $(\lambda/2)$-dimensional subspace A of $\mathbb{Z}_2^\lambda$, and $|\$\rangle_{\mathsf{id}} = |A\rangle$. One possible (quantum-verifier) verification procedure $\mathit{Ver}(x, \mathsf{public}, \mathsf{secret}, \rho_W)$ for these bills parses $\mathsf{secret} = \mathcal{Z}$ and then performs the projective measurement $H^{\otimes\lambda}\mathbb{P}_{A^\perp}H^{\otimes\lambda}\mathbb{P}_A$ on ρ_W (where $\mathbb{P}_A$ is a projection onto all standard basis strings in A, i.e. $\mathbb{P}_A = \sum_{x\in A}|x\rangle\langle x|$, and $\mathbb{P}_{A^\perp}$ is a projection onto all standard basis strings in $A^\perp$), and accepts if and only if the outcome is 1. The scheme (when equipped with this verification procedure) has

[14] The reader should feel free to check that this holds given the previous paragraph.

[15] What we describe here is actually a *private-key* version of the Aaronson-Christiano scheme, equipped with a verification procedure which is similar to a verification procedure used in [BDS16]. Aaronson and Christiano originally proposed this subspace scheme with the idea of making progress towards public-key quantum money. As such, in their original scheme, public is not empty.

completeness parameter 1, and it was shown in [AC12] that its cloning parameter is $\mu_{AC}(\lambda) \leq c^{\lambda}$ for some constant $c < 1$.[16]

As we mentioned in the introduction, we do not know if it is possible to devise a natural proof of quantum knowledge for the Aaronson-Christiano subspace states as they have thus far been described. Nonetheless, we are able to give a proof of knowledge for a version of the subspace scheme in which a (secret) quantum one-time pad has been applied to every subspace state.

Notation. Before we define the associated AaP scenario, we introduce some notation:

- Let $|\$\rangle_{v,\theta}$ be a Wiesner money state representing the string v encoded in bases θ, as in (2).
- Let $\{s_i : i \in \{1,\ldots,\lambda\}\} = \{100...0, 010...0, 001...0, \ldots, 000...1\}$ be the standard basis for $\mathbb{Z}_2^{\lambda}$.
- Let $\mathcal{Z} = \{z_i : i \in \{1,\ldots,\lambda\}\}$ be a basis for $\mathbb{Z}_2^{\lambda}$.
- Let W be the unitary on $(\mathbb{C}^2)^{\otimes\lambda}$ defined as follows:

$$\begin{aligned} W : W|x\rangle &= W|x_1 s_1 + \cdots + x_\lambda s_\lambda\rangle \\ &= |x_1 z_1 + \cdots + x_\lambda z_\lambda\rangle \ . \end{aligned} \tag{3}$$

- Let L_θ for a string $\theta \in \{0,1\}^{\lambda}$ be the subspace of $\mathbb{Z}_2^{\lambda}$ whose elements are always 0 in the positions where $\theta_i = 0$, and can be either 0 or 1 in the positions where $\theta_i = 1$.
- Let $X(a)$ for some vector $a = (a_1, \ldots, a_\lambda) \in \mathbb{Z}_2^{\lambda}$ denote the tensor product of λ single-qubit gates which is Pauli X in those positions i where $a_i = 1$, and I otherwise. Define $Z(b)$ similarly. Let $X_{\mathcal{Z}}(d)$, for a basis $\mathcal{Z} = \{z_j\}$, denote the operator

$$\prod_j \left(X(z_j)\right)^{d_j} ,$$

  where z_j denotes a particular vector from the basis set $\mathcal{Z}$, and d_j denotes the jth bit of d. Define $Z_{\mathcal{Z}}(e)$ similarly.
- Let

$$|\$\rangle_{v,\theta,\mathcal{Z}} \equiv \frac{1}{\sqrt{|L_\theta|}} \sum_{\lambda \in L_\theta} X_{\mathcal{Z}}(d) Z_{\mathcal{Z}}(e) |\lambda_1 z_1 + \cdots + \lambda_n z_n\rangle \ , \tag{4}$$

  with $d_i = v_i$ for i such that $\theta_i = 0$ (and $d_i = 0$ for all other i), and $e_i = v_i$ for i such that $\theta_i = 1$ (and $e_i = 0$ for all other i). Note that the distribution of $|\$\rangle_{v,\theta,\mathcal{Z}}$ over uniform $v, \theta, \mathcal{Z}$ is identical (ignoring global phase) to that of a uniformly random subspace state with a uniformly random Pauli one-time-pad applied to it, because the coordinates of d and e which we have forced to be zero (instead of uniformly random) would only add a global phase to the state.

[16] In fact Aaronson and Christiano show the stronger result that this bound holds even if the adversary is given black-box access to a pair of measurement operators that respectively implement projections on A and $A^{\perp}$.

Scenario 14. *We instantiate the generic AaP scenario for quantum money described in Sect. 3.5 as follows:*

- *Setup functionality* $\mathcal{F}_{AC}(1^\lambda)$*:*
  - $\mathtt{init}_{AC}$ *initializes a random oracle H taking strings of length $2\lambda + \lambda^2$ to strings of length $2\lambda + \lambda^2$.*[17] *In addition, it initializes an empty database B_{AC} that is destined to contain a record of all quantum money bills in circulation.*
  - $\mathcal{O}_{\mathcal{F}_W}(I, \mathtt{getId})$*: generates $v \in \{0,1\}^\lambda$ and $\theta \in \{0,1\}^\lambda$ such that $|\theta|_H = \frac{n}{2}$ uniformly at random and selects $\mathcal{Z} = \{z_i : i \in \{1,\dots,\lambda\}\}$ a uniformly random basis for $\mathbb{Z}_2^\lambda$. Sets $\mathsf{id} = H^{-1}((v,\theta,\mathcal{Z}))$,*[18] *$\mathsf{secret} = (v,\theta,\mathcal{Z})$ and $|\$\rangle_{\mathsf{id}} = |\$\rangle_{v,\theta,\mathcal{Z}}$ defined in (4). Adds $(\mathsf{id}, \mathsf{public}, \mathsf{secret}, |\$\rangle_{\mathsf{id}})$ to B_{AC}. Returns id.*
  - $\mathcal{O}_{\mathcal{F}_{AC}}(\cdot, \mathtt{public}, \mathsf{id})$*,* $\mathcal{O}_{\mathcal{F}_{AC}}(I, \mathtt{getMoney}, \mathsf{id})$*, and* $\mathcal{O}_{\mathcal{F}_{AC}}(V, \mathtt{secret}, \mathsf{id})$*: as described in Sect. 3.5.*
- *Agreement relation* $\mathcal{C}_W^{\mathcal{O}_{\mathcal{F}_{AC}}}(1^\lambda, \mathsf{id})$*: The agreement relation is the same as it is in Sect. 3.5.*
- *Proof relation* $\mathcal{R}_{AC}^{\mathcal{O}_{\mathcal{F}_W}}(1^\lambda, x, \rho_W)$*: The proof relation firstly queries $\mathcal{O}_{\mathcal{F}_W}(V, \mathtt{secret}, x)$ in order to get a tuple $(v,\theta,\mathcal{Z})$. (If $\mathcal{O}_{\mathcal{F}}(V, \mathtt{secret}, x)$ returns $\perp$, then $\mathcal{R}$ rejects.) Then it applies $Z(e)X(d)$ to its quantum input ρ_W, where d and e are defined in terms of (v,θ) the same way that they are below equation (4). Following that, it defines A to be the subspace generated by the vectors $z_i \in \mathcal{Z}$ such that $\theta_i = 1$, and then it follows the subspace money verification procedure: it performs the projective measurement $H^{\otimes\lambda}\mathbb{P}_{A^\perp}H^{\otimes\lambda}\mathbb{P}_A$ on $Z(e)X(d)\rho_W X(d)Z(e)$ (where $\mathbb{P}_A$ is a projection onto all standard basis strings in A, i.e. $\mathbb{P}_A = \sum_{x\in A}|x\rangle\langle x|$, and $\mathbb{P}_{A^\perp}$ is a projection onto all standard basis strings in $A^\perp$), and accepts if and only if the outcome is 1.*

Protocol 15. *We define a proof of knowledge protocol $\mathcal{K}_{AC}$ for the scenario $(\mathcal{F}_{AC}, \mathcal{C}_{AC}, \mathcal{R}_{AC})$. The agreement phase is identical to that in Protocol 13, except that now* id *has length $2\lambda + \lambda^2$. The second phase is similar but not identical, as the verifier's challenge now consists of a single bit:*

1. *V_2 queries $\mathcal{O}_{\mathcal{F}_{AC}}(V, \mathtt{secret}, \mathsf{id})$. If it obtains $\perp$, V_2 aborts. Otherwise, let $\$ = (v,\theta,\mathcal{Z})$ be the classical description obtained.*
2. *V_2 sends a uniformly random bit $c \in \{0,1\}$ to the prover.*
3. *If $c = 0$ the prover P_2 measures the state ρ_{st_P} it received from P_1 in the standard basis, obtaining a λ-bit string of outcomes $m \in \{0,1\}^\lambda$, and sends m to the verifier. If $c = 1$ then P_2 measures in the Hadamard basis and likewise sends the outcomes m to V_2.*
4. *If $c = 0$ the verifier V_2 checks that $m + Wd$ is in the subspace A spanned by $\{z_i : \theta_i = 1\}$, where $\mathcal{Z} = \{z_1, \dots, z_\lambda\}$. If $c = 1$ then V_2 checks that $m + We$ is in $A^\perp$.*

[17] Formally the oracle is implemented in the standard way, recalled in Sect. 2.3.

[18] We use H^{-1} and not H here because we specified in Sect. 3.5 that H maps ids to $(\mathsf{public}, \mathsf{secret})$ pairs.

Finally, the class of input generation algorithms $\mathcal{I}_{AC}$ used for completeness is the same as the class $\mathcal{I}_W$ in Protocol 13.

Lemma 2. *There exists a constant $\kappa < 1$ such that Protocol $\mathcal{K}_{AC}$ (Protocol 15) is secure with completeness 1, up to knowledge error κ, and with extraction distance $\delta = O(\mu^{1/4})$, where $\mu = 1 - p$ and p the prover's success probability, for the subspace AaP scenario $(\mathcal{F}_{AC}, \mathcal{C}_{AC}, \mathcal{R}_{AC})$ (Scenario 14).*

Proof. The proof is similar to that of Lemma 1. Due to space constraints, we refer the reader to the full version [VZ21] for the proof.

6 Arguments of Quantum Knowledge for QMA Relations

The main result of this section is Theorem 1, which gives a classical-verifier protocol to verify any QMA relation (a natural quantum analogue of an NP relation; we recall the definition in Sect. 6.1 below). Since this protocol is only sound against QPT provers, we refer to it as a 'classical argument of quantum knowledge'. We note that, for general QMA relations, the completeness property from Definition 5 requires the honest prover to hold multiple copies of the QMA witness in order to succeed with high probability. It is still possible for completeness to hold with a single witness if one assumes that the QMA relation takes a specific form; see the statement of Theorem 1 below.

Our construction is based on the classical verification protocol for QMA introduced in [Mah18b], which we review in Sect. 6.2. Before doing so we introduce the Agree-and-Prove scenario.

6.1 Agree-and-Prove Scenario for QMA Relations

We first recall the quantum extension of an NP relation $\mathcal{R}$, following [CVZ19, BG19].

Definition 16 (QMA relation). A QMA *relation* is specified by a triple (Q, α, β) where $\alpha, \beta : \mathbb{N} \to [0, 1]$ satisfy $\beta(n) \leq \alpha(n)$ for all $n \in \mathbb{N}$ and $Q = \{Q_n\}_{n \in \mathbb{N}}$ is a uniformly generated family of quantum circuits such that for every n, Q_n takes as input a string $x \in \{0,1\}^n$ and a quantum state $|\psi\rangle$ on $p(n)$ qubits (i.e. Q_n takes $n + p(n)$ input qubits for some polynomial p that is implicitly specified by Q, and is assumed to immediately measure its first n input qubits in the computational basis) and returns a single bit.

To a QMA relation (Q, α, β) we associate two sets

$$R_{Q,\alpha} = \bigcup_{n \in \mathbb{N}} \Big\{ (x, \sigma) \in \{0,1\}^n \times \mathrm{D}(\mathbb{C}^{p(n)}) \,\Big|\, \Pr(Q_n(x, \sigma) = 1) \geq \alpha \Big\}$$

and

$$N_{Q,\beta} = \bigcup_{n \in \mathbb{N}} \Big\{ x \in \{0,1\}^n \,\Big|\, \forall \sigma \in \mathrm{D}(\mathbb{C}^{p(n)}),\ \Pr(Q_n(x, \sigma) = 1) < \beta \Big\}.$$

We say that a (promise) *language* $L = (L_{yes}, L_{no})$ *is specified by the* QMA *relation* (Q, α, β) if

$$L_{yes} \subseteq \left\{ x \in \{0,1\}^* \,\middle|\, \exists \sigma \in \mathrm{D}(\mathbb{C}^{p(n)}),\ (x, \sigma) \in R_{Q,\alpha} \right\}, \tag{5}$$

and $L_{no} \subseteq N_{Q,\beta}$. Note that, whenever $\alpha - \beta > 1/\operatorname{poly}(n)$, any language L that is specified by (Q, α, β) lies in QMA. Conversely, any language in QMA is specified by some QMA relation in a straightforward (non-unique) way.

The local Hamiltonian problem In the following, we make use of Kitaev's circuit-to-Hamiltonian construction [KSVV02,KR03], which associates with any promise language $L = (L_{yes}, L_{no}) \in$ QMA and $x \in L_{yes} \cup L_{no}$ an instance of the *local Hamiltonian problem.* An instance of the local Hamiltonian problem is specified by a local Hamiltonian operator H and two real numbers $\alpha > \beta$. The instance is a 'YES instance' if H has smallest eigenvalue at most α, and a 'NO instance' if it is at least β.

Agree-and-Prove scenario. Fix a QMA relation (Q, α, β). We associate an AaP scenario to Q as follows.

- Setup functionality $\mathcal{F}_Q(1^\lambda)$. We consider a "trivial" setup, i.e. the initialization procedure does nothing and there is no associated oracle $\mathcal{O}_{\mathcal{F}_Q}$.
- Agreement relation $\mathcal{C}_Q(1^\lambda, x)$: returns 1 for any λ and x.[19]
- Proof relation $\mathcal{R}_Q(1^\lambda, x, \rho)$: executes the verification circuit $Q_{|x|}$ on the pair (x, ρ) and returns the outcome.

We end by presenting some assumptions on a QMA relation under which our results will hold. Let (Q, α, β) be a QMA relation. We require that the relation satisfies the following properties:

(Q.1) The completeness parameter α is negligibly close to 1, and the soundness parameter β is bounded away from 1 by an inverse polynomial.

(Q.2) For any $x \in \{0,1\}^n$ there is a local Hamiltonian $H = H_x$ that is efficiently constructible from x and satisfies the following. First, we assume that H is expressed as a linear combination of tensor products of Pauli operators with real coefficients chosen such that $-\mathrm{Id} \leq H \leq \mathrm{Id}$. Second, whenever there is σ such that $(x, \sigma) \in R_{Q,\alpha}$, then $\mathrm{Tr}(H\sigma)$ is negligibly close to -1 and moreover any σ such that $\mathrm{Tr}(H\sigma) \leq -1 + \delta$ satisfies $\Pr(Q_{|x|}(x, \sigma) = 1) \geq 1 - r(|x|)q(\delta)$ for some polynomials q, r depending on the relation only. Third, whenever $x \in N_{Q,\beta}$ then the smallest eigenvalue of H is larger than $-1 + 1/s(|x|)$, where s is another polynomial depending on the relation only.

The first of these assumptions is benign and can be made without loss of generality; the second assumption is a little more restrictive. For a fuller discussion of these assumptions, we refer the reader to the full version [VZ21].

[19] The agreement relation does not even require that $x \in R_{Q,\alpha} \cup N_{Q,\beta}$, as in general this cannot be efficiently verified.

6.2 The Protocol

In the following subsection we recall the high-level structure of the verification protocol from [Mah18b], on which our AaP protocol for the scenario given in Sect. 6.1 will be based.

The verification protocol from [Mah18b]**.** In the protocol from [Mah18b], which we will refer to as the *verification protocol*, the input to the verifier is an n-qubit Hamiltonian H that is expressed as a linear combination of tensor products of σ_X and σ_Z Pauli operators. The input to the prover is a ground state of H. Both parties also receive a security parameter λ. At a high level, the verification protocol has the following structure:

1. The verifier selects a *basis string* $h \in \{0,1\}^n$ according to a distribution that depends on H. The verifier then randomly samples a pair of keys, (pk, sk), consisting of a public key pk and secret key sk. (The distribution according to which (pk, sk) is sampled depends on h.) The choice of keys specifies an integer w of size $\text{poly}(n, \lambda)$. The verifier sends pk to the prover.
2. The prover returns an n-tuple of *commitment strings* $y = (y_1, \ldots, y_n)$, where each y_i lies in some alphabet $\mathcal{Y}$.
3. The verifier selects a *challenge bit* $c \in \{0,1\}$ and sends c to the prover.
4. If $c = 0$ ("test round"), the prover returns a string $b \in \{0,1\}^n$ and $x_1, \ldots, x_n \in \{0,1\}^w$. If $c = 1$ ("Hadamard round"), the prover returns a string $b \in \{0,1\}^n$ and $d_1, \ldots, d_n \in \{0,1\}^w$.
5. In case $c = 0$ the verifier uses pk, y, b and $x_1, \ldots, x_n$ to make a decision to accept or reject. (In a test round the verifier never checks any properties of the prover's state; it only checks that the prover is, loosely speaking, doing the correct operations.) In case $c = 1$ the verifier uses sk to decode y, b and $d_1, \ldots, d_n$ into *decoded measurement outcomes* $(m_1, \ldots, m_n) \in \{0,1\}^n$. (For the case of a honest prover, the decoded outcomes m correspond to the outcomes of measuring a ground state of H in the bases indicated by h, with $h_i = 0$ indicating that the ith qubit should be measured in the computational basis and $h_i = 1$ that the ith qubit should be measured in the Hadamard basis. The prover remains ignorant throughout the entire protocol of the verifier's choice of h.)
6. In case $c = 1$ the verifier makes a decision based on the decoded measurement outcomes and the instance x, as described in [Mah18c, Protocol 8.1].

To model the verifier and prover in the protocol as ITMs, in accordance with the formalism in Definition 6, we introduce registers associated with each party and the messages that they send. Let K and C denote registers that contain the verifier's first and second messages respectively, i.e. the key pk and the challenge bit c. Let T denote the verifier's private space. Let Y denote the register measured by the prover to obtain the prover's first message y, and M the register measured to obtain the prover's second message $(b, x_1, \ldots, x_n)$ or $(b, d_1, \ldots, d_n)$, depending on $c = 0$ or $c = 1$ respectively. Let S denote the prover's private space.

The natural description of the prover as an ITM consists of (i) its initial state $\sigma \in \mathrm{D}(\mathcal{H}_{\mathsf{YMS}})$, (ii) a unitary V_0 acting on KYMS, and (iii) two unitaries V and

V' acting on MS, where V is the action of the prover on challenge $c = 0$ and V' its action on challenge $c = 1$. In either case the register M is measured in the computational basis to obtain the prover's answer.[20]

For convenience we introduce a slightly different representation of the prover, that matches the presentation from [Mah18b] and which can be straightforwardly simulated given black-box access to the natural representation described in the previous paragraph. First, we replace V_0 by the unitary $U_0 = VV_0$. Note that this is well-defined and does not change the prover's first message, since V does not act on Y. Second, we define $U = H^{\otimes(n+nw)}V'V^{\dagger}$, where the Hadamard gates act on the $(n + nw)$ qubits in register M. It is then immediate that given a natural representation of the prover as three unitaries (V_0, V, V') the pair of unitaries (U_0, U) provides a different representation of the same prover, who now behaves as follows:

1. Upon reception of pk, the prover applies U_0 to its initial state (to which $|pk\rangle$ has been appended), measures the first $n \log |\mathcal{Y}|$ qubits in the computational basis and returns the outcome;
2. Upon reception of $c = 0$, the prover directly measures the first (remaining) $n + nw$ qubits in the computational basis and returns the outcome;
3. Upon reception of $c = 1$, the prover applies the unitary U, measures the first (remaining) $n + nw$ qubits in the Hadamard basis and returns the outcome.

In both cases $c = 0$ and $c = 1$ we denote the first n qubits measured by the prover (in step 2 or in step 3, respectively), whose associated measurement outcomes are denoted by b in the protocol, the *committed qubits.*

The Agree-and-Prove Protocol. In this section we define a protocol $\mathcal{K}_Q$ for the AaP scenario $(\mathcal{F}_Q, \mathcal{C}_Q, \mathcal{R}_Q)$ associated to a QMA relation (Q, α, β) as in Sect. 6.1. Recall that an Agree-and-Prove protocol consists of two phases, an "agree" phase and a "prove" phase. The agree phase in protocol $\mathcal{K}_Q$ is simple:

- The prover P_1 takes as input 1^λ and a CQ state ρ_{AUX_P}. It interprets the classical part of ρ as a string $z \in \{0,1\}^n$ and the quantum part as ℓ witnesses $\sigma_1, \ldots, \sigma_\ell$ each of the same number of qubits. (We assume that the integers n and ℓ are both encoded in a canonical way in the state ρ_{AUX_P}.) It sends z to the verifier and outputs the statement $x_p = z$ and the quantum state $\rho_{st_P} = (\sigma_1, \ldots, \sigma_\ell)$ (which may in general be entangled).
- The verifier V_1 takes as input 1^λ and a classical auxiliary input ρ_{AUX_v}. It parses ρ_{AUX_v} as the specification (in binary) of an input length n followed by a string $x \in \{0,1\}^n$. It receives z from P_1. If $z \neq x$ it aborts. Otherwise, it produces the statement $x_v = x$.

[20] This description slightly departs from the 'canonical' formalism introduced in Sect. 2.2 by using different symbols for the prover's unitaries associated with different rounds as well as different challenges. It is not hard to find an equivalent description that uses the language from Sect. 2.2. In this case, the four registers KYCM would all be considered network registers, and are thus accessible to the extractor.

For the proof phase V_2 and P_2 behave exactly as the verifier and prover do in the verification protocol described in Sect. 6.2, first defining the Hamiltonian H_v and H_p from their respective statements x_v and x_p according to assumption (Q.2). Note that H_v (resp. H_p) acts on poly(n) qubits, with $n = |x_v|$ (resp. $n = |x_p|$). Of course, when all parties are honest, $x_v = x_p$.

To complete the description of the protocol we define a class of of input-generation algorithms under which completeness holds. We consider only input generation algorithms that generate positive instances of the language, accompanied with ℓ copies of a valid proof, where $\ell \geq 1$ is a parameter. That is, for any $\ell \geq 1$, $\mathcal{I}_Q^{(\ell)}$ contains any input generation algorithm I that returns a CQ state of the form

$$\sum_{x\in\{0,1\}^*} p_x \, ||x|, x\rangle\langle |x|, x|_{\mathsf{AUX}_V} \otimes \left(|x\rangle\langle x| \otimes \sigma_x^{\otimes \ell} \right)_{\mathsf{AUX}_P} , \tag{6}$$

where (p_x) is any distribution over positive instances for the QMA relation, i.e. the set

$$\{x : \exists \sigma, (x, \sigma) \in R_{Q,\alpha}\} ,$$

and moreover for each x, σ_x is such that $(x, \sigma_x) \in R_{Q,\alpha}$[21].

6.3 Arguments of Quantum Knowledge for QMA Relations

We state the main result of this section.

Theorem 1. *Let* (Q, α, β) *be a* QMA *relation that satisfies properties (Q.1) and (Q.2) described in Sect. 6.1. There exists a polynomially bounded* $\ell = \ell(n)$ *such that the following holds. Under the Learning with Errors assumption the protocol presented in Sect. 6.2 is secure with completeness* c *(for the class of input generation algorithms* $\mathcal{I}_Q^{(\ell)}$*), up to knowledge error* κ *and with extraction distance* δ *for the Agree-and-Prove scenario* $(\mathcal{F}_Q, \mathcal{C}_Q, \mathcal{R}_Q)$*, where:* c *is negligibly close to* 1*;* κ *is bounded away from* 1 *by an inverse polynomial;* $\delta = \text{poly}(1-p)\,\text{poly}(n)$ *(for any prover success probability* $p > \kappa$*).*

Proof. Due to space constraints, we refer the reader to the full version [VZ21] for the proof.

6.4 Sequential Amplification

Due to space constraints, we refer the reader to the full version [VZ21] for a treatment of sequential amplification of the [Mah18c] protocol.

Acknowledgement. We thank Alexandru Gheorghiu for useful feedback and Or Sattath for comments. Thomas Vidick is supported by NSF CAREER Grant CCF-1553477, AFOSR YIP award number FA9550-16-1-0495, MURI Grant FA9550-18-1-0161 and the IQIM, an NSF Physics Frontiers Center (NSF Grant PHY-1125565) with

[21] For clarity we omit explicitly writing out $|x|$ in both registers.

support of the Gordon and Betty Moore Foundation (GBMF-12500028). This material is based upon work supported by DARPA under Agreement No. HR00112020023. Any opinions, findings and conclusions or recommendations expressed in this material are those of the author(s) and do not necessarily reflect the views of the United States Government or DARPA.

References

[AC12] Aaronson, S., Christiano, P.: Quantum money from hidden subspaces. In: Proceedings of the Forty-Fourth Annual ACM Symposium on Theory of Computing (2012)

[AFG+12] Aaronson, S., Farhi, E., Gosset, D., Hassidim, A., Kelner, J., Lutomirski, A.: Quantum money. Commun. ACM **55**(8), 84–92 (2012)

[BCC+20] Badertscher, C., et al.: Security limitations of classical-client delegated quantum computing. arXiv preprint arXiv:2007.01668 (2020)

[BDS16] Ben-David, S., Sattath, O.: Quantum tokens for digital signatures. arXiv preprint arXiv:1609.09047 (2016)

[BG92] Bellare, M., Goldreich, O.: On defining proofs of knowledge. In: Brickell, E.F. (ed.) CRYPTO 1992. LNCS, vol. 740, pp. 390–420. Springer, Heidelberg (1993). https://doi.org/10.1007/3-540-48071-4_28

[BG19] Broadbent, A., Grilo, A.B.: Zero-knowledge for QMA from locally simulatable proofs. arXiv preprint arXiv:1911.07782 (2019)

[BJM19] Badertscher, C., Jost, D., Maurer, U.: Agree-and-prove: generalized proofs of knowledge and applications. IACR Cryptol. ePrint Arch. **2019**, 662 (2019)

[CL06] Chase, M., Lysyanskaya, A.: On signatures of knowledge. In: Dwork, C. (ed.) CRYPTO 2006. LNCS, vol. 4117, pp. 78–96. Springer, Heidelberg (2006). https://doi.org/10.1007/11818175_5

[CVZ19] Coladangelo, A., Vidick, T., Zhang, T.: Non-interactive zero-knowledge arguments for QMA, with preprocessing. arXiv preprint arXiv:1911.07546 (2019)

[FFS88] Feige, U., Fiat, A., Shamir, A.: Zero-knowledge proofs of identity. J. Cryptol. **1**(2), 77–94 (1988)

[GMR89] Goldwasser, S., Micali, S., Rackoff, C.: The knowledge complexity of interactive proof systems. SIAM J. Comput. **18**(1), 186–208 (1989)

[GV19] Gheorghiu, A., Vidick, T.: Computationally-secure and composable remote state preparation. In: 2019 IEEE 60th Annual Symposium on Foundations of Computer Science (FOCS), pp. 1024–1033. IEEE (2019)

[HHJ+17] Haah, J., Harrow, A.W., Ji, Z., Wu, X., Yu, N.: Sample-optimal tomography of quantum states. IEEE Trans. Inf. Theory **63**(9), 5628–5641 (2017)

[KR03] Kempe, J., Regev, O.: 3-local Hamiltonian is QMA-complete. Quantum Inf. Comput. **3**(3), 258–264 (2003)

[KSVV02] Kitaev, A.Y., Shen, A., Vyalyi, M.N., Vyalyi, M.N.: Classical and quantum computation. Number 47. American Mathematical Soc. (2002)

[Mah18a] Mahadev, U.: Classical homomorphic encryption for quantum circuits. In: 2018 IEEE 59th Annual Symposium on Foundations of Computer Science (FOCS), pp. 332–338. IEEE (2018)

[Mah18b] Mahadev, U.: Classical verification of quantum computations. In: 2018 IEEE 59th Annual Symposium on Foundations of Computer Science (FOCS), pp. 259–267, October 2018

[Mah18c] Mahadev, U.: Classical verification of quantum computations. arXiv preprint arXiv:1804.01082 (2018)

[MV20] Metger, T., Vidick, T.: Self-testing of a single quantum device under computational assumptions. arXiv preprint arXiv:2001.09161 (2020)

[MVW12] Molina, A., Vidick, T., Watrous, J.: Optimal counterfeiting attacks and generalizations for Wiesner's quantum money. In: Iwama, K., Kawano, Y., Murao, M. (eds.) TQC 2012. LNCS, vol. 7582, pp. 45–64. Springer, Heidelberg (2013). https://doi.org/10.1007/978-3-642-35656-8_4

[NV16] Natarajan, A., Vidick, T.: Robust self-testing of many-qubit states. arXiv e-prints, page arXiv:1610.03574, October 2016

[SJ00] Claus Schnorr and Markus Jakobsson. Security of signed ElGamal encryption. In International Conference on the Theory and Application of Cryptology and Information Security, volume 1976, pages 73–89, 12 2000

[TW87] Tompa, M., Woll, H.: Random self-reducibility and zero knowledge interactive proofs of possession of information. In: 28th Annual Symposium on Foundations of Computer Science (sfcs 1987), pp. 472–482. IEEE (1987)

[Unr12] Unruh, D.: Quantum proofs of knowledge. In: Pointcheval, D., Johansson, T. (eds.) EUROCRYPT 2012. LNCS, vol. 7237, pp. 135–152. Springer, Heidelberg (2012). https://doi.org/10.1007/978-3-642-29011-4_10

[VZ20] Vidick, T., Zhang, T.: Classical zero-knowledge arguments for quantum computations. Quantum **4**, 266 (2020)

[VZ21] Vidick, T., Zhang, T.: Classical proofs of quantum knowledge (2021)

[Wat09] Watrous, J.: Zero-knowledge against quantum attacks. SIAM J. Comput. **39**(1), 25–58 (2009)

[Wie83] Wiesner, S.: Conjugate coding. ACM SIGACT News **15**(1), 78–88 (1983)

[Zha19] Zhandry, M.: Quantum lightning never strikes the same state twice. In: Ishai, Y., Rijmen, V. (eds.) EUROCRYPT 2019. LNCS, vol. 11478, pp. 408–438. Springer, Cham (2019). https://doi.org/10.1007/978-3-030-17659-4_14

Multiparty Computation

Order-C Secure Multiparty Computation for Highly Repetitive Circuits

Gabrielle Beck[1(✉)], Aarushi Goel[1], Abhishek Jain[1], and Gabriel Kaptchuk[2]

[1] Johns Hopkins University, Baltimore, USA
{gbeck,aarushig,abhishek}@cs.jhu.edu
[2] Boston University, Boston, USA
kaptchuk@bu.edu

Abstract. Running secure multiparty computation (MPC) protocols with hundreds or thousands of players would allow leveraging large volunteer networks (such as blockchains and Tor) and help justify honest majority assumptions. However, most existing protocols have at least a linear (multiplicative) dependence on the number of players, making scaling difficult. Known protocols with asymptotic efficiency independent of the number of parties (excluding additive factors) require expensive circuit transformations that induce large overheads.

We observe that the circuits used in many important applications of MPC such as training algorithms used to create machine learning models have a *highly repetitive structure*. We formalize this class of circuits and propose an MPC protocol that achieves $O(|\mathsf{C}|)$ total complexity for this class. We implement our protocol and show that it is practical and outperforms $O(n|\mathsf{C}|)$ protocols for modest numbers of players.

1 Introduction

Secure Multiparty Computation (MPC) [4,6,23,39] is a technique that allows mutually distrusting parties to compute an arbitrary function without revealing anything about the parties' private inputs, beyond what is revealed by the function output. In this work, we focus on *honest-majority* MPC, where a majority of the participants are assumed to be honest.

As public concern over privacy and data sharing grows, MPC's promise of privacy preserving collaboration becomes increasingly important. In recent years, MPC techniques are being applied to an increasingly complex class of functionalities such as distributed training of machine learning networks. Most current applications of MPC, however, focus on using a *small* number of parties. This is largely because most known (and all implemented) protocols incur a linear

A. Canteaut and F.-X. Standaert (Eds.): EUROCRYPT 2021, LNCS 12697, pp. 663–693, 2021.
https://doi.org/10.1007/978-3-030-77886-6_23

multiplicative overhead in the number of players in the communication and computation complexity, *i.e.* have complexity $O(n|\mathsf{C}|)^1$, where n is the number of players and $|\mathsf{C}|$ is the size of the circuit [7,12,16,27,30,35].

The Need for Large-Scale MPC. Yet, the most exciting MPC applications are at their best when a *large* number of players can participate in the protocol. These include crowd-sourced machine learning and large scale data collection, where widespread participation would result in richer data sets and more robust conclusions. Moreover, when the number of participating players is large, the honest majority assumption – which allows for the most efficient known protocols till date – becomes significantly more believable. Indeed, the honest majority of resources assumptions (a different but closely related set of assumptions) in Bitcoin [34] and TOR [13,36] appear to hold up in practice when there are many protocol participants.

Furthermore, large-scale volunteer networks have recently emerged, like Bitcoin and TOR, that regularly perform incredibly large distributed computations. In the case of cryptocurrencies, it would be beneficial to apply the computational power to more interesting applications than mining, including executions of MPC protocols. Replicating a fraction of the success of these networks could enable massive, crowd-sourced applications that still respect privacy. In fact, attempts to run MPC on such large networks have already started [38], enabling novel measurements.

Our Goal: Order-C MPC. It would be highly advantageous to go beyond the limitation of current protocols and have access to an MPC protocol with total computational and communication complexity $O(|\mathsf{C}|)$.

Such a protocol can support division of the total computation among players which means that using large numbers of players can significantly reduce the burden on each individual participant. In particular, when considering complex functions, with circuit representations containing tens or hundreds of millions of gates, decreasing the workload of each individual party can have a significant impact. Ideally, it would be possible for the data providers themselves, possibly using low power or bandwidth devices, to participate in the computation.

An $O(|\mathsf{C}|)$ MPC protocol can also offer benefits in the design of other cryptographic protocols. In [28], Ishai et al. showed that zero-knowledge (ZK) proofs [24] can be constructed using an "MPC-in-the-head" approach, where the prover simulates an MPC protocol in their mind and the verifier selects a subset of the players views to check for correctness. The efficiency of these proofs is inherited from the complexity of the underlying MPC protocols, and the soundness error is a function of the number of views opened and the number of players for which a malicious prover must have to "cheat" in order to control the protocol's output. This creates a tension: higher number of players can be used to increase the soundness of the ZK proof, but simulating additional players increases the complexity of the protocol. Access to an $O(|\mathsf{C}|)$ MPC protocol would ease this

[1] For sake of simplicity, throughout the introduction, we omit a linear multiplicative factor of the security parameter in all asymptotic notations.

tension, as a large numbers of players could be used to simulate the MPC without incurring additional cost.

Despite numerous motivations and significant effort, there are no known $O(|\mathsf{C}|)$ MPC protocols for "non-SIMD" functionalities.[2] We therefore ask the following:

> *Is it possible to design an MPC protocol with $O(|\mathsf{C}|)$ total computation (supporting division of labor) and $O(|\mathsf{C}|)$ total communication?*

Prior Work: Achieving $\tilde{O}(|\mathsf{C}|)$-MPC. A significant amount of effort has been devoted towards reducing the asymptotic complexity of (honest-majority) MPC protocols, since the initial $O(n^2|\mathsf{C}|)$ protocols [4,6].

Over the years, two primary techniques have been developed for reducing protocol complexity. The first is an *efficient multiplication protocol* combined with batched correlated randomness generation introduced in [12]. Using this multiplication protocol reduces the (amortized) complexity of a multiplication gate from $O(n^2)$ to $O(n)$, effectively shaving a factor of n from the protocol complexity. The second technique is *packed secret sharing* (PSS) [15], a vectorized, single-instruction-multiple-data (SIMD) version of traditional threshold secret sharing. By packing $\Theta(n)$ elements into a single vector, $\Theta(n)$ operations can be performed at once, reducing the protocol complexity by a factor of n when the circuit structure is accommodating to SIMD operations. Using these techniques separately, $O(n|\mathsf{C}|)$ protocols were constructed in [9] and [12].

While it might seem as though combining these two techniques would result in an $O(|\mathsf{C}|)$ protocol, the structural requirements of SIMD operations make it unclear on how to do so. The works of [11] and [10] demonstrate two different approaches to combine these techniques, either by relying on randomizing polynomials or using circuit transformations that involve embedding routing networks within the circuits. These approaches yield $\widetilde{O}(|\mathsf{C}|)$ protocols with large multiplicative constants and additive terms that depend on the circuit depth. (The additive terms were further reduced in the recent work of [20].)

In summary, while both PSS and efficient multiplication techniques have been known for over a decade, no $O(|\mathsf{C}|)$ MPC protocols are known. The best known asymptotic efficiency is $\widetilde{O}(|\mathsf{C}|)$ achieved by [10,11,20]; however, these protocols have never been implemented for reasons discussed above. Instead, the state-of-the-art implemented protocols achieve $O(n|\mathsf{C}|)$ computational and communication efficiency [7,16,35].

1.1 Our Contributions

In this work, we identify a meaningful class of circuits, called (A, B)-repetitive circuits, parameterized by variables A and B. We show that for $(\Omega(n), \Omega(n))$-repetitive circuits, efficient multiplication and PSS techniques can indeed be

[2] SIMD circuits are arithmetic circuits that simultaneously evaluate ℓ copies of the same arithmetic circuit on different inputs. Genkin et al. [20] showed that it is possible to design an $O(|\mathsf{C}|)$ MPC protocol for SIMD circuits, where $\ell = \Theta(n)$.

combined, using new ideas, to achieve $O(|\mathsf{C}|)$ MPC for n parties. To the best of our knowledge, this is the first such construction for a larger class of circuits than SIMD circuits.

We test the practical efficiency of our protocol by means of a preliminary implementation and show via experimental results that for computations involving large number of parties, our protocol outperforms the state-of-the-art implemented MPC protocols. We now discuss our contributions in more detail.

Highly Repetitive Circuits. The class of (A, B)-repetitive circuits are circuits that are composed of an arbitrary number of *blocks* (sets of gates at the same depth) of width at least A, that recur at least B times throughout the circuit. Loosely speaking, we say that an (A, B)-repetitive circuit is *highly repetitive* w.r.t. n parties, if $A \in \Omega(n)$ and $B \in \Omega(n)$.

The most obvious example of this class includes the sequential composition of some (possibly multi-layer) functionality, i.e. $f(f(f(f(\ldots))))$ for some arbitrary f with sufficient width. However, this class also includes many other types of circuits and important functionalities. For example, as we discuss in Sect. 4.3, machine learning model training algorithms (many iterations of gradient descent) are highly repetitive even for large numbers of parties. We also identify block ciphers and collision resistant hash functions as having many iterated rounds; as such functions are likely to be run many times in a large-scale, private computation, they naturally result in highly repetitive circuits for larger numbers of parties. We give formal definition of (A, B)-repetitive circuits in Sect. 4.

Semi-Honest Order-C MPC. Our primary contribution is a semi-honest, honest-majority MPC protocol for highly repetitive circuits with *total computation and communication complexity* $O(|\mathsf{C}|)$. Our protocol only requires communication over point-to-point channels and works in the plain model (i.e., without trusted setup). It achieves unconditional security against $t < n\left(\frac{1}{2} - \frac{2}{\epsilon}\right)$ corruptions, where ϵ is a tunable parameter as in prior works based on PSS.

Our key insight is that the repetitive nature of the circuit can be leveraged to efficiently generate correlated randomness in a way that helps overcome the limitations of PSS. We elaborate on our techniques in Sect. 2.

Malicious Security Compiler. We next consider the case of malicious adversaries. In recent years, significant work [7,16,20,21,25,30,35] has been done on designing efficient malicious security compilers for honest majority MPC. With the exception of [20], all of these works design compilers for protocols based on regular secret sharing (SS) as opposed to PSS. The most recent of these works [7,16,25,35] achieve very small constant multiplicative overhead, and ideally one would like to achieve similar efficiency in the case of PSS-based protocols.

Since our semi-honest protocol is based on PSS, the compilers of [7,16,25,35] are not directly applicable to our protocols. Nevertheless, borrowing upon the insights from [20], we demonstrate that the techniques developed in [7] can in fact be used to design an efficient malicious security compiler for our PSS-based semi-honest protocol. Specifically, our compiler incurs a multiplicative overhead of approximately 1.7–3, depending on the choice of ϵ, over our semi-honest protocol for circuits over large fields (where the field size is exponential in the security parameter).[3] For circuits over smaller fields, the multiplicative overhead incurred is $O(k/\log|\mathbb{F}|)$, where k is the security parameter and $|\mathbb{F}|$ is the field size.

Efficiency. We demonstrate that our protocol is not merely of theoretical interest but is also concretely efficient for various choices of parameters. We give a detailed complexity calculation of our protocols in Sects. 6.2 and 6.3.

For $n = 125$ parties and $t < n/3$, our malicious secure protocol only requires each party to, on average, communicate approximately $3\frac{1}{4}$ *field elements per gate* of a highly repetitive circuit. In contrast, the state-of-the-art [16] (an information-theoretic $O(n|\mathsf{C}|)$ protocol for $t < n/3$) requires each party to communicate approximately $4\frac{2}{3}$ field elements per multiplication gate. Thus, (in theory) we expect our protocol to outperform [16] for circuits with around 75% multiplication gates with just 125 parties. Since the per-party communication in our protocol decreases as the number of parties increase, our protocol is expected to perform better as the number of parties increase.

We confirm our conjecture via a preliminary implementation of our malicious secure protocol and give concrete measurements of running it for up to 300 parties, across multiple network settings. Since state-of-the-art honest-majority MPC protocol have only been tested with smaller numbers of parties, we show that our protocol is comparably efficient even for fewer number of parties. Moreover, our numbers suggest that our protocol would outperform these existing protocols when executed with hundreds or thousands of players at equivalent circuit depths.

Application to Zero-Knowledge Proofs. The *MPC-in-the-head* paradigm of Ishai et al. [28] is a well-known technique for constructing efficient three-round public-coin honest-verifier zero-knowledge proof systems (aka sigma protocols) from (honest-majority) MPC protocols. Such proof systems can be made *non-interactive*, in the random oracle model [3] via the Fiat-Shamir paradigm [14]. Recent works have demonstrated the practical viability of this approach by constructing zero-knowledge proofs [2,5,22,29] where the proof size has linear or sub-linear dependence on the size of the relation circuit.

Our malicious-secure MPC protocol can be used to instantiate the MPC-in-the-head paradigm when the relation circuit has highly repetitive form. The size of the resulting proofs will be comparable to the best-known *linear-sized* proof system constructed via this approach [29]. Importantly, however, it can have more efficient prover and verifier computation time. This is because [29] requires parallel repetition to get negligible soundness, and have computation time linear in the number of simulated players. Our protocol (by virtue of being an Order-C and honest majority protocol), on the other hand, can accommodate massive numbers of (simulated) parties without increasing the protocol simulation time and achieve small soundness error without requiring additional parallel repetition. Finally, we note that sublinear-sized proofs [2] typically require super-linear

[3] We note that for more commonly used corruption thresholds $n/2 > t > n/4$, the overhead incurred by our compiler is somewhere between 2.5–3.

prover time, in which case simulating our protocol may be more computationally efficient for the prover. We leave further exploration of this direction for future work.

Future Directions. Our protocols achieve $O(|\mathsf{C}|)$ complexity for a large class of non-SIMD circuits, namely, highly repetitive circuits. A natural open question is whether it is possible to extend our work to handle other classes of circuits.

Another important direction for future work is to further improve upon the concrete efficiency of our semi-honest $O(|\mathsf{C}|)$ protocol. The multiplicative constant in our protocol complexity is primarily dictated by the tunable parameter ϵ, which is inherent in PSS-based protocols. Thus, achieving improvements on this front will likely require different techniques.

Our malicious security compiler, which builds on ideas from [7], incurs a multiplicative overhead of somewhere between 2.5 and 3, over the semi-honest protocol. Recent works of [16,25] achieve even lower overheads than the compiler of [7]. Another useful direction would be to integrate our ideas with the techniques in [16,25] (possibly for a lower corruption threshold) to obtain more efficient compilers for PSS-based protocols. We leave this for future work.

2 Technical Overview

We begin our technical overview by recalling the key techniques developed in prior works for reducing dependence on the number of parties. We then proceed to describe our main ideas in Sect. 2.2.

2.1 Background

Classical MPC protocols have communication and computation complexity $O(n^2|\mathsf{C}|)$. These protocols, exemplified by [4], leverage Shamir's secret sharing [37] to facilitate distributed computation and require communication for each multiplication gate to enable degree reduction. Typical multiplication subprotocols require that each party send a message to every other party for every multiplication gate, resulting in total communication complexity $O(n^2|\mathsf{C}|)$. As mentioned earlier, two different techniques have been developed to reduce the asymptotic complexity of MPC protocols down to $O(n|\mathsf{C}|)$: efficient multiplication techniques and packed secret sharing.

Efficient Multiplication. In [12], Damgård and Nielsen develop a randomness generation technique that allows for a more efficient multiplication subprotocol. At the beginning of the protocol, the parties generate shares of random values, planning to use one of these values for each multiplication gate. These shares are generated in *batches*, using a subprotocol requiring $O(n^2)$ communication that outputs $\Theta(n)$ shares of random values. This *batched randomness generation* subprotocol can be used to compute $O(|\mathsf{C}|)$ shared values with total complexity $O(n|\mathsf{C}|)$. After locally evaluating a multiplication gate, the players use one of these shared random values to mask the gate output. Players then send the masked gate output to a *leader*, who reconstructs and broadcasts the result back to all players.[4] Finally, players locally remove the mask to get a shared value of the appropriate degree. This multiplication subprotocol has complexity $O(n)$.

Packed Secret Sharing. In [15], Franklin and Yung proposed a vectorized version of Shamir secret sharing called *packed secret sharing* that trades a lower corruption threshold for more efficient representation of secrets. More specifically, their scheme allows a dealer to share a vector of $\Theta(n)$ secrets such that each of the n players still only hold a single field element. Importantly, the resulting shares preserve a SIMD version of the homomorphisms required to run MPC. Specifically, if $X = (x_1, x_2, x_3)$ and $Y = (y_1, y_2, y_3)$ are the vectors that are shared and added or multiplied, the result is a sharing of $X + Y = (x_1 + y_1, x_2 + y_2, x_3 + y_3)$ or $XY = (x_1 y_1, x_2 y_2, x_3 y_3)$ respectively. Like traditional Shamir secret sharing, the degree of the polynomial corresponding to XY is twice that of original packed sharings of X and Y. This allows players to compute over $\Theta(n)$ gates *simultaneously*, provided two properties are satisfied: (1) all of the gates *perform the same operation* and (2) the inputs to each gate *are in identical positions in the respective vectors.* In particular, it is not possible to compute $x_1 y_2$ in the previous example, as x_1 and y_2 are not *aligned.* However, if the circuit has the correct structure, packed secret sharing reduces MPC complexity from $O(n^2|\mathsf{C}|)$ to $O(n|\mathsf{C}|)$.

2.2 Our Approach: Semi-honest Security

A Strawman Protocol. A natural idea towards achieving $O(|\mathsf{C}|)$ MPC is to design a protocol that can take advantage of *both* efficient multiplications and packed secret sharing. As each technique asymptotically shaves off a factor of n, we can expect the resulting protocol to have complexity $O(|\mathsf{C}|)$. A naïve (strawman) protocol combining these techniques might proceed as follows:

- Players engage in a first phase to generate packed shares of random vectors using the batching technique discussed earlier. This subprotocol requires $O(n^2)$ messages to generate $\Theta(n)$ shares of packed random values, each containing $\Theta(n)$ elements. As we need a single random value per multiplication gate, $O(|\mathsf{C}|)$ total messages are sent.
- During the input sharing phase, players generate packed shares of their inputs, distributing shares to all players.
- Players proceed to evaluate the circuit over these packed shares, using a single leader to run the efficient multiplication protocol to reduce the degrees of sharings after multiplication. This multiplication subprotocol requires $O(n)$ communication to evaluate $\Theta(n)$ gates, so the total complexity is $O(|\mathsf{C}|)$.
- Once the outputs have been computed, players broadcast their output shares and reconstruct the output.

[4] The choice of the leader can be rotated amongst the players to divide the total computation.

While natural, this template falls short because the circuit may not satisfy the requirements to perform SIMD computation over packed shares. As mentioned before, packed secret sharing only offers savings if all the simultaneously evaluated gates are the same and all gate inputs are properly aligned. However, this is an unreasonable restriction to impose on the circuits. Indeed, running into this problem, [10,20] show that any circuit can be modified to overcome these limitations, at the cost of a significant blowup in the circuit size, which adversely affects their computation and communication efficiency. (We discuss their approach in more detail later in this section.)

Our Ideas. Without such a circuit transformation, however, it is not immediately clear how to take advantage of packed secret sharing (other than for SIMD circuits). To address this challenge, we devise two conceptual tools, each of which we will "simulate" using existing primitives, as described below:

1. *Differing-operation packed secret sharing*, a variant of packed secret sharing in which different operations can be evaluated for each position in the vector. For example, players holding shares of (x_1, x_2, x_3) and (y_1, y_2, y_3) are unable to compute $(x_1y_1, x_2+y_2, x_3y_3)$. With *differing-operation packed secret sharing*, we imagine the players can generate an operation vector (*e.g.* $(\times, +, \times)$) and apply the corresponding operation to each pair of inputs. Given such a primitive, there would be no need to modify a circuit to ensure that shares are evaluated on the same kind of gate.
2. *A realignment procedure* that allows pre-existing packed secret shares to be modified so previously unaligned vector entries can be moved and aligned properly for continued computation without requiring circuit modification.

We note that highly repetitive circuits are *layered* circuits (that is the inputs to layer $i+1$ of a circuit are all output wires from layer i). For the remainder of this section, we will make the simplifying assumption that circuits contain only multiplication and addition gates and that the circuit is layered. We expand our analysis to cover other gates (e.g. relay gates) in the technical sections.

Simulating Differing-operation Packed Secret Sharing. To realize differing-operation packed secret sharing, we require the parties to compute *both* operations over their input vectors. For instance, if the player hold share of (x_1, x_2, x_3) and (y_1, y_2, y_3) and wish to compute the operation vector $(\times, +, \times)$, they begin by computing both $(x_1 + y_1, x_2 + y_2, x_3 + y_3)$ and (x_1y_1, x_2y_2, x_3y_3). Note that all the entries required for the final result are contained in these vectors, and the players just need to "select" which of the aligned entries will be included in the final result.

Recall that in the multiplication procedure described earlier, the leader reconstructs all masked outputs before resharing them. We modify this procedure to have the leader reconstruct both the sum and product of the input vectors, *i.e.* the unpacked values $x_1 + y_1, x_2 + y_2, x_3 + y_3, x_1y_1, x_2y_2, x_3y_3$ (while masked). The leader then performs this "selection" process, and packs only the required values to get a vector $(x_1y_1, x_2 + y_2, x_3y_3)$, and discards the unused values $x_1 + y_1, x_2y_2, x_3 + y_3$. Shares of this vector are then distributed to the

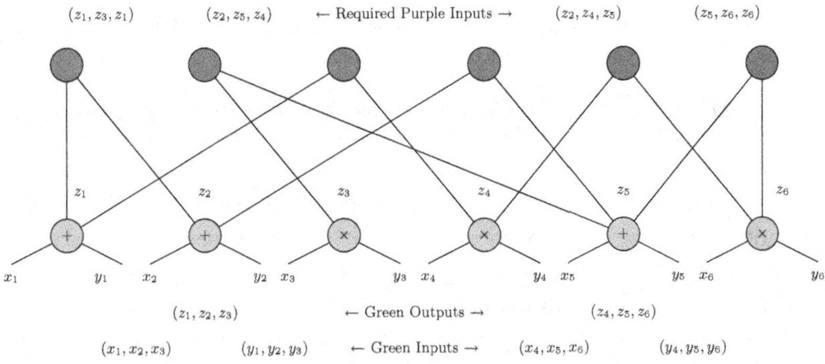

Fig. 1. A simple example pair of circuit layers illustrating the need for differing-operation packed secret sharing and our realignment procedure. Players begin by evaluating both addition and multiplication on each pair of input vectors. However, the resulting vectors are not properly aligned to compute the purple layer. To get properly aligned packings, the vectors $(z_1^{\text{add}}, z_2^{\text{add}}, z_3^{\text{add}}), (z_1^{\text{mult}}, z_2^{\text{mult}}, z_3^{\text{mult}})$ and $(z_4^{\text{add}}, z_5^{\text{add}}, z_6^{\text{add}}), (z_4^{\text{mult}}, z_5^{\text{mult}}, z_6^{\text{mult}})$ are masked and opened to the leader. The leader repacks these values such that the resulting vectors will be properly aligned for computing the purple layer. For instance, in this case the leader would deal shares of $(z_1^{add}, z_3^{mult}, z_1^{add}), (z_2^{add}, z_5^{add}, z_4^{mult}), (z_2^{add}, z_4^{mult}, z_5^{add})$, and $(z_5^{add}, z_6^{mult}, z_6^{mult})$

rest of the players, who unmask their shares. Note that this procedure only has an overhead of 2, as both multiplication and addition must be computed.[5]

Simulating the Realignment Procedure. First note that realigning packed shares may require not only internal permutations of the shares, but also swapping values across vectors. For example, consider the circuit snippet depicted in Fig. 1. The outputs of the green (bottom) layer are not structured correctly to enable computing the purple (top) layer, and require this cross-vector swapping. As such, we require a realignment procedure that takes in all the vectors output by computing a particular circuit layer and outputs multiple properly aligned vectors.

Our realignment procedure builds on the ideas used to realize differing-operation packed secret sharing. Recall that the leader is responsible for reconstructing the masked result values from *all* gates in the previous layer. With access to all these masked values, the leader is not only able to select between a pair of values for each element of a vector (as before), but instead can arbitrarily select the values required from across all outputs. For instance, in the circuit snippet in Fig. 1, the leader has masked, reconstructed values z_i^{add}, z_i^{mult} for $i \in [6]$. Proceeding from left to right of the purple layer, the leader puts the value corresponding to the left input wire of a gate into a vector and the right input wire value into the correctly aligned slot of a corresponding vector. Using

[5] In this toy example only one vector is distributed back to the parties. If layers are approximately of the same size, an approximately equal number of vectors will be returned.

this procedure, the input vectors for the first three gates of the purple layer will be $(z_1^{\text{add}}, z_3^{\text{mult}}, z_1^{\text{add}})$ (left wires) and $(z_2^{\text{add}}, z_5^{\text{add}}, z_4^{\text{mult}})$ (right wires).

Putting it Together. We are now able to refine the strawman protocol into a functional protocol. When evaluating a circuit layer, the players run a protocol to simulate differing-operation packed secret sharing, by evaluating each gate as both an addition gate and multiplication gate. Then, the leader runs the realignment procedure to prepare vectors that are appropriate for the next layer of computation. Finally, the leader secret shares these new vectors, distributing them to all players, and computing the next layer can commence. Conceptually, the protocol uses the leader to "unpack" and "repack" the shares to simultaneously satisfy both requirements of SIMD computation.

Leveraging Circuits with Highly Repetitive Structure. Until this point, we have been using the masking primitive imprecisely, assuming that it could accommodate the procedural changes discussed above without modification. This however, is not the case. Because we need to mask and unmask values while they are in a packed form, *the masks themselves must be generated and handled in packed form.*

Consider the example vectors used to describe differing-operation packed secret sharing, trying to compute $(x_1y_1, x_2 + y_2, x_3y_3)$ given (x_1, x_2, x_3) and (y_1, y_2, y_3). If the same mask (r_1, r_2, r_3) is used to mask both the sum and product of these vectors, privacy will not hold; for example, the leader will open the values $x_1 + y_1 + r_1$ and $x_1y_1 + r_1$, and thus learn something about x_1 and y_1. If (r_1, r_2, r_3) is used to mask addition and (r'_1, r'_2, r'_3) is used for multiplication, there is privacy, but it is unclear how to unmask the result. The shared vector distributed by the leader will correspond to $(x_1y_1 + r_1, x_2 + y_2 + r'_2, x_3y_3 + r_3)$ and the random values cannot be removed with only access to (r_1, r_2, r_3) and (r'_1, r'_2, r'_3). To run the realignment procedure, the same problem arises: the unmasking vectors must have a different structure than the masking vectors, with their relationship determined by the structure of the next circuit layer.

We overcome this problem by making modifications to the batched randomness generation procedure. Instead of generating structurally identical masking and unmasking shares, we instead use the circuit structure to permute the random inputs used during randomness generation so we get outputs of the right form. In the example above, the players will collectively generate the *masking vectors* (r_1, r_2, r_3) and (r'_1, r'_2, r'_3), where each entry is sampled independently at random. The players then generate the *unmasking vector* (r_1, r'_2, r_3) by permuting their inputs to the generation algorithm. For a more complete description of this subprotocol, see Sect. 6.1.

However, it is critical for efficiency that we generate all randomness in *batches.* By permuting the inputs to the randomness generation algorithm, we get $\Theta(n)$ masks that are correctly structured *for a particular part of the circuit structure.* If this particular structure occurs only once in the circuit, only one of the $\Theta(n)$ shares can actually be used during circuit evaluation. In the worst case, if each circuit substructure is *unique*, the resulting randomness generation phase requires $O(n|\mathsf{C}|)$ communication complexity.

This is where the requirement for highly repetitive circuits becomes relevant. This class of circuits guarantees that (1) the circuit layers are wide enough that using packed secret sharing with vectors containing $\Theta(n)$ elements is appropriate, and (2) all $\Theta(n)$ shares of random values generated during the batched randomness generation phase can be used during circuit evaluation. We note that this is a rather simplified version of the definition, we give a formal definition of such circuits in Sect. 4.2.

Non-interactive packed secret sharing from traditional secret shares. Another limitation of the strawman protocol presented above is that the circuit must ensure that all inputs from a single party can be packed into a single packed secret sharing at the beginning of the protocol. We devise a novel strategy (see Sect. 5) that allows parties to secret share each of their inputs individually using regular secret sharing. Parties can then *non-interactively* pack the appropriate inputs according to the circuit structure. This strategy can also be used to efficiently *switch* to $O(n|\mathsf{C}|)$ protocols when parts of the circuit lack highly repetitive structure; the leader omits the repacking step, and the parties compute on traditional secret share until the circuits becomes highly repetitive, at which point they non-interactively re-packing any wire values (see Sect. 4.4).

Existing $O(|\mathsf{C}|)$ protocols like [10] do not explicitly discuss how their protocol handles this input scenario. We posit that this is because there are generic transformations like embedding switching networks at the bottom of the circuit that allow any circuit to be transformed into a circuit in which a player's inputs can be packed together. Unsurprisingly, these transformations significantly increase the size of the circuit. Since [10] is primarily concerned with asymptotic efficiency, such circuit modification strategies are sufficient for their work.

Comparison with [10]. We briefly recall the strategy used in [10], in order to overcome the limitations of working with packed secret sharing that we discussed earlier. They present a generic transformation that transforms any circuit into a circuit that satisfies the following properties:

1. The transformed circuit is layered and each layer only consists of one type of gates.
2. The transformed circuit is such that, when evaluating it over packed secret shares, there is never a need to permute values across different vectors/blocks that are secret shared. While the values within a vector might need to be permuted during circuit evaluation, the transformed circuit has a nice property that only $\log \ell$ (where ℓ is the size of the block) such permutations are needed throughout the circuit.

It is clear that the first property already gets around the first limitation of packed secret sharing. The second property partly resolves the *realignment* requirement from a packed secret sharing scheme by only requiring permutations within a given vector. This is handled in their protocol by generating permuted random blocks that are used for masking and unmasking in the multiplication subprotocol. Since only $\log \ell$ different permutations are required throughout the protocol, they are able to get significant savings by generating random pairs corresponding to the same permutation in *batches*. Our "unpacking" and "repacking" approach can be viewed as a generalization of their technique, in the sense that we enable permutation and duplication of values across different vectors by evaluating the entire layer in one shot.

As noted earlier, this transformation introduces significant overhead to the size of the circuit, and is the primary reason for the large multiplicative and additive terms in the overall complexity of their protocol. As such, it is unclear how to directly use their protocol to compute circuits with highly repetitive structures, while skipping this circuit transformation step. This is primarily because these circuits might not satisfy the first property of the transformed circuit. Moreover, while it is true that the number of possible permutations required in such circuits are very few, they might require permuting values across different vectors, which cannot be handled in their protocol.

2.3 Malicious Security

Significant work has been done in recent years to build compilers that take semi-honest protocols that satisfy common structures and produce efficient malicious protocols, most notably in the "additive attack paradigm" described in [21]. These semi-honest protocols are secure *up to additive attacks*, that is any adversarial strategy is only limited to injecting additive errors onto each of the wires in the circuit that are independent of the "actual" wire values. The current generation of compilers for this class of semi-honest protocols, exemplified by [7,16,25,35], introduce only a small multiplicative overhead (e.g., 2 in the case of [7]) and require only a constant number of additional rounds to perform a single, consolidated check

Genkin et al. showed in [20] (with additional technical details in [19]) that protocols leveraging packed secret sharing schemes do not satisfy the structure required to leverage the compilers designed in the "additive attack paradigm." Instead, they show that most semi-honest protocols that use packed secret sharing are secure up to linear errors, that is the adversary can inject errors onto the output wires of multiplication gates that are *linear functions* of the values contained in the packed sharing of input wires to this gate. We observe that this also holds true for our semi-honest protocol. They present a malicious security compiler for such protocols that introduces a small multiplicative overhead.

To achieve malicious security, we add a new consolidated check onto our semi-honest protocol, reminiscent of the check for circuits over small-fields presented in Sect. 5 of [7]. The resulting maliciously secure protocol has twice the complexity of our semi-honest protocol, plus a constant sized, consolidated check at the end – for the first time matching the efficiency of the compilers designed for protocols secure up to additive attacks.

As in [7], we run two parallel executions of the circuit, maintaining the invariant that for each packed set of wires $z = (z_1, z_2, \dots, z_\ell)$ in C the parties also compute $z' = rz = (rz_1, rz_2, \dots, rz_\ell)$ for a global, secret scalar value r. Once the players have shares of both z and z' for each wire in the circuit, we generate shares of random vectors $\alpha = (\alpha_1, \alpha_2, \ldots, \alpha_\ell)$ (one for each packed sharing vector in the protocol) using a malicious secure sub-protocol and reconstruct the value r. The parties then interactively verify that $r * \alpha * z = \alpha * z'$. Importantly, this check can be carried out simultaneously for all packed wires in the circuit, *i.e.* $r * \sum_{i \in C} \alpha_i * z_i = \sum_{i \in C} \alpha_i * z'_i$. This simplified check relies heavily on the malicious security of the randomness generation sub-protocol. Because of the structure of linear attacks and the fact that α was honestly secret-shared, multiplying z and z' with α injects linear errors chosen by the adversary that are monomials in α only. That is, the equation becomes

$$r * \sum_{i \in C} (\alpha_i * z_i + E(\alpha)) = \sum_{i \in C} (\alpha_i * z'_i + E'(\alpha))$$

for adversarially chosen linear functions E and E'. Because α is independent of r and r is applied to the left hand side of this equation only at the end, this check will only pass if $r * E(\alpha) = E'(\alpha)$. For any functions $E(\cdot), E'(\cdot)$ this only happen if either (1) both are the zero function (in which case there are no errors), or (2) with probability $\frac{1}{|\mathbb{F}|}$. Hence, this technique can also be used with packed secret sharing to get an efficient malicious security compiler.

3 Preliminaries

Model and Notation. We consider a set of parties $\mathcal{P} = \{P_1, \ldots, P_n\}$ in which each party provides inputs to the functionality, participates in the evaluation protocol, and receives an output. We denote an arbitrarily chosen special party P_{leader} for each layer (of the circuit) who will have a special role in the protocol; we note that the choice of P_{leader} may change in each layer to better distribute computation and communication. Each pair of parties are able to communicate over point-to-point private channels.

We consider a functionality that is represented as a circuit C, with maximum width w and total total depth d. We visualize the circuits in a bottom-up setting (like in Merkle trees), where the input gates are at the bottom of the circuit and the output gates are at the top. As we will see later in the definition of highly repetitive circuits, we work with *layered circuits*, which comprise of layers such that the output of layer i are only used as input for the gates in layer $i+1$.

We consider security against a static adversary Adv that corrupts $t \leq n(\frac{1}{2} - \frac{2}{\epsilon})$ players, where ϵ is a tunable parameter of the system. As we will be working with both a packed secret sharing scheme and regular threshold secret sharing scheme, we require additional notation. We denote the packing constant for our protocol as $\ell = \frac{n}{\epsilon}$. Additionally, we will denote the threshold of our packed secret sharing scheme as $D = t + 2\ell - 1$. We will denote vectors of packed values with **bold** alphabets, for instance $\mathbf{x}$. Packed secret shares of a vector $\mathbf{x}$ with respect to degree D are denoted $[\mathbf{x}]$ and with respect to degree $2D$ as $\langle \mathbf{x} \rangle$. We let $e_1, \ldots, e_\ell$ be the fixed x-coordinates on the polynomial used for packed secret sharing, where the ℓ secrets will be stored, and $\alpha_1, \ldots \alpha_n$ be the fixed x-coordinates corresponding to the shares of the parties. For regular threshold secret sharing, we will only require shares w.r.t. degree $t + \ell$. We use the *square bracket* notation to denote a secret sharing w.r.t. degree $t + \ell$. We note that we work with a slightly modified sharing algorithm of the Shamir's secret sharing scheme (see Sect. 5 for details).

4 Highly Repetitive Circuits

In this section, we formalize the class of highly repetitive circuits and discuss some examples of naturally occurring highly repetitive circuits.

4.1 Wire Configuration

We start by formally defining a *gate block*, which is the minimum unit over which we will reason.

Definition 1 (Gate Block). *We call a set of j gates that are all on the same layer a gate block. We say the size of a gate block is j.*

An additional non-standard functionality we require is an explicit wire mapping function. Recall from the technical overview that the leader must repack values according to the structure of the next layer. To reason formally over this procedure, we define the function $\mathsf{WireConfiguration}$, which takes in two blocks of gates block_{m+1} and block_m, such that the output wires of the gates in block_m feed as input to the gates in block_{m+1}. $\mathsf{WireConfiguration}$ outputs two ordered arrays $\mathsf{LeftInputs}$ and $\mathsf{RightInputs}$ that contain the indices corresponding to the left input and right input of each gate in block_{m+1} respectively. In general, we can say that $\mathsf{WireConfiguration}(\mathsf{block}_{m+1}, \mathsf{block}_m)$ will output a correct alignment for block_{m+1}. This is because for all values $j \in [|\mathsf{block}_{m+1}|]$, if the values corresponding to the wire $\mathsf{LeftInputs}[j]$ and $\mathsf{RightInputs}[j]$ are aligned, then computing block_{m+1} is possible. We describe the functionality for $\mathsf{WireConfiguration}$ in Fig. 2. It is easy to see that the blocks $\mathsf{block}_{m+1}, \mathsf{block}_m$ must lie on consecutive layers in the circuit. We say that a pair of gate blocks is *equivalent* to another pair of gate blocks, if the outcome of $\mathsf{WireConfiguration}$ on both pairs is identical.

4.2 (A, B)-Repetitive Circuits

With notation firmly in hand, we can now formalize the class of (A, B)-repetitive circuits, where A, B are the parameters that we explain next. Highly repetitive circuits are a subset of (A, B)-repetitive circuits, which we will define later.

We define an (A, B)-repetitive circuit using a partition function part that decomposes the circuit into blocks of gates, where a block consists of gates on the same layer. Let $\{\mathsf{block}^{\mathsf{child}}_{m,j}\}$ be the output of this partition function, where m indicates the layer of the circuit corresponding to the block and j is its index within layer m. Informally speaking, an (A, B)-repetitive circuit is one that satisfies the following properties:

The Function $\mathsf{WireConfiguration}(\mathsf{block}_{m+1}, \mathsf{block}_m)$

1. Initialize two ordered arrays $\mathsf{LeftInputs} = [\,]$ and $\mathsf{RightInputs} = [\,]$, each with capacity $|\mathsf{block}_{m+1}|$.
2. For a gate g, let $l(g) = (j, \mathsf{type})$ denote the index j and type of the gate in block block_m that feeds the left input of g. Similarly, let $r(g) = (j, \mathsf{type})$ denote the right input gate index and type of g. For gates with fan-in one, *i.e.* relay gates, $r(g) = 0$. For each gate g_j in block_{m+1}, we set $\mathsf{LeftInputs}[j] = l(g_j)$ and $\mathsf{RightInputs}[j] = r(g_j)$
3. Output $\mathsf{LeftInputs}, \mathsf{RightInputs}$.

Fig. 2. A function that computes a proper alignment for evaluating block_{m+1}

1. Each block $\mathsf{block}_{m,j}$ consists of at least A gates.
2. For each pair $(\mathsf{block}_{m,j}, \mathsf{block}_{m+1,j})$, all the gates in $\mathsf{block}_{m+1,j}$ only take in wires that are output wires of gates in $\mathsf{block}_{m,j}$. And the output wires of all the gates in $\mathsf{block}_{m,j}$ only go an input to the gates in $\mathsf{block}_{m+1,j}$.
3. For each pair $(\mathsf{block}_{m,j}, \mathsf{block}_{m+1,j})$, there exist at least B other pairs with identical wiring between the two blocks.

We now give a formal definition.

Definition 2 ((A, B)-Repetitive Circuits). *We say that a layered circuit* C *with depth* d *is called an* (A, B)*-repetitive circuit if there exists a value* $\sigma \geq 1$ *and a partition function* part *which on input* layer_m *(*m^{th} *layer in* C*), outputs disjoint blocks of the form* $\{\mathsf{block}_{m,j}\}_{j\in[\sigma]} \leftarrow \mathsf{part}(m, \mathsf{layer_m})$, *such that the following holds, for each* $m \in [d], j \in [\sigma]$*:*

1. ***Minimum Width:*** *Each* $\mathsf{block}_{m,j}$ *consists of at least* A *gates.*
2. ***Bijective Mapping:*** *All the gates in* $\mathsf{block}_{m,j}$ *only take inputs from the gates in* $\mathsf{block}_{m-1,j}$ *and only give outputs to gates in* $\mathsf{block}_{m+1,j}$.
3. ***Minimum Repetition:*** *For each* $(\mathsf{block}_{m+1,j}, \mathsf{block}_{m,j})$, *there exist pairs* $(m_1, j_1) \neq (m_2, j_2) \neq \ldots \neq (m_B, j_B) \neq (m, j)$ *such that for each* $i \in [B]$, $\mathsf{WireConfiguration}(\mathsf{block}_{m_i+1,j_i}, \mathsf{block}_{m_i,j_i}) = \mathsf{WireConfiguration}(\mathsf{block}_{m+1,j}, \mathsf{block}_{m,j})$.

Intuitively, this says that a circuit is built from an arbitrary number of gate blocks with sufficient size, and that all blocks are repeated often throughout the circuit. Unlike the layer focused example in the introduction, this definition allows layers to comprise of multiple blocks. In fact, these blocks can even *interact* by sharing input values. The limitation of this interaction, captured by the $\mathsf{WireConfiguration}$ check, is that the interacting inputs must come from predictable indices in the previous layer and must have the same gate type.

We also consider a relaxed variant of (A, B)-repetitive circuits, which we call (A, B, C, D)-repetitive circuits. These circuits differ from (A, B)-repetitive circuits in that they allow for a relaxation of the minimum width and repetition requirement. In particular, in an (A, B, C, D)-repetitive circuit, it suffices for all but C blocks to satisfy the minimum width requirement and similarly, all but D

blocks are required to satisfy the minimum repetition requirement. In this work, we focus on the following kind of (A, B, C, D)-repetitive circuits.

Definition 3 (Highly Repetitive Circuits). *We say that (A, B, C, D)-repetitive circuits are highly repetitive w.r.t. n parties, if $A, B \in \Omega(n)$ and C, D are some constants.*

We note that defining a class of circuits w.r.t. to the number of parties that will evaluate the circuit might a priori seem unusual. However, this is common throughout the literature attempting to achieve $O(|\mathsf{C}|)$ MPC that use packed secret sharing. For example, the protocols in [10,11,20] achieve $\tilde{O}(|C|)$ communication for circuits that are $\Omega(n)$ gates wide. Similarly, our work achieves $O(|C|)$ communication and computation for circuits that are $(\Omega(n), \Omega(n), C, D)$-repetitive, where C and D are constants. Alternatively, if the number of input wires are equal to the number of participating parties, we can re-phrase the above definition w.r.t. the number of input wires in a circuit.

It might be useful to see the above definition as putting a limit on the number of parties for which a circuit is highly repetitive: any (A, B, C, D)-repetitive circuit, is highly repetitive for upto $\texttt{min}(O(A), O(B))$ parties. While our MPC protocol can work for any (A, B, C, D)-repetitive circuit, it has $O(|\mathsf{C}|)$ complexity only for highly repetitive circuits. In the next subsection we give examples of such circuits that are highly repetitive for a reasonable range of parties.

For the remainder of this paper, we will use w denote the maximum width of the circuit C, w_m to denote the width of the mth layer and $w_{m,j}$ to denote the width of $\mathsf{block}_{m,j}$.

4.3 Examples of Highly Repetitive Circuits

We give brief overviews of three functionalities with circuit representations that are highly repetitive for up to a large number of parties. Extended discussion of these applications is included in the full version of this paper.

Machine Learning. Machine learning algorithms extract trends from large datasets to facilitate accurate prediction in new, unknown circumstances. A common family of algorithms for training machine learning models is "gradient descent." This algorithm iteratively reduces the models error by making small, greedy changes, terminating when the model quality plateaus. When run with MPC, the number of iterations must be data oblivious and cover the worst case scenario. For a more complete description of gradient descent training algorithms, and their adaptation to MPC, see [31].

It is difficult to compute the exact number of gates for privacy-preserving model training in prior work. In one of the few concrete estimates, Gascón et al. [18] realize coordinate gradient descent training algorithms with approximately 10^{11} gates, which would take 3000 GB to store [32]. Subsequent work instead built a library of sub-circuits that could be loaded as needed. As the amount of data used to train models continues to grow, circuit sizes will continue to increase. While we are not able to accurately estimate the number of gates for this kind of circuit, we can still establish that their structure is highly repetitive; gradient decent algorithm is many iterations of the same functionality. In the implementation of Mohassel et al. [31], the default configuration for training is 10000 iterations, deep enough to accommodate massive numbers of players. Indeed, in the worst case the depth of a gradient descent algorithm must be linear in the input size. This is because gradient descent usually uses a *batching* technique, in which the input data is partitioned into batches and run through the algorithm one at a time.

The width of gradient descent training algorithms is usually roughly proportional to the dimension of the dataset, which is usually quite high for interesting applications. We note that if the width of the data is no wide enough, the natural parallelism of gradient decent training algorithms can be leveraged to provide more width: it is typical to use a *random restart* strategy to avoid getting trapped at local minima, each of which can be execute in parallel.

Table 1. Size of the highly repetitive circuits we consider in this work. We compile these functions into $\mathbb{F}_2$ circuits using Frigate [33] (containerized by [26]). The 64 iterations of the compression function for SHA256 comprise 77% of the gates and the round function of AES comprises 88% of the gates. Both of these metrics are computed for a single block on input.

Circuit	Gates ($\mathbb{F}_2$)	Iterative Loops	Gates per Loop	Percent Repeated Structure
SHA256 (1 Block)	119591	64	1437	77%
AES128 (1 Block)	7458	10	656	88%
Gradient Descent	—	$\geq$ 10000	—	$\sim$ 100%

Cryptographic Hash Functions. All currently deployed cryptographic hash functions rely on iterating over a round function, each iteration of which round function is (typically) *structurally identical.* Moreover, the vast majority of the gates in the circuit representation of a hash function are contained within the iterations of the round function.

Consider SHA256 [1], one of the most widely deployed hash functions; given its common use in applications like Bitcoin [34] and ECDSA [17], SHA256 is an important building block of MPC applications. SHA256 contains 64 rounds of its inner function, with other versions that use larger block size containing 80 rounds. We compiled SHA256 for a single block of input into a circuit using Frigate [33]. As can be seen in Table 1, 77% of all the gates in the compiled SHA256 are repeated structure, that structure repeating at least 64 times. We note that these results were for hashing only a single block of input. When additional blocks of data must be hashed, the percentage of the circuit that is repeated structure will be higher. For example, if there are as few as 10 blocks of input, the circuit is already 97% repeated structure. Common applications of hash functions, like computing a Merkle tree over player inputs, run hash functions in parallel, ensuring there is sufficient width for accommodate large numbers of parties.

Block Ciphers. Modern block ciphers, similar to cryptographic functions, are iterative by nature. For example, Advanced Encryption Standard uses either 10, 12, or 14 iterations of its round function, depending on key length. Performing a similar analysis as with SHA256, we identified that 88% of the gates in AES128 are part of this repeated structure when encrypting a single block of input. Just as with hash functions, more blocks of input lead to increased percentage repeated structure; with 10 blocks of input, 98% of the gates are repeated structure.

4.4 Protocol Switching for Circuits with Partially Repeated Structure

Hash functions and symmetric key cryptography are not comprised of 100% repeated structure. When structure is not repeated, the batched randomness generation step cannot be run efficiently. In the worst case, if a particular piece of structure is only present once in the circuit, $O(n^2)$ messages will be used to generate only a single packet secret share of size $\Theta(n)$. If $0 \leq p \leq 1$ is the fraction of the circuit that is repeated, our protocol has efficiency $O(p|\mathsf{C}| + (1-p)n|\mathsf{C}|)$.

We note that our protocol has worse constants than [7] and [16] when run on the non-repeated portion of the circuit. Specifically, our protocol requires communication for all gates, rather than just multiplication gates. As we are trying to push the constants as low as possible, it would be ideal to run the most efficient known protocols for the portions of the circuit that are linear in the number of players. To do this, we note that our protocol can support mid-evaluation protocol switching.

Recall our simple non-interactive technique to transform normal secret shares into packed secret shares, presented in Sect. 5. This technique can be used in the middle of protocol execution to switch between a traditional, efficient, $O(n|\mathsf{C}|)$ protocol and our protocol. Once the portion of the circuit without repeated structure is computed using another efficient protocol, the players can pause to properly structure their secret shares and non-interactively pack them. The players can then evaluate the circuit using our protocol. If another patch of non-repeated structure is encountered, the leader can reconstruct and re-share normal shares as necessary. Importantly, since all these protocols are linear, it's still possible to use the malicious security compiler of [7].

5 A Non-interactive Protocol for Packing Regular Secret Shares

We now describe a novel, non-interactive transformation that allows a set of parties holding shares corresponding to ℓ secrets $[s_1], \ldots, [s_\ell]$ to compute a single packed secret sharing of the vector $\mathbf{v} = (s_1, \ldots, s_\ell)$. This protocol makes a non-black-box use of Shamir secret sharing to accomplish this non-interactive. As discussed in the technical overview, to achieve efficiency, our protocol computes over packed shares. But, if each player follows the naïve strategy of just packing all their own inputs into a single vector, the values may not be properly aligned for computation. This non-interactive functionality lets players simply share their inputs using Shamir secret sharing (using degree $t+\ell$ polynomials), and then locally pack the values in a way that guarantees alignment.

Let $p_1, \dots, p_\ell$ be the degree $t+\ell$ polynomials that were used for secret sharing secrets $s_1 \dots, s_\ell$ respectively. We require each $p_i(z)$ (for $i \in [\ell]$) to be of the form $s_i + q_i(z) \prod_{j=1}^{\ell}(z - e_j)$, where q_i is a degree t polynomial. Then each party P_j (for $j \in [n]$) holds shares $p_1(\alpha_j), \dots, p_\ell(\alpha_j)$.

Given these shares, each party P_j computes a packed secret share of the vector $(s_1, \dots, s_\ell)$ as follows - $\mathcal{F}_{\textsf{SS-to-PSS}}(\{p_i(\alpha_j)\}_{i\in[\ell]}) = \sum_{i=1}^{\ell} p_i(\alpha_j) L_i(\alpha_j) = p(\alpha_j)$, where $L_i(\alpha_j) = \prod_{j=1, j\neq i}^{\ell} \frac{(\alpha_i - e_j)}{(e_i - e_j)}$ is the Lagrange interpolation constant and p corresponds to a new degree $D = t + 2\ell - 1$ polynomial for the packed secret sharing of vector $\mathbf{v} = (s_1, \dots, s_\ell)$.

Lemma 1. *For each $i \in [\ell]$, let $s_i \in \mathbb{F}$ be secret shared using a degree $t+\ell$ polynomial p_i of the form $s_i + q_i(z) \prod_{j=1}^{\ell}(z - e_j)$, where q_i is a degree t polynomial and $e_1, \dots, e_\ell$ are some pre-determined field elements. Then for each $j \in [n]$, $\mathcal{F}_{\textsf{SS-to-PSS}}(\{p_i(\alpha_j)\}_{i\in[\ell]})$ outputs the jth share corresponding to a valid packed secret sharing of the vector $\mathbf{v} = (s_1, \dots, s_\ell)$, w.r.t. a degree-$D = t + 2\ell - 1$ polynomial.*

Proof. For each $i \in [\ell]$, let $p_i(z)$ be the polynomial used for secret sharing the secret s_i. We know that $p_i(z) = s_i + q_i(z) \prod_{j=1}^{\ell}(z - e_j)$, where q_i is a degree t polynomial. Let $p'_i(z) = q_i(z) \prod_{j=1}^{\ell}(z - e_j)$ and let $p(z)$ be the new polynomial corresponding to the packed secret sharing. From the description of $\mathcal{F}_{\textsf{SS-to-PSS}}$, it follows that:

$$p(z) = \sum_{i=1}^{\ell} p'_i(z) L_i(z) + s_i L_i(z) = \sum_{i=1}^{\ell} p'_i(z) \prod_{j=1, j\neq i}^{\ell} \frac{(z - e_j)}{(e_i - e_j)} + \sum_{i=1}^{\ell} s_i L_i(z)$$
$$= \sum_{i=1}^{\ell} q_i(z) \prod_{j=1, j\neq i}^{\ell} \frac{(z - e_j)}{(e_i - e_j)} \prod_{j=1}^{\ell}(z - e_j) + \sum_{i=1}^{\ell} s_i L_i(z)$$

Let $q'_i(z) = q_i(z) \prod_{j=1, j\neq i}^{\ell} \frac{(z - e_j)}{(e_i - e_j)}$, then,

$$p(z) = \sum_{i=1}^{\ell} q'_i(z) \prod_{j=1}^{\ell}(z - e_j) + \sum_{i=1}^{\ell} s_i L_i(z) = q(z) \prod_{j=1}^{\ell}(z - e_j) + \sum_{i=1}^{\ell} s_i L_i(z)$$

where $q(z) = \sum_{i=1}^{\ell} q'_i(z)$ is a degree $t + \ell - 1$ polynomial and hence $p(z)$ is a degree $D = t + 2\ell - 1$ polynomial. It is now easy to see that for each $i \in [\ell]$, $p(e_i) = s_i$. Hence $\mathcal{F}_{\textsf{SS-to-PSS}}$ computes a valid packed secret sharing of the vector $\mathbf{v} = (s_1, \dots, s_\ell)$.

6 Our Order-C Protocols

6.1 Sub-Functionalities and Protocols

Both our semi-honest and maliciously secure protocols depend on a number of sub-functionalities and protocols which we present in this section.

$f_{\mathsf{pack-input}}$ **functionality.** This functionality takes in the inputs of the players and outputs packed secret shares. Using the circuit information, players can run $\mathsf{WireConfiguration}(\mathsf{block}_{0,j}, \mathsf{block}_{1,j})$ for each $j \in [\sigma]$ to determine the alignment of vectors required to compute the first layer of the circuit. Because each $\mathsf{block}_{1,j}$ in the circuit contains $w_{1,j}/\ell$ gates, the protocol outputs $2w_1/\ell = \sum_{j\in[\sigma]} w_{1,j}$ properly aligned packed secret shares, each containing ℓ values. A detailed description of this functionality appears in Fig. 3. The description of a protocol that makes use of our non-interactive packing protocol from Sect. 5, that securely realizes this functionality is deferred to the full-version of this paper.

The functionality $f_{\mathsf{pack-input}}(\mathcal{P} := \{P_1, \ldots, P_n\},)$

The functionality $f_{\mathsf{pack-input}}$, running with parties $\{P_1, \ldots, P_n\}$ and the ideal adversary Sim proceeds as follows:

- It receives inputs $x_1, \ldots, x_M \in \mathbb{F}$ from the respective parties and the layers $\mathsf{layer}_0, \mathsf{layer}_1$ from all parties.
- It computes $\{\mathsf{block}_{0,j}\}_{j\in[\sigma]} \leftarrow \mathsf{part}(0, \mathsf{layer}_0)$ and $\{\mathsf{block}_{1,j}\}_{j\in[\sigma]} \leftarrow \mathsf{part}(1, \mathsf{layer}_1)$.
- For each $j \in [\sigma]$, it computes $\mathsf{LeftInputs}_j, \mathsf{RightInputs}_j = \mathsf{WireConfiguration}(\mathsf{block}_{1,j}, \mathsf{block}_{0,j})$.
- For each $j \in [\sigma]$ and $q \in [w_{1,j}/\ell]$,
  - Set $\mathbf{x}^{j,q} = (x_{\mathsf{LeftInputs}_j[i]})_{i\in\{(q-1)\ell+1,\ldots,q\ell\}}$ and $\mathbf{y}^{j,q} = (x_{\mathsf{RightInputs}_j[i]})_{i\in\{(q-1)\ell+1,\ldots,q\ell\}}$.
  - Receives from Sim, the shares $[\mathbf{x}^{j,q}]_{\mathcal{A}}, [\mathbf{y}^{j,q}]_{\mathcal{A}}$ of the corrupted parties for the input vectors $\mathbf{x}_{j,q}, \mathbf{y}_{j,q}$.
  - It computes shares $[\mathbf{x}^{j,q}] \leftarrow \mathsf{pshare}(\mathbf{x}^{j,q}, \mathcal{A}, [\mathbf{x}^{j,q}]_{\mathcal{A}}, D)$ and $[\mathbf{y}^{j,q}] \leftarrow \mathsf{pshare}(\mathbf{y}^{j,q}, \mathcal{A}, [\mathbf{y}^{j,q}]_{\mathcal{A}}, D)$ and sends them to the parties.

Fig. 3. Packed secret sharing of all inputs functionality

$f_{\mathsf{corr-rand}}$ **functionality.** This functionality generates correlated randomness for our main construction. Recall from the technical overview that the values in the packed secret shares of random values must be generated according to the circuit structure. More specifically, the unmasking values (degree D shares) for some $\mathsf{block}_{m+1,j}$ must be aligned according to the output of $\mathsf{WireConfiguration}(\mathsf{block}_{m+1,j}, \mathsf{block}_{m,j})$.

Before describing the functionality, we quickly note the number of shares generated, as it is somewhat non-standard. Let $w_{m,j}$ be the number of gates in $\mathsf{block}_{m,j}$ and $w_{m+1,j}$ be the number of gates in $\mathsf{block}_{m+1,j}$. As noted in the technical overview, our protocol treats each gate as though it performs *all* operations (relay, addition and multiplication). This lets the players evaluate different operations on each value in a packed secret share. Each of these operations must be masked with different randomness to ensure privacy. As such, the functionality generates $3w_{m,j}/\ell$ shares of uniformly random vectors. To facilitate unmasking after the leader has run the realignment procedure, the functionality must generate shares of vectors with values selected from these $3w_{m,j}/\ell$ uniformly random

The functionality $f_{\mathsf{corr-rand}}(\{P_1,\ldots,P_n\})$

The n-party functionality $f_{\mathsf{corr-rand}}$, running with parties $\{P_1,\ldots,P_n\}$ and the ideal adversary Sim proceeds as follows:

- Each honest party sends $\mathsf{block}_{m+1,j}$, $\mathsf{block}_{m,j}$ to the functionality.
- The ideal simulator Sim sends $\{\mathbf{u}_i^{q,\mathsf{left}},\mathbf{u}_i^{q,\mathsf{right}}\}_{q\in[w_{m+1}/\ell]}$ and $\{\mathbf{v}_i^{q,\mathsf{mult}},\mathbf{v}_i^{q,\mathsf{add}},\mathbf{v}_i^{q,\mathsf{relay}}\}_{q\in[w_{m,j}/\ell]}$ for each corrupt party $i\in\mathcal{A}$.
- The functionality $f_{\mathsf{corr-rand}}$ samples random vectors $(\{\mathbf{r}^{q,\mathsf{mult}},\mathbf{r}^{q,\mathsf{add}},\mathbf{r}^{q,\mathsf{relay}}\}_{q\in[w_{m,j}/\ell]})\in\mathbb{F}^{\ell\times 3w_{m,j}/\ell}$ of length ℓ and does the following:
  - For each $q\in[w_{m+1,j}/\ell]$, it sets $[\mathbf{r}^{q,\mathsf{left}}]_{\mathcal{A}}=\{\mathbf{u}_i^{q,\mathsf{left}}\}_{i\in\mathcal{A}}$ and $[\mathbf{r}^{q,\mathsf{right}}]_{\mathcal{A}}=\{\mathbf{u}_i^{q,\mathsf{right}}\}_{i\in\mathcal{A}}$. .
  - For each $q\in[w_{m,j}/\ell]$, it sets $\langle\mathbf{r}^{q,\mathsf{mult}}\rangle_{\mathcal{A}}=\{\mathbf{v}_i^{q,\mathsf{mult}}\}_{i\in\mathcal{A}}$ and $\langle\mathbf{r}^{q,\mathsf{add}}\rangle_{\mathcal{A}}=\{\mathbf{v}_i^{q,\mathsf{add}}\}_{i\in\mathcal{A}}$ and $\langle\mathbf{r}^{q,\mathsf{relay}}\rangle_{\mathcal{A}}=\{\mathbf{v}_i^{q,\mathsf{relay}}\}_{i\in\mathcal{A}}$.
  - It computes $\mathsf{LeftInputs},\mathsf{RightInputs}=\mathsf{WireConfiguration}(\mathsf{block}_{m\to m+1})$.
  - For each $q\in[w_{m+1,j}]$ and for each $k\in[\ell]$, let $e_{\mathsf{left}}=\mathsf{LeftInputs}[(q-1)\ell+i]$ and $e_{\mathsf{right}}=\mathsf{RightInputs}[(q-1)\ell+i]$ and set $\mathbf{r}^{q,\mathsf{left}}[k]=\mathbf{r}^{\lfloor e_{\mathsf{left}}/\ell\rfloor,\mathsf{GateType}_k}[e_{\mathsf{left}}-\lfloor e_{\mathsf{left}}/\ell\rfloor]$ and $\mathbf{r}^{q,\mathsf{right}}[k]=\mathbf{r}^{\lfloor e_{\mathsf{right}}/\ell\rfloor,\mathsf{GateType}_k}[e_{\mathsf{right}}-\lfloor e_{\mathsf{right}}/\ell\rfloor]$, where $\mathsf{GateType}_k=\mathsf{mult}$ if gate k on layer m is a multiplication gate, else if it is an addition gate then $\mathsf{GateType}_k=\mathsf{add}$ and for relay gates, $\mathsf{GateType}_k=\mathsf{relay}$.
  - For each $q\in[w_{m,j}/\ell]$, it runs $\mathsf{pshare}(\mathbf{r}^{q,\mathsf{mult}},\mathcal{A},\langle\mathbf{v}^{q,\mathsf{mult}}\rangle_{\mathcal{A}},2D)$, $\mathsf{pshare}(\mathbf{r}^{q,\mathsf{add}},\mathcal{A},\langle\mathbf{v}^{q,\mathsf{add}}\rangle_{\mathcal{A}},2D)$, $\mathsf{pshare}(\mathbf{r}^{q,\mathsf{relay}},\mathcal{A},\langle\mathbf{v}^{q,\mathsf{relay}}\rangle_{\mathcal{A}},2D)$.
  - For each $q\in[w_{m+1,j}/\ell]$, it runs $\mathsf{pshare}(\mathbf{r}^{q,\mathsf{left}},\mathcal{A},[\mathbf{u}^{q,\mathsf{left}}]_{\mathcal{A}},D)$ and $\mathsf{pshare}(\mathbf{r}^{q,\mathsf{right}},\mathcal{A},[\mathbf{u}^{q,\mathsf{right}}]_{\mathcal{A}},D)$.
- It hands each honest party P_i its shares $\{\mathbf{u}_i^{q,\mathsf{left}},\mathbf{u}_i^{q,\mathsf{right}}\}_{q\in[w_{m+1,j}/\ell]}$ and $\{\mathbf{v}_i^{q,\mathsf{mult}},\mathbf{v}_i^{q,\mathsf{add}},\mathbf{v}_i^{q,\mathsf{relay}}\}_{q\in[w_{m,j}/\ell]}$.

Fig. 4. Random share generation functionality

vectors. This selection is governed by $\mathsf{WireConfiguration}(\mathsf{block}_{m+1,j},\mathsf{block}_{m,j})$. As there are $w_{m+1,j}$ gates in $\mathsf{block}_{m+1,j}$, the functionality will output $2w_{m+1,j}/\ell$ of these unmasking shares (with degree D). In total, this is $(3w_{m,j}+2w_{m+1,j})/\ell$ packed secret sharings. A detailed description of this functionality appears in Fig. 4. The description of a protocol that securely realizes this functionality is deferred to the full-version of our paper.

π_{layer} **Protocol.** This sub-protocol takes properly aligned input vectors $\left\{[\mathbf{x}_1^{j,q}],[\mathbf{y}_1^{j,q}]\right\}_{j\in[\sigma],q\in[w_{m,j}/\ell]}$ held by a set of parties, and computes packed shares$[\mathbf{z}^{j,q,\mathsf{left}}]$ and $[\mathbf{z}^{j,q,\mathsf{right}}]$, for each $j\in[\sigma]$ and $q\in[w_{m+1,j}/\ell]$ that can be used to evaluate the next layer. We note that for notational convenience, this protocol takes as input $\left\{[\mathbf{x}_1^{j,q}],[\mathbf{y}_1^{j,q}],[\mathbf{x}_2^{j,q}],[\mathbf{y}_2^{j,q}]\right\}_{j\in[\sigma],q\in[w_{m,j}/\ell]}$ instead of just $\left\{[\mathbf{x}_1^{j,q}],[\mathbf{y}_1^{j,q}]\right\}_{j\in[\sigma],q\in[w_{m,j}/\ell]}$. This is because in our maliciously secure protocol, we invoke this sub-protocol for evaluating the circuit on actual inputs as well as on randomized inputs. When computing on actual inputs, we set $\mathbf{x}_1^{j,q}=\mathbf{x}_2^{j,q}$ and $\mathbf{y}_1^{j,q}=\mathbf{y}_2^{j,q}$ and when computing on randomized inputs, we set $\mathbf{x}_2^{j,q}=\mathbf{r}\mathbf{x}_1^{j,q}$ and $\mathbf{y}_2^{j,q}=\mathbf{r}\mathbf{y}_1^{j,q}$. A detailed description of this sub-protocol appears in Fig. 5.

The protocol $\pi_{\mathsf{layer}}(\{P_1,\ldots,P_n\})$

Input: The parties $\{P_i\}_{i\in[n]}$ hold packed secret sharings $\left\{[\mathbf{x}_1^{j,q}],[\mathbf{y}_1^{j,q}],[\mathbf{x}_2^{j,q}],[\mathbf{y}_2^{j,q}]\right\}_{j\in[\sigma],q\in[w_{m,j}/\ell]}$ and configuration of layers layer_m and layer_{m+1}.
Protocol: For each $j\in[\sigma]$, the parties proceed as follows:

— They invoke $f_{\mathsf{corr-rand}}$ to obtain packed secret shares: $\{[\mathbf{r}^{j,q,\mathsf{left}}],[\mathbf{r}^{j,q,\mathsf{right}}]\}_{j,q\in[w_{m+1,j}/\ell]},\{\langle\mathbf{r}^{j,q,\mathsf{mult}}\rangle,\langle\mathbf{r}^{j,q,\mathsf{add}}\rangle,\langle\mathbf{r}^{j,q,\mathsf{relay}}\rangle\}_{q\in[w_{m,j}/\ell]}$.
— For each $q\in[w_{m,j}/\ell]$, the parties locally compute the following:
$\langle\mathbf{x}_1^{j,q}\cdot\mathbf{y}_2^{j,q}+\mathbf{r}^{j,q,\mathsf{mult}}\rangle=[\mathbf{x}_1^{j,q}]\cdot[\mathbf{y}_2^{j,q}]+\langle\mathbf{r}^{j,q,\mathsf{mult}}\rangle$
$\langle\mathbf{x}_1^{j,q}+\mathbf{y}_1^{j,q}+\mathbf{r}^{j,q,\mathsf{add}}\rangle=[\mathbf{x}_1^{j,q}]+[\mathbf{y}_1^{j,q}]+\langle\mathbf{r}^{j,q,\mathsf{add}}\rangle$
$\langle\mathbf{x}_1^{j,q}+\mathbf{r}^{j,q,\mathsf{relay}}\rangle=[\mathbf{x}_1^{j,q}]+\langle\mathbf{r}^{j,q,\mathsf{relay}}\rangle$
— All the parties send their shares to the designated party P_{leader} for that layer.
— Party P_{leader} reconstructs all the shares to get individual values $\{z_i^{j,\mathsf{mult}},z_i^{j,\mathsf{add}},z_i^{j,\mathsf{relay}}\}_{j\in[\sigma],i\in[w_{m,j}]}$. It then computes the values $z_i^{j,1},\ldots,z_i^{j,w_{m+1}}$ on the outgoing wires from the gates in layer m as follows: For each $j\in[\sigma],i\in[w_{m,j}]$:
  - If gate $g_m^{j,i}$ is a multiplication gate, it sets $z^{j,i}=z_i^{j,\mathsf{mult}}$.
  - If gate $g_m^{j,i}$ is a multiplication gate, it sets $z^{j,i}=z_i^{j,\mathsf{add}}$.
  - If gate $g_m^{j,i}$ is a relay gate, it sets $z^{j,i}=z_i^{j,\mathsf{relay}}$.
— It then computes $\mathsf{LeftInputs}_j,\mathsf{RightInputs}_j=\mathsf{WireConfiguration}(\mathsf{block}_{m+1,j},\mathsf{block}_{m,j})$.
— For each $j\in[\sigma]$ and $q\in[w_{m+1,j}/\ell]$ each $i\in[\ell]$, let $e_{\mathsf{left}}=\mathsf{LeftInputs}[\ell\cdot(j-1)+i]$ and $e_{\mathsf{right}}=\mathsf{RightInputs}[\ell\cdot(j-1)+i]$, it sets $\mathbf{z}^{j,q,\mathsf{left}}[i]=z^{j,e_{\mathsf{left}}}$ and $\mathbf{z}^{j,q,\mathsf{right}}[i]=z^{j,e_{\mathsf{right}}}$.
— For each $j\in[\sigma],q\in[w_{m+1,j}/\ell]$, it then runs $\mathsf{pshare}(\mathbf{z}^{j,q,\mathsf{left}},D)$ to obtain shares $[\mathbf{z}_i^{j,q,\mathsf{left}}]$ and $\mathsf{pshare}(\mathbf{z}^{j,q,\mathsf{right}},D)$ to obtain a shares $[\mathbf{z}^{j,q,\mathsf{right}}]$ for each party.
— For each $j\in[\sigma],q\in[w_{m+1,j}/\ell]$, all parties locally subtract the randomness from these packed secret sharings as follows— $[\mathbf{z}^{j,q,\mathsf{left}}]=[\mathbf{z}^{j,q,\mathsf{left}}]-[\mathbf{r}^{j,q,\mathsf{left}}]$ and $[\mathbf{z}^{j,q,\mathsf{right}}]=[\mathbf{z}^{j,q,\mathsf{right}}]-[\mathbf{r}^{j,q,\mathsf{right}}]$.

Output: The parties output their shares in $[\mathbf{z}^{j,q,\mathsf{left}}]$ and $[\mathbf{z}^{j,q,\mathsf{right}}]$, for each $j\in[\sigma]$ and $q\in[w_{m+1,j}/\ell]$.

Fig. 5. A protocol for secure layer evaluation

6.2 Semi-honest Protocol

In this section, we describe our semi-honest protocol. All parties get a finite field $\mathbb{F}$ and a layered arithmetic circuit C (of width w and no. of gates $|\mathsf{C}|$) over $\mathbb{F}$ that computes the function f on inputs of length n as auxiliary inputs.[6]
Protocol: For each $i\in[n]$, party P_i holds input $x_i\in\mathbb{F}$ and the protocol proceeds as follows:

1. **Input Sharing Phase:** All the parties $\{P_1,\ldots,P_n\}$ collectively invoke $f_{\mathsf{pack-input}}$ as follows—every party P_i for $i\in[n]$, sends each of its input x_i to functionality $f_{\mathsf{pack-input}}$ and records its vector of packed shares $\left\{[\mathbf{x}^{j,q}],[\mathbf{y}^{j,q}]\right\}_{j\in[\sigma],q\in[w_{1,j}/\ell]}$ of the inputs as received from $f_{\mathsf{pack-input}}$. They set $[\mathbf{z}_1^{j,q,\mathsf{left}}]=[\mathbf{x}^{j,q}]$ and $[\mathbf{z}_1^{j,q,\mathsf{right}}]=[\mathbf{y}^{j,q}]$ for each $j\in[\sigma]$ and $q\in[w_{1,j}/\ell]$.

[6] For simplicity we assume that each party has only one input. But our protocol can be trivially extended to accommodate scenarios where each party has multiple inputs.

2. **Circuit Evaluation:** The circuit evaluation proceeds layer-wise, where for each layer $m \in [d]$, where d is the depth of the circuit, the parties evaluate each gate in that layer simultaneously as follows—Given packed input shares $\{[\mathbf{z}_m^{j,q,\mathsf{left}}], [\mathbf{z}_m^{j,q,\mathsf{right}}]\}$ for $j \in [\sigma], q \in [w_{m,j}/\ell]$, the parties run π_{layer} on inputs $\mathsf{layer}_{m+1}, \mathsf{layer}_m, \{[\mathbf{z}_m^{j,q,\mathsf{left}}], [\mathbf{z}_m^{j,q,\mathsf{right}}], [\mathbf{z}_m^{j,q,\mathsf{left}}], [\mathbf{z}_m^{j,q,\mathsf{right}}]\}_{j\in[\sigma],q\in[w_{m,j}/\ell]}$. They record their shares in $\left\{[\mathbf{z}_{m+1}^{j,q,\mathsf{left}}], [\mathbf{z}_{m+1}^{j,q,\mathsf{right}}]\right\}_{j\in[\sigma],q\in[w_{m+1,j}/\ell]}$.
3. **Output Reconstruction:** For each $\left\{[\mathbf{z}_{d+1}^{j,q,\mathsf{left}}], [\mathbf{z}_{d+1}^{j,q,\mathsf{right}}]\right\}_{j\in[\sigma],q\in[w_{d+1,j}/\ell]}$, the parties run the reconstruction algorithm of packed secret sharing to learn the ouput.

We give a proof of security for this protocol in the full-version of our paper. Next we calculate the complexity of this protocol.

Complexity of Our Semi-honest Protocol. For each layer in the protocol, we generate 5 × (width of the layer/ℓ) packed shares, where $\ell = n/\epsilon$. We have $t = n\left(\frac{1}{2} - \frac{2}{\epsilon}\right)$. In the semi-honest setting, $n - t = n(\frac{1}{2} + \frac{2}{\epsilon})$ of these can be computed with n^2 communication (this is because in the semi-honest setting, we do not need to check if the shares were computed honestly). Therefore, overall the total communication required to generate all the correlated random packed shares is $5 \times |\mathsf{C}|2\epsilon^2/(4+\epsilon) = 10|\mathsf{C}|\epsilon^2/(4+\epsilon)$.

Additional communication required to evaluate each layer of the circuit is $5n \times$ (width of the layer/ℓ). Therefore, overall the total communication to generate correlated randomness and to evaluate the circuit is $10|\mathsf{C}|\epsilon^2/(4+\epsilon)+5|\mathsf{C}|\epsilon = \frac{5|\mathsf{C}|\epsilon(3\epsilon+4)}{4+\epsilon}$. An additional overhead to generate packed input shares for all inputs is at most $4n|\mathcal{I}|$, where $|\mathcal{I}|$ is the number of inputs to the protocol. Therefore, the total communication complexity is $\frac{5|\mathsf{C}|\epsilon(3\epsilon+4)}{4+\epsilon} + 4n|\mathcal{I}|$.

6.3 Maliciously Secure Protocol

In this section, we now describe a protocol that achieves security with abort against malicious corruptions. In addition to the sub-functionalities and protocol discussed in Sect. 6.1, this protocol makes use of the following additional functionalities, we defer their description to the full version of our paper due to space constraints:

- Functionality $f_{\mathsf{pack-rand}}$ is realised by a protocol that outputs packed secret sharings of random vectors. Because of our requirements, we assume that this functionality operates in two modes - the independent mode will generate packed sharings of vectors in which each element is independent and the uniform mode will generate packed sharing of vectors in which each element is the same random value.
- Functionality f_{mult} is realised by a protocol that multiplies 2 pack-secret shared vectors.
- Functionality $f_{\mathsf{checkZero}}$ takes a pack-shared vector as input and checks whether or not it corresponds to a 0 vector.

Auxiliary Inputs: A finite field $\mathbb{F}$ and a layered arithmetic circuit C (of width w and $|\mathsf{C}|$ gates) over $\mathbb{F}$ that computes the function f on inputs of length n.
Inputs: For each $i \in [n]$, party P_i holds input $x_i \in \mathbb{F}$.
Protocol: (Throughout the protocol, if any party receives $\perp$ as output from a call to a sub-functionality, then it sends $\perp$ to all other parties, outputs $\perp$ and halts):

1. **Secret-Sharing Inputs:** All the parties $\{P_1, \ldots, P_n\}$ collectively invoke $f_{\mathsf{pack-input}}$ as follows—every party P_i for $i \in [n]$, sends each of its input x_i to functionality $f_{\mathsf{pack-input}}$. and records its vector of packed shares $\{[\mathbf{x}^{j,q}], [\mathbf{y}^{j,q}]\}_{j\in[\sigma],q\in[w_{1,j}/\ell]}$ of the inputs as received from $f_{\mathsf{pack-input}}$. They set $[\mathbf{z}_1^{j,q,\mathsf{left}}] = [\mathbf{x}^{j,q}]$ and $[\mathbf{z}_1^{j,q,\mathsf{right}}] = [\mathbf{y}^{j,q}]$ for each $j \in [\sigma]$ and $q \in [w_{1,j}/\ell]$.
2. **Pre-processing:**
   - Random Input Generation: The parties invoke $f_{\mathsf{pack-rand}}$ on mode $\mathsf{uniform}$ to receive packed sharings $[\mathbf{r}]$ of a vector $\mathbf{r}$, of the form $\mathbf{r} = (r, \ldots, r)$.
   - The parties also invoke $f_{\mathsf{pack-rand}}$ on mode $\mathsf{independent}$ to receive packed sharings $\{[\boldsymbol{\alpha}_m^{j,q,\mathsf{left}}], [\boldsymbol{\alpha}_m^{j,q,\mathsf{right}}]\}_{m\in[d],j\in[\sigma],q\in[w_{m,j}/\ell]}$ of random vectors $\boldsymbol{\alpha}_m^{j,q,\mathsf{left}}, \boldsymbol{\alpha}_m^{j,q,\mathsf{right}}$.
   - Randomizing Inputs: For each packed input sharing $[\mathbf{z}_1^{j,q,\mathsf{left}}], [\mathbf{z}_1^{j,q,\mathsf{right}}]$ (for $j \in [\sigma], q \in [w_{1,j}/\ell]$), the parties invoke f_{mult}, on $[\mathbf{z}_1^{j,q,\mathsf{right}}]$ and $[\mathbf{r}]$ to receive $[\mathbf{r}\mathbf{z}_1^{j,q,\mathsf{left}}]$ and on $[\mathbf{z}_1^{j,q,\mathsf{right}}]$ and $[\mathbf{r}]$ to receive $[\mathbf{r}\mathbf{z}_1^{j,q,\mathsf{right}}]$.
3. **Dual Circuit Evaluation:** The circuit evaluation proceeds layer-wise, where for each layer $m \in [d]$, where d is the depth of the circuit, the parties evaluate each gate in that layer simultaneously as follows:
   - The parties run π_{layer} on inputs $\mathsf{layer}_m, \mathsf{layer}_{m+1}$, $\{[\mathbf{z}_m^{j,q,\mathsf{left}}], [\mathbf{z}_m^{j,q,\mathsf{right}}], [\mathbf{z}_m^{j,q,\mathsf{left}}], [\mathbf{z}_m^{j,q,\mathsf{right}}]\}_{j\in[\sigma],q\in[w_{m,j}/\ell]}$ and obtain their respective shares in $\left\{[\mathbf{z}_{m+1}^{j,q,\mathsf{left}}], [\mathbf{z}_{m+1}^{j,q,\mathsf{right}}]\right\}_{j\in[\sigma],q\in[w_{m,j}/\ell]}$.
   - The parties then run π_{layer} on inputs $\mathsf{layer}_m, \mathsf{layer}_{m+1}$, $\{[\mathbf{z}_m^{j,q,\mathsf{left}}], [\mathbf{z}_m^{j,q,\mathsf{right}}], [\mathbf{r}\mathbf{z}_m^{j,q,\mathsf{left}}], [\mathbf{r}\mathbf{z}_m^{j,q,\mathsf{right}}]\}_{j\in[\sigma],q\in[w_{m,j}/\ell]}$ and obtain their respective shares in $\left\{[\mathbf{r}\mathbf{z}_{m+1}^{j,q,\mathsf{left}}], [\mathbf{r}\mathbf{z}_{m+1}^{j,q,\mathsf{right}}]\right\}_{j\in[\sigma],q\in[w_{m,j}/\ell]}$.
4. **Verification Step:** Each party does the following:
   (a) For each $m \in [d]$, $j \in [\sigma], q \in [w_{m,j}/\ell]$, the parties invoke f_{mult} on their packed shares $([\mathbf{z}_m^{j,q,\mathsf{left}}], [\boldsymbol{\alpha}_m^{j,q,\mathsf{left}}])$, $([\mathbf{r}\mathbf{z}_m^{j,q,\mathsf{left}}], [\boldsymbol{\alpha}_m^{j,q,\mathsf{left}}])$, $([\mathbf{z}_m^{j,q,\mathsf{right}}], [\boldsymbol{\alpha}_m^{j,q,\mathsf{right}}])$ and $([\mathbf{r}\mathbf{z}_m^{j,q,\mathsf{right}}], [\boldsymbol{\alpha}_m^{j,q,\mathsf{right}}])$, and locally compute. [7]

$$[\mathbf{v}] = \sum_{m\in[d]} \sum_{j\in[\sigma],q\in[w_{m,j}/\ell]} [\boldsymbol{\alpha}_m^{j,q,\mathsf{left}}][\mathbf{r}\mathbf{z}_m^{j,q,\mathsf{left}}] + [\boldsymbol{\alpha}_m^{j,q,\mathsf{right}}][\mathbf{r}\mathbf{z}_m^{j,q,\mathsf{right}}]$$

$$[\mathbf{u}] = \sum_{m\in[d]} \sum_{j\in[\sigma],q\in[w_{m,j}/\ell]} [\boldsymbol{\alpha}_m^{j,q,\mathsf{left}}][\mathbf{z}_m^{j,q,\mathsf{left}}] + [\boldsymbol{\alpha}_m^{j,q,\mathsf{right}}][\mathbf{z}_m^{j,q,\mathsf{right}}]$$

[7] We remark that for notational convenience we describe this step as consisting of $4|\mathsf{C}|/\ell$ multiplications (and hence these many degree reduction steps), it can be done with just two degree reduction step, where the parties first locally multiply and add their respective shares to compute $\langle \mathbf{v} \rangle$ and $\langle \mathbf{u} \rangle$ and then communicate to obtain shares of $[\mathbf{v}]$ and $[\mathbf{u}]$ respectively.

(b) The parties open shares $[\mathbf{r}]$ to reconstruct $\mathbf{r} = (r, \ldots, r)$.
(c) Each party then locally computes $[\mathbf{t}] = [\mathbf{v}] - r[\mathbf{u}]$
(d) The parties invoke $f_{\mathsf{checkZero}}$ on $[\mathbf{t}]$. If $f_{\mathsf{checkZero}}$ outputs reject, the output of the parties is $\perp$. Else, if it outputs accept, then the parties proceed.

5. **Output Reconstruction:** For each output vector, the parties run the reconstruction algorithm of packed secret sharing to learn the output. If the reconstruction algorithm outputs $\perp$, then the honest parties output $\perp$ and halt.

Due to space constraints, we defer the proof of security for this protocol to the full version of our paper. We note that the above protocol only works for circuits over large arithmetic fields. In the full version, we also present an extension to a protocol that works for circuits over smaller fields.

Complexity Calculation for our Maliciously Secure Protocol over Large Fields. For each layer in the protocol, we generate $5 \times$ (width of the layer$/\ell$), where $\ell = n/\epsilon$. We have $t = n\left(\frac{1}{2} - \frac{2}{\epsilon}\right)$. In the malicious setting, $n - t - 1 \approx n(\frac{1}{2} + \frac{2}{\epsilon})$ of these packed shares can be computed with $5n^2 + 5n(t+1)$ communication. Therefore, overall the total communication required to generate all the randomness is the following:

- Correlated randomness for evaluating the circuit on actual inputs: $\frac{|C|}{\frac{n}{\epsilon} \times n(\frac{1}{2}+\frac{2}{\epsilon})}\left(5n^2 + 5n^2\left(\frac{1}{2} - \frac{2}{\epsilon}\right)\right) = \frac{5\epsilon|\mathsf{C}|(3\epsilon-4)}{\epsilon+4}$.
- Correlated randomness for evaluating the circuit on randomized inputs: $\frac{5\epsilon|\mathsf{C}|(3\epsilon-4)}{\epsilon+4}$
- Shares of random $\boldsymbol{\alpha}$ vectors: $\frac{2\epsilon|\mathsf{C}|(3\epsilon-4)}{\epsilon+4}$

Additional communication required for dual execution of the circuit is $2 \times 5 \times n \times$ (width of the layer$/\ell$). Therefore, overall the total communication to generate correlated randomness and for the dual evaluate the circuit is $\frac{12\epsilon|\mathsf{C}|(3\epsilon-4)}{\epsilon+4} + 10|\mathsf{C}|\epsilon = \frac{46\epsilon^2|\mathsf{C}|-8\epsilon|\mathsf{C}|}{\epsilon+4}$. An additional overhead to generate packed input shares for all inputs is $n^2|\mathcal{I}|$, where $|\mathcal{I}|$ is the number of inputs to the protocol. The communication required to generate shares of randomized inputs is $n^2|\mathcal{I}|$. Finally, the verification step only requires $2n^2$ communication. Therefore, the total communication complexity is $\frac{46\epsilon^2|\mathsf{C}|-8\epsilon|\mathsf{C}|}{\epsilon+4} + 2n^2|\mathcal{I}|$.

7 Implementation and Evaluation

7.1 Theoretical Comparison to Prior Work

We start by comparing the concrete efficiency of our protocol based on the calculations from Sect. 6.3, where we show that the total communication complexity of our maliciously secure protocol is $\frac{46\epsilon^2|\mathsf{C}|-8\epsilon|\mathsf{C}|}{\epsilon+4} + 2n^2|\mathcal{I}|$. Recall that our protocol achieves security against $t < n\left(\frac{1}{2} - \frac{2}{\epsilon}\right)$ corruptions; we do our comparison with the state-of-the-art using the same corruption threshold as they consider.

The state-of-the-art in this regime is the $O(n|\mathsf{C}|)$ protocol of [16] for $t < n/3$ corruptions, that requires each party to communicate approximately $4\frac{2}{3}$ field elements per multiplication gate. In contrast, for $n = 125$ parties and $t < n/3$ corruptions, our protocol requires each party to send approximately $3\frac{1}{4}$ field elements per gate, in expectation. Notice that while we require parties to communicate for every gate in the circuit, [16] only requires communication per multiplication gate. However, it is easy to see that for circuits with approximately 75% multiplication gates, our protocol is expected (in theory) to outperform [16] for 125 parties.

The advantage of $O(|\mathsf{C}|)$ protocols is that the per-party communication decreases as the number of parties increases. For the same corruption threshold of $t < n/3$, and $n = 150$ parties, our protocol would (on paper) only require each party to communicate $2\frac{2}{3}$ field elements per gate. In this case, our protocol is already expected to perform better than [16] for circuits that have more that 60% multiplication gates. As the number of parties increase, less of the circuit must be comprised of multiplication gates in order to show improvements. Alternatively, because our communication complexity depends on ϵ (that is directly proportional to the corruption threshold t), our protocol outperforms prior work with fewer parties if we reduce the corruption threshold. or $t < n/4$ corruptions and $n = 100$ parties, we require per-party communication of $2\frac{2}{5}$ field elements per gate.

Finally, we remark that the above is a theoretical comparison, and assumes the "best-case scenario", e.g., where the circuit is such that it has exactly $n-t-1$ repetitions of the same kinds of blocks, and that each block has an exact multiple of n/ϵ gates and n is exactly divisible by ϵ, etc. In practice, this may not be the case, and some of the generated randomness will be "wasted" or some packed secret sharings will not be completely filled.

7.2 Implementation Comparison to Prior Work

To make our comparison more concrete, we implement our protocol and evaluate it on different network settings. While we do not get the exact same improvements as derived above (likely due to waste), we clearly demonstrate that our protocol is practical for even small numbers of parties, and becomes more efficient than state-of-the-art for large numbers of parties.

We implemented our maliciously secure protocol from Sect. 6.3. Additional details about our implementation can be found in the full version of the paper. Our implementation is in `C++` and built on top of libscapi [8], which provides communication and circuit parsing. To evaluate our implementation, we generate random layered circuits that satisfy the highly repetitive structural requirements. Benchmarking on random circuits is common, accepted practice for honest majority protocols [7,16]. We also modify the libscapi [8] circuit file format to allow for more succinct representation of highly repetitive circuits.

Table 2. Comparing the runtime of our protocol and that of related work. Results for our circuits are reported for the average protocol execution time over five randomized circuits each with 1,000,000 gates. All times are rounded to seconds due to space constraints. Asterisk denote extrapolated runtimes between LAN setting and WAN setting (see text). On the right side of the table, prior work does not run for this number of parties, so we only include our own results.

Configuration			**Number of Parties**								
Net. Config	t	Depth	30	50	70	90	110	150	200	250	300
LAN (our work)	$n/4$	1000	29	37	49	53	60	-	-	-	-
LAN (our work)	$n/3$	1000	29	41	55	54	63	-	-	-	-
[7]	$n/2$	1000	12	26	33	49	80	-	-	-	-
[16]	$n/3$	20	1	2	3	4	> 4	-	-	-	-
WAN (our work)	$n/4$	1000	261	206	187	278	271	282	263	302	336
WAN (our work)	$n/3$	1000	299	285	215	261	305	315	279	320	378
[7]	$n/2$	20	87	128	164*	204*	257*	-	-	-	-
[7]	$n/2$	100	135	197	251*	355*	478*	-	-	-	-
[7]	$n/2$	1000	376*	816*	1k*	1.5k*	2.4k*	-	-	-	-

We ran tests in two network deployments, LAN and WAN. In our LAN deployment, all parties were co-located on a single, large server with two Intel(R) Xeon(R) CPU E5-2695 @ 2.10 GHz. In our WAN deployment, parties were split evenly across three different AWS regions: us-east-1, us-east-2, and us-west-2. Each party was a separate c4.xlarge instances with 7.5 GB of RAM and a 2.9 GHz Intel Xeon E5-2666 v3 Processor.

We compare our work to the most efficient $O(n|\mathsf{C}|)$ work, as there is no comparable work which has been run for a large number of parties.[8] These works only test for up to 110 parties. Therefore our emphasis is not on direct time result comparisons, but instead on relative efficiency even with small numbers of players.

We compare the runtime of our protocol in both our LAN deployment and WAN deployment to [7,16] in Table 2. Because of differences between our protocol and intended applications, there are several important things to note in this comparison. First, we run all our tests on circuits with depth 1,000 to ensure there is sufficient repetition in the circuit. Furukawa et al. use only a depth 20 circuit in their LAN tests, meaning more parallelism can be leveraged. We note that when Chida et al. increase the depth of their circuits from 20 to 1,000 in their LAN deployment, the runtime for large numbers of parties increases 5–10 [7]. If we assume [16] will act similarly, we see that their runtime is approximately half of ours, when run with small number of parties. This is consistent

[8] The only protocol to be run on large numbers of parties rests on incomparable assumptions like CRS [38].

with their finding that their protocol is about twice as fast as [7]. We emphasise that for larger numbers of parties our protocol is expected to perform better.

Because Chida et al. only run their protocol for up to 30 players and up to circuit depth 100 in their WAN deployment, there is missing data for our comparison. We note that their WAN runtimes are consistently just over 30x higher than their LAN deployment. Using this observation, we extrapolate estimated runtimes for their protocol under different configurations, denoted with an asterisk. We emphasise that this estimation is rough, and all these measurements should be interpreted with a degree of skepticism; we include them only to attempt a more consistent comparison to illustrate the general trends of our preliminary implementation.

Our results show that our protocol, even using an un-optimized implementation, is comparable to these works for small numbers of parties (see left side of Table 2). For larger numbers of parties (see right side Table 2), where we have no comparable results, there is an upward trend in execution time. This could be a result of networking overhead or varying levels of network congestion when each of the experiments was performed. For example, when executing with 250 parties and a corruption threshold of n/4 the difference between the fastest and slowest execution time was over 60,000 ms, whereas in other deployments the difference is as low as 1,000 ms. In general, an increase is also expected as asymptotic complexity has an additive quadratic dependency on n with the input size of the circuit. Overall our experiments demonstrate that our protocol does not introduce an impractical overhead in its effort to achieve $O(|\mathsf{C}|)$ MPC. *As the number of parties continues to grow* (e.g. *hundreds or thousands), the benefits of our protocol will become even more apparent.*

Acknowledgements. The first and second authors are supported in part by NSF under awards CNS-1653110 and CNS-1801479 and the Office of Naval Research under contract N00014-19-1-2292. The first author is also supported in part by DARPA under Contract No. HR001120C0084. The second and third authors are supported in part by an NSF CNS grant 1814919, NSF CAREER award 1942789 and Johns Hopkins University Catalyst award. The third author is additionally partly supported by Office off Naval Research grant N00014-19-1-2294. The forth author is supported by the National Science Foundation under Grant #2030859 to the Computing Research Association for the CIFellows Project. Any opinions, findings and conclusions or recommendations expressed in this material are those of the author(s) and do not necessarily reflect the views of the United States Government or DARPA.

References

1. Fips pub 180–2, secure hash standard (shs), 2002. U.S. Department of Commerce/National Institute of Standards and Technology (2002)
2. Ames, S., Hazay, C., Ishai, Y., Venkitasubramaniam, M.: Ligero: lightweight sublinear arguments without a trusted setup. In: Thuraisingham, B.M., Evans, D., Malkin, T., Xu, D. (eds.) ACM CCS 2017, pp. 2087–2104. ACM Press, October 2017

3. Bellare, M., Rogaway, P.: Random oracles are practical: a paradigm for designing efficient protocols. In: Denning, D.E., Pyle, R., Ganesan, R., Sandhu, R.S., Ashby, V. (eds.) ACM CCS 93, pp. 62–73. ACM Press, November 1993
4. Ben-Or, M., Goldwasser, S., Wigderson, A.: Completeness theorems for non-cryptographic fault-tolerant distributed computation (extended abstract). In: 20th ACM STOC, pp. 1–10. ACM Press, May 1988
5. Chase, M., et al.: Post-quantum zero-knowledge and signatures from symmetric-key primitives. In: Thuraisingham, B.M., Evans, D., Malkin, T., Xu, D. (eds.) ACM CCS 2017, pp. 1825–1842. ACM Press, October 2017
6. Chaum, D., Crépeau, C., Damgård, I.: Multiparty unconditionally secure protocols (Abstract). In: Pomerance, C. (ed.) CRYPTO 1987. LNCS, vol. 293, p. 462. Springer, Heidelberg (1988). https://doi.org/10.1007/3-540-48184-2_43
7. Chida, K., et al.: Fast large-scale honest-majority MPC for malicious adversaries. In: Shacham, H., Boldyreva, A. (eds.) CRYPTO 2018. LNCS, vol. 10993, pp. 34–64. Springer, Cham (2018). https://doi.org/10.1007/978-3-319-96878-0_2
8. Cryptobiu. cryptobiu/libscapi, May 2019
9. Damgård, I., Ishai, Y.: Scalable secure multiparty computation. In: Dwork, C. (ed.) CRYPTO 2006. LNCS, vol. 4117, pp. 501–520. Springer, Heidelberg (2006). https://doi.org/10.1007/11818175_30
10. Damgård, I., Ishai, Y., Krøigaard, M.: Perfectly secure multiparty computation and the computational overhead of cryptography. In: Gilbert, H. (ed.) EUROCRYPT 2010. LNCS, vol. 6110, pp. 445–465. Springer, Heidelberg (2010). https://doi.org/10.1007/978-3-642-13190-5_23
11. Damgård, I., Ishai, Y., Krøigaard, M., Nielsen, J.B., Smith, A.: Scalable multiparty computation with nearly optimal work and resilience. In: Wagner, D. (ed.) CRYPTO 2008. LNCS, vol. 5157, pp. 241–261. Springer, Heidelberg (2008). https://doi.org/10.1007/978-3-540-85174-5_14
12. Damgård, I., Nielsen, J.B.: Scalable and unconditionally secure multiparty computation. In: Menezes, A. (ed.) CRYPTO 2007. LNCS, vol. 4622, pp. 572–590. Springer, Heidelberg (2007). https://doi.org/10.1007/978-3-540-74143-5_32
13. Dingledine, R., Mathewson, N., Syverson, P.: Tor: the second-generation onion router. In: Proceedings of the 13th Conference on USENIX Security Symposium, vol. 13, SSYM 2004, pp. 21, Berkeley, CA, USA. USENIX Association (2004)
14. Fiat, A., Shamir, A.: How to prove yourself: practical solutions to identification and signature problems. In: Odlyzko, A.M. (ed.) CRYPTO 1986. LNCS, vol. 263, pp. 186–194. Springer, Heidelberg (1987). https://doi.org/10.1007/3-540-47721-7_12
15. Franklin, M.K., Yung, M.: Communication complexity of secure computation (extended abstract). In: 24th ACM STOC, pp. 699–710. ACM Press, May 1992
16. Furukawa, J., Lindell, Y.: Two-thirds honest-majority MPC for malicious adversaries at almost the cost of semi-honest. In: Cavallaro, L., Kinder, J., Wang, X., Katz, J. (eds.) ACM CCS 2019, pp. 1557–1571. ACM Press, November 2019
17. Gallagher, P., Foreword, D.D., Director, C.F.: FIPS PUB 186–3 federal information processing standards publication digital signature standard (DSS), June 2009. U.S. Department of Commerce/National Institute of Standards and Technology (2009)
18. Gascon, A., et al.: Secure linear regression on vertically partitioned datasets. Cryptology ePrint Archive, Report 2016/892 (2016). http://eprint.iacr.org/2016/892
19. Genkin, D.: Secure Computation in Hostile Environments. PhD thesis, Technion - Israel Institute of Technology (2016)

20. Genkin, D., Ishai, Y., Polychroniadou, A.: Efficient multi-party computation: from passive to active security via secure SIMD circuits. In: Gennaro, R., Robshaw, M. (eds.) CRYPTO 2015. LNCS, vol. 9216, pp. 721–741. Springer, Heidelberg (2015). https://doi.org/10.1007/978-3-662-48000-7_35
21. Genkin, D., Ishai, Y., Prabhakaran, M., Sahai, A., Tromer, E.: Circuits resilient to additive attacks with applications to secure computation. In: Shmoys, D.B. (ed.) 46th ACM STOC, pp. 495–504. ACM Press, May/June (2014)
22. Giacomelli, I., Madsen, J., Orlandi, C.: ZKBoo: faster zero-knowledge for Boolean circuits. In: Holz, T., Savage, S. (eds.) USENIX Security 2016, pp. 1069–1083. USENIX Association, August 2016
23. Goldreich, O., Micali, S., Wigderson, A.: How to play any mental game or a completeness theorem for protocols with honest majority. In: Aho, A. (ed.), 19th ACM STOC, pp. 218–229. ACM Press, May 1987
24. Goldwasser, S., Micali, S., Rackoff, C.: The knowledge complexity of interactive proof-systems (extended abstract). In: 17th ACM STOC, pp. 291–304. ACM Press, May 1985
25. Goyal, V., Song, Y., Zhu, C.: Guaranteed output delivery comes free in honest majority MPC. In: Micciancio, D., Ristenpart, T. (eds.) CRYPTO 2020. LNCS, vol. 12171, pp. 618–646. Springer, Cham (2020). https://doi.org/10.1007/978-3-030-56880-1_22
26. Hastings, M., Hemenway, B., Noble, D., Zdancewic, S.: SoK: general purpose compilers for secure multi-party computation. In: 2019 IEEE Symposium on Security and Privacy, pp. 1220–1237. IEEE Computer Society Press, May 2019
27. Hirt, M., Nielsen, J.B.: Robust multiparty computation with linear communication complexity. In: Dwork, C. (ed.) CRYPTO 2006. LNCS, vol. 4117, pp. 463–482. Springer, Heidelberg (2006). https://doi.org/10.1007/11818175_28
28. Ishai, Y., Kushilevitz, E., Ostrovsky, R., Sahai, A.: Zero-knowledge from secure multiparty computation. In: Johnson, D.S., Feige, U. (eds.) 39th ACM STOC, pp. 21–30. ACM Press, June 2007
29. Katz, J., Kolesnikov, V., Wang, X.: Improved non-interactive zero knowledge with applications to post-quantum signatures. In: Lie, D., Mannan, M., Backes, M., Wang, X. (eds.) ACM CCS 2018, pp. 525–537. ACM Press, October 2018
30. Lindell, Y., Nof, A.: A framework for constructing fast MPC over arithmetic circuits with malicious adversaries and an honest-majority. In: Thuraisingham, B.M., Evans, D., Malkin, T., Xu, D. (eds.) ACM CCS 2017, pp. 259–276. ACM Press, October 2017
31. Mohassel, P., Rindal, P.: ABY^3: a mixed protocol framework for machine learning. In: Lie, D., Mannan, M., Backes, M., Wang, X. (eds.) ACM CCS 2018, pp. 35–52. ACM Press, October 2018
32. Mohassel, P., Zhang, Y.: SecureML: a system for scalable privacy-preserving machine learning. In: 2017 IEEE Symposium on Security and Privacy, pp. 19–38. IEEE Computer Society Press, May 2017
33. Mood, B., Gupta, D., Carter, H., Butler, K., Traynor, P.: Frigate: a validated, extensible, and efficient compiler and interpreter for secure computation. In: 2016 IEEE European Symposium on Security and Privacy (EuroS&P), pp. 112–127. IEEE (2016)
34. Nakamoto, S.: Bitcoin: a peer-to-peer electronic cash system (2008)
35. Nordholt, P.S., Veeningen, M.: Minimising communication in honest-majority MPC by batchwise multiplication verification. In: Preneel, B., Vercauteren, F. (eds.) ACNS 2018. LNCS, vol. 10892, pp. 321–339. Springer, Cham (2018). https://doi.org/10.1007/978-3-319-93387-0_17

36. Reed, M.G., Syverson, P.F., Goldschlag, D.M.: Anonymous connections and onion routing. IEEE J. Sel. Areas Commun. **16**(4), 482–494 (1998)
37. Shamir, A.: How to share a secret. Commun. Assoc. Comput. Mach. **22**(11), 612–613 (1979)
38. Wails, R., Johnson, A., Starin, D., Yerukhimovich, A., Gordon, S.D.: Stormy: Statistics in tor by measuring securely. In: Cavallaro, L., Kinder, J., Wang, X., Katz, J. (eds.) ACM CCS 2019, pp. 615–632. ACM Press, November 2019
39. Yao, A.C.-C.: How to generate and exchange secrets (extended abstract). In: 27th FOCS, pp. 162–167. IEEE Computer Society Press, October 1986

The More the Merrier: Reducing the Cost of Large Scale MPC

S. Dov Gordon[1(✉)], Daniel Starin[2], and Arkady Yerukhimovich[3]

[1] George Mason University, Fairfax, USA
gordon@gmu.edu
[2] Perspecta Labs, Basking Ridge, USA
dstarin@perspectalabs.com
[3] George Washington University, Washington, D.C., USA
arkady@gwu.edu

Abstract. Secure multi-party computation (MPC) allows multiple parties to perform secure joint computations on their private inputs. Today, applications for MPC are growing with thousands of parties wishing to build federated machine learning models or trusted setups for blockchains. To address such scenarios we propose a suite of novel MPC protocols that maximize throughput when run with large numbers of parties. In particular, our protocols have both communication and computation complexity that decrease with the number of parties. Our protocols buildon prior protocolsbased on packed secret-sharing, introducing new techniques to build more efficient computation for general circuits. Specifically, we introduce a new approach for handling *linear attacks* that arise in protocols using packed secret-sharing and we propose a method for unpacking shared multiplication triples without increasing the asymptotic costs. Compared with prior work, we avoid the $\log |C|$ overhead required when generically compiling circuits of size $|C|$ for use in a SIMD computation, and we improve over folklore "committee-based" solutions by a factor of $O(s)$, the statistical security parameter. In practice, our protocol is up to $10X$ faster than any known construction, under a reasonable set of parameters.

1 Introduction

A major goal in secure multi-party computation (MPC) is to reduce the necessary communication and computation as a function of the number of parties participating in the protocol. Today, most protocols have costs growing linearly and even quadratically as the number of parties increases. This makes MPC prohibitively expensive for applications with very large numbers of parties, and all real-world applications of MPC have focused on use-cases with only a handful of parties. Academic experiments have pushed the limit to a few hundreds of participants [37]. However, today we have use-cases for MPC that naturally have thousands if not millions of participating parties. For example, in secure federated learning, thousands of low-resource devices wish to train a single machine

A. Canteaut and F.-X. Standaert (Eds.): EUROCRYPT 2021, LNCS 12697, pp. 694–723, 2021.
https://doi.org/10.1007/978-3-030-77886-6_24

learning model on their collective data [30]. Another example is that of distributed trusted setup for blockchains where (possibly) millions of miners may wish to participate in the protocol. Finally, a particularly well fitting application for such large-scale MPC is to generate offline material for smaller MPC computation. Such offline material is usually expensive to generate, but enables much faster *online* MPC computations once it is available.

To address such applications we construct a new MPC protocol that scales practically to hundreds of thousands of parties. The amortized cost of our protocol decreases as the number of parties increases, resulting in reduced cost for all parties as more parties join the computation – the more the merrier. This is especially true for applications such as blockchain setup, where the number of inputs does not grow with the number of computing parties. Specifically, assuming that at most $t \leq n(1/2 - \epsilon)$ parties are actively malicious, for any $0 < \epsilon < 1/2$, our protocol requires each party to send $O(|C|/n)$ field elements, where $|C|$ is the size of the circuit we wish to evaluate, and n is the number of parties. It requires each party to perform $O(\log n|C|/n)$ field operations.[1]

While ours is not the only protocol with communication and computation that diminishes with n, our communication complexity is better, asymptotically and concretely, than every construction that we know of. For example, one naive solution in this setting of a strong honest majority is to elect a small committee of size $O(s)$, where s is a statistical security parameter, independent of n, and to run any arbitrary MPC protocol among that committee alone. Technically, the average communication and computation cost reduces with n, since $n - O(s)$ parties that remain idle still reduce the average. However, the committee members carry the worst-case cost, $O(|C|)$. As we will see, even when we consider natural improvements to this approach that spread the worst-case cost among the parties, we out-perform such approaches by a factor of $O(s)$, which, concretely, could be as large as $40X$. More interestingly, several solutions using packed secret sharing are also known [13,23]: we outperform these constructions by a factor of $O(\log |C|)$ by avoiding the use of a general compiler from standard circuits to SIMD circuits. We provide a brief asymptotic comparison with specific prior constructions at the end of this introduction, in Subsect. 1.2, and we provide a thorough analysis of these comparisons in Sect. 5.

We have implemented our protocol and executed it for small numbers of parties. To our knowledge, this is the first implementation with sub-linear costs: among existing implementations, the one with lowest concrete costs that we know of is by Furukawa and Lindell [20], which requires $O(|C|)$ communication per party, and does not benefit from an increase in the number of participants. Missing from our implementation is any large-scale deployment, which would introduce some major engineering challenges (not to mention social and/or financial challenges of finding participants). Most obviously, it would be very difficult

[1] We are ignoring terms that do not depend on $|C|$ or n.

to convincingly simulate the network environment.[2] Additionally, while a single Linux server can efficiently handle tens of millions of TCP connections [39], this is not currently supported by the OS, and requires extensive effort to implement. Nevertheless, our implementation allows us to precisely measure the computational cost for a million participants, which is the bottleneck in our construction. It also allows us to provide an exact extrapolation on the amount of data communicated. What is missing from this extrapolation is any handling of network variance or participant failure. Recognizing these caveats and extrapolating our performance, we estimate that we can achieve a throughput of 500 million multiplication triples per second[3] when 1 million parties participate, even over a relatively slow 10 megabit per second network.

One particularly appealing application for our protocol is as a service for generating offline material for smaller scale computations. The offline phase is the bottleneck for the majority of MPC protocols. If tens of thousands of users can be incentivized[4] to generate billions of computation triples over night, which might require less than 10 min of their time, these triples can be transferred to a small online committee for arbitrary computation the next day, enabling malicious-secure MPC, even with a dishonest majority, at the cost of an efficient online phase.

1.1 Technical Overview

We now give a brief overview of the key ideas and building blocks behind our main protocol.

Damgård-Nielsen: In the honest-majority setting, most modern approaches to MPC build upon the multiplication protocol of Damgård-Nielsen (DN) [15]. This construction begins with an input-independent pre-processing phase in which the parties compute threshold double sharings of random values, $([r]_d, [r]_{2d})$, with thresholds d and $2d$, respectively. During the online phase of the computation, these double sharings can be used to perform multiplication on shared field elements at a communication cost of 2 field elements per party.

To generate these random sharings in the semi-honest setting, the DN protocol proceeds as follows. Each party P_i samples a random r_i and sends two threshold sharings to every other party: $[r_i]_d, [r_i]_{2d}$. This costs n^2 total communication. Naively, each party could locally sum their received shares to recover

[2] Sometimes such experiments are run in cloud environments, which is useful for tens or hundreds of participants. However, we are interested in deployments involving tens or hundreds of *thousands* of participants. AWS has only 64 data centers, so testing with more parties than this would provide an inaccurate simulation of the network environment.

[3] This estimate is for a malicious-secure protocol that generates *unauthenticated* triples, which suffice for semi-honest computation in the online phase. In Sect. 4.1, we present a known result for converting these to authenticated triples. The throughput in that setting is closer to 70 million triples per second.

[4] Or commanded by Google.

a single double sharing of a random r, but the cost per sharing would be $O(n^2)$. Instead, each party assembles an n dimensional vector from the shares that they received, and multiplies this with a Vandermonde matrix, M. Assuming $h = O(n)$ honest parties, this allows them to extract h random double sharings, instead of a single one. This reduces the total communication cost to $O(n)$ per multiplication gate, requiring each party to send only a constant number of field elements per circuit gate.

Moreover, recent work by Genkin et al. [24] showed that this semi-honest DN protocol actually offers a stronger notion of security, called *security up to additive attacks*. This means that the protocol offers privacy against a malicious adversary and only allows an additive attack, wherein an adversary can add an error δ to the result of each multiplication. Several works have since shown how to leverage this property to efficiently achieve full malicious security (with abort) [10,20,33].

Packed secret sharing: To further reduce the cost by a factor of $O(n)$, we use packed secret sharing when we construct our double sharings [13,18,23]. In a standard Shamir sharing, the secret is encoded in the evaluation of a random polynomial at 0. However, if $t = (1/2 - \epsilon)n$, then even after fixing all t adversarial shares, there are still ϵn degrees of freedom in the polynomial (while maintaining the degree $d < n/2$). These can be used for encoding additional secret values. In a packed secret sharing scheme, a vector of $\ell = \epsilon n$ elements are encoded together in a single polynomial by interpolating a random polynomial through those ℓ points, and, as in Shamir sharing, providing point evaluations of the polynomial as shares. By packing $[\mathbf{r}] = [r_1], \ldots, [r_\ell]$ into a single polynomial, and performing the Vandermonde matrix multiplication on the packed shares, we can further reduce the communication and computational costs by a factor of $O(n)$, as was done by Damgård et al., and Genkin et al. [13,23]. When performing ℓ independent computations in parallel, this directly reduces both the communication and the computation by a factor of ℓ, without any cost. When performing only a single evaluation of the circuit (which is the setting we focus on), Damgård et al. [13] show how to compile a circuit C into one of size at most $O(|C| \log |C|)$, that can leverage packed sharing even in a single computation by parallelizing the multiplication gates in groups of size ℓ.

Unpacking the secret shares: Our first contribution is a new way to avoid this $\log |C|$ multiplicative overhead, even in the single execution setting. To do this, we avoid computing on packed values, and instead unpack the random values into fresh secret shares for later use by an "online committee".[5] That committee then uses these values to perform the online phase (i.e., the input dependent portion of the computation). Unpacking the secrets allows us to directly compute an arbitrary circuit. However, if we unpack the ℓ secrets before sending them

[5] There are advantages and disadvantages to varying the size of this committee, which we will discuss in depth in what follows. For now, we can assume that the online committee is in fact the entire network of n parties. In the "standard" approach to executing the online phase with n parties, the communication complexity is $O(|C|)$ per party. We will address this as well.

to the online committee, we ruin our sub-linear communication complexity: for every gate in the circuit, each of the n parties would need to send (at least) one share to the online committee, resulting in a per-party communication complexity of (at least) $O(|C|)$. Instead, we observe that unpacking requires only linear operations (i.e., we need to perform polynomial interpolation, which is a linear operation), and thus can be performed on secret shares of the packed secret sharing. So, the n parties *re-share* each of their packed shares with the online committee. Because they are still packed, the per-party communication of re-sharing is $O(|C|/n)$ instead of $O(|C|)$. The online committee then locally unpacks the "inner" threshold sharing by interpolating the polynomial that is "underneath" the outside sharing. This requires no interaction inside the online committee, and maintains the desired complexity.

Now consider the question of how to re-share the packed sharing. The naive choice here is to stick with a threshold secret sharing scheme, ensuring that after they unpack into the outer scheme, the parties maintain a threshold sharing of the DN double sharings, and can proceed exactly as in the DN protocol. Unfortunately, starting with $([\mathbf{r}]_d, [\mathbf{r}]_{2d})$, we do not know how to efficiently transfer $([\mathbf{r}]_s, [\mathbf{r}]_{2s})$ to an online committee of size s without incurring a communication overhead of $O(s)$: the cost of sending a Shamir share to a committee of size s is, seemingly, $O(s)$. In the case where the "committee" is of size n, this again ruins the claim of sub-linear complexity, even though there are only $O(|C|/n)$ values to be re-shared. Instead, we use an additive secret-sharing for our outer scheme. After establishing pairwise seeds between the senders and the receivers, we can compress the cost of re-sharing: to re-share some value x, party i computes $[x]_s = x + G(r_{i,1}) + \cdots + G(r_{i,s-1})$ and sends this to party s. All other parties fix their shares deterministically using their shared seed. This saves a factor of $O(s)$ in the communication cost, and when the committee size is n, it allows us to maintain the desired complexity. However, with an additive secret sharing, we can no longer use DN for multiplication. Instead, prior to transferring the packed values, we use our double sharings to create packed multiplication triples $([\mathbf{a}]_d, [\mathbf{b}]_d, [\mathbf{ab}]_d)$, and send additive shares of these packed, threshold shares to the online committee. The online committee unpacks these values into additive shares of multiplication triples by interpolating inside the additive sharing.

So far, we have ignored two important points: the cost of the online phase, and computational complexity of the protocol. Using n-out-of-n additive shares of multiplication triples, there is no clear way to achieve sub-linear communication complexity in the online phase. Furthermore, even if we ignore the cost of the online phase, unpacking a single multiplication triple requires $O(n \log n)$ field operations, which, having successfully reduced the communication complexity, becomes the new bottleneck in our protocol. The solution to both problems is one and the same: we parallelize the work of unpacking the triples, using many small committees, each of size $O(s)$, with the guarantee that each has at least one honest participant[6]. The computational cost of unpacking is now reduced to $O(s \log n|C|/n)$ field operations per party. Rather than transfer these shares to a single evaluation committee, we then split $|C|$ among the $O(n/s)$ committees, charging each with evaluating $O(s|C|/n)$ gates.[7] For the online phase, we use the online phase of the SPDZ protocol [16]. In order to use the generated triples in this protocol, each committee first "authenticates" their triples. This is very similar to the protocols found in prior work ([3,14,16,32]), and appears in Sect. 4.1. We stress that the authentication and the SPDZ online protocol have bottleneck communication linear in the number of gates to be evaluated.

Security against linear attacks: Genkin et al. [23] (building on Damgård et al. [13]) present a protocol that begins as ours does, with the construction of packed double sharings. (They do not construct packed triples for use in a malicious majority online committee, but instead use the packed values in a SIMD computation, incurring the $O(\log|C|)$ overhead described above.) In their security analysis, Genkin et al. observed that when computing with packed double sharings, one has to prevent a "linear attack" in which an adversary adds to the output of a multiplication gate some arbitrary linear combination of the values that are packed into the input shares. As the authors note, this is not something that is allowed by an additive attack, since the adversary does not know the packed secrets. Briefly, the linear attack works as follows (See Appendix B of [22]). Consider shares $[\mathbf{a}]_d = a_1, \ldots, a_n$, and $[\mathbf{b}]_d = b_1, \ldots, b_n$ for $n = 2d+1$. Let $\delta_1, \ldots, \delta_{d+1}$ denote the Lagrange coefficients that recover the first element in the packed polynomial: $b^{(1)} = \sum_{i=1}^{d+1} \delta_i b_i$. Let $\gamma_1, \ldots, \gamma_n$ denote the coefficients that recover the second element in the product polynomial: $a^{(2)}b^{(2)} = \sum_{i=1}^{n} \gamma_i a_i b_i$. If an adversary modifies the first $d+1$ shares of $\mathbf{a}$, $[\hat{\mathbf{a}}]^i = [\mathbf{a}]^i + \delta_i/\gamma_i$, then the reconstruction of $a^{(2)}b^{(2)}$ will equal $a^{(2)}b^{(2)} + b^{(1)}$. Such a dependency on $b^{(1)}$ is not allowed in an additive attack.

We avoid linear attacks using two critical properties of our construction. Observe that linear attacks work by modifying at least $d+1$ shares of an input wire to a multiplication gate. Thus, we ensure that this can never happen in our construction. First, as described earlier, we only use packed multiplication to produce triples, thus we only need to deal with a depth-1 circuit of multiplication gates. In particular, the output of any (packed) multiplication gate is never used as an input into another (packed) multiplication gate. Thus, even though an adversary can introduce an arbitrary additive attack to modify all the packed values in the resulting product, these modified values will never be used as an input to a (packed) multiplication gate. There is still one place where the adversary can introduce a linear attack: the original inputs to the triple generation

6 Technically, since we are selecting many such committees, to guarantee that they all have at least one honest party requires a union bound over the number of committees, resulting in committees of size $O(s + \log n)$. However, since $s > \log n$, we drop this $\log n$ term in our asymptotic notation. However, we point out that our experimental results in Sect. 6 do account for this union bound.

7 This can be done regardless of the circuit structure, and does not require a wide circuit.

(i.e., $\mathcal{A}$'s shares of a and b). However, we observe that this requires the adversary to change at least $d+1$ shares of a and thus requires changing at least one share held by an honest party. However, this is detectable by the honest parties if they (collectively) check the degree of the polynomial on which their shares lie. We, therefore, avoid linear attacks on the inputs by performing a degree check on the input shares of $[\mathbf{a}]$ and $[\mathbf{b}]$ using a standard procedure. Moreover, since we can batch all of these checks, doing so is (almost) for free.

1.2 Performance Comparisons

We give here a brief overview of how our protocol compares, asymptotically, to various other protocols. We will give a more detailed description of how we arrive at these numbers in Sect. 5, after presenting our protocol in full; here we only present the alternative protocols used in the comparisons, and present the results. Throughout, we assume we begin the computation with n parties, and $t < n/3$ corruptions by an actively malicious adversary. We use s to denote a statistical security parameter.

Performance metrics: When comparing the communication and computation costs of various protocols, we consider the *bottleneck complexities* [7]. This refers to the maximum communication sent or received[8] by any party taking part in the protocol, and the maximum computation performed by any one party. We believe that this is a more meaningful metric than average or total communication when analyzing protocols that use small committees, since most parties might do nothing after sharing their inputs, and therefore reduce the average artificially. In Sect. 5 we will give a more careful analysis, and, for completeness, we include there the total complexities.

Protocol Variants and Results: In what follows, we consider three variants of our protocol, as each provides insight into various aspects of our design. We begin by considering the simplest variant in which the full network of n participants unpack all $|C|$ triples, and all n parties participate in the online phase. We compare this with two folklore solutions in which a single committee is elected to perform the computation. We then describe two changes that strengthen our protocol, and compare the impact of each improvement to a similar improvement to these folklore solutions.

Baseline comparisons: In Fig. 1, we compare the asymptotic behavior of our protocol to that of Furukawa and Lindell, which is also designed for a corruption threshold of $t < n/3$ [20]. Additionally, with $t < (1/2 - \epsilon)n$, an old folklore approach is to choose a random committee of size $O(s)$ that is guaranteed, with

[8] When analyzing total or average communication, there is no need to consider receiving complexity as the number of bits sent by all parties equals the number of bits received. But, when considering bottleneck complexity, one must make a distinction between the two. For example, if many parties send messages to one party, that party's receiving bandwidth becomes the bottleneck. In fact, there are MPC protocols such as [37] that are bottlenecked by the receiving bandwidth of some of the parties.

Single Online, Single Unpack				
	Ours	$t < n/3$ [20]	$t < n/2$ [10]	$t < n$ [16]
Comm	$O(\|C\|/n)$	$O(\|C\|)$	$O(\|C\|)$	$O(s\|C\|)$
Comp	$O(\log n\|C\|)$	$O(\log n\|C\|)$	$O(\log s\|C\|)$	$O(s\|C\|)$

Fig. 1. Asymptotic complexities for the offline phase of four protocols. In our variant, and in that of [20], all parties participate throughout. In the other two protocols, the state-of-the-art is run by a small committee: with an honest majority in column 4, and a malicious majority in column 5. All values measure bottleneck costs, rather than total costs. The online communication and computation cost for all four protocols is $O(C)$, and is not included.

probability $1 - \mathsf{negl}(s)$, to contain an honest majority. We consider performing the entire computation within that committee, using the state-of-the-art protocol for the $t < n/2$ setting by Chida et al. [10]. Finally, a similar folklore solution is to select a much smaller committee, with the weaker guarantee that at least one honest party is chosen, and then run the entire protocol using the state-of-the-art construction for the $t < n$ setting, such as the protocol by Damgård et al. [16], or any of the follow-up work. Furukawa and Lindell requires $O(|C|)$ communication per party, and the folklore solution using an honest majority committee requires $O(|C|)$ communication for each party on the committee, yielding the same bottleneck complexity. The folklore solution with a malicious majority has bottleneck complexity of $O(s|C|)$. In comparison, our offline phase has bottleneck complexity of $O(|C|/n)$. However, as mentioned previously, our online phase has bottleneck complexity of $O(|C|)$ as well, and our computational cost is higher than that of the first folklore solution. More importantly, computation is the major bottleneck in our performance. In the next two tables, we address these two issues, strengthening the folklore solutions in analogous ways.

Single Online, Distributed Unpack			
	Ours	$t < n/2$	$t < n$
Comm	$O(s\|C\|/n)$	$O(s\|C\|)$	$O(s^2\|C\|/n)$
Comp	$O(s \log n\|C\|/n)$	$O(s \log s\|C\|/n)$	$O(s^2\|C\|/n)$

Fig. 2. In our protocol variant, triples are unpacked in many parallel committees, and then transferred back to the full set of size n. Costs are measured through the transfer step, and exclude the cost of the online phase. In the column labeled $t < n/2$, many parallel committees, each with an honest majority, prepare double-sharings that will be used by a single online committee of size $O(s)$. In the column labeled $t < n$, many parallel committees, each with at least one honest participant, generate multiplication triples that will be used by the full network of size n. The online phase still requires $O(|C|)$ communication and computation for all three protocols, and is not included in the Table.

Distributed triple generation: Instead of unpacking all triples in a single committee, we improve our computational complexity by a factor of $O(n/s)$ by unpacking the triples in $O(n/s)$ small committees, each large enough to guarantee at least one honest member. The resulting triples are then transferred to a single online committee, still of size n.

Making an analogous change to the two folklore solutions,[9] we consider constructing triples in parallel, using $O(n/s)$ committees – honest majority committees in the first variant, and malicious majority committees in the second – each responsible for an $O(s/n)$ fraction of the pre-processing. When using honest majority committees, we analyze the case where the double sharings are transferred to a single online committee of size $O(s)$, which is guaranteed to have an honest majority with all but negligible probability. When using malicious majority committees, we distribute the multiplication triples to the entire network of size n. (In both cases, these choices minimize the bottleneck complexity. We consider using a small online committee, both for ourselves, and for the $t < n$ setting, in Sect. 5. This reduces total communication complexity, but introduces the bottleneck of having a small receiving committee.) We summarize these comparisons in Fig. 2.

Asymptotically, all three protocols improve equally in computational cost, by a factor of $O(s/n)$. However, because honest majority committees are about 18X larger than malicious majority committees, in concrete terms, our computational cost is quite similar to protocol using honest majority committees. We discuss in more detail in Sect. 5.

Distributed online computation: To claim an end-to-end protocol that has sub-linear communication, we present a final set of protocol variants in which we distribute the online computation. These three protocol variants begin as in the previous set of protocols, but they stop short of transferring the multiplication triples to an online committee. Instead, each of the $O(n/s)$ committees is

Distributed Online						
	Ours		$t < n/2$		$t < n$	
	Offline	Online	Offline	Online	Offline	Online
Comm	$O(\|C\|/n)$	$O(s\|C\|/n)$	$O(s\|C\|/n)$	$O(s^2\|C\|/n)$	$O(s^2\|C\|/n)$	$O(s\|C\|/n)$
Comp	$O(s \log n\|C\|/n)$	$O(s\|C\|/n)$	$O(s \log s\|C\|/n)$	$O(s\|C\|/n)$	$O(s^2\|C\|/n)$	$O(s\|C\|/n)$

Fig. 3. Here we distribute the work done in the online phase, assigning $O(s|C|/n)$ gates to each of the $O(n/s)$ committees. In all three protocols, the material generated during pre-processing remains with the same committee for the online phase. The state of the online phase is transfered from one committee to the next.

[9] Note that when we assume $t < n/3$, we cannot construct committees of size $O(s)$ that have the same corruption threshold. We therefore do not consider running Furukawa and Lindell in parallel. We could do so with larger, committees, or we could consider a smaller threshold, but we feel the current set of comparisons suffices for demonstrating the value of our protocol.

responsible for $O(s|C|/n)$ triples (or double sharings, when $t < n/2$), and holds them until the online phase. Each committee is then responsible for a proportionate "chunk" of the circuit during the online evaluation. All three protocols benefit similarly from the reduced cost of the online evaluation.

In Fig. 3, we have separated the online cost in this protocol. In some settings, it might make sense to stop the protocol after the offline phase, leaving the triples in their committees until they are needed by some other group for an online computation. For example, we can imagine using such a protocol in a service that sells computation triples. The cost of producing the triples diminishes with n, and the small unpacking committees can then transfer these triples, as needed, to paying customers. The receiving customers might have a malicious majority, and the cost of receiving the transfer would be minimal in comparison to the cost of securely generating the triples on their own. In this setting, the cost of receiving these triples (which show up in Fig. 3), and the cost of using them in an online evaluation, can both be reasonably ignored by the triple service provider.

This last protocol variant combining distributed unpacking and a distributed online phase gives us the following main theorem.

Theorem 1 (Informal). *Assuming the existence of a PRG, our distributed online protocol generates $|C|$ multiplication triples with $O(\frac{|C|}{n})$ bottleneck complexity and $O(\frac{s \log n |C|}{n})$ bottleneck computation for a statistical security s, achieving security against a static, malicious adversary corrupting $t < n/3$ parties.*

1.3 Related Work

A full survey of the MPC literature is out of scope for this work, so we only discuss the results that are most directly relevant. Damgård and Nielsen [15] introduced the technique of using double sharings for realizing multiplication with $O(|C|)$ per-party communication in the honest majority setting. The technique has been used in many follow-up results [5,10,13,20,23,24,33] for a variety of efficient MPC protocols with honest majority. The technique of using multiplication triples was first introduced by Beaver [4]. Since then this technique has been extremely fruitful in the setting of malicious majority with a number of works proposing improved constructions of multiplication triples based on oblivious transfer (OT) [19,26,27] and based on somewhat-homomorphic encryption [16,32].

Several works have looked into achieving sub-linear communication for MPC in the honest majority setting. In particular, packed secret sharing was originally introduced by Franklin and Yung [18]. We use the packed version of the protocol due to Damgård and Nielsen [15] that was first presented in [13]. Other recent works such as Leviosa [25] and Ligero [2] have also used packed secret sharing to achieve efficiency for MPC-in-the-head [28] and zero-knowledge proofs. Damgård and Ishai [12] present a protocol for MPC in a client/server model that leverages packed secret sharing. Their construction has total communication complexity of $O(n|C|\log|C|)$, but when the number of clients is constant, they can remove a factor of n, achieving performance that improves as they introduce more servers. Very recently, Garay et al. [21] study the feasibility of constructing sub-linear communication MPC and demonstrate some challenges to achieving sub-linear communication in MPC, especially when $|C|$ is small.

Using committees to speed up performance of MPC has been studied starting with the work of Bracha [8]. Since then several works [11,17,29,36,38] have looked into using committees to reduce communication in MPC over large numbers of parties. Additionally, another line of work has leveraged committees to improve the communication locality (i.e., how many parties a party must talk to as part of the protocol) of MPC protocols [6,9]. Finally, similar to our work, Scholl et al. [35] also consider how one can outsource triple generation when an online committee does not want to do the work on its own. They propose several approaches for outsourcing triple generation for MPC.

MPC protocols secure against additive attacks were introduced by Genkin et al. [24]. Then, Genkin, Ishai, and Polychroniadou [23] introduced the notion of a linear attack and showed that the semi-honest variant of packed Damgård-Nielsen given by Damgård et al. [13] is secure up to linear attack. For details see Genkin's thesis [22].

Finally, the notion of bottleneck complexity for MPC communication was originally introduced by Boyle et al. [7].

2 Preliminaries

2.1 Secret Sharing

We use two types of secret sharing schemes. Packed secret sharing, in which a secret share is a single evaluation of a polynomial that encodes ℓ secrets, and additive secret sharing, in which a secret share is a random field element, and the shares sum to the secret. We only define notation here, and do not bother to define security or correctness of secret sharing.

Packed secret sharing:
We let $[\mathbf{r}]_d$ represent a secret sharing of $\mathbf{r}$ using a degree d polynomial, and we denote party P_i's share with $[\mathbf{r}]_d^i$.

$\mathsf{share}(d, \mathbf{r})$: outputs n shares of a degree d polynomial $(d, s^1, \ldots, s^n)$.

$\mathsf{reconstruct}(d, s^1, \ldots, s^j)$: given j shares, with $j > d$, output $\mathbf{r} \in \mathbb{F}^\ell$.

$\mathsf{reconstruct}(d, i, s^1, \ldots, s^j)$: given j shares, with $j > d$, output $r_i \in \mathbb{F}$, which is the value stored in the ith packing slot. In practice, we never extract a single value, as we can unpack all values using a pair of FFT / IFFT operations. However, notationaly, it is convenient to refer to the value recovered from a single slot.

Additive secret sharing:
We fix the size of our additive secret sharing to that of the online committee, Com. Our additive secret shares will always be a sum of $|\mathsf{Com}|$ field elements.

$\mathsf{aShare}(x)$: outputs $x_1, \ldots, x_{\mathsf{Com}}$ such that $x = \sum_i x_i$. In practice, this can be done by generating the first $\mathsf{Com} - 1$ shares pseudorandomly, and then choosing the final share as $x_{\mathsf{Com}} = x - \sum_{i=1}^{\mathsf{Com}-1} x_i$.

$\mathsf{reconstruct}(x_1, \ldots, x_n)$: outputs $\sum_i x_i$.

3 Multiplication Triple Generation

Overview: We describe a maliciously secure protocol with $t = \epsilon n$ corrupted parties, for $\epsilon \in [0, .5)$. We let $h = n - t$ denote the number of honest parties, and we let $\ell = n/2 - \epsilon n$ denote the packing parameter used in our secret sharing scheme. We will use polynomials of degree $d = \lfloor (n-1)/2 \rfloor$, and $d' = n-1$. However, to simplify the notation, we will assume n is odd, and use d and $2d$ as the degrees of these polynomials. For simplicity, we describe only one protocol variant. We describe the protocol as having a single unpacking committee, denoted Com, and, we allow the committee size to be flexible. The extension to multiple, parallel unpacking committees is straightforward. If $|\mathsf{Com}| < n$, we elect a random subset of the parties to the committee. To ensure an honest member with probability 2^{-s}, it suffices to elect a committee of size $|\mathsf{Com}| \leq -s/\log \epsilon$. This is done by performing a secure coin flip among the n parties, and using the result to select parties at random, with replacement, $-s/\log \epsilon$ times. (If the committee happens to be smaller than Com because there are collisions in the sampling, this improves performance without impacting security.)

In steps 1 and 2 of the protocol, the parties exchange secret shares of random values, and use the public Vandermonde matrix M to extract $O(h)$ packed secret values. In step 3, they perform a degree check on all the shares sent in the 1st step, ensuring that the shares of all honest parties lie on a degree d polynomial, as expected. This limits any future modifications by the adversary to $t < d$ shares, eliminating the linear attack described previously, and limiting the adversary to simple additive attacks.

In Step 4, the parties perform local multiplication on their packed shares, doubling the degree of the polynomial, and blind the result using their share of $[\mathbf{r}]_{2d}$. This is sent to the dealer, P_0, who extracts the blinded, packed secrets, and reshares them, reducing the degree back down to d.

The resharing can be sent only to the first $d+1$ parties. At this point in the protocol, any further deviations by the adversary will only create additive attacks, which we do not bother to prevent. (These attacks will be caught in the online phase, through a call to $\mathsf{macCheck}$, before the outputs are revealed.) We therefore do not need the redundancy of extra shares.

In step 6, the $d+1$ parties receiving shares of the blinded product re-share their shares using the additive secret sharing scheme. These additive shares are sent to the committee(s) of size Com, which might be of size n or of size $O(s)$. In step 7, the committee unpacks their shares of the triples, homomorphically, resulting in additive shares $[a]_{\mathsf{a}}, [b]_{\mathsf{a}}$ and $[ab]_{\mathsf{a}}$.

The ideal functionality is presented in Fig. 4. We note that the adversary is allowed to specify what output shares they would like to receive (but learns nothing about the shared value, which is still random). This is because we do not try to prevent a rushing attack in which the adversary sees the messages sent by the honest parties in the first step of the protocol, prior to fixing its own first message. This attack is benign, and is commonly allowed in prior work. More importantly, the adversary is allowed to specify an additive attack for every triple produced. Instead of receiving $[a]_\mathsf{a}, [b]_\mathsf{a}$ and $[ab]_\mathsf{a}$, the output committee instead receives $[a]_\mathsf{a}, [b]_\mathsf{a}$ and $[ab + \delta]_\mathsf{a}$

Ideal functionality for triple generation secure up to additive attack: $\mathcal{F}_{\text{triple}}$

Adversarial Behavior: The adversary gets to specify the share values they receive from the functionality. Additionally, the adversary inputs a vector $\boldsymbol{\delta} \in \mathbb{F}^{h\ell}$.

Input: The functionality takes no input.

Computation: For $i \in \{1, \ldots, h\ell\}$

1. Sample random a_i and b_i and compute $c_i = a_i \cdot b_i + \delta_i$.
2. For each $i \in [h\ell]$, additively secret-share a_i, b_i, c_i to Com.

Output: Each party in Com receives a share of a_i, b_i, and c_i for $i \in \{1, \ldots, h\ell\}$.

Fig. 4. This is a randomized functionality that outputs additive shares of $h\ell = O(n^2)$ multiplication triples to a designated committee, Com. Note that although no parties have input, and only $|\mathsf{Com}| \leq n$ parties have output, the protocol for realizing the functionality is always an n-party protocol. The produced triples are secure up to additive attack.

Theorem 2. *Let $t = \epsilon n$ for some $\epsilon \in [0, .5)$, let $h = n - t$, and let $\ell = n/2 - \epsilon n$. Then the protocol for unauthenticated triple generation in Fig. 5 securely realizes the functionality of Fig. 4 in the presence of an active, computationally unbounded adversary corrupting t parties.*

Proof. We define $\mathcal{A}$ to be the set of corrupted parties, and $\mathcal{H}$ to be the set of honest parties. The simulator begins by selecting randomness on behalf of all honest parties, and executes the protocol on their behalf, exchanging messages with the adversary as needed.

In the first step of the protocol, for each $P_i \in \mathcal{A}$, when P_i calls $\mathsf{share}(d, \tilde{\mathbf{r}}_i)$, $\mathsf{share}(d, \tilde{\mathbf{a}}_i)$ and $\mathsf{share}(d, \tilde{\mathbf{b}}_i)$, the simulator extracts the values $\tilde{\mathbf{r}}_i, \tilde{\mathbf{a}}_i, \tilde{\mathbf{b}}_i$ from the shares sent to the honest parties. If the values are not consistently defined (because the degree of the polynomial is too high), $\mathcal{S}$ sets the shares to $\perp$, and continues the simulation until the degree check in Step 3, at which point $\mathcal{S}$ always aborts. Otherwise, $\mathcal{S}$ computes $(\mathbf{r}^{(1)}, \ldots, \mathbf{r}^{(h)}), (\mathbf{a}^{(1)}, \ldots, \mathbf{a}^{(h)}), (\mathbf{b}^{(1)}, \ldots, \mathbf{b}^{(h)})$ using the extracted values, the honest randomness, and the local multiplication with the Vandermonde matrix, M.

Prior to simulating the final message in which additive shares are sent to the output committee, Com, $\mathcal{S}$ extracts $\boldsymbol{\delta}$, the value used as an additive attack by $\mathcal{A}$, and submits this to the functionality. There are three places in which the adversary might introduce an additive attack; the simulator extracts three values, $\boldsymbol{\delta}_0, \boldsymbol{\delta}_1, \boldsymbol{\delta}_2$, some of which might be 0, and sums them to recover $\boldsymbol{\delta}$.

Triple generation (Π_{triple})

Inputs: No parties have any input.

1. P_i samples random $\tilde{\mathbf{r}}_i$, $\tilde{\mathbf{a}}_i$ and $\tilde{\mathbf{b}}_i$, and calls $\mathsf{share}(d, \tilde{\mathbf{r}}_i)$, $\mathsf{share}(2d, \tilde{\mathbf{r}}_i)$, $\mathsf{share}(d, \tilde{\mathbf{a}}_i)$ and $\mathsf{share}(d, \tilde{\mathbf{b}}_i)$.
2. Party P_i receives: $([\tilde{\mathbf{r}}_1]_d^i, \ldots, [\tilde{\mathbf{r}}_n]_d^i)$, $([\tilde{\mathbf{r}}_1]_{2d}^i, \ldots, [\tilde{\mathbf{r}}_n]_{2d}^i)$, $([\tilde{\mathbf{a}}_1]_d^i, \ldots, [\tilde{\mathbf{a}}_n]_d^i)$ and $([\tilde{\mathbf{b}}_1]_d^i, \ldots, [\tilde{\mathbf{b}}_n]_d^i)$.
and computes:
$\left([\mathbf{r}^{(1)}]_d^i, \ldots, [\mathbf{r}^{(h)}]_d^i\right) = M \cdot ([\tilde{\mathbf{r}}_1]_d^i, \ldots, [\tilde{\mathbf{r}}_n]_d^i)$,
$\left([\mathbf{r}^{(1)}]_{2d}^i, \ldots, [\mathbf{r}^{(h)}]_{2d}^i\right) = M \cdot ([\tilde{\mathbf{r}}_1]_{2d}^i, \ldots, [\tilde{\mathbf{r}}_n]_{2d}^i)$,
$\left([\mathbf{a}^{(1)}]_d^i, \ldots, [\mathbf{a}^{(h)}]_d^i\right) = M \cdot ([\tilde{\mathbf{a}}_1]_d^i, \ldots, [\tilde{\mathbf{a}}_n]_d^i)$, and
$\left([\mathbf{b}^{(1)}]_d^i, \ldots, [\mathbf{b}^{(h)}]_d^i\right) = M \cdot ([\tilde{\mathbf{b}}_1]_d^i, \ldots, [\tilde{\mathbf{b}}_n]_d^i)$
3. The parties call $[\boldsymbol{\gamma}]_d \leftarrow \mathcal{F}_{\mathsf{rand}}$.
The parties call $\mathcal{F}_{\mathsf{coin}}$ to get random coefficients $c_1, \ldots, c_{3h} \leftarrow \mathbb{F}$.
They compute $[\boldsymbol{\zeta}] = [\boldsymbol{\gamma}]_d + \sum_{i=1}^n c_i[\mathbf{a}_i]_d + c_{n+i}[\mathbf{b}_i]_d + c_{2n+i}[\mathbf{r}_i]_d$.
They open $\boldsymbol{\zeta}$, and verify that it is of degree d. If not, they abort.
4. For $j \in \{1, \ldots, h\}$, P_i computes $[\mathbf{m}^{(j)}]_{2d}^i = [\mathbf{a}^{(j)}]_d^i \cdot [\mathbf{b}^{(j)}]_d^i + [\mathbf{r}^{(j)}]_{2d}^i$, and sends $[\mathbf{m}^{(j)}]_{2d}^i$ to P_0.
5. For $j \in \{1, \ldots, h\}$, P_0 receives $([\mathbf{m}^{(j)}]_{2d}^1, \ldots, [\mathbf{m}^{(j)}]_{2d}^n)$. P_0 reconstructs the packed secrets: $\mathbf{m}^{(j)} = \mathsf{reconstruct}(2d, [\mathbf{m}^{(j)}]_{2d}^1, \ldots, [\mathbf{m}^{(j)}]_{2d}^n)$. P_0 then calls $\mathsf{share}(d, \mathbf{m}^{(j)})$ and sends the first $d+1$ shares to $P_1, \ldots, P_{d+1}$.
6. For $j \in \{1, \ldots, h\}$, each $P_i \in \{P_1, \ldots, P_{d+1}\}$ receives $[\mathbf{m}^{(j)}]_d^i$ from P_0, and computes
$[\mathbf{c}^{(j)}]_d^i = [\mathbf{m}^{(j)}]_d^i - [\mathbf{r}^{(j)}]_d^i = [\mathbf{a}^{(j)} \cdot \mathbf{b}^{(j)}]_d^i$.
P_i calls $\mathsf{aShare}([\mathbf{a}^{(j)}]_d^i)$, $\mathsf{aShare}([\mathbf{b}^{(j)}]_d^i)$, and $\mathsf{aShare}([\mathbf{c}^{(j)}]_d^i)$.
7. For each $j \in \{1, \ldots, h\}$, each $P_k \in \mathsf{Com}$ receives $([[\mathbf{a}^{(j)}]_d^1]_{\mathsf{a}}^k, \ldots, [[\mathbf{a}^{(j)}]_d^n]_{\mathsf{a}}^k)$, $([[\mathbf{b}^{(j)}]_d^1]_{\mathsf{a}}^k, \ldots, [[\mathbf{b}^{(j)}]_d^n]_{\mathsf{a}}^k)$, and $([[\mathbf{c}^{(j)}]_d^1]_{\mathsf{a}}^k, \ldots, [[\mathbf{c}^{(j)}]_d^n]_{\mathsf{a}}^k)$.
For $i \in \{1, \ldots, \ell\}$, $j \in \{1, \ldots, h\}$, P_k computes:
$[a^{(i,j)}]_{\mathsf{a}}^k = \mathsf{reconstruct}(d, i, [[\mathbf{a}^{(j)}]_d^1]_{\mathsf{a}}^k, \ldots, [[\mathbf{a}^{(j)}]_d^n]_{\mathsf{a}}^k)$.
$[b^{(i,j)}]_{\mathsf{a}}^k = \mathsf{reconstruct}(d, i, [[\mathbf{b}^{(j)}]_d^1]_{\mathsf{a}}^k, \ldots, [[\mathbf{b}^{(j)}]_d^n]_{\mathsf{a}}^k)$.
$[c^{(i,j)}]_{\mathsf{a}}^k = \mathsf{reconstruct}(d, i, [[\mathbf{c}^{(j)}]_d^1]_{\mathsf{a}}^k, \ldots, [[\mathbf{c}^{(j)}]_d^n]_{\mathsf{a}}^k)$.

Output: Each $P_k \in \mathsf{Com}$ outputs $\left\{[a^{(j)}]_{\mathsf{a}}^k, [b^{(j)}]_{\mathsf{a}}^k, [c^{(j)}]_{\mathsf{a}}^k\right\}_{j=1}^{|h\ell|}$

Fig. 5. Protocol for computing additive shares of $h\ell = O(n^2)$ triples. The shares are delivered to a designated committee, Com. For $|C|$ triples, this protocol must be repeated $|C|/h\ell$ times. $M \in \mathbb{F}^{h \times n}$ is a Van Der Monde matrix.

This is done for each of the h packed shares of triples. For ease of notation, we drop the superscript and only describe the simulation for one of these h values. Recall that P_0 denotes the dealer, and Com is the set of parties receiving output. We let D^+ denote the set $\{P_1, \ldots, P_{d+1}\}$.

If $P_0 \in \mathcal{H}$, $\mathcal{S}$ recovers $\mathbf{m}$ after the malicious parties send shares of $[\mathbf{m}]_{2d}$ to P_0 in Step 4. He then computes $\boldsymbol{\delta}_0 = \mathbf{m} - (\mathbf{ab} + \mathbf{r})$. If $P_0 \in \mathcal{A}$, $\mathcal{S}$ sets $\boldsymbol{\delta}_0 = 0^l$.

If $(P_0 \in \mathcal{A}) \wedge (D^+ \subset \mathcal{H})$:
$\mathcal{S}$ recovers $\mathbf{m}$ by interpolating the shares sent from P_0 to D^+ in Step 5. He computes $\boldsymbol{\delta}_1 = \mathbf{m} - (\mathbf{ab} + \mathbf{r})$. If $P_0 \in \mathcal{H}$, or $D^+ \not\subset \mathcal{H}$, $\mathcal{S}$ sets $\boldsymbol{\delta}_1 = 0^l$.

If $D^+ \not\subset \mathcal{H} \wedge \mathsf{Com} \subset \mathcal{H}$:
$\mathcal{S}$ recovers $\widetilde{\mathbf{ab}}$ by summing the shares sent from the malicious parties in D^+ to Com in Step 6 (using the stored values of any any honest parties in D^+ to fill in the gaps) and interpolating the resulting polynomial shares. He computes $\boldsymbol{\delta}_2 = \widetilde{\mathbf{ab}} - \mathbf{ab}$. If $D^+ \in \mathcal{H}$, or $\mathsf{Com} \not\subset \mathcal{H}$, $\mathcal{S}$ sets $\boldsymbol{\delta}_2 = 0^l$.
$\mathcal{S}$ sets $\boldsymbol{\delta} = \boldsymbol{\delta}_0 + \boldsymbol{\delta}_1 + \boldsymbol{\delta}_2$.

Finally, $\mathcal{S}$ calls $\mathcal{F}_{\mathsf{triple}}(\boldsymbol{\delta})$, and returns the output from the functionality to $\mathcal{A}$.

We now argue that $\mathcal{S}$ produces a joint distribution on the view of $\mathcal{A}$ and the output of honest parties that is statistically close to $\mathcal{A}$'s view in the real world, together with the honest output in a real execution.

We first argue that if $\mathcal{S}$ does not abort, the $\boldsymbol{\delta}$ value extracted by $\mathcal{S}$ is correct. That is, that it matches the $\boldsymbol{\delta}$ imposed in the real world output under the same adversarial behavior. Because $\mathcal{S}$ does not abort, the values $\mathbf{a}, \mathbf{b}$ and $\mathbf{r}$ that are extracted in the first step are well defined. There are only 3 other messages sent in the protocol: $[\mathbf{m}]_{2d}$ sent to P_0, the response $[\mathbf{m}]_d$ sent to D^+, and additive sharing of $[\mathbf{ab}]_d$ sent from D^+ to Com. In each of these 3 cases we show that the δ values that the adversary is able to introduce are independent of the values of $\mathbf{a}$ or $\mathbf{b}$. We note that this is not true when there is a *linear* attack since the $\boldsymbol{\delta}$ value in that case is allowed to be a linear combination of the packed values. Namely, we prove the following claim.

Claim. If $\mathcal{S}$ does not abort, then for any values $\bar{\mathbf{a}}$, $\bar{\mathbf{b}}$, and $\bar{\boldsymbol{\delta}} \in \mathbb{F}^l$, we have that

$$\Pr[\mathbf{a} = \bar{\mathbf{a}} \wedge \mathbf{b} = \bar{\mathbf{b}} | \boldsymbol{\delta} = \bar{\boldsymbol{\delta}}] = \Pr[\mathbf{a} = \bar{\mathbf{a}} \wedge \mathbf{b} = \bar{\mathbf{b}}]$$

Proof. Since $\mathcal{S}$ aborts whenever the degree of the initial sharing is too high, we know that $[\mathbf{a}]$, $[\mathbf{b}]$, and $[\mathbf{r}]$ are all shared via degree t polynomials, and thus the values $\mathbf{a}, \mathbf{b}, \mathbf{r}$ extracted by $\mathcal{S}$ are well defined. We now analyze all the ways in which a malicious $\mathcal{A}$ can introduce a non-zero $\boldsymbol{\delta}$.

If $P_0 \in \mathcal{H}$, then $\boldsymbol{\delta}_0$ is extracted by P_0 after receiving shares of $[\mathbf{m}]_{2d}$ in Step 4. In this case, $P_i \in \mathcal{A}$ can modify his share $[\mathbf{m}]_d^i$ to $[\mathbf{m}']^i = ([\mathbf{a}]_d^i + \delta_a) \cdot ([\mathbf{b}]_d^i + \delta_b) + [\mathbf{r}]_{2d}^i + \delta_m$ for adversarially chosen δ_a, δ_b, and δ_m, where each of these can be arbitrary functions of the $t < d$ shares received by the malicious parties in Step 1. Rewriting this as $[\mathbf{m}']^i = ([\mathbf{a}]_d^i \cdot [\mathbf{b}]_d^i) + (\delta_a \cdot [\mathbf{b}]_d^i) + (\delta_b \cdot [\mathbf{a}]_d^i) + \delta_m$, we see that P_i can contribute a value $\delta^i = (\delta_a \cdot [\mathbf{b}]_d^i) + (\delta_b \cdot [\mathbf{a}]_d^i) + \delta_m$, which is also a function of at most t shares of $\mathbf{a}$ and $\mathbf{b}$. Thus, the jth value in $\boldsymbol{\delta}_0$, $\boldsymbol{\delta}_0^j = \sum_{P_i \in \mathcal{A}} s_i^j \delta^i$ where the s_i^j are the corresponding Lagrange coefficients. Since $\boldsymbol{\delta}_0^j$ is a linear combination of these δ^i values, it follows that it is also independent of $\mathbf{a}$ and $\mathbf{b}$.

If $(P_0 \in \mathcal{A}) \wedge (D^+ \subset \mathcal{H})$, then $\mathcal{S}$ extracts $\boldsymbol{\delta_1}$ from the values sent to D^+ by the dealer in Step 5. Because the sharing is of degree $d = |D^+| - 1$, whatever P_0 sends in this step is a consistent sharing of some value, $\mathbf{m}'$. This value might be some function of $\mathbf{ab} + \mathbf{r}$, but because the P_0 has no information about $\mathbf{r}$, it follows that δ_1 is independent of $\mathbf{ab}$.

Finally, if $D^+ \not\subset \mathcal{H} \wedge \mathsf{Com} \subset \mathcal{H}$, $\boldsymbol{\delta_2}$ is extracted from the shares sent to Com. Thus, $\boldsymbol{\delta_2^j} = \sum_{P_i \in \mathcal{A}} s_i^j \delta_i$ where δ_i is the change introduce by P_i to his Shamir sharing of $\mathbf{ab}$ (during the process of additively sharing the Shamir share). Since this is again a linear combination of at most t shares of $\mathbf{ab}$, it is independent of $\mathbf{a}$ and $\mathbf{b}$.

We can now complete the proof of Theorem 2. It is easy to see that the shares included in $\mathcal{A}$'s view are independent of the values $\mathbf{a_i}, \mathbf{b_i}, \mathbf{r_i}$ chosen by $\mathcal{S}$. Moreover, by Claim 3, we know that, as long as the degree check does not fail, for any $\mathcal{A}$, the value of $\boldsymbol{\delta}$ is also independent of these values. In the real-world, the honest parties would output these shares while in the ideal-world they output the shares chosen by $\mathcal{F}_{\text{triple}}$. Since the view of $\mathcal{A}$ is independent of these values, both sets of honest outputs are consistent with $\mathcal{A}$'s view showing that the simulation is perfect. Finally, since the degree check succeeds with all but negligible probability, we have that the simulated joint distribution is statistically indistinguishable from that of the real world, proving the theorem.

4 Protocols for Circuit Evaluation

For input sharing and the online phase we use the well-known SPDZ protocol [16]. However, as SPDZ uses authenticated triples, the online protocol first needs to "authenticate" the triples produced by our offline phase. This authentication protocol is very similar to the protocols found in prior work ([3,14,16,32]), and appears in Sect. 4.1. We note that while the cost of authenticating the triples is asymptotically the same as the cost of using them for circuit evaluation, this does result in approximately a factor of 7 increase in communication in the online phase, when compare with the online phase of SPDZ. We leave reducing this as an interesting open question.

4.1 Authenticating the Triples

The previous protocol provides triples that are un-authenticated. We now use these unauthenticated triples to construct *authenticated* triples of the form $(a, b, c, \alpha a, \alpha b, \alpha c)$, where $ab = c$, and α, which is unknown to the parties, is used to authenticate all of the triples.

For a committee to generate $m = O(\frac{s|C|}{n})$ authenticated triples, they need to use $8m$ unauthenticated triples. We describe the protocol in the $\mathcal{F}_{\text{triple}}$-hybrid model, allowing the parties on this committee to receive these unauthenticated triples from that functionality. We remind the reader that in practice, the protocol realizing $\mathcal{F}_{\text{triple}}$ is executed in the full network. The remainder of the Π_{TripAuth}

$\mathcal{F}_{\mathsf{TripAuth}}$

Inputs: None.

Computation: Sample $\alpha \leftarrow \mathbb{F}$, and a random additive sharing, $[\alpha]$.

For $i \in [m]$:
- Sample $a_i, b_i \leftarrow \mathbb{F}$, and compute $c_i = a_i b_i$.
- Sample random additive sharings, $[a_i], [b_i], [c_i], [\alpha a_i], [\alpha b_i], [\alpha c_i]$

Output: $[\alpha], \{[a_i], [b_i], [c_i], [\alpha a_i], [\alpha b_i], [\alpha c_i]\}_{i=1}^{m}$

Fig. 6. An ideal functionality for constructing authenticated triples. The functionality is parameterized by an integer m indicating how many authenticated triples should be output.

protocol is carried out only by the smaller committees and only requires a dishonest majority.

Our construction is almost identical to the one used in SPDZ. The parties first choose an additive secret sharing of a random authentication value, α. They take one triple, $([a], [b], [c])$, and compute $([\alpha a], [\alpha b], [\alpha c])$ using 3 other triples, one for each multiplication (as in the classic result by Beaver [4]).[10] We denote this procedure by Mult in the protocol description.

Because the triples are additively shared and unauthenticated, it is important to note that the adversary can modify the shared value at anytime. To verify that we have a valid authenticated triple after performing these multiplications, we sacrifice one authenticated triple against another to catch any malicious modifications, precisely as in prior work.

The only difference between our construction and that of SPDZ (and the follow-up work) is in the way we instantiate the Mult sub-routine. While we use unauthenticated triples, as just described, SPDZ uses somewhat homomorphic encryption to generate these authenticated triples (prior to the sacrifice step). With that approach, once the parties hold $([a], [b], [c])$, the adversary is unable to modify the result of $\mathsf{Mult}(a, \alpha)$ or $\mathsf{Mult}(b, \alpha)$. However, because they need to refresh the ciphertext encrypting c, the adversary can introduce an additive shift, resulting in $\mathsf{Mult}(c + \delta_c, \alpha)$. In our realization of Mult, the adversary can introduce this shift on any of the inputs to Mult. For this reason, we provide a complete proof of security for the authentication step. The functionality and protocol realizing this authentication are given in Figs. 6 and 7 respectively.

Complexity. After receiving the $8M$ unauthenticated triples, each party sends $12M$ field elements in the $6M$ executions to the Mult subroutines, and another

[10] For example, to compute $[\alpha a]$ from $[\alpha]$ and $[a]$ using triple (x, y, z), the parties open $a + x$ and $\alpha + y$. Each locally fixes its share by computing $(a + x)[\alpha] + (\alpha + y)[a] - (a + x)(\alpha + y) + [z]$.

Π_{TripAuth}

Inputs: None.

Protocol:

1. The parties call $[\alpha] \leftarrow \mathcal{F}_{\mathsf{rand}}$.
2. The parties call $\mathcal{F}_{\mathsf{triple}}$ to generate $8m$ triples. We denote the first $2m$ of these triples by $\{[a_i], [b_i], [c_i], [a_i'], [b_i'], [c_i']\}_{i=1}^{m}$.
3. The parties call $[a\alpha] = \mathsf{Mult}(a, \alpha), [b\alpha] = \mathsf{Mult}(b, \alpha), [c\alpha] = \mathsf{Mult}(c, \alpha)$ and $[a'\alpha] = \mathsf{Mult}(a', \alpha), [b'\alpha] = \mathsf{Mult}(b', \alpha), [c'\alpha] = \mathsf{Mult}(c', \alpha)$
4. The parties call $(r_1, \ldots, r_m) \leftarrow \mathcal{F}_{\mathsf{rand}}$.
5. For $i \in [m]$, the parties
   - compute and open $\overline{a}_i = r_i \cdot [a_i] - [a_i']$, and $\overline{b}_i = [b_i] - [b_i']$.
   - The parties compute:

$$[\gamma_i] = r_i[c_i\alpha] - [c_i'\alpha] - \overline{b}_i[a_i'\alpha] - \overline{a}_i[b_i'\alpha] - \overline{a}_i\overline{b}_i[\alpha]$$

$$[\rho_i] = r_i[a_i\alpha] - [a_i'\alpha] - \overline{a}_i[\alpha]$$

$$[\sigma_i] = [b_i\alpha] - [b_i'\alpha] - \overline{b}_i[\alpha]$$

6. The parties call $(\tau_1, \ldots, \tau_{3m}) \leftarrow \mathcal{F}_{\mathsf{rand}}$.
7. The parties compute

$$[\zeta] = \sum_{i=1}^{m} \tau_i[\gamma_i] + \sum_{i=1}^{m} \tau_{m+i}[\rho_i] + \sum_{i=1}^{m} \tau_{2m+i}[\sigma_i]$$

   The parties open $[\zeta]$ using a commit-and-reveal. If $\zeta \neq 0$, abort.

Output: Each party outputs its shares of $[\alpha], ([a_i], [b_i], [c_i])$, and $([a_i\alpha], [b_i\alpha], [c_i\alpha])$.

Fig. 7. Protocol for sacrificing some triples in order to authenticate others. The authenticated triples are then used in the online phase. The protocol is in the $\mathcal{F}_{\mathsf{triple}}$-hybrid model (Fig. 4), and realizes the $\mathcal{F}_{\mathsf{TripAuth}}$ functionality (Fig. 6). The Mult sub-routine is the standard protocol by Beaver [4] for securely computing $[xy]$ from $[x]$ and $[y]$.

$2\,M$ field elements in the sacrifice step. The rest of the communication can be amortized, as it is independent of m.

It is known that we can further reduce the number of unauthenticated triples needed [31]. In the sacrifice step, instead of using 2 independent triples, we can use $(\alpha a, \alpha b, \alpha c)$ and $(\alpha a', \alpha b, \alpha c')$, where b was used twice. In this case, we could reduce communication per triple in our offline phase by 12.5% (by sending half as many b values), and we can reduce the number of triples needed in the Π_{TripAuth} protocol by 12.5% (because we only multiply b with α and not b'.)[11]

[11] Note that our offline phase has a computational bottleneck, so reducing the communication cost per triple might not lead to large improvement in runtime, though it still may reduce the dollar cost of communicating. Reducing the number of triples needed will reduce end-to-end runtime.

Theorem 3. *The protocol Π_{TripAuth} securely realizes $\mathcal{F}_{\mathsf{TripAuth}}$ in the $\mathcal{F}_{\mathsf{triple}}$-hybrid model, in the presence of an active adversary corrupting all but one party.*

Proof. The proof of Theorem 3 follows from prior work and we defer it to the full version.

4.2 Providing Input and MACCheck

For providing input, we note that SPDZ uses authenticated random values $([r], [\alpha r])$ to mask the inputs. We can use the shares of either a or b from an authenticated triple in place of these random values.

Finally, as in SPDZ, prior to reconstructing the output, we perform a MAC-Check on all values opened during the protocol. Specifically, as in SPDZ, we do this by opening α to all parties. The parties can then perform a batched MAC-Check on all values that were publicly opened during multiplication. For the parties providing input, the committee additionally opens $[\alpha r]$ to the relevant party, allowing them to locally MACCheck the masks r that they used to hide their inputs.

As these protocols, and the corresponding functionalities, are exactly as described in SPDZ and we omit their descriptions here.

5 Optimizing Large-Scale MPC

Having presented the components of our protocol in Sects. 3 and 4, we now describe trade-offs that result from various choices of committee sizes. In the process we identify several standard, but critical optimization techniques, and we identify communication and computation bottlenecks. We also provide a more in-depth analysis of the enhanced "folklore" schemes described in Sect. 1.2, explaining how these compare to our work.

5.1 Protocol Optimizations

We make heavy use of the following two standard optimization techniques. While these are not new, we briefly describe them here for completeness.

Pseudorandom share transfer: Our first optimization technique allows us to transfer an additively shared value using very low communication by using a PRG. Suppose a party P wants to additively secret share a value s to a committee Com containing S parties. P pre-shares a PRG seed s_i with each party P_i in Com. Then, for all but the last party in Com, both P and $P_i \in \mathsf{Com}$ compute a share as $[s]_i = G(s_i)$, and P computes $s - \sum_{i=1}^{s-1} [s]_i$ and sends this value to P_S as his share. In this way, P can share a secret with a committee of any size while communicating only one field element. If we start with an additive secret sharing of s across a committee Com_1, using the same technique, we can transfer this shared value to another committee Com_2 (of arbitrary size) by having each party in Com_1 send one field element. We observe that this technique does not work for

Shamir-shared values. Instead, the natural parallel (e.g., as described by [20,34]) can only save, approximately, a factor of 2 in the communication.

Amortization: A second optimization that we use extensively in all of our protocols is amortization. Specifically, we rotate the roles in our protocol to ensure that the communication and computation loads are split equally across all parties. For example, we rotate the party serving as the dealer (P_0) in Steps 4–5 of Fig. 5, and we rotate the party receiving the real share in the pseudorandom share transfer described above.

5.2 Protocol Bottlenecks

To simplify the analysis of both our and related protocols, we decompose our protocol into phases, allowing us to analyze the bottlenecks of each phase separately.

1. The *Vandermonde* phase corresponds to Steps 1–2 of Fig. 5 in which parties generate doubly-shared (packed) random values. This phase is always run by all n parties and produces $O(|C|/n)$ packed secrets. It requires each party to send (and receive) $O(n)$ shares (one to each party) to produce $O(n)$ packed secrets, resulting in $O(|C|/n)$ bottleneck communication.
   For computation, for every n packed secrets, each party must produce its own packed share, requiring $O(n \log n)$ field operations using an FFT, and must perform multiplication by the Vandermonde matrix M, which can be done by an IFFT in the same time. Thus, we have a bottleneck computation of $O(|C|/n^2 \cdot n \log n) = O(\log n |C|/n)$ field multiplications.
2. The *Triple Gen.* phase corresponds to Steps 3–5 in Fig. 5. This phase is again run by all n parties, and we rotate the dealer to ensure that each party plays the role of the dealer in a $1/n$ fraction of the $O(|C|/n)$ executions. Each time a party is the dealer, it receives and sends $O(n)$ shares for each packed triple and also performs an iFFT and an FFT to produce the new sharing. Thus, the bottleneck communication is $O(|C|/n^2 \cdot n) = O(|C|/n)$ field elements and the bottleneck computation is $O(\log n|C|/n)$ field operations. We note that Step 3 (degree check) is only performed once per $O(n^2)$ triples, and thus will not be the bottleneck.
3. The *Transfer* phase corresponds to Step 6 in Fig. 5. In this phase all n parties sub-share their (Shamir-shared) packed triples to the committee Com. The cost of this step varies a good deal in our different protocol variants, so we defer the discussion.
4. The *Unpack* phase corresponds to Step 7 in Fig. 5. In this phase the parties in Com perform local computation to unpack the received triples into additively shared triples. This requires no communication, but requires an IFFT and thus $O(n \log n)$ field operations for every n shares.
5. The *Online* phase corresponds to the online protocols described in Sect. 4.

5.3 Protocol Variants

We now describe several different protocol variants for realizing secure committee-based MPC. For each of these variants, we analyze its asymptotic communication and computation complexity. Additionally, for each of these protocol variants, we analyze analogous committee-based protocols built on top of the existing protocols [10,16,20], as described briefly in Sect. 1.2, to provide an apples-to-apples comparison to our work. For ease of reference, we duplicate the tables that appeared in Sect. 1.2 here.

Single Online, Single Unpack				
	Ours	$t < n/3$ [20]	$t < n/2$ [10]	$t < n$ [16]
Comm	$O(\lvert C\rvert/n)$	$O(\lvert C\rvert)$	$O(\lvert C\rvert)$	$O(s\lvert C\rvert)$
Comp	$O(\log n\lvert C\rvert)$	$O(\log n\lvert C\rvert)$	$O(\log s\lvert C\rvert)$	$O(s\lvert C\rvert)$

Fig. 8. Asymptotic complexities for the offline phase of four protocols. In our variant, and in that of [20], all parties participate throughout. In the other two protocols, the state-of-the-art is run by a small committee: with an honest majority in column 4, and a malicious majority in column 5. All values measure bottleneck costs, rather than total costs. The online communication and computation cost for all four protocols is $O(C)$, and is not included.

Single Committee: The first protocol variant we consider is one that directly follows the protocol specified in Fig. 5. That is, we use a single committee Com for performing both the *unpack* and *online* phases. We consider both a committee of size $O(s)$, and the case where Com is the set of all n parties. In the former case, the communication bottleneck (for the offline portion) is the cost for the committee parties to receive the packed secrets. Since we have $O(|C|/n)$ packed secrets, with n parties holding a share of each, there are a total of $O(|C|)$ shares that need to be transmitted to Com. Using pseudorandom shares and amortizing receiving cost, this requires each party in Com to receive $O(|C|/s)$ field elements. If, on the other hand, we let $|\mathsf{Com}| = n$, then we can split the task of receiving these shares across all n parties, resulting in $O(|C|/n)$ bottleneck communication. We note that in this case, this also matches the bottleneck communication in the Vandermonde and Triple gen. phases. In both of these options, the bottleneck communication of the online phase is $O(|C|)$: given multiplication triples, evaluating a multiplication gate requires $O(1)$ communication by each party in Com. In both cases, the computation bottleneck arises from the unpacking step, where the parties in Com need to unpack $O(|C|/n)$ packed shares, each requiring $O(n \log n)$ field operations (for FFT), resulting in bottleneck computation of $O(\log n|C|)$ field operations.

It is worth exploring the trade-off here between bottleneck complexity and total complexity. We have added Fig. 9 to help do so. Because receiving shares is a bottleneck, we lower the bottleneck complexity in the offline phase if we have a bigger receiving committee. Put another way, using pseudorandom shares, sending to a larger committee does not increase the total communication, but it does distribute the cost of receiving that same data. On the other hand, when we look at the cost of the online phase, computing in a smaller committee does reduce the total communication. The question of which is preferable depends on the application, and possibly on the incentive of the participants and the protocol administrator. In some rough sense, a lower bottleneck complexity implies a shorter run-time, while a lower total complexity implies a cheaper protocol, financially. We note that the same comparison can be made for the protocol using a single malicious majority committee in Fig. 10, and for the two protocols with malicious majority committees in Fig. 11. We avoid the redundancy and do not include the data in our figures.

Single Online, Single Unpack				
	Offline		Online	
	$\lvert\mathsf{Com}\rvert = n$	$\lvert\mathsf{Com}\rvert = O(s)$	$\lvert\mathsf{Com}\rvert = n$	$\lvert\mathsf{Com}\rvert = O(s)$
Bottleneck Comm	$O(\lvert C\rvert/n)$	$O(\lvert C\rvert/s)$	$O(\lvert C\rvert)$	$O(\lvert C\rvert)$
Total Comm	$O(\lvert C\rvert)$	$O(\lvert C\rvert)$	$O(n\lvert C\rvert)$	$O(s\lvert C\rvert)$
Bottleneck Comp	$O(\log n\lvert C\rvert)$	$O(\log n\lvert C\rvert)$	$O(\lvert C\rvert)$	$O(\lvert C\rvert)$
Total Comp	$O(n\log n\lvert C\rvert)$	$O(s\log n\lvert C\rvert)$	$O(n\lvert C\rvert)$	$O(s\lvert C\rvert)$

Fig. 9. We compare two variants of our protocol that was described in Fig. 10. In the first column, the packed triples are re-shared with the full network, and unpacked by all n parties. In the second column, the they are re-shared with a small, malicious majority committee, and unpacked there.

For comparison purposes, we consider analogous protocol variants built from existing protocols. First, consider the protocol of Furukawa and Lindell [20] which is secure for $t < n/3$. Since we only have $t < n/3$, this protocol must use all n parties for the entire computation resulting in an $O(|C|)$ bottleneck communication and $O(|C|\log n)$ computation (from the Vandermonde step). It is easy to see that we achieve significant asymptotic savings in offline communication while matching the online communication and computation bottlenecks. Second, consider the protocol of Genkin et al. [23]. This protocol also requires $t < n/3$ and thus must use all n parties. However, this circuit works by converting the circuit C into a SIMD circuit at the cost of a $O(\log|C|)$ factor increase in circuit size. This results in an offline and online bottleneck communication of $O(|C|\log|C|/n)$, a $O(\log|C|)$ overhead on our protocols.

Next, we build a protocol using the honest majority (i.e., $t < n/2$) protocol from Chida et al. [10]. For this protocol we select random Com of size $O(s)$ that guarantees honest majority within the committee, and use this committee for the entire computation. Since the Chida et al. protocol cannot take advantage of pseudorandom share transfer, there is no benefit to using a committee of size n. This results in a bottleneck communication of $O(|C|)$ for both the offline (i.e., Vandermonde) and online phases and $O(|C|\log s)$ computation (from Vandermonde multiplication). We again significantly improve in the offline communication. However, we are now slightly worse in bottleneck computation.

Finally, we consider a protocol variant using the malicious majority protocol of Damgård et al. [16]. For this setting, we choose a committee of size $O(s)$ to guarantee at least one honest party and run both the offline and online phase inside this committee. Here, the higher complexity of triple generation becomes the bottleneck resulting in $O(s|C|)$ bottleneck communication and computation for the triple generation. This communication is worse than our protocol by a factor of $O(n)$. The online communication of $O(|C|)$ matches our protocol.

Single Online, Distributed Unpack			
	Ours	$t < n/2$	$t < n$
Comm	$O(s\|C\|/n)$	$O(s\|C\|)$	$O(s^2\|C\|/n)$
Comp	$O(s \log n\|C\|/n)$	$O(s \log s\|C\|/n)$	$O(s^2\|C\|/n)$

Fig. 10. In our protocol variant, triples are unpacked in many parallel committees, and then transferred back to the full set of size n. Costs are measured through the transfer step, and exclude the cost of the online phase. In the column labeled $t < n/2$, many parallel committees, each with an honest majority, prepare double-sharings that will be used by a single online committee of size $O(s)$. In the column labeled $t < n$, many parallel committees, each with at least one honest participant, generate multiplication triples that will be used by the full network of size n. The online phase still requires $O(|C|)$ for all three protocols, and is not included in the Table.

Distributed triple generation: We note that the bottleneck computation cost of our protocol grows logarithmically in the number of parties. For our protocol, this bottleneck comes from the cost of the unpacking phase. Thus, our next protocol variant addresses this problem by distributing the unpacking. Specifically, we elect many *unpacking* committees, each of size $O(s)$ to guarantee at least one honest party per committee. These committees split the triples to unpack, and then transfer the unpacked triples to the online committee (which can again be of size $O(s)$ or include all n parties). Now each unpacking committee only needs to unpack a $O(s/n)$ fraction of the triples, requiring $O(|C|/n \cdot s/n \cdot n \log n) = O(s \log n|C|/n)$ field operations. However, we now need to communicate unpacked triples to the online committee. Since there are $O(|C|)$ unpacked triples held by committees that are each of size $O(s)$, we need to receive a total of $O(s|C|)$ shares. If we use a committee of size $O(s)$, this requires $O(|C|)$ bottleneck communication, but if we use an online committee of size $O(n)$, this only requires $O(s|C|/n)$ communication. We note, however, that the total communication of the protocol (across all parties) does not decrease, and in fact, increases for the online computation. However, we still believe that presenting the bottleneck complexity is the correct metric here as it measures the end-to-end computation time for running the protocol, whereas the total (or average) communication is measuring the total monetary cost of running the protocol.

We now describe equivalent protocol variants using the protocols of Chida et al. [10] and Damgård et al. [16]. We do not provide further comparison to Furukawa and Lindell [20] or Genkin et al. [23] as their protocols require $t < n/3$ and thus cannot be used with smaller committees. For both of these base protocols, the equivalent protocol variant is to elect many "offline" committees that generate double-shared values (in the case of Chida et al.) or triples (in the case of Damgård et al.) and then transmit this material to a single online committee. For Chida et al., since this protocol cannot take advantage of the pseudorandom share transfer, the cost of transferring the offline material forms the bottleneck of $O(s|C|)$ field elements, a factor of $O(n)$ worse than our best deployment. However, the ability to use smaller committees, each generating a $O(s/n)$ fraction of the pre-processing material, results in $O(s \log s|C|/n)$ field operations bottleneck computation. While this computation is asymptotically better than what we achieve, we note that, concretely, the two are quite similar. Specifically, the $O(s)$ size committee necessary to guarantee honest majority is much larger than the committee needed to guarantee at least one honest party. Concretely, for 2^{-40} security, a committee of size 25 suffices for dishonest majority, but a committee of size 430 is needed to guarantee honest majority. In comparing computation between these solutions, we need to compare $O(s \log n)$ for dishonest majority to $O(s \log s)$ for the honest majority setting. For $n < 2^{150}$, $25 \log n < 430 \log 430$. Taking other constants into account, our protocol requires roughly 2X more computation.

The equivalent protocol variant using Damgård et al. chooses many triple generation committees of size $O(s)$ and has them all transfer the produced triples to the online committee. Since there are $O(n/s)$ such offline committees, each one is tasked with generating $O(s|C|/n)$ triples for bottleneck communication of $O(s^2|C|/n)$, which is $O(s)$ times worse than what is achieved by our protocol.

Distributed Online						
	Ours		$t < n/2$		$t < n$	
	Offline	Online	Offline	Online	Offline	Online
Comm	$O(\|C\|/n)$	$O(s\|C\|/n)$	$O(s\|C\|/n)$	$O(s^2\|C\|/n)$	$O(s^2\|C\|/n)$	$O(s\|C\|/n)$
Comp	$O(s \log n\|C\|/n)$	$O(s\|C\|/n)$	$O(s \log s\|C\|/n)$	$O(s\|C\|/n)$	$O(s^2\|C\|/n)$	$O(s\|C\|/n)$

Fig. 11. Here we distribute the work done in the online phase, assigning $O(s|C|/n)$ gates to each of the $O(n/s)$ committees. In all three protocols, the material generated during pre-processing remains with the same committee for the online phase. The state of the online phase is transfered from one committee to the next.

Distributed Online Computation: Finally, we note that the online cost of all our protocols considered so far grows linearly with $|C|$, as parties in the online committee must send $O(1)$ bits for each gate. To improve on this, we design a protocol that also distributed the online computation. Specifically, we elect many *online* committees, each of size $O(s)$ to guarantee at least one honest party per committee. These committees split the gates of the circuit to evaluate, with each committees responsible for an $O(s/n)$ fraction of the gates. Of course, the intermediate gate outputs must be communicated to the committee responsible for the next gate. Using pseudorandom share transfer, this can be done with each party sending $O(1)$ field elements per gate. Thus, each party needs $O(s|C|/n)$ communication for computing the gates it is responsible for and the same amount of communication to transfer the results of these gates. We note that this deployment also reduces the communication of the offline phase. The reason for this is that we no longer need to transfer unpacked triples to a single online committee, instead each unpacking committee serves as an online committee using the triples it unpacks. Thus, the cost of transfer in the offline phase disappears, and with triple generation and Vandermonde steps as the new bottleneck, we get $O(|C|/n)$ bottleneck communication. Since the computation in the offline phase is unchanged, this remains $O(s \log n|C|/n)$.

For a comparison, we consider similar protocol variants built using the protocols of Chida et al. [10] and Damgård et al. [16]. While we can similarly partition the online phase in both these protocols, the advantages of doing so for Chida et al. are limited. Since their $t < n/2$ protocol cannot take advantage of pseudorandom share transfer, the cost to transmit the state between gates of the circuit dominates, resulting in online communication of $O(s^2|C|/n)$, a factor of $O(s)$ worse than for our protocol. The Damgård et al. protocol, on the other hand, can benefit from pseudorandom share transfer, and can thus distribute their online phase at the same communication cost as our protocol. However, in their offline phase, the cost of triple generation becomes the bottleneck requiring communication of $O(s^2|C|/n)$, which is $O(s^2)$ times worse than our offline cost. The computational load for the distributed online protocol is the same as in the distributed unpacking protocol regardless of which of the three protocols is used as the building block. Thus, in the distributed online variant, our protocol is strictly better than the variants based on either existing protocol, achieving a factor of at least $O(s)$ improvement in communication in both the online and offline phases for Chida et al., and in the offline phase for Damgård et al.

Triples as a service: A related protocol variant that we wish to mention briefly is that of triples as a service. Here, our protocol would be used to produce triples, distributed across multiple unpacking committees, for use by external parties for their online MPC computation. In this case, we do not need to pay the cost for transferring the triples to the clients or for the online phase. Thus, looking at only the offline costs for our optimal deployment (the distributed online one), we see that for this variant we save a factor of $O(s)$ and $O(s^2)$ in communication costs over Chida et al. and Damgård et al. respectively.

6 Concrete Performance Estimation

In Sect. 5 we analyzed the asymptotic performance of our protocols and compared them to committee-based protocols. Here we look at how these protocols

n	1 mbps		10 mbps		100 mbps		1000 mbps	
	Ours	DN	Ours	DN	Ours	DN	Ours	DN
1024	8898.0	384380.2	1366.2	39286.2	613.0	4776.8	539.6	1325.9
4096	2248.3	85541.2	369.6	8769.4	181.7	1092.2	162.9	324.5
16384	571.0	20274.3	101.6	2086.5	54.7	267.7	50.0	85.8
65536	144.9	5071.6	27.5	524.3	15.8	69.6	14.6	24.1
262144	36.8	1266.5	7.5	131.5	4.6	18.0	4.3	6.7
1048576	9.4	316.6	2.0	33.1	1.3	4.8	1.2	1.9
Ratio	33.8 - 43.2		16.2 - 28.8		3.6 - 7.8		1.6 - 2.5	
Ratio Per Gate	9.7 - 12.3		4.6 - 8.2		1 - 2.2		.5 - .7	

Fig. 12. Ours vs. Damgård-Nielsen Pre-Processing Time. This describes the time, in milliseconds, for n parties to generate one million (unauthenticated) triples (for our protocol) or doubly-shared random values (for DN) as used by Chida et al. [10]. For both we use the multiple unpacking committees protocol. Times are given for four different network bandwidths from 1mbps to 1000mbps. The ratio is a range of ratios between DN and our protocol. In the final row, we consider the fact that the online phase of Chida et al. requires only 2 unauthenticated triples per gate, whereas our online phase requires 7 unauthenticated triples per gate.

might perform in practice, taking into account the constants hidden in the big-O notation, and the incomparable nature of communication and computation. To better understand the concrete performance comparison, we built a prototype to estimate computation and communication time for two of the protocol variants previously described: our own protocol using distributed unpacking and distributed online evaluation, and the comparable protocol that uses parallel honest majority committees for pre-processing (labeled $t < n/2$ in Fig. 11).

In both cases, we only measure the performance of the offline phase, as we view this as our main contribution. Additionally, the offline phase of the distributed online protocol is precisely what is needed for the triples-as-a-service application.

We also do not compare to the cost of parallel triple generation using malicious majority committees. Asymptotically, this protocol is worse than the variant using honest majority committees, in both communication and computation (Fig. 11). When considering the concrete costs reported in Overdrive [32], it seems to compare less favorably than the honest majority protocol that we have chosen for comparison. Also important is that the protocol we implemented looks similar to our own (since both rely on DN). Nevertheless, a concrete comparison with malicious majority committees would be interesting to add in the future.

6.1 Measurement Details

To estimate the performance of these protocols, we use different techniques for computation and communication. For computation, we implement and run a single party doing the full computation of our protocol to give an accurate estimate of the bottleneck complexity. This is done using the implementation of

FFT from the libiop library [1]. All experiments were performed on a machine with a dual core i7 cpu at 2.80 GHz.

To estimate the cost of communication, we took a somewhat different approach. Since we do not have access to millions of compute nodes, instead of building a full, networked test of our protocol, we precisely calculated the necessary communication at each step, and estimated the communication time as a function of the network bandwidth and latency. For this evaluation, we varied the available bandwidth between 1 mbps, 10 mbps, 100 mbps, and 1000 mbps.

6.2 Results

The results of our empirical evaluation are given in Fig. 12 where we report the time (in milliseconds) needed to produce one million (unauthenticated) triples. Recall that our offline protocol generates unauthenticated triples, and we need 7 such triples for each gate in the online phase. In contrast, protocols using honest majority in the online phase require only 2 unauthenticated triples per gate. In the row labeled "Ratio Per Gate" we provide estimates with this distinction in mind. In the remainder of the Table, we consider the costs of generating unauthenticated triples. At the top end of our performance, with approximately $1,000,000$ parties on a 1000 mbps network, we can generate one million triples in only 1.2 milliseconds. But, our best performance improvement over honest majority committees is on lower bandwidth networks, where we can outperform their pre-processing protocol by as much as 43.2X, and 12.3X when considering authenticated triples. This is due to the fact that our biggest improvement is in communication, at a slight cost in computation. We note that when considering deployment of MPC across tens or hundreds of thousands of parties, it is quite unlikely that all parties will have access to a high-speed (e.g., 1000 mbps) network connection. For example, 4G LTE offers roughly 10 mbps. For synchronous protocols such as ours, the bandwidth and latency of the slowest party becomes that of all parties. Thus, we believe that our results for lower network speeds more closely represent the use-cases we envision.

Acknowledgments. The authors would like to thank the anonymous reviewers for many helpful comments. Arkady Yerukhimovich and Dov Gordon are supported by NSF grant 1955264. Arkady Yerukhimovich is also supported by a Facebook Research Award.

References

1. libiop. https://github.com/scipr-lab/libiop
2. Ames, S., Hazay, C., Ishai, Y., Venkitasubramaniam, M.: Ligero: Lightweight sublinear arguments without a trusted setup. In: Thuraisingham, B.M., Evans, D., Malkin, T., Xu, D. (eds.). ACM CCS 2017, pp. 2087–2104. ACM Press, October/November 2017

3. Baum, C., Cozzo, D., Smart, N.P.: Using TopGear in overdrive: a more efficient ZKPoK for SPDZ. In: Paterson, K.G., Stebila, D. (eds.) SAC 2019. LNCS, vol. 11959, pp. 274–302. Springer, Cham (2020). https://doi.org/10.1007/978-3-030-38471-5_12
4. Beaver, D.: Efficient multiparty protocols using circuit randomization. In: Feigenbaum, J. (ed.) CRYPTO 1991. LNCS, vol. 576, pp. 420–432. Springer, Heidelberg (1992). https://doi.org/10.1007/3-540-46766-1_34
5. Beerliová-Trubíniová, Z., Hirt, M.: Perfectly-secure MPC with linear communication complexity. In: Canetti, R. (ed.) TCC 2008. LNCS, vol. 4948, pp. 213–230. Springer, Heidelberg (2008). https://doi.org/10.1007/978-3-540-78524-8_13
6. Boyle, E., Goldwasser, S., Tessaro, S.: Communication locality in secure multiparty computation. In: Sahai, A. (ed.) TCC 2013. LNCS, vol. 7785, pp. 356–376. Springer, Heidelberg (2013). https://doi.org/10.1007/978-3-642-36594-2_21
7. Boyle, E., Jain, A., Prabhakaran, M., Yu, C.-H.: The bottleneck complexity of secure multiparty computation. In: Chatzigiannakis, I., Kaklamanis, C., Marx, D., Sannella, D. (eds.). ICALP 2018, vol. 107. LIPIcs, pp. 24:1–24:16. Schloss Dagstuhl, July 2018
8. Bracha, G.: An o(log n) expected rounds randomized byzantine generals protocol. J. ACM **34**(4), 910–920 (1987)
9. Chandran, N., Chongchitmate, W., Garay, J.A., Goldwasser, S., Ostrovsky, R., Zikas, V.: The hidden graph model: communication locality and optimal resiliency with adaptive faults. In: Roughgarden, T. (ed.) ITCS 2015, pp. 153–162. ACM, January 2015
10. Chida, K., et al.: Fast large-scale honest-majority MPC for malicious adversaries. In: Shacham, H., Boldyreva, A. (eds.) CRYPTO 2018. LNCS, vol. 10993, pp. 34–64. Springer, Cham (2018). https://doi.org/10.1007/978-3-319-96878-0_2
11. Choudhury, A., Patra, A.: Optimally resilient asynchronous MPC with linear communication complexity. In: Proceedings of the 2015 International Conference on Distributed Computing and Networking, ICDCN 2015, Goa, India, 4–7 January 2015, pp. 5:1–5:10 (2015)
12. Damgård, I., Ishai, Y.: Scalable secure multiparty computation. In: Dwork, C. (ed.) CRYPTO 2006. LNCS, vol. 4117, pp. 501–520. Springer, Heidelberg (2006). https://doi.org/10.1007/11818175_30
13. Damgård, I., Ishai, Y., Krøigaard, M.: Perfectly secure multiparty computation and the computational overhead of cryptography. In: Gilbert, H. (ed.) EUROCRYPT 2010. LNCS, vol. 6110, pp. 445–465. Springer, Heidelberg (2010). https://doi.org/10.1007/978-3-642-13190-5_23
14. Damgård, I., Keller, M., Larraia, E., Pastro, V., Scholl, P., Smart, N.P.: Practical covertly secure MPC for dishonest majority - or: Breaking the SPDZ limits. In: Crampton, J., Jajodia, S., Mayes, K. (eds.) ESORICS 2013. LNCS, vol. 8134, pp. 1–18. Springer, Heidelberg (2013)
15. Damgård, I., Nielsen, J.B.: Scalable and unconditionally secure multiparty computation. In: Menezes, A. (ed.) CRYPTO 2007. LNCS, vol. 4622, pp. 572–590. Springer, Heidelberg (2007). https://doi.org/10.1007/978-3-540-74143-5_32
16. Damgård, I., Pastro, V., Smart, N., Zakarias, S.: Multiparty computation from somewhat homomorphic encryption. In: Safavi-Naini, R., Canetti, R. (eds.) CRYPTO 2012. LNCS, vol. 7417, pp. 643–662. Springer, Heidelberg (2012). https://doi.org/10.1007/978-3-642-32009-5_38

17. Dani, V., King, V., Movahedi, M., Saia, J.: Quorums quicken queries: efficient asynchronous secure multiparty computation. In: Chatterjee, M., Cao, J., Kothapalli, K., Rajsbaum, S. (eds.) ICDCN 2014. LNCS, vol. 8314, pp. 242–256. Springer, Heidelberg (2014). https://doi.org/10.1007/978-3-642-45249-9_16
18. Franklin, M.K., Yung, M.: Communication complexity of secure computation (extended abstract). In: 24th ACM STOC, pp. 699–710. ACM Press, May 1992
19. Frederiksen, T.K., Keller, M., Orsini, E., Scholl, P.: A unified approach to MPC with preprocessing using OT. In: Iwata, T., Cheon, J.H. (eds.) ASIACRYPT 2015. LNCS, vol. 9452, pp. 711–735. Springer, Heidelberg (2015). https://doi.org/10.1007/978-3-662-48797-6_29
20. Furukawa, J., Lindell, Y.: Two-thirds honest-majority MPC for malicious adversaries at almost the cost of semi-honest. In: Cavallaro, L., Kinder, J., Wang, X., Katz, J. (eds.) ACM CCS 2019, pp. 1557–1571. ACM Press, November 2019
21. Garay, J., Ishai, Y., Ostrovsky, R., Zikas, V.: The price of low communication in secure multi-party computation. In: Katz, J., Shacham, H. (eds.) CRYPTO 2017. LNCS, vol. 10401, pp. 420–446. Springer, Cham (2017). https://doi.org/10.1007/978-3-319-63688-7_14
22. Genkin, D.: Secure computation in hostile environments (Phd thesis) (2016)
23. Genkin, D., Ishai, Y., Polychroniadou, A.: Efficient multi-party computation: from passive to active security via secure SIMD circuits. In: Gennaro, R., Robshaw, M. (eds.) CRYPTO 2015. LNCS, vol. 9216, pp. 721–741. Springer, Heidelberg (2015). https://doi.org/10.1007/978-3-662-48000-7_35
24. Genkin, D., Ishai, Y., Prabhakaran, M., Sahai, A., Tromer, E.: Circuits resilient to additive attacks with applications to secure computation. In: Shmoys, D.B. (ed.) 46th ACM STOC, pp. 495–504. ACM Press, May/June 2014
25. Hazay, C., Ishai, Y., Marcedone, A., Venkitasubramaniam, M.: LevioSA: lightweight secure arithmetic computation. In: Cavallaro, L., Kinder, J., Wang, X., Katz, J. (eds.) ACM CCS 2019, pp. 327–344. ACM Press, November 2019
26. Hazay, C., Orsini, E., Scholl, P., Soria-Vazquez, E.: Concretely efficient large-scale MPC with active security (or, TinyKeys for TinyOT). In: Peyrin, T., Galbraith, S. (eds.) ASIACRYPT 2018. LNCS, vol. 11274, pp. 86–117. Springer, Cham (2018). https://doi.org/10.1007/978-3-030-03332-3_4
27. Hazay, C., Orsini, E., Scholl, P., Soria-Vazquez, E.: TinyKeys: a new approach to efficient multi-party computation. In: Shacham, H., Boldyreva, A. (eds.) CRYPTO 2018. LNCS, vol. 10993, pp. 3–33. Springer, Cham (2018). https://doi.org/10.1007/978-3-319-96878-0_1
28. Ishai, Y., Kushilevitz, E., Ostrovsky, R., Sahai, A.: Zero-knowledge from secure multiparty computation. In: Johnson, D.S., Feige, U. (eds.) 39th ACM STOC, pp. 21–30. ACM Press, June 2007
29. Jaiyeola, M.O., Patron, K., Saia, J., Young, M., Zhou, Q.M.: Good things come in LogLog(n)-sized packages: robustness with small quorums. CoRR, arXiv:1705.10387 (2017)
30. Kairouz, P., et al.: Advances and open problems in federated learning (2019)
31. Keller, M., Orsini, E., Scholl, P.: MASCOT: faster malicious arithmetic secure computation with oblivious transfer. In: Weippl, E.R., Katzenbeisser, S., Kruegel, C., Myers, A.C., Halevi, S. (eds.) ACM CCS 2016, pp. 830–842. ACM Press, October 2016
32. Keller, M., Pastro, V., Rotaru, D.: Overdrive: making SPDZ great again. In: Nielsen, J.B., Rijmen, V. (eds.) EUROCRYPT 2018. LNCS, vol. 10822, pp. 158–189. Springer, Cham (2018). https://doi.org/10.1007/978-3-319-78372-7_6

33. Lindell, Y., Nof, A.: A framework for constructing fast MPC over arithmetic circuits with malicious adversaries and an honest-majority. In: Thuraisingham, B.M., Evans, D., Malkin, T., Xu, D., (eds.) ACM CCS 2017, pp. 259–276. ACM Press, October/November 2017
34. Nordholt, P.S., Veeningen, M.: Minimising communication in honest-majority MPC by batchwise multiplication verification. In: Preneel, B., Vercauteren, F. (eds.) ACNS 2018. LNCS, vol. 10892, pp. 321–339. Springer, Cham (2018). https://doi.org/10.1007/978-3-319-93387-0_17
35. Scholl, P., Smart, N.P., Wood, T.: When it's all just too much: outsourcing MPC-preprocessing. In: O'Neill, M. (ed.) IMACC 2017. LNCS, vol. 10655, pp. 77–99. Springer, Cham (2017). https://doi.org/10.1007/978-3-319-71045-7_4
36. Wails, R., Johnson, A., Starin, D., Yerukhimovich, A., Gordon, S.D.: Stormy: statistics in tor by measuring securely. In: Cavallaro, L., Kinder, J., Wang, X., Katz, J. (eds.) ACM CCS 2019, pp. 615–632. ACM Press, November 2019
37. Wang, X., Ranellucci, S., Katz, J.: Global-scale secure multiparty computation. In: Thuraisingham, B.M., Evans, D., Malkin, T., Xu, D. (eds.) ACM CCS 2017, pp. 39–56. ACM Press, October/November 2017
38. Zamani, M., Movahedi, M., Saia, J.: Millions of millionaires: multiparty computation in large networks. Cryptology ePrint Archive, Report 2014/149 (2014). http://eprint.iacr.org/2014/149
39. Zheng, C., Tang, Q., Lu, Q., Li, J., Zhou, Z., Liu, Q.: Janus: a user-level TCP stack for processing 40 million concurrent TCP connections. In: 2018 IEEE International Conference on Communications (ICC), pp. 1–7 (2018)

Multiparty Reusable Non-interactive Secure Computation from LWE

Fabrice Benhamouda[1(✉)], Aayush Jain[2,3], Ilan Komargodski[3,4], and Huijia Lin[5]

[1] Algorand Foundation, New York, USA
[2] UCLA, Los Angeles, CA 90095, USA
aayushjain@cs.ucla.edu
[3] NTT Research, Sunnyvale, CA 94085, USA
[4] Hebrew University of Jerusalem, 91904 Jerusalem, Israel
ilank@cs.huji.ac.il
[5] University of Washington, Seattle, WA 98195, USA
rachel@cs.washington.edu

Abstract. Motivated by the goal of designing versatile and flexible secure computation protocols that at the same time require as little interaction as possible, we present new multiparty reusable Non-Interactive Secure Computation (mrNISC) protocols. This notion, recently introduced by Benhamouda and Lin (TCC 2020), is essentially two-round Multi-Party Computation (MPC) protocols where the first round of messages serves as a reusable commitment to the private inputs of participating parties. Using these commitments, any subset of parties can later compute any function of their choice on their respective inputs by just sending a single message to a stateless evaluator, conveying the result of the computation but nothing else. Importantly, the input commitments can be computed without knowing anything about other participating parties (neither their identities nor their number) and they are reusable across any number of desired computations.

We give a construction of mrNISC that achieves standard simulation security, as classical multi-round MPC protocols achieve. Our construction relies on the Learning With Errors (LWE) assumption with polynomial modulus, and on the existence of a pseudorandom function (PRF) in NC^1. We achieve semi-malicious security in the plain model and malicious security by further relying on trusted setup (which is unavoidable for mrNISC). In comparison, the only previously known constructions of mrNISC were either using bilinear maps or using strong primitives such as program obfuscation.

We use our mrNISC to obtain new Multi-Key FHE (MKFHE) schemes with threshold decryption:

- In the CRS model, we obtain threshold MKFHE for NC^1 based on LWE with only *polynomial* modulus and PRFs in NC^1, whereas all previous constructions rely on LWE with super-polynomial modulus-to-noise ratio.
- In the plain model, we obtain threshold levelled MKFHE for P based on LsWE with *polynomial* modulus, PRF in NC^1, and NTRU, and

A. Canteaut and F.-X. Standaert (Eds.): EUROCRYPT 2021, LNCS 12697, pp. 724–753, 2021.
https://doi.org/10.1007/978-3-030-77886-6_25

another scheme for constant number of parties from LWE with subexponential modulus-to-noise ratio. The only known prior construction of threshold MKFHE (Ananth et al., TCC 2020) in the plain model restricts the set of parties who can compute together at the onset.

1 Introduction

Much of the research in secure multiparty computation (MPC) is driven by the goal of minimizing interaction as much as possible. This is first motivated by the fact that network latency is often a major bottleneck to efficiency. Furthermore, having many communication rounds requires participating parties to be stateful and on-line for a long time which is difficult if not possible in some scenarios, especially when the number of participants is large. Soon after the invention of MPC [19,33,48], a large body of works investigated constant-round MPC protocols, or even completely non-interactive ones.

The vision of non-interactive MPC is extremely fascinating. Ideally, it would allow any set of parties to jointly compute an arbitrary function of their respective secret inputs, without any prior interaction or input-dependent setup, by each sending a single message to a public bulletin board, enabling an external evaluator to compute the output of the function based only on these messages.[1] Unfortunately, it is known that such non-interactive protocols cannot satisfy the standard simulation security notion, as they are inherently susceptible to the so called residual-function attack. Therefore, at least another round of communication is necessary.

MrNISC. In a recent work, Benhamouda and Lin [22] introduced a hybrid model between non-interactive MPC and two-round MPC which they called *multiparty reusable Non-Interactive Secure Computation (mrNISC)*. To motivate the model, it is useful to consider the following scenario: users across the world wish to publish an encryption of their DNA on a public bulletin board, once and for all. At a later stage, for the purposes of medical analysis, a subset of them wants to compute some function on their DNAs by sending just a single public message to a doctor, who should be able to compute this function, but nothing else. Furthermore, a user may participate in an unbounded number of medical analyses, reusing the same encryption of DNA, with the same or other subsets of parties on the same or different functions.

More formally, in the mrNISC model, parties publish encodings of their private inputs x_i on a public bulletin board, once and for all, independently of each other and even independently of the total number of parties. Later, any subset I of them can compute *on-the-fly* a function f on their inputs $\boldsymbol{x}_I = \{x_i\}_{i \in I}$

[1] The reconstruction of the output is "public" in the sense that it does not require any secrets. It is w.l.o.g. to consider public output reconstruction, as one can always consider the evaluator as a participant of MPC with a dummy input and uses the all zero string as its random tape.

by just sending a single public message to a stateless evaluator, conveying the result $f(\boldsymbol{x}_I)$ and nothing else. Importantly, the input encodings are reusable across any number of computation sessions, and are generated independently of any information of later computation sessions—each later computation can evaluate any polynomial-time function, among any polynomial-size subset of participants. The security guarantee is that an adversary corrupting a subset of parties, chosen statically at the beginning, learns no information about the private inputs of honest parties, beyond the outputs of the computations they participated in. This holds for any polynomial number of computation sessions. Throughout, each party's input, and the function and participants of each computation session are chosen adaptively by the adversary.

The work of Benhamouda and Lin [22] presents a general-purpose mrNISC for computing polynomial-sized circuits, whose security is based on the SXDH assumption in asymmetric bilinear groups. It is in the plain model (without any trusted setup), and satisfies semi-malicious security.[2] For malicious security, the use of some setup is inevitable; they rely on a CRS. To date, this is the only mrNISC construction in the plain model, based on well-established assumptions. Prior plain-model 2-round MPC protocols either rely on strong primitives like indistinguishability obfuscation or general-purpose witness encryption [29,35,39, 42,50] which have complex constructions from less well-established assumptions, or have first messages that are not reusable [6,7,21,40,41,43,44,60], or only reusable among a fixed set of parties [8,17]. Another line of works leading to two-round MPC, using multi-key fully-homomorphic encryption (MKFHE) [10, 12,25,27,34,56,58], could possibly be made an mrNISC, but even then all known constructions rely on trusted setup even for semi-honest security.

1.1 Our Results

New mrNISC from LWE. Our main result is a new construction of an mrNISC. Our construction is based on the standard Learning-With-Errors (LWE) assumption with polynomial modulus as well as on a PRF in NC^1. The construction is in the plain model, and satisfies semi-malicious security.

Theorem 1.1 (mrNISC from LWE). *Assuming LWE with polynomial modulus and a PRF in* NC^1, *there exists a mrNISC protocol for all polynomial-size functions. The construction is in the plain model (without any trusted setup), and satisfies semi-malicious security. For malicious security, we need to further rely on a CRS.*[3]

We emphasize that our construction requires only LWE with polynomial modulus. This is important both for efficiency as well as for security. First, having

[2] Semi-malicious security is a strengthening of the semi-honest security wherein the adversary is allowed to choose its random tape arbitrarily. [10] showed that any protocol satisfying semi-malicious security can be made maliciously secure by additionally using Non-Interactive Zero-Knowledge proofs (NIZKs).

[3] The CRS is needed for NIZK which exists from LWE with polynomial modulus [59].

a polynomial modulus makes the sizes of keys and ciphertexts shorter. Second, for security, it is known that LWE with polynomial ratio between modulus and noise (which is our case) is at least as hard as (classical) GapSVP with polynomial approximation factor [26,53,54,57,61].

Unfortunately, it is not known whether PRF in NC^1 can be based on LWE with polynomial modulus-to-noise ratio, as all known constructions require super-polynomial modulus-to-noise ratio [15,16,23]. Therefore, the above theorem can also be instantiated using a single assumption of LWE with super-polynomial modulus-to-noise ratio, which is independent of the depths of computations.

New Threshold Multi-key FHE Schemes. We observe that mrNISC can be used to generically boost any multi-key FHE with an "unstructured" decryption function that takes as input the secret key of all participating parties, into a threshold multi-key FHE scheme by just decentralizing the decryption function.

This observation gives us new constructions of threshold multi-key FHE by instantiating the base multi-key FHE scheme with different known constructions. Specifically, we obtain the following three threshold multi-key FHE instantiations.

Theorem 1.2 (Threshold multi-key FHE in the CRS model). *There exists a threshold multi-key FHE scheme in the CRS model for* NC^1 *circuits assuming LWE with* polynomial *modulus and a PRF in* NC^1.

The above theorem follows from the multi-key FHE schemes of [34,56], which require LWE with polynomial modulus for evaluating NC^1 circuits. Here, we rely additionally on a PRF in NC^1. In comparison, all previous constructions of threshold multi-key FHE even for NC^1 require LWE with super-polynomial modulus-to-noise ratio. Since the latter readily implies a PRF in NC^1, our assumption is weaker.

Theorem 1.3 (Threshold multi-key FHE in the plain model). *Let* $d = d(\lambda)$ *and* $N = N(\lambda)$ *be arbitrary polynomial functions of the security parameter.*

1. *There exists a threshold multi-key FHE scheme in the plain model for polynomial-size depth-*d *circuits and supporting* N *keys. The scheme is secure assuming LWE with polynomial modulus, a PRF in* NC^1*, and the DPSR assumption.*[4]
2. *There exists a threshold multi-key FHE scheme in the plain model for polynomial-size depth-*d *circuits and supporting arbitrary constant number of keys. The scheme is secure assuming LWE with sub-exponential modulus-to-noise ratio.*

The first bullet is obtained by using the multi-key FHE scheme of [52]. Recently, Ananth et al. [9] obtained a similar result except that their threshold multi-key FHE definition is somewhat weak in the sense that the set of public-keys under which each evaluation is performed is fixed once and for all. On the other

[4] DSPR stands for the *decision small polynomial ratio* assumption [52] which is used to prove the security of the NTRU encryption scheme.

hand, the original vision for multi-key FHE was to support "on-the-fly" computation [52] on ciphertext encrypted any subset of public-keys. All other multi-key FHE schemes were not in the plain model.

The second bullet is obtained by relying on the folklore multi-key FHE scheme obtained by nesting a constant number of FHE schemes. There was no previously-known scheme supporting constant-many keys without setup just from LWE.

Technical Highlight and an Open Problem. Our construction is obtained in few modular steps. We first identify a "two-party" NISC protocol (denoted 2rNISC henceforth) for a particular functionality that we call "functional OT". This protocol still supports arbitrary polynomially-many parties, but only the function to be computed is specific and involves just two parties. More specifically, the two parties, acting as the OT sender and receiver, respectively, wish to compute OT with two sender's strings $(\ell_0, \ell_1) = g_1(x_1)$ computed from sender's private input x_1, and a receiver's choice bit $c = g_2(x_2)$ computed from the receiver's private input x_2, where g_1, g_2 are arbitrary public polynomial-size circuits that are different for each computation. 2rNISC enables computing ℓ_c with the sender and receiver sending a single message each. We then show that this can be generically turned into a general-purpose mrNISC. We believe that 2rNISC for the functional OT functionality is an interesting primitive that may find other applications.

Lastly, we show a construction of a 2rNISC for the functional OT functionality, from LWE with polynomial modulus-to-noise ratio and PRFs in NC^1. Our construction draws techniques from homomorphic commitments/signatures [49] and 2-message statistically sender-private OT [24] based on LWE. At its core is a weak version of witness encryption for verifying the decommitments of homomorphic commitments, where the decommitments satisfy zero-knowledge property. This partially answers a question left open by the work of [22].

We believe that the above modular approach is a contribution of independent interest, as new constructions of our 2rNISC for the functional OT functionality directly yield new constructions of mrNISC. One intriguing open problem is whether it is possible to base mrNISC on DDH or even CDH. Our reduction shows that, for this purpose, it suffices to build a 2rNISC for a specific functionality from DDH/CDH.

1.2 Related Works

While mrNISC is a new concept that was recently introduced by Benhamouda and Lin [22], it is related to (but differs from) many previously-defined variants of minimal-interaction MPC protocols. We refer to [22] for a comprehensive comparison and merely mention some of the most related notions. mrNISC can be viewed as a generalization of the notion of reusable NISC of Ishai et al. [51] (see also [1,11,14,30,32]) from two parties to multiple parties. mrNISC differs from various completely non-interactive notions such as non-interactive MPC (NIMPC) [18] and Private Simultaneous Messages (PSM) [38,47] which inherently achieve weaker security guarantees or restrict the corruption pattern.

Apart from Benhamouda and Lin's [22] recent mrNISC construction from bilinear maps, all other 2-message MPC protocols either rely on strong primitives like indistinguishability obfuscation or general-purpose witness encryption [39, 50], or fall short of being an mrNISC. For instance, the works of Garg and Srinivasan and Benhamouda and Lin [21,44] constructed 2-round MPC protocols from any 2-round Oblivious Transfer (OT). However, both constructions are not reusable in their first message. This was recently solved by Ananth et al. [8] and Bartusek et al. [17] who constructed a 2-round MPC where the first message is reusable across polynomially-many sessions. The construction of [8] relies on LWE and the construction of [17] relies on DDH. However, both construction requires all computation sessions to be carried out by a fixed set of parties.

The concept of threshold multi-key FHE is very related to mrNISC. It is plausible that threshold multi-key FHE that are used to get 2-round MPC [10,13,34,56], could also be used to get mrNISC. However, proving it is not straightforward. For instance, as pointed out in [22], the current definitions of threshold decryption, e.g., [10,13,34,56] are insufficient for constructing mrNISC, as simulatability only ensures that a single partial decryption can be simulated (hence this definition does not allow to re-use ciphertexts). Even if the proof works out, it would only yield a mrNISC in the CRS model even for semi-honest security.

1.3 Organization of the Paper

We start by a technical overview in Sect. 2. After recalling preliminaries in Sect. 3, we show how to construct a 2rNISC for Functional OT in Sect. 4. We then present our transformation from such a 2rNISC to an mrNISC for any polynomial-time functionality in Sect. 5. Finally, we formally show applications in the full version [20].

2 Technical Overivew

We now give an overview of our construction of mrNISC protocols in the plain model from LWE with polynomial modulus and PRF in NC^1.

2.1 Review of Definition of mrNISC Protocols

Towards constructing mrNISC protocols, the work of [22] defined the notion of mrNISC schemes, with a game-based security definition. Furthermore, they showed that a mrNISC scheme immediately yields a mrNISC protocol that UC-implements an ideal mrNISC functionality that allows for any number of computations over any subsets of inputs registered by parties. Thus, in this work, we focus on implementing mrNISC schemes for polynomial-size circuits.

mrNISC Scheme. An n-party functionality $\mathcal{U}$ is a represented by a Boolean circuit that takes a public input z and n private inputs. If $\mathcal{U}$ is a universal circuit and z specifies the actual function to be computed, then this formalism allows the parties of the mrNISC to compute any function on their private inputs. An mrNISC scheme for $\mathcal{U}$, consists the following three algorithms:

- Input Encoding: A party P_i encodes its private input x_i by invoking $(\hat{x}_i, s_i) \leftarrow \mathsf{Com}(1^\lambda, x_i)$. It then publishes the encoding $\hat{x}_i$ and keeps the secret state s_i.
- Computation: In order for a subset of parties $\{P_i\}_{i \in I}$ to compute the functionality $\mathcal{U}$ on their private inputs $\boldsymbol{x}_I$ and a public input z, each party in I generates a computation encoding $\alpha_i \leftarrow \mathsf{Encode}(z, \{\hat{x}_j\}_{j \in I}, s_i)$ and sends it to the evaluator.
- Output: The evaluator reconstructs the output $y = \mathsf{Eval}(z, \{\hat{x}_i\}_{i \in I}, \{\alpha_i\}_{i \in I})$. (Note that reconstruction is *public* as the evaluator has no secret state.) Correctness requires that $y = \mathcal{U}(z, \{x_i\}_{i \in I})$ when everything is honestly computed.

Simulation-security requires that the view of an adversary corrupting the evaluator and a subset of parties, can be simulated using just the outputs of the computations.[5] Following [22], we consider static corruptions and semi-malicious security. Static corruptions restrict the adversary to corrupt a fixed subset C of parties chosen at the very beginning, and semi-malicious security [10] restricts the corrupted parties $\{P_i\}_{i \in C}$ to follow the protocol specification, but allows the adversary to choose their inputs and randomness $\{x_i, r_i\}_{i \in C}$ arbitrarily. During an execution of the mrNISC scheme for $\mathcal{U}$, honest and corrupted parties P_i can register their inputs by posting input encodings $\hat{x}_i$. Multiple computations, each specified by (z^k, I^k), can be carried out as follows: each P_i for $i \in I^k$ sends the corresponding computation encoding α_i^k, which together reveal $y^k = \mathcal{U}(z^k, \{x_i\}_{i \in I^k})$. All the messages from the honest parties, including $\{\hat{x}_i\}_{i \notin C}$ and $\{\alpha_i^k\}_{k, i \in I^k \setminus C}$, must be simulatable from the outputs $\{y^k\}_k$, the public information of the computations $\{z^k, I^k\}_k$, and the input and randomness of the corrupted parties $\{x_i, r_i\}_{i \in C}$. Furthermore, simulation must hold in the adaptive setting, where the input and computation encodings are interleaved and all x_i and (z^k, I^k) are chosen adaptively by the adversary.

2.2 Step 1: Reusable Functional OT from LWE

We identify a complete 2-party function, called *functional OT* $\mathcal{U}_{\mathrm{fOT}}$, and show 1) how to construct a 2-party reusable NISC scheme for computing $\mathcal{U}_{\mathrm{fOT}}$ in the plain model, and 2) how to bootstrap from $\mathcal{U}_{\mathrm{fOT}}$ to general mrNISC scheme for any circuit $\mathcal{U} \in \mathrm{P}$.

Functional OT. $\mathcal{U}_{\mathrm{fOT}}$ takes three inputs: A public input consisting of two functions $g_1 \colon \{0,1\}^{n_1} \to \{0,1\}^\lambda \times \{0,1\}^\lambda$ and $g_2 \colon \{0,1\}^{n_2} \to \{0,1\}$ represented as Boolean circuits, a private input $x_1 \in \{0,1\}^{n_1}$ from a party P_1 acting as the $\mathcal{U}_{\mathrm{fOT}}$ sender $x_2 \in \{0,1\}^{n_2}$ from a party P_2 acting as the $\mathcal{U}_{\mathrm{fOT}}$ receiver, and computes:

[5] It suffices to simulate only these computations that involve at least one honest party. Computations involving only corrupted parties can be viewed as part of the internal computation of the adversary.

$$\mathcal{U}_{\mathrm{fOT}}((g_1,g_2),x_1,x_2) \;: \text{compute sender's strings } (\ell_0,\ell_1)=g_1(x_1),$$
$$\text{compute receiver's choice } c=g_2(x_2),$$
$$\text{output } \; y=(c,\ell_c)$$

The name functional OT comes from the fact that both the OT sender's strings ℓ_0, ℓ_1 and receiver's choice bit c are functions on sender's and receiver's private inputs x_1 and x_2.

A 2rNISC scheme for computing $\mathcal{U}_{\mathrm{fOT}}$ provides a way to encode the private input x_i of any party P_i, so that later any two parties P_i and P_j can securely compute $\mathcal{U}_{\mathrm{fOT}}$ (acting as sender and receiver respectively) to reveal only (c, ℓ_c) computed according to arbitrarily chosen functions (g_1, g_2) and their private inputs x_i and x_j, by each sending a single message. Importantly, the encoding $\hat{x}_i$ of P_i is reusable in any number of $\mathcal{U}_{\mathrm{fOT}}$ computations with different parties and different functions. Note that different from classical OT where (c, ℓ_c) is private to the receiver, a 2rNISC scheme allows to reconstruct (c, ℓ_c) publicly given all messages sent. Jumping ahead, this feature serves exactly the purpose of achieving the public reconstruction property of mrNISC.

Constructing 2rNISC for $\mathcal{U}_{\mathrm{fOT}}$. We construct 2rNISC for $\mathcal{U}_{\mathrm{fOT}}$ in the plain model from LWE with just *polynomial modulus* and PRF in NC^1 in two steps: We start with designing a scheme $\Pi_{\mathrm{fOT}} = (\mathsf{Com}, \mathsf{Encode}, \mathsf{Eval})$ that handles only circuits g_2 with bounded logarithmic depth $O(\log \lambda)$ (whereas the depth of g_1 is unrestricted), and then bootstrap Π to 2rNISC that handles g_2 with unbounded polynomial depth.

GSW ENCRYPTION AS HOMOMORPHIC COMMITMENTS. Our 2rNISC makes use of the GSW homomorphic encryption scheme [46], which can be turned into a homomorphic commitment scheme (or homomorphic trapdoor functions) as done in [49]. It enables us to commit to a string $\boldsymbol{x} \in \{0,1\}^n$ in a commitment $\mathbf{C}$, and then homomorphically evaluate any circuit f on $\mathbf{C}$ to obtain a commitment $\mathbf{C}_f$ to $f(\boldsymbol{x})$. More concretely, the scheme publishes a CRS $\mathsf{crs} = \mathbf{A}$ containing a matrix of dimension $N \times M$ for $M = \Omega(N \cdot \log q)$; the matrix $\mathbf{A} = [\mathbf{B}^\top | \boldsymbol{b}_1^\top | \ldots | \boldsymbol{b}_k^\top]^\top$ consists of a random submatrix $\mathbf{B} \leftarrow \mathbb{Z}_q^{(N-k)\times M}$, together with k LWE samples $\{b_l = \boldsymbol{t}_l \mathbf{B} + \boldsymbol{e}_l\}_{l\in[k]}$ w.r.t. independently sampled secret $\boldsymbol{t}_l$ and noise $\boldsymbol{e}_l$, where $\boldsymbol{e}_1$ is sampled from a *truncated* discrete Gaussian distribution and always bounded by $|\boldsymbol{e}_l|_\infty \leq B$. Committing to a binary string $\boldsymbol{x}$ simply involves encrypting each bit x_i using GSW encryption and public key $\mathbf{A}$, and the encryption randomness is the decommitment.

$$\text{Commitment to}\boldsymbol{x} : \{\mathbf{C}_i = \mathbf{A}\mathbf{R}_i + x_i \mathbf{G}\}_i \qquad \text{Decommitment: } \{\mathbf{R}_i\}_i$$
$$\text{where } \mathbf{R}_i \leftarrow \{-1,1\}^{M\times N\cdot\lceil \log q\rceil},\ \mathbf{G} \text{ the gadget matrix.}$$

We note two important details: First, the matrix $\mathbf{A}$ corresponds to the public key in GSW encryption; here, we insist on it containing $k > 1$ LWE samples, where k is a parameter that scales with the input length of the parties. Second, when $\mathbf{A}$ is sampled honestly at random, it satisfies the following well-formedness with overwhelming probability: *1)* it is generated as above using some $\mathbf{B}$, $\boldsymbol{t}_l$, and B-bounded $\boldsymbol{e}_l$'s, and *2)* vectors $\boldsymbol{e}_l$'s are linearly independent over the integers. Observe that the well-formedness can be verified efficiently given the random coins used to sample $\mathbf{A}$. For any $\mathbf{A}$ satisfying property 1), commitments w.r.t. $\mathbf{A}$ are statistical binding, and in fact even extractable using the secrets $\boldsymbol{t}_l$'s. We shall see how property 2) is helpful later.

The homomorphism of GSW enables homomorphic evaluation over the commitments to obtain a commitment to $f(\boldsymbol{x})$ as follows

$$\mathsf{GSW.Eval}(f, \{\mathbf{C}_i\}) = \mathbf{C}_f = \mathbf{A}\mathbf{R}_f + f(\boldsymbol{x})\mathbf{G} \ , \qquad \text{where } \mathbf{R}_f = \mathsf{GSW.RandEval}(f, \{\mathbf{R}_i\}, \{\mathbf{C}_i\}, \boldsymbol{x}) \ .$$

The new decommitment $\mathbf{R}_f$ can be evaluated directly from $\{\mathbf{R}_i\}, \{\mathbf{C}_i\}, \boldsymbol{x}$ and in particular is linear in the original decommitments $\mathbf{R}_i$'s.

FROM HOMOMORPHIC COMMITMENTS TO 2RNISC. To construct 2rNISC for functional OT, our idea is letting each player P_i commit to its input $\boldsymbol{x}$ as the input encoding, and keep the decommitment as its private state. Note that the homomorphic commitments require a CRS, but we wish to construct 2rNISC in the plain model. Thus, we let each player choose its own CRS.

$$\mathsf{Com}(1^\lambda, \boldsymbol{x}) \ : \ \hat{\boldsymbol{x}} = (\mathbf{A}, \{\mathbf{C}_i = \mathbf{A}\mathbf{R}_i + x_i\mathbf{G}\}_i), \quad s = \{\mathbf{R}_i\}_i$$

Later two parties, P_1 acting as the sender and P_2 acting as the receiver, wish to compute functional OT w.r.t. (g_1, g_2) on their private inputs denoted as $\boldsymbol{x}_1$ and $\boldsymbol{x}_2$, and have encodings and secret states denoted as $(\hat{\boldsymbol{x}}_b = (\mathbf{A}_b, \{\mathbf{C}_{b,i}\}), s_b = \{\mathbf{R}_{b,i}\})$ with $b = 1$ for P_1 and $b = 2$ for P_2. P_1 can privately compute sender's strings $(\ell_0, \ell_1) = g_1(\boldsymbol{x}_1)$, and P_2 the receiver's choice $c = g_2(\boldsymbol{x}_2)$. In addition, given $\hat{\boldsymbol{x}}_2$, both parties can homomorphically evaluate g_2 to obtain a commitment $\mathbf{C}_{g_2} = \mathbf{A}_2\mathbf{R}_{g_2} + c\mathbf{G}$ to c, while P_2 additionally knows the decommitment $\mathbf{R}_{g_2}$.

At this point, we wish to have the following two components to enable computing ℓ_c non-interactively.

- *Witness Encryption of Sender's Strings* (ℓ_0, ℓ_1): P_1 would like to witness encrypt ℓ_b w.r.t. the statement that, under CRS $\mathbf{A}$, $\mathbf{C}_{g_2}$ is a commitment to bit b, so that, ℓ_b is revealed given a witness that is a decommtiment to b, and is hidden if $\mathbf{C}_{g_2}$ is a commitment to $1-b$. Then the sender's computation encoding is

$$\mathsf{Encode}((g_1, g_2), (\hat{x}_1, \hat{x}_2), s_1) \ : \ \alpha_1 = \{\boldsymbol{w}_b \leftarrow \mathsf{WEnc}((\mathbf{A}_2, \mathbf{C}_{g_2}, b), \ell_b)\}_{b \in \{0,1\}}$$

- *Zero-Knowledge Decommitment to Receiver's Choice* c: P_2 would like to open $\mathbf{C}_{g_2}$ to c by sending a decommitment, in a zero-knowledge way that reveals only c and nothing more about $\boldsymbol{x}_2$. Note that the basic decommitment $\mathbf{R}_{g_2}$ is not zero-knowledge and may reveal information of $\boldsymbol{x}_2$.

$$\mathsf{Encode}((g_1, g_2), (\hat{x}_1, \hat{x}_2), s_2 = \{\mathbf{R}_i\}_i) \ : \ \alpha_2 = (\mathbf{X}_{g_2} \leftarrow \mathsf{ZKDecom}(g_2, \mathbf{C}_{g_2}, \mathbf{R}_{g_2})) \ ,$$

where $\mathsf{ZKDecom}$ produces a zero-knowledge decommitment $\mathbf{X}_{g_2}$.

An evaluator given (α_1, α_2) can witness decrypt to obtain ℓ_c as desired.

SEMI-MALICIOUS SECURITY AND "PROMISE" WE AND ZK DECOMMITMENTS. The main technical challenge is co-designing WE and ZK decommitments so that the latter can decrypt the former. For this we will draw techniques from previous works for constructing context-hiding homomorphic signatures [49] and 2-message statistically sender private OT [24]. At the same time, we crucially rely on the fact that our 2rNISC only need to be secure against semi-malicious adversaries to simplify the requirements on WE and ZK decommitments. The key observation is that a semi-malicious corrupted party P_2 must generate its input encoding $(\mathbf{A}_2, \{\mathbf{C}_{2,i}\}_i)$ using the honest algorithm, albeit using arbitrary randomness. This means that *i)* $\mathbf{A}_2$ must be well-formed and *ii)* $\{\mathbf{C}_{2,i}\}_i$ must be a valid commitment $\{\mathbf{A}_2\mathbf{R}_i + x_{2,i}\mathbf{G}\}_i$ to some input $\boldsymbol{x}_2$ with a decommitement $\mathbf{R}_i$ of $1/-1$ values. As a result, $\mathbf{C}_{g_2} = \mathbf{A}_2\mathbf{R}_{g_2} + g_2(\boldsymbol{x}_2)\mathbf{G}$ must be a valid commitment to $g_2(\boldsymbol{x}_2) = 0/1$ with a decommitment $\mathbf{R}_{g_2}$ of small magnitude[6].

Therefore, the correctness and security of WE and ZK decommitments only need to hold w.r.t. well-formed $\mathbf{A}$ (i.e., $\mathbf{A}_2$) and valid commitment $\mathbf{C}$ (i.e., $\mathbf{C}_{g_2}$) to $0/1$ with small decommitment, and does not need to hold w.r.t. ill-formed $\mathbf{A}$ or invalid commitment $\mathbf{C}$—we refer to this as the *promise* version of WE and ZK decommitments:

- *Yes instances* $(\mathbf{A}, \mathbf{C}, b)$ contain a well-formed $\mathbf{A}$ and a valid commitment $\mathbf{C}$ to bit b, and we require the ZK property of the decommitments and correctness of WE for them.
- *No instances* $(\mathbf{A}, \mathbf{C}, b)$ contain a well-formed $\mathbf{A}$ and a valid commitment $\mathbf{C}$ to bit $1-b$, and we require the hiding property of WE for them.

Thanks to the fact that it suffices to focus on the promise version, we manage to give a relatively simple construction of WE and ZK decommitment. Next we proceed to their description; by default, all matrices $\mathbf{A}$'s are well-formed and commitments $\mathbf{C}$'s are valid $0/1$ commitments.

ZK DECOMMITMENT. The context-hiding homomorphic signature schemes of [49] provides a way to generate zero-knowledge decommtiments. If the committer wishes to open $\mathbf{C}_f = \mathbf{A}\mathbf{R}_f + f(\boldsymbol{x})\mathbf{G}$ to $f(\boldsymbol{x}) = b$ w.r.t. CRS $\mathbf{A}$, it constructs the matrix

$$\mathbf{D}^{(b)} = [\mathbf{A} \mid \mathbf{C}_f + (1-b)\mathbf{G}] = [\mathbf{A} \mid \mathbf{A}\mathbf{R}_f \pm \mathbf{G}] \in \mathbb{Z}_q^{N \times M'},\ M' = M + N\lceil \log q \rceil\ ,$$

and uses $\mathbf{R}_f$ as a right-trapdoor [2,31] of $\mathbf{D}^{(b)}$ to sample a short B'-bounded vector $\boldsymbol{v}$, for appropriately set B' such that, $\mathbf{D}^{(b)}\boldsymbol{v} = \boldsymbol{u}$, where $\boldsymbol{u}$ is a random vector published additionally in the CRS. The vector $\boldsymbol{v}$ is the new decommitment.[7] $\boldsymbol{v}$ together with $\mathbf{A}$ and the original commitment $\{\mathbf{C}_i\}$ to $\boldsymbol{x}$ reveals no

[6] The magnitude scales exponentially with the depth of g_2, which is relatively small if we set the modulus to be sufficiently large.

[7] It can be verified efficiently by checking whether it has small magnitude and $\mathbf{D}^{(b)}\boldsymbol{v} = \boldsymbol{u}$.

more information beyond that $f(\boldsymbol{x}) = b$, since they can be jointly simulated using only (f, b), by sampling $\mathbf{A}$ at random with a trapdoor $\mathbf{T_A}$ [2,54], $\mathbf{C}_i$'s at random, and $\boldsymbol{v}$ using $\mathbf{T_A}$ as a left-trapdoor of $\mathbf{D}^{(b)}$. A random $\mathbf{A}$ is computationally indistinguishable from a well-formed $\mathbf{A}$ by LWE, and $\boldsymbol{v}$ sampled using the left or the right trapdoor is statistically close.

However, we do not know how to construct a matching WE for verifying the above ZK decommitment and need to modify the decommitment as follows. The new decommitment of $\mathbf{A}, \mathbf{C}_f$ to $f(\boldsymbol{x}) = b$ contains a short B'-bounded basis $\mathbf{X}_f \in \mathbb{Z}^{M' \times M'}$ of the lattice $\Lambda_q^{\perp}(\mathbf{D^{(b)}}) = \{\boldsymbol{z} \in \mathbb{Z}^{M'} : \mathbf{D^{(b)}}\boldsymbol{z} = \mathbf{0} \pmod q\}$ over the integers, that is, $\mathbf{D^{(b)}}\mathbf{X}_f = \mathbf{0}^{N \times M'}$ and is $\mathbf{X}_f$ has full rank over the integers. Such a basis can be sampled again using $\mathbf{R}_f$ as a right-trapdoor of $\mathbf{D}^{(b)}$, and can be simulated together with $\mathbf{A}, \{\mathbf{C}_i\}$ by sampling $\mathbf{A}$ without a trapdoor $\mathbf{T_A}$ and using it as a left-trapdoor of $\mathbf{D}^{(b)}$ to sample the basis. In summary, our ZK decommitment is generated as:

$$\mathsf{ZKDecom}(f, b, \mathbf{D}^{(b)}, \mathbf{R}_f) \ : \ \mathbf{X}_f \leftarrow \mathsf{SampleRight}(\mathbf{A}, \pm\mathbf{G}, \mathbf{R_f}, \mathbf{T_G}, \alpha) \ .$$

where $\mathbf{T_G}$ is a trapdoor of the gadget matrix $\mathbf{G}$ and α controls the norm of the trapdoor.

<u>Promise Witness Encryption.</u> To design a compatible WE that can be decrypted using the above ZK decommitments. we crucially rely on the following fundamental properties of lattices defined by a matrix $\mathbf{D} \in \mathbb{Z}_q^{N \times M'}$.

- If the lattice $\Lambda_q^{\perp}(\mathbf{D}) = \{\boldsymbol{z} \in \mathbb{Z}^{M'} : \mathbf{D}\boldsymbol{z} = \mathbf{0} \pmod q\}$ has a B'-bounded basis $\mathbf{X}$ over the integers, then vectors of form $\boldsymbol{s}\mathbf{D} + \boldsymbol{e}$ can be efficiently decoded using $\mathbf{X}$, and $\boldsymbol{s}$ can be recovered, provided that the norm of $\boldsymbol{e}$ is sufficiently smaller than q/B'.
- On the other hand if the lattice $\Lambda_q(\mathbf{D}) = \{\boldsymbol{y} \in \mathbb{Z}^{M'} : \boldsymbol{y} = \boldsymbol{s}\mathbf{D} \pmod q\}$ contains k linearly independent vectors of norm $\ll q/B'$, then vectors of form $\boldsymbol{s}\mathbf{D} + \boldsymbol{e}$ is *lossy* and $\boldsymbol{s}$ has n bits of entropy, if k is sufficiently larger than n. This is essentially because the components of $\boldsymbol{s}\mathbf{A}$ in the direction the short vectors are masked by $\boldsymbol{e}$.

The work of [24] relied on the above properties in their construction of two message statistically sender-private OT from LWE. We here rely on them to achieve respectively the correctness and hiding property of our promise WE. To encrypt a string ℓ_b, under a statement $(\mathbf{A}, \mathbf{C} = \mathbf{C}_f, b)$, our WE does:

$$\begin{aligned} \mathsf{WEnc}((\mathbf{A}, \mathbf{C}, b), \ell_b) \ : \ & \mathbf{D}^{(b)} = [\mathbf{A} \mid \mathbf{C} - (1-b)\mathbf{G}], \ \boldsymbol{w}_b = \boldsymbol{s}_b\mathbf{D}^{(b)} + \boldsymbol{e}_b, \\ & \hat{\ell}_b = \mathsf{Ext}(\mathsf{sd}, \boldsymbol{s}_b) \oplus \ell_b \\ & \text{output } (\boldsymbol{w}_b, \mathsf{sd}, \hat{\ell}_b) \end{aligned}$$

where Ext is a strong seeded extractor and sd is a randomly sampled seed, $\boldsymbol{s}_b$ is a random secret from $\mathbb{Z}_q^N$, and $\boldsymbol{e}_b$ is from a truncated discrete Gaussian distribution with appropriate parameter.

- *Correctness for Yes Instances:* For a well-formed $\mathbf{A}$ and a valid commitment $\mathbf{C} = \mathbf{AR} + b\mathbf{G}$ to b, the ZK decommitment $\mathbf{X}$ is exactly a short-basis of $\Lambda_q^{\perp}(\mathbf{D}^{(b)})$. Therefore, by the first lattice property, given $\mathbf{X}$, the decryptor can efficiently decode $\boldsymbol{w}_b$ to obtain $\boldsymbol{s}_b$ and then recover ℓ_b.
- *Hiding for No Instances:* For a well-formed $\mathbf{A}$ and a valid commitment $\mathbf{C} = \mathbf{AR} + (1-b)\mathbf{G}$ to $1-b$, $\mathbf{D}^{(b)} = [\mathbf{A} \mid \mathbf{AR}]$ and hence the lattice $\Lambda_q(\mathbf{D}^{(b)})$ contains at least k short vectors. This is because, by the structure of a well-formed $\mathbf{A}$, for every $l \in [k]$, $(-\boldsymbol{t}_l||1)\mathbf{D}^{(b)} = (\boldsymbol{e}_l||\boldsymbol{e}_l\mathbf{R})$ is short as $\boldsymbol{e}_l$ and $\mathbf{R}$ are. Moreover, these vectors are independent as long as $\boldsymbol{e}_l$'s are (and $k < \dim(\boldsymbol{e}_l) = M$), where the latter is guaranteed by the (second requirement of) well-formedness of $\mathbf{A}$. Therefore, by the second lattice property, $\boldsymbol{s}_b$ has n bits of entropy conditioned on $\boldsymbol{w}_b$ and the output of the extractor information theoretically hides ℓ_b.

<u>PUTTING PIECES TOGETHER.</u> Combining the homomorphic commitment scheme with ZK decommitments and the witness encryption, we obtain 2rNISC for computing functional OT with semi-malicious security. Let's now examine the magnitude of the modulus, which we wish to be polynomial. Based on LWE, to support homomorphic evaluation of a circuit g_2 of depth d requires the modulus to grow exponentially in d. Therefore, only when d is a fixed logarithmic function in the security parameter λ, would the modulus be a fixed polynomial in λ as desired.

Following a technique used in [22], we can generically bootstrap to 2rNISC supporting circuits g_2 with unbounded polynomial depth, with the help of a PRF in NC^1 and Yao's garbled circuits. At a high-level, P_1 is going to hide the sender's string ℓ_b in a garbled circuit $\hat{G}_{\ell_b}$ for a function $G_{\ell_b}(\Lambda)$ that on input a randomized encoding Λ, outputs ℓ_b iff Λ evaluates to b. At evaluation time, the evaluator will obtain the set of labels $\{\bar{\ell}_j\}$ of $\hat{G}_{\ell_b}$ corresponding exactly to a randomized encoding Λ of $(g_2, \boldsymbol{x}_2)$ generated using pseudorandom coins expanded via PRF on a key k_2 belong to the receiver P_2. Then the evaluator can recover ℓ_b iff $g_2(\boldsymbol{x}_2) = b$. Crucially, the task for revealing the labels corresponding to Λ can exactly be accomplished using 2rNISC for logarithmic-depth receiver's circuits, as every bit of Λ can be computed by a logarithmic-depth circuit evaluated on $(\boldsymbol{x}_2, k_2)$ if $\mathsf{PRF} \in \mathrm{NC}^1$. Correspondingly, every party now needs to commit to their private input $\boldsymbol{x}$ and a PRF key k. This yields our final 2rNISC for functional OT from LWE with polynomial modulus and PRF in NC^1.

2.3 Step 2: 2rNISC for Functional OT to General mrNISC for P

We construct general mrNISC for polynomial-sized circuits from 2rNISC for functional OT following a similar approach as [22], which in turn is based on the round collapsing approach for constructing 2-round MPC protocols started in [39,50]. The *round-collapsing* approach collapses an inner MPC protocol with a polynomial L number of rounds into a 2-round outer MPC protocol, essentially by letting every party garble its next-step message function for computing the inner MPC messages. The challenge lies in how to enable the garbled circuits generated independently by different parties "talk" to each other: the output of one party's garbled circuit is the input of another party's garbled circuit. What is new in this work is that we use 2rNISC for functional OT to enable this, which is weaker than the tools used in previous works. Specifically, the work of [22] proposed and constructed a primitive called Witness Encryption for NIZK of commitments, which is a witness encryption scheme for verifying NIZK proof of the correctness of deterministic computation over committed values. In comparison, 2rNISC is weaker (in particular, is implied by WE for NIZK of commitments) and has a simpler definition, thanks to which we manage to instantiate it from LWE and PRF in NC^1. Next, we give an overview of our mrNISC from 2rNISC for functional OT.

Round Collapsing via 2rNISC for Functional OT. In mrNISC, each party P_i uses 2rNISC for functional OT to encode its private input x_i and a PRF key fk_i, $((\hat{x}_i, \mathrm{fk}\rho_i), s_i) \leftarrow \mathsf{Com}(x_i, \rho_i)$. The PRF key will be used to expand pseudorandom coins for running the inner MPC protocol and generating garbled circuits described below.

A subset I of parties $\{P_i\}_{i \in I}$ wishes to compute $f(z, \{x_i\}_{i \in I})$. Assume that each party P_1 in the inner MPC broadcasts one message m_i^ℓ in each round ℓ; but we now want to carry out this multi-round interaction non-interactively. To do so, each P_i sends one garbled circuit $\hat{\mathsf{F}}_i^\ell$ per round $\ell \in [L]$ of the inner MPC protocol corresponding to the next message function F_i^ℓ of P_i. This garbled circuit takes as input all the messages $\boldsymbol{m}^{<\ell} = \{m_j^l\}_{l<\ell, j \in [n]}$ sent in previous rounds, and outputs the next message m_i^ℓ of P_i of the inner MPC (or the output for the last round $\ell = L$).

For an evaluator to compute the output from these garbled circuits $\{\hat{\mathsf{F}}_i^\ell\}_{\ell \in [L], i \in [n]}$, we need a mechanism to reveal the labels of P_i's garbled circuits $\hat{\mathsf{F}}_i^\ell$ that correspond to the correct messages of the inner MPC. More specifically, let k_0, k_1 be two labels of P_i's garbled circuit $\hat{\mathsf{F}}_i^\ell$ for an input wire that takes in the t'th bit $y = m_{j,t}^l$ of a message from P_j. The goal is revealing only k_y, which can be accomplished using exactly 2rNISC for functional OT.

First, we let k_0, k_1 be expanded from P_i's PRF key ρ_i, that is $(k_0, k_1) = g_1(x_i, \mathrm{fk}_i)$ for some well-chosen g_1. Second, $y = m_j^1$ is P_j's inner MPC message computed from its input x_j and randomness expanded from ρ_j; hence, $y = g_2(x_i, \rho)$ for some g_2. Therefore, to reveal k_y, we can modify garbled circuits of P_i and P_j to additionally output the right 2rNISC computation encodings:

- $\hat{\mathsf{F}}_i^{\ell-1}$ for round $\ell - 1$ additionally outputs $\alpha_i \leftarrow \mathsf{Encode}((g_1, g_2), (\hat{x}_i, \hat{\mathrm{fk}}_i), (\hat{x}_j, \hat{\mathrm{fk}}_j), s_i)$.
- $\hat{\mathsf{F}}_j^l$ for round l where P_j outputs m_j^l additionally outputs $\alpha_j \leftarrow \mathsf{Encode}((g_1, g_2), (\hat{x}_i, \hat{\mathrm{fk}}_i), (\hat{x}_j, \hat{\mathrm{fk}}_j), s_j)$.

By the correctness and security of 2rNISC, the evaluator can recover only k_y as desired.

We do not know however how to prove the above construction secure. The issue is that the PRF key fk_i is used to generate the labels of all the garbled circuits and our security hybrids switch garbled circuits to simulated ones, one by one. Concretely, to switch the garbled circuit for round ℓ into a simulated one, its input labels must first be switched to uniformly random ones (instead of being PRF outputs). The usual solution for that is to use the pseudorandom property of the PRF. Unfortunately, we cannot do that, because the secret key fk_i of the PRF is an input of the 2rNISC for functional OT for the rounds after round ℓ. To solve this issue, our final scheme actually uses $L+1$ PRF keys, one for the randomness of the inner MPC and one for the labels of the garbled circuit for each of the L rounds. To make sure that the input encodings do not depend on the parameters of computations later, we employ a constant round inner MPC protocol, that is, $L = O(1)$.

3 Preliminaries

We denote the security parameter by λ. Let $\mathbb{N}$ be the set of non-negative integers. A function $\mathsf{negl}\colon \mathbb{N} \to \mathbb{N}$ is negligible if for any polynomial $p\colon \mathbb{N} \to \mathbb{N}$, for any large enough $\lambda \in \mathbb{N}$, $\mathsf{negl}(\lambda) < 1/p(\lambda)$.

We make use of garbled circuits, collision-resistant hash functions, and pseudorandom functions. A *garbled circuit* scheme GC is defined as a tuple of four polynomial-time algorithms $\mathsf{GC} = (\mathsf{GC.Gen}, \mathsf{GC.Garble}, \mathsf{GC.Eval}, \mathsf{GC.Sim})$: i) $\mathsf{key} \leftarrow_{\mathrm{R}} \mathsf{GC.Gen}(1^\lambda)$ generates labels or keys $\mathsf{key} = \{\mathsf{key}[i,b]\}_{i,b\in\{0,1\}}$, ii) $\widehat{C} \leftarrow_{\mathrm{R}} \mathsf{GC.Garble}(\mathsf{key}, C)$ garbles the circuit, iii) $y = \mathsf{GC.Eval}(\widehat{C}, \mathsf{key}')$ evaluates the garbled circuit on the input x corresponding to the selected labels $\mathsf{key}' = \{\mathsf{key}[i, x_i]\}_i$, iv) $(\mathsf{key}', \widetilde{C}) \leftarrow_{\mathrm{R}} \mathsf{GC.Sim}(1^\lambda, y)$ simulates a garbled circuit and the corresponding input labels from the output.

3.1 General Lattice Preliminaries

Lattices. An m-dimensional lattice $\mathcal{L}$ is a discrete additive subgroup of $\mathbb{R}^m$. Given positive integers n, m, q and a matrix $\mathbf{A} \in \mathbb{Z}_q^{n\times m}$, we let $\Lambda_q^\perp(\mathbf{A})$ denote the lattice $\{\boldsymbol{x} \in \mathbb{Z}^m \mid \mathbf{A}\boldsymbol{x}^\top = \mathbf{0}^\top \bmod q\}$.

Discrete Gaussians. Let σ be any positive real number. The Gaussian distribution $\mathcal{D}_\sigma$ with parameter σ is defined by the probability distribution function $\rho_\sigma(\boldsymbol{x}) = \exp(-\pi\|x\|^2/\sigma^2)$. For any discrete set $\mathcal{L} \subseteq \mathcal{R}^m$, define $\rho_\sigma(\mathcal{L}) = \sum_{\boldsymbol{x}\in\mathcal{L}} \rho_\sigma(\boldsymbol{x})$. The discrete Gaussian distribution $\mathcal{D}_{\mathcal{L},\sigma}$ over $\mathcal{L}$ with parameter σ is defined by the probability distribution function $\rho_{\mathcal{L},\sigma}(\boldsymbol{x}) = \rho_\sigma(\boldsymbol{x})/\rho_\sigma(\mathcal{L})$.

The following lemma (e.g., [55, Lemma 4.4]) shows that if the parameter σ of a discrete Gaussian distribution is small, then any vector drawn from this distribution will be short (with high probability).

Lemma 3.1. *Let m, n, q be positive integers with $m > n$, $q > 2$. Let $\mathbf{A} \in \mathbb{Z}_q^{n\times m}$ be a matrix of dimensions $n \times m$, $\sigma \in \tilde{\Omega}(n)$, and $\mathcal{L} = \Lambda_q^\perp(\mathbf{A})$. Then, there is a negligible function* $\mathsf{negl}(\cdot)$ *such that*

$$\Pr_{\boldsymbol{x}\leftarrow\mathcal{D}_{\mathcal{L},\sigma}}\left[\|\boldsymbol{x}\| > \sqrt{m}\sigma\right] \leq \mathsf{negl}(n),$$

where $\|\boldsymbol{x}\|$ denotes the ℓ_2 norm of $\boldsymbol{x}$.

Truncated Discrete Gaussians. The truncated discrete Gaussian distribution over $\mathbb{Z}^m$ with parameter σ, denoted by $\widetilde{\mathcal{D}}_{\mathbb{Z}^m,\sigma}$, is the same as the discrete Gaussian distribution $\mathcal{D}_{\mathbb{Z}^m,\sigma}$ except that it outputs 0 whenever the ℓ_∞ norm exceeds $\sqrt{m}\sigma$. By definition, we can say that $\widetilde{\mathcal{D}}_{\mathbb{Z}^m,\sigma}$ is $\sqrt{m}\sigma$-bounded, where a family of distributions $\mathcal{D} = \{\mathcal{D}_\lambda\}_{\lambda \in \mathbb{N}}$ over the integers is B *-bounded* (for $B = B(\lambda) > 0$) if for every $\lambda \in \mathbb{N}$ it holds that $\Pr_{x \leftarrow \mathcal{D}_\lambda}[|x| \leq B(\lambda)] = 1$.

Also, by Lemma 3.1 we get that $\widetilde{\mathcal{D}}_{\mathbb{Z}^m,\sigma}$ and $\mathcal{D}_{\mathbb{Z}^m,\sigma}$ are statistically indistinguishable. Therefore, in the preliminaries below, unless specified, the lemata will apply in the setting where by sampling from discrete Gaussian we mean sampling from truncated discrete Gaussian distribution.

3.2 Learning with Errors

The learning with errors (LWE) problem was defined by Regev [61]. The $\mathsf{LWE}_{n,m,q,\chi}$ problem for parameters $n, m, q \in \mathbb{N}$ and for a distribution χ supported over $\mathbb{Z}$ is to distinguish between the following pair of distributions

$$(\mathbf{A}, \boldsymbol{s}\mathbf{A} + \boldsymbol{e} \bmod q) \quad \text{and} \quad (\mathbf{A}, \boldsymbol{u}),$$

where $\mathbf{A} \leftarrow \mathbb{Z}_q^{n \times m}$, $\boldsymbol{s} \leftarrow \mathbb{Z}_q^{1 \times n}$, $\boldsymbol{e} \leftarrow \chi^{1 \times n}$ and $\boldsymbol{u} \leftarrow \mathbb{Z}_q^{1 \times m}$. Similarly, we can define the matrix version of the problem, which is known to be hard, if the version above is hard. Specifically, let $k \in \mathsf{poly}(n, m)$, then in the matrix the task is to distinguish between the following two distributions

$$(\mathbf{A}, \mathbf{SA} + \mathbf{E} \bmod q) \quad \text{and} \quad (\mathbf{A}, \mathbf{U}),$$

where $\mathbf{A} \leftarrow \mathbb{Z}_q^{n \times m}$, $\mathbf{S} \leftarrow \mathbb{Z}_q^{k \times n}$, $\mathbf{E} \leftarrow \chi^{k \times n}$ and $\mathbf{U} \leftarrow \mathbb{Z}_q^{k \times m}$.

The Gadget Matrix [54]. Fix a dimension n and a modulus q. Define the gadget vector $\boldsymbol{g} = (1, 2, 4, \ldots, 2^{\log q - 1})$ and the gadget function $g^{-1} \colon \mathbb{Z}_q \to \{0, 1\}^{\lceil \log q \rceil}$ to be the function that computes the $(\log q)$th bit decomposition of an integer. For some integer z the function is defined as $g^{-1}(z) = \boldsymbol{v} = (v_1, \ldots, v_{\log q})$ where $v_i \in \{0, 1\}$ such that $z = \langle \boldsymbol{g}, \boldsymbol{v} \rangle$. By extension we define the augmented gadget function $G^{-1} \colon \mathbb{Z}_q^{n \times m} \to \{0, 1\}^{(n \cdot \lceil \log q \rceil) \times m}$ to be the function that computes the $(\log q)$th bit decomposition of every integer in a matrix $\mathbf{A} \in \mathbb{Z}_q^{n \times m}$, and arranges them as a binary matrix of dimension $(n \cdot \log q) \times k$ which we denote $\boldsymbol{G}^{-1}(\mathbf{A})$. Hence, $\mathbf{G}_n \cdot G^{-1}(\boldsymbol{z}) = \mathbf{Z}$, where the gadget matrix $\mathbf{G}_n$ is $\mathbf{G}_n = \boldsymbol{g} \otimes \mathbf{I}_n \in \mathbb{Z}_q^{n \times (n \cdot \lceil \log q \rceil)}$. When n is clear from context, we denote $\mathbf{G}_n$ simply by $\mathbf{G}$.

3.3 Review of Gentry-Sahai-Waters FHE Scheme

We now recall the Gentry-Sahai-Waters FHE scheme [46]. The scheme has the following overall structure:

GSW.Setup: The public key consists of a matrix $\mathbf{A} \in \mathbb{Z}_q^{n \times m}$. This matrix is typically generated by sampling a matrix $\mathbf{B} \in \mathbb{Z}_q^{n_1 \times m}$, a secret $\mathbf{S} \leftarrow \mathbb{Z}_q^{k \times n_1}$, errors $\mathbf{E} \leftarrow \chi^{k \times m}$, and finally setting $\mathbf{A} = [\mathbf{B}^\top | (\mathbf{SB} + \mathbf{E})^\top]^\top \in \mathbb{Z}_q^{n \times m}$ where $n = n_1 + k$ and $m \in \Omega(n \cdot \lceil \log q \rceil))$. The secret key is $\mathbf{S}$.

GSW.Encrypt: To encrypt a message $\mu \in \{0,1\}$, sample randomness $\mathbf{R} \in \{-1,0,1\}^{m\times(n\cdot\lceil\log q\rceil)}$ and finally setting $\mathbf{C} = \mathbf{A}\cdot\mathbf{R} + \mu\cdot\mathbf{G}$. Note that if $\mathbf{A}$ is generated in the manner above, μ is recoverable, and if it is generated at random, then μ is information theoretically lost.

GSW.Eval: Let $f : \{0,1\}^\kappa \to \{0,1\}$ be a depth $d(\kappa)$ boolean circuit, then, given honestly generated ciphertexts $\mathbf{C}_i = \mathbf{A}\cdot\mathbf{R}_i + \mu_i\cdot\mathbf{G}$ for $i \in [\kappa]$. Then $\mathsf{GSW.Eval}(f, \{\mathbf{C}_i\}_{i\in[\kappa]})$ computes the evaluated ciphetext $\tilde{\mathbf{C}} = \mathbf{A}\cdot\tilde{\mathbf{R}} + f(\mu_1,\ldots,\mu_\kappa)\cdot\mathbf{G}$. There are two facts about this computation:

Randomness Homomorphism: There is a polynomial time algorithm GSW.RandEval that on input $\mathbf{A}, \{\mathbf{R}_i, \mu_i\}_{i\in[\kappa]}$, and f, computes $\tilde{\mathbf{R}}$.

Bounds: If $f \in \mathsf{NC}^1$, then $\|\tilde{\mathbf{R}}\|_\infty \le O(4^d\cdot m)$ as shown in [28]. Otherwise, $\|\tilde{\mathbf{R}}\|_\infty \le O(m^d)$ [46].

3.4 Lattice Trapdoors

Definition 3.2 (Lattice trapdoors [4,5,45,54]**).** *There is an efficient randomized algorithm* $\mathsf{TrapGen}(1^n, 1^m, q)$ *that given any integers* $n \ge 1, q \ge 2$ *and* $m \in \Omega(n\log q)$, *outputs a full-rank matrix* $\mathbf{A} \in \mathbb{Z}_q^{n\times m}$ *and a trapdoor matrix* $\mathbf{T_A} \in \mathbb{Z}^{m\times m}$ *such that*

1. $\mathbf{A}\cdot\mathbf{T_A} = \mathbf{0}^{n\times m} \bmod q$.
2. *The distribution of* $\mathbf{A}$ *is* $\mathsf{negl}(n)$*-close to uniform.*
3. $\mathbf{T_A} \in \mathbb{Z}^{m\times m}$ *is a short matrix with linearly independent columns over* $\mathbb{R}$. *More precisely,* $\|\mathbf{T_A}\|_{\mathsf{GS}} = O(\sqrt{n\cdot\log q})$, *where for a matrix* $\mathbf{X}$, $\|\mathbf{X}\|_{\mathsf{GS}}$ *is the operator norm of the matrix obtained by performing Gram-Schmidt (GS) orthogonalization of* $\mathbf{X}$.

The following lemma is standard and follows from the leftover hash lemma.

Lemma 3.3. *For any* $k \in \mathsf{poly}(n)$ *and* $m \in \Omega(n\log q)$, *the following two distributions are* $\mathsf{negl}(n)$*-close in statistical distance:*

$$\{(\mathbf{A}, \mathbf{T_A}, \mathbf{U})\ |(\mathbf{A}, \mathbf{T_A}) \leftarrow \mathsf{TrapGen}(1^n, 1^m, q),\ \mathbf{U} \leftarrow \mathbb{Z}_q^{n\times k}\}$$

and

$$\{(\mathbf{A}, \mathbf{T_A}, \mathbf{A}\cdot\mathbf{R})\ |(\mathbf{A}, \mathbf{T_A}) \leftarrow \mathsf{TrapGen}(1^n, 1^m, q),\ \mathbf{R} \leftarrow \{-1,+1\}_q^{m\times k}\}.$$

We will use the following algorithms for sampling trapdoor matrices.

Algorithm $\mathsf{SampleLeft}(\mathbf{A}, \mathbf{B}, \mathbf{T_A}, \alpha) \mapsto \mathbf{T}_{[\mathbf{A}|\mathbf{B}]}$:] The sample left algorithm takes as input a full rank matrix $\mathbf{A} \in \mathbb{Z}_q^{n\times m_1}$, a matrix $\mathbf{B} \in \mathbb{Z}_q^{n\times m_2}$, a trapdoor $\mathbf{T_A}$ and it outputs a trapdoor $\mathbf{T}_{[\mathbf{A}|\mathbf{B}]}$ of $[\mathbf{A} \mid \mathbf{B}]$.

Algorithm $\mathsf{SampleRight}(\mathbf{A}, \mathbf{B}, \mathbf{R}, \mathbf{T_B}, \alpha) \mapsto \mathbf{T}_{[\mathbf{A}|\mathbf{AR}+\mathbf{B}]}$:] The sample right algorithm takes as input a matrix $\mathbf{A} \in \mathbb{Z}_q^{n\times m_1}$, a full rank matrix $\mathbf{B} \in \mathbb{Z}_q^{n\times m_2}$ and its trapdoor $\mathbf{T_B}$, along with $\mathbf{R} \in \mathbb{Z}_q^{m_1\times m_2}$. It outputs a trapdoor $\mathbf{T}_{[\mathbf{A}|\mathbf{A}\cdot\mathbf{R}+\mathbf{B}]}$ of $[\mathbf{A}|\mathbf{A}\cdot\mathbf{R}+\mathbf{B}]$.

The following lemma says that the process of sampling from SampleLeft and SampleRight produce indistinguishable outputs, when executed on the appropriate inputs. The lemma follows from [2,31].

Lemma 3.4 (Indistinguishability of SampleRight, SampleLeft). *Let* $\mathbf{A} \in \mathbb{Z}_q^{n\times m_1}$ *be a full rank matrix with a trapdoor* $\mathbf{T_A}$. *Let* $\mathbf{B} \in \mathbb{Z}_q^{n\times m_2}$ *be a full rank matrix with a trapdoor* $\mathbf{T_B}$. *Let* $\mathbf{R} \in \mathbb{Z}^{m_1\times m_2}$. *Let*

$$\alpha > \max\left\{\|\mathbf{T_A}\|_{\mathsf{GS}} \cdot \omega(\sqrt{\log(m_1+m_2)}), \|\mathbf{T_B}\|_{\mathsf{GS}} \cdot \|\mathbf{R}\| \cdot \omega(\sqrt{\log(m_2)})\right\}.$$

Then, the following two distributions are statistically close (up to negligible in n distance):

$$\{\mathbf{X} \mid \mathbf{X} \leftarrow \mathsf{SampleLeft}(\mathbf{A}, \mathbf{A}\cdot\mathbf{R}+\mathbf{B}, \mathbf{T_A}, \alpha)\}$$

and

$$\{\mathbf{X} \mid \mathbf{X} \leftarrow \mathsf{SampleRight}(\mathbf{A}, \mathbf{B}, \mathbf{R}, \mathbf{T_B}, \alpha)\}$$

Further, $\|\mathbf{X}\| \in O(\sqrt{m_1+m_2}\cdot\alpha)$.

3.5 Lossy Modes and Unique Decoding

For a given matrix $\mathbf{A} \in \mathbb{Z}_q^{n\times m}$ we consider the function:

$$f_{\mathbf{A}}(\boldsymbol{s}, \boldsymbol{e}) = \boldsymbol{s}\cdot\mathbf{A} + \boldsymbol{e} \bmod q,$$

where $\boldsymbol{s} \in \mathbb{Z}_q^{1\times n}$ and $\boldsymbol{e} \in \mathbb{Z}_q^{1\times m}$. We now consider two settings where in one $f_{\mathbf{A}}$ is invertible and in the other it is lossy.

Invertible Mode. When we have a short trapdoor for $\mathbf{A}$, and if $\boldsymbol{e}$ is short, then $\boldsymbol{s}$ is recoverable. This is captured by the following lemma.

Lemma 3.5 ([54]). *There exist a polynomial time (deterministic) algorithm* RecoverSecret *such that the following holds. Let* $\mathbf{A} \in \mathbb{Z}_q^{n\times m}$ *be any full rank matrix and* $\mathbf{T_A}$ *be a corresponding trapdoor. Let* $\boldsymbol{s} \in \mathbb{Z}_q^{1\times n}$ *and* $\boldsymbol{e} \in \mathbb{Z}^{1\times m}$ *be arbitrary. Then,* $\mathsf{RecoverSecret}(\mathbf{A}, \mathbf{T_A}, \boldsymbol{s}\mathbf{A} + \boldsymbol{e} \bmod q) = \boldsymbol{s}$ *whenever* $q > \|\mathbf{T_A}\| \cdot \|\boldsymbol{e}\|$.

Lossy Mode. In the other extreme when the row span of $\mathbf{A}$ has k linearly independent vectors of short norm, $\boldsymbol{s}$ is chosen at random from $\mathbb{Z}_q^n$, and $\boldsymbol{e} \leftarrow \mathcal{D}_{\mathbb{Z}^m,\sigma}$ is sampled from a wide enough discrete Gaussian, then $\boldsymbol{s}\boldsymbol{A} + \boldsymbol{e} \bmod q$ hides $\boldsymbol{s}$ information theoretically. This is captured by the following lemma.

Lemma 3.6 (From Lemma 4.3 and Lemma 3.2 of [24]). *Let* $\mathbf{A} \in \mathbb{Z}_q^{n\times m}$ *where* $m \in \Omega(n\log q)$. *Assume that there exist* $k \leq n$ *linearly independent vectors in the row span of* $\mathbf{A}$, *each with norm bounded by* γ. *Then,*

$$\tilde{H}_\infty(\boldsymbol{s} \mid (\mathbf{A}, \boldsymbol{s}\mathbf{A} + \boldsymbol{e} \bmod q) \geq k\cdot\log\frac{\sigma}{\gamma} - 1,$$

where $\boldsymbol{s} \leftarrow \mathbb{Z}_q^{1\times n}$ *and* $\boldsymbol{e} \leftarrow \mathcal{D}_{\mathbb{Z}^m,\sigma}$. *(*$\tilde{H}_\infty$ *denotes average-conditional min-entropy; see Definition 3.7.)*

3.6 Other Preliminaries

Definition 3.7 (Average Conditional Min-Entropy). *Let X be a random-variable supported on a finite set $\mathcal{X}$ and Z be a possibly correlated random-variable supported on a finite set $\mathcal{Z}$. The average conditional min-entropy:*

$$\tilde{H}_\infty(X|Z) = -\log\left(\mathop{\mathbb{E}}_{z}\left[\max_{x\in\mathcal{X}} \Pr\left[X = x \mid Z = z\right]\right]\right)$$

Definition 3.8 ((k,ϵ)-average case strong seeded extractor). *A function $\mathsf{Ext}\colon \{0,1\}^{\ell_{\mathsf{Ext}}} \times \mathcal{X} \to \{0,1\}^{\ell}$ is called a seeded strong average-case extractor, if it holds that for all random variables X and Z defined on some domains with a finite support, if $\tilde{H}_\infty(X|Z) \geq k$ then it holds that:*

$$(s, \mathsf{Ext}(s, X), Z) \approx_\epsilon (s, U, Z)$$

where $s \leftarrow \{0,1\}^{\ell_{\mathsf{Ext}}}$ and $U \leftarrow \{0,1\}^{\ell}$.

There exists explicit polynomial-time constructions of seeded strong average-case $(\ell + O(\log(1/\epsilon)), \epsilon)$ extractors [36,37].

Lemma 3.9 (Error vectors are linearly independent). *Let $k, m \in \mathbb{N}$ such that $k < m/2$. Let $\mathbf{e}_i \leftarrow \mathcal{D}_{\mathbb{Z}^m,\sigma}$ for $i \in [k]$, where $\sigma > m$. Except with $\mathsf{negl}(m)$ probability, the vectors $\{\mathbf{e}_i\}_{i\in[k]}$ are linearly independent.*

Proof. First observe that the column rank of the matrix $\mathbf{E} = [\mathbf{e}_1^\top|\ldots|\mathbf{e}_k^\top]$ is at least as much as the column rank of the matrix $\mathbf{E}$ mod 2 (over the field $\mathbb{Z}_2$). Due to the smoothing lemma [55], it is known that the statistical distance between $\mathbf{e}$ mod 2 and $\mathbb{Z}_2^m$ is at most $2^{-\Omega(m)}$ as $\sigma > m$. Finally, the claim holds since for a matrix $\mathbf{A} \leftarrow \mathbb{Z}_2^{k\times m}$ sampled uniformly at random

$$\Pr[\mathsf{rank}(\mathbf{A}) = k] > 1 - O(k \cdot 2^{k-m}).$$

4 Construction of 2rNISC

In this section, we give a construction of $\mathsf{2rNISC}$ for the functionality:

$$\mathcal{U}_{\mathsf{fOT}} = \{\mathcal{U}_{\mathsf{fOT},\lambda}\}_{\lambda\in\mathbb{N}}$$

This functionality takes three inputs. The public input consists of two polynomial sized (in λ) functions $g_1\colon \{0,1\}^{n_1} \to \{0,1\}^{\lambda} \times \{0,1\}^{\lambda}$ and $g_2\colon \{0,1\}^{n_2} \to \{0,1\}$. (We assume that functions are given in the form of Boolean circuits). The functionality is evaluated as in the specifications described in Fig. 1.

We recall that a 2rNISC is a mrNISC where the functionality to be evaluated is restricted to 2 parties. A 2rNISC allows for an arbitrary number of parties to commit or encode their inputs. The notion of mrNISC was recalled in the overview (Sect. 2.1). A formal definition can be found in the full version [20].

The main result of this section is a semi-malicious $\mathsf{2rNISC}$ scheme for $\mathcal{U}_{\mathsf{fOT},\lambda}$ assuming LWE and a PRF in NC^1.

Functionality $\mathcal{U}_{\mathsf{fOT},\lambda}$

Public Input: Polynomial-sized functions $g_1 \colon \{0,1\}^{n_1} \to \{0,1\}^\lambda \times \{0,1\}^\lambda$ and $g_1 \colon \{0,1\}^{n_2} \to \{0,1\}$.
Input of the First Party: $x_1 \in \{0,1\}^{n_1}$.
Input of the Second Party: $x_2 \in \{0,1\}^{n_2}$.
Output to both Parties: Compute $(y_0, y_1) = g_1(x_1)$ where $y_0, y_1 \in \{0,1\}^\lambda$. Output $(g_2(x_2), y_{g_2(x_2)})$.

Fig. 1. The functionality $\mathcal{U}_{\mathsf{fOT},\lambda,d}$

Theorem 4.1. *Assume LWE with polynomial modulus and a PRF in* NC^1*. Then, there exists a semi-malicious* 2rNISC *for* $\mathcal{U}_{\mathsf{fOT}}$.

The construction that gives Theorem 4.1 is obtained in two modular steps. In the first step (see Sect. 4.1 and Theorem 4.2), we construct a 2rNISC for a subset of all functions in the functionality $\mathcal{U}_{\mathsf{fOT},\lambda}$. Specifically, we restrict the circuit depth of g_2 to be an a priori fixed $d = d(\lambda)$ and obtain a protocol based solely on LWE. In the next step (see Sect. 4.2 and Theorem 4.3), using standard bootstrapping techniques using randomized encodings, we obtain our final 2rNISC without any restriction on d. This step relies, in addition to LWE, on a PRF in NC^1.[8]

4.1 2rNISC for Depth-Bounded Functions

In this section, we give a construction of a semi-malicious 2rNISC for the restricted functionality, where g_2 has a priori bounded depth $d = d(\lambda)$. We denote this functionality by $\{\mathcal{U}_{\mathsf{fOT},\lambda,d}\}_{\lambda,d\in\mathbb{N}}$.

Theorem 4.2. *Assuming LWE with polynomial modulus, there exists a semi-malicious* 2rNISC *for* $\mathcal{U}_{\mathsf{fOT},\lambda,d}$ *for all (a priori) bounded* $d \in O(\log\lambda)$*. Further, assuming LWE assumption holds with modulus-to-noise ratio* 2^{N^ϵ} *for any constant* ϵ*, where* N *is the dimension, the same protocol is a semi-malicious* 2rNISC *protocol for* $\mathcal{U}_{\mathsf{fOT},\lambda,d}$ *for any (a priori) bounded polynomial* $d(\lambda)$.

Before presenting the protocol, we list various parameters used in the scheme. We will explain how to set these parameters to achieve correctness and security in the full version [20].

[8] The common definition of a PRF in NC^1 is a PRF whose circuit representation is in NC^1 when viewed as a function of both the input and the seed. We actually need a slightly weaker condition, namely, that the circuit computing $F_x(\cdot) = \mathsf{PRF.Eval}(\cdot, x)$ with the hardwired input x, as a function of the PRF key is in NC^1.

Parameters.

- λ is the security parameter,
- n_i is the length of the input of party i,
- d is the depth parameter,
- N_1 is a lattice dimension involved,
- k is the number of secrets used to generate the commitment key,
- $N := N_1 + k$,
- q is a modulus,
- $M \in \Omega(N \cdot \log q)$ is a dimension involved,
- σ, σ' are discrete Gaussian parameters,
- ρ is a parameter for trapdoor sampling,
- ℓ_{Ext} is the seed length of an average-case strong-seeded extractor (Definition 3.8).

The Protocol. We now describe the protocol which consists of three phases. The first phase is a commitment phase where any party can publish a commitment to its input. The second phase is when two parties decide to execute the functionality $\mathcal{U}_{\mathsf{fOT},\lambda,d}$ with their respective commitments from the first phase. In this phase, one message is published from each of these parties. In the third and last phase, each party locally computes their output, given the public transcript. No communication is involved in this phase.

We present the protocol from the point of view of a given party which we call P. This party first commits to its input on a public board. Later, P can engage in a computation phase with some other party P', by each broadcasting just one message. For this phase, we distinguish between two cases: whether P is the "first" or "second" party among P, P', where the ordering is given by the functionality. Lastly, each party can recover the output of the computation just from the public messages.

Commit on input $(1^\lambda, x)$**:** On input $x \in \{0,1\}^*$ perform the following steps:
- Sample a matrix $\mathbf{B} \leftarrow \mathbb{Z}_q^{N_1 \times M}$ uniformly at random.
- Sample secrets $\boldsymbol{t}_l \leftarrow \mathbb{Z}_q^{1 \times N_1}$ for $l \in [k]$.
- For $l \in [k]$, compute $\boldsymbol{b}_l = \boldsymbol{t}_l \cdot \mathbf{B} + \boldsymbol{e}_l$ where $\boldsymbol{e}_l$ is sampled from $\mathcal{D}_\sigma^M$.
- Set $\mathsf{flag} = 0$ if $\{\boldsymbol{e}_l\}_{l \in [k]}$ are not linearly independent. Otherwise set $\mathsf{flag} = 1$. Observe that due to Lemma 3.9, with overwhelming probability $\mathsf{flag} = 1$.
- Denote $\mathbf{A} = [\mathbf{B}^\top | \boldsymbol{b}_1^\top | \dots | \boldsymbol{b}_k^\top]^\top \in \mathbb{Z}_q^{N \times M}$.
- Compute commitments of input x. Parse $x = (x_1, \dots, x_n)$, where $n = |x|$. Compute matrices $\mathbf{C}_\ell = \mathbf{A} \cdot \mathbf{R}_\ell + x_\ell \mathbf{G}$ for $\ell \in [n]$. Here $\mathbf{R}_\ell \leftarrow \{-1,+1\}^{M \times (N \lceil \log q \rceil)}$ is chosen uniformly at random and $\mathbf{G} \in \mathbb{Z}_q^{N \times (N \lceil \log q \rceil)}$ is the gadget matrix.
- Output $\hat{x} = (\mathsf{flag}, \mathbf{A}, \{\mathbf{C}_\ell\}_{\ell \in [n]})$ as a public string and remember $s = (\{\mathbf{R}_\ell\}_{\ell \in [n]}, x)$ as a private string.

Encode: There are two cases, depending on the "order" of the parties involved, denoted P and P'. In both cases, the view of party P (or its query) consists of $\hat{x}, \hat{x}', s$ and the view of P' consists of $\hat{x}, \hat{x}', s'$. The descriptions of g_1, g_2 are public. In both cases, party P first parses the public message of P' as follows:

- Parse $\hat{x}' = (\mathsf{flag}', \mathbf{A}', \{\mathbf{C}'_\ell\}_{\ell \in [n']})$, where n' is the input length of party P'. If $\mathsf{flag}' = 0$, output $\perp$. Otherwise, proceed.

Party P proceeds as follows, depending on whether it is the "first" party or the "second".

Case 1: Party P is the "first" party.

- Compute $(y_0, y_1) = g_1(x)$.
- Compute $\tilde{\mathbf{C}}'_{g_2} = \mathsf{GSW.Eval}(g_2, \{\mathbf{C}'_\ell\}_{\ell \in [n_j]})$.
- Sample two secrets $\boldsymbol{u}_0, \boldsymbol{u}_1 \leftarrow \mathbb{Z}_q^{1 \times N}$.
- Compute $\boldsymbol{w}_b = \boldsymbol{u}_b \cdot [\mathbf{A}' | \tilde{\mathbf{C}}'_{g_2} - (1-b) \cdot \mathbf{G}] + \tilde{\boldsymbol{e}} \bmod q$ for $b \in \{0, 1\}$. Here $\tilde{\boldsymbol{e}}$ is sampled from $\mathcal{D}_{\sigma'}^{1 \times (M + N\lceil \log q \rceil)}$.
- Let $\mathsf{Ext}\colon \{0,1\}^{\ell_{\mathsf{Ext}}} \times \{0,1\}^{N \log q} \to \{0,1\}^\lambda$ be a $(\lambda, 2^{-\lambda})$-strong seeded extractor. Sample a seed sd of the extractor. Output $\alpha = (\mathsf{sd}, \boldsymbol{w}_0, \boldsymbol{w}_1, v_0 = \mathsf{Ext}(\mathsf{sd}, \boldsymbol{u}_0) \oplus y_0, v_1 = \mathsf{Ext}(\mathsf{sd}, \boldsymbol{u}_1) \oplus y_1)$.

Case 2: Party P is the "second" party.

- Compute $\tilde{\mathbf{C}}_{g_2} = \mathsf{GSW.Eval}(g_2, \{\mathbf{C}_\ell\}_{\ell \in [n]})$.
- Compute $\mathsf{GSW.RandEval}(\mathbf{A}, \{\mathbf{R}_\ell, x_\ell\}_{\ell \in [n]}) \to \tilde{\mathbf{R}}_{g_2}$ such that $\tilde{\mathbf{C}}_{g_2} = \mathbf{A} \cdot \tilde{\mathbf{R}}_{g_2} + g_2(x) \cdot \mathbf{G}$.
- Compute a matrix $\mathbf{X}_{g_2}$ as:

$$\mathbf{X}_{g_2} = \begin{cases} \mathsf{SampleRight}(\mathbf{A}, -\mathbf{G}, \tilde{\mathbf{R}}_{g_2}, \mathbf{T}_\mathbf{G}, \rho) \text{ when } g_2(x) = 0 \\ \mathsf{SampleRight}(\mathbf{A}, \mathbf{G}, \tilde{\mathbf{R}}_{g_2}, \mathbf{T}_\mathbf{G}, \rho) \text{ when } g_2(x) = 1 \end{cases}$$

  Observe that $\mathbf{X}_{g_2}$ is a trapdoor of $[\mathbf{A} \mid \tilde{\mathbf{C}}_{g_2} - (1 - g_2(x))\mathbf{G}]$.
- Output $\alpha = (g_2(x), \mathbf{X}_{g_2})$.

Eval on input $(z = (g_1, g_2), \hat{x}, \hat{x}', \alpha, \alpha')$**:** Let P be the first party and P' be the second party.

- Parse $\hat{x} = (\mathsf{flag}, \mathbf{A}, \{\mathbf{C}_\ell\}_{\ell \in [n]})$ and $\hat{x}' = (\mathsf{flag}', \mathbf{A}', \{\mathbf{C}'_\ell\}_{\ell \in [n']})$. If $\alpha = \perp$ or $\alpha' = \perp$, then output $\perp$. Otherwise,
- Parse $\alpha = (\mathsf{sd}, \boldsymbol{w}_0, \boldsymbol{w}_1, v_0, v_1)$ and $\alpha' = (\alpha'_1, \mathbf{X})$ where α'_1 is a bit.
- Compute $\boldsymbol{u} = \mathsf{RecoverSecret}([\mathbf{A}' | \tilde{\mathbf{C}}'_{g_2} - (1-\alpha'_1)\mathbf{G})], \mathbf{X}, \boldsymbol{w}_{\alpha'_1})$, where recall that $\tilde{\mathbf{C}}'_{g_2} = \mathsf{GSW.Eval}(g_2, \{\mathbf{C}'_\ell\}_{\ell \in [n]})$.
- Compute $\mathsf{out}_2 = \mathsf{Ext}(\mathsf{sd}, \boldsymbol{u}) \oplus v_{\alpha'_1}$. Set $\mathsf{out}_1 = \alpha'_1$
- Output $\mathsf{out} = (\mathsf{out}_1, \mathsf{out}_2)$.

In the full version, we derive a concrete setting of parameters with which we can instantiate the scheme as well as prove the correctness as well as the security.

4.2 Bootstrapping 2rNISC for All Depths

In this section, we use a PRF in NC^1 to bootstrap a 2rNISC protocol for the functionality $\mathcal{U}_{\mathsf{fOT},\lambda,c\log\lambda}$ for some fixed large enough constant c to a 2rNISC for $\mathcal{U}_{\mathsf{fOT},\lambda}$, as required in Theorem 4.1. Namely, the theorem we prove is:

Theorem 4.3. *Assuming a* 2rNISC *protocol for the functionality* $\mathcal{U}_{f\mathsf{OT},\lambda,c\log\lambda}$ *for a large enough constant* $c > 0$*, a* PRF *in* NC^1*, and a collision resistant hash function, there exist a* 2rNISC *for the functionality* $\mathcal{U}_{f\mathsf{OT},\lambda}$.

By combining Theorems 4.2 and 4.2, and using the fact that LWE (with polynomial modulus) imply collision-resistant hash functions [3], imply Theorem 4.1.

We prove Theorem 4.3 in the full version [20]. An overview of the construction is provided at the end of Sect. 2.2.

5 Construction of MrNISC Schemes

Let us now show our construction of mrNISC schemes. We recall the mrNISC notion from the overview (Sect. 2.1) and the definition of Functional OT ($\mathcal{U}_{\mathrm{fOT}}$, Fig. 1).

We have the following theorem.

Theorem 5.1. *Assuming the existence of a semi-malicious 2rNISC for Functional OT there exists an mrNISC scheme for any polynomial-time functionality.*

Our construction of mrNISC for a polynomial-time functionality $\mathcal{U}$ uses the following building blocks:

- A 2rNISC $\mathsf{2rNISC} = (\mathsf{Com}', \mathsf{Encode}', \mathsf{Eval}')$ for Functional OT (fOT).
- A semi-malicious output-delayed simulatable L-round MPC protocol Π = $(\mathsf{Next}, \mathsf{Output})$ for f. Output-delayed simulatability was introduced in [22] and ensures that the transcript excluding the last messages can be simulated for all-but-one honest parties before knowing the output. Formal definitions and constructions from standard semi-malicious MPC are recalled in the full version [20]. We require the number of rounds L to be constant. The reason behind this requirement is that in an mrNISC protocol, only when all the honest parties agreed to provide a computation encoding, the adversary (and so the simulator) should be able to learn the output. Without loss of generality, we will assume that in each round ℓ of Π, each party P_i broadcasts a single message that depends on its input x_i, randomness r_i and on the messages $\mathsf{Msg}^{<\ell} = \{\mathsf{msg}_j^{\ell'}\}_{j\in[n],\ell'<\ell}$ that it received from all parties in all previous rounds such that $\mathsf{msg}_j^{\ell} = \mathsf{Next}_j(z, x_j, r_j, \mathsf{Msg}^{<\ell})$, where z is the public input. In other words, Next_j is the next message function that computes the message broadcast by P_j. In the last round L of Π anybody computes the public output $y = \mathsf{Output}(z, \mathsf{Msg}) = \mathcal{U}(z, \{x_i\})$, from the messages $\mathsf{Msg} = \{\mathsf{msg}_j^{\ell}\}_{j\in[n],\ell\in[L]}$. We denote by ν_r the number of bits of r_i and by ν_m the number of bits of messages msg_i^{ℓ} (without loss of generality, we suppose that these numbers

are independent of i and ℓ, but they may depend on z and the security parameter). Next_j and Output implicitly take as input a unary representation of the security parameter 1^λ.

- A garbled circuit scheme $\mathsf{GC} = (\mathsf{GC.Gen}, \mathsf{GC.Garble}, \mathsf{GC.Eval}, \mathsf{GC.Sim})$ for P. The keys (aka labels) of the garbled circuits have κ bits.
- A pseudorandom function PRF. Each party will generate $L+1$ PRF keys $\mathrm{fk}_i^0, \ldots, \mathrm{fk}_i^L$. The key fk_i^0 is used to generate the randomness for the internal MPC (via $\mathsf{PRF}(\mathrm{fk}_i, 0\|z\|\ldots)$), while the keys $\mathrm{fk}_i^1, \ldots, \mathrm{fk}_i^L$ are used to encrypt (via a one-time pad) the labels of the used garbled circuits for rounds $1, \ldots, L$ respectively (via $\mathsf{PRF}(\mathrm{fk}_i, 1\|z\|\ldots)$).

Our mrNISC scheme is constructed as follows:

- Input: $(\hat{x}_i, s_i) \leftarrow \mathsf{Com}(1^\lambda, x_i)$ samples $L+1$ PRF key $\mathrm{fk}_i^0, \ldots, \mathrm{fk}_i^L \leftarrow_{\mathrm{R}} \{0,1\}^\lambda$.For each $\ell \in L$, Com also generates 2rNISC input encodings and associated secret state for $x_i\|\mathrm{fk}_i^0\|\mathrm{fk}_i^\ell$:
$$(\hat{x}_i^\ell, s_i^\ell) \leftarrow_{\mathrm{R}} \mathsf{Com}'(x_i\|\mathrm{fk}_i^0\|\mathrm{fk}_i^\ell) \ . \tag{1}$$
In other words, party P_i make L 2rNISC input encodings. When we need to differentiate these encodings, we say that the ℓ-th such input encoding is made by the virtual party P_i^ℓ. Finally, Com sets $\hat{x}_i := \{\hat{x}_i^\ell\}_{\ell\in[L]}$ and $s_i := (x_i, \{\mathrm{fk}_i^\ell\}_{\ell\in[0,L]}, \{s_i^\ell\}_{\ell\in[L]})$.
- Computation of $\mathcal{U}(z,\star)$: $\alpha_i \leftarrow \mathsf{Encode}(z, \{\hat{x}_j\}_{j\in[n]}, s_i)$ proceeds as follows:[9]
  - For $\ell \in [L]$, generate input labels that will be used to garble the evaluation circuit F_i^ℓ defined in Fig. 2:
  $$(\mathbf{stateKey}_i^\ell,\ \{\mathbf{msgKey}_{i,j}^\ell\}_j) \leftarrow_{\mathrm{R}} \mathsf{GC.Gen}(1^\lambda) \ .$$
  For $\ell = 1$, all the input labels are empty, as F_i^1 does not take any input. We also define $\mathbf{stateKey}_i^{L+1}$ and $\{\mathbf{msgKey}_{i,j}^{L+1}\}_j$ to be empty strings.
  - For $\ell \in [L]$, $j \in [n]$, $k \in [\nu_m]$, $b \in \{0,1\}$, compute the following ciphertexts
  $$\mathsf{ct}_{i,j,k,b}^\ell \leftarrow_{\mathrm{R}} \mathbf{msgKey}_{i,j}^{\ell+1}[k,b] \oplus \mathsf{PRF}(\mathrm{fk}_i^\ell, 1\|z\|j\|k\|b\|[\kappa]) \ . \tag{2}$$
  If $\ell = L$, these ciphertexts are set to be empty strings.
  - For $\ell \in [L]$, garble the evaluation circuit F_i^ℓ:
  $$\hat{\mathsf{F}}_i^\ell \leftarrow_{\mathrm{R}} \mathsf{GC.Garble}((\mathbf{stateKey}_i^\ell,\ \{\mathbf{msgKey}_{i,j}^\ell\}_{j\in[n]}),\ \mathsf{F}_i^\ell) \ .$$
  - Set $\alpha_i := (\{\hat{\mathsf{F}}_i^\ell\}_{\ell\in[L]}, \{\mathsf{ct}_{i,j,k,b}^{\ell+1}\}_{j,k,b})$.
- Output $y = \mathsf{Eval}(z, \{\hat{x}_i\}_{i\in[n]}, \{\alpha_i\}_{i\in[n]})$ proceeds as follows in L iterations, for $\ell = 1, \ldots, L$:

[9] For simplicity, we suppose that the set of parties participating in the computation is $I = [n]$.

Circuit F_i^ℓ

Hardwired Values: 1^λ, ℓ, i, z, $\{\widehat{x}_j = \{\widehat{x}_j^\ell\}_{\ell\in[L]}\}_{j\in[n]}$, $s_i = (x_i, \{\mathrm{fk}_i^\ell\}_{\ell\in[0,L]}, \{s_i^\ell\}_{\ell\in[L]})$, $\mathbf{stateKey}_i^{\ell+1}$, $\{\mathbf{msgKey}_{i,j}^{\ell+1}\}_{j\in[n]}$.

Inputs: $(\mathsf{Msg}^{<\ell-1}, \mathbf{msg}^{\ell-1})$ where for $\ell > 1$:
- The input messages $\mathsf{Msg}^{<\ell-1}$ are the messages of protocol Π of the first $\ell-2$ rounds. Corresponding garble labels are denoted by $\mathbf{stateKey}_i^\ell$.
- The input messages $\mathbf{msg}^{\ell-1} := \{\mathsf{msg}_j^{\ell-1}\}_{j\in[n]}$ are the $\ell-1$ round messages of protocol Π. Corresponding garble labels are denoted by $\{\mathbf{msgKey}_{i,j}^\ell\}_{j\in[n]}$.

Procedure: (for randomized algorithms, randomness is implicitly hardwired)
1. For $j \in [n]$, $k \in [\nu_m]$, and $b \in \{0,1\}$, define the functions $g_{1,j,k}^\ell$ and $g_{2,j}^\ell$ by:
$$g_{1,j,k}^\ell(x\|\mathrm{fk}^0\|\mathrm{fk}^\ell) := \{\mathsf{PRF}(\mathrm{fk}^\ell, 1\|z\|j\|k\|b\|[\kappa])\}_{b\in\{0,1\}} ,$$
$$g_{2,j}^\ell(x\|\mathrm{fk}^0\|\mathrm{fk}^\ell) := \mathsf{Next}_j(z, x, \mathsf{PRF}(\mathrm{fk}^0, 0\|z\|[\nu_r]), \mathsf{Msg}^{<\ell-1}, \mathbf{msg}^{\ell-1}) ,$$
and define the functions $g_{2,j,k}^\ell$ to output the k'th bit of $g_{2,j}^\ell$, for $k \in [\nu_m]$.
2. Compute the ℓ-th round message $\mathsf{msg}_i^\ell = \mathsf{msg}_{i,1}^\ell\|\cdots\|\mathsf{msg}_{i,\nu_m}^\ell := g_{2,i}^\ell(x_i\|\mathrm{fk}_i)$ of P_i in the inner protocol Π, and associated 2rNISC encodings, for $j \in [n]$, $k \in [\nu_m]$
$$\alpha_{i,j,k,1}^\ell \leftarrow_{\mathrm{R}} \mathsf{Encode}'((g_{1,j,k}^\ell, g_{2,j,k}^\ell), (\widehat{x}_i^\ell, \widehat{x}_j^\ell), s_i^\ell) \quad (3)$$
$$\alpha_{j,i,k,2}^\ell \leftarrow_{\mathrm{R}} \mathsf{Encode}'((g_{1,i,k}^\ell, g_{2,i,k}^\ell), (\widehat{x}_j^\ell, \widehat{x}_i^\ell), s_i^\ell) \quad (4)$$
3. Select the input labels $\mathbf{stateKey}_i^{\ell+1}[\mathsf{Msg}^{<\ell-1}\|\mathbf{msg}^{\ell-1}]$ for the next round $(\ell+1)$, corresponding to the messages $\mathsf{Msg}^{<\ell-1}\|\mathbf{msg}^{\ell-1}$. If $\ell = L$, these values are set to be empty strings.

Output: $(\mathbf{stateKey}_i^{\ell+1}[\mathsf{Msg}^{<\ell-1}\|\mathbf{msg}^{\ell-1}]$, msg_i^ℓ, $\{\alpha_{i,j,k,1}^\ell\}_{j,k}$, $\{\alpha_{j,i,k,2}^\ell\}_{j,k})$.

Fig. 2. Circuit F_i^ℓ for the construction of mrNISC in Sect. 5

- Evaluate the garbled circuits for round ℓ, for $i \in [n]$:

$$\left(\mathbf{stateKey}_i'^{\ell+1},\ \mathsf{msg}_i^\ell,\ \{\alpha_{i,j,k,1}^\ell\}_{j,k},\ \{\alpha_{j,i,k,2}^\ell\}_{j,k}\right) := \mathsf{GC.Eval}(\hat{\mathsf{F}}_i,\ (\mathbf{stateKey}_i'^{\ell},\ \{\mathbf{msgKey}_{i,j}^\ell[\mathsf{msg}_j^{\ell-1}]\}_{j\in[n]})) .$$

We recall that for round $\ell = 1$, all the input labels are empty strings, so the evaluation can be performed.

- If $\ell \neq L$, decrypt the input labels for the next round, for $i, j \in [n]$ and $k \in [\nu_m]$, define $g^\ell_{1,j,k}, g^\ell_{2,i,k}$ as in Fig. 2 and compute:

$$(\_, K^\ell_{i,j,k}) := \mathsf{Eval}'((g^\ell_{1,j,k}, g^\ell_{2,j,k}), (\hat{x}'_i, \hat{x}'_j), (\alpha^\ell_{i,j,k,1}, \alpha^\ell_{i,j,k,2})) ,$$
$$\mathbf{msgKey}^{\ell+1}_{i,j}[\mathsf{msg}^\ell_j] := \{\mathsf{ct}^\ell_{i,j,k}, \oplus K^\ell_{i,j,k}\}_{k\in[\nu_m]} ,$$

where _ just indicates that we ignore the output.

At the end, Eval got the full transcript of the inner MPC $\mathsf{Msg} = \{\mathsf{msg}^\ell_j\}_{j\in[n],\ell\in[L]}$ and set $y := \mathsf{Output}(z, \mathsf{Msg})$.

The correctness of the mrNISC scheme is follows from the perfect correctness properties of the inner MPC protocol, of the garbled circuit scheme, and the following fact (if everything is generated as specified in the description above):

$$\begin{aligned}\mathsf{Eval}'((g^\ell_{1,j,k}, g^\ell_{2,j,k}), (\hat{x}'_i, \hat{x}'_j), (\alpha^\ell_{i,j,k,1}, \alpha^\ell_{i,j,k,2})) &= (\beta, y_\beta)\\ \text{where } \beta = g^\ell_{2,j,k}(x_j \| \mathrm{fk}^0_j \| \mathrm{fk}^\ell_j) &= \text{the } k\text{-th bit of } \mathsf{msg}^\ell_j\\ \text{and } (y_0, y_1) &= g^\ell_{1,j,k}(x_i \| \mathrm{fk}^0_i \| \mathrm{fk}^\ell_i)\end{aligned}$$

thus:

$$K^\ell_{i,j,k} = y_b = \mathsf{PRF}(\mathrm{fk}_j, 1\|z\|j\|k\|\beta\|[\kappa]) .$$

The proof is similar to the security proof of the mrNISC in [22] and is formally presented in the full version [20].

Acknowledgments. Aayush Jain was supported by a Google PhD fellowship in the area of security and privacy (2018) and in part from DARPA SAFEWARE and SIEVE awards, NTT Research, NSF Frontier Award 1413955, and NSF grant 1619348, BSF grant 2012378, a Xerox Faculty Research Award, a Google Faculty Research Award, an equipment grant from Intel, and an Okawa Foundation Research Grant. This material is based upon work supported by the Defense Advanced Research Projects Agency through Award HR00112020024 and the ARL under Contract W911NF-15-C- 0205.

Ilan Komargodski is supported in part by an Alon Young Faculty Fellowship and by an ISF grant (No. 1774/20).

Huijia Lin was supported by NSF grants CNS-1528178, CNS-1929901, CNS-1936825 (CAREER), CNS-2026774, a Hellman Fellowship, a JP Morgan AI Research Award, a Simons Collaboration grant on the Theory of Algorithmic Fairness, the Defense Advanced Research Projects Agency (DARPA) and Army Research Office (ARO) under Contract No. W911NF-15-C-0236, and a subcontract No. 2017-002 through Galois.

The views expressed are those of the authors and do not reflect the official policy or position of the Department of Defense, DARPA, the National Science Foundation, or the U.S. Government.

References

1. Afshar, A., Mohassel, P., Pinkas, B., Riva, B.: Non-interactive secure computation based on cut-and-choose. In: Nguyen, P.Q., Oswald, E. (eds.) EUROCRYPT 2014. LNCS, vol. 8441, pp. 387–404. Springer, Heidelberg (2014). https://doi.org/10.1007/978-3-642-55220-5_22

2. Agrawal, S., Boneh, D., Boyen, X.: Efficient lattice (H)IBE in the standard model. In: Gilbert, H. (ed.) EUROCRYPT 2010. LNCS, vol. 6110, pp. 553–572. Springer, Heidelberg (2010). https://doi.org/10.1007/978-3-642-13190-5_28
3. Ajtai, M.: Generating hard instances of lattice problems (extended abstract). In: 28th ACM STOC, pp. 99–108. ACM Press (May 1996). https://doi.org/10.1145/237814.237838
4. Ajtai, M.: Generating hard instances of the short basis problem. In: Wiedermann, J., van Emde Boas, P., Nielsen, M. (eds.) ICALP 1999. LNCS, vol. 1644, pp. 1–9. Springer, Heidelberg (1999). https://doi.org/10.1007/3-540-48523-6_1
5. Alwen, J., Peikert, C.: Generating shorter bases for hard random lattices. In: Albers, S., Marion, J. (eds.) Proceedings of the 26th International Symposium on Theoretical Aspects of Computer Science, STACS 2009. LIPIcs, 26–28 February 2009, Freiburg, Germany, vol. 3, pp. 75–86. Schloss Dagstuhl - Leibniz-Zentrum fuer Informatik, Germany (2009). https://doi.org/10.4230/LIPIcs.STACS.2009.1832
6. Ananth, P., Badrinarayanan, S., Jain, A., Manohar, N., Sahai, A.: From FE combiners to secure MPC and back. In: Hofheinz, D., Rosen, A. (eds.) TCC 2019. LNCS, vol. 11891, pp. 199–228. Springer, Cham (2019). https://doi.org/10.1007/978-3-030-36030-6_9
7. Ananth, P., Choudhuri, A.R., Goel, A., Jain, A.: Round-optimal secure multiparty computation with honest majority. In: Shacham, H., Boldyreva, A. (eds.) CRYPTO 2018. LNCS, vol. 10992, pp. 395–424. Springer, Cham (2018). https://doi.org/10.1007/978-3-319-96881-0_14
8. Ananth, P., Jain, A., Jin, Z.: Multiparty homomorphic encryption (or: on removing setup in multi-key FHE). IACR Cryptology ePrint Archive: 2020/169 (2020)
9. Ananth, P., Jain, A., Jin, Z., Malavolta, G.: Multi-key fully-homomorphic encryption in the plain model. In: Pass, R., Pietrzak, K. (eds.) TCC 2020. LNCS, vol. 12550, pp. 28–57. Springer, Cham (2020). https://doi.org/10.1007/978-3-030-64375-1_2
10. Asharov, G., Jain, A., López-Alt, A., Tromer, E., Vaikuntanathan, V., Wichs, D.: Multiparty computation with low communication, computation and interaction via threshold FHE. In: Pointcheval, D., Johansson, T. (eds.) EUROCRYPT 2012. LNCS, vol. 7237, pp. 483–501. Springer, Heidelberg (2012). https://doi.org/10.1007/978-3-642-29011-4_29
11. Badrinarayanan, S., Garg, S., Ishai, Y., Sahai, A., Wadia, A.: Two-message witness indistinguishability and secure computation in the plain model from new assumptions. In: Takagi, T., Peyrin, T. (eds.) ASIACRYPT 2017. LNCS, vol. 10626, pp. 275–303. Springer, Cham (2017). https://doi.org/10.1007/978-3-319-70700-6_10
12. Badrinarayanan, S., Jain, A., Manohar, N., Sahai, A.: Secure MPC: laziness leads to GOD. IACR Cryptology ePrint Archive: Report 2018/580 (2018). https://eprint.iacr.org/2018/580
13. Badrinarayanan, S., Jain, A., Manohar, N., Sahai, A.: Secure MPC: laziness leads to GOD. In: Moriai, S., Wang, H. (eds.) ASIACRYPT 2020. LNCS, vol. 12493, pp. 120–150. Springer, Cham (2020). https://doi.org/10.1007/978-3-030-64840-4_5
14. Badrinarayanan, S., Jain, A., Ostrovsky, R., Visconti, I.: Non-interactive secure computation from one-way functions. In: Peyrin, T., Galbraith, S. (eds.) ASIACRYPT 2018. LNCS, vol. 11274, pp. 118–138. Springer, Cham (2018). https://doi.org/10.1007/978-3-030-03332-3_5
15. Banerjee, A., Peikert, C.: New and improved key-homomorphic pseudorandom functions. In: Garay, J.A., Gennaro, R. (eds.) CRYPTO 2014. LNCS, vol. 8616, pp. 353–370. Springer, Heidelberg (2014). https://doi.org/10.1007/978-3-662-44371-2_20

16. Banerjee, A., Peikert, C., Rosen, A.: Pseudorandom functions and lattices. In: Pointcheval, D., Johansson, T. (eds.) EUROCRYPT 2012. LNCS, vol. 7237, pp. 719–737. Springer, Heidelberg (2012). https://doi.org/10.1007/978-3-642-29011-4_42
17. Bartusek, J., Garg, S., Masny, D., Mukherjee, P.: Reusable two-round MPC from DDH. In: Pass, R., Pietrzak, K. (eds.) TCC 2020. LNCS, vol. 12551, pp. 320–348. Springer, Cham (2020). https://doi.org/10.1007/978-3-030-64378-2_12
18. Beimel, A., Gabizon, A., Ishai, Y., Kushilevitz, E., Meldgaard, S., Paskin-Cherniavsky, A.: Non-interactive secure multiparty computation. In: Garay, J.A., Gennaro, R. (eds.) CRYPTO 2014. LNCS, vol. 8617, pp. 387–404. Springer, Heidelberg (2014). https://doi.org/10.1007/978-3-662-44381-1_22
19. Ben-Or, M., Goldwasser, S., Wigderson, A.: Completeness theorems for non-cryptographic fault-tolerant distributed computation (extended abstract). In: 20th ACM STOC, pp. 1–10. ACM Press (May 1988). https://doi.org/10.1145/62212.62213
20. Benhamouda, F., Jain, A., Komargodski, I., Lin, H.: Multiparty reusable non-interactive secure computation from LWE. IACR Cryptology ePrint Archive (2021)
21. Benhamouda, F., Lin, H.: k-round multiparty computation from k-round oblivious transfer via garbled interactive circuits. In: Nielsen, J.B., Rijmen, V. (eds.) EUROCRYPT 2018. LNCS, vol. 10821, pp. 500–532. Springer, Cham (2018). https://doi.org/10.1007/978-3-319-78375-8_17
22. Benhamouda, F., Lin, H.: Mr NISC: multiparty reusable non-interactive secure computation. In: Pass, R., Pietrzak, K. (eds.) TCC 2020. LNCS, vol. 12551, pp. 349–378. Springer, Cham (2020). https://doi.org/10.1007/978-3-030-64378-2_13
23. Boneh, D., Lewi, K., Montgomery, H., Raghunathan, A.: Key homomorphic PRFs and their applications. In: Canetti, R., Garay, J.A. (eds.) CRYPTO 2013. LNCS, vol. 8042, pp. 410–428. Springer, Heidelberg (2013). https://doi.org/10.1007/978-3-642-40041-4_23
24. Brakerski, Z., Döttling, N.: Two-message statistically sender-private OT from LWE. In: Beimel, A., Dziembowski, S. (eds.) TCC 2018. LNCS, vol. 11240, pp. 370–390. Springer, Cham (2018). https://doi.org/10.1007/978-3-030-03810-6_14
25. Brakerski, Z., Halevi, S., Polychroniadou, A.: Four round secure computation without setup. In: Kalai, Y., Reyzin, L. (eds.) TCC 2017. LNCS, vol. 10677, pp. 645–677. Springer, Cham (2017). https://doi.org/10.1007/978-3-319-70500-2_22
26. Brakerski, Z., Langlois, A., Peikert, C., Regev, O., Stehlé, D.: Classical hardness of learning with errors. In: Boneh, D., Roughgarden, T., Feigenbaum, J. (eds.) 45th ACM STOC, pp. 575–584. ACM Press (June 2013). https://doi.org/10.1145/2488608.2488680
27. Brakerski, Z., Perlman, R.: Lattice-based fully dynamic multi-key FHE with short ciphertexts. In: Robshaw, M., Katz, J. (eds.) CRYPTO 2016. LNCS, vol. 9814, pp. 190–213. Springer, Heidelberg (2016). https://doi.org/10.1007/978-3-662-53018-4_8
28. Brakerski, Z., Vaikuntanathan, V.: Lattice-based FHE as secure as PKE. In: Naor, M. (ed.) ITCS 2014, pp. 1–12. ACM (January 2014). https://doi.org/10.1145/2554797.2554799
29. Canetti, R., Goldwasser, S., Poburinnaya, O.: Adaptively secure two-party computation from indistinguishability obfuscation. In: Dodis, Y., Nielsen, J.B. (eds.) TCC 2015. LNCS, vol. 9015, pp. 557–585. Springer, Heidelberg (2015). https://doi.org/10.1007/978-3-662-46497-7_22

30. Canetti, R., Jain, A., Scafuro, A.: Practical UC security with a global random oracle. In: Ahn, G.J., Yung, M., Li, N. (eds.) ACM CCS 2014, pp. 597–608. ACM Press (November 2014). https://doi.org/10.1145/2660267.2660374
31. Cash, D., Hofheinz, D., Kiltz, E., Peikert, C.: Bonsai trees, or how to delegate a lattice basis. In: Gilbert, H. (ed.) EUROCRYPT 2010. LNCS, vol. 6110, pp. 523–552. Springer, Heidelberg (2010). https://doi.org/10.1007/978-3-642-13190-5_27
32. Chase, M., et al.: Reusable non-interactive secure computation. In: Boldyreva, A., Micciancio, D. (eds.) CRYPTO 2019. LNCS, vol. 11694, pp. 462–488. Springer, Cham (2019). https://doi.org/10.1007/978-3-030-26954-8_15
33. Chaum, D., Crépeau, C., Damgård, I.: Multiparty unconditionally secure protocols (extended abstract). In: 20th ACM STOC, pp. 11–19. ACM Press (May 1988). https://doi.org/10.1145/62212.62214
34. Clear, M., McGoldrick, C.: Multi-identity and multi-key leveled FHE from learning with errors. In: Gennaro, R., Robshaw, M. (eds.) CRYPTO 2015. LNCS, vol. 9216, pp. 630–656. Springer, Heidelberg (2015). https://doi.org/10.1007/978-3-662-48000-7_31
35. Dachman-Soled, D., Katz, J., Rao, V.: Adaptively secure, universally composable, multiparty computation in constant rounds. In: Dodis, Y., Nielsen, J.B. (eds.) TCC 2015. LNCS, vol. 9015, pp. 586–613. Springer, Heidelberg (2015). https://doi.org/10.1007/978-3-662-46497-7_23
36. Dodis, Y., Ostrovsky, R., Reyzin, L., Smith, A.D.: Fuzzy extractors: how to generate strong keys from biometrics and other noisy data. SIAM J. Comput. **38**(1), 97–139 (2008)
37. Dodis, Y., Reyzin, L., Smith, A.: Fuzzy extractors: how to generate strong keys from biometrics and other noisy data. In: Cachin, C., Camenisch, J.L. (eds.) EUROCRYPT 2004. LNCS, vol. 3027, pp. 523–540. Springer, Heidelberg (2004). https://doi.org/10.1007/978-3-540-24676-3_31
38. Feige, U., Kilian, J., Naor, M.: A minimal model for secure computation (extended abstract). In: 26th ACM STOC, pp. 554–563. ACM Press (May 1994). https://doi.org/10.1145/195058.195408
39. Garg, S., Gentry, C., Halevi, S., Raykova, M.: Two-round secure MPC from indistinguishability obfuscation. In: Lindell, Y. (ed.) TCC 2014. LNCS, vol. 8349, pp. 74–94. Springer, Heidelberg (2014). https://doi.org/10.1007/978-3-642-54242-8_4
40. Garg, S., Ishai, Y., Srinivasan, A.: Two-round MPC: information-theoretic and black-box. In: Beimel, A., Dziembowski, S. (eds.) TCC 2018. LNCS, vol. 11239, pp. 123–151. Springer, Cham (2018). https://doi.org/10.1007/978-3-030-03807-6_5
41. Garg, S., Miao, P., Srinivasan, A.: Two-round multiparty secure computation minimizing public key operations. In: Shacham, H., Boldyreva, A. (eds.) CRYPTO 2018. LNCS, vol. 10993, pp. 273–301. Springer, Cham (2018). https://doi.org/10.1007/978-3-319-96878-0_10
42. Garg, S., Polychroniadou, A.: Two-round adaptively secure MPC from indistinguishability obfuscation. In: Dodis, Y., Nielsen, J.B. (eds.) TCC 2015. LNCS, vol. 9015, pp. 614–637. Springer, Heidelberg (2015). https://doi.org/10.1007/978-3-662-46497-7_24
43. Garg, S., Srinivasan, A.: Garbled protocols and two-round MPC from bilinear maps. In: Umans, C. (ed.) 58th FOCS, pp. 588–599. IEEE Computer Society Press (October 2017). https://doi.org/10.1109/FOCS.2017.60
44. Garg, S., Srinivasan, A.: Two-round multiparty secure computation from minimal assumptions. In: Nielsen, J.B., Rijmen, V. (eds.) EUROCRYPT 2018. LNCS, vol. 10821, pp. 468–499. Springer, Cham (2018). https://doi.org/10.1007/978-3-319-78375-8_16

45. Gentry, C., Peikert, C., Vaikuntanathan, V.: Trapdoors for hard lattices and new cryptographic constructions. In: Ladner, R.E., Dwork, C. (eds.) 40th ACM STOC, pp. 197–206. ACM Press (May 2008). https://doi.org/10.1145/1374376.1374407
46. Gentry, C., Sahai, A., Waters, B.: Homomorphic encryption from learning with errors: conceptually-simpler, asymptotically-faster, attribute-based. In: Canetti, R., Garay, J.A. (eds.) CRYPTO 2013. LNCS, vol. 8042, pp. 75–92. Springer, Heidelberg (2013). https://doi.org/10.1007/978-3-642-40041-4_5
47. Gertner, Y., Ishai, Y., Kushilevitz, E., Malkin, T.: Protecting data privacy in private information retrieval schemes. In: 30th ACM STOC, pp. 151–160. ACM Press (May 1998). https://doi.org/10.1145/276698.276723
48. Goldreich, O., Micali, S., Wigderson, A.: How to play any mental game or a completeness theorem for protocols with honest majority. In: Aho, A. (ed.) 19th ACM STOC, pp. 218–229. ACM Press (May 1987). https://doi.org/10.1145/28395.28420
49. Gorbunov, S., Vaikuntanathan, V., Wichs, D.: Leveled fully homomorphic signatures from standard lattices. In: Servedio, R.A., Rubinfeld, R. (eds.) 47th ACM STOC, pp. 469–477. ACM Press (June 2015). https://doi.org/10.1145/2746539.2746576
50. Dov Gordon, S., Liu, F.-H., Shi, E.: Constant-round MPC with fairness and guarantee of output delivery. In: Gennaro, R., Robshaw, M. (eds.) CRYPTO 2015. LNCS, vol. 9216, pp. 63–82. Springer, Heidelberg (2015). https://doi.org/10.1007/978-3-662-48000-7_4
51. Ishai, Y., Kushilevitz, E., Ostrovsky, R., Prabhakaran, M., Sahai, A.: Efficient non-interactive secure computation. In: Paterson, K.G. (ed.) EUROCRYPT 2011. LNCS, vol. 6632, pp. 406–425. Springer, Heidelberg (2011). https://doi.org/10.1007/978-3-642-20465-4_23
52. López-Alt, A., Tromer, E., Vaikuntanathan, V.: On-the-fly multiparty computation on the cloud via multikey fully homomorphic encryption. In: Karloff, H.J., Pitassi, T. (eds.) 44th ACM STOC, pp. 1219–1234. ACM Press (May 2012). https://doi.org/10.1145/2213977.2214086
53. Micciancio, D., Mol, P.: Pseudorandom Knapsacks and the sample complexity of LWE search-to-decision reductions. In: Rogaway, P. (ed.) CRYPTO 2011. LNCS, vol. 6841, pp. 465–484. Springer, Heidelberg (2011). https://doi.org/10.1007/978-3-642-22792-9_26
54. Micciancio, D., Peikert, C.: Trapdoors for lattices: simpler, tighter, faster, smaller. In: Pointcheval, D., Johansson, T. (eds.) EUROCRYPT 2012. LNCS, vol. 7237, pp. 700–718. Springer, Heidelberg (2012). https://doi.org/10.1007/978-3-642-29011-4_41
55. Micciancio, D., Regev, O.: Worst-case to average-case reductions based on Gaussian measures. In: 45th FOCS, pp. 372–381. IEEE Computer Society Press (October 2004). https://doi.org/10.1109/FOCS.2004.72
56. Mukherjee, P., Wichs, D.: Two round multiparty computation via multi-key FHE. In: Fischlin, M., Coron, J.-S. (eds.) EUROCRYPT 2016. LNCS, vol. 9666, pp. 735–763. Springer, Heidelberg (2016). https://doi.org/10.1007/978-3-662-49896-5_26
57. Peikert, C.: Public-key cryptosystems from the worst-case shortest vector problem: extended abstract. In: Mitzenmacher, M. (ed.) Proceedings of the 41st Annual ACM Symposium on Theory of Computing, STOC 2009, Bethesda, MD, USA, 31 May–2 June 2009, pp. 333–342. ACM (2009)
58. Peikert, C., Shiehian, S.: Multi-key FHE from LWE, revisited. In: Hirt, M., Smith, A. (eds.) TCC 2016. LNCS, vol. 9986, pp. 217–238. Springer, Heidelberg (2016). https://doi.org/10.1007/978-3-662-53644-5_9

59. Peikert, C., Shiehian, S.: Noninteractive zero knowledge for np from (plain) learning with errors. In: Boldyreva, A., Micciancio, D. (eds.) CRYPTO 2019. LNCS, vol. 11692, pp. 89–114. Springer, Cham (2019). https://doi.org/10.1007/978-3-030-26948-7_4
60. Quach, W., Wee, H., Wichs, D.: Laconic function evaluation and applications. In: Thorup, M. (ed.) 59th FOCS, pp. 859–870. IEEE Computer Society Press (October 2018). https://doi.org/10.1109/FOCS.2018.00086
61. Regev, O.: On lattices, learning with errors, random linear codes, and cryptography. In: STOC, pp. 84–93 (2005)

Unbounded Multi-party Computation from Learning with Errors

Prabhanjan Ananth[1(✉)], Abhishek Jain[2], Zhengzhong Jin[2], and Giulio Malavolta[3]

[1] University of California, Santa Barbara, CA, USA
[2] Johns Hopkins University, Baltimore, MD, USA
{abhishek,zzjin}@cs.jhu.edu
[3] Max Planck Institute for Security and Privacy, Bochum, Germany

Abstract. We consider the problem of round-optimal *unbounded MPC*: in the first round, parties publish a message that depends only on their input. In the second round, any subset of parties can jointly and securely compute any function f over their inputs in a single round of broadcast. We do not impose any a-priori bound on the number of parties nor on the size of the functions that can be computed.

Our main result is a semi-honest two-round protocol for unbounded MPC in the plain model from the hardness of the standard learning with errors (LWE) problem. Prior work in the same setting assumes the hardness of problems over bilinear maps. Thus, our protocol is the first example of unbounded MPC that is post-quantum secure.

The central ingredient of our protocol is a new scheme of attribute-based secure function evaluation (AB-SFE) with *public decryption*. Our construction combines techniques from the realm of homomorphic commitments with delegation of lattice basis. We believe that such a scheme may find further applications in the future.

1 Introduction

A multi-party computation (MPC) protocol [20] allows a set of n mutually distrustful parties to evaluate any circuit C over their inputs $(x_1, \ldots, x_n)$, while leaking nothing beyond the circuit output $C(x_1, \ldots, x_n)$. MPC is one of the pillars of modern cryptography and the study of its round complexity (and the necessary assumptions) has motivated a large body of research. A series of recent works has established that two rounds are necessary and sufficient to securely compute any function, under a variety of cryptographic assumptions [8,15,17,18,24,29].

A recent line of work [2,7,9] focuses on constructing round-optimal MPC with *reusable* first message, i.e. where the first message of the MPC can be reused an unbounded number of times for computing different functions over the committed inputs. However, out of these works only [9] achieves the "dream version" of two round MPC, i.e. an MPC that simultaneously satisfies *all* of the following properties:

A. Canteaut and F.-X. Standaert (Eds.): EUROCRYPT 2021, LNCS 12697, pp. 754–781, 2021.
https://doi.org/10.1007/978-3-030-77886-6_26

- No trusted setup is required.
- In the first round, each party publishes a first message that depends only on their input and does *not* depend on the number of parties nor on the size of the circuit being evaluated.
- In the second round, any subset of parties can evaluate a circuit C over their first messages. The output can be publicly reconstructed given all the second messages.
- The second round can be repeated arbitrarily many times (with different circuits and different sets of parties), without the need to recompute a first message. Parties can join the system at any time by posting a first message.

Throughout this work, we refer to such an MPC protocol as *unbounded MPC.*

Among all works on round-optimal protocols, only [9] achieves the notion of truly unbounded MPC without the need for a trusted setup. In particular, the works of [2,7] fall short in satisfying this notion because they impose a bound on the number of participants that needs to be fixed once and for all in the first round and needs to be shared across all parties. The earlier work of [29] does not suffer from this limitation, but requires a trusted setup.

The work of [9] assumes the hardness of standard problems over bilinear maps. While the veracity of such assumptions is well-established in the classical settings, the lurking threat of quantum computing renders such a solution immediately insecure in the presence of a scalable quantum machine. This motivates us to ask the following question:

Can we construct unbounded MPC from Learning with Errors (LWE)?

1.1 Our Results

We consider the problem of unbounded MPC with security against semi-honest adversaries in the dishonest majority setting. In our communication model, parties publish their first message through a broadcast channel which is immediately delivered to all participants. At any point in time, any subset S of participants (with a dishonest majority) can gather together and evaluate a circuit C over their inputs $(x_1, \ldots, x_{|S|})$ in a *single round* of broadcast. The output $C(x_1, \ldots, x_{|S|})$ can then be publicly reconstructed from the messages of all parties. This phase can be repeated arbitrarily many times without having to re-initialize the first message (i.e. the first message is reusable). We do not impose any a-priori bound on the number of participants nor on the size of the circuits.

We prove the following theorem:

Theorem 1 (Informal). *If the learning with errors (LWE) problem is hard, then there exist a two-round unbounded MPC in the plain model.*

By additionally assuming the quantum hardness of LWE, we obtain the first post-quantum secure protocol for (semi-honest) unbounded MPC in two rounds. Our main technical ingredient is a new construction of attribute-based secure function evaluation (AB-SFE) [27] where the output can be *publicly reconstructed* at the end of the second round. On a technical level, our scheme combines the homomorphic commitment scheme from [23] with techniques to delegate a lattice basis. We believe that such a scheme may find further applications in the future.

Semi-malicious Security. In the full version of the paper, we extend our results to the semi-malicious setting by building on techniques in [10].

2 Technical Overview

In the following, we summarize the main technical innovations of our work. This outline can be roughly split in three components: First we introduce the notion of AB-SFE [27] with public decryption and we recall the security properties that we want to guarantee. Then we show an instantiation of AB-SFE with public decryption from LWE, building on the construction of homomorphic commitments from [23]. Finally, we show how AB-SFE functions as the main ingredient (alongside garbled circuits) for constructing unbounded MPC.

2.1 AB-SFE with Public Decryption

We begin by recalling the notion of AB-SFE [27]. AB-SFE was introduced in the context of designated-verifier non-interactive zero-knowledge proof to obtain constructions from new assumptions. However the work of [27] focused on the notion where decrypting a message requires a *secret state* (that might leak some information about the attribute). Here we augment the syntax of AB-SFE with a *public decryption* procedure. For the purpose of our work, it is going to be useful to cast this primitive as a two-party protocol between an "authority" and a "sender." The interaction proceeds as follows:

- **Key Generation:** On input an attribute x, the authority locally runs a setup algorithm $\mathsf{crs} \leftarrow \mathsf{Setup}(1^\lambda)$ and generates a secret/public key pair $(\mathsf{msk}, \mathsf{pk}) \leftarrow \mathsf{KeyGen}(\mathsf{crs}, x)$.[1]
- **Encryption:** Given the public key pk (generated as above), a circuit C and a message μ, the sender computes a ciphertext $\mathsf{ct} \leftarrow \mathsf{Enc}(\mathsf{pk}, C, \mu)$.
- **Decryption Hint:** To enable public decryption, the authority crafts a circuit-specific decryption hint $\mathsf{sk}_C \leftarrow \mathsf{Hint}(\mathsf{msk}, C)$.
- **Public Decryption:** Anyone who possesses the ciphertext ct and the decryption hint sk_C can recover the message μ by running $\mathsf{Dec}(\mathsf{sk}_C, \mathsf{ct})$. The procedure succeeds if and only if $C(x) = 1$.

One way to intepret this primitive is as a secure two-party computation protocol where the interaction consists only of two rounds and where only one party speaks in the first round. Looking ahead, this latter property is going to be crucial to achieve unbounded secure MPC, since it will allow *multiple (unbounded) parties to simultaneously play the role of the sender.*

[1] Note that we could have merged the Setup and the KeyGen algorithms in a single subroutine, however we refrained to do so in order to match the original syntax from [27].

Security of AB-SFE. As for the security of AB-SFE we define two properties: (1) We require that nothing beyond $C(x)$ is revealed about the attribute x. This requirement must hold even for polynomially many circuits $(C_1, \ldots, C_q)$ and in the presence of the corresponding decryption hints $(\mathsf{sk}_{C_1}, \ldots, \mathsf{sk}_{C_q})$, for any polynomial q. (2) We require that for all circuits C such that $C(x) = 0$ it holds that

$$\mathsf{Enc}(\mathsf{pk}, C, \mu_0) \approx \mathsf{Enc}(\mathsf{pk}, C, \mu_1)$$

are computationally indistinguishable. This is required to hold *even if the distinguisher is given the random coins used in the key generation procedure.* In other words, if the circuit outputs 0, even the key authority should not be able to learn the message of the sender. This is in stark contrast with the standard attribute-based encryption settings [25,31] where typically semantic security does *not* hold against a corrupted authority.

2.2 AB-SFE from Learning with Errors

The problem of constructing AB-SFE was considered in [27] where they obtained schemes from a variety of assumptions in the private decryption settings, based on 2-round oblivious transfer. However, none of their schemes support *public decryption* (without adding an extra round of interaction).

In this work we take a different route. Our starting point is the fully homomorphic commitment scheme from [23], which we briefly recall in the following.

Homomorphic Commitments. The commitment key is a uniform matrix $\mathbf{A} \leftarrow \mathbb{Z}_q^{n \times m}$ and committing to a multi-bit string $(x_1, \ldots, x_u)$ corresponds to the computation of a set of

$$\mathbf{C}_i = \mathsf{Com}(\mathbf{A}, x_i; \mathbf{R}_i) = \mathbf{A} \cdot \mathbf{R}_i + x_i \mathbf{G}$$

where $\mathbf{R}_i \leftarrow \{0,1\}^{m \times m}$ and $\mathbf{G}$ is the gadget matrix from [28]. Here $\mathbf{R}_i$ is a low-norm vector and plays the role of the decommitment. In [23] it is shown that one can homomorphically evaluate any (depth-bounded) circuit C over committed value and still obtain a well-formed commitment $\mathbf{C}_C$. The exact details of the algorithm are irrelevant for the purpose of this overview, except for the fact that one can define a (deterministic) homomrphic computation over the decommitments and obtain a low-norm vector $\mathbf{R}_{C,x}$, which is a valid decommitment for $\mathbf{C}_C$.

At this point it is instructive to take a step back and think how we could implement AB-SFE if we had a general-purpose witness encryption [16] scheme. A witness encryption scheme, associated with a NP language, consists of an encryption and a decryption algorithm: Anyone can encrypt their message μ under an NP instance and the decryption algorithm can obtain μ using the witness to this instance. We use witness encryption as follows: The sender encrypts μ under the instance $\mathbf{A} \cdot \mathbf{R}_{C,x} + C(x)\mathbf{G}$ which is obtained by homomorphically evaluating upon the commitments using the circuit C. The authority releases the decommitment $\mathbf{R}_{C,x}$ as witness which would then allow anyone to recover μ if and only if $C(x) = 1$. Temporarily glossing over the fact that $\mathbf{R}_{C,x}$ might leak some information about x, we are going to show how to implement this idea without resorting to the power of general-purpose witness encryption.

Computing Hints via Basis Delegation. Our first observation is that, when $C(x) = 1$, the matrix $\left[\mathbf{A}\ \mathbf{C}_C\right] = \left[\mathbf{A}\ \mathbf{A}\mathbf{R}_{C,x} + \mathbf{G}\right]$ matches the construction of lattice trapdoor in [28]. Hence, $\mathbf{R}_{C,x}$ allows us to compute a short basis (a trapdoor) for the dual lattice spanned by $\left[\mathbf{A}\ \mathbf{C}_C\right]$. Following [28], such a trapdoor $\mathbf{T}$ can be efficiently computed in the following way

$$\mathbf{T} = \begin{bmatrix} \mathbf{I} & -\mathbf{R}_{C,x} \\ \mathbf{0} & \mathbf{I} \end{bmatrix} \cdot \begin{bmatrix} \mathbf{I} & \mathbf{0} \\ -\mathbf{G}^{-1}[\mathbf{A}] & \mathbf{T}_{\mathbf{G}} \end{bmatrix}$$

where $\mathbf{T}_{\mathbf{G}}$ is a short basis for the lattice $\Lambda_q^{\perp}(\mathbf{G})$, which is publicly computable. At this point it is tempting to view $\left[\mathbf{A}\ \mathbf{C}_C\right]$ as the public-key of the witness encryption and $\mathbf{T}$ as the witness. After all, $\mathbf{T}$ has low norm if and only if $\mathbf{R}_{C,x}$ does, which implies that $\mathbf{R}_{C,x}$ is a valid decommitment for $\mathbf{C}_C$.

However we are not yet done. The adversary receives $\mathbf{R}_{C,x}$, for multiple circuits, where each decommitment is a deterministic function of the decommitments $(\mathbf{R}_1, \ldots, \mathbf{R}_u)$ and enough number of such decommitments will leak some information about x. Recall that we are interested in the public decryption setting, which would require us to publicly release $\mathbf{T}$, which is again a deterministic function of $\mathbf{R}_{C,x}$.

Our next idea is to *randomize* the trapdoor $\mathbf{T}$ using the basis delegation procedure of [12]. In the literature, this process is also referred to as *SampleRight*. First we add a uniformly sampled matrix $\widehat{\mathbf{A}} \leftarrow \mathbb{Z}_q^{n \times 2m}$ and a uniform vector $\mathbf{y} \leftarrow \mathbb{Z}_q^n$ to the public parameters. Given the trapdoor $\mathbf{T}$ for $\left[\mathbf{A}\ \mathbf{C}_C\right]$, the inverse sampling algorithm allows us to probabilistically sample a low-norm vector $\mathbf{e}$ such that

$$\left[\widehat{\mathbf{A}}\ \mathbf{A}\ \mathbf{C}_C\right] \cdot \mathbf{e} = \mathbf{y}$$

and $\mathbf{e}$ carries no information about $\mathbf{T}$. At this point we have all ingredients to instantiate our witness encryption: After recomputing $\mathbf{C}_C$ homomorphically, the encryptor parses

$$\widehat{\mathsf{pk}} = \left[\mathbf{y}\ \widehat{\mathbf{A}}\ \mathbf{A}\ \mathbf{C}_C\right]$$

as a public key for a dual Regev encryption scheme [19] (with appropriate dimensions) and uses $\widehat{\mathsf{pk}}$ to encrypt μ in a canonical way. The decryption hint $\mathbf{e}$ can be computed from $\mathbf{R}_{C,x}$ as described above and allows anyone to recover μ, since it has low norm. Some care is needed in setting the parameters for the noise, but it is not hard to prove that the scheme is secure assuming the hardness of the LWE problem.

To see why we achieve security against a corrupted sender, we first switch from using a trapdoor for $\left[\mathbf{A}\ \mathbf{C}_C\right]$ to generate the matrix $\mathbf{R}_{C,x}$ to instead use a trapdoor for $\widehat{\mathbf{A}}$ (using a process referred to as *SampleLeft*)[2]; this switch is statistically indistinguishable and follows from the standard lattice trapdoor lemmas. We do this switch for every circuit. Once we do this, we then invoke leftover hash lemma to instead generate the commitment as $\mathbf{U_i} + x_i\mathbf{G}$, where $\mathbf{U_i}$ is generated uniformly at random. At this point, the input of the receiver is information-theoretically hidden from the sender.

The security against a corrupted receiver follows from the noise smudging lemma and learning with errors.

2.3 From AB-SFE with Public Decryption to Unbounded MPC

We are now ready to show how AB-SFE with public decryption readily gives us a construction of unbounded MPC.

Building Blocks. In addition to AB-SFE with public decryption, we are going to assume the existence of any semi-malicious secure two-round MPC, denoted by mpc, such as the protocols proposed in [8,18]. We note that we do not place any additional restrictions on mpc: For instance, it need not guarantee any reusability property and moreover, the total number of parties in the MPC protocol can be fixed before the first round message. Furthermore we are going to make use of garbled circuits [32]. For the reader unfamiliar with the notion, a garbling scheme allows one to compute a garbled version of a circuit C together with set of label pairs $(\mathsf{lab}_{i,0}, \mathsf{lab}_{i,1})$. Given an input z, its encoding consists of the labels corresponding to its bit representation $(\mathsf{lab}_{1,z_1}, \ldots, \mathsf{lab}_{|z|,z_{|z|}})$ and security requires that nothing is revealed about z, besides the output of the computation $C(z)$.

It is also going to be convenient to consider an augmented notion of AB-SFE, that we denote by 2AB-SFE, following the convention from [22]. A 2AB-SFE with public decryption is identical to AB-SFE with public decryption except that the encryption algorithm takes as input two messages (μ_0, μ_1) and the public decryption returns μ_0 if $C(x) = 0$ and μ_1 if $C(x) = 1$. Given an AB-SFE, it is easy to construct a 2AB-SFE by just encrypting μ_0 under the complement of C.

The Unbounded MPC Protocol. We provide a simplified description of our unbounded MPC in the following.

- **First Message:** Given an input x_i, the first message of each party simply consists of the generation of a public key pk_i for the 2AB-SFE scheme, where the attribute is set to the input x_i.
- **Second Message:** Each party P_i is given as input set of parties S and a circuit C. First, it computes a garbled version of the circuit that takes as input S (specifying the subset of parties participating in the protocol), any first

[2] In the technical sections, instead of using the terms SampleLeft and SampleRight, we use the algorithm GenSamplePre that captures the functionality of both these algorithms.

round messages $(m_1, \ldots, m_{|S|})$ of mpc and computes the ith party's second round messages of mpc (the input x_i is hardwired in the computation). After it computes the garbled circuit, it then takes each pair of labels $(\mathsf{lab}_{i,0}, \mathsf{lab}_{i,1})$ and computes a 2AB-SFE encryption for the corresponding participant P_j under the circuit $\Gamma_{i,j}$, defined as follows.

$$\Gamma_{i,j} : \text{Compute the } i\text{-th bit of } m_j.$$

Finally, for all $j = 1 \ldots |S|$ compute the decryption hints for the 2AB-SFE encryption corresponding to the circuit $\Gamma_{j,i}$.

- **Reconstruction:** The public reconstruction algorithm works by using all the decryption hints to recover all the labels, which in turn are used to evaluate the garbled circuits. This results in a set of second round messages $(p_1, \ldots, p_{|S|})$ for the underlying two-round MPC. The reconstruction algorithm then returns the result of the reconstruction procedure of the one-time MPC.

Since the first message consists only of the key of the 2AB-SFE scheme, it is clear that the resulting MPC does not impose a bound on the parties. Also note that the underlying two-round secure MPC, namely mpc, is freshly re-initialized for each second message and therefore the security of the reusable protocol is not affected. One subtlety that we ignored in the above description is that the computation of the messages for the one-time MPC is randomized and we need to ensure that the same randomness is used consistently in the first and second message for each party. This can be done routinely by adding a PRF key alongside the input and drawing all necessary random coins by evaluating the PRF on some public input.

2.4 Related Work

Ishai et al. [26] introduced the notion of reusable non-interactive secure computation (rNISC), where a receiver can publish a reusable encoding of its input y and any sender can enable computation of $f(x, y)$ by computing a message using input x and sending it to the receiver. This notion has subsequently been studied in many follow-up works; see, e.g., [1,5,6,11,13].

The recent work of Benhamouda and Lin [9] extends this notion to the *multiparty* setting, and refer to it as multiparty reusable NISC (mrNISC). Unlike rNISC which is primarily challenging in the malicious adversary model (from the viewpoint of black-box constructions), mrNISC is non-trivial even in the semi-honest adversary model. Unbounded MPC seeks the same goals as mrNISC; we use the former terminology to emphasize the key property that the first round messages do not depend on the number of parties or the size of the circuit or the size of the subset of parties involved in the actual computation.

3 Preliminaries

3.1 Notations

For any integer n, we use $[n]$ to denote the set $\{1, 2, \ldots, n\}$. We use $\mathbb{Z}$ to denote the sets of integers, and use $\mathbb{Z}_q$ to denote $\mathbb{Z}/q\mathbb{Z}$.

For any sets $S_1, S_2, \ldots, S_n$ of integers, and any tuple $(i_1^*, i_2^*, \ldots, i_n^*) \in S_1 \times S_2 \times \cdots \times S_n$, we use the notation $(i_1^*, i_2^*, \ldots, i_n^*) + 1$ (resp. $(i_1^*, i_2^*, \ldots, i_n^*) - 1$) to denote the lexicographical smallest (resp. biggest) element in $S_1 \times S_2 \times \cdots \times S_n$ that is lexicographical greater (resp. less) than $(i_1^*, i_2^*, \ldots, i_n^*)$.

Statistical Distance. For any two discrete distributions P, Q, the statistical distance between P and Q is defined as $\mathsf{SD}(P, Q) = \sum_i \big| \Pr[P = i] - \Pr[Q = i] \big| / 2$ where i takes all the values in the support of P and Q.

3.2 Lattice and LWE Assumption

Let m be an integer, a lattice is a discrete additive group in $\mathbb{R}^m$. We say that a set of linear independent vectors $\mathbf{B} = \{\mathbf{b}_1, \mathbf{b}_2, \ldots, \mathbf{b}_k\}$ is a basis of a lattice Λ, if $\Lambda = \{\mathbf{Bz} \mid \mathbf{z} \in \mathbb{Z}^k\}$. Let $\widetilde{\mathbf{B}} = \{\widetilde{\mathbf{b}_1}, \widetilde{\mathbf{b}_2}, \ldots, \widetilde{\mathbf{b}_k}\}$ be the Gram-Schmidt basis derived from $\mathbf{B}$. We denote $\|\widetilde{\mathbf{B}}\| = \max_{i \in [k]} \|\widetilde{\mathbf{b}}_i\|$.

For any integer $n, m, q \geq 2$ and $\mathbb{Z}_q^{n \times m}$, we define the q-ary lattice

$$\Lambda_q(\mathbf{A}) = \{\mathbf{z} \in \mathbb{Z}_q^m \mid \exists \mathbf{s} \in \mathbb{Z}^n, \mathbf{z} = \mathbf{A}^T \mathbf{s} \pmod{q}\}$$
$$\Lambda_q^{\perp}(\mathbf{A}) = \{\mathbf{z} \in \mathbb{Z}_q^m \mid \mathbf{Az} = \mathbf{0} \pmod{q}\}$$

Similarly, for any $\mathbf{y} \in \mathbb{Z}_q^n$, we define the coset $\Lambda_q^{\mathbf{y}}(\mathbf{A}) = \{\mathbf{z} \in \mathbb{Z}_q^m \mid \mathbf{Az} = \mathbf{y} \pmod{q}\}$.

Discrete Gaussian. For any integer n and real $s > 0$, define the Gaussian function $\rho_s : \mathbb{R} \to \mathbb{R}^+$ of parameter s as $\rho_s(\mathbf{x}) = \exp(-\pi \|\mathbf{x}\|^2 / s^2)$. For any lattice Λ, any vector $\mathbf{c} \in \mathbb{R}^m$, and real $s > 0$, we denote $\rho_s(\Lambda + \mathbf{c}) = \sum_{\mathbf{x} \in \Lambda} \rho_s(\mathbf{x} + \mathbf{c})$. The discrete Gaussian probabilistic distribution $D_{\Lambda + \mathbf{c}, s}$ is a distribution over Λ with density function $\rho_s(\mathbf{x}) / \rho_s(\Lambda + \mathbf{c})$, for any $\mathbf{x} \in \Lambda$.

Theorem 2 (Noise Flooding [4,14,21,30]). For any $c \in \mathbb{Z}$, and real $s > 0$, $\mathsf{SD}(D_{\mathbb{Z},s}, D_{c+\mathbb{Z},s}) < O(c/s)$.

Definition 1 (LWE Assumption). *Let $n = n(\lambda), m = m(\lambda), \ell = \ell(\lambda)$ be polynomials in λ, and let the modulus $q = 2^{\lambda^{O(1)}}$ be a function of λ, and $\chi = \chi(\lambda)$ be a noise distribution. The Learning with Error (LWE) assumption states that for any PPT distinguisher $\mathcal{D}$, there exists a negligible function $\nu(\lambda)$ such that for any sufficiently large λ,*

$$\left| \Pr\left[\mathcal{D}(1^\lambda, (\mathbf{A}, \mathbf{S} \cdot \mathbf{A} + \mathbf{E})) = 1\right] - \Pr\left[\mathcal{D}(1^\lambda, (\mathbf{A}, \mathbf{U})) = 1\right] \right| < \nu(\lambda)$$

where $\mathbf{A} \leftarrow \mathbb{Z}_q^{n \times m}, \mathbf{S} \leftarrow \mathbb{Z}_q^{\ell \times n}, \mathbf{U} \leftarrow \mathbb{Z}_q^{\ell \times m}, \mathbf{E} \leftarrow \chi^{\ell \times m}$.

Lattice Trapdoor and Preimage Sampling

Theorem 3 (**[28], Theorem 5.1). ** There is an efficient randomized algorithm $\mathsf{TrapGen}(1^n, 1^m, q)$, that given any integer $n \geq 1, q \geq 2$, and sufficiently large $m = O(n \log q)$, outputs a (partity-check) matrix $\mathbf{A} \in \mathbb{Z}_q^{n\times m}$, and a short basis $\mathbf{T}$ for $\Lambda_q^{\perp}(\mathbf{A})$, such that $\mathbf{A}$ is statistically close to uniform.

Theorem 4 (**[12], Theorem 3.4, Special Case). ** Let n, q, m be positive integers with $q \geq 2$, and $m \geq 2n \log q$, there exists a PPT algorithm $\mathsf{GenSamplePre}$ on input of $\mathbf{A} = \left[\mathbf{A}_1\ \mathbf{A}_2\right] \in \mathbb{Z}_q^{n\times 2m}$, and $S \in \{1, 2\}$, a basis $\mathbf{B}_S$ for $\Lambda_q^{\perp}(\mathbf{A}_S)$, a vector $\mathbf{y} \in \mathbb{Z}_q^n$, and an integer $r > \|\widetilde{\mathbf{B}_S}\| \cdot \omega(\sqrt{\log 2m})$, outputs $\mathbf{e} \leftarrow \mathsf{GenSamplePre}(\mathbf{A}, \mathbf{B}_S, S, \mathbf{y}, r)$, such that for overwhelming fraction of $\mathbf{A}$, $\mathbf{e}$ is statistically close to $D_{\Lambda_q^{\mathbf{y}}(\mathbf{A}),r}$.

3.3 Garbling Scheme

A garbling scheme is a pair of algorithms $(\mathsf{Garble}, \mathsf{Eval})$, which works as follows.

- $\mathsf{Garble}(1^\lambda, C)$: The garbling algorithm takes as input a security parameter λ, and a circuit C with input length ℓ_{in} and output length ℓ_{out}. Then it outputs a garbled circuit $\widetilde{C}$ and some labels $\mathsf{lab} = \{\mathsf{lab}_{b,i}\}_{b\in\{0,1\}, i\in[\ell_{\mathsf{in}}]}$.
- $\mathsf{Eval}(\widetilde{C}, \mathsf{lab}_x)$: For any $x \in \ell_{\mathsf{in}}$, let lab_x denote $\{\mathsf{lab}_{x_i,i}\}_{i\in[\ell_{\mathsf{in}}]}$. On input $\widetilde{C}$ and lab_x, it outputs a y.

We require a garbling scheme to satisfy the following properties.

- **Correctness:** For any circuit $C : \{0, 1\}^{\ell_{\mathsf{in}}} \rightarrow \{0, 1\}^{\ell_{\mathsf{out}}}$, and any input $x \in \{0, 1\}^{\ell_{\mathsf{in}}}$, we have

$$\Pr\left[(\widetilde{C}, \mathsf{lab}) \leftarrow \mathsf{Garble}(1^\lambda, C), y \leftarrow \mathsf{Eval}(\widetilde{C}, \mathsf{lab}_x) : y = C(x)\right] = 1$$

- **Simulation Security:** There exists a simulator Sim such that for any n.u. PPT distinguisher $\mathcal{D}$, there exists a negligible function $\nu(\lambda)$ such that

$$\Big| \Pr\left[(\widetilde{C}, \mathsf{lab}) \leftarrow \mathsf{Garble}(1^\lambda, C) : \mathcal{D}(1^\lambda, \widetilde{C}, \mathsf{lab}_x) = 1\right] - \Pr\left[(\overline{C}, \overline{\mathsf{lab}}) \leftarrow \mathsf{Sim}(1^\lambda, C(x)) : \mathcal{D}(1^\lambda, \overline{C}, \overline{\mathsf{lab}}) = 1\right] \Big| < \nu(\lambda)$$

3.4 Semi-malicious 2-Round MPC in Plain Model

A (one-time useable, selective secure) semi-malicious 2-round MPC in the plain model is a tuple of algorithms $(\mathsf{Round}_1, \mathsf{Round}_2, \mathsf{Rec})$, which work as follows.

There are N parties who want to jointly compute $f(x_1, x_2, \ldots, x_N)$, where x_i is the input of i-th party.

- **Round 1:** For each $i \in [N]$, the i-th party sets fresh random coins r_i, and executes $\mathsf{msg}_i \leftarrow \mathsf{Round}_1(1^\lambda, x_i, f; r_i)$.
- **Round 2:** For each $i \in [N]$, the i-th party executes $p_i \leftarrow \mathsf{Round}_2(x_i, r_i, \{\mathsf{msg}_j\}_{j \in [N]})$.
- **Output Recovery:** Any one with $\{p_i\}_{i \in [N]}$ executes $y \leftarrow \mathsf{Rec}(\{p_i\}_{i \in [N]})$.

We require the protocol to satisfy the following property.

- **Semi-Malicious Simulation Security:** There exists a simulator Sim such that, for any input $\{x_i\}_{i \in [N]}$, for any subset of honest parties $H \subseteq [N]$, and any dishonest parties' random coins $\{r_i\}_{i \in [N] \setminus H}$, any PPT distinguisher $\mathcal{D}$, there exists a negligible function $\nu(\lambda)$ such that for any sufficiently large λ,

$$\left| \Pr\left[\begin{smallmatrix} \forall i \in H, r_i \leftarrow \{0,1\}^*, \forall i \in [N], \mathsf{msg}_i = \mathsf{Round}_1(1^\lambda, x_i; r_i), \\ p_i = \mathsf{Round}_2(x_i, r_i, \{\mathsf{msg}_j\}_{j \in [N]}) \end{smallmatrix} : \mathcal{D}(1^\lambda, \{\mathsf{msg}_i, p_i\}_{i \in [N]}) = 1 \right] - \Pr\left[\mathcal{D}(1^\lambda, \mathsf{Sim}(1^\lambda, H, \{x_i, r_i\}_{i \notin H}, f, f(\{x_i\}_{i \in [N]}))) = 1\right] \right| < \nu(\lambda)$$

Here, without loss of generality, we assume the Round_1 and Round_2 use the same random coins.

3.5 Homomorphic Commitment

A homomorphic commitment scheme is a tuple of algorithms $(\mathsf{Setup}, \mathsf{Com}, \mathsf{Eval})$, with the following syntax.

- $\mathsf{Gen}(1^\lambda)$: A CRS generation algorithm that takes as input a security parameter λ, and it outputs a common random string crs.
- $\mathsf{Com}(\mathsf{crs}, \mu; r)$: A commitment algorithm that takes as input the CRS crs, a message $\mu \in \{0,1\}$, and randomness r, it outputs a commitment c.
- $\mathsf{Eval}(C, (c_1, c_2, \ldots, c_u))$: The (fully) homomorphic evaluation algorithm Eval takes as input a circuit C, and some commitments $c_1, c_2, \ldots, c_u$, and it outputs an evaluated commitment $\mathsf{Com}(C(x); r_{C,x})$, where $x = (x_1, x_2, \ldots, x_u)$ is the message that $c_1, c_2, \ldots, c_u$ committed. Furthermore, the randomness $r_{C,x}$ can be efficiently computed from the randomness used to compute $c_1, c_2, \ldots c_u$ and x.

We require it to satisfy the following properties.

Statistical Hiding. There exists a negligible function $\nu(\lambda)$ such that,

$$\mathsf{SD}((\mathsf{crs}, \mathsf{Com}(\mathsf{crs}, 0)), (\mathsf{crs}, \mathsf{Com}(\mathsf{crs}, 1))) < \nu(\lambda),$$

where the randomness is over the CRS crs and the randomness used to compute the commitment.

Construction. Let $n = n(\lambda)$ be a polynomial in λ, $q = 2^{ADD}$, and $m = 2n \log q$.

- $\mathsf{Gen}(1^\lambda)$: It samples $\mathbf{A} \leftarrow \mathbb{Z}_q^{n \times m}$ uniformly at random, and output $\mathsf{crs} = \mathbf{A}$.

- $\mathsf{Com}(\mathsf{crs} = \mathbf{A}, \mu \in \{0,1\}; \mathbf{R})$: It outputs a commitment $\mathbf{C} = \mathbf{AR} + \mu\mathbf{G}$.
- $\mathsf{Eval}(C, (\mathbf{C}_1, \mathbf{C}_2, \ldots, \mathbf{C}_u))$: For each gate in the circuit C, the homomorphic evaluation algorithm performs the following:
  - For each addition gate, let the commitment of the input wires to be $\mathbf{C}_l, \mathbf{C}_r$, it computes the commitment for the output wire as follows.

$$\mathbf{C}_o = \mathbf{C}_l + \mathbf{C}_r$$

  - For each multiplication gate, let the commitment of the input wires to be $\mathbf{C}_l, \mathbf{C}_r$, it computes the commitment for the output wire as follows.

$$\mathbf{C}_o = \mathbf{C}_l\mathbf{G}^{-1}[\mathbf{C}_r]$$

Lemma 1 (Bound on Homomorphic Evaluation). *Let $\mathbf{A} \in \mathbb{Z}_q^{n\times m}$ be a matrix, $x = (x_1, x_2, \ldots, x_u)$ be a binary string, and C be a boolean circuit of depth d. Let*

$$\mathbf{C} = \mathsf{Eval}(C, (\mathsf{Com}(\mathbf{A}, x_1; \mathbf{R}_1), \mathsf{Com}(\mathbf{A}, x_2; \mathbf{R}_1), \ldots, \mathsf{Com}(\mathbf{A}, x_u; \mathbf{R}_u))),$$

where $x_1, x_2, \ldots, x_u \in \{0,1\}$, and $\mathbf{R}_1, \mathbf{R}_2, \ldots, \mathbf{R}_u \in \{0,1\}^{m\times m}$. Then there exists a $\mathbf{R}_{C,x}$ that can be efficiently computed from $x_1, x_2, \ldots, x_u$ and $\mathbf{R}_1, \mathbf{R}_2, \ldots, \mathbf{R}_u$ such that $\mathbf{C} = \mathsf{Com}(\mathbf{A}, C(x_1, x_2, \ldots, x_u); \mathbf{R}_{C,x})$ and $\|\mathbf{R}_{C,x}\|_{\max} < 2^{O(d\log m)}$.

Proof. We analysis for each gate. For each addition gate, if $\mathbf{C}_l = \mathbf{AR}_l + \mu_l\mathbf{G}$, and $\mathbf{C}_r = \mathbf{AR}_r + \mu_r\mathbf{G}$, then $\mathbf{C}_o = \mathbf{A}(\mathbf{R}_l + \mathbf{R}_r) + (\mu_r + \mu_l)\mathbf{G}$. Hence, if we let $\mathbf{R}_o = \mathbf{R}_l + \mathbf{R}_r$, then $\|\mathbf{R}_o\|_{\max} \le \|\mathbf{R}_l\|_{\max} + \|\mathbf{R}_r\|_{\max}$.

For each multiplication gate, $\mathbf{C}_o = \mathbf{C}_l\mathbf{G}^{-1}[\mathbf{C}_r] = \mathbf{A}(\mathbf{R}_l\mathbf{G}^{-1}[\mathbf{C}_r] + \mu_r\mathbf{R}_r) + \mu_l\mu_r\mathbf{G}$. Let $\mathbf{R}_o = \mathbf{R}_l\mathbf{G}^{-1}[\mathbf{C}_r] + \mu_r\mathbf{G}_r$. Hence, $\|\mathbf{R}_o\|_{\max} \le m\|\mathbf{R}_l\|_{\max} + \|\mathbf{R}_r\|_{\max}$.

Hence, by induction on the depth of the circuit, we have that $\|\mathbf{R}_{C,x}\|_{\max} \le (m+1)^{O(d)}$.

4 Secure Function Evaluation with Public Decryption

4.1 Definition

An AB-SFE with public decryption is a tuple of algorithms ($\mathsf{Setup}, \mathsf{KeyGen}, \mathsf{Enc}, \mathsf{Hint}, \mathsf{Dec}$), with the following syntax.

- $\mathsf{Setup}(1^\lambda)$: On input the security parameter λ, output a common random string crs.
- $\mathsf{KeyGen}(\mathsf{crs}, x)$: On input the crs, and a binary string x, it outputs a public key pk and a master secret key msk.
- $\mathsf{Enc}(\mathsf{pk}, C, \mu)$: On input the public key pk, a boolean circuit $C : \{0,1\}^{|x|} \to \{0,1\}$, and a message $\mu \in \{0,1\}$, it outputs a ciphertext ct.
- $\mathsf{Hint}(\mathsf{msk}, C)$: On input the master secret key, and the circuit C, output a hint sk_C.

- $\mathsf{Dec}(\mathsf{sk}_C, \mathsf{ct})$: On input a hint sk_C, and a ciphertext ct, it outputs a message μ'.

We require the AB-SFE to satisfy the following properties.

- **Correctness.** For any binary string x, circuit $C : \{0,1\}^{|x|} \to \{0,1\}$ with $C(x) = 1$, and any message $\mu \in \{0,1\}$, there exists a negligible function $\nu(\lambda)$ such that for any sufficiently large λ,

$$\Pr\left[\substack{\mathsf{crs} \leftarrow \mathsf{Setup}(1^\lambda), (\mathsf{pk}, \mathsf{msk}) \leftarrow \mathsf{KeyGen}(\mathsf{crs}, x), \mathsf{ct} \leftarrow \mathsf{Enc}(\mathsf{pk}, C, \mu) \\ \mathsf{sk}_C \leftarrow \mathsf{Hint}(\mathsf{msk}, C), \mu' \leftarrow \mathsf{Dec}(\mathsf{sk}_C, \mathsf{ct})} : \mu = \mu'\right] \geq 1 - \nu(\lambda)$$

- **Statistical Indistinguishability of Public Keys.** There exists a negligible function $\nu(\lambda)$ such that, with $1 - \mathsf{negl}(\lambda)$ probability over the randomness of $\mathsf{crs} \leftarrow \mathsf{Setup}(1^\lambda)$, for any x_0, x_1 with $|x_0| = |x_1|$, and any sufficiently large λ,

$$\mathsf{SD}(\mathsf{pk}_0, \mathsf{pk}_1) < \nu(\lambda)$$

where pk_b is generated by $\mathsf{KeyGen}(\mathsf{crs}, x_b)$ for $b \in \{0,1\}$.
- **Statistical Simulation of Hints.** There exists a negligible function $\nu(\lambda)$, a PPT crs generating function $\overline{\mathsf{Setup}}(1^\lambda)$ and a PPT simulator Sim such that, for any input string x, any circuit C, let $(\overline{\mathsf{crs}}, \mathsf{tr}) \leftarrow \overline{\mathsf{Setup}}(1^\lambda)$, $(\mathsf{pk}, \mathsf{msk}) \leftarrow \mathsf{KeyGen}(\overline{\mathsf{crs}}, x)$, we have

$$\mathsf{SD}\left(\mathsf{Setup}(1^\lambda), \overline{\mathsf{crs}}\right) < \nu(\lambda) \tag{1}$$

$$\mathsf{SD}\left(\mathsf{Hint}(\mathsf{msk}, f), \mathsf{Sim}(1^\lambda, \mathsf{pk}, \mathsf{tr}, C, C(x))\right) < \nu(\lambda) \tag{2}$$

where the randomness in Eq. 1 is over the randomness of Setup. The randomness in Equation 2 is *only* over the randomness of Hint, and all other random values are fixed.
- **Adaptive Sender Computational Indistinguishable Security.** For any input string x, any boolean circuit $C : \{0,1\}^{|x|} \to \{0,1\}$ with $C(x) = 0$, any adaptive n.u. PPT adversary $\mathcal{A}$, there exists a negligible function $\nu(\lambda)$ such that

$$\left|\Pr\left[\substack{\mathsf{crs} \leftarrow \mathsf{Setup}(1^\lambda), r \leftarrow \{0,1\}^* \\ (\mathsf{pk}, \mathsf{msk}) = \mathsf{KeyGen}(\mathsf{crs}, x; r)} : C \leftarrow \mathcal{A}(1^\lambda, \mathsf{crs}, r), \mathcal{A}(\mathsf{Enc}(\mathsf{pk}, C, 0)) = 1\right] - \right.$$
$$\left.\Pr\left[\substack{\mathsf{crs} \leftarrow \mathsf{Setup}(1^\lambda), r \leftarrow \{0,1\}^* \\ (\mathsf{pk}, \mathsf{msk}) = \mathsf{KeyGen}(\mathsf{crs}, x; r)} : C \leftarrow \mathcal{A}(1^\lambda, \mathsf{crs}, r), \mathcal{A}(\mathsf{Enc}(\mathsf{pk}, C, 1)) = 1\right]\right| < \nu(\lambda)$$

2AB-SFE.A 2AB-SFE scheme with public decryption has the same syntax as AB-SFE with public decryption, except that Enc and Dec are replaced by the following two algorithms:

- $\mathsf{2Enc}(\mathsf{pk}, C, \{\mu_{i,0}, \mu_{i,1}\}_{i \in [\ell_{\mathsf{out}}]})$: On input the public key pk, a multi-bit output circuit $C : \{0,1\}^{|x|} \to \{0,1\}^{\ell_{\mathsf{out}}}$, and ℓ_{out} pair of labels, it output a ciphertext ct.

- $\mathsf{2Dec}(\mathsf{sk}_C, \mathsf{ct})$: On input a hint sk_C, and a ciphertext ct, output $\{\mu'_i\}_{i\in[\ell_{\mathsf{out}}]}$.

We also extend the correctness and sender's security to the following.

- **Correctness:** For any binary string x, circuit $C : \{0,1\}^{|x|} \to \{0,1\}^{\ell_{\mathsf{out}}}$, and any messages $(\mu_{i,0}, \mu_{i,1})_{i\in[\ell_{\mathsf{out}}]}$, there exists a negligible function $\nu(\lambda)$ such that for any sufficiently large λ,

$$\Pr\left[\begin{matrix}\mathsf{crs}\leftarrow\mathsf{Setup}(1^\lambda),(\mathsf{pk},\mathsf{msk})\leftarrow\mathsf{KeyGen}(\mathsf{crs},x),\mathsf{ct}\leftarrow\mathsf{2Enc}(\mathsf{pk},C,(\mu_{i,0},\mu_{i,1})_{i\in[\ell_{\mathsf{out}}]})\\ \mathsf{sk}_C\leftarrow\mathsf{Hint}(\mathsf{msk},C),(\mu'_i)_{i\in[\ell_{\mathsf{out}}]}\leftarrow\mathsf{2Dec}(\mathsf{sk}_C,\mathsf{ct})\end{matrix} : \forall i \in [\ell_{\mathsf{out}}], \mu'_i = \mu_{i,C_i(x)}\right] \geq 1 - \nu(\lambda)$$

where $C_i(x)$ is the i-th output bit of $C(x)$.
- **Adaptive Sender's Computational Indistinguishable Security:** For any input string x, any circuit $C : \{0,1\}^{|x|} \to \{0,1\}^{\ell_{\mathsf{out}}}$, any messages $(\mu_{i,0}, \mu_{i,1})_{i\in[\ell_{\mathsf{out}}]}$, any n.u. PPT adversary $\mathcal{A}$, there exists a negligible function $\nu(\lambda)$ such that for any sufficiently large λ,

$$\Bigg|\Pr\left[\begin{matrix}\mathsf{crs}\leftarrow\mathsf{Setup}(1^\lambda),r\leftarrow\{0,1\}^*\\ (\mathsf{pk},\mathsf{msk})=\mathsf{KeyGen}(\mathsf{crs},x;r)\end{matrix} : C \leftarrow \mathcal{A}(1^\lambda, \mathsf{crs}, r), \mathcal{A}(\mathsf{2Enc}(\mathsf{pk}, C, (\mu_{i,0}, \mu_{i,1})_{i\in[\ell_{\mathsf{out}}]})) = 1\right] - \Pr\left[\begin{matrix}\mathsf{crs}\leftarrow\mathsf{Setup}(1^\lambda),r\leftarrow\{0,1\}^*\\ (\mathsf{pk},\mathsf{msk})=\mathsf{KeyGen}(\mathsf{crs},x;r)\end{matrix} : C \leftarrow \mathcal{A}(1^\lambda, \mathsf{crs}, r), \mathcal{A}(\mathsf{2Enc}(\mathsf{pk}, C, (\mu_{i,C_i(x)}, \mu_{i,C_i(x)})_{i\in[\ell_{\mathsf{out}}]})) = 1\right]\Bigg| < \nu(\lambda)$$

From AB-SFE to 2AB-SFE with Public Decryption. Given an AB-SFE scheme with public decryption, it is straightforward to construct a 2AB-SFE scheme with public decryption, following the methodology in [22] (where it was described in the context of attribute-based encryption). Roughly speaking, the idea is to encrypt one of the messages under the *complement* of C. We refer the reader to [22] for details.

4.2 Construction

Our construction uses the following parameters and algorithms.

- λ, the security parameter.
- n, the dimension of LWE.
- $q = 2^{\Theta(d \log^3 \lambda)}$, the LWE modulus, where d is the bound for the depth of the circuit.
- χ, the discrete Gaussian of deviation $\mathsf{poly}(\lambda)$.
- χ', the descrete Gaussian of deviation $2^{\Theta(d \log^2 \lambda)}$.
- $m = 2n \log q$, the number of columns in the commitment.
- A homomorphic commitment scheme $(\mathsf{Gen}, \mathsf{Com}, \mathsf{Eval})$. See Sect. 3.5.

- Preimage sampling algorithm GenSamplePre, with $r = 2^{\Theta(d \log^2 m)}$. See Sect. 3.2.

The construction is described in Fig. 1. Now we proceed to prove the properties.

Removing the Depth Dependence. In the construction Fig. 1, the parameters depends on the depth of the circuit. However, one can use the randomized encoding [3] to remove the depth dependence. Specifically, instead of evaluate the circuit C on input x directly, we evaluate the randomized encoding of C and x. Since the randomized encoding can be computed in NC^1, we can set the parameters to be large enough to work for any circuit in NC^1, and thus remove the depth dependence.

Lemma 2 (Correctness). *The construction in Fig. 1 satisfies correctness.*

Proof. For any binary string x, any circuit C with $C(x) = 1$ and depth at most d, and any message $\mu \in \{0,1\}$, by Lemma 1, $\mathbf{R}_{C,x}$ is bounded by $2^{O(d \log m)}$. Hence, $\|\mathbf{T}_{\mathbf{A}'}\|_{\max} \leq 2\|\mathbf{R}_{C,x}\|_{\max}(2m) = 2^{O(d \log m)}$, and thus $\|\widetilde{\mathbf{T}_{\mathbf{A}'}}\| \leq \sqrt{2m}\|\mathbf{T}_{\mathbf{A}'}\|_{\max} = 2^{O(d \log m)}$. Since the matrix $\mathbf{T}_{\mathbf{A}'}$ is basis for $\Lambda_q^{\perp}(\mathbf{A}')$ and we set the parameter $r = 2^{\Theta(d \log^2 m)} > \|\widetilde{\mathbf{T}_{\mathbf{A}'}}\| \cdot \omega(\sqrt{\log 2m})$. From Theorem 4, $\mathbf{e}$ is statistically close to $D_{\Lambda_q^{\mathbf{y}}(\mathbf{A}'),r}$. Hence, we have

$$\langle \mathsf{ct}, (1, -\mathbf{e}^T) \rangle = \mathbf{s}^T \cdot [\mathbf{y}\ \mathbf{A}''] \begin{bmatrix} 1 \\ -\mathbf{e} \end{bmatrix} + [\mathbf{e}_1^T\ \mathbf{e}_2^T] \begin{bmatrix} 1 \\ -\mathbf{e} \end{bmatrix} + \frac{q}{2}\mu = \frac{q}{2}\mu + [\mathbf{e}_1^T\ \mathbf{e}_2^T] \begin{bmatrix} 1 \\ -\mathbf{e} \end{bmatrix},$$

where the second equality follows from $\mathbf{e} \approx_s D_{\Lambda_q^{\mathbf{y}}(\mathbf{A}''),r}$, and thus $\mathbf{A}''\mathbf{e} = \mathbf{y}$ with overwhelming probability.

Since the second term can be bounded by

$$|\langle (\mathbf{e}_1^T, \mathbf{e}_2^T), (1, -\mathbf{e}) \rangle| \leq \sqrt{\|\mathbf{e}_1\|^2 + \|\mathbf{e}_2\|^2} \cdot \sqrt{\|\mathbf{e}\|^2 + 1} < q/4,$$

with overwhelming probability, the scheme is correct.

Lemma 3 (Statistical Indistinguishability of Public Keys). *The construction satisfies statistical public key indistinguishability security.*

Proof. For any x_0, x_1 with $|x_0| = |x_1|$, and $b \in \{0,1\}$, we have $\mathsf{pk}_b = (\mathsf{crs}, \mathsf{Com}(\mathbf{A}, x_b))$. From the statistical hiding property of the commitment scheme, we have $\mathsf{SD}(\mathsf{pk}_0, \mathsf{pk}_1) < \nu(\lambda)$.

Lemma 4 (Statistical Simulation of Hints). *The construction satisfies statistical hint simulation security.*

AB-SFE with Public Decryption

- $\mathsf{Setup}(1^\lambda)$: Sample $\mathbf{y} \leftarrow \mathbb{Z}_q^n, \mathbf{A} \leftarrow \mathbb{Z}_q^{n \times m}, \widehat{\mathbf{A}} \leftarrow \mathbb{Z}_q^{n \times 2m}$. Output $\mathsf{crs} = (\mathbf{y}, \mathbf{A}, \widehat{\mathbf{A}})$.
- $\mathsf{KeyGen}(\mathsf{crs}, x = (x_1, \ldots, x_u) \in \{0,1\}^u)$:
  - Parse $\mathsf{crs} = (\mathbf{y}, \mathbf{A}, \widehat{\mathbf{A}})$. Sample $\mathbf{R}_i \leftarrow \{0,1\}^{m \times m}$.
  - For all $i \in [u]$, compute $\mathbf{C}_i = \mathsf{Com}(\mathbf{A}, x_i; \mathbf{R}_i) = \mathbf{A} \cdot \mathbf{R}_i + x_i \mathbf{G}$.
  - Let $\mathsf{pk} = (\mathsf{crs}, \{\mathbf{C}_i\}_{i \in [u]})$, and $\mathsf{msk} = (\mathsf{pk}, \{\mathbf{R}_i\}_{i \in [u]})$.
  - Output $(\mathsf{pk}, \mathsf{msk})$.
- $\mathsf{Enc}(\mathsf{pk}, C, \mu \in \{0,1\})$:
  - Parse $\mathsf{pk} = (\mathsf{crs}, \{\mathbf{C}_i\}_{i \in [u]})$ and $\mathsf{crs} = (\mathbf{y}, \mathbf{A}, \widetilde{\mathbf{A}})$.
  - Deterministically homomorphically compute $\mathbf{C}_C = \mathsf{Eval}(C, \{\mathbf{C}_i\}_{i \in [u]})$.
  - Let $\mathbf{A}' = [\mathbf{A}\ \mathbf{C}_C]$, and $\mathbf{A}'' = [\widehat{\mathbf{A}}\ \mathbf{A}']$.
  - Samples $\mathbf{s} \leftarrow \mathbb{Z}_q^n$ and $\mathbf{e}_1 \leftarrow \chi^{3m+1}, \mathbf{e}_2 \leftarrow \chi'^{m}$.
  - Output $\mathsf{ct} = \mathbf{s}^T \cdot [\mathbf{y}\ \mathbf{A}''] + [\mathbf{e}_1^T\ \mathbf{e}_2^T] + \mu \cdot [\frac{q}{2}\ \mathbf{0}_{1 \times 4m}]$.
- $\mathsf{Hint}(\mathsf{msk}, C)$:
  - Parse $\mathsf{msk} = (\mathsf{pk}, \{\mathbf{R}_i\}_{i \in [u]})$, and $\mathsf{pk} = ((\mathbf{y}, \mathbf{A}, \widehat{\mathbf{A}}), \{\mathbf{C}\}_{i \in [u]})$
  - Deterministically homomorphically compute $\mathbf{C}_C = \mathsf{Eval}(C, \{\mathbf{C}_i\}_{i \in [u]})$.
  - Let $\mathbf{A}' = [\mathbf{A}\ \mathbf{C}_C]$, and $\mathbf{A}'' = [\widehat{\mathbf{A}}\ \mathbf{A}']$.
  - If $C(x) = 0$, Let $\mathsf{sk}_C = \perp$. Otherwise, parse $\mathbf{C}_C = \mathbf{A} \cdot \mathbf{R}_{C,x} + \mathbf{G}$, where $\mathbf{R}_{C,x}$ can be obtained deterministically from $\{\mathbf{R}_i\}_{i \in [u]}$ and C.
  - Let $\mathbf{T}_{\mathbf{A}'} = \begin{bmatrix} \mathbf{I} & -\mathbf{R}_{C,x} \\ \mathbf{0} & \mathbf{I} \end{bmatrix} \cdot \begin{bmatrix} \mathbf{I} & \mathbf{0} \\ -\mathbf{G}^{-1}[\mathbf{A}] & \mathbf{T}_{\mathbf{G}} \end{bmatrix}$, where $\mathbf{T}_{\mathbf{G}}$ is the short basis for $\Lambda_q^{\perp}(\mathbf{G})$.
  - Sample $\mathbf{e} \leftarrow \mathsf{GenSamplePre}(\mathbf{A}'', \mathbf{T}_{\mathbf{A}'}, 2, \mathbf{y}, r)$.
  - Output $\mathsf{sk}_C = \mathbf{e}$.
- $\mathsf{Dec}(\mathsf{sk}_C, \mathsf{ct})$:
  - If $\mathsf{sk}_C = \perp$, output $\perp$.
  - Otherwise, parse $\mathsf{sk}_C = \mathbf{e}$, if $|\langle \mathsf{ct}, (1, -\mathbf{e}^T) \rangle| < q/4$, then let $\mu' = 0$, otherwise $\mu' = 1$, and output μ'.

Fig. 1. Description of AB-SFE with public decryption.

Proof. We construct the following simulator $(\overline{\mathsf{Setup}}, \mathsf{Sim})$.

We now prove the two properties. For any $x \in \{0,1\}^n$, let $\mathsf{crs} \leftarrow \mathsf{Setup}(1^\lambda)$, $(\mathsf{pk}, \mathsf{msk}) \leftarrow \mathsf{KeyGen}(\mathsf{crs}, x)$, and $(\overline{\mathsf{crs}}, \mathsf{tr}) \leftarrow \overline{\mathsf{Setup}}(1^\lambda)$.

Simulator $(\overline{\mathsf{Setup}}, \mathsf{Sim})$

- $\overline{\mathsf{Setup}}(1^\lambda)$:
  - Sample $\mathbf{y} \leftarrow \mathbb{Z}_q^n, \mathbf{A} \leftarrow \mathsf{Gen}(1^\lambda)$.
  - Let $(\widehat{\mathbf{A}}, \mathbf{T}) \leftarrow \mathsf{TrapGen}(1^n, 1^{2m})$.
  - Output $\overline{\mathsf{crs}} = (\mathbf{y}, \mathbf{A}, \widehat{\mathbf{A}})$, and trapdoor $\mathsf{tr} = \mathbf{T}$.
- $\mathsf{Sim}(1^\lambda, \mathsf{pk}, \mathsf{tr}, C, C(x))$:
  - Parse $\mathsf{pk} = (\overline{\mathsf{crs}}, (\mathbf{C}_i)_{i\in[u]})$, $\overline{\mathsf{crs}} = (\mathbf{y}, \mathbf{A}, \widehat{\mathbf{A}})$, and $\mathsf{tr} = \mathbf{T}$.
  - Deterministically homomorphically compute $\mathbf{C}_C = \mathsf{Eval}(C, (\mathbf{C}_i)_{i\in[u]})$.
  - Denote $\mathbf{A}' = \left[\mathbf{A}\ \mathbf{C}_C\right]$, and $\mathbf{A}'' = \left[\widehat{\mathbf{A}}\ \mathbf{A}'\right]$.
  - If $C(x) = 0$, Let $\overline{\mathsf{sk}_C} = \perp$.
  - Otherwise, Sample $\mathbf{e} \leftarrow \mathsf{GenSamplePre}(\mathbf{A}'', \mathsf{tr}, 1, \mathbf{y}, r)$.
  - Output $\overline{\mathsf{sk}_C} = \mathbf{e}$.

Fig. 2. Description of the simulator.

- $\mathsf{SD}(\mathsf{crs}, \overline{\mathsf{crs}}) < \mathsf{negl}(\lambda)$: This follows from the property that $\widehat{\mathbf{A}}$ sampled by $\mathsf{TrapGen}$ is statistically close to uniform random.
- $\mathsf{SD}\left(\mathsf{Hint}(\mathsf{msk}, C), \mathsf{Sim}(1^\lambda, \mathsf{pk}, \mathsf{tr}, C, C(x))\right) < \mathsf{negl}(\lambda)$: Note that the matrices $\mathbf{A}''$ in Sim and Hint are the same. Follow the argument in Lemma 2, the parameters r satisfies the condition for Theorem 4. Hence, from Theorem 4, we have

$$\mathsf{SD}\left(\mathsf{GenSamplePre}(\mathbf{A}'', \mathbf{T}_{\mathbf{A}'}, 2, \mathbf{y}, r), \mathsf{GenSamplePre}(\mathbf{A}'', \mathbf{T}, 1, \mathbf{y}, r)\right) < \mathsf{negl}(\lambda)$$

  Hence, $\mathsf{SD}(\mathsf{sk}_C, \overline{\mathsf{sk}_C}) < \mathsf{negl}(\lambda)$.

Lemma 5 (Sender's Indistinguishability Security). *The construction satisfies sender's indistinguishability security.*

Proof. For any input $x_1, \ldots, x_u$ and circuit C with $C(x_1, x_2, \ldots, x_u) = 0$, we build the following hybrids.

- Hybrid_0: In this hybrid, the adversary is given a ciphertext of $\mathsf{Enc}(\mathsf{pk}, C, 0)$.
- Hybrid_1: This hybrid is almost the same as Hybrid_0, except that we use $\mathbf{R}_{C,x}$ to generate the ciphertext ct. Specifically, we replace the ct as follows.
  - Let $\mathbf{C}_C = \mathbf{A} \cdot \mathbf{R}_{C,x}$, where $\mathbf{R}_{C,x}$ can be computed deterministically from $\{\mathbf{R}_i\}_{i\in[u]}$.
  - Samples $\mathbf{s} \leftarrow \mathbb{Z}_q^n$ and $e \leftarrow \chi, \mathbf{e}_1' \leftarrow \chi^{2m}, \mathbf{e}_2' \leftarrow \chi^m, \mathbf{e}_2 \leftarrow \chi'^m$.
  - Output
    $\mathsf{ct} = \left[\mathbf{s}^T \cdot \mathbf{y} + e + \frac{q}{2}\mu\ \mathbf{s}^T\widehat{\mathbf{A}} + \mathbf{e}_1'^T\ \mathbf{s}^T\mathbf{A} + \mathbf{e}_2'^T\ (\mathbf{s}^T\mathbf{A} + \mathbf{e}_2'^T) \cdot \mathbf{R}_{C,x} + \mathbf{e}_2^T\right]$.

- Hybrid_2: This hybrid is the same as Hybrid_1, except that we replace the first, the second, and the third component of ct as uniformly random matrices. Specifically, we replace the ct as follows.
  - Let $\mathbf{C}_C = \mathbf{A} \cdot \mathbf{R}_{C,x}$, where $\mathbf{R}_{C,x}$ can be computed deterministically from $(\mathbf{R}_i)_{i \in [u]}$.
  - Samples $u \leftarrow \mathbb{Z}_q, \mathbf{u}_1 \leftarrow \mathbb{Z}_q^{2m}$ and $\mathbf{u}_2 \leftarrow \mathbb{Z}_q^m, \mathbf{e}_2 \leftarrow \chi'^m$.
  - Output $\mathsf{ct} = \left[u \ \mathbf{u}_1 \ \mathbf{u}_2 \ \mathbf{u}_2 \cdot \mathbf{R}_{C,x} + \mathbf{e}_2^T\right]$.
- Hybrid_3: This hybrid is almost the same as Hybrid_0, except that the adversary is given a ciphertext of $\mathsf{Enc}(\mathsf{pk}, C, 1)$.

Now we prove that these hybrids are indistinguishable.

- $\mathsf{Hybrid}_0 \approx_s \mathsf{Hybrid}_1$: In the hybrid Hybrid_0, parse $\mathbf{e}_1^T = \left[e \ \mathbf{e}_1'^T \ \mathbf{e}_2'^T\right]$, where $e \in \mathbb{Z}_q, \mathbf{e}_1' \in \mathbb{Z}_q^{2m}, \mathbf{e}_2' \in \mathbb{Z}_q^m$. Then we can express ct as

$$\begin{aligned}\mathsf{ct} &= \mathbf{s}^T \cdot \left[\mathbf{y} \ \widehat{\mathbf{A}} \ \mathbf{A} \ \mathbf{C}_C\right] + \left[e \ \mathbf{e}_1' \ \mathbf{e}_2' \ \mathbf{e}_2\right] + \mu \left[\tfrac{q}{2} \ \mathbf{0} \ \mathbf{0} \ \mathbf{0}\right] \\ &= \left[\mathbf{s}^T\mathbf{y} + \mathbf{e} + \tfrac{q}{2}\mu, \ \mathbf{s}^T\widehat{\mathbf{A}} + \mathbf{e}_1'^T, \ \mathbf{s}^T\mathbf{A} + \mathbf{e}_2'^T, \ (\mathbf{s}^T\mathbf{A} + \mathbf{e}_2'^T)\mathbf{R}_{C,x} + \mathbf{e}_2^T + (-\mathbf{e}_2'^T\mathbf{R}_{C,x})\right]\end{aligned}$$

  Since $|-\mathbf{e}_2'^T \cdot \mathbf{R}_{C,x}| \leq \|\mathbf{e}_2'\|\|\mathbf{R}_{C,x}\|_2$, by the noise flooding Theorem 2, we have

$$\mathsf{SD}(\mathsf{Hybrid}_0, \mathsf{Hybrid}_1) = \mathsf{SD}(\mathbf{e}_2^T + (-\mathbf{e}_2'^T\mathbf{R}_{C,x}), \chi'^m) < O(\|\mathbf{e}_2'\|\|\mathbf{R}_{C,x}\|_2/r') = \mathsf{negl}(\lambda)$$

- $\mathsf{Hybrid}_1 \approx_c \mathsf{Hybrid}_2$: Since the only difference between Hybrid_1 and Hybrid_2 is the first, the second, and third component of ct. Also note that, in Hybrid_1, $\mathbf{s}^T \cdot \mathbf{y} + e$, $\mathbf{s}^T\widehat{\mathbf{A}} + \mathbf{e}_1'^T$ and $\mathbf{s}^T\mathbf{A} + \mathbf{e}_2'^T$ are LWE instance, and hence is indistinguishable with the uniformly random $u, \mathbf{u}_1, \mathbf{u}_2$ in Hybrid_2. Hence, Hybrid_1 and Hybrid_2 are computationally indistinguishable by LWE assumption.
- $\mathsf{Hybrid}_2 \approx_c \mathsf{Hybrid}_3$: Since Hybrid_2 does not use any message μ to generat the ciphertext ct, we can reverse Hybrid_0 to Hybrid_2, and obtain $\mathsf{Hybrid}_2 \approx_c \mathsf{Hybrid}_3$.

By the hyrbid argument, we finish the proof.

5 Unbounded MPC

5.1 Definition

A (semi-honest) unbounded MPC protocol is a 2-round MPC protocol (Round_1, $\mathsf{Round}_2, \mathsf{Rec}$) satisfying the following syntax.

- **First Round:** The i-th party's input is x_i. It sets the random coins r_i, and executes $\mathsf{msg}_i \leftarrow \mathsf{Round}_1(1^\lambda, x_i; r_i)$. Then the i-th party broadcasts msg_i.
- **Second Round:** After receiving the first round messages, a subset of parties $S \subseteq [N]$ decide to jointly compute a ℓ_{out}-bit output circuit $f : \prod_{i \in S}\{0,1\}^{|x_i|} \to \{0,1\}^{\ell_{\mathsf{out}}}$.
  For each $i \in S$, the i-th party executes $p_i \leftarrow \mathsf{Round}_2(x_i, r_i, \{\mathsf{msg}_j\}_{j \in S}, S, f)$, and broadcasts p_i.

- **Public Recovery:** Anyone with $\{p_i\}_{i\in S}$ can execute $y \leftarrow \mathsf{Rec}(\{p_i\}_{i\in S}, S)$.

Efficiency. The running time of Round_1 is polynomial in λ and $|x_i|$, and is independent of N or the size of the circuit they want to compute later. The runing time of Round_2 is polynomial in λ, $|S|$ and $|C|$.

Unbounded-Party Semi-honest Security. For any PPT adversary $\mathcal{A}$, there exists a simulator $(\mathsf{Sim}_1, \mathsf{Sim}_2)$ such that

$$\left|\Pr\left[\mathcal{A}^{\mathsf{Regstr}(\cdot,\cdot),\mathsf{Eval}(\cdot,\cdot)}(1^\lambda) = 1\right] - \Pr\left[\mathcal{A}^{\overline{\mathsf{Regstr}}(\cdot,\cdot),\overline{\mathsf{Eval}}(\cdot,\cdot)}(1^\lambda) = 1\right]\right| \leq \mathsf{negl}(\lambda)$$

where the oracles $\mathsf{Regstr}(\cdot,\cdot)$ and $\mathsf{Eval}(\cdot,\cdot)$ are defined as follows.

- $\mathsf{Regstr}(\mathsf{flag} \in \{\mathsf{Honest}, \mathsf{Dishonest}\}, x)$:
  - Set random coins r_N, and let $\mathsf{msg}_i \leftarrow \mathsf{Round}_1(1^\lambda, x; r_N)$.
  - If flag is Honest, then let $H = H \cup \{i\}$ and output msg_N. Otherwise, output (msg, r_N).
  - Let $x_N = x$ and $N = N + 1$.
- $\mathsf{Eval}(S, f)$:
  - If $S \not\subseteq [N]$, then abort.
  - For each $i \in S \cap H$, let $p_i \leftarrow \mathsf{Round}_2(x_i, r_i, \{\mathsf{msg}_j\}_{j\in S}, S, f)$.
  - Output $\{p_i\}_{i\in S}$.
- $\overline{\mathsf{Regstr}}(\mathsf{flag} \in \{\mathsf{Honest}, \mathsf{Dishonest}\}, x)$:
  - If flag is Honest, then let $H = H \cup \{N\}$, compute $(\mathsf{msg}_N, \mathsf{st}_N) \leftarrow \mathsf{Sim}_1(1^\lambda, 1^{|x|})$, and output msg_N. Otherwise, set fresh randomness r_N, output $(\mathsf{Round}_1(1^\lambda, x; r_N), r_N)$.
  - Let $x_N = x$, and $N = N + 1$.
- $\overline{\mathsf{Eval}}(S, f)$:
  - If $S \not\subseteq [N]$, then abort.
  - Output $\{p_i\}_{i\in S\cap H} \leftarrow \mathsf{Sim}_2(\{\mathsf{st}_i\}_{i\in S\cap H}, S, H, f, f(\{x_i\}_{i\in S\cap H}))$.

5.2 Construction

We present our unbounded MPC protocol $\Pi = (\mathsf{Round}_1, \mathsf{Round}_2, \mathsf{Rec})$ in Fig. 3. Our construction uses the following ingredients:

- An AB-SFE scheme $\mathsf{ABSFE} = (\mathsf{ABSFE.Setup}, \mathsf{ABSFE.KGen}, \mathsf{ABSFE.2Enc}, \mathsf{ABSFE.Hint}, \mathsf{ABSFE.2Dec})$ with public decryption.
- A *one-time use* two-round semi-malicious MPC protocol $\mathsf{One} = (\mathsf{One.Round}_1, \mathsf{One.Round}_2, \mathsf{One.Rec})$ in the plain model.
- A pseudorandom function $\mathsf{PRF} = (\mathsf{PRF.Gen}, \mathsf{PRF.Eval})$.
- A garbling scheme $\mathsf{GC} = (\mathsf{GC.Garble}, \mathsf{GC.Eval})$.

$\underline{\mathsf{Round}_1(1^\lambda, x_i)}$: Party i performs the following steps:

- Sample a CRS $\mathsf{crs}_i \leftarrow \mathsf{ABSFE.Setup}(1^\lambda)$ and a PRF key $k_i \leftarrow \mathsf{PRF.Gen}(1^\lambda)$.
- Compute $(\mathsf{pk}_i, \mathsf{msk}_i) \leftarrow \mathsf{ABSFE.KGen}(\mathsf{crs}_i, (x_i, k_i))$
- Output $\mathsf{msg}_i = \mathsf{pk}_i$.

$\underline{\mathsf{Round}_2(x_i, r_i, \{\mathsf{msg}_j\}_{j\in S}, S, f)}$: Party i performs the following steps:

- Compute crs_i, k_i and msk_i from r_i, and parse $\mathsf{msg}_j = \mathsf{pk}_j$.
- Compute $(\widetilde{C}_i, \widetilde{\mathsf{lab}}) \leftarrow \mathsf{GC.Garble}(C_{[x_i,k_i]})$, where the circuit $C_{[x_i,k_i]}$ on input a tuple $\{\widetilde{\mathsf{msg}_j}\}_{j\in S}$ does the following:
  - $r_i = \mathsf{PRF.Eval}(k_i, (S \parallel f))$.
  - Output $\widetilde{p}_i = \mathsf{One.Round}_2(x_i, r_i, \{\widetilde{\mathsf{msg}_j}\}_{j\in S}, f)$.
- Parse $\widetilde{\mathsf{lab}} = \{\widetilde{\mathsf{lab}_{j,k,b}}\}_{j\in S, k\in[|\widetilde{\mathsf{msg}_j}|], b\in\{0,1\}}$.
- For $j \in S \setminus \{i\}$, compute $c_{i,j} \leftarrow \mathsf{ABSFE.2Enc}\left(\mathsf{pk}_j, G_{S,f}, \{\widetilde{\mathsf{lab}_{j,k,0}}, \widetilde{\mathsf{lab}_{j,k,1}}\}_{k\in[|\widetilde{\mathsf{msg}_j}|]}\right)$, where the circuit $G_{S,f}$ on input (x_i, k_i) does the following:
  - $r_i = \mathsf{PRF.Eval}(k_i, (S \parallel f))$.
  - $\widetilde{\mathsf{msg}_i} = \mathsf{One.Round}_1(1^\lambda, x_i, f; r_i)$.
  - Output $\widetilde{\mathsf{msg}_i}$.
- $h_i \leftarrow \mathsf{ABSFE.Hint}(\mathsf{msk}_i, G_{S,f})$, $\widetilde{\mathsf{msg}_i} = G_{S,f}(x_i, k_i)$.
- Output $p_i = \left(\{c_{i,j}\}_{j\in S\setminus\{i\}}, h_i, \widetilde{C}_i, \{\widetilde{\mathsf{lab}_{i,k,\widetilde{\mathsf{msg}_i}[k]}}\}_{k\in[|\widetilde{\mathsf{msg}_i}|]}\right)$.

$\underline{\mathsf{Rec}(\{p_j\}_{j\in S}, S)}$: Party i performs the following steps:

- For each $i \in S$, parse $p_i = \left(\{c_{i,j}\}_{j\in S\setminus\{i\}}, h_i, \widetilde{C}_i, \{\widetilde{\mathsf{lab}_{i,k,\widetilde{\mathsf{msg}_i}[k]}}\}_{k\in[|\widetilde{\mathsf{msg}_i}|]}\right)$.
- For each $i \in S$ and $j \in S \setminus \{i\}$, compute $\widetilde{\mathsf{lab}}_{i,j} \leftarrow \mathsf{ABSFE.2Dec}(h_i, c_{i,j})$. Set $\widetilde{\mathsf{lab}}_{i,i} = \{\widetilde{\mathsf{lab}_{i,k,\widetilde{\mathsf{msg}_i}[k]}}\}_{k\in[|\widetilde{\mathsf{msg}_i}|]}$. Compute $\widetilde{p}_i = \mathsf{GC.Eval}(\widetilde{C}_i, \{\widetilde{\mathsf{lab}}_j\}_{j\in S})$.
- Output $y = \mathsf{One.Rec}(\{\widetilde{p}_i\}_{i\in S})$.

Fig. 3. Description of unbounded-party reusable MPC Π.

5.3 Security

Lemma 6 (Unbounded-Party Simulation Security). *The construction in Sect. 5.2 satisfies semi-honest unbounded-party simulation security.*

Proof. For any n.u. PPT adversary $\mathcal{A}$, let $N(\lambda)$ be the upper bound for the number of parties N, and $Q(\lambda)$ be the upper bound for the number of queries the $\mathcal{A}$ made to Eval. For any $i^* \in [N(\lambda)]$, and $q^* \in [Q(\lambda)]$, we build the following hybrids.

- Hybrid_0: This hybrid is the same as $\mathcal{A}^{\mathsf{Regstr}(\cdot,\cdot),\mathsf{Eval}(\cdot,\cdot)}$.

- $\mathsf{Hybrid}_1^{(i^*,j^*,q^*)}$: This hybrid is almost the same as the Hybrid_0, except that we replace the labels used by ABSFE.2Enc to the same labels. Specifically, we replace the ABSFE.2Enc encryption in $\mathsf{Eval}(\cdot,\cdot)$ as follows.
  - For $j \in S \setminus \{i\}$, if $(i,j,q) < (i^*,j^*,q^*)$, $\widetilde{\mathsf{msg}}_j = G_{S,f}(x_j, k_j)$, $c_{i,j} \leftarrow \mathsf{ABSFE.2Enc}(\mathsf{pk}_j, G_{S,f}, (\mathsf{lab}_{j,k,\widetilde{\mathsf{msg}}_j[k]}, \mathsf{lab}_{j,k,\widetilde{\mathsf{msg}}_j[k]})_{k\in[|\widetilde{\mathsf{msg}}_j|]})$.
    If $(i,j,q) \geq (i^*,j^*,q^*)$, $c_{i,j} \leftarrow \mathsf{ABSFE.2Enc}(\mathsf{pk}_j, G_{S,f}, (\widetilde{\mathsf{lab}}_{j,k,0}, \widetilde{\mathsf{lab}}_{j,k,1})_{k\in[|\widetilde{\mathsf{msg}}_j|]})$.
- $\mathsf{Hybrid}_2^{(i^*,q^*)}$: This hybrid is almost the same as the $\mathsf{Hybrid}_1^{(N,N,Q)+1}$, except that we generate the labels of the garbled circuits by the simulator. Specifically, we replace the garbled circuits generation in $\mathsf{Eval}(\cdot,\cdot)$ as follows.
  - If $(i,q) < (i^*,q^*)$, then $(\overline{C_i}, \overline{\mathsf{lab}}) \leftarrow \mathsf{GC.Sim}(1^\lambda, C_{[x_i,k_i]}(\{\widetilde{\mathsf{msg}}_j\}_{j\in S}))$, let $\widetilde{C}_i = \overline{C_i}$, and parse $\overline{\mathsf{lab}} = (\mathsf{lab}_{j,k,\widetilde{\mathsf{msg}}_j[k]})_{j\in S,k\in[|\widetilde{\mathsf{msg}}_j|]}$.
    If $(i,q) \geq (i^*,q^*)$, then $(\widetilde{C}_i, \widetilde{\mathsf{lab}}) \leftarrow \mathsf{Garble}(C_{[x_i,k_i]})$.
- $\mathsf{Hybrid}_3^{i^*}$: This hybrid is almost the same as $\mathsf{Hybrid}_2^{(N,Q)+1}$, except that we generate the replace the CRS generation of $\mathsf{Round}_1(1^\lambda, x_i)$ in $\mathsf{Regstr}(\cdot,\cdot)$ as follows.
  - If $i < i^*$ and $i \in H$, generate $(\mathsf{crs}_i, \mathsf{tr}_i) \leftarrow \mathsf{ABSFE.}\overline{\mathsf{Setup}}(1^\lambda)$.
  - If $i \geq i^*$ or $i \notin H$, generate $\mathsf{crs}_i \leftarrow \mathsf{ABSFE.Setup}(1^\lambda)$.
- $\mathsf{Hybrid}_4^{(i^*,q^*)}$: This hybrid is almost the same as Hybrid_3^{N+1}, except that we replace the hint generation in $\mathsf{Eval}(\cdot,\cdot)$ by the simulator. Specifically, let q be the number of queries to $\mathsf{Eval}(\cdot,\cdot)$, we replace the generation of h_i as follows.
  - If $(i,q) < (i^*,q^*)$ and $i \in H$, $h_i \leftarrow \mathsf{ABSFE.Sim}(1^\lambda, \mathsf{pk}_i, \mathsf{tr}_i, G_{S,f}, \widetilde{\mathsf{msg}}_i)$.
  - If $(i,q) \geq (i^*,q^*)$ or $i \in \bar{H}$, $h_i \leftarrow \mathsf{ABSFE.Hint}(\mathsf{msk}_i, G_{S,f})$.
- $\mathsf{Hybrid}_5^{i^*}$: This hybrid is almost the same with $\mathsf{Hybrid}_4^{(N,Q)+1}$, except that we replace the PRF with random function. Specifically, we replace the randomness r_i generation in $\mathsf{Eval}(\cdot,\cdot)$ with the following. Let (S,f) be the q-th query,
  - For each $i \in S$, if $i < i^*$ and $i \in H$, let $r_i = \mathsf{PRF}_i.\mathsf{F}(S \,||\, f)$.
  - If $i \geq i^*$ or $i \notin H$, let $r_i = \mathsf{PRF.Eval}(k_i, (S \,||\, f))$.
  - Let $\widetilde{\mathsf{msg}}_i = \mathsf{One.Round}_1(1^\lambda, x_i, f; r_i)$, $\widetilde{p}_i = \mathsf{One.Round}_2(x_i, r_i, \{\widetilde{\mathsf{msg}}_j\}_{j\in S}, f)$.

  where $\mathsf{PRF}_i.\mathsf{F}$ is a random function for each $i < i^*, i \in H$.
- $\mathsf{Hybrid}_6^{q^*}$: This hybrid is almost the same with Hybrid_5^{N+1}, except that we replace the $\{\widetilde{\mathsf{msg}}_i, \widetilde{p}_i\}_{i\in S\cap H}$ using One.Sim. Specifically, we replace the generation of $\{\widetilde{\mathsf{msg}}_i, \widetilde{p}_i\}_{i\in S\cap H}$ in $\mathsf{Eval}(\cdot,\cdot)$ as follows.
  At the beginning of $\mathsf{Eval}(\cdot,\cdot)$, we initialize an empty map $\mathsf{Map} : \phi \rightarrow \phi$.
  Let (S,f) be the q-th query to $\mathsf{Eval}(\cdot,\cdot)$.
  - If $\mathsf{Map}(S,f)$ is defined before, let $\{\widetilde{\mathsf{msg}}_i, \widetilde{p}_i\}_{i\in S\cap H} = \mathsf{Map}(S,f)$.
  - Otherwise, if $q < q^*$, let $r_i = \mathsf{PRF.Eval}(k_i, (S||f))$ for each $i \in S \setminus H$,
  - $\{\widetilde{\mathsf{msg}}_i, \widetilde{p}_i\}_{i\in S\cap H} \leftarrow \mathsf{One.Sim}(1^\lambda, S\cap H, \{x_i, r_i\}_{i\in S\setminus H}, f, f(\{x_i\}_{i\in S}))$,

• and if $q \geq q^*$, for each $i \in S \cap H$, set fresh randomness r_i, let $\widetilde{\mathsf{msg}}_i = \mathsf{One.Round}_1(1^\lambda, x_i, f; r_i)$, $\widetilde{p_i} = \mathsf{One.Round}_2(x_i, r_i, \{\widetilde{\mathsf{msg}_j}\}_{j \in S}, f)$, and define $\mathsf{Map}(S, f) = \{\widetilde{\mathsf{msg}}_i, \widetilde{p_i}\}_{i \in S \cap H}$.

- Ideal: This hybrid is the same as Hybrid_6^{Q+1}, except that we replace each KGen of real input (x_i, k_i) with the dummy $(0^{|x_i|}, 0^{|k_i|})$, for each $i \in H$. This hybrid is the same as $\mathcal{A}^{\overline{\mathsf{Regstr}}(\cdot,\cdot),\overline{\mathsf{Eval}}(\cdot,\cdot)}(1^\lambda)$. See the simulator in Fig. 4.

Lemma 7. Hybrid_0 *is identical to* $\mathsf{Hybrid}_1^{(1,1,1)}$. *Moreover, there exists a negligible function* $\nu(\lambda)$ *such that for any sufficiently large* λ,

$$\left| \Pr_{\mathsf{Hybrid}_1^{(i^*,j^*,q^*)}} \left[\mathcal{A}^{\mathsf{Regstr}(\cdot,\cdot),\mathsf{Eval}(\cdot,\cdot)}(1^\lambda) = 1 \right] - \Pr_{\mathsf{Hybrid}_1^{(i^*,j^*,q^*)+1}} \left[\mathcal{A}^{\mathsf{Regstr}(\cdot,\cdot),\mathsf{Eval}(\cdot,\cdot)}(1^\lambda) = 1 \right] \right| < \nu(\lambda).$$

Proof. We build the following adversary $\mathcal{A}'$ trying to break the sender's indistinguishability security. $\mathcal{A}'$ sets the randomness and runs the adversary $\mathcal{A}^{\mathsf{Regstr}(\cdot,\cdot),\mathsf{Eval}(\cdot,\cdot)}$, where the oracles $\mathsf{Regstr}(\cdot,\cdot)$ and $\mathsf{Eval}(\cdot,\cdot)$ are implemented as follows.

- $\mathsf{Regstr}(\cdot,\cdot)$: For each query, the adversary $\mathcal{A}'$ does the same thing as the Hybrid_0.
- $\mathsf{Eval}(\cdot,\cdot)$: Let q the q-th query be (S, f). The adversary does the following. For each $i \in H \cap S$, it generates the garbled circuit and labels $(\widetilde{C}_i, \widetilde{\mathsf{lab}})$ for $C_{[x_i,k_i]}$. Then for each $j \in S \setminus \{i\}$, it considers three cases.
  • If $(i, j, q) < (i^*, j^*, q^*)$, $\mathcal{A}'$ uses ABSFE.2Enc to encrypt the same labels.
  • If $(i, j, q) = (i^*, j^*, q^*)$, it queries the challenger with the circuit $G_{S,f}$, and obtains a challenge ciphertext ct. Let $c_{i,j} = \mathsf{ct}$.
  • If $(i, j, q) > (i^*, j^*, q^*)$, $\mathcal{A}'$ uses ABSFE.2Enc to encrypt different labels.
  Finally $\mathcal{A}'$ computes and outputs $\{p_i\}_{i \in S \cap H}$ by the same way as Hybrid_0.

Now for the challenge ciphertext ct, we consider two cases. When ct is obtained by ABSFE.2Enc of different labels, then the adversary $\mathcal{A}'$ simulates the environment of $\mathsf{Hybrid}_1^{(i^*,j^*,q^*)}$. Hence,

$$\Pr\left[\mathsf{ct} \leftarrow \mathsf{ABSFE.2Enc}(\mathsf{pk}, G_{S,f}, (\widetilde{\mathsf{lab}_{j,k,0}}, \widetilde{\mathsf{lab}_{j,k,1}})_{k \in [|\widetilde{\mathsf{msg}_j}|]}) : \mathcal{A}'(1^\lambda, \mathsf{crs}, r) = 1\right] = \Pr_{\mathsf{Hybrid}_1^{(i^*,j^*,q^*)}} \left[\mathcal{A}^{\mathsf{Regstr}(\cdot,\cdot),\mathsf{Eval}(\cdot,\cdot)}(1^\lambda) = 1 \right]$$

When ct is generated with the same labels, then the adversary $\mathcal{A}'$ simulates the environment of $\mathsf{Hybrid}_1^{(i^*,j^*,q^*)+1}$. Hence,

$$\Pr\left[\mathsf{ct} \leftarrow \mathsf{ABSFE.2Enc}(\mathsf{pk}, G_{S,f}, (\widetilde{\mathsf{lab}_{j,k,\widetilde{\mathsf{msg}_j}[k]}}, \widetilde{\mathsf{lab}_{j,k,\widetilde{\mathsf{msg}_j}[k]}})_{k \in [|\widetilde{\mathsf{msg}_j}|]}) : \mathcal{A}'(1^\lambda, \mathsf{crs}, r) = 1\right] = \Pr_{\mathsf{Hybrid}_1^{(i^*,j^*,q^*)+1}} \left[\mathcal{A}^{\mathsf{Regstr}(\cdot,\cdot),\mathsf{Eval}(\cdot,\cdot)}(1^\lambda) = 1 \right]$$

$\underline{\mathsf{Sim}_1(1^\lambda, 1^{|x|})}$:

- Let $(\overline{\mathsf{crs}_N}, \mathsf{tr}_N) \leftarrow \overline{\mathsf{Setup}}(1^\lambda)$, and $(\mathsf{pk}_N, \mathsf{msk}_N) \leftarrow \mathsf{KGen}(\overline{\mathsf{crs}}_N, (0^{|x|}, 0^\lambda))$.
- Output $\mathsf{msg}_N = \mathsf{pk}_N$, and $\mathsf{st}_N = \mathsf{tr}_N$.

Sim_2 initialization: an empty map $\mathsf{Map} : \phi \to \phi$.

$\underline{\mathsf{Sim}_2(\{\mathsf{st}_i\}_{i \in S \cap H}, S, H, f, f(\{x_i\}_{i \in S \cap H}))}$:

- For the q-the query (S, f), if $\mathsf{Map}(S, f)$ is defined before, then let
$$\{\widetilde{\mathsf{msg}_i}, \widetilde{p_i}\}_{i \in S \cap H} = \mathsf{Map}(S, f).$$
- Otherwise, let $r_i = \mathsf{PRF.Eval}(k_i, (S||f))$ for each $i \in S \setminus H$, and
$$\{\widetilde{\mathsf{msg}_i}, \widetilde{p_i}\}_{i \in S \cap H} \leftarrow \mathsf{One.Sim}(1^\lambda, S \cap H, \{x_i, r_i\}_{i \in S \setminus H}, f, f(\{x_i\}_{i \in S})),$$
define $\mathsf{Map}(S, f) = \{\widetilde{\mathsf{msg}_i}, \widetilde{p_i}\}_{i \in S \cap H}$.
- For each $i \in S \cap H$
  * Let $(\widetilde{C_i}, \widetilde{\mathsf{lab}}) \leftarrow \mathsf{GC.Sim}(1^\lambda, \widetilde{p_i})$, parse $\widetilde{\mathsf{lab}} = \{\widetilde{\mathsf{lab}_{j,k,\widetilde{\mathsf{msg}_j}[k]}}\}_{j \in S, k \in [|\widetilde{\mathsf{msg}_j}|]}$.
  * For each $j \in S \setminus \{i\}$, compute
$$c_{i,j} \leftarrow \mathsf{ABSFE.2Enc}(\mathsf{pk}_j, G_{S,f}, \{\widetilde{\mathsf{lab}_{j,k,\widetilde{\mathsf{msg}_j}[k]}}, \widetilde{\mathsf{lab}_{j,k,\widetilde{\mathsf{msg}_j}[k]}}\}_{k \in [|\widetilde{\mathsf{msg}_j}|]}).$$
  * $h_i \leftarrow \mathsf{ABSFE.Sim}(1^\lambda, \mathsf{pk}_i, \mathsf{tr}_i = \mathsf{st}_i, G_{S,f}, \widetilde{\mathsf{msg}_i})$.
- Output $p_i = \Big((c_{i,j})_{j \in S}, h_i, \widetilde{C_i}, \{\widetilde{\mathsf{lab}_{i,k,\widetilde{\mathsf{msg}_i}[k]}}\}_{k \in [|\widetilde{\mathsf{msg}_i}|]}\Big)$.

Fig. 4. Description of the simulator $(\mathsf{Sim}_1, \mathsf{Sim}_2)$.

From the adaptive sender's computational indistinguishable security of AB-SFE, we derive that $\mathsf{Hybrid}_1^{(i^*,j^*,q^*)}$ and $\mathsf{Hybrid}_1^{(i^*,j^*,q^*)+1}$ are indistinguishable.

Lemma 8. *$\mathsf{Hybrid}_1^{(N,N,Q)+1}$ is identical to $\mathsf{Hybrid}_2^{(1,1)}$. Moreover, there exists a negligible function $\nu(\lambda)$ such that for any sufficiently large λ,*

$$\left| \Pr_{\mathsf{Hybrid}_2^{(i^*,q^*)}}\left[\mathcal{A}^{\mathsf{Regstr}(\cdot,\cdot),\mathsf{Eval}(\cdot,\cdot)}(1^\lambda) = 1\right] - \Pr_{\mathsf{Hybrid}_2^{(i^*,q^*)+1}}\left[\mathcal{A}^{\mathsf{Regstr}(\cdot,\cdot),\mathsf{Eval}(\cdot,\cdot)}(1^\lambda) = 1\right] \right| < \nu(\lambda)$$

Proof. We build the following distinguisher $\mathcal{D}$ for the garbled scheme GC. $\mathcal{D}$ takes as input $(1^\lambda, \widetilde{C}, \mathsf{lab})$, sets the randomness and runs the adversary $\mathcal{A}^{\mathsf{Regstr}(\cdot,\cdot),\mathsf{Eval}(\cdot,\cdot)}$, where the oracles $\mathsf{Regstr}(\cdot,\cdot)$ and $\mathsf{Eval}(\cdot,\cdot)$ are implemented as follows.

- $\mathsf{Regstr}(\cdot,\cdot)$: For each query, the adversary $\mathcal{A}'$ does the same thing as the Hybrid_0.
- $\mathsf{Eval}(\cdot,\cdot)$: Let q the q-th query be (S, f). The adversary does the following. For each $i \in H \cap S$, it considers three cases.
  - If $(i, q) < (i^*, q^*)$, then it generates $\widetilde{C_i}, \widetilde{\mathsf{lab}}$ by the simulator GC.Sim.

- If $(i, q) = (i^*, q^*)$, then it sets $\widetilde{C_i}, \widetilde{\mathsf{lab}}$ to be the input $\widetilde{C}$, lab.
- If $(i, q) > (i^*, q^*)$, then it generates $\widetilde{C_i}, \widetilde{\mathsf{lab}}$ by honestly garbling $C_{[x_i, k_i]}$.

Finally, it computes and outputs $\{p_i\}_{i \in S \cap H}$ by the same way as $\mathsf{Hybrid}_1^{(N,N,Q)+1}$.

When $(\widetilde{C}, \mathsf{lab}) \leftarrow \mathsf{GC.Garble}(1^\lambda, C_{[\mathsf{sk}_{i^*}, k_{i^*}]})$, then the distinguisher $\mathcal{D}$ simulates the environment of $\mathsf{Hybrid}_2^{(i^*,q^*)}$ for $\mathcal{A}$. Hence, we have

$$\Pr\left[(\widetilde{C}, \mathsf{lab}) \leftarrow \mathsf{GC.Garble}(1^\lambda, C_{[\mathsf{sk}_{i^*}, k_{i^*}]}) : \mathcal{D}(1^\lambda, \widetilde{C}, \mathsf{lab}) = 1\right] = \Pr_{\mathsf{Hybrid}_2^{(i^*,q^*)}}\left[\mathcal{A}^{\mathsf{Regstr}(\cdot,\cdot),\mathsf{Eval}(\cdot,\cdot)}(1^\lambda) = 1\right].$$

When $(\widetilde{C}, \mathsf{lab}) \leftarrow \mathsf{GC.Sim}(1^\lambda, C_{[\mathsf{sk}_{i^*}, k_{i^*}]}(\{\widetilde{\mathsf{msg}_j}\}_{j \in S}))$, the distinguisher simulates the environment of $\mathsf{Hybrid}_2^{(i^*,q^*)+1}$ for $\mathcal{A}$. Hence,

$$\Pr\left[(\widetilde{C}, \mathsf{lab}) \leftarrow \mathsf{GC.Sim}(1^\lambda, C_{[\mathsf{sk}_{i^*}, k_{i^*}]}(\{\mathsf{msg}_j\}_{j \in S})) : \mathcal{D}(1^\lambda, \widetilde{C}, \mathsf{lab}) = 1\right] = \Pr_{\mathsf{Hybrid}_2^{(i^*,q^*)+1}}\left[\mathcal{A}^{\mathsf{Regstr}(\cdot,\cdot),\mathsf{Eval}(\cdot,\cdot)}(1^\lambda) = 1\right].$$

From the security of the garbling scheme, we derive that $\mathsf{Hybrid}_2^{(i^*,q^*)}$ and $\mathsf{Hybrid}_2^{(i^*,q^*)+1}$ are indistinguishable.

Lemma 9. $\mathsf{Hybrid}_2^{(N,Q)+1}$ *is identical to* Hybrid_3^1*. Moreover, there exists a negligible function* $\nu(\lambda)$ *such that for any sufficiently large* λ*,* $\mathsf{SD}(\mathsf{Hybrid}_3^{i^*}, \mathsf{Hybrid}_3^{i^*+1}) < \nu(\lambda)$*.*

Proof. We build the following function g. The function g takes as input the crs, and for each $i < i^*$, g generates the crs_i using $\mathsf{ABSFE}.\overline{\mathsf{Setup}}$. For each $i > i^*$, g generates crs_i using $\mathsf{ABSFE.Setup}$. For i^*, if $i^* \in H$, then sets crs_{i^*} as crs. Otherwise, it generates crs_{i^*} using $\mathsf{ABSFE.Setup}$. Then g invokes $\mathcal{A}$ and simulates $\mathsf{Regstr}(\cdot,\cdot)$ and $\mathsf{Eval}(\cdot,\cdot)$ in the same way as $\mathsf{Hybrid}_2^{(N,Q)+1}$.

When $\mathsf{crs} \leftarrow \mathsf{ABSFE.Setup}(1^\lambda)$, then $g(\mathsf{crs})$ is identical to $\mathsf{Hybrid}_3^{i^*}$. When crs is generated by $\mathsf{ABSFE}.\overline{\mathsf{Setup}}(1^\lambda)$, then $g(\mathsf{crs})$ is identical to $\mathsf{Hybrid}_3^{i^*+1}$. From the statistical public key indistinguisbaility property, we derive that $\mathsf{SD}(\mathsf{Hybrid}_3^{i^*}, \mathsf{Hybrid}_3^{i^*+1}) < \mathsf{negl}(\lambda)$.

Lemma 10. Hybrid_3^{N+1} *is identical to* $\mathsf{Hybrid}_4^{(1,1)}$*. Moreover, there exists a negligible function* $\nu(\lambda)$ *such that for sufficiently large* λ*,* $\mathsf{SD}(\mathsf{Hybrid}_4^{(i^*,q^*)}, \mathsf{Hybrid}_4^{(i^*,q^*)+1}) < \nu(\lambda)$*.*

Proof. Since the only difference between $\mathsf{Hybrid}_4^{(i^*,q^*)}$ and $\mathsf{Hybrid}_4^{(i^*,q^*)+1}$ is the way that h_i is generated in q-th query of $\mathcal{O}$, from the statistical hint simulation security of AB-SFE, we have $\mathsf{SD}(\mathsf{Hybrid}_4^{(i^*,q^*)}, \mathsf{Hybrid}_4^{(i^*,q^*)+1}) < \mathsf{negl}(\lambda)$.

Lemma 11. $\mathsf{Hybrid}_4^{(N,Q)+1}$ *and* Hybrid_5^1 *are identical. There exists a negligible function* $\nu(\lambda)$ *such that for any sufficiently large* λ,

$$\left| \Pr_{\mathsf{Hybrid}_5^{i^*}} \left[\mathcal{A}^{\mathsf{Regstr}(\cdot,\cdot),\mathsf{Eval}(\cdot,\cdot)}(1^\lambda) = 1 \right] - \Pr_{\mathsf{Hybrid}_5^{i^*+1}} \left[\mathcal{A}^{\mathsf{Regstr}(\cdot,\cdot),\mathsf{Eval}(\cdot,\cdot)}(1^\lambda) = 1 \right] \right| < \nu(\lambda).$$

Proof. We construct the following adversary $\mathcal{A}'$ for the PRF. $\mathcal{A}'^{\mathcal{O}}(1^\lambda)$ is given access to a PRF oracle, and it invokes the adversary $\mathcal{A}^{\mathsf{Regstr}(\cdot,\cdot),\mathsf{Eval}(\cdot,\cdot)}(1^\lambda)$ by implementing the oracles $\mathsf{Regstr}(\cdot,\cdot)$ and $\mathsf{Eval}(\cdot,\cdot)$ as follows.

- $\mathsf{Regstr}(\cdot,\cdot)$: For the i-th query, only sample $k_i \leftarrow \mathsf{PRF.Gen}(1^\lambda)$ when $i \geq i^*$ or $i \notin H$.
- $\mathsf{Eval}(\cdot,\cdot)$: For each query (S, f), do the same thing as Eval in $\mathsf{Hybrid}_4^{(N,Q)+1}$, except the generation of r_i. We generate r_i as follows. For each $i \in S$,
  - if $i < i^*$ and $i \in H$, let $r_i = \mathsf{PRF}_i.\mathsf{F}(S||f)$.
  - If $i = i^*$ and $i^* \in H$, let $r_i \leftarrow \mathcal{O}(S||f)$.
  - If $i > i^*$ or $i \notin H$, $r_i = \mathsf{PRF.Eval}(k_i, (S||f))$.

When $\mathcal{O}'$ is $\mathsf{PRF.Eval}(k,\cdot)$ for a uniform random PRF key k, the adversary $\mathcal{A}'$ simulates the environment of $\mathsf{Hybrid}_5^{i^*}$ for $\mathcal{A}$. Hence,

$$\Pr\left[k \leftarrow \{0,1\}^\lambda : \mathcal{A}'^{\mathsf{PRF.Eval}(k,\cdot)}(1^\lambda) = 1\right] = \Pr_{\mathsf{Hybrid}_5^{i^*}} \left[\mathcal{A}^{\mathsf{Regstr}(\cdot,\cdot),\mathsf{Eval}(\cdot,\cdot)}(1^\lambda) = 1\right].$$

When $\mathcal{O}'$ is a random function $\mathsf{F}(\cdot)$, the adversary $\mathcal{A}'$ simulates the environment of $\mathsf{Hybrid}_5^{i^*}$ for $\mathcal{A}$. Hence,

$$\Pr[\mathcal{A}'^{\mathsf{F}(\cdot)}(1^\lambda) = 1] = \Pr_{\mathsf{Hybrid}_5^{i^*+1}} \left[\mathcal{A}^{\mathsf{Regstr}(\cdot,\cdot),\mathsf{Eval}(\cdot,\cdot)}(1^\lambda) = 1\right].$$

From the security of PRF, we derive that $\mathsf{Hybrid}_5^{i^*}$ and $\mathsf{Hybrid}_5^{i^*+1}$ are indistinguishable.

Lemma 12. Hybrid_5^{N+1} *is identical to* Hybrid_6^1*. Moreover, there exists a negligible function* $\nu(\lambda)$ *such that for any sufficiently large* λ,

$$\left| \Pr_{\mathsf{Hybrid}_6^{q^*}} \left[\mathcal{A}^{\mathsf{Regstr}(\cdot,\cdot),\mathsf{Eval}(\cdot,\cdot)}(1^\lambda) = 1 \right] - \Pr_{\mathsf{Hybrid}_6^{q^*+1}} \left[\mathcal{A}^{\mathsf{Regstr}(\cdot,\cdot),\mathsf{Eval}(\cdot,\cdot)}(1^\lambda) = 1 \right] \right| < \nu(\lambda).$$

Proof. We build the following distinguisher $\mathcal{D}$ for the semi-malicous MPC security. The adversary $\mathcal{D}$ invokes the adversary $\mathcal{A}^{\mathsf{Regstr}(\cdot,\cdot),\mathsf{Eval}(\cdot,\cdot)}(1^\lambda)$, where the oracle $\mathsf{Regstr}(\cdot,\cdot)$ is the same as in Hybrid_5^{N+1}, and the oracle $\mathsf{Eval}(\cdot,\cdot)$ is implemented as follows.

Let the q-th query be (S, f), the oracle $\mathsf{Eval}(\cdot,\cdot)$ performs the same executions as in Hybrid_5^{N+1}, except the generation of $(\widetilde{\mathsf{msg}}_i, \widetilde{p}_i)$ is replaced as follows.

- If $\mathsf{Map}(S, f)$ is defined before, then let $\{\widetilde{\mathsf{msg}}_i, \widetilde{p}_i\}_{i \in S \cap H} \leftarrow \mathsf{Map}(S, f)$. Othwerwise,
  - If $q < q^*$, let $\{\widetilde{\mathsf{msg}}_i, \widetilde{p}_i\}_{i \in S \cap H} \leftarrow \mathsf{One.Sim}(1^\lambda, S \cap H, \{x_i, r_i\}_{i \in S \setminus H}, f, f(\{x_i\}_{i \in S}))$.

- If $q = q^*$, query the challenger with the number of parties $|S|$, the inputs $\{x_i\}_{i\in S}$, the honest party subset $H \cap S$, the randomness for dishonest parties $\{r_i\}_{i\in S\setminus H}$, and obtains the challenge $\{\mathsf{msg}_i, p_i\}_{i\in S\cap H}$. Let $\{\widetilde{\mathsf{msg}_i}, \widetilde{p_i}\}_{i\in S\cap H} = \{\mathsf{msg}_i, p_i\}_{i\in S\cap H}$, and define $\mathsf{Map}(S, f) = \{\mathsf{msg}_i, p_i\}_{i\in S\cap H}$.
- If $q > q^*$, for each $i \in S \cap H$, set fresh randomness r_i. Let $\widetilde{\mathsf{msg}_i} = \mathsf{One.Round}_1(1^\lambda, x_i, f; r_i)$, $\widetilde{p_i} = \mathsf{One.Round}_2(x_i, r_i, \{\widetilde{\mathsf{msg}_j}\}_{j\in S}, f)$, and define $\mathsf{Map}(S, f) = \{\widetilde{\mathsf{msg}_i}, \widetilde{p_i}\}_{i\in S\cap H}$.

When $\{\mathsf{msg}_i, p_i\}_{i\in S\cap H}$ is obtained from real world execution, with dishonest parties' random coins $\{r_i\}_{i\in S\setminus H}$, the distinguisher $\mathcal{D}$ simulates the environment of $\mathsf{Hybrid}_6^{q^*}$ for $\mathcal{A}$. Hence,

$$\Pr\left[\begin{smallmatrix}\forall i\in S\cap H, r_i \leftarrow \{0,1\}^* \\ \forall i\in S, \mathsf{msg}_i = \mathsf{One.Round}_1(1^\lambda, x_i; r_i), \\ p_i = \mathsf{One.Round}_2(x_i, r_i, \{\mathsf{msg}_j\}_{j\in S})\end{smallmatrix} : \mathcal{D}(1^\lambda, \{\mathsf{msg}_i, p_i\}_{i\in S}) = 1\right] = \Pr\left[\mathcal{D}(1^\lambda, \mathsf{Hybrid}_6^{q^*}) = 1\right]$$

When $\{\mathsf{msg}_i, p_i\}_{i\in S\cap H}$ is obtained from the ideal simulation, then the distinguisher $\mathcal{D}$ simulates the environment of Hybrid_6^{q*+1} for $\mathcal{A}$. Hence,

$$\Pr\left[\{\mathsf{msg}_i, p_i\}_{i\in S\cap H} \leftarrow \mathsf{Sim}(1^\lambda, S\cap H, \{x_i, r_i\}_{i\in S\setminus H}, f, f(\{x_i\}_{i\in S})) : \mathcal{D}(1^\lambda, \{\mathsf{msg}_i, p_i\}_{i\in S}) = 1\right] = \Pr\left[\mathcal{D}(1^\lambda, \mathsf{Hybrid}_6^{q^*+1})\right].$$

Hence, from the semi-malicious security of the MPC protocol, we derive that $\mathsf{Hybrid}_6^{q^*}$ and $\mathsf{Hybrid}_6^{q^*+1}$ are indistinguishable.

Lemma 13. *There exists a negligible function $\nu(\lambda)$ such that for any sufficiently large λ, $\mathsf{SD}(\mathsf{Hybrid}_6^{Q+1}, \mathsf{Ideal}) < \nu(\lambda)$.*

Proof. Similar to Lemma 10, this Lemma follows from the statistical public key indistinguishability.

Combining Lemma 7 to Lemma 13, we finish the proof.

References

1. Afshar, A., Mohassel, P., Pinkas, B., Riva, B.: Non-interactive secure computation based on cut-and-choose. In: Nguyen, P.Q., Oswald, E. (eds.) EUROCRYPT 2014. LNCS, vol. 8441, pp. 387–404. Springer, Heidelberg (2014). https://doi.org/10.1007/978-3-642-55220-5_22
2. Ananth, P., Jain, A., Jin, Z., Malavolta, G.: Multikey FHE in the plain model. Cryptology ePrint Archive, Report 2020/180 (2020). https://eprint.iacr.org/2020/180

3. Applebaum, B., Ishai, Y., Kushilevitz, E.: Cryptography in NC^0. In: 45th FOCS, Rome, Italy, pp. 166–175. IEEE Computer Society Press, 17–19 October 2004. https://doi.org/10.1109/FOCS.2004.20
4. Applebaum, B., Ishai, Y., Kushilevitz, E.: How to garble arithmetic circuits. In: Ostrovsky, R. (ed.) 52nd FOCS, Palm Springs, CA, USA, pp. 120–129. IEEE Computer Society Press, 22–25 October 2011. https://doi.org/10.1109/FOCS.2011.40
5. Badrinarayanan, S., Garg, S., Ishai, Y., Sahai, A., Wadia, A.: Two-message witness indistinguishability and secure computation in the plain model from new assumptions. In: Takagi, T., Peyrin, T. (eds.) ASIACRYPT 2017. LNCS, vol. 10626, pp. 275–303. Springer, Cham (2017). https://doi.org/10.1007/978-3-319-70700-6_10
6. Badrinarayanan, S., Jain, A., Ostrovsky, R., Visconti, I.: Non-interactive secure computation from one-way functions. In: Peyrin, T., Galbraith, S. (eds.) ASIACRYPT 2018. LNCS, vol. 11274, pp. 118–138. Springer, Cham (2018). https://doi.org/10.1007/978-3-030-03332-3_5
7. Bartusek, J., Garg, S., Masny, D., Mukherjee, P.: Reusable two-round MPC from DDH. Cryptology ePrint Archive, Report 2020/170 (2020) https://eprint.iacr.org/2020/170
8. Benhamouda, F., Lin, H.: k-round multiparty computation from k-round oblivious transfer via garbled interactive circuits. In: Nielsen, J.B., Rijmen, V. (eds.) EUROCRYPT 2018. LNCS, vol. 10821, pp. 500–532. Springer, Cham (2018). https://doi.org/10.1007/978-3-319-78375-8_17
9. Benhamouda, F., Lin, H.: Multiparty reusable non-interactive secure computation. Cryptology ePrint Archive, Report 2020/221 (2020). https://eprint.iacr.org/2020/221
10. Brakerski, Z., Döttling, N.: Two-message statistically sender-private OT from LWE. In: Beimel, A., Dziembowski, S. (eds.) TCC 2018. LNCS, vol. 11240, pp. 370–390. Springer, Cham (2018). https://doi.org/10.1007/978-3-030-03810-6_14
11. Canetti, R., Jain, A., Scafuro, A.: Practical UC security with a global random oracle. In: Ahn, G.J., Yung, M., Li, N. (eds.) ACM CCS 2014, Scottsdale, AZ, USA, pp. 597–608. ACM Press, 3–7 November 2014. https://doi.org/10.1145/2660267.2660374
12. Cash, D., Hofheinz, D., Kiltz, E.: How to delegate a lattice basis. Cryptology ePrint Archive, Report 2009/351 (2009) https://eprint.iacr.org/2009/351
13. Chase, M., et al.: Reusable non-interactive secure computation. In: Boldyreva, A., Micciancio, D. (eds.) CRYPTO 2019. LNCS, vol. 11694, pp. 462–488. Springer, Cham (2019). https://doi.org/10.1007/978-3-030-26954-8_15
14. Dodis, Y., Goldwasser, S., Tauman Kalai, Y., Peikert, C., Vaikuntanathan, V.: Public-key encryption schemes with auxiliary inputs. In: Micciancio, D. (ed.) TCC 2010. LNCS, vol. 5978, pp. 361–381. Springer, Heidelberg (2010). https://doi.org/10.1007/978-3-642-11799-2_22
15. Garg, S., Gentry, C., Halevi, S., Raykova, M.: Two-round secure MPC from indistinguishability obfuscation. In: Lindell, Y. (ed.) TCC 2014. LNCS, vol. 8349, pp. 74–94. Springer, Heidelberg (2014). https://doi.org/10.1007/978-3-642-54242-8_4
16. Garg, S., Gentry, C., Sahai, A., Waters, B.: Witness encryption and its applications. In: Boneh, D., Roughgarden, T., Feigenbaum, J. (eds.) 45th ACM STOC, Palo Alto, CA, USA, pp. 467–476. ACM Press, 1–4 June 2013. https://doi.org/10.1145/2488608.2488667
17. Garg, S., Srinivasan, A.: Garbled protocols and two-round MPC from bilinear maps. In: Umans, C. (ed.) 58th FOCS, Berkeley, CA, USA, pp. 588–599. IEEE Computer Society Press, 15–17 October 2017. https://doi.org/10.1109/FOCS.2017.60

18. Garg, S., Srinivasan, A.: Two-round multiparty secure computation from minimal assumptions. In: Nielsen, J.B., Rijmen, V. (eds.) EUROCRYPT 2018. LNCS, vol. 10821, pp. 468–499. Springer, Cham (2018). https://doi.org/10.1007/978-3-319-78375-8_16
19. Gentry, C., Peikert, C., Vaikuntanathan, V.: Trapdoors for hard lattices and new cryptographic constructions. In: Ladner, R.E., Dwork, C. (eds.) 40th ACM STOC, Victoria, BC, Canada, pp. 197–206. ACM Press, 17–20 May 2008. https://doi.org/10.1145/1374376.1374407
20. Goldreich, O., Micali, S., Wigderson, A.: How to play any mental game or A completeness theorem for protocols with honest majority. In: Aho, A. (ed.) 19th ACM STOC, New York City, NY, USA, pp. 218–229. ACM Press, 25–27 May 1987. https://doi.org/10.1145/28395.28420
21. Goldwasser, S., Kalai, Y.T., Peikert, C., Vaikuntanathan, V.: Robustness of the learning with errors assumption. In: Yao, A.C.C. (ed.) ICS 2010, pp. 230–240. Tsinghua University Press, Tsinghua University, Beijing, China, 5–7 January 2010
22. Goldwasser, S., Kalai, Y.T., Popa, R.A., Vaikuntanathan, V., Zeldovich, N.: Reusable garbled circuits and succinct functional encryption. In: Boneh, D., Roughgarden, T., Feigenbaum, J. (eds.) 45th ACM STOC, Palo Alto, CA, USA, pp. 555–564. ACM Press, 1–4 June 2013. https://doi.org/10.1145/2488608.2488678
23. Gorbunov, S., Vaikuntanathan, V., Wichs, D.: Leveled fully homomorphic signatures from standard lattices. In: Servedio, R.A., Rubinfeld, R. (eds.) 47th ACM STOC, Portland, OR, USA, pp. 469–477. ACM Press, 14–17 June 2015. https://doi.org/10.1145/2746539.2746576
24. Dov Gordon, S., Liu, F.-H., Shi, E.: Constant-round MPC with fairness and guarantee of output delivery. In: Gennaro, R., Robshaw, M. (eds.) CRYPTO 2015. LNCS, vol. 9216, pp. 63–82. Springer, Heidelberg (2015). https://doi.org/10.1007/978-3-662-48000-7_4
25. Goyal, V., Pandey, O., Sahai, A., Waters, B.: Attribute-based encryption for fine-grained access control of encrypted data. In: Juels, A., Wright, R.N., De Capitani di Vimercati, S. (eds.) ACM CCS 2006, Alexandria, Virginia, USA, pp. 89–98. ACM Press, 30 October–3 November 2006. https://doi.org/10.1145/1180405.1180418. Cryptology ePrint Archive Report 2006/309
26. Ishai, Y., Kushilevitz, E., Ostrovsky, R., Prabhakaran, M., Sahai, A.: Efficient non-interactive secure computation. In: Paterson, K.G. (ed.) EUROCRYPT 2011. LNCS, vol. 6632, pp. 406–425. Springer, Heidelberg (2011). https://doi.org/10.1007/978-3-642-20465-4_23
27. Lombardi, A., Quach, W., Rothblum, R.D., Wichs, D., Wu, D.J.: New constructions of reusable designated-verifier NIZKs. In: Boldyreva, A., Micciancio, D. (eds.) CRYPTO 2019. LNCS, vol. 11694, pp. 670–700. Springer, Cham (2019). https://doi.org/10.1007/978-3-030-26954-8_22
28. Micciancio, D., Peikert, C.: Trapdoors for lattices: simpler, tighter, faster, smaller. In: Pointcheval, D., Johansson, T. (eds.) EUROCRYPT 2012. LNCS, vol. 7237, pp. 700–718. Springer, Heidelberg (2012). https://doi.org/10.1007/978-3-642-29011-4_41
29. Mukherjee, P., Wichs, D.: Two round multiparty computation via multi-key FHE. In: Fischlin, M., Coron, J.-S. (eds.) EUROCRYPT 2016. LNCS, vol. 9666, pp. 735–763. Springer, Heidelberg (2016). https://doi.org/10.1007/978-3-662-49896-5_26
30. O'Neill, A., Peikert, C., Waters, B.: Bi-deniable public-key encryption. In: Rogaway, P. (ed.) CRYPTO 2011. LNCS, vol. 6841, pp. 525–542. Springer, Heidelberg (2011). https://doi.org/10.1007/978-3-642-22792-9_30

31. Sahai, A., Waters, B.: Fuzzy identity-based encryption. In: Cramer, R. (ed.) EUROCRYPT 2005. LNCS, vol. 3494, pp. 457–473. Springer, Heidelberg (2005). https://doi.org/10.1007/11426639_27
32. Yao, A.C.C.: How to generate and exchange secrets (extended abstract). In: 27th FOCS, Toronto, Ontario, Canada, pp. 162–167. IEEE Computer Society Press, 27–29 October 1986. https://doi.org/10.1109/SFCS.1986.25

Generic Compiler for Publicly Verifiable Covert Multi-Party Computation

Sebastian Faust[1], Carmit Hazay[2], David Kretzler[1(✉)], and Benjamin Schlosser[1(✉)]

[1] Technical University of Darmstadt, Darmstadt, Germany
{sebastian.faust,david.kretzler,benjamin.schlosser}@tu-darmstadt.de
[2] Bar-Ilan University, Ramat Gan, Israel
carmit.hazay@biu.ac.il

Abstract. Covert security has been introduced as a compromise between semi-honest and malicious security. In a nutshell, covert security guarantees that malicious behavior can be detected by the honest parties with some probability, but in case detection fails all bets are off. While the security guarantee offered by covert security is weaker than full-fledged malicious security, it comes with significantly improved efficiency. An important extension of covert security introduced by Asharov and Orlandi (ASIACRYPT'12) is *public verifiability*, which allows the honest parties to create a publicly verifiable certificate of malicious behavior. Public verifiability significantly strengthen covert security as the certificate allows punishment via an external party, e.g., a judge.

Most previous work on publicly verifiable covert (PVC) security focuses on the two-party case, and the multi-party case has mostly been neglected. In this work, we introduce a novel compiler for multi-party PVC secure protocols with no private inputs. The class of supported protocols includes the preprocessing of common multi-party computation protocols that are designed in the offline-online model. Our compiler leverages time-lock encryption to offer high probability of cheating detection (often also called deterrence factor) independent of the number of involved parties. Moreover, in contrast to the only earlier work that studies PVC in the multi-party setting (CRYPTO'20), we provide the first full formal security analysis.

Keywords: Covert security · Multi-party computation · Public verifiability · Time-lock puzzles

1 Introduction

Secure multi-party computation (MPC) allows a set of n parties P_i to jointly compute a function f on their inputs such that nothing beyond the output of that function is revealed. Privacy of the inputs and correctness of the outputs need to be guaranteed even if some subset of the parties is corrupted by an

A. Canteaut and F.-X. Standaert (Eds.): EUROCRYPT 2021, LNCS 12697, pp. 782–811, 2021.
https://doi.org/10.1007/978-3-030-77886-6_27

adversary. The two most prominent adversarial models considered in the literature are the *semi-honest* and *malicious* adversary model. In the semi-honest model, the adversary is passive and the corrupted parties follow the protocol description. Hence, the adversary only learns the inputs and incoming/outgoing messages including the internal randomness of the corrupted parties. In contrast, the adversarial controlled parties can arbitrarily deviate from the protocol specification under malicious corruption.

Since in most cases it seems hard (if not impossible) to guarantee that a corrupted party follows the protocol description, malicious security is typically the desired security goal for the design of multi-party computation protocols. Unfortunately, compared to protocols that only guarantee semi-honest security, protection against malicious adversaries results into high overheads in terms of communication and computation complexity. For protocols based on distributed garbling techniques in the oblivious transfer (OT)-hybrid model, the communication complexity is inflated by a factor of $\frac{s}{\log|\mathrm{C}|}$ [WRK17b], where C is the computed circuit and s is a statistical security parameter. For secret sharing-based protocols, Hazay et al. [HVW20] have recently shown a constant communication overhead over the semi-honest GMW-protocol [GMW87]. In most techniques, the computational overhead grows with an order of s.

In order to mitigate the drawbacks of the overhead required for malicious secure function evaluation, one approach is to split protocols into an input-independent offline and an input-dependent online phase. The input-independent offline protocol carries out pre-computations that are utilized to speed up the input-dependent online protocol which securely evaluates the desired function. Examples for such offline protocols are the circuit generation of garbling schemes as in authenticated garbling [WRK17a, WRK17b] or the generation of correlated randomness in form of Beaver triples [Bea92] in secret sharing-based protocols such as in SPDZ [DPSZ12]. The main idea of this approach is that the offline protocol can be executed continuously *in the background* and the online protocol is executed ad-hoc once input data becomes available or output data is required. Since the performance requirements for the online protocol are usually much stricter, the offline part should cover the most expensive protocol steps, as for example done in [WRK17a, WRK17b, DPSZ12].

A middle ground between the design goals of security and efficiency has been proposed with the notion of *covert security*. Introduced by Aumann and Lindell [AL07], covert security allows the adversary to take full control over a party and let her deviate from the protocol specification in an arbitrary way. The protocol, however, is designed in such a way that honest parties can detect cheating with some probability ϵ (often called the deterrence factor). However, if cheating is not detected all bets are off. This weaker security notion comes with the benefit of significantly improved efficiency, when compared to protocols in the full-fledged malicious security model. The motivation behind covert security is that in many real-world scenarios, parties are able to actively deviate from the protocol instructions (and as such are not semi-honest), but due to reputation concerns only do so if they are not caught. In the initial work of Aumann and

Lindell, the focus was on the two-party case. This has been first extended to the multi-party case by Goyal et al. [GMS08] and later been adapted to a different line of MPC protocols by Damgård et al. [DKL+13].

While the notion of covert security seems appealing at first glance it has one important shortcoming. If an honest party detects cheating, then she cannot reliably transfer her knowledge to other parties, which makes the notion of covert security significantly less attractive for many applications. This shortcoming of covert security was first observed by Asharov and Orlandi [AO12], and addressed with the notion of *public verifiability.* Informally speaking, public verifiability guarantees that if an honest party detects cheating, she can create a certificate that uniquely identifies the cheater, and can be verified by an external party. Said certificate can be used to punish cheaters for misbehavior, e.g., via a smart contract [ZDH19], thereby disincentivizing misbehavior.

Despite being a natural security notion, there has been relatively little work on covert security with public verifiability. In particular, starting with the work of Asharov and Orlandi [AO12] most works have explored publicly verifiable covert security in the two-party setting [KM15, HKK+19, ZDH19, DOS20]. These works use a publicly checkable cut-and-choose approach for secure two-party computation based on garbled circuits. Here a random subset of size $t-1$ out of t garbled circuits is opened to verify if cheating occurred, while the remaining unopened garbled circuit is used for the actual secure function evaluation. The adversary needs to guess which circuit is used for the final evaluation and only cheat in this particular instance. If her guess is false, she will be detected. Hence, there is a deterrence factor of $\frac{t-1}{t}$.

For the extension to the multi-party case of covert security even less is known. Prior work mainly focuses on the restricted version of covert security that does not offer public verifiability [GMS08, DGN10, LOP11, DKL+13]. The only work that we are aware of that adds public verifiability to covert secure multi-party computation protocols is the recent work of Damgård et al. [DOS20]. While [DOS20] mainly focuses on a compiler for the two-party case, they also sketch how their construction can be extended to the multi-party setting.

1.1 Our Contribution

In contrast to most prior research, we focus on the multi-party setting. Our main contribution is a novel compiler for transforming input-independent multi-party computation protocols with semi-honest security into protocols that offer covert security with public verifiability. Our construction achieves a high deterrence factor of $\frac{t-1}{t}$, where t is the number of semi-honest instances executed in the cut-and-choose protocol. In contrast, the only prior work that sketches a solution for publicly verifiable covert security for the multi-part setting [DOS20] achieves $\approx \frac{t-1}{nt}$, which in particular for a large number of parties n results in a low deterrence factor. [DOS20] states that the deterrence factor can be increased at the cost of multiple protocol repetitions, which results into higher complexity and can be abused to amplify denial-of-service attacks. A detail discussion of the main differences between [DOS20] and our work is given in Sect. 6. We emphasize that our work is also the first that provides a full formal security proof of the multi-party case in the model of covert security with public verifiability.

Our results apply to a large class of input-independent offline protocols for carrying out pre-computation. Damgård et al. [DOS20] have shown that an offline-online protocol with a publicly verifiable covert secure offline phase and a maliciously secure online phase constitutes a publicly verifiable covert secure protocol in total. Hence, by applying our compiler to a passively secure offline protocol and combining it with an actively secure online protocol, we obtain a publicly verifiable covert secure protocol in total. Since offline protocols are often the most expensive part of the secure multi-party computation protocol, e.g., in protocols like [YWZ20] and [DPSZ12], our approach has the potential of significantly improving efficiency of multi-party computation protocols in terms of computation and communication overhead.

An additional contribution of our work (which is of independent interest) is to introduce a novel mechanism for achieving public verifiability in protocols with covert security. Our approach is based on *time-lock encryption* [RSW96, MT19, MMV11, BGJ+16], a primitive that enables encryption of messages into the future and has previously been discussed in the context of delayed digital cash payments, sealed-bid auctions, key escrow, and e-voting. Time-lock encryption can be used as a building block to guarantee that in case of malicious behavior each honest party can construct a publicly verifiable cheating certificate without further interaction. The use of time-lock puzzles in a simulation-based security proof requires us to overcome several technical challenges that do not occur for proving game-based security notions.

In order to achieve efficient verification of the cheating certificates, we also show how to add verifiability to the notion of time-lock encryption by using techniques from verifiable delay functions [BBBF18]. While our construction can be instantiated with any time-lock encryption satisfying our requirements, we present a concrete extension of the RSW time-lock encryption scheme. Since RSW-based time-lock encryption [RSW96, MT19] requires a one-time trusted setup, an instantiation of our construction using the RSW-based time-lock encryption inherits this assumption. We can implement the one-time trusted setup using a maliciously secure multi-party computation protocol similar to the MPC ceremony used, e.g., by the cryptocurrency ZCash.

1.2 Technical Overview

In this section, we give a high-level overview of the main techniques used in our work. To this end, we start by briefly recalling how covert security is typically achieved. Most covert secure protocols take a semi-honest protocol and execute t instances of it in parallel. They then check the correctness of $t-1$ randomly chosen instances by essentially revealing the used inputs and randomness and finally take the result of the last unopened execution as protocol output. The above requires that (a) checking the correctness of the $t-1$ instances can be carried out efficiently, and (b) the private inputs of the parties are not revealed.

In order to achieve the first goal, one common approach is to derandomize the protocol, i.e., let the parties generate a random seed from which they derive their internal randomness. Once the protocol is derandomized, correctness can efficiently be checked by the other parties. To achieve the second goal, the protocol is divided into an offline and an online protocol as described above. The output of the offline phase (e.g., a garbling scheme) is just some correlated randomness. As this protocol is input-independent, the offline phase does not leak information about the parties' private inputs. The online phase (e.g., evaluating a garbled circuit) is maliciously secure and hence protects the private inputs.

Public Verifiability. To add public verifiability to the above-described approach, the basic idea is to let the parties sign all transcripts that have been produced during the protocol execution. This makes them accountable for cheating in one of the semi-honest executions. One particular challenge for public verifiability is to ensure that once a malicious party notices that its cheating attempt will be detected it cannot prevent (e.g., by aborting) the creation of a certificate proving its misbehavior. Hence, the trivial idea of running a shared coin tossing protocol to select which of the instances will be checked does not work because the adversary can abort before revealing her randomness and inputs used in the checked instances. To circumvent this problem, the recent work of Damgård et al. [DOS20] proposes the following technique. Each party locally chooses a subset I of the t semi-honest instances whose computation it wants to check (this is often called a watchlist [IPS08]). Next, it obliviously asks the parties to explain their execution in those instances (i.e., by revealing the random coins used in the protocol execution). While this approach works well in the two-party case, in the multi-party case it either results in a low deterrence factor or requires that the protocol execution is repeated many times. This is due to the fact that each party chooses its watchlist independently; in the worst case, all watchlists are mutually disjoint. Hence, the size of each watchlist is set to be lower or equal than $\frac{t-1}{n}$ (resulting in a deterrence factor of $\frac{t-1}{nt}$) to guarantee that one instance remains unchecked or parties repeat the protocol several times until there is a protocol execution with an unchecked instance.

Public Verifiability from Time-Lock Encryption. Our approach avoids the above shortcomings by using time-lock encryption. Concretely, we follow the shared coin-tossing approach mentioned above but prevent the rushing attack by locking the shared coin (selecting which semi-honest executions shall be opened) and the seeds of the opened executions in time-lock encryption. Since the time-lock ciphertexts are produced before the selection-coin is made public, it will be too late for the adversary to abort the computation. Moreover, since the time-lock encryption can be solved even without the participation of the adversary, the honest parties can produce a publicly verifiable certificate to prove misbehavior. This approach has the advantage that we can always check all but one instance of the semi-honest executions, thereby significantly improving the deterrence factor and the overall complexity. One may object that solving time-lock encryption adds additional computational overhead to the honest parties. We emphasize, however, that the time-lock encryption has to be solved only in the pessimistic case when one party aborts after the puzzle generation. Moreover, in our construction, the time-lock parameter can be chosen rather small, since the encryption has to hide the selection-coin and the seeds only for two communication rounds. See Sect. 6 for a more detailed analysis of the overhead introduced by the time-lock puzzle generation and a comparison to prior work.

Creating the Time-Lock Encryption. There are multiple technical challenges that we need to address to make the above idea work. First, current constructions of time-lock encryption matching our requirements require a trusted setup for generating the public parameters. In particular, we need to generate a strong RSA modulus N without leaking its factorization, and produce a base-puzzle that later can be used for efficiency reasons. Both of these need to be generated just once and can be re-used for all protocol executions. Hence, one option is to replace the trusted setup by a maliciously secure MPC similar to what has been done for the MPC ceremony used by the cryptocurrency ZCash. Another alternative is to investigate if time-lock puzzles matching the requirements of our compiler can be constructed from hidden order groups with public setup such as ideal class groups of imaginary quadratic fields [BW88] or Jacobians of hyperelliptic curves [DG20]. An additional challenge is that we cannot simply time-lock the seeds of all semi-honest protocol executions (as one instance needs to remain unopened). To address this problem, we use a maliciously secure MPC protocol to carry out the shared coin-tossing protocol and produce the time-lock encryptions of the seeds for the semi-honest protocol instance that are later opened. We emphasize that the complexity of this step only depends on t and n, and is in particular independent of the complexity of the functionality that we want to compute. Hence, for complex functionalities the costs of the maliciously secure puzzle generation are amortized over the protocol costs[1].

2 Secure Multi-Party Computation

Secure computation in the standalone model is defined via the real world/ideal world paradigm. In the real world, all parties interact in order to jointly execute the protocol Π. In the ideal world, the parties send their inputs to a trusted party called ideal functionality and denoted by $\mathcal{F}$ which computes the desired function f and returns the result back to the parties. It is easy to see that in the ideal world the computation is correct and reveals only the intended information by definition. The security of a protocol Π is analyzed by comparing the ideal-world execution with the real-world execution. Informally, protocol Π is said to securely realize $\mathcal{F}$ if for every real-world adversary $\mathcal{A}$, there exists an ideal-world

[1] Concretely, for each instantiation we require two exponentiations and a small number of symmetric key encryptions. The latter can be realized using tailored MPC-ciphers like LowMC [ARS+15].

adversary $\mathcal{S}$ such that the joint output distribution of the honest parties and the adversary $\mathcal{A}$ in the real-world execution of Π is indistinguishable from the joint output distribution of the honest parties and $\mathcal{S}$ in the ideal-world execution.

We denote the number of parties executing a protocol Π by n. Let $f : (\{0,1\}^*)^n \rightarrow (\{0,1\}^*)^n$, where $f = (f_1, \ldots, f_n)$, be the function realized by Π. For every input vector $\bar{x} = (x_1, \ldots, x_n)$ the output vector is $\bar{y} = (f_1(\bar{x}), \ldots, f_n(\bar{x}))$ and the i-th party P_i with input x_i obtains output $f_i(\bar{x})$.

An adversary can corrupt any subset $I \subseteq [n]$ of parties. We further set $\mathsf{REAL}_{\Pi,\mathcal{A}(z),I}(\bar{x}, 1^\kappa)$ to be the output vector of the protocol execution of Π on input $\bar{x} = (x_1, \ldots, x_n)$ and security parameter κ, where the adversary $\mathcal{A}$ on auxiliary input z corrupts the parties $I \subseteq [n]$. By $\mathsf{OUTPUT}_i(\mathsf{REAL}_{\Pi,\mathcal{A}(z),I}(\bar{x}, 1^\kappa))$, we specify the output of party P_i for $i \in [n]$.

2.1 Covert Security

Aumann and Lindell introduced the notion of *covert security with ϵ-deterrence factor* in 2007 [AL07]. We focus on the strongest given formulation of covert security that is the *strong explicit cheat formulation*, where the ideal-world adversary only learns the honest parties' inputs if cheating is undetected. However, we slightly modify the original notion of covert security to capture realistic effects that occur especially in input-independent protocols and are disregarded by the notion of [AL07]. The changes are explained and motivated below.

As in the standard secure computation model, the execution of a real-world protocol is compared to the execution within an ideal world. The real world is exactly the same as in the standard model but the ideal model is slightly adapted in order to allow the adversary to cheat. Cheating will be detected by some fixed probability ϵ, which is called the deterrence factor. Let $\epsilon : \mathbb{N} \rightarrow [0, 1]$ be a function, then the execution in the ideal model works as follows.

Inputs: Each party obtains an input; the ith party's input is denoted by x_i. We assume that all inputs are of the same length. The adversary receives an auxiliary input z.

Send Inputs to Trusted Party: Any honest party P_j sends its received input x_j to the trusted party. The corrupted parties, controlled by $\mathcal{S}$, may either send their received input, or send some other input of the same length to the trusted party. This decision is made by $\mathcal{S}$ and may depend on the values x_i for $i \in I$ and auxiliary input z. If there are no inputs, the parties send ok_i instead of their inputs to the trusted party.

Trusted Party Answers Adversary: If the trusted party receives inputs from all parties, the trusted party computes $(y_1, \ldots, y_m) = f(\bar{w})$ and sends y_i to $\mathcal{S}$ for all $i \in I$.

Abort Options: If the adversary sends abort to the trusted party as additional input (before or after the trusted party sends the potential output to the adversary), then the trusted party sends abort to all the honest parties and halts. If a corrupted party sends additional input $w_i = \mathsf{corrupted}_i$ to the trusted party, then the trusted party sends $\mathsf{corrupted}_i$ to all of the honest parties and halts. If multiple parties send $\mathsf{corrupted}_i$, then the trusted party disregards all but one

of them (say, the one with the smallest index i). If both $\mathsf{corrupted}_i$ and abort messages are sent, then the trusted party ignores the $\mathsf{corrupted}_i$ message.
Attempted Cheat Option: If a corrupted party sends additional input $w_i = \mathsf{cheat}_i$ to the trusted party (as above: if there are several messages $w_i = \mathsf{cheat}_i$ ignore all but one - say, the one with the smallest index i), then the trusted party works as follows:

1. With probability ϵ, the trusted party sends $\mathsf{corrupted}_i$ to the adversary and all of the honest parties.
2. With probability $1 - \epsilon$, the trusted party sends $\mathsf{undetected}$ to the adversary along with the honest parties inputs $\{x_j\}_{j \notin I}$. Following this, the adversary sends the trusted party abort or output values $\{y_j\}_{j \notin I}$ of its choice for the honest parties. If the adversary sends abort, the trusted party sends abort to all honest parties. Otherwise, for every $j \notin I$, the trusted party sends y_j to P_j.

The ideal execution then ends at this point. Otherwise, if no w_i equals abort_i, $\mathsf{corrupted}_i$ or cheat_i, the ideal execution continues below.
Trusted Party Answers Honest Parties: If the trusted party did not receive $\mathsf{corrupted}_i$, cheat_i or abort from the adversary or a corrupted party then it sends y_j for all honest parties P_j (where $j \notin I$).
Outputs: An honest party always outputs the message it obtained from the trusted party. The corrupted parties outputs nothing. The adversary $\mathcal{S}$ outputs any arbitrary (probabilistic) polynomial-time computable function of the initial inputs $\{x_i\}_{i \in I}$, the auxiliary input z, and the received messages.

We denote by $\mathsf{IDEALC}^{\epsilon}_{f,\mathcal{S}(z),I}(\bar{x}, 1^{\kappa})$ the output of the honest parties and the adversary in the execution of the ideal model as defined above, where $\bar{x}$ is the input vector and the adversary $\mathcal{S}$ runs on auxiliary input z.

Definition 1 (Covert security with ϵ-deterrent). *Let f, Π, and ϵ be as above. Protocol Π is said to* securely compute f in the presence of covert adversaries with ϵ-deterrent *if for every non-uniform probabilistic polynomial-time adversary $\mathcal{A}$ for the real model, there exists a non-uniform probabilistic polynomial-time adversary $\mathcal{S}$ for the ideal model such that for every $I \subseteq [n]$, every balanced vector $\bar{x} \in (\{0,1\}^*)^n$, and every auxiliary input $z \in \{0,1\}^*$:*

$$\{\mathsf{IDEALC}^{\epsilon}_{f,\mathcal{S}(z),I}(\bar{x}, 1^{\kappa})\}_{\kappa \in \mathbb{N}} \stackrel{c}{\equiv} \{\mathsf{REAL}_{\Pi,\mathcal{A}(z),I}(\bar{x}, 1^{\kappa})\}_{\kappa \in \mathbb{N}}$$

Notice that the definition of the ideal world given above differs from the original definition of Aumann and Lindell in four aspects. First, we add the support of functions with no private inputs from the parties to model input-independent functionalities. In this case, the parties send ok instead of their inputs to the trusted party. Second, whenever a corrupted party aborts, the trusted party sends abort to all honest parties. Note that this message does not include the index of the aborting party which differs from the original model. The security notion of *identifiable abort* [IOZ14], where the aborting party is identified, is an independent research area, and is not achieved by our compiler.

Third, we allow a corrupted party to abort after undetected cheating, which does not weaken the security guarantees.

Finally, we allow the adversary to learn the output of the function f before it decides to cheat or to act honestly. In the original notion the adversary has to make this decision without seeing the potential output. Although this modification gives the adversary additional power, it captures the real world more reliably in regard to standalone input-independent protocols.

Covert security is typically achieved by executing several semi-honest instances and checking some of them via cut-and-choose while utilizing an unchecked instance for the actual output generation. The result of the semi-honest instances is often an input-independent precomputation in the form of correlated randomness, e.g., a garbled circuit or multiplication triples, which is consumed in a maliciously secure input-dependent online phase, e.g., the circuit evaluation or a SPDZ-style [DKL+13] online phase. Typically, the precomputation is explicitly designed not to leak any information about the actual output of the online phase, e.g., a garbled circuit obfuscates the actual circuit gate tables and multiplication triples are just random values without any relation to the output or even the function computed in the online phase. Thus, in such protocols, the adversary does not learn anything about the output when executing the semi-honest instances and therefore when deciding to cheat, which makes the original notion of covert security realistic for such input-dependent protocols.

However, if covert security is applied to the standalone input-independent precomputation phase, as done by our compiler, the actual output is the correlated randomness provided by one of the semi-honest instances. Hence, the adversary learns potential outputs when executing the semi-honest instances. Considering a rushing adversary that learns the output of a semi-honest instance first and still is capable to cheat with its last message, the adversary can base its decision to cheat on potential outputs of the protocol. Although this scenario is simplified and there is often a trade-off between output determination and cheating opportunities, the adversary potentially learns something about the output before deciding to cheat. This is a power that the adversary might have in all cut-and-choose-based protocols that do not further process the output of the semi-honest instances, also in the input-independent covert protocols compiled by Damgård et al. [DOS20].

Additionally, as we have highlighted above, the result of the precomputation typically does not leak any information about an input-dependent phase which uses this precomputation. Hence, in such offline-online protocols, the adversary has only little benefit of seeing the result of the precomputation before deciding to cheat or to act honestly.

Instead of adapting the notion of covert security, we could also focus on protocols that first obfuscate the output of the semi-honest instances, e.g., by secret sharing it, and then de-obfuscate the output in a later stage. However, this restricts the compiler to a special class of protocols but has basically the same effect. If we execute such a protocol with our notion of security up to the obfuscation stage but without de-obfuscating, the adversary learns the potential output, that is just some obfuscated output and therefore does not provide any benefit to the adversary's cheat decision. Next, we only have to ensure that the de-obfuscating is done in a malicious or covert secure way, which can be achieved, e.g., by committing to all output shares after the semi-honest instances and then open them when the cut-and-choose selection is done.

For the above reasons, we think it is a realistic modification to the covert notion to allow the adversary to learn the output of the function f before she decides to cheat or to act honestly. Note that the real-world adversary in cut-and-choose-based protocols does only see a list of potential outputs but the ideal-world adversary receives a single output which is going to be the protocol output if the adversary does not cheat or abort. However, we have chosen to be more generous to the adversary and model the ideal world like this in order to keep it simpler and more general. For the same reason we ignore the trade-off between output determination and cheating opportunities observed in real-world protocols.

In the rest of this work, we denote the trusted party computing function f in the ideal-world description by $\mathcal{F}_{\mathsf{Cov}}$.

2.2 Covert Security with Public Verifiability

As discussed in the introduction Asharov and Orlandi introduced to notion of *covert security with ϵ-deterrent and public verifiability* (PVC) in the two-party setting [AO12]. We give an extension of their formal definition to the multi-party setting in the following.

In addition to the covert secure protocol Π, we define two algorithms Blame and Judge. Blame takes as input the view of an honest party P_i after P_i outputs $\mathsf{corrupted}_j$ in the protocol execution for $j \in I$ and returns a certificate Cert, i.e., $\mathsf{Cert} := \mathsf{Blame}(\mathsf{view}_i)$. The Judge-algorithm takes as input a certificate Cert and outputs the identity id_j if the certificate is valid and states that party P_j behaved maliciously; otherwise, it returns none to indicate that the certificate was invalid.

Moreover, we require that the protocol Π is slightly adapted such that an honest party P_i computes $\mathsf{Cert} = \mathsf{Blame}(\mathsf{view}_i)$ and broadcasts it after cheating has been detected. We denote the modified protocol by Π'. Notice that due to this change, the adversary gets access to the certificate. By requiring simulatability, it is guaranteed that the certificate does not reveal any private information.

We now continue with the definition of covert security with ϵ-deterrent and public verifiability in the multi-party case.

Definition 2 (Covert security with ϵ-deterrent and public verifiability in the multi-party case (PVC-MPC)). *Let* f, Π', Blame, *and* Judge *be as above. The triple* (Π', Blame, Judge) securely computes f in the presence of covert adversaries with ϵ-deterrent and public verifiability *if the following conditions hold:*

1. *(Simulatability) The protocol Π' securely computes f in the presence of covert adversaries with ϵ-deterrent according to the strong explicit cheat formulation (see Definition 1).*
2. *(Public Verifiability) For every* PPT *adversary $\mathcal{A}$ corrupting parties P_i for $i \in I \subseteq [n]$, there exists a negligible function $\mu(\cdot)$ such that for all $(\bar{x}, z) \in (\{0,1\}^*)^{n+1}$ the following holds:*
If $\mathsf{OUTPUT}_j(\mathsf{REAL}_{\Pi,\mathcal{A}(z),I}(\bar{x}, 1^\kappa)) = \mathsf{corrupted}_i$ *for $j \in [n] \setminus I$ and $i \in I$ then:*

$$\Pr[\mathsf{Judge}(\mathsf{Cert}) = \mathsf{id}_i] > 1 - \mu(n),$$

where Cert *is the output certificate of the honest party P_j in the execution.*
3. *(Defamation Freeness) For every* PPT *adversary $\mathcal{A}$ corrupting parties P_i for $i \in I \subseteq [n]$, there exists a negligible function $\mu(\cdot)$ such that for all $(\bar{x}, z) \in (\{0,1\}^*)^{n+1}$ and all $j \in [n] \setminus I$:*

$$\Pr[\mathsf{Cert}^* \leftarrow \mathcal{A}; \mathsf{Judge}(\mathsf{Cert}^*) = \mathsf{id}_j] < \mu(n).$$

3 Preliminaries

3.1 Communication Model and Notion of Time

We assume the existence of authenticated channels between every pair of parties. Further, we assume synchronous communication between all parties participating in the protocol execution. This means the computation proceeds in rounds, where each party is aware of the current round. All messages sent in one round are guaranteed to arrive at the other parties at the end of this round. We further consider rushing adversaries which in each round are able to learn the messages sent by other parties before creating and sending their own messages. This allows an adversary to create messages depending on messages sent by other parties in the same round.

We denote the time for a single communication round by T_c. In order to model the time, it takes to compute algorithms, we use the approach presented by Wesolowski [Wes19]. Suppose the adversary works in computation model $\mathcal{M}$. The model defines a cost function C and a time-cost function T. $C(\mathcal{A}, x)$ denotes the overall cost to execute algorithm $\mathcal{A}$ on input x. Similar, the time-cost function $T(\mathcal{A}, x)$ abstracts the notion of time of running $\mathcal{A}(x)$. Considering circuits as computational model, one may consider the cost function denoting the overall number of gates of the circuit and the time-cost function being the circuit's depth.

Let $\mathcal{S}$ be an algorithm that for any RSA modulus N generated with respect to the security parameter κ on input N and some element $g \in \mathbb{Z}_N$ outputs the square of g. We define the time-cost function $\delta_{\mathsf{Sq}}(\kappa) = T(\mathcal{S}, (N, g))$, i.e., the time it takes for the adversary to compute a single squaring modulo N.

3.2 Verifiable Time-Lock Puzzle

Time-lock puzzles (TLP) provide a mean to encrypt messages to the future. The message is kept secret at least for some predefined time. The concept of a time-lock puzzle was first introduced by Rivest et al. [RSW96] presenting an elegant construction using sequential squaring modulo a composite integer $N = p \cdot q$, where p and q are primes. The puzzle is some $x \in \mathbb{Z}_N^*$ with corresponding solution $y = x^{2^T}$. The conjecture about this construction is that it requires T sequential squaring to find the solution. Based on the time to compute a single squaring modulo N, the hardness parameter $\mathcal{T}$ denotes the amount of time required to decrypt the message. (See Sect. 3.1 for a notion of time.)

We extend the notion of time-lock puzzle by a verifiability notion. This property allows a party who solved a puzzle to generate a proof which can be efficiently verified by any third party. Hence, a solver is able to create a verifiable statement about the solution of a puzzle. Boneh et al. [BBBF18] introduced the notion of verifiable delay functions (VDF). Similar to solving a TLP, the evaluation of a VDF on some input x takes a predefined number of sequential steps. Together with the output y, the evaluator obtains a short proof π. Any other party can use π to verify that y was obtained by evaluating the VDF on input x. Besides the sequential evaluation, a VDF provides no means to obtain the output more efficiently. Since we require a primitive that allows a party using some trapdoor information to perform the operation more efficiently, we cannot use a VDF but start with a TLP scheme and add verifiability using known techniques.

We present a definition of verifiable time-lock puzzles. We include a setup algorithm in the definition which generates public parameters required to efficiently construct a new puzzle. This way, we separate expensive computation required as a one-time setup from the generation of puzzles.

Definition 3. *Verifiable time-lock puzzle (VTLP) A verifiable time-lock puzzle scheme over some finite domain $\mathcal{S}$ consists of four probabilistic polynomial-time algorithms* $(\mathsf{TL.Setup}, \mathsf{TL.Generate}, \mathsf{TL.Solve}, \mathsf{TL.Verify})$ *defined as follows.*

- $(pp) \leftarrow \mathsf{TL.Setup}(1^\lambda, \mathcal{T})$ *takes as input the security parameter* 1^λ *and a hardness parameter* $\mathcal{T}$, *and outputs public parameter* pp.
- $p \leftarrow \mathsf{TL.Generate}(pp, s)$ *takes as input public parameters* pp *and a solution* $s \in \mathcal{S}$ *and outputs a puzzle* p.
- $(s, \pi) \leftarrow \mathsf{TL.Solve}(pp, p)$ *is a deterministic algorithm that takes as input public parameters* pp *and a puzzle* p *and outputs a solution* s *and a proof* π.
- $b := \mathsf{TL.Verify}(pp, p, s, \pi)$ *is a deterministic algorithm that takes as input public parameters* pp, *a puzzle* p, *a solution* s, *and a proof* π *and outputs a bit* b, *with* $b = 1$ *meaning valid and* $b = 0$ *meaning invalid. Algorithm* $\mathsf{TL.Verify}$ *must run in total time polynomial in* $\log \mathcal{T}$ *and* λ.

We require the following properties of a verifiable time-lock puzzle scheme.

Completeness. *For all* $\lambda \in \mathbb{N}$, *for all* $\mathcal{T}$, *for all* $pp \leftarrow \mathsf{TL.Setup}(1^\lambda, \mathcal{T})$, *and for all* s, *it holds that*

$$(s, \cdot) \leftarrow \mathsf{TL.Solve}(\mathsf{TL.Generate}(pp, s)).$$

Correctness. *For all* $\lambda \in \mathbb{N}$, *for all* $\mathcal{T}$, *for all* $pp \leftarrow \mathsf{TL.Setup}(1^\lambda, \mathcal{T})$, *for all* s, *and for all* $p \leftarrow \mathsf{TL.Generate}(pp, s)$, *if* $(s, \pi) \leftarrow \mathsf{TL.Solve}(p)$, *then*

$$\mathsf{TL.Verify}(pp, p, s, \pi) = 1.$$

Soundness. *For all* $\lambda \in \mathbb{N}$, *for all* $\mathcal{T}$, *and for all PPT algorithms* $\mathcal{A}$

$$\Pr\left[\begin{array}{c} \mathsf{TL.Verify}(pp, p', s', \pi') = 1 \\ s' \neq s \end{array} \middle| \begin{array}{c} pp \leftarrow \mathsf{TL.Setup}(1^\lambda, \mathcal{T}) \\ (p', s', \pi') \leftarrow \mathcal{A}(1^\lambda, pp, \mathcal{T}) \\ (s, \cdot) \leftarrow \mathsf{TL.Solve}(pp, p') \end{array}\right] \leq \mathsf{negl}(\lambda)$$

Security. *A VTLP scheme is secure with gap* $\epsilon < 1$ *if there exists a polynomial* $\tilde{\mathcal{T}}(\cdot)$ *such that for all polynomials* $\mathcal{T}(\cdot) \geq \tilde{\mathcal{T}}(\cdot)$ *and every polynomial-size adversary* $(\mathcal{A}_1, \mathcal{A}_2) = \{(\mathcal{A}_1, \mathcal{A}_2)_\lambda\}_{\lambda \in \mathbb{N}}$ *where the depth of* $\mathcal{A}_2$ *is bounded from above by* $\mathcal{T}^\epsilon(\lambda)$, *there exists a negligible function* $\mu(\cdot)$, *such that for all* $\lambda \in \mathbb{N}$ *it holds that*

$$\Pr\left[b \leftarrow \mathcal{A}_2(pp, p, \tau) \middle| \begin{array}{c} (\tau, s_0, s_1) \leftarrow \mathcal{A}_1(1^\lambda) \\ pp \leftarrow \mathsf{TL.Setup}(1^\lambda, \mathcal{T}(\lambda)) \\ b \xleftarrow{\$} \{0,1\} \\ p \leftarrow \mathsf{TL.Generate}(pp, s_b) \end{array}\right] \leq \frac{1}{2} + \mu(\lambda)$$

and $(s_0, s_1) \in \mathcal{S}^2$.

Although our compiler can be instantiated with any TLP scheme satisfying Definition 3, we present a concrete construction based on the RSW time-lock puzzle [RSW96]. We leave it to further research to investigate if a time-lock puzzle scheme matching our requirements, i.e., verifiability and efficient puzzle generation, can be constructed based on hidden order groups with public setup such as ideal class groups of imaginary quadratic fields [BW88] or Jacobians of hyperelliptic curves [DG20]. Due to the public setup, such constructions might be more efficient than our RSW-based solution.

In order to make the decrypted value verifiable we integrate the generation of a proof as introduced by Wesolowski [Wes19] for verifiable delay functions. The technique presented by Wesolowski provides a way to generate a small proof which can be efficiently verified. However, proof generation techniques from other verifiable delay functions, e.g., presented by Pietrzak [Pie19] can be used as well. The approach of Wesolowski utilizes a function bin, which maps an integer to its binary representation, and a hash function H_{prime} that maps any string to an element of $\mathsf{Primes}(2k)$. The set $\mathsf{Primes}(2k)$ contains the first 2^{2k} prime numbers, where k denotes the security level (typically 128, 192 or 256).

The $\mathsf{TL.Setup}$-algorithm takes the security and hardness parameter and outputs public parameter. This includes an RSA modulus of two strong primes, the number of sequential squares corresponding to the hardness parameter, and a base puzzle. The computation can be executed efficiently if the prime numbers are know. Afterwards, the primes are not needed anymore and can be thrown away. Note that any party knowing the factorization of the RSA modulus can efficiently solve puzzles. Hence, the TL.Setup-algorithm should be executed in a trusted way.

The TL.Generate-algorithm allows any party to generate a time-lock puzzle over some secret s. In the construction given below, we assume s to be an element in $\mathbb{Z}_N^*$. However, one can use a hybrid approach where the secret is encrypted with some symmetric key which is then mapped to an element in $\mathbb{Z}_N^*$. This allows the generator to time-lock large secrets as well. Note that the puzzle generation can be done efficiently and does not depend on the hardness parameter $\mathcal{T}$.

The TL.Solve-algorithm solves a time-lock puzzle p by performing sequential squaring, where the number of steps depend on the hardness parameter $\mathcal{T}$. Along with the solution, it outputs a verifiable proof π. This proof is used as additional input to the TL.Verify-algorithm outputting true if the given secret was time-locked by the given puzzle.

We state the formal definition of our construction next.

Construction Verifiable Time-Lock Puzzle

$\mathsf{TL.Setup}(1^\lambda, \mathcal{T})$:

- Sample two strong primes (p, q) and set $N := p \cdot q$.
- Set $\mathcal{T}' := \mathcal{T}/\delta_{\mathsf{Sq}}(\lambda)$.
- Sample uniform $\tilde{g} \xleftarrow{\$} \mathbb{Z}_N^*$ and set $g := -\tilde{g}^2(\mod N)$.
- Compute $h := g^{2^{\mathcal{T}'}}$, which can be optimized by reducing $2^{\mathcal{T}'}$ module $\phi(N)$ first.
- Set $Z := (g, h)$.
- Output $(\mathcal{T}', N, Z)$.

$\mathsf{TL.Generate}(pp, s)$:

- Parse $pp := (\mathcal{T}', N, Z)$ and $Z := (g, h)$.
- Sample uniform $r \xleftarrow{\$} \{1, \ldots, N^2\}$.
- Compute $g^* := g^r$ and $h^* := h^r$.
- Set $c^* := h^* \cdot s \mod N$.
- Output $p := (g^*, c^*)$.

$\mathsf{TL.Solve}(pp, p)$:

- Parse $pp := (\mathcal{T}', N, Z)$ and $p := (g^*, c^*)$.
- Compute $h := g^{*2^{\mathcal{T}'}}(\mod N)$ by repeated squaring.
- Compute $s := \frac{c^*}{h} \mod N$ as the solution.
- Compute $\ell = H_{\mathsf{prime}}(\mathsf{bin}(g^*)||\star||\mathsf{bin}(s)) \in \mathsf{Primes}(2k)$ as the challenge.
- Compute $\pi = g^{*\lfloor 2^{\mathcal{T}'}/\ell \rfloor}$ as the proof.
- Output (s, π).

$\mathsf{TL.Verify}(pp, p, s, \pi)$:

- Parse $pp := (\mathcal{T}', N, Z)$.

- Parse $p := (g^*, c^*)$.
- Compute $\ell = H_{\mathsf{prime}}(\mathsf{bin}(g^*)||\star||\mathsf{bin}(s)) \in \mathsf{Primes}(2k)$ as the challenge.
- Compute $r = 2^{T'} \mod \ell$.
- Compute $h' = \pi^{\ell} g^{*r}$.
- Compute $s' := \frac{c^*}{h'}$.
- If $s = s'$, output 1, otherwise output 0.

The security of the presented construction is based on the conjecture that it requires T' sequential squarings to solve a puzzle. Moreover, the soundness of the proof generation is based on the number-theoretic assumption that it is hard to find the ℓ-th root modulo an RSA modulus N of an integer $x \notin \{-1, 0, +1\}$ where ℓ is uniformly sampled from $\mathsf{Primes}(2k)$ and the factorization of N is unknown. See [Wes19] for a detailed description of the security assumption.

3.3 Commitment

Our protocol makes use of an extractable commitment scheme which is *computationally binding and hiding.* For ease of description, we assume the scheme to be non-interactive. We will use the notation $(c, d) \leftarrow \mathsf{Commit}(m)$ to commit to message m, where c is the commitment value and d denotes the decommitment or opening value. Similarly, we use $m' \leftarrow \mathsf{Open}(c, d)$ to open commitment c with opening value d to $m' = m$ or $m' = \bot$ in case of incorrect opening. The extractability property allows the simulator to extract the committed message m and the opening value d from the commitment c by using some trapdoor information.

Such a scheme can be implemented in the random oracle model by defining $\mathsf{Commit}(x) = H(i, x, r)$ where i is the identity of the committer, $H : \{0,1\}^* \to \{0,1\}^{2\kappa}$ is a random oracle and $r \xleftarrow{\$} \{0,1\}^{\kappa}$.

3.4 Signature Scheme

We use a signature scheme $(\mathsf{Gen}, \mathsf{Sign}, \mathsf{Verify})$ that is *existentially unforgeable under chosen-message attacks.* Before the start of our protocol, each party executes the Gen-algorithm to obtain a key pair $(\mathsf{pk}, \mathsf{sk})$. While the secret key sk is kept private, we assume that each other party is aware of the party's public key pk.

3.5 Semi-honest Base Protocol

Our compiler is designed to transform a semi-honest secure n-party protocol with no private input tolerating $n-1$ corruptions, Π_{SH}, that computes a probabilistic function $(y^1, \dots, y^n) \leftarrow f()$, where y^i is the output for party P_i, into a publicly verifiable covert protocol, Π_{PVC}, that computes the same function. In order to compile Π_{SH}, it is necessary that all parties that engage in the protocol Π_{SH} receive a protocol transcript, which is the same if all parties act honestly. This means that there needs to be a fixed ordering for the sent messages and that each message needs to be sent to all involved parties[2].

We stress that any protocol can be adapted to fulfill the compilation requirements. Adding a fixed order to the protocol messages is trivial and just a matter of specification. Furthermore, parties can send all of their outgoing messages to all other parties without harming the security. This is due to the fact, that the protocol tolerates $n-1$ corruptions which implies that the adversary is allowed to learn all messages sent by the honest party anyway. Note that the transferred messages do not need to be securely broadcasted, because our compiler requires the protocol to produce a consistent transcript only if all parties act honestly.

3.6 Coin Tossing Functionality

We utilize a maliciously secure coin tossing functionality $\mathcal{F}_{\mathsf{coin}}$ parameterized with the security parameter κ and the number of parties n. The functionality receives ok_i from each party P_i for $i \in [n]$ and outputs a random κ-bit string $\mathsf{seed} \xleftarrow{\$} \{0,1\}^\kappa$ to all parties.

Functionality $\mathcal{F}_{\mathsf{coin}}$

Inputs: Each party P_i with $i \in [n]$ inputs ok_i.

- Sample $\mathsf{seed} \xleftarrow{\$} \{0,1\}^\kappa$.
- Send seed to $\mathcal{A}$.
  - If $\mathcal{A}$ returns abort, send abort to all honest parties and stop.
  - Otherwise, send seed to all honest parties.

3.7 Puzzle Generation Functionality

The maliciously secure puzzle generation functionality $\mathcal{F}_{\mathsf{PG}}$ is parameterized with the computational security parameter κ, the number of involved parties n, the cut-and-choose parameter t and public TLP parameters pp. It receives a coin share r^i, a puzzle randomness share u^i, and the seed-share decommitments for all instances $\{d_j^i\}_{j \in [t]}$ as input from each party P_i. $\mathcal{F}_{\mathsf{PG}}$ calculates the random coin r and the puzzle randomness u using the shares of all parties. Then, it generates a time-lock puzzle p of r and all seed-share decommitments expect the ones with index r. In the first output round it sends p to all parties. In the second output round it reveals the values locked within p to all parties. As we assume a rushing adversary, $\mathcal{A}$ receives the outputs first in both rounds and can decide if the other parties should receive the outputs as well.

The functionality $\mathcal{F}_{\mathsf{PG}}$ can be instantiated with a general purpose maliciously secure MPC-protocol such as the ones specified by [DKL+13] or [YWZ20].

[2] This requirement is inherent to all known publicly verifiable covert secure protocols.

Functionality $\mathcal{F}_{\mathsf{PG}}$

Inputs: Each party P_i with $i \in [n]$ inputs $(r^i, u^i, \{d^i_j\}_{j\in[t]})$, where $r^i \in [t]$, $u^i \in \{0,1\}^\kappa$, and $d^i_j \in \{0,1\}^\kappa$.

- Compute $r := \sum_{i=1}^n r^i \mod t$ and $u := \bigoplus_{i=1}^n u^i$.
- Generate puzzle $p \leftarrow \mathsf{TL.Generate}(pp, (r, \{d^i_j\}_{i\in[n],j\in[t]\setminus r}))$ using randomness u.
- Send p to $\mathcal{A}$.
  - If $\mathcal{A}$ returns abort, send abort to all honest parties and stop.
  - Otherwise, send p to all honest parties.[3]
- Upon receiving continue from each party, send $(r, \{d^i_j\}_{i\in[n],j\in[t]\setminus r})$ to $\mathcal{A}$.
  - If $\mathcal{A}$ returns abort or some party does not send continue, send abort to all honest parties and stop.
  - Otherwise, send $(r, \{d^i_j\}_{i\in[n],j\in[t]\setminus r})$ to all honest parties.

4 PVC Compiler

In the following, we present our compiler for multi-party protocols with no private input from semi-honest to publicly verifiable covert security. We start with presenting a distributed seed computation which is used as subprotocol in our compiler. Next, we state the detailed description of our compiler. Lastly, we provide information about the Blame- and Judge-algorithm required by the notion of publicly verifiable covert security.

4.1 Distributed Seed Computation

The execution of the semi-honest protocol instances Π_{SH} within our PVC compiler requires each party to use a random tape that is uniform at random. In order to ensure this requirement, the parties execute several instances of a distributed seed computation subprotocol Π_{SG} at the beginning. During this subprotocol, each party P_h selects a uniform κ-bit string as private seed share $\mathsf{seed}^{(1,h)}$. Additionally, P_h and all other parties get uniform κ-bit strings $\{\mathsf{seed}^{(2,i)}\}_{i\in[n]}$, which are the public seed shares of all parties. The randomness used by P_h in the semi-honest protocol will be derived from $\mathsf{seed}^h := \mathsf{seed}^{(1,h)} \oplus \mathsf{seed}^{(2,h)}$. This way seed^h is distributed uniformly. Note that if protocol Π_{SH} is semi-malicious instead of semi-honest secure then each party may choose the randomness arbitrarily and there is no need to run the seed generation.

As the output, party P_h obtains its own private seed, commitments to all private seeds, a decommitment for its own private seed, and all public seed shares. We state the detailed protocol steps next. The protocol is executed by each party P_h, parameterized with the number of parties n and the security parameter κ.

[3] The honest parties receive p or abort in the same communication round as $\mathcal{A}$.

Protocol Π_{SG}

(a) **Commit-phase**
Party P_h chooses a uniform κ-bit string $\mathsf{seed}^{(1,h)}$, sets $(c^h, d^h) \leftarrow \mathsf{Commit}(\mathsf{seed}^{(1,h)})$, and sends c^h to all parties.

(b) **Public coin-phase**
For each $i \in [n]$, party P_h sends ok to $\mathcal{F}_{\mathsf{coin}}$ and receives $\mathsf{seed}^{(2,i)}$.
Output
If P_h has not received all messages in the expected communication rounds or any $\mathsf{seed}^{(2,i)} = \bot$, it sends abort to all parties and outputs abort.
Otherwise, it outputs $(\mathsf{seed}^{(1,h)}, d^h, \{\mathsf{seed}^{(2,i)}, c^i\}_{i \in [n]})$.

4.2 The PVC Compiler

Starting with a n-party semi-honest secure protocol Π_{SH} we compile a publicly verifiable covert secure protocol Π_{PVC}. The compiler works for protocols that receive no private input.

The compiler uses a signature scheme, a verifiable time-lock puzzle scheme, and a commitment scheme as building blocks. Moreover, the communication model is as defined in Sect. 3.1. We assume each party generated a signature key pair $(\mathsf{sk}, \mathsf{pk})$ and all parties know the public keys of the other parties. Furthermore, we suppose the setup of the verifiable time-lock puzzle scheme $\mathsf{TL.Setup}$ was executed in a trusted way beforehand. This means in particular that all parties are aware of the public parameters pp. We stress that this setup needs to be executed once and may be used by many protocol executions. The hardness parameter $\mathcal{T}$ used as input to the $\mathsf{TL.Setup}$-algorithm needs to be defined as $\mathcal{T} > 2 \cdot T_c$, where T_c denotes the time for a single communication round (see Sect. 3.1). In particular, the hardness parameter is independent of the complexity of Π_{SH}.

From a high-level perspective, our compiler works in five phases. At the beginning, all parties jointly execute the seed generation to set up seeds from which the randomness in the semi-honest protocol instances is derived. Second, the parties execute t instances of the semi-honest protocol Π_{SH}. By executing several instances, the parties' honest behavior can be later on checked in all but one instance. Since checking reveals the confidential outputs of the other parties, there must be one instance that is unchecked. The index of this one is jointly selected in a random way in the third phase. Moreover, publicly verifiable evidence is generated such that an honest party can blame any malicious behavior afterwards. To this end, we use the puzzle generation functionality $\mathcal{F}_{\mathsf{PG}}$ to generate a time-lock puzzle first. Next, each party signs all information required for the other parties to blame this party. In the fourth phase, the parties either honestly reveal secret information for all but one semi-honest execution or abort. In case of abort, the honest parties execute the fifth phase. By solving the time-lock puzzle, the honest parties obtain the required information to create a certificate about malicious behavior. Since this phase is only required to be executed in case any party aborted before revealing the information, we call this the pessimistic case. We stress that no honest party is required to solve a time-lock puzzle in case all parties behave honestly.

A corrupted party may cheat in two different ways in the compiled protocol. Either the party inputs decommitment values into the puzzle generation functionality which open the commitments created during the seed generation to $\perp$ or the party misbehaved in the execution of Π_{SH}. The later means that a party uses different randomness than derived from the seeds generated at the beginning.

The first cheat attempt may be detected in two ways. In the optimistic execution, all parties receive the inputs to $\mathcal{F}_{\mathsf{PG}}$ and can verify that opening the commitments is successful. In the pessimistic case, solving the time-lock puzzle reveals the input to $\mathcal{F}_{\mathsf{PG}}$. Since we do not want the Judge to solve the puzzle itself, we provide a proof along with the solution of the time-lock puzzle. To this end, we require a verifiable time-lock puzzle as modeled in Sect. 3. Even in the optimistic case, if an honest party detects cheating, the time-lock puzzle needs to be solved in order to generate a publicly verifiable certificate.

If all decommitments open the commitments successfully, an honest party can recompute the seeds used by all other parties in an execution of Π_{SH} and re-run the execution. The resulting transcript is compared with the one signed by all parties beforehand. In case any party misbehaved, a publicly verifiable certificate can be created. For the sake of exposition, we compress the detection of malicious behavior and the generation of the certificate into the Blame-algorithm.

The protocol defined as follows is executed by each honest party P_h.

Protocol Π_{PVC}

Public input: All parties agree on κ, n, t, Π_{SH} and pp and know all parties' public keys $\{pk_i\}_{i\in[n]}$.
Private input: P_h knows its own secret key sk_h.

Distributed seed computation:
We abuse notation here and assume that the parties execute the seed generation protocol from above.

1. For each instance $j \in [t]$ party P_h interacts with all other parties to receive

$$(\mathsf{seed}_j^{(1,h)}, d_j^h, \{\mathsf{seed}_j^{(2,i)}, c_j^i\}_{i\in[n]}) \leftarrow \Pi_{\mathsf{SG}}$$

and computes $\mathsf{seed}_j^h := \mathsf{seed}_j^{(1,h)} \oplus \mathsf{seed}_j^{(2,h)}$.

Semi-honest protocol execution:

2. Party P_h engages in t instances of the protocol Π_{SH} with all other parties. In the j-th instance, party P_h uses randomness derived from seed_j^h and receives a transcript and output:

$$(\mathsf{trans}_j, y_j^h) \leftarrow \Pi_{\mathsf{SH}}.$$

Create publicly verifiable evidence:

3. Party P_h samples a coin share $r^h \xleftarrow{\$} [t]$, a randomness share $u^h \xleftarrow{\$} \{0,1\}^\kappa$, sends the message $(r^h, u^h, \{d_j^h\}_{j\in[t]})$ to $\mathcal{F}_{\mathsf{PG}}$ and receives time-lock puzzle p as response.
4. For each $j \in [t]$, Party P_h creates a signature $\sigma_j^h \leftarrow \mathsf{Sign}_{\mathsf{sk}_h}(\mathsf{data}_j)$, where the signed data is defined as

$$\mathsf{data}_j := (h, j, \{\mathsf{seed}_j^{(2,i)}\}_{i\in[n]}, \{c_j^i\}_{i\in[n]}, p, \mathsf{trans}_j).$$

   P_h broadcasts its signatures and verifies the received signatures.

Optimistic case:

5. If any of the following cases happens
   - P_h has not received valid messages in the first protocol steps in the expected communication round.
   - $\mathcal{F}_{\mathsf{PG}}$ returned abort, or
   - any other party has sent abort

   party P_h broadcasts and outputs abort.
6. Otherwise, P_h sends $\mathsf{continue}_h$ to $\mathcal{F}_{\mathsf{PG}}$, receives $(r, \{d_j^{*i}\}_{i\in[n],j\in[t]\setminus r})$ as response and calculates

$$(m, \mathsf{cert}) := \mathsf{Blame}(\mathsf{view}^h)$$

   where view^h is the view of P_h.
   If $\mathsf{cert} \neq \perp$, broadcast cert and output $\mathsf{corrupted}_m$. Otherwise, P_h outputs y_r^h.

Pessimistic case:

7. If $\mathcal{F}_{\mathsf{PG}}$ returned abort in step 6, P_h solves the time-lock puzzle

$$((r, \{d_j^{*i}\}_{i\in[n],j\in[t]\setminus r}), \pi) := \mathsf{TL.Solve}(pp, p)$$

   and calculates

$$(m, \mathsf{cert}) := \mathsf{Blame}(\mathsf{view}^h)$$

   where view^h is the view of P_h.
   If $\mathsf{cert} \neq \perp$, broadcast cert and output $\mathsf{corrupted}_m$. Otherwise, output abort.

4.3 Blame-Algorithm

Our PVC compiler uses an algorithm Blame in order to verify the behavior of all parties in the opened protocol instances and to generate a certificate of misbehavior if cheating has been detected. It takes the view of a party as input and outputs the index of the corrupted party in addition to the certificate. If there are several malicious parties the algorithm selects the one with the minimal index.

Algorithm Blame

On input the view view of a party which contains:

- public parameters (n, t)
- public seed shares $\{\mathsf{seed}_j^{(2,i)}\}_{i\in[n]}$
- shared coin r
- private seed share commitments and decommitments $\{c_j^i, d_j^i\}_{i\in[n],j\in[t]\setminus r}$
- additional certificate information $(\{\mathsf{pk}_j\}_{i\in[n]}, \{\mathsf{data}_j\}_{j\in[t]}, \pi, \{\sigma_j^i\}_{i\in[n],j\in[t]})$

do:

1. Calculate $\mathsf{seed}_j^{(1,i)} := \mathsf{Open}(c_j^i, d_j^i)$ for each $i \in [n], j \in [t] \setminus r$.
2. Let $M_1 := \{(i,j) \in ([n], [t] \setminus r) : \mathsf{seed}_j^{(1,i)} = \bot\}$. If $M_1 \neq \emptyset$, choose the tuple $(m,l) \in M_1$ with minimal m and l, prioritized by m, compute $(\cdot, \pi) := \mathsf{TL.Solve}(pp, p)$, if $\pi = \bot$, set $\mathsf{cert} := (\mathsf{pk}_m, \mathsf{data}_j, \pi, r, \{d_j^i\}_{i\in[n],j\in[t]\setminus r}, \sigma_l^m)$ and output (m, cert).
3. Set $\mathsf{seed}_j^i := \mathsf{seed}_j^{(1,i)} \oplus \mathsf{seed}_j^{(2,i)}$ for all $i \in [n]$ and $j \in [t] \setminus r$.
4. Re-run Π_{SH} for all $j \in [t] \setminus r$ by simulating the view of all other parties: In the j-th instance simulate all parties P_i with randomness seed_j^i for $i \in [n]$ and receive $(\mathsf{trans}'_j, \cdot)$.
5. Let $M_2 := \{j \in [t] \setminus r : \mathsf{trans}'_j \neq \mathsf{trans}_j\}$. If $M_2 \neq \emptyset$, determine the minimal index m such that P_m is the first party that has deviated from the protocol description in an instance $l \in M_2$. If P_m has deviated from the protocol description in several instances $l \in M_2$, choose the smallest such l. Then, set $\mathsf{cert} := (\mathsf{pk}_m, \mathsf{data}_l, \{d_l^i\}_{i\in[n]}, \sigma_l^m)$ and output (m, cert).
6. Output $(0, \bot)$.

4.4 Judge-Algorithm

The Judge-algorithm receives the certificate and outputs either the identity of the corrupted party or $\bot$. The execution of this algorithm requires no interaction with the parties participating in the protocol execution. Therefore, it can also be executed by any third party which possesses a certificate cert. If the output is pk_m for $m \in [n]$, the executing party is convinced that party P_m misbehaved during the protocol execution. The Judge-algorithm is parameterized with n, t, pp, and Π_{SH}.

Algorithm Judge(cert)

Inconsistency certificate:
On input $\mathsf{cert} = (\mathsf{pk}_m, \mathsf{data}, \pi, r, \{d_j^i\}_{i\in[n],j\in[t]\setminus r}, \sigma_l^m)$ do:

- If $\mathsf{Verify}_{\mathsf{pk}_m}(\mathsf{data}; \sigma_l^m) = \bot$, output $\bot$.
- Parse data to $(m, l, \cdot, \{c_l^i\}_{i\in[n]}, p, \cdot)$.

- If $\mathsf{TL.Verify}(pp, p, (r, \{d_j^i\}_{i,j}), \pi) = 0$ output $\perp$.
- If $r = l$, output $\perp$.
- If $\mathsf{Open}(c_l^m, d_l^m) \neq \perp$, output $\perp$. Else output pk_m.

Deviation certificate:
On input $\mathsf{cert} = (\mathsf{pk}_m, \mathsf{data}, \{d_l^i\}_{i\in[n]}, \sigma_l^m)$.

- If $\mathsf{Verify}_{\mathsf{pk}_m}(\mathsf{data}; \sigma_l^m) = \perp$, output $\perp$.
- Parse data to $(m, l, \{\mathsf{seed}_l^{(2,i)}\}_{i\in[n]}, \{c_l^i\}_{i\in[n]}, \cdot, \mathsf{trans}_l)$.
- Set $\mathsf{seed}_l^{(1,i)} \leftarrow \mathsf{Open}(c_l^i, d_l^i)$ for each $i \in [n]$. If any $\mathsf{seed}_l^{(1,i)} = \perp$, output $\perp$.
- Set $\mathsf{seed}_l^i := \mathsf{seed}_l^{(1,i)} \oplus \mathsf{seed}_l^{(2,i)}$ for each i.
- Simulate Π_{SH} using the seeds seed_l^i as randomness of party P_i and get result $(\mathsf{trans}_l', \cdot)$.
- If $\mathsf{trans}_l' = \mathsf{trans}_l$, output $\perp$. Otherwise, determine the index m' of the first party that has deviated from the protocol description. If $m \neq m'$, output $\perp$. Otherwise, output pk_m.

Ill formatted: If the cert cannot be parsed to neither of the two above cases, output $(\perp)$.

5 Security

In this section, we show the security of the compiled protocol described in Sect. 4. To this end, we state the security guarantee in Theorem 1 and prove its correctness in the following.

Theorem 1. *Let Π_{SH} be a n-party protocol, receiving no private inputs, which is secure against a passive adversary that corrupts up to $n-1$ parties. Let the signature scheme* $(\mathsf{Gen}, \mathsf{Sign}, \mathsf{Verify})$ *be existentially unforgettable under chosen-message attacks and let the verifiable time-lock puzzle scheme* TL *be secure with hardness parameter $\mathcal{T} > 2 \cdot T_c$. Let* $(\mathsf{Commit}, \mathsf{Open})$ *be an extractable commitment scheme which is computationally binding and hiding. Then protocol Π_{PVC} along with algorithms* Blame *and* Judge *is secure against a covert adversary that corrupts up to $n-1$ parties with deterrence $\epsilon = 1 - \frac{1}{t}$ and public verifiability according to Definition 2 in the $(\mathcal{F}_{\mathsf{coin}}, \mathcal{F}_{\mathsf{PG}})$-hybrid model.*[4]

Proof. We prove security of the compiled protocol Π_{PVC} by showing simulatability, public verifiability, and defamation freeness according to Definition 2 separately.

5.1 Simulatability

In order to prove that Π_{PVC} meets covert security with ϵ-deterrent, we define an ideal-world simulator $\mathcal{S}$ using the adversary $\mathcal{A}$ in a black-box way as a subroutine

[4] See Sect. 3.1, for details on the notion of time and the communication model.

and playing the role of the parties corrupted by $\mathcal{A}$ when interacting with the ideal covert-functionality $\mathcal{F}_{\mathsf{Cov}}$.

The simulator and the proof that the joint distribution of the honest parties' outputs and the view of $\mathcal{A}$ in the ideal world is computationally indistinguishable from the honest parties' outputs and the view of $\mathcal{A}$ in the real world are given in the full version of the paper.

5.2 Public Verifiability

We first argue that an adversary is not able to perform what we call a *detection dependent abort.* This means that once an adversary learns if its cheating will be detected, it can no longer prevent honest parties from generating a certificate.

In order to see this, note that withholding valid signatures by corrupted parties in step 4 results in an abort of all honest parties. In contrast, if all honest parties receive valid signatures from all other parties in step 4, then they are guaranteed to obtain the information encapsulated in the time-lock puzzle, i.e., the coin r and the decommitments of all parties $\{d_j^i\}_{i\in[n],j\in[t]\setminus r}$. Either, all parties jointly trigger the puzzle generation functionality $\mathcal{F}_{\mathsf{PG}}$ to output the values or in case any corrupted party aborts, an honest party can solve the time-lock puzzle without interaction. Thus, it is not possible for a rushing adversary that gets the output of $\mathcal{F}_{\mathsf{PG}}$ in step 6 first, to prevent the other parties from learning it at some time as well. Moreover, the adversary also cannot extract the values from the puzzles before making the decision if it wants to continue or abort, as the decision has to be made in time smaller than the time required to solve the puzzle. Thus, the adversary's decision to continue or abort is independent from the coin r and therefore independent from the event of being detected or not.

Secondly, we show that the Judge-algorithm will accept a certificate, created by an honest party, expect with negligible probability. Assume without loss of generality that some malicious party P_m has cheated, cheating has been detected and a certificate (blaming party P_m) has been generated. As we have two types of certificates, we will look at them separately.

If an honest party outputs an *inconsistency certificate*, it has received an inconsistent commitment-opening pair (c_l^m, d_l^m) for some $l \neq r$. The value c_l^m is signed directly by P_m and d_l^m indirectly via the signed time-lock puzzle p. Hence, Judge can verify the signatures and detect the inconsistent commitment of P_m as well. Note that due to the verifiability of our time-lock construction, the Judge-algorithm does not have to solve the time-lock puzzle itself but just needs to verify a given solution. This enables the algorithm to be executed efficiently.

If an honest party outputs a *deviation certificate*, it has received consistent openings for all $j \neq r$ from all other parties, but party P_m was the first party who deviated from the specification of Π_{SH} in some instance $l \in [t] \setminus r$. Since Π_{SH} requires no input from the parties, deviating from its specification means using different randomness than derived from the seeds generated at the beginning of the compiled protocol. As P_m has signed the transcript trans_l, the private seed-commitments of all parties $\{c_l^i\}_{i\in[n]}$, the public seeds $\{\mathsf{seed}^{(2,i)}\}_{i\in[n]}$, and the certificate contains the valid openings $\{d_l^i\}_{i\in[n]}$, the Judge-algorithm can verify that P_m was the first party who misbehaved in instance l the same way the honest party does. Note that it is not necessary for Judge to verify that $j \neq r$, because the certificate generating party can only gain valid openings $\{d_l^i\}_{i \in [n]}$ for $j \neq r$.

5.3 Defamation Freeness

Assume, without loss of generality, that some honest party P_h is blamed by the adversary. We show defamation freeness for the two types of certificates separately via a reduction to the security of the commitment scheme, the signature scheme and the time-lock puzzle scheme.

First, assume there is a valid *inconsistency certificate* cert^* blaming P_h. This means that there is a valid signatures of P_h on a commitment c_j^{*h} and a time-lock puzzle p^* that has a solution s^* which contains an opening d_j^{*h} such that $\mathsf{Open}(c_j^{*h}, d_j^{*h}) = \bot$ and $j \neq r$. As P_h is honest, P_h only signs a commitment c_j^{*h} which equals the commitment honestly generated by P_h during the seed generation. We call such a c_j^{*h} *correct.* Thus, c_j^{*h} is either correct or the adversary can forge signatures. Similar, P_h does only sign the puzzle p^* received by $\mathcal{F}_{\mathsf{PG}}$. This puzzle is generated on the opening value provided by all parties. Since P_h is honest, correct opening values are inserted. Therefore, the signed puzzle p^* either contains the correct opening value or the adversary can forge signatures. Due to the security guarantees of the puzzle, the adversary has to either provide the correct solution s^* or can break the soundness of the time-lock puzzle scheme. To sum it up, an adversary creating a valid *inconsistency certificate* contradicts to the security assumptions specified in Theorem 1.

Second, assume there is a valid *deviation certificate* cert^* blaming P_h. This means, there is a protocol transcript trans_j^* in which P_h is the first party that has sent a message which does not correspond to the next-message function of Π_{SH} and the randomness, seed_j^h used by the judge to simulate P_h. As P_h is honest, either trans^* or seed_j^h needs to be incorrect. Also, P_h does not create a signature for an invalid trans^*. Thus, trans^* is either correct or the adversary can forge signatures. The seed_j^h is calculated as $\mathsf{seed}_j^h := \mathsf{seed}_j^{(1,h)} \oplus \mathsf{seed}_j^{(2,h)}$. The public seed $\mathsf{seed}_j^{(2,h)}$ is signed by P_h and provided directly. The private seed of P_h is provided via a commitment-opening pair (c_j^h, d_j^h), where c_j^h is signed by P_h. As above, c_j^h and $\mathsf{seed}_j^{(2,h)}$ are either correct or the adversary can forge signatures. Similar, d_j^h is either correct or the adversary can break the binding property of the commitment scheme. If the certificate contains correct $(\mathsf{trans}_j^*, c_j^h, d_j^h, \mathsf{seed}_j^{(2,h)})$ the certificate is not valid. Thus, when creating an accepting cert^*, the adversary has either broken the signature or the commitment scheme which contradicts to the assumption of Theorem 1.

□

6 Evaluation

6.1 Efficiency of Our Compiler

In Sect. 4, we presented a generic compiler for transforming input-independent multi-party computation protocols with semi-honest security into protocols that offer covert security with public verifiability. We elaborate on efficiency parameters of our construction in the following.

The deterrence factor $\epsilon = \frac{t-1}{t}$ only depends on the number of semi-honest protocol executions t. In particular, ϵ is independent of the number of parties. This property allows for achieving the same deterrence factor for a fixed number of semi-honest executions while the number of parties increases. Our compiler therefore facilitates secure computation with a large number of parties. Furthermore, the deterrence factor grows with the number of semi-honest instances (t), similar to previous work based on cut-and-choose (e.g., [AL07, AO12, DOS20]). Concretely, this means that for only five semi-honest instances, our compiler achieves a cheating detection probability of 80%. Moreover, the semi-honest instances are independent of each other and, hence, can be executed in parallel. This means, that the communication and computation complexity in comparison to a semi-honest protocol increases by factor t. However, our compiler preserves the round complexity of the semi-honest protocol. Hence, it is particularly useful for settings and protocols in which the round complexity constitutes the major efficiency bottleneck. Similarly, the requirement of sending all messages to all parties further increases the communication overhead by a factor of $n - 1$ but does not affect the round complexity. Since this requirement is inherent to all known publicly verifiable covert secure protocols, e.g., [DOS20], these protocols incur a similar communication overhead.

While our compiler requires a maliciously secure puzzle generation functionality, we stress that the complexity of the puzzle generation is independent of the cost of the semi-honest protocol. Therefore, the relative overhead of the puzzle generation shrinks for more complex semi-honest protocols. One application where our result may be particular useful is for the preprocessing phase of multi-party computation, e.g., protocols for generating garbled circuits or multiplication triples. In such protocols, one can generate several circuits resp. triples that are used in several online instances but require just one puzzle generation.

For the sake of concreteness, we constructed a boolean circuit for the puzzle generation functionality and estimated its complexity in terms of the number of AND-gates. The construction follows a naive design and should not constitute an efficient solution but should give a first impression on the circuit complexity. We present some intuition on how to improve the circuit complexity afterwards.

We utilize the RSW VTLP construction described in Sect. 3.2 with a hybrid construction, in which a symmetric encryption key is locked within the actual time-lock puzzle and is used to encrypt the actual secret. Note that the RSW VTLP is not optimized for MPC scenarios. Since our compiler can be instantiated with an arbitrary VTLP satisfying Definition 3, any achievements in the area of MPC-friendly TLP can result into an improved puzzle generation functionality for our compiler. To instantiate the symmetric encryption operation, we use the LowMC [ARS+15] cipher, an MPC-friendly cipher tailored for boolean circuits.

Let n be the number of parties, t being the number of semi-honest instances, κ denoting the computational security parameter, and N represents the RSA modulus used for the RSW VTLP. We use the notation $|x|$ to denote the bit length of x. The total number of AND-gates of our naive circuit is calculated as follows:

$$\begin{aligned}&(n-1)\cdot(11|t|+22\,N|+12)\\&+nt\cdot(4|t|+2\kappa+755)\\&+192\,N|^3+112\,N|^2+22|N|\end{aligned}$$

It is easy to see that the number of AND-gates is linear in both n and t. The most expensive part of the puzzle generation is the computation of two exponentiations required for the RSW VTLP, since the number of required AND-gates is cubic in $|N|$ for an exponentiation. However, we can slightly adapt our puzzle generation functionality and protocol to remove these exponentiations from the maliciously secure puzzle generation protocol. For the sake of brevity, we just give an intuition here.

Instead of performing the exponentiations g^u and h^u required for the puzzle creation within the puzzle generation functionality, we let each party P_i input a 0-puzzle consisting of the two values $g_i = g^{u_i}$ and $h_i = h^{u_i}$. The products of all g_i respectively h_i are used as g^* and h^* for the VTLP computation. Since we replace the exponentiations with multiplications, the number of AND-gates is quadratic instead of cubic in $|N|$.

Note that this modification enables a malicious party to modify the resulting puzzle by inputting a non-zero puzzle. Intuitively, the attacker can render the puzzle invalid such that no honest party can create a valid certificate or the puzzle can be modified such that a corrupted party can create a valid certificate defaming an honest party. Concretely, one possible attack is to input inconsistent values g_i and h_i, i.e., to use different exponents for the two exponentiations. As such an attack must be executed without knowledge of the coin r, it is sufficient to detect invalid inputs and consider such behavior as an early abort. To this end, parties have to provide u_i to the puzzle generation functionality and the functionality outputs $u = \Sigma\, u_i$, g^* and h^* in the second output round together with the coin and the seed openings. By comparing if $g^* = g^u$ and $h^* = h^u$, each party can check the validity of the puzzle. Finally, we need to ensure that a manipulated puzzle cannot be used to create an inconsistency certificate blaming an honest party. Such false accusation can easily be prevented, e.g., by adding some zero padding to the value inside the puzzle such that any invalid puzzle input renders the whole puzzle invalid.

6.2 Comparison with Prior Work

To the best of our knowledge, our work is the first to provide a fully specified publicly verifiable multi-party computation protocol against covert adversaries. Hence, we cannot compare to existing protocols directly. However, Damgård et al. [DOS20] have recently presented two compilers for constructing publicly verifiable covert secure protocols from semi-honest secure protocols in the two-party setting, one for input-independent and one for input-dependent protocols. For the latter, they provide an intuition on how to extend the compiler to the multi-party case. However, there is no full compiler specification for neither input-dependent nor input-independent protocols. Still, there exist a natural extension for the input-independent compiler, which we can compare to.

The major difference between our input-independent protocol and their input-independent protocol, is the way the protocols prevent *detection dependent abort*. In the natural extension to Damgård et al. [DOS20], which we call the *watchlist approach* in the following, each party independently selects a subset of instances it wants to check and receives the corresponding seeds via oblivious transfer. The transcript of the oblivious transfer together with the receiver's randomness can be used by the receiver to prove integrity of its watchlist to the judge; similar to the seed commitments and openings used in our protocol. The watchlists are only revealed after each party receives the data required to create a certificate in case of cheating detection, i.e., the signatures by the other parties. Once a party detects which instances are checked, it is too late to prevent the creation of a certificate. Our approach utilizes time-lock puzzles for the same purpose.

In the watchlist approach, all parties have different watchlists. For t semi-honest instances and watchlists of size $s \geq \frac{t}{n}$, there is a constant probability $\mathsf{Pr}[\mathsf{bad}]$ that no semi-honest instance remains unwatched which leads to a failure of the protocol. Thus, parties either need to choose $s < \frac{t}{n}$ and hence $\epsilon = \frac{s}{t} < \frac{1}{n}$ or run several executions of the protocol. For the latter, the probability of a protocol failure $\mathsf{Pr}[\mathsf{bad}]$ and the expected number of protocol runs runs are calculated based on the inclusion-exclusion principle as follows:

$$\begin{aligned}
\mathsf{Pr}[\mathsf{bad}] &= 1 - \frac{\sum_{k=1}^{t}(-1)^{(k-1)} * \binom{t}{k} * (\prod_{j=0}^{s-1}(t-j-k))^n}{\prod_{j=0}^{s-1}(t-j))^n} \\
&= 1 - \sum_{k=1}^{t}(-1)^{(k-1)} \cdot \binom{t}{k} \cdot \left(\frac{(t-k)! \cdot (t-s)!}{(t-k-s)! \cdot t!}\right)^n \\
\mathsf{runs} &= \mathsf{Pr}[\mathsf{bad}]^{-1}
\end{aligned}$$

Setting the watchlist size $s \geq \frac{t}{n}$ such that there is a constant failure probability has the additional drawback that the repetition can be abused to amplify denial-of-service attacks. An adversary can enforce a high failure probability by selecting its watchlists strategically. If $s \geq \frac{t}{(n-1)}$ and $n-1$ parties are corrupted, the adversary can cause an error with probability 1 which enables an infinite DoS-attack.

This restriction of the deterrence factor seems to be a major drawback of the watchlist approach. Although our approach has an additional overhead due to the puzzle generation, which is independent of the complexity of the transformed protocol and thus amortizes over the complexity of the base protocols, it has the benefit that it immediately supports an arbitrary deterrence factor ϵ. This is due to the fact that the hidden shared coin toss determines a single watchlist shared by all parties. In Table 1, we display the maximal deterrence factor of our approach ϵ in comparison to the maximal deterrence factor of the watchlist approach without protocol repetitions ϵ' for different settings. Additionally, we provide the number of expected runs required to achieve ϵ in the watchlist approach with repetitions.

Table 1. Maximal deterrence factor or expected number of runs of the watchlist approach in comparison to our approach.

n	t	Our approach	Watchlist approach	
		ϵ	ϵ' or	runs
2	2	1/2	-	2
	3	2/3	1/3	3
	10	9/10	4/10	10
3	2	1/2	-	4
	4	3/4	1/4	16
	10	9/10	3/10	100
5	2	1/2	-	16
	6	5/6	1/6	1296

Acknowledgments. The first, third, and fourth authors were supported by the German Federal Ministry of Education and Research (BMBF) *iBlockchain project* (grant nr. 16KIS0902), by the Deutsche Forschungsgemeinschaft (DFG, German Research Foundation) *SFB 1119 – 236615297 (CROSSING Project S7)*, by the BMBF and the Hessian Ministry of Higher Education, Research, Science and the Arts within their joint support of the *National Research Center for Applied Cybersecurity ATHENE*, and by Robert Bosch GmbH, by the Economy of Things Project. The second author was supported by the BIU Center for Research in Applied Cryptography and Cyber Security in conjunction with the Israel National Cyber Bureau in the Prime Minister's Office, and by ISF grant No. 1316/18.

References

[AL07] Aumann, Y., Lindell, Y.: Security against covert adversaries: efficient protocols for realistic adversaries. In: Vadhan, S.P. (ed.) TCC 2007. LNCS, vol. 4392, pp. 137–156. Springer, Heidelberg (2007). https://doi.org/10.1007/978-3-540-70936-7_8

[AO12] Asharov, G., Orlandi, C.: Calling out cheaters: covert security with public verifiability. In: Wang, X., Sako, K. (eds.) ASIACRYPT 2012. LNCS, vol. 7658, pp. 681–698. Springer, Heidelberg (2012). https://doi.org/10.1007/978-3-642-34961-4_41

[ARS+15] Albrecht, M.R., Rechberger, C., Schneider, T., Tiessen, T., Zohner, M.: Ciphers for MPC and FHE. In: Oswald, E., Fischlin, M. (eds.) EUROCRYPT 2015. LNCS, vol. 9056, pp. 430–454. Springer, Heidelberg (2015). https://doi.org/10.1007/978-3-662-46800-5_17

[BBBF18] Boneh, D., Bonneau, J., Bünz, B., Fisch, B.: Verifiable delay functions. In: Shacham, H., Boldyreva, A. (eds.) CRYPTO 2018. LNCS, vol. 10991, pp. 757–788. Springer, Cham (2018). https://doi.org/10.1007/978-3-319-96884-1_25

[Bea92] Beaver, D.: Efficient multiparty protocols using circuit randomization. In: Feigenbaum, J. (ed.) CRYPTO 1991. LNCS, vol. 576, pp. 420–432. Springer, Heidelberg (1992). https://doi.org/10.1007/3-540-46766-1_34

[BGJ+16] Bitansky, N., Goldwasser, S., Jain, A., Paneth, O., Vaikuntanathan, V., Waters, B.: Time-lock puzzles from randomized encodings. In: ITCS (2016)

[BW88] Buchmann, J., Williams, H.C.: A key-exchange system based on imaginary quadratic fields. J. Cryptol. **1**(2), 107–118 (1988). https://doi.org/10.1007/BF02351719

[DG20] Dobson, S., Galbraith, S.D.: Trustless groups of unknown order with hyperelliptic curves. IACR Cryptology ePrint Archive 2020 (2020)

[DGN10] Damgård, I., Geisler, M., Nielsen, J.B.: From passive to covert security at low cost. In: Micciancio, D. (ed.) TCC 2010. LNCS, vol. 5978, pp. 128–145. Springer, Heidelberg (2010). https://doi.org/10.1007/978-3-642-11799-2_9

[DKL+13] Damgård, I., Keller, M., Larraia, E., Pastro, V., Scholl, P., Smart, N.P.: Practical covertly secure MPC for dishonest majority – or: breaking the SPDZ limits. In: Crampton, J., Jajodia, S., Mayes, K. (eds.) ESORICS 2013. LNCS, vol. 8134, pp. 1–18. Springer, Heidelberg (2013). https://doi.org/10.1007/978-3-642-40203-6_1

[DOS20] Damgård, I., Orlandi, C., Simkin, M.: Black-box transformations from passive to covert security with public verifiability. In: Micciancio, D., Ristenpart, T. (eds.) CRYPTO 2020. LNCS, vol. 12171, pp. 647–676. Springer, Cham (2020). https://doi.org/10.1007/978-3-030-56880-1_23

[DPSZ12] Damgård, I., Pastro, V., Smart, N., Zakarias, S.: Multiparty computation from somewhat homomorphic encryption. In: Safavi-Naini, R., Canetti, R. (eds.) CRYPTO 2012. LNCS, vol. 7417, pp. 643–662. Springer, Heidelberg (2012). https://doi.org/10.1007/978-3-642-32009-5_38

[GMS08] Goyal, V., Mohassel, P., Smith, A.: Efficient two party and multi party computation against covert adversaries. In: Smart, N. (ed.) EUROCRYPT 2008. LNCS, vol. 4965, pp. 289–306. Springer, Heidelberg (2008). https://doi.org/10.1007/978-3-540-78967-3_17

[GMW87] Goldreich, O., Micali, S., Wigderson, A.: How to play any mental game or a completeness theorem for protocols with honest majority. In: 19th ACM STOC 1987 (1987)

[HKK+19] Hong, C., Katz, J., Kolesnikov, V., Lu, W., Wang, X.: Covert security with public verifiability: faster, leaner, and simpler. In: Ishai, Y., Rijmen, V. (eds.) EUROCRYPT 2019. LNCS, vol. 11478, pp. 97–121. Springer, Cham (2019). https://doi.org/10.1007/978-3-030-17659-4_4

[HVW20] Hazay, C., Venkitasubramaniam, M., Weiss, M.: The price of active security in cryptographic protocols. In: Canteaut, A., Ishai, Y. (eds.) EUROCRYPT 2020. LNCS, vol. 12106, pp. 184–215. Springer, Cham (2020). https://doi.org/10.1007/978-3-030-45724-2_7

[IOZ14] Ishai, Y., Ostrovsky, R., Zikas, V.: Secure multi-party computation with identifiable abort. In: Garay, J.A., Gennaro, R. (eds.) CRYPTO 2014. LNCS, vol. 8617, pp. 369–386. Springer, Heidelberg (2014). https://doi.org/10.1007/978-3-662-44381-1_21

[IPS08] Ishai, Y., Prabhakaran, M., Sahai, A.: Founding cryptography on oblivious transfer – efficiently. In: Wagner, D. (ed.) CRYPTO 2008. LNCS, vol. 5157, pp. 572–591. Springer, Heidelberg (2008). https://doi.org/10.1007/978-3-540-85174-5_32

[KM15] Kolesnikov, V., Malozemoff, A.J.: Public verifiability in the covert model (almost) for free. In: Iwata, T., Cheon, J.H. (eds.) ASIACRYPT 2015. LNCS, vol. 9453, pp. 210–235. Springer, Heidelberg (2015). https://doi.org/10.1007/978-3-662-48800-3_9

[LOP11] Lindell, Y., Oxman, E., Pinkas, B.: The IPS compiler: optimizations, variants and concrete efficiency. In: Rogaway, P. (ed.) CRYPTO 2011. LNCS, vol. 6841, pp. 259–276. Springer, Heidelberg (2011). https://doi.org/10.1007/978-3-642-22792-9_15

[MMV11] Mahmoody, M., Moran, T., Vadhan, S.: Time-lock puzzles in the random oracle model. In: Rogaway, P. (ed.) CRYPTO 2011. LNCS, vol. 6841, pp. 39–50. Springer, Heidelberg (2011). https://doi.org/10.1007/978-3-642-22792-9_3

[MT19] Malavolta, G., Thyagarajan, S.A.K.: Homomorphic time-lock puzzles and applications. In: Boldyreva, A., Micciancio, D. (eds.) CRYPTO 2019. LNCS, vol. 11692, pp. 620–649. Springer, Cham (2019). https://doi.org/10.1007/978-3-030-26948-7_22

[Pie19] Pietrzak, K.: Simple verifiable delay functions. In: ITCS 2019 (2019)

[RSW96] Rivest, R.L., Shamir, A., Wagner, D.A.: Time-lock puzzles and timed-release crypto. Technical report, Massachusetts Institute of Technology. Laboratory for Computer Science (1996)

[Wes19] Wesolowski, B.: Efficient verifiable delay functions. In: Ishai, Y., Rijmen, V. (eds.) EUROCRYPT 2019. LNCS, vol. 11478, pp. 379–407. Springer, Cham (2019). https://doi.org/10.1007/978-3-030-17659-4_13

[WRK17a] Wang, X., Ranellucci, S., Katz, J.: Authenticated garbling and efficient maliciously secure two-party computation. In: ACM CCS 2017 (2017)

[WRK17b] Wang, X., Ranellucci, S., Katz, J.: Global-scale secure multiparty computation. In: ACM CCS 2017 (2017)

[YWZ20] Yang, K., Wang, X., Zhang, J.: More efficient MPC from improved triple generation and authenticated garbling. In: ACM CCS 2020 (2020)

[ZDH19] Zhu, R., Ding, C., Huang, Y.: Efficient publicly verifiable 2PC over a blockchain with applications to financially-secure computations. In: ACM CCS 2019 (2019)

Constant-Overhead Unconditionally Secure Multiparty Computation Over Binary Fields

Antigoni Polychroniadou[1] and Yifan Song[2(✉)]

[1] J.P. Morgan AI Research, New York, USA
[2] Carnegie Mellon University, Pittsburgh, USA
yifans2@andrew.cmu.edu

Abstract. We study the communication complexity of unconditionally secure multiparty computation (MPC) protocols in the honest majority setting. Despite tremendous efforts in achieving efficient protocols for binary fields under computational assumptions, there are no efficient unconditional MPC protocols in this setting. In particular, there are no n-party protocols with constant overhead admitting communication complexity of $O(n)$ bits per gate. Cascudo, Cramer, Xing and Yuan (CRYPTO 2018) were the first ones to achieve such an overhead in the amortized setting by evaluating $O(\log n)$ copies of the same circuit in the binary field in parallel. In this work, we construct the first unconditional MPC protocol secure against a malicious adversary in the honest majority setting evaluating just a *single* boolean circuit with amortized communication complexity of $O(n)$ bits per gate.

1 Introduction

Secure multiparty computation (MPC) [Yao82, GMW87, CCD88, BOGW88] allows n parties to compute any function of their local inputs while guaranteeing the privacy of the inputs and the correctness of the outputs even if t of the parties are corrupted by an adversary.

A. Polychroniadou—This paper was prepared in part for information purposes by the Artificial Intelligence Research group of JPMorgan Chase & Co and its affiliates ("JP Morgan"), and is not a product of the Research Department of JP Morgan. JP Morgan makes no representation and warranty whatsoever and disclaims all liability, for the completeness, accuracy or reliability of the information contained herein. This document is not intended as investment research or investment advice, or a recommendation, offer or solicitation for the purchase or sale of any security, financial instrument, financial product or service, or to be used in any way for evaluating the merits of participating in any transaction, and shall not constitute a solicitation under any jurisdiction or to any person, if such solicitation under such jurisdiction or to such person would be unlawful.
Y. Song—Work done in part while at J.P. Morgan AI Research. Supported in part by the NSF award 1916939, DARPA SIEVE program, a gift from Ripple, a DoE NETL award, a JP Morgan Faculty Fellowship, a PNC center for financial services innovation award, and a Cylab seed funding award.

A. Canteaut and F.-X. Standaert (Eds.): EUROCRYPT 2021, LNCS 12697, pp. 812–841, 2021.
https://doi.org/10.1007/978-3-030-77886-6_28

Given that point-to-point secure channels are established across the parties, any function can be computed with unconditional (perfect) security, against a semi-honest adversary if $n \geq 2t+1$ and against a malicious adversary if $n \geq 3t+1$ [BOGW88, CCD88]. If we accept small error probability, $n \geq 2t+1$ is sufficient to get malicious security [RBO89, Bea89].

The methods used in unconditional secure protocols tend to be computationally much more efficient than the cryptographic machinery required for computational security. So unconditionally secure protocols are very attractive from a computational point of view, but they seem to require a lot of interaction. In fact, such protocols require communication complexity proportional to the size of the (arithmetic) circuit computing the function. In this work we focus on the communication complexity per multiplication of unconditional MPC protocols in the honest majority setting.

Known unconditional secure MPC protocols represent the inputs as elements of a finite field F_q and represent the function as an arithmetic circuit over that finite field. Moreover, protocols that are efficient in the circuit size of the evaluated function process the circuit gate-by-gate using Shamir secret sharing [Sha79]. This approach usually allows non-interactive processing of addition gates but requires communication for every multiplication gate. However, secret-sharing-based protocols require that the size of the underlying finite field is larger than the number of parties, i.e., $q > n$. The work of [BTH08] based on hyper-invertible matrices requires the underlying finite field to be $q \geq 2n$.[1] Other types of protocols with unconditional online phase based on message authentication codes, such as the SPDZ-based protocol [DPSZ12], require the size of the underlying finite field to be large, i.e., $q > 2^{\kappa}$, where κ is the security parameter. This is based on the fact that the cheating probability of the adversary needs to be inverse proportional to the size of the field.

In this paper, we ask a very natural question for unconditionally secure protocols which, to the best of our knowledge, has not been studied in detail before:

Is it possible to construct unconditional MPC protocols for $t < n/2$ for computing an arithmetic circuit over a small field F_q (such as $q = 2$) with amortized communication complexity $O(n)$ field elements (bits) per gate?

Note that the standard solution of applying the existing protocols to functions which are already represented as binary circuits requires to lift the circuit to a large enough extension field. That said, in such a scenario the communication complexity incurs a multiplicative overhead of $\log n$.

Recently, Cascudo, et al. [CCXY18] revisited the amortized complexity of unconditional MPC. At a high level, the authors leverage the large extension field to evaluate more than one instance of the same binary circuit in parallel. In particular, the authors compile an MPC protocol for a circuit over an extension

[1] In [CCXY18], Cascudo, et al. show that the requirement $q \geq 2n$ of using hyper-invertible matrices can be relaxed to any field size. However, $q > n$ is still necessary to use Shamir secret sharing in [BTH08].

field to a parallel MPC protocol of the same circuit but with inputs defined over its base field. That said, their protocol can evaluate $O(\log n)$ copies of the same circuit in the binary field in parallel and achieve communication complexity of $O(Cn)$ bits where C is the size of the circuit. However, such an overhead cannot be achieved for a single copy of the circuit. The works of [DZ13, CG20] also allow efficient parallel computation of several evaluations of the same binary circuits with a special focus on the dishonest majority. Note that these works are based on packed secret sharing for SIMD circuits, however this induces an extra overhead of $\log C$ in the circuit size when using for a single binary circuit.

Our Results. We answer the above question in the affirmative, obtaining an unconditional MPC protocol in the honest majority setting for calculations over $\mathbb{F}_2$. Informally, we prove the following:

Theorem 1 (informal). *There exists an unconditional MPC protocol for n parties secure against $t < n/2$ corruptions in the presence of a malicious adversary evaluating a single boolean circuit with an amortized communication complexity of $O(n)$ bits per gate.*

We formally state our results and communication overhead in Theorem 5. To establish our result, we propose an online phase based on additive sharings where we are able to authenticate the shares with $O(Cn)$ communication overhead as opposed to prior works which achieve an overhead of $O(Cn\kappa)$ for a single boolean circuit, where κ is the security parameter.

We are aware that the works of Hazay et al. [HVW20] and Boyle et al. [BGIN20] (building on Boneh et al. [BBCG+19]) provide general compilers from semi-honest security to malicious security in the honest-majority setting, with at most a constant communication overhead. We leave the possibility of an alternative approach to achieve malicious security by applying these compilers to a semi-honest protocol which communicates $O(n)$ field elements per gate, such as our semi-honest protocol, to future work.

2 Technical Overview

In the following, we will use n to denote the number of parties and t to denote the number of corrupted parties. In the setting of the honest majority, we have $n = 2t + 1$.

Our construction will utilize two kinds of secret sharing schemes:

- The standard Shamir secret sharing scheme [Sha79]: We will use $[x]_t$ to denote a degree-t Shamir sharing, or a $(t + 1)$-out-of-n Shamir sharing. It requires at least $t + 1$ shares to reconstruct the secret and any t shares do not leak any information about the secret.
- An additive sharing among the first $t + 1$ parties: We will use $\langle x \rangle$ to denote an additive sharing, which satisfies that the summation of the shares held by the first $t+1$ parties is the secret x, and the shares of the rest of parties are 0.

In this paper, we are interested in the information-theoretic setting. Our goal is to construct a secure-with-abort MPC protocol for a *single* arithmetic circuit over the binary field $\mathbb{F}_2$, such that the communication complexity is $O(Cn)$ bits (ignoring terms which are sub-linear in the circuit size), where C is the circuit size and n is the number of parties. The structure of our overview is as follows:

1. We first provide an overview of related works and discuss why their protocols cannot achieve $O(Cn)$ bits for a single binary circuit.
2. Then we introduce a high-level structure of our construction. Very informally, our protocol uses additive sharings to achieve high efficiency in the online phase. However, using additive sharings requires authentications of the secrets to detect malicious behaviors. Based on the prior works, directly generating an authentication for each sharing already requires the communication of $O(Cn\kappa)$ bits, where κ is the security parameter. The main difficulty is how to efficiently authenticate the secrets of additive sharings.
3. Next we review the notion of reverse multiplication-friendly embeddings (RMFE) introduced in [CCXY18], which is an important building block of our protocol.
4. Finally, we introduce our main technique. Our idea stems from a new way to authenticate the secret of an additive sharing. Combining with RMFEs, we can authenticate the secret of a single additive sharing with the communication of $O(n)$ bits. Relying on this new technique, we can obtain a secure-with-abort MPC protocol for a single binary circuit with the communication complexity of $O(Cn)$ bits.

How Previous Constructions Work. In the honest majority setting, the best-known semi-honest protocol is introduced in the work of Damgård and Nielsen [DN07] in 2007 (hereafter referred to as the DN protocol). The communication complexity of the DN protocol is $O(Cn\phi)$ bits, where ϕ is the size of a field element. A beautiful line of works [GIP+14, LN17, CGH+18, NV18, GSZ20] have shown how to compile the DN protocol to achieve security-with-abort. In particular, the recent work [GSZ20] gives the first construction where the communication complexity matches the DN protocol. At a high-level, these protocols follow the idea of computing a degree-t Shamir sharing for each wire, and making use of the properties of the Shamir secret sharing scheme to evaluate addition gates and multiplication gates. However, the Shamir secret sharing scheme requires the field size to be at least $n+1$. It means that the size of a field element $\phi \geq \log n$. When we want to evaluate a binary circuit by using these protocols, we need to use a large enough extension field so that the Shamir secret sharing scheme is well-defined, which results in $O(Cn\log n)$ bits in the communication complexity.

[CCXY18] revisited the amortized complexity of information-theoretically secure MPC. Their idea is to compile an MPC for a circuit over an extension field to a parallel MPC of the same circuit but with inputs defined over its base field. In this way, we can evaluate $O(\log n)$ copies of the same circuit in the binary field at the same time and achieve $O(Cn)$ bits per circuit. The main technique is the notion of reverse multiplication-friendly embeddings (RMFE) introduced in this work [CCXY18]. At a high-level, RMFE allows us to perform a coordinate-wise product between two vectors of bits by multiplying two elements in the extension field. When evaluating $O(\log n)$ copies of the same circuit in the binary field, each multiplication is just a coordinate-wise product between the vectors of bits associated with the input wires. Relying on RMFE, all parties can transform the computation to one multiplication between two elements in the extension field, which can be handled by the DN protocol. This is the first paper which sheds light on the possibility of evaluating a binary circuit with communication complexity of $O(Cn)$ bits. However, it is unclear how to use this technique to evaluate a *single* binary circuit.

In the setting of the dishonest majority, the well-known work SPDZ [DPSZ12] shows that, with necessary correlated randomness prepared in the preprocessing phase, we can use an information-theoretic protocol in the online phase to achieve high efficiency. The high-level idea of the online phase protocol is to use the notion of Beaver tuples to transform a multiplication operation to two reconstructions. We will elaborate this technique at a later point. In the online phase, all parties will compute an additive sharing for each wire. One benefit of the additive secret sharing scheme is that it is well-defined in the binary field and each party holds a single bit as its share. As a result, the communication complexity in the online phase is just $O(Cn)$ bits. However, unlike the honest majority setting where the shares of honest parties can determine the secret of a degree-t Shamir sharing, the secret of an additive sharing can be easily altered by a corrupted party changing its own share. Therefore, a secure MAC is required to authenticate the secret of each additive sharing. To make the MAC effective, the MAC size should be proportional to the security parameter κ. Although it does not necessarily affect the sharing space, e.g., the work TinyOT [NNOB12] uses an additive sharing in the binary field with a secure MAC in the extension field, generating a secure MAC for each sharing in the preprocessing phase brings in an overhead of κ, which results in $O(Cn\kappa)$ bits in the overall communication complexity. We however note that, this protocol achieves a highly efficient online phase, which is $O(Cn)$ bits. Our starting idea is the online phase protocol in [DPSZ12]. In the honest majority setting, the preprocessing phase can also be done by an information-theoretic protocol. In fact, the idea of using Beaver tuples has been used in several previous works [BTH08, BSFO12, CCXY18] in the honest majority setting. We first describe a prototype protocol of using Beaver tuples in this setting.

A Prototype Protocol of Using Beaver Tuples. This protocol follows the same structure as the protocol in [DPSZ12], but in the honest majority setting. Recall that we use $\langle x \rangle$ to denote an additive sharing among the first $t+1$ parties. We use $\mathsf{MAC}(x)$ to denote an abstract MAC for x. It satisfies that all parties can use $\mathsf{MAC}(x)$ to check the correctness of x. We further require that $\mathsf{MAC}(\cdot)$ is linear homomorphic, i.e., $\mathsf{MAC}(x) + \mathsf{MAC}(y) = \mathsf{MAC}(x+y)$. Let $[\![x]\!] := (\langle x \rangle, \mathsf{MAC}(x))$.

In the preprocessing phase, all parties prepare a batch of Beaver tuples in the form of $([\![a]\!], [\![b]\!], [\![c]\!])$, where a, b are random bits and $c := a \cdot b$. These tuples will be used in the online phase to evaluate multiplication gates.

In the online phase, all parties start with holding $[\![x]\!]$ for each input wire. Addition gates and multiplication gates are evaluated in a predetermined topological order.

- For an addition gate with input sharings $[\![x]\!]$ and $[\![y]\!]$, all parties can locally compute

$$[\![z]\!] := (\langle z \rangle, \mathsf{MAC}(z)) = (\langle x \rangle, \mathsf{MAC}(x)) + (\langle y \rangle, \mathsf{MAC}(y)) = [\![x]\!] + [\![y]\!].$$

- For a multiplication gate with input sharings $[\![x]\!]$ and $[\![y]\!]$, let $([\![a]\!], [\![b]\!], [\![c]\!])$ be the first unused Beaver tuple. Note that:

$$\begin{aligned} z = x \cdot y &= (x + a - a) \cdot (y + b - b) \\ &= (x + a) \cdot (y + b) - (x + a) \cdot b - (y + b) \cdot a + a \cdot b \end{aligned}$$

  Therefore, if all parties know $x + a$ and $y + b$, $[\![z]\!]$ can be locally computed by

$$[\![z]\!] := (x + a) \cdot (y + b) - (x + a) \cdot [\![b]\!] - (y + b) \cdot [\![a]\!] + [\![c]\!].$$

  The task of computing $[\![z]\!]$ becomes to reconstruct $[\![x]\!] + [\![a]\!]$ and $[\![y]\!] + [\![b]\!]$. We will use $\langle x + a \rangle$ and $\langle y + b \rangle$ to do the reconstructions. All parties send their shares of $\langle x + a \rangle, \langle y + b \rangle$ to the first party. Then, the first party reconstructs the $x + a, y + b$, and sends the result back to other parties.

To check the correctness of the computation, it is sufficient to verify the reconstructions. For each $x + a$, all parties use $[\![x]\!], [\![a]\!]$ to compute $\mathsf{MAC}(x + a)$, which can be used to verify the reconstruction.

Note that we only need to communicate $O(n)$ bits per multiplication gates. Therefore, the communication complexity is $O(Cn)$ bits in the online phase. The main bottleneck of this approach is how to generate Beaver tuples efficiently. Our protocol relies on the notion of reverse multiplication-friendly embeddings and a novel MAC to achieve high efficiency in generating Beaver tuples.

Review of the Reverse Multiplication-Friendly Embeddings [CCXY18]. We note that a Beaver tuple can be prepared by the following two steps: (1) prepare two random sharings $[\![a]\!], [\![b]\!]$, and (2) compute $[\![c]\!]$ such that $c := a \cdot b$. Note that a, b are random bits. It naturally connects to the idea of RMFE, which allows us to perform a coordinate-wise product between two vector of bits by multiplying two elements in the extension field. We first give a quick review of this notion.

Let $\mathbb{F}_2^k$ denote a vector space of $\mathbb{F}_2$ of dimension k, and $\mathbb{F}_{2^m}$ denote the extension field of $\mathbb{F}_2$ of degree m. A reverse multiplication-friendly embedding is a pair of $\mathbb{F}_2$-linear maps (ϕ, ψ), where $\phi : \mathbb{F}_2^k \to \mathbb{F}_{2^m}$ and $\psi : \mathbb{F}_{2^m} \to \mathbb{F}_2^k$, such that for all $\boldsymbol{x}, \boldsymbol{y} \in \mathbb{F}_2^k$,

$$\boldsymbol{x} * \boldsymbol{y} = \psi(\phi(\boldsymbol{x}) \cdot \phi(\boldsymbol{y})),$$

where $*$ denotes the coordinate-wise product. In [CCXY18], it has been shown that there exists a family of RMFEs such that $m = \Theta(k)$.

In [CCXY18], recall that $k = O(\log n)$ copies of the same circuit are evaluated together. For each wire, there is a vector of k bits associated with this wire, where the i-th bit is the wire value of the i-th copy of the circuit. Thus, an addition gate corresponds to a coordinate-wise addition, and a multiplication gate corresponds to a coordinate-wise product. In the construction of [CCXY18], for each wire, the vector $\boldsymbol{x}$ associated with this wire is encoded to $\phi(\boldsymbol{x}) \in \mathbb{F}_{2^m}$. All parties hold a degree-t Shamir sharing $[\phi(\boldsymbol{x})]_t$. Since $\phi(\cdot)$ is an $\mathbb{F}_2$-linear map, addition gates can be computed locally. The main task is to evaluate multiplication gates:

- For a multiplication gate with input sharings $[\phi(\boldsymbol{x})]_t, [\phi(\boldsymbol{y})]_t$, the goal is to compute a degree-t Shamir sharing $[\phi(\boldsymbol{z})]_t$ such that $\boldsymbol{z} = \boldsymbol{x} * \boldsymbol{y}$.
- Relying on the DN protocol [DN07], all parties can compute a degree-t Shamir sharing $[w]_t := [\phi(\boldsymbol{x}) \cdot \phi(\boldsymbol{y})]_t$. By the property of the RMFE, we have $\boldsymbol{z} = \psi(w)$. Therefore, all parties need to transform $[w]_t$ to $[\phi(\psi(w))]_t$.
- In [CCXY18], this is done by using a pair of random sharings $([r]_t, [\phi(\psi(r))]_t)$. All parties reconstruct $[w + r]_t$ and compute $[\phi(\psi(w))]_t := \phi(\psi(w + r)) - [\phi(\psi(r))]_t$. The correctness follows from the fact that ϕ and ψ are $\mathbb{F}_2$-linear maps.
- Finally, all parties set $[\phi(\boldsymbol{z})]_t := [\phi(\psi(w))]_t$.

As analyzed in [CCXY18], the communication complexity per multiplication gate is $O(m \cdot n)$ bits. Since each multiplication gate corresponds to k multiplications in the binary field, the amortized communication complexity per multiplication is $O(m/k \cdot n) = O(n)$ bits.

Following the idea in [CCXY18], we can prepare a random tuple of sharings $([\phi(\boldsymbol{a})]_t, [\phi(\boldsymbol{b})]_t, [\phi(\mathbf{c})]_t)$, where $\boldsymbol{a}, \boldsymbol{b}$ are random vectors in $\mathbb{F}_2^k$, and $\mathbf{c} = \boldsymbol{a} * \boldsymbol{b}$. In particular, the communication complexity per tuple is $O(m \cdot n)$ bits. Suppose that $\boldsymbol{a} = (a_1, a_2, \ldots, a_k), \boldsymbol{b} = (b_1, b_2, \ldots, b_k)$, and $\mathbf{c} = (c_1, c_2, \ldots, c_k)$. If we can transform a random tuple $([\phi(\boldsymbol{a})]_t, [\phi(\boldsymbol{b})]_t, [\phi(\mathbf{c})]_t)$ to k Beaver tuples:

$$([\![a_1]\!], [\![b_1]\!], [\![c_1]\!]), ([\![a_2]\!], [\![b_2]\!], [\![c_2]\!]), \ldots, ([\![a_k]\!], [\![b_k]\!], [\![c_k]\!]),$$

then the communication complexity per Beaver tuple is $O(m/k \cdot n) = O(n)$ bits! More concretely, our goal is to efficiently separate a degree-t Shamir sharing $[\phi(\boldsymbol{a})]_t$ to k sharings $[\![a_1]\!], [\![a_2]\!], \ldots, [\![a_k]\!]$. For all $i \in [k]$, recall that $[\![a_i]\!] = (\langle a_i \rangle, \mathsf{MAC}(a_i))$. Therefore, we need to efficiently obtain *an additive sharing* $\langle a_i \rangle$ and *a secure* $\mathsf{MAC}(a_i)$ from a degree-t Shamir sharing $[\phi(\boldsymbol{a})]_t$.

Establish a Connection between $[\phi(\boldsymbol{x})]_t$ *and* $\{[\![x_i]\!]\}_{i=1}^k$. We first consider the following question: Given $\phi(\boldsymbol{x})$, how can we obtain the i-th bit x_i from $\phi(\boldsymbol{x})$? Let $\mathbf{e}^{(i)}$ be a vector in $\mathbb{F}_2^k$ such that all entries are 0 except that the i-th entry is 1. Then $\mathbf{e}^{(i)} * \boldsymbol{x}$ is a vector in $\mathbb{F}_2^k$ such that all entries are 0 except that the i-th entry is x_i. According to the definition of RMFEs, we have

$$\mathbf{e}^{(i)} * \boldsymbol{x} = \psi(\phi(\mathbf{e}^{(i)}) \cdot \phi(\boldsymbol{x})).$$

To obtain x_i from $\mathbf{e}^{(i)} * \boldsymbol{x}$, we can compute the summation of all entries in $\mathbf{e}^{(i)} * \boldsymbol{x}$. We define an $\mathbb{F}_2$-linear map $\mathsf{val}(\cdot) : \mathbb{F}_{2^m} \to \mathbb{F}_2$ as follows:

- For an input element $y \in \mathbb{F}_{2^m}$, suppose $\psi(y) = (y_1, y_2, \ldots, y_k)$.
- $\mathsf{val}(y)$ is defined to be $\sum_{i=1}^{k} y_i$.

Therefore, we have

$$x_i := \mathsf{val}(\phi(\boldsymbol{e}^{(i)}) \cdot \phi(\boldsymbol{x})).$$

Note that $\phi(\boldsymbol{e}^{(i)})$ is an element in $\mathbb{F}_{2^m}$ and is known to all parties. Therefore, all parties can locally compute $[y^{(i)}]_t := \phi(\boldsymbol{e}^{(i)}) \cdot [\phi(\boldsymbol{x})]_t$. In particular, we have $\mathsf{val}(y^{(i)}) = x_i$. In the honest majority setting, a degree-t Shamir sharing satisfies that the secret is determined by the shares of honest parties. In particular, corrupted parties cannot alter the secret of this sharing. Therefore, $[y^{(i)}]_t$ can be seen as a secure MAC for x_i. Thus for an element $x \in \mathbb{F}_2$, we set $\mathsf{MAC}(x) := [y]_t$, where $y \in \mathbb{F}_{2^m}$ satisfies that $\mathsf{val}(y) = x$. Note that $[y]_t$ can be used to check the correctness of x, and for all $x, x' \in \mathbb{F}_2$,

$$\mathsf{MAC}(x) + \mathsf{MAC}(x') = [y]_t + [y']_t = [y + y']_t = \mathsf{MAC}(x + x'),$$

where the last step follows from the fact that $\mathsf{val}(y + y') = \mathsf{val}(y) + \mathsf{val}(y')$.

Recall that $[\![x_i]\!] = (\langle x_i \rangle, \mathsf{MAC}(x_i))$. So far, we have obtained $\mathsf{MAC}(x_i)$ from $[\phi(\boldsymbol{x})]_t$. Therefore, the only task is to obtain $\langle x_i \rangle$. Let $\langle \boldsymbol{x} \rangle := (\langle x_1 \rangle, \langle x_2 \rangle, \ldots, \langle x_k \rangle)$ denote a vector of additive sharings of $\boldsymbol{x} \in \mathbb{F}_2^k$. For each party, its share of $\langle \boldsymbol{x} \rangle$ is a vector in $\mathbb{F}_2^k$. For the last t parties, they take the all-0 vector as their shares.

We note that for a degree-t Shamir sharing $[\phi(\boldsymbol{x})]_t$, the secret $\phi(\boldsymbol{x})$ can be written as a linear combination of the shares of the first $t+1$ parties. Therefore, the first $t+1$ parties can locally transform their shares of $[\phi(\boldsymbol{x})]_t$ to an additive sharing of $\phi(\boldsymbol{x})$, denoted by $\langle \phi(\boldsymbol{x}) \rangle$. Let u_i denote the i-th share of $\langle \phi(\boldsymbol{x}) \rangle$. Then we have $\phi(\boldsymbol{x}) = \sum_{i=1}^{t+1} u_i$. In Sect. 3.3, we give an explicit construction of an $\mathbb{F}_2$-linear map $\tilde{\phi}^{-1} : \mathbb{F}_{2^m} \to \mathbb{F}_2^k$ which satisfies that for all $\boldsymbol{x} \in \mathbb{F}_2^k$, $\tilde{\phi}^{-1}(\phi(\boldsymbol{x})) = \boldsymbol{x}$. Utilizing $\tilde{\phi}^{-1}$, we have

$$\sum_{i=1}^{t+1} \tilde{\phi}^{-1}(u_i) = \tilde{\phi}^{-1}(\sum_{i=1}^{t+1} u_i) = \tilde{\phi}^{-1}(\phi(\boldsymbol{x})) = \boldsymbol{x}.$$

Thus, the i-th party takes $\tilde{\phi}^{-1}(u_i)$ as its share of $\langle \boldsymbol{x} \rangle$.

In summary, we show that given $[\phi(\boldsymbol{x})]_t$, all parties can *locally* obtain $\{[\![x_i]\!]\}_{i=1}^{k}$. Together with RMFEs, the communication complexity per Beaver tuple is $O(n)$ bits. Relying on the prototype protocol of using Beaver tuples, we obtain a secure-with-abort MPC protocol for a *single* binary circuit which has communication complexity $O(Cn)$ bits. We note that these k sharings $\{[\![x_i]\!]\}_{i=1}^{k}$ are correlated since they are computed from a single degree-t Shamir sharing $[\phi(\boldsymbol{x})]_t$. Our protocol will make use of additional randomness as mask to protect the secrecy of these sharings when they are used. The preparation of this additional randomness is done in a batch way at the beginning of the protocol and does not affect the asymptotic communication complexity of the main protocol. We refer the readers to Sect. 6.3 and Sect. 6.4 for the additional randomness we need in the construction.

An Overview of Our Main Construction. Our main protocol follows the same structure as the prototype protocol of using Beaver tuples. Recall that for $x \in \mathbb{F}_2$, we use $\langle x \rangle$ to denote an additive sharing of x among the first $t+1$ parties, and the shares of the rest of parties are 0. Let (ϕ, ψ) be a RMFE, where $\phi : \mathbb{F}_2^k \rightarrow \mathbb{F}_{2^m}$ and $\psi : \mathbb{F}_{2^m} \rightarrow \mathbb{F}_2^k$ are $\mathbb{F}_2$-linear maps. Recall that $\mathsf{val}(\cdot) : \mathbb{F}_{q^m} \rightarrow \mathbb{F}_q$ is an $\mathbb{F}_q$-linear map, defined by $\mathsf{val}(y) = \sum_{i=1}^{k} y_i$, where $(y_1, y_2, \ldots, y_k) = \psi(y)$. For $x \in \mathbb{F}_2$, let $[\![x]\!] := (\langle x \rangle, [y]_t)$, where $\langle x \rangle$ is an additive sharing among the first $t+1$ parties in $\mathbb{F}_2$, and $[y]_t$ is a degree-t Shamir sharing of $y \in \mathbb{F}_{2^m}$ such that $\mathsf{val}(y) = x$.

In the preprocessing phase, all parties prepare a batch of Beaver tuples in the form of $([\![a]\!], [\![b]\!], [\![c]\!])$, where a, b are random bits and $c := a \cdot b$. The Beaver tuples are prepared by the following steps:

- All parties first prepare a batch of random tuples of sharings in the form of $([\phi(\boldsymbol{a})]_t, [\phi(\boldsymbol{b})]_t, [\phi(\boldsymbol{c})]_t)$, where $\boldsymbol{a}, \boldsymbol{b}$ are random vectors in $\mathbb{F}_2^k$ and $\boldsymbol{c} = \boldsymbol{a} * \boldsymbol{b}$. In our protocol, preparing such a random tuple of sharings require the communication of $O(m \cdot n)$ bits.
- For each tuple of sharings $([\phi(\boldsymbol{a})]_t, [\phi(\boldsymbol{b})]_t, [\phi(\boldsymbol{c})]_t)$, all parties locally transform it to k Beaver tuples in the form of $([\![a]\!], [\![b]\!], [\![c]\!])$.

Note that the amortized cost per Beaver tuple is $O(n)$ bits.

In the online phase, all parties start with holding $[\![x]\!]$ for each input wire. Addition gates and multiplication gates are evaluated in a predetermined topological order.

- For an addition gate with input sharings $[\![x]\!]$ and $[\![y]\!]$, all parties locally compute $[\![z]\!] := [\![x]\!] + [\![y]\!]$.
- For a multiplication gate with input sharings $[\![x]\!]$ and $[\![y]\!]$, let $([\![a]\!], [\![b]\!], [\![c]\!])$ be the first unused Beaver tuple. All parties use the additive sharings $\langle x + a \rangle, \langle y + b \rangle$ to reconstruct $x + a$ and $y + b$. Then all parties compute

  $$[\![z]\!] := (x + a) \cdot (y + b) - (x + a) \cdot [\![b]\!] - (y + b) \cdot [\![a]\!] + [\![c]\!].$$

  All parties also locally compute $[\![x + a]\!] := [\![x]\!] + [\![a]\!]$ and $[\![y + b]\!] := [\![y]\!] + [\![b]\!]$. These sharings will be used to verify the reconstructions at the end of the protocol.

After evaluating the whole circuit, all parties together verify the value-sharing pairs in the form of $(x + a, [\![x + a]\!])$, where $x + a$ is the reconstruction of $[\![x + a]\!]$. In Sect. 7.3, we show that all the value-sharing pairs can be verified together with sub-linear communication complexity in the number of pairs.

Note that addition gates can be computed locally, and the communication complexity per multiplication gate is $O(n)$ bits. Therefore, the communication complexity of our protocol is $O(Cn)$ bits.

Other Building Blocks and Security Issues. We note that the work [CCXY18] only focuses on the setting of 1/3 corruption. These protocols cannot be used directly in the honest majority setting. Some techniques even fail when the corruption threshold increases. In this work, we rebuild the protocols in [CCXY18] to fit the honest majority setting by combining known techniques in [BSFO12, GSZ20]. Concretely,

- We follow the definition of a general linear secret sharing scheme (GLSSS) in [CCXY18]. Following the idea in [BSFO12] of preparing random degree-t Shamir sharings, we introduce a protocol to allow all parties efficiently prepare random sharings of a given GLSSS. We use this protocol to prepare various kinds of random sharings in our main construction. Let $\mathcal{F}_{\text{rand}}$ denote the functionality of this protocol.
- To prepare Beaver tuples, we first prepare a random tuple of sharings

$$([\phi(\boldsymbol{a})]_t, [\phi(\boldsymbol{b})]_t, [\phi(\boldsymbol{c})]_t),$$

  where $\boldsymbol{a}, \boldsymbol{b}$ are random vectors in $\mathbb{F}_2^k$ and $\boldsymbol{c} = \boldsymbol{a} * \boldsymbol{b}$. This random tuple of sharings is prepared as follows:
  - The first step is to prepare random sharings $[\phi(\boldsymbol{a})]_t, [\phi(\boldsymbol{b})]_t$. We show that they can be prepared by using $\mathcal{F}_{\text{rand}}$.
  - Then all parties compute $[\phi(\boldsymbol{a}) \cdot \phi(\boldsymbol{b})]_t$. We rely on the multiplication protocol and the efficient multiplication verification in [GSZ20].
  - Finally, all parties need to transform a sharing $[w]_t$ to $[\phi(\psi(w))]_t$, where $w = \phi(\boldsymbol{a}) \cdot \phi(\boldsymbol{b})$. We model this process in the functionality $\mathcal{F}_{\text{re-encode}}$. We extend the idea in [CCXY18] from the 1/3 corruption setting to the honest majority setting, and construct an efficient protocol for the functionality $\mathcal{F}_{\text{re-encode}}$.

More details can be found in Sect. 4 and Sect. 6.

We note that the idea of using Beaver tuples to construct an MPC protocol in the honest majority setting has been used in several previous works [BTH08, BSFO12, CCXY18]. These protocols all have an additional term $O(D \cdot n^2)$ in the communication complexity, where D is the circuit depth. It is due to a verification of the computation in each layer. Recall that relying on Beaver tuples, an multiplication can be transformed to two reconstructions. In [GLS19], Goyal, et al. show that, without verification of the computation in each layer, corrupted parties can learn extra information when doing reconstructions for multiplications in the next layer. It turns out that our protocol has a similar security issue.

To avoid the verification of the computation per layer, Goyal, et al. [GLS19] rely on an n-out-of-n secret sharing to protect the shares of honest parties. In this way, even without verifications, the share of each honest party is uniformly distributed. It allows Goyal, et al. to only check the correctness at the end of the protocol. We follows the idea in [GLS19]. Concretely, we want to protect the shares of honest parties when using $\langle x+a \rangle, \langle y+b \rangle$ to do reconstructions. To this end, we add a uniformly random additive sharing of 0 for each reconstruction. In this way, each honest party simply sends a uniformly random element to the first party. It allows us to delay the verification to the end of the protocol. More details can be found in Sect. 7.

3 Preliminaries

3.1 The Model

In this work, we focus on functions that can be represented as arithmetic circuits over a finite field $\mathbb{F}_q$ of size q with input, addition, multiplication, and output gates. We use κ to denote the security parameter and C to denote the size of the circuit. In the following, we will use an extension field of $\mathbb{F}_q$ denoted by $\mathbb{F}_{q^m}$ (of size q^m). We always assume that $|\mathbb{F}_{q^m}| = q^m \geq 2^\kappa$.

For the secure multi-party computation, we use the *client-server* model. In the client-server model, clients provide inputs to the functionality and receive outputs, and servers can participate in the computation but do not have inputs or get outputs. Each party may have different roles in the computation. Note that, if every party plays a single client and a single server, this corresponds to a protocol in the standard MPC model. Let c denote the number of clients and $n = 2t + 1$ denote the number of servers. For all clients and servers, we assume that every two of them are connected via a secure (private and authentic) synchronous channel so that they can directly send messages to each other. The communication complexity is measured by the number of bits via private channels.

An adversary $\mathcal{A}$ can corrupt at most c clients and t servers, provide inputs to corrupted clients, and receive all messages sent to corrupted clients and servers. Corrupted clients and servers can deviate from the protocol arbitrarily. We refer the readers to Sect. 3.1 in the full version of this paper [PS20] for the security definition.

Benefits of the Client-Server Model. In our construction, the clients only participate in the input phase and the output phase. The main computation is conducted by the servers. For simplicity, we use $\{P_1, \ldots, P_n\}$ to denote the n servers, and refer to the servers as parties. Let $\mathcal{C}$ denote the set of all corrupted parties and $\mathcal{H}$ denote the set of all honest parties. One benefit of the client-server model is the following theorem shown in [GIP+14].

Theorem 2 (Lemma 5.2 [GIP+14]**).** *Let Π be a protocol computing a c-client circuit C using $n = 2t + 1$ parties. Then, if Π is secure against any adversary controlling exactly t parties, then Π is secure against any adversary controlling at most t parties.*

This theorem allows us to only consider the case where the adversary controls exactly t parties. Therefore in the following, we assume that there are exactly t corrupted parties.

3.2 Secret Sharing Scheme

Shamir Secret Sharing Scheme. In this work, we will use the standard Shamir Secret Sharing Scheme [Sha79]. Let n be the number of parties and $\mathbb{G}$ be a finite field of size $|\mathbb{G}| \geq n + 1$. Let $\alpha_1, \ldots, \alpha_n$ be n distinct non-zero elements in $\mathbb{G}$.

A *degree-d* Shamir sharing of $x \in \mathbb{G}$ is a vector $(x_1, \ldots, x_n)$ which satisfies that, there exists a polynomial $f(\cdot) \in \mathbb{G}[X]$ of degree at most d such that $f(0) = x$ and $f(\alpha_i) = x_i$ for $i \in \{1, \ldots, n\}$. Each party P_i holds a share x_i and the whole sharing is denoted by $[x]_d$.

We recall the properties of a degree-d Shamir sharing: (1) It requires $d+1$ shares to reconstruct the secret x, and (2) any d shares do not leak any information about x.

Abstract General Linear Secret Sharing Schemes. We adopt the notion of an abstract definition of a general linear secret sharing scheme (GLSSS) in [CCXY18]. The following notations are borrowed from [CCXY18].

For non-empty sets U and $\mathcal{I}$, $U^{\mathcal{I}}$ denotes the indexed Cartesian product $\prod_{i \in \mathcal{I}} U$. For a non-empty set $A \subset \mathcal{I}$, the natural projection π_A maps a tuple $u = (u_i)_{i \in \mathcal{I}} \in U^{\mathcal{I}}$ to the tuple $(u_i)_{i \in A} \in U^A$. Let K be a field.

Definition 1 (Abstract K-GLSSS [CCXY18]). *A general K-linear secret sharing scheme Σ consists of the following data:*

- *A set of parties $\mathcal{I} = \{1, \ldots, n\}$*
- *A finite-dimensional K-vector space Z, the secret space.*
- *A finite-dimensional K-vector space U, the share space.*
- *A K-linear subspace $C \subset U^{\mathcal{I}}$, where the latter is considered a K-vector space in the usual way (i.e., direct sum).*
- *A surjective K-linear map $\Phi : C \to Z$, its defining map.*

Definition 2 ([CCXY18]). *Suppose $A \subset \mathcal{I}$ is nonempty. Then A is a privacy set if the K-linear map*

$$(\Phi, \pi_A) : C \longrightarrow Z \times \pi_A(C), \quad x \mapsto (\Phi(x), \pi_A(x))$$

is surjective. Finally, A is a reconstruction set if, for all $x \in C$, it holds that

$$\pi_A(x) = 0 \Rightarrow \Phi(x) = 0.$$

A Tensoring-up Lemma. We follow the definition of interleaved GLSSS: the m-fold interleaved GLSSS $\Sigma^{\times m}$ is an n-party scheme which corresponds to m Σ-sharings. We have the following proposition from [CCXY18]:

Proposition 1 ([CCXY18]). *Let L be a degree-m extension field of K and let Σ be a K-GLSSS. Then the m-fold interleaved K-GLSSS $\Sigma^{\times m}$ is naturally viewed as an L-GLSSS, compatible with its K-linearity.*

Let $[x]$ denote a sharing in Σ. This proposition allows us to define $\lambda : \Sigma^{\times m} \to \Sigma^{\times m}$ for every $\lambda \in L$ such that for all $[\boldsymbol{x}] = ([x_1], \ldots, [x_m]) \in \Sigma^{\times m}$:

- for all $\lambda \in K$, $\lambda \cdot ([x_1], \ldots, [x_m]) = (\lambda \cdot [x_1], \ldots, \lambda \cdot [x_m])$;
- for all $\lambda_1, \lambda_2 \in L$, $\lambda_1 \cdot [\boldsymbol{x}] + \lambda_2 \cdot [\boldsymbol{x}] = (\lambda_1 + \lambda_2) \cdot [\boldsymbol{x}]$;
- for all $\lambda_1, \lambda_2 \in L$, $\lambda_1 \cdot (\lambda_2 \cdot [\boldsymbol{x}]) = (\lambda_1 \cdot \lambda_2) \cdot [\boldsymbol{x}]$.

An Example of a GLSSS and Using the Tensoring-up Lemma. We will use the standard Shamir secret sharing scheme as an example of a GLSSS and show how to use the tensoring-up lemma. For a field K (of size $|K| \geq n+1$), we may define a secret sharing Σ which takes an input $x \in K$ and outputs $[x]_t$, i.e., a degree-t Shamir sharing. The secret space and the share space of Σ are K. According to the Lagrange interpolation, the secret x can be written as a K-linear combination of all the shares. Therefore, the defining map of Σ is K-linear. Thus Σ is a K-GLSSS.

A sharing $[\boldsymbol{x}]_t = ([x_1]_t, [x_2]_t, \ldots, [x_m]_t) \in \Sigma^{\times m}$ is a vector of m sharings in Σ. Let L be a degree-m extension field of K. The tensoring-up lemma says that $\Sigma^{\times m}$ is a L-GLSSS. Therefore we can perform L-linear operations to the sharings in $\Sigma^{\times m}$.

3.3 Reverse Multiplication Friendly Embeddings

Definition 3 ([CCXY18]). *Let k, m be integers and $\mathbb{F}_q$ be a finite field. A pair (ϕ, ψ) is called an $(k, m)_q$-reverse multiplication friendly embedding (RMFE) if $\phi : \mathbb{F}_q^k \to \mathbb{F}_{q^m}$ and $\psi : \mathbb{F}_{q^m} \to \mathbb{F}_q^k$ are two $\mathbb{F}_q$-linear maps satisfying*

$$\boldsymbol{x} * \boldsymbol{y} = \psi(\phi(\boldsymbol{x}) \cdot \phi(\boldsymbol{y}))$$

for all $\boldsymbol{x}, \boldsymbol{y} \in \mathbb{F}_q^k$, where $*$ denotes coordinate-wise product.

Note that when picking $\mathbf{1} = (1, 1, \ldots, 1)$, we have $\boldsymbol{x} * \mathbf{1} = \boldsymbol{x}$ and therefore, $\boldsymbol{x} = \psi(\phi(\boldsymbol{x}) \cdot \phi(\mathbf{1}))$. It implies that ϕ is injective. Therefore, there exists ϕ^{-1} : $\mathrm{Im}(\phi) \to \mathbb{F}_q^k$ such that for all $\boldsymbol{x} \in \mathbb{F}_q^k$, it satisfies that

$$\phi^{-1}(\phi(\boldsymbol{x})) = \boldsymbol{x}.$$

It is easy to verify that ϕ^{-1} is also $\mathbb{F}_q$-linear.

Now we show that there exists an $\mathbb{F}_q$-linear map $\tilde{\phi}^{-1} : \mathbb{F}_{q^m} \to \mathbb{F}_q^k$ such that for all $\boldsymbol{x} \in \mathbb{F}_q^k$,

$$\tilde{\phi}^{-1}(\phi(\boldsymbol{x})) = \boldsymbol{x}.$$

Lemma 1. *Let k, m be integers and $\mathbb{F}_q$ be a finite field. Suppose (ϕ, ψ) is an $(k, m)_q$-reverse multiplication friendly embedding. Then there exists an $\mathbb{F}_q$-linear map $\tilde{\phi}^{-1} : \mathbb{F}_{q^m} \to \mathbb{F}_q^k$ such that for all $\boldsymbol{x} \in \mathbb{F}_q^k$,*

$$\tilde{\phi}^{-1}(\phi(\boldsymbol{x})) = \boldsymbol{x}.$$

Proof. Let $\mathbf{1} = (1, 1, \ldots, 1) \in \mathbb{F}_q^k$. We explicitly construct $\tilde{\phi}^{-1}$ as follows:

$$\tilde{\phi}^{-1} : \mathbb{F}_{q^m} \longrightarrow \mathbb{F}_q^k, \quad x \mapsto \psi(\phi(\mathbf{1}) \cdot x)$$

It is clear that $\tilde{\phi}^{-1}$ is $\mathbb{F}_q$-linear. For all $\boldsymbol{x} \in \mathbb{F}_q^k$, by the definition of RMFE, we have

$$\tilde{\phi}^{-1}(\phi(\boldsymbol{x})) = \psi(\phi(\mathbf{1}) \cdot \phi(\boldsymbol{x})) = \mathbf{1} * \boldsymbol{x} = \boldsymbol{x}.$$

□

In [CCXY18], Cascudo et al. show that there exist constant rate RMFEs, which is summarized in Theorem 3.

Theorem 3. *For every finite prime power q, there exists a family of constant rate $(k, m)_q$-RMFE where $m = \Theta(k)$.*

3.4 Useful Building Blocks

In this part, we will introduce three functionalities which will be used in our main construction.

- The first functionality $\mathcal{F}_{\text{coin}}$ allows all parties to generate a random element. An instantiation of this functionality can be found in [GSZ20] (Protocol 6 in Sect. 3.5 of [GS20]), which has communication complexity $O(n^2)$ elements in $\mathbb{F}_{q^m}$ (i.e., $O(n^2 \cdot m)$ elements in $\mathbb{F}_q$).
- The second functionality $\mathcal{F}_{\text{mult}}$ allows all parties to evaluate a multiplication with inputs being shared by degree-t Shamir sharings. While $\mathcal{F}_{\text{mult}}$ protects the secrets of the input sharings, it allows the adversary to add an arbitrary fixed value to the multiplication result. This functionality can be instantiated by the multiplication protocol in the semi-honest DN protocol [DN07]. In [GSZ20], Goyal et al. also provide a detailed proof of the security of the multiplication protocol in [DN07] (Lemma 4 in Sect. 4.1 of [GS20]). The amortized communication complexity per multiplication is $O(n)$ field elements per party.
- The third functionality $\mathcal{F}_{\text{multVerify}}$ allows all parties to verify the correctness of multiplications computed by $\mathcal{F}_{\text{mult}}$. An instantiation of $\mathcal{F}_{\text{multVerify}}$ can be found in [GSZ20] (Protocol 17 in Sect. 5.4 of [GS20]), which has communication complexity $O(n^2 \cdot \log N \cdot \kappa)$ bits, where n is the number of parties and κ is the security parameter. Note that the amortized communication per multiplication tuple is sub-linear.

We refer the readers to Sect. 3.4 in the full version of this paper [PS20] for the descriptions of these functionalities.

4 Preparing Random Sharings for $\mathbb{F}_q$-GLSSS

In this section, we present the protocol for preparing random sharings for a given general $\mathbb{F}_q$-linear secret sharing scheme, denoted by Σ. Let $[x]$ denote a sharing in Σ of secret x. For a set $A \subset \mathcal{I}$, recall that $\pi_A([x])$ refers to the shares of $[x]$ held by parties in A. We assume that Σ satisfies the following property:

- Given a set $A \subset \mathcal{I}$ and a set of shares $\{a_i\}_{i \in A}$ for parties in A, let

$$\Sigma(A, (a_i)_{i \in A}) := \{[x] \| \ [x] \in \Sigma \text{ and } \pi_A([x]) = (a_i)_{i \in A}\}.$$

Then, there is an efficient algorithm which outputs that either $\Sigma(A, (a_i)_{i \in A}) = \emptyset$, or a random sharing $[x]$ in $\Sigma(A, (a_i)_{i \in A})$.

The description of the functionality $\mathcal{F}_{\text{rand}}$ appears in Functionality 1. In short, $\mathcal{F}_{\text{rand}}$ allows the adversary to specify the shares held by corrupted parties. Based on these shares, $\mathcal{F}_{\text{rand}}$ generates a random sharing in Σ and distributes the shares to honest parties. Note that, when the set of corrupted parties is a privacy set, the secret is independent of the shares chosen by the adversary.

Functionality 1: $\mathcal{F}_{\text{rand}}$

1. $\mathcal{F}_{\text{rand}}$ receives from the adversary the set of corrupted parties, denoted by $\mathcal{C}$, and a set of shares $(s_i)_{i\in\mathcal{C}}$ such that $\Sigma(\mathcal{C},(s_i)_{i\in\mathcal{C}}) \neq \emptyset$. Then $\mathcal{F}_{\text{rand}}$ randomly samples $[r] \in \Sigma(\mathcal{C},(s_i)_{i\in\mathcal{C}})$.
2. $\mathcal{F}_{\text{rand}}$ asks the adversary whether it should continue or not.
   - If the adversary replies `abort`, $\mathcal{F}_{\text{rand}}$ sends `abort` to honest parites.
   - If the adversary replies `continue`, for each honest party P_i, $\mathcal{F}_{\text{rand}}$ sends the i-th share of $[r]$ to P_i.

We will follow the idea in [BSFO12] of preparing random degree-t Shamir sharings to prepare random sharings in Σ. At a high-level, each party first deals a batch of random sharings in Σ. For each party, all parties together verify that the sharings dealt by this party have the correct form. Then all parties locally convert the sharings dealt by each party to random sharings such that the secrets are not known to any single party.

We refer the readers to Sect. 4 in the full version of this paper [PS20] for the construction for $\mathcal{F}_{\text{rand}}$. Suppose the share size of a sharing in Σ is sh field elements in $\mathbb{F}_q$. The communication complexity of preparing N random sharings in Σ is $O(N \cdot n \cdot \mathsf{sh} + n^3 \cdot m)$ elements in $\mathbb{F}_q$.

5 Hidden Additive Secret Sharing

Let (ϕ, ψ) be an $(k, m)_q$-RMFE. Recall that n denotes the number of parties and $\phi : \mathbb{F}_q^k \to \mathbb{F}_{q^m}$ is an $\mathbb{F}_q$-linear map. Recall that $|\mathbb{F}_{q^m}| = q^m \geq 2^\kappa \geq n+1$. Thus, the Shamir secret sharing scheme is well-defined in $\mathbb{F}_{q^m}$. In our construction, we will use ϕ to encode a vector $\boldsymbol{x} = (x^{(1)}, \ldots, x^{(k)}) \in \mathbb{F}_q^k$. All parties will hold a degree-t Shamir sharing of $\phi(\boldsymbol{x})$, denoted by $[\phi(\boldsymbol{x})]_t$.

Defining Additive Sharings and Couple Sharings. For $x \in \mathbb{F}_q$, we use $\langle x \rangle$ to denote an additive sharing of x among the first $t+1$ parties in $\mathbb{F}_q$. Specifically, $\langle x \rangle = (x_1, \ldots, x_n)$ where the party P_i holds the share $x_i \in \mathbb{F}_q$ such that $x = \sum_{i=1}^{t+1} x_i$ and the last t shares $x_{t+2}, \ldots, x_n$ are all 0.

Recall that $\psi : \mathbb{F}_{q^m} \to \mathbb{F}_q^k$ is an $\mathbb{F}_q$-linear map. For all $y \in \mathbb{F}_{q^m}$, if $\psi(y) = (y_1, y_2, \ldots, y_k)$, we define $\mathsf{val}(y) := \sum_{i=1}^k y_i$. Note that $\mathsf{val}(\cdot)$ is an $\mathbb{F}_q$-linear map from $\mathbb{F}_{q^m}$ to $\mathbb{F}_q$. We say a pair of sharings $(\langle x \rangle, [y]_t)$ is a pair of *couple sharings* if

- $\langle x \rangle$ is an additive sharing of $x \in \mathbb{F}_q$;
- $[y]_t$ is a degree-t Shamir sharing of $y \in \mathbb{F}_{q^m}$;
- $\mathsf{val}(y) = x$.

In the following, we will use $[\![x]\!] := (\langle x \rangle, [y]_t)$ to denote a pair of couple sharings of $x \in \mathbb{F}_q$. Note that for the additive sharing $\langle x \rangle$, a corrupted party in the first $t+1$ parties can easily change the secret by changing its own share. However, the secret of $[y]_t$ is determined by the shares of honest parties and cannot be altered by corrupted parties. Therefore, $[y]_t$ can be seen as a robust version of the sharing $\langle x \rangle$.

Properties of Couple Sharings. We note that couple sharings are $\mathbb{F}_q$-linear. Concretely, for all couple sharings $[\![x]\!] = (\langle x \rangle, [y]_t)$ and $[\![x']\!] = (\langle x' \rangle, [y']_t)$, and for all $\alpha, \beta \in \mathbb{F}_q$, the linear combination

$$\alpha \cdot [\![x]\!] + \beta \cdot [\![x']\!] := (\alpha \cdot \langle x \rangle + \beta \cdot \langle x' \rangle, \alpha \cdot [y]_t + \beta \cdot [y']_t)$$

is still a pair of couple sharings. This property follows from the fact that $\mathsf{val}(\cdot)$ is an $\mathbb{F}_q$-linear map.

We can also define the addition operation between a pair of couple sharings $[\![x]\!]$ and a field element x' in $\mathbb{F}_q$. This is done by transforming x' to a pair of couple sharings of x'. For $\langle x' \rangle$, we set the share of the first party to be x', and the shares of the rest of parties to be 0. For the degree-t Shamir sharing, we first need to find $y' \in \mathbb{F}_{q^m}$ such that $\mathsf{val}(y') = x'$. This is done by choosing two vectors $\boldsymbol{a}, \boldsymbol{b} \in \mathbb{F}_q^k$ such that:

- For $\boldsymbol{a}$, the first entry is 1 and the rest of entries are 0.
- For $\boldsymbol{b}$, the first entry is x' and the rest of entries are 0.

By the property of RMFE, $\psi(\phi(\boldsymbol{a}) \cdot \phi(\boldsymbol{b})) = \boldsymbol{a} * \boldsymbol{b}$. In particular, the first entry of $\boldsymbol{a} * \boldsymbol{b}$ is x' and the rest of entries are 0. Therefore $y' := \phi(\boldsymbol{a}) \cdot \phi(\boldsymbol{b})$ satisfies that $\mathsf{val}(y') = x'$. For $[y']_t$, we set the share of each party to be y'. Finally, the addition operation between $[\![x]\!]$ and $x' \in \mathbb{F}_q$ is defined by

$$[\![x]\!] + x' := (\langle x \rangle, [y]_t) + (\langle x' \rangle, [y']_t).$$

Generating Couple Sharings from $[\phi(\boldsymbol{x})]_t$. In this part, we show how to *non-interactively* obtain k pairs of couple sharings $[\![x^{(1)}]\!], [\![x^{(2)}]\!], \ldots, [\![x^{(k)}]\!]$ from a degree-t Shamir sharing $[\phi(\boldsymbol{x})]_t$, where $\boldsymbol{x} = (x^{(1)}, x^{(2)}, \ldots, x^{(k)}) \in \mathbb{F}_q^k$. It allows us to prepare k pairs of random couple sharings with the cost of preparing one random sharing $[\phi(\boldsymbol{x})]_t$.

We first show how to obtain $[y^{(i)}]_t$ such that $\mathsf{val}(y^{(i)}) = x^{(i)}$ for all $i \in [k]$. Let $\boldsymbol{e}^{(i)}$ be a vector in $\mathbb{F}_q^k$ such that all entries are 0 except that the i-th entry is 1. By the property of RMFE, we have

$$\psi(\phi(\boldsymbol{e}^{(i)}) \cdot \phi(\boldsymbol{x})) = \boldsymbol{e}^{(i)} * \boldsymbol{x}.$$

For $\boldsymbol{e}^{(i)} * \boldsymbol{x}$, all entries are 0 except that the i-th entry is $x^{(i)}$. Therefore by the definition of $\mathsf{val}(\cdot)$, we have $\mathsf{val}(\phi(\boldsymbol{e}^{(i)}) \cdot \phi(\boldsymbol{x})) = x^{(i)}$. To obtain $[y^{(i)}]_t$, all parties compute

$$[y^{(i)}]_t := \phi(\boldsymbol{e}^{(i)}) \cdot [\phi(\boldsymbol{x})]_t.$$

Now we show how to obtain $\langle x^{(i)} \rangle$ from $[\phi(\boldsymbol{x})]$. Let $\langle \boldsymbol{x} \rangle := (\langle x^{(1)} \rangle, \ldots, \langle x^{(k)} \rangle)$ denote a vector of additive sharings of $\boldsymbol{x} \in \mathbb{F}_q^k$. For each party, its share of $\langle \boldsymbol{x} \rangle$ is a vector in $\mathbb{F}_q^k$. For the last t parties, they take the all-0 vector as their shares.

Recall that the degree-t Shamir sharing $[\phi(\boldsymbol{x})]_t$ corresponds to a degree-t polynomial $f(\cdot) \in \mathbb{F}_{q^m}[X]$ such that $f(\alpha_i)$ is the share of the i-th party P_i and $f(0) = \phi(\boldsymbol{x})$, where $\alpha_1, \ldots, \alpha_n$ are distinct non-zero elements in $\mathbb{F}_{q^m}$. In particular, relying on Lagrange interpolation, $f(0)$ can be written as a linear combination of the first $t+1$ shares. For $i \in \{1, \ldots, t+1\}$, let $c_i = \prod_{j \neq i, j \in [t+1]} \frac{\alpha_j}{\alpha_j - \alpha_i}$. We have

$$f(0) = \sum_{i=1}^{t+1} c_i f(\alpha_i).$$

Therefore, the Shamir sharing $[\phi(\boldsymbol{x})]_t$ can be locally converted to an additive sharing of $\phi(\boldsymbol{x})$ among the first $t+1$ parties by letting P_i take $c_i f(\alpha_i)$ as its share. For each $i \in \{1, \ldots, t+1\}$, P_i locally applies $\tilde{\phi}^{-1}(c_i f(\alpha_i))$, which outputs a vector in $\mathbb{F}_q^k$. It is sufficient to show that these $t+1$ shares correspond to an additive sharing of $\boldsymbol{x}$. Note that

$$\sum_{i=1}^{t+1} \tilde{\phi}^{-1}(c_i f(\alpha_i)) = \tilde{\phi}^{-1}(\sum_{i=1}^{t+1} c_i f(\alpha_i)) = \tilde{\phi}^{-1}(f(0)) = \boldsymbol{x}.$$

The description of SEPARATE appears in Protocol 2.

Protocol 2: SEPARATE($[\phi(\boldsymbol{x})]_t$)

1. For all $i \in [k]$, let $\boldsymbol{e}^{(i)}$ be a vector in $\mathbb{F}_q^k$ such that all entries are 0 except that the i-th entry is 1. All parties locally compute $[y^{(i)}]_t := \phi(\boldsymbol{e}^{(i)}) \cdot [\phi(\boldsymbol{x})]_t$.
2. Let $\alpha_1, \ldots, \alpha_n$ be n distinct elements in $\mathbb{F}_{q^m}$ defined in the Shamir secret sharing scheme.
   - For each $i \in \{1, \ldots, t+1\}$, P_i locally computes $c_i = \prod_{j \neq i, j \in [t+1]} \frac{\alpha_j}{\alpha_j - \alpha_i}$. Let $f(\alpha_i)$ denote the i-th share of $[\phi(\boldsymbol{x})]_t$. P_i locally computes $\tilde{\phi}^{-1}(c_i f(\alpha_i))$ and regards the result as the i-th share of $\langle \boldsymbol{x} \rangle = (\langle x^{(1)} \rangle, \ldots, \langle x^{(k)} \rangle)$.
   - For each $i \in \{t+2, \ldots, n\}$, P_i takes the all-0 vector as its share of $\langle \boldsymbol{x} \rangle$.
3. For all $i \in [k]$, all parties set $[\![x^{(i)}]\!] := (\langle x^{(i)} \rangle, [y^{(i)}]_t)$. All parties take the following k pairs of couple sharings as output:

$$[\![x^{(1)}]\!], [\![x^{(2)}]\!], \ldots, [\![x^{(k)}]\!]$$

6 Building Blocks for Preprocessing Phase

In this section, we will introduce 4 functionalities which are used to prepare necessary correlated-randomness for the computation.

- The first functionality $\mathcal{F}_{\text{random}}$ allows all parties to prepare random sharings in the form of $[\phi(\boldsymbol{r})]_t$, where (ϕ, ψ) is a RMFE, and $\boldsymbol{r}$ is a random vector in $\mathbb{F}_q^k$.
- The second functionality $\mathcal{F}_{\text{tuple}}$ allows all parties to prepare random tuple of sharings in the form of $([\phi(\boldsymbol{a})]_t, [\phi(\boldsymbol{b})]_t, [\phi(\boldsymbol{c})]_t)$, where $\boldsymbol{a}, \boldsymbol{b}$ are random vectors in $\mathbb{F}_q^k$, and $\boldsymbol{c} = \boldsymbol{a} * \boldsymbol{b}$. For each tuple, relying on Separate, all parties can locally obtain k multiplication tuples in the form of $([\![a]\!], [\![b]\!], [\![c]\!])$, where a, b are random elements in $\mathbb{F}_q$, and $c = a \cdot b$. Such a multiplication tuple is referred to as a Beaver tuple. In the online phase, one Beaver tuple will be consumed to compute a multiplication gate.
- Recall that we use $\langle x \rangle$ to denote an additive sharing of $x \in \mathbb{F}_q$ among the first $t+1$ parties, and the shares of the rest of parties are 0. The third functionality $\mathcal{F}_{\text{zero}}$ allows all parties to prepare random additive sharings of 0. When evaluating a multiplication gate in the online phase, we will use random additive sharings of 0 to protect the shares of honest parties.
- Recall that $\mathsf{val}(\cdot) : \mathbb{F}_{q^m} \to \mathbb{F}_q$ is an $\mathbb{F}_q$-linear map, defined by $\mathsf{val}(y) = \sum_{i=1}^k y_i$, where $(y_1, y_2, \ldots, y_k) = \psi(y)$. The last functionality $\mathcal{F}_{\text{parity}}$ allows all parties to prepare random sharings in the form of $[p]_t$, where $\mathsf{val}(p) = 0$. These random sharings are used at the end of the protocol to verify the computation.

6.1 Preparing Random Sharings

In this part, we introduce the functionality to let all parties prepare random sharings in the form of $[\phi(\boldsymbol{r})]_t$. Recall that (ϕ, ψ) is an $(k, m)_q$-RMFE. Here each $[\phi(\boldsymbol{r})]_t$ is a random degree-t Shamir sharing of the secret $\phi(\boldsymbol{r})$ where $\boldsymbol{r}$ is a random vector in $\mathbb{F}_q^k$. The description of $\mathcal{F}_{\text{random}}$ appears in Functionality 3. In Sect. 6.1 of the full version of this paper [PS20], we show how to use $\mathcal{F}_{\text{rand}}$ to instantiate $\mathcal{F}_{\text{random}}$. Relying on the protocol (Sect. 4 in [PS20]) for $\mathcal{F}_{\text{rand}}$, we can generate N random sharings in the form of $[\phi(\boldsymbol{r})]_t$ with communication of $O(N \cdot n \cdot m + n^3 \cdot m)$ elements in $\mathbb{F}_q$.

6.2 Preparing Beaver Tuples

In this part, we show how to prepare random tuples of sharings in $\mathbb{F}_{q^m}$ in the form of $([\phi(\boldsymbol{a})]_t, [\phi(\boldsymbol{b})]_t, [\phi(\boldsymbol{c})]_t)$ where $\boldsymbol{a}, \boldsymbol{b}$ are random vectors in $\mathbb{F}_q^k$, and $\boldsymbol{c} = \boldsymbol{a} * \boldsymbol{b}$. The description of $\mathcal{F}_{\text{tuple}}$ appears in Functionality 4. In Sect. 6.2 of the full version of this paper [PS20], we introduce an instantiation of $\mathcal{F}_{\text{tuple}}$. The communication complexity of preparing N tuples of sharings in the form of $([\phi(\boldsymbol{a})]_t, [\phi(\boldsymbol{b})]_t, [\phi(\boldsymbol{c})]_t)$ is $O(N \cdot n \cdot m + n^3 \cdot m + n^2 \cdot \log N \cdot m)$ elements in $\mathbb{F}_q$.

In the online phase, each tuple $([\phi(\boldsymbol{a})]_t, [\phi(\boldsymbol{b})]_t, [\phi(\boldsymbol{c})]_t)$ will be separated by Separate (Protocol 2) to k Beaver tuples

$$([\![a^{(1)}]\!], [\![b^{(1)}]\!], [\![c^{(1)}]\!]), ([\![a^{(2)}]\!], [\![b^{(2)}]\!], [\![c^{(2)}]\!]), \ldots, ([\![a^{(k)}]\!], [\![b^{(k)}]\!], [\![c^{(k)}]\!]).$$

Functionality 3: $\mathcal{F}_{\text{random}}$

1. $\mathcal{F}_{\text{random}}$ receives $\{s_i\}_{i \in \mathcal{C}}$ from the adversary, where $\mathcal{C}$ is the set of corrupted parties. Then $\mathcal{F}_{\text{random}}$ randomly samples $\boldsymbol{r} \in \mathbb{F}_q^k$ and generates a degree-t Shamir sharing $[\phi(\boldsymbol{r})]_t$ such that the share of $P_i \in \mathcal{C}$ is s_i.
2. $\mathcal{F}_{\text{random}}$ asks the adversary whether it should continue or not.
   - If the adversary replies `abort`, $\mathcal{F}_{\text{random}}$ sends `abort` to honest parties.
   - If the adversary replies `continue`, for each honest party P_i, $\mathcal{F}_{\text{random}}$ sends the i-th share of $[\phi(\boldsymbol{r})]_t$ to P_i.

A Beaver tuple $([\![a^{(i)}]\!], [\![b^{(i)}]\!], [\![c^{(i)}]\!])$ satisfies that $a^{(i)}, b^{(i)}$ are random elements in $\mathbb{F}_q$ and $c^{(i)} = a^{(i)} \cdot b^{(i)}$. A multiplication gate is then evaluated by consuming one Beaver tuple. More details can be found in Sect. 7.2.

Functionality 4: $\mathcal{F}_{\text{tuple}}$

1. $\mathcal{F}_{\text{tuple}}$ receives $\{(u_i, v_i, w_i)\}_{i \in \mathcal{C}}$ from the adversary, where $\mathcal{C}$ is the set of corrupted parties. Then $\mathcal{F}_{\text{tuple}}$ randomly samples $\boldsymbol{a}, \boldsymbol{b} \in \mathbb{F}_q^k$ and computes $\boldsymbol{c} = \boldsymbol{a} * \boldsymbol{b}$. Finally, $\mathcal{F}_{\text{tuple}}$ generates 3 degree-t Shamir sharings $[\phi(\boldsymbol{a})]_t, [\phi(\boldsymbol{b})]_t, [\phi(\boldsymbol{c})]_t$ such that the shares of $P_i \in \mathcal{C}$ are u_i, v_i, w_i respectively.
2. $\mathcal{F}_{\text{tuple}}$ asks the adversary whether it should continue or not.
   - If the adversary replies `abort`, $\mathcal{F}_{\text{tuple}}$ sends `abort` to honest parties.
   - If the adversary replies `continue`, for each honest party P_i, $\mathcal{F}_{\text{tuple}}$ sends the i-th shares of $[\phi(\boldsymbol{a})]_t, [\phi(\boldsymbol{b})]_t, [\phi(\boldsymbol{c})]_t$ to P_i.

6.3 Preparing Zero Additive Sharings

With Beaver tuples prepared in the preprocessing phase, all parties only need to do reconstructions in the online phase. To protect the shares held by honest parties, for each reconstruction, we will prepare a random additive sharing of 0 among the first $t+1$ parties. We summarize the functionality for zero additive sharings in Functionality 5. In Sect. 6.3 of the full version of this paper [PS20], we show how to use $\mathcal{F}_{\text{rand}}$ to instantiate $\mathcal{F}_{\text{zero}}$. Relying on the protocol (Sect. 4 in [PS20]) for $\mathcal{F}_{\text{rand}}$, we can generate N random sharings in the form of $\langle o \rangle$ with communication of $O(N \cdot n + n^3 \cdot m)$ elements in $\mathbb{F}_q$.

Functionality 5: $\mathcal{F}_{\text{zero}}$

1. $\mathcal{F}_{\text{zero}}$ receives $\{s_i\}_{i \in \mathcal{C} \bigcap \{1,\ldots,t+1\}}$ from the adversary, where $\mathcal{C}$ is the set of corrupted parties. Then $\mathcal{F}_{\text{zero}}$ randomly samples an additive sharing $\langle o \rangle$ such that $o = 0$, and for each $i \in \mathcal{C} \bigcap \{1, \ldots, t+1\}$, the i-th share of $\langle o \rangle$ is s_i.
2. $\mathcal{F}_{\text{zero}}$ asks the adversary whether it should continue or not.
   - If the adversary replies `abort`, $\mathcal{F}_{\text{zero}}$ sends `abort` to honest parties.
   - If the adversary replies `continue`, $\mathcal{F}_{\text{zero}}$ distributes the shares of $\langle o \rangle$ to parties in $\mathcal{H} \bigcap \{1, \ldots, t+1\}$, where $\mathcal{H}$ is the set of honest parties.

6.4 Preparing Parity Sharings

Recall that all parties only need to do reconstructions in the online phase. At the end of the online phase, it is sufficient to only verify the reconstructions. To this end, we first define what we call parity elements and parity sharings.

Recall that $\mathsf{val}(\cdot) : \mathbb{F}_{q^m} \rightarrow \mathbb{F}_q$ is an $\mathbb{F}_q$-linear map, defined by $\mathsf{val}(y) = \sum_{i=1}^{k} y_i$, where $(y_1, y_2, \ldots, y_k) = \psi(y)$. For an element $p \in \mathbb{F}_{q^m}$, we say p is a parity element if $\mathsf{val}(p) = 0$. A parity sharing is a degree-t Shamir sharing of a parity element. At the end of the protocol, we will use uniformly random parity sharings as masks when checking the correctness of the reconstructions. We summarize the functionality for preparing random parity sharings in Functionality 6. In Sect. 6.4 of the full version of this paper [PS20], we show how to use $\mathcal{F}_{\text{rand}}$ to instantiate $\mathcal{F}_{\text{parity}}$. Relying on the protocol (Sect. 4 in [PS20]) for $\mathcal{F}_{\text{rand}}$, we can generate N random parity sharings with communication of $O(N \cdot n \cdot m + n^3 \cdot m)$ elements in $\mathbb{F}_q$.

Functionality 6: $\mathcal{F}_{\text{parity}}$

1. $\mathcal{F}_{\text{parity}}$ receives $\{u_i\}_{i \in \mathcal{C}}$ from the adversary, where $\mathcal{C}$ is the set of corrupted parties. Then $\mathcal{F}_{\text{parity}}$ randomly samples $p \in \mathbb{F}_{q^m}$ such that $\mathsf{val}(p) = 0$. Finally, $\mathcal{F}_{\text{parity}}$ generates a degree-t sharing $[p]_t$ such that the share of $P_i \in \mathcal{C}$ is u_i.
2. $\mathcal{F}_{\text{parity}}$ asks the adversary whether it should continue or not.
   - If the adversary replies `abort`, $\mathcal{F}_{\text{parity}}$ sends `abort` to honest parties.
   - If the adversary replies `continue`, for each honest party P_i, $\mathcal{F}_{\text{parity}}$ sends the i-th share of $[p]_t$ to P_i.

7 Online Phase

Let (ϕ, ψ) be an $(k, m)_q$-RMFE. Recall that

- $\mathsf{val}(\cdot) : \mathbb{F}_{q^m} \to \mathbb{F}_q$ is defined by $\mathsf{val}(y) = \sum_{i=1}^{k} y_i$, where $(y_1, \ldots, y_k) = \psi(y)$.
- We use $\langle x \rangle$ to denote an additive sharing of $x \in \mathbb{F}_q$ among the first $t+1$ parties, and the shares of the rest of parties are 0.
- A pair of couple sharings $[\![x]\!] := (\langle x \rangle, [y]_t)$ contains an additive sharing of $x \in \mathbb{F}_q$ and a degree-t Shamir sharing of $y \in \mathbb{F}_{q^m}$ such that $\mathsf{val}(y) = x$.

In the online phase, our idea is to compute a pair of couple sharings for each wire. For an addition gate, given two pairs of couple sharings as input, all parties can locally compute the addition of these two sharings. For a multiplication gate, relying on Beaver tuples prepared in the preprocessing phase, all parties only need to reconstruct two pairs of couple sharings. We note that for the two sharings in a pair of couple sharings:

- The first sharing is an additive sharing in $\mathbb{F}_q$. The share of each party is just a field element in $\mathbb{F}_q$. We will use this sharing to do reconstruction. However, the correctness cannot be guaranteed since a single corrupted party can change the secret by changing its own share.
- The second sharing is a degree-t Shamir sharing in $\mathbb{F}_{q^m}$. The share of each party is a field element in $\mathbb{F}_{q^m}$. Note that the secret is determined by the shares of honest parties, and cannot be altered by corrupted parties. However, using this sharing to do reconstruction is expensive. Therefore, we will use this sharing to verify the correctness of reconstruction at the end of the protocol.

7.1 Input Gates

Recall that we are in the client-server model. In particular, all the inputs belong to the clients. In this part, we introduce a protocol INPUT, which allows a client to share k inputs to all parties. In the main protocol, we will invoke INPUT for every client with k inputs.

The description of INPUT appears in Protocol 7. The communication complexity of INPUT(Client, $\{x^{(1)}, \ldots, x^{(k)}\}$) is $O(m+k)$ elements in $\mathbb{F}_q$ plus one call of $\mathcal{F}_{\text{random}}$. Note that this protocol guarantees the security of the inputs of honest clients. This is because the input of honest clients are masked by random vectors $\boldsymbol{r}$'s which are chosen by $\mathcal{F}_{\text{random}}$. However, a corrupted client can send different values to different parties, which leads to incorrect or inconsistent couple sharings in the final step. We will address this issue by checking consistency of the values distributed by all clients at the end of the protocol.

7.2 Addition Gates and Multiplication Gates

For each fan-in two addition gate with input sharings $[\![x^{(1)}]\!], [\![x^{(2)}]\!]$, all parties locally compute

$$[\![x^{(0)}]\!] := [\![x^{(1)} + x^{(2)}]\!] = [\![x^{(1)}]\!] + [\![x^{(2)}]\!].$$

Protocol 7: INPUT(Client, $\{x^{(1)}, \ldots, x^{(k)}\}$)

1. All parties invoke $\mathcal{F}_{\text{random}}$ to prepare a random sharing $[\phi(\boldsymbol{r})]_t$, where $\boldsymbol{r}$ is a random vector in $\mathbb{F}_q^k$. Then, all parties send their shares of $[\phi(\boldsymbol{r})]_t$ to the Client.
2. After receiving the shares of $[\phi(\boldsymbol{r})]_t$, the Client checks whether all the shares lie on a polynomial of degree at most t in $\mathbb{F}_{q^m}$. If not, the Client aborts. Otherwise, the Client reconstructs the secret $\phi(\boldsymbol{r})$.
3. The Client computes $\boldsymbol{r}$ from $\phi(\boldsymbol{r})$. Then, the Client sets $\boldsymbol{x} = (x^{(1)}, \ldots, x^{(k)})$, where $x^{(1)}, \ldots, x^{(k)}$ are its input. The Client sends $\boldsymbol{x} + \boldsymbol{r}$ to all parties.
4. After receiving $\boldsymbol{x} + \boldsymbol{r}$ from the Client, all parties locally compute $[\phi(\boldsymbol{x})]_t := \phi(\boldsymbol{x} + \boldsymbol{r}) - [\phi(\boldsymbol{r})]_t$.
5. All parties invoke SEPARATE on $[\phi(\boldsymbol{x})]_t$ to obtain couple sharings for the input of the Client:
$$(\langle x^{(1)}\rangle, [y^{(1)}]_t), \ldots, (\langle x^{(k)}\rangle, [y^{(k)}]_t)$$

For each multiplication gate with input sharings $[\![x^{(1)}]\!], [\![x^{(2)}]\!]$, we want to obtain a pair of couple sharings $[\![x^{(0)}]\!]$ such that $x^{(0)} = x^{(1)} \cdot x^{(2)}$. To this end, we will use one Beaver tuple $([\![a]\!], [\![b]\!], [\![c]\!])$ prepared in Sect. 6.2. It satisfies that a, b are random field elements in $\mathbb{F}_q$ and $c = a \cdot b$. Note that

$$\begin{aligned} x^{(0)} &= x^{(1)} \cdot x^{(2)} \\ &= (a + x^{(1)} - a) \cdot (b + x^{(2)} - b) \\ &= (a + x^{(1)}) \cdot (b + x^{(2)}) - (b + x^{(2)}) \cdot a - (a + x^{(1)}) \cdot b + a \cdot b \\ &= (a + x^{(1)}) \cdot (b + x^{(2)}) - (b + x^{(2)}) \cdot a - (a + x^{(1)}) \cdot b + c. \end{aligned}$$

Therefore, all parties only need to reconstruct the sharings $[\![a]\!] + [\![x^{(1)}]\!]$ and $[\![b]\!] + [\![x^{(2)}]\!]$, and the resulting sharing can be computed by

$$[\![x^{(0)}]\!] = (a + x^{(1)}) \cdot (b + x^{(2)}) - (b + x^{(2)}) \cdot [\![a]\!] - (a + x^{(1)}) \cdot [\![b]\!] + [\![c]\!].$$

To reconstruct $[\![a]\!] + [\![x^{(1)}]\!]$, we will use the additive sharing $\langle a + x^{(1)}\rangle := \langle a\rangle + \langle x^{(1)}\rangle$. We first add a random additive sharing $\langle o\rangle$ of 0 (prepared in Sect. 6.3) to protect the shares of honest parties. The first $t+1$ parties locally compute $\langle a\rangle + \langle x^{(1)}\rangle + \langle o\rangle$ and send their shares to P_1. P_1 reconstructs the secret $a + x^{(1)}$ and sends the result to all other parties. Similar process is done when reconstructing $\langle b + x^{(2)}\rangle := \langle b\rangle + \langle x^{(2)}\rangle$.

Note that $\langle a\rangle + \langle o\rangle$ is a random additive sharing. The share of each honest party in $\{P_1, \ldots, P_{t+1}\}$ is uniformly distributed. Essentially, each honest party in $\{P_1, \ldots, P_{t+1}\}$ uses a random element as mask to protect its own share. The protocol MULT appears in Protocol 8. The communication complexity of MULT is $O(n)$ elements in $\mathbb{F}_q$ plus two calls of $\mathcal{F}_{\text{zero}}$. The protocol MULT can go wrong at three places:

Protocol 8: $\text{MULT}([\![x^{(1)}]\!], [\![x^{(2)}]\!], ([\![a]\!], [\![b]\!], [\![c]\!]))$

1. All parties invoke $\mathcal{F}_{\text{zero}}$ to prepare two random additive sharings $\langle o^{(1)} \rangle, \langle o^{(2)} \rangle$ where $o^{(1)} = o^{(2)} = 0$.
2. Let $\langle x^{(1)} + a \rangle, \langle x^{(2)} + b \rangle$ denote the additive sharings in $[\![x^{(1)} + a]\!], [\![x^{(2)} + b]\!]$ respectively. The first $t+1$ parties locally compute $\langle u^{(1)} \rangle := \langle x^{(1)} + a \rangle + \langle o^{(1)} \rangle$ and $\langle u^{(2)} \rangle := \langle x^{(2)} + b \rangle + \langle o^{(2)} \rangle$. Then, they send their shares of $\langle u^{(1)} \rangle, \langle u^{(2)} \rangle$ to the first party P_1.
3. P_1 reconstructs the secrets $u^{(1)}, u^{(2)}$ by computing the summation of the shares of $\langle u^{(1)} \rangle$ and $\langle u^{(2)} \rangle$ respectively. Then, P_1 sends $u^{(1)}, u^{(2)}$ to all other parties (including the last t parties).
4. After receiving $u^{(1)}, u^{(2)}$, all parties locally compute the resulting couple sharings
$$[\![x^{(0)}]\!] = u^{(1)} \cdot u^{(2)} - u^{(2)} \cdot [\![a]\!] - u^{(1)} \cdot [\![b]\!] + [\![c]\!],$$
and take $[\![x^{(0)}]\!]$ as output.

- A corrupted party may send an incorrect share to P_1.
- P_1 is corrupted and distributes an incorrect reconstruction result to all other parties.
- P_1 is corrupted and distributes different values to different parties.

Note that, relying on the random additive sharing of 0, honest parties in the first $t+1$ parties only send random elements to P_1. Therefore, MULT does not leak any information about the shares of honest parties *even if the input sharings of the multiplication gate are not in the correct form*. It allows us to delay the verification of the values distributed by P_1 to the end of the protocol. It also allows us to delay the verification of the values distributed by clients in the input phase to the end of the protocol since a corrupted client distributing different values to different parties has the same effect as P_1 distributing different values to different parties. During the verification of the computation, we will first check whether all parties receive the same values to resolve the third issue. Then, for the first two issues, it is sufficient to check the correctness of the reconstructions.

7.3 Verification of the Computation

Before all parties revealing the outputs, we need to verify the computation. Concretely, we need to verify that (1) the clients distributed the same values in the input phase, and P_1 distributed the same values when evaluating multiplication gates, and (2) the reconstructions are correct.

Checking the Correctness of Distribution. All parties first check whether they receive the same values when handling input gates and multiplication gates. Note that these values are all in $\mathbb{F}_q$. Assume that these values are denoted by

$x^{(1)}, x^{(2)}, \ldots, x^{(N)}$. The protocol CHECKCONSISTENCY appears in Protocol 9. The communication complexity of CHECKCONSISTENCY$(N, \{x^{(1)}, \ldots, x^{(N)}\})$ is $O(n^2 \cdot m)$ elements in $\mathbb{F}_q$.

Protocol 9: CHECKCONSISTENCY$(N, \{x^{(1)}, \ldots, x^{(N)}\})$

1. All parties invoke $\mathcal{F}_{\text{coin}}(\mathbb{F}_{q^m})$ to generate a random element $r \in \mathbb{F}_{q^m}$. All parties locally compute
$$x := x^{(1)} + x^{(2)} \cdot r + \ldots + x^{(N)} \cdot r^{N-1}.$$
2. All parties exchange their results x's and check whether they are the same. If a party P_i receives different x's, P_i aborts.

Lemma 2. *If there exists two honest parties who receive different set of values* $\{x^{(1)}, \ldots, x^{(N)}\}$, *then with overwhelming probability, at least one honest party will abort in the protocol* CHECKCONSISTENCY.

We refer the readers to Sect. 7.3 in the full version of this paper [PS20] for the proof of Lemma 2.

This step makes sure that all (honest) parties receive the same values from clients and P_1. Therefore, the remaining task is to verify the correctness of the reconstructions.

Verification of Reconstructions. Recall that a pair of couple sharings $[\![x]\!] := (\langle x \rangle, [y]_t)$ satisfies that $\langle x \rangle$ is an additive sharing of x and $[y]_t$ is a degree-t Shamir sharing of y such that $\mathsf{val}(y) = x$. For a multiplication gate with input sharings $(\langle x^{(1)} \rangle, [y^{(1)}]_t), (\langle x^{(2)} \rangle, [y^{(2)}]_t)$, one Beaver tuple $((\langle a \rangle, [\alpha]_t), (\langle b \rangle, [\beta]_t), (\langle c \rangle, [\gamma]_t))$ is consumed to compute the resulting sharing. All parties reconstruct

$$(\langle x^{(1)} \rangle, [y^{(1)}]_t) + (\langle a \rangle, [\alpha]_t) \text{ and } (\langle x^{(2)} \rangle, [y^{(2)}]_t) + (\langle b \rangle, [\beta]_t),$$

and learn $x^{(1)} + a$ and $x^{(2)} + b$. Note that, the secret of a degree-t Shamir sharing is determined by the shares held by honest parties. Therefore, the correctness can be verified by checking $\mathsf{val}(y^{(1)} + \alpha) = x^{(1)} + a$ and $\mathsf{val}(y^{(2)} + \beta) = x^{(2)} + b$.

This task can be summarized as follows: Given N value-sharing pairs

$$(u^{(1)}, [w^{(1)}]_t), \ldots, (u^{(N)}, [w^{(N)}]_t),$$

where $u^{(i)} \in \mathbb{F}_q$ and $w^{(i)} \in \mathbb{F}_{q^m}$ for all $i \in [N]$, we want to verify that for all $i \in [N]$, $\mathsf{val}(w^{(i)}) = u^{(i)}$. Here $u^{(i)}$ corresponds to $x^{(1)} + a$ and $[w^{(i)}]_t$ corresponds to $[y^{(1)} + \alpha]_t$. The functionality $\mathcal{F}_{\text{checkRecon}}$ appears in Functionality 10. In Sect. 7.3 of the full version of this paper [PS20], we introduce an instantiation of $\mathcal{F}_{\text{checkRecon}}$. The communication complexity of this instantiation is $O(n^2 \cdot m^2)$ elements in $\mathbb{F}_q$ plus m calls of $\mathcal{F}_{\text{parity}}$.

Functionality 10: $\mathcal{F}_{\text{checkRecon}}$

1. Let N denote the number of value-sharing pairs. These value-sharing pairs are denoted by
$$(u^{(1)}, [w^{(1)}]_t), (u^{(2)}, [w^{(2)}]_t), \ldots, (u^{(N)}, [w^{(N)}]_t).$$
$\mathcal{F}_{\text{checkRecon}}$ will check whether $\mathsf{val}(w^{(i)}) = u^{(i)}$ for all $i \in [N]$.
2. For all $i \in [N]$, $\mathcal{F}_{\text{checkRecon}}$ receives from honest parties their shares of $[w^{(i)}]_t$. Then $\mathcal{F}_{\text{checkRecon}}$ reconstructs the secret $w^{(i)}$. $\mathcal{F}_{\text{checkRecon}}$ further computes the shares of $[w^{(i)}]_t$ held by corrupted parties and sends these shares to the adversary.
3. For all $i \in [N]$, $\mathcal{F}_{\text{checkRecon}}$ computes $\mathsf{val}(w^{(i)})$ and sends $u^{(i)}, \mathsf{val}(w^{(i)})$ to the adversary.
4. Finally, let $b \in \{\texttt{abort}, \texttt{accept}\}$ denote whether there exists $i \in [N]$ such that $\mathsf{val}(w^{(i)}) \neq u^{(i)}$. $\mathcal{F}_{\text{checkRecon}}$ sends b to the adversary and waits for its response.
   - If the adversary replies `abort`, $\mathcal{F}_{\text{checkRecon}}$ sends `abort` to honest parties.
   - If the adversary replies `continue`, $\mathcal{F}_{\text{checkRecon}}$ sends b to honest parties.

7.4 Output Gates

Recall that we are in the client-server model. In particular, only the clients receive the outputs. In this part, we will introduce a functionality $\mathcal{F}_{\text{output}}$ which reconstructs the output couple sharings to the client who should receive them. In the main protocol, we will invoke $\mathcal{F}_{\text{output}}$ for every client.

Suppose we need to reconstruct the following N pairs of couple sharings to the Client:
$$[\![x^{(1)}]\!], [\![x^{(2)}]\!], \ldots, [\![x^{(N)}]\!].$$
Recall that a pair of couple sharings $[\![x]\!] := (\langle x \rangle, [y]_t)$ satisfies that $\langle x \rangle$ is an additive sharing of x, and $[y]_t$ is a degree-t Shamir sharing of y such that $\mathsf{val}(y) = x$. The functionality $\mathcal{F}_{\text{output}}$ appears in Functionality 11. In Sect. 7.4 of the full version of this paper [PS20], we introduce an instantiation of $\mathcal{F}_{\text{output}}$. The communication complexity of this instantiation is $O(N \cdot n + n^2 \cdot m + n \cdot m^2)$ elements in $\mathbb{F}_q$ plus N calls of $\mathcal{F}_{\text{zero}}$ and m calls of $\mathcal{F}_{\text{parity}}$.

7.5 Main Protocol

Now we are ready to introduce our main construction. Recall that we are in the client-server model. In particular, all the inputs belong to the clients, and only the clients receive the outputs. The functionality $\mathcal{F}_{\text{main}}$ is described in Functionality 12. The protocol MAIN appears in Protocol 13.

Theorem 4. *Let c be the number of clients and $n = 2t+1$ be the number of parties. The protocol* MAIN *securely computes $\mathcal{F}_{main}$ with abort in $\{\mathcal{F}_{tuple}, \mathcal{F}_{random},$*

Functionality 11: $\mathcal{F}_{\text{output}}$

1. Let N denote the number of output gates belonging to the Client. The couple sharings are denoted by
$$[\![x^{(1)}]\!], [\![x^{(2)}]\!], \ldots, [\![x^{(N)}]\!].$$
$\mathcal{F}_{\text{output}}$ will reconstruct $x^{(1)}, x^{(2)}, \ldots, x^{(N)}$ to the Client.
2. For all $i \in [N]$, suppose $[\![x^{(i)}]\!] = (\langle x^{(i)} \rangle, [y^{(i)}]_t)$. $\mathcal{F}_{\text{output}}$ receives from honest parties their shares of $(\langle x^{(i)} \rangle, [y^{(i)}]_t)$. Then $\mathcal{F}_{\text{output}}$ reconstructs the secret $y^{(i)}$ and computes $\mathsf{val}(y^{(i)})$.
   - For $[y^{(i)}]_t$, $\mathcal{F}_{\text{output}}$ computes the shares of $[y^{(i)}]_t$ held by corrupted parties and sends these shares to the adversary.
   - For $\langle x^{(i)} \rangle$, note that the summation of all the shares should be $\mathsf{val}(y^{(i)})$. $\mathcal{F}_{\text{output}}$ computes the summation of the shares of corrupted parties, denoted by $x_{\mathcal{C}}^{(i)}$, which can be computed from $\mathsf{val}(y^{(i)})$ and the shares of $\langle x^{(i)} \rangle$ held by honest parties. $\mathcal{F}_{\text{output}}$ sends $x_{\mathcal{C}}^{(i)}$ to the adversary.
3. Depending on whether the Client is honest, there are two cases:
   - If the Client is corrupted, $\mathcal{F}_{\text{output}}$ sends $\{\mathsf{val}(y^{(i)})\}_{i=1}^{N}$ to the adversary. If the adversary replies `abort`, $\mathcal{F}_{\text{output}}$ sends `abort` to all honest parties.
   - If the Client is honest, $\mathcal{F}_{\text{output}}$ asks the adversary whether it should continue. If the adversary replies `abort`, $\mathcal{F}_{\text{output}}$ sends `abort` to the Client and all honest parties. If the adversary replies `continue`, $\mathcal{F}_{\text{output}}$ sends $\{\mathsf{val}(y^{(i)})\}_{i=1}^{N}$ to the Client.

Functionality 12: $\mathcal{F}_{\text{main}}$

1. $\mathcal{F}_{\text{main}}$ receives from all clients their inputs.
2. $\mathcal{F}_{\text{main}}$ evaluates the circuit and computes the outputs. $\mathcal{F}_{\text{main}}$ first sends the outputs of corrupted clients to the adversary.
   - If the adversary replies `continue`, $\mathcal{F}_{\text{main}}$ distributes the outputs to honest clients.
   - If the adversary replies `abort`, $\mathcal{F}_{\text{main}}$ sends `abort` to honest clients.

$\mathcal{F}_{zero}, \mathcal{F}_{coin}, \mathcal{F}_{checkRecon}, \mathcal{F}_{output}\}$*-hybrid model in the presence of a fully malicious adversary controlling up to c clients and t parties.*

We refer the readers to Sect. 7.5 in the full version of this paper [PS20] for the proof of Theorem 4.

Analysis of the Communication Complexity of MAIN. Let c_I, c_M, c_O denote the numbers of input gates, multiplication gates, and output gates. Recall that c is the number of clients. In MAIN, we need to invoke

Protocol 13: MAIN

Let (ϕ, ψ) be an $(k, m)_q$-RMFE. Recall that $\mathsf{val}(\cdot) : \mathbb{F}_{q^m} \to \mathbb{F}_q$ is an $\mathbb{F}_q$-linear map, which is defined by $\mathsf{val}(y) = \sum_{i=1}^{k} y_i$ where $(y_1, \ldots, y_k) = \psi(y)$. A pair of couple sharings $[\![x]\!] := (\langle x \rangle, [y]_t)$ satisfies that $\mathsf{val}(y) = x$.

1. **Preparing Beaver Tuples**: Let c_M denote the number of multiplication gates in the circuit. All parties invoke $\mathcal{F}_{\text{tuple}}$ to prepare c_M/k random tuples in the form of
$$([\phi(\boldsymbol{a})]_t, [\phi(\boldsymbol{b})]_t, [\phi(\boldsymbol{c})]_t),$$
where $\boldsymbol{a}, \boldsymbol{b}$ are random vectors in $\mathbb{F}_q^k$ and $\boldsymbol{c} = \boldsymbol{a} * \boldsymbol{b}$. Then all parties invoke SEPARATE to locally transform these c_M/k tuples into c_M random Beaver tuples in the form of
$$([\![a]\!], [\![b]\!], [\![c]\!]),$$
where a, b are random elements in $\mathbb{F}_q$ and $c = a \cdot b$.
2. **Input Phase**: For every Client with k inputs $x^{(1)}, \ldots, x^{(k)} \in \mathbb{F}_q$, all parties and the Client invoke INPUT(Client, $\{x^{(1)}, \ldots, x^{(k)}\}$). At the end of the protocol, all parties take the couple sharings $[\![x^{(1)}]\!], [\![x^{(2)}]\!], \ldots, [\![x^{(k)}]\!]$ as output.
3. **Computation Phase**: All parties start with holding a pair of couple sharings for each input gate. The circuit is evaluated in a predetermined topological order.
   - For each addition gate with input sharings $[\![x^{(1)}]\!], [\![x^{(2)}]\!]$, all parties locally compute $[\![x^{(0)}]\!] := [\![x^{(1)} + x^{(2)}]\!] = [\![x^{(1)}]\!] + [\![x^{(2)}]\!]$.
   - For each multiplication gate with input sharings $[\![x^{(1)}]\!], [\![x^{(2)}]\!]$, all parties invoke MULT with the first *unused* Beaver tuple $([\![a]\!], [\![b]\!], [\![c]\!])$ to compute $[\![x^{(0)}]\!]$. Let $u^{(1)}, u^{(2)}$ denote the reconstruction results of $[\![x^{(1)} + a]\!], [\![x^{(2)} + b]\!]$ sent by P_1 in Step 3 of MULT.
   Suppose $[w^{(1)}]_t$ is the degree-t Shamir sharing in $[\![x^{(1)} + a]\!]$, and $[w^{(2)}]_t$ is the degree-t Shamir sharing in $[\![x^{(2)} + b]\!]$. All parties will use $(u^{(1)}, [w^{(1)}]_t)$ and $(u^{(2)}, [w^{(2)}]_t)$ to verify the reconstructions.
4. **Verification phase**:
   - Suppose that $u^{(1)}, u^{(2)}, \ldots, u^{(c_I)}$ are the values all parties receive from the clients in INPUT, and $u^{(c_I+1)}, \ldots, u^{(c_I+2\cdot c_M)}$ are the values all parties receive from P_1 in MULT, where c_I denotes the number of inputs and c_M denotes the number of multiplications. All parties invoke CHECKCONSISTENCY($c_I + 2 \cdot c_M, \{u^{(1)}, \ldots, u^{(c_I+2\cdot c_M)}\}$) to verify that they receive the same values.
   - Suppose $(u^{(1)}, [w^{(1)}]_t), \ldots, (u^{(2\cdot c_M)}, [w^{(2\cdot c_M)}]_t)$ are the value-sharing pairs generated when evaluating multiplication gates. All parties invoke $\mathcal{F}_{\text{checkRecon}}$ to verify that for all $i \in [2 \cdot c_M]$, $\mathsf{val}(w^{(i)}) = u^{(i)}$.
5. **Output Phase**: For every Client, let $[\![x^{(1)}]\!], [\![x^{(2)}]\!], \ldots, [\![x^{(N)}]\!]$ denote the sharings associated with the output gates, which should be reconstructed to the Client. All parties and the Client invoke $\mathcal{F}_{\text{output}}$ on these N pairs of couple sharings.

- c_M/k times of $\mathcal{F}_{\text{tuple}}$ in Step 1, which has communication complexity $O(c_M \cdot n \cdot m/k + n^3 \cdot m + n^2 \cdot \log(c_M/k) \cdot m)$ elements in $\mathbb{F}_q$,
- c_I/k times of INPUT in Step 2, which has communication complexity $O(c_I \cdot (m+k)/k)$ elements in $\mathbb{F}_q$ and c_I/k calls of $\mathcal{F}_{\text{random}}$,
- c_M times of MULT in Step 3, which has communication complexity $O(c_M \cdot n)$ elements in $\mathbb{F}_q$ and $2 \cdot c_M$ calls of $\mathcal{F}_{\text{zero}}$,
- one time of CHECKCONSISTENCY in Step 4, which has communication complexity $O(n^2 \cdot m)$ elements in $\mathbb{F}_q$,
- one time of $\mathcal{F}_{\text{checkRecon}}$ in Step 4, which has communication complexity $O(n^2 \cdot m^2)$ elements in $\mathbb{F}_q$ plus m calls of $\mathcal{F}_{\text{parity}}$,
- c times of $\mathcal{F}_{\text{output}}$ in Step 5, which has communication complexity $O(c_O \cdot n + c \cdot n^2 \cdot m + c \cdot n \cdot m^2)$ elements in $\mathbb{F}_q$ plus c_O calls of $\mathcal{F}_{\text{zero}}$ and $c \cdot m$ calls of $\mathcal{F}_{\text{parity}}$.

For $\mathcal{F}_{\text{random}}, \mathcal{F}_{\text{zero}}, \mathcal{F}_{\text{parity}}$, we will instantiate them using RAND with suitable secret sharing schemes. As analyzed in Sect. 6,

- the communication complexity for c_I/k calls of $\mathcal{F}_{\text{random}}$ is $O(c_I \cdot n \cdot m/k + n^3 \cdot m)$ elements in $\mathbb{F}_q$,
- the communication complexity for $2 \cdot c_M + c_O$ calls of $\mathcal{F}_{\text{zero}}$ is $O((2 \cdot c_M + c_O) \cdot n + n^3 \cdot m)$ elements in $\mathbb{F}_q$,
- the communication complexity for $(c+1) \cdot m$ calls of $\mathcal{F}_{\text{parity}}$ is $O((c+1) \cdot n \cdot m^2 + n^3 \cdot m)$ elements in $\mathbb{F}_q$.

Let $C = c_I + c_M + c_O$ be the size of the circuit. In summary, the communication complexity of MAIN is

$$O(C \cdot n \cdot m/k + n^2 \cdot \log(C/k) \cdot m + n^3 \cdot m + n^2 \cdot m^2 + c \cdot (n^2 \cdot m + n \cdot m^2))$$

elements in $\mathbb{F}_q$. Recall that we require the extension field $\mathbb{F}_{q^m}$ to satisfy that $q^m \geq 2^\kappa$. Therefore, we use κ as an upper bound of m. According to Theorem 3, there exists a family of constant rate $(k,m)_q$-RMFEs with $m = \Theta(k)$. Thus, m/k is a constant. The communication complexity becomes

$$O(C \cdot n + n^2 \cdot \log C \cdot \kappa + n^3 \cdot \kappa + n^2 \cdot \kappa^2 + c \cdot (n^2 \cdot \kappa + n \cdot \kappa^2)) = O(C \cdot n + \mathsf{poly}(c, n, \kappa, \log C))$$

elements in $\mathbb{F}_q$.

Theorem 5. *In the client-server model, let c denote the number of clients, and $n = 2t+1$ denote the number of parties (servers). Let κ denote the security parameter, and $\mathbb{F}_q$ denote a finite field of size q. For an arithmetic circuit over $\mathbb{F}_q$ of size C, there exists an information-theoretic MPC protocol which securely computes the arithmetic circuit with abort in the presence of a fully malicious adversary controlling up to c clients and t parties. The communication complexity of this protocol is $O(C \cdot n + \mathsf{poly}(c, n, \kappa, \log C))$ elements in $\mathbb{F}_q$.*

References

BBCG+19. Boneh, D., Boyle, E., Corrigan-Gibbs, H., Gilboa, N., Ishai, Y.: Zero-knowledge proofs on secret-shared data via fully linear PCPs. In: Boldyreva, A., Micciancio, D. (eds.) CRYPTO 2019, Part III. LNCS, vol. 11694, pp. 67–97. Springer, Cham (2019). https://doi.org/10.1007/978-3-030-26954-8_3

Bea89. Beaver, D.: Multiparty protocols tolerating half faulty processors. In: Brassard, G. (ed.) CRYPTO 1989. LNCS, vol. 435, pp. 560–572. Springer, New York (1990). https://doi.org/10.1007/0-387-34805-0_49

BGIN20. Boyle, E., Gilboa, N., Ishai, Y., Nof, A.: Efficient fully secure computation via distributed zero-knowledge proofs. In: Moriai, S., Wang, H. (eds.) ASIACRYPT 2020, Part III. LNCS, vol. 12493, pp. 244–276. Springer, Cham (2020). https://doi.org/10.1007/978-3-030-64840-4_9

BOGW88. Ben-Or, M., Goldwasser, S., Wigderson, A.: Completeness theorems for non-cryptographic fault-tolerant distributed computation. In: Proceedings of the Twentieth Annual ACM Symposium on Theory of Computing, pp. 1–10. ACM (1988)

BSFO12. Ben-Sasson, E., Fehr, S., Ostrovsky, R.: Near-linear unconditionally-secure multiparty computation with a dishonest minority. In: Safavi-Naini, R., Canetti, R. (eds.) CRYPTO 2012. LNCS, vol. 7417, pp. 663–680. Springer, Heidelberg (2012). https://doi.org/10.1007/978-3-642-32009-5_39

BTH08. Beerliová-Trubíniová, Z., Hirt, M.: Perfectly-secure MPC with linear communication complexity. In: Canetti, R. (ed.) TCC 2008. LNCS, vol. 4948, pp. 213–230. Springer, Heidelberg (2008). https://doi.org/10.1007/978-3-540-78524-8_13

CCD88. Chaum, D., Crépeau, C., Damgard, I.: Multiparty unconditionally secure protocols. In: Proceedings of the Twentieth Annual ACM Symposium on Theory of Computing, pp. 11–19. ACM (1988)

CCXY18. Cascudo, I., Cramer, R., Xing, C., Yuan, C.: Amortized complexity of information-theoretically secure MPC revisited. In: Shacham, H., Boldyreva, A. (eds.) CRYPTO 2018, Part III. LNCS, vol. 10993, pp. 395–426. Springer, Cham (2018). https://doi.org/10.1007/978-3-319-96878-0_14

CG20. Cascudo, I., Gundersen, J.S.: A secret-sharing based MPC protocol for boolean circuits with good amortized complexity. Cryptology ePrint Archive, Report 2020/162 (2020). https://eprint.iacr.org/2020/162

CGH+18. Chida, K., et al.: Fast large-scale honest-majority MPC for malicious adversaries. In: Shacham, H., Boldyreva, A. (eds.) CRYPTO 2018, Part III. LNCS, vol. 10993, pp. 34–64. Springer, Cham (2018). https://doi.org/10.1007/978-3-319-96878-0_2

DN07. Damgård, I., Nielsen, J.B.: Scalable and unconditionally secure multiparty computation. In: Menezes, A. (ed.) CRYPTO 2007. LNCS, vol. 4622, pp. 572–590. Springer, Heidelberg (2007). https://doi.org/10.1007/978-3-540-74143-5_32

DPSZ12. Damgård, I., Pastro, V., Smart, N., Zakarias, S.: Multiparty computation from somewhat homomorphic encryption. In: Safavi-Naini, R., Canetti, R. (eds.) CRYPTO 2012. LNCS, vol. 7417, pp. 643–662. Springer, Heidelberg (2012). https://doi.org/10.1007/978-3-642-32009-5_38

DZ13. Damgård, I., Zakarias, S.: Constant-overhead secure computation of boolean circuits using preprocessing. In: Sahai, A. (ed.) TCC 2013. LNCS, vol. 7785, pp. 621–641. Springer, Heidelberg (2013). https://doi.org/10.1007/978-3-642-36594-2_35

GIP+14. Genkin, D., Ishai, Y., Prabhakaran, M.M., Sahai, A., Tromer, E.: Circuits resilient to additive attacks with applications to secure computation. In: Proceedings of the Forty-Sixth Annual ACM Symposium on Theory of Computing, STOC 2014, New York, NY, USA, pp. 495–504. ACM (2014)

GLS19. Goyal, V., Liu, Y., Song, Y.: Communication-efficient unconditional MPC with guaranteed output delivery. In: Boldyreva, A., Micciancio, D. (eds.) CRYPTO 2019, Part II. LNCS, vol. 11693, pp. 85–114. Springer, Cham (2019). https://doi.org/10.1007/978-3-030-26951-7_4

GMW87. Goldreich, O., Micali, S., Wigderson, A.: How to play any mental game. In: Proceedings of the Nineteenth Annual ACM Symposium on Theory of Computing, pp. 218–229. ACM (1987)

GS20. Goyal, V., Song, Y.: Malicious security comes free in honest-majority MPC. Cryptology ePrint Archive, Report 2020/134 (2020). https://eprint.iacr.org/2020/134

GSZ20. Goyal, V., Song, Y., Zhu, C.: Guaranteed output delivery comes free in honest majority MPC. In: Micciancio, D., Ristenpart, T. (eds.) CRYPTO 2020, Part II. LNCS, vol. 12171, pp. 618–646. Springer, Cham (2020). https://doi.org/10.1007/978-3-030-56880-1_22

HVW20. Hazay, C., Venkitasubramaniam, M., Weiss, M.: The price of active security in cryptographic protocols. In: Canteaut, A., Ishai, Y. (eds.) EUROCRYPT 2020, Part II. LNCS, vol. 12106, pp. 184–215. Springer, Cham (2020). https://doi.org/10.1007/978-3-030-45724-2_7

LN17. Lindell, Y., Nof, A.: A framework for constructing fast MPC over arithmetic circuits with malicious adversaries and an honest-majority. In: Proceedings of the 2017 ACM SIGSAC Conference on Computer and Communications Security, pp. 259–276. ACM (2017)

NNOB12. Nielsen, J.B., Nordholt, P.S., Orlandi, C., Burra, S.S.: A new approach to practical active-secure two-party computation. In: Safavi-Naini, R., Canetti, R. (eds.) CRYPTO 2012. LNCS, vol. 7417, pp. 681–700. Springer, Heidelberg (2012). https://doi.org/10.1007/978-3-642-32009-5_40

NV18. Nordholt, P.S., Veeningen, M.: Minimising communication in honest-majority MPC by batchwise multiplication verification. In: Preneel, B., Vercauteren, F. (eds.) ACNS 2018. LNCS, vol. 10892, pp. 321–339. Springer, Cham (2018). https://doi.org/10.1007/978-3-319-93387-0_17

PS20. Polychroniadou, A., Song, Y.: Constant-overhead unconditionally secure multiparty computation over binary fields. Cryptology ePrint Archive, Report 2020/1412 (2020). https://eprint.iacr.org/2020/1412

RBO89. Rabin, T., Ben-Or, M.: Verifiable secret sharing and multiparty protocols with honest majority. In: Proceedings of the Twenty-First Annual ACM Symposium on Theory of Computing, pp. 73–85. ACM (1989)

Sha79. Shamir, A.: How to share a secret. Commun. ACM **22**(11), 612–613 (1979)

Yao82. Yao, A.C.: Protocols for secure computations. In: 23rd Annual Symposium on Foundations of Computer Science, 1982, SFCS 2008, pp. 160–164. IEEE (1982)

Breaking the Circuit Size Barrier for Secure Computation Under Quasi-Polynomial LPN

Geoffroy Couteau[1(✉)] and Pierre Meyer[2(✉)]

[1] CNRS, IRIF, Université de Paris, Paris, France
couteau@irif.fr
[2] École Normale Supérieure de Lyon and IDC Herzliya, Herzliya, Israel
pierre.meyer@ens-lyon.fr

Abstract. In this work we introduce a new (circuit-dependent) *homomorphic secret sharing* (HSS) scheme for all $\log / \log\log$-local circuits, with communication proportional only to the width of the circuit, and polynomial computation, assuming the super-polynomial hardness of learning parity with noise (LPN). At the heart of our new construction is a *pseudorandom correlation generator* (PCG), which allows two partie to locally stretch, from short seeds, pseudorandom instances of an arbitrary $\log / \log\log$-local additive correlation.

Our main application, and the main motivation behind this work, is a generic two-party secure computation protocol for every layered (boolean or arithmetic) circuit of size s with total communication $O(s/\log\log s)$ and polynomial computation, assuming the super-polynomial hardness of the standard learning parity with noise assumption (a circuit is layered if its nodes can be partitioned in layers, such that any wire connects adjacent layers). This expands the set of assumptions under which the 'circuit size barrier' can be broken, for a large class of circuits. The strength of the underlying assumption is tied to the sublinearity factor: we achieve communication $O(s/k(s))$ under the $s^{2^{k(s)}}$-hardness of LPN, for any $k(s) \leq \log\log s/4$.

Previously, the set of assumptions known to imply a PCG for correlations of degree $\omega(1)$ or generic secure computation protocols with sublinear communication was restricted to LWE, DDH, and a circularly secure variant of DCR.

Keywords: Homomorphic secret sharing · Multiparty computation · Sublinear communication · Learning parity with noise · Pseudorandom correlation generators

1 Introduction

In this work, we present a novel (circuit dependent) *homomorphic secret sharing* (HSS) scheme for any $(\log / \log\log)$-local circuit which is secure under the super-polynomial hardness of the learning parity with noise (LPN) assumption. The

A. Canteaut and F.-X. Standaert (Eds.): EUROCRYPT 2021, LNCS 12697, pp. 842–870, 2021.
https://doi.org/10.1007/978-3-030-77886-6_29

main application, and motivation for this work, is a new protocol for securely computing layered arithmetic and boolean circuits with communication sublinear in the circuit size, under the quasi-polynomial hardness of LPN.

*Homomorphic Secret Sharing (*HSS*).* An HSS is a compact secret sharing scheme equipped with homomorphism: the parties can locally convert compact (additive) shares of an input into (additive) shares of some function of it, without interaction. Compactness here means that the input shares should be much smaller than, and ideally independent of, the size of the evaluated circuit. More precisely, HSS for a circuit class allows the parties to homomorphically convert their shares for any circuit in the class. This powerful primitive has been instantiated for all circuits under LWE [BKS19], or for NC^1 under DDH [BGI16a], or a circularly secure variant of DCR [FGJS17], and for the class of constant degree polynomials from LPN [BCG+19b].

The Circuit Size Barrier in Secure Computation. Secure computation allows mutually distrustful parties to securely compute a public function of their joint private inputs, concealing all information beyond the output. Since its introduction in the seminal works of Yao [Yao86], and Goldreich, Micali, and Wigderson [GMW87b,GMW87a], secure computation has received a constant attention. For a long time, however, all standard approaches to secure computation have been stuck at an intriguing *circuit-size barrier*, in that they require an amount of communication (at least) proportional to the size of the circuit being computed. In contrast, insecure computation only requires exchanging the inputs, which might be considerably smaller than the entire circuit. Getting beyond this limitation has been a major challenge in secure computation. Early positive results required exponential computation [BFKR91,NN01], or were limited to very simple functions such as point functions [CGKS95,KO97,CG97] or constant-depth circuits [BI05].

The situation changed with the breakthrough result of Gentry [Gen09] on fully-homomorphic encryption (FHE), which led to optimal communication protocols in the computational setting [DFH12,AJL+12]. On the downside, the set of assumptions under which we know how to build FHE is very narrow; it is restricted to lattice-based assumptions such as LWE, and in particular does not include any of the traditional assumptions which were used in the 20th century. More recently, the elegant work of [BGI16a] showed for the first time that secure computation with sublinear communication could be based on assumptions not known to imply FHE, by building a two-party secure computation protocol under the DDH assumption, with communication $O(s/\log s)$ for *layered* circuits of size s.[1] [FGJS17] later followed this blueprint and switched out the DDH assumption for the circular security of the Pallier encryption scheme. It remains open whether secure computation with sublinear communication can be based on any other traditional and well-studied assumption, such as code-based assumptions.

[1] A depth-d circuit is layered if it can be divided into d layers such that any wire connects adjacent layers.

1.1 Our Contribution

We show that circuit-dependent homomorphic secret sharing, *i.e.*HSS where the share generation requires knowing in advance the circuit to be evaluated homomorphically, for the class of log-local circuits exists, conditioned on (the quasi-polynomial hardness of) a well-studied 20th century assumption: the learning parity with noise (LPN) assumption [BFKL94]. Informally, the LPN assumption captures the hardness of solving an overdetermined system of linear equations over $\mathbb{F}_2$, when a small subset of the equations is perturbed with a random noise. The LPN assumption has a long history in computational learning theory, where it emerged. Furthermore, our results only require a flavour of LPN where the adversary is given a very limited number of samples (typically, $O(n)$ equations in n indeterminates). In this regime, LPN is equivalent to the hardness of decoding random linear codes over $\mathbb{F}_2$, which is the well-known *syndrome decoding* problem in the coding theory community, where it has been studied since the 60's [Pra62].

Details on the Underlying Assumption. In a bit more detail, given a security parameter λ, the (T, n, N, r)-LPN assumption with dimension $n = n(\lambda)$, number of samples $N = N(\lambda)$ and noise rate $r = r(\lambda)$ states that for every adversary Adv running in time at most $T = T(\lambda)$,

$$\Pr\left[A \xleftarrow{\$} \mathbb{F}_2^{N\times n}, \vec{e} \xleftarrow{\$} \mathsf{Ber}_r^N, \vec{s} \xleftarrow{\$} \mathbb{F}_2^n \;:\; \mathsf{Adv}(A, A\cdot\vec{s}+\vec{e}) = \vec{s}\right] = \mathrm{negl}(\lambda),$$

where Ber_r denotes the Bernouilli distribution which outputs 1 with probability r, and negl denote some negligible function. When T can be any polynomial (resp. any super-polynomial function, some super-polynomial function), we say that we assume the polynomial (resp. quasi-polynomial, super-polynomial) hardness of LPN. For arithmetic circuits, we need to assume LPN over large fields, or equivalently syndrome decoding for random linear codes over large fields; this is also a well-founded and well-studied assumption, used in several previous works, e.g. [BCGI18, BCG+19b].

HSS for Any Loglog-Depth Circuit. We introduce a new circuit-dependent HSS scheme for the class of all log log-depth circuits. More precisely,

Main Theorem 1 (HSS for any loglog-Depth Circuit, Informal). *Let C be a size-s, n-input, m-output, $(\epsilon \cdot \log\log)$-depth arithmetic circuit over $\mathbb{F}$ (for some $\epsilon < 1/4$). If the $\mathbb{F}$-LPN assumption with super-polynomial dimension ℓ, $O(\ell)$ samples, and inverse super-polynomial rate holds, then there exists a secure HSS scheme for the class $\{C\}$ with share size $n + O(m\cdot s\cdot \log s / c^{\log^{1-\epsilon} s - \log^{1-2\epsilon} s})$ (for some constant c) and computational complexity $O(m\cdot \mathsf{poly}(s)\cdot(\log|\mathbb{F}|)^2)$.*

Restricting the circuit class to depth-k size-s circuits where $k(s) \le \log\log s/4$ leads to quantitative improvements in the size of the shares, the computational complexity of expanding shares, and the strength of the LPN assumption.

Application to Sublinear Computation. Our HSS scheme has (non black-box) implications for sublinear computation. As in [BGI16a], our results holds for all layered (boolean or arithmetic) circuits, in the two-party setting.

Main Theorem 2 (Sublinear Computation of Layered Circuits, Informal). *For any layered arithmetic circuit C of polynomial size $s = s(\lambda)$ with n inputs and m outputs, for any function $k(s) \leq \log\log s - \log\log\log s + O(1)$, there exists a two party protocol for securely computing C in the honest-but-curious model, with total communication $\lceil 2(n + m + s/k)\rceil \cdot \log|\mathbb{F}| + o(s/k)$ and computation bounded by $s^3 \cdot \mathsf{polylog} s \cdot (\log|\mathbb{F}|)^2$ under a set of* LPN *assumptions, the exact nature of which depends on the sublinearity factor k.*

In particular, setting $k \leftarrow O(\log\log s)$ leads to a protocol with total communication $O(n + m + s/\log\log s)$, secure under the super-polynomial hardness of:

- $\mathbb{F}$-LPN *with super-polynomial dimension ℓ, $O(\ell)$ samples, and inverse super-polynomial rate,*
- $\mathbb{F}_2$-LPN *with super-polynomial dimension ℓ', $O(\ell')$ samples, and inverse polynomial rate $1/s^{O(1)}$ (which is implied by the above if $\mathbb{F} = \mathbb{F}_2$).*

Furthermore (but with a slighly different choice of parameters than the one described above), as k is reduced to an arbitrarily small $k = \omega(1)$, we need only assume the quasi-polynomial hardness of:

- $\mathbb{F}$-LPN *with quasi-polynomial dimension ℓ, $O(\ell)$ samples, and inverse quasi-polynomial rate,*
- $\mathbb{F}_2$-LPN *with quasi-polynomial dimension ℓ', $O(\ell')$ samples, and inverse polynomial rate $1/s^{O(1)}$ (which is implied by the above if $\mathbb{F} = \mathbb{F}_2$).*

and the computation is reduced to $O(s^{1+o(1)} \cdot (\log|\mathbb{F}|)^2)$.

Remark 1. While we require security against super-polynomial-time adversaries, this remains a relatively weak flavour of LPN where the dimension is very high, i.e. super-polynomial as well (and the adversary is allowed to run in time $O(\ell^2)$ where ℓ is the dimension), and the number of samples which the adversary gets is very limited, $O(\ell)$. On the other hand, we require a very small noise rate λ/N. For example, instantiating the above with $k = (\log\log s)/5$, we obtain a secure computation protocol with total communication $O(\ell + m + s/\log\log s)$ (sublinear in s) and polynomial computation, assuming that LPN is hard against adversaries running in super-polynomial time $\lambda^{O(\log\lambda)}$, with dimension $\ell = \lambda^{O(\log\lambda)}$, $N = 2\ell$ samples, and noise rate λ/N. More generally, for any super-constant function $\omega(1)$, there is a two-party protocol with communication $O(n + m + s/\log\omega(1))$ assuming the $\lambda^{\omega(1)}$-hardness of LPN (i.e., the quasi-polynomial hardness of LPN).

We note that, in this regime of parameters, the best known attacks are the information set decoding attack [Pra62] and its variants (which only shave constant in the exponents, hence have the same asymptotic complexity), which require time $2^{O(\lambda)}$.[2] Therefore, assuming hardness against $\lambda^{O(\log \lambda)}$-time adversaries is a very plausible assumption.

Remark 2 (On the Generality of Layered Circuits). Our construction is restricted to the class of (boolean or arithmetic) layered circuits. This restriction stems from the blockwise structure of the construction, and was also present in the previous works of [BGI16a] and [Cou19]. As noted in [Cou19], layered circuits are a relatively large and general class of circuits, which furthermore capture many "real-world" circuits such as FFT-like circuits (used in signal processing, integer multiplication, or permutation networks [Wak68]), Symmetric crypto primitives (e.g. AES and algorithms that proceed in sequences of low-complexity rounds are naturally "layered by blocks"), or dynamic-programming algorithm (e.g. the Smith-Waterman distance, or the Levenshtein distance and its variants).

Generalisation to the Malicious Setting. Our result can directly be generalised to the malicious setting using a generic GMW-style compiler [GMW87a], which is communication preserving when instantiated with succinct zero-knowledge arguments [NN01]. Such arguments exist under collision-resistant hash functions; hence, Theorem 2 extends to the malicious setting as well, at the cost of further assuming collision-resistant hash functions (which is a mild assumption). We note that CRHFs have recently been built from (sub-exponentially strong) flavours of LPN [AHI+17, YZW+19, BLVW19].

1.2 Our Techniques

Our starting point is the construction of *pseudorandom generator* (PCG) from the work of [BCG+19b], under the LPN assumption. At a high level, a PCG allows to distributively generate long pseudorandom instances of a correlation. More precisely, a PCG for a correlation corr (seen as a distribution over pairs of elements) is a pair (Gen, Expand) where $\mathsf{Gen}(1^\lambda)$ generates a pair of seeds $(\mathsf{k}_0, \mathsf{k}_1)$ and $\mathsf{Expand}(b, \mathsf{k}_b)$ output a string R_b. A PCG must satisfy two properties: (correctness) (R_0, R_1) is indistinguishable from a random sample from corr, and (security) for $b \in \{0,1\}$, the string R_b is indistinguishable, even given k_{1-b}, from a string R'_b sampled randomly conditioned on satisfying the correlation with R_{1-b}.

The technical contribution at the heart of this paper is to show that, under a certain LPN assumption, there exists a 2-party PCG for the following correlation, which we call *substrings tensor powers* (stp) correlation. It is (publicly) parametrised by

- a string length n;
- subsets $S_1, \ldots, S_{\mathsf{n_s}} \in \binom{[n]}{\leq K}$ of at most $K = \log n / \log\log n$ many coordinates each;

[2] BKW and its variants [BKW00, Lyu05] do not improve over information set decoding attacks in this regime of parameters, due to the very low number of samples.

– a tensor power parameter tpp (which can be super-constant, as high as K);

and generates additive shares of all the tensor powers of the prescribed substrings of a random string, *i.e.*

$$(\vec{r}, ((1_{\mathbb{F}} \mid\mid \vec{r}[S_i])^{\otimes \mathsf{tpp}})_{1 \leq i \leq \mathsf{n_s}}), \text{ where } \vec{r} \in \mathbb{F}^n \text{ is (pseudo)random.}$$

In the above, $\vec{a}^{\otimes b}$ denotes a vector $\vec{a}$ tensored with itself b rimes. In order to build shares of $(\vec{r}, \vec{r}^{\otimes 2})$ for some (pseudo)random $\vec{r} \in \mathbb{F}^n$ (the bilinear correlation), the PCG of [BCG+19b] uses a multi-point function secret sharing scheme (MPFSS) (defined in Sect. 3.1) to give the parties small seeds which can be expanded locally to shares of $(\vec{e}, \vec{e}^{\otimes 2})$ for some random sparse vector $\vec{e} \in \mathbb{F}^n$. Thence, if H is some suitable public matrix the parties can get shares of $\vec{r} := H \cdot \vec{e}$, which is pseudorandom under LPN, and of $\vec{r}^{\otimes 2} = H^{\otimes 2} \cdot \vec{e}^{\otimes 2}$ by locally multiplying their shares of $\vec{e}$ and $\vec{e}^{\otimes 2}$ by H and $H^{\otimes 2}$ respectively. The main issue in using this approach directly is that performing the expanding $\vec{r}^{\otimes \mathsf{tpp}} = H[S_i]^{\otimes \mathsf{tpp}} \cdot \vec{e}^{\otimes \mathsf{tpp}}$ (where $H[S_i]$–abusively–denotes the submatrix of H with only the rows indexed by elements of S_i) would require super-polynomial computation, as $H[S_i]$ has n columns.

The core idea of our work is to develop a very careful modified strategy. Instead of letting each $\vec{r}$ be a (pseudo)random mask, we construct $\vec{r}$ as a sum of $n \cdot \log n$ vectors $\vec{r}_j$, each associated with a public subset of at most K coordinates: these K coordinates are random, but all others are zero. The crucial property achieved by this construction is the following: with high probability, the sum of these sparse vectors will be pseudorandom, but every size-K substring of $\vec{r}$ (and in particular $S_1, \ldots, S_{\mathsf{n_s}}$) will be expressible as a sum of 'not too many' of the $\vec{r}_j$. This allows the expanding to be done by raising to the tensor power tpp a matrix whose dimensions are both $K^{O(1)}$, and not n as before. Thus computation remains polynomial.

If we were to stop here, the size of the seeds would grow linearly with $\mathsf{n_s}$, the number of subsets; this would violate the compactness requirement. Instead, we show that we can batch the subsets into $\mathsf{n_s}/\beta$ groups of at most β subsets each, for some parameter β to be refined, to reduce the share size and recover compactness, without harming computational efficiency. Indeed, so long as β is not too large, the substring of $\vec{r}$ associated with the union of any β size-K subsets of coordinates will still be expressible as a sum of 'not too many' of the $\vec{r}_j$. Our computations reveal a sweet spot for the choice of β, for which the PCG seeds are compact and yet the complexity of expanding them remains polynomial.

1.3 Related Work

Pseudorandom correlation generators were first studied (under the name of cryptocapsules) in [BCG+17]. Constructions of PCGs for various correlations, under variants of the LPN assumptions, and applications of PCGs to low-communication secure computation, have been described in [BCGI18, BCG+19b, BCG+19a, SGRR19, BCG+20b, BCG+20a].

Early works on sublinear-communication secure computation either incurred some exponential cost, or were restricted to very limited types of computations. The first protocols to break the circuit size barriers was shown in [BFKR91] (which gave a protocol with optimal communication, albeit with exponential computation and only for a number of parties linear in the input size). The work of [NN01] gave a sublinear protocol, but with exponential complexity. The work of [BI05] gives a low-communication protocol for constant-depth circuit, for a number of parties polylogarithmic in the circuit size, and the works of [CGKS95,KO97,CG97] gave sublinear protocols for the special case of point functions. The result of Gentry [Gen09] led to the first optimal communication protocols in the computational setting [DFH12,AJL+12] under LWE-style assumptions, for all circuits and without incurring any exponential cost. The work of [IKM+13] gave an optimal communication protocol in the correlated randomness model, albeit using an exponential amount of correlated randomness. More recently, [Cou19] constructed an unconditionally secure MPC protocol with sublinear communication for layered circuits, in the two-party setting, with a polynomial amount of correlated randomness. Finally, progress in breaking the circuit-size barrier for layered circuits in the computational setting is closely tied to the advances in HSS for super-constant depth circuits [BGI16a,FGJS17].

2 Technical Overview

Notations. We say that a function negl: $\mathbb{N} \rightarrow \mathbb{R}^+$ is *negligible* if it vanishes faster than every inverse polynomial. For two families of distributions $X = \{X_\lambda\}$ and $Y = \{Y_\lambda\}$ indexed by a security parameter $\lambda \in \mathbb{N}$, we write $X \overset{c}{\approx} Y$ if X and Y are *computationally indistinguishable* (*i.e.* any family of circuits of size $\mathsf{poly}(\lambda)$ has a negligible distinguishing advantage), $X \overset{s}{\approx} Y$ if they are *statistically indistinguishable* (*i.e.* the above holds for arbitrary, unbounded, distinguishers), and $X \equiv Y$ if the two families are identically distributed.

We usually denote matrices with capital letters (A, B, C) and vectors with bold lowercase $(\vec{x}, \vec{y})$. By default, vectors are assumed to be column vectors. If $\vec{x}$ and $\vec{y}$ are two (column) vectors, we use $\vec{x}||\vec{y}$ to denote the (column) vector obtained by their concatenation. We write $\vec{x} \otimes \vec{y}$ to denote the tensor product between $\vec{x}$ and $\vec{y}$, i.e., the vector of length $n_x n_y$ with coordinates $x_i y_j$ (where n_x is the length of $\vec{x}$ and n_y is the length of $\vec{y}$). We write $\vec{x}^{\otimes 2}$ for $\vec{x} \otimes \vec{x}$, and more generally, $\vec{x}^{\otimes n}$ for the *n-th tensor power* of $\vec{x}$, $\vec{x} \otimes \vec{x} \otimes \cdots \otimes \vec{x}$. Given a vector $\vec{x}$ of length $|\vec{x}| = n$, the notation $\mathsf{HW}(x)$ denotes the Hamming weight $\vec{x}$, *i.e.*, the number of its nonzero entries. Let k be an integer. We let $\{0,1\}^k$ denote the set of bitstrings of length k. For two strings (x, y) in $\{0,1\}^k$, we denote by $x \oplus y$ their bitwise xor.

Circuits. An arithmetic circuit C with n inputs and m outputs over a field $\mathbb{F}$ is a directed acyclic graph with two types of nodes: the *input nodes* are labelled according to variables $\{x_1, \cdots, x_n\}$; the *(computation) gates* are labelled according to a base B of arithmetic functions. In this work, we will focus on arithmetic circuits with indegree two, over the standard basis $\{+, \times\}$. C contains m gates with no children, which are called *output gates*. If there is a path between two nodes (v, v'), we say that v is an *ancestor* of v'. In this work, we will consider a special type of arithmetic circuits, called *layered arithmetic circuits* (LBC). An LBC is a arithmetic circuit C whose nodes can be partitioned into $D = \mathsf{depth}(C)$ layers $(L_1, \cdots, L_d)$, such that any edge (u, v) of C satisfies $u \in L_i$ and $v \in L_{i+1}$ for some $i \leq d-1$. Note that the width of a layered arithmetic circuit is also the maximal number of non-output gates contained in any single layer. Evaluating a circuit C on input $\vec{x} \in \mathbb{F}^n$ is done by assigning the coordinates of $\vec{x}$ to the variables $\{x_1, \cdots, x_n\}$, and then associating to each gate g of C (seen as an arithmetic function) the value obtained by evaluating g on the values associated to its parent nodes. The output of C on input $\vec{x}$, denoted $C(\vec{x})$, is the vector of values associated to the output gates.

2.1 PCG and HSS

Much like a PCG for the bilinear correlation yields an HSS for degree-two circuits [BCG+19b], given a PCG for the stp correlation with $\mathsf{tpp} = K$, it is almost immediate to build an HSS scheme for any singleton class comprised of a log/loglog-local circuit C (which is the case in particular if its depth is at most $\log\log - \log\log\log$, since the gates have in-degree at most 2). Since the circuit to be homomorphically evaluated on the input shares is known, the Share procedure can depend on it (which is not usually the case for HSS). Let $S_1, \ldots, S_m$ be the subsets of inputs on which each output depends, and let K denote the locality of C; we build a (circuit dependent) HSS scheme as follows:

- HSS.Share($\vec{x}$): Generates compact PCG key (k_0, k_1) which expand to shares of $(\vec{r}, ((1_\mathbb{F} \mid\mid \vec{r}[S_i])^{\otimes \mathsf{tpp}})_{1 \leq i \leq m})$, set $\vec{x}' \leftarrow \vec{x} \oplus \vec{r}$, and give to each party P_σ a share $s_\sigma = (k_\sigma, \vec{x}')$.
- HSS.Eval(σ, s_σ): Expand s_σ and, for each $i = 1 \ldots m$, extract a share of $(1_\mathbb{F} \mid\mid \vec{r}[S_i])^{\otimes \mathsf{tpp}}$. Use it to generate shares of the coefficients of the "degree-K polynomial" on $|S_i| \leq K$ variables P_i satisfying $P_i(X) = C(X - \vec{r}[S_i])$. Output the inner product of the vector of coefficient shares with the vector $(1_\mathbb{F} \mid\mid \vec{x}')^{\otimes K}$. (This linear product is a share of $P_i(\vec{x}')$.)

Correctness and security follow from inspection, along the same lines as [BCG+19b]. Usually, HSS.Share is given only a circuit class as auxiliary input, not a specific circuit, and the parties should be able to homomorphically evaluate any circuit in the class. In our case however the HSS is circuit-dependent, because the subsets $S_1, \ldots, S_m$ are intrinsically tied to the evaluated circuit. An alternative formulation is that our HSS scheme supports singleton circuit classes (or, more generally, local circuits with the same pattern of subsets).

2.2 Generating Correlated Randomness from a PCG

From now on, we set the number of parties to $N = 2$. The work of [BCG+19b, Section 6] provides a pseudorandom correlation generator under the LPN assumption, generates correlated (pseudo) random strings for the low-degree polynomial correlation, *i.e.* shares of $(\vec{r}, \vec{r}^{\otimes 2}, \ldots, \vec{r}^{\otimes d})$ for some constant d, where $\vec{r}$ is a (pseudo)random vector. With the construction from the previous paragraph, this yields an HSS for constant-depth circuits. Our goal is to design a PCG which would lead to an HSS for super-constant depth circuits. More specifically, and keeping our end application in mind, we would like for our PCG to have short enough seeds to lead to a *compact* HSS scheme (i.e., shares of an input x should be at most $O(x)$). This is fundamental when using the scheme to generate correlated randomness in the protocol of [Cou19], which achieves sublinear communication in the correlated randomness model, and which is the starting point of our application to sublinear secure computation.

Our approach is therefore to directly plug in the construction of [BCG+19b] and see where it fails. Two issues emerge: the computation is super-polynomial, and the communication not sublinear. Below, we outline each of these issues, and explain how we overcome them.

First Issue: Too Many Polynomials. The first problem which appears when plugging the PCG of [BCG+19b] in the protocol of [Cou19] is that the latter requires distributing *many* shares of multivariate polynomials $\hat{Q}$ – more precisely, s/k such polynomials (one for each coordinate of each first layer of a bloc). While the PCG of [BCG+19b] allows to compress pseudorandom pairs $(\vec{r}, Q(\vec{X} - \vec{r}))$ into short seeds, these seeds will still be of length at least $\omega(\log \lambda)$, where λ is the security parameter, for the PCG to have any hope of being secure. That means that even if we could manage to securely distribute all these seeds with optimal communication protocols, the overall communication would still be at the very least $\omega((s \log \lambda)/\log\log s)$, which cannot be sublinear since $\log\log s = o(\log \lambda)$ (as s is polynomial in λ).

We solve this first issue as follows: we fix a parameter β, and partition each $\vec{y}_i$ into w/β subvectors, each containing β consecutive coordinates of $\vec{y}_i$. Then, the core observation is that a simple variant of the PCG of [BCG+19b] allows in fact to generate shares of $(\vec{r}, \vec{r}^{\otimes 2}, \cdots, \vec{r}^{\otimes 2^k})$ for some pseudorandom r, where $\vec{r}^{\otimes j}$ denotes the tensor product of $\vec{r}$ with itself j times (which we call from now on the *j-th tensor power of $\vec{r}$*): this correlation is enough to generate shares of all degree-2^k polynomial in $\vec{r}$ rather than a single one. We will build upon this observation to show how to generate a batch of β shares of multivariate polynomials from a single tensor-power correlation, thus reducing the number of PCG seeds required in the protocol by a factor of β, at the tolerable cost of slightly increasing the size of each seed.

Solution: Batching β Multivariate Polynomials. Consider the first length-β subvector of $\vec{y}_{i+1}$, which we denote $\vec{v}$. Observe that the entire subvector $\vec{v}$ can depend on at most $\beta \cdot 2^k$ coordinates of $\vec{y}_i$, since each coordinate of $\vec{v}$ depends on at most 2^k coordinates of $\vec{y}_i$. Therefore, we can now see the computation of $\vec{v}$ from $\vec{y}_i$ as evaluating β multivariate polynomials $(Q_1 \cdots, Q_\beta)$, where all multivariate polynomials take as input the same size-$(\beta 2^k)$ subset of coordinates of $\vec{y}_i$. To securely compute shares of $\vec{v}$ from shares of $\vec{y}_i$, the parties can use the following type of correlated randomness: they will have shares of $(\vec{r}, \vec{r}^{\otimes 2}, \cdots \vec{r}^{\otimes 2^k})$, where $\vec{r}$ is a random mask of length $\beta \cdot 2^k$. Consider the following polynomials:

$$(\hat{Q}_1(\vec{X}), \cdots, \hat{Q}_\beta(\vec{X})) \stackrel{\mathsf{def}}{=} (Q_1(\vec{X} - \vec{r}), \cdots, Q_\beta(\vec{X} - \vec{r})).$$

Each coefficient of each $\hat{Q}$ can be computed as a degree-2^k multivariate poynomial in the coordinates of $\vec{r}$ – or, equivalently, as a linear combination of the coordinates of $(\vec{r}, \vec{r}^{\otimes 2}, \cdots \vec{r}^{\otimes 2^k})$. Hence, given additive shares of $(\vec{r}, \vec{r}^{\otimes 2}, \cdots \vec{r}^{\otimes 2^k})$, the parties can locally compute additive shares of the coefficients of *all* the polynomials $(\hat{Q}_1, \cdots \hat{Q}_\beta)$. Using the PCG of [BCG+19b], the seeds for generating pseudorandom correlations of the form $(\vec{r}, \vec{r}^{\otimes 2}, \cdots \vec{r}^{\otimes 2^k})$ have length:

$$O\left(\lambda^{2^k} \cdot \log\left(\left(\beta \cdot 2^k\right)^{2^k}\right)\right),$$

where λ is some security parameter related to the hardness of the underlying LPN assumption. Or more simply, using the fact the computational cost of generating the correlations contains the term $\left(\beta \cdot 2^k\right)^{2^k}$ which must remain polynomial in s. Therefore, the total number of bits which the parties have to distribute (for all $(d/k) \cdot (w/\beta) = s/(\beta k)$ such seeds) is $O((s/k) \cdot (\lambda^{2^k} \cdot \log s)/\beta)$.

Choosing the Parameter β. Suppose for simplicity that we already have at hand an MPC protocol allowing to securely distribute such seeds between the parties, with linear overhead over the total length of the seeds generated. This means that generating the full material will require a total communication of $c \cdot s \cdot \lambda^{2^k} \cdot \log s/(\beta k)$. By setting β to be larger than $c \cdot \lambda^{2^k} \cdot \log s$, the total communication will be upper bounded by $O(s/k) = O(s/\log\log s)$ when setting $k \leftarrow O(\log\log s)$, which is the highest our techniques will allow it to be pushed. The most important remaining question is whether we can execute this process in polynomial time given such a large β. Put more simply, the core issue is that the *computational complexity* of expanding short seeds to shares of $(\vec{r}, \vec{r}^{\otimes 2}, \cdots \vec{r}^{\otimes 2^k})$ with the PCG of [BCG+19b] contains a term of the form $(\beta \cdot 2^k)^{2^k}$. To make the computation polynomial, we must therefore ensure that β is at most $s^{O(2^{-k})}$, which is subpolynomial. Fortunately, this can be done by setting the security parameter λ of the underlying PCG to be $s^{O(2^{-2k})}$. For instance, for any constant $\epsilon \in]0, 1[$, we can set $\lambda \leftarrow 2^{\log^\epsilon s}$, $k \leftarrow \log\log s/c_\epsilon$, and $\beta \leftarrow s^{O(2^{-k})}$ for some explicit constant $c_\epsilon > 2$, at the cost of now having to assume the *quasi-polynomial security* of the LPN assumption.

Second Issue: Too Much Communication. In the previous paragraphs, we focused on generating the appropriate correlated random coins using sublinear total communication. But doing so, we glossed over the fact that in the full protocol, the parties must *also* broadcast (shares of) values of the form $\vec{y} + \vec{r}$, where $\vec{y}$ contains values of some layer, and $\vec{r}$ is some mask. Recall that with the method which we just outlined, the parties must generate such a length-$(\beta 2^k)$

mask $\vec{r}$ for the k-ancestors of each length-β subvector of each last layer of a block. Since there are d/k blocks, whose first layers contain w/β subvector each, and since each $\vec{y} + \vec{r}$ is of length $\beta \cdot 2^k$, this requires to communicate a total of $(d/k) \cdot (w/\beta) \cdot \beta 2^k = s \cdot 2^k/k$ values – and this cannot possibly be sublinear in s. In fact, this issue already appears in [Cou19], where it was solved as follows: rather than picking an independent mask for each vector of ancestors of a node on a layer (or, in our case, of a length-β block of nodes), pick a single $\vec{r}_i$ to mask a full layer $\vec{y}_i$, and define the mask for the subset $S_{i,j}$ of ancestors of a target value $y_{i+1,j}$ to be $\vec{r}_i[S_{i,j}]$. This implies that the parties must mow broadcast a single masked vector $\vec{y}_i + \vec{r}_i$ for each first layer of a block, reducing the overall communication back to $O(s/k)$. The correlated randomness which the parties must securely distribute now consists of tensor powers of many subsets of the coordinates of each mask.

Using the PCG of [BCG+19b] *for 'Subvectors Tensor Powers Correlations'.* However, attemping to construct a PCG for generating this kind of correlated randomness from the PCG of [BCG+19b] blows up the computation to the point that it can no longer be polynomial. To explain this issue, we briefly recall the high level construction of the PCG of [BCG+19b]. To share a pseudorandom vector $(\vec{r}, \cdots, \vec{r}^{\otimes 2^k})$ where $\vec{r}$ is of length w, the PCG will first generate a *very sparse* vector $\vec{r}'$, with some number t of nonzero coordinates. Then, each $(\vec{r'})^{\otimes n}$ for some $n \leq 2^k$ is itself a t^n-sparse vector, of length w^n. Using multi-point function secret sharing (MPFSS, a primitive which was developed in a recent line of work [GI14,BGI15,BGI16b,BCGI18] and can be built from one way functions), one can compress shares of $(\vec{r'})^{\otimes n}$ to length-$t^n \cdot \log w$ seeds. Then, the final pseudorandom correlation is obtained by letting the parties locally compress $\vec{r}'$ by multiplying it with a large public matrix H, giving a vector $\vec{r} = H \cdot \vec{r}'$. Similarly, $\vec{r}^{\otimes n}$ can be reconstructed by computing $H^{\otimes n} \cdot (\vec{r'})^{\otimes n} = (H \cdot \vec{r}')^{\otimes n} = \vec{r}^{\otimes n}$, using the multilinearity of tensor powers. The security relies on the fact that if H is a large compressing public random matrix, then its product with a random sparse noise vector $\vec{r}'$ is indistinguishable from random, under the dual LPN assumption (which is equivalent to the standard LPN assumption). Concretely, one can think of $\vec{r}'$ as being of length $2w$, and of H as being a matrix from $\mathbb{F}^{w \times 2w}$ which compresses $\vec{r}'$ to a pseudorandom length-w vector.

Now, the issue with this construction is that even if we need only tensor powers of small subvectors (of length $\beta \cdot 2^k$ in our construction) of the vector $\vec{r}$, the computation for expanding the seed to these pseudorandom tensor powers will grow super-polynomially with the length of *entire* vector w. Indeed, consider generating the 2^k-th tensor power of a subvector $\vec{r}[S]$ of $\vec{r}$, for some size-$\beta \cdot 2^k$ subset S of $[w]$. Then with the PCG of [BCG+19b], this requires computing $(H[S])^{\otimes 2^k} \cdot (\vec{r}'[S])^{\otimes 2^k}$, where the share of $(\vec{r}'[S])^{\otimes 2^k}$ are obtained from a short seed using MPFSS, and $H[S] \in \mathbb{F}^{|S| \times 2w}$ is the submatrix of H whose columns are indexed by S. The core issue becomes now visible: even though $H[S]$ has only $|S|$ rows, it still has $2w$ columns, and computing $H[S]^{\otimes 2^k}$ requires roughly $(|S| \cdot w)^{2^k}$ arithmetic operation. But since we want ultimately to have k be some increasing function of s, the above will contain a term of the form $w^{2^k} = w^{\omega(1)}$, where w (the circuit width) can be polynomial in the circuit size s, leading to an overall computational complexity of $s^{\omega(1)}$, which is super-polynomial.

Solution: Covering the Private Values with the Sum of Separable Masks. Our solution to circumvent the above problem is to generate $\vec{r}$ as the sum of a certain number m of shorter masks $\vec{r}^1, \vec{r}^2, \ldots$ which each only cover θ values (note that they may – and will – overlap). This way the 2^k-th tensor power of a subvector $\vec{v}$ can be obtained from appropriate linear combinations of coordinates of the 2^k-th tensor power of the concatenation of *only* the $\vec{r}^j$ which overlap with $\vec{v}$. The amount of computation grows super-polynomially in the length of this concatenated vector only (instead of w as before).

More formally, we have a list of w/β target subsets $S_1, \ldots, S_{w/\beta}$ (each one corresponding to the $2^k\beta$ ancestors of a batch of β outputs) for which we want to compute the 2^k-th tensor power of $\vec{r}[S_i]$, for some random $\vec{r} \in \mathbb{F}^w$. We want to find M size-K sets $\alpha_1, \alpha_2, \ldots, \alpha_M \in \binom{[w]}{K}$ such that each S_i intersects with a small number B of α_js, while $\cup_{i=1}^{M} \alpha_i = [w]$. We associate each α_j with a vector $\vec{r}^j \in \mathbb{F}^K$: together they define a sparse subvector of $\mathbb{F}^w$. If we let $\vec{r}$ be the sum of these sparse vectors, it is clear that for any $i \in [w/\beta]$, each element of $(1_{\mathbb{F}} \mid\mid \vec{r}[S_i])^{\otimes 2^k}$ can be obtained by a linear combination of the elements of the 2^k-th tensor power of the vector of size $(1+BK)$ obtained by concatenating $(1_{\mathbb{F}})$ and the $\vec{r}^j$s such that $\alpha_j \cap S_i \neq \emptyset$. The amount of computation required is then of the order $(BK)^{2^k}$.

The problem of deterministically finding such subsets $\alpha_1, \ldots, \alpha_M$ – which we call a *B-Good Cover* of $(S_i)_{i\in[w/\beta]}$ – turns out to be difficult in the general case. Fortunately, there is a straightforward probabilistic solution: choosing them independently and at random works with high probability. More specifically, taking $M \leftarrow O(w \cdot \ln w)$ i.i.d. uniformly random submasks covering $K \leftarrow \beta 2^k$ values each means that the $\beta 2^k$ ancestral inputs of any batch of β outputs will be covered by only a total of roughly $B = \log w$ submasks (the proof of this relies on standard concentration bounds). This effectively lifts the cost of the computation from being super-polynomial in w to being only super-polynomial in $\beta 2^k \log w$, which remains polynomial overall when setting β and k to be appropriately small.

2.3 Application to Sublinear Secure Computation

The work of [Cou19] gives a generic secure protocol with sublinear communication for layered circuits. It works in the *corruptible correlated randomness model*: before the protocol, a trusted dealer lets the adversary choose the strings that the corrupted parties will get, samples the correlated random coins of the remaining parties afterwards, and distributes them to the parties. As shown in [BCG+19b], generating this corruptible randomness using a PCG leads to a secure protocol in the standard model. In a bit more detail, the parties use a generic secure protocol to generate the short seeds $(\mathsf{k}_0, \mathsf{k}_1)$ then expand them locally; it might have a high overhead, but it will not be a bottleneck since the seeds are very small. We show that our new PCG can be used for just this purpose.

The general idea is to split a layered circuit of size s into carefully chosen blocks, each containing $O(\log\log s)$ consecutive layers. The precise block decomposition is detailed in [Cou19]. Using our PCG cast as an HSS scheme for $O(\log\log s)$-depth circuits (with the duality described in Sect. 2.1) allows the parties to evaluate the circuit in a block-by-clock fashion: for each block the parties start with additive shares of

- the inputs of the circuit;
- the values of the first layer of the block;

and, using HSS, compute additive shares of

- the outputs of the circuit which are in the block;
- the values of the last layer, which are also the values of the first layer of the next block.

Let us note that since the circuit and its blocks are publicly known to both parties, so the fact our HSS scheme is circuit-dependent is not an issue here. This block-by-block approach allows the parties to 'skip' a fraction $O(\log\log(s))$ of the gates when computing the circuit, by communicating at each block rather than at each gate. Unfortunately, combining all these blocks together involves pesky technicalities which prohibit a very modular approach and require us to consider the protocol in its entirety. Indeed, the inputs can appear arbitrarily many times–up to $O(s)$ even–across many blocks, so the randomness used to mask them has to be reused, and we cannot deal with each block using an independent instance of HSS. However, dealing with this problem does not require any additional insight, only more cumbersome notations.

In the above outline, we assumed that we had access to a sufficiently low-communication MPC protocol to distribute the generation of the seeds to our new PCG. To obtain our claimed result, it remains to show that this building block can be instantiated under the quasi-polynomial hardness of LPN. In fact, this MPC protocol needs not have linear communication in the seed size; it turns out that by tuning the parameters appropriately, any fixed polynomial in the seed size suffices to guarantee the existence of a "soft spot" for the parameters of our PCG such that we simultaneously get sublinear total communication $O(s/\log\log s)$ and polynomial computation. Distributing the generation procedure of our PCG essentially boils down to generating (many) seeds for a multi-point function secret sharing scheme, which itself boils down mainly to securely generating seeds for a standard length-doubling pseudorandom generator (PRG), and securely executing about $\log(\mathsf{domsize})$ expansions of these short seeds, where $\mathsf{domsize}$ denotes the domain size of the MPFSS. Using a standard LPN-based PRG and GMW-style secure computation, instantiated with an LPN-based oblivious transfer protocol, suffices to securely generate the MPFSS seeds we need.

3 Preliminaries

3.1 Function Secret Sharing

Informally, an FSS scheme for a class of functions $\mathscr{C}$ is a pair of algorithms $\mathsf{FSS} = (\mathsf{FSS.Gen}, \mathsf{FSS.Eval})$ such that:

- $\mathsf{FSS.Gen}$ given a function $f \in \mathscr{C}$ outputs a pair of keys (K_0, K_1);
- $\mathsf{FSS.Eval}$, given K_b and input x, outputs y_b such that y_0 and y_1 form additive shares of $f(x)$.

The security requirement is that each key K_b computationally hide f, except for revealing the input and output domains of f. For the formal definition of FSS, we refer the reader to the full version of this paper. Our application of FSS requires applying the evaluation algorithm on *all inputs*. Following [BGI16b, BCGI18, BCG+19b, BCG+19a], given an FSS scheme $(\mathsf{FSS.Gen}, \mathsf{FSS.Eval})$, we denote by $\mathsf{FSS.FullEval}$ an algorithm which, on input a bit b, and an evaluation key K_b (which defines the input domain I), outputs a list of $|I|$ elements of $\mathbb{G}$ corresponding to the evaluation of $\mathsf{FSS.Eval}(b, K_b, \cdot)$ on every input $x \in I$ (in some predetermined order). Below, we recall some results from [BGI16b] on FSS schemes for useful classes of functions.

Distributed Point Functions. A distributed point function (DPF) [GI14] is an FSS scheme for the class of point functions $f_{\alpha,\beta} : \{0,1\}^\ell \to \mathbb{G}$ which satisfies $f_{\alpha,\beta}(\alpha) = \beta$, and $f_{\alpha,\beta}(x) = 0$ for any $x \neq \alpha$. A sequence of works [GI14, BGI15, BGI16b] has led to highly efficient constructions of DPF schemes from any pseudorandom generator (PRG).

Theorem 3 (PRG-based DPF [BGI16b]**).** *Given a PRG $G : \{0,1\}^\lambda \to \{0,1\}^{2\lambda+2}$, there exists a DPF for point functions $f_{\alpha,\beta} : \{0,1\}^\ell \to \mathbb{G}$ with key size $\ell\cdot(\lambda+2)+\lambda+\lceil \log_2 |\mathbb{G}|\rceil$ bits. For $m = \lceil \frac{\log |\mathbb{G}|}{\lambda+2} \rceil$, the key generation algorithm* Gen *invokes G at most $2(\ell+m)$ times, the evaluation algorithm* Eval *invokes G at most $\ell+m$ times, and the full evaluation algorithm* $\mathsf{FullEval}$ *invokes G at most $2^\ell(1+m)$ times.*

FSS for Multi-Point Functions. Similarly to [BCGI18, BCG+19b, BCG+19a], we use FSS for *multi-point functions.* A k-point function evaluates to 0 everywhere, except on k specified points. When specifying multi-point functions we often view the domain of the function as $[n]$ for $n = 2^\ell$ instead of $\{0,1\}^\ell$.

Definition 4 (Multi-Point Function [BCGI18]**).** *An (n,t)-multi-point function over an abelian group $(\mathbb{G}, +)$ is a function $f_{S,\vec{y}} : [n] \to \mathbb{G}$, where $S = (s_1, \cdots, s_t)$ is an ordered subset of $[n]$ of size t and $\vec{y} = (y_1, \cdots, y_t) \in \mathbb{G}^t$, defined by $f_{S,\vec{y}}(s_i) = y_i$ for any $i \in [t]$, and $f_{S,y}(x) = 0$ for any $x \in [n] \setminus S$.*

We assume that the description of S includes the input domain $[n]$ so that $f_{S,\vec{y}}$ is fully specified. A *Multi-Point Function Secret Sharing* (MPFSS) is an FSS scheme for the class of multi-point functions, where a point function $f_{S,\vec{y}}$ is represented in a natural way. We assume that an MPFSS scheme leaks not only the input and output domains but also the number of points t that the multi-point function specifies. An MPFSS can be easily obtained by adding t instances of a DPF.

3.2 Learning Parity with Noise

Our constructions rely on the Learning Parity with Noise assumption [BFKL93] (LPN) over a field $\mathbb{F}$ (the most standard variant of LPN typically assumes $\mathbb{F} = \mathbb{F}_2$, but other fields can be considered). Unlike the LWE assumption, in LPN over $\mathbb{F}$ the noise is assumed to have a small Hamming weight. Concretely, the noise is a random field element in a small fraction of the coordinates and 0 elsewhere. Given a field $\mathbb{F}$, $\mathsf{Ber}_r(\mathbb{F})$ denote the distribution which outputs a uniformly random element of $\mathbb{F} \setminus \{0\}$ with probability r, and 0 with probability $1 - r$.

Definition 5 (LPN). *For dimension $k = k(\lambda)$, number of samples (or block length) $q = q(\lambda)$, noise rate $r = r(\lambda)$, and field $\mathbb{F} = \mathbb{F}(\lambda)$, the $\mathbb{F}$-$\mathsf{LPN}(k, q, r)$ assumption states that*

$$\begin{aligned} &\{(A, \vec{b}) \mid A \xleftarrow{\$} \mathbb{F}^{q \times k}, \vec{e} \xleftarrow{\$} \mathsf{Ber}_r(\mathbb{F})^q, \vec{s} \xleftarrow{\$} \mathbb{F}^k, \vec{b} \leftarrow A \cdot \vec{s} + \vec{e}\} \\ \overset{c}{\approx} &\{(A, \vec{b}) \mid A \xleftarrow{\$} \mathbb{F}^{q \times k}, \vec{b} \xleftarrow{\$} \mathbb{F}^q\} \end{aligned}$$

Here and in the following, all parameters are functions of the security parameter λ and computational indistinguishability is defined with respect to λ. Note that the search LPN problem, of finding the vector can be reduced to the decisional LPN assumption [BFKL93, AIK09]. In this paper, our protocols will mostly rely on a variant of LPN, called *exact LPN* (xLPN) [JKPT12]. In this variant, the noise vector $\vec{e}$ is not sampled from $\mathsf{Ber}_r(\mathbb{F})^q$, but it is sampled uniformly from the set $\mathsf{HW}_{rq}(\mathbb{F}^q)$ of length-q vectors over $\mathbb{F}$ with *exactly* rq nonzero coordinates (in contrast, a sample from $\mathsf{Ber}_r(\mathbb{F})^q$ has an *expected* number $r \cdot q$ of nonzero coordinates). While standard LPN is usually preferred since the Bernouilli distribution is convenient to analyze, xLPN is often preferred in concrete implementations, since it offers a potentially higher level of security for similar parameters (by avoiding weak instances with a low amount of noise). Furthermore, as outlined in [JKPT12], xLPN and LPN are equivalent: xLPN reduces to its search version using the sample-preserving reduction of [AIK07], and search-xLPN is easily seen to be polynomially equivalent to search-LPN.

Dual LPN. In our protocols, it will also prove convenient to work with the (equivalent) alternative *dual* formulation of LPN.

Definition 6 (Dual LPN). *For dimension $k = k(\lambda)$, number of samples (or block length) $q = q(\lambda)$, noise rate $r = r(\lambda)$, and field $\mathbb{F} = \mathbb{F}(\lambda)$, the dual-$\mathbb{F}$-$\mathsf{LPN}(k, q, r)$ assumption states that*

$$\{(H, \vec{b}) \mid H \xleftarrow{\$} \mathbb{F}^{q-k \times q}, \vec{e} \xleftarrow{\$} \mathsf{Ber}_r(\mathbb{F})^q, \vec{b} \leftarrow H \cdot \vec{e}\}$$
$$\stackrel{c}{\approx}\{(H, \vec{b}) \mid H \xleftarrow{\$} \mathbb{F}^{q-k \times q}, \vec{b} \xleftarrow{\$} \mathbb{F}^q\}$$

Solving the dual LPN assumption is easily seen to be at least as hard as solving LPN: given a sample $(A, \vec{b})$, define $H \in \mathbb{F}^{q-k \times q}$ to be the parity-check matrix of A (hence $H \cdot A = 0$), and feed $(H, H \cdot \vec{b})$ to the dual LPN solver. Note that the parity check matrix of a random matrix is distributed as a random matrix. Furthermore, when $\vec{b} = A \cdot \vec{s} + \vec{e}$, we have $H \cdot \vec{b} = H \cdot (A \cdot \vec{s} + \vec{e}) = H \cdot \vec{e}$. For discussions regarding existing attacks on LPN and their efficiency, we refer the reader to [BCGI18, BCG+19b].

3.3 Pseudorandom Correlation Generators

Pseudorandom correlation generators (PCG) have been introduced in [BCG+19b]. Informally, a pseudorandom correlation generator allows to generate pairs of short keys (or seeds) $(\mathsf{k}_0, \mathsf{k}_1)$ such that each key k_σ can be expanded to a long string $R_\sigma = \mathsf{Expand}(\sigma, \mathsf{k}_\sigma)$, with the following guarantees: given the key $\mathsf{k}_{1-\sigma}$, the string R_σ is indistinguishable from a random string sampled conditioned on satisfying the target correlation with the string $R_{1-\sigma} = \mathsf{Expand}(1 - \sigma, \mathsf{k}_{1-\sigma})$. The formal definition of PCGs is given in the full version of this paper

4 Secure Computation from Super-Constant-Degree Low-Locality Polynomial Correlated Randomness

4.1 Block Decomposition of Layered Circuits

Given an arithmetic circuit C and an input vector $\vec{x}$, we call *value of the gate g on input $\vec{x}$* the value carried by the output wire of a given gate g of C during the evaluation of $C(\vec{x})$. The following decomposition of layered circuits is implicit in [Cou19]; for completeness, we give the proof in the full version.

Lemma 7 (Block-Decomposition of Layered Circuits). *Let C be a layered arithmetic circuit over a field $\mathbb{F}$ with n inputs and m outputs, of size s and depth $d = d(n)$. For any integer k, denoting $t = t(k) = \lceil d/k \rceil$, there exists $2t+1$ integers $(s_0 = 0, s_1, \cdots, s_{t-1}, s_t = 0)$, $(m_0, \cdots, m_{t-1})$, and functions $(f_0, \cdots, f_{t-1})$ with $f_i : \mathbb{F}^n \times \mathbb{F}^{s_i} \to \mathbb{F}^{s_{i+1}} \times \mathbb{F}^{m_i}$, such that:*

- *The algorithm A given below satisfies, for any input vector $\vec{x} \in \mathbb{F}^n$, $A(\vec{x}) = C(\vec{x})$ (that is, A computes C);*

  ***function** $A(\vec{x})$*

$\vec{x}_0 \leftarrow \vec{x}$
for $i = 0$ *to* $t-1$ ***do*** $(\vec{x}_{i+1}, \vec{y}_i) \leftarrow f_i(\vec{x}_i)$
$\vec{y} \leftarrow \vec{y}_0 || \cdots || \vec{y}_{t-1}$
return $\vec{y}$

- *For any* $i \in [\![0, t-1]\!]$, $j \le s_{i+1} + m_i$, *the* j*-th output*[3] *of* $f_i : \mathbb{F}^n \times \mathbb{F}^{s_i} \mapsto \mathbb{F}^{s_{i+1}} \times \mathbb{F}^{m_i}$ *can be computed by a multivariate polynomial* $P_{i,j}$ *over* $\mathbb{F}^{2^k}$ *of degree* $\deg P_{i,j} \le 2^k$*;*
- $\sum_{i=0}^{t-1} s_i \le s/k$ *and* $\sum_{i=0}^{t-1} m_i = m$.

4.2 Securely Computing C in the Correlated Randomness Model

We represent in Fig. 1 the ideal functionality for securely evaluating the layered arithmetic circuit C.

Ideal Functionality $\mathscr{F}_C$

- **Parameters.** The functionality is parametrised with an arithmetic circuit C with n inputs over a finite field $\mathbb{F}$.
- **Parties.** An adversary $\mathscr{A}$ and N parties $P_1, \cdots, P_N$. Each party P_ℓ has $p_\ell \in [0, n]$ inputs over $\mathbb{F}$, with $\sum_{\ell \le N} p_\ell = n$.

The functionality aborts if it receives any incorrectly formatted message.

1. On input a message $(\mathsf{input}, \vec{x}_\ell)$ from each party P_ℓ where $\vec{x}_\ell \in \mathbb{F}^{p_\ell}$, set
$$\vec{x} \leftarrow \vec{x}_1 || \cdots || \vec{x}_N \in \mathbb{F}^n.$$
2. Compute $\vec{y} \leftarrow C(\vec{x})$. Output $\vec{y}$ to all parties, and terminate.

Fig. 1. Ideal functionality $\mathscr{F}_C$ for securely evaluating an arithmetic circuit C among N parties.

We represent on Fig. 2 an ideal functionality for distributing (function-dependent) correlated randomness between the parties.

Theorem 8. *Let* $k \le \log\log s - \log\log\log s$*. There exists a protocol* Π_C *which (perfectly) securely implements the* N*-party functionality* $\mathscr{F}_C$ *in the* $\mathscr{F}_{\mathsf{corr}}$*-hybrid model, against a static, passive, non-aborting adversary corrupting at most* $N-1$ *out of* N *parties, with communication complexity upper bounded by* $O(N \cdot (n + \frac{s}{k} + m) \cdot \log|\mathbb{F}|)$ *and polynomial computation.*

The protocol follows closely the construction of [Cou19], with some tedious technical adaptations which are necessary to rely on the specific type of correlated randomness which we will manage to securely generate with low communication overhead. The protocol and its security analysis are given in the full version.

[3] *i.e.* the jth coordinate of the image by f_i, seen as $f_i : \mathbb{F}^n \times \mathbb{F}^{s_i} \to \mathbb{F}^{s_{i+1}+m_i}$.

Ideal Functionality $\mathscr{F}_{\mathsf{corr}}$

- **Parameters.** For every $i = 0, \dots, \lceil d/k \rceil - 1$, functionality is parameterised with subsets $(U_{i,j}^{\mathsf{in}}, U_{i,j})_{1 \le j \le \lceil s_{i+1}/\beta \rceil}$ and $(V_{i,j}^{\mathsf{in}}, V_{i,j})_{1 \le j \le \lceil m_i/\beta \rceil}$.
- **Parties.** An adversary $\mathscr{A}$ and N parties $P_1, \cdots, P_N$.

The functionality aborts if it receives any incorrectly formatted message.

1. On input a message $(\mathsf{corrupt}, D)$ with $D \subsetneq [N]$ from $\mathscr{A}$, set $H \leftarrow [N] \setminus D$ and store (H, D).
2. On input a message input with from each party P_ℓ, send ready to $\mathscr{A}$.
3. *Setup input masks:* On input a message $(\mathsf{setinputshare}, (\vec{r}_{\mathsf{in},\ell})_{\ell \in D})$ from $\mathscr{A}$ with $\forall \ell \in D, \vec{r}_{\mathsf{in},\ell} \in \mathbb{F}^n$, sample $(\vec{r}_{\mathsf{in},\ell})_{\ell \in H} \stackrel{\$}{\leftarrow} (\mathbb{F}^n)^{|H|}$, and set $\vec{r}_{\mathsf{in}} \leftarrow \sum_{\ell \in [N]} \vec{r}_{\mathsf{in},\ell}$.
4. For $i = 1$ to $\lceil d/k \rceil - 1$:
   (a) *Setup masks for the computation gates of the first layer of the ith chunk:* On input a message $(\mathsf{setblockshare}, i, (\vec{r}_{i,\ell})_{\ell \in D})$ from $\mathscr{A}$ with $\forall \ell \in D, \vec{r}_{i,\ell} \in \mathbb{F}^{s_i}$, sample $(\vec{r}_{i,\ell})_{\ell \in H} \stackrel{\$}{\leftarrow} (\mathbb{F}^{s_i})^{|H|}$, and set $\vec{r}_{\mathsf{in}} \leftarrow \sum_{\ell \in [N]} \vec{r}_{\mathsf{in},\ell}$.
   (b) *Setup evaluation of the computation gates on the final layer of the ith chunk:*
      - For $j = 1$ to $\lceil s^{i+1}/\beta \rceil$, set:
      $$\vec{\pi}^{(i,j)} \leftarrow \left(1 \,\|\, \vec{r}_{\mathtt{in}}[U_{i,j}^{\mathtt{in}}] \,\|\, \vec{r}_i[U_{i,j}]\right)^{\otimes 2^k}.$$
      - Wait for a message $(\mathsf{setshare}, (i,j), (\vec{\pi}_\ell^{(i,j)})_{\ell \in D})$ from $\mathscr{A}$ with $\vec{\pi}_\ell^{(i,j)} \in \mathbb{F}^\delta$;
      - Compute uniformly random shares $(\vec{\pi}_\ell^{(i,j)})_{\ell \in |H|}$ of $\vec{\pi}^{(i,j)} - \sum_{\ell \in D} \vec{\pi}_\ell^{(i,j)}$.
   (c) *Setup evaluation of the output gates in the ith chunk:*
      - For $j = 1$ to $\lceil m_i/\beta \rceil$, set:
      $$\vec{\pi}^{(i,j)} \leftarrow \left(1 \,\|\, \vec{r}_{\mathtt{in}}[V_{i,j}^{\mathtt{in}}] \,\|\, \vec{r}_i[V_{i,j}]\right)^{\otimes 2^k}.$$
      - Wait for a message $(\mathsf{setoutputshare}, (i,j), (\vec{\pi}_\ell^{(i,j)})_{\ell \in D})$ from $\mathscr{A}$ with $\vec{\pi}_\ell^{(i,j)} \in \mathbb{F}^\delta$;
      - Compute uniformly random shares $(\vec{\pi}_\ell^{(i,j)})_{\ell \in |H|}$ of $\vec{\pi}^{(i,j)} - \sum_{\ell \in D} \vec{\pi}_\ell^{(i,j)}$.
5. Output $(\vec{r}_{\mathsf{in},\ell}, (\vec{r}_{i,\ell}, (\vec{\pi}_\ell^{(i,j)})_{1 \le j \le \lceil s_{i+1}/\beta \rceil}, (\vec{\pi}_{\mathsf{out},\ell}^{(i,j)})_{1 \le j \le \lceil m_i/\beta \rceil})_{0 \le i < \lceil d/k \rceil})$ to each party P_ℓ.

Fig. 2. Ideal corruptible functionality $\mathscr{F}_{\mathsf{corr}}$ to deal out correlated randomness to the parties.

5 Generating Correlated Randomness from LPN

In this section, we construct a protocol Π_{corr}, which implements the ideal functionality $\mathscr{F}_{\mathsf{corr}}$ with small communication, under the quasi-polynomial LPN assumption. A very natural approach to realise a functionality that distributes correlated random coins using a small amount of communication is to rely on *pseudorandom correlation generators*, a primitive recently defined an constructed (for various types of correlations, and under a variety of assumptions) in [BCG+19b]. At a high level, [BCG+19b] suggests to distribute correlated randomness with the following approach:

- Use a generic secure computation protocol Π_{Gen} to distributively execute the PCG.Gen functionality of the pseudorandom correlation generator. Note that PCG.Gen outputs short seeds, much smaller than the correlated pseudorandom strings which can be stretched from these seeds. Therefore, Π_{Gen} can potentially have a relatively high communication overhead in its inputs and outputs, while maintaining the overall communication overhead of Π_{corr} small.
- Expand the distributively generated seeds locally using the Expand algorithm of the PCG. Each such string is guaranteed, by the security of the PCG, to be indistinguishable (from the viewpoint of the other parties) from a uniformly random string sampled conditioned on satisfying the target correlation with the expanded strings held by the other parties.

While this approach does not necessarily leads to a secure implementation of an ideal functionality generating correlated random coins, it was shown in [BCG+19b] (Theorem 19 in [BCG+19b]) that it provides a provably secure implementation for all *corruptible* ideal functionalities for distributing correlated random coins. Note that this property is satisfied by our functionality $\mathscr{F}_{\mathsf{corr}}$. Our protocol Π_{corr} will follow this approach. We start by constructing a pseudorandom correlation generator for the type of correlated randomness produced by $\mathscr{F}_{\mathsf{corr}}$, building upon an LPN-based construction of [BCG+19b].

5.1 Substrings Tensor Powers Correlations (stp)

We now describe our construction of a PCG for generating the type of correlated randomness produced by $\mathscr{F}_{\mathsf{corr}}$. As all constructions of [BCG+19b], our construction will be restricted to the two-party setting; hence, we focus on $N = 2$ parties from now on. Abstracting out the unnecessary details, the functionality $\mathscr{F}_{\mathsf{corr}}$ does the following. It is parametrised with a vector length w, subsets $(S_i)_{1\leq i\leq \mathsf{n_s}} \in \binom{[w]}{\leq K}^{\mathsf{n_s}}$, a tensor power parameter tpp, and generates shares of:

$$(\vec{r}, ((1_{\mathbb{F}} \mid\mid \vec{r}[S_i])^{\otimes \mathsf{tpp}})_{1\leq i\leq \mathsf{n_s}}), \text{ where } \vec{r} \in \mathbb{F}^w \text{ is random.}$$

We call $\mathscr{C}$ the correlation generator associated with $\mathscr{F}_{\mathsf{corr}}$, i.e. the PPT algorithm that, on input the security parameter in unary 1^λ, samples correlated random string as above (where the parameters $(\mathsf{n_s}, K, \mathsf{tpp})$ are functions of λ). It is straightforward to see that $\mathscr{C}$ is a reverse-samplable correlation generator , since it is an additive correlation: given any fixed share share_0, a matching share can be reverse-sampled by sampling $\vec{r}$ and setting $\mathsf{share}_1 \leftarrow (\vec{r}, ((1_{\mathbb{F}} \mid\mid \vec{r}[S_i])^{\otimes \mathsf{tpp}})_{1\leq i\leq \mathsf{n_s}}) - \mathsf{share}_0$. We call this type of correlated randomness a *subsets tensor powers* (stp). Below, we describe a pseudorandom correlation generator for such correlations.

5.2 Good Cover

Before we proceed with the description of a PCG to generate such correlations, we need to introduce a concept, that of a *good cover*. The notations in this subsection are completely self-contained, and may conflict with the parameters defined for the main protocol. In the course of our construction we will want to solve the following problem: given a vector $\vec{v}$ of size n, a family $(S_i)_{i\in[t]} \in \mathscr{P}([n])^t$ of t (*short*) subsets of coordinates of $\vec{v}$, and a (*small*) bound $B > 0$, the problem is to find a family $(\vec{v}_j)_{j\in[M]}$ of some number m of size-K subvectors of $\vec{v}$ such that:

1. The subvectors collectively cover $\vec{v}$;
2. For each $i \in [t]$, there are at most B subvectors in $(\vec{v}_j)_{j\in[M]}$ whose coordinates intersect S_i.

We call such a family a B-*Good Cover* of $(\vec{v}, (S_i)_{i\in[t]})$. First of all we note that the values of the vectors and subvectors do not matter, so we will conflate them with sets and subsets (of coordinates) for simplicity, which leads to a more natural formulation.

Definition 9 (Good Cover – Set Formulation). *Let* $n, B, K, t, q, M \in \mathbb{N}$ *and* $(S_i)_{i\in[t]} \in \binom{[n]}{\le q}^t$ *a family of* t *subsets of* $[n]$ *of size at most* q *each. A family* $A = (\vec{\alpha}^j)_{j\in[M]} \in \binom{[n]}{K}^M$ *is a* B-Good Cover *of* $(S_i)_{i\in[t]}$ *if:*

1. A covers $[n]$: $\bigcup_{j=1}^M \vec{\alpha}^j = [n]$
2. Each S_i intersects at most B elements of A: $\forall i \in [t], |\{j \in [M] \colon \vec{\alpha}^j \cap S_i \neq \emptyset\}| \le B$.

We abusively conflate the two views, where a good cover is just a family of subsets $A \in \binom{[n]}{K}^M$ and where the good cover is a family of sparse vectors—given by a set of coordinates and a short vector of values—$A \in (\binom{[n]}{K} \times \mathbb{F}^K)^M$.

Lemma 10 (Random Covers are Good Covers.). *Let* $n, \kappa, \kappa' \in \mathbb{N} \setminus \{0, 1\}$, *and* $(S_i)_{i\in[t]} \in \binom{[n]}{\le q}^t$ *a family of* t *subsets of* $[n]$ *of size at most* q *each. Let* $A = (\vec{\alpha}^j)_{j\in[M]} \in \binom{[n]}{K}^M$ *be a sequence of* M i.i.d. *uniform random size-*K *subsets of* $[n]$, *with* $M = \kappa \cdot n \ln n / K$. *Let* $B \leftarrow \kappa'\kappa \cdot q \cdot \ln n$.

It holds that $A = (\vec{\alpha}^j)_{j\in[M]}$ *is a* B-*Good Cover of* $(S_i)_{i\in[t]}$ *with probability at least:*

$$1 - \frac{1}{n^{\kappa-1}} - \frac{t}{n^{(\kappa'-2)\kappa \cdot q/2}}.$$

The proof is given in the full version.

5.3 PCG for Subsets Tensor Powers ($\mathsf{PCG_{stp}}$)

We now proceed with the description of a pseudorandom correlation generator for subsets tensor powers.

PCG for Low-Degree Polynomials from [BCG+19b]. We start by recalling a natural variant of pseudorandom correlation generator of [BCG+19b, Section 6], which generates shares of $\vec{r}^{\otimes \mathsf{tpp}}$, for a parameter tpp and a pseudorandom $\vec{r}$. It relies on the xLPN assumption with dimension n, number of samples $n' > n$, and a number λ of noisy coordinates. In our instantiation, we will typically consider $n' = O(n)$, e.g. $n' = 12n$; this corresponds to a particularly conservative variant of LPN with a very limited number of samples, and is equivalent to the hardness of decoding a random constant-rate linear code (which is known as the *syndrome decoding* problem). As discussed in Sect. 3, all known attacks on the syndrome decoding problem for constant-rate codes have complexity $2^{O(\lambda)}$. The PCG of [BCG+19b] is parametrised by integers $1^\lambda, n, n', \lambda, \mathsf{tpp} \in \mathbb{N}$ (where $n' > n$), a field $\mathbb{F}$, and a random parity-check matrix $H_{n',n} \xleftarrow{\$} \mathbb{F}^{(n'-n)\times n'}$ (Fig. 3).

PCG for Degree-tpp Polynomial Correlations

PCG.Gen: On input 1^λ:

1. Pick a random λ-sparse vector $\vec{e} \xleftarrow{\$} \mathsf{HW}_\lambda(\mathbb{F}^{n'})$. Note that $\vec{e}^{\otimes \mathsf{tpp}} \in \mathsf{HW}_{\lambda^{\mathsf{tpp}}}(\mathbb{F}^{(n')^{\mathsf{tpp}}})$. Let $f : [(n')^{\mathsf{tpp}}] \mapsto \mathbb{F}$ be the multi-point function with λ^{tpp} points, such that $f(i)$ returns the i-th coordinate of $\vec{e}^{\otimes \mathsf{tpp}}$.
2. Compute $(K_0^{\mathsf{fss}}, K_1^{\mathsf{fss}}) \xleftarrow{\$} \mathsf{MPFSS.Gen}(1^\lambda, f)$. Output $\mathsf{k}_0 \leftarrow (n, K_0^{\mathsf{fss}})$ and $\mathsf{k}_1 \leftarrow (n, K_1^{\mathsf{fss}})$.

PCG.Expand: On input $(\sigma, \mathsf{k}_\sigma)$, compute $\vec{v}_\sigma \leftarrow \mathsf{MPFSS.FullEval}(\sigma, K_\sigma^{\mathsf{fss}})$ in $\mathbb{F}^{(n')^{\mathsf{tpp}}}$ and set $\vec{r}_\sigma \leftarrow H_{n',n}^{\otimes \mathsf{tpp}} \cdot \vec{v}_\sigma$. Output $\vec{r}_\sigma$.

Fig. 3. PCG for low-degree polynomials from [BCG+19b].

Correctness follows from the fact that $\vec{v}_0 + \vec{v}_1 = \vec{e}^{\otimes \mathsf{tpp}}$ by the correctness of MPFSS, and $H_{n',n}^{\otimes \mathsf{tpp}} \cdot \vec{e}^{\otimes \mathsf{tpp}} = (H_{n',n} \cdot \vec{e})^{\otimes \mathsf{tpp}}$ by multilinearity of the tensor product. Hence, denoting $\vec{r} = H_{n',n} \cdot \vec{e}$, it holds that $\vec{r}_0 + \vec{r}_1 = \vec{r}^{\otimes \mathsf{tpp}}$. For security, we must show that the following distributions are indistinguishable for any $\sigma = 0, 1$:

$$\begin{aligned} &\{(\mathsf{k}_\sigma, \vec{r}_{1-\sigma}) : (\mathsf{k}_0, \mathsf{k}_1) \xleftarrow{\$} \mathsf{Gen}(1^\lambda), \vec{r}_{1-\sigma} \leftarrow \mathsf{Expand}(1-\sigma, \mathsf{k}_{1-\sigma})\} \\ \overset{c}{\approx} &\{(\mathsf{k}_\sigma, \vec{r}_{1-\sigma}) : (\mathsf{k}_0, \mathsf{k}_1) \xleftarrow{\$} \mathsf{Gen}(1^\lambda), \vec{r}_\sigma \leftarrow \mathsf{Expand}(\sigma, \mathsf{k}_\sigma), \vec{r} \xleftarrow{\$} \mathbb{F}^n, \\ &\qquad \vec{r}_{1-\sigma} \leftarrow \vec{r}^{\otimes \mathsf{tpp}} - \vec{r}_\sigma\} \end{aligned}$$

Proof. We sketch the analysis for the sake of completeness; the full proof is given in [BCG+19b]. Security is shown with the following sequence of hybrids: first generate $(\mathsf{k}_\sigma, \vec{r}_{1-\sigma})$ as in the first distribution above. Then, generate $(\mathsf{k}_\sigma, \vec{r}_{1-\sigma})$ as before, and generate an alternative key k'_σ solely from the parameters $(1^\lambda, \mathbb{F}, n, n', t, \mathsf{tpp})$, using the simulator of the MPFSS. Output $(\mathsf{k}'_\sigma, \vec{r}_{1-\sigma})$; under the security of the MPFSS, this distribution is indistinguishable from the previous one. Note that k'_σ does not depend anymore on the noise vector $\vec{e}$. In the next hybrid, generate $\vec{r} \stackrel{\$}{\leftarrow} H_{n',n} \cdot \vec{e}$ and set $\vec{r}_{1-\sigma} \leftarrow \vec{r}^{\otimes \mathsf{tpp}} - \mathsf{Expand}(\sigma, \mathsf{k}_\sigma)$; this game is perfectly indistinguishable from the previous one. Finally, replace $\vec{r} \stackrel{\$}{\leftarrow} H_{n',n} \cdot \vec{e}$ by $\vec{r} \stackrel{\$}{\leftarrow} \mathbb{F}^n$; under the LPN assumption, this last game (which correspond exactly to the second distribution) is computationally indistinguishable from the previous one, and security follows. □

Our New PCG. We now describe a variant of the above PCG, tailored to computing the tensor powers of many short subsets. The PCG is parametrised by $(S_i)_{i\in[K]} \in \binom{[w]}{\leq K}^{\mathsf{n_s}}$, $\mathsf{n_s}$ subsets of at most K indices taken from $[w]$. We assume for simplicity, but morally without loss of generality[4], that $\bigcup_{i=1}^{\mathsf{n_s}} S_i = [w]$. Our goal is for the parties to obtain shares of some pseudorandom vector $\vec{r} \in \mathbb{F}^w$ as well as shares of $(1 \mid\mid \vec{r}[S_i])^{\otimes \mathsf{tpp}} \in \mathbb{F}^{w\cdot \mathsf{tpp}}$ for each $i \in [\mathsf{n_s}]$.

We start by generating a B-good cover (for some integer B) of the $(S_i)_i$ of the form $(\alpha_j, \vec{r}_j)_{j\in[m]} \in (\binom{[w]}{\theta} \times \mathbb{F}^\theta)^m$ where each $\vec{r}_j$ is pseudorandom. We generate each of the m pseudorandom masks $\vec{r}_j$ using a different instance of xLPN, *i.e.* $\vec{r}_j \leftarrow H_j \cdot \vec{e}_j$, where $\vec{e}_j \in \mathbb{F}^{\theta'}$ is λ-sparse and $H_j \stackrel{\$}{\leftarrow} \mathbb{F}^{\theta\times\theta'}$ for some $\theta' = O(\theta)$. For each S_i, we denote $I_i := \{j \in [m] \colon \alpha_j \cap S_i \neq \emptyset\} = \{j_1, \ldots, j_{|I_i|}\}$ the set of the indices of the masks which 'intersect' with S_i. Note that $\forall i \in [\mathsf{n_s}], |I_i| \leq B$ by definition of a B-good cover. We can now proceed with our main goal: generating shares of a subsets tensor powers correlation.

We define $\vec{r} := \sum_{j=1}^m f_{\alpha_j,\vec{r}_j} \in \mathbb{F}^w$, where $f_{\alpha_j,\vec{r}_j} \in \mathbb{F}^w$ is the sparse vector defined by $(f_{\alpha_j,\vec{r}_j})_{|\alpha_j} = \vec{r}_j$ (and which is equal to $0_\mathbb{F}$ on $[w] \smallsetminus \alpha_j$). Since $\bigcup_{i=1}^{\mathsf{n_s}} S_i = [w]$ and each of the $\vec{r}_j$ is pseudorandom, $\vec{r}$ is also pseudorandom.

Note that for any given $i \in [\mathsf{n_s}]$, $(1_\mathbb{F} \mid\mid \vec{r}[S_i])$ is a subvector of the vector $\tilde{\vec{r}}_i$ obtained by multiplying the block-diagonal matrix $H'_i = \mathsf{Diag}((1_\mathbb{F}), H_{j_1}, \ldots, H_{j_{|I_i|}})$ with the vector $\vec{e}'_i = (1_\mathbb{F} || e_{j_1} || \cdots || e_{j_{|I_i|}})$. Therefore for any tensor power tpp (*i.e.* the degree of the polynomial correlation), $\tilde{\vec{r}}_i^{\otimes \mathsf{tpp}} = (H'_i \cdot \vec{e}'_i)^{\otimes \mathsf{tpp}} = (H'_i)^{\otimes \mathsf{tpp}} \cdot (\vec{e}'_i)^{\otimes \mathsf{tpp}}$. If the parties use an MPFSS scheme to generate small seeds which expand to $(\vec{e}'_i)^{\otimes \mathsf{tpp}}$, they can then locally obtain shares of $\tilde{\vec{r}}_i^{\otimes \mathsf{tpp}}$ (since $(H'_i)^{\otimes \mathsf{tpp}}$ is public), and therefore of $(1_\mathbb{F} \mid\mid \vec{r}[S_i])^{\otimes \mathsf{tpp}}$. From all these shares of all the $(1_\mathbb{F} \mid\mid \vec{r}[S_i])^{\otimes \mathsf{tpp}}, i \in [\mathsf{n_s}]$ the parties can locally extract shares of all the $\vec{r}[S_i]$ and thence shares of $\vec{r}$ (since $\bigcup_{i=1}^{\mathsf{n_s}} S_i = [w]$). The protocol is given in Fig. 4.

[4] If $\bigcup_{i=1}^{\mathsf{n_s}} S_i \neq \emptyset$, and with the notations of the rest of the section, the vector $\vec{r}$ we generate is equal to $0_\mathbb{F}$ on $[w] \smallsetminus \bigcup_{i=1}^{\mathsf{n_s}} S_i$, hence not pseudorandom. However, we can simply have the parties generate another mask $\vec{r}' = H' \cdot \vec{e}'$, pseudorandom under xLPN, to cover $[w] \smallsetminus \bigcup_{i=1}^{\mathsf{n_s}} S_i$. Since the parties do not need shares of $(\vec{r}')^{\otimes \mathsf{tpp}}$, the communication complexity of generating the λ-sparse $\vec{e}'$ using an MPFSS is not an issue.

Pseudorandom Correlation Generator $\mathsf{PCG}_{\mathsf{stp}}$

Parameters: $w, \mathsf{tpp}, \lambda \in \mathbb{N}$ and $(S_i)_{1\leq i\leq \mathsf{n_s}} \subseteq [w]^{\mathsf{n_s}}$.

Gen: On input 1^λ:

1. Generate a family of subsets $(\alpha_j)_{1\leq j\leq m} \in \binom{[m]}{\theta'}^m$ which form a B-good cover of the $(S_i)_{i\in[\mathsf{n_s}]}$ (when the α_j are paired with length-θ' vectors in $\mathbb{F}^{\theta'}$), and contracting matrices[a] $(H_j)_{j\in[m]} \in (\mathbb{F}^{\theta\times\theta'})^m$.
2. Pick m random λ-sparse vectors $\vec{e}_j \stackrel{\$}{\leftarrow} \mathsf{HW}_\lambda(\mathbb{F}^{\theta'}), j \in [m]$ and define:
$$\vec{r}_j \leftarrow H_j \cdot \vec{e}_j^{\intercal}, \text{ for all } j \in [m].$$
3. For each $i = 1 \dots \mathsf{n_s}$:
   (a) Denoting $I_i := \{j \in [m] : \alpha_j \cap S_i \neq \emptyset\} = \{j_1, \cdots, j_{m_i}\}$ (with $m_i \leq B$), set:
   $$\tilde{\vec{r}}_i \leftarrow (1_{\mathbb{F}} \,||\, H_{j_1} \cdot \vec{e}_{j_1}^{\intercal} \,||\, \cdots \,||\, H_{j_{m_i}} \cdot \vec{e}_{j_{m_i}}^{\intercal})^{\intercal}.$$
   (b) Let $f_i : [(1 + m_i \cdot \theta')^{\mathsf{tpp}}] \to \mathbb{F}$ be the multi-point function with $(1 + m_i \cdot \lambda)^{\mathsf{tpp}}$ points, such that $f_i(x) = (1_{\mathbb{F}}||\vec{e}_{j_1}||\cdots||\vec{e}_{j_{m_i}})^{\otimes \mathsf{tpp}}[x]$. Compute $(K^{\mathsf{fss}}_{i,0}, K^{\mathsf{fss}}_{i,1}) \stackrel{\$}{\leftarrow} \mathsf{MPFSS.Gen}(1^\lambda, f_i)$.
4. Output $\mathsf{k}_0 \leftarrow (w, (K^{\mathsf{fss}}_{i,0})_{i\leq \mathsf{n_s}})$ and $\mathsf{k}_1 \leftarrow (w, (K^{\mathsf{fss}}_{i,1})_{i\leq \mathsf{n_s}})$.

Expand: On input $(\sigma, \mathsf{k}_\sigma)$, parse k_σ as $(w, (K^{\mathsf{fss}}_{i,\sigma})_{i\leq \mathsf{n_s}})$.

1. For each $i = 1 \dots \mathsf{n_s}$:
   Set $H'_i \leftarrow \mathsf{Diag}((1_{\mathbb{F}}), H_{j_1}, \dots, H_{j_{m_i}})$, compute
   $$\vec{v}_{i,\sigma} \leftarrow \mathsf{MPFSS.FullEval}(\sigma, K^{\mathsf{fss}}_{i,\sigma}) \in \mathbb{F}^{(1+m_i\lambda)^{\mathsf{tpp}}}$$
   and set $\vec{y}_\sigma \leftarrow ((H'_i)^{\otimes \mathsf{tpp}} \cdot \vec{v}_\sigma)_{1\leq i\leq \mathsf{n_s}}$.
2. Extract from $\vec{y}_\sigma$ the appropriate linear combinations of its elements corresponding to a share of $(\vec{r}, ((1_{\mathbb{F}} \,||\, \vec{r}[S_i])^{\otimes tpp})_{i\in[\mathsf{n_s}]})$. // If there are several ways to do so, it must be consistent accross $\sigma \in \{0, 1\}$.

[a] Implicitly, the H_j are supposed to be 'suitably chosen' for xLPN to be presumed hard, e.g. that they were randomly and independently sampled.

Fig. 4. Pseudorandom correlation generator $\mathsf{PCG}_{\mathsf{stp}}$ for generating pseudorandom instances of the subsets tensor powers correlation over a field $\mathbb{F}$.

Theorem 11. *Let $w > 0$, and $(S_i)_{i\in[\mathsf{n_s}]}$ a list of $\mathsf{n_s}$ subsets of $[w]$. Let B, θ' such that there exists a B-good cover of $(S_i)_{i\in[\mathsf{n_s}]}$ comprised of size-θ' vectors, and let $\theta < \theta'$. Assume that the $\mathbb{F}$-xLPN$(\theta, \theta', \lambda)$ assumption holds, and that MPFSS is a secure multi-point function secret-sharing scheme for the family of $(1 + \mu \cdot \lambda)^{\mathsf{tpp}}$-point functions from $[(1 + \mu \cdot \theta')^{\mathsf{tpp}}]$ to $\mathbb{F}$ for all $\mu \in [B]$. Then $\mathsf{PCG}_{\mathsf{stp}}$ is a secure pseudorandom correlation generator, which generates pseudorandom shares of a subsets tensor powers correlation $(\vec{r}, ((1_{\mathbb{F}} \,||\, \vec{r}[S_i])^{\otimes \mathsf{tpp}})_{1\leq i\leq \mathsf{n_s}})$ where $\vec{r} \in \mathbb{F}^w$.*

- Communication: *If the* MPFSS *seeds have size* $O[\lambda \cdot (1 + B\lambda)^{\mathsf{tpp}} \cdot \log((1 + B\theta')^{\mathsf{tpp}})]$ *and* $\mathsf{MPFSS.FullEval}$ *can be computed with* $O((1+B\lambda)^{\mathsf{tpp}} \cdot (1+B\theta')^{\mathsf{tpp}} \cdot \frac{\log |\mathbb{F}|}{\lambda})$ *invocations of a pseudorandom generator* $\mathsf{PRG} : \{0,1\}^\lambda \mapsto \{0,1\}^{2\lambda+2}$, *then* $\mathsf{PCG_{stp}.Gen}$ *outputs seeds of size:*

$$|\mathsf{k}_\sigma| = O\left(\mathsf{n_s} \cdot \lambda \cdot (1 + B\lambda)^{\mathsf{tpp}} \cdot \log\left((1 + B\theta')^{\mathsf{tpp}}\right)\right).$$

- Computation: *The computational complexity of* $\mathsf{PCG_{stp}.Expand}$ *is predominantly that of* $O(\mathsf{n_s} \cdot (1 + B\lambda)^{\mathsf{tpp}} \cdot (1 + B\theta') \cdot \frac{\log |\mathbb{F}|}{\lambda})$ *invocations of a PRG, plus* $\mathsf{n_s}$ *matrix-vector products with a matrix of dimensions* $(1+B\theta)^{\mathsf{tpp}} \times (1+B\theta')^{\mathsf{tpp}}$ *which requires at most* $O(\mathsf{n_s} \cdot (B\theta)^{\mathsf{tpp}} \cdot (B\theta')^{\mathsf{tpp}}) \subseteq O(\mathsf{n_s} \cdot (B\theta')^{2 \cdot \mathsf{tpp}})$ *arithmetic operations over* $\mathbb{F}$.

The proof of the above theorem is omitted in this version of the paper.

5.4 Instantiating the MPFSS

Theorem 11 assumes the existence of an MPFSS scheme MPFSS for the family of all $(1 + \mu \cdot \lambda)^{\mathsf{tpp}}$-point functions from $[(1 + \mu \cdot \theta')^{\mathsf{tpp}}]$ to $\mathbb{F}$ for some $\mu \in [B]$ (or, equivalently, an MPFSS for each μ which can then all be combined into one scheme), with the following efficiency guarantees: $\mathsf{MPFSS.Gen}(1^\lambda)$ outputs seeds of size $O((1 + B\lambda)^{\mathsf{tpp}} \cdot \lambda \cdot \log((1 + B\theta')^{\mathsf{tpp}}))$, and $\mathsf{MPFSS.FullEval}$ can be computed with $O((1+B\lambda)^{\mathsf{tpp}} \cdot (1+B\theta')^{\mathsf{tpp}} \cdot \frac{\log |\mathbb{F}|}{\lambda})$ invocations of a pseudorandom generator $\mathsf{PRG} : \{0,1\}^\lambda \mapsto \{0,1\}^{2\lambda+2}$. The works of [BGI16b,BCGI18] provides exactly such a construction, which makes a black box use of any pseudorandom generator $\mathsf{PRG} : \{0,1\}^\lambda \mapsto \{0,1\}^{2\lambda+2}$. We instantiate the PRG using the LPN-based construction of [BKW03], which we recall in the full version of the paper.

5.5 Securely Distributing MPFSS.Gen an Π_{stp}

The seeds of the MPFSS scheme of [BCGI18] can be securely generated by using parallel instances of a generic secure computation protocols to securely evaluate the above PRG. Using GMW to instantiate the generic protocol, we have:

Corollary 12. *There exists a semi-honest secure two-party protocol* Π_{MPFSS} *which distributes the seeds of a multi-point function secret-sharing scheme* MPFSS *for the family of* t'*-point functions from* $[(1+B\theta')^{\mathsf{tpp}}]$ *to* $\mathbb{F}$, *using* $O(t' \cdot \nu \cdot \lambda^2)$ *calls to an ideal oblivious transfer functionality, where* $\nu = \log((1 + B\theta')^{\mathsf{tpp}})$ *and* $t' = (1+B\lambda')^{\mathsf{tpp}}$, *with an additional communication of* $O(t' \cdot \nu \cdot \lambda^2)$ *bits, and total computation polynomial in* $t' \cdot \nu \cdot \lambda$.

We prove the above corollary by exhibiting Π_{MPFSS} in the full version. As a direct corollary of Corollary 12, since the seeds of $\mathsf{PCG_{stp}}$ contain exactly $\mathsf{n_s}$ independent MPFSS seeds, we have:

Corollary 13. *There exists a semi-honest secure two-party protocol* Π_{stp} *which distributes the seeds of the pseudorandom correlation generator* $\mathsf{PCG_{stp}}$ *represented on Fig. 4, using* $O(\mathsf{n_s} \cdot t' \cdot \nu \cdot \lambda^2)$ *calls to an ideal oblivious transfer functionality, where* $\nu = \log((B\theta' + 1)^{\mathsf{tpp}})$ *and* $t' = (1 + B\lambda)^{\mathsf{tpp}}$, *with an additional communication of* $O(\mathsf{n_s} \cdot t' \cdot \nu \cdot \lambda^2)$ *bits, and total computation* $O(\mathsf{n_s} \cdot \mathsf{poly}(t' \cdot \nu \cdot \lambda))$.

Instantiating the oblivious transfer. To execute the GMW protocol, we need an oblivious transfer. Under the $\mathbb{F}_2$-$\mathsf{LPN}(\lambda, O(\lambda), 1/\lambda^\delta)$ assumption (δ is any small constant), there exists oblivious transfers (with simulation security) with $\mathsf{poly}(\lambda)$ communication and computation; see for example [DGH+20].

Constructing Π_{corr}. The work of [BCG+19b] shows that any corruptible functionality distributing the output of a correlation generator $\mathscr{C}$ can be secure instantiated using any semi-honest secure two-party protocol Π for distributing the Gen procedure of a PCG for $\mathscr{C}$, with the same communication as Π, and with computational complexity dominated by the computational complexity of Π plus the computational complexity for computing the $\mathsf{PCG.Expand}$ procedure. Therefore, using their result together with our protocol Π_{stp} for generating the seeds of a PCG for subsets tensor powers correlation allows to securely instantiate $\mathscr{F}_{\mathsf{corr}}$ (with $N = 2$).

Recall that the computation of $\mathsf{PCG}_{\mathsf{stp}}.\mathsf{Expand}$ is dominated by $O(\mathsf{n_s} \cdot (1 + B\lambda)^{\mathsf{tpp}} \cdot (1 + B\theta')^{\mathsf{tpp}} \cdot \frac{\log|\mathbb{F}|}{\lambda})$ invocations of a PRG – which requires at most $O(\lambda^2 \cdot \mathsf{n_s} \cdot (1+B\lambda)^{\mathsf{tpp}} \cdot (1+B\theta')^{\mathsf{tpp}} \cdot \frac{\log|\mathbb{F}|}{\lambda})$ operations over $\mathbb{F}_2$ using the simple LPN-based PRG from [BKW03] –, plus an additional $O(\mathsf{n_s} \cdot (1 + B\theta)^{\mathsf{tpp}} \cdot (1 + B\theta')^{\mathsf{tpp}})$ arithmetic operations over $\mathbb{F}$. Since each operation over $\mathbb{F}$ can be computed with $O(\log|\mathbb{F}|)^2)$ boolean operations, combining the two, we get computation $O(\lambda \cdot \mathsf{n_s} \cdot (1 + B\theta)^{\mathsf{tpp}} \cdot (1 + B\theta')^{\mathsf{tpp}} \cdot (\log|\mathbb{F}|)^2)$.

All that remains is for the parties to generate the necessary material for $\mathsf{PCG}_{\mathsf{stp}}$: m random $\mathbb{F}^{\theta \times \theta'}$ matrices and m size-θ' subsets of $[w]$. At its core, this is just a matter for the parties to generate and hold the same $m \cdot (\theta \cdot \theta' \cdot \log|\mathbb{F}| + \log\binom{w}{\theta'})$ (pseudo)-random bits. This can be achieved by having one party sample a seed of size λ, send it to the other, and both parties can expand it locally by calling the length-doubling PRG from [BKW03] (and used above) $m \cdot \theta' \cdot (\theta \cdot \log|\mathbb{F}| + \log w)/\lambda$ times (in a GGM tree-like approach). This requires λ bits of communication and $O(m \cdot \theta' \cdot (\theta \cdot \log|\mathbb{F}| + \log w) \cdot \lambda)$ bits of local computation. This is summarised in an intermediate theorem, omitted from this version. Wrapping up, using Π_{stp} with an appropriate good cover suffices to construct a protocol Π_{corr} for securely implementing the functionality $\mathscr{F}_{\mathsf{corr}}$. The detailed choice of parameters is deferred to the full version. Below, we describe a specific choice of parameters for the full construction which suffices to arrive at the claimed result.

6 Choice of Parameters

In this section, we tune the parameters of our protocol. We want to ensure the scheme is correct with all but negligible probability, that it is secure, that the communication is sublinear, and that the computation is polynomial. We make two sets of choices for the parameters: the first optimising for communication, and the other for computation (and incidentally for the strength of the security assumption). The full discussion is deferred to the full version.

Combining Theorem 8–which provides a secure protocol in the $\mathscr{F}_{\mathsf{corr}}$-hybrid model–and the instantiation of the $\mathscr{F}_{\mathsf{corr}}$ as provided in the full version, with an appropriate choice of parameters, also made explicit in the full version, we get our main theorem, Main Theorem 1 below.

Main Theorem 1 (Sublinear Computation of Layered Circuits – Optimised for Communication). *Assuming the super-polynomial security of*

- $\mathbb{F}$-LPN *with super-polynomial dimension* ℓ, $O(\ell)$ *samples, and inverse super-polynomial rate,*
- $\mathbb{F}_2$-LPN *with super-polynomial dimension* $\ell' = s^{O((1))}$, $O(\ell')$ *samples, and inverse polynomial rate (which is implied by the above if* $\mathbb{F} = \mathbb{F}_2$*),*

there exists a probabilistic semi-honest two-party protocol which securely evaluates any layered arithmetic circuit over $\mathbb{F}$ *with success probability* $1 - \text{negl}(s)$ *and which uses* $O([n + s/\log\log s + m] \cdot \log|\mathbb{F}|)$ *bits of communication and* $s^3 \cdot \mathsf{polylog}s \cdot (\log|\mathbb{F}|)^2$ *bits of computation (where* s*,* n*, and* m *are respectively the number of gates, inputs, and outputs of the circuit).*

Instantiating the protocol with an alternative choice of parameters, also detailed in the full version, instead yields the following.

Main Theorem 2 (Sublinear Computation of Layered Circuits – Optimised for Computation). *Assuming the quasi-polynomial security of*

- $\mathbb{F}$-LPN *with quasi-polynomial dimension* ℓ, $O(\ell)$ *samples, and inverse quasi-polynomial rate,*
- $\mathbb{F}_2$-LPN *with quasi-polynomial dimension* ℓ', $O(\ell')$ *samples, and inverse polynomial rate (which is implied by the above if* $\mathbb{F} = \mathbb{F}_2$*),*

there exists a probabilistic semi-honest two-party protocol which securely evaluates any layered arithmetic circuit over $\mathbb{F}$ *with success probability* $1 - \text{negl}(s)$ *and which uses* $O([n + o(s) + m] \cdot \log|\mathbb{F}|)$ *bits of communication and* $s^{1+o(1)} \cdot (\log|\mathbb{F}|)^2$ *bits of computation (where* s*,* n*, and* m *are respectively the number of gates, inputs, and outputs of the circuit).*

References

AHI+17. Applebaum, B., Haramaty-Krasne, N., Ishai, Y., Kushilevitz, E., Vaikuntanathan, V.: Low-complexity cryptographic hash functions, pp. 7:1–7:31 (2017)

AIK07. Applebaum, B., Ishai, Y., Kushilevitz, E.: Cryptography with constant input locality. In: Menezes, A. (ed.) CRYPTO 2007. LNCS, vol. 4622, pp. 92–110. Springer, Heidelberg (2007). https://doi.org/10.1007/978-3-540-74143-5_6

AIK09. Applebaum, B., Ishai, Y., Kushilevitz, E.: J. Cryptol. Cryptography with constant input locality. **22**(4), 429–469 (2009)

AJL+12. Asharov, G., Jain, A., López-Alt, A., Tromer, E., Vaikuntanathan, V., Wichs, D.: Multiparty computation with low communication, computation and interaction via threshold FHE. In: Pointcheval, D., Johansson, T. (eds.) EUROCRYPT 2012. LNCS, vol. 7237, pp. 483–501. Springer, Heidelberg (2012). https://doi.org/10.1007/978-3-642-29011-4_29

BCG+17. Boyle, E., Couteau, G., Gilboa, N., Ishai, Y., Orrù, M.: Homomorphic secret sharing: Optimizations and applications, pp. 2105–2122 (2017)

BCG+19a. Boyle, E., et al.: Efficient two-round OT extension and silent non-interactive secure computation, pp. 291–308 (2019)

BCG+19b. Boyle, E., Couteau, G., Gilboa, N., Ishai, Y., Kohl, L., Scholl, P.: Efficient pseudorandom correlation generators: silent OT extension and more. In: Boldyreva, A., Micciancio, D. (eds.) CRYPTO 2019. LNCS, vol. 11694, pp. 489–518. Springer, Cham (2019). https://doi.org/10.1007/978-3-030-26954-8_16

BCG+20a. Boyle, E., Couteau, G., Gilboa, N., Ishai, Y., Kohl, L., Scholl, P.: Correlated pseudorandom functions from variable-density LPN, pp. 1069–1080 (2020)

BCG+20b. Boyle, E., Couteau, G., Gilboa, N., Ishai, Y., Kohl, L., Scholl, P.: Efficient pseudorandom correlation generators from ring-LPN. In: Micciancio, D., Ristenpart, T. (eds.) CRYPTO 2020. LNCS, vol. 12171, pp. 387–416. Springer, Cham (2020). https://doi.org/10.1007/978-3-030-56880-1_14

BCGI18. Boyle, E., Couteau, G., Gilboa, N., Ishai, Y.: Compressing vector OLE, pp. 896–912 (2018)

BFKL93. Blum, A., Furst, M., Kearns, M., Lipton, R.J.: Cryptographic primitives based on hard learning problems. In: Stinson, D.R. (ed.) CRYPTO 1993. LNCS, vol. 773, pp. 278–291. Springer, Heidelberg (1994). https://doi.org/10.1007/3-540-48329-2_24

BFKL94. Blum, A., Furst, M.L., Kearns, M.J., Lipton, R.J.: Cryptographic primitives based on hard learning problems, pp. 278–291 (1994)

BFKR91. Beaver, D., Feigenbaum, J., Kilian, J., Rogaway, P.: Security with low communication overhead. In: Menezes, A.J., Vanstone, S.A. (eds.) CRYPTO 1990. LNCS, vol. 537, pp. 62–76. Springer, Heidelberg (1991). https://doi.org/10.1007/3-540-38424-3_5

BGI15. Boyle, E., Gilboa, N., Ishai, Y.: Function secret sharing. In: Oswald, E., Fischlin, M. (eds.) EUROCRYPT 2015. LNCS, vol. 9057, pp. 337–367. Springer, Heidelberg (2015). https://doi.org/10.1007/978-3-662-46803-6_12

BGI16a. Boyle, E., Gilboa, N., Ishai, Y.: Breaking the circuit size barrier for secure computation under DDH. In: Robshaw, M., Katz, J. (eds.) CRYPTO 2016. LNCS, vol. 9814, pp. 509–539. Springer, Heidelberg (2016). https://doi.org/10.1007/978-3-662-53018-4_19

BGI16b. Boyle, E., Gilboa, N., Ishai, Y.: Function secret sharing: improvements and extensions, pp. 1292–1303 (2016)

BI05. Barkol, O., Ishai, Y.: Secure computation of constant-depth circuits with applications to database search problems. In: Shoup, V. (ed.) CRYPTO 2005. LNCS, vol. 3621, pp. 395–411. Springer, Heidelberg (2005). https://doi.org/10.1007/11535218_24

BKS19. Boyle, E., Kohl, L., Scholl, P.: Homomorphic secret sharing from lattices without FHE. In: Ishai, Y., Rijmen, V. (eds.) EUROCRYPT 2019. Homomorphic secret sharing from lattices without FHE, vol. 11477, pp. 3–33. Springer, Cham (2019). https://doi.org/10.1007/978-3-030-17656-3_1

BKW00. Blum, A., Kalai, A., Wasserman, H.: Noise-tolerant learning, the parity problem, and the statistical query model, pp. 435–440 (2000)

BKW03. Blum, A., Kalai, A., Wasserman, H.: Noise-tolerant learning, the parity problem, and the statistical query model. J. ACM (JACM) **50**(4), 506–519 (2003)

BLVW19. Brakerski, Z., Lyubashevsky, V., Vaikuntanathan, V., Wichs, D.: Worst-case hardness for LPN and cryptographic hashing via code smoothing. In: Ishai, Y., Rijmen, V. (eds.) EUROCRYPT 2019. LNCS, vol. 11478, pp. 619–635. Springer, Cham (2019). https://doi.org/10.1007/978-3-030-17659-4_21

CG97. Chor, B., Gilboa, N.: Computationally private information retrieval (extended abstract), pp. 304–313 (1997)

CGKS95. Chor, B., Goldreich, O., Kushilevitz, E., Sudan, M.: Private information retrieval, pp. 41–50 (1995)

Cou19. Couteau, G.: A note on the communication complexity of multiparty computation in the correlated randomness model. In: Ishai, Y., Rijmen, V. (eds.) EUROCRYPT 2019. LNCS, vol. 11477, pp. 473–503. Springer, Cham (2019). https://doi.org/10.1007/978-3-030-17656-3_17

DFH12. Damgård, I., Faust, S., Hazay, C.: Secure two-party computation with low communication. In: Cramer, R. (ed.) TCC 2012. LNCS, vol. 7194, pp. 54–74. Springer, Heidelberg (2012). https://doi.org/10.1007/978-3-642-28914-9_4

DGH+20. Döttling, N., Garg, S., Hajiabadi, M., Masny, D., Wichs, D.: Two-round oblivious transfer from CDH or LPN. In: Canteaut, A., Ishai, Y. (eds.) EUROCRYPT 2020. LNCS, vol. 12106, pp. 768–797. Springer, Cham (2020). https://doi.org/10.1007/978-3-030-45724-2_26

FGJS17. Fazio, N., Gennaro, R., Jafarikhah, T., Skeith, W.E.: Homomorphic secret sharing from Paillier encryption. In: Okamoto, T., Yu, Y., Au, M.H., Li, Y. (eds.) ProvSec 2017. LNCS, vol. 10592, pp. 381–399. Springer, Cham (2017). https://doi.org/10.1007/978-3-319-68637-0_23

Gen09. Gentry, C.: Fully homomorphic encryption using ideal lattices, pp. 169–178 (2009)

GI14. Gilboa, N., Ishai, Y.: Distributed point functions and their applications. In: Nguyen, P.Q., Oswald, E. (eds.) EUROCRYPT 2014. LNCS, vol. 8441, pp. 640–658. Springer, Heidelberg (2014). https://doi.org/10.1007/978-3-642-55220-5_35

GMW87a. Goldreich, O., Micali, S., Wigderson, A.: How to play any mental game or a completeness theorem for protocols with honest majority, pp. 218–229 (1987)

GMW87b. Goldreich, O., Micali, S., Wigderson, A.: How to prove all NP statements in zero-knowledge and a methodology of cryptographic protocol design (Extended Abstract). In: Odlyzko, A.M. (ed.) CRYPTO 1986. LNCS, vol. 263, pp. 171–185. Springer, Heidelberg (1987). https://doi.org/10.1007/3-540-47721-7_11

IKM+13. Ishai, Y., Kushilevitz, E., Meldgaard, S., Orlandi, C., Paskin-Cherniavsky, A.: On the power of correlated randomness in secure computation. In: Sahai, A. (ed.) TCC 2013. LNCS, vol. 7785, pp. 600–620. Springer, Heidelberg (2013). https://doi.org/10.1007/978-3-642-36594-2_34

JKPT12. Jain, A., Krenn, S., Pietrzak, K., Tentes, A.: Commitments and efficient zero-knowledge proofs from learning parity with noise. In: Wang, X., Sako, K. (eds.) ASIACRYPT 2012. LNCS, vol. 7658, pp. 663–680. Springer, Heidelberg (2012). https://doi.org/10.1007/978-3-642-34961-4_40

KO97. Kushilevitz, E., Ostrovsky, R.: Replication is NOT needed: SINGLE database, computationally-private information retrieval, pp. 364–373 (1997)

Lyu05. Lyubashevsky, V.: The parity problem in the presence of noise, decoding random linear codes, and the subset sum problem. In: Chekuri, C., Jansen, K., Rolim, J.D.P., Trevisan, L. (eds.) APPROX/RANDOM -2005. LNCS, vol. 3624, pp. 378–389. Springer, Heidelberg (2005). https://doi.org/10.1007/11538462_32

NN01. Naor, M., Nissim, K.: Communication preserving protocols for secure function evaluation, pp. 590–599 (2001)

Pra62. Prange, E.: The use of information sets in decoding cyclic codes. IRE Trans. Inf. Theory **8**(5), 5–9 (1962)

SGRR19. Schoppmann, P., Gascón, A., Reichert, L., Raykova, M.: Distributed vector-OLE: improved constructions and implementation, pp. 1055–1072 (2019)

Wak68. Waksman, A.: A permutation network. J. ACM (JACM) **15**(1), 159–163 (1968)

Yao86. Yao, A.C.C.: How to generate and exchange secrets (extended abstract), pp. 162–167 (1986)

YZW+19. Yu, Yu., Zhang, J., Weng, J., Guo, C., Li, X.: Collision resistant hashing from sub-exponential learning parity with noise. In: Galbraith, S.D., Moriai, S. (eds.) ASIACRYPT 2019. LNCS, vol. 11922, pp. 3–24. Springer, Cham (2019). https://doi.org/10.1007/978-3-030-34621-8_1

Function Secret Sharing for Mixed-Mode and Fixed-Point Secure Computation

Elette Boyle[1(✉)], Nishanth Chandran[2(✉)], Niv Gilboa[3], Divya Gupta[2], Yuval Ishai[4], Nishant Kumar[5], and Mayank Rathee[6]

[1] IDC Herzliya, Herzliya, Israel
eboyle@alum.mit.edu
[2] Microsoft Research, Bengaluru, India
nichandr@microsoft.com
[3] Ben-Gurion University of the Negev, Beersheba, Israel
[4] Technion, Haifa, Israel
[5] University of Illinois at Urbana-Champaign, Champaign, USA
[6] University of California, Berkeley, USA

Abstract. Boyle *et al.* (TCC 2019) proposed a new approach for secure computation in the *preprocessing model* building on *function secret sharing* (FSS), where a gate g is evaluated using an FSS scheme for the related *offset family* $g_r(x) = g(x + r)$. They further presented efficient FSS schemes based on any pseudorandom generator (PRG) for the offset families of several useful gates g that arise in "mixed-mode" secure computation. These include gates for zero test, integer comparison, ReLU, and spline functions. The FSS-based approach offers significant savings in online communication and round complexity compared to alternative techniques based on garbled circuits or secret sharing.

In this work, we improve and extend the previous results of Boyle *et al.* by making the following three kinds of contributions:

- **Improved Key Size.** The preprocessing and storage costs of the FSS-based approach directly depend on the FSS key size. We improve the key size of previous constructions through two steps. First, we obtain roughly 4× reduction in key size for Distributed Comparison Function (DCF), i.e., FSS for the family of functions $f^{<}_{\alpha,\beta}(x)$ that output β if $x < \alpha$ and 0 otherwise. DCF serves as a central building block in the constructions of Boyle *et al.*. Second, we improve the number of DCF instances required for realizing useful gates g. For example, whereas previous FSS schemes for ReLU and m-piece spline required 2 and $2m$ DCF instances, respectively, ours require only a *single instance of DCF* in both cases. This improves the FSS key size by $6-22\times$ for commonly used gates such as ReLU and sigmoid.
- **New Gates.** We present the first PRG-based FSS schemes for arithmetic and logical shift gates, as well as for bit-decomposition where both the input and outputs are shared over $\mathbb{Z}_{2^n}$. These gates are crucial for many applications related to fixed-point arithmetic and machine learning.

N. Kumar and M Rathee—Work done while at Microsoft Research, India.

A. Canteaut and F.-X. Standaert (Eds.): EUROCRYPT 2021, LNCS 12697, pp. 871–900, 2021.
https://doi.org/10.1007/978-3-030-77886-6_30

- **A Barrier.** The above results enable a 2-round PRG-based secure evaluation of "multiply-then-truncate," a central operation in fixed-point arithmetic, by sequentially invoking FSS schemes for multiplication and shift. We identify a barrier to obtaining a 1-round implementation via a single FSS scheme, showing that this would require settling a major open problem in the area of FSS: namely, a PRG-based FSS for the class of bit-conjunction functions.

1 Introduction

Secure multi-party computation (or MPC) [8,20,29,53] allows two or more parties to compute any function on their private inputs without revealing anything other than the output. A useful intermediate construction goal is that of MPC *in the preprocessing model*, wherein the parties receive *correlated randomness* from a trusted dealer in an offline input-independent phase, and then use this correlated randomness in the online phase once the inputs are known. Such protocols can be directly converted to ones in the standard model (without a dealer) via an assortment of general transformations, e.g. emulating the role of the dealer jointly using a targeted MPC protocol between the parties (see discussion in Appendix A in full version [9]). This modular design approach facilitates significant performance benefits, and indeed is followed by essentially all concretely efficient MPC protocols to date. Common types of correlated randomness include Beaver triples for multiplication [6], garbled circuit correlations [25,53], OT [16,31,35] and OLE [32,42] correlations, and one-time truth tables [23,30].

When used to evaluate "pure" Boolean or arithmetic circuits, MPC protocols in the preprocessing model have the benefit of a very fast online phase in which the local computation performed by the parties is comparable to computing the circuit in the clear. Furthermore, the online *communication* is roughly the same as communicating the values of all wires in the circuit, and the number of online *rounds* is equal to the circuit depth.

Unfortunately, typical applications of MPC in areas such as machine learning and scientific computing apply computations that cannot be succinctly represented by pure Boolean or arithmetic circuits. Instead, they involve a mixture of arithmetic operations (additions and multiplications over a large field or ring) and "non-arithmetic" operations such as truncation, rounding, integer comparison, ReLU, bit-decomposition, or piecewise-polynomial functions known as splines. The cost of naively emulating such mixed computations by pure Boolean or arithmetic circuits is prohibitively high.

This motivated a long line of work on "mixed-mode" MPC, which supports efficient inter-conversions between arithmetic and Boolean domains and supports the above kinds of non-arithmetic operations. General frameworks such as [15,19,25,36,40] allow mixing of arithmetic gates (additions and multiplications) and Boolean gates (such as integer comparison), performing a suitable conversion whenever the type of gate changes. Together with MPC protocols for Boolean circuits based on garbled circuits or secret sharing, they can support the above kinds of non-arithmetic operations. However, the efficiency of these techniques leaves much to be desired, as they typically incur a significant overhead in communication and rounds even when ignoring the cost of input-independent preprocessing.

Recently, Boyle *et al.* [13] proposed a powerful approach for mixed-mode MPC in the preprocessing model, using *function secret sharing* (FSS) [10,12] (their approach can be seen as a generalization of an earlier truth-table based protocol of Damgård *et al.* [23]). The FSS-based approach to MPC with preprocessing can support arithmetic operations that are mixed with the above kinds of non-arithmetic operations with the same online communication and round complexity as pure arithmetic computations, and while only making use of *symmetric* cryptography. In the present work, we significantly improve the efficiency of this FSS-based approach and extend it by supporting useful new types of non-arithmetic operations. Before giving a more detailed account of our results, we give an overview of the FSS-based approach to MPC with preprocessing.

1.1 MPC with Preprocessing Through FSS

At a high level, a (2-party) FSS scheme [10,12] for a function family $\mathcal{F}$ splits a function $f \in \mathcal{F}$ into two *additive* shares f_0, f_1, such that each f_σ hides f and $f_0(x) + f_1(x) = f(x)$ for every input x. Here we assume that the output domain of f is a finite Abelian group $\mathbb{G}$, where addition is taken over $\mathbb{G}$. While this can be trivially solved by secret-sharing the truth-table of f, the goal of FSS is to obtain *succinct* descriptions of f_0 and f_1 using short keys k_0 and k_1, while still allowing their efficient evaluation.

For simplicity, consider *semi-honest* 2-party secure computation (2PC) with a *trusted dealer* – in the full version [9] we discuss how to emulate the trusted dealer with 2PC (building upon [27]) as well as extensions to malicious security, in Appendix A and B, respectively. The main idea, from [13], to obtain 2PC with trusted dealer is as follows. Consider a mixed circuit whose wires take values from (possibly different) Abelian groups and where each gate g maps a single input wire to a single output wire. We can additionally make free use of fan-out gates that duplicate wires, "splitters" that break a wire from a product group $\mathbb{G}_1 \times \mathbb{G}_2$ into two wires, and "joiners" that concatenate two wires into a single wire from the product group. This allows us to view a two-input gate (such as addition or multiplication) as a single-input gate applied on top of a joiner gate.

The FSS-based evaluation of such a circuit proceeds by maintaining the following invariant: for every wire w_i in the circuit, both parties learn the *masked* wire value $w_i + r_i$, where r_i is a random secret mask (from the group associated with w_i) which is picked by the dealer and is not revealed to any of the parties. The only exceptions are input wires, where the mask r_i is revealed to the party owning the input, and the circuit output wires, where the masks are revealed to both parties.

This above is easy to achieve for input wires by simply letting the dealer send to each party the masks of the inputs owned by this party, and having the parties reveal the masked inputs to each other. The challenge is to maintain the invariant when evaluating a gate g with input wire w_i and output wire $w_j = g(w_i)$ without revealing any information about the wire values. The idea is to consider the function mapping the masked input $w'_i = w_i + r_i$ to the masked output $w'_j = g(w_i) + r_j$ as a *secret* function f determined by r_i and r_j, applied to the *public* input w'_i. Concretely, $f(w'_i) = g(w'_i - r_i) + r_j$.

Since the secret function f is known to the dealer (who picks all random masks), the dealer can securely delegate the evaluation of f to the two parties by splitting it into f_0 and f_1 via FSS and sending to each party σ its corresponding FSS key k_σ. Letting party σ evaluate $f_\sigma(w'_i)$, the parties obtain additive shares of w'_j, which they can safely exchange and recover the masked output w'_j. Finally, the circuit output wires are unmasked by having the dealer provide their masks to both parties.

The key observation is that given a gate g, the secret function f comes from the family of *offset* functions $\mathcal{F}_g$ that includes all functions of the form $g^{[\mathsf{r}^{\mathsf{in}},\mathsf{r}^{\mathsf{out}}]}(x) = g(x - \mathsf{r}^{\mathsf{in}}) + \mathsf{r}^{\mathsf{out}}$. (Alternatively, up to a slight loss of efficiency, it is enough to use FSS for the simpler class of functions of the form $g_r(x) = g(x+r)$, together with separate shares of the masks.) We refer to an FSS scheme for the offset function family $\mathcal{F}_g$ as an *FSS gate* for g. The key technical challenge in implementing the approach of [13] is in efficiently realizing FSS gates for useful types of gates g.

For addition and multiplication gates over a finite ring, the FSS gates are information-theoretic and essentially coincide with Beaver's protocol [6] (more accurately, its circuit-dependent variant from [7,21,23]). A key observation of [13] is that for a variety of useful non-arithmetic gates, including zero test, integer comparison, ReLU, splines, and bit-decomposition (mapping an input in $\mathbb{Z}_{2^n}$ to the corresponding output in $\mathbb{Z}_2^n$), FSS gates can be efficiently constructed using a small number of invocations of FSS schemes from [12]. The latter FSS schemes have the appealing feature of making a black-box use of any pseudorandom generator (PRG). This gives rise to relatively short keys and fast implementations using hardware support for AES.

Alternative Variants. The above protocol uses *circuit-dependent* correlated randomness, since a wire mask is used in two or more gates incident to this wire, and this incidence relation depends on the circuit topology. At a small additional cost, one can break the correlations between FSS gates and obtain a circuit independent variant; see [13] for details. Another variant, which corresponds to how standard MPC protocols are typically described, is to use an FSS gate for mapping a *secret-shared* input to a *secret-shared* output (rather than a masked input to a masked output). This variant proceeds as described above, except that the parties start by reconstructing the masked input using a single round of interaction, and then use the FSS gate to locally compute shares of the output (without any interaction). With this variant, one can seamlessly use FSS gates in combination with other kinds of MPC protocols are based on garbled circuits, secret sharing, or homomorphic encryption.

Efficiency. When mapping a masked input to a masked output, processing a gate g requires only a *single* round of interaction, where each party sends a message to the other party. This message consists of a single element in the output group of g. Similarly, the variant mapping a secret-shared input to a secret-shared output still requires only a single round of interaction, where the message here consists of a single element in the input group of g. Assuming a single round of interaction, this online communication complexity is optimal [13]. Overall, when evaluating a full circuit the communication by each party (using either the masked-input to masked-output or the shared-input to shared-output variant) is equal to that of communicating all wire values. The round complexity is equal to the circuit depth, no matter how complex the gates g are. The only complexity measures which are sensitive to the FSS gate implementation are the evaluation time and, typically more significantly, the size of the correlated randomness communicated by the dealer and stored by the parties. Optimizing the latter is a central focus of our work.

When is the FSS-Based Approach Attractive? It is instructive to compare the efficiency features of the above FSS-based approach with that of the two main approaches for MPC with preprocessing: a Yao-style protocol based on garbled circuits (GC) [53] and a GMW-style protocol based on secret sharing [29].[1] Consider the goal of securely converting input shares for g into output shares when g is a nontrivial gate, say ReLU, over elements of $\mathbb{Z}_N$ for $N = 2^n$.

The FSS-based online protocol requires only *one* round of interaction in which each party sends only n bits (as argued above, this is optimal). In contrast, in a GC-based protocol the online phase (as used in several related works [15,19, 25,33,39–41]) requires one of the parties to communicate $256n$ bits (a pair of AES keys for each input), which is $128\times$ bigger. Furthermore, the parties need to interact in *two* sequential rounds. In the full version of this paper [9], we discuss a way to reduce the online communication of a GC-based protocol by $2\times$, which still leaves a $64\times$ overhead in communication and $2\times$ overhead in rounds over the FSS-based protocol. A GMW-style protocol typically requires a large number of rounds (depending on the multiplicative depth of a Boolean circuit implementing g), and has online per-party communication which is bigger than n by a multiplicative factor which depends on the number of multiplication gates in the circuit. See full version for a more concrete comparison with previous works taking the GC-based or GMW-based approach.

Even when considering MPC *without* preprocessing, namely, when the offline and online phases are combined, the FSS-based approach can still maintain some of its advantages. For instance, since keys for all FSS gates in a deep circuit can be generated in parallel, the advantage in round complexity is maintained. In the 3PC setting where one party emulates the role of the dealer, or in the 2PC setting with a relatively small input length n (see Appendix A of full version [9]), one can potentially beat the communication complexity of a GC-based protocol, depending on the FSS key size. This will be further discussed below.

---

[1] Here we only consider protocols whose online phase is based on *symmetric* cryptography. This excludes protocols based on homomorphic encryption, whose concrete costs are typically much higher.

To conclude, FSS-based protocols will typically outperform competing approaches in two common scenarios: (1) when offline communication is cheaper than online communication, or alternatively (2) when latency is the bottleneck and minimizing rounds is a primary goal. In the setting of MPC with preprocessing, the FSS-based approach beats *all* previous practical approaches to mixed-mode secure computation with respect to *both* online communication and round complexity.

Finally, we stress that while the above discussion mainly focuses on semi-honest 2PC with a trusted dealer, most of the above benefits also apply to malicious security (see full version), and when emulating the trusted dealer using the different options we discuss: third party, 2PC protocol (full version), or semi-trusted hardware [43].

Bottlenecks for the FSS-Based Approach. Given the optimality of rounds and communication in the online evaluation of a gate g, the main bottleneck in the FSS-based approach lies in the size of the correlated randomness provided by the trusted dealer, namely the size of the FSS keys k_σ. This affects both *offline communication* and *online storage*. In the 3PC setting, where the trusted dealer is emulated by a third party, the FSS key size directly translates to offline communication from the third party to the other two parties. In the 2PC setting, where the dealer is emulated by an offline protocol for securely generating correlated randomness (see full version [9] for more details), the communication and computation costs of the offline protocol grow significantly with the key size. Thus, minimizing key size of useful FSS gates is strongly motivated by all application scenarios of FSS-based MPC.

Many compelling use-cases of MPC, such as privacy-preserving machine learning, finance, and scientific computing, involve numerical computation with finite precision, also known as "fixed-point arithmetic." Arithmetic over fixed-point numbers not only requires arithmetic operations such as additions and multiplications, for which efficient protocols can be based on traditional techniques, but also other kinds of operations that cannot be efficiently reduced to arithmetic operations over large rings. These include Boolean shift operators needed for adjusting the "scale" of fixed-point numbers. Concretely, for $N = 2^n$, a logical (resp., arithmetic) right shift by s converts an element $x \in \mathbb{Z}_N$ representing an n-bit unsigned (resp., signed) number to $y \in \mathbb{Z}_N$ representing $\lfloor x/2^s \rfloor$. To date, there are no PRG-based realizations of FSS gates for these Boolean operations,[2] and hence, fixed-point arithmetic operations cannot be realized securely using existing lightweight FSS machinery.

We now discuss our contributions that address these bottlenecks.

[2] An FSS-based protocol for right-shift can be obtained using the FSS gate for bit-decomposition from [13]. However, their construction only allows output shares of bits over $\mathbb{Z}_2$, whereas such a reduction (as well as other applications) requires output shares over $\mathbb{Z}_N$. Conversion of shares from $\mathbb{Z}_2$ to $\mathbb{Z}_N$ would thus require an additional round of interaction. Furthermore, this approach would require key size quadratic in input length: $O(n^2\lambda)$ for $N = 2^n$ (i.e., n-bit numbers) and PRG seed length λ.

1.2 Our Contributions

In this work, we make the following contributions:

- **Improved Key Size.** We obtain both concrete and asymptotic improvements in key size for widely applicable FSS gates such as integer comparisons, interval containment, bit-decomposition, and splines.
- **New Gates.** We extend the scope of FSS-based MPC by providing the first efficient FSS gates for several useful function families that include (logical and arithmetic) right shift, as well as bit-decomposition with outputs shared in $\mathbb{Z}_N$ (rather than $\mathbb{Z}_2$ in the construction from [13]).
- **A Barrier.** We provide a barrier result explaining the difficulty of obtaining PRG-based FSS gates for functions such as fixed-point multiplication.

We now give more details about these three kinds of contributions.

Improved Key Size. In Table 1 we summarize our improvements in key size over [13] and compare our improved FSS key size with garbled circuit size for the same gates. We provide the key size both as a function of input bitlength n and for the special case $n = 16$. Compared to [13], we observe a reduction in key size ranging from 6$\times$ for ReLU to 22$\times$ for splines and 77$\times$ for multiple interval containment (MIC) with 12 intervals. (Please refer to Appendix D in full version [9] for precise definitions of all gate types.) As can be observed, for all of the FSS gates considered in [13], their key size was significantly larger than the garbled circuit size. With our constructions, the key size is significantly *lower* than garbled circuits, for all gates except bit-decomposition (with output in $\mathbb{Z}_2^n$). For instance, our key size is at least 2$\times$ better than garbled circuits for ReLU and 15$\times$ and 27$\times$ better for splines and MIC, respectively. Recall that when compared to MPC protocols that use garbled circuits for preprocessing, protocols that follow the FSS-based approach have 64$\times$ lower online communication and 2$\times$ less rounds. So with our new schemes, FSS-based MPC with preprocessing will typically become more efficient in storage as well. The offline cost can also be smaller in some MPC settings (such as the 3PC case).

Our improvements in key size are obtained in two steps. The first step is a roughly 4$\times$ improvement for a central building block of useful FSS gates that we call Distributed Comparison Function (DCF). A DCF is an FSS scheme for the family of functions $f^{<}_{\alpha,\beta}(x)$ that output β if $x < \alpha$ and 0 otherwise, where $\alpha, \beta \in \mathbb{Z}_N$. This improvement is independently motivated by several other applications, including Yao's millionaires' problem and 2-server PIR with range queries. However, our primary motivation is the fact that previous FSS gate constructions from [13] are cast as *reductions* that invoke multiple instances of DCF. As a second step, we significantly improve the previous reductions from [13] of useful non-arithmetic FSS gates to DCF. We describe these two types of improvements in more detail below.

Optimized DCF. The best previous DCF construction is an instance of an FSS scheme for decision trees from [12]. Instead, we provide a tighter direct construction that reduces the key size by roughly 4×. Concretely, the total key size is improved from $\approx 2n(4\lambda + n)$ to $\approx 2n(\lambda + n)$ for input and output domains of size $N = 2^n$ and PRG seed length λ, with similar savings for general input and output domains.[3]

Better Reductions to DCF. We significantly reduce the number of DCF instances required by most of the non-arithmetic FSS gates from [13]. The main new building block is a new FSS scheme for the offset families of interval containment (IC for short) and splines (piecewise polynomial functions) when the comparison points are public. Our construction uses only one DCF instance compared to the analogous constructions from [13] that require 2 and $2m$ DCF instances for IC and splines with m pieces, respectively, but can hide the comparison points. We note that comparison points are public for almost all important applications - e.g. the popular activation function in machine learning, ReLU,[4] absolute value, as well as approximations of transcendental functions [38,41].

Concretely, for $n = 16$ (where inputs and outputs are in $\mathbb{Z}_N$ for $N = 2^n$), including our improvement in DCF key size, we improve the key size from [13] by roughly 6×, 12×, and 22× for the spline functions ReLU, absolute value and sigmoid, respectively, where the sigmoid function is approximated using 12 pieces [38]. Moreover, this improvement in key size makes the FSS-based construction beat garbled circuits not only in terms of online communication but also in terms of per-gate storage requirements. See Table 1 for a more detailed comparison.

The main technical idea that enables the above improvement is that an FSS scheme for the offset family of a *public* IC function $f_{[p,q]}$ (that outputs is 1 if $p \leq x \leq q$ and 0 otherwise) can be reduced to a single DCF instance with $\alpha = N - 1 + \mathsf{r}^{\mathsf{in}}$. We build on this construction to reduce FSS keys for multiple intervals (and hence splines with constant payload) to this single DCF instance. See Sect. 4 for details. Constructions for splines with general polynomial outputs employ additional techniques to embed secret payloads (see Sect. 5.1).

Another kind of FSS gate for which we get an asymptotic improvement in key size over [13] is *bit-decomposition* with outputs shared over $\mathbb{Z}_2$. Here an input $x \in \mathbb{Z}_N$ is split to its bit-representation $(x_{n-1}, \cdots, x_0) \in \{0,1\}^n$, where each x_i is individually shared over $\mathbb{Z}_2$. (This type of "arithmetic to Boolean" conversion can be useful for applying a garbled circuit to compute a complex function of x that is not efficiently handled by FSS gates.) Non-trivial protocols for bit-decomposition have been proposed in different MPC models [22,44,49,50]. An FSS gate for the above flavor of bit-decomposition was given in [13] with $O(n^2\lambda)$

[3] A concurrent work by Ryffel *et al.* [48] on privacy-preserving machine learning using FSS also proposes an optimized DCF scheme. Our construction is around 1.7× better in key size than theirs.

[4] A ReLU operator, or Rectified Linear Unit, is a function on signed numbers defined by $g(x) = \max(x, 0)$.

Table 1. Comparison of our FSS gate key sizes, with those of [13], and Garbled Circuits (GC) [52]. For FSS (i.e., our work and [13]), we list total key size for *both* P_0, P_1. For GC, we under-approximate and consider only the size of garbled circuit. The table only captures the size of correlated randomness (offline communication in the 3PC case); the online communication corresponding to both FSS columns is at least $\frac{\lambda}{2}\times$ better than GC (and rounds $2\times$ better). $\mathbb{U}_N$, $\mathbb{S}_N$ denote unsigned and signed n-bit integers, respectively. We consider gates for: Interval containment (IC), multiple interval containment (MIC) with m intervals, splines with m intervals and d-degree polynomial outputs, ReLU, Absolute value (ABS), Bit Decomposition (BD), Logical/Arithmetic Right Shifts (LRS/ARS) by s. Syntax and definitions of all gates are described in appendix D in our full version [9]. We provide cost in terms of number of $\mathsf{DCF}_{n,\mathbb{G}}$ keys for DCF with input bitlength n and output group $\mathbb{G}$. To disambiguate between our optimized DCF and DCF used in [13], we use $\mathsf{DCF}^{\mathsf{BGI}}_{n,\mathbb{G}}$ for the latter. Let $\ell = \lceil \log |\mathbb{G}| \rceil$. Size of our optimized $\mathsf{DCF}_{n,\mathbb{G}}$ key is total $2\,(n(\lambda+\ell+2)+\lambda+\ell)$ bits. Size of $\mathsf{DCF}^{\mathsf{BGI}}_{n,\mathbb{G}}$ key (using [12]) is $2\,(4n(\lambda+1)+n\ell+\lambda)$ bits. For our BD scheme (with output over $\mathbb{U}_2^n$), w is a parameter (here we assume $w \mid n$) and compute grows exponentially with w. We provide approximate key size expressions here by ignoring lower order terms; refer to Table 2 in Appendix C.2 of full version [9] for exact expressions. The values in parenthesis give exact key size in bits for $\lambda = 128$, $n = 16$, $m = 12$, $d = 1$, $w = 4$, $s = 7$.

Gate	This work	BGI'19 [13]	GC
IC (n)	$\mathsf{DCF}_{n,\mathbb{U}_N}$ (4992)	$2\times\mathsf{DCF}^{\mathsf{BGI}}_{n,\mathbb{U}_N}$ (34592)	$8\lambda n$ (15616)
MIC (n,m)	$\mathsf{DCF}_{n,\mathbb{U}_N}+2mn$ (5344)	$2m\times\mathsf{DCF}^{\mathsf{BGI}}_{n,\mathbb{U}_N}$ (415104)	$6\lambda mn$ (145152)
Splines (n,m,d)	$\mathsf{DCF}_{n,\mathbb{U}_N^{m(d+1)}}+4mn(d+1)$ (19040)	$2m\times\mathsf{DCF}^{\mathsf{BGI}}_{n,\mathbb{U}_N^{(d+1)}}$ (427008)	$4\lambda mn(d+2)$ (289536)
ReLU (n)	$\mathsf{DCF}_{n,\mathbb{U}_N^2}$ (5664)	$2\times\mathsf{DCF}^{\mathsf{BGI}}_{n,\mathbb{U}_N^2}$ (35616)	$6\lambda n$ (11776)
ABS (n)	$\mathsf{DCF}_{n,\mathbb{U}_N^2}$ (5728)	$4\times\mathsf{DCF}^{\mathsf{BGI}}_{n,\mathbb{U}_N^2}$ (71168)	$8\lambda n$ (15616)
BD (n,w)	$\frac{n}{w}\times\mathsf{DCF}_{\frac{n+w}{2},\mathbb{U}_2}$ (11544)	$(n-1)\times\mathsf{DCF}^{\mathsf{BGI}}_{\frac{n}{2},\mathbb{U}_2}$ (127952)	$2\lambda n$ (3840)
LRS (n,s)	$\mathsf{DCF}_{s,\mathbb{U}_N}+\mathsf{DCF}_{n,\mathbb{U}_N}$ (7324)	– (–)	$4\lambda n$ (7680)
ARS (n,s)	$\mathsf{DCF}_{s,\mathbb{S}_N}+\mathsf{DCF}_{n-1,\mathbb{S}_N^2}$ (7608)	– (–)	$4\lambda n$ (7680)

key size. Here we substantially improve the hidden constant by reducing the bit-decomposition problem to a series of public interval containments. Moreover, we show how to further reduce the key size by an extra factor of w at the cost of computational overhead that grows exponentially with w. Setting $w = \log n$, we get an asymptotic improvement in key size over [13], while maintaining poly(n) computation time.

New FSS Gates. A central operation that underlies fixed-point arithmetic with bounded precision is a Boolean *right shift* operation that maps a number $x \in \mathbb{Z}_N$ to $y \in \mathbb{Z}_N$ representing $\lfloor x/2^s \rfloor$ for shift amount s. This operation comes in two flavors: *logical* that applies to unsigned numbers and *arithmetic* that applies to signed numbers in 2's complement representation. These operations are typically applied following a multiplication operation to enable further computations while keeping the significant bits. Previous results from the literature do not give rise to efficient PRG-based FSS gates for these shift operators. We present a new design approach to FSS for right shift that uses only two invocations of DCF, obtaining asymptotic key size of $O(n\lambda + n^2)$. See Sect. 6 for definitions and construction details and Table 1 for comparison of key size with garbled circuits.

Another new feasibility result is related to the bit-decomposition problem discussed above. The FSS gate for bit-decomposition from [13] crucially relies on the output bits x_i being shared over $\mathbb{Z}_2$, whereas in some applications one needs the bits x_i to be individually shared over $\mathbb{Z}_N$ (or a different $\mathbb{Z}_{N'}$). While a conversion from $\mathbb{Z}_2$ to $\mathbb{Z}_N$ can be done directly using another FSS gate or oblivious transfer, this costs at least one more round of interaction. We realize this generalized form of bit-decomposition directly by a single FSS gate, via a similar approach of reducing the problem to a series of public interval containments.

A Barrier. Most applications of MPC in the areas of machine learning (see [40,41,46] and references therein) and scientific computing (see [4,5,17,18] and references therein) use fixed-point arithmetic for efficiently obtaining an approximate output. Fixed-point addition is defined to be the same as integer addition; however, fixed-point multiplication requires an integer multiplication followed by an appropriate right shift operation for preventing integer overflows (see Sect. 6). Many prior works, for efficiency reasons, implement this right shift (or truncation) through a non-interactive "local truncation" procedure [26,37,40,41,51]. This has two issues. First, the truncated output can be *totally* incorrect, in the sense of being random, with some (small) probability. Since this probability accumulates with the number of such multiplications (and hence truncations), it necessitates an increase of the modulus N that can take a toll on efficiency. While this overhead is reasonable in some cases [2,47], local truncation may be too costly for large scale applications [46]. Second, even when a big error does not occur, the least significant bit resulting from local truncation is erroneous with high probability. Such small errors are aggregated over the course of the computation. This makes the correctness of the implementation more difficult to verify, and can potentially lead to fraud through salami slicing (or penny shaving) in financial applications [1], where the adversary ensures that the small errors are biased in its favorable direction.

Our new FSS gate constructions for right shifts provide an effective solution for performing fixed-point multiplication operations in two rounds by sequentially invoking two FSS gates: one FSS gate for performing multiplication over $\mathbb{Z}_N$ (implemented via [13] or a standard multiplication triple), followed by a second FSS gate to perform an arithmetic right shift for signed integers (or logical shift for unsigned integers). This approach gives a faithful error-free implementation of secure fixed-point multiplication for inputs of all bitlengths. A natural question is whether it is possible to replace the two FSS gates by a single FSS gate, avoiding the additional round of communication, using only cheap symmetric cryptographic primitives such as a PRG.

We demonstrate a barrier toward this goal, showing that this requires settling a major open problem in the area of FSS: namely, whether the family of conjunctions of a subset of n bits has an FSS scheme based on symmetric cryptography. Currently, FSS schemes for this family are known only under structured, public-key computational hardness assumptions such as Decisional Diffie-Hellman [11], Paillier [28] or Learning With Errors [14,26], that imply homomorphic public key encryption. Such FSS schemes are less efficient than the PRG-based schemes considered in this work by several orders of magnitude, with respect to both communication and computation.

2 Preliminaries

We provide an abbreviated version of preliminaries and notation. A more detailed formal treatment can be found in Appendix E in our full version [9].

Notation. We use arithmetic operations in the ring $\mathbb{Z}_N$ for $N = 2^n$. We naturally identify elements of $\mathbb{Z}_N$ with their n-bit binary representation, where 0 is represented by 0^n and $N-1$ by 1^n. Unless otherwise specified, we parse $x \in \{0,1\}^n$ as $x_{[n-1]}, \ldots, x_{[0]}$, where $x_{[n-1]}$ is the most significant bit (MSB) and $x_{[0]}$ is the least significant bit (LSB). For $0 \leq j < k \leq n$, $z = x_{[j,k)} \in \mathbb{Z}_{2^{k-j}}$ denotes the ring element corresponding to the bit-string $x_{[k-1]}, \ldots, x_{[j]}$. $||$ denotes string concatenation. *Function family* denotes an infinite collection of functions specified by the same representation. λ denotes computational security parameter.

2.1 Data Types and Operators

Unsigned and Signed Integers. We consider computations over finite bit unsigned and signed integers, denoted by $\mathbb{U}_N$ and $\mathbb{S}_N$, respectively, over n-bits. We note that $\mathbb{U}_N = \{0, \ldots, N-1\}$ is isomorphic to $\mathbb{Z}_N$. Moreover, $\mathbb{S}_N = \{-N/2, \ldots, 0, \ldots, N/2-1\}$ can be encoded into $\mathbb{Z}_N$ or $\mathbb{U}_N$ using 2's complement notation or mod N operation. The positive values $\{0, \ldots, N/2-1\}$ are mapped identically to $\{0, \ldots, N/2-1\}$ and negative values $\{-N/2, \ldots, -1\}$ are mapped to $\{N/2, \ldots, N-1\}$. In this notation, the MSB of (the binary representation of) x is 0 if $x \geq 0$ and 1 if $x < 0$. Note that addition, subtraction and multiplication of signed integers modulo N respect this representation as long as the result is in the range $[-N/2, N/2)$. Our work also considers fixed-point representation of numbers and its associated arithmetic. Section 6 provides a more detailed description of the mapping of rationals into the fixed-point space as well as fixed-point arithmetic.

Operators. We consider several standard operators, which can be thought of as applying to (signed or unsigned) integers. Each operator is defined by a *gate*: a function family parameterized by input and output domains and possibly other parameters. Some of the operators we consider are single and multiple interval containments (Sect. 4), splines and applications to ReLU and absolute value (Sect. 5.1), bit decomposition (Sect. 5.2 in full version [9]), as well as operators required for the realization of fixed-point arithmetic - such as fixed-point addition and multiplication (Sect. 6.1), logical right shifts (Sect. 6.2), arithmetic right shifts, and comparison (Sect. 6.3 and 6.4 in full version [9]).

2.2 Function Secret Sharing

We follow the definition of function secret sharing (FSS) from [12]. Intuitively, a (2-party) FSS scheme is an efficient algorithm that splits a function $f \in \mathcal{F}$ into two *additive* shares f_0, f_1, such that: (1) each f_σ hides f; (2) for every input x, $f_0(x) + f_1(x) = f(x)$. The main challenge is to make the descriptions of f_0 and f_1 compact, while still allowing their efficient evaluation. As in [10,12,13], we insist on an additive representation of the output that is critical for applications.

Definition 1 (FSS: Syntax). *A (2-party)* function secret sharing (FSS) scheme *is a pair of algorithms* $(\mathsf{Gen}, \mathsf{Eval})$ *such that:*

- $\mathsf{Gen}(1^\lambda, \hat{f})$ *is a PPT* key generation algorithm *that given* 1^λ *and* $\hat{f} \in \{0,1\}^*$ *(description of a function* f*) outputs a pair of keys* (k_0, k_1)*. We assume that* $\hat{f}$ *explicitly contains descriptions of input and output groups* $\mathbb{G}^{\mathsf{in}}, \mathbb{G}^{\mathsf{out}}$.
- $\mathsf{Eval}(\sigma, k_\sigma, x)$ *is a polynomial-time* evaluation algorithm *that given* $\sigma \in \{0,1\}$ *(party index),* k_σ *(key defining* $f_\sigma : \mathbb{G}^{\mathsf{in}} \to \mathbb{G}^{\mathsf{out}}$*) and* $x \in \mathbb{G}^{\mathsf{in}}$ *(input for* f_σ*) outputs a group element* $y_\sigma \in \mathbb{G}^{\mathsf{out}}$ *(the value of* $f_\sigma(x)$*).*

Definition 2 (FSS: Correctness and Security). *Let* $\mathcal{F} = \{f\}$ *be a function family and* Leak *be a function specifying the allowable leakage about* $\hat{f}$*. When* Leak *is omitted, it is understood to output only* $\mathbb{G}^{\mathsf{in}}$ *and* $\mathbb{G}^{\mathsf{out}}$*. We say that* $(\mathsf{Gen}, \mathsf{Eval})$ *as in Definition 1 is an* FSS scheme for $\mathcal{F}$ *(with respect to leakage* Leak*) if it satisfies the following requirements.*

- **Correctness:** *For all* $\hat{f} \in P_{\mathcal{F}}$ *describing* $f : \mathbb{G}^{\mathsf{in}} \to \mathbb{G}^{\mathsf{out}}$*, and every* $x \in \mathbb{G}^{\mathsf{in}}$*, if* $(k_0, k_1) \leftarrow \mathsf{Gen}(1^\lambda, \hat{f})$ *then* $\Pr[\mathsf{Eval}(0, k_0, x) + \mathsf{Eval}(1, k_1, x) = f(x)] = 1$.
- **Security:** *For each* $\sigma \in \{0,1\}$ *there is a PPT algorithm* Sim_σ *(simulator), such that for every sequence* $(\hat{f}_\lambda)_{\lambda \in \mathbb{N}}$ *of polynomial-size function descriptions from* $\mathcal{F}$ *and polynomial-size input sequence* x_λ *for* f_λ*, the outputs of the following experiments* Real *and* Ideal *are computationally indistinguishable:*
  - Real_λ*:* $(k_0, k_1) \leftarrow \mathsf{Gen}(1^\lambda, \hat{f}_\lambda)$*; Output* k_σ.
  - Ideal_λ*: Output* $\mathsf{Sim}_\sigma(1^\lambda, \mathsf{Leak}(\hat{f}_\lambda))$.

A central building block for many of our constructions is an FSS scheme for a *special interval function* referred to as a *distributed comparison function* (DCF) as defined below. We formalize it below.

Definition 3 (DCF). *A special interval* function $f^{<}_{\alpha,\beta}$*, also referred to as a* comparison *function, outputs* β *if* $x < \alpha$ *and 0 otherwise. We refer to an FSS schemes for comparison functions as* distributed comparison function *(DCF). Analogously, function* $f^{\leq}_{\alpha,\beta}$ *outputs* β *if* $x \leq \alpha$ *and* 0 *otherwise. In all of these cases, we allow the default leakage* $\mathsf{Leak}(\hat{f}) = (\mathbb{G}^{\mathsf{in}}, \mathbb{G}^{\mathsf{out}})$.

The following theorem captures the concrete costs of the best known construction of DCF from a PRG (Theorem 3.17 in the full version of [12]):

Theorem 1 (Concrete cost of DCF [12]**).** *Given a PRG* $G : \{0,1\}^{\lambda} \to \{0,1\}^{2\lambda+2}$*, there exists a DCF for* $f^{<}_{\alpha,\beta} : \mathbb{G}^{\mathsf{in}} \to \mathbb{G}^{\mathsf{out}}$ *with key size* $4n \cdot (\lambda + 1) + n\ell + \lambda$*, where* $n = \lceil \log |\mathbb{G}^{\mathsf{in}}| \rceil$ *and* $\ell = \lceil \log |\mathbb{G}^{\mathsf{out}}| \rceil$*. For* $\ell' = \lceil \frac{\ell}{\lambda+2} \rceil$*, the key generation algorithm* Gen *invokes* G *at most* $n \cdot (4 + \ell')$ *times and the algorithm* Eval *invokes* G *at most* $n \cdot (2 + \ell')$ *times.*

We use $\mathbf{DCF}_{n,\mathbb{G}}$ to denote the total key size, i.e. $|k_0| + |k_1|$, of the DCF key with input length n and output group $\mathbb{G}$ (see Table 1). This captures the output length of Gen algorithm. On the other hand, we use $\mathsf{DCF}_{n,\mathbb{G}}$ (non-bold) to denote the key size per party, i.e., $|k_b|, b \in \{0,1\}$. This captures the key size used in Eval algorithm. In the rest of the paper, we use $\mathsf{DCF}_{n,\mathbb{G}}$ to count number of invocations/evaluations as well as key size per evaluator P_b, $b \in \{0,1\}$.

2.3 FSS Gates

The recent work of Boyle *et al.* [13] provided general-purpose transformations for obtaining efficient secure computation protocols in the preprocessing model via FSS schemes for corresponding function families.

The key idea is the following FSS-based gate evaluation procedure. For each gate $g : \mathbb{G}^{\mathsf{in}} \to \mathbb{G}^{\mathsf{out}}$ in the circuit to be securely evaluated, the dealer uses an FSS scheme for the class of *offset* functions $\hat{\mathcal{G}}$ that includes all functions of the form $g^{[\mathsf{r}^{\mathsf{in}},\mathsf{r}^{\mathsf{out}}]}(x) = g(x - \mathsf{r}^{\mathsf{in}}) + \mathsf{r}^{\mathsf{out}}$. If the input to gate g is wire i and the output is wire j, the dealer uses the FSS scheme for $\hat{\mathcal{G}}$ to split the function $g^{[\mathsf{r}^{\mathsf{in}},\mathsf{r}^{\mathsf{out}}]}$ into two functions with keys k_0, k_1, and delivers each key k_σ to party P_σ. Now, evaluating their FSS shares on the common masked input $w_i + r_i$, the parties obtain additive shares of the masked output $w_j + r_j$, which they can exchange and maintain the invariant for wire j. Finally, the outputs are reconstructed by having the dealer reveal to both parties the masks of the output wires. We defer a formal statement of the corresponding transformation to Appendix E in our full version [9]. In what follows we introduce necessary terminology.

Definition 4 (Offset function family and FSS gates). *Let* $\mathcal{G} = \{g : \mathbb{G}^{\mathsf{in}} \to \mathbb{G}^{\mathsf{out}}\}$ *be a computation gate (parameterized by input and output groups* $\mathbb{G}^{\mathsf{in}}, \mathbb{G}^{\mathsf{out}}$*). The* family of offset functions $\hat{\mathcal{G}}$ *of* $\mathcal{G}$ *is given by*

$$\hat{\mathcal{G}} := \left\{ g^{[\mathsf{r}^{in},\mathsf{r}^{out}]} : \mathbb{G}^{\mathsf{in}} \to \mathbb{G}^{\mathsf{out}} \;\middle|\; \begin{array}{c} g : \mathbb{G}^{\mathsf{in}} \to \mathbb{G}^{\mathsf{out}} \in \mathcal{G}, \\ \mathsf{r}^{in} \in \mathbb{G}^{\mathsf{in}}, \mathsf{r}^{out} \in \mathbb{G}^{\mathsf{out}} \end{array} \right\}, \text{ where}$$

$$g^{[\mathsf{r}^{in},\mathsf{r}^{out}]}(x) := g(x - \mathsf{r}^{in}) + \mathsf{r}^{out},$$

and $g^{[\mathsf{r}^{in},\mathsf{r}^{out}]}$ *contains an explicit description of* $\mathsf{r}^{in}, \mathsf{r}^{out}$. *Finally, we use the term* FSS gate for $\mathcal{G}$ *to denote an FSS scheme for the corresponding offset family* $\hat{\mathcal{G}}$.

As explained above, an FSS gate for $\mathcal{G}$ implies an "online-optimal" protocol for converting a masked input x to a masked output $g(x)$ for $g \in \mathcal{G}$. Concretely, the online phase consists of only one round in which each party sends a message of length $|g(x)|$. Alternatively, we can have a similar one-round protocol converting additively shared input to additively shared output, where here the message length is $|x|$. The offline communication and storage correspond to the FSS key size produced by Gen, and the online compute time corresponds to the computational cost of Eval.

Boyle *et al.* [13] constructed FSS gates for most of the operators from Sect. 2.1 by reducing them to multiple invocations of DCF. In this work we will improve the efficiency of previous DCF constructions, and provide better reductions (both asymptotically and concretely) from gates in Sect. 2.1 to DCF.

3 Optimized Distributed Comparison Function

A Distributed Comparison Function (DCF), as formalized in Definition 3, is an FSS scheme for the family of comparison functions. We reduce the key size of prior best known construction of [12] from roughly $n(4\lambda+n)$ to roughly $n(\lambda+n)$, i.e. roughly $4\times$, for input and output domains of size $N = 2^n$ and security parameter λ, with similar savings for general input and output domains.

Our construction draws inspiration from the DPF of [12]. The Gen algorithm uses a PRG G and generates two keys (k_0, k_1) such that $\forall b \in \{0,1\}$, k_b includes a random PRG seed s_b and $n+1$ shared *correction words.* A key implicitly defines a binary tree with $N = 2^n$ leaves where a node u is associated with a tuple (s_b, V_b, t_b), for a PRG seed s_b, an output group element $V_b \in \mathbb{G}$ and a bit t_b. The construction ensures that the sum $V_0 + V_1$ over all nodes leading to an input x is exactly equal to $f^{<}_{\alpha,\beta}(x)$. Therefore, evaluating a key k_b on an input x requires traversing the tree generated by k_b from the root to the leaf representing x, computing (s_b, V_b, t_b) at each node and summing up the values V_b.

The tuple (s_b, V_b, t_b) associated with u is a function of the seed associated with the parent of u and the correction words. Therefore, if $s_0 = s_1$ then for any descendent of u, k_0 and k_1 generate identical tuples. The correction words are chosen such that when a path to x departs from the path to α, the two seeds s_0 and s_1 on the first node off the path are identical, and the sum of $V_0 + V_1$ along the whole path to u is exactly zero if the departure is to the right of the path to α, i.e. $x > \alpha$, and is β if the departure is to the left of the path to α. Finally, along the path to α any seed s_b is computationally indistinguishable from a random string given the key k_{1-b}, which ensures the security of the construction.

The DCF scheme is presented in Fig. 1, and a formal statement of the scheme's complexity appears in Theorem 2 (see Appendix F.1 in full version [9] for detailed security proof). The scheme uses the function $\mathsf{Convert}_{\mathbb{G}} : \{0,1\}^{\lambda} \to \mathbb{G}$

Distributed Comparison Function $(\mathsf{Gen}_n^<, \mathsf{Eval}_n^<)$
Let $G : \{0,1\}^\lambda \to \{0,1\}^{2(2\lambda+1)}$ be a pseudorandom generator.
Let $\mathsf{Convert}_{\mathbb{G}} : \{0,1\}^\lambda \to \mathbb{G}$ be a map converting a random λ-bit string to a pseudorandom group element of $\mathbb{G}$.

$\mathsf{Gen}_n^<(1^\lambda, \alpha, \beta, \mathbb{G})$:

Let $\alpha = \alpha_1, \ldots, \alpha_n \in \{0,1\}^n$ be the bit decomposition of α
Sample random $s_0^{(0)} \leftarrow \{0,1\}^\lambda$ and $s_1^{(0)} \leftarrow \{0,1\}^\lambda$
Let $V_\alpha = 0 \in \mathbb{G}$, let $t_0^{(0)} = 0$ and $t_1^{(0)} = 1$
for $i = 1$ to n **do**
  $s_0^L || v_0^L || t_0^L \;||\; s_0^R || v_0^R || t_0^R \leftarrow G(s_0^{(i-1)})$
  $s_1^L || v_1^L || t_1^L \;||\; s_1^R || v_1^R || t_1^R \leftarrow G(s_1^{(i-1)})$
  if $\alpha_i = 0$ **then** $\mathsf{Keep} \leftarrow L$, $\mathsf{Lose} \leftarrow R$
  else $\mathsf{Keep} \leftarrow R$, $\mathsf{Lose} \leftarrow L$
  end if
  $s_{CW} \leftarrow s_0^{\mathsf{Lose}} \oplus s_1^{\mathsf{Lose}}$
  $V_{CW} \leftarrow (-1)^{t_1^{(i-1)}} \cdot [\mathsf{Convert}_{\mathbb{G}}(v_1^{\mathsf{Lose}}) - \mathsf{Convert}_{\mathbb{G}}(v_0^{\mathsf{Lose}}) - V_\alpha]$
  if $\mathsf{Lose} = L$ **then** $V_{CW} \leftarrow V_{CW} + (-1)^{t_1^{(i-1)}} \cdot \beta$
  end if
  $V_\alpha \leftarrow V_\alpha - \mathsf{Convert}_{\mathbb{G}}(v_1^{\mathsf{Keep}}) + \mathsf{Convert}_{\mathbb{G}}(v_0^{\mathsf{Keep}}) + (-1)^{t_1^{(i-1)}} \cdot V_{CW}$
  $t_{CW}^L \leftarrow t_0^L \oplus t_1^L \oplus \alpha_i \oplus 1$ and $t_{CW}^R \leftarrow t_0^R \oplus t_1^R \oplus \alpha_i$
  $CW^{(i)} \leftarrow s_{CW} || V_{CW} || t_{CW}^L || t_{CW}^R$
  $s_b^{(i)} \leftarrow s_b^{\mathsf{Keep}} \oplus t_b^{(i-1)} \cdot s_{CW}$ for $b = 0, 1$
  $t_b^{(i)} \leftarrow t_b^{\mathsf{Keep}} \oplus t_b^{(i-1)} \cdot t_{CW}^{\mathsf{Keep}}$ for $b = 0, 1$
end for
$CW^{(n+1)} \leftarrow (-1)^{t_1^n} \cdot [\mathsf{Convert}_{\mathbb{G}}(s_1^{(n)}) - \mathsf{Convert}_{\mathbb{G}}(s_0^{(n)}) - V_\alpha]$
Let $k_b = s_b^{(0)} || CW^{(1)} || \cdots || CW^{(n+1)}$
return (k_0, k_1)

$\mathsf{Eval}_n^<(b, k_b, x)$:

Parse $k_b = s^{(0)} || CW^{(1)} || \cdots || CW^{(n+1)}$, $x = x_1, \ldots, x_n$, let $V = 0 \in \mathbb{G}$, $t^{(0)} = b$.
for $i = 1$ to n **do**
  Parse $CW^{(i)} = s_{CW} || V_{CW} || t_{CW}^L || t_{CW}^R$
  Parse $G(s^{(i-1)}) = \hat{s}^L || \hat{v}^L || \hat{t}^L \;||\; \hat{s}^R || \hat{v}^R || \hat{t}^R$
  $\tau^{(i)} \leftarrow (\hat{s}^L || \hat{t}^L \;||\; \hat{s}^R || \hat{t}^R) \oplus (t^{(i-1)} \cdot [s_{CW} || t_{CW}^L || s_{CW} || t_{CW}^R])$
  Parse $\tau^{(i)} = s^L || t^L \;||\; s^R || t^R \in \{0,1\}^{2(\lambda+1)}$
  if $x_i = 0$ **then** $V \leftarrow V + (-1)^b \cdot [\mathsf{Convert}_{\mathbb{G}}(\hat{v}^L) + t^{(i-1)} \cdot V_{CW}]$
    $s^{(i)} \leftarrow s^L$, $t^{(i)} \leftarrow t^L$
  else $V \leftarrow V + (-1)^b \cdot [\mathsf{Convert}_{\mathbb{G}}(\hat{v}^R) + t^{(i-1)} \cdot V_{CW}]$
    $s^{(i)} \leftarrow s^R$, $t^{(i)} \leftarrow t^R$
  end if
end for
$V \leftarrow V + (-1)^b \cdot [\mathsf{Convert}_{\mathbb{G}}(s^{(n)}) + t^{(n)} \cdot CW^{(n+1)}]$
Return V

Fig. 1. Optimized FSS scheme for the class $\mathcal{F}_{n,\mathbb{G}}^<$ of comparison functions $f_{\alpha,\beta}^< : \{0,1\}^n \to \mathbb{G}$, outputting β for $0 \le x < \alpha$ and 0 for $x \ge \alpha$. $||$ denotes string concatenation. b refers to party id. All s and v values are λ-bit strings, V values are elements in $\mathbb{G}$, which are represented in $\lceil \log |\mathbb{G}| \rceil$ bits and t values are single bits. α_1 and x_1 refer to MSBs of α and x, respectively. Similarly, α_n and x_n are the corresponding LSBs.

[12] that converts a pseudo-random string to a pseudo-random group element. When $|\mathbb{G}| = 2^k$ and $k \leq \lambda$, the function simply outputs the first k bits of the input. In any other case, the function expands the input s to a string $G(s)$ of length at least $\log|\mathbb{G}|$ using a PRG G, regards $G(s)$ as an integer and returns $G(s) \bmod |\mathbb{G}|$.

Theorem 2. *Let λ be a security parameter, let $\mathbb{G}$ be an Abelian group, $\ell = \lceil \log|\mathbb{G}| \rceil$, and let $G : \{0,1\}^\lambda \to \{0,1\}^{4\lambda+2}$ be a PRG. The scheme in Fig. 1 is a DCF for $f^<_{\alpha,\beta} : \{0,1\}^n \to \mathbb{G}$ with key size $n(\lambda+\ell+2)+\lambda+\ell$ bits. For $\ell' = \lceil \frac{\ell}{4\lambda+2} \rceil$, the key generation algorithm* Gen *invokes G at most $2n(1+2\ell')+2\ell'$ times and the evaluation algorithm* Eval *invokes G at most $n(1+\ell')+\ell'$ times. In the special case that $|\mathbb{G}| = 2^c$ for $c \leq \lambda$ the number of PRG invocations in* Gen *is $2n$ and the number of PRG invocations in* Eval *is n.*

Dual Distributed Comparison Function (DDCF). Consider a variant of DCF, called *Dual Distributed Comparison Function*, denoted by $\mathcal{F}^{\mathsf{DDCF}}_{n,\mathbb{G}}$. It is a class of comparison functions $f_{\alpha,\beta_1,\beta_2} : \{0,1\}^n \to \mathbb{G}$, that outputs β_1 for $0 \leq x < \alpha$ and β_2 for $x \geq \alpha$. The FSS scheme for DDCF, denoted by $\mathsf{DDCF}_{n,\mathbb{G}}$, follows easily from DCF using $f_{\alpha,\beta_1,\beta_2}(x) = \beta_2 + f^<_{\alpha,\beta_1-\beta_2}(x)$. We provide a formal construction in Fig. 12 of Appendix F.2 in our full version [9].

4 Public Intervals and Multiple Interval Containments

Computing interval containment for a secret value w.r.t. a publicly known interval, that is, whether $x \in [p, q]$, is an important building block for many tasks occurring in scientific computations [4] as well as machine learning [37,41,51]. Moreover, many popular functions such as splines (Sect. 5.1) and most significant non-zero bit (MSNZB) (Appendix H.1 of full version [9]) reduce to computing multiple interval containments on the same secret value x. The work of [13] provided the first constructions of an FSS gate for interval containment as well as splines. In their work, the key size of an FSS gate for interval containment was $\approx$ 2 DCF keys. They build on this to construct an FSS gate for splines and multiple interval containment with m different intervals using key size proportional to $2m$ DCF keys, which is quite expensive. We provide the following constructions:

- In Sect. 4.1, we show how to reduce the key size required for a single interval containment to a *single* DCF key, compared to two DCF keys needed in [13]. Including the gains from our optimized DCF, we get around 7× reduction in key size over [13] for $n = 32$.
- In Sect. 4.2 of our full version [9], we show how to *compress* the FSS keys for multiple interval containments to that of an FSS key for a *single* interval containment (and ring elements proportional to m). More concretely, over inputs of length n, and for computing the output of m interval containment functions on the same input, we reduce the FSS key size from $\approx 2m(4n\lambda + n^2 + 4n) + mn$ to $\approx n\lambda + n^2 + mn$ (including gains from our optimized DCF construction). As an example, taking $n = 32$, we reduce the key size by up to 1100× and for instance, for $m = 10$, the reduction is about 62×.

While the construction from [13] also works when the interval boundaries are secret, i.e., known only to the dealer, our techniques crucially rely on the interval boundaries being public. However, we show that our techniques enable the reduction of key size for several important applications, such as splines (Sect. 5.1), bit decomposition and MSNZB (Sect. 5.2 and Appendix H.1 of full version [9]).

We start by setting notation for single and multiple interval containments. For ease of exposition, in this section, we only consider the ring $\mathbb{U}_N$; however our ideas easily extend to $\mathbb{S}_N$ as well. In particular, for signed intervals checking whether $x \in [p, q]$, where $p, q \in \mathbb{S}_N$, can be reduced to the following unsigned interval containment: $(x+N/2 \bmod N) \in [(p+N/2 \bmod N), (q+N/2 \bmod N)]$. We define $\mathbf{1}\{b\}$ as 1 when b is true and 0 otherwise.

Interval Containment Gate. The (single) interval containment gate $\mathcal{G}_{\mathsf{IC}}$ is the family of functions $g_{\mathsf{IC},n,p,q} : \mathbb{U}_N \rightarrow \mathbb{U}_N$ parameterized by input and output groups $\mathbb{G}^{\mathsf{in}} = \mathbb{G}^{\mathsf{out}} = \mathbb{U}_N$, and given by

$$\mathcal{G}_{\mathsf{IC}} = \left\{ g_{\mathsf{IC},n,p,q} : \mathbb{U}_N \rightarrow \mathbb{U}_N \right\}_{0 \leq p \leq q \leq N-1}, g_{\mathsf{IC},n,p,q}(x) = \mathbf{1}\{p \leq x \leq q\}.$$

Multiple Interval Containment Gate. The multiple interval containment gate $\mathcal{G}_{\mathsf{MIC}}$ is the family of functions $g_{\mathsf{MIC},n,m,P,Q} : \mathbb{U}_N \rightarrow \mathbb{U}_N^m$ for m interval containments parameterized by input and output groups $\mathbb{G}^{\mathsf{in}} = \mathbb{U}_N$ and $\mathbb{G}^{\mathsf{out}} = \mathbb{U}_N^m$, respectively, and for $P = \{p_1, p_2, \ldots, p_m\}$ and $Q = \{q_1, q_2, \ldots, q_m\}$, given by

$$\mathcal{G}_{\mathsf{MIC}} = \left\{ g_{\mathsf{MIC},n,m,P,Q} : \mathbb{U}_N \rightarrow \mathbb{U}_N^m \right\}_{0 \leq p_i \leq q_i \leq N-1}, g_{\mathsf{MIC},n,m,P,Q}(x) = \left\{ \mathbf{1}\{p_i \leq x \leq q_i\} \right\}_{1 \leq i \leq m},$$

Next, we describe our construction for single interval containment that reduces to universal comparison function $f^{<}_{(N-1)+\mathsf{r}^{\mathsf{in}},1}$ and this is the key idea that allows us to compress keys for multiple interval containments.

4.1 Realizing FSS Gate for $[p, q]$ Using FSS Scheme for $f^{<}_{(N-1)+\mathsf{r}^{\mathsf{in}},1}$

First, in Fig. 2, we describe a construction of an FSS gate for $\mathcal{G}_{\mathsf{IC}}$ that is a slight modification of the construction in [13]. This will enable us to build upon it to obtain an FSS gate for $\mathcal{G}_{\mathsf{IC}}$ with a reduced key size (when the intervals are public). The modification that we make is as follows: in [13], the FSS keys for $\mathcal{G}_{\mathsf{IC}}$ were generated differently in the case when only $q + \mathsf{r}^{\mathsf{in}}$ wraps around in $\mathbb{U}_N$ as opposed to when either both or none of $p + \mathsf{r}^{\mathsf{in}}$ and $q + \mathsf{r}^{\mathsf{in}}$ wrap around. In our construction (Fig. 2), we unify these cases, except that the dealer additionally includes an additive correction term $\mathbf{1}\{(p + \mathsf{r}^{\mathsf{in}} \bmod N) > (q + \mathsf{r}^{\mathsf{in}} \bmod N)\}$ in the key, which makes up for the difference between the cases. For completeness, we provide a correctness proof in Appendix G.1 of full version [9]. We note that the key size of our construction in Fig. 2 is identical to the scheme presented in [13], that is, 2 DCF keys and a ring element in $\mathbb{U}_N$.

Next, we present an alternate construction of FSS gate for $\mathcal{G}_{\mathsf{IC}}$ again using two DCF keys that are *independent of interval* $[p, q]$. Later, we will optimize this construction to use only a single DCF key.

Interval Containment Gate $(\mathsf{Gen}^{\mathsf{IC}}_{n,p,q}, \mathsf{Eval}^{\mathsf{IC}}_{n,p,q})$

$\mathsf{Gen}^{\mathsf{IC}}_{n,p,q}(1^\lambda, \mathsf{r}^{\mathsf{in}}, \mathsf{r}^{\mathsf{out}})$:

1: $(k_0^{(p)}, k_1^{(p)}) \leftarrow \mathsf{Gen}^{<}_{n}(1^\lambda, \alpha^{(p)}, N-1, \mathbb{U}_N)$, $\alpha^{(p)} = p + \mathsf{r}^{\mathsf{in}} \in \mathbb{U}_N$.
2: $(k_0^{(q)}, k_1^{(q)}) \leftarrow \mathsf{Gen}^{\leqslant}_{n}(1^\lambda, \alpha^{(q)}, 1, \mathbb{U}_N)$, $\alpha^{(q)} = q + \mathsf{r}^{\mathsf{in}} \in \mathbb{U}_N$.
3: Sample random $w_0, w_1 \leftarrow \mathbb{U}_N$ s.t. $w_0 + w_1 = \mathsf{r}^{\mathsf{out}} + \mathbf{1}\{\alpha^{(p)} > \alpha^{(q)}\}$.
4: For $b \in \{0,1\}$, let $k_b = k_b^{(p)} || k_b^{(q)} || w_b$.
5: **return** (k_0, k_1).

$\mathsf{Eval}^{\mathsf{IC}}_{n,p,q}(b, k_b, x)$:

1: Parse $k_b = k_b^{(p)} || k_b^{(q)} || w_b$.
2: Set $t_b^{(p)} \leftarrow \mathsf{Eval}^{<}_{n}(b, k_b^{(p)}, x)$.
3: Set $t_b^{(q)} \leftarrow \mathsf{Eval}^{\leqslant}_{n}(b, k_b^{(q)}, x)$.
4: **return** $t_b^{(p)} + t_b^{(q)} + w_b$.

Fig. 2. FSS Gate for $\mathcal{G}_{\mathsf{IC}}$ using 2 DCFs [13], b refers to party id.

Using 2 DCF keys independent of *p* and *q*. Below, we state our main technical lemma that allows us to give an alternate construction of FSS gate for $g_{\mathsf{IC},n,p,q}$ using 2 keys for comparison that are *independent of the interval* $[p,q]$ and only depend on r^{in}. More concretely, we will use FSS keys for $f^{<}_{(N-1)+\mathsf{r}^{\mathsf{in}},N-1}$ and $f^{\leq}_{(N-1)+\mathsf{r}^{\mathsf{in}},1}$. In the lemma statement and its proof (Appendix G.2 of full version [9]), unless explicitly stated using mod N, all expressions and equations are over $\mathbb{Z}$ and we consider the natural embedding of $\mathbb{U}_N$ into $\mathbb{Z}$.

Lemma 1. *Let $a, \tilde{a}, b, \tilde{b}, r \in \mathbb{U}_N$, where $a \leq b$, $\tilde{a} = a + r \bmod N$ and $\tilde{b} = b + r \bmod N$. Define 4 boolean predicates over $\mathbb{U}_N \to \{0,1\}$ as follows: $P(x)$ denotes $x < \tilde{a}$, $P'(x)$ denotes $x \leq \tilde{a}$, $Q(x)$ denotes $(x + (b-a) \bmod N) < \tilde{b}$, $Q'(x)$ denotes $(x + (b-a) \bmod N) \leq \tilde{b}$. Then, the following holds:*

$$P(x) = Q(x) + (e_a - e_x) \text{ and } P'(x) = Q'(x) + (e_a - e_x)$$

$$\text{where } e_a = \mathbf{1}\{\tilde{a} + (b-a) > N-1\} \text{ and } e_x = \mathbf{1}\{x + (b-a) > N-1\}$$

Intuitively, Lemma 1 allows us to reduce comparison of x with $\tilde{a}$ (both $<$ and $\leq$) to similar comparison with $\tilde{b}$ modulo some additive correction terms, i.e. e_a and e_x. Our next observation is that in the FSS setting, e_a can be computed by the dealer (with the knowledge of r) and e_x can be locally computed by P_0, P_1 (with the knowledge of x at runtime). Using Lemma 1 and this observation, we can construct an FSS gate for $g_{\mathsf{IC},n,p,q}$ using 2 DCF keys, for functions $f^{<}_{(N-1)+\mathsf{r}^{\mathsf{in}},N-1}$ and $f^{\leq}_{(N-1)+\mathsf{r}^{\mathsf{in}},1}$ (see Appendix G.4 of full version [9] for this).

Reducing to 1 DCF Key. We now optimize the key size of our construction to a single DCF key using Lemma 2 (proof in Appendix G.3 of full version).

Interval Containment Gate $(\mathsf{Gen}^{\mathsf{IC}}_{n,p,q}, \mathsf{Eval}^{\mathsf{IC}}_{n,p,q})$

$\mathsf{Gen}^{\mathsf{IC}}_{n,p,q}(1^\lambda, \mathsf{r}^{\mathsf{in}}, \mathsf{r}^{\mathsf{out}})$:

1: Set $\gamma = (N-1) + \mathsf{r}^{\mathsf{in}} \in \mathbb{U}_N$.
2: $(k_0^{(N-1)}, k_1^{(N-1)}) \leftarrow \mathsf{Gen}^{<}_n(1^\lambda, \gamma, 1, \mathbb{U}_N)$.
3: Set $q' = q + 1 \in \mathbb{U}_N$, $\alpha^{(p)} = p + \mathsf{r}^{\mathsf{in}} \in \mathbb{U}_N$, $\alpha^{(q)} = q + \mathsf{r}^{\mathsf{in}} \in \mathbb{U}_N$ and $\alpha^{(q')} = q + 1 + \mathsf{r}^{\mathsf{in}} \in \mathbb{U}_N$.
4: Sample random $z_0, z_1 \leftarrow \mathbb{U}_N$ s.t. $z_0 + z_1 = \mathsf{r}^{\mathsf{out}} + \mathbf{1}\{\alpha^{(p)} > \alpha^{(q)}\} - \mathbf{1}\{\alpha^{(p)} > p\} + \mathbf{1}\{\alpha^{(q')} > q'\} + \mathbf{1}\{\alpha^{(q)} = N-1\}$.
5: For $b \in \{0,1\}$, let $k_b = k_b^{(N-1)} || z_b$.
6: **return** (k_0, k_1).

$\mathsf{Eval}^{\mathsf{IC}}_{n,p,q}(b, k_b, x)$:

1: Parse $k_b = k_b^{(N-1)} || z_b$.
2: Set $q' = q + 1 \in \mathbb{U}_N$, $x^{(p)} = x + (N - 1 - p) \in \mathbb{U}_N$ and $x^{(q')} = x + (N - 1 - q') \in \mathbb{U}_N$.
3: Set $s_b^{(p)} \leftarrow \mathsf{Eval}^{<}_n(b, k_b^{(N-1)}, x^{(p)})$.
4: Set $s_b^{(q')} \leftarrow \mathsf{Eval}^{<}_n(b, k_b^{(N-1)}, x^{(q')})$.
5: **return** $y_b = b \cdot (\mathbf{1}\{x > p\} - \mathbf{1}\{x > q'\}) - s_b^{(p)} + s_b^{(q')} + z_b$.

Fig. 3. FSS Gate for $\mathcal{G}_{\mathsf{IC}}$ using DCF key for $f^{<}_{(N-1)+\mathsf{r}^{\mathsf{in}},1}$, b refers to party id.

Lemma 2. *Let $c, c' \in \mathbb{U}_N$, where $c' = c + 1 \bmod N$. Define 2 boolean predicates over $\mathbb{U}_N \to \{0,1\}$ as follows: $R(x)$ denotes $x \leq c$ and $S(x)$ denotes $x < c'$. Then the following holds: $R(x) = S(x) + \mathbf{1}\{c = N-1\}$*

This lemma lets us get rid of the DCF key for $f^{\leq}_{(N-1)+\mathsf{r}^{\mathsf{in}},1}$ and work with the key for $f^{<}_{(N-1)+\mathsf{r}^{\mathsf{in}},1}$ using an additional correction term which can be computed by the dealer. Formally, we have the following theorem.

Theorem 3. *There is an FSS Gate $(\mathsf{Gen}^{\mathsf{IC}}_{n,p,q}, \mathsf{Eval}^{\mathsf{IC}}_{n,p,q})$ for $\mathcal{G}_{\mathsf{IC}}$ that requires 2 invocations of $\mathsf{DCF}_{n,\mathbb{U}_N}$, and has a total key size of n bits plus key size of $\mathsf{DCF}_{n,\mathbb{U}_N}$.*

Proof. We present our construction formally in Fig. 3. For arguing correctness we need to prove that $y = y_0 + y_1 \bmod N = \mathbf{1}\{p \leq (x - \mathsf{r}^{\mathsf{in}} \bmod N) \leq q\} + \mathsf{r}^{\mathsf{out}}$. We use correctness of FSS gate in Fig. 2 and prove that output of Fig. 3 is identical to output of Fig. 2. In Fig. 2, using correctness of FSS schemes for $f^{<}_{\alpha,\beta}$ and $f^{\leq}_{\alpha,\beta}$,

$$t^{(p)} = t_0^{(p)} + t_1^{(p)} \bmod N = -1 \cdot \mathbf{1}\{x < \alpha^{(p)}\} \text{ and}$$
$$t^{(q)} = t_0^{(q)} + t_1^{(q)} \bmod N = \mathbf{1}\{x \leq \alpha^{(q)}\}$$

Also, from correctness of FSS gate in Fig. 2, $t^{(p)} + t^{(q)} + \mathbf{1}\{\alpha^{(p)} > \alpha^{(q)}\} + \mathsf{r}^{\mathsf{out}} = \mathbf{1}\{p \leq (x - \mathsf{r}^{\mathsf{in}} \bmod N) \leq q\} + \mathsf{r}^{\mathsf{out}}$.

First, we look at $t^{(q)} = \mathbf{1}\{x \leq \alpha^{(q)}\}$. From Lemma 2, we can write $t^{(q)} = \mathbf{1}\{x < \alpha^{(q')}\} + \mathbf{1}\{\alpha^{(q)} = N-1\}$, where $\alpha^{(q')} = \alpha^{(q)} + 1 \bmod N$. Now, using

Lemma 1 with $a = q'$, $b = N-1$, $r = \mathsf{r}^{\mathsf{in}}$, $\tilde{a} = \alpha^{(q')}$, and $\tilde{b} = \gamma$:

$$\begin{aligned} t^{(q)} &= \mathbf{1}\{x < \alpha^{(q')}\} + \mathbf{1}\{\alpha^{(q)} = N-1\} \\ &= \mathbf{1}\{x + (N-1-q') \bmod N < \gamma\} + \mathbf{1}\{\alpha^{(q')} + (N-1-q') > (N-1)\} \\ &\qquad - \mathbf{1}\{x + (N-1-q') > (N-1)\} + \mathbf{1}\{\alpha^{(q)} = N-1\} \\ &= \mathbf{1}\{x^{(q')} < \gamma\} + \mathbf{1}\{\alpha^{(q')} > q'\} - \mathbf{1}\{x > q'\} + \mathbf{1}\{\alpha^{(q)} = N-1\} \\ &= s_0^{(q')} + s_1^{(q')} + \mathbf{1}\{\alpha^{(q')} > q'\} - \mathbf{1}\{x > q'\} + \mathbf{1}\{\alpha^{(q)} = N-1\} \end{aligned}$$

Similarly, using Lemma 1, it can be proven that: $t^{(p)} = -1\cdot(s_0^{(p)} + s_1^{(p)}) - \mathbf{1}\{\alpha^{(p)} > p\} + \mathbf{1}\{x > p\}$. Therefore, in Fig. 3, $y = y_0 + y_1 = t^{(p)} + t^{(q)} + \mathbf{1}\{\alpha^{(p)} > \alpha^{(q)}\} + \mathsf{r}^{\mathsf{out}}$ matches the output of Fig. 2.

5 Applications of Public Intervals

5.1 Splines with Public Intervals

A spline is a special function defined piecewise by polynomials. Formally, consider $P = \{p_i\}_i \in \mathbb{U}_N^m$ such that $0 \leq p_1 < p_2 < \ldots < p_{m-1} < p_m$ ($p_m = N-1$) and $d-$*degree* univariate polynomials $F = \{f_i\}_i$. Then, a spline function $h_{n,m,d,P,F} : \mathbb{U}_N \rightarrow \mathbb{U}_N$ parameterized by input and output rings $\mathbb{U}_N$, list of m interval boundaries P and degree d polynomials F is defined as

$$h_{n,m,d,P,F}(x) = \begin{cases} f_1(x) & \text{if } x \in [0, p_1] \\ f_2(x) & \text{if } x \in [p_1+1, p_2] \\ & \vdots \\ f_m(x) & \text{if } x \in [p_{m-1}+1, p_m] \end{cases}$$

Commonly used functions such as Rectified Linear Unit (ReLU) and Absolute value are special cases of splines. Moreover, splines have been used to approximate transcendental functions such as sigmoid [38,41], sometimes with up to $m = 12$ intervals. Boyle *et al.* [13], gave a construction of an FSS gate for splines by reducing it to m instances of interval containment, resulting in both key size and online evaluation cost being proportional to the cost of $2m$ DCF keys. In this work, building upon our techniques for multiple interval containment[5], we reduce both the key size as well as online evaluation. More concretely, [13] requires $2m$ $\mathsf{DCF}_{n,\mathbb{Z}_N^{d+1}}$ keys and each key is evaluated once during online phase. We provide a construction using a *single* $\mathsf{DCF}_{n,\mathbb{Z}_N^{(d+1)m}}$ key that is evaluated m times and additional $2m(d+1)+1$ ring elements. Hence, including our improved DCF construction, we reduce the overall key size from $\approx 2m\left(4n(\lambda+1) + n^2(d+1)\right)$ to $\approx \left(\lambda(n+1) + mn^2(d+1)\right) + 2mn(d+1)$ bits. As an example, for $n = 32$,

[5] As we explain later, our FSS gate for splines requires secret payload (function of r^{in}) in DCF known only to the dealer and hence, it does not black-box reduce to $\mathcal{G}_{\mathsf{MIC}}$.

$m \geq 2$ and degree 1 polynomials, this represents a reduction in key size of about $8-17\times$, and for instance, for $m=10$, the reduction is $14\times$.

The spline gate $\mathcal{G}_{\mathsf{spline}}$ is the family of functions $g_{\mathsf{spline},n,m,d,P,F}: \mathbb{U}_N \rightarrow \mathbb{U}_N$ with m intervals parameterized by input and output rings $\mathbb{U}_N$, and for $P = \{p_1, p_2, \ldots, p_m\}$ and $F = \{f_1, f_2, \ldots, f_m\}$, given by

$$\mathcal{G}_{\mathsf{spline}} = \left\{ g_{\mathsf{spline},n,m,d,P,F} : \mathbb{U}_N \rightarrow \mathbb{U}_N \right\}_{\substack{0 \leq p_i < p_{i+1} \leq N-1 \\ p_0 = p_m = N-1}}, g_{\mathsf{spline},n,m,d,P,F}(x) = h_{n,m,d,P,F}(x).$$

Construction Overview. Our FSS gate for splines builds upon our techniques from multiple interval containment to incorporate secret payloads as required. At a high level, the basic idea, also used in [13], is to check for interval containment $[p_{i-1}+1, p_i]$ and output the coefficients of the polynomial $f_i' = f_i(x - \mathsf{r}^{\mathsf{in}})$ as payload. Once the evaluators P_0 and P_1 learn the shares of the correct coefficients, they compute an inner product with $(x^d, \ldots, x^0)$ to learn shares of final output. We note that coefficients of f_i' depend on the randomness r^{in} that is secret and known only to the dealer. Due to this, we cannot invoke our FSS gate for multiple interval containment $\mathcal{G}_{\mathsf{MIC}}$ directly. Next, [13] used a different interval containment key for each interval with payload as the corresponding coefficients of the polynomials. In our construction, we only use a single DCF key for all intervals, and hence, the payload of this key has to encode the coefficients of all the polynomials. Moreover, naively building on $\mathcal{G}_{\mathsf{MIC}}$, the online computation would require $2m$ evaluations of the DCF key. However, for the case of splines, we use the property that the intervals are consecutive, that is, of the form $[p_{i-1}+1, p_i]$, to reduce this to m evaluations.

We present our final construction in 2 steps. First, we present the construction for a simpler spline gate, $\mathcal{G}_{\mathsf{spline\text{-}one}}$ that is a family of functions $h_{n,d,p,f}$ with only 1 interesting interval i.e., it outputs $f(x)$ on $[0, p]$ and 0 otherwise. With this construction, we describe our techniques for embedding secret payloads in our optimized FSS gate for $\mathcal{G}_{\mathsf{IC}}$ that uses a single DCF key. Note that ReLU function, the most commonly used activation in machine learning, is a function in $\mathcal{G}_{\mathsf{spline\text{-}one}}$. We discuss about ReLU and absolute value function in the full version of this paper [9]. Then, we will give our construction for general splines using our ideas of common payload for all intervals and reducing number of DCF evaluations.

Spline with One Interesting Interval. The simple spline gate $\mathcal{G}_{\mathsf{spline\text{-}one}}$ is a family of functions $h_{n,d,p,f}: \mathbb{U}_N \rightarrow \mathbb{U}_N$ such that $p \in \mathbb{U}_N$, f is a d-degree univariate polynomial and $h_{n,d,p,f}(x) = f(x)$ for $x \in [0, p]$ and 0 otherwise. We give a formal construction for FSS gate for $\mathcal{G}_{\mathsf{spline\text{-}one}}$ in Fig. 4. At a high level, we build on our construction for $\mathcal{G}_{\mathsf{IC}}$ and modify it to allow for secret payloads as follows: Recall that in FSS gate for $\mathcal{G}_{\mathsf{IC}}$, we give out a DCF key with payload 1 and shares of a correction term that depends on r^{in}, say c_r. Also, during evaluation, P_0, P_1 compute a correction term, say c_x, that depends on x. Overall, at the time of evaluation, P_0, P_1 evaluate the DCF key and add c_r and c_x. Now we desire the payload to be coefficients of $f' = f(x - \mathsf{r}^{\mathsf{in}})$, say β. To enable this, the dealer sets the payload of the DCF key as β. But now, this β

also needs to be multiplied with c_r and c_x. For this the dealer gives out shares of $c_r \cdot \beta$ and shares of β. Shares of β allow P_0 and P_1 to compute shares of $c_x \cdot \beta$, as c_x can be computed locally.

Spline Gate $(\mathsf{Gen}^{\mathsf{spline\text{-}one}}_{n,d,p}, \mathsf{Eval}^{\mathsf{spline\text{-}one}}_{n,d,p})$

$\mathsf{Gen}^{\mathsf{spline\text{-}one}}_{n,d,p}(1^\lambda, f, \mathsf{r}^{\mathsf{in}}, \mathsf{r}^{\mathsf{out}})$:

Let $(f'_d, \ldots, f'_0) \in \mathbb{U}_N^{(d+1)}$ be coefficients of f' such that $f'(x) = f(x - \mathsf{r}^{\mathsf{in}})$.
Set $\beta = (f'_d, \ldots, f'_0) \in \mathbb{U}_N^{(d+1)}$ and $\gamma = (N-1) + \mathsf{r}^{\mathsf{in}} \in \mathbb{U}_N$.
$(k_0^{(N-1)}, k_1^{(N-1)}) \leftarrow \mathsf{Gen}^{<}_n(1^\lambda, \gamma, \beta, \mathbb{U}_N^{(d+1)})$.
Set $\alpha^{(L)} = \mathsf{r}^{\mathsf{in}} \in \mathbb{U}_N$, $\alpha^{(R)} = p + \mathsf{r}^{\mathsf{in}} \in \mathbb{U}_N$ and $\alpha^{(R')} = p + 1 + \mathsf{r}^{\mathsf{in}} \in \mathbb{U}_N$.
Set
$c_r = \mathbf{1}\{\alpha^{(L)} > \alpha^{(R)}\} - \mathbf{1}\{\alpha^{(L)} > 0\} + \mathbf{1}\{\alpha^{(R')} > (p+1 \bmod N)\} + \mathbf{1}\{\alpha^{(R)} = N-1\}$.
Sample random $e_0, e_1 \leftarrow \mathbb{U}_N^{(d+1)}$ s.t. $e_0 + e_1 = c_r \cdot \beta$.
Sample random $\beta_0, \beta_1 \leftarrow \mathbb{U}_N^{(d+1)}$ s.t. $\beta_0 + \beta_1 = \beta$.
Sample random $r_0, r_1 \leftarrow \mathbb{U}_N$ s.t. $r_0 + r_1 = \mathsf{r}^{\mathsf{out}}$.
For $b \in \{0, 1\}$, let $k_b = k_b^{(N-1)} || e_b || \beta_b || r_b$.
return (k_0, k_1).

$\mathsf{Eval}^{\mathsf{spline\text{-}one}}_{n,d,p}(b, k_b, x)$:

Parse $k_b = k_b^{(N-1)} || e_b || \beta_b || r_b$.
Set $x^{(L)} = x + (N-1) \in \mathbb{U}_N$ and $x^{(R')} = x + (N - 1 - (p+1)) \in \mathbb{U}_N$.
Set $s_b^{(L)} \leftarrow \mathsf{Eval}^{<}_n(b, k_b^{(N-1)}, x^{(L)})$.
Set $s_b^{(R')} \leftarrow \mathsf{Eval}^{<}_n(b, k_b^{(N-1)}, x^{(R')})$.
Set $c_x = (\mathbf{1}\{x > 0\} - \mathbf{1}\{x > (p+1 \bmod N)\})$.
$w_b = (w_{d,b}, \ldots, w_{0,b}) = c_x \cdot \beta_b - s_b^{(L)} + s_b^{(R')} + e_b$.
return $u_b = r_b + \sum_{i=0}^{d}(w_{i,b} \cdot x^i) \bmod N$.

Fig. 4. FSS Gate for single interval splines $\mathcal{G}_{\mathsf{spline\text{-}one}}$, b refers to party id.

Theorem 4. *There is an FSS Gate* $(\mathsf{Gen}^{\mathsf{spline\text{-}one}}_{n,d,p}, \mathsf{Eval}^{\mathsf{spline\text{-}one}}_{n,d,p})$ *for* $\mathcal{G}_{\mathsf{spline\text{-}one}}$ *that requires 2 invocations of* $\mathsf{DCF}_{n,\mathbb{U}_N^{(d+1)}}$, *and has a total key size of* $n(2d+3)$ *bits plus the key size of* $\mathsf{DCF}_{n,\mathbb{U}_N^{(d+1)}}$.

Proof. We present our construction of FSS Gate for single interval spline formally in Fig. 4. To prove correctness of our scheme it suffices to show that $w = w_0 + w_1$ is β when $(x - \mathsf{r}^{\mathsf{in}}) \in [0, p]$ and 0^{d+1} otherwise. In our scheme, $w = \sum_b (c_x \cdot \beta_b - s_b^{(L)} + s_b^{(R')} + e_b) = c_x \cdot \beta - s^{(L)} + s^{(R')} + c_r \cdot \beta$. Now, by correctness of DCF keys, $s^{(L)} = \beta \cdot \mathbf{1}\{x^{(L)} < \gamma\}$ and $s^{(R')} = \beta \cdot \mathbf{1}\{x^{(R')} < \gamma\}$. Using these, we get that $w = \left(c_x - \mathbf{1}\{x^{(L)} < \gamma\} + \mathbf{1}\{x^{(R')} < \gamma\} + c_r\right) \cdot \beta = \mathbf{1}\{0 \leq (x - \mathsf{r}^{\mathsf{in}}) \leq p\} \cdot \beta$ as required, by using similar arguments as in correctness of $\mathcal{G}_{\mathsf{IC}}$ in Fig. 3.

General Splines. To construct an FSS gate for general splines, we make two modifications to the previous construction. First, we change the payload of our DCF key to be the long vector containing coefficients of all polynomials $\{f_i'\}_i$, where $f_i' = f(x - \mathsf{r}^{\mathsf{in}})$. Now, during evaluation, we do DCF evaluations similar to $\mathcal{G}_{\mathsf{MIC}}$ separately for each interval. For each interval, output would be over $\mathbb{U}_N^{m(d+1)}$. While considering the ith interval, i.e., $[p_{i-1}+1, p_i]$, we will only use the ith segment of $(d+1)$ ring elements. These would either be shares of coefficients of f_i' (if $(x - \mathsf{r}^{\mathsf{in}}) \in [p_{i-1}+1, p_i]$) or 0^{d+1}. Next, to reduce number of evaluations from $2m$ to m, we rely on intervals in splines being consecutive, i.e., an interval ends at p_i and next interval starts at $p_i + 1$. Recall from our construction of $\mathcal{G}_{\mathsf{MIC}}$, that we need to do two DCF evaluations for each interval of interest, one for the left point and one for the right point. This is also true for Fig. 4, where we do one DCF evaluation each for $x^{(L)}$ and $x^{(R')}$. In general splines, for the ith interval $[p_{i-1}+1, p_i]$, let these points be $x_i^{(L)}$ and $x_i^{(R')}$. Now, observe that since $x_i^{(R')} = x_{i+1}^{(L)}$, we need to evaluate the DCF only once for them. For consistency of notation, we set $p_0 = p_m = N - 1$, so that the first interval, i.e., $[0, p_1]$ can also be written as $[p_0+1, p_1]$ and similarly the last interval, i.e., $[p_{m-1}+1, N-1]$ can be written as $[p_{m-1} + 1, p_m]$. In our construction, we do DCF evaluations for all points $x_i = x_i^{(L)} = x + (N - 1 - (p_{i-1} + 1))$ for $i \in \{1, \ldots, m\}$.

Theorem 5. *There is an FSS Gate* $(\mathsf{Gen}^{\mathsf{spline}}_{n,m,d,\{p_i\}_i}, \mathsf{Eval}^{\mathsf{spline}}_{n,m,d,\{p_i\}_i})$ *for* $\mathcal{G}_{\mathsf{spline}}$ *that requires* m *invocations of* $\mathsf{DCF}_{n,\mathbb{U}_N^{m(d+1)}}$*, and has a total key size of* $2mn(d+1) + n$ *bits plus the key size of* $\mathsf{DCF}_{n,\mathbb{U}_N^{m(d+1)}}$.

We provide our scheme and its proof formally in the full version [9].

6 FSS Gates for Fixed-Point Arithmetic

Fixed-point representation allows us to embed rational numbers into fixed bit-width integers. Let $\mathbb{Q}^{\mathsf{u}}$ denote non-negative rational numbers. Assuming no overflows, the unsigned (resp. signed) forward mapping $f^{\mathsf{ufix}}_{n,s} : \mathbb{Q}^{\mathsf{u}} \to \mathbb{U}_N$ (resp. $f^{\mathsf{sfix}}_{n,s} : \mathbb{Q} \to \mathbb{S}_N$) is defined by $\lfloor x \cdot 2^s \rfloor$ and the reverse mapping $h^{\mathsf{ufix}}_{n,s} : \mathbb{U}_N \to \mathbb{Q}^{\mathsf{u}}$ (resp. $h^{\mathsf{sfix}}_{n,s} : \mathbb{S}_N \to \mathbb{Q}$) is defined by $x/2^s$, where x is lifted to $\mathbb{Q}$ and "/" denotes the regular division over $\mathbb{Q}$. The value s associated with a fixed-point representation is called the "scale" which defines the precision, i.e., the number of bits after the decimal point, that the fixed-point number preserves. When 2 fixed-point numbers are added or multiplied in n-bit integer ring, the bits at the top (significant bits) can overflow leading to incorrect results. To prevent this from happening, these operations are accompanied by a "scale adjustment" step where the scale of operands are appropriately reduced to create enough room in the top bits for the computation to fit. Scale adjustment is also used in multiplication to maintain the scale of the output at s instead of getting doubled for every multiplication performed. Many applications of secure computation require computing over the rational numbers. One such application is privacy-preserving machine learning where most prior works use fixed-point representation to deal with rational numbers [33,37,39–41,46,51][6,7].

In this section we build efficient FSS gates for realizing secure fixed-point arithmetic. In particular, we consider the following operations: addition, multiplication, and comparison. We begin (in Sect. 6.1) by first describing how fixed-point addition and multiplication work given access to a FSS gates for secure right shift operations. We then describe the FSS gate constructions for right shift operator - logical right shift (LRS) in Sect. 6.2, which enables scale adjustment, and hence fixed-point multiplication, over unsigned integers. We defer the details on arithmetic right shift (ARS) and fixed-point comparison to Sects. 6.3 and 6.4 respectively of our full version [9].

6.1 Fixed-Point Addition and Multiplication

We describe the case when the scales of both operands is the same, i.e. s - the case of different scales is similar[8]. Fixed-point addition is a local operation where the corresponding shares of the operands are added together by each party and no scale adjustment is typically performed. This is same as the construction of FSS gate for addition from [13] as described in Fig. 17, Appendix I.1 (of full version [9]). Fixed-point multiplication involves 2 steps: first, using the FSS gate for multiplication from [13] (presented in Fig. 18, Appendix I.2 of full version for completeness) the operands are multiplied resulting in an output of scale $2s$, and second, using our FSS gate for right shift, values are shifted (ARS/LRS for signed/unsigned operands respectively) by s to reduce the scale back to s.

6.2 Logical Right Shift

Logical right shift of unsigned integers is done by shifting the integer by a prescribed number of bits to the right while removing the low-order bits and inserting zeros as the high order bits. Implementing the shift operation on secret shared values is a nontrivial task even when the shift s is public, and is typically achieved via an expensive secure bit-decomposition operation. Prior FSS gate for bit-decomposition [13] output shares of bits in $\mathbb{U}_2$ (which must then be converted into shares over $\mathbb{U}_N$, if it is to be used in computing logical right shift). Hence, this leads to construction for right shift that has 2 online rounds. Here we provide a much more efficient construction, which a) requires only 1 online round

[6] Although there are a handful of works outside the secure ML context that give secure protocols directly for floating-point numbers [3,24,34,45], they are usually orders of magnitude slower than the ones based on fixed-point.

[7] All of these works except [24,45] consider simplified variants of the IEEE 754 floating-point standard.

[8] When scales of the operands differ, they need to be aligned before addition can happen. For this, a common practice is to left shift (locally) the operand with smaller scale by the difference of the scales. Fixed-point multiplication remains the same and shift parameter for the right shift at the end can be chosen depending on the scale required for the output.

of communication of a single group element; and b) further, improves upon the key size of the approach based on bit-decomposition, by roughly a factor of n (when $n \leq \lambda$), i.e. $O(n\lambda + n^2)$ vs $O(n^2\lambda)$.

If an integer $x \in \mathbb{U}_N$ ($N = 2^n$) is additively shared into $x \equiv x_0 + x_1 \bmod N$ with one party holding x_0 and the other holding x_1 then locally shifting x_0 and x_1 by s bits is not sufficient to additively share a logically shifted x. Lemma 3 (proof appears in Appendix I.3 of full version [9]) gives an identity showing that the LRS of a secret shared x can be computed as the sum of the LRS of the shares and the output of two comparison functions. This identity is the basis for an FSS gate realizing the offset family associated with LRS.

Notation. *Given integers* $0 < n, 0 \leq s \leq n$*, let* $(\gg_L s) : \mathbb{U}_N \to \mathbb{U}_N, 0 \leq s \leq n$ *be the logical right shift function with action on input* x *denoted by* $(\gg_L s)(x) = (x \gg_L s)$ *and defined by* $(x \gg_L s) = \frac{x-(x \bmod 2^s)}{2^s}$ *over* $\mathbb{Z}$.

Lemma 3. *For any integers* $0 < n, 0 \leq s \leq n$*, any* $x \in \mathbb{U}_N$ *and any* $x_0, x_1 \in \mathbb{U}_N$ *such that* $x_0 + x_1 \equiv x \bmod N$*, the following holds over* $\mathbb{Z}$ *(and in particular over* $\mathbb{U}_N$*)* $(x \gg_L s) = (x_0 \gg_L s) + (x_1 \gg_L s) + t^{(s)} - 2^{n-s} \cdot t^{(n)}$*, where for any* $0 \leq i \leq n$*,* $t^{(i)}$ *is defined by:*

$$t^{(i)} = \begin{cases} 1 & (x_0 \bmod 2^i) + (x_1 \bmod 2^i) > 2^i - 1 \\ 0 & \textit{otherwise} \end{cases},$$

The logical right-shift gate $\mathcal{G}_{\gg_L}$ is the family of functions $g_{\gg_L,s,n} : \mathbb{U}_N \to \mathbb{U}_N$ parameterized by input/output groups $\mathbb{G}^{\mathsf{in}} = \mathbb{G}^{\mathsf{out}} = \mathbb{U}_N$, shift s and given by

$$\mathcal{G}_{\gg_L} = \left\{ g_{\gg_L,s,n} : \mathbb{U}_N \to \mathbb{U}_N \right\}_{0 \leq s \leq n}, g_{\gg_L,s,n}(x) = (x \gg_L s).$$

We denote the corresponding offset gate class by $\hat{\mathcal{G}}_{\gg_L}$ and the offset functions by $\hat{g}^{[\mathsf{r}^{\mathsf{in}},\mathsf{r}^{\mathsf{out}}]}_{\gg_L,s,n}(x) = g_{\gg_L,s,n}(x - \mathsf{r}^{\mathsf{in}}) + \mathsf{r}^{\mathsf{out}} = ((x - \mathsf{r}^{\mathsf{in}}) \gg_L s) + \mathsf{r}^{\mathsf{out}}$. We use Lemma 3 to construct our FSS gate for LRS (as described in Fig. 6 of full version [9]) and which satisfies the following theorem.

Theorem 6 (LRS from DCF). *There is an FSS Gate* $(\mathsf{Gen}^{\gg_L}_{n,s}, \mathsf{Eval}^{\gg_L}_{n,s})$ *for* $\mathcal{G}_{\gg_L}$ *that requires a single invocation each of* $\mathsf{DCF}_{n,\mathbb{U}_N}$ *and* $\mathsf{DCF}_{s,\mathbb{U}_N}$*, and has a total key size of* n *bits plus the key sizes of* $\mathsf{DCF}_{n,\mathbb{U}_N}$ *and* $\mathsf{DCF}_{s,\mathbb{U}_N}$.

7 FSS Barrier for Fixed-Point Multiplication

In the previous sections, we presented FSS gates for several fixed-point operations, enabling secure computation of fixed-point multiplication $\mathcal{F}_{\mathsf{FPM}}$ with "FSS depth 2": namely, one FSS gate for performing multiplication of the two integer inputs over $\mathbb{U}_N$ (resp. $\mathbb{S}_N$), followed by a second FSS gate to perform a logical right shift (resp. arithmetic right shift). While this provides an effective solution, a downside of two sequential FSS gates is that the resulting secure computation protocol requires information communicated between parties via two sequential rounds, and a natural goal would be to construct a *single* FSS gate to perform both steps of the fixed-point multiplication together. Such a single FSS gate would not only lead to optimal round complexity (one instead of two rounds), but also to optimal online communication complexity (a factor-2 improvement over the current implementation). In this section, we demonstrate a barrier toward achieving this goal using only symmetric-key cryptography.

More specifically, we show that the existence of any FSS gate construction for fixed-point multiplication, denoted by $\mathcal{G}_{\mathsf{uFPM}}$ (resp. $\mathcal{G}_{\mathsf{sFPM}}$) for operation over unsigned (resp. signed) integers, (with polynomial key size) directly implies the existence of FSS scheme for the class of all bitwise conjunction formulas (with polynomial key size), from the same underlying assumptions. As discussed below, FSS schemes for conjunctions from symmetric-key primitives have remained elusive despite significant research effort. As such, this constitutes a barrier toward symmetric-key constructions for fixed-point multiplication.

FSS for Conjunctions. We will denote by $\mathcal{F}^{\wedge}_{n,\mathbb{U}_N}$ the collection of bit-conjunction functions on n-bit inputs, each parameterized by a subset $S \subseteq [n]$, where $[n] = \{i \mid (0 \le i \le n-1) \wedge (i \in \mathbb{Z})\}$), of input bits, evaluating to a given nonzero value if the corresponding input bits are all 1.

Definition 5. *The family* $\mathcal{F}^{\wedge}_{n,\mathbb{U}_N}$ *of conjunction functions is*

$$\mathcal{F}^{\wedge}_{n,\mathbb{U}_N} = \left\{ f_S : \{0,1\}^n \to \mathbb{U}_N \right\}_{S \subseteq [n]}, \text{ where } f_S(x) = \begin{cases} \beta & \bigwedge_{i \in S} x_{[i]} = 1 \\ 0 & \text{otherwise} \end{cases}.$$

Presently the only existing construction of FSS scheme for $\mathcal{F}^{\wedge}_{n,\mathbb{U}_N}$ with negligible correctness error relies on the Learning With Errors (LWE) assumption [14,26]. A construction with inverse-polynomial correctness error can be obtained from the Decisional Diffie-Hellman (DDH) assumption [11] or from the Paillier assumption [28]. All assumptions are specific structured assumptions, and corresponding constructions require heavy public-key cryptographic machinery. It remains a highly motivated open question to attain such an FSS construction using only symmetric-key cryptography, even in the case when payload β is public.

Open Question (FSS for conjunctions)**.** *Construct FSS scheme for the class* $\mathcal{F}^{\wedge}_{n,\mathbb{U}_N}$ *of bit-conjunction functions (with key size polynomial in the security parameter and input length n) based on symmetric-key cryptographic primitives.*

The Barrier Result. We prove the desired barrier result via an intermediate function family: $\mathcal{F}^{\times\mathsf{MSB}}_{\eta,\mathbb{U}_N}$, a simplified version of fixed-point multiplication.

Definition 6. *The family* $\mathcal{F}^{\times\mathsf{MSB}}_{\eta,\mathbb{U}_N}$ *of multiply-then-MSB functions is given by*

$$\mathcal{F}^{\times\mathsf{MSB}}_{\eta,\mathbb{U}_N} = \left\{ f_c : \mathbb{U}_{2^\eta} \to \mathbb{U}_N \right\}_{c \in \mathbb{U}_{2^\eta}}, \text{ where } f_c(x) = \mathsf{MSB}(c \cdot x),$$

and where $n \le \eta$ *and* $c \cdot x$ *is multiplication over* $\mathbb{U}_{2^\eta}$*.*

The description of a function f_c above is assumed to explicitly contain a description of the respective parameter $c \in \mathbb{U}_{2^\eta}$ (similarly for $f_S \in \mathcal{F}^{\wedge}_{n,\mathbb{U}_N}$ and $S \subseteq [n]$).

Our overall barrier result will proceed in two steps. First, we build an FSS scheme for conjunctions $\mathcal{F}^{\wedge}_{n,\mathbb{U}_N}$ from an FSS scheme for multiply-then-MSB $\mathcal{F}^{\times \mathsf{MSB}}_{n(\lceil \log n \rceil+1),\mathbb{U}_N}$. Next, we give a reduction from the FSS scheme for $\mathcal{F}^{\times \mathsf{MSB}}_{\eta,\mathbb{U}_N}$ to the FSS gate for unsigned fixed-point multiplication, $\mathcal{G}_{\mathsf{uFPM}}$ over $\mathbb{U}_{2^n}$, and set $\eta = n(\lceil \log n \rceil + 1)$. We now focus only on the case of unsigned fixed point multiplication - the case of signed fixed point multiplication follows in an analogous manner (details of the changes needed can be found in the full version [9]).

Step One of the Barrier Result. Intuitively, for a function $f_S \in \mathcal{F}^{\wedge}_{n,\mathbb{U}_N}$, the input/output behavior will be emulated by a corresponding function $f_{c_S} \in \mathcal{F}^{\times \mathsf{MSB}}_{n(\lceil \log n \rceil+1),\mathbb{U}_N}$, i.e., $f_S(x) = f_{c_S}(x) = \mathsf{MSB}(x' \cdot c_S)$, where x' is a public encoding of the input x, and c_S is a (secret) constant determined as a function of S. The Gen algorithm of FSS scheme for $f_S \in \mathcal{F}^{\wedge}_{n,\mathbb{U}_N}$ will output FSS keys for $f_{c_S} \in \mathcal{F}^{\times \mathsf{MSB}}_{n(\lceil \log n \rceil+1),\mathbb{U}_N}$, where c_S is determined from S. The Eval algorithm will encode the public $x \in \mathbb{U}_{2^n}$ to $x' \in \mathbb{U}_{2^{n(\lceil \log n \rceil+1)}}$ and evaluate the given FSS key for f_{c_S}.

More concretely, the new FSS evaluation will encode the input x to x' by "spacing out" the bits of x with $m = \lceil \log n \rceil$ zeros with $x_{[0]}$ as the least significant bit (as depicted below). Now, c_S is carefully crafted to "extract" and add the bits in x at indices in S such that: the value $x' \cdot c_S$ will have most significant bit (MSB) as 1 if and only if bits of x in all indices of S are equal to 1. For ease of exposition, first consider the case when size $h = |S|$ is a power of 2 and let $\ell = \log h$. Moreover, consider an alternate representation of $S \subseteq [n]$ as $(s_{n-1}, \ldots, s_0) \in \{0,1\}^n$ such that $s_i = 1$ iff $i \in S$, else 0. Then, $c_S \in \mathbb{U}_{2^{n(m+1)}}$ (depicted below) will be constructed by spacing out the bits s_i by m zeros and put in reverse order, and has ℓ leading zeros and $m - \ell$ trailing zeros.

Mathematically, we can write, $x' = \sum_{i=0}^{n-1} x_{[i]} \cdot 2^{i(m+1)} \in \mathbb{U}_{2^{n(m+1)}}$ and $c_S = 2^{n(m+1)-\ell-1} \cdot \sum_{i=0}^{n-1} s_i \cdot 2^{-i(m+1)} \in \mathbb{U}_{2^{n(m+1)}}$. We will make use of these equations in formal construction and correctness of reduction.

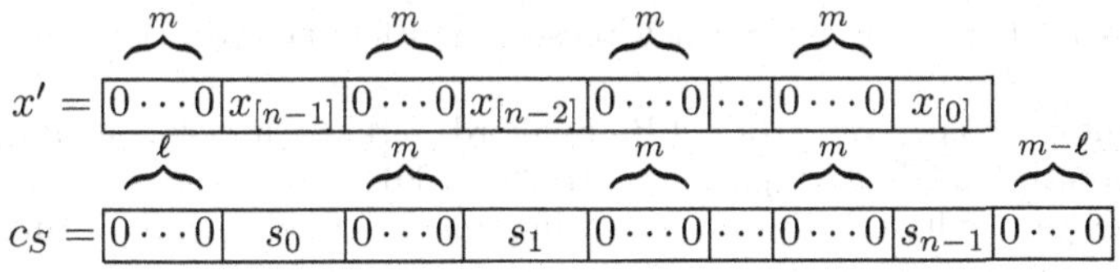

$$x' = \boxed{\overbrace{0\cdots0}^{m}}\boxed{x_{[n-1]}}\boxed{\overbrace{0\cdots0}^{m}}\boxed{x_{[n-2]}}\boxed{\overbrace{0\cdots0}^{m}}\boxed{\cdots}\boxed{\overbrace{0\cdots0}^{m}}\boxed{x_{[0]}}$$

$$c_S = \boxed{\overbrace{0\cdots0}^{\ell}}\boxed{s_0}\boxed{\overbrace{0\cdots0}^{m}}\boxed{s_1}\boxed{\overbrace{0\cdots0}^{m}}\boxed{\cdots}\boxed{\overbrace{0\cdots0}^{m}}\boxed{s_{n-1}}\boxed{\overbrace{0\cdots0}^{m-\ell}}$$

The interesting part in the product $x' \cdot c_S$ is the upper $\ell + 1$ bits which will capture the sum $\sum_{i=0}^{n-1} x_{[i]} \cdot s_i$. Things have been structured so that none of the other terms in $x' \cdot c_S$ affect these upper bits due to the large spacing of 0s (preventing additive carries), as shown in the proof of Theorem 7. Therefore, $\mathsf{MSB}(x' \cdot c_S) = \mathsf{MSB}(\sum_{i=0}^{n-1} x_{[i]} \cdot s_i) = \mathsf{MSB}(\sum_{i \in S} x_{[i]})$ (because $s_i = 1$ for $i \in S$, else 0), which is equal to 1 precisely if all bits $\{x_{[i]}\}_{i \in S}$ are equal to 1. Namely, precisely if $f_S(x) = 1$, as desired.

The more general case where $h = |S|$ is not necessarily a power of 2 can be addressed by replacing $s_i \in \{0, 1\}$ with arbitrary positive integer values such that the sum of *all* terms $\sum_{i \in S} s_i$ is precisely equal to 2^ℓ, where $\ell = \lceil \log h \rceil$, and $\{s_i\}_{i \notin S} = 0$. The analysis remains the same.

Theorem 7. *Assume the existence of an FSS scheme for the function class* $\mathcal{F}^{\times \mathsf{MSB}}_{n(m+1), \mathbb{U}_N}$, *where* $m = \lceil \log n \rceil$. *Then there exists an FSS scheme for* $\mathcal{F}^{\wedge}_{n, \mathbb{U}_N}$.

Proof. Details of this proof can be found in our full version [9].

Step two of the barrier result. In the full version, we give a formal reduction from the FSS scheme for $\mathcal{F}^{\times \mathsf{MSB}}_{\eta, \mathbb{U}_N}$ to $\mathcal{G}_{\mathsf{uFPM}}$ over $\mathbb{U}_{2^\eta}$. Setting $\eta = n(\lceil \log n \rceil + 1)$ completes the barrier result for unsigned fixed-point multiplication. The high level idea is as follows: we set the shift parameter of $\mathcal{G}_{\mathsf{uFPM}}$ as $s = \eta - 1$ and include $c + r$ as a part of the FSS key (along with the key for $\mathcal{G}_{\mathsf{uFPM}}$) which still hides the secret constant c of member functions in $\mathcal{F}^{\times \mathsf{MSB}}_{\eta, \mathbb{U}_N}$, where r is randomly sampled from $\mathbb{U}_{2^\eta}$ and known only to the Gen algorithm. Then using these FSS keys, the evaluation algorithm computes $((x \cdot c) \gg_L \eta - 1) = \mathsf{MSB}(x \cdot c)$, as desired.

Acknowledgments. E. Boyle supported by ISF grant 1861/16, AFOSR Award FA9550-17-1-0069, and ERC Project HSS (852952). N. Gilboa supported by ISF grant 2951/20, ERC grant 876110, and a grant by the BGU Cyber Center. Y. Ishai supported by ERC Project NTSC (742754), ISF grant 2774/20, NSF-BSF grant 2015782, and BSF grant 2018393.

References

1. Salami slicing – Wikipedia. https://en.wikipedia.org/w/index.php?title=Salami_slicing&oldid=943583075 (2020) Accessed 1 Nov 2020
2. Agrawal, N., Shamsabadi, A.S., Kusner, M.J., Gascón, A.: QUOTIENT: two-party secure neural network training and prediction. In: CCS (2019)
3. Aliasgari, M., Blanton, M., Zhang, Y., Steele, A.: Secure computation on floating point numbers. In: NDSS (2013)
4. Aly, A., Smart, N.P.: Benchmarking privacy preserving scientific operations. In: ACNS 2019 (2019)
5. Atallah, M.J., Pantazopoulos, K.N., Rice, J.R., Spafford, E.H.: Secure outsourcing of scientific computations. Adv. Comput. **54**, 247–264 (2001)
6. Beaver, D.: Efficient multiparty protocols using circuit randomization. In: CRYPTO (1991)
7. Ben-Efraim, A., Nielsen, M., Omri, E.: Turbospeedz: double your online SPDZ! improving SPDZ using function dependent preprocessing. In: ACNS (2019)
8. Ben-Or, M., Goldwasser, S., Wigderson, A.: Completeness theorems for non-cryptographic fault-tolerant distributed computation. In: STOC (1988)
9. Boyle, E., et al.: Function secret sharing for mixed-mode and fixed-point secure computation. IACR Cryptol. ePrint Arch. (2020)
10. Boyle, E., Gilboa, N., Ishai, Y.: Function secret sharing. In: EUROCRYPT (2015)

11. Boyle, E., Gilboa, N., Ishai, Y.: Breaking the circuit size barrier for secure computation under DDH. In: CRYPTO (2016)
12. Boyle, E., Gilboa, N., Ishai, Y.: Function secret sharing: Improvements and extensions. In: CCS (2016)
13. Boyle, E., Gilboa, N., Ishai, Y.: Secure computation with preprocessing via function secret sharing. In: TCC (2019)
14. Boyle, E., Kohl, L., Scholl, P.: Homomorphic secret sharing from lattices without FHE. In: EUROCRYPT (2019)
15. Büscher, N., Demmler, D., Katzenbeisser, S., Kretzmer, D., Schneider, T.: HyCC: compilation of hybrid protocols for practical secure computation. In: CCS (2018)
16. Canetti, R., Lindell, Y., Ostrovsky, R., Sahai, A.: Universally composable two-party and multi-party secure computation. In: STOC (2002)
17. Catrina, O., de Hoogh, S.: Secure multiparty linear programming using fixed-point arithmetic. In: ESORICS (2010)
18. Catrina, O., Saxena, A.: Secure computation with fixed-point numbers. In: FC (2010)
19. Chandran, N., Gupta, D., Rastogi, A., Sharma, R., Tripathi, S.: EzPC: programmable and efficient secure two-party computation for machine learning. In: IEEE EuroS&P (2019)
20. Chaum, D., Crépeau, C., Damgård, I.: Multiparty unconditionally secure protocols (extended abstract). In: STOC (1988)
21. Couteau, G.: A note on the communication complexity of multiparty computation in the correlated randomness model. In: EUROCRYPT, Part II (2019)
22. Damgård, I., Fitzi, M., Kiltz, E., Nielsen, J.B., Toft, T.: Unconditionally secure constant-rounds multi-party computation for equality, comparison, bits and exponentiation. In: TCC (2006)
23. Damgård, I., Nielsen, J.B., Nielsen, M., Ranellucci, S.: The tinytable protocol for 2-party secure computation, or: Gate-scrambling revisited. In: CRYPTO, Part I (2017)
24. Demmler, D., Dessouky, G., Koushanfar, F., Sadeghi, A., Schneider, T., Zeitouni, S.: Automated synthesis of optimized circuits for secure computation. In: CCS (2015)
25. Demmler, D., Schneider, T., Zohner, M.: ABY-a framework for efficient mixed-protocol secure two-party computation. In: NDSS (2015)
26. Dodis, Y., Halevi, S., Rothblum, R.D., Wichs, D.: Spooky encryption and its applications. In: CRYPTO (2016)
27. Doerner, J., Shelat, A.: Scaling ORAM for secure computation. In: CCS (2017)
28. Fazio, N., Gennaro, R., Jafarikhah, T., III, W.E.S.: Homomorphic secret sharing from paillier encryption. In: Provable Security (2017)
29. Goldreich, O., Micali, S., Wigderson, A.: How to play any mental game or a completeness theorem for protocols with honest majority. In: STOC (1987)
30. Ishai, Y., Kushilevitz, E., Meldgaard, S., Orlandi, C., Paskin-Cherniavsky, A.: On the power of correlated randomness in secure computation. In: TCC (2013)
31. Ishai, Y., Prabhakaran, M., Sahai, A.: Founding cryptography on oblivious transfer - efficiently. In: CRYPTO (2008)
32. Ishai, Y., Prabhakaran, M., Sahai, A.: Secure arithmetic computation with no honest majority. In: TCC (2009)
33. Juvekar, C., Vaikuntanathan, V., Chandrakasan, A.: GAZELLE: a low latency framework for secure neural network inference. In: USENIX Security (2018)
34. Kerik, L., Laud, P., Randmets, J.: Optimizing MPC for robust and scalable integer and floating-point arithmetic. In: FC (2016)

35. Kilian, J.: More general completeness theorems for secure two-party computation. In: STOC (2000)
36. Kiltz, E., Damgaard, I., Fitzi, M., Nielsen, J.B., Toft, T.: Unconditionally secure constant round multi-party computation for equality, comparison, bits and exponentiation. IACR Cryptology ePrint Archive **2005**, (2005)
37. Kumar, N., Rathee, M., Chandran, N., Gupta, D., Rastogi, A., Sharma, R.: Cryptflow: secure tensor flow inference. In: IEEE S&P (2020)
38. Liu, J., Juuti, M., Lu, Y., Asokan, N.: Oblivious neural network predictions via minionn transformations. In: CCS (2017)
39. Mishra, P., Lehmkuhl, R., Srinivasan, A., Zheng, W., Popa, R.A.: Delphi: a cryptographic inference service for neural networks. In: USENIX Security (2020)
40. Mohassel, P., Rindal, P.: ABY3: a mixed protocol framework for machine learning. In: CCS (2018)
41. Mohassel, P., Zhang, Y.: Secure ML: a system for scalable privacy-preserving machine learning. In: IEEE S&P (2017)
42. Naor, M., Pinkas, B.: Oblivious polynomial evaluation. SIAM J. Comput.**35**(5), 1254–1281 (2006)
43. Nawaz, M., Gulati, A., Liu, K., Agrawal, V., Ananth, P., Gupta, T.: Accelerating 2PC-based ML with limited trusted hardware. arXiv preprint:2009.05566 (2020)
44. Nishide, T., Ohta, K.: Multiparty computation for interval, equality, and comparison without bit-decomposition protocol. In: PKC (2007)
45. Pullonen, P., Siim, S.: Combining secret sharing and garbled circuits for efficient private IEEE 754 floating-point computations. In: FC (2015)
46. Rathee, D., et al.: CrypTFlow2: pactical 2-party secure inference. In: CCS (2020)
47. Riazi, M.S., Samragh, M., Chen, H., Laine, K., Lauter, K.E., Koushanfar, F.: XONN: xnor-based oblivious deep neural network inference. In: USENIX Security (2019)
48. Ryffel, T., Pointcheval, D., Bach, F.: ARIANN: Low-interaction privacy-preserving deep learning via function secret sharing. arXiv preprint:2006.04593 (2020)
49. Schoenmakers, B., Tuyls, P.: Efficient binary conversion for paillier encrypted values. In: EUROCRYPT (2006)
50. Toft, T.: Constant-rounds, almost-linear bit-decomposition of secret shared values. In: CT-RSA (2009)
51. Wagh, S., Gupta, D., Chandran, N.: SecureNN: 3-party secure computation for neural network training. PoPETs **2019**(3), 26–49 (2019)
52. Wang, X., Malozemoff, A.J., Katz, J.: EMP-toolkit: Efficient MultiParty computation toolkit. https://github.com/emp-toolkit (2016)
53. Yao, A.C.: How to generate and exchange secrets. In: FOCS (1986)

VOLE-PSI: Fast OPRF and Circuit-PSI from Vector-OLE

Peter Rindal[1(✉)] and Phillipp Schoppmann[2]

[1] Visa Research, Palo Alto, USA
[2] Humboldt-Universität zu Berlin, Berlin, Germany
schoppmann@informatik.hu-berlin.de

Abstract. In this work we present a new construction for a batched Oblivious Pseudorandom Function (OPRF) based on Vector-OLE and the PaXoS data structure. We then use it in the standard transformation for achieving Private Set Intersection (PSI) from an OPRF. Our overall construction is highly efficient with $O(n)$ communication and computation. We demonstrate that our protocol can achieve malicious security at only a very small overhead compared to the semi-honest variant. For input sizes $n = 2^{20}$, our malicious protocol needs 6.2 s and less than 59 MB communication. This corresponds to under 450 bits per element, which is the lowest number for any published PSI protocol (semi-honest or malicious) to date. Moreover, in theory our semi-honest (resp. malicious) protocol can achieve as low as 219 (resp. 260) bits per element for $n = 2^{20}$ at the added cost of interpolating a polynomial over n elements.

As a second contribution, we present an extension where the output of the PSI is secret-shared between the two parties. This functionality is generally referred to as Circuit-PSI. It allows the parties to perform a subsequent MPC protocol on the secret-shared outputs, e.g., train a machine learning model. Our circuit PSI protocol builds on our OPRF construction along with another application of the PaXoS data structure. It achieves semi-honest security and allows for a highly efficient implementation, up to 3x faster than previous work.

1 Introduction

We consider the problem of private set intersection (PSI) in a two-party setting. Here, two mutually distrusting parties, a receiver and a sender, each hold a set of identifiers X, Y respectively. The goal of the two parties is for the receiver to learn the intersection $X \cap Y$ without revealing any additional information to the parties. In particular, the sender should not learn any information about X beyond the size of it. Similarly, the receiver should not learn anything about $Y \setminus X$ beyond the size of Y.

A common approach to PSI is based on oblivious pseudo-random functions (OPRFs). An OPRF allows the receiver to input x and learn $F_k(x)$, where F is a PRF, and k is known to the sender. A straight-forward PSI protocol can be obtained by running an OPRF protocol for each $x \in X$, and then having

A. Canteaut and F.-X. Standaert (Eds.): EUROCRYPT 2021, LNCS 12697, pp. 901–930, 2021.
https://doi.org/10.1007/978-3-030-77886-6_31

the sender send $\{F_k(y) \mid y \in Y\}$ to the receiver. The receiver can then locally compare the sender's OPRF values to her own to learn which elements of X are in the intersection. This is the basis of several PSI protocols (see Sect. 1.4), and our first contribution also follows this paradigm.

While PSI alone has interesting applications, such as private contact discovery [Dem+18, Kal+19, Kis+17], other variants of PSI are gaining traction from a practical perspective. For example, both Google [Ion+20] and Facebook [Bud+20] have implemented variants of PSI that allow them to compute functions of the intersection, where only the result of the function evaluation and the intersection size is revealed, but not the intersection itself.

A generalization of these PSI-with-computation protocols yields *circuit PSI*, where the output isn't revealed to either party, but instead is secret-shared between the parties. More precisely, the receiver learns a random vector $\boldsymbol{Q}^{\mathbf{0}}$ and the sender learns $\boldsymbol{Q}^{\mathbf{1}}$ such that $(q_i^0 \oplus q_i^1) = 1$ if i corresponds to an element $x \in X$ in the intersection, and $(q_i^0 \oplus q_i^1) = 0$ otherwise. Note that this means that not even the intersection size is revealed to either party. We additionally can allow the sender (resp. receiver) to input an "associated value" $\tilde{y}_j$ (resp. $\tilde{x}_i$) for each $y_j \in Y$ (resp. $x_i \in X$). In this case, the output also includes a random vector $\boldsymbol{Z}^{\mathbf{0}}$ to the receiver and $\boldsymbol{Z}^{\mathbf{1}}$ to the sender such that $(z_i^0 \oplus z_i^1) = (\tilde{y}_j || \tilde{x}_i)$ if $x_i = y_j$.

1.1 Contributions

PSI: We present a protocol for private set intersection (Sect. 4) based on two building blocks. The first building block is a protocol known as Vector OLE and presented in Fig. 2. Multiple implementations of VOLE have recently been presented [Boy+19, Sch+19a, Wen+20, Yan+20]. We use an improved version of [Sch+19a] in this paper. The second building block is a linear system solver, e.g. PaXoS [Pin+20], which we adapt for our purposes as shown in Fig. 1. Combining these two primitives in a novel way, we obtain an OPRF protocol (Fig. 4). This construction is highly efficient, requiring an amortized 2.4κ bits of communication per input in our computationally efficient version or just κ bits when optimized for communication. We also demonstrate that malicious security can be obtained with only a very small overhead.

From an OPRF it is easy to obtain an PSI protocol which is our final goal. This final step is shown in Fig. 6. We show that the malicious variant of this well known transformation can be optimized which reduces its overhead by as much as 50% compared to prior art [Pin+20, CKT10]. Our final PSI protocol is secure against both semi-honest and malicious adversaries, and we provide an implementation for both threat models. It is also highly efficient, requiring just 5.4 (resp. 6.2) seconds and less than 54 (resp. 59) MB communication in the semi-honest (resp. malicious) setting.

Circuit PSI: Our second contribution is a protocol for circuit PSI. In Sect. 5, we show that using our variant of the PaXoS solver along with any OPRF protocol yields an Oblivious Programmable PRF (OPPRF) protocol. Given this, we then construct the final protocol in Sect. 6 with the additional help of data structure known as a cuckoo hash table. We also implement two variants of our circuit PSI protocol in the semi-honest model and show that they outperform the best previous approach [Pin+19a].

1.2 Notation

We use κ as the computational security parameter and λ for statistical security. The receiver's set is detonated as X while the sender's is Y. Their respective sizes are $n_{\mathsf{x}}, n_{\mathsf{y}}$. Often we will just assume both set are of size n. $[a, b]$ denotes the set $\{a, a+1, ..., b\}$ and $[b]$ is shorthand for $[1, b]$. We denote row vectors $\boldsymbol{A} = (a_1, ..., a_n)$ using the arrow notation while the elements are indexed without it. A set $S = \{s_1, ..., s_n\}$ will use similar notation. For a matrix M, we use $\boldsymbol{M}_i$ to denote its i-th row vector, and $M_{i,j}$ for the element at row i and column j. $\langle \boldsymbol{A}, \boldsymbol{B} \rangle$ denotes the inner product of $\boldsymbol{A}, \boldsymbol{B}$. We use $=$ to denote the statement that the values are equal. Assignment is denoted as $:=$ and for some set S, the notation $s \leftarrow S$ means that s is assigned a uniformly random element from S. If a function F is deterministic then we write $y := F(x)$ while if F is randomized we use $y \leftarrow F(x)$ to denote $y := F(x; r)$ for $r \leftarrow \{0,1\}^*$.

1.3 Overview

OPRF. We now present a simplified version of our main protocols. Our core building block is a functionality known as (random) vector OLE which allows the parties to sample random vectors $\boldsymbol{A}, \boldsymbol{B}, \boldsymbol{C} \in \mathbb{F}^m$ and element $\Delta \in \mathbb{F}$ such that $\boldsymbol{C} = \Delta\boldsymbol{A} + \boldsymbol{B}$. The PSI receiver will hold $\boldsymbol{A}, \boldsymbol{C}$ while the sender will hold $\boldsymbol{B}, \Delta$. We note that in the vector OLE literature, the sender/receiver roles are typically reversed.

The parties (implicitly) sample an exponentially large random matrix $M^* \in \{0,1\}^{|\mathbb{F}| \times m}$. The receiver defines $M \in \{0,1\}^{n \times m}$ which is the submatrix indexed by the rows $x \in X$. The receiver then solves the linear system

$$M\boldsymbol{P}^{\intercal} = (0, ..., 0)^{\intercal}$$

for the unknown $\boldsymbol{P} \in \mathbb{F}^m$. For now let us assume $\boldsymbol{P}$ is some random solution and not the trivial $(0, ..., 0)$ solution[1]. The protocol proceeds by having the receiver send $\boldsymbol{A} + \boldsymbol{P}$ to the sender who defines

$$\boldsymbol{K} := \boldsymbol{B} + \Delta(\boldsymbol{A} + \boldsymbol{P})$$

[1] In our malicious OPRF construction (Sect. 3.2), we will instead use a random oracle H, and set $M\boldsymbol{P}^{\intercal} = (\mathsf{H}(x_0), \mathsf{H}(x_1), \ldots, \mathsf{H}(x_n))^{\intercal}$. We stick to the semi-honest variant here for ease of presentation.

The crucial observation is that

$$\begin{aligned} M\boldsymbol{K}^\intercal =& M\boldsymbol{B}^\intercal + \Delta(M\boldsymbol{A}^\intercal + M\boldsymbol{P}^\intercal)\\ =& M\boldsymbol{B}^\intercal + \Delta M\boldsymbol{A}^\intercal\\ =& M\boldsymbol{C}^\intercal \end{aligned}$$

In particular, for each $x \in X$ it holds that $\langle \boldsymbol{M}^*_x, \boldsymbol{K}\rangle = \langle \boldsymbol{M}^*_x, \boldsymbol{C}\rangle$ where $\boldsymbol{M}^*_x$ is the x'th row of M^*. An OPRF can then be obtained by having the receiver apply a random oracle as

$$\mathsf{H}(\langle \boldsymbol{M}^*_x, \boldsymbol{C}\rangle), \qquad x \in X$$

while the sender computes the output at any y as

$$F_{\boldsymbol{K}}(y) := \mathsf{H}(\langle \boldsymbol{M}^*_y, \boldsymbol{K}\rangle)$$

To ensure efficiency we will require M^* to be of a special form such that solving $M\boldsymbol{P}^\intercal = (0, ..., 0)^\intercal$ is efficient while also computing $\langle \boldsymbol{M}^*_x, \boldsymbol{V}\rangle$ in $O(1)$ time. Specifically, we will use the PaXoS solver [Pin+20] to enable these properties.

To achieve security it is crucial that the receiver can not compute the OPRF F at any other point $x \notin X$. In the formulation above this effectively means that it is hard to find a $x \notin X$, such that $\langle \boldsymbol{M}^*_x, \boldsymbol{P}\rangle = 0$. We demonstrate how such a property can be obtained at little to no overhead.

PSI. We then employ our OPRF construction as a subroutine to obtain a PSI protocol. This traditional transformation instructs the receiver to input their set X into an OPRF protocol to obtain $F(x)$ for $x \in X$. The sender can then send $Y' = \{F(y) \mid y \in Y\}$ which allows the receiver to identify the common items. In the malicious setting, one must show how the simulator extracts the set Y from observing Y'. The traditional analysis [Pin+20, CKT10] effectively achieves this by requiring the OPRF F to be second-preimage resistant and as such each $y' \in Y'$ must be of length $2\kappa \approx 256$ bits. We demonstrate that in fact preimage resistance is sufficient which allows the OPRF to have κ bit output which reduces the communication overhead by approximately 33%, or as much as 50% when $|Y| \gg |X|$.

Programmable OPRF. We present extension of our OPRF protocol to achieve a functionality known as a Programmable OPRF (OPPRF) [Pin+19a]. This building block will allow the sender to sample an OPPRF key k such that $F_k(y_i) = v_i$ for their choice of y_i, v_i. At all other locations the output of F_k will be random.

The parties first perform a normal OPRF protocol for an OPRF F', where the receiver inputs their set X and receive $F'(x)$ for $x \in X$. The sender solves the system

$$M\boldsymbol{P}^\intercal = (v_1 - F'(y_1), ..., v_n - F'(y_n))^\intercal$$

where $M \in \{0,1\}^{n\times m}$ the submatrix of M^* indexed by the rows y_i. The sender will send $\boldsymbol{P}$ to the receiver who outputs

$$x' := F'(x) + \langle \boldsymbol{M}^*_x, \boldsymbol{P}\rangle$$

for $x \in X$. Observe that at $x = y_i \in Y$

$$\begin{aligned} x' :=& F'(x) + \langle \boldsymbol{M}^*_x, \boldsymbol{P} \rangle \\ =& F'(y_i) + v_i - F'(y_i) \\ =& v_i \end{aligned}$$

as desired. It can be shown that at all other points $y \notin Y$, the output is completely random. One security concern is that $\boldsymbol{P}$ might leak information about Y. Indeed, the PaXoS solver requires m larger than n, therefore several solutions could exist, and which $\boldsymbol{P}$ is output by PaXoS may leak information. We show that this is the case for PaXoS and then present an extension which is uniformly distributed under some constraints. We call our extension XoPaXoS and present it in Sect. 2. Our full OPPRF protocol is presented in Sect. 5.

Circuit-PSI. Finally, we present our Circuit PSI extension which allows the output of the PSI to be secret shared between the two parties. Our protocol builds on the previous approach of Pinkas et al. [Pin+19a] by replacing their OPPRF construction with ours. For completeness we present this construction in Sect. 6.

1.4 Related Work

Early PSI protocols based on OPRFs/Diffie–Hellman (DH) have been around since the 1980s [Mea86], and they still form the basis of many modern PSI protocols [Bud+20,CT10,Ion+20]. The advantage of DH-based protocols is their low communication cost and constant round complexity, which however comes at the cost of high computational overhead. A more computationally efficient protocol based on oblivious transfer extension [Ish+03] (as opposed to OPRF based) was presented by Schneider et al. [Pin+15] along with many derivatives [Kol+16,OOS17,PSZ14,RR17b].

More recently, these two paradigms have begun to merge, and various OPRF constructions have been proposed [CM20,DCW13,Kol+16,Pin+19b,Pin+20, RR17a] which more closely resemble [Ish+03]. All of these come with higher communication cost than [Mea86], but they significantly reduce computation. However, as the evaluation of Chase and Miao [CM20] has shown, the optimal choice of protocol often depends on the network setting. Our work also follows the OPRF-based approach, building on the recent PSI protocol of Pinkas et al.[Pin+20], but significantly reducing communication. As our experiments in Sect. 7 show, our protocol works particularly well in settings with limited bandwidth and large input sizes. For an extended overview of the different approaches to PSI, see [Ion+20, Section 4.1] and [PSZ18, Section 1.2].

The first circuit PSI protocols were based entirely on generic techniques such as garbled circuits [HEK12] or GMW [Pin+15,PSZ18]. Subsequent works improved computation and communication [CO18,Pin+18,Pin+19a], and the linear-complexity protocol of Pinkas et al. [Pin+19a] forms the current state of the art. Their protocol combines an oblivious *programmable* PRF (OPPRF) based on polynomial interpolation with a relatively small GMW circuit. Our circuit PSI protocol follows a similar approach, but uses our new OPRF construction, as well as a novel way to program it based on PaXoS [Pin+20].

2 Linear Solvers and PaXoS

Our constructions makes use of linear system solvers. As discussed before, we will use these solvers to encode our input sets $(z_1, ..., z_n) = Z$ and values $(v_1, ..., v_n) = V$ as a vector $\boldsymbol{P} \in \mathbb{G}^m$. There will exist a function Decode such that $\mathsf{Decode}(\boldsymbol{P}, z_i) = v_i$ for $i \in [n]$ and is linear with respect to $\boldsymbol{P}$. There are three main performance metrics that we are concerted with. The first is the rate $\rho = m/n$ which denotes how compact the encoding is, i.e. n items can be encoded as m element vector. The last two metrics are the running time of the encoder/solver and that of the decoder/matrix multiplier.

Each instance of a solver is parameterized by a finite group $\mathbb{G}$, integer $m \geq n$, security parameter λ and an implicit random matrix $M^* \in \mathbb{G}^{|\mathbb{G}| \times m}$. The instance is fixed by sampling $M^* \leftarrow \mathcal{M}$ from some set $\mathcal{M}$ which depends on the particular solver. For any set $Z \subset \mathbb{G}$ s.t. $|Z| = n$, the solver will output $\boldsymbol{P} \in \mathbb{G}^m$ s.t.

$$M\boldsymbol{P}^{\mathsf{T}} = (v_1, ..., v_n)^{\mathsf{T}}$$

where $M \in \{0,1\}^{n \times m}$ is the submatrix of M^* obtained by taking the rows indexed by $z \in Z$. The target values $v_1, ..., v_n \in \mathbb{G}$ can be arbitrary. Our application will require the solver to output a solution with probability $1 - O(2^{-\lambda})$.

Since M^* is exponential in size, it is more efficient to represent it as a random seed $r \in \{0,1\}^\kappa$ and define the i-th row as being the output of the random function $\mathsf{row}(i, r)$. Therefore we will have the property $\langle \mathsf{row}(x_i, r), \boldsymbol{P} \rangle = v_i$. For easy of presentation we will further abstract this via the Decode function defined as $\mathsf{Decode}(\boldsymbol{P}, x_i, r) := \langle \mathsf{row}(x_i, r), \boldsymbol{P} \rangle$. We note that this is a very general encoding framework and encompasses several schemes, e.g. PaXoS, interpolation, bloom filters, and many others.

The Vandermonde Solver. One example of this general approach is polynomial interpolation. In this case we require $\mathbb{G}$ to also be a field and $\mathcal{M}$ contains only the Vandermonde matrix, i.e. $\mathsf{row}(i, r) = (1, i, i^2, ..., i^{n-1})$ for all r. As such it achieves an optimal rate of $\rho = 1$, i.e. $m = n$. In this case, solving the system requires $O(n \log^2 n)$ time using polynomial interpolation and decoding n points also requires $O(n \log^2 n)$ time [BM74]. For large n it is also possible to construct row in such a way that t smaller systems of size $O(\lambda)$ are constructed and solved independently [Pin+19a]. This so called binning technique effectively results in a $O(n \log^2 \lambda)$ running time while also maintaining near optimal rate $\rho \approx 1$.

The PaXoS Solver. The PaXoS solver [Pin+20] significantly improves on polynomial interpolation in that it achieves $O(n)$ running time. However, it comes at the cost of rate $\rho \approx 2.4$, i.e., $m \approx 2.4n$. The scheme of Pinkas et al. [Pin+20] defines row as outputting a binary vector s.t. the first $m' := 2.4n$ elements have

Parameters:

- Statistical security parameter λ and computational security parameter κ.
- Input length n.
- A finite group $\mathbb{G}$.
- For $m' = 2.4n$, let $d = O(\lambda)$ upper bound the size of 2-core of a (m', n)-Cuckoo graph [Pin+20].
- Output length $m = m' + d + \lambda$.
- A random function $\mathsf{row} : \mathbb{G} \times \{0,1\}^\kappa \to \{0,1\}^m$ s.t. $\forall x$, the weight of the first m' bits of $\mathsf{row}(x)$ is 2.

$\underline{\mathsf{Encode}\ ((z_1, v_1), ..., (z_n, v_n); r):}$

1. Define $\mathsf{row}' : \mathbb{G} \to \{0,1\}^{m'}$ and $\tilde{\mathsf{row}}(z)$ s.t. $\mathsf{row}'(z) || \tilde{\mathsf{row}}(z) = \mathsf{row}(z, r)$ for all z. Let
$$M := \begin{bmatrix} \mathsf{row}(z_1, r) \\ ... \\ \mathsf{row}(z_n, r) \end{bmatrix} \in \{0,1\}^{n \times m}$$
and let $M' \in \{0,1\}^{n \times m'}, \tilde{M} \in \{0,1\}^{n \times d + \lambda}$ s.t. $M' || \tilde{M} = M$.
2. Let $\mathcal{G} = (\mathcal{V}, \mathcal{E})$ be a graph with vertex set $\mathcal{V} = [m']$ and edge set $\mathcal{E} = \{(c_0, c_1) \mid i \in [n], M'_{i,c_0} = M'_{i,c_1} = 1\}$. Let $\tilde{\mathcal{G}} = (\tilde{\mathcal{V}}, \tilde{\mathcal{E}})$ be the 2-core of $\mathcal{G}$.
3. Let $R \subset [n]$ index the rows of M in the 2-core, i.e. $R = \{i \mid M'_{i,c_0} = M'_{i,c_1} = 1 \wedge (c_0, c_1) \in \tilde{\mathcal{E}}\}$. Let $\tilde{d} := |R|$ and abort if $\tilde{d} > d$.
4. Let $\tilde{M}' \in \{0,1\}^{\tilde{d} \times (d+\lambda)}$ be the submatrix of $\tilde{M}$ obtained by taking the row indexed by R. Abort if $\tilde{M}'$ does not contain an invertible $\tilde{d} \times \tilde{d}$ matrix. Otherwise let $\tilde{M}^*$ be one such matrix and $C \subset [d + \lambda]$ index the corresponding columns of $\tilde{M}'$.
5. Let $C' := \{j \mid i \in R, M'_{i,j} = 1\} \cup ([d + \lambda] \setminus C + m')$ and for $i \in C'$ assign $P_i \leftarrow \mathbb{G}$. For $i \in R$, define $v'_i := v_i - (M\boldsymbol{P}^\intercal)_i$ where P_i is assumed to be zero if unassigned.
6. Using Gaussian elimination solve the system $\tilde{M}^*(P_{m'+C_1}, ..., P_{m'+C_{\tilde{d}}})^\intercal = (v'_{R_1}, ..., v'_{R_{\tilde{d}}})^\intercal$.
7. Let $T \subset [m']$ such that each tree in $\mathcal{G}$ has a single vertex in T. For $i \in T$, assign $P_i \leftarrow \mathbb{G}$.
8. Let $I := \{j \mid i \in R, M'_{i,j} = 1\} \cup T$ and $\overline{I} := [m'] \setminus I$.
9. While $I \neq \emptyset$, select an $i \in I$ and do the following: Update $I := I \setminus \{i\}$ and $\overline{I} := \overline{I} \cup \{i\}$. For all $j \in \{j \mid (j, i) \in \mathcal{E} \wedge j \notin \overline{I}\}$. Identify k s.t. $\{h_0(z_k, r), h_1(z_k, r)\} = \{i, j\}$ and assign $P_j := v_k - P_i$.
10. Return $\boldsymbol{P}$.

$\underline{\mathsf{Decode}\ (\boldsymbol{P}, z, r):}$

1. Return $\langle \mathsf{row}(z, r), \boldsymbol{P} \rangle$.

Fig. 1. XoPaXoS algorithm.

weight 2 while the last $m - m' = O(\lambda)$ bits are distributed uniformly. There is also a PaXoS variant which achieves a slightly better rate of $\rho = 2$ but at an increased running time. In this paper, we only make use of the first scheme.

Other Solvers. Other solvers have also been considered in the context of PSI and OPRF. A garbled bloom filter [DCW13, RR17a] where $\mathsf{row}(i, r)$ is a random weight κ vector of length $m = 2\kappa n$. Another options is to let $\mathsf{row} : \mathbb{G} \times \{0,1\}^\kappa \rightarrow \mathbb{G}^m$ be a random function with $m = n + O(\lambda)$. The Bloom filter has a linear time solver but very poor rate while the latter requires $O(n^3)$ time (via Gaussian elimination) and near optimal rate. Constructing more efficient solvers remains an open question. With the advent of PaXoS we believe significant progress can be made at achieving improved rates, i.e., $\rho < 2$, while at the same time maintaining a linear running time. Evidence of this is that PaXoS is based on cuckoo hashing which is known to achieve a significantly better rate when the matrix has weight 3 instead of weight 2 used by PaXoS [Dem+18, PSZ18]. Moreover, solvers for such systems have been presented [Dem+18, KS12], but it is unclear whether they can be made robust enough to succeed with probability $1 - O(2^\lambda)$. As we will see in Sect. 7, our communication overhead is dominated by $\rho\kappa n$, so the performance of the solver has a direct impact.

PaXoS Details. We now present the PaXoS solver [Pin+20] in detail. Let $M' \in \{0,1\}^{n \times m'}$ be the submatrix formed by the first $m' = 2.4n$ columns of M which itself consists of rows $\mathsf{row}(z_1, r), ..., \mathsf{row}(z_n, r)$. As such, each row of M' has weight 2. The solver first analyses the sparse system formed by M' as follows. Let $\mathcal{G}$ be the graph consisting of m' vertices $\mathcal{V} = [m']$ and the edge set $\mathcal{E} = \{(c_0, c_1) \mid i \in [n] \wedge M'_{i,c_0} = M'_{i,c_1} = 1\}$. That is, for each constraint $v_i = \langle \boldsymbol{P}, \mathsf{row}(z_i, r) \rangle = P_{c_0} + P_{c_1} + ...$ there is an edge between vertices $(c_0, c_1) = e_i$. $\mathcal{G}$ is called the cuckoo-graph [Pin+20].

First, let us assume that $\mathcal{G}$ has no cycles and therefore consists of one or more trees. This case can be solved by doing a linear pass over the nodes along tree edges, and assigning values on the way. In particular: (1) Initialize $P_i := 0$ for $i \in [m]$. (2) Let $I \subseteq \mathcal{V}$ s.t. each tree in $\mathcal{G}$ has a single vertex in I and $\overline{I} := \mathcal{V} \setminus I$. (3) Pick an $i \in I$ and for each edge $(j, i) \in \mathcal{E}$ such that $j \in \overline{I}$, identify $e_k \in \mathcal{E}$, i.e. $M'_{k,i} = M'_{k,j} = 1$, and update $P_j := v_k - P_i$. Note that because $\mathcal{G}$ is acyclic, P_i will not change value later. Update $I := I \cup \{j\}$. Finally, define $I := I \setminus \{i\}$, $\overline{I} := \overline{I} \cup \{i\}$ and if $I \neq \emptyset$, go back to (3).

Observe that this algorithm does not work if $\mathcal{G}$ contains a cycle since at some point in step (3) P_j will have already been updated. To address this, the solver first identifies the so called 2-core graph $\tilde{\mathcal{G}}$ which is the subgraph of $\mathcal{G}$ which only contains the cycles along with any paths between these cycles. Observe that the graph formed by $\mathcal{G} \setminus \tilde{\mathcal{G}}$ is acyclic.

The solver uses Gaussian elimination to solve the constraints contained in $\tilde{\mathcal{G}} = (\tilde{\mathcal{V}}, \tilde{\mathcal{E}})$ with the use of the $m - m'$ additional columns of M. In particular, Pinkas et al. [Pin+20] show that for $m' = 2.4n$, the size of $\tilde{\mathcal{E}}$ is bounded by $d = O(\lambda)$ with overwhelming probability. Let the actual number of edges in $\tilde{\mathcal{G}}$ be $\tilde{d} < d$. They then consider the submatix $\tilde{M}$ formed by the last $m - m'$ columns of

M and the $\tilde{d}$ rows corresponding to edges in $\tilde{\mathcal{G}}$. In their parameterization they set $m = d+\lambda+m'$. As such $\tilde{M}$ is a $(d+\lambda)\times\tilde{d}$ random binary matrix. With probability $1-O(2^{-\lambda})$ there exists an invertible $\tilde{d}\times\tilde{d}$ submatrix $\tilde{M}^*$ within $\tilde{M}$ [Pin+20]. The $\tilde{d}$ constraints in $\tilde{\mathcal{G}}$ can then be solved for using Gaussian elimination on $\tilde{M}^*$ which requires $O(\tilde{d}^3) = O(\lambda^3)$ time. The remaining P_i values corresponding to $\tilde{\mathcal{G}}$ and $\tilde{M}$ are assigned the value zero, and the remaining constraints in $\mathcal{G}\setminus\tilde{\mathcal{G}}$ can then be solved using the linear time algorithm described above.

X-oblivious PaXoS. We now present a modified scheme detailed in Fig. 1 which we denote as XoPaXoS. Looking forward our Circuit PSI protocol will require an additional simulation property of the encode algorithm. Informally, given that the v_i values are uniform, we require the distribution of $\boldsymbol{P}$ is independent of the z_i values. More formally, we will require that the distributions

$$\begin{aligned}
\mathcal{D}_0(z_1,...,z_n) &:= (\mathsf{Encode}((z_1,v_1),...,(z_n,v_n),r),r) \\
&\qquad\qquad\qquad \text{where } r\leftarrow\{0,1\}^\kappa; v_i\leftarrow\mathbb{G}, \forall i\in[n] \\
\mathcal{D}_1(z_1,...,z_n) &:= (\boldsymbol{P},r), \quad \text{where } r\leftarrow\{0,1\}^\kappa; \boldsymbol{P}\leftarrow\mathbb{G}^m
\end{aligned}$$

be indistinguishable for any PPT adversary except with probability $2^{-\lambda}$.

However, this does not hold for the [Pin+20] construction outlined above. In particular, the PaXoS algorithm assigns zero to P_i values in two locations. When solving the 2-core using Gaussian elimination some of the column of $\tilde{M}$ are not used and therefore the corresponding P_i are assigned zero. The XoPaXoS scheme rectifies this in Step 5 of Fig. 1 by first assigning random values to the redundant P_i positions and then solving the remaining (fully constrained) system using Gaussian elimination. It is easy to verify that the P_i values output by Gaussian elimination have the desired distribution.

Secondly, when performing the linear pass over the trees of $\mathcal{G}$, a vertex i from each tree is picked and P_i is assigned zero. In Step 7 of XoPaXoS, we again replace this assignment with sampling P_i uniformly from $\mathbb{G}$. Finally, the remaining assignments have the form $P_i := v_k + P_j + ...$ where each assignment contains a distinct uniform v_k value and therefore P_i is uniform as desired. These modifications make the Encode algorithm randomized even for a fixed r. In particular, we assume Encode takes an addition random tape as input from which the uniform P_i values are sampled. We note that the original PaXoS algorithm can be obtained by omitting these addition steps and instead initializing all P_i to zero.

3 Vole Based OPRF

3.1 Vector OLE

The VOLE functionality $\mathcal{F}_{\mathsf{vole}}$ is presented in Fig. 2. Let $\mathbb{F}$ be some finite field, e.g., $\mathbb{F} = GF(2^\kappa)$. The parties have no input. The Sender obtains a random value $\Delta\in\mathbb{F}$ and a random vector $\boldsymbol{B}\in\mathbb{F}^m$. The Receiver obtains a random vector $\boldsymbol{A}'\in\mathbb{F}^m$ and the vector

$$\boldsymbol{C} = \boldsymbol{A}'\Delta + \boldsymbol{B}.$$

That is, the i-th position of $\boldsymbol{C}$ is equal to $A'_i\Delta + B_i$. We note that several definitions of VOLE have been introduced in the literature, for both chosen-input and random variants [App+17,Boy+18,Boy+19,Wen+20]. In the context of these previous works, the functionality described here can be seen as *random reversed vector OLE.* We refer to it as VOLE for simplicity.

A naive implementation of a VOLE generator would be to run a two-party multiplication protocol (e.g., Gilboa multiplication [Gil99]) for each $i \in [m]$. The drawback here is that communication is linear in m. Recently, significant advances have been made in developing VOLE generators with *sub-linear* communication. Boyle et al. [Boy+18] presented the first protocols in that direction based on the LPN assumption. Their two protocols, a *primal* and a *dual* variant, rely on two different flavors of LPN. While the primal variant can be instantiated from LPN with cheap local linear codes, its communication grows asymptotically with the square-root of the output size. The dual variant, on the other hand, allows for logarithmic communication, but requires more computation.

A first implementation of a primal VOLE generator was provided in [Sch+19a], while concurrently, Boyle et al. [Boy+19] provide an implementation of dual VOLE over binary fields. Recently, Yang et al. [Yan+20] improved on the protocols of [Sch+19a], significantly reducing the communication overhead. Their main observation is that the primal VOLE generator works by expanding a size-$O(\sqrt{m})$ random seed correlation to a size-m pseudorandom correlation. Now by applying this expansion iteratively, they manage to get VOLE correlations of size m from a much shorter seed. Each expansion still takes $O(\sqrt{m})$ communication, but as Yang et al. [Yan+20] show, the LPN security parameters can be optimized so that the concrete communication complexity is still far below the non-iterative approach. Since they focus on the application of VOLE to correlated OT, the implementation of Yang et al. [Yan+20] is limited to binary fields. However, Weng et al. [Wen+20] extend this paradigm to VOLE over general fields, for which they also provide a consistency check for malicious security. In our implementation (Sect. 7), we use an improved version of the library of Schoppmann et al. [Sch+19a], incorporating the iterative approach of Yang et al. [Yan+20] and the consistency check of Weng et al. [Wen+20].

3.2 Malicious Secure Oblivious PRF

We now present our main (multi-input) OPRF construction in the $\mathcal{F}_{\mathsf{vole}}$-hybrid model. Our construction Π_{oprf} is detailed in Fig. 4 and realizes the functionality $\mathcal{F}_{\mathsf{oprf}}$ from Fig. 3 in the malicious setting. Our protocol will make use of two random oracles, $\mathsf{H} : \mathbb{F} \times \mathbb{F} \rightarrow \{0,1\}^{\mathsf{out}}, \mathsf{H}^{\mathbb{F}} : \mathbb{F} \rightarrow \mathbb{F}$.

First, the receiver will solve the system

$$\begin{bmatrix} \mathsf{row}(x_1) \\ \dots \\ \mathsf{row}(x_n) \end{bmatrix} \boldsymbol{P}^{\intercal} = (\mathsf{H}^{\mathbb{F}}(x_1), \dots, \mathsf{H}^{\mathbb{F}}(x_n))^{\intercal}$$

as a function of the set X. Depending on the choice of row this can correspond to polynomial interpolation, a bloom filter solver, PaXoS or some other fast solver,

Parameters: There are two parties, a Sender and a Receiver. Let $\mathbb{F}$ be a field. Let m denote the size of the output vectors.

Functionality: Upon receiving $(\mathsf{sender}, \mathsf{sid})$ from the Sender and $(\mathsf{receiver}, \mathsf{sid})$ from the Receiver.

- If the Receiver is malicious, wait for them to send $\boldsymbol{C}, \boldsymbol{A} \in \mathbb{F}^m$. Sample $\Delta \leftarrow \mathbb{F}$ and compute $\boldsymbol{B} := \boldsymbol{C} - \boldsymbol{A}\Delta$. Otherwise,
- If the Sender is malicious, wait for them to send $\boldsymbol{B} \in \mathbb{F}^m, \Delta \in \mathbb{F}$. Sample $\boldsymbol{A} \leftarrow \mathbb{F}^m$ and compute $\boldsymbol{C} := \boldsymbol{B} + \boldsymbol{A}\Delta$. Otherwise,
- Sample $\boldsymbol{A}, \boldsymbol{B} \leftarrow \mathbb{F}^m, \Delta \leftarrow \mathbb{F}$ and compute $\boldsymbol{C} := \boldsymbol{B} + \boldsymbol{A}\Delta$.

The functionality sends $\Delta, \boldsymbol{B}$ to the Sender and $\boldsymbol{C} := \boldsymbol{A}\Delta + \boldsymbol{B}, \boldsymbol{A}$ to the Receiver.

Fig. 2. Ideal functionality $\mathcal{F}_{\mathsf{vole}}$ of random reversed Vector-OLE (vole).

see Sect. 2. Recall that for all $x \in X$ it holds that $\mathsf{Decode}(\boldsymbol{P}, x) = \langle \mathsf{row}(x), \boldsymbol{P} \rangle = \mathsf{H}^{\mathbb{F}}(x)$ and that Decode is a linear function in $\boldsymbol{P}$. Another important property is that $\mathsf{Decode}(\boldsymbol{P}, x) = \mathsf{H}^{\mathbb{F}}(x)$ only for the elements in the set X, except the negligible probability[2].

The parties first invoke $\mathcal{F}_{\mathsf{vole}}$ where the Receiver obtains $\boldsymbol{A}', \boldsymbol{C} \in \mathbb{F}^m$ while the Sender obtains $\Delta \in \mathbb{F}, \boldsymbol{B} \in \mathbb{F}^m$. Recall that $\boldsymbol{C} = \boldsymbol{A}'\Delta + \boldsymbol{B}$. The Receiver computes $\boldsymbol{A} := \boldsymbol{P} + \boldsymbol{A}'$ and sends this to the Sender who computes $\boldsymbol{K} := \boldsymbol{B} + \boldsymbol{A}\Delta$. The parties will run a coin flipping protocol to then choose a random $w \leftarrow \mathbb{F}$.

The Sender defines their the PRF function as

$$F(x) = \mathsf{H}(\mathsf{Decode}(\boldsymbol{K}, x) - \Delta \mathsf{H}^{\mathbb{F}}(x) + w, x).$$

The Receiver outputs the values

$$X' := \{\mathsf{H}(\mathsf{Decode}(\boldsymbol{C}, x) + w, x) \mid x \in X\}.$$

To understand why $F(x) = \mathsf{H}(\mathsf{Decode}(\boldsymbol{C}, x) + w, x)$ for $x \in X$, observe that

$$\begin{aligned}
\mathsf{Decode}(\boldsymbol{K}, x) - \Delta \mathsf{H}^{\mathbb{F}}(x) =& \mathsf{Decode}(\boldsymbol{B} + \boldsymbol{P}\Delta + \boldsymbol{A}'\Delta, x) - \Delta \mathsf{H}^{\mathbb{F}}(x) \\
=& \langle \boldsymbol{B} + \boldsymbol{P}\Delta + \boldsymbol{A}'\Delta, \mathsf{row}(x) \rangle - \Delta \mathsf{H}^{\mathbb{F}}(x) \\
=& \langle \boldsymbol{B} + \boldsymbol{A}'\Delta, \mathsf{row}(x) \rangle + \langle \boldsymbol{P}\Delta, \mathsf{row}(x) \rangle - \Delta \mathsf{H}^{\mathbb{F}}(x) \\
=& \langle \boldsymbol{C}, \mathsf{row}(x) \rangle + \Delta \langle \boldsymbol{P}, \mathsf{row}(x) \rangle - \Delta \mathsf{H}^{\mathbb{F}}(x) \\
=& \langle \boldsymbol{C}, \mathsf{row}(x) \rangle + \Delta \mathsf{H}^{\mathbb{F}}(x) - \Delta \mathsf{H}^{\mathbb{F}}(x), \qquad \forall x \in X \\
=& \mathsf{Decode}(\boldsymbol{C}, x), \qquad \forall x \in X
\end{aligned}$$

When this is decoded at any $x \in X$ recall that $\mathsf{Decode}(\boldsymbol{P}, x) = \mathsf{H}^{\mathbb{F}}(x)$ and therefore the receiver will compute the correct value $\mathsf{Decode}(\boldsymbol{C}, x)$. Also recall that

[2] In the case of a malicious Receiver and depending on the choice of row, it may be possible for $|X| > n$ with noticeable probability. However, for PaXoS this can be bounded as $|X| \le m \approx 2.4n$ while interpolation ensures that $|X| \le m = n$.

this encoding has the property that at all other locations $x' \notin X$ it holds that $\mathsf{Decode}(\boldsymbol{P}\Delta, x') \neq \mathsf{H}^{\mathbb{F}}(x')$ and therefore the outputs will disagree. Finally, we obtain an OPRF by hashing away the linear correlation using the hash function H.

The final random oracle H call also contains to x to facilitate extraction in the case of a malicious Sender. In particular, our functionality requires the OPRF to effectively behave like a random oracle for the Sender. This differs from a normal PRF where there is no security with respect to the party holding the secret key.

Parameters: There are two parties, a Sender and a Receiver. Let $n, n' \in \mathbb{Z}$ be parameters such that if Receiver is malicious then $|X| < n'$ and otherwise $|X| = n$. Let $\mathsf{out} \in \mathbb{Z}$ be the output bit length.

Functionality: Upon input $(\mathsf{sender}, \mathsf{sid})$ from the Sender and $(\mathsf{receiver}, \mathsf{sid}, X)$ from the Receiver, the functionality samples $F : \mathbb{F} \to \{0,1\}^{\mathsf{out}}$ and sends $X' := \{F(x) \mid x \in X\}$ to the Receiver.
Subsequently, upon input $(\mathsf{sender}, \mathsf{sid}, y)$ from the Sender, the functionality returns $F(y)$ to the Sender.

Fig. 3. Ideal functionality $\mathcal{F}_{\mathsf{oprf}}$ batched oblivious PRF.

Theorem 1. *The Protocol Π_{oprf} realizes the $\mathcal{F}_{\mathsf{oprf}}$ functionality against a Malicious adversary in the random oracle, $\mathcal{F}_{\mathsf{vole}}$-hybrid model.*

Proof. First observe that the protocol is correct. We prove the following two Lemmas:

Lemma 1. *The Protocol Π_{oprf} realizes the $\mathcal{F}_{\mathsf{oprf}}$ functionality against a Malicious Sender $\mathcal{A}$ in the random oracle, $\mathcal{F}_{\mathsf{vole}}$-hybrid model.*

Proof. The simulator $\mathcal{S}$ interacts with the Sender as follows:

- $\mathcal{S}$ plays the role of $\mathcal{F}_{\mathsf{vole}}$. When $\mathcal{A}$ sends $(\mathsf{sender}, \mathsf{sid})$ to $\mathcal{F}_{\mathsf{vole}}$, $\mathcal{S}$ waits for $\mathcal{A}$ to send $\Delta, \boldsymbol{B}$.
- On behalf of the Receiver, $\mathcal{S}$ sends uniform $r, \boldsymbol{A}$ to $\mathcal{A}$.
- Whenever $\mathcal{A}$ queries $\mathsf{H}(q, y)$, if $q = \langle \boldsymbol{K}, \mathsf{row}(y, r)\rangle - \Delta\mathsf{H}^{\mathbb{F}}(y) + w$ and $\mathsf{H}(q, y)$ has not previously been queried, $\mathcal{S}$ sends $(\mathsf{sender}, \mathsf{sid}, y)$ to $\mathcal{F}_{\mathsf{oprf}}$ and programs $\mathsf{H}(q, y)$ to the response. Otherwise H responds normally.

To prove that this simulation is indistinguishable consider the following hybrids:

- Hybrid 0: The same as the real protocol except $\mathcal{S}$ in this hybrid plays the role of $\mathcal{F}_{\mathsf{vole}}$.
- Hybrid 1: $\mathcal{S}$ in this hybrid samples $\boldsymbol{A}$ uniformly as opposed to $\boldsymbol{A} := \boldsymbol{P} + \boldsymbol{A}'$. Since $\boldsymbol{A}'$ is distributed uniformly in the view of the $\mathcal{A}$, this hybrid has an identical distribution.

Parameters: There are two parties, a Sender and a Receiver with a set $X \subseteq \mathbb{F}$ where $|X| = n$.

Protocol: Upon input $(\text{sender}, \text{sid})$ from the Sender and $(\text{receiver}, \text{sid}, X)$ from the Receiver, the protocol specifies the following:

1. The Sender samples $w^{\mathsf{s}} \leftarrow \mathbb{F}$ and sends $c^{\mathsf{s}} := \mathsf{H}^{\mathbb{F}}(w^{\mathsf{s}})$ to the Receiver.
2. The Receiver samples $r \leftarrow \{0,1\}^{\kappa}, w^{\mathsf{r}} \leftarrow \mathbb{F}$ and solves the systems
$$\begin{bmatrix} \mathsf{row}(x_1, r) \\ \dots \\ \mathsf{row}(x_n, r) \end{bmatrix} \boldsymbol{P} = (\mathsf{H}^{\mathbb{F}}(x_1), ..., \mathsf{H}^{\mathbb{F}}(x_n))$$
for $\boldsymbol{P}$ as a function of their set $\{x_1, ..., x_n\} = X \subset \mathbb{F}$.
3. The Sender sends $(\text{sender}, \text{sid})$ and the Receiver sends $(\text{receiver}, \text{sid})$ to $\mathcal{F}_{\text{vole}}$ with dimension m and $|\mathbb{F}| \approx 2^{\kappa}$. The parties respectively receive $\Delta, \boldsymbol{B}$ and $\boldsymbol{C} := \boldsymbol{A}'\Delta + \boldsymbol{B}, \boldsymbol{A}'$.
4. The Receiver sends $r, w^{\mathsf{r}}, \boldsymbol{A} := \boldsymbol{P} + \boldsymbol{A}'$ to the Sender who defines $\boldsymbol{K} := \boldsymbol{B} + \boldsymbol{A}\Delta$.
5. The Sender sends w^{s} to the Receiver who aborts if $c^{\mathsf{s}} \neq \mathsf{H}^{\mathbb{F}}(w^{\mathsf{s}})$. Both parties define $w := w^{\mathsf{r}} + w^{\mathsf{s}}$.
6. The Receiver outputs $X' := \{\mathsf{H}(\mathsf{Decode}(\boldsymbol{C}, x) + w, x) \mid x \in X\}$.

Subsequently, upon each input $(\text{sender}, \text{sid}, y)$ from the Sender, the protocol specifies that the Sender outputs $F(y) = \mathsf{H}(\mathsf{Decode}(\boldsymbol{K}, y, r) - \Delta\mathsf{H}^{\mathbb{F}}(y) + w, y)$.

Fig. 4. Protocol Π_{oprf} which realizes the oblivious PRF functionality $\mathcal{F}_{\text{oprf}}$.

- Hybrid 2: When $\mathcal{S}$ in this hybrid samples r, it aborts if any of the $\mathsf{row}(\cdot, r)$ queries have previously been made. Since r is sampled uniformly the probability of this is $O(2^{-\kappa})$ and therefore this hybrid is indistinguishable from the previous.
- Hybrid 3: $\mathcal{S}$ in this hybrid does not call Encode, and so does not abort if Encode fails. Since none of $\mathsf{row}(\cdot, r)$ queries have previously been made, the PaXoS cuckoo-graph is uniformly sampled from all (n, m)-cuckoo graphs and therefore the probability of abort is bounded by $2^{-\lambda}$ [Pin+20]. Therefore this hybrid is statistically indistinguishable from the previous. Observe that this hybrid no longer uses the Receiver's input.
- Hybrid 4: Whenever $\mathcal{A}$ queries $\mathsf{H}(q, y)$ after receiving $\boldsymbol{A}$, if $q = \langle \boldsymbol{K}, \mathsf{row}(y, r) \rangle + w$ and $\mathsf{H}(q, y)$ has previously been queried, this hybrid aborts. Otherwise it sends $(\text{sender}, \text{sid}, y)$ to $\mathcal{F}_{\text{oprf}}$ and programs $\mathsf{H}(q, y)$ to the response.
  Observe that r is uniformly distributed prior to it being sent. Therefore, any given $q = \langle \boldsymbol{K}, \mathsf{row}(y, r) \rangle - \mathsf{H}^{\mathbb{F}}(y)\Delta + w$ is similarly distributed and $\mathcal{A}$ has a negligible probability of previously querying $\mathsf{H}(q, y)$. We conclude that this hybrid is indistinguishable from the simulation.

Lemma 2. *The Protocol Π_{oprf} realizes the $\mathcal{F}_{\mathsf{oprf}}$ functionality against a Malicious Receiver $\mathcal{A}$ in the random oracle, $\mathcal{F}_{\mathsf{vole}}$-hybrid model.*

Proof. The simulator $\mathcal{S}$ interacts with the Receiver as follows:

- $\mathcal{S}$ plays the role of $\mathcal{F}_{\mathsf{vole}}$ and receives $\boldsymbol{A}', \boldsymbol{C}$ from $\mathcal{A}$.
- When $\mathcal{A}$ sends $r, \boldsymbol{A}$, $\mathcal{S}$ computes $\boldsymbol{P} := \boldsymbol{A} - \boldsymbol{A}'$. For each of the previous $\mathsf{H}^{\mathbb{F}}(x)$ queries made by $\mathcal{A}$, $\mathcal{S}$ checks if $\mathsf{Decode}(\boldsymbol{P}, x, r) = \mathsf{H}^{\mathbb{F}}(x)$ and if so adds x to set X. $\mathcal{S}$ sends $(\mathsf{Receiver}, \mathsf{sid}, X)$ to $\mathcal{F}_{\mathsf{oprf}}$ and receives $\{F(x) \mid x \in X\}$ in response.
- $\mathcal{S}$ samples $w \leftarrow \{0,1\}^{\kappa}$. For each $x \in X$, $\mathcal{S}$ programs $\mathsf{H}(\mathsf{Decode}(\boldsymbol{C}, x, r) + w, x) := F(x)$. $\mathcal{S}$ sends w to $\mathcal{A}$.

To prove that this simulation is indistinguishable consider the following hybrids:

- Hybrid 0: The same as the real protocol except the $\mathcal{S}$ plays the role of $\mathcal{F}_{\mathsf{vole}}$. When $\mathcal{A}$ sends $(\mathsf{receiver}, \mathsf{sid})$ to $\mathcal{F}_{\mathsf{vole}}$, $\mathcal{S}$ waits to receive $\boldsymbol{A}', \boldsymbol{C}$.
- Hybrid 1: When $\mathcal{A}$ sends $r, \boldsymbol{A}$, $\mathcal{S}$ in this hybrid computes $\boldsymbol{P} := \boldsymbol{A} - \boldsymbol{A}'$. For each of the previous $\mathsf{H}^{\mathbb{F}}(x)$ queries made by $\mathcal{A}$, this hybrid checks if $\mathsf{Decode}(\boldsymbol{P}, x, r) = \mathsf{H}^{\mathbb{F}}(x)$ and if so adds x to set X. This hybrid sends $(\mathsf{Receiver}, \mathsf{sid}, X)$ to $\mathcal{F}_{\mathsf{oprf}}$ and receives $\{F(x) \mid x \in X\}$ in response.
- Hybrid 2: $\mathcal{S}$ in this hybrid does not sample w^{s} at the beginning of the protocol and sends a random value for c^{s} instead $H(w^{\mathsf{s}})$. Right before w^{s} is should be sent, $\mathcal{S}$ samples w^{s} and programs $H(w^{\mathsf{s}}) := c^{\mathsf{s}}$. Conditioned on $H(w^{\mathsf{s}})$ not previously being queried, this hybrid is identically distributed and therefore indistinguishable in general since w^{s} is uniform.
- Hybrid 3: When $w^{\mathsf{s}} \leftarrow \{0,1\}^{\kappa}$ is sampled, $\mathcal{S}$ in this hybrid aborts if any $\mathsf{H}(\mathsf{Decode}(\boldsymbol{C}, x, r) + w, x)$ has been made by $\mathcal{A}$. Since w^{s} was just sampled, each $\mathsf{Decode}(...) + ... + w^{\mathsf{s}}$ is uniform and therefore the probability of abort is at most $O(2^{-\kappa})$.
  $\mathcal{S}$ in this hybrid programs $\mathsf{H}(\mathsf{Decode}(\boldsymbol{C}, x, r) + w, x) := F(x)$ for all $x \in X$ and sends w^{s} to $\mathcal{A}$. Since the $F(x)$ are uniform, programming H does not change the distribution.
- Hybrid 4: $\mathcal{S}$ in this hybrid aborts if $\mathcal{A}$ ever makes an $\mathsf{H}(v, x)$ query such that $(v, x) \in \{(\mathsf{Decode}(\boldsymbol{K}, x, r) - \Delta \mathsf{H}^{\mathbb{F}}(x) + w, x) \mid x \in \mathbb{F} \setminus X\}$. Observe that

$$\begin{aligned}\mathsf{Decode}(\boldsymbol{K}, x, r) - \Delta \mathsf{H}^{\mathbb{F}}(x) &= \langle \boldsymbol{K}, \mathsf{row}(x, r)\rangle - \Delta \mathsf{H}^{\mathbb{F}}(x)\\ &= \langle \boldsymbol{B} + \boldsymbol{P}\Delta + \boldsymbol{A}'\Delta, \mathsf{row}(x, r)\rangle - \Delta \mathsf{H}^{\mathbb{F}}(x)\\ &= \langle \boldsymbol{C} + \boldsymbol{P}\Delta, \mathsf{row}(x, r)\rangle - \Delta \mathsf{H}^{\mathbb{F}}(x)\\ &= \Delta(\langle \boldsymbol{P}, \mathsf{row}(x, r)\rangle - \mathsf{H}^{\mathbb{F}}(x)) + \langle \boldsymbol{C}, \mathsf{row}(x, r)\rangle\end{aligned}$$

  and recall that Δ is uniformly distributed in the view of $\mathcal{A}$. So for all x s.t. $\langle \boldsymbol{P}, \mathsf{row}(x, r)\rangle \neq \mathsf{H}^{\mathbb{F}}(x)$, the distribution of $\Delta(\langle \boldsymbol{P}, \mathsf{row}(x, r)\rangle - \mathsf{H}^{\mathbb{F}}(x))$ is uniform in the view of $\mathcal{A}$. Now consider the case that $\langle \boldsymbol{P}, \mathsf{row}(x, r)\rangle = \mathsf{H}^{\mathbb{F}}(x)$. W.l.o.g., let us assume that all $\mathsf{H}^{\mathbb{F}}(x)$ queries are made prior to sending $\boldsymbol{A}$ and that for any given set $(x_1, ..., x_m) = X \subset \mathbb{F}$ and $r \in \{0,1\}^{\kappa}$, the matrix with rows $\mathsf{row}(x_1, r), ..., \mathsf{row}(x_m, r)$ is invertible. Recall that $\boldsymbol{P} \in \mathbb{F}^m$ where

$m \approx 2.4n$ for PaXoS. Therefore, for any X s.t. $|X| \leq m$, $\mathcal{A}$ can trivially construct the unique $\boldsymbol{P}$ such that $\langle \boldsymbol{P}, \mathsf{row}(x,r)\rangle = \mathsf{H}^{\mathbb{F}}(x)$ for all $x \in X$. Now consider the probability for any $x' \in \mathbb{F} \setminus X$, that $\langle \boldsymbol{P}, \mathsf{row}(x',r)\rangle = \mathsf{H}^{\mathbb{F}}(x')$. Since $\mathsf{H}^{\mathbb{F}}(x)$ is a random function and all $\langle \boldsymbol{P}, \mathsf{row}(x',r)\rangle$ values are fixed, the probability is $O(1/|\mathbb{F}|) = O(2^{-\kappa})$. Therefore we conclude that this hybrid aborts with negligible probability and that the size of X is at most $n' = m$.

4 Private Set Intersection

Using our OPRF protocol from the previous section, we now obtain a PSI protocol via the well known transformation shown in Fig. 6. The ideal functionality for PSI is given in Fig. 5. Given a malicious or semi-honest OPRF, this transformation achieves malicious or semi-honest security, respectively. While the general transformation is known and implicitly or explicitly used by used by [CKT10, CM20, DCW13, Pin+19b, Pin+20, RR17a], we provide a tight analysis in the malicious setting which reduces our communication by 20% to 50% compared to [CKT10, Pin+20].

The OPRF to PSI transformation works as follows. The PSI receiver sends their set X to the OPRF functionality $\mathcal{F}_{\mathsf{oprf}}$ and receives back $F(x)$ for all $x \in X$. The sender queries $\mathcal{F}_{\mathsf{oprf}}$ to learn $F(y)$ for their y. The sender sends $Y' := \{F(y) \mid y \in Y\}$ to the receiver who can compute $X \cap Y := \{x \mid x \in X \wedge F(x) \in Y'\}$.

To ensure the correctness of this protocol it is crucial that there are not any spurious collisions between the $F(x)$ and $F(y)$ values. In particular, since F is a random function it is possible that $x \neq y \wedge F(x) = F(y)$. In the semi-honest setting, the standard approach is to define the output domain of F to be $\{0,1\}^{\mathsf{out}}$ where $\mathsf{out} := \lambda + \log_2(n_{\mathsf{x}} n_{\mathsf{y}})$. Since the X, Y are fixed prior to randomly sampling F, the probability for any $x \notin Y$ to result in $F(x) \in Y'$ is purely a statistical problem[3]. In particular,

$$\Pr_{x,Y,F}[F(x) \in \{F(y) \mid y \in Y\} \wedge x \notin Y] = 2^{-\mathsf{out}} n_{\mathsf{y}} = 2^{-\mathsf{out} + \log_2(n_{\mathsf{y}})}.$$

If we take the union bound over $x \in X$, the overall probability of a collision is $n_{\mathsf{x}} 2^{-\mathsf{out}+\log_2(n_{\mathsf{y}})} = 2^{-\mathsf{out}+\log_2(n_{\mathsf{y}} n_{\mathsf{x}})} = 2^{-\lambda}$.

In the malicious setting the situation is complicated by the fact that the simulator must extract the sender's set Y by observing the sender's $\mathcal{F}_{\mathsf{oprf}}$ queries and the value of Y'. The folklore approach is to extract $Y := \{y \mid y \in Y^* \wedge F(y) \in Y'\}$ where Y^* is the set of inputs the sender queried the $\mathcal{F}_{\mathsf{oprf}}$ at. However, in the event that there exists distinct $y, y' \in Y^*$ s.t. $F(y) = F(y')$, then more than one y is extracted for each $y^* \in Y^*$.

The probability that there exists distinct $y, y' \in Y^*$ s.t. $F(y) = F(y')$ is at most $2^{-\mathsf{out}+2\log_2(n_{\mathsf{y}}{}^*)}$ where $n_{\mathsf{y}}{}^* := |Y^*|$. Therefore, it is expected to occur when $n_{\mathsf{y}}{}^* \geq 2^{\mathsf{out}/2}$. As such, in the folklore analysis and that of [CKT10, Pin+20], it is required that $\mathsf{out} := 2\kappa$ in order for the security argument to hold.

[3] In the $\mathcal{F}_{\mathsf{oprf}}$ hybrid where F is truly random.

We now present a new extraction procedure which allows $\mathsf{out} = \kappa$. In our protocol this effectively reduces the sender's communication by half, therefore reducing the overall communication by half when $|X| \ll |Y|$.

Our extraction procedure is to only extract $y \in Y^*$ if it is distinct. Intuitively, the reason security still holds is that collisions within Y^* are unlikely to collide with the receiver's set X. In particular, the receiver's set X is first fixed and then the function F is sampled. Thus, the probability that there exists a $y \in Y^*$ and $y \notin X$, yet $F(x) = F(y)$ is at most

$$2^{-\mathsf{out}+\log_2(n_{\mathsf{x}} n_{\mathsf{y}}{}^*)} = O(2^{-\mathsf{out}+\log_2(\kappa)+\log_2(n_{\mathsf{y}}{}^*)})$$

and therefore if $\mathsf{out} := \kappa$ the probability is $O(2^{-\kappa+\log(\kappa)+\log(n_{\mathsf{y}}{}^*)})$. Concretely, if $\kappa = 128, n_{\mathsf{x}} = 2^{30}$ then the sender would have to make an expected $n_{\mathsf{y}}{}^* = 2^{98}$ $\mathcal{F}_{\mathsf{oprf}}$ queries in order to expect to distinguish as opposed to 2^{49} queries via the folklore analysis.

Parameters: There are two parties, a sender with set $Y \subset \mathbb{F}$ and a receiver with a set of key $X \subseteq \mathbb{F}$. Let $n_{\mathsf{y}}, n_{\mathsf{x}}, n_{\mathsf{x}}{}' \in \mathbb{Z}$ be public parameters where $n_{\mathsf{x}} \leq n_{\mathsf{x}}{}'$.

Functionality: Upon receiving $(\mathsf{sender}, \mathsf{sid}, Y)$ from the sender and $(\mathsf{receiver}, \mathsf{sid}, X)$ from the receiver. If $|Y| > n_{\mathsf{y}}$, abort. If the receiver is malicious and $|X| > n_{\mathsf{x}}{}'$, then abort. If the receiver is honest and $|X| > n_{\mathsf{x}}$, then abort.
The functionality outputs $X \cap Y$ to the receiver.

Fig. 5. Ideal functionality $\mathcal{F}_{\mathsf{psi}}$ of Private Set Intersection.

Parameters: There are two parties, a sender with set $Y \subset \mathbb{F}$ and a receiver with a set of key $X \subseteq \mathbb{F}$.
In the Semi-honest setting, let $\mathsf{out} := \lambda + \log_2(n_{\mathsf{x}}) + \log_2(n_{\mathsf{y}})$. In the malicious setting let $\mathsf{out} := \kappa$. Let $\mathcal{F}_{\mathsf{oprf}}$ be the OPRF functionality with $n = n_{\mathsf{x}}$ and $n_{\mathsf{x}}{}' := n'$ and the output length out.

Protocol:

1. The sender sends $(\mathsf{sender}, \mathsf{sid})$ and receiver sends $(\mathsf{receiver}, \mathsf{sid}, X)$ to $\mathcal{F}_{\mathsf{oprf}}$. The receiver receives $X' = \{F(x) \mid x \in X\}$.
2. For $y \in Y$, the sender sends $(\mathsf{sender}, \mathsf{sid}, y)$ to $\mathcal{F}_{\mathsf{oprf}}$ and receives back $F(y)$.
3. The sender sends $Y' := \{F(y) \mid y \in Y\}$ to the receiver in a random order.
4. The receiver outputs $\{x \mid F(x) \in Y', x \in X\}$.

Fig. 6. Protocol Π_{psi} which realizes the PSI functionality $\mathcal{F}_{\mathsf{psi}}$.

Theorem 2. *The Protocol Π_{psi} realizes the $\mathcal{F}_{\mathsf{psi}}$ functionality against a Malicious adversary in the $\mathcal{F}_{\mathsf{oprf}}$-hybrid model.*

Proof. Consider a malicious sender. The simulator interacts with the sender as:

- The simulator plays the role of $\mathcal{F}_{\mathsf{oprf}}$. The simulator observes all the $(\mathsf{sender}, \mathsf{sid}, y)$ messages. Let Y^* be the set of all such y.
- When the sender sends Y', the simulator computes $\hat{Y} := \{y \mid y \in Y^* \wedge \nexists y' \in Y^* \ s.t.\ y \neq y' \wedge F(y) = F(y')\}$ and extracts $Y := \{y \mid y \in \hat{Y} \wedge F(y) \in Y'\}$ and sends Y to $\mathcal{F}_{\mathsf{psi}}$.

First, conditioned on there not being any $F(y) = F(y')$ collisions, it is easy to verify that the simulation above is correct and indistinguishable.

Now consider some collision $F(y) = F(y')$. Observe that the simulator only needs to extract y, y' if there is a noticeable probability of one of them being in X. W.l.o.g., let us assume $y \in X$. Therefore, consider the probability of $F(y') = F(x)$ for some $x \in X$. Since $|X| = n_{\mathsf{x}} = O(\kappa)$, the probability of the sender finding such a (target preimage) collision is $O(2^{-\kappa})$.

Consider a malicious receiver. The simulator is as follows:

- The simulator plays the role of $\mathcal{F}_{\mathsf{oprf}}$.
- When the receiver sends $(\mathsf{receiver}, \mathsf{sid}, X)$ to $\mathcal{F}_{\mathsf{oprf}}$, the simulator observes X and sends X' back as the $\mathcal{F}_{\mathsf{oprf}}$ would.
- The simulator forwards X to $\mathcal{F}_{\mathsf{psi}}$ and receives $Z = X \cap Y$ in response.
- The simulator computes Y' as containing all $\{F(z) \mid z \in Z\}$ along with $n_{\mathsf{y}} - |Z|$ uniform values from $\{0,1\}^{\mathsf{out}} \setminus X'$. The simulator sends Y'.

This simulation is identical to the real protocol except for the dummy items being sampled from $\{0,1\}^{\mathsf{out}} \setminus X'$ instead of $\{0,1\}^{\mathsf{out}}$. However, since $2^{\mathsf{out}} - |X| = O(2^{\kappa})$ this change is indistinguishable.

5 Oblivious Programmable PRF

We now turn our attention to constructing our circuit PSI protocol. To achieve this, we first construct a type of protocol known as an oblivious programmable PRF (OPPRF). The functionality is shown in Fig. 7. The sender has a set of input pairs $(y_1, z_1), ..., (y_n, z_n)$. The functionality samples a key k such that $F_k(y_i) = z_i$ and at all other input points it outputs a random value. The receiver on input points $x_1, ..., x_n$ then obtains $F_k(x_i)$ for all i.

We instantiate this functionality using an OPRF protocol, and the XoPaXoS solver. The parties call the OPRF functionality $\mathcal{F}_{\mathsf{oprf}}$ with X being the receiver's input. The sender obtains k while the receiver obtains $X' = \{F_k(x_1), ..., F_k(x_n)\}$. The sender constructs a solver for $\boldsymbol{P}$ such that $\mathsf{Decode}(\boldsymbol{P}, y_i) = z_i - F_k(y_i)$ using XoPaXoS and sends $\boldsymbol{P}$ to the receiver who then outputs $x_i^* := x_i' + \mathsf{Decode}(\boldsymbol{P}, x_i)$ for all i. When $x_i = y_j$, then

$$x^* := F_k(x_i) + \mathsf{Decode}(\boldsymbol{P}, x_i) = F_k(x_i) + z_j - F_k(x_i) = z_j.$$

Parameters: There are two parties, a sender with input $L = \{(y_1, z_1), ..., (y_{n_y}, z_{n_y})\}$ where $y_i \in \mathbb{F}, z_i \in \{0,1\}^{\text{out}}$ and a receiver with a set $X \subseteq \mathbb{F}$ where $|X| = n_x$.

Functionality: Upon input $(\mathsf{sender}, \mathsf{sid}, L)$ from the sender and $(\mathsf{receiver}, \mathsf{sid}, X)$ from the receiver, the functionality samples a random function $F : \mathbb{F} \to \{0,1\}^{\text{out}}$ such that $F_k(y) = z$ for each $(y, z) \in L$ and sends $X' := \{F_k(x) \mid x \in X\}$ to the receiver.
Subsequently, upon input $(\mathsf{sender}, \mathsf{sid}, y)$ from the sender, the functionality returns $F(y)$ to the sender.

Fig. 7. Ideal functionality $\mathcal{F}_{\mathsf{opprf}}$ of Oblivious Programmable PRF.

The sender outputs the key $k^* := (k, \boldsymbol{P})$ where the OPPRF function is defined as $F^*_{k^*}(x) := F_k(x) + \mathsf{Decode}(P, x)$.

With respect to security, first observe that the v_i values outside the intersection are information theoretically hidden in the $\mathcal{F}_{\mathsf{oprf}}$ hybrid. What remains to be shown is that the distribution of $\boldsymbol{P}$ does not depend on $Y \setminus X$. Recall from Sect. 2 that this is the exact issue XoPaXoS addresses compared to PaXoS. Intuitively, XoPaXoS ensures that each position of $\boldsymbol{P}$ is either assigned a uniformly random value or is the sum of previous positions and some $z_i - F_k(y_i)$. We prove security of this protocol in Theorem 3 (Fig. 8).

Parameters: There are two parties, a sender with $L = \{(y_1, z_1), ..., (y_\ell, z_\ell)\}$ and a receiver with a set $X \subseteq \mathbb{F}$ where $|X| = n$.

Protocol: Upon input $(\mathsf{sender}, \mathsf{sid}, L)$ from the sender and $(\mathsf{receiver}, \mathsf{sid}, X)$ from the receiver, the parties do the following:

1. The sender sends $(\mathsf{sender}, \mathsf{sid}, L)$ and the receiver sends $(\mathsf{receiver}, \mathsf{sid}, X)$ to $\mathcal{F}_{\mathsf{oprf}}$ with $|\hat{\mathbb{F}}| \approx 2^\kappa$. The parties respectively receive k and $X' = \{F_k(x) \mid x \in X\}$.
2. The sender uses the XoPaXoS solver to compute $\boldsymbol{P} \in \mathbb{F}^m$ over the field $\mathbb{F}$ such that $\boldsymbol{P} \leftarrow \mathsf{Encode}((y_1, z_1 - F_k(y_1)), ..., (y_\ell, z_\ell - F_k(y_\ell)))$ and sends it to the receiver.
3. The receiver outputs $\{x_1^*, ..., x_n^*\}$ such that $x_i^* := x_i' + \mathsf{Decode}(P, x_i)$.

Subsequently, upon input $(\mathsf{sender}, \mathsf{sid}, y)$ from the sender, output: $F_k(x) + \mathsf{Decode}(P, x)$.

Fig. 8. Protocol Π_{opprf} which realizes the Oblivious Programmable PRF functionality $\mathcal{F}_{\mathsf{opprf}}$.

Theorem 3. *The Protocol Π_{opprf} realizes the $\mathcal{F}_{\mathsf{opprf}}$ functionality against a semi-honest adversary in the $\mathcal{F}_{\mathsf{oprf}}$-hybrid model.*

Proof. Consider a semi-honest sender. Observe that the protocol is correct. Since the receiver does not send any messages the simulation is trivial.

Consider a malicious receiver. The simulator generates the receiver's transcript as follows:

- The simulator samples uniform values $F_k(x)$ for $x \in X$.
- The simulator sends X to $\mathcal{F}_{\mathsf{opprf}}$ functionality and receives back $x'_1, ..., x'_n$.
- Samples $\boldsymbol{P}$ uniformly from all vectors such that $\mathsf{Decode}(\boldsymbol{P}, x_i) = x'_i - F_k(x_i)$.
- The simulator outputs $(\{F_k(x) \mid x \in X\}, \boldsymbol{P})$ as the transcript.

Clearly the $\mathbb{F}_k(x)$ values are identically distributed. What remains to be shown is that $\boldsymbol{P}$ has the same distribution as it would in the real protocol. Recall from Sect. 2 that XoPaXoS assign values to $\boldsymbol{P}$ in four ways

- During Step 5, $P_i \leftarrow \mathbb{G}$ for $i \in C'$. Recall that Step 4 identifies $\tilde{d}$ of the last $d + \lambda$ columns which form an invertible matrix for the 2-core. These columns are indexed by C. Then C' is defined as $C' = \{j \mid i \in R, M'_{i,j} = 1\} \cup ([d+\lambda] \setminus C + m')$ indexes all positions of $\boldsymbol{P}$ which interact with the 2-core along with all of the last $d + \lambda$ columns which are not used to invert.
- Next, in Step 6, the remaining $\tilde{d}$ positions of $\boldsymbol{P}$ corresponding are assigned a value such that $\mathsf{Decode}(\boldsymbol{P}, y_i) = v'_i - F_k(y_i)$ for the i in the 2-core which is equivalent to solving

$$\tilde{M}^*(P_{C_1+m'}, ..., P_{C_{\tilde{d}}+m'})^\intercal = (y'_{R_1}, ..., y'_{R_{\tilde{d}}})^\intercal.$$

  Since this is a fully determined system, there is exactly one solution.
- In Step 7 a single node i from each tree in G is assigned a uniform value.
- Lastly, observe that the rest of the system is fully determined. That is, each the the remaining P_i position are assigned a value with the form

$$P_i := v'_k - F_k(y_k) - \sum_{j \in \{...\}} P_j.$$

The analysis above can be reordered such that Step 5, 7 are performed first. Then there is exactly one solution to the correctness constraint.

6 Circuit PSI

We now construct a circuit PSI protocol from our OPPRF. Our construction (Fig. 10) builds on the approach of Pinkas et al. [Pin+19a], using our novel XoPaXoS and VOLE-based OPPRF from the previous section. As we will see in the experiments (Sect. 7), this translates into a significant speedup compared to [Pin+19a]. The ideal functionality for circuit PSI is given in Fig. 9. It allows both sender and receiver to input a set of associated values, which will be secret-shared alongside the elements in the intersection. The associated values corresponding to elements in the intersection can then be used in any subsequent MPC phase, and could for example be used to compute sums [Ion+20] or inner products [Sch+19b] of the intersection. Since our protocol is effectively the same as [Pin+19a] with the substitution of our OPPRF and $\mathcal{F}_{\mathsf{2pc}}$ implementation, we defer the proof of security to [Pin+19a].

Parameters: There are two parties, a sender with set $Y \subset \mathbb{F}$, associated values $\tilde{Y} \subset \{0,1\}^{\sigma_y}$ and a receiver with a set of keys $X \subseteq \mathbb{F}$, associated values $\tilde{X} \subset \{0,1\}^{\sigma_x}$ where $|Y| = |\tilde{Y}| = n_y, |X| = |\tilde{X}| = n_x$. The functionality is parameterized by $\mathsf{Reorder} : \mathbb{F}^n \rightarrow (\pi : [n] \rightarrow [m])$ which on input X outputs a injective function π.

Functionality: Upon receiving $(\mathsf{sender}, \mathsf{sid}, Y, \tilde{Y})$ from the sender and $(\mathsf{receiver}, \mathsf{sid}, X, \tilde{X})$ the functionality computes $\pi \leftarrow \mathsf{Reorder}(X)$ and uniformly samples $Q^0, Q^1 \in \{0,1\}^m, Z^0, Z^1 \in \{0,1\}^{(\sigma_x+\sigma_y)\times m}$ such that

$$
\begin{aligned}
&q_{i'}^0 \oplus q_{i'}^1 = 1, \;\; z_{i'}^0 \oplus z_{i'}^1 = (\tilde{x}_{i'} || \tilde{y}_i) && \text{if } \exists x_i \in X, y_j \in Y \text{ s.t. } x_i = y_j, \\
&q_{i'}^0 \oplus q_{i'}^1 = 0, \;\; z_{i'}^0 \oplus z_{i'}^1 = 0 && \text{otherwise}
\end{aligned}
$$

where $i' = \pi(i)$. Output Q^0, Z^0, π to the receiver and Q^1, Z^1 to the sender.

Fig. 9. Ideal functionality $\mathcal{F}_{\mathsf{cpsi}}$ of circuit private set intersection.

Cuckoo Hashing. We make use of a data structure known as a cuckoo hash table. Given a set X, one can create a hash table T of size $m = \epsilon|X|$. This table is parameterized by k hash functions $h_1, \ldots, h_k : \{0,1\}^* \rightarrow \{1, 2, ..., m\}$. There is a procedure [PSZ18, Dem+18] s.t. with overwhelming probability for all $x \in X$, x can be storied in T at $T[h_j(x)]$ for a $j \in [k]$, and only one item will be stored at any position of T. We discuss concrete parameter choices for ϵ and k in Sect. 7.2.

We will also refer to a procedure known as *simple hashing* of a set Y where we store $y \in Y$ at *all* locations $T[h_j(y)]$. For simple hashing, each position of T may hold more than one value. It can be shown that if the table has $m = O(|Y|)$ positions, then any given location of the table will hold at most $O(\log |Y|)$ items.

Protocol. The full circuit PSI protocol is constructed using the OPPRF and cuckoo hashing. The receiver will construct a cuckoo hash table T_x of their set X. The sender will construct a simple has table T_y of their set Y.

For each $i \in [m]$ the sender will sample a random value $r_i \leftarrow \{0,1\}^\ell$ where $\ell := \lambda + \log_2 m$. For all i and $y \in T_y[i]$, the sender will construct a list $L = \{(y', r_i)\}$ where $y' = H(y, j)$ and j is defined such that $i = h_j(y)$. That is, j is the hash function index that mapped y to this bin. The receiver constructs set X' which is defined as the collection of all $H(x, j)$ such that x is stored at $T_x[h_j(x)]$. The sender then provides L as their input to $\mathcal{F}_{\mathsf{opprf}}$ while the receiver inputs X'. In response the receiver obtains the set X^*.

As an explanation of this, let us focus on some bin index i such that x was mapped to bin $T_x[i]$ due to hash function h_j, i.e., $T_x[i] = x$ and $h_j(x) = i$. Furthermore, let us assume that there is some $y \in Y$ s.t. $x = y$. Since the sender did simple hashing, they too mapped y to bin $T_y[i]$ since $h_j(y) = i$. For this y, they programmed the OPPRF with the pair $(H(y, j), r_i)$. When the receiver inputs $H(x, j)$ to the OPPRF they receive the value r_i in response. If $x \notin Y$, then the receiver will receive a random value. Therefore, for each i, the receiver now has a value r_i' which is equal to r_i (held by the sender) if $T_x[i] \in Y$ and otherwise r_i' is random per the OPPRF security definition.

Parameters: There are two parties, a sender with set $Y \subset \mathbb{F}$, associated values $\tilde{Y} \subset \{0,1\}^{\sigma_y}$ and a receiver with a set of key $X \subseteq \mathbb{F}$, associated values $\tilde{X} \subset \{0,1\}^{\sigma_x}$ where $|Y| = |\tilde{Y}| = n_y, |X| = |\tilde{X}| = n_x$. The protocol is parameterized by an expansion factor ϵ, cuckoo hash table size $m = \epsilon n_x$, and k hash functions $h_j : \{0,1\}^* \to m$.

Protocol:

1. The receiver constructs a cuckoo hash table T_x of X such that $x \in X$, there exists a $j \in [k]$ such that $H(x||j) = T_x[h_j(x)]$.
2. The sender constructs a simple hash table T_y of Y such that $y \in Y$, for all $j \in [k]$ it holds that $H(y||j) \in T_y[h_j(y)]$.
3. For all i, the sender samples random $r_i \in \{0,1\}^\ell, w_i \in \{0,1\}^{\sigma_y}$ and for all $y' \in T_y[i]$, the receiver defines $L := \{(y', r_i||\tilde{y} \oplus w_i)\} \in (\mathbb{F} \times \{0,1\}^{\ell+\sigma_y})^m$ where $\tilde{y}$ is associated value for y s.t. $y' = H(y,j)$.
4. The sender sends $(\mathsf{sender}, \mathsf{sid}, L)$ and the receiver sends $(\mathsf{receiver}, \mathsf{sid}, T_x')$ to $\mathcal{F}_{\mathsf{opprf}}$ where $T_x' := (H(1, T_x[1]), ..., H(m, T_x[m]))$. The receiver receives $X^* = \{(r_i'||w_i') \mid i \in [m]\}$.
5. For each i, the sender sends $(\mathsf{receiver}, \mathsf{sid}, r_i'||w_i')$ and the receiver sends $(\mathsf{sender}, \mathsf{sid}, r_i||w_i||\tilde{x})$ to $\mathcal{F}_{\mathsf{2pc}}$ where $\tilde{x}$ is the associated value with $x = T_x[i]$ (or zero if $T_x[i]$ is empty). $\mathcal{F}_{\mathsf{2pc}}$ computes a circuit $\mathcal{C}$ that for each $i \in [m]$:
   (a) Sets $q_i := 1$ if $r_i' = r_i$ and $q_i := 0$ otherwise,
   (b) Outputs secret shares q_i^0, q_i^1 of q_i and z_i^0, z_i^1 of $z_i := q_i \cdot ((w_i' \oplus w_i)||\tilde{x})$.

Fig. 10. Protocol Π_{cpsi} which realizes the circuit PSI functionality $\mathcal{F}_{\mathsf{cpsi}}$.

The final step of the protocol is to use a generic MPC protocol to compare each r_i' with r_i to check if they are equal. The output of this generic MPC will be secret shared which will be the output of the protocol.

In the event that the sender has "associated values", they will program the OPPRF with $L = \{(y', r_i||\tilde{y} \oplus w_i)\}$ where $\tilde{y}$ is the associated value for y', and w_i is an random value that the sender samples for each bin $i \in \{1, 2, ..., m\}$ in the same way as r_i. The receiver will then obtain $r_i'||w_i'$ from the OPPRF protocol for each i. The generic MPC will then take as input $\{(r_i', w_i')\}$ from the receiver and $\{(r_i, w_i, \tilde{x})\}$ from the sender. For each i the MPC computation will compute

Parameters: There are two parties, a sender and a receiver. The functionality is parameterized by a circuit $\mathcal{C} : \{0,1\}^{\mathsf{in}_1+\mathsf{in}_2} \to \{0,1\}^{\mathsf{out}_1+\mathsf{out}_2}$.

Functionality: Upon receiving $(\mathsf{sender}, \mathsf{sid}, X)$ from the sender and $(\mathsf{receiver}, \mathsf{sid}, Y)$ where $X \in \{0,1\}^{\mathsf{in}_1}$ and $Y \in \{0,1\}^{\mathsf{in}_2}$, the functionality computes $(Z_1, Z_2) := \mathcal{C}(X, Y)$ and returns $Z_1 \in \{0,1\}^{\mathsf{in}_1}$ to the receiver and $Z_2 \in \{0,1\}^{\mathsf{in}_2}$ to the sender.

Fig. 11. Ideal functionality $\mathcal{F}_{\mathsf{2pc}}$ of generic two party computation.

Table 1. Comparison of theoretical communication cost of various PSI protocols. Several protocols have additional parameters which have been *approximated* in terms of κ, λ. In particular, the coefficients shown below often vary (non-linearly) as a function of n, κ, λ. In these cases we chose representative values. The third column contains the overhead for fixed $\lambda = 40, \kappa = 128$ while the last three columns also fix the set sizes.

Protocol	Communication		$n = n_y = n_x$		
			2^{16}	2^{20}	2^{24}
Semi-Honest					
DH-PSI	$4\kappa n_x + (\lambda + \log(n_x n_y))n_y$	$512n_x + 40n_y + \log(n_x n_y)n_y$	$584n$	$592n$	$600n$
[Kol+16]	$6\kappa n_x + 3(\lambda + \log(n_x n_y))n_y$	$768n_x + 120n_y + 3\log(n_x n_y)n_y$	$984n$	$1008n$	$1032n$
[Pin+19b] Low-Comm	$3.5\kappa n_x + 1.02(2 + \lambda + \log(n_x))n_y$	$450n_x + 43n_y + 1.02\log(n_x)n_y$	**509n**	$513n$	$517n$
[Pin+19b] Fast	$3.5(1 + 1/\lambda)\kappa n_x + 2(\lambda + \log(n_x n_y))n_y$	$461n_x + 80n_y + 2\log(n_x n_y)n_y$	$603n$	$619n$	$635n$
[Pin+20]	$9.3\kappa n_x + (\lambda + \log(n_x n_y))n_y$	$461n_x + 40n_y + \log(n_x n_y)n_y$	$1208n$	$1268n$	$1302n$
[CM20]	$4.8\kappa n_x + (\lambda + \log(n_x n_y))n_y$	$620n_x + 40n_y + \log(n_x n_y)n_y$	$678n$	$694n$	$702n$
Ours total (PaXoS)	$2.4\kappa n_x + (\lambda + \log(n_x n_y))n_y + 2^{17}\kappa {n_x}^{0.05}$	$2^{24}{n_x}^{0.05} + 307n_x + 40n_y + \log(n_x n_y)n_y$	$914n$	$426n$	$398n$
Ours total (interpolation)	$\kappa n_x + (\lambda + \log(n_x n_y))n_y + 2^{17}\kappa {n_x}^{0.05}$	$2^{24}{n_x}^{0.05} + 128n_x + 40n_y + \log(n_x n_y)n_y$	$702n$	**245n**	**219n**
Ours online (PaXoS)	$2.4\kappa n_x + (\lambda + \log(n_x n_y))n_y + 2^{13}\kappa {n_x}^{0.13}$	$2^{20}{n_x}^{0.13} + 307n_x + 40n_y + \log(n_x n_y)n_y$	$502n$	$398n$	$396n$
Ours online (interpolation)	$\kappa n_x + (\lambda + \log(n_x n_y))n_y + 2^{13}\kappa {n_x}^{0.13}$	$2^{20}{n_x}^{0.13} + 128n_x + 40n_y + \log(n_x n_y)n_y$	$310n$	$218n$	$217n$
Malicious					
[Pin+20]	$11.8\kappa n_x + 2\kappa n_y$	$1512n_x + 256n_y$	$1766n$	$1766n$	$1766n$
Ours total (PaXoS)	$2.4\kappa n_x + (\lambda + \log(n_x n_y))n_y + 2^{17}\kappa {n_x}^{0.05}$	$2^{24}{n_x}^{0.05} + 307n_x + 128n_y$	$960n$	$474n$	$438n$
Ours total (interpolation)	$\kappa n_x + (\lambda + \log(n_x n_y))n_y + 2^{17}\kappa {n_x}^{0.05}$	$2^{24}{n_x}^{0.05} + 128n_x + 128n_y$	**754n**	**293n**	**259n**
Ours online (PaXoS)	$2.4\kappa n_x + \kappa n_y + 2^{13}\kappa {n_x}^{0.13}$	$2^{20}{n_x}^{0.13} + 307n_x + 128n_y$	$558n$	$446n$	$436n$
Ours online (interpolation)	$\kappa n_x + \kappa n_y + 2^{13}\kappa {n_x}^{0.13}$	$2^{20}{n_x}^{0.13} + 128n_x + 128n_y$	$366n$	$266n$	$257n$

$q_i := (r'_i = r_i)$ and $z_i := q_i \cdot ((w'_i \oplus w_i)||\tilde{x})$ and then output secret shares of q_i and z_i (Fig. 11).

7 Performance Evaluation

7.1 Theoretical Comparison

All protocols compared here are largely based on efficient symmetric key primitives – with the exception of the DH-PSI protocol – and can be instantiated with $O(n_x + n_y)$ running time. Since these protocols are asymptotically similar, it becomes difficult to compare them. As we do below, one metric is to implement the protocol and compare their running times. However, the quality of the implementation has a large impact on running time. Arguably a more objective metric is the total communication which is independent of the implementation.

Table 1 shows a theoretical comparison of the communication required by various PSI protocols. We present the communication overhead in three ways. The general case in terms of $n_x, n_y, \kappa, \lambda$; when we fix $\kappa = 128, \lambda = 40$; and when we fix all the parameters. Many protocols contain addition parameters that allow a for some type of tradeoff. For these we chose representative values.

Our semi-honest protocol requires sending $\rho\kappa n_x + (\lambda + \log(n_y n_y))n_y$ bits plus the overhead of performing a VOLE of size ρn_x. Here, ρ is the rate of the linear system solver which is being employed by the protocol. We consider two values of ρ. The first is $\rho = 2.4$ which corresponds to the PaXoS solver while the second is $\rho = 1$ when Vandermonde/interpolation solver is used.

To estimate the overhead of the VOLE protocol we experimentally determined that our implementation requires a total of $2^{17}\kappa \sqrt[20]{n_{\mathsf{x}}}$ bits. We note that this is the approximate overhead of our implementation and may not be asymptotically correct for $n_{\mathsf{x}} \gg 2^{24}$. Since the cost of the VOLE is highly sublinear, the overhead it contributes quickly diminishes as n_{x} increase. For example, the VOLE requires 27,800 bits per element for $n_{\mathsf{x}} = 2^{10}$ while only requiring 38 bits per element for $n_{\mathsf{x}} = 2^{20}$. From this we can conclude that our protocol works best for large sets, e.g. $n_{\mathsf{x}} \geq 2^{16}$.

We also consider a setting where we perform a one time VOLE preprocessing phase. In this case the bulk of the VOLE computation can be performed before the X, Y sets or their sizes $n_{\mathsf{x}}, n_{\mathsf{y}}$ are known. This is akin to performing base OTs ahead of time as is done by all the protocols compared below (except DH-PSI). With preprocessing the online overhead of the VOLE decreases to approximately $2^{13}\kappa \sqrt[8]{n_{\mathsf{x}}}$ bits, an improvement of $16\times$. In addition, sublinear VOLE constructions are relatively new and there are likely more optimizations opportunities, like the recent work of Yang et al. [Yan+20] which we utilize.

As the table shows, our protocol outperforms prior work, especially for large inputs. The three protocols of [Pin+19b, Pin+20] mostly differ in their linear system encoding rates. [Pin+19b] considers two different types of Vandermonde/interpolation solvers which achieve rate $\rho \approx 1$ while [Pin+20] achieves rate $\rho = 2.4$ via their PaXoS solver and a significantly improved running time. Both of these works use an OT-extension type protocol which results in sending approximately 3.5κ bits per element in their encoding. We on the other hand depart from this OT-extension based technique and utilize sublinear VOLE. This has the advantage that we send only κ bits per item in the encoding. For the final PSI-from-OPRF construction, the sender will additionally send their set encoded under the OPRF which requires $\lambda + \log(n_{\mathsf{x}}n_{\mathsf{y}})$ bits per item in Y.

[Kol+16] does not encode their input into a linear system and instead uses cuckoo hashing which has a rate of $\rho \approx 1.7$. This work is also a OT-extension type protocol which requires sending 3.5κ bits per hash table element which results in an overhead of $6\kappa n_{\mathsf{x}}$. However, the cuckoo hashing approach results in the sender needing to send 3 OPRF values per item in Y. The core advantage of [Kol+16] is that cuckoo hashing is extremely efficient compared to solving a linear system and as such obtains very small running times.

In the case of malicious security, the overhead of our protocol is effectively identical except that the sender now must send larger OPRF values, i.e. κ bits per element in Y as opposed to $\lambda + \log(n_{\mathsf{x}}n_{\mathsf{y}})$ bits. On the other hand, the protocol of [Pin+20] requires increasing the number of bits per item in the linear encoding from 3.5κ to 5κ. This has the effect that they must send an overall encoding size of $11.8\kappa n_{\mathsf{x}}$. Our protocol more naturally achieves malicious security and only requires sending κ per encoding position. In addition, the [Pin+20] analysis states the sender must send OPRF values of size 2κ. However, we demonstrate that our protocol remains secure when only κ bits are sent.

7.2 Experimental Evaluation

Implementation. We implement all our protocols in C++. We use an extended version of the VOLE implementation of Schoppmann et al. [Sch+19a], supporting iterative bootstrapping [Yan+20] and a consistency check for malicious security [Wen+20], and assuming LPN with regular noise [see Boy+18, Wen+20]. For computing the 2-core of the cuckoo graph in our PaXoS implementation, we use igraph [Bud+20], and we rely on libOTe [Rin] for oblivious transfers and the GMW implementation used in our circuit PSI protocol.

To compare our protocols to previous work [CM20, Kol+16, Pin+20, Pin+19a], we perform experiments in different network settings. To that end, we use two Amazon EC2 M5.2xlarge VMs, each featuring 8 cores at 2.5 GHz and 32 GiB of RAM. For comparability, we limit each protocol to a single core. In the LAN, without any artificial constraints, we measured a bandwidth of 5 Gbps between our machines. For settings with lower bandwidth, we use Wondershaper [HGS] to limit incoming and outgoing traffic.

PSI. Here, we compare our semi-honest and malicious PSI implementations against the works of Kolesnikov et al. [Kol+16], Chase and Miao [CM20], and Pinkas et al. [Pin+20]. The protocol of Kolesnikov et al. [Kol+16] is particularly fast, but comes with a comparatively large communication overhead. The semi-honest protocol of Kolesnikov et al. [CM20] on the other hand comes with a lower communication overhead, but more expensive computation. Finally, the PaXoS protocol of Pinkas et al. [Pin+20] features fast computation, but increased communication compared to [CM20]. We do not compare against the SpOT-light protocol [Pin+19b], since [CM20] outperforms it in high-bandwidth settings[4], and our protocol has even lower communication than SpOT-low.

The results of our evaluation in the semi-honest setting are shown in Table 2. As expected, [Kol+16] outperforms all other protocols in the LAN setting, but is less effective with reduced bandwidth. For medium input sizes and bandwidths, [CM20] and [Pin+20] sometimes outperform our protocols and [Pin+20]. Our protocols particularly shine in medium to low bandwidth settings, and with large input sizes, which is to be expected given its low communication cost.

In the malicious setting, the state of the art is presented by [Pin+20]. Again, we compare communication and running time in different bandwidth settings, and present our results in Table 3. While in the LAN, [Pin+20] sometimes outperforms our implementation, we are consistently faster as bandwidth decreases.

Since the vector OLE implementation underlying our protocols uses the iterative bootstrapping approach of Yang et al. [Yan+20], our protocols have the

[4] In low communication settings (10 Mbps and 1 Mbps), [CM20] takes 15% longer than [Pin+19b], but at the same time up to 75% longer than our protocol.

distinctive feature that a part of the computation can be performed in a one-time, data-independent setup phase. Our implementation of this setup phase could be improved by tuning the LPN parameters (and thus the bootstrapping iteration sizes) to the input set sizes. Currently we use the parameters from [Boy+18, Yan+20] without any additional tuning. In our tables, we highlight the best protocols when setup is amortized in gray. It can be seen that in that case, our protocol more consistently outperforms previous work.

Table 2. Comparison of our PSI protocols to previous works in the semi-honest setting. We compare the amount of data sent by both parties, as well as the total running time with different bandwidths. A dash (–) indicates experiments that either crashed or did not finish, or where only the total communication is reported. The best protocol within a setting is marked in blue if setup is included, and in gray if setup is excluded.

n	Protocol	Communication (MB)			Total running time (s)			
		P_1	P_2	Total	LAN	100 Mbps	10 Mbps	1 Mbps
2^{16}	[KKRT16]	–	–	7.730	0.1106	0.7250	6.884	68.82
	[CM20]	0.5790	4.764	5.343	0.5853	0.6437	4.870	47.49
	[PRTY20]	12.62	0.5898	13.21	0.6460	1.682	11.86	112.8
	Ours	0.9965	2.702	3.699	0.1720	0.4510	3.277	31.18
	Ours (w/setup)	1.171	3.062	4.232	0.5030	1.067	6.742	63.33
2^{18}	[KKRT16]	–	–	31.88	0.5850	2.968	28.46	283.6
	[CM20]	2.520	19.23	21.75	2.017	2.194	19.50	193.8
	[PRTY20]	51.94	2.621	54.56	1.517	5.976	47.66	464.2
	Ours	3.066	10.30	13.37	1.227	2.192	12.26	114.1
	Ours (w/setup)	3.622	10.68	14.31	1.985	3.279	16.65	151.5
2^{20}	[KKRT16]	–	–	128.5	2.441	11.928	114.8	1143
	[CM20]	10.03	77.63	87.66	8.148	9.071	78.38	780.0
	[PRTY20]	214.0	10.49	224.5	5.885	24.09	195.6	1910
	Ours	12.06	40.55	52.61	4.398	8.496	48.69	449.7
	Ours (w/setup)	12.062	40.93	53.55	5.396	9.850	53.35	487.7
2^{22}	[KKRT16]	–	–	530.1	10.19	49.30	473.6	4718
	[CM20]	44.08	313.5	357.6	34.70	41.54	319.4	3182
	[PRTY20]	815.7	46.14	861.9	22.94	93.67	751.3	–
	Ours	47.28	161.7	208.9	23.93	40.67	199.0	1794
	Ours (w/setup)	47.84	162.0	209.9	25.88	42.97	204.7	1834
2^{24}	[KKRT16]	–	–	2137	43.90	199.1	1909	–
	[CM20]	176.3	1266	1442	189.6	198.1	1289	12860
	[PRTY20]	3364	184.5	3548	101.7	392.0	–	–
	Ours	204.2	645.7	849.9	90.741	156.4	814.2	7296
	Ours (w/setup)	204.7	646.1	850.9	92.81	158.7	819.9	7335

Table 3. Comparison of our PSI protocols to [Pin+20] in the malicious setting.

n	Protocol	Communication (MB)			Total running time (s)			
		P_1	P_2	Total	LAN	100 Mbps	10 Mbps	1 Mbps
2^{16}	[PRTY20]	12.62	2.097	14.71	0.6510	1.808	13.13	125.5
	Ours	1.390	2.702	4.092	0.2250	0.5260	3.627	34.77
	Ours (w/setup)	1.564	3.062	4.626	0.5560	1.147	7.109	66.72
2^{18}	[PRTY20]	51.94	8.389	60.33	1.556	6.469	52.57	513.1
	Ours	4.639	10.30	14.94	1.279	2.464	13.96	127.6
	Ours (w/setup)	5.195	10.68	15.88	2.046	3.558	18.37	165.0
2^{20}	[PRTY20]	214.0	33.55	247.6	6.119	26.12	215.2	2410
	Ours	17.31	40.55	57.85	5.150	9.599	54.090	494.0
	Ours (w/setup)	17.86	40.93	58.79	6.157	10.94	58.76	532.6
2^{22}	[PRTY20]	815.7	134.2	950.0	23.37	101.2	826.1	–
	Ours	68.25	161.7	229.9	26.50	45.19	222.5	1975
	Ours (w/setup)	68.81	162.0	230.9	28.46	47.50	228.3	2015
2^{24}	[PRTY20]	3364	536.9	3901	102.8	422.1	–	–
	Ours	271.3	645.7	917.0	104.0	174.5	881.0	7876
	Ours (w/setup)	271.9	646.1	918.0	106.0	176.8	886.7	7914

Circuit PSI. We also compare our circuit-PSI implementation to the state of the art protocol [Pin+19a]. We use the same cuckoo hashing parameters as [Pin+19a], $\epsilon = 1.27$ and $k = 3$ hash functions, following the analysis of [PSZ18]. We note, however, that there is some disagreement in the literature regarding the correct cuckoo hashing parameters for a given statistical security level λ. For example, for $k = 3, n = 2^{20}$, and $\lambda = 40$, [PSZ18] and [Dem+18] report quite different expansion factors (1.27 vs. 1.54). In our own experiments, we found the security level to be approximated by $\lambda = 240\epsilon - 256 - \log_2 n$, which requires $\epsilon = 1.32$ for $n = 2^{20}$ and $\lambda = 40$. Still, we stick to the parameters used by Pinkas et al. [Pin+19a] for comparability.

Like [Pin+19a], our construction uses a generic two-party computation phase in the end (Step 5 in Fig. 10). We implement two variants of this step: one using the standard IKNP OT extension [Ish+03] to implement the GMW offline phase, and one using the more recent SilentOT [Boy+19].

Our results in Table 4 show that our protocols outperform [Pin+19a] in both high and low-bandwidth settings. Since the main communication bottleneck is the GMW phase, the SilentOT variant works particularly well in the low-communication setting. In the LAN, our IKNP variant still outperforms [Pin+19a] (who also used IKNP) in terms of running time, which showcases the efficiency of our novel OPPRF construction.

Table 4. Comparison of our Circuit-PSI protocol to Pinkas et al. [Pin+19a]. Values marked with an asterisk (*) were not measured, but computed from the theoretical communication costs [Section 7.3][Pin+19a].

n	Protocol	Total comm. (MB)	Total running time (s)	
			5 Gbps	100 Mbps
2^{12}	[PSTY19]	9*	0.965	1.34
	Ours (IKNP)	13.4	0.495	1.19
	Ours (SilentOT)	4.79	0.737	1.07
2^{16}	[PSTY19]	149*	5.01	11.3
	Ours (IKNP)	171	1.52	9.03
	Ours (SilentOT)	21.1	4.0	5.34
2^{20}	[PSTY19]	2540*	72.0	172
	Ours (IKNP)	2830	23.3	149
	Ours (SilentOT)	277	103	120

8 Conclusion

In this paper, we have shown how to combine two cryptographic primitives, namely Vector-OLE and linear system solvers like (Xo)PaXoS, into highly efficient O(P)PRF and PSI protocols. Our final protocols outperform previous work in terms of communication, and as a consequence, in terms of running time in bandwidth-constrained environments. From a theoretical perspective, we provide a more efficient reduction from OPRF to PSI.

As discussed in Sect. 2, there are many ways to implement the linear system solvers we require for VOLE-PSI. One approach, based on polynomial interpolation, promises to result in the lowest communication complexity, but as previous work has shown, this comes at the cost of expensive computation. The approach presented in this paper, using PaXoS, allows for fast computation, but incurs a higher communication blowup of asymptotically $2.4\kappa n$. It remains an open question whether there are more efficient (i.e., smaller) data structures that also allow for linear encoding and decoding. Should these become available, they will directly improve the communication complexity of our protocols.

References

App+17. Applebaum, B., Damgård, I., Ishai, Y., Nielsen, M., Zichron, L.: Secure arithmetic computation with constant computational overhead. In: Katz, J., Shacham, H. (eds.) CRYPTO 2017. LNCS, vol. 10401, pp. 223–254. Springer, Cham (2017). https://doi.org/10.1007/978-3-319-63688-7_8

BM74. Borodin, A., Moenck, R.: Fast modular transforms. J. Comput. Syst. Sci. **8**(3), 366–386 (1974)

Boy+18. Boyle, E., Couteau, G., Gilboa, N., Ishai, Y.: Compressing vector OLE. In: ACM Conference on Computer and Communications Security, pp. 896–912. ACM (2018)

Boy+19. Boyle, E., et al.: Efficient two-round OT extension and silent non-interactive secure computation. In: ACM Conference on Computer and Communications Security, pp. 291–308. ACM (2019)

Bud+20. Buddhavarapu, P., Knox, A., Mohassel, P., Sengupta, S., Taubeneck, E., Vlaskin, V.: Private matching for compute. IACR Cryptology ePrint Archive 2020, p. 599 (2020)

CKT10. De Cristofaro, E., Kim, J., Tsudik, G.: Linear-complexity private set intersection protocols secure in malicious model. In: Abe, M. (ed.) ASIACRYPT 2010. LNCS, vol. 6477, pp. 213–231. Springer, Heidelberg (2010). https://doi.org/10.1007/978-3-642-17373-8_13

CM20. Chase, M., Miao, P.: Private set intersection in the internet setting from lightweight oblivious PRF. In: Micciancio, D., Ristenpart, T. (eds.) CRYPTO 2020. LNCS, vol. 12172, pp. 34–63. Springer, Cham (2020). https://doi.org/10.1007/978-3-030-56877-1_2

CO18. Ciampi, M., Orlandi, C.: Combining private set-intersection with secure two-party computation. In: Catalano, D., De Prisco, R. (eds.) SCN 2018. LNCS, vol. 11035, pp. 464–482. Springer, Cham (2018). https://doi.org/10.1007/978-3-319-98113-0_25

CT10. De Cristofaro, E., Tsudik, G.: Practical private set intersection protocols with linear complexity. In: Sion, R. (ed.) FC 2010. LNCS, vol. 6052, pp. 143–159. Springer, Heidelberg (2010). https://doi.org/10.1007/978-3-642-14577-3_13

DCW13. Dong, C., Chen, L., Wen, Z.: When private set intersection meets big data: an efficient and scalable protocol. In: ACM Conference on Computer and Communications Security, pp. 789–800. ACM (2013)

Dem+18. Demmler, D., Rindal, P., Rosulek, M., Trieu, N.: PIRPSI: scaling private contact discovery. Proc. Priv. Enhancing Technol. **2018**(4), 159–178 (2018)

Gil99. Gilboa, N.: Two party RSA key generation. In: Wiener, M. (ed.) CRYPTO 1999. LNCS, vol. 1666, pp. 116–129. Springer, Heidelberg (1999). https://doi.org/10.1007/3-540-48405-1_8

HEK12. Huang, Y., Evans, D., Katz, J.: Private set intersection: are garbled circuits better than custom protocols? In: NDSS. The Internet Society (2012)

HGS. Hubert, B., Geul, J., Séhier, S.: wondershaper: Command-line utility for limiting an adapter bandwidth. https://github.com/magnific0/wondershaper

Igr. igraph: Library for the analysis of networks. https://github.com/igraph/igraph

Ion+20. Ion, M., et al.: On deploying secure computing: private intersection- sum-with-cardinality. In: EuroS&P, pp. 370–389. IEEE (2020)

Ish+03. Ishai, Y., Kilian, J., Nissim, K., Petrank, E.: Extending oblivious transfers efficiently. In: Boneh, D. (ed.) CRYPTO 2003. LNCS, vol. 2729, pp. 145–161. Springer, Heidelberg (2003). https://doi.org/10.1007/978-3-540-45146-4_9

Kal+19. Kales, D., Rechberger, C., Schneider, T., Senker, M., Weinert, C.: Mobile private contact discovery at scale. In: USENIX Security Symposium, pp. 1447–1464. USENIX Association (2019)

Kis+17. Kiss, Á., Liu, J., Schneider, T., Asokan, N., Pinkas, B.: Private set intersection for unequal set sizes with mobile applications. Proc. Priv. Enhancing Technol. **2017**(4), 177–197 (2017)

Kol+16. Kolesnikov, V., Kumaresan, R., Rosulek, M., Trieu, N.: Efficient batched oblivious PRF with applications to private set intersection. In: ACM Conference on Computer and Communications Security, pp. 818–829. ACM (2016)

KS12. Kobayashi, K., Shibuya, T.: Generalization of Lu's linear time encoding algorithm for LDPC codes. In: ISITA, pp. 16–20. IEEE (2012)

LM10. Lu, J., Moura, J.M.F.: Linear time encoding of LDPC codes. IEEE Trans. Inf. Theory **56**(1), 233–249 (2010)

Mea86. Meadows, C.A.: A more efficient cryptographic matchmaking protocol for use in the absence of a continuously available third party. In: IEEE Symposium on Security and Privacy, pp. 134–137. IEEE Computer Society (1986)

OOS17. Orrù, M., Orsini, E., Scholl, P.: Actively secure 1-out-of-N OT extension with application to private set intersection. In: Handschuh, H. (ed.) CT-RSA 2017. LNCS, vol. 10159, pp. 381–396. Springer, Cham (2017). https://doi.org/10.1007/978-3-319-52153-4_22

Pin+15. Pinkas, B., Schneider, T., Segev, G., Zohner, M.: Phasing: private set intersection using permutation-based hashing. In: USENIX Security Symposium, pp. 515–530. USENIX Association (2015)

Pin+18. Pinkas, B., Schneider, T., Weinert, C., Wieder, U.: Efficient circuit-based PSI via cuckoo hashing. In: Nielsen, J.B., Rijmen, V. (eds.) EUROCRYPT 2018. LNCS, vol. 10822, pp. 125–157. Springer, Cham (2018). https://doi.org/10.1007/978-3-319-78372-7_5

Pin+19a. Pinkas, B., Schneider, T., Tkachenko, O., Yanai, A.: Efficient circuit-based PSI with linear communication. In: Ishai, Y., Rijmen, V. (eds.) EUROCRYPT 2019. LNCS, vol. 11478, pp. 122–153. Springer, Cham (2019). https://doi.org/10.1007/978-3-030-17659-4_5

Pin+19b. Pinkas, B., Rosulek, M., Trieu, N., Yanai, A.: SpOT-light: lightweight private set intersection from sparse OT extension. In: Boldyreva, A., Micciancio, D. (eds.) CRYPTO 2019. LNCS, vol. 11694, pp. 401–431. Springer, Cham (2019). https://doi.org/10.1007/978-3-030-26954-8_13

Pin+20. Pinkas, B., Rosulek, M., Trieu, N., Yanai, A.: PSI from PaXoS: fast, malicious private set intersection. In: Canteaut, A., Ishai, Y. (eds.) EUROCRYPT 2020. LNCS, vol. 12106, pp. 739–767. Springer, Cham (2020). https://doi.org/10.1007/978-3-030-45724-2_25

PSZ14. Pinkas, B., Schneider, T., Zohner, M.: Faster private set intersection based on OT extension. In: USENIX Security Symposium, pp. 797–812. USENIX Association (2014)

PSZ18. Pinkas, B., Schneider, T., Zohner, M.: Scalable private set intersection based on OT extension. ACM Trans. Priv. Secur. **21**(2), 71–735 (2018)

Rin. Rindal, P.: libOTe: A fast, portable, and easy to use Oblivious Transfer Library. https://github.com/osu-crypto/libOTe

RR17a. Rindal, P., Rosulek, M.: Improved private set intersection against malicious adversaries. In: Coron, J.-S., Nielsen, J.B. (eds.) EUROCRYPT 2017. LNCS, vol. 10210, pp. 235–259. Springer, Cham (2017). https://doi.org/10.1007/978-3-319-56620-7_9

RR17b. Rindal, P., Rosulek, M.: Malicious-secure private set intersection via dual execution. In: ACM Conference on Computer and Communications Security, pp. 1229–1242. ACM (2017)

Sch+19a. Schoppmann, P., Gascón, A., Reichert, L., Raykova, M.: Distributed vector-OLE: improved constructions and implementation. In: ACM Conference on Computer and Communications Security, pp. 1055–1072. ACM (2019)

Sch+19b. Schoppmann, P., Gascón, A., Raykova, M., Pinkas, B.: Make some ROOM for the zeros: data sparsity in secure distributed machine learning. In: ACM Conference on Computer and Communications Security, pp. 1335–1350. ACM (2019)

Wen+20. Weng, C., Yang, K., Katz, J., Wang, X.: Wolverine: fast, scalable, and communication-efficient zero- knowledge proofs for Boolean and arithmetic circuits. IACR Cryptology ePrint Archive 2020, p. 925 (2020)

Yan+20. Yang, K., Weng, C., Lan, X., Zhang, J., Wang, X.: Ferret: fast extension for correlated OT with small communication. In: CCS, pp. 1607–1626. ACM (2020)

Author Index